Bill James presents . . .

STATS™ 1992 Major League Handbook

STATS, Inc. • Bill James

Published by Sports Team Analysis & Tracking Systems, Inc.
Dr. Richard Cramer, Chairman • John Dewan, President

Cover by John Grimwade, New York, NY

Photo by Tony Inzerillo, Bensenville, IL

First Edition: November, 1991

Printed in the United States of America

ISBN 0-9625581-3-3

This book is dedicated to

Jean Berken, Shawn Dawson, Tom Dozier, Don Hartack,
Rollie Loewen, Jim Rogde, Tim Rumoshosky and Rick Soos.

MVR's (Most Valuable Reporters) in 1991.

Acknowledgments

Another season has come and gone and, not one, but two Cinderella stories have developed. Both the Atlanta Braves and the Minnesota Twins leaped from last place to first place in one season. As I write this, these two underdogs are battling to face each other in the World Series. By now you know the outcome, and you probably had a chance to relax in front of your TV or radio, or if you are really lucky, sit in the stadium and watch history unfold.

The staff in the STATS office, however, is not so relaxed. The office buzzes with activity while the playoff games can be heard on a background radio or TV. There is no time for relaxing now. This book must be to the printer one week after the regular season ends. And so I'd like to acknowledge all those who sacrificed their TV, lounge chair and peanuts during the playoffs in order to make this timely book possible.

Dr. Richard Cramer, Chairman of STATS, is the creator of the baseball system which gives us the ability to look at statistics in a million different ways. Dick began working with the design of this system about 13 years ago. The rest of us are mere rookies compared to Dick considering the time and energy he has put into the design and improvements of the System. Thanks Dick, for creating such a great tool.

John Dewan, President and CEO, has been a catalyst in making things happen at STATS. His faith in the talents of the STATS staff, his innovative way of looking at baseball and his personal motivation encourages us to get things done that we didn't know we could do. John also dug in and got his hands dirty, toiling on this book as he worked with Bill James to program and refine the 1992 Projections.

Bob Mecca, has been a pillar of STATS, Inc. since 1988. He is responsible for the accuracy of all the baseball data in our computer which, in turn, produces the statistics in this book. Once again, Bob took wicked cuts at the statistics with his bat to come up with the Leader Boards and Player Profiles in this book.

Steve Moyer, a rookie at STATS (not unlike Jeff Bagwell), has done a yeoman's job coordinating all the parts of the book, ensuring that all the pieces fit and are put together on time. He also worked on rehabbing this year's Fielding Section.

Ross Schaufelberger coordinated the advertising, while still covering his many other jobs here at STATS. Ross is a real STATS All-Star.

Many others in the office worked less directly on this book, but were extremely important in getting this book done.:

Art Ashley, Assistant Vice President, wears many different hats for long hours each day. Besides using his computer expertise to keep our System up to snuff, he has been working on expanding STATS' product line.

Bob Meyerhoff, Assistant Vice President, keeps us afloat as he watches over our financial matters. He is also responsible for the coordination of our Reporters Network. Along with Steve Moyer, he makes sure that we have at least three accounts of every game — an important fact in ensuring accuracy.

Jim Musso, Chuck Miller and Jonathan Forman are new names at STATS this year. Each has brought his own baseball background and insights. Nadine Jenkins, Marge Morra and Suzette Neily keep the administrative side of the office running smoothly.

David Pinto brings STATS' information into your living room through his daily support of the ESPN broadcasts. Don Zminda's handiwork can be seen in other upcoming publications: **The Scouting Report: 1992** and **STATS 1992 Baseball Scoreboard.** Craig Wright continues to oversee our Major League Operations.

This book is dedicated to eight of STATS' very talented reporters of 1991. They are the eyes and ears of STATS at the games. STATS is lucky to have an extremely talented group of reporters. These eight are some of the best and they embody the qualities that we think are characteristic of our Reporter Team as a whole. Here are some of the other "Iron men and women" of STATS: Marc Bowman, Marco Bresba, Jeff Burhans, Mike Cassin, Ken Kozyra, Don Kriss, Rob Kuron, Brad Lucht, Steve Lysogorski, Brian Macomber, Dan McIlroy, Ray Pinter, Greg Porzucek, Dave Schultz, Lee Starr, Steve Utter, Chris Weber, and Ken Zakel. We wish we had room to list everyone, but our thanks goes out to every member of the Reporter Team.

Special acknowledgment to John Doucette (who was an outstanding relief reporter), to Steve Fillebrown (who never made an error) and to Dave Schultz (whose daughter decided to be born into this world during the Milwaukee game he was covering at the park).

Rob Neyer once again assisted Bill James and John Dewan in refining the Minor League Equivalencies used in the 1992 Projections. Thanks Rob.

Finally, thanks to Bill James for the conception and design of this book as well as the major effort he puts into refining the Major League Equivalencies and Projections. Never satisfied until it reaches perfection, Bill continues to improve on his formulas. We think he's designed a winner in this book; we hope you do too.

— Sue Dewan, Vice President

Table of Contents

Introduction

"Jeff Bagwell, the 1991 National League Batting Champ! C'mon, you gotta be kidding me. Who is this guy? He hasn't even played a major league game yet!"

That was one of the many reactions we received when last year's Handbook was released. The very last chart in the book which projected Jeff Bagwell to hit .318 wasn't added until the day the book went to print. Frankly, it never really dawned on us that maybe this would make him the NL batting champ based on all the projections for National League players! With that kind of publicity regarding the projections, it became an absolute requirement for everyone associated with STATS, Inc. to root heavily for Jeff Bagwell to take the league by storm.

Well, Jeff didn't win the batting title, but he did win a regular job, hit a solid .294 and most certainly will be the National League's Rookie of the Year.

Call us talented — the most impressive crew of analysts and statisticians this side of the equator. Call us pyschic — no one better since Karnak the Magnificent. Or, most likely, call us lucky! As my bowling buddy tells me every time I get a strike, "Even a blind dog finds a bone once in a while."

Welcome to the 1992 Handbook! This is our third year, and yes, we are going to do projections again. They're a lot of fun and we've had some success — see Bill James' comments later in the book. Plus, we've tried to improve this year's edition in many ways:

- We've added minor league statistics for all players who qualified as rookies in 1991, courtesy of Howe Sportsdata International once again.

- We've improved our presentation of fielding statistics, organizing them in a more useful style.

- We've revised the format of lefty-righty data to make them easier to read.

- We've expanded the Leader Boards and Player Profiles to provide more information.

- We've labored over projections hoping to maintain our level of success.

Hope you enjoy it!

What's Official and What's Not

The stats in this book are technically unofficial. The Official Major League Baseball Averages are not released until December. But once again, we (and our readers) can't wait that long. We've found in the past that if you compare these stats with those that come out in December, you'll find no major differences. We take extraordinary efforts to insure accuracy.

In the interest of completeness, we'd like to point out a couple of differences between our stats and those printed by the MLB-IBM system and the USA Today in early October. We have an extra game played for Lance Johnson of the Chicago White Sox. On April 13 in Detroit, Johnson came in as a defensive replacement in the top of the 9th of a winning effort by the White Sox (with Sammy Sosa moving to right field). The change was not announced in the Detroit pressbox, but the televised coverage in Chicago clearly showed Johnson playing center field in the 9th inning.

The other difference we noted involved an intentional walk issued to Jose Canseco in the 4th inning of the Oakland/Minnesota game on April 23. All four accounts of the game we received showed that the fourth ball was thrown intentionally after a 3-0 count.

—John Dewan

Career Stats

Each year we strive to make the best career numbers available even better. This year we are including minor league career data back to 1984, not only for players who debuted in the last two years (1990 or 1991), but also for any players who still maintained rookie status in 1991. This will provide more reference data for a player such as Dean Palmer, who had nineteen at bats in 1989 and whose minor league data would have been excluded under our previous method. Otherwise, everything else should look familiar.

For newcomers:

- **Age** is seasonal age based on July 1, 1992. This means our age is the player's age as of July 1. By choosing this particular date, almost exactly mid-season, we get the age at which each player will play during most of the 1992 season.

- **Hm** and **Rd** in the batters' tables stand for home runs hit at home and home runs hit on the road, respectively.

- **TBB** and **IBB** are Total Bases on Balls and Intentional Bases on Balls.

- **SB%** is Stolen Base Percentage (stolen bases divided by attempts). **OBP** and **SLG** are On-Base Percentage and Slugging Percentage.

- **BFP**, **Bk**, and **ShO** are Batters Faced Pitcher, Balks, and Shutouts.

- For pitchers, thirds of an inning were not officially kept prior to 1982. Therefore, there are no thirds of an inning for 1981 and before for older pitchers.

- For players who played for more than one major league team in a season, stats for each team are shown just above the bottom line career totals.

Jim Abbott

Pitches: Left **Bats:** Left **Pos:** SP   **Ht:** 6' 3" **Wt:** 210 **Born:** 09/19/67 **Age:** 24

		HOW MUCH HE PITCHED						WHAT HE GAVE UP									THE RESULTS				
Year Team	Lg	G	GS	CG	GF	IP	BFP	H	R	ER	HR	SH	SF	HB	TBB	IBB	SO	WP	Bk	W	L	Pct.	ShO	Sv	ERA
1989 California	AL	29	29	4	0	181.1	788	190	95	79	13	11	5	4	74	3	115	8	2	12	12	.500	2	0	3.92
1990 California	AL	33	33	4	0	211.2	925	246	116	106	16	9	6	5	72	6	105	4	3	10	14	.417	1	0	4.51
1991 California	AL	34	34	5	0	243	1002	222	85	78	14	7	7	5	73	6	158	1	4	18	11	.621	1	0	2.89
3 ML YEARS		96	96	13	0	636	2715	658	296	263	43	27	18	14	219	15	378	13	9	40	37	.519	4	0	3.72

Kyle Abbott

Pitches: Left **Bats:** Left **Pos:** SP   **Ht:** 6' 4" **Wt:** 195 **Born:** 02/18/68 **Age:** 24

		HOW MUCH HE PITCHED						WHAT HE GAVE UP									THE RESULTS				
Year Team	Lg	G	GS	CG	GF	IP	BFP	H	R	ER	HR	SH	SF	HB	TBB	IBB	SO	WP	Bk	W	L	Pct.	ShO	Sv	ERA
1989 Quad City	A	13	12	0	1	73.2	303	55	26	21	5	0	4	0	30	0	95	3	5	5	4	.556	0	0	2.57
1990 Midland	AA	24	24	2	0	128.1	565	124	75	59	8	4	4	8	73	0	91	6	3	6	9	.400	0	0	4.14
Edmonton	AAA	3	3	0	0	10.1	61	26	18	17	4	0	1	0	4	0	14	4	0	1	0	1.000	0	0	14.81
1991 Edmonton	AAA	27	27	4	0	180.1	732	173	84	80	22	7	6	1	46	1	120	7	1	14	10	.583	2	0	3.99
1991 California	AL	5	3	0	0	19.2	90	22	11	10	2	3	0	1	13	0	12	1	1	1	2	.333	0	0	4.58

Paul Abbott

Pitches: Right **Bats:** Right **Pos:** RP/SP   **Ht:** 6' 3" **Wt:** 193 **Born:** 09/15/67 **Age:** 24

		HOW MUCH HE PITCHED						WHAT HE GAVE UP									THE RESULTS				
Year Team	Lg	G	GS	CG	GF	IP	BFP	H	R	ER	HR	SH	SF	HB	TBB	IBB	SO	WP	Bk	W	L	Pct.	ShO	Sv	ERA
1985 Elizabethtn	R	10	10	1	0	35	172	33	32	27	3	1	0	0	32	0	34	7	1	1	5	.167	0	0	6.94
1986 Kenosha	A	25	15	1	7	98	462	102	62	49	13	3	2	2	73	3	73	7	0	6	10	.375	0	0	4.50
1987 Kenosha	A	26	25	1	0	145.1	620	102	76	59	11	5	6	3	103	0	138	11	2	13	6	.684	0	0	3.65
1988 Visalia	A	28	28	4	0	172.1	799	141	95	80	9	8	6	4	143	5	205	12	9	11	9	.550	2	0	4.18
1989 Orlando	AA	17	17	1	0	90.2	389	71	46	44	6	2	1	0	48	0	102	7	7	9	3	.750	0	0	4.37
1990 Portland	AAA	23	23	4	0	128.1	568	110	75	65	9	3	3	1	82	0	129	8	5	5	14	.263	1	0	4.56
1991 Portland	AAA	8	8	1	0	44	193	36	19	19	2	0	1	3	28	0	40	1	0	2	3	.400	1	0	3.89
1990 Minnesota	AL	7	7	0	0	34.2	162	37	24	23	0	1	1	1	28	0	25	1	0	0	5	.000	0	0	5.97
1991 Minnesota	AL	15	3	0	1	47.1	210	38	27	25	5	7	3	0	36	1	43	5	0	3	1	.750	0	0	4.75
2 ML YEARS		22	10	0	1	82	372	75	51	48	5	8	4	1	64	1	68	6	0	3	6	.333	0	0	5.27

Shawn Abner

Bats: Right **Throws:** Right **Pos:** CF   **Ht:** 6' 1" **Wt:** 194 **Born:** 06/17/66 **Age:** 26

		BATTING																	BASERUNNING			PERCENTAGES		
Year Team	Lg	G	AB	H	2B	3B	HR	(Hm	Rd)	TB	R	RBI	TBB	IBB	SO	HBP	SH	SF	SB	CS	SB%	GDP	Avg	OBP	SLG
1987 San Diego	NL	16	47	13	3	1	2	(1	1)	24	5	7	2	0	8	0	0	0	1	0	1.00	0	.277	.306	.511
1988 San Diego	NL	37	83	15	3	0	2	(2	0)	24	6	5	4	1	19	1	0	1	0	1	.00	1	.181	.225	.289
1989 San Diego	NL	57	102	18	4	0	2	(1	1)	28	13	14	5	2	20	0	0	1	1	0	1.00	1	.176	.213	.275
1990 San Diego	NL	91	184	45	9	0	1	(1	0)	57	17	15	9	1	28	2	2	1	2	3	.40	3	.245	.286	.310
1991 2 ML Teams		94	216	42	10	2	3	(2	1)	65	27	14	11	4	43	1	1	1	1	2	.33	6	.194	.236	.301
1991 San Diego	NL	53	115	19	4	1	1	(1	0)	28	15	5	7	4	25	1	1	1	0	0	.00	3	.165	.218	.243
California	AL	41	101	23	6	1	2	(1	1)	37	12	9	4	0	18	0	0	0	1	2	.33	3	.228	.257	.366
5 ML YEARS		295	632	133	29	3	10	(7	3)	198	68	55	31	8	118	4	4	4	5	6	.45	11	.210	.250	.313

Jim Acker

Pitches: Right **Bats:** Right **Pos:** RP/SP   **Ht:** 6' 2" **Wt:** 215 **Born:** 09/24/58 **Age:** 33

		HOW MUCH HE PITCHED						WHAT HE GAVE UP									THE RESULTS				
Year Team	Lg	G	GS	CG	GF	IP	BFP	H	R	ER	HR	SH	SF	HB	TBB	IBB	SO	WP	Bk	W	L	Pct.	ShO	Sv	ERA
1983 Toronto	AL	38	5	0	8	97.2	426	103	52	47	7	1	2	8	38	1	44	1	0	5	1	.833	0	1	4.33
1984 Toronto	AL	32	3	0	9	72	312	79	39	35	3	4	1	6	25	3	33	5	0	3	5	.375	0	1	4.38
1985 Toronto	AL	61	0	0	26	86.1	370	86	35	31	7	1	2	3	43	1	42	2	0	7	2	.778	0	10	3.23
1986 2 ML Teams		44	19	0	9	155	661	163	81	69	13	12	9	3	48	6	69	5	1	5	12	.294	0	0	4.01
1987 Atlanta	NL	68	0	0	41	114.2	491	109	57	53	11	3	3	4	51	4	68	1	0	4	9	.308	0	14	4.16
1988 Atlanta	NL	21	1	0	7	42	184	45	26	22	6	5	3	1	14	3	25	2	0	0	4	.000	0	0	4.71
1989 2 ML Teams		73	0	0	26	126	499	108	36	34	6	6	3	2	32	11	92	3	0	2	7	.222	0	2	2.43
1990 Toronto	AL	59	0	0	19	91.2	403	103	49	39	9	3	1	3	30	5	54	4	1	4	4	.500	0	1	3.83
1991 Toronto	AL	54	4	0	11	88.1	374	77	53	51	16	7	5	2	36	5	44	7	0	3	5	.375	0	1	5.20
1986 Toronto	AL	23	5	0	6	60	259	63	34	29	6	6	5	2	22	3	32	3	1	2	4	.333	0	0	4.35
Atlanta	NL	21	14	0	3	95	402	100	47	40	7	6	4	1	26	3	37	2	0	3	8	.273	0	0	3.79
1989 Atlanta	NL	59	0	0	23	97.2	383	84	29	29	5	5	3	1	20	8	68	2	0	0	6	.000	0	2	2.67
Toronto	AL	14	0	0	3	28.1	116	24	7	5	1	1	0	1	12	3	24	1	0	2	1	.667	0	0	1.59
9 ML YEARS		450	32	0	156	873.2	3720	873	428	381	78	42	29	32	317	39	471	30	2	33	49	.402	0	30	3.92

Troy Afenir

Bats: Right **Throws:** Right **Pos:** C   **Ht:** 6' 4" **Wt:** 195 **Born:** 09/21/63 **Age:** 28

								BATTING											BASERUNNING				PERCENTAGES		
Year Team	Lg	G	AB	H	2B	3B	HR	(Hm Rd)	TB	R	RBI	TBB	IBB	SO	HBP	SH	SF	SB	CS	SB%	GDP	Avg	OBP	SLG
1984 Asheville	A	115	358	69	16	0	16	-- --	133	44	69	39	1	125	2	4	6	1	2	.33	9	.193	.272	.372
1985 Osceola	A	99	323	80	19	1	6	-- --	119	38	41	20	1	86	0	2	2	3	1	.75	4	.248	.290	.368
1986 Columbus	AA	91	313	68	15	3	14	-- --	131	50	45	22	0	90	3	4	3	0	5	.00	6	.217	.273	.419
1987 Columbus	AA	31	99	20	8	0	2	-- --	34	15	11	6	0	20	0	2	0	0	0	.00	0	.202	.248	.343
Osceola	A	79	294	81	20	1	14	-- --	145	60	68	33	1	75	2	0	8	1	0	1.00	5	.276	.344	.493
1988 Columbus	AA	137	494	122	21	5	16	-- --	201	61	66	45	0	131	5	0	5	11	6	.65	6	.247	.313	.407
1989 Huntsville	AA	65	225	57	15	1	13	-- --	113	31	45	28	0	63	1	0	4	1	3	.25	3	.253	.333	.502
1990 Tacoma	AAA	88	289	72	14	2	15	-- --	135	44	47	30	0	81	1	4	1	1	1	.50	5	.249	.321	.467
1991 Tacoma	AAA	80	262	64	12	3	10	-- --	112	35	38	22	1	59	3	3	6	0	0	.00	5	.244	.304	.427
1987 Houston	NL	10	20	6	1	0	0	(0 0)	7	1	1	0	0	12	0	0	0	0	0	.00	0	.300	.300	.350
1990 Oakland	AL	14	14	2	0	0	0	(0 0)	2	0	2	0	0	6	0	0	1	0	0	.00	1	.143	.133	.143
1991 Oakland	AL	5	11	1	0	0	0	(0 0)	1	0	0	0	0	2	0	0	0	0	0	.00	0	.091	.091	.091
3 ML YEARS		29	45	9	1	0	0	(0 0)	10	1	3	0	0	20	0	0	1	0	0	.00	1	.200	.196	.222

Juan Agosto

Pitches: Left **Bats:** Left **Pos:** RP   **Ht:** 6' 2" **Wt:** 190 **Born:** 02/23/58 **Age:** 34

		HOW MUCH HE PITCHED						WHAT HE GAVE UP												THE RESULTS					
Year Team	Lg	G	GS	CG	GF	IP	BFP	H	R	ER	HR	SH	SF	HB	TBB	IBB	SO	WP	Bk	W	L	Pct.	ShO	Sv	ERA
1981 Chicago	AL	2	0	0	1	6	22	5	3	3	1	0	0	1	0	0	3	0	0	0	0	.000	0	0	4.50
1982 Chicago	AL	1	0	0	1	2	13	7	4	4	0	0	0	0	0	0	1	0	0	0	0	.000	0	0	18.00
1983 Chicago	AL	39	0	0	13	41.2	166	41	20	19	2	5	4	1	11	1	29	2	0	2	2	.500	0	7	4.10
1984 Chicago	AL	49	0	0	18	55.1	243	54	20	19	2	5	1	3	34	7	26	1	0	2	1	.667	0	7	3.09
1985 Chicago	AL	54	0	0	21	60.1	246	45	27	24	3	3	3	3	23	1	39	0	0	4	3	.571	0	1	3.58
1986 2 ML Teams		26	1	0	4	25	139	49	30	24	1	2	0	2	18	0	12	1	0	1	4	.200	0	1	8.64
1987 Houston	NL	27	0	0	13	27.1	118	26	12	8	1	3	0	0	10	1	6	1	0	1	1	.500	0	2	2.63
1988 Houston	NL	75	0	0	33	91.2	371	74	27	23	6	9	5	0	30	13	33	3	5	10	2	.833	0	4	2.26
1989 Houston	NL	71	0	0	28	83	361	81	32	27	3	5	6	2	32	10	46	4	1	4	5	.444	0	1	2.93
1990 Houston	NL	82	0	0	29	92.1	404	91	46	44	4	7	2	7	39	8	50	1	0	9	8	.529	0	4	4.29
1991 St. Louis	NL	72	0	0	22	86	377	92	52	46	4	11	3	8	39	4	34	6	0	5	3	.625	0	2	4.81
1986 Chicago	AL	9	0	0	1	4.2	24	6	5	4	0	0	0	0	4	0	3	0	0	0	2	.000	0	0	7.71
Minnesota	AL	17	1	0	3	20.1	115	43	25	20	1	2	0	2	14	0	9	1	0	1	2	.333	0	1	8.85
11 ML YEARS		498	1	0	183	570.2	2460	565	273	241	27	50	24	27	236	45	279	19	6	38	29	.567	0	29	3.80

Rick Aguilera

Pitches: Right **Bats:** Right **Pos:** RP   **Ht:** 6' 5" **Wt:** 205 **Born:** 12/31/61 **Age:** 30

		HOW MUCH HE PITCHED						WHAT HE GAVE UP												THE RESULTS					
Year Team	Lg	G	GS	CG	GF	IP	BFP	H	R	ER	HR	SH	SF	HB	TBB	IBB	SO	WP	Bk	W	L	Pct.	ShO	Sv	ERA
1985 New York	NL	21	19	2	1	122.1	507	118	49	44	8	7	4	2	37	2	74	5	2	10	7	.588	0	0	3.24
1986 New York	NL	28	20	2	2	141.2	605	145	70	61	15	6	5	7	36	1	104	5	3	10	7	.588	0	0	3.88
1987 New York	NL	18	17	1	0	115	494	124	53	46	12	7	2	3	33	2	77	9	0	11	3	.786	0	0	3.60
1988 New York	NL	11	3	0	2	24.2	111	29	20	19	2	2	0	1	10	2	16	1	1	0	4	.000	0	0	6.93
1989 2 ML Teams		47	11	3	19	145	594	130	51	45	8	7	1	3	38	4	137	4	3	9	11	.450	0	7	2.79
1990 Minnesota	AL	56	0	0	54	65.1	268	55	27	20	5	0	0	4	19	6	61	3	0	5	3	.625	0	32	2.76
1991 Minnesota	AL	63	0	0	60	69	275	44	20	18	3	1	1	3	30	6	61	4	0	4	5	.444	0	42	2.35
1989 New York	NL	36	0	0	19	69.1	284	59	19	18	3	5	1	2	21	3	80	3	3	6	6	.500	0	7	2.34
Minnesota	AL	11	11	3	0	75.2	310	71	32	27	5	2	0	1	17	1	57	1	0	3	5	.375	0	0	3.21
7 ML YEARS		244	70	8	138	683	2854	645	290	253	53	30	15	21	203	23	530	30	9	49	40	.551	0	81	3.33

Darrel Akerfelds

Pitches: Right **Bats:** Right **Pos:** RP   **Ht:** 6' 2" **Wt:** 218 **Born:** 06/12/62 **Age:** 30

		HOW MUCH HE PITCHED						WHAT HE GAVE UP												THE RESULTS					
Year Team	Lg	G	GS	CG	GF	IP	BFP	H	R	ER	HR	SH	SF	HB	TBB	IBB	SO	WP	Bk	W	L	Pct.	ShO	Sv	ERA
1986 Oakland	AL	2	0	0	2	5.1	26	7	5	4	2	0	0	0	3	1	5	2	0	0	0	.000	0	0	6.75
1987 Cleveland	AL	16	13	1	0	74.2	347	84	60	56	18	2	4	7	38	1	42	7	0	2	6	.250	0	0	6.75
1989 Texas	AL	6	0	0	2	11	50	11	6	4	1	0	1	0	5	2	9	1	0	0	1	.000	0	0	3.27
1990 Philadelphia	NL	71	0	0	18	93	395	65	45	39	10	9	5	3	54	8	42	7	1	5	2	.714	0	3	3.77
1991 Philadelphia	NL	30	0	0	11	49.2	229	49	30	29	5	6	2	3	27	4	31	4	0	2	1	.667	0	0	5.26
5 ML YEARS		125	13	1	33	233.2	1047	216	146	132	36	17	12	13	127	16	129	21	1	9	10	.474	0	3	5.08

Scott Aldred

Pitches: Left **Bats:** Left **Pos:** SP **Ht:** 6' 4" **Wt:** 215 **Born:** 06/12/68 **Age:** 24

Year Team	Lg	G	GS	CG	GF	IP	BFP	H	R	ER	HR	SH	SF	HB	TBB	IBB	SO	WP	Bk	W	L	Pct.	ShO	Sv	ERA
1987 Fayetteville	A	21	20	0	0	111	485	101	56	44	5	2	7	3	69	0	91	8	1	4	9	.308	0	0	3.57
1988 Lakeland	A	25	25	1	0	131.1	583	122	61	52	6	3	3	8	72	1	102	5	4	8	7	.533	1	0	3.56
1989 London	AA	20	20	3	0	122	513	98	55	52	11	3	3	5	59	0	97	9	2	10	6	.625	1	0	3.84
1990 Toledo	AAA	29	29	2	0	158	687	145	93	86	16	2	10	4	81	1	133	9	4	6	15	.286	0	0	4.90
1991 Toledo	AAA	22	20	2	2	135.1	581	127	65	59	7	8	3	4	72	1	95	4	0	8	8	.500	0	1	3.92
1990 Detroit	AL	4	3	0	0	14.1	63	13	6	6	0	2	1	1	10	1	7	0	0	1	2	.333	0	0	3.77
1991 Detroit	AL	11	11	1	0	57.1	253	58	37	33	9	3	2	0	30	2	35	3	1	2	4	.333	0	0	5.18
2 ML YEARS		15	14	1	0	71.2	316	71	43	39	9	5	3	1	40	3	42	3	1	3	6	.333	0	0	4.90

Mike Aldrete

Bats: Left **Throws:** Left **Pos:** 1B/LF **Ht:** 5'11" **Wt:** 185 **Born:** 01/29/61 **Age:** 31

Year Team	Lg	G	AB	H	2B	3B	HR	(Hm	Rd)	TB	R	RBI	TBB	IBB	SO	HBP	SH	SF	SB	CS	SB%	GDP	Avg	OBP	SLG
1986 San Francisco	NL	84	216	54	18	3	2	(1	1)	84	27	25	33	4	34	2	4	1	1	3	.25	3	.250	.353	.389
1987 San Francisco	NL	126	357	116	18	2	9	(7	2)	165	50	51	43	5	50	0	4	2	6	0	1.00	6	.325	.396	.462
1988 San Francisco	NL	139	389	104	15	0	3	(3	0)	128	44	50	56	13	65	0	1	3	6	5	.55	10	.267	.357	.329
1989 Montreal	NL	76	136	30	8	1	1	(0	1)	43	12	12	19	0	30	1	1	2	1	3	.25	4	.221	.316	.316
1990 Montreal	NL	96	161	39	7	1	1	(0	1)	51	22	18	37	2	31	1	0	1	1	2	.33	2	.242	.385	.317
1991 2 ML Teams		97	198	48	6	1	1	(0	1)	59	24	20	39	1	41	0	1	2	1	3	.25	1	.242	.364	.298
1991 San Diego	NL	12	15	0	0	0	0	(0	0)	0	2	1	3	0	4	0	0	0	0	1	.00	1	.000	.167	.000
Cleveland	AL	85	183	48	6	1	1	(0	1)	59	22	19	36	1	37	0	1	2	1	2	.33	0	.262	.380	.322
6 ML YEARS		618	1457	391	72	8	17	(11	6)	530	179	176	227	25	251	4	11	11	16	16	.50	26	.268	.366	.364

Gerald Alexander

Pitches: Right **Bats:** Right **Pos:** RP/SP **Ht:** 5'11" **Wt:** 190 **Born:** 03/26/68 **Age:** 24

Year Team	Lg	G	GS	CG	GF	IP	BFP	H	R	ER	HR	SH	SF	HB	TBB	IBB	SO	WP	Bk	W	L	Pct.	ShO	Sv	ERA
1989 Rangers	R	6	0	0	5	6.1	19	3	0	0	0	0	0	0	0	0	9	0	0	0	0	.000	0	4	0.00
Charlotte	A	14	6	0	5	53	215	36	12	10	1	2	1	2	16	0	41	5	0	2	3	.400	0	2	1.70
1990 Charlotte	A	7	7	0	0	42.2	163	24	7	3	0	0	0	1	14	0	39	2	0	6	1	.857	0	0	0.63
Okla City	AAA	20	20	2	0	118.2	510	126	58	54	6	2	4	3	45	0	94	6	1	13	2	.867	1	0	4.10
1991 Okla City	AAA	2	2	0	0	10.2	46	10	5	5	0	1	0	0	4	0	10	0	0	1	1	.500	0	0	4.22
1990 Texas	AL	3	2	0	1	7	39	14	6	6	0	0	1	1	5	0	8	0	0	0	0	.000	0	0	7.71
1991 Texas	AL	30	9	0	4	89.1	402	93	56	52	11	6	3	3	48	7	50	3	1	5	3	.625	0	0	5.24
2 ML YEARS		33	11	0	5	96.1	441	107	62	58	11	6	4	4	53	7	58	3	1	5	3	.625	0	0	5.42

Luis Alicea

Bats: Both **Throws:** Right **Pos:** 2B **Ht:** 5' 9" **Wt:** 165 **Born:** 07/29/65 **Age:** 26

Year Team	Lg	G	AB	H	2B	3B	HR	(Hm	Rd)	TB	R	RBI	TBB	IBB	SO	HBP	SH	SF	SB	CS	SB%	GDP	Avg	OBP	SLG
1988 St. Louis	NL	93	297	63	10	4	1	(1	0)	84	20	24	25	4	32	2	4	2	1	1	.50	12	.212	.276	.283
1991 St. Louis	NL	56	68	13	3	0	0	(0	0)	16	5	0	8	0	19	0	0	0	1	0	.00	0	.191	.276	.235
2 ML YEARS		149	365	76	13	4	1	(1	0)	100	25	24	33	4	51	2	4	2	2	1	.33	12	.208	.276	.274

Andy Allanson

Bats: Right **Throws:** Right **Pos:** C **Ht:** 6' 5" **Wt:** 220 **Born:** 12/22/61 **Age:** 30

Year Team	Lg	G	AB	H	2B	3B	HR	(Hm	Rd)	TB	R	RBI	TBB	IBB	SO	HBP	SH	SF	SB	CS	SB%	GDP	Avg	OBP	SLG
1986 Cleveland	AL	101	293	66	7	3	1	(0	1)	82	30	29	14	0	36	1	11	4	10	1	.91	7	.225	.260	.280
1987 Cleveland	AL	50	154	41	6	0	3	(2	1)	56	17	16	9	0	30	0	4	5	1	1	.50	2	.266	.298	.364
1988 Cleveland	AL	133	434	114	11	0	5	(4	1)	140	44	50	25	2	63	3	8	4	5	9	.36	6	.263	.305	.323
1989 Cleveland	AL	111	323	75	9	1	3	(1	2)	95	30	17	23	2	47	4	6	3	4	4	.50	7	.232	.289	.294
1991 Detroit	AL	60	151	35	10	0	1	(0	1)	48	10	16	7	0	31	0	2	0	1	0	.00	3	.232	.266	.318
5 ML YEARS		455	1355	331	43	4	13	(7	6)	421	131	128	78	4	207	8	31	16	20	16	.56	25	.244	.286	.311

Dana Allison

Pitches: Left **Bats:** Right **Pos:** RP **Ht:** 6' 3" **Wt:** 215 **Born:** 08/14/66 **Age:** 25

Year Team	Lg	G	GS	CG	GF	IP	BFP	H	R	ER	HR	SH	SF	HB	TBB	IBB	SO	WP	Bk	W	L	Pct.	ShO	Sv	ERA
1989 Madison	A	13	0	0	11	24	100	24	6	3	0	3	0	0	3	2	16	1	0	2	3	.400	0	1	1.13
Sou Oregon	A	11	2	0	6	29.1	108	17	8	6	0	0	1	1	4	0	27	2	1	0	2	.000	0	4	1.84

6

Year	Team	Lg	G	GS	CG	GF	IP	BFP	H	R	ER	HR	SH	SF	HB	TBB	IBB	SO	WP	Bk	W	L	Pct.	ShO	Sv	ERA
1990	Modesto	A	10	0	0	8	19.1	76	13	9	5	0	0	1	0	3	0	19	0	1	0	0	.000	0	4	2.33
	Huntsville	AA	35	0	0	14	52.2	216	52	14	14	2	7	2	0	6	3	36	1	0	7	1	.875	0	2	2.39
	Tacoma	AAA	2	0	0	1	1.1	6	1	0	0	0	0	0	0	1	0	2	0	0	0	0	.000	0	0	0.00
1991	Tacoma	AAA	18	0	0	4	22.2	101	25	12	11	2	2	0	1	11	2	13	0	1	3	1	.750	0	0	4.37
1991	Oakland	AL	11	0	0	4	11	49	16	9	9	0	1	1	0	5	1	4	0	0	1	1	.500	0	0	7.36

Beau Allred

Bats: Left **Throws:** Left **Pos:** RF/LF **Ht:** 6' 0" **Wt:** 193 **Born:** 06/04/65 **Age:** 27

							BATTING													BASERUNNING				PERCENTAGES		
Year	Team	Lg	G	AB	H	2B	3B	HR	(Hm	Rd)	TB	R	RBI	TBB	IBB	SO	HBP	SH	SF	SB	CS	SB%	GDP	Avg	OBP	SLG
1987	Burlington	R	54	167	57	14	1	10	--	--	103	39	38	35	3	33	1	2	4	4	0	1.00		.341	.449	.617
1988	Kinston	A	126	397	100	23	3	15	--	--	174	66	74	59	4	112	5	0	8	6	0	1.00	5	.252	.350	.438
1989	Canton-Akrn	AA	118	412	125	23	5	14	--	--	200	67	75	56	2	88	2	2	8	16	5	.76	8	.303	.383	.485
	Colo Sprngs	AAA	11	47	13	3	0	1	--	--	19	8	4	2	1	10	0	0	0	0	3	.00	2	.277	.306	.404
1990	Colo Sprngs	AAA	115	378	105	23	6	13	--	--	179	79	74	60	1	54	4	2	7	6	3	.67	5	.278	.376	.474
1991	Colo Sprngs	AAA	53	148	37	12	3	6	--	--	73	39	21	34	1	55	3	0	2	1	1	.50	0	.250	.396	.493
1989	Cleveland	AL	13	24	6	3	0	0	(0	0)	9	0	1	2	0	10	0	0	0	0	0	.00	0	.250	.308	.375
1990	Cleveland	AL	4	16	3	1	0	1	(0	1)	7	2	2	2	0	3	0	0	0	0	0	.00	0	.188	.278	.438
1991	Cleveland	AL	48	125	29	3	0	3	(0	3)	41	17	12	25	2	35	1	3	2	2	2	.50	2	.232	.359	.328
3 ML YEARS			65	165	38	7	0	4	(0	4)	57	19	15	29	2	48	1	3	2	2	2	.50	2	.230	.345	.345

Roberto Alomar

Bats: Both **Throws:** Right **Pos:** 2B **Ht:** 6' 0" **Wt:** 175 **Born:** 02/05/68 **Age:** 24

							BATTING													BASERUNNING				PERCENTAGES		
Year	Team	Lg	G	AB	H	2B	3B	HR	(Hm	Rd)	TB	R	RBI	TBB	IBB	SO	HBP	SH	SF	SB	CS	SB%	GDP	Avg	OBP	SLG
1988	San Diego	NL	143	545	145	24	6	9	(5	4)	208	84	41	47	5	83	3	16	0	24	6	.80	15	.266	.328	.382
1989	San Diego	NL	158	623	184	27	1	7	(3	4)	234	82	56	53	4	76	1	17	8	42	17	.71	10	.295	.347	.376
1990	San Diego	NL	147	586	168	27	5	6	(4	2)	223	80	60	48	1	72	2	5	5	24	7	.77	16	.287	.340	.381
1991	Toronto	AL	161	637	188	41	11	9	(6	3)	278	88	69	57	3	86	4	16	5	53	11	.83	5	.295	.354	.436
4 ML YEARS			609	2391	685	119	23	31	(18	13)	943	334	226	205	13	317	10	54	18	143	41	.78	46	.286	.343	.394

Sandy Alomar Jr

Bats: Right **Throws:** Right **Pos:** C **Ht:** 6' 5" **Wt:** 215 **Born:** 06/18/66 **Age:** 26

							BATTING													BASERUNNING				PERCENTAGES		
Year	Team	Lg	G	AB	H	2B	3B	HR	(Hm	Rd)	TB	R	RBI	TBB	IBB	SO	HBP	SH	SF	SB	CS	SB%	GDP	Avg	OBP	SLG
1988	San Diego	NL	1	1	0	0	0	0	(0	0)	0	0	0	0	0	1	0	0	0	0	0	.00	0	.000	.000	.000
1989	San Diego	NL	7	19	4	1	0	1	(1	0)	8	1	6	3	1	3	0	0	0	0	0	.00	1	.211	.318	.421
1990	Cleveland	AL	132	445	129	26	2	9	(5	4)	186	60	66	25	2	46	2	5	6	4	1	.80	10	.290	.326	.418
1991	Cleveland	AL	51	184	40	9	0	0	(0	0)	49	10	7	8	1	24	2	2	1	0	4	.00	4	.217	.264	.266
4 ML YEARS			191	649	173	36	2	10	(6	4)	243	71	79	36	4	74	6	7	7	4	5	.44	15	.267	.308	.374

Wilson Alvarez

Pitches: Left **Bats:** Left **Pos:** SP **Ht:** 6' 1" **Wt:** 175 **Born:** 03/24/70 **Age:** 22

			HOW MUCH HE PITCHED						WHAT HE GAVE UP												THE RESULTS				
Year	Team	Lg	G	GS	CG	GF	IP	BFP	H	R	ER	HR	SH	SF	HB	TBB	IBB	SO	WP	Bk	W	L	Pct.	ShO	Sv	ERA
1987	Gastonia	A	8	6	0	1	32	153	39	24	23	5	0	1	4	23	0	19	0	0	1	5	.167	0	0	6.47
	Rangers	R	10	10	0	0	44.2	193	41	29	26	6	1	1	3	21	0	46	3	0	2	5	.286	0	0	5.24
1988	Gastonia	A	23	23	1	0	127	552	113	63	42	5	4	6	7	49	1	134	5	10	4	11	.267	0	0	2.98
	Okla City	AAA	5	3	0	1	16.2	71	17	8	7	2	0	2	1	6	0	9	0	0	1	1	.500	0	0	3.78
1989	Charlotte	A	13	13	3	0	81	331	68	29	19	2	3	3	4	21	0	51	4	0	7	4	.636	2	0	2.11
	Tulsa	AA	7	7	1	0	48	196	40	14	11	1	2	2	0	16	3	29	1	4	2	2	.500	1	0	2.06
	Birmingham	AA	6	6	0	0	35.2	193	32	12	12	2	2	0	1	16	0	18	1	1	2	1	.667	0	0	3.03
1990	Vancouver	AAA	17	15	1	0	75	350	91	54	50	7	2	3	4	51	0	35	1	2	7	7	.500	0	0	6.00
	Birmingham	AA	7	7	1	0	46.1	204	44	24	22	5	0	0	0	25	0	36	2	2	5	1	.833	0	0	4.27
1991	Birmingham	AA	23	23	3	0	152.1	634	109	46	31	6	7	3	3	74	0	165	9	3	10	6	.625	0	0	1.83
1989	Texas	AL	1	1	0	0	0	5	3	3	3	2	0	0	0	2	0	0	0	0	0	1	.000	0	0	0.00
1991	Chicago	AL	10	9	2	0	56.1	237	47	26	22	9	3	1	0	29	0	32	2	0	3	2	.600	0	0	3.51
2 ML YEARS			11	10	2	0	56.1	242	50	29	25	11	3	1	0	31	0	32	2	0	3	3	.500	0	0	3.99

Rich Amaral

Bats: Right **Throws:** Right **Pos:** 2B **Ht:** 6' 0" **Wt:** 175 **Born:** 04/01/62 **Age:** 30

							BATTING													BASERUNNING				PERCENTAGES		
Year	Team	Lg	G	AB	H	2B	3B	HR	(Hm	Rd)	TB	R	RBI	TBB	IBB	SO	HBP	SH	SF	SB	CS	SB%	GDP	Avg	OBP	SLG
1984	Quad City	A	34	119	25	1	0	0	--	--	26	21	7	24	0	29	1	0	0	12	0	1.00	0	.210	.343	.218
1985	Winston-Sal	A	124	428	116	15	5	3	--	--	150	62	36	59	1	68	2	5	1	26	7	.79	11	.271	.361	.350
1986	Pittsfield	AA	114	355	89	12	0	0	--	--	101	43	24	39	1	65	4	5	2	25	8	.76	5	.251	.330	.285
1987	Pittsfield	AA	104	315	80	8	5	0	--	--	98	45	28	43	2	50	3	6	1	28	6	.82	1	.254	.348	.311

Year Team	Lg	G	AB	H	2B	3B	HR	(Hm	Rd)	TB	R	RBI	TBB	IBB	SO	HBP	SH	SF	SB	CS	SB%	GDP	Avg	OBP	SLG
1988 Pittsfield	AA	122	422	117	15	4	4	--	--	152	66	47	56	1	53	1	5	5	54	5	.92	2	.277	.360	.360
1989 Birmingham	AA	122	432	123	15	6	4	--	--	162	90	48	88	2	66	2	7	4	57	14	.80	6	.285	.405	.375
1990 Vancouver	AAA	130	462	139	39	5	4	--	--	200	87	56	88	3	68	4	9	4	20	14	.59	4	.301	.414	.433
1991 Calgary	AAA	86	347	120	26	2	3	--	--	159	79	36	53	0	37	3	3	3	30	8	.79	6	.346	.433	.458
1991 Seattle	AL	14	16	1	0	0	0	(0	0)	1	2	0	1	0	5	1	0	0	0	0	.00	1	.063	.167	.063

Ruben Amaro

Bats: Both **Throws:** Right **Pos:** 2B   **Ht:** 5'10" **Wt:** 170 **Born:** 02/12/65 **Age:** 27

							BATTING												BASERUNNING				PERCENTAGES		
Year Team	Lg	G	AB	H	2B	3B	HR	(Hm	Rd)	TB	R	RBI	TBB	IBB	SO	HBP	SH	SF	SB	CS	SB%	GDP	Avg	OBP	SLG
1987 Salem	A	71	241	68	7	3	3	--	--	90	51	31	49	5	28	7	3	6	27	11	.71	5	.282	.409	.373
1988 Midland	AA	13	31	4	1	0	0	--	--	5	5	2	4	0	5	1	0	0	4	0	1.00	1	.129	.250	.161
Palm Sprngs	A	115	417	111	13	3	4	--	--	142	96	50	105	2	61	8	5	2	44	20	.69	13	.266	.421	.341
1989 Quad City	A	59	200	72	9	4	3	--	--	98	50	27	42	4	25	7	0	1	20	8	.71	5	.360	.484	.490
Midland	AA	29	110	42	9	2	3	--	--	64	28	9	10	1	19	1	2	2	7	1	.88	0	.382	.431	.582
1990 Midland	AA	57	224	80	15	6	4	--	--	119	50	38	29	1	23	9	2	2	8	8	.50	4	.357	.447	.531
Edmonton	AAA	82	318	92	15 .	4	3	--	--	124	53	32	40	2	43	7	5	3	32	14	.70	2	.289	.378	.390
1991 Edmonton	AAA	121	472	154	42	6	3	--	--	217	95	42	63	2	50	6	9	2	36	18	.67	6	.326	.411	.460
1991 California	AL	10	23	5	1	0	0	(0	0)	6	0	2	3	1	3	0	0	0	0	0	.00	1	.217	.308	.261

Larry Andersen

Pitches: Right **Bats:** Right **Pos:** RP   **Ht:** 6'3" **Wt:** 205 **Born:** 05/06/53 **Age:** 39

		HOW MUCH HE PITCHED						WHAT HE GAVE UP										THE RESULTS					
Year Team	Lg	G	GS	CG	GF	IP	BFP	H	R	ER	HR	SH	SF	HB	TBB	IBB	SO	WP	Bk	W	L	Pct.	ShO	Sv	ERA
1975 Cleveland	AL	3	0	0	1	6	23	4	3	3	0	0	1	0	2	0	4	2	0	0	0	.000	0	0	4.50
1977 Cleveland	AL	11	0	0	7	14	62	10	7	5	1	3	0	0	9	3	8	1	0	0	1	.000	0	0	3.21
1979 Cleveland	AL	8	0	0	4	17	77	25	14	14	3	1	2	0	4	0	7	0	0	0	0	.000	0	0	7.41
1981 Seattle	AL	41	0	0	23	68	273	57	27	20	4	0	3	2	18	2	40	0	0	3	3	.500	0	5	2.65
1982 Seattle	AL	40	1	0	14	79.2	354	100	56	53	16	2	3	4	23	1	32	2	0	0	0	.000	0	1	5.99
1983 Philadelphia	NL	17	0	0	4	26.1	106	19	7	7	0	1	1	0	9	1	14	1	1	1	0	1.000	0	0	2.39
1984 Philadelphia	NL	64	0	0	25	90.2	376	85	32	24	5	4	4	0	25	6	54	2	1	3	7	.300	0	4	2.38
1985 Philadelphia	NL	57	0	0	19	73	318	78	41	35	5	3	1	3	26	4	50	1	1	3	3	.500	0	3	4.32
1986 2 ML Teams		48	0	0	8	77.1	323	83	30	26	2	10	5	1	26	10	42	1	0	2	1	.667	0	1	3.03
1987 Houston	NL	67	0	0	31	101.2	440	95	46	39	7	7	4	2	41	10	94	1	1	9	5	.643	0	5	3.45
1988 Houston	NL	53	0	0	25	82.2	350	82	29	27	3	3	3	1	20	8	66	1	2	2	4	.333	0	5	2.94
1989 Houston	NL	60	0	0	21	87.2	351	63	19	15	2	4	5	0	24	4	85	2	1	4	4	.500	0	3	1.54
1990 2 ML Teams		65	0	0	24	95.2	387	79	22	19	2	5	5	2	27	5	93	4	0	5	2	.714	0	7	1.79
1991 San Diego	NL	38	0	0	24	47	188	39	13	12	0	4	2	0	13	3	40	1	0	3	4	.429	0	13	2.30
1986 Philadelphia	NL	10	0	0	1	12.2	55	19	8	6	0	2	1	0	3	0	9	0	0	0	0	.000	0	0	4.26
Houston	NL	38	0	0	7	64.2	268	64	22	20	2	8	4	1	23	10	33	1	0	2	1	.667	0	1	2.78
1990 Houston	NL	50	0	0	20	73.2	301	61	19	16	2	5	5	1	24	5	68	2	0	5	2	.714	0	6	1.95
Boston	AL	15	0	0	4	22	86	18	3	3	0	0	0	1	3	0	25	2	0	0	0	.000	0	1	1.23
14 ML YEARS		572	1	0	230	866.2	3628	819	346	299	50	47	39	15	267	57	629	19	9	35	34	.507	0	47	3.11

Allan Anderson

Pitches: Left **Bats:** Left **Pos:** SP/RP   **Ht:** 6'0" **Wt:** 201 **Born:** 01/07/64 **Age:** 28

		HOW MUCH HE PITCHED						WHAT HE GAVE UP										THE RESULTS					
Year Team	Lg	G	GS	CG	GF	IP	BFP	H	R	ER	HR	SH	SF	HB	TBB	IBB	SO	WP	Bk	W	L	Pct.	ShO	Sv	ERA
1986 Minnesota	AL	21	10	1	3	84.1	371	106	54	52	11	2	3	1	30	3	51	2	2	3	6	.333	0	0	5.55
1987 Minnesota	AL	4	2	0	0	12.1	61	20	15	15	3	0	0	0	10	2	3	0	0	1	0	1.000	0	0	10.95
1988 Minnesota	AL	30	30	3	0	202.1	815	199	70	55	14	3	5	7	37	1	83	1	4	16	9	.640	1	0	2.45
1989 Minnesota	AL	33	33	4	0	196.2	846	214	97	83	15	4	5	7	53	1	69	5	0	17	10	.630	1	0	3.80
1990 Minnesota	AL	31	31	5	0	188.2	797	214	106	95	20	4	8	5	39	1	82	4	3	7	18	.280	1	0	4.53
1991 Minnesota	AL	29	22	2	4	134.1	584	148	82	74	24	4	6	5	42	4	51	3	0	5	11	.313	0	0	4.96
6 ML YEARS		148	128	15	7	818.2	3474	901	424	374	87	17	27	25	211	12	339	15	9	49	54	.476	3	0	4.11

Brady Anderson

Bats: Left **Throws:** Left **Pos:** LF/CF   **Ht:** 6'1" **Wt:** 185 **Born:** 01/18/64 **Age:** 28

							BATTING												BASERUNNING				PERCENTAGES		
Year Team	Lg	G	AB	H	2B	3B	HR	(Hm	Rd)	TB	R	RBI	TBB	IBB	SO	HBP	SH	SF	SB	CS	SB%	GDP	Avg	OBP	SLG
1988 2 ML Teams		94	325	69	13	4	1	(1	0)	93	31	21	23	0	75	4	11	1	10	6	.63	3	.212	.272	.286
1989 Baltimore	AL	94	266	55	12	2	4	(2	2)	83	44	16	43	6	45	3	5	0	16	4	.80	4	.207	.324	.312
1990 Baltimore	AL	89	234	54	5	2	3	(1	2)	72	24	24	31	2	46	5	4	5	15	2	.88	5	.231	.327	.308
1991 Baltimore	AL	113	256	59	12	3	2	(1	1)	83	40	27	38	0	44	5	11	3	12	5	.71	1	.230	.338	.324
1988 Boston	AL	41	148	34	5	3	0	(0	0)	45	14	12	15	0	35	4	4	1	4	2	.67	2	.230	.315	.304
Baltimore	AL	53	177	35	8	1	1	(1	0)	48	17	9	8	0	40	0	7	0	6	4	.60	1	.198	.232	.271
4 ML YEARS		390	1081	237	42	11	10	(5	5)	331	139	88	135	8	210	17	31	9	53	17	.76	13	.219	.313	.306

Dave Anderson

Bats: Right **Throws:** Right **Pos:** SS/1B **Ht:** 6' 2" **Wt:** 184 **Born:** 08/01/60 **Age:** 31

Year	Team	Lg	G	AB	H	2B	3B	HR	(Hm	Rd)	TB	R	RBI	TBB	IBB	SO	HBP	SH	SF	SB	CS	SB%	GDP	Avg	OBP	SLG
1983	Los Angeles	NL	61	115	19	4	2	1	(1	0)	30	12	2	12	1	15	0	4	0	6	3	.67	1	.165	.244	.261
1984	Los Angeles	NL	121	374	94	16	2	3	(2	1)	123	51	34	45	4	55	2	7	5	15	5	.75	8	.251	.331	.329
1985	Los Angeles	NL	77	221	44	6	0	4	(1	3)	62	24	18	35	3	42	1	4	1	5	4	.56	4	.199	.310	.281
1986	Los Angeles	NL	92	216	53	9	0	1	(0	1)	65	31	15	22	1	39	0	2	1	5	1	.83	11	.245	.314	.301
1987	Los Angeles	NL	108	265	62	12	3	1	(0	1)	83	32	13	24	1	43	1	6	1	9	5	.64	2	.234	.299	.313
1988	Los Angeles	NL	116	285	71	10	2	2	(1	1)	91	31	20	32	4	45	1	5	2	4	2	.67	9	.249	.325	.319
1989	Los Angeles	NL	87	140	32	2	0	1	(1	0)	37	15	14	17	1	26	0	5	1	2	0	1.00	1	.229	.310	.264
1990	San Francisco	NL	60	100	35	5	1	1	(1	0)	45	14	6	3	0	20	0	1	0	1	2	.33	2	.350	.369	.450
1991	San Francisco	NL	100	226	56	5	2	2	(1	1)	71	24	13	12	2	35	0	2	0	2	4	.33	8	.248	.286	.314
9 ML YEARS			822	1942	466	69	12	16	(8	8)	607	234	135	202	17	320	5	36	11	49	26	.65	46	.240	.312	.313

Eric Anthony

Bats: Left **Throws:** Left **Pos:** RF **Ht:** 6' 2" **Wt:** 195 **Born:** 11/08/67 **Age:** 24

Year	Team	Lg	G	AB	H	2B	3B	HR	(Hm	Rd)	TB	R	RBI	TBB	IBB	SO	HBP	SH	SF	SB	CS	SB%	GDP	Avg	OBP	SLG
1989	Houston	NL	25	61	11	2	0	4	(2	2)	25	7	7	9	2	16	0	0	0	0	0	.00	1	.180	.286	.410
1990	Houston	NL	84	239	46	8	0	10	(5	5)	84	26	29	29	3	78	2	1	6	5	0	1.00	4	.192	.279	.351
1991	Houston	NL	39	118	18	6	0	1	(0	1)	27	11	7	12	1	41	0	0	2	1	0	1.00	2	.153	.227	.229
3 ML YEARS			148	418	75	16	0	15	(7	8)	136	44	43	50	6	135	2	1	8	6	0	1.00	7	.179	.266	.325

Kevin Appier

Pitches: Right **Bats:** Right **Pos:** SP **Ht:** 6' 2" **Wt:** 200 **Born:** 12/06/67 **Age:** 24

			HOW	MUCH	HE	PITCHED			WHAT	HE	GAVE	UP					THE	RESULTS			
Year	Team	Lg	G	GS	CG	GF	IP	BFP	H	R	ER	HR	SH	SF	HB	TBB	IBB	SO	WP	Bk	W	L	Pct.	ShO	Sv	ERA
1989	Kansas City	AL	6	5	0	0	21.2	106	34	22	22	3	0	3	0	12	1	10	0	0	1	4	.200	0	0	9.14
1990	Kansas City	AL	32	24	3	1	185.2	784	179	67	57	13	5	9	6	54	2	127	6	1	12	8	.600	3	0	2.76
1991	Kansas City	AL	34	31	6	1	207.2	881	205	97	79	13	8	6	2	61	3	158	7	1	13	10	.565	3	0	3.42
3 ML YEARS			72	60	9	2	415	1771	418	186	158	29	13	18	8	127	6	295	13	2	26	22	.542	6	0	3.43

Luis Aquino

Pitches: Right **Bats:** Right **Pos:** RP/SP **Ht:** 6' 1" **Wt:** 195 **Born:** 05/19/65 **Age:** 27

Year	Team	Lg	G	GS	CG	GF	IP	BFP	H	R	ER	HR	SH	SF	HB	TBB	IBB	SO	WP	Bk	W	L	Pct.	ShO	Sv	ERA
1986	Toronto	AL	7	0	0	3	11.1	50	14	8	8	2	0	1	0	3	1	5	1	0	1	1	.500	0	0	6.35
1988	Kansas City	AL	7	5	1	0	29	136	33	15	9	1	0	1	1	17	0	11	1	1	1	0	1.000	1	0	2.79
1989	Kansas City	AL	34	16	2	1	141.1	591	148	62	55	6	2	4	4	35	4	68	4	0	6	8	.429	1	0	3.50
1990	Kansas City	AL	20	3	1	3	68.1	287	59	25	24	6	5	2	4	27	6	28	3	1	4	1	.800	0	0	3.16
1991	Kansas City	AL	38	18	1	9	157	661	152	67	60	10	2	7	4	47	5	80	1	0	8	4	.667	1	3	3.44
5 ML YEARS			106	42	5	22	407	1725	406	177	156	25	9	15	13	129	16	192	10	2	20	14	.588	3	3	3.45

Jack Armstrong

Pitches: Right **Bats:** Right **Pos:** SP **Ht:** 6' 5" **Wt:** 215 **Born:** 03/07/65 **Age:** 27

Year	Team	Lg	G	GS	CG	GF	IP	BFP	H	R	ER	HR	SH	SF	HB	TBB	IBB	SO	WP	Bk	W	L	Pct.	ShO	Sv	ERA
1988	Cincinnati	NL	14	13	0	0	65.1	293	63	44	42	8	4	5	0	38	2	45	3	2	4	7	.364	0	0	5.79
1989	Cincinnati	NL	9	8	0	1	42.2	187	40	24	22	5	2	1	0	21	4	23	0	0	2	3	.400	0	0	4.64
1990	Cincinnati	NL	29	27	2	1	166	704	151	72	63	9	8	5	6	59	7	110	7	5	12	9	.571	1	0	3.42
1991	Cincinnati	NL	27	24	1	1	139.2	611	158	90	85	25	6	9	2	54	2	93	2	1	7	13	.350	0	0	5.48
4 ML YEARS			79	72	3	3	413.2	1795	412	230	212	47	20	20	8	172	15	271	12	8	25	32	.439	1	0	4.61

Brad Arnsberg

Pitches: Right **Bats:** Right **Pos:** RP **Ht:** 6' 4" **Wt:** 210 **Born:** 08/20/63 **Age:** 28

Year	Team	Lg	G	GS	CG	GF	IP	BFP	H	R	ER	HR	SH	SF	HB	TBB	IBB	SO	WP	Bk	W	L	Pct.	ShO	Sv	ERA
1986	New York	AL	2	1	0	1	8	39	13	3	3	1	0	0	0	1	0	3	0	0	0	0	.000	0	0	3.38
1987	New York	AL	6	2	0	2	19.1	91	22	12	12	5	0	2	0	13	3	14	1	0	1	3	.250	0	0	5.59
1989	Texas	AL	16	1	0	3	48	209	45	27	22	6	1	1	3	22	0	26	6	2	2	1	.667	0	1	4.13
1990	Texas	AL	53	0	0	20	62.2	277	56	20	15	4	2	2	2	33	1	44	8	1	6	1	.857	0	5	2.15
1991	Texas	AL	9	0	0	2	9.2	44	10	9	9	5	0	0	0	5	0	8	1	1	0	1	.000	0	0	8.38
5 ML YEARS			86	4	0	28	147.2	660	146	71	61	21	3	5	5	74	4	95	16	3	9	6	.600	0	6	3.72

Andy Ashby

Pitches: Right **Bats:** Right **Pos:** SP **Ht:** 6' 5" **Wt:** 180 **Born:** 07/11/67 **Age:** 24

Year Team	Lg	G	GS	CG	GF	IP	BFP	H	R	ER	HR	SH	SF	HB	TBB	IBB	SO	WP	Bk	W	L	Pct.	ShO	Sv	ERA
1986 Bend	A	16	6	0	4	60	0	56	40	33	3	0	0	2	34	1	45	3	1	1	2	.333	0	2	4.95
1987 Spartanburg	A	13	13	1	0	64.1	301	73	45	40	8	3	1	2	38	2	52	9	1	4	6	.400	0	0	5.60
Utica	A	13	13	0	0	60	264	56	38	27	3	2	1	1	36	3	51	7	0	3	7	.300	0	0	4.05
1988 Batavia	A	6	6	2	0	44.2	174	25	11	8	3	2	0	1	16	0	32	0	2	3	1	.750	1	0	1.61
Spartanburg	A	3	3	0	0	16.2	68	13	7	5	0	0	0	0	7	0	16	2	3	1	1	.500	0	0	2.70
1989 Spartanburg	A	17	17	3	0	106.2	463	95	48	34	8	3	0	5	49	0	100	8	0	5	9	.357	1	0	2.87
Clearwater	A	6	6	2	0	43.2	173	28	9	6	0	1	0	0	21	0	44	4	1	1	4	.200	1	0	1.24
1990 Reading	AA	23	23	4	0	139.2	591	134	65	53	3	5	4	4	48	0	94	10	2	10	7	.588	1	0	3.42
1991 Scranton-Wb	AAA	26	26	6	0	161.1	691	144	78	62	12	3	4	9	60	2	113	6	0	11	11	.500	3	0	3.46
1991 Philadelphia	NL	8	8	0	0	42	186	41	28	28	5	1	3	3	19	0	26	6	0	1	5	.167	0	0	6.00

Paul Assenmacher

Pitches: Left **Bats:** Left **Pos:** RP **Ht:** 6' 3" **Wt:** 200 **Born:** 12/10/60 **Age:** 31

Year Team	Lg	G	GS	CG	GF	IP	BFP	H	R	ER	HR	SH	SF	HB	TBB	IBB	SO	WP	Bk	W	L	Pct.	ShO	Sv	ERA
1986 Atlanta	NL	61	0	0	27	68.1	287	61	23	19	5	7	1	0	26	4	56	2	3	7	3	.700	0	7	2.50
1987 Atlanta	NL	52	0	0	10	54.2	251	58	41	31	8	2	1	1	24	4	39	0	0	1	1	.500	0	2	5.10
1988 Atlanta	NL	64	0	0	32	79.1	329	72	28	27	4	8	1	1	32	11	71	7	0	8	7	.533	0	5	3.06
1989 2 ML Teams		63	0	0	17	76.2	331	74	37	34	3	9	3	1	28	8	79	3	1	3	4	.429	0	0	3.99
1990 Chicago	NL	74	1	0	21	103	426	90	33	32	10	10	3	1	36	8	95	2	0	7	2	.778	0	10	2.80
1991 Chicago	NL	75	0	0	31	102.2	427	85	41	37	10	8	4	3	31	6	117	4	0	7	8	.467	0	15	3.24
1989 Atlanta	NL	49	0	0	14	57.2	247	55	26	23	2	7	2	1	16	7	64	3	1	1	3	.250	0	0	3.59
Chicago	NL	14	0	0	3	19	84	19	11	11	1	2	1	0	12	1	15	0	0	2	1	.667	0	0	5.21
6 ML YEARS		389	1	0	138	484.2	2051	440	203	180	40	44	13	7	177	41	457	18	4	33	25	.569	0	39	3.34

Don August

Pitches: Right **Bats:** Right **Pos:** SP/RP **Ht:** 6' 3" **Wt:** 190 **Born:** 07/03/63 **Age:** 28

Year Team	Lg	G	GS	CG	GF	IP	BFP	H	R	ER	HR	SH	SF	HB	TBB	IBB	SO	WP	Bk	W	L	Pct.	ShO	Sv	ERA
1988 Milwaukee	AL	24	22	6	0	148.1	614	137	55	51	12	4	3	0	48	6	66	5	0	13	7	.650	1	0	3.09
1989 Milwaukee	AL	31	25	2	2	142.1	648	175	93	84	17	2	7	2	58	2	51	3	1	12	12	.500	1	0	5.31
1990 Milwaukee	AL	5	0	0	1	11	51	13	10	8	0	2	0	0	5	0	2	2	0	0	3	.000	0	0	6.55
1991 Milwaukee	AL	28	23	1	3	138.1	613	166	87	84	18	9	3	3	47	2	62	5	0	9	8	.529	1	0	5.47
4 ML YEARS		88	70	9	6	440	1926	491	245	227	47	17	13	5	158	10	181	15	1	34	30	.531	3	0	4.64

Jim Austin

Pitches: Right **Bats:** Right **Pos:** RP **Ht:** 6' 2" **Wt:** 200 **Born:** 12/07/63 **Age:** 28

Year Team	Lg	G	GS	CG	GF	IP	BFP	H	R	ER	HR	SH	SF	HB	TBB	IBB	SO	WP	Bk	W	L	Pct.	ShO	Sv	ERA
1986 Spokane	A	28	0	0	19	59.2	0	53	24	15	1	0	0	1	22	2	74	7	0	5	4	.556	0	5	2.26
1987 Chston-Sc	A	31	21	2	3	152	642	138	89	71	10	4	1	1	56	2	123	20	1	7	10	.412	1	0	4.20
1988 Riverside	A	12	12	2	0	80	333	65	31	24	5	2	3	0	35	0	73	2	0	6	2	.750	1	0	2.70
Wichita	AA	12	12	4	0	73	313	76	46	39	9	2	3	0	23	0	52	10	0	5	6	.455	1	0	4.81
1989 Stockton	A	7	7	0	0	48.1	204	51	19	14	3	2	1	0	14	0	44	2	0	3	3	.500	0	0	2.61
El Paso	AA	22	13	2	5	85	406	121	60	55	6	2	3	4	34	1	69	4	0	3	10	.231	0	1	5.82
1990 El Paso	AA	38	3	0	24	92.1	384	91	36	25	5	2	3	1	26	4	77	8	0	11	3	.786	0	6	2.44
1991 Denver	AAA	20	3	0	10	44	184	35	12	12	4	2	0	2	24	3	37	1	0	6	3	.667	0	3	2.45
1991 Milwaukee	AL	5	0	0	1	8.2	46	8	8	8	1	2	1	3	11	1	3	1	0	0	0	.000	0	0	8.31

Steve Avery

Pitches: Left **Bats:** Left **Pos:** SP **Ht:** 6' 4" **Wt:** 190 **Born:** 04/14/70 **Age:** 22

Year Team	Lg	G	GS	CG	GF	IP	BFP	H	R	ER	HR	SH	SF	HB	TBB	IBB	SO	WP	Bk	W	L	Pct.	ShO	Sv	ERA
1988 Pulaski	R	10	10	3	0	66	249	38	16	11	2	1	1	1	19	0	80	5	1	7	1	.875	2	0	1.50
1989 Durham	A	13	13	0	0	86.2	337	59	22	14	5	5	0	1	20	1	90	4	1	6	4	.600	1	0	1.45
Greenville	AA	13	13	1	0	84.1	341	68	32	26	3	4	1	1	34	0	75	4	0	6	3	.667	0	0	2.77
1990 Richmond	AAA	13	13	3	0	82.1	343	85	35	32	7	6	2	2	21	0	69	5	0	5	5	.500	0	0	3.50
1990 Atlanta	NL	21	20	1	1	99	466	121	79	62	7	14	4	2	45	2	75	5	1	3	11	.214	1	0	5.64
1991 Atlanta	NL	35	35	3	0	210.1	868	189	89	79	21	8	4	3	65	0	137	4	1	18	8	.692	1	0	3.38
2 ML YEARS		56	55	4	1	309.1	1334	310	168	141	28	22	8	5	110	2	212	9	2	21	19	.525	2	0	4.10

Oscar Azocar

Bats: Left **Throws:** Left **Pos:** LF **Ht:** 6' 1" **Wt:** 195 **Born:** 02/21/65 **Age:** 27

Year Team	Lg	G	AB	H	2B	3B	HR	(Hm	Rd)	TB	R	RBI	TBB	IBB	SO	HBP	SH	SF	SB	CS	SB%	GDP	Avg	OBP	SLG
1987 Ft.Laudrdle	A	53	192	69	11	3	6	--	--	104	25	39	3	0	18	0	0	0	5	5	.50	6	.359	.369	.542
1988 Albany	AA	138	543	148	22	9	6	--	--	206	60	66	12	6	48	2	4	4	21	6	.78	15	.273	.289	.379
1989 Albany	AA	92	362	101	15	2	4	--	--	132	50	47	10	4	31	0	8	4	11	6	.65	6	.279	.295	.365
Columbus	AAA	37	130	38	9	3	1	--	--	56	14	12	7	0	10	1	1	0	3	1	.75	1	.292	.333	.431
1990 Columbus	AAA	94	374	109	20	5	5	--	--	154	49	52	9	2	26	2	4	7	8	8	.50	15	.291	.306	.412
1991 Las Vegas	AAA	107	361	107	23	3	7	--	--	157	51	50	21	3	26	1	1	5	4	4	.50	12	.296	.332	.435
1990 New York	AL	65	214	53	8	0	5	(3	2)	76	18	19	2	0	15	1	0	1	7	0	1.00	1	.248	.257	.355
1991 San Diego	NL	38	57	14	2	0	0	(0	0)	16	5	9	1	1	9	1	0	1	2	0	1.00	1	.246	.267	.281
2 ML YEARS		103	271	67	10	0	5	(3	2)	92	23	28	3	1	24	2	0	2	9	0	1.00	2	.247	.259	.339

Wally Backman

Bats: Both **Throws:** Right **Pos:** 2B/3B **Ht:** 5' 9" **Wt:** 168 **Born:** 09/22/59 **Age:** 32

Year Team	Lg	G	AB	H	2B	3B	HR	(Hm	Rd)	TB	R	RBI	TBB	IBB	SO	HBP	SH	SF	SB	CS	SB%	GDP	Avg	OBP	SLG
1980 New York	NL	27	93	30	1	1	0	(0	0)	33	12	9	11	1	14	1	4	1	2	3	.40	3	.323	.396	.355
1981 New York	NL	26	36	10	2	0	0	(0	0)	12	5	0	4	0	7	0	2	0	1	0	1.00	1	.278	.350	.333
1982 New York	NL	96	261	71	13	2	3	(1	2)	97	37	22	49	1	47	0	2	0	8	7	.53	6	.272	.387	.372
1983 New York	NL	26	42	7	0	1	0	(0	0)	9	6	3	2	0	8	0	1	0	0	0	.00	2	.167	.205	.214
1984 New York	NL	128	436	122	19	2	1	(0	1)	148	68	26	56	2	63	0	5	2	32	9	.78	13	.280	.360	.339
1985 New York	NL	145	520	142	24	5	1	(0	1)	179	77	38	36	1	72	1	14	3	30	12	.71	3	.273	.320	.344
1986 New York	NL	124	387	124	18	2	1	(1	0)	149	67	27	36	1	32	0	14	3	13	7	.65	3	.320	.376	.385
1987 New York	NL	94	300	75	6	1	1	(0	1)	86	43	23	25	0	43	0	9	1	11	3	.79	5	.250	.307	.287
1988 New York	NL	99	294	89	12	0	0	(0	1)	101	44	17	41	1	49	1	9	2	9	5	.64	6	.303	.388	.344
1989 Minnesota	AL	87	299	69	9	2	1	(0	1)	85	33	26	32	0	45	1	4	1	1	1	.50	4	.231	.306	.284
1990 Pittsburgh	NL	104	315	92	21	3	2	(0	2)	125	62	28	42	1	53	1	0	3	6	3	.67	5	.292	.374	.397
1991 Philadelphia	NL	94	185	45	12	0	0	(0	0)	57	20	15	30	0	30	0	2	3	3	2	.60	2	.243	.344	.308
12 ML YEARS		1050	3168	876	137	19	10	(2	8)	1081	474	234	364	8	463	5	66	19	116	52	69	52	.277	.350	.341

Carlos Baerga

Bats: Both **Throws:** Right **Pos:** 3B/2B **Ht:** 5'11" **Wt:** 165 **Born:** 11/04/68 **Age:** 23

Year Team	Lg	G	AB	H	2B	3B	HR	(Hm	Rd)	TB	R	RBI	TBB	IBB	SO	HBP	SH	SF	SB	CS	SB%	GDP	Avg	OBP	SLG
1986 Charleston	A	111	378	102	14	4	7	--	--	145	57	41	26	1	60	5	2	5	6	1	.86	4	.270	.323	.384
1987 Chston-Sc	A	134	515	157	23	9	7	--	--	219	83	50	38	7	107	12	6	2	26	21	.55	10	.305	.365	.425
1988 Wichita	AA	122	444	121	28	1	12	--	--	187	67	65	31	2	83	9	0	3	4	4	.50	8	.273	.331	.421
1989 Las Vegas	AAA	132	520	143	28	2	10	--	--	205	63	74	30	5	98	6	0	6	6	6	.50	10	.275	.319	.394
1990 Colo Sprngs	AAA	12	50	19	2	1	1	--	--	26	11	11	5	2	4	0	0	0	1	0	1.00	4	.380	.436	.520
1990 Cleveland	AL	108	312	81	17	2	7	(3	4)	123	46	47	16	2	57	4	1	5	0	2	.00	4	.260	.300	.394
1991 Cleveland	AL	158	593	171	28	2	11	(2	9)	236	80	69	48	5	74	6	4	3	3	2	.60	12	.288	.346	.398
2 ML YEARS		266	905	252	45	4	18	(5	13)	359	126	116	64	7	131	10	5	8	3	4	.43	16	.278	.330	.397

Jeff Bagwell

Bats: Right **Throws:** Right **Pos:** 1B **Ht:** 6' 0" **Wt:** 195 **Born:** 05/27/68 **Age:** 24

Year Team	Lg	G	AB	H	2B	3B	HR	(Hm	Rd)	TB	R	RBI	TBB	IBB	SO	HBP	SH	SF	SB	CS	SB%	GDP	Avg	OBP	SLG
1989 Red Sox	R	5	19	6	1	0	0	--	--	7	3	3	3	0	0	0	0	0	0	0	.00	1	.316	.409	.368
Winter Havn	A	64	210	65	13	2	2	--	--	88	27	19	23	0	25	3	3	1	1	1	.50	7	.310	.384	.419
1990 New Britain	AA	136	481	160	34	7	4	--	--	220	63	61	72	12	57	7	3	6	5	7	.42	15	.333	.422	.457
1991 Houston	NL	156	554	163	26	4	15	(6	9)	242	79	82	75	5	116	13	1	7	7	4	.64	12	.294	.387	.437

Scott Bailes

Pitches: Left **Bats:** Left **Pos:** RP **Ht:** 6' 2" **Wt:** 184 **Born:** 12/18/62 **Age:** 29

Year Team	Lg	G	GS	CG	GF	IP	BFP	H	R	ER	HR	SH	SF	HB	TBB	IBB	SO	WP	Bk	W	L	Pct.	ShO	Sv	ERA
1986 Cleveland	AL	62	10	0	22	112.2	500	123	70	62	12	7	4	1	43	5	60	4	2	10	10	.500	0	7	4.95
1987 Cleveland	AL	39	17	0	15	120.1	551	145	75	62	21	4	6	4	47	1	65	3	0	7	8	.467	0	6	4.64
1988 Cleveland	AL	37	21	5	7	145	617	149	89	79	22	5	4	2	46	0	53	2	3	9	14	.391	2	0	4.90
1989 Cleveland	AL	34	11	0	9	113.2	473	116	57	54	7	5	5	3	29	4	47	3	0	5	9	.357	0	0	4.28
1990 California	AL	27	0	0	6	35.1	173	46	30	25	8	1	5	1	20	0	16	0	0	2	0	1.000	0	0	6.37
1991 California	AL	42	0	0	14	51.2	219	41	26	24	5	3	2	4	22	5	41	2	0	1	2	.333	0	0	4.18
6 ML YEARS		241	59	5	73	578.2	2533	620	347	306	75	25	26	15	207	15	282	14	5	34	43	.442	2	13	4.76

11

Harold Baines

Bats: Left   **Throws:** Left   **Pos:** DH   **Ht:** 6' 2"   **Wt:** 195   **Born:** 03/15/59   **Age:** 33

								BATTING											BASERUNNING				PERCENTAGES		
Year Team	Lg	G	AB	H	2B	3B	HR	(Hm Rd)	TB	R	RBI	TBB	IBB	SO	HBP	SH	SF	SB	CS	SB%	GDP	Avg	OBP	SLG
1980 Chicago	AL	141	491	125	23	6	13	(3 10)	199	55	49	19	7	65	1	2	5	2	4	.33	15	.255	.281	.405
1981 Chicago	AL	82	280	80	11	7	10	(3 7)	135	42	41	12	4	41	2	0	2	6	2	.75	6	.286	.318	.482
1982 Chicago	AL	161	608	165	29	8	25	(11 14)	285	89	105	49	10	95	0	2	9	10	3	.77	12	.271	.321	.469
1983 Chicago	AL	156	596	167	33	2	20	(12 8)	264	76	99	49	13	85	1	3	6	7	5	.58	15	.280	.333	.443
1984 Chicago	AL	147	569	173	28	10	29	(16 13)	308	72	94	54	9	75	0	1	5	1	2	.33	12	.304	.361	.541
1985 Chicago	AL	160	640	198	29	3	22	(13 9)	299	86	113	42	8	89	1	0	10	1	1	.50	23	.309	.348	.467
1986 Chicago	AL	145	570	169	29	2	21	(8 13)	265	72	88	38	9	89	2	0	8	2	1	.67	14	.296	.338	.465
1987 Chicago	AL	132	505	148	26	4	20	(12 8)	242	59	93	46	2	82	1	0	2	0	0	.00	12	.293	.352	.479
1988 Chicago	AL	158	599	166	39	1	13	(5 8)	246	55	81	67	14	109	1	0	7	0	0	.00	21	.277	.347	.411
1989 2 ML Teams		146	505	156	29	1	16	(5 11)	235	73	72	73	13	79	1	0	4	0	3	.00	15	.309	.395	.465
1990 2 ML Teams		135	415	118	15	1	16	(9 7)	183	52	65	67	10	80	0	0	7	0	3	.00	17	.284	.378	.441
1991 Oakland	AL	141	488	144	25	1	20	(11 9)	231	76	90	72	22	67	1	0	5	0	1	.00	12	.295	.383	.473
1989 Chicago	AL	96	333	107	20	1	13	(4 9)	168	55	56	60	13	52	1	0	3	0	1	.00	11	.321	.423	.505
Texas	AL	50	172	49	9	0	3	(1 2)	67	18	16	13	0	27	0	0	1	0	2	.00	4	.285	.333	.390
1990 Texas	AL	103	321	93	10	1	13	(6 7)	144	41	44	47	9	63	0	0	3	0	1	.00	13	.290	.377	.449
Oakland	AL	32	94	25	5	0	3	(3 0)	39	11	21	20	1	17	0	0	4	0	2	.00	4	.266	.381	.415
12 ML YEARS		1704	6266	1809	316	46	225	(108 117)	2892	807	990	588	121	956	11	8	70	29	25	.54	174	.289	.347	.462

Jeff Ballard

Pitches: Left   **Bats:** Left   **Pos:** SP   **Ht:** 6' 2"   **Wt:** 203   **Born:** 08/13/63   **Age:** 28

			HOW MUCH HE PITCHED						WHAT HE GAVE UP										THE RESULTS					
Year Team	Lg	G	GS	CG	GF	IP	BFP	H	R	ER	HR	SH	SF	HB	TBB	IBB	SO	WP	Bk	W	L	Pct.	ShO	Sv	ERA
1987 Baltimore	AL	14	14	0	0	69.2	327	100	60	51	15	0	1	0	35	1	27	0	1	2	8	.200	0	0	6.59
1988 Baltimore	AL	25	25	6	0	153.1	654	167	83	75	15	3	3	6	42	2	41	2	2	8	12	.400	1	0	4.40
1989 Baltimore	AL	35	35	4	0	215.1	912	240	95	82	16	10	5	4	57	5	62	3	0	18	8	.692	1	0	3.43
1990 Baltimore	AL	44	17	0	6	133.1	578	152	79	73	22	5	2	3	42	6	50	2	1	2	11	.154	0	0	4.93
1991 Baltimore	AL	26	22	0	1	123.2	540	153	91	77	16	1	3	2	28	2	37	1	1	6	12	.333	0	0	5.60
5 ML YEARS		144	113	10	7	695.1	3011	812	408	358	84	19	14	15	204	16	217	10	5	36	51	.414	2	0	4.63

Jeff Banister

Bats: Right   **Throws:** Right   **Pos:** PH   **Ht:** 6' 2"   **Wt:** 200   **Born:** 01/15/65   **Age:** 27

								BATTING											BASERUNNING				PERCENTAGES		
Year Team	Lg	G	AB	H	2B	3B	HR	(Hm Rd)	TB	R	RBI	TBB	IBB	SO	HBP	SH	SF	SB	CS	SB%	GDP	Avg	OBP	SLG
1986 Watertown	A	41	124	18	4	0	0	-- --	22	9	8	12	0	27	1	0	1	4	0	1.00	9	.145	.225	.177
1987 Macon	A	101	307	78	20	0	6	-- --	116	39	37	27	0	70	2	3	3	1	0	1.00	7	.254	.316	.378
1988 Harrisburg	AA	71	205	53	6	0	6	-- --	77	9	26	10	4	38	1	4	0	0	0	.00	4	.259	.296	.376
1989 Harrisburg	AA	102	336	80	13	0	12	-- --	129	48	48	30	0	57	4	1	2	2	1	.67	11	.238	.306	.384
1990 Buffalo	AAA	12	25	8	2	0	1	-- --	13	3	3	3	1	5	0	0	1	0	0	.00	2	.320	.379	.520
Harrisburg	AA	101	368	99	13	0	10	-- --	142	43	57	23	0	71	3	0	5	2	0	1.00	6	.269	.313	.386
1991 Buffalo	AAA	79	234	57	7	1	2	-- --	72	23	21	28	2	57	1	0	0	1	2	.33	7	.244	.327	.308
1991 Pittsburgh	NL	1	1	1	0	0	0	(0 0)	1	0	0	0	0	0	0	0	0	0	0	.00	0	1.000	1.000	1.000

Scott Bankhead

Pitches: Right   **Bats:** Right   **Pos:** SP/RP   **Ht:** 5'10"   **Wt:** 185   **Born:** 07/31/63   **Age:** 28

			HOW MUCH HE PITCHED						WHAT HE GAVE UP										THE RESULTS					
Year Team	Lg	G	GS	CG	GF	IP	BFP	H	R	ER	HR	SH	SF	HB	TBB	IBB	SO	WP	Bk	W	L	Pct.	ShO	Sv	ERA
1986 Kansas City	AL	24	17	0	2	121	517	121	66	62	14	5	5	3	37	7	94	1	0	8	9	.471	0	0	4.61
1987 Seattle	AL	27	25	2	1	149.1	642	168	96	90	35	4	6	3	37	0	95	2	2	9	8	.529	0	0	5.42
1988 Seattle	AL	21	21	2	0	135	557	115	53	46	8	3	1	1	38	5	102	3	1	7	9	.438	1	0	3.07
1989 Seattle	AL	33	33	3	0	210.1	862	187	84	78	19	4	8	3	63	1	140	2	0	14	6	.700	2	0	3.34
1990 Seattle	AL	4	4	0	0	13	63	18	16	16	2	0	2	0	7	0	10	1	0	0	2	.000	0	0	11.08
1991 Seattle	AL	17	9	0	2	60.2	271	73	35	33	8	0	2	2	21	2	28	0	0	3	6	.333	0	0	4.90
6 ML YEARS		126	109	7	5	689.1	2912	682	350	325	86	15	24	12	203	15	469	9	3	41	40	.506	3	0	4.24

Willie Banks

Pitches: Right   **Bats:** Right   **Pos:** SP   **Ht:** 6' 1"   **Wt:** 190   **Born:** 02/27/69   **Age:** 23

			HOW MUCH HE PITCHED						WHAT HE GAVE UP										THE RESULTS					
Year Team	Lg	G	GS	CG	GF	IP	BFP	H	R	ER	HR	SH	SF	HB	TBB	IBB	SO	WP	Bk	W	L	Pct.	ShO	Sv	ERA
1987 Elizabethtn	R	13	13	0	0	65.2	332	73	71	51	3	3	4	3	62	0	71	28	3	1	8	.111	0	0	6.99
1988 Kenosha	A	24	24	0	0	125.2	580	109	73	52	3	2	5	4	107	2	113	14	2	10	10	.500	0	0	3.72
1989 Visalia	A	27	27	7	0	174	723	122	70	50	5	2	7	10	85	0	173	22	1	12	9	.571	4	0	2.59
Orlando	AA	1	1	0	0	7	30	10	4	4	0	0	0	0	0	0	9	2	0	1	0	1.000	0	0	5.14
1990 Orlando	AA	28	28	1	0	162.2	737	161	93	71	15	1	8	7	98	0	114	6	1	7	9	.438	0	0	3.93

| 1991 Portland | AAA | 25 | 24 | 1 | 1 | 146.1 | 653 | 156 | 81 | 74 | 6 | 2 | 4 | 6 | 76 | 1 | 63 | 14 | 1 | 9 | 8 | .529 | 1 | 0 | 4.55 |
| 1991 Minnesota | AL | 5 | 3 | 0 | 2 | 17.1 | 85 | 21 | 15 | 11 | 1 | 0 | 0 | 0 | 12 | 0 | 16 | 3 | 0 | 1 | 1 | .500 | 0 | 0 | 5.71 |

Floyd Bannister

Pitches: Left **Bats:** Left **Pos:** RP **Ht:** 6' 1" **Wt:** 190 **Born:** 06/10/55 **Age:** 37

| | | HOW MUCH HE PITCHED | | | | | | WHAT HE GAVE UP | | | | | | | | | | | THE RESULTS | | | | | |
Year Team	Lg	G	GS	CG	GF	IP	BFP	H	R	ER	HR	SH	SF	HB	TBB	IBB	SO	WP	Bk	W	L	Pct.	ShO	Sv	ERA
1977 Houston	NL	24	23	4	0	143	622	138	70	64	11	2	4	4	68	1	112	6	2	8	9	.471	1	0	4.03
1978 Houston	NL	28	16	2	3	110	502	120	59	59	13	7	3	1	63	4	94	7	2	3	9	.250	2	0	4.83
1979 Seattle	AL	30	30	6	0	182	792	185	92	82	25	5	3	4	68	4	115	1	0	10	15	.400	2	0	4.05
1980 Seattle	AL	32	32	8	0	218	918	200	96	84	24	8	5	2	66	6	155	7	0	9	13	.409	0	0	3.47
1981 Seattle	AL	21	20	5	0	121	522	128	62	60	14	2	0	3	39	0	85	7	1	9	9	.500	2	0	4.46
1982 Seattle	AL	35	35	5	0	247	1022	225	112	94	32	10	5	3	77	0	209	6	0	12	13	.480	3	0	3.43
1983 Chicago	AL	34	34	5	0	217.1	902	191	88	81	19	4	4	2	71	3	193	8	1	16	10	.615	2	0	3.35
1984 Chicago	AL	34	33	4	0	218	936	211	127	117	30	3	10	6	80	2	152	10	0	14	11	.560	0	0	4.83
1985 Chicago	AL	34	34	4	0	210.2	928	211	121	114	30	9	8	4	100	5	198	11	0	10	14	.417	1	0	4.87
1986 Chicago	AL	28	27	6	0	165.1	688	162	81	65	17	7	5	2	48	0	92	5	0	10	14	.417	1	0	3.54
1987 Chicago	AL	34	34	11	0	228.2	939	216	100	91	38	9	3	0	49	0	124	5	1	16	11	.593	2	0	3.58
1988 Kansas City	AL	31	31	2	0	189.1	816	182	102	91	22	8	2	5	68	6	113	6	2	12	13	.480	0	0	4.33
1989 Kansas City	AL	14	14	0	0	75.1	323	87	40	39	8	2	2	1	18	1	35	1	0	4	1	.800	0	0	4.66
1991 California	AL	16	0	0	2	25	104	25	12	11	5	0	0	0	10	1	16	1	0	0	0	.000	0	0	3.96
14 ML YEARS		395	363	62	5	2350.2	10014	2281	1162	1052	288	76	54	37	825	33	1693	81	9	133	142	.484	16	0	4.03

Bret Barberie

Bats: Both **Throws:** Right **Pos:** SS **Ht:** 5'11" **Wt:** 185 **Born:** 08/16/67 **Age:** 24

| | | BATTING | | | | | | | | | | | | | | | | | BASERUNNING | | | | PERCENTAGES | | |
Year Team	Lg	G	AB	H	2B	3B	HR	(Hm	Rd)	TB	R	RBI	TBB	IBB	SO	HBP	SH	SF	SB	CS	SB%	GDP	Avg	OBP	SLG
1989 Wst Plm Bch	A	124	457	122	16	4	4	--	--	158	63	34	64	7	39	10	5	4	10	4	.71	9	.267	.366	.346
1990 Jacksnville	AA	133	431	112	18	3	7	--	--	157	71	56	87	6	64	11	3	5	20	7	.74	3	.260	.393	.364
1991 Indianapols	AAA	71	218	68	10	4	10	--	--	116	45	48	59	2	47	3	1	2	10	5	.67	4	.312	.461	.532
1991 Montreal	NL	57	136	48	12	2	2	(2	0)	70	16	18	20	2	22	2	1	3	0	1	.00	4	.353	.435	.515

Jesse Barfield

Bats: Right **Throws:** Right **Pos:** RF **Ht:** 6' 1" **Wt:** 206 **Born:** 10/29/59 **Age:** 32

| | | BATTING | | | | | | | | | | | | | | | | | BASERUNNING | | | | PERCENTAGES | | |
Year Team	Lg	G	AB	H	2B	3B	HR	(Hm	Rd)	TB	R	RBI	TBB	IBB	SO	HBP	SH	SF	SB	CS	SB%	GDP	Avg	OBP	SLG
1981 Toronto	AL	25	95	22	3	2	2	(1	1)	35	7	9	4	0	19	1	0	0	4	3	.57	4	.232	.270	.368
1982 Toronto	AL	139	394	97	13	2	18	(11	7)	168	54	58	42	3	79	3	6	1	1	4	.20	7	.246	.323	.426
1983 Toronto	AL	128	388	98	13	3	27	(22	5)	198	58	68	22	0	110	4	1	5	2	5	.29	8	.253	.296	.510
1984 Toronto	AL	110	320	91	14	1	14	(10	4)	149	51	49	35	5	81	2	1	2	8	2	.80	5	.284	.357	.466
1985 Toronto	AL	155	539	156	34	9	27	(15	12)	289	94	84	66	5	143	4	0	3	22	8	.73	14	.289	.369	.536
1986 Toronto	AL	158	589	170	35	2	40	(16	24)	329	107	108	69	5	146	8	0	5	8	8	.50	9	.289	.368	.559
1987 Toronto	AL	159	590	155	25	3	28	(11	17)	270	89	84	58	7	141	3	1	2	3	5	.38	13	.263	.331	.458
1988 Toronto	AL	137	468	114	21	5	18	(12	6)	199	62	56	41	6	108	1	4	6	7	3	.70	10	.244	.302	.425
1989 2 ML Teams		150	521	122	23	1	23	(7	16)	216	79	67	87	6	150	3	1	3	5	5	.50	8	.234	.345	.415
1990 New York	AL	153	476	117	21	2	25	(12	13)	217	69	78	82	4	150	5	2	5	4	3	.57	6	.246	.359	.456
1991 New York	AL	84	284	64	12	0	17	(11	6)	127	37	48	36	6	80	0	0	1	1	0	1.00	11	.225	.312	.447
1989 Toronto	AL	21	80	16	4	0	5	(1	4)	35	8	11	5	0	28	1	0	0	0	2	.00	0	.200	.256	.438
New York		129	441	106	19	1	18	(6	12)	181	71	56	82	6	122	2	1	3	5	3	.63	8	.240	.360	.410
11 ML YEARS		1398	4664	1206	214	30	239	(128	111)	2197	707	709	542	47	1207	34	16	33	65	46	.59	95	.259	.338	.471

John Barfield

Pitches: Left **Bats:** Left **Pos:** RP/SP **Ht:** 6' 1" **Wt:** 195 **Born:** 10/15/64 **Age:** 27

| | | HOW MUCH HE PITCHED | | | | | | WHAT HE GAVE UP | | | | | | | | | | | THE RESULTS | | | | | |
Year Team	Lg	G	GS	CG	GF	IP	BFP	H	R	ER	HR	SH	SF	HB	TBB	IBB	SO	WP	Bk	W	L	Pct.	ShO	Sv	ERA
1989 Texas	AL	4	2	0	1	11.2	52	15	10	8	0	1	0	0	4	0	9	1	0	0	1	.000	0	0	6.17
1990 Texas	AL	33	0	0	10	44.1	178	42	25	23	2	3	4	1	13	3	17	1	1	4	3	.571	0	1	4.67
1991 Texas	AL	28	9	0	4	83.1	361	96	51	42	11	3	4	0	22	3	27	0	2	4	4	.500	0	1	4.54
3 ML YEARS		65	11	0	15	139.1	591	153	86	73	13	7	8	1	39	6	53	2	3	8	8	.500	0	2	4.72

Brian Barnes

Pitches: Left **Bats:** Left **Pos:** SP **Ht:** 5' 9" **Wt:** 170 **Born:** 03/25/67 **Age:** 25

| | | HOW MUCH HE PITCHED | | | | | | WHAT HE GAVE UP | | | | | | | | | | | THE RESULTS | | | | | |
Year Team	Lg	G	GS	CG	GF	IP	BFP	H	R	ER	HR	SH	SF	HB	TBB	IBB	SO	WP	Bk	W	L	Pct.	ShO	Sv	ERA
1989 Jamestown	A	2	2	0	0	9	33	4	1	1	0	0	0	0	3	0	15	1	1	1	0	1.000	0	0	1.00

	Lg																									
Wst Plm Bch	A	7	7	4	0	50	187	25	9	4	0	3	1	0	16	0	67	4	0	4	3	.571	3	0	0.72
Indianapols	AAA	1	1	0	0	6	24	5	1	1	0	0	0	0	2	0	5	0	0	1	0	1.000	0	0	1.50
1990 Jacksonville	AA	29	28	3	0	201.1	828	144	78	62	12	7	5	9	87	2	213	8	1	13	7	.650	0	0	2.77
1991 Wst Plm Bch	A	2	2	0	0	7	27	3	0	0	0	0	0	0	4	0	6	3	0	0	0	.000	0	0	0.00
Indianapols	AAA	2	2	0	0	11	44	6	2	2	0	1	0	1	8	0	10	0	0	2	0	1.000	0	0	1.64
1990 Montreal	NL	4	4	1	0	28	115	25	10	9	2	2	0	0	7	0	23	2	0	1	1	.500	0	0	2.89
1991 Montreal	NL	28	27	1	0	160	684	135	82	75	16	9	5	6	84	2	117	5	1	5	8	.385	0	0	4.22
2 ML YEARS		32	31	2	0	188	799	160	92	84	18	11	5	6	91	2	140	7	1	6	9	.400	0	0	4.02

Skeeter Barnes

Bats: Right **Throws:** Right **Pos:** 3B/LF/RF **Ht:** 5'11" **Wt:** 175 **Born:** 03/07/57 **Age:** 35

						BATTING													BASERUNNING				PERCENTAGES		
Year Team	Lg	G	AB	H	2B	3B	HR	(Hm	Rd)	TB	R	RBI	TBB	IBB	SO	HBP	SH	SF	SB	CS	SB%	GDP	Avg	OBP	SLG
1983 Cincinnati	NL	15	34	7	0	0	1	(1	0)	10	5	4	7	0	3	2	0	0	2	2	.50	0	.206	.372	.294
1984 Cincinnati	NL	32	42	5	0	0	1	(1	0)	8	5	3	4	1	6	0	0	0	0	0	.00	1	.119	.196	.190
1985 Montreal	NL	19	26	4	1	0	0	(0	0)	5	0	0	0	0	2	0	0	0	0	1	.00	1	.154	.154	.192
1987 St. Louis	NL	4	4	1	0	0	1	(0	1)	4	1	3	0	0	0	0	0	0	0	0	.00	0	.250	.250	1.000
1989 Cincinnati	NL	5	3	0	0	0	0	(0	0)	0	1	0	0	0	0	0	0	0	0	1	.00	0	.000	.000	.000
1991 Detroit	AL	75	159	46	13	2	5	(1	4)	78	28	17	9	1	24	0	2	1	10	7	.59	1	.289	.325	.491
6 ML YEARS		150	268	63	14	2	8	(3	5)	105	40	27	20	2	35	2	2	1	12	11	.52	3	.235	.292	.392

Marty Barrett

Bats: Right **Throws:** Right **Pos:** 2B **Ht:** 5'10" **Wt:** 175 **Born:** 06/23/58 **Age:** 34

						BATTING													BASERUNNING				PERCENTAGES		
Year Team	Lg	G	AB	H	2B	3B	HR	(Hm	Rd)	TB	R	RBI	TBB	IBB	SO	HBP	SH	SF	SB	CS	SB%	GDP	Avg	OBP	SLG
1982 Boston	AL	8	18	1	0	0	0	(0	0)	1	0	0	0	0	1	0	0	0	0	0	.00	1	.056	.056	.056
1983 Boston	AL	33	44	10	1	1	0	(0	0)	13	7	2	3	0	1	0	0	1	0	0	.00	1	.227	.271	.295
1984 Boston	AL	139	475	144	23	3	3	(1	2)	182	56	45	42	2	25	1	4	4	5	3	.63	9	.303	.358	.383
1985 Boston	AL	156	534	142	26	0	5	(3	2)	183	59	56	56	3	50	2	12	4	7	5	.58	14	.266	.336	.343
1986 Boston	AL	158	625	179	39	4	4	(4	0)	238	94	60	65	0	31	1	18	4	15	7	.68	13	.286	.353	.381
1987 Boston	AL	137	559	164	23	0	3	(2	1)	196	72	43	51	0	38	1	22	5	15	2	.88	11	.293	.351	.351
1988 Boston	AL	150	612	173	28	1	1	(1	0)	206	83	65	40	1	35	7	20	8	7	3	.70	16	.283	.330	.337
1989 Boston	AL	86	336	86	18	0	1	(0	1)	107	31	27	32	0	12	2	15	5	4	1	.80	12	.256	.320	.318
1990 Boston	AL	62	159	36	4	0	0	(0	0)	40	15	13	15	1	13	1	11	2	4	0	1.00	4	.226	.294	.252
1991 San Diego	NL	12	16	3	1	0	1	(1	0)	7	1	3	0	0	3	1	0	0	0	0	.00	0	.188	.235	.438
10 ML YEARS		941	3378	938	163	9	18	(12	6)	1173	418	314	304	7	209	16	102	33	57	21	.73	81	.278	.337	.347

Kevin Bass

Bats: Both **Throws:** Right **Pos:** RF/LF **Ht:** 6' 0" **Wt:** 190 **Born:** 05/12/59 **Age:** 33

						BATTING													BASERUNNING				PERCENTAGES		
Year Team	Lg	G	AB	H	2B	3B	HR	(Hm	Rd)	TB	R	RBI	TBB	IBB	SO	HBP	SH	SF	SB	CS	SB%	GDP	Avg	OBP	SLG
1982 2 ML Teams		30	33	1	0	0	0	(0	0)	1	6	1	1	0	9	0	1	0	0	0	.00	1	.030	.059	.030
1983 Houston	NL	88	195	46	7	3	2	(0	1)	65	25	18	6	1	27	0	4	1	2	2	.50	2	.236	.257	.333
1984 Houston	NL	121	331	86	17	5	2	(1	1)	119	33	29	6	1	57	3	2	0	5	5	.50	2	.260	.279	.360
1985 Houston	NL	150	539	145	27	5	16	(9	7)	230	72	68	31	1	63	6	4	2	19	8	.70	10	.269	.315	.427
1986 Houston	NL	157	591	184	33	5	20	(5	15)	287	83	79	38	11	72	6	1	4	22	13	.63	15	.311	.357	.486
1987 Houston	NL	157	592	168	31	5	19	(10	9)	266	83	85	53	13	77	4	0	5	21	8	.72	15	.284	.344	.449
1988 Houston	NL	157	541	138	27	2	14	(5	9)	211	57	72	42	10	65	6	3	3	31	6	.84	16	.255	.314	.390
1989 Houston	NL	87	313	94	19	4	5	(2	3)	136	42	44	29	3	44	1	1	4	11	4	.73	2	.300	.357	.435
1990 San Francisco	NL	61	214	54	9	1	7	(4	3)	86	25	32	14	3	26	2	2	1	2	2	.50	5	.252	.303	.402
1991 San Francisco	NL	124	361	84	10	4	10	(5	5)	132	43	40	36	8	56	4	2	3	7	4	.64	12	.233	.307	.366
1982 Milwaukee	AL	18	9	0	0	0	0	(0	0)	0	4	0	1	0	1	0	1	0	0	0	.00	0	.000	.100	.000
Houston	NL	12	24	1	0	0	0	(0	0)	1	2	1	0	0	8	0	0	0	0	0	.00	1	.042	.042	.042
10 ML YEARS		1132	3710	1000	180	34	95	(42	53)	1533	469	468	256	51	496	32	20	23	120	52	.70	80	.270	.320	.413

Kim Batiste

Bats: Right **Throws:** Right **Pos:** SS **Ht:** 6' 0" **Wt:** 175 **Born:** 03/15/68 **Age:** 24

						BATTING													BASERUNNING				PERCENTAGES		
Year Team	Lg	G	AB	H	2B	3B	HR	(Hm	Rd)	TB	R	RBI	TBB	IBB	SO	HBP	SH	SF	SB	CS	SB%	GDP	Avg	OBP	SLG
1987 Utica	A	46	150	26	8	1	2	--	--	42	15	10	7	3	65	0	0	0	4	0	1.00	3	.173	.210	.280
1988 Spartanburg	A	122	430	107	19	6	6	--	--	156	51	52	14	1	101	1	5	1	16	9	.64	13	.249	.274	.363
1989 Clearwater	A	114	385	90	12	4	3	--	--	119	36	33	17	1	67	4	11	1	13	7	.65	7	.234	.273	.309
1990 Reading	AA	125	486	134	14	4	6	--	--	174	57	33	13	1	73	2	5	2	28	14	.67	11	.276	.296	.358
1991 Scranton-Wb	AAA	122	462	135	25	6	1	--	--	175	54	41	11	0	72	4	10	4	18	12	.60	5	.292	.312	.379
1991 Philadelphia	NL	10	27	6	0	0	0	(0	0)	6	2	1	1	1	8	0	0	0	0	1	.00	0	.222	.250	.222

Jose Bautista

Pitches: Right **Bats:** Right **Pos:** RP **Ht:** 6' 2" **Wt:** 207 **Born:** 07/25/64 **Age:** 27

Year	Team	Lg	G	GS	CG	GF	IP	BFP	H	R	ER	HR	SH	SF	HB	TBB	IBB	SO	WP	Bk	W	L	Pct.	ShO	Sv	ERA
1988	Baltimore	AL	33	25	3	5	171.2	721	171	86	82	21	2	3	7	45	3	76	4	5	6	15	.286	0	0	4.30
1989	Baltimore	AL	15	10	0	4	78	325	84	46	46	17	1	1	1	15	0	30	0	0	3	4	.429	0	0	5.31
1990	Baltimore	AL	22	0	0	9	26.2	112	28	15	12	4	1	1	0	7	3	15	2	0	1	0	1.000	0	0	4.05
1991	Baltimore	AL	5	0	0	3	5.1	34	13	10	10	1	0	0	1	5	0	3	1	0	0	1	.000	0	0	16.88
	4 ML YEARS		75	35	3	21	281.2	1192	296	157	150	43	4	5	9	72	6	124	7	5	10	20	.333	0	0	4.79

Chris Beasley

Pitches: Right **Bats:** Right **Pos:** RP **Ht:** 6' 2" **Wt:** 190 **Born:** 06/23/62 **Age:** 30

Year	Team	Lg	G	GS	CG	GF	IP	BFP	H	R	ER	HR	SH	SF	HB	TBB	IBB	SO	WP	Bk	W	L	Pct.	ShO	Sv	ERA
1984	Batavia	A	14	13	4	0	89.2	399	97	54	40	11	1	3	1	33	2	70	8	1	6	5	.545	1	0	4.01
1985	Waterloo	A	17	17	6	0	120	511	110	55	44	6	3	2	2	47	2	87	7	1	6	7	.462	1	0	3.30
	Waterbury	AA	9	9	4	0	56	238	44	28	26	4	4	0	3	35	1	27	1	0	2	6	.250	0	0	4.18
1986	Waterbury	AA	27	25	5	0	155.2	675	152	83	66	10	3	4	7	67	2	105	10	2	8	9	.471	2	0	3.82
1987	Williamsprt	AA	11	11	1	0	66.1	316	93	63	49	8	2	3	3	30	1	37	5	0	2	6	.250	0	0	6.65
	Chattanooga	AA	14	8	0	4	56.1	250	73	33	23	4	0	2	1	22	0	26	2	0	2	4	.333	0	0	3.67
1989	Palm Sprngs	A	10	10	3	0	71	294	60	31	21	1	1	2	8	18	0	44	5	1	4	3	.571	0	0	2.66
	Midland	AA	16	15	4	1	104.1	442	101	53	45	2	3	4	4	33	0	48	6	1	8	4	.667	1	1	3.88
1990	Edmonton	AAA	28	27	5	0	176.1	792	201	107	88	15	2	5	16	70	5	108	5	0	12	9	.571	0	0	4.49
1991	Edmonton	AAA	23	10	1	3	89	377	99	55	52	10	1	4	5	26	3	51	3	0	3	5	.375	1	1	5.26
1991	California	AL	22	0	0	8	26.2	113	26	14	10	2	0	1	1	10	1	14	2	0	0	1	.000	0	0	3.38

Blaine Beatty

Pitches: Left **Bats:** Left **Pos:** RP **Ht:** 6' 2" **Wt:** 185 **Born:** 04/25/64 **Age:** 28

Year	Team	Lg	G	GS	CG	GF	IP	BFP	H	R	ER	HR	SH	SF	HB	TBB	IBB	SO	WP	Bk	W	L	Pct.	ShO	Sv	ERA
1986	Newark	A	15	15	8	0	119.1	475	98	37	28	6	5	2	1	30	3	93	6	0	11	3	.786	3	0	2.11
1987	Hagerstown	A	13	13	4	0	100	389	81	32	28	7	3	1	1	11	0	65	5	0	11	1	.917	1	0	2.52
	Charlotte	AA	15	15	3	0	105.2	438	110	38	36	2	1	4	1	20	2	57	4	0	6	5	.545	1	0	3.07
1988	Jackson	AA	30	28	12	1	208.2	824	191	64	57	13	12	6	0	34	3	103	3	7	16	8	.667	5	0	2.46
1989	Tidewater	AAA	27	27	6	0	185	764	173	86	68	14	4	8	1	43	0	90	3	2	12	10	.545	3	0	3.31
1991	Tidewater	AAA	28	28	3	0	175.1	750	192	86	80	18	7	4	5	43	6	74	0	1	12	9	.571	1	0	4.11
1989	New York	NL	2	1	0	0	6	25	5	1	1	1	0	0	0	2	0	3	0	0	0	0	.000	0	0	1.50
1991	New York	NL	5	0	0	1	9.2	42	9	3	3	0	1	1	0	4	1	7	1	0	0	0	.000	0	0	2.79
	2 ML YEARS		7	1	0	1	15.2	67	14	4	4	1	1	1	0	6	1	10	1	0	0	0	.000	0	0	2.30

Rod Beck

Pitches: Right **Bats:** Right **Pos:** RP **Ht:** 6' 1" **Wt:** 215 **Born:** 08/03/68 **Age:** 23

Year	Team	Lg	G	GS	CG	GF	IP	BFP	H	R	ER	HR	SH	SF	HB	TBB	IBB	SO	WP	Bk	W	L	Pct.	ShO	Sv	ERA
1986	Medford	A	13	6	0	5	32.2	0	47	25	19	4	0	0	1	11	1	21	4	0	1	3	.250	0	1	5.23
1987	Medford	A	17	12	2	1	92	431	106	74	53	5	4	4	4	26	0	69	12	1	5	8	.385	0	0	5.18
1988	Clinton	A	28	23	5	1	177	706	177	68	59	11	4	1	0	27	2	123	3	5	12	7	.632	0	0	3.00
1989	San Jose	A	13	13	4	0	97.1	402	91	29	26	5	1	3	1	26	0	88	2	1	11	2	.846	0	0	2.40
	Shreveport	AA	16	14	4	0	99	416	108	45	39	6	2	2	3	16	3	74	3	2	7	3	.700	1	0	3.55
1990	Phoenix	AAA	12	12	2	0	76.2	345	100	51	42	8	2	4	1	18	1	43	6	0	4	7	.364	0	0	4.93
	Shreveport	AA	14	14	2	0	93	366	85	26	23	4	4	1	1	17	1	71	7	0	10	3	.769	1	0	2.23
1991	Phoenix	AAA	23	5	3	14	71.1	280	56	18	16	3	2	4	2	13	2	35	2	0	4	3	.571	0	6	2.02
1991	San Francisco	NL	31	0	0	10	52.1	214	53	22	22	4	4	2	1	13	2	38	0	0	1	1	.500	0	1	3.78

Steve Bedrosian

Pitches: Right **Bats:** Right **Pos:** RP **Ht:** 6' 3" **Wt:** 205 **Born:** 12/06/57 **Age:** 34

Year	Team	Lg	G	GS	CG	GF	IP	BFP	H	R	ER	HR	SH	SF	HB	TBB	IBB	SO	WP	Bk	W	L	Pct.	ShO	Sv	ERA
1981	Atlanta	NL	15	1	0	5	24	0	15	14	12	2	0	1	1	15	2	9	0	0	1	2	.333	0	0	4.50
1982	Atlanta	NL	64	3	0	30	137.2	567	102	39	37	7	9	2	4	57	5	123	0	0	8	6	.571	0	11	2.42
1983	Atlanta	NL	70	1	0	52	120	504	100	50	48	11	8	4	4	51	8	114	2	0	9	10	.474	0	19	3.60
1984	Atlanta	NL	40	4	0	28	83.2	345	65	23	22	5	1	1	1	33	5	81	4	0	9	6	.600	0	11	2.37
1985	Atlanta	NL	37	37	0	0	206.2	907	198	101	88	17	6	7	5	111	0	134	6	0	7	15	.318	0	0	3.83
1986	Philadelphia	NL	68	0	0	56	90.1	381	79	39	34	12	3	3	0	34	10	82	5	2	8	6	.571	0	29	3.39
1987	Philadelphia	NL	65	0	0	56	89	366	79	31	28	11	2	1	1	28	5	74	3	1	5	3	.625	0	40	2.83
1988	Philadelphia	NL	57	0	0	49	74.1	322	75	34	31	6	0	3	0	27	5	61	0	0	6	6	.500	0	28	3.75
1989	2 ML Teams		68	0	0	60	84.2	342	56	31	27	12	1	4	1	39	5	58	0	0	3	7	.300	0	23	2.87

15

1990 San Francisco	NL	68	0	0	53	79.1	349	72	40	37	6	3	1	2	44	9	43	3	0	9	9	.500	0	17	4.20
1991 Minnesota	AL	56	0	0	22	77.1	332	70	42	38	11	2	4	3	35	6	44	2	0	5	3	.625	0	6	4.42
1989 Philadelphia	NL	28	0	0	27	33.2	135	21	13	12	7	0	2	1	17	1	24	0	0	2	3	.400	0	6	3.21
San Francisco	NL	40	0	0	33	51	207	35	18	15	5	1	2	0	22	4	34	2	0	1	4	.200	0	17	2.65
11 ML YEARS		608	46	0	411	1067	4521	911	444	402	100	35	31	22	474	66	823	27	3	70	73	.490	0	184	3.39

Tim Belcher

Pitches: Right **Bats:** Right **Pos:** SP **Ht:** 6' 3" **Wt:** 223 **Born:** 10/19/61 **Age:** 30

		HOW MUCH HE PITCHED						WHAT HE GAVE UP											THE RESULTS					
Year Team	Lg	G	GS	CG	GF	IP	BFP	H	R	ER	HR	SH	SF	HB	TBB	IBB	SO	WP	Bk	W	L	Pct.	ShO	Sv	ERA
1987 Los Angeles	NL	6	5	0	1	34	135	30	11	9	2	2	1	0	7	0	23	0	1	4	2	.667	0	0	2.38
1988 Los Angeles	NL	36	27	4	5	179.2	719	143	65	58	8	6	1	2	51	7	152	4	0	12	6	.667	1	4	2.91
1989 Los Angeles	NL	39	30	10	6	230	937	182	81	72	20	6	6	7	80	5	200	7	2	15	12	.556	8	1	2.82
1990 Los Angeles	NL	24	24	5	0	153	627	136	76	68	17	5	6	2	48	0	102	6	1	9	9	.500	2	0	4.00
1991 Los Angeles	NL	33	33	2	0	209.1	880	189	76	61	10	11	3	2	75	3	156	7	0	10	9	.526	1	0	2.62
5 ML YEARS		138	119	21	12	806	3298	680	309	268	57	30	17	13	261	15	633	24	4	50	38	.568	12	5	2.99

Stan Belinda

Pitches: Right **Bats:** Right **Pos:** RP **Ht:** 6' 3" **Wt:** 200 **Born:** 08/06/66 **Age:** 25

		HOW MUCH HE PITCHED						WHAT HE GAVE UP											THE RESULTS					
Year Team	Lg	G	GS	CG	GF	IP	BFP	H	R	ER	HR	SH	SF	HB	TBB	IBB	SO	WP	Bk	W	L	Pct.	ShO	Sv	ERA
1989 Pittsburgh	NL	8	0	0	2	10.1	46	13	8	7	0	0	0	0	2	0	10	1	0	0	1	.000	0	0	6.10
1990 Pittsburgh	NL	55	0	0	17	58.1	245	48	23	23	4	2	2	1	29	3	55	1	0	3	4	.429	0	8	3.55
1991 Pittsburgh	NL	60	0	0	37	78.1	318	50	30	30	10	4	3	4	35	4	71	2	0	7	5	.583	0	16	3.45
3 ML YEARS		123	0	0	56	147	609	111	61	60	14	6	5	5	66	7	136	4	0	10	10	.500	0	24	3.67

Derek Bell

Bats: Right **Throws:** Right **Pos:** LF **Ht:** 6' 2" **Wt:** 200 **Born:** 12/11/68 **Age:** 23

		BATTING															BASERUNNING				PERCENTAGES		
Year Team	Lg	G	AB	H	2B	3B	HR	(Hm | Rd)	TB	R	RBI	TBB	IBB	SO	HBP	SH	SF	SB	CS	SB%	GDP	Avg	OBP	SLG
1987 St.Cathrnes	A	74	273	72	11	3	10	--	--	119	46	42	18	1	60	6	2	3	12	4	.75	5	.264	.320	.436
1988 Myrtle Bch	A	91	352	121	29	5	12	--	--	196	55	60	15	3	67	6	0	4	18	6	.75	9	.344	.377	.557
Knoxville	AA	14	52	13	3	1	0	--	--	18	5	4	1	0	14	0	0	0	2	1	.67	1	.250	.264	.346
1989 Knoxville	AA	136	513	124	22	6	16	--	--	206	72	75	26	4	92	6	0	4	15	7	.68	6	.242	.284	.402
1990 Syracuse	AAA	109	402	105	13	5	7	--	--	149	57	56	23	0	75	3	0	6	21	7	.75	8	.261	.302	.371
1991 Syracuse	AAA	119	457	158	22	12	13	--	--	243	89	93	57	7	69	9	0	5	27	11	.71	16	.346	.424	.532
1991 Toronto	AL	18	28	4	0	0	0	(0 | 0)	4	5	1	6	0	5	1	0	0	3	2	.60	0	.143	.314	.143

Eric Bell

Pitches: Left **Bats:** Left **Pos:** RP **Ht:** 6' 0" **Wt:** 165 **Born:** 10/27/63 **Age:** 28

		HOW MUCH HE PITCHED						WHAT HE GAVE UP											THE RESULTS					
Year Team	Lg	G	GS	CG	GF	IP	BFP	H	R	ER	HR	SH	SF	HB	TBB	IBB	SO	WP	Bk	W	L	Pct.	ShO	Sv	ERA
1985 Baltimore	AL	4	0	0	3	5.2	24	4	3	3	1	0	0	0	4	0	4	0	0	0	0	.000	0	0	4.76
1986 Baltimore	AL	4	4	0	0	23.1	105	23	14	13	4	1	1	0	14	0	18	0	0	1	2	.333	0	0	5.01
1987 Baltimore	AL	33	29	2	1	165	729	174	113	100	32	4	2	2	78	0	111	11	1	10	13	.435	0	0	5.45
1991 Cleveland	AL	10	0	0	3	18	61	5	2	1	0	0	0	1	5	0	7	0	0	4	0	1.000	0	0	0.50
4 ML YEARS		51	33	2	7	212	919	206	132	117	37	5	3	3	101	0	140	11	1	15	15	.500	0	0	4.97

George Bell

Bats: Right **Throws:** Right **Pos:** LF **Ht:** 6' 1" **Wt:** 202 **Born:** 10/21/59 **Age:** 32

		BATTING															BASERUNNING				PERCENTAGES		
Year Team	Lg	G	AB	H	2B	3B	HR	(Hm | Rd)	TB	R	RBI	TBB	IBB	SO	HBP	SH	SF	SB	CS	SB%	GDP	Avg	OBP	SLG
1981 Toronto	AL	60	163	38	2	1	5	(3 | 2)	57	19	12	5	1	27	0	0	0	3	2	.60	1	.233	.256	.350
1983 Toronto	AL	39	112	30	5	4	2	(1 | 1)	49	5	17	4	1	17	2	0	0	1	1	.50	4	.268	.305	.438
1984 Toronto	AL	159	606	177	39	4	26	(12 | 14)	302	85	87	24	2	86	8	0	3	11	2	.85	14	.292	.326	.498
1985 Toronto	AL	157	607	167	28	6	28	(10 | 18)	291	87	95	43	6	90	8	0	8	21	6	.78	8	.275	.327	.479
1986 Toronto	AL	159	641	198	38	6	31	(15 | 16)	341	101	108	41	3	62	2	0	6	7	8	.47	15	.309	.349	.532
1987 Toronto	AL	156	610	188	32	4	47	(19 | 28)	369	111	134	39	9	75	7	0	9	5	1	.83	17	.308	.352	.605
1988 Toronto	AL	156	614	165	27	5	24	(9 | 15)	274	78	97	34	5	66	1	0	8	4	2	.67	21	.269	.304	.446
1989 Toronto	AL	153	613	182	41	2	18	(8 | 10)	281	88	104	33	3	60	4	0	14	4	3	.57	18	.297	.330	.458
1990 Toronto	AL	142	562	149	25	0	21	(11 | 10)	237	67	86	32	7	80	3	0	11	3	2	.60	14	.265	.303	.422
1991 Chicago	NL	149	558	159	27	0	25	(9 | 16)	261	63	86	32	6	62	4	0	9	2	6	.25	10	.285	.323	.468
10 ML YEARS		1330	5086	1453	264	32	227	(97 | 130)	2462	704	826	287	43	625	39	0	68	61	33	.65	122	.286	.325	.484

Jay Bell

Bats: Right **Throws:** Right **Pos:** SS   **Ht:** 6' 1" **Wt:** 185 **Born:** 12/11/65 **Age:** 26

Year Team	Lg	G	AB	H	2B	3B	HR	(Hm	Rd)	TB	R	RBI	TBB	IBB	SO	HBP	SH	SF	SB	CS	SB%	GDP	Avg	OBP	SLG
1986 Cleveland	AL	5	14	5	2	0	1	(0	1)	10	3	4	2	0	3	0	0	0	0	0	.00	0	.357	.438	.714
1987 Cleveland	AL	38	125	27	9	1	2	(1	1)	44	14	13	8	0	31	1	3	0	2	0	1.00	0	.216	.269	.352
1988 Cleveland	AL	73	211	46	5	1	2	(2	0)	59	23	21	21	0	53	1	1	2	4	2	.67	3	.218	.289	.280
1989 Pittsburgh	NL	78	271	70	13	3	2	(1	1)	95	33	27	19	0	47	1	10	2	5	3	.63	9	.258	.307	.351
1990 Pittsburgh	NL	159	583	148	28	7	7	(1	6)	211	93	52	65	0	109	3	39	6	10	6	.63	14	.254	.329	.362
1991 Pittsburgh	NL	157	608	164	32	8	16	(7	9)	260	96	67	52	1	99	4	30	3	10	6	.63	15	.270	.330	.428
6 ML YEARS		510	1812	460	89	20	30	(12	18)	679	262	184	167	1	342	10	83	13	31	17	.65	41	.254	.318	.375

Juan Bell

Bats: Both **Throws:** Right **Pos:** 2B   **Ht:** 5'11" **Wt:** 170 **Born:** 03/29/68 **Age:** 24

Year Team	Lg	G	AB	H	2B	3B	HR	(Hm	Rd)	TB	R	RBI	TBB	IBB	SO	HBP	SH	SF	SB	CS	SB%	GDP	Avg	OBP	SLG
1985 Dodgers	R	42	106	17	0	0	0	--	--	17	11	8	12	0	20	1	2	0	2	1	.67	1	.160	.252	.160
1986 Dodgers	R	59	217	52	6	2	0	--	--	62	38	26	29	1	28	1	0	3	12	2	.86	2	.240	.328	.286
1988 San Antonio	AA	61	215	60	4	2	5	--	--	83	37	21	16	2	37	2	3	1	11	3	.79	3	.279	.333	.386
Albuquerque	AAA	73	257	77	9	3	8	--	--	116	42	45	16	1	70	1	6	3	7	10	.41	3	.300	.339	.451
1989 Rochester	AAA	116	408	107	15	6	2	--	--	140	50	32	39	0	92	1	2	4	17	10	.63	8	.262	.325	.343
1990 Rochester	AAA	82	326	93	12	5	6	--	--	133	59	35	36	1	59	3	0	2	16	12	.57	9	.285	.360	.408
1989 Baltimore	AL	8	4	0	0	0	0	(0	0)	0	2	0	0	0	1	0	0	0	1	0	1.00	0	.000	.000	.000
1990 Baltimore	AL	5	2	0	0	0	0	(0	0)	0	1	0	0	0	1	0	0	0	0	0	.00	0	.000	.000	.000
1991 Baltimore	AL	100	209	36	9	2	1	(0	1)	52	26	15	8	0	51	0	4	2	0	0	.00	1	.172	.201	.249
3 ML YEARS		113	215	36	9	2	1	(0	1)	52	29	15	8	0	53	0	4	2	1	0	1.00	1	.167	.196	.242

Mike Bell

Bats: Left **Throws:** Left **Pos:** 1B   **Ht:** 6' 1" **Wt:** 175 **Born:** 04/22/68 **Age:** 24

Year Team	Lg	G	AB	H	2B	3B	HR	(Hm	Rd)	TB	R	RBI	TBB	IBB	SO	HBP	SH	SF	SB	CS	SB%	GDP	Avg	OBP	SLG
1987 Sumter	A	133	443	108	17	3	5	--	--	146	54	51	54	3	95	3	0	1	11	9	.55	10	.244	.329	.330
1988 Durham	A	126	440	113	18	3	17	--	--	188	72	84	58	3	91	6	2	6	11	3	.79	5	.257	.347	.427
Greenville	AA	4	12	3	1	0	0	--	--	4	1	4	1	0	1	0	0	0	0	0	.00	0	.250	.308	.333
1989 Greenville	AA	132	472	115	26	3	6	--	--	165	63	57	62	6	91	2	1	1	10	5	.67	8	.244	.333	.350
1990 Greenville	AA	106	405	118	24	2	6	--	--	164	50	42	41	6	63	5	4	2	10	4	.71	3	.291	.362	.405
1991 Richmond	AAA	91	341	85	12	2	5	--	--	116	37	29	26	2	68	2	2	2	2	3	.40	8	.249	.292	.467
1990 Atlanta	NL	36	45	11	5	1	1	(0	1)	21	8	5	2	0	9	1	0	0	1	0	1.00	2	.244	.292	.467
1991 Atlanta	NL	17	30	4	0	0	1	(1	0)	7	4	1	2	0	7	0	0	0	0	0	.00	4	.133	.188	.233
2 ML YEARS		53	75	15	5	1	2	(1	1)	28	12	6	4	0	16	1	0	0	1	1	.50	6	.200	.250	.373

Albert Belle

Bats: Right **Throws:** Right **Pos:** LF/DH   **Ht:** 6' 2" **Wt:** 200 **Born:** 08/25/66 **Age:** 25

Year Team	Lg	G	AB	H	2B	3B	HR	(Hm	Rd)	TB	R	RBI	TBB	IBB	SO	HBP	SH	SF	SB	CS	SB%	GDP	Avg	OBP	SLG
1989 Cleveland	AL	62	218	49	8	4	7	(3	4)	86	22	37	12	0	55	2	0	2	2	2	.50	4	.225	.269	.394
1990 Cleveland	AL	9	23	4	0	0	1	(1	0)	7	1	3	1	0	6	0	1	0	0	0	.00	1	.174	.208	.304
1991 Cleveland	AL	123	461	130	31	2	28	(8	20)	249	60	95	25	2	99	5	0	5	3	1	.75	24	.282	.323	.540
3 ML YEARS		194	702	183	39	6	36	(12	24)	342	83	135	38	2	160	7	1	7	5	3	.63	29	.261	.302	.487

Rafael Belliard

Bats: Right **Throws:** Right **Pos:** SS   **Ht:** 5' 6" **Wt:** 160 **Born:** 10/24/61 **Age:** 30

Year Team	Lg	G	AB	H	2B	3B	HR	(Hm	Rd)	TB	R	RBI	TBB	IBB	SO	HBP	SH	SF	SB	CS	SB%	GDP	Avg	OBP	SLG
1982 Pittsburgh	NL	9	2	1	0	0	0	(0	0)	1	3	0	0	0	0	0	0	0	1	0	1.00	0	.500	.500	.500
1983 Pittsburgh	NL	4	1	0	0	0	0	(0	0)	0	1	0	0	0	1	0	0	0	0	0	.00	0	.000	.000	.000
1984 Pittsburgh	NL	20	22	5	0	0	0	(0	0)	5	3	0	0	0	1	0	0	0	4	1	.80	0	.227	.227	.227
1985 Pittsburgh	NL	17	20	4	0	0	0	(0	0)	4	1	1	0	0	5	0	0	0	0	0	.00	0	.200	.200	.200
1986 Pittsburgh	NL	117	309	72	5	2	0	(0	0)	81	33	31	26	6	54	3	11	1	12	2	.86	8	.233	.298	.262
1987 Pittsburgh	NL	81	203	42	4	3	1	(0	1)	55	26	15	20	6	25	3	2	1	5	1	.83	4	.207	.286	.271
1988 Pittsburgh	NL	122	286	61	0	4	0	(0	0)	69	28	11	26	3	47	4	5	0	7	1	.88	10	.213	.288	.241
1989 Pittsburgh	NL	67	154	33	4	0	0	(0	0)	37	10	8	8	2	22	0	3	0	5	2	.71	1	.214	.253	.240
1990 Pittsburgh	NL	47	54	11	3	0	0	(0	0)	14	10	6	5	0	13	1	1	0	1	2	.33	2	.204	.283	.259
1991 Atlanta	NL	149	353	88	9	2	0	(0	0)	101	36	27	22	2	63	2	7	1	3	1	.75	4	.249	.296	.286
10 ML YEARS		633	1404	317	25	11	1	(0	1)	367	151	99	107	19	231	13	29	3	38	10	.79	29	.226	.286	.261

Esteban Beltre

Bats: Right **Throws:** Right **Pos:** SS **Ht:** 5'10" **Wt:** 155 **Born:** 12/26/67 **Age:** 24

Year	Team	Lg	G	AB	H	2B	3B	HR	(Hm	Rd)	TB	R	RBI	TBB	IBB	SO	HBP	SH	SF	SB	CS	SB%	GDP	Avg	OBP	SLG
1984	Calgary	R	18	20	4	0	0	0	--	--	4	1	2	2	0	8	0	0	0	1	0	1.00	1	.200	.273	.200
1985	Utica	A	72	241	48	6	2	0	--	--	58	19	22	18	0	58	3	8	1	8	7	.53	4	.199	.262	.241
1986	Wst Plm Bch	A	97	285	69	11	1	1	--	--	85	24	20	16	2	59	0	4	1	4	2	.67	9	.242	.281	.298
1987	Jacksnville	AA	142	491	104	15	4	4	--	--	139	55	34	40	0	98	3	10	0	9	8	.53	7	.212	.275	.283
1988	Jacksnville	AA	35	113	17	2	0	0	--	--	19	5	6	3	0	28	0	0	0	1	0	1.00	1	.150	.172	.168
	Wst Plm Bch	A	69	226	63	5	6	0	--	--	80	23	15	11	0	38	1	11	1	4	0	1.00	1	.279	.314	.354
1989	Rockford	A	104	375	80	15	3	2	--	--	107	42	33	33	1	83	0	5	1	9	3	.75	8	.213	.276	.285
1990	Indianapols	AAA	133	407	92	11	2	1	--	--	110	33	37	32	1	77	2	5	4	8	2	.80	9	.226	.283	.270
1991	Denver	AAA	27	78	14	1	3	0	--	--	21	11	9	9	0	16	0	0	0	3	2	.60	5	.179	.264	.269
	Vancouver	AAA	88	347	94	11	3	0	--	--	111	48	30	23	0	61	0	7	1	8	7	.53	7	.271	.315	.320
1991	Chicago	AL	8	6	1	0	0	0	(0	0)	1	0	0	1	0	1	0	0	0	1	0	1.00	0	.167	.286	.167

Freddie Benavides

Bats: Right **Throws:** Right **Pos:** SS **Ht:** 6' 2" **Wt:** 180 **Born:** 04/07/66 **Age:** 26

Year	Team	Lg	G	AB	H	2B	3B	HR	(Hm	Rd)	TB	R	RBI	TBB	IBB	SO	HBP	SH	SF	SB	CS	SB%	GDP	Avg	OBP	SLG
1987	Cedar Rapds	A	5	15	2	1	0	0	--	--	3	2	0	0	0	7	0	0	0	0	1	.00	1	.133	.133	.200
1988	Cedar Rapds	A	88	314	70	9	2	1	--	--	86	38	32	35	3	75	2	4	4	18	7	.72	7	.223	.301	.274
1989	Chattanooga	AA	88	284	71	14	3	0	--	--	91	25	27	22	0	46	2	2	3	1	4	.20	2	.250	.305	.320
	Nashville	AAA	31	94	16	4	0	1	--	--	23	9	12	6	0	24	0	1	0	0	0	.00	1	.170	.220	.245
1990	Chattanooga	AA	55	197	51	10	1	1	--	--	66	20	28	11	0	25	2	3	2	4	2	.67	4	.259	.302	.335
	Nashville	AAA	77	266	56	7	3	2	--	--	75	30	20	12	3	50	3	4	1	3	1	.75	4	.211	.252	.282
1991	Nashville	AAA	94	331	80	8	0	0	--	--	88	24	21	16	3	55	0	3	0	7	7	.50	10	.242	.277	.266
1991	Cincinnati	NL	24	63	18	1	0	0	(0	0)	19	11	3	1	1	15	1	1	1	1	0	1.00	1	.286	.303	.302

Andy Benes

Pitches: Right **Bats:** Right **Pos:** SP **Ht:** 6' 6" **Wt:** 238 **Born:** 08/20/67 **Age:** 24

Year	Team	Lg	G	GS	CG	GF	IP	BFP	H	R	ER	HR	SH	SF	HB	TBB	IBB	SO	WP	Bk	W	L	Pct.	ShO	Sv	ERA
1989	San Diego	NL	10	10	0	0	66.2	280	51	28	26	7	6	2	1	31	0	66	0	3	6	3	.667	0	0	3.51
1990	San Diego	NL	32	31	2	0	192.1	811	177	87	77	18	5	6	1	69	5	140	2	5	10	11	.476	0	0	3.60
1991	San Diego	NL	33	33	4	0	223	908	194	76	75	23	5	4	4	59	7	167	3	4	15	11	.577	1	0	3.03
	3 ML YEARS		75	74	6	1	482	1999	422	191	178	48	16	12	6	159	12	373	5	12	31	25	.554	1	0	3.32

Mike Benjamin

Bats: Right **Throws:** Right **Pos:** SS **Ht:** 6' 3" **Wt:** 195 **Born:** 11/22/65 **Age:** 26

Year	Team	Lg	G	AB	H	2B	3B	HR	(Hm	Rd)	TB	R	RBI	TBB	IBB	SO	HBP	SH	SF	SB	CS	SB%	GDP	Avg	OBP	SLG
1987	Fresno	A	64	212	51	6	4	6	--	--	83	25	24	24	1	71	2	2	0	6	2	.75	1	.241	.324	.392
1988	Shreveport	AA	89	309	73	19	5	6	--	--	120	48	37	22	1	63	0	5	2	14	6	.70	5	.236	.285	.388
	Phoenix	AAA	37	106	18	4	1	0	--	--	24	13	6	13	0	32	2	2	1	2	1	.67	3	.170	.270	.226
1989	Phoenix	AAA	113	363	94	17	6	3	--	--	132	44	36	18	1	82	6	12	2	10	4	.71	6	.259	.303	.364
1990	Phoenix	AAA	118	419	105	21	7	5	--	--	155	61	39	25	3	89	5	2	5	13	7	.65	6	.251	.297	.370
1991	Phoenix	AAA	64	226	46	13	2	6	--	--	81	34	31	20	3	67	2	1	4	3	2	.60	5	.204	.270	.358
1989	San Francisco	NL	14	6	1	0	0	0	(0	0)	1	6	0	0	0	1	0	0	0	0	0	.00	0	.167	.167	.167
1990	San Francisco	NL	22	56	12	3	1	2	(2	0)	23	7	3	3	1	10	0	0	0	1	0	1.00	2	.214	.254	.411
1991	San Francisco	NL	54	106	13	3	0	2	(0	2)	22	12	8	7	2	26	2	3	2	3	0	1.00	1	.123	.188	.208
	3 ML YEARS		90	168	26	6	1	4	(2	2)	46	25	11	10	3	37	2	3	2	4	0	1.00	3	.155	.209	.274

Todd Benzinger

Bats: Both **Throws:** Right **Pos:** 1B/LF **Ht:** 6' 1" **Wt:** 190 **Born:** 02/11/63 **Age:** 29

Year	Team	Lg	G	AB	H	2B	3B	HR	(Hm	Rd)	TB	R	RBI	TBB	IBB	SO	HBP	SH	SF	SB	CS	SB%	GDP	Avg	OBP	SLG
1987	Boston	AL	73	223	62	11	1	8	(5	3)	99	36	43	22	3	41	2	3	3	5	4	.56	5	.278	.344	.444
1988	Boston	AL	120	405	103	28	1	13	(6	7)	172	47	70	22	4	80	1	6	2	2	3	.40	8	.254	.293	.425
1989	Cincinnati	NL	161	628	154	28	3	17	(6	11)	239	79	76	44	13	120	2	4	8	3	7	.30	5	.245	.293	.381
1990	Cincinnati	NL	118	376	95	14	2	5	(4	1)	128	35	46	19	4	69	4	2	7	3	4	.43	5	.253	.291	.340
1991	2 ML Teams		129	416	109	18	5	3	(2	1)	146	36	51	27	4	66	3	2	3	4	6	.40	7	.262	.310	.351
1991	Cincinnati	NL	51	123	23	3	2	1	(1	0)	33	7	11	10	2	20	0	1	2	2	0	1.00	2	.187	.244	.268
	Kansas City	AL	78	293	86	15	3	2	(1	1)	113	29	40	17	2	46	3	1	1	2	6	.25	5	.294	.338	.386
	5 ML YEARS		601	2048	523	99	12	46	(23	23)	784	233	286	134	28	376	12	17	23	17	24	.41	28	.255	.302	.383

18

Juan Berenguer

Pitches: Right   **Bats:** Right   **Pos:** RP   **Ht:** 5'11"   **Wt:** 223   **Born:** 11/30/54   **Age:** 37

			HOW MUCH HE PITCHED						WHAT HE GAVE UP									THE RESULTS					
Year	Team	Lg	G	GS	CG	GF	IP	BFP	H	R	ER	HR	SH	SF	HB	TBB	IBB	SO	WP	Bk	W	L	Pct.	ShO	Sv	ERA
1978	New York	NL	5	3	0	1	13	65	17	12	12	1	0	1	1	11	0	8	0	0	0	2	.000	0	0	8.31
1979	New York	NL	5	5	0	0	31	126	28	13	10	2	1	1	1	12	0	25	0	2	1	1	.500	0	0	2.90
1980	New York	NL	6	0	0	4	9	46	9	9	6	1	0	0	0	10	2	7	0	0	1	0	.000	0	0	6.00
1981	2 ML Teams		20	14	1	4	91	405	84	62	53	11	2	7	5	51	1	49	2	0	2	13	.133	0	0	5.24
1982	Detroit	AL	2	1	0	0	6.2	34	5	5	5	0	0	0	0	9	1	8	0	0	0	0	.000	0	0	6.75
1983	Detroit	AL	37	19	2	7	157.2	650	110	58	55	19	1	2	6	71	3	129	3	1	9	5	.643	1	1	3.14
1984	Detroit	AL	31	27	2	0	168.1	720	146	75	65	14	2	6	5	79	2	118	7	2	11	10	.524	1	0	3.48
1985	Detroit	AL	31	13	0	9	95	424	96	67	59	12	1	4	1	48	3	82	4	1	5	6	.455	0	0	5.59
1986	San Francisco	NL	46	4	0	17	73.1	314	64	23	22	4	2	1	2	44	3	72	4	2	2	3	.400	0	4	2.70
1987	Minnesota	AL	47	6	0	13	112	473	100	51	49	10	2	4	0	47	7	110	6	0	8	1	.889	0	4	3.94
1988	Minnesota	AL	57	1	0	27	100	428	74	44	44	7	5	4	1	61	7	99	3	5	8	4	.667	0	2	3.96
1989	Minnesota	AL	56	0	0	17	106	452	96	44	41	11	7	5	2	47	0	93	5	3	9	3	.750	0	3	3.48
1990	Minnesota	AL	51	0	0	13	100.1	434	85	43	38	9	5	2	2	58	4	77	5	0	8	5	.615	0	0	3.41
1991	Atlanta	NL	49	0	0	35	64.1	255	43	18	16	5	2	2	3	20	2	53	0	0	0	3	.000	0	17	2.24
1981	Kansas City	AL	8	3	0	4	20	97	22	21	19	4	0	3	2	16	0	20	1	0	0	4	.000	0	0	8.55
	Toronto	AL	12	11	1	0	71	308	62	41	34	7	2	4	3	35	1	29	1	0	2	9	.182	0	0	4.31
	14 ML YEARS		443	93	5	147	1127.2	4826	957	524	475	106	30	39	29	568	35	930	39	16	63	57	.525	2	31	3.79

Dave Bergman

Bats: Left   **Throws:** Left   **Pos:** 1B   **Ht:** 6' 2"   **Wt:** 195   **Born:** 06/06/53   **Age:** 39

			BATTING															BASERUNNING				PERCENTAGES		
Year	Team	Lg	G	AB	H	2B	3B	HR	(Hm | Rd)	TB	R	RBI	TBB	IBB	SO	HBP	SH	SF	SB	CS	SB%	GDP	Avg	OBP	SLG
1975	New York	AL	7	17	0	0	0	0	(0 | 0)	0	0	0	2	0	4	0	0	0	0	0	.00	0	.000	.105	.000
1977	New York	NL	5	4	1	0	0	0	(0 | 0)	1	1	1	0	0	0	0	0	1	0	0	.00	0	.250	.200	.250
1978	Houston	NL	104	186	43	5	1	0	(0 | 0)	50	15	12	39	9	32	0	1	2	2	0	1.00	5	.231	.361	.269
1979	Houston	NL	13	15	6	0	0	1	(0 | 1)	9	4	2	0	0	3	0	0	0	0	0	.00	0	.400	.400	.600
1980	Houston	NL	90	78	20	6	1	0	(0 | 0)	28	12	3	10	2	10	0	3	0	1	0	1.00	1	.256	.341	.359
1981	2 ML Teams		69	151	38	9	0	4	(1 | 3)	59	17	14	19	3	18	0	2	1	2	0	1.00	4	.252	.333	.391
1982	San Francisco	NL	100	121	33	3	1	4	(2 | 2)	50	22	14	18	3	11	0	0	1	3	0	1.00	1	.273	.364	.413
1983	San Francisco	NL	90	140	40	4	1	6	(3 | 3)	64	16	24	24	2	21	1	2	0	2	1	.67	5	.286	.394	.457
1984	Detroit	AL	120	271	74	8	5	7	(4 | 3)	113	42	44	33	2	40	3	3	6	3	4	.43	4	.273	.351	.417
1985	Detroit	AL	69	140	25	2	0	3	(2 | 1)	36	8	7	14	0	15	0	1	2	0	0	.00	6	.179	.250	.257
1986	Detroit	AL	65	130	30	6	1	1	(0 | 1)	41	14	9	21	0	16	0	0	0	0	0	.00	3	.231	.338	.315
1987	Detroit	AL	91	172	47	7	3	6	(4 | 2)	78	25	22	30	4	23	1	1	3	0	1	.00	1	.273	.379	.453
1988	Detroit	AL	116	289	85	14	0	5	(4 | 1)	114	37	35	38	2	34	0	2	4	0	2	.00	7	.294	.372	.394
1989	Detroit	AL	137	385	103	13	1	7	(6 | 1)	139	38	37	44	3	44	2	4	1	1	3	.25	5	.268	.345	.361
1990	Detroit	AL	100	205	57	10	1	2	(1 | 1)	75	21	26	33	3	17	0	1	2	3	2	.60	7	.278	.375	.366
1991	Detroit	AL	86	194	46	10	1	7	(2 | 5)	79	23	29	35	2	40	0	0	2	1	1	.50	2	.237	.351	.407
1981	Houston	NL	6	6	1	0	0	1	(0 | 1)	4	1	1	0	0	0	0	0	0	0	0	.00	0	.167	.167	.667
	San Francisco	NL	63	145	37	9	0	3	(1 | 2)	55	16	13	19	3	18	0	2	1	2	0	1.00	4	.255	.339	.379
	16 ML YEARS		1262	2498	648	97	16	53	(29 | 24)	936	295	279	360	35	328	7	20	25	18	14	.56	51	.259	.351	.375

Tony Bernazard

Bats: Both   **Throws:** Right   **Pos:** 2B   **Ht:** 5' 9"   **Wt:** 170   **Born:** 08/24/56   **Age:** 35

			BATTING															BASERUNNING				PERCENTAGES		
Year	Team	Lg	G	AB	H	2B	3B	HR	(Hm | Rd)	TB	R	RBI	TBB	IBB	SO	HBP	SH	SF	SB	CS	SB%	GDP	Avg	OBP	SLG
1979	Montreal	NL	22	40	12	2	0	1	(0 | 1)	17	11	8	15	0	12	1	2	0	1	2	.33	2	.300	.500	.425
1980	Montreal	NL	82	183	41	7	1	5	(2 | 3)	65	26	18	17	4	41	0	1	1	9	2	.82	3	.224	.289	.355
1981	Chicago	AL	106	384	106	14	4	6	(3 | 3)	146	53	34	54	6	66	2	9	1	4	4	.50	7	.276	.367	.380
1982	Chicago	AL	137	540	138	25	9	11	(1 | 10)	214	90	56	67	0	88	2	16	5	11	0	1.00	9	.256	.337	.396
1983	2 ML Teams		139	533	141	34	3	8	(6 | 2)	205	65	56	55	3	97	2	9	7	23	9	.72	9	.265	.332	.385
1984	Cleveland	AL	140	439	97	15	4	2	(1 | 1)	126	44	38	43	0	70	2	7	6	20	13	.61	10	.221	.290	.287
1985	Cleveland	AL	153	500	137	26	3	11	(4 | 7)	202	73	59	69	2	72	1	5	4	17	9	.65	11	.274	.361	.404
1986	Cleveland	AL	146	562	169	28	4	17	(9 | 8)	256	88	73	53	5	77	6	7	8	17	8	.68	6	.301	.362	.456
1987	2 ML Teams		140	507	127	26	2	14	(3 | 11)	199	73	49	55	2	79	1	7	3	11	8	.58	10	.250	.323	.393
1991	Detroit	AL	6	12	2	0	0	0	(0 | 0)	2	0	0	0	0	4	0	0	0	0	0	.00	0	.167	.167	.167
1983	Chicago	AL	59	233	61	16	2	2	(2 | 0)	87	30	26	17	0	45	0	4	5	2	1	.67	5	.262	.306	.373
	Seattle	AL	80	300	80	18	1	6	(4 | 2)	118	35	30	38	3	52	2	5	2	21	8	.72	4	.267	.351	.393
1987	Cleveland	AL	79	293	70	12	1	11	(3 | 8)	117	39	30	25	2	49	1	4	1	7	4	.64	4	.239	.300	.399
	Oakland	AL	61	214	57	14	1	3	(0 | 3)	82	34	19	30	0	30	0	3	2	4	4	.50	6	.266	.354	.383
	10 ML YEARS		1071	3700	970	177	30	75	(29 | 46)	1432	523	391	428	22	606	17	63	35	113	55	.67	67	.262	.339	.387

Sean Berry

Bats: Right **Throws:** Right **Pos:** 3B   **Ht:** 5'11" **Wt:** 210 **Born:** 03/22/66 **Age:** 26

							BATTING												BASERUNNING				PERCENTAGES		
Year Team	Lg	G	AB	H	2B	3B	HR	(Hm	Rd)	TB	R	RBI	TBB	IBB	SO	HBP	SH	SF	SB	CS	SB%	GDP	Avg	OBP	SLG
1986 Eugene	A	65	238	76	20	2	5	--	--	115	53	44	44	0	73	5	1	2	10	1	.91	2	.319	.433	.483
1987 Ft. Myers	A	66	205	52	7	2	2	--	--	69	26	30	43	2	65	3	1	1	4	4	.50	1	.254	.389	.337
1988 Baseball Cy	A	94	304	71	6	4	4	--	--	97	34	30	31	1	62	2	3	3	24	11	.69	3	.234	.306	.319
1989 Baseball Cy	A	116	399	106	19	7	4	--	--	151	67	44	44	1	68	6	5	5	37	11	.77	6	.266	.344	.378
1990 Memphis	AA	135	487	142	25	4	14	--	--	217	73	77	44	1	89	5	7	5	18	9	.67	10	.292	.353	.446
1991 Omaha	AAA	103	368	97	21	9	11	--	--	169	62	54	48	2	70	3	0	5	8	6	.57	8	.264	.349	.459
1990 Kansas City	AL	8	23	5	1	1	0	(0	0)	8	2	4	2	0	5	0	0	0	0	0	.00	0	.217	.280	.348
1991 Kansas City	AL	31	60	8	3	0	0	(0	0)	11	5	1	5	0	23	1	0	0	0	0	.00	1	.133	.212	.183
2 ML YEARS		39	83	13	4	1	0	(0	0)	19	7	5	7	0	28	1	0	0	0	0	.00	1	.157	.231	.229

Damon Berryhill

Bats: Both **Throws:** Right **Pos:** C   **Ht:** 6' 0" **Wt:** 205 **Born:** 12/03/63 **Age:** 28

							BATTING												BASERUNNING				PERCENTAGES		
Year Team	Lg	G	AB	H	2B	3B	HR	(Hm	Rd)	TB	R	RBI	TBB	IBB	SO	HBP	SH	SF	SB	CS	SB%	GDP	Avg	OBP	SLG
1987 Chicago	NL	12	28	5	1	0	0	(0	0)	6	2	1	3	0	5	0	0	0	0	1	.00	1	.179	.258	.214
1988 Chicago	NL	95	309	80	19	1	7	(5	2)	122	19	38	17	5	56	0	3	3	1	0	1.00	11	.259	.295	.395
1989 Chicago	NL	91	334	86	13	0	5	(2	3)	114	37	41	16	4	54	2	4	5	1	0	1.00	13	.257	.291	.341
1990 Chicago	NL	17	53	10	4	0	1	(1	0)	17	6	9	5	1	14	0	0	1	0	0	.00	3	.189	.254	.321
1991 2 ML Teams		63	160	30	7	0	5	(3	2)	52	13	14	11	1	42	1	0	1	1	2	.33	2	.188	.243	.325
1991 Chicago	NL	62	159	30	7	0	5	(3	2)	52	13	14	11	1	41	1	0	1	1	2	.33	2	.189	.244	.327
Atlanta	NL	1	1	0	0	0	0	(0	0)	0	0	0	0	0	1	0	0	0	0	0	.00	0	.000	.000	.000
5 ML YEARS		278	884	211	44	1	18	(11	7)	311	77	103	52	11	171	3	7	10	3	3	.50	30	.239	.280	.352

Dante Bichette

Bats: Right **Throws:** Right **Pos:** RF   **Ht:** 6' 3" **Wt:** 225 **Born:** 11/18/63 **Age:** 28

							BATTING												BASERUNNING				PERCENTAGES		
Year Team	Lg	G	AB	H	2B	3B	HR	(Hm	Rd)	TB	R	RBI	TBB	IBB	SO	HBP	SH	SF	SB	CS	SB%	GDP	Avg	OBP	SLG
1988 California	AL	21	46	12	2	0	0	(0	0)	14	1	8	0	0	7	0	0	4	0	0	.00	0	.261	.240	.304
1989 California	AL	48	138	29	7	0	3	(2	1)	45	13	15	6	0	24	0	0	2	3	0	1.00	3	.210	.240	.326
1990 California	AL	109	349	89	15	1	15	(8	7)	151	40	53	16	1	79	3	1	2	5	2	.71	9	.255	.292	.433
1991 Milwaukee	AL	134	445	106	18	3	15	(6	9)	175	53	59	22	4	107	1	1	6	14	8	.64	9	.238	.272	.393
4 ML YEARS		312	978	236	42	4	33	(16	17)	385	107	135	44	5	217	4	2	14	22	10	.69	21	.241	.273	.394

Mike Bielecki

Pitches: Right **Bats:** Right **Pos:** SP/RP   **Ht:** 6' 3" **Wt:** 195 **Born:** 07/31/59 **Age:** 32

		HOW MUCH HE PITCHED						WHAT HE GAVE UP										THE RESULTS					
Year Team	Lg	G	GS	CG	GF	IP	BFP	H	R	ER	HR	SH	SF	HB	TBB	IBB	SO	WP	Bk	W	L	Pct.	ShO	Sv	ERA
1984 Pittsburgh	NL	4	0	0	1	4.1	17	4	0	0	0	1	0	0	0	0	1	0	1	0	0	.000	0	0	0.00
1985 Pittsburgh	NL	12	7	0	1	45.2	211	45	26	23	5	4	0	1	31	1	22	1	1	2	3	.400	0	0	4.53
1986 Pittsburgh	NL	31	27	0	0	148.2	667	149	87	77	10	7	6	2	83	3	83	7	5	6	11	.353	0	0	4.66
1987 Pittsburgh	NL	8	8	2	0	45.2	192	43	25	24	6	5	2	1	12	0	25	3	0	2	3	.400	0	0	4.73
1988 Chicago	NL	19	5	0	7	48.1	215	55	22	18	4	1	4	0	16	1	33	3	3	2	2	.500	0	0	3.35
1989 Chicago	NL	33	33	4	0	212.1	882	187	82	74	16	9	3	0	81	8	147	9	4	18	7	.720	3	0	3.14
1990 Chicago	NL	36	29	0	6	168	749	188	101	92	13	16	4	5	70	11	103	11	0	8	11	.421	0	0	4.93
1991 2 ML Teams		41	25	0	9	173.2	727	171	91	86	18	10	6	2	56	6	75	6	0	13	11	.542	0	1	4.46
1991 Chicago	NL	39	25	0	8	172	718	169	91	86	18	10	6	2	54	6	72	6	0	13	11	.542	0	0	4.50
Atlanta	NL	2	0	0	1	1.2	9	2	0	0	0	0	0	0	2	0	3	0	0	0	0	.000	0	0	0.00
8 ML YEARS		184	134	6	24	846.2	3660	842	434	394	72	53	25	11	349	30	489	40	14	51	48	.515	3	1	4.19

Craig Biggio

Bats: Right **Throws:** Right **Pos:** C   **Ht:** 5'11" **Wt:** 180 **Born:** 12/14/65 **Age:** 26

							BATTING												BASERUNNING				PERCENTAGES		
Year Team	Lg	G	AB	H	2B	3B	HR	(Hm	Rd)	TB	R	RBI	TBB	IBB	SO	HBP	SH	SF	SB	CS	SB%	GDP	Avg	OBP	SLG
1988 Houston	NL	50	123	26	6	1	3	(1	2)	43	14	5	7	2	29	0	1	0	6	1	.86	1	.211	.254	.350
1989 Houston	NL	134	443	114	21	2	13	(6	7)	178	64	60	49	8	64	6	6	5	21	3	.88	7	.257	.336	.402
1990 Houston	NL	150	555	153	24	2	4	(2	2)	193	53	42	53	1	79	3	9	1	25	11	.69	11	.276	.342	.348
1991 Houston	NL	149	546	161	23	4	4	(0	4)	204	79	46	53	3	71	2	5	3	19	6	.76	2	.295	.358	.374
4 ML YEARS		483	1667	454	74	9	24	(9	15)	618	210	153	162	14	243	11	21	9	71	21	.77	21	.272	.339	.371

Dann Bilardello

Bats: Right **Throws:** Right **Pos:** C **Ht:** 6' 0" **Wt:** 190 **Born:** 05/26/59 **Age:** 33

Year	Team	Lg	G	AB	H	2B	3B	HR	(Hm	Rd)	TB	R	RBI	TBB	IBB	SO	HBP	SH	SF	SB	CS	SB%	GDP	Avg	OBP	SLG
1983	Cincinnati	NL	109	298	71	18	0	9	(7	2)	116	27	38	15	3	49	1	2	4	2	1	.67	9	.238	.274	.389
1984	Cincinnati	NL	68	182	38	7	0	2	(2	0)	51	16	10	19	3	34	1	4	0	0	1	.00	6	.209	.287	.280
1985	Cincinnati	NL	42	102	17	0	0	1	(1	0)	20	6	9	4	1	15	1	1	0	0	0	.00	5	.167	.206	.196
1986	Montreal	NL	79	191	37	5	0	4	(1	3)	54	12	17	14	3	32	0	7	0	1	0	1.00	5	.194	.249	.283
1989	Pittsburgh	NL	33	80	18	6	0	2	(1	1)	30	11	8	2	0	18	0	1	0	1	2	.33	1	.225	.244	.375
1990	Pittsburgh	NL	19	37	2	0	0	0	(0	0)	2	1	3	4	1	10	0	2	0	0	0	.00	0	.054	.146	.054
1991	San Diego	NL	15	26	7	2	1	0	(0	0)	11	4	5	3	0	4	0	0	0	0	0	.00	0	.269	.345	.423
	7 ML YEARS		365	916	190	38	1	18	(12	6)	284	77	90	61	11	162	3	17	4	4	4	.50	26	.207	.258	.310

Joe Bitker

Pitches: Right **Bats:** Right **Pos:** RP **Ht:** 6' 1" **Wt:** 175 **Born:** 02/12/64 **Age:** 28

Year	Team	Lg	G	GS	CG	GF	IP	BFP	H	R	ER	HR	SH	SF	HB	TBB	IBB	SO	WP	Bk	W	L	Pct.	ShO	Sv	ERA
1984	Spokane	A	14	14	2	0	87	0	85	48	33	2	0	0	2	33	0	60	8	0	4	4	.500	0	0	3.41
1985	Charleston	A	13	13	6	0	90.1	380	74	35	26	3	4	3	2	31	0	85	3	3	9	3	.750	4	0	2.59
	Beaumont	AA	15	14	4	0	98	422	91	43	34	3	3	4	2	41	2	64	3	1	8	1	.889	1	0	3.12
1986	Beaumont	AA	18	17	2	1	114.2	497	114	55	45	2	5	4	6	52	4	91	4	1	7	7	.500	2	0	3.53
	Las Vegas	AAA	5	4	0	0	27.1	112	24	10	10	3	2	0	2	9	0	19	4	0	2	0	1.000	0	0	3.29
1987	Las Vegas	AAA	36	27	3	2	160.1	736	184	97	86	14	9	3	7	79	1	80	9	1	11	9	.550	0	1	4.83
1988	Las Vegas	AAA	28	27	3	0	178.1	769	195	98	71	11	7	10	4	41	3	106	4	4	8	10	.444	1	0	3.58
1989	Las Vegas	AAA	18	0	0	10	22.2	104	29	12	10	1	2	1	0	8	1	11	1	1	0	1	.000	0	2	3.97
	Tacoma	AAA	24	2	0	6	51	207	38	26	20	3	3	0	3	12	1	37	3	0	3	3	.500	0	1	3.53
1990	Tacoma	AAA	48	0	0	43	56.1	235	51	22	20	6	3	1	0	20	0	52	2	0	2	3	.400	0	26	3.20
1991	Okla City	AAA	23	0	0	20	26.2	115	30	16	12	1	1	0	0	9	2	33	1	0	0	5	.000	0	7	4.05
1990	2 ML Teams		6	0	0	5	12	48	8	3	3	0	0	1	1	4	0	8	0	0	0	0	.000	0	0	2.25
1991	Texas	AL	9	0	0	2	14.2	70	17	11	11	4	0	0	0	8	3	16	2	0	1	0	1.000	0	0	6.75
1990	Oakland	AL	1	0	0	1	3	10	1	0	0	0	0	0	0	1	0	2	0	0	0	0	.000	0	0	0.00
	Texas	AL	5	0	0	4	9	38	7	3	3	0	0	1	1	3	0	6	0	0	0	0	.000	0	0	3.00
	2 ML YEARS		15	0	0	7	26.2	118	25	14	14	4	0	1	1	12	3	24	2	0	1	0	1.000	0	0	4.72

Bud Black

Pitches: Left **Bats:** Left **Pos:** SP **Ht:** 6' 2" **Wt:** 185 **Born:** 06/30/57 **Age:** 35

Year	Team	Lg	G	GS	CG	GF	IP	BFP	H	R	ER	HR	SH	SF	HB	TBB	IBB	SO	WP	Bk	W	L	Pct.	ShO	Sv	ERA
1981	Seattle	AL	2	2	0	0	1	7	2	0	0	0	0	0	0	3	1	0	1	0	0	0	.000	0	0	0.00
1982	Kansas City	AL	22	14	0	2	88.1	386	92	48	45	10	4	3	3	34	6	40	4	7	4	6	.400	0	0	4.58
1983	Kansas City	AL	24	24	3	0	161.1	672	159	75	68	19	4	5	2	43	1	58	4	0	10	7	.588	0	0	3.79
1984	Kansas City	AL	35	35	8	0	257	1045	226	99	89	22	6	1	4	64	2	140	2	2	17	12	.586	1	0	3.12
1985	Kansas City	AL	33	33	5	0	205.2	885	216	111	99	17	8	4	8	59	4	122	9	1	10	15	.400	2	0	4.33
1986	Kansas City	AL	56	4	0	26	121	503	100	49	43	14	4	4	7	43	5	68	2	2	5	10	.333	0	9	3.20
1987	Kansas City	AL	29	18	0	4	122.1	520	126	63	49	16	1	3	5	35	2	61	6	0	8	6	.571	0	1	3.60
1988	2 ML Teams		33	7	0	9	81	358	82	47	45	8	6	3	4	34	3	63	5	6	4	4	.500	0	1	5.00
1989	Cleveland	AL	33	32	6	0	222.1	912	213	95	83	14	9	5	1	52	0	88	13	5	12	11	.522	3	0	3.36
1990	2 ML Teams		32	31	5	1	206.2	857	181	86	82	19	6	7	5	61	1	106	6	1	13	11	.542	2	0	3.57
1991	San Francisco	NL	34	34	3	0	214.1	893	201	104	95	25	11	7	4	71	8	104	6	6	12	16	.429	3	0	3.99
1988	Kansas City	AL	17	0	0	5	22	98	23	12	12	2	1	0	0	11	2	19	0	2	2	1	.667	0	0	4.91
	Cleveland	AL	16	7	0	4	59	260	59	35	33	6	5	3	4	23	1	44	5	4	2	3	.400	0	1	5.03
1990	Cleveland	AL	29	29	5	0	191	796	171	79	75	17	4	5	4	58	1	103	6	1	11	10	.524	2	0	3.53
	Toronto	AL	3	2	0	1	15.2	61	10	7	7	2	2	2	1	3	0	3	0	0	2	1	.667	0	0	4.02
	11 ML YEARS		333	232	30	42	1681	7038	1598	777	698	164	59	42	43	499	33	850	58	30	95	98	.492	11	11	3.74

Willie Blair

Pitches: Right **Bats:** Right **Pos:** RP/SP **Ht:** 6' 1" **Wt:** 185 **Born:** 12/18/65 **Age:** 26

Year	Team	Lg	G	GS	CG	GF	IP	BFP	H	R	ER	HR	SH	SF	HB	TBB	IBB	SO	WP	Bk	W	L	Pct.	ShO	Sv	ERA
1986	St.Cathrnes	A	21	0	0	18	53.2	204	32	10	10	1	1	0	0	20	1	55	3	0	5	0	1.000	0	12	1.68
1987	Dunedin	A	50	0	0	45	85.1	375	99	51	42	5	5	6	1	29	0	72	9	0	2	9	.182	0	13	4.43
1988	Dunedin	A	4	0	0	1	6.2	26	5	2	2	0	1	0	0	4	1	5	2	0	2	0	1.000	0	0	4.05
	Knoxville	AA	34	9	0	14	102	429	94	49	41	7	1	5	4	35	2	76	4	2	5	5	.500	0	3	3.62
1989	Syracuse	AAA	19	17	3	2	106.2	451	94	55	47	10	2	2	1	38	1	76	1	2	5	6	.455	1	0	3.97

Year	Team	Lg	G	GS	CG	GF	IP	BFP	H	R	ER	HR	SH	SF	HB	TBB	IBB	SO	WP	Bk	W	L	Pct.	ShO	Sv	ERA
1990	Syracuse	AAA	3	3	1	0	19	83	20	13	10	1	1	1	0	8	1	6	0	0	0	2	.000	0	0	4.74
1991	Colo Sprngs	AAA	26	15	0	10	113.2	496	130	74	63	10	3	3	2	30	2	57	3	1	9	6	.600	0	4	4.99
1990	Toronto	AL	27	6	0	8	68.2	297	66	33	31	4	0	4	1	28	4	43	3	0	3	5	.375	0	0	4.06
1991	Cleveland	AL	11	5	0	1	36	168	58	27	27	7	1	2	1	10	0	13	1	0	2	3	.400	0	0	6.75
	2 ML YEARS		38	11	0	9	104.2	465	124	60	58	11	1	6	2	38	4	56	4	0	5	8	.385	0	0	4.99

Lance Blankenship

Bats: Right **Throws:** Right **Pos:** 2B/3B/LF **Ht:** 6' 0" **Wt:** 185 **Born:** 12/06/63 **Age:** 28

									BATTING										BASERUNNING				PERCENTAGES		
Year	Team	Lg	G	AB	H	2B	3B	HR	(Hm	Rd)	TB	R	RBI	TBB	IBB	SO	HBP	SH	SF	SB	CS	SB%	GDP	Avg	OBP	SLG
1988	Oakland	AL	10	3	0	0	0	0	(0	0)	0	1	0	0	0	1	0	0	0	0	1	.00	0	.000	.000	.000
1989	Oakland	AL	58	125	29	5	1	1	(1	0)	39	22	4	8	0	31	0	3	1	5	1	.83	0	.232	.276	.312
1990	Oakland	AL	86	136	26	3	0	0	(0	0)	29	18	10	20	0	23	0	6	0	9	2	.82	6	.191	.295	.213
1991	Oakland	AL	90	185	46	8	0	3	(0	3)	63	33	21	23	0	42	3	2	3	12	3	.80	2	.249	.336	.341
	4 ML YEARS		244	449	101	16	1	4	(1	3)	131	74	35	51	0	97	3	11	4	20	6	.77	8	.225	.306	.292

Jeff Blauser

Bats: Right **Throws:** Right **Pos:** SS/2B/3B **Ht:** 6' 1" **Wt:** 180 **Born:** 11/08/65 **Age:** 26

									BATTING										BASERUNNING				PERCENTAGES		
Year	Team	Lg	G	AB	H	2B	3B	HR	(Hm	Rd)	TB	R	RBI	TBB	IBB	SO	HBP	SH	SF	SB	CS	SB%	GDP	Avg	OBP	SLG
1987	Atlanta	NL	51	165	40	6	3	2	(1	1)	58	11	15	18	1	34	3	1	0	7	3	.70	4	.242	.328	.352
1988	Atlanta	NL	18	67	16	3	1	2	(2	0)	27	7	7	2	0	11	1	3	1	0	1	.00	1	.239	.268	.403
1989	Atlanta	NL	142	456	123	24	2	12	(5	7)	187	63	46	38	2	101	1	8	4	5	2	.71	7	.270	.325	.410
1990	Atlanta	NL	115	386	104	24	3	8	(3	5)	158	46	39	35	1	70	5	3	0	3	5	.38	4	.269	.338	.409
1991	Atlanta	NL	129	352	91	14	3	11	(7	4)	144	49	54	54	4	59	2	4	3	5	6	.45	4	.259	.358	.409
	5 ML YEARS		455	1426	374	71	12	35	(18	17)	574	176	161	147	8	275	12	19	8	20	17	.54	20	.262	.335	.403

Mike Blowers

Bats: Right **Throws:** Right **Pos:** 3B **Ht:** 6' 2" **Wt:** 210 **Born:** 04/24/65 **Age:** 27

									BATTING										BASERUNNING				PERCENTAGES		
Year	Team	Lg	G	AB	H	2B	3B	HR	(Hm	Rd)	TB	R	RBI	TBB	IBB	SO	HBP	SH	SF	SB	CS	SB%	GDP	Avg	OBP	SLG
1989	New York	AL	13	38	10	0	0	0	(0	0)	10	2	3	3	0	13	0	0	0	0	0	.00	1	.263	.317	.263
1990	New York	AL	48	144	27	4	0	5	(1	4)	46	16	21	12	1	50	1	0	0	1	0	1.00	3	.188	.255	.319
1991	New York	AL	15	35	7	0	0	1	(0	1)	10	3	1	4	0	3	0	1	0	0	0	.00	0	.200	.282	.286
	3 ML YEARS		76	217	44	4	0	6	(1	5)	66	21	25	19	1	66	1	1	0	1	0	1.00	5	.203	.270	.304

Mike Boddicker

Pitches: Right **Bats:** Right **Pos:** SP **Ht:** 5'11" **Wt:** 185 **Born:** 08/23/57 **Age:** 34

			HOW MUCH HE PITCHED						WHAT HE GAVE UP												THE RESULTS				
Year	Team	Lg	G	GS	CG	GF	IP	BFP	H	R	ER	HR	SH	SF	HB	TBB	IBB	SO	WP	Bk	W	L	Pct.	ShO	Sv	ERA
1980	Baltimore	AL	1	1	0	0	7	34	6	6	5	1	0	0	0	5	0	4	0	0	0	1	.000	0	0	6.43
1981	Baltimore	AL	2	0	0	1	6	25	6	4	3	1	0	0	0	2	0	2	2	0	0	0	.000	0	0	4.50
1982	Baltimore	AL	7	0	0	4	25.2	110	25	10	10	2	1	0	0	12	2	20	0	0	1	0	1.000	0	0	3.51
1983	Baltimore	AL	27	26	10	1	179	711	141	65	55	13	4	3	0	52	1	120	5	0	16	8	.667	5	0	2.77
1984	Baltimore	AL	34	34	16	0	261.1	1051	218	95	81	23	2	7	5	81	1	128	6	1	20	11	.645	4	0	2.79
1985	Baltimore	AL	32	32	9	0	203.1	899	227	104	92	13	9	2	5	89	7	135	5	0	12	17	.414	2	0	4.07
1986	Baltimore	AL	33	33	7	0	218.1	934	214	125	114	30	3	6	11	74	4	175	7	0	14	12	.538	0	0	4.70
1987	Baltimore	AL	33	33	7	0	226	950	212	114	105	29	7	4	7	78	4	152	10	0	10	12	.455	2	0	4.18
1988	2 ML Teams	AL	36	35	5	0	236	1001	234	102	89	17	4	12	14	77	6	156	6	4	13	15	.464	1	0	3.39
1989	Boston	AL	34	34	3	0	211.2	912	217	101	94	19	8	10	10	71	4	145	4	1	15	11	.577	2	0	4.00
1990	Boston	AL	34	34	4	0	228	956	225	92	85	16	3	1	10	69	6	143	10	0	17	8	.680	0	0	3.36
1991	Kansas City	AL	30	29	1	1	180.2	775	188	89	82	13	10	1	13	59	0	79	3	2	12	12	.500	0	0	4.08
1988	Baltimore	AL	21	21	4	0	147	636	149	72	63	14	3	8	11	51	5	100	3	4	6	12	.333	0	0	3.86
	Boston	AL	15	14	1	0	89	365	85	30	26	3	1	4	3	26	1	56	3	0	7	3	.700	1	0	2.63
	12 ML YEARS		303	291	62	7	1983	8358	1913	907	815	177	51	46	75	669	35	1259	58	8	130	107	.549	16	0	3.70

Joe Boever

Pitches: Right **Bats:** Right **Pos:** RP **Ht:** 6' 1" **Wt:** 212 **Born:** 10/04/60 **Age:** 31

			HOW MUCH HE PITCHED						WHAT HE GAVE UP												THE RESULTS				
Year	Team	Lg	G	GS	CG	GF	IP	BFP	H	R	ER	HR	SH	SF	HB	TBB	IBB	SO	WP	Bk	W	L	Pct.	ShO	Sv	ERA
1985	St. Louis	NL	13	0	0	5	16.1	69	17	8	8	3	1	1	0	4	1	20	1	0	0	0	.000	0	0	4.41
1986	St. Louis	NL	11	0	0	4	21.2	93	19	5	4	2	0	0	0	11	0	8	1	0	0	0	.000	0	0	1.66
1987	Atlanta	NL	14	0	0	10	18.1	93	29	15	15	4	1	1	0	12	1	18	1	0	1	0	1.000	0	0	7.36
1988	Atlanta	NL	16	0	0	13	20.1	70	12	4	4	1	2	0	1	1	0	7	0	0	0	2	.000	0	1	1.77
1989	Atlanta	NL	66	0	0	53	82.1	349	78	37	36	6	5	0	1	34	5	68	5	0	4	11	.267	0	21	3.94
1990	2 ML Teams		67	0	0	34	88.1	388	77	35	33	6	4	2	0	51	12	75	3	2	3	6	.333	0	14	3.36

Year	Team	Lg	G	GS	CG	GF	IP	BFP	H	R	ER	HR	SH	SF	HB	TBB	IBB	SO	WP	Bk	W	L	Pct.	ShO	Sv	ERA
1991	Philadelphia	NL	68	0	0	27	98.1	431	90	45	42	10	3	6	0	54	11	89	6	1	3	5	.375	0	0	3.84
1990	Atlanta	NL	33	0	0	21	42.1	198	40	23	22	6	2	2	0	35	10	35	2	0	1	3	.250	0	8	4.68
	Philadelphia	NL	34	0	0	13	46	190	37	12	11	0	2	0	0	16	2	40	1	2	2	3	.400	0	6	2.15
	7 ML YEARS		255	0		146	345.2	1493	322	149	142	32	16	10	2	167	30	285	17	3	11	25	.306	0	36	3.70

Wade Boggs

Bats: Left **Throws:** Right **Pos:** 3B **Ht:** 6' 2" **Wt:** 197 **Born:** 06/15/58 **Age:** 34

| | | | | | | BATTING | | | | | | | | | | | | | | BASERUNNING | | | | PERCENTAGES | | |
Year	Team	Lg	G	AB	H	2B	3B	HR	(Hm	Rd)	TB	R	RBI	TBB	IBB	SO	HBP	SH	SF	SB	CS	SB%	GDP	Avg	OBP	SLG
1982	Boston	AL	104	338	118	14	1	5	(4	1)	149	51	44	35	4	21	0	4	4	1	0	1.00	9	.349	.406	.441
1983	Boston	AL	153	582	210	44	7	5	(2	3)	283	100	74	92	2	36	1	3	7	3	3	.50	15	.361	.444	.486
1984	Boston	AL	158	625	203	31	4	6	(5	1)	260	109	55	89	6	44	0	8	4	3	2	.60	13	.325	.407	.416
1985	Boston	AL	161	653	240	42	3	8	(6	2)	312	107	78	96	5	61	4	3	2	2	1	.67	20	.368	.450	.478
1986	Boston	AL	149	580	207	47	2	8	(3	5)	282	107	71	105	14	44	0	4	4	0	4	.00	11	.357	.453	.486
1987	Boston	AL	147	551	200	40	6	24	(10	14)	324	108	89	105	19	48	2	1	8	1	3	.25	13	.363	.461	.588
1988	Boston	AL	155	584	214	45	6	5	(4	1)	286	128	58	125	18	34	3	0	7	2	3	.40	23	.366	.476	.490
1989	Boston	AL	156	621	205	51	7	3	(2	1)	279	113	54	107	19	51	7	0	7	2	6	.25	19	.330	.430	.449
1990	Boston	AL	155	619	187	44	5	6	(3	3)	259	89	63	87	19	68	1	0	14	0	0	.00	14	.302	.386	.418
1991	Boston	AL	144	546	181	42	2	8	(6	2)	251	93	51	89	25	32	0	0	6	1	2	.33	16	.332	.421	.460
	10 ML YEARS		1482	5699	1965	400	43	78	(45	33)	2685	1005	637	930	131	439	18	23	55	15	24	.38	153	.345	.435	.471

Brian Bohanon

Pitches: Left **Bats:** Left **Pos:** SP **Ht:** 6' 2" **Wt:** 215 **Born:** 08/01/68 **Age:** 23

| | | | | | | | HOW MUCH HE PITCHED | | | | WHAT HE GAVE UP | | | | | | | | | THE RESULTS | | | | | |
Year	Team	Lg	G	GS	CG	GF	IP	BFP	H	R	ER	HR	SH	SF	HB	TBB	IBB	SO	WP	Bk	W	L	Pct.	ShO	Sv	ERA
1987	Rangers	R	5	4	0	0	21	84	15	13	11	1	0	0	0	5	0	21	2	0	0	2	.000	0	0	4.71
1988	Charlotte	A	2	2	0	0	6.2	31	6	4	4	0	0	0	0	5	0	9	0	1	0	1	.000	0	0	5.40
1989	Charlotte	A	11	7	0	3	54.2	213	40	16	11	1	1	1	2	20	0	33	1	1	0	3	.000	0	1	1.81
	Tulsa	AA	11	11	1	0	73.2	292	59	20	18	3	3	2	3	27	0	44	2	1	5	0	1.000	1	0	2.20
1990	Okla City	AAA	14	4	0	4	32	135	35	16	13	0	2	1	0	8	0	22	2	1	1	2	.333	0	1	3.66
1991	Charlotte	A	2	2	0	0	11.2	47	6	5	5	0	2	2	2	4	0	7	1	0	1	0	1.000	0	0	3.86
	Tulsa	AA	2	2	0	0	11.2	54	9	8	3	0	1	0	0	11	0	6	0	0	0	1	.000	0	0	2.31
	Okla City	AAA	7	7	0	0	46.1	197	49	19	15	2	2	2	1	18	1	37	2	0	0	4	.000	0	0	2.91
1990	Texas	AL	11	6	0	1	34	158	40	30	25	6	0	3	2	18	0	15	1	0	0	3	.000	0	0	6.62
1991	Texas	AL	11	11	1	0	61.1	273	66	35	33	4	2	5	2	23	0	34	3	1	4	3	.571	0	0	4.84
	2 ML YEARS		22	17	1	1	95.1	431	106	65	58	10	2	8	4	41	0	49	4	1	4	6	.400	0	0	5.48

Tom Bolton

Pitches: Left **Bats:** Left **Pos:** SP/RP **Ht:** 6' 3" **Wt:** 175 **Born:** 05/06/62 **Age:** 30

| | | | | | | | HOW MUCH HE PITCHED | | | | WHAT HE GAVE UP | | | | | | | | | THE RESULTS | | | | | |
Year	Team	Lg	G	GS	CG	GF	IP	BFP	H	R	ER	HR	SH	SF	HB	TBB	IBB	SO	WP	Bk	W	L	Pct.	ShO	Sv	ERA
1987	Boston	AL	29	0	0	5	61.2	287	83	33	30	5	3	3	2	27	2	49	3	0	1	0	1.000	0	0	4.38
1988	Boston	AL	28	0	0	8	30.1	140	35	17	16	1	2	1	0	14	1	21	2	1	1	3	.250	0	1	4.75
1989	Boston	AL	4	4	0	0	17.1	83	21	18	16	1	0	1	0	10	1	9	1	0	0	4	.000	0	0	8.31
1990	Boston	AL	21	16	3	2	119.2	501	111	46	45	6	3	5	3	47	3	65	1	1	10	5	.667	0	0	3.38
1991	Boston	AL	25	19	0	4	110	499	136	72	64	16	2	4	1	51	2	64	3	0	8	9	.471	0	0	5.24
	5 ML YEARS		107	39	3	19	339	1510	386	186	171	29	10	14	6	149	9	208	10	2	20	21	.488	0	1	4.54

Barry Bonds

Bats: Left **Throws:** Left **Pos:** LF **Ht:** 6' 1" **Wt:** 190 **Born:** 07/24/64 **Age:** 27

| | | | | | | BATTING | | | | | | | | | | | | | | BASERUNNING | | | | PERCENTAGES | | |
Year	Team	Lg	G	AB	H	2B	3B	HR	(Hm	Rd)	TB	R	RBI	TBB	IBB	SO	HBP	SH	SF	SB	CS	SB%	GDP	Avg	OBP	SLG
1986	Pittsburgh	NL	113	413	92	26	3	16	(9	7)	172	72	48	65	2	102	2	2	2	36	7	.84	4	.223	.330	.416
1987	Pittsburgh	NL	150	551	144	34	9	25	(12	13)	271	99	59	54	3	88	3	0	3	32	10	.76	4	.261	.329	.492
1988	Pittsburgh	NL	144	538	152	30	5	24	(14	10)	264	97	58	72	14	82	2	0	2	17	11	.61	3	.283	.368	.491
1989	Pittsburgh	NL	159	580	144	34	6	19	(7	12)	247	96	58	93	22	93	1	1	4	32	10	.76	9	.248	.351	.426
1990	Pittsburgh	NL	151	519	156	32	3	33	(14	19)	293	104	114	93	15	83	3	0	6	52	13	.80	8	.301	.406	.565
1991	Pittsburgh	NL	153	510	149	28	5	25	(12	13)	262	95	116	107	25	73	4	0	13	43	13	.77	8	.292	.410	.514
	6 ML YEARS		870	3111	837	184	31	142	(68	74)	1509	563	453	484	81	521	15	3	30	212	64	.77	36	.269	.367	.485

Ricky Bones

Pitches: Right **Bats:** Right **Pos:** SP **Ht:** 5'10" **Wt:** 175 **Born:** 04/07/69 **Age:** 23

| | | | | | | | HOW MUCH HE PITCHED | | | | WHAT HE GAVE UP | | | | | | | | | THE RESULTS | | | | | |
Year	Team	Lg	G	GS	CG	GF	IP	BFP	H	R	ER	HR	SH	SF	HB	TBB	IBB	SO	WP	Bk	W	L	Pct.	ShO	Sv	ERA
1986	Spokane	A	18	9	0	0	58	0	63	44	36	3	0	0	1	29	1	46	7	2	1	3	.250	0	0	5.59
1987	Chston-Sc	A	26	26	4	0	170.1	729	183	81	69	9	4	1	6	45	4	130	5	2	12	5	.706	1	0	3.65
1988	Riverside	A	25	25	5	0	175.1	742	162	80	71	11	2	2	4	64	3	129	14	5	15	6	.714	2	0	3.64

1989 Wichita	AA	24	24	2	0	136.1	611	162	103	87	22	4	3	2	47	5	88	7	3	10	9	.526	0	0	5.74
1990 Wichita	AA	21	21	2	0	137	591	138	66	53	15	7	5	5	45	0	96	6	4	6	4	.600	1	0	3.48
Las Vegas	AAA	5	5	0	0	36.1	158	45	17	14	2	0	3	1	10	0	25	1	0	2	1	.667	0	0	3.47
1991 Las Vegas	AAA	23	23	1	0	136.1	611	155	90	64	10	2	4	4	43	3	95	6	3	8	6	.571	0	0	4.22
1991 San Diego	NL	11	11	0	0	54	234	57	33	29	3	0	4	0	18	0	31	4	0	4	6	.400	0	0	4.83

Bobby Bonilla

Bats: Both   **Throws:** Right   **Pos:** RF/3B   **Ht:** 6' 3"   **Wt:** 240   **Born:** 02/23/63   **Age:** 29

							BATTING												BASERUNNING				PERCENTAGES		
Year Team	Lg	G	AB	H	2B	3B	HR	(Hm	Rd)	TB	R	RBI	TBB	IBB	SO	HBP	SH	SF	SB	CS	SB%	GDP	Avg	OBP	SLG
1986 2 ML Teams		138	426	109	16	4	3	(2	1)	142	55	43	62	3	88	2	5	1	8	5	.62	9	.256	.352	.333
1987 Pittsburgh	NL	141	466	140	33	3	15	(7	8)	224	58	77	39	4	64	2	0	8	3	5	.38	8	.300	.351	.481
1988 Pittsburgh	NL	159	584	160	32	7	24	(9	15)	278	87	100	85	19	82	4	0	8	3	5	.38	4	.274	.366	.476
1989 Pittsburgh	NL	163	616	173	37	10	24	(13	11)	302	96	86	76	20	93	1	0	5	8	8	.50	10	.281	.358	.490
1990 Pittsburgh	NL	160	625	175	39	7	32	(13	19)	324	112	120	45	9	103	1	0	15	4	3	.57	10	.280	.322	.518
1991 Pittsburgh	NL	157	577	174	44	6	18	(9	9)	284	102	100	90	8	67	2	0	11	2	4	.33	14	.302	.391	.492
1986 Chicago	AL	75	234	63	10	2	2	(2	0)	83	27	26	33	2	49	1	2	1	4	1	.80	4	.269	.361	.355
Pittsburgh	NL	63	192	46	6	2	1	(0	1)	59	28	17	29	1	39	1	3	0	4	4	.50	5	.240	.342	.307
6 ML YEARS		918	3294	931	201	37	116	(53	63)	1554	510	526	397	63	497	12	5	48	28	30	.48	55	.283	.357	.472

Rod Booker

Bats: Left   **Throws:** Right   **Pos:** SS   **Ht:** 6' 0"   **Wt:** 178   **Born:** 09/04/58   **Age:** 33

							BATTING												BASERUNNING				PERCENTAGES		
Year Team	Lg	G	AB	H	2B	3B	HR	(Hm	Rd)	TB	R	RBI	TBB	IBB	SO	HBP	SH	SF	SB	CS	SB%	GDP	Avg	OBP	SLG
1987 St. Louis	NL	44	47	13	1	1	0	(0	0)	16	9	8	7	1	7	0	2	0	2	0	1.00	0	.277	.370	.340
1988 St. Louis	NL	18	35	12	3	0	0	(0	0)	15	6	3	4	0	3	0	0	0	2	2	.50	0	.343	.410	.429
1989 St. Louis	NL	10	8	2	0	0	0	(0	0)	2	1	0	0	0	1	0	0	0	0	0	.00	0	.250	.250	.250
1990 Philadelphia	NL	73	131	29	5	2	0	(0	0)	38	19	10	15	7	26	0	2	0	3	1	.75	7	.221	.301	.290
1991 Philadelphia	NL	28	53	12	1	0	0	(0	0)	13	3	7	1	1	7	0	1	1	0	0	.00	1	.226	.236	.245
5 ML YEARS		173	274	68	10	3	0	(0	0)	84	38	28	27	9	44	0	5	1	7	3	.70	8	.248	.315	.307

Pat Borders

Bats: Right   **Throws:** Right   **Pos:** C   **Ht:** 6' 2"   **Wt:** 200   **Born:** 05/14/63   **Age:** 29

							BATTING												BASERUNNING				PERCENTAGES		
Year Team	Lg	G	AB	H	2B	3B	HR	(Hm	Rd)	TB	R	RBI	TBB	IBB	SO	HBP	SH	SF	SB	CS	SB%	GDP	Avg	OBP	SLG
1988 Toronto	AL	56	154	42	6	3	5	(2	3)	69	15	21	3	0	24	0	2	1	0	0	.00	5	.273	.285	.448
1989 Toronto	AL	94	241	62	11	1	3	(1	2)	84	22	29	11	2	45	1	1	2	2	1	.67	7	.257	.290	.349
1990 Toronto	AL	125	346	99	24	2	15	(10	5)	172	36	49	18	2	57	0	1	3	0	1	.00	17	.286	.319	.497
1991 Toronto	AL	105	291	71	17	0	5	(2	3)	103	22	36	11	1	45	1	6	3	0	0	.00	8	.244	.271	.354
4 ML YEARS		380	1032	274	58	6	28	(15	13)	428	95	135	43	5	171	2	10	9	2	2	.50	37	.266	.294	.415

Mike Bordick

Bats: Right   **Throws:** Right   **Pos:** SS   **Ht:** 5'11"   **Wt:** 175   **Born:** 07/21/65   **Age:** 26

							BATTING												BASERUNNING				PERCENTAGES		
Year Team	Lg	G	AB	H	2B	3B	HR	(Hm	Rd)	TB	R	RBI	TBB	IBB	SO	HBP	SH	SF	SB	CS	SB%	GDP	Avg	OBP	SLG
1986 Medford	A	46	187	48	3	1	0	--	--	53	30	19	40	0	21	1	1	1	6	0	1.00	5	.257	.389	.283
1987 Modesto	A	133	497	133	17	0	3	--	--	159	73	75	87	3	92	5	4	8	8	8	.50	13	.268	.377	.320
1988 Huntsville	AA	132	481	130	13	2	0	--	--	147	48	38	87	0	50	4	9	3	7	9	.44	11	.270	.384	.306
1989 Tacoma	AAA	136	487	117	17	1	1	--	--	139	55	43	58	0	51	7	15	2	4	9	.31	14	.240	.329	.285
1990 Tacoma	AAA	111	348	79	16	1	2	--	--	103	49	30	46	0	40	3	7	2	3	0	1.00	6	.227	.321	.296
1991 Tacoma	AAA	26	81	22	4	1	2	--	--	34	15	14	17	0	10	1	1	0	0	1	.00	0	.272	.404	.420
1990 Oakland	AL	25	14	1	0	0	0	(0	0)	1	0	0	1	0	4	0	0	0	0	0	.00	0	.071	.133	.071
1991 Oakland	AL	90	235	56	5	1	0	(0	0)	63	21	21	14	0	37	3	12	1	3	4	.43	3	.238	.289	.268
2 ML YEARS		115	249	57	5	1	0	(0	0)	64	21	21	15	0	41	3	12	1	3	4	.43	3	.229	.280	.257

Chris Bosio

Pitches: Right   **Bats:** Right   **Pos:** SP   **Ht:** 6' 3"   **Wt:** 225   **Born:** 04/03/63   **Age:** 29

		HOW MUCH HE PITCHED						WHAT HE GAVE UP											THE RESULTS					
Year Team	Lg	G	GS	CG	GF	IP	BFP	H	R	ER	HR	SH	SF	HB	TBB	IBB	SO	WP	Bk	W	L	Pct.	ShO	Sv	ERA
1986 Milwaukee	AL	10	4	0	3	34.2	154	41	27	27	9	1	0	0	13	0	29	2	1	0	4	.000	0	0	7.01
1987 Milwaukee	AL	46	19	2	8	170	734	187	102	99	18	3	3	1	50	3	150	14	2	11	8	.579	1	2	5.24
1988 Milwaukee	AL	38	22	9	15	182	766	190	80	68	13	7	9	2	38	6	84	1	2	7	15	.318	1	6	3.36
1989 Milwaukee	AL	33	33	8	0	234.2	969	225	90	77	16	5	5	6	48	1	173	4	2	15	10	.600	2	0	2.95
1990 Milwaukee	AL	20	20	4	0	132.2	557	131	67	59	15	4	4	3	38	1	76	7	0	4	9	.308	1	0	4.00
1991 Milwaukee	AL	32	32	5	0	204.2	840	187	80	74	15	2	6	8	58	0	117	5	0	14	10	.583	1	0	3.25
6 ML YEARS		179	130	28	26	958.2	4020	961	446	404	86	22	27	20	245	11	629	33	7	51	56	.477	6	8	3.79

Shawn Boskie

Pitches: Right **Bats:** Right **Pos:** SP/RP **Ht:** 6' 3" **Wt:** 205 **Born:** 03/28/67 **Age:** 25

				HOW	MUCH	HE	PITCHED			WHAT	HE	GAVE	UP							THE	RESULTS			
Year	Team	Lg	G	GS	CG	GF	IP	BFP	H	R	ER	HR	SH	SF	HB	TBB	IBB	SO	WP	Bk	W	L	Pct.	ShO	Sv	ERA
1986	Wytheville	R	14	12	1	0	54	268	42	41	32	4	0	1	7	57	1	40	15	0	4	4	.500	0	0	5.33
1987	Peoria	A	26	25	1	0	149	657	149	91	72	12	4	5	17	56	2	100	7	5	9	11	.450	0	0	4.35
1988	Winston-Sal	A	27	27	4	0	186	825	176	83	70	9	4	7	17	89	1	164	14	4	12	7	.632	2	0	3.39
1989	Charlotte	AA	28	28	5	0	181	813	196	105	88	10	3	8	19	84	3	164	11	1	11	8	.579	0	0	4.38
1990	Iowa	AAA	8	8	1	0	51	217	46	22	18	1	2	1	2	21	1	51	1	0	4	2	.667	0	0	3.18
1991	Iowa	AAA	7	6	2	0	45.1	186	43	19	18	1	5	1	2	11	0	29	1	1	2	2	.500	0	0	3.57
1990	Chicago	NL	15	15	1	0	97.2	415	99	42	40	8	8	2	1	31	3	49	3	2	5	6	.455	0	0	3.69
1991	Chicago	NL	28	20	0	2	129	582	150	78	75	14	8	6	5	52	4	62	1	1	4	9	.308	0	0	5.23
	2 ML YEARS		43	35	1	2	226.2	997	249	120	115	22	16	8	6	83	7	111	4	3	9	15	.375	0	0	4.57

Daryl Boston

Bats: Left **Throws:** Left **Pos:** CF/RF **Ht:** 6' 3" **Wt:** 205 **Born:** 01/04/63 **Age:** 29

						BATTING													BASERUNNING				PERCENTAGES		
Year	Team	Lg	G	AB	H	2B	3B	HR	(Hm	Rd)	TB	R	RBI	TBB	IBB	SO	HBP	SH	SF	SB	CS	SB%	GDP	Avg	OBP	SLG
1984	Chicago	AL	35	83	14	3	1	0	(0	0)	19	8	3	4	0	20	0	0	0	6	0	1.00	0	.169	.207	.229
1985	Chicago	AL	95	232	53	13	1	3	(1	2)	77	20	15	14	1	44	0	1	1	8	6	.57	3	.228	.271	.332
1986	Chicago	AL	56	199	53	11	3	5	(1	4)	85	29	22	21	3	33	0	3	1	9	5	.64	4	.266	.335	.427
1987	Chicago	AL	103	337	87	21	2	10	(5	5)	142	51	29	25	2	68	0	4	3	12	6	.67	5	.258	.307	.421
1988	Chicago	AL	105	281	61	12	2	15	(6	9)	122	37	31	21	5	44	0	2	1	9	3	.75	5	.217	.271	.434
1989	Chicago	AL	101	218	55	3	4	5	(3	2)	81	34	23	24	3	31	0	4	1	7	2	.78	1	.252	.325	.372
1990	2 ML Teams		120	367	100	21	2	12	(4	8)	161	65	45	28	2	50	2	0	0	19	7	.73	7	.272	.327	.439
1991	New York	NL	137	255	70	16	4	4	(2	2)	106	40	21	30	0	42	0	0	1	15	8	.65	2	.275	.350	.416
1990	Chicago	AL	5	1	0	0	0	0	(0	0)	0	0	0	0	0	0	0	0	0	1	0	1.00	0	.000	.000	.000
	New York	NL	115	366	100	21	2	12	(4	8)	161	65	45	28	2	50	2	0	0	18	7	.72	7	.273	.328	.440
	8 ML YEARS		752	1972	493	100	19	54	(22	32)	793	284	189	167	16	332	2	14	8	85	37	.70	27	.250	.308	.402

Denis Boucher

Pitches: Left **Bats:** Right **Pos:** SP **Ht:** 6' 1" **Wt:** 195 **Born:** 03/07/68 **Age:** 24

					HOW	MUCH	HE	PITCHED			WHAT	HE	GAVE	UP							THE	RESULTS			
Year	Team	Lg	G	GS	CG	GF	IP	BFP	H	R	ER	HR	SH	SF	HB	TBB	IBB	SO	WP	Bk	W	L	Pct.	ShO	Sv	ERA
1988	Myrtle Bch	A	33	32	1	0	196.2	809	161	81	62	11	7	6	8	63	1	169	15	21	13	12	.520	2	0	2.84
1989	Dunedin	A	33	28	1	1	164.2	675	142	80	56	6	3	6	6	58	2	117	13	8	10	10	.500	1	0	3.06
1990	Dunedin	A	9	9	2	0	60	226	45	8	5	1	0	0	2	8	0	62	4	0	7	0	1.000	2	0	0.75
	Syracuse	AAA	17	17	2	0	107.2	449	100	51	46	7	4	4	2	37	2	80	6	0	8	5	.615	1	0	3.85
1991	Syracuse	AAA	8	8	1	0	56.2	241	57	24	20	5	4	1	3	19	1	28	2	0	2	1	.667	0	0	3.18
	Colo Sprngs	AAA	3	3	0	0	14.1	59	14	8	8	1	0	1	0	2	0	9	0	0	1	0	1.000	0	0	5.02
1991	2 ML Teams		12	12	0	0	58	270	74	41	39	12	3	1	2	24	1	29	1	4	1	7	.125	0	0	6.05
1991	Toronto	AL	7	7	0	0	35.1	162	39	20	18	6	3	1	2	16	1	16	0	4	0	3	.000	0	0	4.58
	Cleveland	AL	5	5	0	0	22.2	108	35	21	21	6	0	0	0	8	0	13	1	0	1	4	.200	0	0	8.34

Ryan Bowen

Pitches: Right **Bats:** Right **Pos:** SP **Ht:** 6' 0" **Wt:** 185 **Born:** 02/10/68 **Age:** 24

					HOW	MUCH	HE	PITCHED			WHAT	HE	GAVE	UP							THE	RESULTS			
Year	Team	Lg	G	GS	CG	GF	IP	BFP	H	R	ER	HR	SH	SF	HB	TBB	IBB	SO	WP	Bk	W	L	Pct.	ShO	Sv	ERA
1987	Asheville	A	26	26	6	0	160.1	704	143	86	72	12	7	4	5	78	1	126	8	2	12	5	.706	2	0	4.04
1988	Osceola	A	4	4	0	0	13.2	65	12	8	6	0	1	0	1	10	0	12	2	0	1	0	1.000	0	0	3.95
1989	Columbus	AA	27	27	1	0	139.2	655	123	83	66	11	7	4	8	116	0	136	12	0	8	6	.571	1	0	4.25
1990	Tucson	AAA	10	7	0	0	34.2	177	41	36	36	5	2	0	0	38	1	29	0	0	1	3	.250	0	0	9.35
	Columbus	AA	18	18	2	0	113	491	103	59	47	7	4	6	0	49	0	109	5	1	8	4	.667	2	0	3.74
1991	Tucson	AAA	18	18	2	0	98.2	450	114	56	48	3	3	0	3	56	2	78	9	0	5	5	.500	2	0	4.38
1991	Houston	NL	14	13	0	0	71.2	319	73	43	41	4	2	6	3	36	1	49	8	1	6	4	.600	0	0	5.15

Oil Can Boyd

Pitches: Right **Bats:** Right **Pos:** SP **Ht:** 6' 1" **Wt:** 160 **Born:** 10/06/59 **Age:** 32

					HOW	MUCH	HE	PITCHED			WHAT	HE	GAVE	UP							THE	RESULTS			
Year	Team	Lg	G	GS	CG	GF	IP	BFP	H	R	ER	HR	SH	SF	HB	TBB	IBB	SO	WP	Bk	W	L	Pct.	ShO	Sv	ERA
1982	Boston	AL	3	1	0	0	8.1	37	11	5	5	2	0	0	0	2	0	2	1	0	0	1	.000	0	0	5.40
1983	Boston	AL	15	13	5	2	98.2	413	103	46	36	9	1	5	1	23	0	43	3	1	4	8	.333	1	0	3.28
1984	Boston	AL	29	26	10	0	197.2	835	207	109	96	18	4	8	1	53	5	134	5	1	12	12	.500	3	0	4.37
1985	Boston	AL	35	35	13	0	272.1	1132	273	117	112	26	9	7	4	67	3	154	1	1	15	13	.536	3	0	3.70
1986	Boston	AL	30	30	10	0	214.1	893	222	99	90	32	3	6	2	45	1	129	3	0	16	10	.615	0	0	3.78

25

Year Team	Lg	G	GS	CG	GF	IP	BFP	H	R	ER	HR	SH	SF	HB	TBB	IBB	SO	WP	Bk	W	L	Pct.	ShO	Sv	ERA
1987 Boston	AL	7	7	0	0	36.2	167	47	31	24	6	4	3	2	9	1	12	0	2	1	3	.250	0	0	5.89
1988 Boston	AL	23	23	1	0	129.2	561	147	82	77	25	3	6	2	41	2	71	0	5	9	7	.563	0	0	5.34
1989 Boston	AL	10	10	0	0	59	246	57	31	29	8	0	2	0	19	0	26	2	0	3	2	.600	0	0	4.42
1990 Montreal	NL	31	31	3	0	190.2	774	164	64	62	19	12	4	3	52	10	113	3	3	10	6	.625	3	0	2.93
1991 2 ML Teams		31	31	1	0	182.1	773	196	96	93	21	4	4	0	57	3	115	2	4	8	15	.348	1	0	4.59
1991 Montreal	NL	19	19	1	0	120.1	496	115	49	47	9	2	4	0	40	2	82	2	3	6	8	.429	1	0	3.52
Texas	AL	12	12	0	0	62	277	81	47	46	12	2	0	0	17	1	33	0	1	2	7	.222	0	0	6.68
10 ML YEARS		214	207	43	4	1389.2	5831	1427	680	624	166	40	45	15	368	25	799	20	17	78	77	.503	10	0	4.04

Scott Bradley

Bats: Left   **Throws:** Right   **Pos:** C   **Ht:** 5'11"   **Wt:** 185   **Born:** 03/22/60   **Age:** 32

							BATTING													BASERUNNING				PERCENTAGES		
Year Team	Lg	G	AB	H	2B	3B	HR	(Hm	Rd)	TB	R	RBI	TBB	IBB	SO	HBP	SH	SF	SB	CS	SB%	GDP	Avg	OBP	SLG
1984 New York	AL	9	21	6	1	0	0	(0	0)	7	3	2	1	0	1	0	0	0	0	0	.00	0	.286	.318	.333
1985 New York	AL	19	49	8	2	1	0	(0	0)	12	4	1	1	0	5	1	0	0	0	0	.00	2	.163	.196	.245
1986 2 ML Teams		77	220	66	8	3	5	(4	1)	95	20	28	13	4	7	4	2	2	1	2	.33	13	.300	.347	.432
1987 Seattle	AL	102	342	95	15	1	5	(5	0)	127	34	43	15	1	18	3	2	1	0	1	.00	13	.278	.310	.371
1988 Seattle	AL	103	335	86	17	1	4	(3	1)	117	45	33	17	1	16	2	3	2	1	1	.50	11	.257	.295	.349
1989 Seattle	AL	103	270	74	16	0	3	(1	2)	99	21	37	21	4	23	1	1	6	1	1	.50	5	.274	.322	.367
1990 Seattle	AL	101	233	52	9	0	1	(1	0)	64	11	28	15	2	20	0	3	6	0	1	.00	6	.223	.264	.275
1991 Seattle	AL	83	172	35	7	0	0	(0	0)	42	10	11	19	2	19	0	5	2	0	0	.00	6	.203	.280	.244
1986 Chicago	AL	9	21	6	0	0	0	(0	0)	6	3	0	1	0	0	2	0	0	0	2	.00	1	.286	.375	.286
Seattle	AL	68	199	60	8	3	5	(4	1)	89	17	28	12	4	7	2	2	2	1	0	1.00	12	.302	.344	.447
8 ML YEARS		597	1642	422	75	6	18	(14	4)	563	148	183	102	14	109	11	16	22	3	6	.33	52	.257	.301	.343

Glenn Braggs

Bats: Right   **Throws:** Right   **Pos:** LF/RF   **Ht:** 6'4"   **Wt:** 220   **Born:** 10/17/62   **Age:** 29

							BATTING													BASERUNNING				PERCENTAGES		
Year Team	Lg	G	AB	H	2B	3B	HR	(Hm	Rd)	TB	R	RBI	TBB	IBB	SO	HBP	SH	SF	SB	CS	SB%	GDP	Avg	OBP	SLG
1986 Milwaukee	AL	58	215	51	8	2	4	(2	2)	75	19	18	11	0	47	1	2	3	1	1	.50	6	.237	.274	.349
1987 Milwaukee	AL	132	505	136	28	7	13	(4	9)	217	67	77	47	7	96	4	2	7	12	5	.71	20	.269	.332	.430
1988 Milwaukee	AL	72	272	71	14	0	10	(6	4)	115	30	42	14	0	60	5	1	2	6	4	.60	6	.261	.307	.423
1989 Milwaukee	AL	144	514	127	12	3	15	(8	7)	190	77	66	42	4	111	4	3	7	17	5	.77	13	.247	.305	.370
1990 2 ML Teams		109	314	88	14	1	9	(5	4)	131	39	41	38	3	64	6	0	4	8	7	.53	4	.280	.365	.417
1991 Cincinnati	NL	85	250	65	10	0	11	(8	3)	108	36	39	23	3	46	2	0	4	11	3	.79	11	.260	.323	.432
1990 Milwaukee	AL	37	113	28	5	0	3	(1	2)	42	17	13	12	2	21	3	0	3	5	3	.63	1	.248	.328	.372
Cincinnati	NL	72	201	60	9	1	6	(4	2)	89	22	28	26	1	43	3	0	1	3	4	.43	3	.299	.385	.443
6 ML YEARS		600	2070	538	86	13	62	(33	29)	836	268	283	175	17	424	22	8	27	55	25	.69	53	.260	.320	.404

Cliff Brantley

Pitches: Right   **Bats:** Right   **Pos:** SP   **Ht:** 6'1"   **Wt:** 190   **Born:** 04/12/68   **Age:** 24

						HOW MUCH HE PITCHED		WHAT HE GAVE UP												THE RESULTS					
Year Team	Lg	G	GS	CG	GF	IP	BFP	H	R	ER	HR	SH	SF	HB	TBB	IBB	SO	WP	Bk	W	L	Pct.	ShO	Sv	ERA
1986 Utica	A	11	11	0	0	60.2	280	68	37	29	5	2	4	4	25	1	42	5	1	3	5	.375	0	0	4.30
1987 Spartanburg	A	20	20	3	0	110.1	494	114	69	59	2	2	2	9	58	2	86	10	3	3	10	.231	0	0	4.81
1988 Clearwater	A	24	24	6	0	166.2	689	126	55	48	2	4	6	5	74	6	124	20	9	8	11	.421	1	0	2.59
Reading	AA	1	1	0	0	6	26	5	4	4	1	0	1	1	2	0	5	0	0	1	0	1.000	0	0	6.00
1989 Reading	AA	11	9	0	1	49	227	49	29	18	1	1	2	2	28	0	35	2	1	3	4	.429	0	1	3.31
Clearwater	A	8	8	1	0	49.2	228	60	31	24	3	1	3	0	19	1	33	6	2	0	5	.000	0	0	4.35
1990 Clearwater	A	8	8	2	0	49	201	44	20	16	3	4	0	1	17	0	37	5	0	1	4	.200	0	0	2.94
Reading	AA	17	17	0	0	87	386	93	51	44	4	3	3	3	39	0	69	4	1	4	9	.308	0	0	4.55
1991 Reading	AA	11	11	2	0	69.2	279	50	17	15	3	8	0	4	25	1	51	2	1	4	3	.571	1	0	1.94
Scranton-Wb	AAA	8	8	0	0	47.1	206	44	26	20	2	1	0	2	25	0	28	0	2	2	4	.333	0	0	3.80
1991 Philadelphia	NL	6	5	0	0	31.2	140	26	12	12	2	3	2	1	19	0	25	2	0	2	2	.500	0	0	3.41

Jeff Brantley

Pitches: Right   **Bats:** Right   **Pos:** RP   **Ht:** 5'11"   **Wt:** 190   **Born:** 09/05/63   **Age:** 28

						HOW MUCH HE PITCHED		WHAT HE GAVE UP												THE RESULTS					
Year Team	Lg	G	GS	CG	GF	IP	BFP	H	R	ER	HR	SH	SF	HB	TBB	IBB	SO	WP	Bk	W	L	Pct.	ShO	Sv	ERA
1988 San Francisco	NL	9	1	0	2	20.2	88	22	13	13	2	1	0	2	6	1	11	0	1	0	1	.000	0	1	5.66
1989 San Francisco	NL	59	1	0	15	97.1	422	101	50	44	10	7	3	2	37	8	69	3	2	7	1	.875	0	4	4.07
1990 San Francisco	NL	55	0	0	32	86.2	361	77	18	15	3	2	3	2	33	6	61	0	3	5	3	.625	0	19	1.56
1991 San Francisco	NL	67	0	0	39	95.1	411	78	27	26	8	4	4	5	52	10	81	6	0	5	2	.714	0	15	2.45
4 ML YEARS		190	2	0	88	300	1282	278	108	98	23	14	9	11	128	25	222	9	6	17	7	.708	0	35	2.94

Sid Bream

Bats: Left   **Throws:** Left   **Pos:** 1B   **Ht:** 6' 4"   **Wt:** 220   **Born:** 08/03/60   **Age:** 31

Year	Team	Lg	G	AB	H	2B	3B	HR	(Hm	Rd)	TB	R	RBI	TBB	IBB	SO	HBP	SH	SF	SB	CS	SB%	GDP	Avg	OBP	SLG
1983	Los Angeles	NL	15	11	2	0	0	0	(0	0)	2	0	2	2	0	2	0	0	0	0	0	.00	1	.182	.308	.182
1984	Los Angeles	NL	27	49	9	3	0	0	(0	0)	12	2	6	6	2	9	0	1	2	1	0	1.00	1	.184	.263	.245
1985	2 ML Teams		50	148	34	7	0	6	(2	4)	59	18	21	18	5	24	0	3	2	0	2	.00	4	.230	.310	.399
1986	Pittsburgh	NL	154	522	140	37	5	16	(5	11)	235	73	77	60	5	73	1	1	7	13	7	.65	14	.268	.341	.450
1987	Pittsburgh	NL	149	516	142	25	3	13	(10	3)	212	64	65	49	11	69	0	3	4	9	8	.53	19	.275	.336	.411
1988	Pittsburgh	NL	148	462	122	37	0	10	(6	4)	189	50	65	47	6	64	1	4	8	9	9	.50	11	.264	.328	.409
1989	Pittsburgh	NL	19	36	8	3	0	0	(0	0)	11	3	4	12	0	10	0	2	0	0	4	.00	0	.222	.417	.306
1990	Pittsburgh	NL	147	389	105	23	2	15	(8	7)	177	39	67	48	5	65	2	4	5	8	4	.67	6	.270	.349	.455
1991	Atlanta	NL	91	265	67	12	0	11	(3	8)	112	32	45	25	5	31	0	4	4	0	3	.00	8	.253	.313	.423
1985	Los Angeles	NL	24	53	7	0	0	3	(2	1)	16	4	6	7	3	10	0	2	1	0	0	.00	1	.132	.230	.302
	Pittsburgh	NL	26	95	27	7	0	3	(0	3)	43	14	15	11	2	14	0	1	1	0	2	.00	4	.284	.355	.453
	9 ML YEARS		800	2398	629	147	10	71	(34	37)	1009	281	352	267	39	347	4	22	32	40	37	.52	64	.262	.333	.421

George Brett

Bats: Left   **Throws:** Right   **Pos:** DH   **Ht:** 6' 0"   **Wt:** 205   **Born:** 05/15/53   **Age:** 39

Year	Team	Lg	G	AB	H	2B	3B	HR	(Hm	Rd)	TB	R	RBI	TBB	IBB	SO	HBP	SH	SF	SB	CS	SB%	GDP	Avg	OBP	SLG
1973	Kansas City	AL	13	40	5	2	0	0	(0	0)	7	2	0	0	0	5	0	1	0	0	0	.00	0	.125	.125	.175
1974	Kansas City	AL	133	457	129	21	5	2	(0	2)	166	49	47	21	3	38	0	6	2	8	5	.62	9	.282	.313	.363
1975	Kansas City	AL	159	634	195	35	13	11	(2	9)	289	84	89	46	6	49	2	9	6	13	10	.57	8	.308	.353	.456
1976	Kansas City	AL	159	645	215	34	14	7	(6	1)	298	94	67	49	4	36	1	2	8	21	11	.66	8	.333	.377	.462
1977	Kansas City	AL	139	564	176	32	13	22	(9	13)	300	105	88	55	9	24	2	3	3	14	12	.54	12	.312	.373	.532
1978	Kansas City	AL	128	510	150	45	8	9	(4	5)	238	79	62	39	6	35	1	3	5	23	7	.77	6	.294	.342	.467
1979	Kansas City	AL	154	645	212	42	20	23	(11	12)	363	119	107	51	14	36	0	1	4	17	10	.63	8	.329	.376	.563
1980	Kansas City	AL	117	449	175	33	9	24	(13	11)	298	87	118	58	16	22	1	0	7	15	6	.71	11	.390	.454	.664
1981	Kansas City	AL	89	347	109	27	7	6	(2	4)	168	42	43	27	7	23	1	0	4	14	6	.70	7	.314	.361	.484
1982	Kansas City	AL	144	552	166	32	9	21	(9	12)	279	101	82	71	14	51	1	0	5	6	1	.86	12	.301	.378	.505
1983	Kansas City	AL	123	464	144	38	2	25	(7	18)	261	90	93	57	13	39	1	0	3	0	1	.00	9	.310	.385	.563
1984	Kansas City	AL	104	377	107	21	3	13	(6	7)	173	42	69	38	6	37	0	0	7	0	2	.00	11	.284	.344	.459
1985	Kansas City	AL	155	550	184	38	5	30	(15	15)	322	108	112	103	31	49	3	0	9	9	1	.90	12	.335	.436	.585
1986	Kansas City	AL	124	441	128	28	4	16	(8	8)	212	70	73	80	18	45	4	0	4	1	2	.33	6	.290	.401	.481
1987	Kansas City	AL	115	427	124	18	2	22	(14	8)	212	71	78	72	14	47	1	0	8	6	3	.67	10	.290	.388	.496
1988	Kansas City	AL	157	589	180	42	3	24	(13	11)	300	90	103	82	15	51	3	0	7	14	3	.82	15	.306	.389	.509
1989	Kansas City	AL	124	457	129	26	3	12	(3	9)	197	67	80	59	14	47	3	0	9	14	4	.78	18	.282	.362	.431
1990	Kansas City	AL	142	544	179	45	7	14	(3	11)	280	82	87	56	14	63	0	0	7	9	2	.82	17	.329	.387	.515
1991	Kansas City	AL	131	505	129	40	2	10	(3	7)	203	77	61	58	11	75	0	1	8	2	0	1.00	20	.255	.327	.402
	19 ML YEARS		2410	9197	2836	599	129	291	(128	163)	4566	1459	1459	1022	214	772	24	26	106	186	86	.68	199	.308	.375	.496

Rod Brewer

Bats: Left   **Throws:** Left   **Pos:** 1B   **Ht:** 6' 3"   **Wt:** 208   **Born:** 02/24/66   **Age:** 26

Year	Team	Lg	G	AB	H	2B	3B	HR	(Hm	Rd)	TB	R	RBI	TBB	IBB	SO	HBP	SH	SF	SB	CS	SB%	GDP	Avg	OBP	SLG
1987	Johnson Cty	R	67	238	60	11	2	10	--	--	105	33	42	36	5	40	3	0	2	2	2	.50	4	.252	.355	.441
1988	Springfield	A	133	457	136	25	2	8	--	--	189	57	64	63	7	52	5	1	4	6	4	.60	22	.298	.386	.414
1989	Arkansas	AA	128	470	130	25	2	10	--	--	189	71	93	46	3	46	7	0	3	2	3	.40	8	.277	.348	.402
1990	Louisville	AAA	144	514	129	15	5	12	--	--	190	60	83	54	7	62	9	0	6	0	2	.00	9	.251	.329	.370
1991	Louisville	AAA	104	382	86	21	1	8	--	--	133	39	52	35	1	57	6	0	1	4	0	1.00	10	.225	.300	.348
1990	St. Louis	NL	14	25	6	1	0	0	(0	0)	7	4	2	0	0	4	0	0	0	0	0	.00	1	.240	.240	.280
1991	St. Louis	NL	19	13	1	0	0	0	(0	0)	1	0	1	0	0	5	0	0	0	0	0	.00	0	.077	.077	.077
	2 ML YEARS		33	38	7	1	0	0	(0	0)	8	4	3	0	0	9	0	0	0	0	0	.00	1	.184	.184	.211

Greg Briley

Bats: Left   **Throws:** Right   **Pos:** LF/RF   **Ht:** 5' 8"   **Wt:** 165   **Born:** 05/24/65   **Age:** 27

Year	Team	Lg	G	AB	H	2B	3B	HR	(Hm	Rd)	TB	R	RBI	TBB	IBB	SO	HBP	SH	SF	SB	CS	SB%	GDP	Avg	OBP	SLG
1988	Seattle	AL	13	36	9	2	0	1	(0	1)	14	6	4	5	1	6	0	0	1	0	1	.00	0	.250	.333	.389
1989	Seattle	AL	115	394	105	22	4	13	(5	8)	174	52	52	39	1	82	5	1	5	11	5	.69	6	.266	.336	.442
1990	Seattle	AL	126	337	83	18	2	5	(4	1)	120	40	29	37	0	48	1	1	4	16	4	.80	6	.246	.319	.356
1991	Seattle	AL	139	381	99	17	3	2	(2	0)	128	39	26	27	0	51	0	1	3	23	11	.68	7	.260	.307	.336
	4 ML YEARS		393	1148	296	59	9	21	(11	10)	436	137	111	108	2	187	6	3	13	50	21	.70	22	.258	.322	.380

John Briscoe

Pitches: Right **Bats:** Right **Pos:** RP **Ht:** 6' 3" **Wt:** 185 **Born:** 09/22/67 **Age:** 24

		HOW MUCH HE PITCHED						WHAT HE GAVE UP										THE RESULTS					
Year	Team	Lg	G	GS	CG	GF	IP	BFP	H	R	ER	HR	SH	SF	HB	TBB	IBB	SO	WP	Bk	W	L	Pct.	ShO	Sv	ERA
1988	Athletics	R	7	6	0	0	25.2	105	26	14	10	1	0	1	1	6	0	23	3	3	1	1	.500	0	0	3.51
1989	Madison	A	21	20	1	1	117.2	524	121	66	55	7	10	9	9	57	0	69	11	1	7	5	.583	0	0	4.21
1990	Modesto	A	29	12	1	12	86.1	373	72	50	44	12	4	1	2	52	0	66	6	0	3	6	.333	0	4	4.59
	Huntsville	AA	3	0	0	0	4.2	30	9	7	7	1	0	0	0	7	0	7	1	0	0	0	.000	0	0	13.50
1991	Huntsville	AA	2	0	0	2	4.1	19	1	2	0	0	0	0	0	2	0	6	0	0	2	0	1.000	0	0	0.00
	Tacoma	AAA	22	9	0	6	76.1	342	73	35	31	7	2	2	5	44	1	66	3	0	3	5	.375	0	1	3.66
1991	Oakland	AL	11	0	0	9	14	62	12	11	11	3	0	1	0	10	0	9	3	0	0	0	.000	0	0	7.07

Greg Brock

Bats: Left **Throws:** Right **Pos:** 1B **Ht:** 6' 3" **Wt:** 205 **Born:** 06/14/57 **Age:** 35

							BATTING												BASERUNNING				PERCENTAGES		
Year	Team	Lg	G	AB	H	2B	3B	HR	(Hm	Rd)	TB	R	RBI	TBB	IBB	SO	HBP	SH	SF	SB	CS	SB%	GDP	Avg	OBP	SLG
1982	Los Angeles	NL	18	17	2	1	0	0	(0	0)	3	1	1	1	1	5	0	0	0	0	0	.00	0	.118	.167	.176
1983	Los Angeles	NL	146	455	102	14	2	20	(14	6)	180	64	66	83	12	81	1	0	4	5	1	.83	13	.224	.343	.396
1984	Los Angeles	NL	88	271	61	6	0	14	(8	6)	109	33	34	39	3	37	0	0	3	8	0	1.00	6	.225	.319	.402
1985	Los Angeles	NL	129	438	110	19	0	21	(7	14)	192	64	66	54	4	72	0	2	2	4	2	.67	9	.251	.332	.438
1986	Los Angeles	NL	115	325	76	13	0	16	(5	11)	137	33	52	37	5	60	0	1	4	2	5	.29	5	.234	.309	.422
1987	Milwaukee	AL	141	532	159	29	3	13	(5	8)	233	81	85	57	4	63	6	4	3	5	4	.56	9	.299	.371	.438
1988	Milwaukee	AL	115	364	77	16	1	6	(4	2)	113	53	50	63	16	48	3	3	4	6	2	.75	11	.212	.329	.310
1989	Milwaukee	AL	107	373	99	16	0	12	(7	5)	151	40	52	43	8	49	3	2	1	6	1	.86	10	.265	.345	.405
1990	Milwaukee	AL	123	367	91	23	0	7	(3	4)	135	42	50	43	9	45	2	2	8	4	2	.67	6	.248	.324	.368
1991	Milwaukee	AL	31	60	17	4	0	1	(0	1)	24	9	6	14	1	9	0	1	0	1	1	.50	1	.283	.419	.400
	10 ML YEARS		1013	3202	794	141	6	110	(53	57)	1277	420	462	434	63	469	15	15	29	41	18	.69	70	.248	.338	.399

Hubie Brooks

Bats: Right **Throws:** Right **Pos:** RF **Ht:** 6' 0" **Wt:** 205 **Born:** 09/24/56 **Age:** 35

							BATTING												BASERUNNING				PERCENTAGES		
Year	Team	Lg	G	AB	H	2B	3B	HR	(Hm	Rd)	TB	R	RBI	TBB	IBB	SO	HBP	SH	SF	SB	CS	SB%	GDP	Avg	OBP	SLG
1980	New York	NL	24	81	25	2	1	1	(0	1)	32	8	10	5	0	9	2	1	0	1	1	.50	1	.309	.364	.395
1981	New York	NL	98	358	110	21	2	4	(2	2)	147	34	38	23	2	65	1	1	6	9	5	.64	9	.307	.345	.411
1982	New York	NL	126	457	114	21	2	2	(1	1)	145	40	40	28	5	76	5	3	5	6	3	.67	11	.249	.297	.317
1983	New York	NL	150	586	147	18	4	5	(4	1)	188	53	58	24	2	96	4	7	3	6	4	.60	14	.251	.284	.321
1984	New York	NL	153	561	159	23	2	16	(12	4)	234	61	73	48	15	79	2	0	2	6	5	.55	17	.283	.341	.417
1985	Montreal	NL	156	605	163	34	7	13	(4	9)	250	67	100	34	6	79	5	0	8	6	9	.40	20	.269	.310	.413
1986	Montreal	NL	80	306	104	18	5	14	(3	11)	174	50	58	25	3	60	2	0	5	4	2	.67	11	.340	.388	.569
1987	Montreal	NL	112	430	113	22	3	14	(9	5)	183	57	72	24	2	72	1	0	4	4	3	.57	7	.263	.301	.426
1988	Montreal	NL	151	588	164	35	2	20	(9	11)	263	61	90	35	3	108	1	0	4	7	3	.70	21	.279	.318	.447
1989	Montreal	NL	148	542	145	30	1	14	(7	7)	219	56	70	39	2	108	4	0	8	6	11	.35	15	.268	.317	.404
1990	Los Angeles	NL	153	568	151	28	1	20	(9	11)	241	74	91	33	10	108	6	0	11	2	5	.29	13	.266	.307	.424
1991	New York	NL	103	357	85	11	1	16	(4	12)	146	48	50	44	8	62	3	0	3	3	1	.75	7	.238	.324	.409
	12 ML YEARS		1454	5439	1480	263	31	139	(64	75)	2222	609	750	362	58	922	36	12	59	60	52	.54	146	.272	.319	.409

Scott Brosius

Bats: Right **Throws:** Right **Pos:** RF **Ht:** 6' 1" **Wt:** 185 **Born:** 08/15/66 **Age:** 25

							BATTING												BASERUNNING				PERCENTAGES		
Year	Team	Lg	G	AB	H	2B	3B	HR	(Hm	Rd)	TB	R	RBI	TBB	IBB	SO	HBP	SH	SF	SB	CS	SB%	GDP	Avg	OBP	SLG
1987	Medford	A	65	255	73	18	1	3	--	--	102	34	49	26	0	36	0	1	7	5	2	.71	7	.286	.344	.400
1988	Madison	A	132	504	153	28	2	9	--	--	212	82	58	56	1	67	3	4	4	13	12	.52	7	.304	.374	.421
1989	Huntsville	AA	128	461	125	22	2	7	--	--	172	68	60	58	3	62	5	6	6	4	6	.40	11	.271	.355	.373
1990	Huntsville	AA	142	547	162	39	2	23	--	--	274	94	88	81	2	81	1	7	9	12	3	.80	8	.296	.382	.501
	Tacoma	AAA	3	7	1	0	1	0	--	--	3	2	0	1	0	3	0	0	0	0	0	.00	0	.143	.250	.429
1991	Tacoma	AAA	65	245	70	16	3	8	--	--	116	28	31	18	0	29	2	1	2	4	2	.67	7	.286	.337	.473
1991	Oakland	AL	36	68	16	5	0	2	(1	1)	27	9	4	3	0	11	0	1	0	3	1	.75	2	.235	.268	.397

Terry Bross

Pitches: Right **Bats:** Right **Pos:** RP **Ht:** 6' 9" **Wt:** 230 **Born:** 03/30/66 **Age:** 26

				HOW MUCH HE PITCHED					WHAT HE GAVE UP												THE RESULTS			
Year	Team	Lg	G	GS	CG	GF	IP	BFP	H	R	ER	HR	SH	SF	HB	TBB	IBB	SO	WP	Bk	W	L	Pct.	ShO	Sv	ERA
1987	Little Fls	A	10	6	0	1	28	129	22	23	12	3	2	1	0	20	0	21	1	1	2	0	1.000	0	0	3.86
1988	Little Fls	A	20	6	0	8	55.1	248	43	25	19	2	1	2	1	38	0	59	2	2	2	1	.667	0	1	3.09
1989	St.Lucie	A	35	0	0	26	58	234	39	21	18	1	0	4	1	26	3	47	3	1	8	2	.800	0	11	2.79
1990	Jackson	AA	58	0	0	48	71.2	289	46	21	21	4	5	3	2	40	5	51	4	4	3	4	.429	0	28	2.64

1991 Tidewater	AAA	27	0	0	10	33	159	31	21	16	0	1	1	1	32	2	23	3	2	2	0	1.000	0	2	4.36
Williamsprt	AA	20	0	0	16	25.1	98	13	12	7	1	2	1	0	11	0	28	1	1	2	0	1.000	0	5	2.49
1991 New York	NL	8	0	0	4	10	39	7	2	2	1	1	0	0	3	0	5	0	0	0	0	.000	0	0	1.80

Jarvis Brown

Bats: Right **Throws:** Right **Pos:** RF **Ht:** 5' 7" **Wt:** 165 **Born:** 03/26/67 **Age:** 25

								BATTING										BASERUNNING				PERCENTAGES		
Year Team	Lg	G	AB	H	2B	3B	HR	(Hm	Rd)	TB	R	RBI	TBB	IBB	SO	HBP	SH	SF	SB	CS	SB%	GDP	Avg	OBP	SLG
1986 Elizabethtn	R	49	180	41	4	0	3	--	--	54	28	23	18	0	41	4	5	1	15	3	.83	3	.228	.310	.300
1987 Elizabethtn	R	67	258	63	9	1	1	--	--	77	52	15	48	1	50	5	3	0	30	2	.94	3	.244	.373	.298
Kenosha	A	43	117	22	4	1	3	--	--	37	17	16	19	0	24	2	1	2	6	2	.75	2	.188	.307	.316
1988 Kenosha	A	138	531	156	25	7	7	--	--	216	108	45	71	0	89	10	7	5	72	15	.83	10	.294	.384	.407
1989 Visalia	A	141	545	131	21	6	4	--	--	176	95	46	73	0	112	13	4	4	49	13	.79	12	.240	.342	.323
1990 Orlando	AA	135	527	137	22	7	14	--	--	215	104	57	80	1	79	9	5	2	33	19	.63	13	.260	.366	.408
1991 Portland	AAA	108	436	126	5	8	3	--	--	156	62	37	36	1	66	6	3	1	26	12	.68	6	.289	.351	.358
1991 Minnesota	AL	38	37	8	0	0	0	(0	0)	8	10	0	2	0	8	0	0	1	7	1	.88	0	.216	.256	.216

Keith Brown

Pitches: Right **Bats:** Both **Pos:** RP **Ht:** 6' 4" **Wt:** 215 **Born:** 02/14/64 **Age:** 28

			HOW MUCH HE PITCHED					WHAT HE GAVE UP										THE RESULTS					
Year Team	Lg	G	GS	CG	GF	IP	BFP	H	R	ER	HR	SH	SF	HB	TBB	IBB	SO	WP	Bk	W	L	Pct.	ShO	Sv	ERA
1986 Reds	R	7	7	1	0	47.1	179	29	15	5	0	2	1	2	5	1	26	3	0	4	1	.800	0	0	0.95
Billings	R	4	3	0	1	21.1	0	18	6	5	0	0	0	1	7	0	14	1	0	2	0	1.000	0	0	2.11
Vermont	AA	4	2	1	0	14	58	12	10	8	2	1	1	0	8	0	11	1	0	1	1	.500	0	0	5.14
1987 Cedar Rapds	A	17	17	3	0	124.1	481	91	28	22	5	2	1	3	27	0	86	3	0	13	4	.765	1	0	1.59
1988 Chattanooga	AA	10	10	2	0	69.2	273	47	11	11	3	2	1	4	20	1	34	1	0	9	1	.900	0	0	1.42
Nashville	AAA	12	12	3	0	85.1	354	72	33	18	1	6	2	1	28	2	43	2	1	6	3	.667	1	0	1.90
1989 Nashville	AAA	29	27	4	0	161.1	695	171	99	86	13	10	4	1	51	2	85	5	2	8	13	.381	2	0	4.80
1990 Nashville	AAA	39	9	1	26	94.1	379	83	37	25	6	8	2	4	24	2	50	4	1	7	8	.467	0	9	2.39
1991 Nashville	AAA	47	1	0	32	62	274	64	26	24	3	5	2	2	32	4	53	5	0	2	5	.286	0	16	3.48
1988 Cincinnati	NL	4	3	0	1	16.1	63	14	5	5	1	0	0	0	4	0	6	1	0	2	1	.667	0	0	2.76
1990 Cincinnati	NL	8	0	0	2	11.1	46	12	6	6	2	1	0	0	3	0	8	0	0	0	0	.000	0	0	4.76
1991 Cincinnati	NL	11	0	0	3	12	56	15	4	3	0	1	0	0	6	1	4	1	0	0	0	.000	0	0	2.25
3 ML YEARS		23	3	0	6	39.2	165	41	15	14	3	2	0	0	13	1	18	2	0	2	1	.667	0	0	3.18

Kevin Brown

Pitches: Right **Bats:** Right **Pos:** SP **Ht:** 6' 4" **Wt:** 195 **Born:** 03/14/65 **Age:** 27

			HOW MUCH HE PITCHED					WHAT HE GAVE UP										THE RESULTS					
Year Team	Lg	G	GS	CG	GF	IP	BFP	H	R	ER	HR	SH	SF	HB	TBB	IBB	SO	WP	Bk	W	L	Pct.	ShO	Sv	ERA
1986 Texas	AL	1	1	0	0	5	19	6	2	2	0	0	0	0	0	0	4	0	0	1	0	1.000	0	0	3.60
1988 Texas	AL	4	4	1	0	23.1	110	33	15	11	2	1	0	1	8	0	12	1	0	1	1	.500	0	0	4.24
1989 Texas	AL	28	28	7	0	191	798	167	81	71	10	3	6	4	70	2	104	7	2	12	9	.571	0	0	3.35
1990 Texas	AL	26	26	6	0	180	757	175	84	72	13	2	7	3	60	3	88	9	2	12	10	.545	2	0	3.60
1991 Texas	AL	33	33	0	0	210.2	934	233	116	103	17	6	4	13	90	5	96	12	3	9	12	.429	0	0	4.40
5 ML YEARS		92	92	14	0	610	2618	614	298	259	42	12	17	21	228	10	304	29	7	35	32	.522	2	0	3.82

Kevin D. Brown

Pitches: Left **Bats:** Left **Pos:** SP/RP **Ht:** 6' 1" **Wt:** 185 **Born:** 03/05/66 **Age:** 26

			HOW MUCH HE PITCHED					WHAT HE GAVE UP										THE RESULTS					
Year Team	Lg	G	GS	CG	GF	IP	BFP	H	R	ER	HR	SH	SF	HB	TBB	IBB	SO	WP	Bk	W	L	Pct.	ShO	Sv	ERA
1986 Idaho Falls	R	12	12	1	0	68	0	65	48	38	5	0	0	4	41	0	44	2	0	3	6	.333	0	0	5.03
1987 Sumter	A	9	9	0	0	56	232	53	14	12	2	2	1	1	19	0	45	5	0	7	1	.875	0	0	1.93
Durham	A	13	12	1	1	72.2	330	78	46	42	6	0	1	0	42	0	48	5	2	4	4	.500	0	0	5.20
1988 Jackson	AA	5	5	1	0	32.2	129	24	9	8	1	1	2	0	11	0	24	2	0	2	4	.333	1	0	2.20
St. Lucie	A	20	20	5	0	134	533	96	42	27	4	3	2	6	37	1	113	10	2	5	7	.417	1	0	1.81
1989 Jackson	AA	8	8	2	0	51.2	216	51	15	13	0	1	1	4	11	0	40	4	4	5	2	.714	2	0	2.26
Tidewater	AAA	13	13	4	0	75	326	81	41	37	2	3	1	0	31	0	46	2	0	6	6	.500	0	0	4.44
1990 Tidewater	AAA	26	24	3	0	134.1	592	138	71	53	4	7	0	2	60	0	109	3	2	10	6	.625	0	0	3.55
1991 Denver	AAA	12	11	1	1	61.2	277	71	36	32	4	3	0	2	34	0	31	2	2	4	3	.571	0	0	4.67
1990 2 ML Teams		7	3	0	2	23	96	16	7	6	1	1	1	1	8	1	12	2	0	1	1	.500	0	0	2.35
1991 Milwaukee	AL	15	10	0	0	63.2	285	66	39	39	6	5	1	1	34	2	30	6	0	2	4	.333	0	0	5.51
1990 New York	NL	2	0	0	1	2	9	2	0	0	0	0	0	0	1	0	0	0	0	0	0	.000	0	0	0.00
Milwaukee	AL	5	3	0	1	21	87	14	7	6	1	1	1	1	7	1	12	2	0	1	1	.500	0	0	2.57
2 ML YEARS		22	13	0	2	86.2	381	82	46	45	7	6	2	2	42	3	42	8	0	3	5	.375	0	0	4.67

Jerry Browne

Bats: Both **Throws:** Right **Pos:** 2B/3B/LF — **Ht:** 5'10" **Wt:** 170 **Born:** 02/13/66 **Age:** 26

Year Team	Lg	G	AB	H	2B	3B	HR	(Hm	Rd)	TB	R	RBI	TBB	IBB	SO	HBP	SH	SF	SB	CS	SB%	GDP	Avg	OBP	SLG
1986 Texas	AL	12	24	10	2	0	0	(0	0)	12	6	3	1	0	4	0	0	0	0	2	.00	0	.417	.440	.500
1987 Texas	AL	132	454	123	16	6	1	(1	0)	154	63	38	61	0	50	2	7	2	27	17	.61	6	.271	.358	.339
1988 Texas	AL	73	214	49	9	2	1	(1	0)	65	26	17	25	0	32	0	3	1	7	5	.58	5	.229	.308	.304
1989 Cleveland	AL	153	598	179	31	4	5	(1	4)	233	83	45	68	10	64	1	14	4	14	6	.70	9	.299	.370	.390
1990 Cleveland	AL	140	513	137	26	5	6	(2	4)	191	92	50	72	1	46	2	12	11	12	7	.63	12	.267	.353	.372
1991 Cleveland	AL	107	290	66	5	2	1	(1	0)	78	28	29	27	0	29	1	12	4	2	4	.33	5	.228	.292	.269
6 ML YEARS		617	2093	564	89	19	14	(6	8)	733	298	182	254	11	225	6	48	22	62	41	.60	37	.269	.347	.350

Tom Browning

Pitches: Left **Bats:** Left **Pos:** SP — **Ht:** 6'1" **Wt:** 195 **Born:** 04/28/60 **Age:** 32

			HOW MUCH HE PITCHED					WHAT HE GAVE UP									THE RESULTS					
Year Team	Lg	G	GS	CG	GF	IP	BFP	H	R	ER	HR	SH	SF	HB	TBB	IBB	SO	WP	Bk	W	L	Pct.	ShO	Sv	ERA
1984 Cincinnati	NL	3	3	0	0	23.1	95	27	4	4	0	1	0	0	5	0	14	1	0	1	0	1.000	0	0	1.54
1985 Cincinnati	NL	38	38	6	0	261.1	1083	242	111	103	29	13	7	3	73	8	155	2	0	20	9	.690	4	0	3.55
1986 Cincinnati	NL	39	39	4	0	243.1	1016	225	123	103	26	14	12	1	70	6	147	3	0	14	13	.519	2	0	3.81
1987 Cincinnati	NL	32	31	2	1	183	791	201	107	102	27	10	7	5	61	7	117	2	4	10	13	.435	0	0	5.02
1988 Cincinnati	NL	36	36	5	0	250.2	1001	205	98	95	36	6	8	7	64	3	124	2	4	18	5	.783	2	0	3.41
1989 Cincinnati	NL	37	37	9	0	249.2	1031	241	109	94	31	12	6	3	64	10	118	2	1	15	12	.556	2	0	3.39
1990 Cincinnati	NL	35	35	2	0	227.2	957	235	98	96	24	13	5	5	52	13	99	5	1	15	9	.625	1	0	3.80
1991 Cincinnati	NL	36	36	1	0	230.1	983	241	124	107	32	8	9	4	56	4	115	3	1	14	14	.500	0	0	4.18
8 ML YEARS		256	255	29	1	1669.1	6957	1617	774	704	205	77	54	28	445	51	889	20	11	107	75	.588	11	0	3.80

Mike Brumley

Bats: Both **Throws:** Right **Pos:** SS/3B — **Ht:** 5'10" **Wt:** 165 **Born:** 04/09/63 **Age:** 29

Year Team	Lg	G	AB	H	2B	3B	HR	(Hm	Rd)	TB	R	RBI	TBB	IBB	SO	HBP	SH	SF	SB	CS	SB%	GDP	Avg	OBP	SLG
1987 Chicago	NL	39	104	21	2	2	1	(0	1)	30	8	9	10	1	30	1	1	1	7	1	.88	2	.202	.276	.288
1989 Detroit	AL	92	212	42	5	2	1	(1	0)	54	33	11	14	0	45	1	3	0	8	4	.67	4	.198	.251	.255
1990 Seattle	AL	62	147	33	5	4	0	(0	0)	46	19	7	10	0	22	0	4	1	2	0	1.00	5	.224	.272	.313
1991 Boston	AL	63	118	25	5	0	0	(0	0)	30	16	5	10	0	22	0	4	0	2	0	1.00	0	.212	.273	.254
4 ML YEARS		256	581	121	17	8	2	(1	1)	160	76	32	44	1	119	2	12	2	19	5	.79	11	.208	.266	.275

Tom Brunansky

Bats: Right **Throws:** Right **Pos:** RF — **Ht:** 6'4" **Wt:** 216 **Born:** 08/20/60 **Age:** 31

Year Team	Lg	G	AB	H	2B	3B	HR	(Hm	Rd)	TB	R	RBI	TBB	IBB	SO	HBP	SH	SF	SB	CS	SB%	GDP	Avg	OBP	SLG
1981 California	AL	11	33	5	0	0	3	(1	2)	14	7	6	8	0	10	0	0	0	1	0	1.00	4	.152	.317	.424
1982 Minnesota	AL	127	463	126	30	1	20	(10	10)	218	77	46	71	0	101	8	1	2	1	2	.33	12	.272	.377	.471
1983 Minnesota	AL	151	542	123	24	5	28	(8	20)	241	70	82	61	4	95	4	1	3	2	5	.29	13	.227	.308	.445
1984 Minnesota	AL	155	567	144	21	0	32	(14	18)	261	75	85	57	2	94	0	0	4	4	5	.44	15	.254	.320	.460
1985 Minnesota	AL	157	567	137	28	4	27	(12	15)	254	71	90	71	7	86	0	0	13	5	3	.63	12	.242	.320	.448
1986 Minnesota	AL	157	593	152	28	1	23	(15	8)	251	69	75	53	4	98	1	1	7	12	4	.75	15	.256	.315	.423
1987 Minnesota	AL	155	532	138	22	2	32	(19	13)	260	83	85	74	5	104	4	0	4	11	11	.50	12	.259	.352	.489
1988 2 ML Teams		157	572	137	23	4	23	(7	16)	237	74	85	86	6	93	4	1	6	17	8	.68	17	.240	.340	.414
1989 St. Louis	NL	158	556	133	29	3	20	(4	16)	228	67	85	59	3	107	2	0	5	5	9	.36	10	.239	.312	.410
1990 2 ML Teams		148	518	132	27	5	16	(13	3)	217	66	73	66	7	115	4	0	9	5	10	.33	13	.255	.338	.419
1991 Boston	AL	142	459	105	24	1	16	(10	6)	179	54	70	49	2	72	3	0	8	1	2	.33	8	.229	.303	.390
1988 Minnesota	AL	14	49	9	1	0	1	(0	1)	13	5	6	7	0	11	0	0	0	1	2	.33	0	.184	.286	.265
St. Louis	NL	143	523	128	22	4	22	(7	15)	224	69	79	79	6	82	4	1	6	16	6	.73	17	.245	.345	.428
1990 St. Louis	NL	19	57	9	3	0	1	(0	1)	15	5	2	12	0	10	1	0	1	0	0	.00	1	.158	.310	.263
Boston	AL	129	461	123	24	5	15	(13	2)	202	61	71	54	7	105	3	0	8	5	10	.33	12	.267	.342	.438
11 ML YEARS		1518	5402	1332	256	26	240	(113	127)	2360	713	782	655	40	975	30	4	61	64	59	.52	127	.247	.328	.437

Steve Buechele

Bats: Right **Throws:** Right **Pos:** 3B/2B — **Ht:** 6'2" **Wt:** 200 **Born:** 09/26/61 **Age:** 30

Year Team	Lg	G	AB	H	2B	3B	HR	(Hm	Rd)	TB	R	RBI	TBB	IBB	SO	HBP	SH	SF	SB	CS	SB%	GDP	Avg	OBP	SLG
1985 Texas	AL	69	219	48	6	3	6	(5	1)	78	22	21	14	2	38	2	0	1	3	2	.60	11	.219	.271	.356
1986 Texas	AL	153	461	112	19	2	18	(6	12)	189	54	54	35	1	98	5	9	3	5	8	.38	10	.243	.302	.410
1987 Texas	AL	136	363	86	20	0	13	(6	7)	145	45	50	28	3	66	1	4	4	2	2	.50	7	.237	.290	.399
1988 Texas	AL	155	503	126	21	4	16	(8	8)	203	68	58	65	6	79	5	6	0	2	4	.33	8	.250	.342	.404

30

1989 Texas	AL	155	486	114	22	2	16	(7	9)	188	60	59	36	0	107	5	2	1	1	3	.25	21	.235	.294	.387
1990 Texas	AL	91	251	54	10	0	7	(5	2)	85	30	30	27	1	63	2	7	2	1	0	1.00	5	.215	.294	.339
1991 2 ML Teams		152	530	139	22	3	22	(9	13)	233	74	85	49	4	97	7	11	3	0	5	.00	14	.262	.331	.440
1991 Texas	AL	121	416	111	17	2	18	(7	11)	186	58	66	39	4	69	5	10	2	0	4	.00	11	.267	.335	.447
Pittsburgh	NL	31	114	28	5	1	4	(2	2)	47	16	19	10	0	28	2	1	1	0	1	.00	3	.246	.315	.412
7 ML YEARS		911	2813	679	120	14	98	(46	52)	1121	353	357	254	17	548	27	39	14	14	24	.37	76	.241	.309	.399

Jay Buhner

Bats: Right **Throws:** Right **Pos:** RF   **Ht:** 6' 3" **Wt:** 205 **Born:** 08/13/64 **Age:** 27

						BATTING													BASERUNNING				PERCENTAGES		
Year Team	Lg	G	AB	H	2B	3B	HR	(Hm	Rd)	TB	R	RBI	TBB	IBB	SO	HBP	SH	SF	SB	CS	SB%	GDP	Avg	OBP	SLG
1987 New York	AL	7	22	5	2	0	0	(0	0)	7	0	1	1	0	6	0	0	0	0	0	.00	1	.227	.261	.318
1988 2 ML Teams		85	261	56	13	1	13	(8	5)	110	36	38	28	1	93	6	1	3	1	1	.50	5	.215	.302	.421
1989 Seattle	AL	58	204	56	15	1	9	(7	2)	100	27	33	19	0	55	2	0	1	1	4	.20	0	.275	.341	.490
1990 Seattle	AL	51	163	45	12	0	7	(2	5)	78	16	33	17	1	50	4	0	1	2	2	.50	6	.276	.357	.479
1991 Seattle	AL	137	406	99	14	4	27	(14	13)	202	64	77	53	5	117	6	1	4	0	1	.00	10	.244	.337	.498
1988 New York	AL	25	69	13	0	0	3	(1	2)	22	8	13	3	0	25	3	0	1	0	0	.00	1	.188	.250	.319
Seattle	AL	60	192	43	13	1	10	(7	3)	88	28	25	25	1	68	3	1	2	1	1	.50	4	.224	.320	.458
5 ML YEARS		338	1056	261	56	6	56	(31	25)	497	143	182	118	7	321	18	3	9	4	8	.33	22	.247	.331	.471

Scott Bullett

Bats: Both **Throws:** Left **Pos:** LF   **Ht:** 6' 2" **Wt:** 200 **Born:** 12/25/68 **Age:** 23

						BATTING													BASERUNNING				PERCENTAGES		
Year Team	Lg	G	AB	H	2B	3B	HR	(Hm	Rd)	TB	R	RBI	TBB	IBB	SO	HBP	SH	SF	SB	CS	SB%	GDP	Avg	OBP	SLG
1988 Pirates	R	21	61	11	1	0	0	--	--	12	6	8	7	1	9	0	1	1	2	5	.29	0	.180	.261	.197
1989 Pirates	R	46	165	42	7	3	1	--	--	58	24	16	12	2	31	5	1	0	15	5	.75	2	.255	.324	.352
1990 Welland	A	74	256	77	11	4	3	--	--	105	46	33	13	2	50	2	1	0	30	6	.83	7	.301	.339	.410
1991 Augusta	A	95	384	109	21	6	1	--	--	145	61	36	27	2	79	2	1	1	48	17	.74	1	.284	.333	.378
Salem	A	39	156	52	7	5	2	--	--	75	22	15	8	1	29	0	0	0	15	7	.68	0	.333	.366	.481
1991 Pittsburgh	NL	11	4	0	0	0	0	(0	0)	0	2	0	0	0	3	1	0	0	1	1	.50	0	.000	.200	.000

Eric Bullock

Bats: Left **Throws:** Left **Pos:** LF   **Ht:** 5'11" **Wt:** 185 **Born:** 02/16/60 **Age:** 32

						BATTING													BASERUNNING				PERCENTAGES		
Year Team	Lg	G	AB	H	2B	3B	HR	(Hm	Rd)	TB	R	RBI	TBB	IBB	SO	HBP	SH	SF	SB	CS	SB%	GDP	Avg	OBP	SLG
1985 Houston	NL	18	25	7	2	0	0	(0	0)	9	3	2	1	0	3	0	0	0	0	1	.00	0	.280	.308	.360
1986 Houston	NL	6	21	1	0	0	0	(0	0)	1	0	1	0	0	3	0	0	0	2	0	1.00	0	.048	.048	.048
1988 Minnesota	AL	16	17	5	0	0	0	(0	0)	5	3	3	3	0	1	0	0	0	1	0	1.00	0	.294	.400	.294
1989 Philadelphia	NL	6	4	0	0	0	0	(0	0)	0	1	0	0	0	2	0	0	0	0	0	.00	0	.000	.000	.000
1990 Montreal	NL	4	2	1	0	0	0	(0	0)	1	0	0	0	0	0	0	0	0	0	0	.00	0	.500	.500	.500
1991 Montreal	NL	73	72	16	4	0	1	(1	0)	23	6	6	9	0	13	0	0	1	6	1	.86	3	.222	.305	.319
6 ML YEARS		123	141	30	6	0	1	(1	0)	39	13	12	13	0	22	0	0	1	9	2	.82	3	.213	.277	.277

Dave Burba

Pitches: Right **Bats:** Right **Pos:** RP   **Ht:** 6' 4" **Wt:** 220 **Born:** 07/07/66 **Age:** 25

		HOW MUCH HE PITCHED						WHAT HE GAVE UP									THE RESULTS					
Year Team	Lg	G	GS	CG	GF	IP	BFP	H	R	ER	HR	SH	SF	HB	TBB	IBB	SO	WP	Bk	W	L	Pct.	ShO	Sv	ERA
1987 Bellingham	A	5	5	0	0	23.1	97	20	10	5	0	0	0	0	3	0	24	4	0	3	1	.750	0	0	1.93
Salinas	A	9	9	0	0	54.2	246	53	31	28	3	3	2	2	29	0	46	3	0	1	6	.143	0	0	4.61
1988 San Berndno	A	20	20	1	0	114	485	106	41	34	4	4	2	4	54	1	102	5	2	5	7	.417	0	0	2.68
1989 Williamsprt	AA	25	25	5	0	156.2	651	138	69	55	7	5	3	3	55	0	89	4	5	11	7	.611	1	0	3.16
1990 Calgary	AAA	31	18	1	8	113.2	493	124	64	59	11	4	3	2	45	0	47	5	3	10	6	.625	0	2	4.67
1991 Calgary	AAA	23	9	0	9	71.1	315	82	35	28	4	4	1	4	27	0	42	3	2	6	4	.600	0	4	3.53
1990 Seattle	AL	6	0	0	2	8	35	8	6	4	0	2	0	1	2	0	4	0	0	0	0	.000	0	0	4.50
1991 Seattle	AL	22	2	0	11	36.2	153	34	16	15	6	0	0	0	14	3	16	1	0	2	2	.500	0	1	3.68
2 ML YEARS		28	2	0	13	44.2	188	42	22	19	6	2	0	1	16	3	20	1	0	2	2	.500	0	1	3.83

Tim Burke

Pitches: Right **Bats:** Right **Pos:** RP   **Ht:** 6' 3" **Wt:** 205 **Born:** 02/19/59 **Age:** 33

		HOW MUCH HE PITCHED						WHAT HE GAVE UP									THE RESULTS					
Year Team	Lg	G	GS	CG	GF	IP	BFP	H	R	ER	HR	SH	SF	HB	TBB	IBB	SO	WP	Bk	W	L	Pct.	ShO	Sv	ERA
1985 Montreal	NL	78	0	0	31	120.1	483	86	32	32	9	8	3	7	44	14	87	7	0	9	4	.692	0	8	2.39
1986 Montreal	NL	68	2	0	25	101.1	451	103	37	33	7	4	2	4	46	13	82	4	0	9	7	.563	0	4	2.93
1987 Montreal	NL	55	0	0	30	91	354	64	18	12	3	8	2	0	17	6	58	2	0	7	0	1.000	0	18	1.19
1988 Montreal	NL	61	0	0	39	82	350	84	36	31	7	8	5	3	25	13	42	3	1	3	5	.375	0	18	3.40
1989 Montreal	NL	68	0	0	52	84.2	333	68	24	24	6	4	5	0	22	7	54	1	0	9	3	.750	0	28	2.55

Year	Team	Lg	G	GS	CG	GF	IP	BFP	H	R	ER	HR	SH	SF	HB	TBB	IBB	SO	WP	Bk	W	L	Pct.	ShO	Sv	ERA
1990	Montreal	NL	58	0	0	35	75	316	71	29	21	6	3	3	2	21	6	47	1	1	3	3	.500	0	20	2.52
1991	2 ML Teams		72	0	0	31	101.2	421	96	46	38	8	3	3	4	26	8	59	3	0	6	7	.462	0	6	3.36
1991	Montreal	NL	37	0	0	16	46	190	41	24	21	3	2	1	4	14	6	25	1	0	3	4	.429	0	5	4.11
	New York	NL	35	0	0	15	55.2	231	55	22	17	5	1	2	0	12	2	34	2	0	3	3	.500	0	1	2.75
	7 ML YEARS		460	2	0	243	656	2708	572	222	191	46	40	23	20	201	67	429	21	2	46	29	.613	0	102	2.62

John Burkett

Pitches: Right **Bats:** Right **Pos:** SP   **Ht:** 6' 2" **Wt:** 210 **Born:** 11/28/64 **Age:** 27

			HOW MUCH HE PITCHED						WHAT HE GAVE UP											THE RESULTS					
Year	Team	Lg	G	GS	CG	GF	IP	BFP	H	R	ER	HR	SH	SF	HB	TBB	IBB	SO	WP	Bk	W	L	Pct.	ShO	Sv	ERA
1987	San Francisco	NL	3	0	0	1	6	28	7	4	3	2	1	0	1	3	0	5	0	0	0	0	.000	0	0	4.50
1990	San Francisco	NL	33	32	2	1	204	857	201	92	86	18	6	5	4	61	7	118	3	3	14	7	.667	0	1	3.79
1991	San Francisco	NL	36	34	3	0	206.2	890	223	103	96	19	8	8	10	60	2	131	5	0	12	11	.522	1	0	4.18
	3 ML YEARS		72	66	5	2	416.2	1775	431	199	185	39	15	13	15	124	9	254	8	3	26	18	.591	1	1	4.00

Ellis Burks

Bats: Right **Throws:** Right **Pos:** CF   **Ht:** 6' 2" **Wt:** 202 **Born:** 09/11/64 **Age:** 27

			BATTING															BASERUNNING				PERCENTAGES		
Year	Team	Lg	G	AB	H	2B	3B	HR	(Hm | Rd)	TB	R	RBI	TBB	IBB	SO	HBP	SH	SF	SB	CS	SB%	GDP	Avg	OBP	SLG
1987	Boston	AL	133	558	152	30	2	20	(11 | 9)	246	94	59	41	0	98	2	4	1	27	6	.82	1	.272	.324	.441
1988	Boston	AL	144	540	159	37	5	18	(8 | 10)	260	93	92	62	1	89	3	4	6	25	9	.74	8	.294	.367	.481
1989	Boston	AL	97	399	121	19	6	12	(6 | 6)	188	73	61	36	2	52	5	2	4	21	5	.81	8	.303	.365	.471
1990	Boston	AL	152	588	174	33	8	21	(10 | 11)	286	89	48	48	4	82	1	2	2	9	11	.45	18	.296	.349	.486
1991	Boston	AL	130	474	119	33	3	14	(8 | 6)	200	56	56	39	2	81	6	2	3	6	11	.35	7	.251	.314	.422
	5 ML YEARS		656	2559	725	152	24	85	(43 | 42)	1180	405	357	226	9	402	17	14	16	88	42	.68	42	.283	.344	.461

Todd Burns

Pitches: Right **Bats:** Right **Pos:** RP   **Ht:** 6' 2" **Wt:** 195 **Born:** 07/06/63 **Age:** 28

			HOW MUCH HE PITCHED						WHAT HE GAVE UP											THE RESULTS					
Year	Team	Lg	G	GS	CG	GF	IP	BFP	H	R	ER	HR	SH	SF	HB	TBB	IBB	SO	WP	Bk	W	L	Pct.	ShO	Sv	ERA
1988	Oakland	AL	17	14	2	3	102.2	425	93	38	36	8	2	2	1	34	1	57	3	6	8	2	.800	0	1	3.16
1989	Oakland	AL	50	2	0	22	96.1	374	66	27	24	3	7	1	1	28	5	49	4	0	6	5	.545	0	8	2.24
1990	Oakland	AL	43	2	0	9	78.2	337	78	28	26	8	5	3	0	32	4	43	5	0	3	3	.500	0	3	2.97
1991	Oakland	AL	9	0	0	5	13.1	57	10	5	5	2	1	2	0	8	1	3	1	0	1	0	1.000	0	0	3.38
	4 ML YEARS		119	18	2	39	291	1193	247	98	91	21	15	8	2	102	11	152	13	6	18	10	.643	0	12	2.81

Randy Bush

Bats: Left **Throws:** Left **Pos:** RF   **Ht:** 6' 1" **Wt:** 190 **Born:** 10/05/58 **Age:** 33

			BATTING															BASERUNNING				PERCENTAGES		
Year	Team	Lg	G	AB	H	2B	3B	HR	(Hm | Rd)	TB	R	RBI	TBB	IBB	SO	HBP	SH	SF	SB	CS	SB%	GDP	Avg	OBP	SLG
1982	Minnesota	AL	55	119	29	6	1	4	(2 | 2)	49	13	13	8	0	28	3	0	1	0	0	.00	1	.244	.305	.412
1983	Minnesota	AL	124	373	93	24	3	11	(4 | 7)	156	43	56	34	8	51	7	0	1	0	1	.00	7	.249	.323	.418
1984	Minnesota	AL	113	311	69	17	1	11	(8 | 3)	121	46	43	31	6	60	4	0	10	1	2	.33	1	.222	.292	.389
1985	Minnesota	AL	97	234	56	13	3	10	(5 | 5)	105	26	35	24	1	30	5	0	2	3	0	1.00	3	.239	.321	.449
1986	Minnesota	AL	130	357	96	19	7	7	(6 | 1)	150	50	45	39	2	63	4	1	1	5	3	.63	7	.269	.347	.420
1987	Minnesota	AL	122	293	74	10	2	11	(3 | 8)	121	46	46	43	5	49	3	5	5	10	3	.77	6	.253	.349	.413
1988	Minnesota	AL	136	394	103	20	3	14	(10 | 4)	171	51	51	58	14	49	9	0	5	8	6	.57	8	.261	.365	.434
1989	Minnesota	AL	141	391	103	17	4	14	(6 | 8)	170	60	54	48	6	73	3	0	5	5	8	.38	16	.263	.347	.435
1990	Minnesota	AL	73	181	44	8	0	6	(4 | 2)	70	17	18	21	2	27	6	0	2	0	3	.00	2	.243	.338	.387
1991	Minnesota	AL	93	165	50	10	1	6	(2 | 4)	80	21	23	24	3	25	3	0	0	0	2	.00	5	.303	.401	.485
	10 ML YEARS		1084	2818	717	144	25	94	(50 | 44)	1193	373	384	330	47	455	47	6	29	32	28	.53	56	.254	.339	.423

Brett Butler

Bats: Left **Throws:** Left **Pos:** CF   **Ht:** 5'10" **Wt:** 160 **Born:** 06/15/57 **Age:** 35

			BATTING															BASERUNNING				PERCENTAGES		
Year	Team	Lg	G	AB	H	2B	3B	HR	(Hm | Rd)	TB	R	RBI	TBB	IBB	SO	HBP	SH	SF	SB	CS	SB%	GDP	Avg	OBP	SLG
1981	Atlanta	NL	40	126	32	2	3	0	(0 | 0)	40	17	4	19	0	17	0	0	0	9	1	.90	0	.254	.352	.317
1982	Atlanta	NL	89	240	52	2	0	0	(0 | 0)	54	35	7	25	0	35	0	3	0	21	8	.72	1	.217	.291	.225
1983	Atlanta	NL	151	549	154	21	13	5	(4 | 1)	216	84	37	54	3	56	2	3	5	39	23	.63	5	.281	.344	.393
1984	Cleveland	AL	159	602	162	25	9	3	(1 | 2)	214	108	49	86	1	62	4	11	6	52	22	.70	4	.269	.361	.355
1985	Cleveland	AL	152	591	184	28	14	5	(1 | 4)	255	106	50	63	2	42	1	8	3	47	20	.70	8	.311	.377	.431
1986	Cleveland	AL	161	587	163	17	14	4	(0 | 4)	220	92	51	70	1	65	4	17	5	32	15	.68	8	.278	.356	.375
1987	Cleveland	AL	137	522	154	25	8	9	(4 | 5)	222	91	41	91	0	55	1	2	2	33	16	.67	3	.295	.399	.425
1988	San Francisco	NL	157	568	163	27	9	6	(1 | 5)	226	109	43	97	4	64	4	8	2	43	20	.68	2	.287	.393	.398
1989	San Francisco	NL	154	594	168	22	4	4	(2 | 2)	210	100	36	59	2	69	3	13	3	31	16	.66	4	.283	.349	.354
1990	San Francisco	NL	160	622	192	20	9	3	(3 | 0)	239	108	44	90	1	62	6	7	7	51	19	.73	3	.309	.397	.384

Year	Team	Lg	G	AB	H	2B	3B	HR	(Hm	Rd)	TB	R	RBI	TBB	IBB	SO	HBP	SH	SF	SB	CS	SB%	GDP	Avg	OBP	SLG
1991	Los Angeles	NL	161	615	182	13	5	2	(2	0)	211	112	38	108	4	79	1	4	2	38	28	.58	3	.296	.401	.343
11 ML YEARS			1521	5616	1606	202	88	41	(18	23)	2107	962	400	762	18	606	26	76	35	396	188	.68	43	.286	.372	.375

Francisco Cabrera

Bats: Right Throws: Right Pos: C/1B Ht: 6' 4" Wt: 193 Born: 10/10/66 Age: 25

						BATTING														BASERUNNING				PERCENTAGES		
Year	Team	Lg	G	AB	H	2B	3B	HR	(Hm	Rd)	TB	R	RBI	TBB	IBB	SO	HBP	SH	SF	SB	CS	SB%	GDP	Avg	OBP	SLG
1989 2 ML Teams			7	26	5	3	0	0	(0	0)	8	1	0	1	0	6	0	0	0	0	0	.00	0	.192	.222	.308
1990 Atlanta	NL		63	137	38	5	1	7	(4	3)	66	14	25	5	0	21	0	0	1	1	0	1.00	4	.277	.301	.482
1991 Atlanta	NL		44	95	23	6	0	4	(2	2)	41	7	23	6	0	20	0	0	1	1	1	.50	5	.242	.284	.432
1989 Toronto	AL		3	12	2	1	0	0	(0	0)	3	1	0	1	0	3	0	0	0	0	0	.00	0	.167	.231	.250
Atlanta	NL		4	14	3	2	0	0	(0	0)	5	0	0	0	0	3	0	0	0	0	0	.00	0	.214	.214	.357
3 ML YEARS			114	258	66	14	1	11	(6	5)	115	22	48	12	0	47	0	0	2	2	1	.67	9	.256	.287	.446

Greg Cadaret

Pitches: Left Bats: Left Pos: RP/SP Ht: 6' 3" Wt: 214 Born: 02/27/62 Age: 30

			HOW MUCH HE PITCHED					WHAT HE GAVE UP										THE RESULTS					
Year	Team	Lg	G	GS	CG	GF	IP	BFP	H	R	ER	HR	SH	SF	HB	TBB	IBB	SO	WP	Bk	W	L	Pct.	ShO	Sv	ERA
1987 Oakland	AL		29	0	0	7	39.2	176	37	22	20	6	2	2	1	24	1	30	1	0	6	2	.750	0	0	4.54
1988 Oakland	AL		58	0	0	16	71.2	311	60	26	23	2	5	3	1	36	1	64	5	3	5	2	.714	0	3	2.89
1989 2 ML Teams			46	13	3	7	120	531	130	62	54	7	3	5	2	57	4	80	6	2	5	5	.500	1	0	4.05
1990 New York	AL		54	6	0	9	121.1	525	120	62	56	8	9	4	1	64	5	80	14	0	5	4	.556	0	3	4.15
1991 New York	AL		68	5	0	17	121.2	517	110	52	49	8	6	3	2	59	6	105	3	1	8	6	.571	0	3	3.62
1989 Oakland	AL		26	0	0	6	27.2	119	21	9	7	0	0	2	0	19	3	14	0	0	0	0	.000	0	0	2.28
New York	AL		20	13	3	1	92.1	412	109	53	47	7	3	3	2	38	1	66	6	2	5	5	.500	1	0	4.58
5 ML YEARS			255	24	3	56	474.1	2060	457	224	202	31	25	17	7	240	17	359	29	6	29	19	.604	1	9	3.83

Ivan Calderon

Bats: Right Throws: Right Pos: LF Ht: 6' 1" Wt: 221 Born: 03/19/62 Age: 30

						BATTING														BASERUNNING				PERCENTAGES		
Year	Team	Lg	G	AB	H	2B	3B	HR	(Hm	Rd)	TB	R	RBI	TBB	IBB	SO	HBP	SH	SF	SB	CS	SB%	GDP	Avg	OBP	SLG
1984 Seattle	AL		11	24	5	1	0	1	(0	1)	9	2	1	2	0	5	0	0	0	1	0	1.00	1	.208	.269	.375
1985 Seattle	AL		67	210	60	16	4	8	(6	2)	108	37	28	19	1	45	2	1	1	2	2	.67	10	.286	.349	.514
1986 2 ML Teams			50	164	41	7	1	2	(1	1)	56	16	15	9	1	39	1	0	0	3	1	.75	1	.250	.293	.341
1987 Chicago	AL		144	542	159	38	2	28	(15	13)	285	93	83	60	6	109	1	0	4	10	5	.67	13	.293	.362	.526
1988 Chicago	AL		73	264	56	14	0	14	(6	8)	112	40	35	34	2	66	0	0	3	4	4	.50	6	.212	.299	.424
1989 Chicago	AL		157	622	178	34	9	14	(2	12)	272	83	87	43	7	94	3	2	6	7	1	.88	20	.286	.332	.437
1990 Chicago	AL		158	607	166	44	2	14	(6	8)	256	85	74	51	7	79	1	0	8	32	16	.67	26	.273	.327	.422
1991 Montreal	NL		134	470	141	22	3	19	(7	12)	226	69	75	53	4	64	3	1	10	31	16	.66	7	.300	.368	.481
1986 Seattle	AL		37	131	31	5	0	2	(1	1)	42	13	13	6	0	33	1	0	0	3	1	.75	1	.237	.275	.321
Chicago	AL		13	33	10	2	1	0	(0	0)	14	3	2	3	1	6	0	0	0	0	0	.00	0	.303	.361	.424
8 ML YEARS			794	2903	806	176	21	100	(43	57)	1324	425	398	271	28	501	11	4	32	92	45	.67	86	.278	.338	.456

Ken Caminiti

Bats: Both Throws: Right Pos: 3B Ht: 6' 0" Wt: 200 Born: 04/21/63 Age: 29

						BATTING														BASERUNNING				PERCENTAGES		
Year	Team	Lg	G	AB	H	2B	3B	HR	(Hm	Rd)	TB	R	RBI	TBB	IBB	SO	HBP	SH	SF	SB	CS	SB%	GDP	Avg	OBP	SLG
1987 Houston	NL		63	203	50	7	1	3	(2	1)	68	10	23	12	1	44	0	2	1	0	0	.00	6	.246	.287	.335
1988 Houston	NL		30	83	15	2	0	1	(0	1)	20	5	7	5	0	18	0	0	1	0	0	.00	3	.181	.225	.241
1989 Houston	NL		161	585	149	31	3	10	(3	7)	216	71	72	51	9	93	3	3	4	4	1	.80	8	.255	.316	.369
1990 Houston	NL		153	541	131	20	2	4	(2	2)	167	52	51	48	7	97	0	3	4	9	4	.69	14	.242	.302	.309
1991 Houston	NL		152	574	145	30	3	13	(9	4)	220	65	80	46	7	85	5	3	4	4	5	.44	18	.253	.312	.383
5 ML YEARS			559	1986	490	90	9	31	(16	15)	691	203	233	162	24	337	8	11	14	17	10	.63	49	.247	.304	.348

Kevin Campbell

Pitches: Right Bats: Right Pos: RP Ht: 6' 2" Wt: 225 Born: 12/06/64 Age: 27

			HOW MUCH HE PITCHED					WHAT HE GAVE UP										THE RESULTS					
Year	Team	Lg	G	GS	CG	GF	IP	BFP	H	R	ER	HR	SH	SF	HB	TBB	IBB	SO	WP	Bk	W	L	Pct.	ShO	Sv	ERA
1986 Great Falls	R		15	15	3	0	85	0	99	62	44	5	0	0	3	32	0	66	6	0	5	6	.455	0	0	4.66
1987 Vero Beach	A		28	28	5	0	184	807	200	100	80	11	6	6	9	64	4	112	11	4	7	14	.333	1	0	3.91
1988 Vero Beach	A		26	26	5	0	163.2	677	166	67	50	6	10	4	3	49	2	115	6	1	8	12	.400	1	0	2.75
1989 Bakersfield	A		31	0	0	17	60.1	255	43	23	17	0	2	5	1	28	1	63	3	0	5	3	.625	0	6	2.54
San Antonio	AA		17	0	0	7	27	127	29	22	20	3	2	2	0	16	1	28	1	0	1	5	.167	0	2	6.67
1990 San Antonio	AA		49	0	0	29	81	329	67	29	21	1	3	3	1	25	6	84	5	1	2	6	.250	0	8	2.33
1991 Tacoma	AAA		35	0	0	12	75	304	53	18	15	1	3	1	3	35	1	56	5	0	9	2	.818	0	2	1.80
1991 Oakland	AL		14	0	0	2	23	94	13	7	7	4	1	0	1	14	0	16	0	0	1	0	1.000	0	0	2.74

Sil Campusano

Bats: Right **Throws:** Right **Pos:** CF **Ht:** 6' 0" **Wt:** 178 **Born:** 12/31/66 **Age:** 25

Year	Team	Lg	G	AB	H	2B	3B	HR	(Hm	Rd)	TB	R	RBI	TBB	IBB	SO	HBP	SH	SF	SB	CS	SB%	GDP	Avg	OBP	SLG
1988	Toronto	AL	73	142	31	10	2	2	(1	1)	51	14	12	9	0	33	4	2	1	0	0	.00	0	.218	.282	.359
1990	Philadelphia	NL	66	85	18	1	1	2	(2	0)	27	10	9	6	0	16	1	0	1	1	0	1.00	1	.212	.269	.318
1991	Philadelphia	NL	15	35	4	0	0	1	(0	1)	7	2	2	1	0	10	0	1	0	0	0	.00	0	.114	.139	.200
	3 ML YEARS		154	262	53	11	3	5	(3	2)	85	26	23	16	0	59	5	3	2	1	0	1.00	1	.202	.260	.324

George Canale

Bats: Left **Throws:** Right **Pos:** 1B **Ht:** 6' 1" **Wt:** 190 **Born:** 08/11/65 **Age:** 26

Year	Team	Lg	G	AB	H	2B	3B	HR	(Hm	Rd)	TB	R	RBI	TBB	IBB	SO	HBP	SH	SF	SB	CS	SB%	GDP	Avg	OBP	SLG
1986	Helena	R	65	221	72	19	0	9	--	--	118	48	49	54	0	65	0	2	5	6	4	.60	2	.326	.450	.534
1987	Stockton	A	66	246	69	18	1	7	--	--	110	42	48	38	3	59	1	2	2	5	4	.56	8	.280	.376	.447
	El Paso	AA	65	253	65	10	2	7	--	--	100	38	36	20	1	69	2	0	0	3	2	.60	4	.257	.316	.395
1988	El Paso	AA	132	496	120	23	2	23	--	--	216	77	93	59	5	152	2	0	2	9	3	.75	12	.242	.324	.435
1989	Denver	AAA	144	503	140	33	9	18	--	--	245	80	71	71	1	134	2	2	6	5	8	.38	3	.278	.366	.487
1990	Denver	AAA	134	468	119	18	6	12	--	--	185	76	60	69	4	103	1	3	3	12	5	.71	10	.254	.349	.395
1991	Denver	AAA	88	274	64	10	2	10	--	--	108	36	47	51	0	49	2	0	3	6	2	.75	6	.234	.355	.394
1989	Milwaukee	AL	13	26	5	1	0	1	(0	1)	9	5	3	2	0	3	0	1	0	0	1	.00	0	.192	.250	.346
1990	Milwaukee	AL	10	13	1	1	0	0	(0	0)	2	4	0	2	0	6	0	0	0	0	1	.00	0	.077	.200	.154
1991	Milwaukee	AL	21	34	6	2	0	3	(1	2)	17	6	10	8	0	6	0	0	2	0	0	.00	5	.176	.318	.500
	3 ML YEARS		44	73	12	4	0	4	(1	3)	28	15	13	12	0	15	0	1	2	0	2	.00	5	.164	.276	.384

Casey Candaele

Bats: Both **Throws:** Right **Pos:** 2B/LF **Ht:** 5' 9" **Wt:** 165 **Born:** 01/12/61 **Age:** 31

Year	Team	Lg	G	AB	H	2B	3B	HR	(Hm	Rd)	TB	R	RBI	TBB	IBB	SO	HBP	SH	SF	SB	CS	SB%	GDP	Avg	OBP	SLG
1986	Montreal	NL	30	104	24	4	1	0	(0	0)	30	9	6	5	0	15	0	0	1	3	5	.38	3	.231	.264	.288
1987	Montreal	NL	138	449	122	23	4	1	(1	0)	156	62	23	38	3	28	2	4	2	7	10	.41	5	.272	.330	.347
1988	2 ML Teams		57	147	25	8	1	0	(0	0)	35	11	5	11	1	17	0	3	0	1	1	.50	7	.170	.224	.238
1990	Houston	NL	130	262	75	8	6	3	(1	2)	104	30	22	31	5	42	1	4	0	7	5	.58	4	.286	.364	.397
1991	Houston	NL	151	461	121	20	7	4	(1	3)	167	44	50	40	7	49	0	1	3	9	3	.75	5	.262	.319	.362
1988	Montreal	NL	36	116	20	5	1	0	(0	0)	27	9	4	10	1	11	0	2	0	1	0	1.00	1	.172	.238	.233
	Houston	NL	21	31	5	3	0	0	(0	0)	8	2	1	1	0	6	0	1	0	0	1	.00	0	.161	.188	.258
	5 ML YEARS		506	1423	367	63	19	8	(3	5)	492	156	106	125	16	151	3	12	6	27	24	.53	24	.258	.318	.346

John Candelaria

Pitches: Left **Bats:** Right **Pos:** RP **Ht:** 6' 6" **Wt:** 225 **Born:** 11/06/53 **Age:** 38

Year	Team	Lg	G	GS	CG	GF	IP	BFP	H	R	ER	HR	SH	SF	HB	TBB	IBB	SO	WP	Bk	W	L	Pct.	ShO	Sv	ERA
1975	Pittsburgh	NL	18	18	4	0	121	497	95	47	37	8	6	4	2	36	9	95	1	0	8	6	.571	1	0	2.75
1976	Pittsburgh	NL	32	31	11	1	220	881	173	87	77	22	13	6	2	60	5	138	0	0	16	7	.696	4	1	3.15
1977	Pittsburgh	NL	33	33	6	0	231	917	197	64	60	29	9	6	2	50	2	133	1	2	20	5	.800	1	0	2.34
1978	Pittsburgh	NL	30	29	3	1	189	796	191	73	68	15	8	2	5	49	6	94	3	3	12	11	.522	1	1	3.24
1979	Pittsburgh	NL	33	30	8	2	207	850	201	83	74	25	4	7	3	41	6	101	2	0	14	9	.609	0	0	3.22
1980	Pittsburgh	NL	35	34	7	1	233	969	246	114	104	14	14	12	3	50	4	97	0	2	11	14	.440	0	1	4.02
1981	Pittsburgh	NL	6	6	0	0	41	168	42	17	16	3	1	1	0	11	1	14	0	0	2	2	.500	0	0	3.51
1982	Pittsburgh	NL	31	30	1	1	174.2	704	166	62	57	13	5	6	4	37	3	133	1	0	12	7	.632	1	1	2.94
1983	Pittsburgh	NL	33	32	2	0	197.2	797	191	73	71	15	4	4	2	45	3	157	3	2	15	8	.652	0	0	3.23
1984	Pittsburgh	NL	33	28	3	4	185.1	751	179	69	56	19	10	6	1	34	3	133	1	1	12	11	.522	1	2	2.72
1985	2 ML Teams		50	13	1	26	125.1	530	127	56	52	14	7	7	4	38	3	100	2	0	9	7	.563	1	9	3.73
1986	California	AL	16	16	1	0	91.2	365	68	30	26	4	3	3	3	26	2	81	2	1	10	2	.833	1	0	2.55
1987	2 ML Teams		23	23	0	0	129	544	144	78	69	18	8	6	1	23	0	84	0	1	10	6	.625	0	0	4.81
1988	New York	AL	25	24	6	1	157	640	150	69	59	18	4	6	2	23	2	121	2	12	13	7	.650	2	1	3.38
1989	2 ML Teams		22	6	1	3	65.1	274	66	36	34	11	3	5	0	16	3	51	2	1	3	5	.375	0	0	4.68
1990	2 ML Teams		47	3	0	15	79.2	345	87	36	35	11	2	6	2	20	5	63	5	0	7	6	.538	0	5	3.95
1991	Los Angeles	NL	59	0	0	10	33.2	138	31	16	14	3	1	3	0	11	2	38	1	1	1	1	.500	0	2	3.74
1985	Pittsburgh	NL	37	0	0	26	54.1	229	57	23	22	7	3	4	1	14	2	47	0	0	2	4	.333	0	9	3.64
	California	AL	13	13	1	0	71	301	70	33	30	7	4	3	3	24	1	53	2	0	7	3	.700	1	0	3.80
1987	California	AL	20	20	0	0	116.2	487	127	70	61	17	6	5	1	20	0	74	0	0	8	6	.571	0	0	4.71
	New York	NL	3	3	0	0	12.1	57	17	8	8	1	2	1	0	3	0	10	0	1	2	0	1.000	0	0	5.84
1989	New York	AL	10	6	1	1	49	206	49	28	28	8	2	2	0	12	1	37	2	1	3	3	.500	0	0	5.14
	Montreal	NL	12	0	0	2	16.1	68	17	8	6	3	1	3	0	4	2	14	0	0	0	2	.000	0	0	3.31
1990	Minnesota	AL	34	1	0	10	58.1	239	55	23	22	9	2	3	0	9	2	44	3	0	7	3	.700	0	0	3.39
	Toronto	AL	13	2	0	5	21.1	106	32	13	13	2	0	3	2	11	3	19	2	0	0	3	.000	0	1	5.48
	17 ML YEARS		526	356	54	65	2481.1	10166	2354	1010	909	242	102	90	36	570	59	1633	26	26	175	114	.606	13	23	3.30

Tom Candiotti

Pitches: Right **Bats:** Right **Pos:** SP
Ht: 6' 2" **Wt:** 200 **Born:** 08/31/57 **Age:** 34

| | | HOW MUCH HE PITCHED | | | | | | WHAT HE GAVE UP | | | | | | | | | | | | THE RESULTS | | | | | |
Year Team	Lg	G	GS	CG	GF	IP	BFP	H	R	ER	HR	SH	SF	HB	TBB	IBB	SO	WP	Bk	W	L	Pct.	ShO	Sv	ERA
1983 Milwaukee	AL	10	8	2	1	55.2	233	62	21	20	4	0	2	2	16	0	21	0	0	4	4	.500	1	0	3.23
1984 Milwaukee	AL	8	6	0	0	32.1	147	38	21	19	5	0	0	0	10	0	23	1	0	2	2	.500	0	0	5.29
1986 Cleveland	AL	36	34	17	1	252.1	1078	234	112	100	18	3	9	8	106	0	167	12	4	16	12	.571	3	0	3.57
1987 Cleveland	AL	32	32	7	0	201.2	888	193	132	107	28	8	10	4	93	2	111	13	2	7	18	.280	2	0	4.78
1988 Cleveland	AL	31	31	11	0	216.2	903	225	86	79	15	12	5	6	53	3	137	5	7	14	8	.636	1	0	3.28
1989 Cleveland	AL	31	31	4	0	206	847	188	80	71	10	6	4	4	55	5	124	4	8	13	10	.565	0	0	3.10
1990 Cleveland	AL	31	29	3	1	202	856	207	92	82	23	4	3	6	55	1	128	9	3	15	11	.577	1	0	3.65
1991 2 ML Teams		34	34	6	0	238	981	202	82	70	12	4	11	6	73	1	167	11	0	13	13	.500	2	0	2.65
1991 Cleveland	AL	15	15	3	0	108.1	442	88	35	27	6	1	7	2	28	0	86	6	0	7	6	.538	0	0	2.24
Toronto	AL	19	19	3	0	129.2	539	114	47	43	6	3	4	4	45	1	81	5	0	6	7	.462	0	0	2.98
8 ML YEARS		213	205	50	3	1404.2	5933	1349	626	548	115	37	44	36	461	12	878	55	24	84	78	.519	8	0	3.51

Jose Canseco

Bats: Right **Throws:** Right **Pos:** RF/DH
Ht: 6' 4" **Wt:** 240 **Born:** 07/02/64 **Age:** 27

| | | BATTING | | | | | | | | | | | | | | | | | BASERUNNING | | | | PERCENTAGES | | |
Year Team	Lg	G	AB	H	2B	3B	HR	(Hm	Rd)	TB	R	RBI	TBB	IBB	SO	HBP	SH	SF	SB	CS	SB%	GDP	Avg	OBP	SLG
1985 Oakland	AL	29	96	29	3	0	5	(4	1)	47	16	13	4	0	31	0	0	0	1	1	.50	1	.302	.330	.490
1986 Oakland	AL	157	600	144	29	1	33	(14	19)	274	85	117	65	1	175	8	0	9	15	7	.68	12	.240	.318	.457
1987 Oakland	AL	159	630	162	35	3	31	(16	15)	296	81	113	50	2	157	2	0	9	15	3	.83	16	.257	.310	.470
1988 Oakland	AL	158	610	187	34	0	42	(16	26)	347	120	124	78	10	128	10	1	6	40	16	.71	15	.307	.391	.569
1989 Oakland	AL	65	227	61	9	1	17	(8	9)	123	40	57	23	4	69	2	0	6	6	3	.67	4	.269	.333	.542
1990 Oakland	AL	131	481	132	14	2	37	(18	19)	261	83	101	72	8	158	5	0	5	19	10	.66	9	.274	.371	.543
1991 Oakland	AL	154	572	152	32	1	44	(16	28)	318	115	122	78	8	152	9	0	6	26	6	.81	16	.266	.359	.556
7 ML YEARS		853	3216	867	156	8	209	(92	117)	1666	540	647	370	33	870	36	1	41	122	46	.73	73	.270	.348	.518

Mike Capel

Pitches: Right **Bats:** Right **Pos:** RP
Ht: 6' 2" **Wt:** 175 **Born:** 10/13/61 **Age:** 30

| | | HOW MUCH HE PITCHED | | | | | | WHAT HE GAVE UP | | | | | | | | | | | | THE RESULTS | | | | | |
Year Team	Lg	G	GS	CG	GF	IP	BFP	H	R	ER	HR	SH	SF	HB	TBB	IBB	SO	WP	Bk	W	L	Pct.	ShO	Sv	ERA
1988 Chicago	NL	22	0	0	11	29.1	134	34	19	16	5	2	0	3	13	2	19	5	0	2	1	.667	0	0	4.91
1990 Milwaukee	AL	2	0	0	0	0.1	9	6	6	5	0	0	0	1	1	0	1	0	0	0	0	.000	0	0	99.99
1991 Houston	NL	25	0	0	13	32.2	143	33	14	11	3	3	1	0	15	1	23	0	0	1	3	.250	0	3	3.03
3 ML YEARS		49	0	0	24	62.1	286	73	39	32	8	5	1	4	29	3	43	5	0	3	4	.429	0	3	4.62

Nick Capra

Bats: Right **Throws:** Right **Pos:** CF
Ht: 5' 8" **Wt:** 165 **Born:** 03/08/58 **Age:** 34

| | | BATTING | | | | | | | | | | | | | | | | | BASERUNNING | | | | PERCENTAGES | | |
Year Team	Lg	G	AB	H	2B	3B	HR	(Hm	Rd)	TB	R	RBI	TBB	IBB	SO	HBP	SH	SF	SB	CS	SB%	GDP	Avg	OBP	SLG
1982 Texas	AL	13	15	4	0	0	1	(0	1)	7	2	1	3	0	4	1	0	0	2	1	.67	0	.267	.421	.467
1983 Texas	AL	8	2	0	0	0	0	(0	0)	0	2	0	0	0	0	0	0	0	0	0	.00	0	.000	.000	.000
1985 Texas	AL	8	8	1	0	0	0	(0	0)	1	1	0	0	0	3	0	0	0	1	0	1.00	3	.125	.125	.125
1988 Kansas City	AL	14	29	4	1	0	0	(0	0)	5	3	0	2	0	3	0	0	0	0	0	.00	0	.138	.194	.172
1991 Texas	AL	2	0	0	0	0	0	(0	0)	0	1	0	1	0	0	0	0	0	0	0	.00	0	.000	1.000	.000
5 ML YEARS		45	54	9	1	0	1	(0	1)	13	9	1	6	0	7	1	0	0	3	1	.75	4	.167	.262	.241

Don Carman

Pitches: Left **Bats:** Left **Pos:** RP
Ht: 6' 3" **Wt:** 201 **Born:** 08/14/59 **Age:** 32

| | | HOW MUCH HE PITCHED | | | | | | WHAT HE GAVE UP | | | | | | | | | | | | THE RESULTS | | | | | |
Year Team	Lg	G	GS	CG	GF	IP	BFP	H	R	ER	HR	SH	SF	HB	TBB	IBB	SO	WP	Bk	W	L	Pct.	ShO	Sv	ERA
1983 Philadelphia	NL	1	0	0	1	1	3	0	0	0	0	0	0	0	0	0	0	0	0	0	0	.000	0	1	0.00
1984 Philadelphia	NL	11	0	0	8	13.1	61	14	9	8	2	0	0	0	6	4	16	3	0	0	1	.000	0	0	5.40
1985 Philadelphia	NL	71	0	0	33	86.1	342	52	25	20	6	5	5	2	38	3	87	1	0	9	4	.692	0	7	2.08
1986 Philadelphia	NL	50	14	2	13	134.1	545	113	50	48	11	5	3	3	52	11	98	6	2	10	5	.667	1	1	3.22
1987 Philadelphia	NL	35	35	3	0	211	886	194	110	99	34	11	5	5	69	7	125	3	1	13	11	.542	2	0	4.22
1988 Philadelphia	NL	36	32	2	0	201.1	873	211	101	96	20	9	8	4	70	6	116	8	3	10	14	.417	0	0	4.29
1989 Philadelphia	NL	49	20	0	5	149.1	683	152	98	87	21	5	5	3	86	6	81	7	3	5	15	.250	0	0	5.24
1990 Philadelphia	NL	59	1	0	11	86.2	368	69	43	40	13	6	4	4	38	7	58	6	1	6	2	.750	0	1	4.15
1991 Cincinnati	NL	28	0	0	10	36	164	40	23	21	8	3	1	1	19	1	15	2	0	0	2	.000	0	0	5.25
9 ML YEARS		340	102	7	82	919.1	3925	845	459	419	115	44	31	22	378	45	596	36	10	53	54	.495	3	11	4.10

Cris Carpenter

Pitches: Right **Bats: Right** **Pos: RP** **Ht: 6' 1"** **Wt: 185** **Born: 04/05/65** **Age: 27**

		HOW MUCH HE PITCHED						WHAT HE GAVE UP										THE RESULTS					
Year Team	Lg	G	GS	CG	GF	IP	BFP	H	R	ER	HR	SH	SF	HB	TBB	IBB	SO	WP	Bk	W	L	Pct.	ShO	Sv	ERA
1988 St. Louis	NL	8	8	1	0	47.2	203	56	27	25	3	1	4	1	9	2	24	1	0	2	3	.400	0	0	4.72
1989 St. Louis	NL	36	5	0	10	68	303	70	30	24	4	4	4	2	26	9	35	1	0	4	4	.500	0	0	3.18
1990 St. Louis	NL	4	0	0	1	8	32	5	4	4	2	0	0	0	2	1	6	0	0	0	0	.000	0	0	4.50
1991 St. Louis	NL	59	0	0	19	66	266	53	31	31	6	3	2	0	20	9	47	1	0	10	4	.714	0	0	4.23
4 ML YEARS		107	13	1	30	189.2	804	184	92	84	15	8	10	3	57	21	112	3	0	16	11	.593	0	0	3.99

Chuck Carr

Bats: Both **Throws: Right** **Pos: CF** **Ht: 5'10"** **Wt: 165** **Born: 08/10/68** **Age: 23**

		BATTING																BASERUNNING				PERCENTAGES		
Year Team	Lg	G	AB	H	2B	3B	HR	(Hm	Rd)	TB	R	RBI	TBB	IBB	SO	HBP	SH	SF	SB	CS	SB%	GDP	Avg	OBP	SLG
1986 Reds	R	44	123	21	5	0	0	--	--	26	13	10	10	0	27	0	5	2	9	1	.90	2	.171	.230	.211
1987 Bellingham	A	44	165	40	1	1	1	--	--	46	31	11	12	0	38	1	3	0	20	1	.95	2	.242	.298	.279
1988 Wausau	A	82	304	91	14	2	6	--	--	127	58	30	14	0	49	1	3	5	41	11	.79	5	.299	.327	.418
Vermont	AA	41	159	39	4	2	1	--	--	50	26	13	8	0	33	0	3	1	21	9	.70	0	.245	.280	.314
1989 Jackson	AA	116	444	107	13	1	0	--	--	122	45	22	27	2	66	1	7	2	47	20	.70	3	.241	.285	.275
1990 Tidewater	AAA	20	81	21	5	1	0	--	--	28	13	8	4	0	12	0	0	2	6	4	.60	0	.259	.287	.346
Jackson	AA	93	360	93	20	9	3	--	--	140	60	24	44	2	77	2	3	2	47	15	.76	2	.258	.341	.389
1991 Tidewater	AAA	64	246	48	6	1	1	--	--	59	34	11	18	0	37	1	1	0	27	8	.77	3	.195	.253	.240
1990 New York	NL	4	2	0	0	0	0	(0	0)	0	0	0	0	0	2	0	0	0	1	0	1.00	0	.000	.000	.000
1991 New York	NL	12	11	2	0	0	0	(0	0)	2	1	1	0	0	2	0	0	0	1	0	1.00	0	.182	.182	.182
2 ML YEARS		16	13	2	0	0	0	(0	0)	2	1	1	0	0	4	0	0	0	2	0	1.00	0	.154	.154	.154

Amalio Carreno

Pitches: Right **Bats: Right** **Pos: RP** **Ht: 6' 0"** **Wt: 170** **Born: 04/11/64** **Age: 28**

		HOW MUCH HE PITCHED						WHAT HE GAVE UP										THE RESULTS					
Year Team	Lg	G	GS	CG	GF	IP	BFP	H	R	ER	HR	SH	SF	HB	TBB	IBB	SO	WP	Bk	W	L	Pct.	ShO	Sv	ERA
1984 Yankees	R	9	7	1	2	33	166	37	28	18	1	1	2	0	26	0	31	4	2	1	6	.143	0	0	4.91
1985 Yankees	R	1	0	0	0	2	9	1	1	1	0	0	0	0	1	0	1	2	1	0	0	.000	0	0	4.50
1986 Yankees	R	7	7	2	0	47.2	184	36	12	9	1	0	2	1	12	0	27	1	0	5	0	1.000	1	0	1.70
Ft.Lauderdle	A	3	3	1	0	15.2	70	16	11	7	0	0	0	0	7	1	8	3	0	1	1	.500	0	0	4.02
1987 Columbus	AAA	11	0	0	5	17.1	80	26	15	15	2	0	1	0	5	0	11	0	0	1	1	.500	0	1	7.79
Pr William	A	26	4	2	14	62.1	271	53	30	21	2	1	3	1	30	2	49	14	0	5	2	.714	0	2	3.03
Albany	AA	9	3	0	4	24	116	32	23	21	6	1	0	0	15	1	18	1	0	0	3	.000	0	0	7.88
1988 Columbus	AAA	1	0	0	0	3.1	18	8	4	4	0	0	0	1	0	0	2	1	0	0	0	.000	0	0	10.80
Albany	AA	9	7	1	2	38.1	175	38	20	15	3	1	1	3	21	2	24	1	1	2	4	.333	0	0	3.52
Reading	AA	5	4	0	1	21.1	93	22	12	12	2	0	0	1	11	0	7	1	1	1	0	1.000	0	0	5.06
1989 Reading	AA	31	11	2	11	101.2	443	99	57	49	9	3	6	4	41	2	56	9	0	5	7	.417	1	1	4.34
1990 Reading	AA	25	23	3	1	128	565	137	62	52	5	3	3	5	47	4	86	8	0	4	13	.235	1	1	3.66
1991 Scranton-Wb	AAA	33	8	1	12	81	358	88	51	48	7	4	1	6	26	2	52	4	1	4	8	.333	0	0	5.33
1991 Philadelphia	NL	3	0	0	1	3.1	20	5	6	6	1	0	2	1	3	0	2	0	0	0	0	.000	0	0	16.20

Mark Carreon

Bats: Right **Throws: Left** **Pos: LF/CF/RF** **Ht: 6' 0"** **Wt: 195** **Born: 07/09/63** **Age: 28**

		BATTING																BASERUNNING				PERCENTAGES		
Year Team	Lg	G	AB	H	2B	3B	HR	(Hm	Rd)	TB	R	RBI	TBB	IBB	SO	HBP	SH	SF	SB	CS	SB%	GDP	Avg	OBP	SLG
1987 New York	NL	9	12	3	0	0	0	(0	0)	3	0	1	1	0	1	0	0	0	0	0	.00	0	.250	.308	.250
1988 New York	NL	7	9	5	2	0	1	(0	1)	10	5	1	2	0	1	0	0	0	0	0	.00	0	.556	.636	1.111
1989 New York	NL	68	133	41	6	0	6	(4	2)	65	20	16	12	0	17	1	0	0	2	3	.40	1	.308	.370	.489
1990 New York	NL	82	188	47	12	0	10	(1	9)	89	30	26	15	0	29	2	0	0	1	0	1.00	1	.250	.312	.473
1991 New York	NL	106	254	66	6	0	4	(3	1)	84	18	21	12	2	26	2	1	1	2	1	.67	14	.260	.297	.331
5 ML YEARS		272	596	162	26	0	21	(8	13)	251	73	65	42	2	74	5	1	1	5	5	.50	16	.272	.325	.421

Matias Carrillo

Bats: Left **Throws: Left** **Pos: PH** **Ht: 5'11"** **Wt: 190** **Born: 02/24/63** **Age: 29**

		BATTING																BASERUNNING				PERCENTAGES		
Year Team	Lg	G	AB	H	2B	3B	HR	(Hm	Rd)	TB	R	RBI	TBB	IBB	SO	HBP	SH	SF	SB	CS	SB%	GDP	Avg	OBP	SLG
1990 Denver	AAA	21	75	20	6	2	2	--	--	36	15	10	2	0	16	0	0	1	0	2	.00	2	.267	.282	.480
1991 Denver	AAA	120	421	116	18	5	8	--	--	168	56	56	32	2	84	0	5	3	11	13	.46	11	.276	.325	.399
1991 Milwaukee	AL	3	0	0	0	0	0	(0	0)	0	0	0	0	0	0	0	0	0	0	0	.00	0	.000	.000	.000

Gary Carter

Bats: Right **Throws:** Right **Pos:** C   **Ht:** 6' 2" **Wt:** 214 **Born:** 04/08/54 **Age:** 38

								BATTING												BASERUNNING				PERCENTAGES		
Year Team	Lg	G	AB	H	2B	3B	HR	(Hm	Rd)	TB	R	RBI	TBB	IBB	SO	HBP	SH	SF	SB	CS	SB%	GDP	Avg	OBP	SLG
1974 Montreal	NL	9	27	11	0	1	1	(1	0)	16	5	6	1	0	2	0	0	1	2	0	1.00	0	.407	.414	.593
1975 Montreal	NL	144	503	136	20	1	17	(9	8)	209	58	68	72	8	83	1	10	4	5	2	.71	7	.270	.360	.416
1976 Montreal	NL	91	311	68	8	1	6	(5	1)	96	31	38	30	2	43	1	2	3	0	2	.00	7	.219	.287	.309
1977 Montreal	NL	154	522	148	29	2	31	(22	9)	274	86	84	58	5	103	5	3	7	5	5	.50	9	.284	.356	.525
1978 Montreal	NL	157	533	136	27	1	20	(7	13)	225	76	72	62	11	70	5	2	5	10	6	.63	10	.255	.336	.422
1979 Montreal	NL	141	505	143	26	5	22	(12	10)	245	74	75	40	3	62	5	2	7	3	2	.60	11	.283	.338	.485
1980 Montreal	NL	154	549	145	25	5	29	(12	17)	267	76	101	58	11	78	1	1	8	3	2	.60	9	.264	.331	.486
1981 Montreal	NL	100	374	94	20	2	16	(7	9)	166	48	68	35	4	35	1	3	6	1	5	.17	6	.251	.313	.444
1982 Montreal	NL	154	557	163	32	1	29	(16	13)	284	91	97	78	11	64	6	4	8	2	5	.29	16	.293	.381	.510
1983 Montreal	NL	145	541	146	37	3	17	(6	11)	240	63	79	51	7	57	7	2	8	1	1	.50	14	.270	.336	.444
1984 Montreal	NL	159	596	175	32	1	27	(14	13)	290	75	106	64	9	57	6	0	3	2	2	.50	8	.294	.366	.487
1985 New York	NL	149	555	156	17	1	32	(12	20)	271	83	100	69	16	46	6	0	3	1	1	.50	18	.281	.365	.488
1986 New York	NL	132	490	125	14	2	24	(13	11)	215	81	105	62	9	63	6	0	15	1	0	1.00	14	.255	.337	.439
1987 New York	NL	139	523	123	18	2	20	(9	11)	205	55	83	42	1	73	1	1	6	0	0	.00	14	.235	.290	.392
1988 New York	NL	130	455	110	16	2	11	(5	6)	163	39	46	34	1	52	7	1	6	0	2	.00	8	.242	.301	.358
1989 New York	NL	50	153	28	8	0	2	(1	1)	42	14	15	12	0	15	0	0	1	0	0	.00	5	.183	.241	.275
1990 San Francisco	NL	92	244	62	10	0	9	(6	3)	99	24	27	25	3	31	1	0	2	1	1	.50	2	.254	.324	.406
1991 Los Angeles	NL	101	248	61	14	0	6	(3	3)	93	22	26	22	1	26	7	1	2	2	2	.50	11	.246	.323	.375
18 ML YEARS		2201	7686	2030	353	30	319	(160	159)	3400	1001	1196	815	102	960	66	32	95	39	38	.51	176	.264	.336	.442

Jeff Carter

Pitches: Right **Bats:** Right **Pos:** RP   **Ht:** 6' 3" **Wt:** 195 **Born:** 12/03/64 **Age:** 27

		HOW MUCH HE PITCHED						WHAT HE GAVE UP										THE RESULTS					
Year Team	Lg	G	GS	CG	GF	IP	BFP	H	R	ER	HR	SH	SF	HB	TBB	IBB	SO	WP	Bk	W	L	Pct.	ShO	Sv	ERA
1987 Jamestown	A	31	0	0	20	42.1	178	39	15	11	1	1	3	0	17	0	42	5	0	2	3	.400	0	5	2.34
1988 Rockford	A	39	11	1	11	107.1	447	100	38	33	8	0	0	1	35	3	91	7	3	11	5	.688	0	3	2.77
1989 Wst Plm Bch	A	7	7	0	0	35	148	36	14	10	0	1	2	1	8	0	29	1	0	4	1	.800	0	0	2.57
Jacksnville	AA	6	6	1	0	36	143	23	11	10	2	1	0	0	14	1	21	2	1	1	4	.200	0	0	2.50
1990 Jacksnville	AA	52	7	2	30	117.1	466	90	36	24	4	10	4	1	33	1	76	3	1	8	3	.727	1	15	1.84
1991 Vancouver	AAA	41	4	0	26	79.2	344	78	33	27	3	7	3	1	35	5	40	3	0	3	7	.300	0	4	3.05
1991 Chicago	AL	5	2	0	1	12	49	8	8	7	1	0	0	0	5	0	2	0	0	0	0	.000	0	0	5.25

Joe Carter

Bats: Right **Throws:** Right **Pos:** RF/LF   **Ht:** 6' 3" **Wt:** 215 **Born:** 03/07/60 **Age:** 32

								BATTING												BASERUNNING				PERCENTAGES		
Year Team	Lg	G	AB	H	2B	3B	HR	(Hm	Rd)	TB	R	RBI	TBB	IBB	SO	HBP	SH	SF	SB	CS	SB%	GDP	Avg	OBP	SLG
1983 Chicago	NL	23	51	9	1	1	0	(0	0)	12	6	1	0	0	21	0	1	0	1	0	1.00	1	.176	.176	.235
1984 Cleveland	AL	66	244	67	6	1	13	(9	4)	114	32	41	11	0	48	1	0	1	2	4	.33	2	.275	.307	.467
1985 Cleveland	AL	143	489	128	27	0	15	(5	10)	200	64	59	25	2	74	2	3	4	24	6	.80	9	.262	.298	.409
1986 Cleveland	AL	162	663	200	36	9	29	(14	15)	341	108	121	32	3	95	5	1	8	29	7	.81	8	.302	.335	.514
1987 Cleveland	AL	149	588	155	27	2	32	(9	23)	282	83	106	27	6	105	9	1	4	31	6	.84	8	.264	.304	.480
1988 Cleveland	AL	157	621	168	36	6	27	(16	11)	297	85	98	35	6	82	7	1	6	27	5	.84	6	.271	.314	.478
1989 Cleveland	AL	162	651	158	32	4	35	(16	19)	303	84	105	39	8	112	8	2	5	13	5	.72	6	.243	.292	.465
1990 San Diego	NL	162	634	147	27	1	24	(12	12)	248	79	115	48	18	93	7	0	8	22	6	.79	12	.232	.290	.391
1991 Toronto	AL	162	638	174	42	3	33	(23	10)	321	89	108	49	12	112	10	0	9	20	9	.69	7	.273	.330	.503
9 ML YEARS		1186	4579	1206	234	27	208	(104	104)	2118	630	754	266	55	742	49	9	45	169	48	.78	59	.263	.308	.463

Chuck Cary

Pitches: Left **Bats:** Left **Pos:** SP   **Ht:** 6' 4" **Wt:** 216 **Born:** 03/03/60 **Age:** 32

		HOW MUCH HE PITCHED						WHAT HE GAVE UP										THE RESULTS					
Year Team	Lg	G	GS	CG	GF	IP	BFP	H	R	ER	HR	SH	SF	HB	TBB	IBB	SO	WP	Bk	W	L	Pct.	ShO	Sv	ERA
1985 Detroit	AL	16	0	0	6	23.2	95	16	9	9	2	0	1	2	8	1	22	0	0	0	1	.000	0	2	3.42
1986 Detroit	AL	22	0	0	6	31.2	140	33	18	12	3	2	2	0	15	4	21	1	1	1	2	.333	0	0	3.41
1987 Atlanta	NL	13	0	0	6	16.2	70	17	7	7	3	1	0	1	4	3	15	1	0	1	1	.500	0	1	3.78
1988 Atlanta	NL	7	0	0	1	8.1	39	8	6	6	1	2	0	1	4	0	7	1	0	0	0	.000	0	0	6.48
1989 New York	AL	22	11	2	4	99.1	404	78	42	36	13	1	1	0	29	6	79	6	1	4	4	.500	0	0	3.26
1990 New York	AL	28	27	2	1	156.2	661	155	77	73	21	3	5	1	55	1	134	11	2	6	12	.333	0	0	4.19
1991 New York	AL	10	9	0	0	53.1	247	61	35	35	6	1	0	0	32	2	34	2	1	1	6	.143	0	0	5.91
7 ML YEARS		118	47	4	24	389.2	1656	368	194	178	49	10	9	5	147	17	312	22	5	13	26	.333	0	3	4.11

Larry Casian

Pitches: Left Bats: Right Pos: RP Ht: 6' 0" Wt: 170 Born: 10/28/65 Age: 26

Year	Team	Lg	G	GS	CG	GF	IP	BFP	H	R	ER	HR	SH	SF	HB	TBB	IBB	SO	WP	Bk	W	L	Pct.	ShO	Sv	ERA
1987	Visalia	A	18	15	2	3	97	400	89	35	27	3	1	2	7	49	0	96	7	0	10	3	.769	1	2	2.51
1988	Orlando	AA	27	26	4	0	174	723	165	72	57	14	6	4	7	62	1	104	12	8	9	9	.500	1	0	2.95
	Portland	AAA	1	0	0	1	2.2	14	5	3	0	1	1	0	0	0	0	2	0	0	0	1	.000	0	0	0.00
1989	Portland	AAA	28	27	0	0	169.1	738	201	97	85	13	5	6	6	63	0	65	5	2	7	12	.368	0	0	4.52
1990	Portland	AAA	37	23	1	4	156.2	682	171	90	78	14	8	4	3	59	5	89	2	2	9	9	.500	0	0	4.48
1991	Portland	AAA	34	6	0	10	52	215	51	25	20	3	0	2	1	16	1	24	0	0	3	2	.600	0	2	3.46
1990	Minnesota	AL	5	3	0	1	22.1	90	26	9	8	2	0	1	0	4	0	11	0	0	2	1	.667	0	0	3.22
1991	Minnesota	AL	15	0	0	4	18.1	87	28	16	15	4	0	0	1	7	2	6	2	0	0	0	.000	0	0	7.36
	2 ML YEARS		20	3	0	5	40.2	177	54	25	23	6	0	1	1	11	2	17	2	0	2	1	.667	0	0	5.09

Vinny Castilla

Bats: Right Throws: Right Pos: SS Ht: 6' 1" Wt: 175 Born: 07/04/67 Age: 24

Year	Team	Lg	G	AB	H	2B	3B	HR	(Hm	Rd)	TB	R	RBI	TBB	IBB	SO	HBP	SH	SF	SB	CS	SB%	GDP	Avg	OBP	SLG
1990	Sumter	A	93	339	91	15	2	9	--	--	137	47	53	28	1	54	8	1	5	2	5	.29	8	.268	.334	.404
	Greenville	AA	46	170	40	5	1	4	--	--	59	20	16	13	3	23	2	0	1	4	4	.50	7	.235	.296	.347
1991	Greenville	AA	66	259	70	17	3	7	--	--	114	34	44	9	1	35	2	2	4	0	1	.00	4	.270	.296	.440
	Richmond	AAA	67	240	54	7	4	7	--	--	90	25	36	14	2	31	3	0	5	1	1	.50	4	.225	.271	.375
1991	Atlanta	NL	12	5	1	0	0	0	(0	0)	1	1	0	0	0	2	0	1	0	0	0	.00	0	.200	.200	.200

Braulio Castillo

Bats: Right Throws: Right Pos: CF Ht: 6' 0" Wt: 160 Born: 05/13/68 Age: 24

Year	Team	Lg	G	AB	H	2B	3B	HR	(Hm	Rd)	TB	R	RBI	TBB	IBB	SO	HBP	SH	SF	SB	CS	SB%	GDP	Avg	OBP	SLG
1990	San Antonio	AA	75	241	55	11	3	3	--	--	81	34	24	14	2	72	2	0	1	11	6	.65	5	.228	.275	.336
1991	San Antonio	AA	87	297	89	19	3	8	--	--	138	49	48	32	2	73	6	1	3	22	10	.69	7	.300	.376	.465
	Scranton-Wb	AAA	16	60	21	9	1	0	--	--	32	14	15	6	0	7	0	0	1	2	1	.67	0	.350	.403	.533
1991	Philadelphia	NL	28	52	9	3	0	0	(0	0)	12	3	2	1	0	15	0	0	0	1	1	.50	1	.173	.189	.231

Carmen Castillo

Bats: Right Throws: Right Pos: RF Ht: 6' 1" Wt: 201 Born: 06/08/58 Age: 34

Year	Team	Lg	G	AB	H	2B	3B	HR	(Hm	Rd)	TB	R	RBI	TBB	IBB	SO	HBP	SH	SF	SB	CS	SB%	GDP	Avg	OBP	SLG
1982	Cleveland	AL	47	120	25	4	0	2	(2	0)	35	11	11	6	2	17	2	1	0	0	0	.00	2	.208	.258	.292
1983	Cleveland	AL	23	36	10	2	1	1	(1	0)	17	9	3	4	0	6	1	0	0	1	1	.50	0	.278	.366	.472
1984	Cleveland	AL	87	211	55	9	2	10	(7	3)	98	36	36	21	0	32	2	0	3	1	3	.25	7	.261	.329	.464
1985	Cleveland	AL	67	184	45	5	1	11	(4	7)	85	27	25	11	0	40	3	0	0	3	0	1.00	6	.245	.298	.462
1986	Cleveland	AL	85	205	57	9	0	8	(4	4)	90	34	32	9	0	48	1	1	1	2	1	.67	9	.278	.310	.439
1987	Cleveland	AL	89	220	55	17	0	11	(8	3)	105	27	31	16	0	52	0	1	4	1	1	.50	0	.250	.296	.477
1988	Cleveland	AL	66	176	48	8	0	4	(2	2)	68	12	14	5	1	31	1	0	0	6	2	.75	4	.273	.297	.386
1989	Minnesota	AL	94	218	56	13	3	8	(2	6)	99	23	33	15	1	40	1	4	2	1	2	.33	5	.257	.305	.454
1990	Minnesota	AL	64	137	30	4	0	0	(0	0)	34	11	12	3	1	23	1	0	1	0	1	.00	1	.219	.239	.248
1991	Minnesota	AL	9	12	2	0	1	0	(0	0)	4	0	0	0	0	2	1	0	0	0	0	.00	0	.167	.231	.333
	10 ML YEARS		631	1519	383	71	8	55	(30	25)	635	190	197	90	5	291	13	7	11	15	11	.58	34	.252	.298	.418

Frank Castillo

Pitches: Right Bats: Right Pos: SP Ht: 6' 1" Wt: 180 Born: 04/01/69 Age: 23

Year	Team	Lg	G	GS	CG	GF	IP	BFP	H	R	ER	HR	SH	SF	HB	TBB	IBB	SO	WP	Bk	W	L	Pct.	ShO	Sv	ERA
1987	Wytheville	R	12	12	5	0	90.1	372	86	31	23	4	3	2	5	21	0	83	2	1	9	1	.909	0	0	2.29
	Geneva	A	1	1	0	0	6	23	3	1	0	0	0	0	0	1	0	6	0	0	1	0	1.000	0	0	0.00
1988	Peoria	A	9	8	2	0	51	186	25	5	4	1	0	0	1	10	0	58	0	0	6	1	.857	2	0	0.71
1989	Winston-Sal	A	18	18	8	0	129.1	521	118	42	36	5	2	1	3	24	1	114	1	1	9	6	.600	1	0	2.51
	Charlotte	AA	10	10	4	0	68	283	73	35	29	7	4	2	1	12	3	43	1	0	3	4	.429	0	0	3.84
1990	Charlotte	AA	18	18	4	0	111.1	471	113	54	48	8	6	3	8	27	4	112	5	1	6	6	.500	1	0	3.88
1991	Iowa	AAA	4	4	1	0	25	98	20	7	7	0	0	1	1	7	0	20	2	0	3	1	.750	0	0	2.52
1991	Chicago	NL	18	18	4	0	111.2	467	107	56	54	5	6	3	0	33	2	73	5	1	6	7	.462	0	0	4.35

Tony Castillo

Pitches: Left **Bats:** Left **Pos:** RP/SP   **Ht:** 5'10" **Wt:** 188 **Born:** 03/01/63 **Age:** 29

		HOW MUCH HE PITCHED						WHAT HE GAVE UP										THE RESULTS					
Year Team	Lg	G	GS	CG	GF	IP	BFP	H	R	ER	HR	SH	SF	HB	TBB	IBB	SO	WP	Bk	W	L	Pct.	ShO	Sv	ERA
1988 Toronto	AL	14	0	0	6	15	54	10	5	5	2	0	2	0	2	0	14	0	0	1	0	1.000	0	0	3.00
1989 2 ML Teams		29	0	0	9	27	127	31	19	17	0	3	4	1	14	6	15	3	0	1	2	.333	0	1	5.67
1990 Atlanta	NL	52	3	0	7	76.2	337	93	41	36	5	4	4	1	20	3	64	2	2	5	1	.833	0	1	4.23
1991 2 ML Teams		17	3	0	6	32.1	148	40	16	12	4	3	1	0	11	1	18	0	0	2	1	.667	0	0	3.34
1989 Toronto	AL	17	0	0	8	17.2	86	23	14	12	0	2	4	1	10	5	10	3	0	1	1	.500	0	1	6.11
Atlanta	NL	12	0	0	1	9.1	41	8	5	5	0	1	0	0	4	1	5	0	0	0	1	.000	0	0	4.82
1991 Atlanta	NL	7	0	0	5	8.2	44	13	9	7	3	1	0	0	5	0	8	0	0	1	1	.500	0	0	7.27
New York	NL	10	3	0	1	23.2	104	27	7	5	1	2	1	0	6	1	10	0	0	1	0	1.000	0	0	1.90
4 ML YEARS		112	6	0	28	151	666	174	81	70	11	10	11	2	47	10	111	5	2	9	4	.692	0	2	4.17

Andujar Cedeno

Bats: Right **Throws:** Right **Pos:** SS   **Ht:** 6' 1" **Wt:** 168 **Born:** 08/21/69 **Age:** 22

		BATTING																		BASERUNNING				PERCENTAGES		
Year Team	Lg	G	AB	H	2B	3B	HR	(Hm	Rd)	TB	R	RBI	TBB	IBB	SO	HBP	SH	SF	SB	CS	SB%	GDP	Avg	OBP	SLG
1988 Astros	R	46	165	47	5	2	1	--	--	59	25	20	11	0	34	1	0	4	10	4	.71	1	.285	.326	.358
1989 Asheville	A	126	487	146	23	6	14	--	--	223	76	93	29	0	124	1	2	5	23	10	.70	10	.300	.337	.458
1990 Columbus	AA	132	495	119	21	11	19	--	--	219	57	64	33	1	135	6	7	5	6	10	.38	11	.240	.293	.442
1991 Tucson	AAA	93	347	105	19	6	7	--	--	157	49	55	19	2	67	5	3	7	5	3	.63	9	.303	.341	.452
1990 Houston	NL	7	8	0	0	0	0	(0	0)	0	0	0	0	0	5	0	0	0	0	0	.00	0	.000	.000	.000
1991 Houston	NL	67	251	61	13	2	9	(4	5)	105	27	36	9	1	74	1	1	2	4	3	.57	3	.243	.270	.418
2 ML YEARS		74	259	61	13	2	9	(4	5)	105	27	36	9	1	79	1	1	2	4	3	.57	3	.236	.262	.405

Rick Cerone

Bats: Right **Throws:** Right **Pos:** C   **Ht:** 5'11" **Wt:** 195 **Born:** 05/19/54 **Age:** 38

		BATTING																		BASERUNNING				PERCENTAGES		
Year Team	Lg	G	AB	H	2B	3B	HR	(Hm	Rd)	TB	R	RBI	TBB	IBB	SO	HBP	SH	SF	SB	CS	SB%	GDP	Avg	OBP	SLG
1975 Cleveland	AL	7	12	3	1	0	0	(0	0)	4	1	0	1	0	0	0	1	0	0	0	.00	0	.250	.308	.333
1976 Cleveland	AL	7	16	2	0	0	0	(0	0)	2	1	1	1	0	2	0	0	0	0	0	.00	0	.125	.125	.125
1977 Toronto	AL	31	100	20	4	0	1	(0	1)	27	7	10	6	0	12	0	1	0	0	0	.00	3	.200	.245	.270
1978 Toronto	AL	88	282	63	8	2	3	(2	1)	84	25	20	23	0	32	1	4	0	1	3	.00	5	.223	.284	.298
1979 Toronto	AL	136	469	112	27	4	7	(3	4)	168	47	61	37	1	40	1	3	4	1	4	.20	5	.239	.294	.358
1980 New York	AL	147	519	144	30	4	14	(7	7)	224	70	85	32	2	56	6	8	10	1	3	.25	14	.277	.321	.432
1981 New York	AL	71	234	57	13	2	2	(2	0)	80	23	21	12	0	24	0	4	4	0	2	.00	10	.244	.276	.342
1982 New York	AL	89	300	68	10	0	5	(1	4)	93	29	28	19	1	27	1	4	5	0	2	.00	12	.227	.271	.310
1983 New York	AL	80	246	54	7	0	2	(0	2)	67	18	22	15	1	29	1	4	0	0	0	.00	5	.220	.267	.272
1984 New York	AL	38	120	25	3	0	2	(0	2)	34	8	13	9	0	15	1	2	0	1	0	1.00	5	.208	.269	.283
1985 Atlanta	NL	96	282	61	9	0	3	(3	0)	79	15	25	29	1	25	1	0	4	0	3	.00	15	.216	.288	.280
1986 Milwaukee	AL	68	216	56	14	0	4	(3	1)	82	22	18	15	0	28	1	5	5	1	1	.50	5	.259	.304	.380
1987 New York	AL	113	284	69	12	1	4	(1	3)	95	28	23	30	0	46	4	5	4	0	1	.00	8	.243	.320	.335
1988 Boston	AL	84	264	71	13	1	3	(0	3)	95	31	27	20	0	32	3	1	1	0	0	.00	6	.269	.326	.360
1989 Boston	AL	102	296	72	16	1	4	(2	2)	102	28	48	34	1	40	2	4	5	0	0	.00	10	.243	.320	.345
1990 New York	AL	49	139	42	6	0	2	(1	1)	54	12	11	5	0	13	0	1	1	0	0	.00	4	.302	.324	.388
1991 New York	NL	90	227	62	13	0	2	(1	1)	81	18	16	30	2	24	1	0	0	1	1	.50	9	.273	.360	.357
17 ML YEARS		1296	4006	981	186	15	58	(29	29)	1371	383	429	317	9	445	23	47	43	5	20	.20	118	.245	.301	.342

John Cerutti

Pitches: Left **Bats:** Left **Pos:** RP/SP   **Ht:** 6' 2" **Wt:** 200 **Born:** 04/28/60 **Age:** 32

		HOW MUCH HE PITCHED						WHAT HE GAVE UP										THE RESULTS					
Year Team	Lg	G	GS	CG	GF	IP	BFP	H	R	ER	HR	SH	SF	HB	TBB	IBB	SO	WP	Bk	W	L	Pct.	ShO	Sv	ERA
1985 Toronto	AL	4	1	0	1	6.2	36	10	7	4	1	0	0	1	4	0	5	2	0	0	2	.000	0	0	5.40
1986 Toronto	AL	34	20	2	3	145.1	616	150	73	67	25	4	5	1	47	2	89	8	0	9	4	.692	1	1	4.15
1987 Toronto	AL	44	21	2	6	151.1	638	144	75	74	30	3	2	1	59	5	92	5	1	11	4	.733	0	0	4.40
1988 Toronto	AL	46	12	0	11	123.2	524	120	56	43	12	8	3	3	42	6	65	7	3	6	7	.462	0	1	3.13
1989 Toronto	AL	33	31	3	1	205.1	856	214	90	70	19	7	5	6	53	2	69	4	2	11	11	.500	1	0	3.07
1990 Toronto	AL	30	23	0	1	140	609	162	77	74	23	5	5	4	49	3	49	4	0	9	9	.500	0	0	4.76
1991 Detroit	AL	38	8	1	10	88.2	389	94	49	45	9	7	3	2	37	9	29	4	1	3	6	.333	0	2	4.57
7 ML YEARS		229	116	8	33	861	3668	894	427	377	119	34	23	18	291	27	398	34	8	49	43	.533	2	4	3.94

Wes Chamberlain

Bats: Right **Throws:** Right **Pos:** LF | **Ht:** 6' 2" **Wt:** 215 **Born:** 04/13/66 **Age:** 26

Year	Team	Lg	G	AB	H	2B	3B	HR	(Hm	Rd)	TB	R	RBI	TBB	IBB	SO	HBP	SH	SF	SB	CS	SB%	GDP	Avg	OBP	SLG
1987	Watertown	A	66	258	67	13	4	5	--	--	103	50	35	25	2	48	1	0	3	22	7	.76	6	.260	.324	.399
1988	Augusta	A	27	107	36	7	2	1	--	--	50	22	17	11	0	11	1	2	0	1	3	.25	4	.336	.403	.467
	Salem	A	92	365	100	15	1	11	--	--	150	66	50	38	2	59	0	0	2	14	4	.78	7	.274	.341	.411
1989	Harrisburg	AA	129	471	144	26	3	21	--	--	239	65	87	32	4	82	2	0	7	11	10	.52	14	.306	.348	.507
1990	Buffalo	AAA	123	416	104	24	2	6	--	--	150	43	52	34	0	58	0	0	5	14	19	.42	19	.250	.315	.361
1991	Scranton-Wb	AAA	39	144	37	7	2	2	--	--	54	12	20	8	1	13	0	0	4	7	4	.64	6	.257	.288	.375
1990	Philadelphia	NL	18	46	13	3	0	2	(0	2)	22	9	4	1	0	9	0	0	0	4	0	1.00	0	.283	.298	.478
1991	Philadelphia	NL	101	383	92	16	3	13	(9	4)	153	51	50	31	0	73	2	1	0	9	4	.69	8	.240	.300	.399
	2 ML YEARS		119	429	105	19	3	15	(9	6)	175	60	54	32	0	82	2	1	0	13	4	.76	8	.245	.300	.408

Darrin Chapin

Pitches: Right **Bats:** Right **Pos:** RP | **Ht:** 6' 0" **Wt:** 170 **Born:** 02/01/66 **Age:** 26

Year	Team	Lg	G	GS	CG	GF	IP	BFP	H	R	ER	HR	SH	SF	HB	TBB	IBB	SO	WP	Bk	W	L	Pct.	ShO	Sv	ERA
1986	Yankees	R	13	13	2	0	83.1	341	71	42	30	2	3	3	2	27	1	67	10	1	4	3	.571	2	0	3.24
1987	Oneonta	A	25	0	0	21	40	170	31	8	3	1	2	1	0	17	5	26	6	0	1	1	.500	0	12	0.68
1988	Albany	AA	3	0	0	3	4	26	11	7	5	0	0	0	1	2	0	4	0	0	0	0	.000	0	0	11.25
	Ft.Laurdrle	A	38	0	0	33	63	234	39	8	6	1	4	1	0	19	5	57	3	1	6	4	.600	0	15	0.86
1989	Albany	AA	7	0	0	7	8.2	32	5	0	0	0	0	0	0	1	1	16	2	0	1	0	1.000	0	3	0.00
	Columbus	AAA	27	0	0	21	40	167	33	15	13	3	3	1	1	15	4	38	3	1	2	4	.333	0	5	2.93
1990	Columbus	AAA	6	0	0	5	8.2	41	10	8	7	0	0	0	0	6	0	8	1	0	0	1	.000	0	2	7.27
	Albany	AA	43	0	0	40	52.2	223	43	20	16	2	1	4	1	21	1	61	4	0	3	2	.600	0	21	2.73
1991	Columbus	AAA	55	0	0	28	78.1	328	54	23	17	5	5	3	1	40	3	69	5	1	10	3	.769	0	12	1.95
1991	New York	AL	3	0	0	2	5.1	25	3	3	3	0	0	0	0	6	0	5	2	1	0	0	.000	0	0	5.06

Norm Charlton

Pitches: Left **Bats:** Both **Pos:** RP/SP | **Ht:** 6' 3" **Wt:** 200 **Born:** 01/06/63 **Age:** 29

Year	Team	Lg	G	GS	CG	GF	IP	BFP	H	R	ER	HR	SH	SF	HB	TBB	IBB	SO	WP	Bk	W	L	Pct.	ShO	Sv	ERA
1988	Cincinnati	NL	10	10	0	0	61.1	259	60	27	27	6	1	2	2	20	2	39	3	2	4	5	.444	0	0	3.96
1989	Cincinnati	NL	69	0	0	23	95.1	393	67	38	31	5	9	2	2	40	7	98	2	4	8	3	.727	0	0	2.93
1990	Cincinnati	NL	56	16	1	13	154.1	650	131	53	47	10	7	2	4	70	4	117	9	1	12	9	.571	1	2	2.74
1991	Cincinnati	NL	39	11	0	10	108.1	438	92	37	35	6	7	1	6	34	4	77	11	0	3	5	.375	0	1	2.91
	4 ML YEARS		174	37	1	50	419.1	1740	350	155	140	27	24	7	14	164	17	331	25	7	27	22	.551	1	3	3.00

Scott Chiamparino

Pitches: Right **Bats:** Left **Pos:** SP | **Ht:** 6' 2" **Wt:** 200 **Born:** 08/22/66 **Age:** 25

Year	Team	Lg	G	GS	CG	GF	IP	BFP	H	R	ER	HR	SH	SF	HB	TBB	IBB	SO	WP	Bk	W	L	Pct.	ShO	Sv	ERA
1987	Medford	A	13	11	3	1	67.2	288	64	29	19	2	1	3	3	20	0	65	6	0	5	4	.556	1	0	2.53
1988	Modesto	A	16	16	5	0	106.2	456	89	40	32	1	2	2	0	56	0	117	17	4	5	7	.417	3	0	2.70
	Huntsville	AA	13	13	4	0	84	365	88	36	30	3	1	7	1	26	2	49	5	1	4	5	.444	0	0	3.21
1989	Huntsville	AA	17	17	2	0	101.2	440	109	60	52	8	4	3	4	29	0	87	8	0	8	6	.571	1	0	4.60
1990	Tacoma	AAA	26	26	4	0	173	744	174	79	63	10	5	4	5	72	1	110	9	1	13	9	.591	0	3	3.28
1990	Texas	AL	6	6	0	0	37.2	160	36	14	11	1	1	1	2	12	0	19	5	0	1	2	.333	0	0	2.63
1991	Texas	AL	5	5	0	0	22.1	101	26	11	10	1	1	0	0	12	0	8	0	0	1	0	1.000	0	0	4.03
	2 ML YEARS		11	11	0	0	60	261	62	25	21	2	2	1	2	24	0	27	5	0	2	2	.500	0	0	3.15

Steve Chitren

Pitches: Right **Bats:** Right **Pos:** RP | **Ht:** 6' 0" **Wt:** 180 **Born:** 06/08/67 **Age:** 25

Year	Team	Lg	G	GS	CG	GF	IP	BFP	H	R	ER	HR	SH	SF	HB	TBB	IBB	SO	WP	Bk	W	L	Pct.	ShO	Sv	ERA
1989	Sou Oregon	A	2	0	0	1	5	20	3	2	1	0	0	1	0	2	0	3	0	0	0	0	.000	0	0	1.80
	Madison	A	20	0	0	18	22.2	85	13	3	3	1	0	2	2	4	0	17	0	0	2	1	.667	0	7	1.19
1990	Huntsville	AA	48	0	0	39	53.2	218	32	18	10	4	0	3	3	22	1	61	2	0	2	4	.333	0	27	1.68
	Tacoma	AAA	1	0	0	1	0.2	3	1	0	0	0	0	0	0	0	0	2	0	0	0	0	.000	0	0	0.00
1990	Oakland	AL	8	0	0	4	17.2	64	7	2	2	0	0	0	0	4	0	19	2	0	1	0	1.000	0	0	1.02
1991	Oakland	AL	56	0	0	20	60.1	271	59	31	29	8	4	2	4	32	4	47	2	1	1	4	.200	0	4	4.33
	2 ML YEARS		64	0	0	24	78	335	66	33	31	8	4	2	4	36	4	66	4	1	2	4	.333	0	4	3.58

Mike Christopher

Pitches: Right **Bats:** Right **Pos:** RP **Ht:** 6' 5" **Wt:** 205 **Born:** 11/03/63 **Age:** 28

		HOW MUCH HE PITCHED					WHAT HE GAVE UP										THE RESULTS					
Year Team	Lg	G	GS	CG	GF	IP	BFP	H	R	ER	HR	SH	SF	HB	TBB	IBB	SO	WP	Bk	W	L	Pct.	ShO	Sv	ERA
1985 Oneonta	A	15	9	2	3	80.1	317	58	21	13	2	1	2	3	22	0	84	3	0	8	1	.889	2	0	1.46
1986 Albany	AA	11	11	2	0	60.2	273	75	48	34	6	2	4	3	12	1	34	3	0	3	5	.375	0	0	5.04
Ft.Laudrdle	A	15	14	3	0	102.2	421	92	37	30	2	4	2	1	36	0	56	1	1	7	3	.700	1	0	2.63
1987 Ft.Laudrdle	A	24	24	9	0	169.1	694	183	63	46	5	6	4	0	28	1	81	4	0	13	8	.619	4	0	2.44
1988 Albany	AA	24	24	5	0	152.2	648	166	75	65	7	4	5	6	44	3	67	2	4	13	7	.650	1	0	3.83
1989 Columbus	AAA	13	11	1	0	73	331	95	45	39	6	6	5	3	21	3	42	1	0	5	6	.455	0	0	4.81
Albany	AA	8	8	3	0	53.2	213	48	17	15	1	0	1	1	7	0	33	0	0	6	1	.857	0	0	2.52
1990 Albuquerque	AAA	54	0	0	25	68.2	287	62	20	15	3	5	4	2	23	3	47	0	0	6	1	.857	0	8	1.97
1991 Albuquerque	AAA	63	0	0	34	77.1	334	73	25	21	2	4	1	3	30	5	67	7	1	7	2	.778	0	16	2.44
1991 Los Angeles	NL	3	0	0	2	4	15	2	0	0	0	0	0	0	3	0	2	0	0	0	0	.000	0	0	0.00

Jim Clancy

Pitches: Right **Bats:** Right **Pos:** RP **Ht:** 6' 4" **Wt:** 220 **Born:** 12/18/55 **Age:** 36

		HOW MUCH HE PITCHED					WHAT HE GAVE UP										THE RESULTS					
Year Team	Lg	G	GS	CG	GF	IP	BFP	H	R	ER	HR	SH	SF	HB	TBB	IBB	SO	WP	Bk	W	L	Pct.	ShO	Sv	ERA
1977 Toronto	AL	13	13	4	0	77	346	80	47	43	7	6	7	0	47	1	44	4	0	4	9	.308	1	0	5.03
1978 Toronto	AL	31	30	7	0	194	846	199	96	88	10	8	10	1	91	1	106	10	0	10	12	.455	0	0	4.08
1979 Toronto	AL	12	11	2	0	64	278	65	44	39	8	3	5	0	31	0	33	2	0	2	7	.222	0	0	5.48
1980 Toronto	AL	34	34	15	0	251	1075	217	108	92	19	9	4	2	128	4	152	10	0	13	16	.448	2	0	3.30
1981 Toronto	AL	22	22	2	0	125	556	126	77	68	12	2	4	5	64	0	56	12	0	6	12	.333	0	0	4.90
1982 Toronto	AL	40	40	11	0	266.2	1100	251	122	110	26	5	4	2	77	1	139	6	0	16	14	.533	3	0	3.71
1983 Toronto	AL	34	34	11	0	223	955	238	115	97	23	4	12	1	61	0	99	3	0	15	11	.577	1	0	3.91
1984 Toronto	AL	36	36	5	0	219.2	966	249	132	125	25	4	4	3	88	2	118	10	0	13	15	.464	0	0	5.12
1985 Toronto	AL	23	23	1	0	128.2	527	117	54	54	15	0	5	0	37	0	66	2	0	9	6	.600	0	0	3.78
1986 Toronto	AL	34	34	6	0	219.1	913	202	100	96	24	5	9	4	63	0	126	4	0	14	14	.500	3	0	3.94
1987 Toronto	AL	37	37	5	0	241.1	1008	234	103	95	24	5	4	1	80	5	180	12	1	15	11	.577	1	0	3.54
1988 Toronto	AL	36	31	4	5	196.1	827	207	106	98	26	7	4	9	47	3	118	7	0	11	13	.458	0	1	4.49
1989 Houston	NL	33	26	1	3	147	655	155	100	83	13	9	4	0	66	15	91	6	3	7	14	.333	0	0	5.08
1990 Houston	NL	33	10	0	8	76	352	100	58	55	4	1	4	3	33	9	44	3	0	2	8	.200	0	1	6.51
1991 2 ML Teams		54	0	0	22	89.2	368	73	42	39	8	2	4	1	34	4	50	10	0	3	5	.375	0	8	3.91
1991 Houston	NL	30	0	0	13	55	215	37	19	17	5	1	2	0	20	3	33	5	0	0	3	.000	0	5	2.78
Atlanta	NL	24	0	0	9	34.2	153	36	23	22	3	1	2	1	14	1	17	5	0	3	2	.600	0	3	5.71
15 ML YEARS		472	381	74	38	2518.2	10772	2513	1304	1182	244	70	84	32	947	45	1422	101	4	140	167	.456	11	10	4.22

Dave Clark

Bats: Left **Throws:** Right **Pos:** PH **Ht:** 6' 2" **Wt:** 210 **Born:** 09/03/62 **Age:** 29

		BATTING																	BASERUNNING			PERCENTAGES		
Year Team	Lg	G	AB	H	2B	3B	HR	(Hm	Rd)	TB	R	RBI	TBB	IBB	SO	HBP	SH	SF	SB	CS	SB%	GDP	Avg	OBP	SLG
1986 Cleveland	AL	18	58	16	1	0	3	(1	2)	26	10	9	7	0	11	0	2	1	1	0	1.00	1	.276	.348	.448
1987 Cleveland	AL	29	87	18	5	0	3	(1	2)	32	11	12	2	0	24	0	0	0	1	0	1.00	4	.207	.225	.368
1988 Cleveland	AL	63	156	41	4	1	3	(2	1)	56	11	18	17	2	28	0	0	1	0	2	.00	6	.263	.333	.359
1989 Cleveland	AL	102	253	60	12	0	8	(4	4)	96	21	29	30	5	63	0	0	1	0	2	.00	7	.237	.317	.379
1990 Chicago	NL	84	171	47	4	2	5	(3	2)	70	22	20	8	1	40	0	0	2	7	1	.88	4	.275	.304	.409
1991 Kansas City	AL	11	10	2	0	0	0	(0	0)	2	1	1	1	0	1	0	0	0	0	0	.00	0	.200	.273	.200
6 ML YEARS		307	735	184	26	3	22	(11	11)	282	76	89	65	8	167	0	3	5	9	5	.64	24	.250	.309	.384

Jack Clark

Bats: Right **Throws:** Right **Pos:** DH **Ht:** 6' 3" **Wt:** 205 **Born:** 11/10/55 **Age:** 36

		BATTING																	BASERUNNING			PERCENTAGES		
Year Team	Lg	G	AB	H	2B	3B	HR	(Hm	Rd)	TB	R	RBI	TBB	IBB	SO	HBP	SH	SF	SB	CS	SB%	GDP	Avg	OBP	SLG
1975 San Francisco	NL	8	17	4	0	0	0	(0	0)	4	3	2	1	0	2	0	0	1	1	0	1.00	0	.235	.263	.235
1976 San Francisco	NL	26	102	23	6	2	2	(2	0)	39	14	10	8	0	18	0	3	2	6	2	.75	0	.225	.277	.382
1977 San Francisco	NL	136	413	104	17	4	13	(7	6)	168	64	51	49	2	73	2	1	3	12	4	.75	7	.252	.332	.407
1978 San Francisco	NL	156	592	181	46	8	25	(10	15)	318	90	98	50	8	72	3	3	9	15	11	.58	15	.306	.358	.537
1979 San Francisco	NL	143	527	144	25	2	26	(10	16)	251	84	86	63	6	95	1	1	6	11	8	.58	9	.273	.348	.476
1980 San Francisco	NL	127	437	124	20	8	22	(8	14)	226	77	82	74	13	52	2	1	10	2	5	.29	12	.284	.382	.517
1981 San Francisco	NL	99	385	103	19	2	17	(7	10)	177	60	53	45	6	45	1	0	6	1	1	.50	12	.268	.341	.460
1982 San Francisco	NL	157	563	154	30	3	27	(9	18)	271	90	103	90	7	91	1	0	5	6	9	.40	20	.274	.372	.481
1983 San Francisco	NL	135	492	132	25	0	20	(11	9)	217	82	66	74	6	79	1	0	7	5	3	.63	14	.268	.361	.441
1984 San Francisco	NL	57	203	65	9	1	11	(4	7)	109	33	44	43	7	29	0	0	3	1	1	.50	9	.320	.434	.537
1985 St. Louis	NL	126	442	124	26	3	22	(8	14)	222	71	87	83	14	88	2	0	5	1	4	.20	10	.281	.393	.502

Year Team	Lg	G	AB	H	2B	3B	HR	(Hm	Rd)	TB	R	RBI	TBB	IBB	SO	HBP	SH	SF	SB	CS	SB%	GDP	Avg	OBP	SLG
1986 St. Louis	NL	65	232	55	12	2	9	(4	5)	98	34	23	45	4	61	1	0	1	1	1	.50	4	.237	.362	.422
1987 St. Louis	NL	131	419	120	23	1	35	(17	18)	250	93	106	136	13	139	0	0	3	1	2	.33	5	.286	.459	.597
1988 New York	AL	150	496	120	14	0	27	(13	14)	215	81	93	113	6	141	2	0	5	3	2	.60	14	.242	.381	.433
1989 San Diego	NL	142	455	110	19	1	26	(11	15)	209	76	94	132	18	145	1	0	5	6	2	.75	10	.242	.410	.459
1990 San Diego	NL	115	334	89	12	1	25	(16	9)	178	59	62	104	11	91	2	0	2	4	3	.57	13	.266	.441	.533
1991 Boston	AL	140	481	120	18	1	28	(18	10)	224	75	87	96	3	133	3	0	5	0	2	.00	17	.249	.374	.466
17 ML YEARS		1913	6590	1772	321	39	335	(155	180)	3176	1086	1147	1206	124	1354	22	9	78	76	60	.56	171	.269	.380	.482

Jerald Clark

Bats: Right **Throws:** Right **Pos:** LF/1B/RF **Ht:** 6' 4" **Wt:** 202 **Born:** 08/10/63 **Age:** 28

		BATTING																	BASERUNNING				PERCENTAGES		
Year Team	Lg	G	AB	H	2B	3B	HR	(Hm	Rd)	TB	R	RBI	TBB	IBB	SO	HBP	SH	SF	SB	CS	SB%	GDP	Avg	OBP	SLG
1988 San Diego	NL	6	15	3	1	0	0	(0	0)	4	0	3	0	0	4	0	0	0	0	0	.00	0	.200	.200	.267
1989 San Diego	NL	17	41	8	2	0	1	(1	0)	13	5	7	3	0	9	0	0	0	0	1	.00	0	.195	.250	.317
1990 San Diego	NL	52	101	27	4	1	5	(2	3)	48	12	11	5	0	24	0	0	1	0	0	.00	3	.267	.299	.475
1991 San Diego	NL	118	369	84	16	0	10	(8	2)	130	26	47	31	2	90	6	1	4	2	1	.67	10	.228	.295	.352
4 ML YEARS		193	526	122	23	1	16	(11	5)	195	43	68	39	2	127	6	1	5	2	2	.50	13	.232	.290	.371

Mark Clark

Pitches: Right **Bats:** Right **Pos:** RP **Ht:** 6' 5" **Wt:** 225 **Born:** 05/12/68 **Age:** 24

		HOW MUCH HE PITCHED						WHAT HE GAVE UP										THE RESULTS					
Year Team	Lg	G	GS	CG	GF	IP	BFP	H	R	ER	HR	SH	SF	HB	TBB	IBB	SO	WP	Bk	W	L	Pct.	ShO	Sv	ERA
1988 Hamilton	A	15	15	2	0	94.1	385	88	39	32	10	4	3	0	32	2	60	2	1	6	7	.462	0	0	3.05
1989 Savannah	A	27	27	4	0	173.2	712	143	61	47	8	4	4	1	52	0	132	11	3	14	9	.609	2	0	2.44
1990 St. Pete	A	10	10	1	0	62	254	63	33	21	3	2	2	1	14	0	58	3	1	3	2	.600	1	0	3.05
Arkansas	AA	19	19	5	0	115.1	479	111	56	49	11	6	4	0	37	2	87	6	1	5	11	.313	0	0	3.82
1991 Arkansas	AA	15	15	4	0	92.1	398	99	50	41	2	3	2	2	30	4	76	0	0	5	5	.500	1	0	4.00
Louisville	AAA	7	6	1	0	45.1	189	43	17	15	4	1	3	0	15	0	29	2	0	3	2	.600	1	0	2.98
1991 St. Louis	NL	7	2	0	1	22.1	93	17	10	10	3	0	3	0	11	0	13	2	0	1	1	.500	0	0	4.03

Will Clark

Bats: Left **Throws:** Left **Pos:** 1B **Ht:** 6' 1" **Wt:** 190 **Born:** 03/13/64 **Age:** 28

		BATTING																	BASERUNNING				PERCENTAGES		
Year Team	Lg	G	AB	H	2B	3B	HR	(Hm	Rd)	TB	R	RBI	TBB	IBB	SO	HBP	SH	SF	SB	CS	SB%	GDP	Avg	OBP	SLG
1986 San Francisco	NL	111	408	117	27	2	11	(7	4)	181	66	41	34	10	76	3	9	4	4	7	.36	3	.287	.343	.444
1987 San Francisco	NL	150	529	163	29	5	35	(22	13)	307	89	91	49	11	98	5	3	2	5	17	.23	2	.308	.371	.580
1988 San Francisco	NL	162	575	162	31	6	29	(14	15)	292	102	109	100	27	129	4	0	10	9	1	.90	9	.282	.386	.508
1989 San Francisco	NL	159	588	196	38	9	23	(9	14)	321	104	111	74	14	103	5	0	8	8	3	.73	6	.333	.407	.546
1990 San Francisco	NL	154	600	177	25	5	19	(8	11)	269	91	95	62	9	97	3	0	13	8	2	.80	7	.295	.357	.448
1991 San Francisco	NL	148	565	170	32	7	29	(17	12)	303	84	116	51	12	91	2	0	4	4	2	.67	5	.301	.359	.536
6 ML YEARS		884	3265	985	182	34	146	(77	69)	1673	536	563	370	83	594	22	12	41	38	32	.54	32	.302	.372	.512

Royce Clayton

Bats: Right **Throws:** Right **Pos:** SS **Ht:** 6' 0" **Wt:** 175 **Born:** 01/02/70 **Age:** 22

		BATTING																	BASERUNNING				PERCENTAGES		
Year Team	Lg	G	AB	H	2B	3B	HR	(Hm	Rd)	TB	R	RBI	TBB	IBB	SO	HBP	SH	SF	SB	CS	SB%	GDP	Avg	OBP	SLG
1988 Everett	A	60	212	55	4	0	3	--	--	68	35	29	27	0	54	3	1	2	10	4	.71	8	.259	.348	.321
1989 Clinton	A	104	385	91	13	3	0	--	--	110	39	24	39	0	101	4	4	5	28	16	.64	6	.236	.309	.286
San Jose	A	28	92	11	2	0	0	--	--	13	5	4	13	0	27	1	0	0	10	1	.91	5	.120	.236	.141
1990 San Jose	A	123	460	123	15	10	7	--	--	179	80	71	68	3	98	4	0	4	33	15	.69	13	.267	.364	.389
1991 Shreveport	AA	126	485	136	22	8	5	--	--	189	84	68	61	7	102	3	3	5	36	10	.78	7	.280	.361	.390
1991 San Francisco	NL	9	26	3	1	0	0	(0	0)	4	0	2	1	0	6	0	0	0	0	0	.00	1	.115	.148	.154

Roger Clemens

Pitches: Right **Bats:** Right **Pos:** SP **Ht:** 6' 4" **Wt:** 220 **Born:** 08/04/62 **Age:** 29

		HOW MUCH HE PITCHED						WHAT HE GAVE UP										THE RESULTS					
Year Team	Lg	G	GS	CG	GF	IP	BFP	H	R	ER	HR	SH	SF	HB	TBB	IBB	SO	WP	Bk	W	L	Pct.	ShO	Sv	ERA
1984 Boston	AL	21	20	5	0	133.1	575	146	67	64	13	2	3	2	29	3	126	4	0	9	4	.692	1	0	4.32
1985 Boston	AL	15	15	3	0	98.1	407	83	38	36	5	7	1	0	37	0	74	1	0	7	5	.583	1	0	3.29
1986 Boston	AL	33	33	10	0	254	997	179	77	70	21	4	6	4	67	0	238	11	3	24	4	.857	1	0	2.48
1987 Boston	AL	36	36	18	0	281.2	1157	248	100	93	19	6	4	9	83	4	256	4	3	20	9	.690	7	0	2.97
1988 Boston	AL	35	35	14	0	264	1063	217	93	86	17	6	3	6	62	4	291	4	7	18	12	.600	8	0	2.93
1989 Boston	AL	35	35	8	0	253.1	1044	215	101	88	20	9	5	8	93	5	230	7	0	17	11	.607	3	0	3.13
1990 Boston	AL	31	31	7	0	228.1	920	193	59	49	7	7	5	7	54	3	209	8	0	21	6	.778	4	0	1.93
1991 Boston	AL	35	35	13	0	271.1	1077	219	93	79	15	6	8	5	65	12	241	6	0	18	10	.643	4	0	2.62
8 ML YEARS		241	240	78	0	1784.1	7240	1500	628	565	117	41	36	44	490	31	1665	45	16	134	61	.687	29	0	2.85

42

Pat Clements

Pitches: Left Bats: Right Pos: RP Ht: 6' 0" Wt: 180 Born: 02/02/62 Age: 30

Year Team	Lg	G	GS	CG	GF	IP	BFP	H	R	ER	HR	SH	SF	HB	TBB	IBB	SO	WP	Bk	W	L	Pct.	ShO	Sv	ERA
1985 2 ML Teams		68	0	0	19	96.1	400	86	37	37	6	6	1	2	40	5	36	3	0	5	2	.714	0	3	3.46
1986 Pittsburgh	NL	65	0	0	19	61	256	53	20	19	1	7	4	2	32	6	31	2	0	0	4	.000	0	2	2.80
1987 New York	AL	55	0	0	20	80	347	91	45	44	4	6	4	3	30	2	36	8	2	3	3	.500	0	7	4.95
1988 New York	AL	6	1	0	1	8.1	41	12	8	6	1	0	2	0	4	0	3	1	0	0	0	.000	0	0	6.48
1989 San Diego	NL	23	1	0	8	39	167	39	17	17	4	5	1	0	15	5	18	1	0	4	1	.800	0	3	3.92
1990 San Diego	NL	9	0	0	3	13	63	20	9	6	1	0	0	0	7	1	6	1	0	0	0	.000	0	0	4.15
1991 San Diego	NL	12	0	0	4	14.1	63	13	8	6	0	0	3	0	9	4	8	0	0	1	0	1.000	0	0	3.77
1985 California	AL	41	0	0	12	62	247	47	23	23	4	4	0	2	25	2	19	1	0	5	0	1.000	0	1	3.34
Pittsburgh	NL	27	0	0	7	34.1	153	39	14	14	2	2	1	0	15	3	17	2	0	0	0	.000	0	2	3.67
7 ML YEARS		238	2	0	74	312	1337	314	144	135	17	24	15	7	137	23	138	16	2	13	10	.565	0	12	3.89

Dave Cochrane

Bats: Both Throws: Right Pos: LF/C/3B Ht: 6' 2" Wt: 180 Born: 01/31/63 Age: 29

Year Team	Lg	G	AB	H	2B	3B	HR	(Hm	Rd)	TB	R	RBI	TBB	IBB	SO	HBP	SH	SF	SB	CS	SB%	GDP	Avg	OBP	SLG
1986 Chicago	AL	19	62	12	2	0	1	(1	0)	17	4	2	5	1	22	0	1	0	0	0	.00	2	.194	.254	.274
1989 Seattle	AL	54	102	24	4	1	3	(3	0)	39	13	7	14	0	27	1	0	0	0	2	.00	2	.235	.333	.382
1990 Seattle	AL	15	20	3	0	0	0	(0	0)	3	0	0	0	0	8	0	0	0	0	0	.00	0	.150	.150	.150
1991 Seattle	AL	65	178	44	13	0	2	(1	1)	63	16	22	9	0	38	1	1	1	0	1	.00	3	.247	.286	.354
4 ML YEARS		153	362	83	19	1	6	(5	1)	122	33	31	28	1	95	2	2	1	0	3	.00	7	.229	.288	.337

Alex Cole

Bats: Left Throws: Left Pos: CF Ht: 6' 2" Wt: 185 Born: 08/17/65 Age: 26

Year Team	Lg	G	AB	H	2B	3B	HR	(Hm	Rd)	TB	R	RBI	TBB	IBB	SO	HBP	SH	SF	SB	CS	SB%	GDP	Avg	OBP	SLG
1985 Johnson Cty	R	66	232	61	5	1	1	--	--	71	60	13	30	0	27	1	0	1	46	8	.85	4	.263	.348	.306
1986 St. Pete	A	74	286	98	9	1	0	--	--	109	76	26	54	1	37	2	2	1	56	22	.72	2	.343	.449	.381
Louisville	AAA	63	200	50	2	4	1	--	--	63	25	16	17	0	30	1	0	1	24	13	.65	3	.250	.311	.315
1987 Arkansas	AA	125	477	122	12	4	2	--	--	148	68	27	44	5	55	0	5	1	68	29	.70	3	.256	.318	.310
1988 Louisville	AAA	120	392	91	7	8	0	--	--	114	44	24	42	1	59	1	6	1	40	15	.73	2	.232	.307	.291
1989 St.Pete	A	8	32	6	0	0	0	--	--	6	2	1	3	0	7	0	0	0	4	1	.80	1	.188	.257	.188
Louisville	AAA	127	455	128	5	5	2	--	--	149	75	29	71	1	76	1	4	1	47	19	.71	3	.281	.379	.327
1990 Las Vegas	AAA	90	341	99	7	4	0	--	--	114	58	28	47	1	62	1	8	2	32	15	.68	4	.290	.376	.334
Colo Spngs	AAA	14	49	21	2	0	0	--	--	23	13	3	8	0	7	1	0	0	6	4	.60	1	.429	.509	.469
1991 Colo Spngs	AAA	8	32	6	0	1	0	--	--	8	6	3	4	0	3	1	0	0	1	3	.25	0	.188	.297	.250
1990 Cleveland	AL	63	227	68	5	4	0	(0	0)	81	43	13	28	0	38	1	0	0	40	9	.82	2	.300	.379	.357
1991 Cleveland	AL	122	387	114	17	3	0	(0	0)	137	58	21	58	2	47	1	4	2	27	17	.61	8	.295	.386	.354
2 ML YEARS		185	614	182	22	7	0	(0	0)	218	101	34	86	2	85	2	4	2	67	26	.72	10	.296	.384	.355

Stu Cole

Bats: Right Throws: Right Pos: 2B Ht: 6' 1" Wt: 175 Born: 02/07/66 Age: 26

Year Team	Lg	G	AB	H	2B	3B	HR	(Hm	Rd)	TB	R	RBI	TBB	IBB	SO	HBP	SH	SF	SB	CS	SB%	GDP	Avg	OBP	SLG
1987 Eugene	A	63	243	74	17	1	3	--	--	102	42	51	34	1	45	1	3	4	3	1	.75	3	.305	.387	.420
1988 Virginia	A	70	257	70	10	0	1	--	--	83	41	22	32	0	52	4	0	2	10	5	.67	6	.272	.359	.323
Baseball Cy	A	15	41	6	0	0	0	--	--	6	7	4	9	0	10	0	1	1	2	1	.67	4	.146	.294	.146
1989 Memphis	AA	90	299	64	8	3	6	--	--	96	30	32	25	0	67	0	4	2	11	3	.79	7	.214	.273	.321
1990 Memphis	AA	113	357	110	18	2	1	--	--	135	61	49	55	2	55	3	4	3	20	5	.80	8	.308	.402	.378
1991 Omaha	AAA	120	441	115	13	7	3	--	--	151	64	39	42	0	60	1	5	2	11	10	.52	12	.261	.325	.342
1991 Kansas City	AL	9	7	1	0	0	0	(0	0)	1	1	0	2	0	2	0	0	0	0	0	.00	0	.143	.333	.143

Vince Coleman

Bats: Both Throws: Right Pos: CF Ht: 6' 1" Wt: 185 Born: 09/22/61 Age: 30

Year Team	Lg	G	AB	H	2B	3B	HR	(Hm	Rd)	TB	R	RBI	TBB	IBB	SO	HBP	SH	SF	SB	CS	SB%	GDP	Avg	OBP	SLG
1985 St. Louis	NL	151	636	170	20	10	1	(1	0)	213	107	40	50	1	115	0	5	1	110	25	.81	3	.267	.320	.335
1986 St. Louis	NL	154	600	139	13	8	0	(0	0)	168	94	29	60	0	98	2	3	5	107	14	.88	4	.232	.301	.280
1987 St. Louis	NL	151	623	180	14	10	3	(3	0)	223	121	43	70	0	126	3	5	1	109	22	.83	7	.289	.363	.358
1988 St. Louis	NL	153	616	160	20	10	3	(2	1)	209	77	38	49	4	111	1	8	5	81	27	.75	4	.260	.313	.339
1989 St. Louis	NL	145	563	143	21	9	2	(1	1)	188	94	28	50	0	90	2	7	2	65	10	.87	4	.254	.316	.334

Year	Team	Lg	G	AB	H	2B	3B	HR	(Hm	Rd)	TB	R	RBI	TBB	IBB	SO	HBP	SH	SF	SB	CS	SB%	GDP	Avg	OBP	SLG
1990	St. Louis	NL	124	497	145	18	9	6	(5	1)	199	73	39	35	1	88	2	4	1	77	17	.82	6	.292	.340	.400
1991	New York	NL	72	278	71	7	5	1	(0	1)	91	45	17	39	0	47	0	1	0	37	14	.73	3	.255	.347	.327
	7 ML YEARS		950	3813	1008	113	61	16	(12	4)	1291	611	234	353	6	675	10	33	15	586	129	.82	31	.264	.327	.339

Darnell Coles

Bats: Right **Throws:** Right **Pos:** RF

Ht: 6' 1" **Wt:** 185 **Born:** 06/02/62 **Age:** 30

							BATTING															BASERUNNING			PERCENTAGES		
Year	Team	Lg	G	AB	H	2B	3B	HR	(Hm	Rd)	TB	R	RBI	TBB	IBB	SO	HBP	SH	SF	SB	CS	SB%	GDP	Avg	OBP	SLG
1983	Seattle	AL	27	92	26	7	0	1	(0	1)	36	9	6	7	0	12	0	1	0	0	3	.00	8	.283	.333	.391
1984	Seattle	AL	48	143	23	3	1	0	(0	0)	28	15	6	17	0	26	2	3	0	2	1	.67	5	.161	.259	.196
1985	Seattle	AL	27	59	14	4	0	1	(0	1)	21	8	5	9	0	17	1	0	2	1	0	1.00	0	.237	.338	.356
1986	Detroit	AL	142	521	142	30	2	20	(12	8)	236	67	86	45	3	84	6	7	8	6	2	.75	8	.273	.333	.453
1987	2 ML Teams		93	268	54	13	1	10	(8	2)	99	34	39	34	3	43	3	5	3	1	4	.20	4	.201	.295	.369
1988	2 ML Teams		123	406	106	23	2	15	(10	5)	178	52	70	37	1	67	7	2	10	4	3	.57	8	.261	.326	.438
1989	Seattle	AL	146	535	135	21	3	10	(4	6)	192	54	59	27	1	61	6	2	3	5	4	.56	13	.252	.294	.359
1990	2 ML Teams		89	215	45	7	1	3	(3	0)	63	22	20	16	2	38	1	1	2	0	4	.00	4	.209	.265	.293
1991	San Francisco	NL	11	14	3	0	0	0	(0	0)	3	1	0	0	0	2	0	0	0	0	0	.00	1	.214	.214	.214
1987	Detroit	AL	53	149	27	5	1	4	(3	1)	46	14	15	15	1	23	2	2	1	0	1	.00	1	.181	.263	.309
	Pittsburgh	NL	40	119	27	8	0	6	(5	1)	53	20	24	19	2	20	1	3	2	1	3	.25	3	.227	.333	.445
1988	Pittsburgh	NL	68	211	49	13	1	5	(1	4)	79	20	36	20	1	41	3	0	7	1	1	.50	3	.232	.299	.374
	Seattle	AL	55	195	57	10	1	10	(9	1)	99	32	34	17	0	26	4	2	3	3	2	.60	5	.292	.356	.508
1990	Seattle	AL	37	107	23	5	1	2	(2	0)	36	9	14	4	1	17	1	0	1	0	0	.00	1	.215	.248	.336
	Detroit	AL	52	108	22	2	0	1	(1	0)	27	13	4	12	1	21	0	1	1	0	4	.00	3	.204	.281	.250
	9 ML YEARS		706	2253	548	108	10	60	(37	23)	856	262	291	192	10	350	26	21	28	18	22	.45	51	.243	.307	.380

Pat Combs

Pitches: Left **Bats:** Left **Pos:** SP

Ht: 6' 4" **Wt:** 207 **Born:** 10/29/66 **Age:** 25

			HOW MUCH HE PITCHED						WHAT HE GAVE UP								THE RESULTS				
Year	Team	Lg	G	GS	CG	GF	IP	BFP	H	R	ER	HR	SH	SF	HB	TBB	IBB	SO	WP	Bk	W	L	Pct.	ShO	Sv	ERA
1989	Philadelphia	NL	6	6	1	0	38.2	153	36	10	9	2	2	0	0	6	1	30	5	0	4	0	1.000	1	0	2.09
1990	Philadelphia	NL	32	31	3	0	183.1	800	179	80	83	12	7	7	4	86	7	108	9	1	10	10	.500	2	0	4.07
1991	Philadelphia	NL	14	13	1	0	64.1	300	64	41	35	7	1	2	2	43	1	41	7	0	2	6	.250	0	0	4.90
	3 ML YEARS		52	50	5	0	286.1	1253	279	141	127	21	10	9	6	135	9	179	21	1	16	16	.500	3	0	3.99

Keith Comstock

Pitches: Left **Bats:** Left **Pos:** RP

Ht: 6' 0" **Wt:** 175 **Born:** 12/23/55 **Age:** 36

			HOW MUCH HE PITCHED						WHAT HE GAVE UP								THE RESULTS				
Year	Team	Lg	G	GS	CG	GF	IP	BFP	H	R	ER	HR	SH	SF	HB	TBB	IBB	SO	WP	Bk	W	L	Pct.	ShO	Sv	ERA
1984	Minnesota	AL	4	0	0	2	6.1	28	6	6	6	2	1	0	0	4	0	2	0	0	0	0	.000	0	0	8.53
1987	2 ML Teams		41	0	0	15	56.2	244	52	30	29	5	3	4	0	31	5	59	6	1	2	1	.667	0	1	4.61
1988	San Diego	NL	7	0	0	3	8	35	8	6	6	1	0	0	0	3	1	9	2	1	0	0	.000	0	0	6.75
1989	Seattle	AL	31	0	0	7	25.2	111	26	8	8	2	2	2	0	10	2	22	2	0	1	2	.333	0	0	2.81
1990	Seattle	AL	60	0	0	19	56	228	40	22	18	4	5	3	0	26	5	50	2	1	7	4	.636	0	2	2.89
1991	Seattle	AL	1	0	0	0	0.1	4	2	2	2	0	0	0	0	1	0	0	0	0	0	0	.000	0	0	54.00
1987	San Francisco	NL	15	0	0	3	20.2	87	19	8	7	1	1	1	0	10	2	21	3	1	2	0	1.000	0	1	3.05
	San Diego	NL	26	0	0	12	36	157	33	22	22	4	2	3	0	21	3	38	3	0	0	1	.000	0	0	5.50
	6 ML YEARS		144	0	0	46	153	650	134	74	69	14	9	9	0	75	13	142	12	3	10	7	.588	0	3	4.06

David Cone

Pitches: Right **Bats:** Left **Pos:** SP

Ht: 6' 1" **Wt:** 190 **Born:** 01/02/63 **Age:** 29

			HOW MUCH HE PITCHED						WHAT HE GAVE UP								THE RESULTS				
Year	Team	Lg	G	GS	CG	GF	IP	BFP	H	R	ER	HR	SH	SF	HB	TBB	IBB	SO	WP	Bk	W	L	Pct.	ShO	Sv	ERA
1986	Kansas City	AL	11	0	0	5	22.2	108	29	14	14	2	0	0	1	13	1	21	3	0	0	0	.000	0	0	5.56
1987	New York	NL	21	13	1	2	99.1	420	87	46	41	11	4	3	5	44	1	68	2	4	5	6	.455	0	1	3.71
1988	New York	NL	35	28	8	0	231.1	936	178	67	57	10	11	5	4	80	7	213	10	10	20	3	.870	4	0	2.22
1989	New York	NL	34	33	7	0	219.2	910	183	92	86	20	6	4	4	74	6	190	14	4	14	8	.636	2	0	3.52
1990	New York	NL	31	30	6	1	211.2	860	177	84	76	21	4	6	1	65	1	233	10	4	14	10	.583	2	0	3.23
1991	New York	NL	34	34	5	0	232.2	966	204	95	85	13	13	7	5	73	2	241	17	1	14	14	.500	2	0	3.29
	6 ML YEARS		166	138	27	9	1017.1	4200	858	398	359	77	38	25	20	349	18	966	56	23	67	41	.620	10	1	3.18

Dennis Cook

Pitches: Left **Bats:** Left **Pos:** RP

Ht: 6' 3" **Wt:** 185 **Born:** 10/04/62 **Age:** 29

			HOW MUCH HE PITCHED						WHAT HE GAVE UP								THE RESULTS				
Year	Team	Lg	G	GS	CG	GF	IP	BFP	H	R	ER	HR	SH	SF	HB	TBB	IBB	SO	WP	Bk	W	L	Pct.	ShO	Sv	ERA
1988	San Francisco	NL	4	4	1	0	22	86	9	8	7	1	0	3	0	11	1	13	1	0	2	1	.667	1	0	2.86
1989	2 ML Teams		23	18	2	1	121	499	110	59	50	18	5	2	2	38	6	67	4	2	7	8	.467	1	0	3.72
1990	2 ML Teams		47	16	2	4	156	663	155	74	68	20	7	7	2	56	9	64	6	3	9	4	.692	1	1	3.92

Year	Team	Lg	G	GS	CG	GF	IP	BFP	H	R	ER	HR	SH	SF	HB	TBB	IBB	SO	WP	Bk	W	L	Pct.	ShO	Sv	ERA
1991	Los Angeles	NL	20	1	0	5	17.2	69	12	3	1	0	1	2	0	7	1	8	0	0	1	0	1.000	0	0	0.51
1989	San Francisco	NL	2	2	1	0	15	58	13	3	3	1	0	0	0	5	0	9	1	0	1	0	1.000	0	0	1.80
	Philadelphia	NL	21	16	1	1	106	441	97	56	47	17	5	2	2	33	6	58	3	2	6	8	.429	1	0	3.99
1990	Philadelphia	NL	42	13	2	4	141.2	594	132	61	56	13	5	5	2	54	9	58	6	3	8	3	.727	1	1	3.56
	Los Angeles	NL	5	3	0	0	14.1	69	23	13	12	7	2	2	0	2	0	6	0	0	1	1	.500	0	0	7.53
	4 ML YEARS		94	39	5	10	316.2	1317	286	144	126	39	13	14	4	112	17	152	11	5	19	13	.594	3	1	3.58

Scott Coolbaugh

Bats: Right **Throws:** Right **Pos:** 3B   **Ht:** 5'11" **Wt:** 195 **Born:** 06/13/66 **Age:** 26

			BATTING																		BASERUNNING				PERCENTAGES		
Year	Team	Lg	G	AB	H	2B	3B	HR	(Hm	Rd)	TB	R	RBI	TBB	IBB	SO	HBP	SH	SF	SB	CS	SB%	GDP	Avg	OBP	SLG
1989	Texas	AL	25	51	14	1	0	2	(1	1)	21	7	7	4	0	12	0	1	1	0	0	.00	2	.275	.321	.412
1990	Texas	AL	67	180	36	6	0	2	(1	1)	48	21	13	15	0	47	1	4	1	1	0	1.00	2	.200	.264	.267
1991	San Diego	NL	60	180	39	8	1	2	(1	1)	55	12	15	19	2	45	1	4	1	0	3	.00	8	.217	.294	.306
	3 ML YEARS		152	411	89	15	1	6	(3	3)	124	40	35	38	2	104	2	9	3	1	3	.25	12	.217	.284	.302

Gary Cooper

Bats: Right **Throws:** Right **Pos:** 3B   **Ht:** 6'1" **Wt:** 200 **Born:** 08/13/64 **Age:** 27

			BATTING																		BASERUNNING				PERCENTAGES		
Year	Team	Lg	G	AB	H	2B	3B	HR	(Hm	Rd)	TB	R	RBI	TBB	IBB	SO	HBP	SH	SF	SB	CS	SB%	GDP	Avg	OBP	SLG
1986	Auburn	A	76	275	86	16	3	11	--	--	141	52	54	47	0	47	2	0	2	16	4	.80	5	.313	.414	.513
1987	Osceola	A	123	427	119	17	4	4	--	--	156	66	74	66	2	69	5	4	5	14	5	.74	12	.279	.378	.365
1988	Columbus	AA	140	474	128	25	7	7	--	--	188	65	69	87	0	87	4	4	7	13	7	.65	20	.270	.383	.397
1989	Tucson	AAA	118	376	102	23	3	1	--	--	134	51	50	48	2	69	4	1	5	5	7	.42	2	.271	.356	.356
1990	Osceola	A	8	26	4	4	0	0	--	--	8	4	2	3	0	3	1	0	1	0	0	.00	1	.154	.258	.308
	Columbus	AA	54	160	42	7	0	8	--	--	73	29	30	30	0	32	1	0	1	1	2	.33	5	.263	.380	.456
1991	Tucson	AAA	120	406	124	25	6	14	--	--	203	86	75	66	5	108	3	2	5	7	8	.47	11	.305	.402	.500
1991	Houston	NL	9	16	4	1	0	0	(0	0)	5	1	2	3	0	6	0	0	0	0	0	.00	0	.250	.368	.313

Scott Cooper

Bats: Left **Throws:** Right **Pos:** 3B   **Ht:** 6'3" **Wt:** 200 **Born:** 10/13/67 **Age:** 24

			BATTING																		BASERUNNING				PERCENTAGES		
Year	Team	Lg	G	AB	H	2B	3B	HR	(Hm	Rd)	TB	R	RBI	TBB	IBB	SO	HBP	SH	SF	SB	CS	SB%	GDP	Avg	OBP	SLG
1986	Elmira	A	51	191	55	9	0	9	--	--	91	23	43	19	2	32	0	1	4	1	4	.20	6	.288	.346	.476
1987	Greensboro	A	119	370	93	21	2	15	--	--	163	52	63	58	7	69	2	0	6	1	0	1.00	5	.251	.351	.441
1988	Lynchburg	A	130	497	148	45	7	9	--	--	234	90	73	58	0	74	2	2	4	0	0	.00	11	.298	.371	.471
1989	New Britain	AA	124	421	104	24	2	7	--	--	153	50	39	55	2	84	6	5	5	1	1	.50	5	.247	.339	.363
1990	Pawtucket	AAA	124	433	115	17	1	12	--	--	170	56	44	39	3	75	7	4	3	2	0	1.00	9	.266	.334	.393
1991	Pawtucket	AAA	137	483	134	21	2	15	--	--	204	55	72	50	11	58	7	4	6	3	4	.43	13	.277	.350	.422
1990	Boston	AL	2	1	0	0	0	0	(0	0)	0	0	0	0	0	1	0	0	0	0	0	.00	0	.000	.000	.000
1991	Boston	AL	14	35	16	4	2	0	(0	0)	24	6	7	2	0	2	0	0	0	0	0	.00	0	.457	.486	.686
	2 ML YEARS		16	36	16	4	2	0	(0	0)	24	6	7	2	0	3	0	0	0	0	0	.00	0	.444	.474	.667

Joey Cora

Bats: Both **Throws:** Right **Pos:** 2B   **Ht:** 5'8" **Wt:** 152 **Born:** 05/14/65 **Age:** 27

			BATTING																		BASERUNNING				PERCENTAGES		
Year	Team	Lg	G	AB	H	2B	3B	HR	(Hm	Rd)	TB	R	RBI	TBB	IBB	SO	HBP	SH	SF	SB	CS	SB%	GDP	Avg	OBP	SLG
1987	San Diego	NL	77	241	57	7	2	0	(0	0)	68	23	13	28	1	26	1	5	1	15	11	.58	4	.237	.317	.282
1989	San Diego	NL	12	19	6	1	0	0	(0	0)	7	5	1	1	0	0	0	0	0	1	0	1.00	0	.316	.350	.368
1990	San Diego	NL	51	100	27	3	0	0	(0	0)	30	12	2	6	1	9	0	0	0	8	3	.73	1	.270	.311	.300
1991	Chicago	AL	100	228	55	2	3	0	(0	0)	63	37	18	20	0	21	5	8	3	11	6	.65	1	.241	.313	.276
	4 ML YEARS		240	588	145	13	5	0	(0	0)	168	77	34	55	2	56	6	13	4	35	20	.64	6	.247	.315	.286

Archie Corbin

Pitches: Right **Bats:** Right **Pos:** RP   **Ht:** 6'4" **Wt:** 190 **Born:** 12/30/67 **Age:** 24

			HOW MUCH HE PITCHED						WHAT HE GAVE UP												THE RESULTS					
Year	Team	Lg	G	GS	CG	GF	IP	BFP	H	R	ER	HR	SH	SF	HB	TBB	IBB	SO	WP	Bk	W	L	Pct.	ShO	Sv	ERA
1986	Kingsport	R	18	1	0	9	30.1	149	31	23	16	3	0	1	0	28	0	30	8	1	1	1	.500	0	0	4.75
1987	Kingsport	R	6	6	0	0	25.2	128	24	21	18	3	0	0	2	26	0	17	6	0	2	3	.400	0	0	6.31
1988	Kingsport	R	11	10	4	0	69.1	277	47	23	12	5	2	0	3	17	0	47	1	1	7	2	.778	1	0	1.56
1989	Columbia	A	27	23	4	3	153.2	664	149	86	77	16	4	4	5	72	0	130	2	0	9	9	.500	2	1	4.51
1990	St. Lucie	A	20	18	3	2	118	494	97	47	39	2	4	3	7	59	0	105	10	0	7	8	.467	0	0	2.97
1991	Memphis	AA	28	25	1	0	156.1	692	139	90	81	7	4	6	8	90	1	166	13	0	8	8	.500	0	0	4.66
1991	Kansas City	AL	2	0	0	2	2.1	12	3	1	1	0	0	0	0	2	0	1	1	1	0	0	.000	0	0	3.86

Rheal Cormier

Pitches: Left   Bats: Left   Pos: SP　　Ht: 5'10" Wt: 185 Born: 04/23/67 Age: 25

Year Team	Lg	G	GS	CG	GF	IP	BFP	H	R	ER	HR	SH	SF	HB	TBB	IBB	SO	WP	Bk	W	L	Pct.	ShO	Sv	ERA
1989 St.Pete	A	26	26	4	0	169.2	669	141	63	42	9	6	3	0	33	2	122	4	7	12	7	.632	2	0	2.23
1990 Arkansas	AA	22	21	3	1	121.1	530	133	81	68	9	6	2	5	30	2	102	5	1	5	12	.294	1	0	5.04
Louisville	AAA	4	4	0	0	24	92	18	8	6	1	0	0	0	3	0	9	4	0	1	1	.500	0	0	2.25
1991 Louisville	AAA	21	21	3	0	127.2	543	140	64	60	5	10	6	6	31	1	74	6	1	7	9	.438	3	0	4.23
1991 St.Louis	NL	11	10	2	1	67.2	281	74	35	31	5	1	3	2	8	1	38	2	1	4	5	.444	0	0	4.12

Jim Corsi

Pitches: Right   Bats: Right   Pos: RP　　Ht: 6'1" Wt: 210 Born: 09/09/61 Age: 30

Year Team	Lg	G	GS	CG	GF	IP	BFP	H	R	ER	HR	SH	SF	HB	TBB	IBB	SO	WP	Bk	W	L	Pct.	ShO	Sv	ERA
1988 Oakland	AL	11	0	0	7	21.1	89	20	10	8	1	3	3	0	6	1	10	1	1	0	1	.000	0	0	3.80
1989 Oakland	AL	22	0	0	14	38.1	149	26	8	8	2	2	2	1	10	0	21	0	0	1	2	.333	0	0	1.88
1991 Houston	NL	47	0	0	15	77.2	322	76	37	32	6	3	2	0	23	5	53	1	1	0	5	.000	0	0	3.71
3 ML YEARS		80	1	0	36	137.1	560	122	55	49	9	8	7	1	39	6	84	2	2	1	8	.111	0	0	3.21

John Costello

Pitches: Right   Bats: Right   Pos: RP　　Ht: 6'1" Wt: 180 Born: 12/24/60 Age: 31

Year Team	Lg	G	GS	CG	GF	IP	BFP	H	R	ER	HR	SH	SF	HB	TBB	IBB	SO	WP	Bk	W	L	Pct.	ShO	Sv	ERA
1988 St.Louis	NL	36	0	0	15	49.2	214	44	15	10	3	1	1	0	25	4	38	0	1	5	2	.714	0	1	1.81
1989 St.Louis	NL	48	0	0	11	62.1	252	48	24	23	5	0	5	2	20	7	40	0	0	5	4	.556	0	3	3.32
1990 2 ML Teams		8	0	0	4	10.2	47	12	8	7	3	0	1	1	2	1	2	0	1	0	0	.000	0	0	5.91
1991 San Diego	NL	27	0	0	6	35	157	37	15	12	2	4	2	0	17	3	24	2	0	1	0	1.000	0	0	3.09
1990 St.Louis	NL	4	0	0	3	4.1	21	7	3	3	1	0	0	1	1	1	1	0	0	0	0	.000	0	0	6.23
Montreal	NL	4	0	0	1	6.1	26	5	5	4	2	0	1	0	1	0	1	0	1	0	0	.000	0	0	5.68
4 ML YEARS		119	0	0	36	157.2	670	141	62	52	13	5	9	3	64	15	104	2	2	11	6	.647	0	4	2.97

Henry Cotto

Bats: Right   Throws: Right   Pos: LF/CF　　Ht: 6'2" Wt: 180 Born: 01/05/61 Age: 31

Year Team	Lg	G	AB	H	2B	3B	HR	(Hm	Rd)	TB	R	RBI	TBB	IBB	SO	HBP	SH	SF	SB	CS	SB%	GDP	Avg	OBP	SLG
1984 Chicago	NL	105	146	40	5	0	0	(0	0)	45	24	8	10	2	23	1	3	0	9	3	.75	1	.274	.325	.308
1985 New York	AL	34	56	17	1	0	1	(0	1)	21	4	3	6	0	12	0	1	0	1	1	.50	1	.304	.339	.375
1986 New York	AL	35	80	17	3	0	1	(0	1)	23	11	6	2	0	17	0	0	1	3	0	1.00	3	.213	.229	.288
1987 New York	AL	68	149	35	10	0	5	(5	0)	60	21	20	6	0	35	1	0	0	4	2	.67	7	.235	.269	.403
1988 Seattle	AL	133	386	100	18	1	8	(5	3)	144	50	33	23	0	53	2	4	3	27	3	.90	8	.259	.302	.373
1989 Seattle	AL	100	295	78	11	2	9	(5	4)	120	44	33	12	3	44	3	0	0	10	4	.71	4	.264	.300	.407
1990 Seattle	AL	127	355	92	14	3	4	(2	2)	124	40	33	22	2	52	4	6	3	21	3	.88	13	.259	.307	.349
1991 Seattle	AL	66	177	54	6	2	6	(2	4)	82	35	23	10	0	27	2	2	1	16	3	.84	7	.305	.347	.463
8 ML YEARS		668	1644	433	68	8	34	(19	15)	619	229	162	88	7	263	13	16	8	91	19	.83	44	.263	.305	.377

Danny Cox

Pitches: Right   Bats: Right   Pos: SP/RP　　Ht: 6'4" Wt: 225 Born: 09/21/59 Age: 32

Year Team	Lg	G	GS	CG	GF	IP	BFP	H	R	ER	HR	SH	SF	HB	TBB	IBB	SO	WP	Bk	W	L	Pct.	ShO	Sv	ERA
1983 St.Louis	NL	12	12	0	0	83	352	92	38	30	6	6	1	0	23	2	36	2	0	3	6	.333	0	0	3.25
1984 St.Louis	NL	29	27	1	0	156.1	668	171	81	70	9	10	5	7	54	6	70	2	4	9	11	.450	1	0	4.03
1985 St.Louis	NL	35	35	10	0	241	989	226	91	77	19	12	9	3	64	6	131	3	1	18	9	.667	4	0	2.88
1986 St.Louis	NL	32	32	8	0	220	881	189	85	71	14	8	3	2	60	6	108	3	0	12	13	.480	0	0	2.90
1987 St.Louis	NL	31	31	2	0	199.1	864	224	99	86	17	14	4	3	71	6	101	5	1	11	9	.550	0	0	3.88
1988 St.Louis	NL	13	13	0	0	86	361	89	40	38	6	5	3	1	25	7	47	4	3	3	8	.273	0	0	3.98
1991 Philadelphia	NL	23	17	0	2	102.1	433	98	57	52	14	6	7	1	39	2	46	7	1	4	6	.400	0	0	4.57
7 ML YEARS		175	167	21	2	1088	4548	1089	491	424	85	61	32	17	336	34	539	26	14	60	62	.492	5	0	3.51

Steve Crawford

Pitches: Right   Bats: Right   Pos: RP　　Ht: 6'6" Wt: 240 Born: 04/29/58 Age: 34

Year Team	Lg	G	GS	CG	GF	IP	BFP	H	R	ER	HR	SH	SF	HB	TBB	IBB	SO	WP	Bk	W	L	Pct.	ShO	Sv	ERA
1980 Boston	AL	6	4	2	1	32	142	41	14	13	3	0	4	0	8	2	10	0	0	2	0	1.000	0	0	3.66
1981 Boston	AL	14	11	0	2	58	257	69	38	32	10	3	4	3	18	0	29	2	0	0	5	.000	0	0	4.97
1982 Boston	AL	5	0	0	4	9	41	14	3	2	0	0	0	0	0	0	2	0	0	1	0	1.000	0	0	2.00
1984 Boston	AL	35	0	0	19	62	268	69	31	23	6	1	4	1	21	5	21	2	0	5	0	1.000	0	1	3.34
1985 Boston	AL	44	1	0	26	91	394	103	47	38	5	3	1	0	28	8	58	5	0	6	5	.545	0	12	3.76

Year	Team	Lg	G	GS	CG	GF	IP	BFP	H	R	ER	HR	SH	SF	HB	TBB	IBB	SO	WP	Bk	W	L	Pct.	ShO	Sv	ERA
1986	Boston	AL	40	0	0	15	57.1	248	69	29	25	5	3	2	0	19	7	32	2	0	0	2	.000	0	4	3.92
1987	Boston	AL	29	0	0	7	72.2	324	91	48	43	13	0	0	2	32	2	43	2	0	5	4	.556	0	0	5.33
1989	Kansas City	AL	25	0	0	5	54	224	48	19	17	2	3	1	3	19	3	33	0	0	3	1	.750	0	0	2.83
1990	Kansas City	AL	46	0	0	14	80	341	79	38	37	7	2	2	3	23	3	54	1	0	5	4	.556	0	1	4.16
1991	Kansas City	AL	33	0	0	17	46.2	216	60	31	31	3	1	3	1	18	5	38	5	0	3	2	.600	0	1	5.98
10 ML YEARS			277	16	2	110	562.2	2455	643	298	261	54	19	19	13	186	35	320	19	0	30	23	.566	0	19	4.17

Tim Crews

Pitches: Right **Bats:** Right **Pos:** RP **Ht:** 6' 0" **Wt:** 195 **Born:** 04/03/61 **Age:** 31

			HOW MUCH HE PITCHED						WHAT HE GAVE UP											THE RESULTS					
Year	Team	Lg	G	GS	CG	GF	IP	BFP	H	R	ER	HR	SH	SF	HB	TBB	IBB	SO	WP	Bk	W	L	Pct.	ShO	Sv	ERA
1987	Los Angeles	NL	20	0	0	7	29	124	30	9	8	2	1	1	2	8	1	20	0	0	1	1	.500	0	3	2.48
1988	Los Angeles	NL	42	0	0	12	71.2	301	77	29	25	3	3	5	0	16	7	45	1	0	4	0	1.000	0	1	3.14
1989	Los Angeles	NL	44	0	0	16	61.2	275	69	27	22	7	7	0	2	23	9	56	1	0	0	1	.000	0	1	3.21
1990	Los Angeles	NL	66	2	0	18	107.1	440	98	40	33	9	1	3	1	24	6	76	2	0	4	5	.444	0	5	2.77
1991	Los Angeles	NL	60	0	0	17	76	318	75	30	29	7	4	2	0	19	11	53	3	1	2	3	.400	0	6	3.43
5 ML YEARS			232	2	0	70	345.2	1458	349	135	117	28	16	11	5	90	34	250	7	1	11	10	.524	0	15	3.05

Chuck Crim

Pitches: Right **Bats:** Right **Pos:** RP **Ht:** 6' 0" **Wt:** 185 **Born:** 07/23/61 **Age:** 30

			HOW MUCH HE PITCHED						WHAT HE GAVE UP											THE RESULTS					
Year	Team	Lg	G	GS	CG	GF	IP	BFP	H	R	ER	HR	SH	SF	HB	TBB	IBB	SO	WP	Bk	W	L	Pct.	ShO	Sv	ERA
1987	Milwaukee	AL	53	5	0	18	130	549	133	60	53	15	6	1	3	39	5	56	2	1	6	8	.429	0	12	3.67
1988	Milwaukee	AL	70	0	0	25	105	425	95	38	34	11	5	6	2	28	3	58	9	2	7	6	.538	0	9	2.91
1989	Milwaukee	AL	76	0	0	31	117.2	487	114	42	37	7	3	6	2	36	9	59	5	0	9	7	.563	0	7	2.83
1990	Milwaukee	AL	67	0	0	25	85.2	367	88	39	33	7	1	4	2	23	4	39	0	1	3	5	.375	0	11	3.47
1991	Milwaukee	AL	66	0	0	29	91.1	408	115	52	47	9	3	1	2	25	9	39	3	3	8	5	.615	0	3	4.63
5 ML YEARS			332	5	0	128	529.2	2236	545	231	204	49	18	18	11	151	30	251	19	7	33	31	.516	0	42	3.47

Warren Cromartie

Bats: Left **Throws:** Left **Pos:** 1B **Ht:** 6' 0" **Wt:** 180 **Born:** 09/29/53 **Age:** 38

			BATTING																BASERUNNING				PERCENTAGES		
Year	Team	Lg	G	AB	H	2B	3B	HR	(Hm	Rd)	TB	R	RBI	TBB	IBB	SO	HBP	SH	SF	SB	CS	SB%	GDP	Avg	OBP	SLG
1974	Montreal	NL	8	17	3	0	0	0	(0	0)	3	2	0	3	0	3	0	0	0	1	0	1.00	0	.176	.300	.176
1976	Montreal	NL	33	81	17	1	0	0	(0	0)	18	8	2	1	0	5	0	0	0	1	2	.33	2	.210	.220	.222
1977	Montreal	NL	155	620	175	41	7	5	(3	2)	245	64	50	33	3	40	4	2	3	10	3	.77	15	.282	.321	.395
1978	Montreal	NL	159	607	180	32	6	10	(5	5)	254	77	56	33	5	60	7	2	6	8	8	.50	15	.297	.337	.418
1979	Montreal	NL	158	659	181	46	5	8	(3	5)	261	84	46	38	19	78	1	6	6	8	7	.53	11	.275	.313	.396
1980	Montreal	NL	162	597	172	33	5	14	(7	7)	257	74	70	51	24	64	2	4	3	8	8	.50	24	.288	.345	.430
1981	Montreal	NL	99	358	109	19	2	6	(4	2)	150	41	42	39	12	27	0	0	3	2	3	.40	8	.304	.370	.419
1982	Montreal	NL	144	497	126	24	3	14	(4	10)	198	59	62	69	15	60	3	1	4	3	0	1.00	10	.254	.346	.398
1983	Montreal	NL	120	360	100	26	2	3	(0	3)	139	37	43	43	7	48	1	1	5	8	3	.73	11	.278	.352	.386
1991	Kansas City	AL	69	131	41	7	2	1	(0	1)	55	13	20	15	0	18	0	1	1	3	3	.25	3	.313	.381	.420
10 ML YEARS			1107	3927	1104	229	32	61	(26	35)	1580	459	391	325	85	403	18	17	31	50	37	.57	99	.281	.336	.402

Chris Cron

Bats: Right **Throws:** Right **Pos:** 1B **Ht:** 6' 2" **Wt:** 200 **Born:** 03/31/64 **Age:** 28

			BATTING																BASERUNNING				PERCENTAGES		
Year	Team	Lg	G	AB	H	2B	3B	HR	(Hm	Rd)	TB	R	RBI	TBB	IBB	SO	HBP	SH	SF	SB	CS	SB%	GDP	Avg	OBP	SLG
1984	Pulaski	R	32	114	42	8	0	7	--	--	71	22	37	17	1	20	6	0	2	2	0	1.00	2	.368	.468	.623
1985	Sumter	A	119	425	102	20	0	7	--	--	143	53	59	51	2	98	18	0	1	5	2	.71	8	.240	.345	.336
1986	Durham	A	90	265	55	10	0	7	--	--	86	26	34	29	0	60	6	2	2	0	2	.00	2	.208	.298	.325
1987	Quad City	A	111	398	110	20	1	11	--	--	165	53	62	44	2	88	17	0	1	1	3	.25	5	.276	.372	.415
	Palm Sprngs	A	26	92	25	3	0	2	--	--	34	6	9	9	0	27	2	1	2	2	2	.50	3	.272	.343	.370
1988	Palm Sprngs	A	127	467	117	28	3	14	--	--	193	71	84	68	1	147	27	2	6	4	3	.57	10	.251	.373	.413
1989	Midland	AA	128	491	148	33	3	22	--	--	253	80	103	39	5	126	14	1	6	0	1	.00	10	.301	.365	.515
1990	Edmonton	AAA	104	401	115	31	0	17	--	--	197	54	75	28	1	92	5	1	5	7	5	.58	9	.287	.337	.491
1991	Edmonton	AAA	123	461	134	21	1	22	--	--	223	74	91	47	3	103	10	2	11	6	5	.55	12	.291	.361	.484
1991	California	AL	6	15	2	0	0	0	(0	0)	2	0	0	0	0	5	0	0	0	0	0	.00	0	.133	.235	.133

Milt Cuyler

Bats: Both **Throws:** Right **Pos:** CF **Ht:** 5'10" **Wt:** 185 **Born:** 10/07/68 **Age:** 23

			BATTING																BASERUNNING				PERCENTAGES		
Year	Team	Lg	G	AB	H	2B	3B	HR	(Hm	Rd)	TB	R	RBI	TBB	IBB	SO	HBP	SH	SF	SB	CS	SB%	GDP	Avg	OBP	SLG
1986	Bristol	R	45	174	40	3	5	1	--	--	56	24	11	15	0	35	5	2	0	12	4	.75	1	.230	.309	.322
1987	Fayettevlle	A	94	366	107	8	4	2	--	--	129	65	34	34	4	78	7	17	2	27	13	.68	3	.292	.362	.352
1988	Lakeland	A	132	483	143	11	3	2	--	--	166	100	32	71	2	83	4	14	1	50	25	.67	3	.296	.390	.344

47

1989 Toledo	AAA	24	83	14	3	2	0	--	--	21	4	6	8	0	27	0	3	1	4	1	.80	1	.169	.239	.253
London	AA	98	366	96	8	7	7	--	--	139	69	34	47	2	74	4	4	0	32	5	.86	2	.262	.353	.380
1990 Toledo	AAA	124	461	119	11	8	2	--	--	152	77	42	60	1	77	5	7	2	52	14	.79	6	.258	.348	.330
1990 Detroit	AL	19	51	13	3	1	0	(0	0)	18	8	8	5	0	10	0	2	1	1	2	.33	1	.255	.316	.353
1991 Detroit	AL	154	475	122	15	7	3	(1	2)	160	77	33	52	0	92	5	12	2	41	10	.80	4	.257	.335	.337
2 ML YEARS		173	526	135	18	8	3	(1	2)	178	85	41	57	0	102	5	14	3	42	12	.78	5	.257	.333	.338

Mike Dalton

Pitches: Left **Bats:** Right **Pos:** RP **Ht:** 6' 0" **Wt:** 215 **Born:** 03/27/63 **Age:** 29

		HOW MUCH HE PITCHED						WHAT HE GAVE UP								THE RESULTS					
Year Team	Lg	G	GS	CG	GF	IP	BFP	H	R	ER	HR	SH	SF	HB	TBB	IBB	SO	WP	Bk	W	L	Pct.	ShO	Sv	ERA
1983 Elmira	R	21	1	0	0	51	0	48	19	15	0	0	0	0	15	0	49	0	0	3	1	.750	0	5	2.65
1984 Winter Havn	A	38	9	2	23	107.2	476	115	56	38	2	5	8	2	52	4	43	8	1	5	8	.385	0	6	3.18
1985 Winter Havn	A	49	0	0	42	72	281	45	14	9	0	5	3	0	27	3	41	1	0	2	3	.400	0	18	1.13
1986 Pawtucket	AAA	37	6	0	22	71.2	324	84	43	40	4	1	3	4	34	3	49	7	0	6	2	.750	0	1	5.02
1987 New Britain	AA	4	0	0	4	5	18	1	0	0	0	0	0	0	2	0	7	0	0	1	0	1.000	0	1	0.00
Pawtucket	AAA	39	1	0	19	88.2	375	83	49	41	10	4	2	0	40	2	45	6	1	1	2	.333	0	2	4.16
1988 New Britain	AA	52	1	1	38	84.1	356	65	32	21	2	6	2	1	39	10	61	3	0	6	5	.545	0	8	2.24
1989 New Britain	AA	18	1	1	7	32.2	135	25	13	9	0	1	1	2	15	3	15	1	0	3	1	.750	1	3	2.48
Pawtucket	AAA	26	3	1	10	45.2	206	55	26	26	2	6	1	2	16	0	20	1	0	1	3	.250	1	4	5.12
1990 Pawtucket	AAA	49	2	1	21	99	412	94	42	28	6	9	5	3	22	2	49	2	0	7	4	.636	0	5	2.55
1991 Toledo	AAA	39	0	0	18	65.1	294	72	33	30	7	5	1	2	24	4	28	6	0	3	3	.500	0	4	4.13
1991 Detroit	AL	4	0	0	1	8	38	12	3	3	2	0	0	0	2	0	4	2	0	0	0	.000	0	0	3.38

Kal Daniels

Bats: Left **Throws:** Right **Pos:** LF **Ht:** 5'11" **Wt:** 205 **Born:** 08/20/63 **Age:** 28

		BATTING																	BASERUNNING				PERCENTAGES		
Year Team	Lg	G	AB	H	2B	3B	HR	(Hm	Rd)	TB	R	RBI	TBB	IBB	SO	HBP	SH	SF	SB	CS	SB%	GDP	Avg	OBP	SLG
1986 Cincinnati	NL	74	181	58	10	4	6	(3	3)	94	34	23	22	1	30	2	1	1	15	2	.88	4	.320	.398	.519
1987 Cincinnati	NL	108	368	123	24	1	26	(13	13)	227	73	64	60	11	62	1	1	0	26	8	.76	6	.334	.429	.617
1988 Cincinnati	NL	140	495	144	29	1	18	(12	6)	229	95	64	87	10	94	3	0	4	27	6	.82	11	.291	.397	.463
1989 2 ML Teams		55	171	42	13	0	4	(2	2)	67	33	17	43	1	33	2	0	2	9	4	.69	2	.246	.399	.392
1990 Los Angeles	NL	130	450	133	23	1	27	(12	15)	239	81	94	68	1	104	3	2	3	4	3	.57	10	.296	.389	.531
1991 Los Angeles	NL	137	461	115	15	1	17	(12	5)	183	54	73	63	4	116	1	0	6	6	1	.86	9	.249	.337	.397
1989 Cincinnati	NL	44	133	29	11	0	2	(1	1)	46	26	9	36	1	28	2	0	1	6	4	.60	1	.218	.390	.346
Los Angeles	NL	11	38	13	2	0	2	(1	1)	21	7	8	7	0	5	0	0	1	3	0	1.00	1	.342	.435	.553
6 ML YEARS		644	2126	615	114	8	98	(54	44)	1039	370	335	343	28	439	12	4	16	87	24	.78	42	.289	.388	.489

Ron Darling

Pitches: Right **Bats:** Right **Pos:** SP **Ht:** 6' 3" **Wt:** 195 **Born:** 08/19/60 **Age:** 31

		HOW MUCH HE PITCHED						WHAT HE GAVE UP								THE RESULTS					
Year Team	Lg	G	GS	CG	GF	IP	BFP	H	R	ER	HR	SH	SF	HB	TBB	IBB	SO	WP	Bk	W	L	Pct.	ShO	Sv	ERA
1983 New York	NL	5	5	1	0	35.1	148	31	11	11	0	3	0	3	17	1	23	3	2	1	3	.250	0	0	2.80
1984 New York	NL	33	33	2	0	205.2	884	179	97	87	17	7	6	5	104	2	136	7	1	12	9	.571	2	0	3.81
1985 New York	NL	36	35	4	1	248	1043	214	93	80	21	13	4	3	114	1	167	7	1	16	6	.727	2	0	2.90
1986 New York	NL	34	34	4	0	237	967	203	84	74	21	10	6	3	81	2	184	7	3	15	6	.714	2	0	2.81
1987 New York	NL	32	32	2	0	207.2	891	183	111	99	24	5	3	3	96	3	167	6	3	12	8	.600	0	0	4.29
1988 New York	NL	34	34	7	0	240.2	971	218	97	87	24	10	8	5	60	2	161	7	2	17	9	.654	4	0	3.25
1989 New York	NL	33	33	4	0	217.1	922	214	100	85	19	7	13	3	70	7	153	12	4	14	14	.500	0	0	3.52
1990 New York	NL	33	18	1	3	126	554	135	73	63	20	7	3	5	44	4	99	5	1	7	9	.438	0	0	4.50
1991 3 ML Teams		32	32	0	0	194.1	827	185	100	92	22	12	8	9	71	3	129	16	5	8	15	.348	0	0	4.26
1991 New York	NL	17	17	0	0	102.1	427	96	50	44	9	7	4	6	28	1	58	9	4	5	6	.455	0	0	3.87
Montreal	NL	3	3	0	0	17	81	25	16	14	6	0	0	1	5	0	11	4	0	0	2	.000	0	0	7.41
Oakland	AL	12	12	0	0	75	319	64	34	34	7	5	4	2	38	2	60	3	1	3	7	.300	0	0	4.08
9 ML YEARS		272	256	25	4	1712	7207	1562	766	678	168	74	51	39	657	25	1219	70	22	102	79	.564	10	0	3.56

Danny Darwin

Pitches: Right **Bats:** Right **Pos:** SP **Ht:** 6' 3" **Wt:** 190 **Born:** 10/25/55 **Age:** 36

		HOW MUCH HE PITCHED						WHAT HE GAVE UP								THE RESULTS					
Year Team	Lg	G	GS	CG	GF	IP	BFP	H	R	ER	HR	SH	SF	HB	TBB	IBB	SO	WP	Bk	W	L	Pct.	ShO	Sv	ERA
1978 Texas	AL	3	1	0	2	9	36	11	4	4	0	0	1	0	1	0	8	0	0	1	0	1.000	0	0	4.00
1979 Texas	AL	20	6	1	4	78	313	50	36	35	5	3	6	5	30	2	58	0	1	4	4	.500	0	0	4.04
1980 Texas	AL	53	2	0	35	110	468	98	37	32	4	5	7	2	50	7	104	3	0	13	4	.765	0	8	2.62
1981 Texas	AL	22	22	6	0	146	601	115	67	59	12	8	3	6	57	5	98	1	0	9	9	.500	2	0	3.64
1982 Texas	AL	56	1	0	41	89	394	95	38	34	6	10	5	2	37	8	61	2	1	10	8	.556	0	7	3.44
1983 Texas	AL	28	26	9	0	183	780	175	86	71	9	7	7	3	62	3	92	2	0	8	13	.381	2	0	3.49

Year	Team	Lg	G	GS	CG	SHO	IP	BFP	H	R	ER	HR	SH	SF	HB	BB	IBB	SO	WP	BK	W	L	Pct	ShO	Sv	ERA
1984	Texas	AL	35	32	5	2	223.2	955	249	110	98	19	3	3	4	54	2	123	3	0	8	12	.400	1	0	3.94
1985	Milwaukee	AL	39	29	11	8	217.2	919	212	112	92	34	7	9	4	65	4	125	6	0	8	18	.308	1	2	3.80
1986	2 ML Teams		39	22	6	6	184.2	759	170	81	65	16	6	9	3	44	1	120	7	1	11	10	.524	1	0	3.17
1987	Houston	NL	33	30	3	0	195.2	833	184	87	78	17	8	3	5	69	12	134	3	1	9	10	.474	1	0	3.59
1988	Houston	NL	44	20	3	9	192	804	189	86	82	20	10	9	7	48	9	129	1	2	8	13	.381	0	3	3.84
1989	Houston	NL	68	0	0	26	122	482	92	34	32	8	8	5	2	33	9	104	2	3	11	4	.733	0	7	2.36
1990	Houston	NL	48	17	3	14	162.2	646	136	42	40	11	4	2	4	31	4	109	0	2	11	4	.733	0	2	2.21
1991	Boston	AL	12	12	0	0	68	292	71	39	39	15	1	2	4	15	1	42	2	0	3	6	.333	0	0	5.16
1986	Milwaukee	AL	27	14	5	4	130.1	537	120	62	51	13	5	6	3	35	1	80	5	0	6	8	.429	1	0	3.52
	Houston	NL	12	8	1	2	54.1	222	50	19	14	3	1	3	0	9	0	40	2	1	5	2	.714	0	0	2.32
	14 ML YEARS		500	220	47	147	1981.1	8282	1847	859	761	176	80	71	51	596	67	1307	32	11	114	115	.498	8	29	3.46

Doug Dascenzo

Bats: Both **Throws:** Left **Pos:** CF/LF **Ht:** 5' 8" **Wt:** 160 **Born:** 06/30/64 **Age:** 28

					BATTING														BASERUNNING				PERCENTAGES		
Year	Team	Lg	G	AB	H	2B	3B	HR	(Hm Rd)	TB	R	RBI	TBB	IBB	SO	HBP	SH	SF	SB	CS	SB%	GDP	Avg	OBP	SLG
1988	Chicago	NL	26	75	16	3	0	0	(0 0)	19	9	4	9	1	4	0	1	0	6	1	.86	2	.213	.298	.253
1989	Chicago	NL	47	139	23	1	0	1	(0 1)	27	20	12	13	0	13	0	3	2	6	3	.67	2	.165	.234	.194
1990	Chicago	NL	113	241	61	9	5	1	(1 0)	83	27	26	21	2	18	1	5	3	15	6	.71	3	.253	.312	.344
1991	Chicago	NL	118	239	61	11	0	1	(0 1)	75	40	18	24	2	26	2	6	1	14	7	.67	3	.255	.327	.314
	4 ML YEARS		304	694	161	24	5	3	(1 2)	204	96	60	67	5	61	3	15	6	41	17	.71	10	.232	.300	.294

Jack Daugherty

Bats: Both **Throws:** Left **Pos:** LF **Ht:** 6' 0" **Wt:** 190 **Born:** 07/03/60 **Age:** 31

					BATTING														BASERUNNING				PERCENTAGES		
Year	Team	Lg	G	AB	H	2B	3B	HR	(Hm Rd)	TB	R	RBI	TBB	IBB	SO	HBP	SH	SF	SB	CS	SB%	GDP	Avg	OBP	SLG
1987	Montreal	NL	11	10	1	1	0	0	(0 0)	2	1	1	0	0	3	0	2	0	0	0	.00	0	.100	.100	.200
1989	Texas	AL	52	106	32	4	2	1	(1 0)	43	15	10	11	0	21	0	1	3	2	1	.67	1	.302	.364	.406
1990	Texas	AL	125	310	93	20	2	6	(5 1)	135	36	47	22	0	49	2	2	3	0	0	1.00	4	.300	.347	.435
1991	Texas	AL	58	144	28	3	2	1	(0 1)	38	8	11	16	1	23	0	4	3	1	0	1.00	4	.194	.270	.264
	4 ML YEARS		246	570	154	28	6	8	(6 2)	218	60	69	49	1	96	2	9	9	3	1	.75	7	.270	.326	.382

Darren Daulton

Bats: Left **Throws:** Right **Pos:** C **Ht:** 6' 2" **Wt:** 200 **Born:** 01/03/62 **Age:** 30

					BATTING														BASERUNNING				PERCENTAGES		
Year	Team	Lg	G	AB	H	2B	3B	HR	(Hm Rd)	TB	R	RBI	TBB	IBB	SO	HBP	SH	SF	SB	CS	SB%	GDP	Avg	OBP	SLG
1983	Philadelphia	NL	2	3	1	0	0	0	(0 0)	1	1	0	1	0	1	0	0	0	0	0	.00	0	.333	.500	.333
1985	Philadelphia	NL	36	103	21	3	1	4	(0 4)	38	14	11	16	0	37	0	0	0	3	0	1.00	0	.204	.311	.369
1986	Philadelphia	NL	49	138	31	4	0	8	(4 4)	59	18	21	38	3	41	1	2	2	2	3	.40	1	.225	.391	.428
1987	Philadelphia	NL	53	129	25	6	0	3	(1 2)	40	10	13	16	1	37	0	4	1	2	1	.67	2	.194	.281	.310
1988	Philadelphia	NL	58	144	30	6	0	1	(0 1)	39	13	12	17	1	26	0	0	2	2	1	.67	2	.208	.288	.271
1989	Philadelphia	NL	131	368	74	12	2	8	(2 6)	114	29	44	52	8	58	2	1	1	2	1	.67	4	.201	.303	.310
1990	Philadelphia	NL	143	459	123	30	1	12	(5 7)	191	62	57	72	9	72	2	3	4	7	1	.88	6	.268	.367	.416
1991	Philadelphia	NL	89	285	56	12	0	12	(8 4)	104	36	42	41	4	66	2	2	5	5	0	1.00	4	.196	.297	.365
	8 ML YEARS		561	1629	361	73	4	48	(20 28)	586	183	200	253	26	338	7	12	15	21	6	.78	18	.222	.326	.360

Mark Davidson

Bats: Right **Throws:** Right **Pos:** LF/RF **Ht:** 6' 2" **Wt:** 190 **Born:** 02/15/61 **Age:** 31

					BATTING														BASERUNNING				PERCENTAGES		
Year	Team	Lg	G	AB	H	2B	3B	HR	(Hm Rd)	TB	R	RBI	TBB	IBB	SO	HBP	SH	SF	SB	CS	SB%	GDP	Avg	OBP	SLG
1986	Minnesota	AL	36	68	8	3	0	0	(0 0)	11	5	2	6	0	22	0	3	0	2	3	.40	1	.118	.189	.162
1987	Minnesota	AL	102	150	40	4	1	1	(0 1)	49	32	14	13	1	26	0	4	2	9	2	.82	4	.267	.321	.327
1988	Minnesota	AL	100	106	23	7	0	1	(0 1)	33	22	10	10	0	20	1	1	1	3	3	.50	3	.217	.288	.311
1989	Houston	NL	33	65	13	2	1	1	(0 1)	20	7	5	7	0	14	0	1	0	1	0	1.00	1	.200	.278	.308
1990	Houston	NL	57	130	38	5	1	1	(0 1)	48	12	11	10	1	18	0	0	1	3	0	.00	1	.292	.340	.369
1991	Houston	NL	85	142	27	6	0	2	(1 1)	39	10	15	12	0	28	2	0	0	0	0	.00	2	.190	.263	.275
	6 ML YEARS		413	661	149	27	3	6	(1 5)	200	88	57	58	2	128	3	10	4	15	11	.58	12	.225	.289	.303

Alvin Davis

Bats: Left **Throws:** Right **Pos:** DH/1B **Ht:** 6' 1" **Wt:** 190 **Born:** 09/09/60 **Age:** 31

					BATTING														BASERUNNING				PERCENTAGES		
Year	Team	Lg	G	AB	H	2B	3B	HR	(Hm Rd)	TB	R	RBI	TBB	IBB	SO	HBP	SH	SF	SB	CS	SB%	GDP	Avg	OBP	SLG
1984	Seattle	AL	152	567	161	34	3	27	(15 12)	282	80	116	97	16	78	7	0	7	5	4	.56	7	.284	.391	.497
1985	Seattle	AL	155	578	166	33	1	18	(11 7)	255	78	78	90	7	71	2	0	7	1	2	.33	14	.287	.381	.441
1986	Seattle	AL	135	479	130	18	1	18	(14 4)	204	66	72	76	10	68	3	2	2	0	3	.00	11	.271	.373	.516
1987	Seattle	AL	157	580	171	37	2	29	(18 11)	299	86	100	72	6	84	2	0	8	0	0	.00	17	.295	.370	.516
1988	Seattle	AL	140	478	141	24	1	18	(12 6)	221	67	69	95	13	53	4	0	5	1	1	.50	14	.295	.412	.462

1989 Seattle	AL	142	498	152	30	1	21	(13	8)	247	84	95	101	15	49	6	0	6	0	1	.00	15	.305	.424	.496
1990 Seattle	AL	140	494	140	21	0	17	(12	5)	212	63	68	85	10	68	4	0	9	0	2	.00	9	.283	.387	.429
1991 Seattle	AL	145	462	102	15	1	12	(6	6)	155	39	69	56	9	78	0	0	10	0	3	.00	8	.221	.299	.335
8 ML YEARS		1166	4136	1163	212	10	160	(101	59)	1875	563	667	672	86	549	28	2	54	7	16	.30	95	.281	.381	.453

Butch Davis

Bats: Right **Throws:** Right **Pos:** PH   **Ht:** 6' 0" **Wt:** 185 **Born:** 06/19/58 **Age:** 34

Year Team	Lg	G	AB	H	2B	3B	HR	(Hm	Rd)	TB	R	RBI	TBB	IBB	SO	HBP	SH	SF	SB	CS	SB%	GDP	Avg	OBP	SLG
1983 Kansas City	AL	33	122	42	2	6	2	(0	2)	62	13	18	4	0	19	0	2	2	4	3	.57	3	.344	.359	.508
1984 Kansas City	AL	41	116	17	3	0	2	(1	1)	26	11	12	10	0	19	0	0	0	4	3	.57	2	.147	.211	.224
1987 Pittsburgh	NL	7	7	1	1	0	0	(0	0)	2	3	0	1	0	3	0	0	0	0	0	.00	0	.143	.250	.286
1988 Baltimore	AL	13	25	6	1	0	0	(0	0)	7	2	0	0	0	8	0	0	0	1	0	1.00	2	.240	.240	.280
1989 Baltimore	AL	5	6	1	1	0	0	(0	0)	2	1	0	0	0	3	0	0	0	0	0	.00	0	.167	.167	.333
1991 Los Angeles	NL	1	1	0	0	0	0	(0	0)	0	0	0	0	0	0	0	0	0	0	0	.00	0	.000	.000	.000
6 ML YEARS		100	277	67	8	6	4	(1	3)	99	30	30	15	0	52	0	2	4	9	6	.60	7	.242	.277	.357

Chili Davis

Bats: Both **Throws:** Right **Pos:** DH   **Ht:** 6' 3" **Wt:** 210 **Born:** 01/17/60 **Age:** 32

Year Team	Lg	G	AB	H	2B	3B	HR	(Hm	Rd)	TB	R	RBI	TBB	IBB	SO	HBP	SH	SF	SB	CS	SB%	GDP	Avg	OBP	SLG
1981 San Francisco	NL	8	15	2	0	0	0	(0	0)	2	1	0	1	0	2	0	0	0	2	0	1.00	1	.133	.188	.133
1982 San Francisco	NL	154	641	167	27	6	19	(6	13)	263	86	76	45	2	115	2	7	6	24	13	.65	13	.261	.308	.410
1983 San Francisco	NL	137	486	113	21	2	11	(7	4)	171	54	59	55	6	108	0	3	9	10	12	.45	9	.233	.305	.352
1984 San Francisco	NL	137	499	157	21	6	21	(7	14)	253	87	81	42	6	74	1	2	2	12	8	.60	13	.315	.368	.507
1985 San Francisco	NL	136	481	130	25	2	13	(7	6)	198	53	56	62	12	74	0	1	7	15	7	.68	16	.270	.349	.412
1986 San Francisco	NL	153	526	146	28	3	13	(7	6)	219	71	70	84	23	96	1	2	5	16	13	.55	11	.278	.375	.416
1987 San Francisco	NL	149	500	125	22	1	24	(9	15)	221	80	76	72	15	109	2	0	4	16	9	.64	8	.250	.344	.442
1988 California	AL	158	600	161	29	3	21	(11	10)	259	81	93	56	14	118	0	1	10	9	10	.47	13	.268	.326	.432
1989 California	AL	154	560	152	24	1	22	(6	16)	244	81	90	61	12	109	0	3	6	3	0	1.00	21	.271	.340	.436
1990 California	AL	113	412	109	17	1	12	(10	2)	164	58	58	61	4	89	0	0	3	1	2	.33	14	.265	.357	.398
1991 Minnesota	AL	153	534	148	34	1	29	(14	15)	271	84	93	95	13	117	1	0	4	5	6	.45	9	.277	.385	.507
11 ML YEARS		1452	5254	1410	248	26	185	(84	101)	2265	736	752	634	107	1011	7	19	56	113	80	.59	128	.268	.345	.431

Eric Davis

Bats: Right **Throws:** Right **Pos:** CF   **Ht:** 6' 3" **Wt:** 185 **Born:** 05/29/62 **Age:** 30

Year Team	Lg	G	AB	H	2B	3B	HR	(Hm	Rd)	TB	R	RBI	TBB	IBB	SO	HBP	SH	SF	SB	CS	SB%	GDP	Avg	OBP	SLG
1984 Cincinnati	NL	57	174	39	10	1	10	(3	7)	81	33	30	24	0	48	1	0	1	10	2	.83	1	.224	.320	.466
1985 Cincinnati	NL	56	122	30	3	3	8	(1	7)	63	26	18	7	0	39	0	2	0	16	3	.84	1	.246	.287	.516
1986 Cincinnati	NL	132	415	115	15	3	27	(12	15)	217	97	71	68	5	100	1	0	3	80	11	.88	6	.277	.378	.523
1987 Cincinnati	NL	129	474	139	23	4	37	(17	20)	281	120	100	84	8	134	1	0	3	50	6	.89	8	.293	.399	.593
1988 Cincinnati	NL	135	472	129	18	3	26	(14	12)	231	81	93	65	10	124	3	0	3	35	3	.92	11	.273	.363	.489
1989 Cincinnati	NL	131	462	130	14	2	34	(15	19)	250	74	101	68	12	116	1	0	11	21	7	.75	16	.281	.367	.541
1990 Cincinnati	NL	127	453	118	26	2	24	(13	11)	220	84	86	60	6	100	2	0	3	21	3	.88	7	.260	.347	.486
1991 Cincinnati	NL	89	285	67	10	0	11	(5	6)	110	39	33	48	5	92	5	0	2	14	2	.88	4	.235	.353	.386
8 ML YEARS		856	2857	767	119	18	177	(80	97)	1453	554	532	424	46	753	14	2	26	247	37	.87	52	.268	.363	.509

Glenn Davis

Bats: Right **Throws:** Right **Pos:** 1B/DH   **Ht:** 6' 3" **Wt:** 200 **Born:** 03/28/61 **Age:** 31

Year Team	Lg	G	AB	H	2B	3B	HR	(Hm	Rd)	TB	R	RBI	TBB	IBB	SO	HBP	SH	SF	SB	CS	SB%	GDP	Avg	OBP	SLG
1984 Houston	NL	18	61	13	5	0	2	(1	1)	24	6	8	4	0	12	0	2	1	0	0	.00	0	.213	.258	.393
1985 Houston	NL	100	350	95	11	0	20	(8	12)	166	51	64	27	6	68	7	2	4	0	0	.00	12	.271	.332	.474
1986 Houston	NL	158	574	152	32	3	31	(17	14)	283	91	101	64	6	72	9	0	7	3	1	.75	11	.265	.344	.493
1987 Houston	NL	151	578	145	35	2	27	(12	15)	265	70	93	47	10	84	5	0	5	4	1	.80	16	.251	.310	.458
1988 Houston	NL	152	561	152	26	0	30	(15	15)	268	78	99	53	20	77	11	0	9	4	3	.57	11	.271	.341	.478
1989 Houston	NL	158	581	156	26	1	34	(15	19)	286	87	89	69	17	123	7	0	6	4	2	.67	9	.269	.350	.492
1990 Houston	NL	93	327	82	15	4	22	(4	18)	171	44	64	46	17	54	8	0	3	8	3	.73	5	.251	.357	.523
1991 Baltimore	AL	49	176	40	9	1	10	(3	7)	81	29	28	16	0	29	5	0	2	4	0	1.00	2	.227	.307	.460
8 ML YEARS		879	3208	835	159	11	176	(75	101)	1544	456	546	326	76	519	52	4	34	27	10	.73	66	.260	.335	.481

Mark Davis

Pitches: Left **Bats:** Left **Pos:** RP/SP **Ht:** 6' 4" **Wt:** 210 **Born:** 10/19/60 **Age:** 31

				HOW	MUCH	HE	PITCHED			WHAT	HE	GAVE	UP								THE	RESULTS			
Year	Team	Lg	G	GS	CG	GF	IP	BFP	H	R	ER	HR	SH	SF	HB	TBB	IBB	SO	WP	Bk	W	L	Pct.	ShO	Sv	ERA
1980	Philadelphia	NL	2	1	0	0	7	30	4	2	2	0	0	0	0	5	0	5	0	0	0	0	.000	0	0	2.57
1981	Philadelphia	NL	9	9	0	0	43	194	49	37	37	7	2	4	0	24	0	29	1	1	1	4	.200	0	0	7.74
1983	San Francisco	NL	20	20	2	0	111	469	93	51	43	14	2	4	3	50	4	83	8	1	6	4	.600	2	0	3.49
1984	San Francisco	NL	46	27	1	6	174.2	766	201	113	104	25	10	10	5	54	12	124	8	4	5	17	.227	0	0	5.36
1985	San Francisco	NL	77	1	0	38	114.1	465	89	49	45	13	13	1	3	41	7	131	6	1	5	12	.294	0	7	3.54
1986	San Francisco	NL	67	2	0	20	84.1	342	63	33	28	6	5	5	1	34	7	90	3	0	5	7	.417	0	4	2.99
1987	2 ML Teams		63	11	1	18	133	566	123	64	59	14	7	2	6	59	8	98	6	2	9	8	.529	0	2	3.99
1988	San Diego	NL	62	0	0	52	98.1	402	70	24	22	2	7	1	0	42	11	102	9	1	5	10	.333	0	28	2.01
1989	San Diego	NL	70	0	0	65	92.2	370	66	21	19	6	3	4	2	31	1	92	8	0	4	3	.571	0	44	1.85
1990	Kansas City	AL	53	3	0	28	68.2	334	71	43	39	9	2	2	4	52	3	73	6	0	2	7	.222	0	6	5.11
1991	Kansas City	AL	29	5	0	8	62.2	276	55	36	31	6	2	5	1	39	0	47	1	0	6	3	.667	0	1	4.45
1987	San Francisco	NL	20	11	1	1	70.2	301	55	38	37	9	3	2	4	28	1	51	4	2	4	5	.444	0	0	4.71
	San Diego		43	0	0	17	62.1	265	51	26	22	5	4	0	2	31	7	47	2	0	5	3	.625	0	2	3.18
	11 ML YEARS		498	79	4	235	989.2	4214	884	473	429	102	53	38	25	431	53	874	56	10	48	75	.390	2	92	3.90

Mark Davis

Bats: Right **Throws:** Right **Pos:** RF **Ht:** 6' 0" **Wt:** 180 **Born:** 11/25/64 **Age:** 27

						BATTING														BASERUNNING				PERCENTAGES		
Year	Team	Lg	G	AB	H	2B	3B	HR	(Hm	Rd)	TB	R	RBI	TBB	IBB	SO	HBP	SH	SF	SB	CS	SB%	GDP	Avg	OBP	SLG
1986	Appleton	A	77	272	62	10	4	3	--	--	89	37	22	54	0	70	4	1	0	19	8	.70	4	.228	.364	.327
1987	Peninsula	A	134	507	149	24	6	16	--	--	233	91	72	63	2	115	6	2	5	37	11	.77	8	.294	.375	.460
1988	Birmingham	AA	66	248	72	18	3	6	--	--	114	52	27	38	0	55	7	0	0	32	13	.71	9	.290	.399	.460
	Vancouver	AAA	68	241	51	9	2	4	--	--	76	24	29	28	0	65	2	6	1	8	10	.44	8	.212	.298	.315
1989	Vancouver	AAA	39	123	16	4	1	0	--	--	22	13	8	13	0	38	5	0	0	6	2	.75	4	.130	.241	.179
	Birmingham	AA	56	192	49	10	3	5	--	--	80	35	26	25	1	52	1	3	0	16	7	.70	3	.255	.344	.417
	Midland	AA	19	58	14	1	0	1	--	--	18	9	7	6	0	18	1	3	0	6	1	.86	1	.241	.323	.310
1990	Midland	AA	92	353	94	16	1	12	--	--	148	66	41	48	2	96	6	3	3	16	8	.67	9	.266	.361	.419
	Edmonton	AAA	35	133	49	10	5	9	--	--	96	30	34	17	0	23	0	2	2	7	8	.47	3	.368	.434	.722
1991	Edmonton	AAA	115	421	117	20	6	13	--	--	188	86	56	70	0	112	8	8	2	32	13	.71	8	.278	.389	.447
1991	California	AL	3	2	0	0	0	0	(0	0)	0	0	0	0	0	0	0	0	0	0	0	.00	0	.000	.000	.000

Storm Davis

Pitches: Right **Bats:** Right **Pos:** RP/SP **Ht:** 6' 4" **Wt:** 225 **Born:** 12/26/61 **Age:** 30

				HOW	MUCH	HE	PITCHED			WHAT	HE	GAVE	UP								THE	RESULTS			
Year	Team	Lg	G	GS	CG	GF	IP	BFP	H	R	ER	HR	SH	SF	HB	TBB	IBB	SO	WP	Bk	W	L	Pct.	ShO	Sv	ERA
1982	Baltimore	AL	29	8	1	9	100.2	412	96	40	39	8	4	6	0	28	4	67	2	1	8	4	.667	0	0	3.49
1983	Baltimore	AL	34	29	6	0	200.1	831	180	90	80	14	5	4	2	64	4	125	7	2	13	7	.650	1	0	3.59
1984	Baltimore	AL	35	31	10	3	225	923	205	86	78	7	7	9	5	71	6	105	6	1	14	9	.609	2	1	3.12
1985	Baltimore	AL	31	28	8	0	175	750	172	92	88	11	3	3	1	70	5	93	2	1	10	8	.556	1	0	4.53
1986	Baltimore	AL	25	25	2	0	154	657	166	70	62	16	3	2	0	49	2	96	5	0	9	12	.429	0	0	3.62
1987	2 ML Teams		26	15	0	5	93	420	98	61	54	8	2	3	2	47	6	65	9	1	3	8	.273	0	0	5.23
1988	Oakland	AL	33	33	1	0	201.2	872	211	86	83	16	3	8	1	91	2	127	16	2	16	7	.696	0	3	3.70
1989	Oakland	AL	31	31	1	0	169.1	733	187	91	82	19	5	7	3	68	1	91	8	1	19	7	.731	0	0	4.36
1990	Kansas City	AL	21	20	0	0	112	498	129	66	59	9	1	3	0	35	1	62	8	1	7	10	.412	0	0	4.74
1991	Kansas City	AL	51	9	1	22	114.1	515	140	69	63	11	6	4	1	46	9	53	1	0	3	9	.250	1	2	4.96
1987	San Diego	NL	21	10	0	5	62.2	292	70	48	43	5	2	2	2	36	6	37	7	1	2	7	.222	0	0	6.18
	Oakland	AL	5	5	0	0	30.1	128	28	13	11	3	0	1	0	11	0	28	2	0	1	1	.500	0	0	3.26
	10 ML YEARS		316	229	30	39	1545.1	6611	1584	751	688	119	39	49	15	569	40	884	64	10	102	81	.557	5	3	4.01

Andre Dawson

Bats: Right **Throws:** Right **Pos:** RF **Ht:** 6' 3" **Wt:** 195 **Born:** 07/10/54 **Age:** 37

						BATTING														BASERUNNING				PERCENTAGES		
Year	Team	Lg	G	AB	H	2B	3B	HR	(Hm	Rd)	TB	R	RBI	TBB	IBB	SO	HBP	SH	SF	SB	CS	SB%	GDP	Avg	OBP	SLG
1976	Montreal	NL	24	85	20	4	1	0	(0	0)	26	9	7	5	1	13	0	2	0	1	2	.33	2	.235	.278	.306
1977	Montreal	NL	139	525	148	26	9	19	(7	12)	249	64	65	34	4	93	2	1	4	21	7	.75	6	.282	.326	.474
1978	Montreal	NL	157	609	154	24	8	25	(12	13)	269	84	72	30	3	128	12	4	5	28	11	.72	7	.253	.299	.442
1979	Montreal	NL	155	639	176	24	12	25	(13	12)	299	90	92	27	5	115	6	8	4	35	10	.78	10	.275	.309	.468
1980	Montreal	NL	151	577	178	41	7	17	(7	10)	284	96	87	44	7	69	6	1	10	34	9	.79	9	.308	.358	.492
1981	Montreal	NL	103	394	119	21	3	24	(9	15)	218	71	64	35	14	50	7	0	5	26	4	.87	6	.302	.365	.553
1982	Montreal	NL	148	608	183	37	7	23	(9	14)	303	107	83	34	4	96	8	4	6	39	10	.80	8	.301	.343	.498
1983	Montreal	NL	159	633	189	36	10	32	(10	22)	341	104	113	38	12	81	9	0	18	25	11	.69	14	.299	.338	.539
1984	Montreal	NL	138	533	132	23	6	17	(6	11)	218	73	86	41	2	80	2	1	6	13	5	.72	12	.248	.301	.409

1985 Montreal	NL	139	529	135	27	2	23	(11	12)	235	65	91	29	8	92	4	1	7	13	4	.76	12	.255	.295	.444
1986 Montreal	NL	130	496	141	32	2	20	(11	9)	237	65	78	37	11	79	6	1	6	18	12	.60	13	.284	.338	.478
1987 Chicago	NL	153	621	178	24	2	49	(27	22)	353	90	137	32	7	103	7	0	2	11	3	.79	15	.287	.328	.568
1988 Chicago	NL	157	591	179	31	8	24	(12	12)	298	78	79	37	12	73	4	1	7	12	4	.75	13	.303	.344	.504
1989 Chicago	NL	118	416	105	18	6	21	(6	15)	198	62	77	35	13	62	1	0	7	8	5	.62	16	.252	.307	.476
1990 Chicago	NL	147	529	164	28	5	27	(14	13)	283	72	100	42	21	65	2	0	8	16	2	.89	12	.310	.358	.535
1991 Chicago	NL	149	563	153	21	4	31	(22	9)	275	69	104	22	3	80	5	0	6	4	5	.44	10	.272	.302	.488
16 ML YEARS		2167	8348	2354	417	92	377	(176	201)	4086	1199	1335	522	127	1279	81	24	101	304	104	.75	163	.282	.327	.489

Ken Dayley

Pitches: Left **Bats:** Left **Pos:** RP **Ht:** 6' 0" **Wt:** 180 **Born:** 02/25/59 **Age:** 33

			HOW MUCH HE PITCHED						WHAT HE GAVE UP									THE RESULTS					
Year Team	Lg	G	GS	CG	GF	IP	BFP	H	R	ER	HR	SH	SF	HB	TBB	IBB	SO	WP	Bk	W	L	Pct.	ShO	Sv	ERA
1982 Atlanta	NL	20	11	0	3	71.1	313	79	39	36	9	7	5	0	25	2	34	2	0	5	6	.455	0	0	4.54
1983 Atlanta	NL	24	16	0	3	104.2	436	100	59	50	12	3	3	2	39	2	70	3	0	5	8	.385	0	0	4.30
1984 2 ML Teams		7	6	0	1	23.2	124	44	28	21	6	4	0	1	11	1	10	0	0	0	5	.000	0	0	7.99
1985 St. Louis	NL	57	0	0	27	65.1	271	65	24	20	2	4	2	0	18	9	62	4	0	4	4	.500	0	11	2.76
1986 St. Louis	NL	31	0	0	13	38.2	170	42	19	14	1	4	1	1	11	3	33	0	0	0	3	.000	0	5	3.26
1987 St. Louis	NL	53	0	0	29	61	260	52	21	18	2	2	1	2	33	8	63	5	0	9	5	.643	0	4	2.66
1988 St. Louis	NL	54	0	0	21	55.1	226	48	20	17	2	4	1	1	19	7	38	2	0	2	7	.222	0	5	2.77
1989 St. Louis	NL	71	0	0	28	75.1	310	63	26	24	3	3	1	0	30	10	40	2	1	4	3	.571	0	12	2.87
1990 St. Louis	NL	58	0	0	17	73.1	307	63	32	29	5	2	5	0	30	7	51	6	0	4	4	.500	0	2	3.56
1991 Toronto	AL	8	0	0	3	4.1	26	7	3	3	0	0	1	1	5	0	3	2	0	0	0	.000	0	0	6.23
1984 Atlanta	NL	4	4	0	0	18.2	92	28	18	11	5	3	0	1	6	1	10	0	0	0	3	.000	0	0	5.30
St. Louis	NL	3	2	0	1	5	32	16	10	10	1	1	0	0	5	0	0	0	0	0	2	.000	0	0	18.00
10 ML YEARS		383	33	0	145	573	2443	563	271	232	42	33	20	8	221	49	404	26	1	33	45	.423	0	39	3.64

Francisco de la Rosa

Pitches: Right **Bats:** Both **Pos:** RP **Ht:** 5'11" **Wt:** 185 **Born:** 03/03/66 **Age:** 26

			HOW MUCH HE PITCHED						WHAT HE GAVE UP									THE RESULTS					
Year Team	Lg	G	GS	CG	GF	IP	BFP	H	R	ER	HR	SH	SF	HB	TBB	IBB	SO	WP	Bk	W	L	Pct.	ShO	Sv	ERA
1985 Blue Jays	R	16	0	0	13	31	148	43	24	19	1	2	4	2	5	1	19	0	2	0	1	.000	0	1	5.52
1988 Hagerstown	A	29	1	0	16	41	182	34	21	21	2	1	2	1	29	4	47	0	2	3	4	.429	0	2	4.61
1989 Frederick	A	23	0	0	19	22.2	101	17	9	6	1	0	1	2	11	2	31	0	0	3	4	.429	0	5	2.38
Hagerstown	AA	18	0	0	15	29.2	133	27	15	15	1	3	1	1	20	0	34	0	0	1	1	.500	0	8	4.55
1990 Hagerstown	AA	23	20	2	2	131	531	97	42	30	5	3	4	4	51	0	105	1	1	9	5	.643	0	0	2.06
Rochester	AAA	2	0	0	1	0.2	4	0	0	0	0	0	0	0	1	0	1	0	0	0	0	.000	0	1	0.00
1991 Rochester	AAA	38	4	0	16	84.1	342	71	28	25	6	2	1	0	33	1	61	2	2	4	1	.800	0	3	2.67
1991 Baltimore	AL	2	0	0	1	4	20	6	3	2	0	0	1	0	2	0	1	0	0	0	0	.000	0	0	4.50

Luis de los Santos

Bats: Right **Throws:** Right **Pos:** DH **Ht:** 6' 5" **Wt:** 225 **Born:** 12/29/66 **Age:** 25

			BATTING									BASERUNNING				PERCENTAGES		
Year Team	Lg	G	AB	H	2B	3B	HR	(Hm | Rd)	TB	R	RBI	TBB	IBB	SO	HBP	SH	SF	SB	CS	SB%	GDP	Avg	OBP	SLG
1988 Kansas City	AL	11	22	2	1	1	0	(0 | 0)	5	1	1	4	0	4	0	0	0	0	0	.00	3	.091	.231	.227
1989 Kansas City	AL	28	87	22	3	1	0	(0 | 0)	27	6	6	5	0	14	0	0	0	0	0	.00	2	.253	.293	.310
1991 Detroit	AL	16	30	5	2	0	0	(0 | 0)	7	1	0	2	0	4	0	0	0	0	0	.00	2	.167	.219	.233
3 ML YEARS		55	139	29	6	2	0	(0 | 0)	39	8	7	11	0	22	0	0	0	0	0	.00	7	.209	.267	.281

Steve Decker

Bats: Right **Throws:** Right **Pos:** C **Ht:** 6' 3" **Wt:** 205 **Born:** 10/25/65 **Age:** 26

			BATTING									BASERUNNING				PERCENTAGES		
Year Team	Lg	G	AB	H	2B	3B	HR	(Hm	Rd)	TB	R	RBI	TBB	IBB	SO	HBP	SH	SF	SB	CS	SB%	GDP	Avg	OBP	SLG
1988 Everett	A	13	42	22	2	0	2	--	--	30	11	13	7	0	5	1	0	3	0	0	.00	1	.524	.566	.714
San Jose	A	47	175	56	9	0	4	--	--	77	31	34	21	1	21	1	1	0	2	0	.00	4	.320	.396	.440
1989 San Jose	A	64	225	65	12	0	3	--	--	86	27	46	44	3	36	0	0	5	8	5	.62	9	.289	.398	.382
Shreveport	AA	44	142	46	8	0	1	--	--	57	19	18	11	0	24	0	1	1	0	3	.00	5	.324	.370	.401
1990 Shreveport	AA	116	403	118	22	1	15	--	--	187	52	80	40	2	64	2	0	7	3	7	.30	11	.293	.354	.464
1991 Phoenix	AAA	31	111	28	5	1	6			53	20	14	13	0	29				0	0	.00	1	.252	.336	.477
1990 San Francisco	NL	15	54	16	2	0	3	(1	2)	27	5	8	1	0	10	0	1	0	0	0	.00	1	.296	.309	.500
1991 San Francisco	NL	79	233	48	7	1	5	(4	1)	72	11	24	16	1	44	3	2	4	0	1	.00	7	.206	.262	.309
2 ML YEARS		94	287	64	9	1	8	(5	3)	99	16	32	17	1	54	3	3	4	0	1	.00	8	.223	.270	.345

Rob Deer

Bats: Right **Throws:** Right **Pos:** RF **Ht:** 6' 3" **Wt:** 225 **Born:** 09/29/60 **Age:** 31

Year	Team	Lg	G	AB	H	2B	3B	HR	(Hm	Rd)	TB	R	RBI	TBB	IBB	SO	HBP	SH	SF	SB	CS	SB%	GDP	Avg	OBP	SLG
1984	San Francisco	NL	13	24	4	0	0	3	(2	1)	13	5	3	7	0	10	1	0	0	1	1	.50	0	.167	.375	.542
1985	San Francisco	NL	78	162	30	5	1	8	(5	3)	61	22	20	23	0	71	0	0	2	0	1	.00	0	.185	.283	.377
1986	Milwaukee	AL	134	466	108	17	3	33	(19	14)	230	75	86	72	3	179	3	2	3	5	2	.71	4	.232	.336	.494
1987	Milwaukee	AL	134	474	113	15	2	28	(11	17)	216	71	80	86	6	186	5	0	1	12	4	.75	4	.238	.360	.456
1988	Milwaukee	AL	135	492	124	24	0	23	(12	11)	217	71	85	51	4	153	7	0	5	9	5	.64	4	.252	.328	.441
1989	Milwaukee	AL	130	466	98	18	2	26	(15	11)	198	72	65	60	5	158	4	0	2	4	8	.33	8	.210	.305	.425
1990	Milwaukee	AL	134	440	92	15	1	27	(11	16)	190	57	69	64	6	147	4	0	3	2	3	.40	0	.209	.313	.432
1991	Detroit	AL	134	448	80	14	2	25	(12	13)	173	64	64	89	1	175	0	0	2	1	3	.25	3	.179	.314	.386
	8 ML YEARS		892	2972	649	108	11	173	(87	86)	1298	437	472	452	25	1079	24	2	18	34	27	.56	23	.218	.325	.437

Jose DeJesus

Pitches: Right **Bats:** Right **Pos:** SP **Ht:** 6' 5" **Wt:** 213 **Born:** 01/06/65 **Age:** 27

Year	Team	Lg	G	GS	CG	GF	IP	BFP	H	R	ER	HR	SH	SF	HB	TBB	IBB	SO	WP	Bk	W	L	Pct.	ShO	Sv	ERA
1988	Kansas City	AL	2	1	0	0	2.2	19	6	10	8	0	0	0	0	5	1	2	0	0	0	1	.000	0	0	27.00
1989	Kansas City	AL	3	1	0	1	8	37	7	4	4	1	0	0	0	8	0	2	0	0	0	0	.000	0	0	4.50
1990	Philadelphia	NL	22	22	3	0	130	544	97	63	54	10	8	0	2	73	3	87	4	0	7	8	.467	1	0	3.74
1991	Philadelphia	NL	31	29	3	1	181.2	801	147	74	69	7	11	3	4	128	4	118	10	0	10	9	.526	0	1	3.42
	4 ML YEARS		58	53	6	2	322.1	1401	257	151	135	18	19	3	6	214	8	209	14	0	17	18	.486	1	1	3.77

Jose DeLeon

Pitches: Right **Bats:** Right **Pos:** SP **Ht:** 6' 3" **Wt:** 215 **Born:** 12/20/60 **Age:** 31

Year	Team	Lg	G	GS	CG	GF	IP	BFP	H	R	ER	HR	SH	SF	HB	TBB	IBB	SO	WP	Bk	W	L	Pct.	ShO	Sv	ERA
1983	Pittsburgh	NL	15	15	3	0	108	438	75	36	34	5	4	3	1	47	2	118	5	2	7	3	.700	2	0	2.83
1984	Pittsburgh	NL	30	28	5	0	192.1	795	147	86	80	10	7	7	3	92	5	153	6	2	7	13	.350	1	0	3.74
1985	Pittsburgh	NL	31	25	1	5	162.2	700	138	93	85	15	7	4	3	89	4	149	7	1	2	19	.095	0	3	4.70
1986	2 ML Teams		22	14	1	5	95.1	408	66	46	41	9	5	1	5	59	3	79	7	0	5	8	.385	0	1	3.87
1987	Chicago	AL	33	31	2	0	206	889	177	106	92	24	6	6	10	97	4	153	6	1	11	12	.478	0	0	4.02
1988	St. Louis	NL	34	34	3	0	225.1	940	198	95	92	13	10	7	2	86	7	208	10	0	13	10	.565	1	0	3.67
1989	St. Louis	NL	36	36	5	0	244.2	972	173	96	83	16	5	3	6	80	5	201	2	0	16	12	.571	3	0	3.05
1990	St. Louis	NL	32	32	0	0	182.2	793	168	96	90	15	11	8	5	86	9	164	5	0	7	19	.269	0	0	4.43
1991	St. Louis	NL	28	28	1	0	162.2	679	144	57	49	15	5	4	6	61	1	118	1	1	5	9	.357	0	0	2.71
1986	Pittsburgh	NL	9	1	0	5	16.1	83	17	16	15	2	1	0	1	17	3	11	1	0	1	3	.250	0	1	8.27
	Chicago	AL	13	13	1	0	79	325	49	30	26	7	4	1	4	42	0	68	6	0	4	5	.444	0	0	2.96
	9 ML YEARS		261	243	21	10	1579.2	6614	1286	711	646	122	60	43	41	697	39	1343	49	7	73	105	.410	7	4	3.68

Rich Delucia

Pitches: Right **Bats:** Right **Pos:** SP **Ht:** 6' 0" **Wt:** 180 **Born:** 10/07/64 **Age:** 27

Year	Team	Lg	G	GS	CG	GF	IP	BFP	H	R	ER	HR	SH	SF	HB	TBB	IBB	SO	WP	Bk	W	L	Pct.	ShO	Sv	ERA
1986	Bellingham	A	13	11	1	0	74	0	44	20	14	4	0	0	1	24	0	69	3	0	8	2	.800	1	0	1.70
1988	San Berndno	A	22	22	0	0	127.2	541	110	57	44	4	2	6	1	59	3	118	6	2	7	8	.467	0	0	3.10
1989	Williamsprt	AA	10	10	0	0	54.2	234	59	28	23	5	3	2	1	13	0	41	5	0	3	4	.429	0	0	3.79
1990	San Berndno	A	5	5	1	0	30.2	116	19	9	7	4	1	0	4	3	0	35	1	0	4	1	.800	0	0	2.05
	Williamsprt	AA	18	18	2	0	115	447	92	30	27	7	3	3	2	30	2	76	1	0	6	6	.500	1	0	2.11
	Calgary	AAA	5	5	1	0	32.1	139	30	17	13	2	0	3	2	12	0	23	3	0	2	2	.500	0	0	3.62
1990	Seattle	AL	5	5	1	0	36	144	30	9	8	2	2	0	0	9	0	20	0	0	1	2	.333	0	0	2.00
1991	Seattle	AL	32	31	0	0	182	779	176	107	103	31	5	14	4	78	4	98	10	0	12	13	.480	0	0	5.09
	2 ML YEARS		37	36	1	0	218	923	206	116	111	33	7	14	4	87	4	118	10	0	13	15	.464	0	0	4.58

Rick Dempsey

Bats: Right **Throws:** Right **Pos:** C **Ht:** 6' 0" **Wt:** 184 **Born:** 09/13/49 **Age:** 42

Year	Team	Lg	G	AB	H	2B	3B	HR	(Hm	Rd)	TB	R	RBI	TBB	IBB	SO	HBP	SH	SF	SB	CS	SB%	GDP	Avg	OBP	SLG
1969	Minnesota	AL	5	6	3	1	0	0	(0	0)	4	1	0	1	0	0	0	0	0	0	0	.00	0	.500	.571	.667
1970	Minnesota	AL	5	7	0	0	0	0	(0	0)	0	1	0	1	0	1	0	0	0	0	0	.00	1	.000	.125	.000
1971	Minnesota	AL	6	13	4	1	0	0	(0	0)	5	2	0	1	0	0	0	0	0	0	0	.00	0	.308	.357	.385
1972	Minnesota	AL	25	40	8	1	0	0	(0	0)	9	0	0	6	0	8	0	1	0	0	0	.00	2	.200	.304	.225
1973	New York	AL	6	11	2	0	0	0	(0	0)	2	0	0	1	0	3	0	1	0	0	0	.00	1	.182	.250	.182
1974	New York	AL	43	109	26	3	0	2	(1	1)	35	12	12	8	0	7	0	1	1	1	0	1.00	5	.239	.288	.321

Year	Team	Lg	G	AB	H	2B	3B	HR	(Hm	Rd)	TB	R	RBI	TBB	IBB	SO	HBP	SH	SF	SB	CS	SB%	GDP	Avg	OBP	SLG
1975	New York	AL	71	145	38	8	0	1	(0	1)	49	18	11	21	1	15	0	3	1	0	0	.00	5	.262	.353	.338
1976	2 ML Teams		80	216	42	2	0	0	(0	0)	44	12	12	18	0	21	2	4	0	1	1	.50	2	.194	.263	.204
1977	Baltimore	AL	91	270	61	7	4	3	(1	2)	85	27	34	34	1	34	2	5	3	2	3	.40	9	.226	.314	.315
1978	Baltimore	AL	136	441	114	25	0	6	(4	2)	157	41	32	48	2	54	0	3	6	7	3	.70	11	.259	.327	.356
1979	Baltimore	AL	124	368	88	23	0	6	(1	5)	129	48	41	38	1	37	0	3	4	0	1	.00	12	.239	.307	.351
1980	Baltimore	AL	119	362	95	26	3	9	(5	4)	154	51	40	36	1	45	3	4	1	3	1	.75	11	.262	.333	.425
1981	Baltimore	AL	92	251	54	10	1	6	(4	2)	84	24	15	32	1	36	1	3	0	0	1	.00	5	.215	.306	.335
1982	Baltimore	AL	125	344	88	15	1	5	(2	3)	120	35	36	46	1	37	0	7	5	0	3	.00	10	.256	.339	.349
1983	Baltimore	AL	128	347	80	16	2	4	(3	1)	112	33	32	40	1	54	3	5	5	1	1	.50	9	.231	.311	.323
1984	Baltimore	AL	109	330	76	11	0	11	(6	5)	120	37	34	40	0	58	1	5	4	1	2	.33	11	.230	.312	.364
1985	Baltimore	AL	132	362	92	19	0	12	(4	8)	147	54	52	50	0	87	1	5	2	0	1	.00	2	.254	.345	.406
1986	Baltimore	AL	122	327	68	15	1	13	(7	6)	124	42	29	45	0	78	3	7	0	1	0	1.00	5	.208	.309	.379
1987	Cleveland	AL	60	141	25	10	0	1	(1	0)	38	16	9	23	0	29	1	4	1	0	0	.00	4	.177	.295	.270
1988	Los Angeles	NL	77	167	42	13	0	7	(3	4)	76	25	30	25	0	44	0	0	6	1	0	1.00	4	.251	.338	.455
1989	Los Angeles	NL	79	151	27	7	0	4	(2	2)	46	16	16	30	3	37	1	1	0	1	0	1.00	5	.179	.319	.305
1990	Los Angeles	NL	62	128	25	5	0	2	(2	0)	36	13	15	23	0	29	0	0	0	1	0	1.00	8	.195	.318	.281
1991	Milwaukee	AL	60	147	34	5	0	4	(2	2)	51	15	21	23	1	20	0	1	3	0	2	.00	7	.231	.329	.347
1976	New York	AL	21	42	5	0	0	0	(0	0)	5	1	2	5	0	4	0	1	0	0	0	.00	0	.119	.213	.119
	Baltimore		59	174	37	2	0	0	(0	0)	39	11	10	13	0	17	2	3	0	1	1	.50	2	.213	.275	.224
	23 ML YEARS		1757	4683	1092	223	12	96	(48	48)	1627	523	471	590	13	735	18	63	42	20	19	.51	130	.233	.319	.347

Jim Deshaies

Pitches: Left **Bats:** Left **Pos:** SP **Ht:** 6' 4" **Wt:** 220 **Born:** 06/23/60 **Age:** 32

| | | | HOW MUCH HE PITCHED | | | | | WHAT HE GAVE UP | | | | | | | | | | | THE RESULTS | | | | | |
Year	Team	Lg	G	GS	CG	GF	IP	BFP	H	R	ER	HR	SH	SF	HB	TBB	IBB	SO	WP	Bk	W	L	Pct.	ShO	Sv	ERA
1984	New York	AL	2	2	0	0	7	40	14	9	9	1	0	1	0	7	0	5	0	0	0	1	.000	0	0	11.57
1985	Houston	NL	2	0	0	0	3	10	1	0	0	0	0	0	0	0	0	2	0	0	0	0	.000	0	0	0.00
1986	Houston	NL	26	26	1	0	144	599	124	58	52	16	4	3	2	59	2	128	0	7	12	5	.706	1	0	3.25
1987	Houston	NL	26	25	1	0	152	648	149	81	78	22	9	3	0	57	7	104	4	5	11	6	.647	0	0	4.62
1988	Houston	NL	31	31	3	0	207	847	164	77	69	20	8	13	2	72	5	127	1	6	11	14	.440	2	0	3.00
1989	Houston	NL	34	34	6	0	225.2	928	180	80	73	15	11	5	4	79	8	153	8	1	15	10	.600	3	0	2.91
1990	Houston	NL	34	34	2	0	209.1	881	180	88	81	21	17	12	8	84	9	119	3	3	7	12	.368	0	0	3.78
1991	Houston	NL	28	28	1	0	161	686	156	90	89	19	4	7	1	72	5	98	0	5	5	12	.294	0	0	4.98
	8 ML YEARS		183	180	14	0	1109	4639	974	488	458	114	53	44	17	430	36	736	16	27	61	60	.504	6	0	3.72

Delino DeShields

Bats: Left **Throws:** Right **Pos:** 2B **Ht:** 6' 1" **Wt:** 170 **Born:** 01/15/69 **Age:** 23

| | | | BATTING | | | | | | | | | | | | | | | | BASERUNNING | | | | PERCENTAGES | | |
Year	Team	Lg	G	AB	H	2B	3B	HR	(Hm	Rd)	TB	R	RBI	TBB	IBB	SO	HBP	SH	SF	SB	CS	SB%	GDP	Avg	OBP	SLG
1987	Expos	R	31	111	24	5	2	1	--	--	36	17	4	21	0	30	2	0	0	16	5	.76	0	.216	.351	.324
	Jamestown	A	34	96	21	1	2	1	--	--	29	16	5	24	1	28	1	2	1	14	4	.78	0	.219	.377	.302
1988	Rockford	A	129	460	116	26	6	12	--	--	190	97	46	95	3	110	2	2	3	59	18	.77	4	.252	.380	.413
1989	Jacksnville	AA	93	307	83	10	6	3	--	--	114	55	35	76	0	80	1	4	3	37	12	.76	3	.270	.413	.371
	Indianapls	AAA	47	181	47	8	4	2	--	--	69	29	14	16	0	53	0	1	1	16	7	.70	0	.260	.320	.381
1990	Montreal	NL	129	499	144	28	6	4	(3	1)	196	69	45	66	3	96	4	1	2	42	22	.66	10	.289	.375	.393
1991	Montreal	NL	151	563	134	15	4	10	(3	7)	187	83	51	95	2	151	2	8	5	56	23	.71	6	.238	.347	.332
	2 ML YEARS		280	1062	278	43	10	14	(6	8)	383	152	96	161	5	247	6	9	7	98	45	.69	16	.262	.360	.361

Mike Devereaux

Bats: Right **Throws:** Right **Pos:** CF **Ht:** 6' 0" **Wt:** 193 **Born:** 04/10/63 **Age:** 29

| | | | BATTING | | | | | | | | | | | | | | | | BASERUNNING | | | | PERCENTAGES | | |
Year	Team	Lg	G	AB	H	2B	3B	HR	(Hm	Rd)	TB	R	RBI	TBB	IBB	SO	HBP	SH	SF	SB	CS	SB%	GDP	Avg	OBP	SLG
1987	Los Angeles	NL	19	54	12	3	0	0	(0	0)	15	7	4	3	0	10	0	1	0	3	1	.75	0	.222	.263	.278
1988	Los Angeles	NL	30	43	5	1	0	0	(0	0)	6	4	2	2	0	10	0	0	0	0	1	.00	0	.116	.156	.140
1989	Baltimore	AL	122	391	104	14	3	8	(4	4)	148	55	46	36	0	60	2	2	3	22	11	.67	7	.266	.329	.379
1990	Baltimore	AL	108	367	88	18	1	12	(6	6)	144	48	49	28	0	48	0	4	4	13	12	.52	10	.240	.291	.392
1991	Baltimore	AL	149	608	158	27	10	19	(10	9)	262	82	59	47	2	115	2	7	4	16	9	.64	13	.260	.313	.431
	5 ML YEARS		428	1463	367	63	14	39	(20	19)	575	196	160	116	2	243	4	14	11	54	34	.61	30	.251	.306	.393

Mario Diaz

Bats: Right **Throws:** Right **Pos:** SS/2B **Ht:** 5'10" **Wt:** 160 **Born:** 01/10/62 **Age:** 30

| | | | BATTING | | | | | | | | | | | | | | | | BASERUNNING | | | | PERCENTAGES | | |
Year	Team	Lg	G	AB	H	2B	3B	HR	(Hm	Rd)	TB	R	RBI	TBB	IBB	SO	HBP	SH	SF	SB	CS	SB%	GDP	Avg	OBP	SLG
1987	Seattle	AL	11	23	7	0	1	0	(0	0)	9	4	3	0	0	4	0	0	0	0	0	.00	0	.304	.304	.391
1988	Seattle	AL	28	72	22	5	0	0	(0	0)	27	6	9	3	0	5	0	0	1	0	0	.00	0	.306	.329	.375
1989	Seattle	AL	52	74	10	0	0	1	(0	1)	13	9	7	7	0	7	0	0	5	0	0	.00	2	.135	.210	.176

Year	Team	Lg	G	AB	H	2B	3B	HR	(Hm	Rd)	TB	R	RBI	TBB	IBB	SO	HBP	SH	SF	SB	CS	SB%	GDP	Avg	OBP	SLG
1990	New York	NL	16	22	3	1	0	0	(0	0)	4	0	1	0	0	3	0	0	1	0	0	.00	0	.136	.130	.182
1991	Texas	AL	96	182	48	7	0	1	(1	0)	58	24	22	15	0	18	0	4	1	0	1	.00	5	.264	.318	.319
5 ML YEARS			203	373	90	13	1	2	(1	1)	111	43	42	25	0	37	0	9	3	0	1	.00	10	.241	.287	.298

Rob Dibble

Pitches: Right **Bats:** Left **Pos:** RP   Ht: 6' 4" Wt: 230 **Born:** 01/24/64 **Age:** 28

			HOW MUCH HE PITCHED						WHAT HE GAVE UP									THE RESULTS					
Year	Team	Lg	G	GS	CG	GF	IP	BFP	H	R	ER	HR	SH	SF	HB	TBB	IBB	SO	WP	Bk	W	L	Pct.	ShO	Sv	ERA
1988	Cincinnati	NL	37	0	0	6	59.1	235	43	12	12	2	2	3	1	21	5	59	3	2	1	1	.500	0	0	1.82
1989	Cincinnati	NL	74	0	0	18	99	401	62	23	23	4	3	4	3	39	11	141	3	1	10	5	.667	0	2	2.09
1990	Cincinnati	NL	68	0	0	29	98	384	62	22	19	3	4	6	1	34	3	136	3	1	8	3	.727	0	11	1.74
1991	Cincinnati	NL	67	0	0	57	82.1	334	67	32	29	5	5	3	0	25	2	124	5	0	3	5	.375	0	31	3.17
4 ML YEARS			246	0	0	110	338.2	1354	234	89	83	14	14	16	5	119	21	460	18	3	22	14	.611	0	44	2.21

Gary Disarcina

Bats: Right **Throws:** Right **Pos:** SS   Ht: 6' 1" Wt: 178 **Born:** 11/19/67 **Age:** 24

			BATTING															BASERUNNING				PERCENTAGES		
Year	Team	Lg	G	AB	H	2B	3B	HR	(Hm	Rd)	TB	R	RBI	TBB	IBB	SO	HBP	SH	SF	SB	CS	SB%	GDP	Avg	OBP	SLG
1988	Bend	A	71	295	90	11	5	2	--	--	117	40	39	27	1	34	2	4	4	7	4	.64	6	.305	.363	.397
1989	Midland	AA	126	441	126	18	7	4	--	--	170	65	54	24	3	54	4	7	5	11	6	.65	17	.286	.325	.385
1990	Edmonton	AAA	97	330	70	12	2	4	--	--	98	46	37	25	0	46	4	5	2	5	3	.63	6	.212	.274	.297
1991	Edmonton	AAA	119	390	121	21	4	4	--	--	162	61	58	29	1	32	9	4	3	16	5	.76	12	.310	.369	.415
1989	California	AL	2	0	0	0	0	0	(0	0)	0	0	0	0	0	0	0	0	0	0	0	.00	0	.000	.000	.000
1990	California	AL	18	57	8	1	1	0	(0	0)	11	8	0	3	0	10	0	1	0	1	0	1.00	3	.140	.183	.193
1991	California	AL	18	57	12	2	0	0	(0	0)	14	5	3	3	0	4	2	2	0	0	0	.00	0	.211	.274	.246
3 ML YEARS			38	114	20	3	1	0	(0	0)	25	13	3	6	0	14	2	3	0	1	0	1.00	3	.175	.230	.219

Chris Donnels

Bats: Left **Throws:** Right **Pos:** 1B/3B   Ht: 6' 0" Wt: 185 **Born:** 04/21/66 **Age:** 26

			BATTING															BASERUNNING				PERCENTAGES		
Year	Team	Lg	G	AB	H	2B	3B	HR	(Hm	Rd)	TB	R	RBI	TBB	IBB	SO	HBP	SH	SF	SB	CS	SB%	GDP	Avg	OBP	SLG
1987	Kingsport	R	26	86	26	4	0	3	--	--	39	18	16	17	1	17	1	0	2	4	1	.80	1	.302	.415	.453
	Columbia	A	41	136	35	7	0	2	--	--	48	20	17	24	1	27	1	0	1	3	1	.75	1	.257	.370	.353
1988	St. Lucie	A	65	198	43	14	2	3	--	--	70	25	22	32	1	53	2	2	1	4	3	.57	4	.217	.330	.354
	Columbia	A	42	133	32	6	0	2	--	--	44	19	13	30	2	25	1	2	1	5	0	1.00	3	.241	.382	.331
1989	St.Lucie	A	117	386	121	23	1	17	--	--	197	70	78	83	15	65	6	2	3	18	4	.82	5	.313	.439	.510
1990	Jackson	AA	130	419	114	24	0	12	--	--	174	66	63	111	5	81	1	5	7	11	8	.58	12	.272	.420	.415
1991	Tidewater	AAA	84	287	87	18	2	8	--	--	133	45	56	62	3	55	1	0	3	1	4	.20	13	.303	.425	.463
1991	New York	NL	37	89	20	2	0	0	(0	0)	22	7	5	14	1	19	0	1	0	1	1	.50	2	.225	.330	.247

John Dopson

Pitches: Right **Bats:** Left **Pos:** RP   Ht: 6' 4" Wt: 225 **Born:** 07/14/63 **Age:** 28

			HOW MUCH HE PITCHED						WHAT HE GAVE UP									THE RESULTS					
Year	Team	Lg	G	GS	CG	GF	IP	BFP	H	R	ER	HR	SH	SF	HB	TBB	IBB	SO	WP	Bk	W	L	Pct.	ShO	Sv	ERA
1985	Montreal	NL	4	3	0	0	13	70	25	17	16	4	0	0	0	4	0	4	2	0	0	2	.000	0	0	11.08
1988	Montreal	NL	26	26	1	0	168.2	704	150	69	57	15	5	2	1	58	3	101	3	1	3	11	.214	0	0	3.04
1989	Boston	AL	29	28	2	0	169.1	727	166	84	75	14	5	4	2	69	0	95	7	15	12	8	.600	0	0	3.99
1990	Boston	AL	4	4	0	0	17.2	75	13	7	4	2	0	1	0	9	0	9	0	0	0	0	.000	0	0	2.04
1991	Boston	AL	1	0	0	1	1	6	2	2	2	0	0	1	0	1	0	0	0	0	0	0	.000	0	0	18.00
5 ML YEARS			64	61	3	1	369.2	1582	356	179	154	35	10	8	3	141	3	209	12	16	15	21	.417	0	0	3.75

Billy Doran

Bats: Both **Throws:** Right **Pos:** 2B   Ht: 6' 0" Wt: 175 **Born:** 05/28/58 **Age:** 34

			BATTING															BASERUNNING				PERCENTAGES		
Year	Team	Lg	G	AB	H	2B	3B	HR	(Hm	Rd)	TB	R	RBI	TBB	IBB	SO	HBP	SH	SF	SB	CS	SB%	GDP	Avg	OBP	SLG
1982	Houston	NL	26	97	27	3	0	0	(0	0)	30	11	6	11	0	11	0	0	1	5	0	1.00	6	.278	.304	.309
1983	Houston	NL	154	535	145	12	7	8	(1	7)	195	70	39	86	11	67	0	7	1	12	12	.50	6	.271	.371	.364
1984	Houston	NL	147	548	143	18	11	4	(2	2)	195	92	41	66	7	69	2	7	3	21	12	.64	6	.261	.341	.356
1985	Houston	NL	148	578	166	31	6	14	(5	9)	251	84	59	71	6	69	0	3	5	23	15	.61	10	.287	.362	.434
1986	Houston	NL	145	550	152	29	3	6	(3	3)	205	92	37	81	7	57	2	4	5	42	19	.69	10	.276	.368	.373
1987	Houston	NL	162	625	177	23	3	16	(7	9)	254	82	79	82	3	64	3	2	7	31	11	.74	11	.283	.365	.406
1988	Houston	NL	132	480	119	18	1	7	(2	5)	160	66	53	65	3	60	1	4	2	17	4	.81	7	.248	.338	.333
1989	Houston	NL	142	507	111	25	2	8	(3	5)	164	65	58	59	2	63	2	3	3	22	3	.88	8	.219	.301	.323
1990	2 ML Teams		126	403	121	29	2	7	(4	3)	175	59	37	79	2	58	0	1	5	23	9	.72	3	.300	.411	.434
1991	Cincinnati	NL	111	361	101	12	2	6	(3	3)	135	51	35	46	1	39	0	0	3	5	4	.56	4	.280	.359	.374
1990	Houston	NL	109	344	99	21	2	6	(3	3)	142	49	32	71	1	53	0	1	5	18	9	.67	2	.288	.405	.413
	Cincinnati	NL	17	59	22	8	0	1	(1	0)	33	10	5	8	1	5	0	0	0	5	0	1.00	1	.373	.448	.559
10 ML YEARS			1293	4684	1262	200	37	76	(30	46)	1764	672	444	639	42	557	10	31	35	201	89	.69	65	.269	.356	.377

55

Brian Dorsett

Bats: Right **Throws:** Right **Pos:** 1B   **Ht:** 6' 3" **Wt:** 215 **Born:** 04/09/61 **Age:** 31

Year Team	Lg	G	AB	H	2B	3B	HR	(Hm	Rd)	TB	R	RBI	TBB	IBB	SO	HBP	SH	SF	SB	CS	SB%	GDP	Avg	OBP	SLG
1987 Cleveland	AL	5	11	3	0	0	1	(1	0)	6	2	3	0	0	3	1	0	0	0	0	.00	0	.273	.333	.545
1988 California	AL	7	11	1	0	0	0	(0	0)	1	0	2	1	0	5	0	0	0	0	0	.00	0	.091	.167	.091
1989 New York	AL	8	22	8	1	0	0	(0	0)	9	3	4	1	0	3	0	0	0	0	0	.00	0	.364	.391	.409
1990 New York	AL	14	35	5	2	0	0	(0	0)	7	2	0	2	0	4	0	0	0	0	0	.00	2	.143	.189	.200
1991 San Diego	NL	11	12	1	0	0	0	(0	0)	1	0	1	0	0	3	0	0	0	0	0	.00	0	.083	.083	.083
5 ML YEARS		45	91	18	3	0	1	(1	0)	24	7	10	4	0	18	1	0	0	0	0	.00	2	.198	.240	.264

Brian Downing

Bats: Right **Throws:** Right **Pos:** DH   **Ht:** 5'10" **Wt:** 194 **Born:** 10/09/50 **Age:** 41

Year Team	Lg	G	AB	H	2B	3B	HR	(Hm	Rd)	TB	R	RBI	TBB	IBB	SO	HBP	SH	SF	SB	CS	SB%	GDP	Avg	OBP	SLG
1973 Chicago	AL	34	73	13	1	0	2	(1	1)	20	5	4	10	1	17	0	2	0	0	0	.00	3	.178	.277	.274
1974 Chicago	AL	108	293	66	12	1	10	(6	4)	110	41	39	51	3	72	2	4	0	0	1	.00	11	.225	.344	.375
1975 Chicago	AL	138	420	101	12	1	7	(5	2)	136	58	41	76	5	75	3	11	6	13	4	.76	12	.240	.356	.324
1976 Chicago	AL	104	317	81	14	0	3	(0	3)	104	38	30	40	0	55	1	4	3	7	3	.70	2	.256	.338	.328
1977 Chicago	AL	69	169	48	4	2	4	(1	3)	68	28	25	34	0	21	2	5	4	1	2	.33	3	.284	.402	.402
1978 California	AL	133	412	105	15	0	7	(2	5)	141	42	46	52	2	47	6	4	2	3	2	.60	14	.255	.345	.342
1979 California	AL	148	509	166	27	3	12	(3	9)	235	87	75	77	4	57	5	3	2	3	3	.50	17	.326	.418	.462
1980 California	AL	30	93	27	6	0	2	(2	0)	39	5	25	12	1	12	0	1	2	0	2	.00	6	.290	.364	.419
1981 California	AL	93	317	79	14	0	9	(6	3)	120	47	41	46	1	35	4	3	0	1	1	.50	11	.249	.351	.379
1982 California	AL	158	623	175	37	2	28	(15	13)	300	109	84	86	1	58	5	3	8	2	1	.67	14	.281	.368	.482
1983 California	AL	113	403	99	15	1	19	(10	9)	173	68	53	62	4	59	5	1	2	1	2	.33	8	.246	.352	.429
1984 California	AL	156	539	148	28	2	23	(9	14)	249	65	91	70	3	66	7	3	9	0	4	.00	18	.275	.360	.462
1985 California	AL	150	520	137	23	1	20	(10	10)	222	80	85	78	3	61	13	5	4	5	3	.63	12	.263	.371	.427
1986 California	AL	152	513	137	27	4	20	(13	7)	232	90	95	90	2	84	17	3	8	4	4	.50	14	.267	.389	.452
1987 California	AL	155	567	154	29	3	29	(11	18)	276	110	77	106	6	85	17	2	3	5	5	.50	10	.272	.400	.487
1988 California	AL	135	484	117	18	2	25	(11	14)	214	80	64	81	5	63	14	5	6	3	4	.43	12	.242	.362	.442
1989 California	AL	142	544	154	25	2	14	(10	4)	225	59	59	56	3	87	6	0	4	0	2	.00	6	.283	.354	.414
1990 California	AL	96	330	90	18	2	14	(11	3)	154	47	51	50	2	45	6	0	4	0	0	.00	11	.273	.374	.467
1991 Texas	AL	123	407	113	17	2	17	(8	9)	185	76	49	58	7	70	8	1	2	1	1	.50	7	.278	.377	.455
19 ML YEARS		2237	7533	2010	342	28	265	(134	131)	3203	1135	1034	1135	53	1069	121	60	69	49	44	.53	190	.267	.369	.425

Kelly Downs

Pitches: Right **Bats:** Right **Pos:** RP/SP   **Ht:** 6' 4" **Wt:** 205 **Born:** 10/25/60 **Age:** 31

Year Team	Lg	G	GS	CG	GF	IP	BFP	H	R	ER	HR	SH	SF	HB	TBB	IBB	SO	WP	Bk	W	L	Pct.	ShO	Sv	ERA
1986 San Francisco	NL	14	14	1	0	88.1	372	78	29	27	5	4	4	3	30	7	64	3	2	4	4	.500	0	0	2.75
1987 San Francisco	NL	41	28	4	4	186	797	185	83	75	14	7	1	4	67	11	137	12	4	12	9	.571	3	1	3.63
1988 San Francisco	NL	27	26	6	0	168	685	140	67	62	11	4	9	3	47	8	118	7	4	13	9	.591	3	0	3.32
1989 San Francisco	NL	18	15	0	1	82.2	349	82	47	44	7	4	4	1	26	4	49	3	3	4	8	.333	0	0	4.79
1990 San Francisco	NL	13	9	0	1	63	265	56	26	24	2	2	1	2	20	4	31	2	1	3	2	.600	0	0	3.43
1991 San Francisco	NL	45	11	0	4	111.2	479	99	59	52	12	4	4	3	53	9	62	4	1	10	4	.714	0	0	4.19
6 ML YEARS		158	103	11	10	699.2	2947	640	311	284	51	25	23	16	243	43	461	31	15	46	36	.561	6	1	3.65

Doug Drabek

Pitches: Right **Bats:** Right **Pos:** SP   **Ht:** 6' 1" **Wt:** 185 **Born:** 07/25/62 **Age:** 29

Year Team	Lg	G	GS	CG	GF	IP	BFP	H	R	ER	HR	SH	SF	HB	TBB	IBB	SO	WP	Bk	W	L	Pct.	ShO	Sv	ERA
1986 New York	AL	27	21	0	2	131.2	561	126	64	60	13	5	2	3	50	1	76	2	0	7	8	.467	0	0	4.10
1987 Pittsburgh	NL	29	28	1	0	176.1	721	165	86	76	22	3	4	0	46	2	120	5	1	11	12	.478	1	0	3.88
1988 Pittsburgh	NL	33	32	3	0	219.1	880	194	83	75	21	7	5	6	50	4	127	4	1	15	7	.682	1	0	3.08
1989 Pittsburgh	NL	35	34	8	1	244.1	994	215	83	76	21	13	7	3	69	3	123	3	0	14	12	.538	5	0	2.80
1990 Pittsburgh	NL	33	33	9	0	231.1	918	190	78	71	15	10	3	3	56	2	131	6	0	22	6	.786	3	0	2.76
1991 Pittsburgh	NL	35	35	5	0	234.2	977	245	92	80	16	12	6	3	62	6	142	5	0	15	14	.517	2	0	3.07
6 ML YEARS		192	183	26	3	1237.2	5051	1135	486	438	108	50	27	18	333	18	719	25	2	84	59	.587	12	0	3.19

Brian Drahman

Pitches: Right **Bats:** Right **Pos:** RP   **Ht:** 6' 3" **Wt:** 205 **Born:** 11/07/66 **Age:** 25

Year Team	Lg	G	GS	CG	GF	IP	BFP	H	R	ER	HR	SH	SF	HB	TBB	IBB	SO	WP	Bk	W	L	Pct.	ShO	Sv	ERA
1986 Helena	R	18	10	0	5	65.1	0	79	49	43	4	0	0	0	33	1	40	4	0	4	6	.400	0	2	5.92

1987	Beloit	A	46	0	0	41	79	318	63	28	19	2	4	2	3	22	3	60	5	1	6	5	.545	0	18	2.16
1988	Stockton	A	44	0	0	40	62.1	266	57	17	14	2	1	0	1	27	3	50	3	0	4	5	.444	0	14	2.02
1989	El Paso	AA	19	0	0	8	31	151	52	31	25	3	3	0	1	11	1	23	3	0	3	4	.429	0	2	7.26
	Stockton	A	12	0	0	10	27.2	112	22	11	10	0	1	0	2	9	0	30	2	0	3	2	.600	0	4	3.25
	Sarasota	A	7	2	0	3	16.2	73	18	9	6	1	1	0	1	5	1	9	1	0	0	1	.000	0	1	3.24
1990	Birmingham	AA	50	1	0	31	90.1	383	90	50	41	6	9	4	3	24	2	72	12	1	6	4	.600	0	17	4.08
1991	Vancouver	AAA	22	0	0	21	24.1	106	21	12	12	2	4	0	0	13	1	17	1	1	2	3	.400	0	12	4.44
1991	Chicago	AL	28	0	0	8	30.2	125	21	12	11	4	2	1	0	13	1	18	0	0	3	2	.600	0	0	3.23

Tom Drees

Pitches: Left   Bats: Both   Pos: RP   **Ht: 6' 6"   Wt: 210   Born: 06/17/63   Age: 29**

			HOW MUCH HE PITCHED						WHAT HE GAVE UP											THE RESULTS					
Year	Team	Lg	G	GS	CG	GF	IP	BFP	H	R	ER	HR	SH	SF	HB	TBB	IBB	SO	WP	Bk	W	L	Pct.	ShO	Sv	ERA
1985	Sara Wsox	R	12	12	2	0	74.1	314	75	29	23	1	2	2	4	17	0	75	6	1	6	3	.667	0	0	2.78
1986	Peninsula	A	37	10	1	14	94.2	440	108	64	50	5	2	3	4	61	1	54	7	1	5	7	.417	0	2	4.75
1987	Daytona Bch	A	27	26	8	1	168.2	747	195	87	70	10	5	7	6	58	4	76	9	1	10	14	.417	3	0	3.74
1988	Birmingham	AA	22	21	6	0	158	664	149	63	49	5	5	3	4	52	0	94	3	10	9	7	.563	2	0	2.79
1989	Vancouver	AAA	26	26	4	0	168.1	701	142	76	63	12	8	5	4	72	2	66	2	10	12	11	.522	3	0	3.37
1990	Vancouver	AAA	17	16	4	0	97.1	430	94	49	43	3	0	2	4	51	0	63	1	0	8	5	.615	1	0	3.98
1991	Vancouver	AAA	22	22	3	0	143	619	130	70	56	15	3	7	3	62	0	89	2	1	8	8	.500	3	0	3.52
1991	Chicago	AL	4	0	0	1	7.1	37	10	10	10	4	1	1	0	6	0	2	2	0	0	0	.000	0	0	12.27

Kirk Dressendorfer

Pitches: Right   Bats: Right   Pos: SP   **Ht: 5'11"   Wt: 190   Born: 04/08/69   Age: 23**

			HOW MUCH HE PITCHED						WHAT HE GAVE UP											THE RESULTS					
Year	Team	Lg	G	GS	CG	GF	IP	BFP	H	R	ER	HR	SH	SF	HB	TBB	IBB	SO	WP	Bk	W	L	Pct.	ShO	Sv	ERA
1990	Sou Oregon	A	7	4	0	0	19.1	78	18	7	5	0	1	1	1	2	0	22	1	0	0	1	.000	0	0	2.33
1991	Tacoma	AAA	8	7	0	0	24	120	31	29	29	4	1	2	1	20	0	19	2	0	1	3	.250	0	0	10.88
1991	Oakland	AL	7	7	0	0	34.2	159	33	28	21	5	2	1	0	21	0	17	3	0	3	3	.500	0	0	5.45

Rob Ducey

Bats: Left   Throws: Right   Pos: LF   **Ht: 6' 2"   Wt: 180   Born: 05/24/65   Age: 27**

			BATTING															BASERUNNING				PERCENTAGES		
Year	Team	Lg	G	AB	H	2B	3B	HR	(Hm | Rd)	TB	R	RBI	TBB	IBB	SO	HBP	SH	SF	SB	CS	SB%	GDP	Avg	OBP	SLG
1987	Toronto	AL	34	48	9	1	0	1	(1 | 0)	13	12	6	8	0	10	0	0	1	2	0	1.00	0	.188	.298	.271
1988	Toronto	AL	27	54	17	4	1	0	(0 | 0)	23	15	6	5	0	7	0	2	2	1	0	1.00	1	.315	.361	.426
1989	Toronto	AL	41	76	16	4	0	0	(0 | 0)	20	5	7	9	1	25	0	1	0	2	1	.67	2	.211	.294	.263
1990	Toronto	AL	19	53	16	5	0	0	(0 | 0)	21	7	7	7	0	15	1	0	1	1	1	.50	0	.302	.387	.396
1991	Toronto	AL	39	68	16	2	2	1	(0 | 1)	25	8	4	6	0	26	0	1	0	2	0	1.00	1	.235	.297	.368
	5 ML YEARS		160	299	74	16	3	2	(1 | 1)	102	47	30	35	1	83	1	4	4	8	2	.80	4	.247	.324	.341

Mariano Duncan

Bats: Right   Throws: Right   Pos: 2B/SS   **Ht: 6' 0"   Wt: 185   Born: 03/13/63   Age: 29**

			BATTING															BASERUNNING				PERCENTAGES		
Year	Team	Lg	G	AB	H	2B	3B	HR	(Hm	Rd)	TB	R	RBI	TBB	IBB	SO	HBP	SH	SF	SB	CS	SB%	GDP	Avg	OBP	SLG
1985	Los Angeles	NL	142	562	137	24	6	6	(1	5)	191	74	39	38	4	113	3	13	4	38	8	.83	9	.244	.293	.340
1986	Los Angeles	NL	109	407	93	7	0	8	(2	6)	124	47	30	30	1	78	2	5	1	48	13	.79	6	.229	.284	.305
1987	Los Angeles	NL	76	261	56	8	1	6	(3	3)	84	31	18	17	1	62	2	6	1	11	1	.92	4	.215	.267	.322
1989	2 ML Teams		94	258	64	15	2	3	(2	1)	92	32	21	8	0	51	5	2	0	9	5	.64	3	.248	.284	.357
1990	Cincinnati	NL	125	435	133	22	11	10	(5	5)	207	67	55	24	4	67	4	4	4	13	7	.65	10	.306	.345	.476
1991	Cincinnati	NL	100	333	86	7	4	12	(10	2)	137	46	40	12	0	57	3	5	3	5	4	.56	0	.258	.288	.411
1989	Los Angeles	NL	49	84	21	5	1	0	(0	0)	28	9	8	0	0	15	2	1	0	3	3	.50	1	.250	.267	.333
	Cincinnati	NL	45	174	43	10	1	3	(2	1)	64	23	13	8	0	36	3	1	0	6	2	.75	2	.247	.292	.368
	6 ML YEARS		646	2256	569	83	24	45	(23	22)	835	297	203	129	10	428	19	35	13	124	38	.77	32	.252	.297	.370

Shawon Dunston

Bats: Right   Throws: Right   Pos: SS   **Ht: 6' 1"   Wt: 175   Born: 03/21/63   Age: 29**

			BATTING															BASERUNNING				PERCENTAGES		
Year	Team	Lg	G	AB	H	2B	3B	HR	(Hm	Rd)	TB	R	RBI	TBB	IBB	SO	HBP	SH	SF	SB	CS	SB%	GDP	Avg	OBP	SLG
1985	Chicago	NL	74	250	65	12	4	4	(3	1)	97	40	18	19	3	42	0	1	2	11	3	.79	3	.260	.310	.388
1986	Chicago	NL	150	581	145	37	3	17	(10	7)	239	66	68	21	5	114	3	4	2	13	11	.54	5	.250	.278	.411
1987	Chicago	NL	95	346	85	18	3	5	(3	2)	124	40	22	10	1	68	1	0	2	12	3	.80	6	.246	.267	.358
1988	Chicago	NL	155	575	143	23	6	9	(5	4)	205	69	56	16	8	108	2	4	2	30	9	.77	6	.249	.271	.357
1989	Chicago	NL	138	471	131	20	6	9	(3	6)	190	52	60	30	15	86	1	6	4	19	11	.63	7	.278	.320	.403

Year	Team	Lg	G	AB	H	2B	3B	HR	(Hm	Rd)	TB	R	RBI	TBB	IBB	SO	HBP	SH	SF	SB	CS	SB%	GDP	Avg	OBP	SLG
1990	Chicago	NL	146	545	143	22	8	17	(7	10)	232	73	66	15	1	87	3	4	6	25	5	.83	9	.262	.283	.426
1991	Chicago	NL	142	492	128	22	7	12	(7	5)	200	59	50	23	5	64	4	4	11	21	6	.78	9	.260	.292	.407
	7 ML YEARS		900	3260	840	154	37	73	(38	35)	1287	399	340	134	38	569	14	23	29	131	48	.73	45	.258	.287	.395

Lenny Dykstra

Bats: Left **Throws:** Left **Pos:** CF **Ht:** 5'10" **Wt:** 186 **Born:** 02/10/63 **Age:** 29

| | | | | | | | | | BATTING | | | | | | | | | | | BASERUNNING | | | | PERCENTAGES | | |
Year	Team	Lg	G	AB	H	2B	3B	HR	(Hm	Rd)	TB	R	RBI	TBB	IBB	SO	HBP	SH	SF	SB	CS	SB%	GDP	Avg	OBP	SLG
1985	New York	NL	83	236	60	9	3	1	(0	1)	78	40	19	30	0	24	1	4	2	15	2	.88	4	.254	.338	.331
1986	New York	NL	147	431	127	27	7	8	(4	4)	192	77	45	58	1	55	0	7	2	31	7	.82	4	.295	.377	.445
1987	New York	NL	132	431	123	37	3	10	(7	3)	196	86	43	40	3	67	4	4	0	27	7	.79	1	.285	.352	.455
1988	New York	NL	126	429	116	19	3	8	(3	5)	165	57	33	30	2	43	3	2	2	30	8	.79	3	.270	.321	.385
1989	2 ML Teams		146	511	121	32	4	7	(5	2)	182	66	32	60	1	53	3	5	5	30	12	.71	7	.237	.318	.356
1990	Philadelphia	NL	149	590	192	35	3	9	(6	3)	260	106	60	89	14	48	7	2	3	33	5	.87	5	.325	.418	.441
1991	Philadelphia	NL	63	246	73	13	5	3	(3	0)	105	48	12	37	1	20	1	0	0	24	4	.86	1	.297	.391	.427
1989	New York	NL	56	159	43	12	1	3	(2	1)	66	27	13	23	0	15	2	4	4	13	1	.93	2	.270	.362	.415
	Philadelphia	NL	90	352	78	20	3	4	(3	1)	116	39	19	37	1	38	1	1	1	17	11	.61	5	.222	.297	.330
	7 ML YEARS		846	2874	812	172	28	46	(28	18)	1178	480	244	344	22	310	19	24	14	190	45	.81	25	.283	.361	.410

Dennis Eckersley

Pitches: Right **Bats:** Right **Pos:** RP **Ht:** 6'2" **Wt:** 195 **Born:** 10/03/54 **Age:** 37

| | | | HOW MUCH HE PITCHED | | | | | | WHAT HE GAVE UP | | | | | | | | | | THE RESULTS | | | | | |
Year	Team	Lg	G	GS	CG	GF	IP	BFP	H	R	ER	HR	SH	SF	HB	TBB	IBB	SO	WP	Bk	W	L	Pct.	ShO	Sv	ERA
1975	Cleveland	AL	34	24	6	5	187	794	147	61	54	16	6	7	7	90	8	152	4	2	13	7	.650	2	2	2.60
1976	Cleveland	AL	36	30	9	3	199	821	155	82	76	13	10	4	5	78	2	200	6	1	13	12	.520	3	1	3.44
1977	Cleveland	AL	33	33	12	0	247	1006	214	100	97	31	11	6	7	54	11	191	3	0	14	13	.519	3	0	3.53
1978	Boston	AL	35	35	16	0	268	1121	258	99	89	30	7	8	7	71	8	162	3	0	20	8	.714	3	0	2.99
1979	Boston	AL	33	33	17	0	247	1018	234	89	82	29	10	6	6	59	4	150	1	1	17	10	.630	2	0	2.99
1980	Boston	AL	30	30	8	0	198	818	188	101	94	25	7	8	2	44	7	121	0	0	12	14	.462	0	0	4.27
1981	Boston	AL	23	23	8	0	154	649	160	82	73	9	6	5	3	35	2	79	0	0	9	8	.529	2	0	4.27
1982	Boston	AL	33	33	11	0	224.1	926	228	101	93	31	4	4	2	43	3	127	1	0	13	13	.500	3	0	3.73
1983	Boston	AL	28	28	2	0	176.1	787	223	119	110	27	1	5	6	39	4	77	1	0	9	13	.409	0	0	5.61
1984	2 ML Teams		33	33	4	0	225	932	223	97	90	21	11	9	5	49	9	114	3	2	14	12	.538	0	0	3.60
1985	Chicago	NL	25	25	6	0	169.1	664	145	61	58	15	6	2	3	19	4	117	0	3	11	7	.611	2	0	3.08
1986	Chicago	NL	33	32	1	0	201	862	226	109	102	21	13	10	3	43	3	137	2	5	6	11	.353	0	0	4.57
1987	Oakland	AL	54	2	0	33	115.2	460	99	41	39	11	3	3	1	17	3	113	1	0	6	8	.429	0	16	3.03
1988	Oakland	AL	60	0	0	53	72.2	279	52	20	19	5	1	3	1	11	2	70	0	0	4	2	.667	0	45	2.35
1989	Oakland	AL	51	0	0	46	57.2	206	32	10	10	5	0	4	1	3	0	55	0	0	4	0	1.000	0	33	1.56
1990	Oakland	AL	63	0	0	61	73.1	262	41	9	5	2	0	1	0	4	1	73	0	0	4	2	.667	0	48	0.61
1991	Oakland	AL	67	0	0	59	76	299	60	26	25	11	1	0	1	9	3	87	1	0	5	4	.556	0	43	2.96
1984	Boston	AL	9	9	2	0	64.2	270	71	38	36	10	3	3	1	13	2	33	2	0	4	4	.500	0	0	5.01
	Chicago	NL	24	24	2	0	160.1	662	152	59	54	11	8	6	4	36	7	81	1	2	10	8	.556	0	0	3.03
	17 ML YEARS		671	361	100	260	2891.1	11904	2685	1207	1116	302	97	85	62	668	74	2025	26	16	174	144	.547	20	188	3.47

Tom Edens

Pitches: Right **Bats:** Right **Pos:** SP **Ht:** 6'3" **Wt:** 185 **Born:** 06/09/61 **Age:** 31

| | | | HOW MUCH HE PITCHED | | | | | | WHAT HE GAVE UP | | | | | | | | | | THE RESULTS | | | | | |
Year	Team	Lg	G	GS	CG	GF	IP	BFP	H	R	ER	HR	SH	SF	HB	TBB	IBB	SO	WP	Bk	W	L	Pct.	ShO	Sv	ERA
1987	New York	NL	2	2	0	0	8	42	15	6	6	2	2	0	0	4	0	4	2	0	0	0	.000	0	0	6.75
1990	Milwaukee	AL	35	6	0	9	89	387	89	52	44	8	6	4	4	33	3	40	1	0	4	5	.444	0	2	4.45
1991	Minnesota	AL	8	6	0	0	33	143	34	15	15	2	0	0	0	10	1	19	1	0	2	2	.500	0	0	4.09
	3 ML YEARS		45	14	0	9	130	572	138	73	65	12	8	4	4	47	4	63	4	0	6	7	.462	0	2	4.50

Wayne Edwards

Pitches: Left **Bats:** Left **Pos:** RP **Ht:** 6'5" **Wt:** 185 **Born:** 03/07/64 **Age:** 28

| | | | HOW MUCH HE PITCHED | | | | | | WHAT HE GAVE UP | | | | | | | | | | THE RESULTS | | | | | |
Year	Team	Lg	G	GS	CG	GF	IP	BFP	H	R	ER	HR	SH	SF	HB	TBB	IBB	SO	WP	Bk	W	L	Pct.	ShO	Sv	ERA
1989	Chicago	AL	7	0	0	2	7.1	30	7	3	3	1	0	1	0	3	0	9	0	0	0	0	.000	0	0	3.68
1990	Chicago	AL	42	5	0	8	95	396	81	39	34	6	4	2	3	41	2	63	1	0	5	3	.625	0	2	3.22
1991	Chicago	AL	13	0	0	3	23.1	106	22	14	10	2	2	2	0	17	3	12	2	0	0	2	.000	0	0	3.86
	3 ML YEARS		62	5	0	13	125.2	532	110	56	47	9	6	5	3	61	5	84	3	0	5	5	.500	0	2	3.37

Bruce Egloff

Pitches: Right **Bats:** Right **Pos:** RP   **Ht:** 6' 2" **Wt:** 215 **Born:** 04/10/65 **Age:** 27

		HOW	MUCH	HE	PITCHED			WHAT	HE	GAVE	UP						THE	RESULTS		
Year Team	Lg	G	GS	CG	GF	IP	BFP	H	R	ER	HR	SH	SF	HB	TBB	IBB	SO	WP	Bk	W	L	Pct.	ShO	Sv	ERA
1986 Batavia	A	12	12	1	0	70	302	79	42	31	8	0	1	3	17	0	62	7	0	1	2	.333	0	0	3.99
1987 Waterloo	A	7	7	0	0	22.2	106	30	14	13	1	2	1	4	10	0	14	1	1	1	2	.333	0	0	5.16
1989 Watertown	A	22	0	0	17	48.2	207	33	19	14	2	3	1	1	24	1	63	9	2	1	1	.500	0	8	2.59
1990 Canton-Akrn	AA	34	0	0	24	54.2	226	44	16	12	5	0	0	3	15	1	53	4	1	3	2	.600	0	15	1.98
1991 Colo Sprngs	AAA	15	0	0	7	29.1	126	31	14	11	2	3	0	1	13	2	17	1	3	1	2	.333	0	2	3.38
1991 Cleveland	AL	6	0	0	2	5.2	28	8	3	3	0	0	0	0	4	1	8	2	0	0	0	.000	0	0	4.76

Mark Eichhorn

Pitches: Right **Bats:** Right **Pos:** RP   **Ht:** 6' 3" **Wt:** 210 **Born:** 11/21/60 **Age:** 31

		HOW	MUCH	HE	PITCHED			WHAT	HE	GAVE	UP						THE	RESULTS		
Year Team	Lg	G	GS	CG	GF	IP	BFP	H	R	ER	HR	SH	SF	HB	TBB	IBB	SO	WP	Bk	W	L	Pct.	ShO	Sv	ERA
1982 Toronto	AL	7	7	0	0	38	171	40	28	23	4	1	2	0	14	1	16	3	0	0	3	.000	0	0	5.45
1986 Toronto	AL	69	0	0	38	157	612	105	32	30	8	9	2	7	45	14	166	2	1	14	6	.700	0	10	1.72
1987 Toronto	AL	89	0	0	27	127.2	540	110	47	45	14	7	4	6	52	13	96	3	1	10	6	.625	0	4	3.17
1988 Toronto	AL	37	0	0	17	66.2	302	79	32	31	3	8	1	6	27	4	28	3	6	0	3	.000	0	1	4.18
1989 Atlanta	NL	45	0	0	13	68.1	286	70	36	33	6	7	4	1	19	8	49	0	1	5	5	.500	0	0	4.35
1990 California	AL	60	0	0	40	84.2	374	98	36	29	2	2	4	6	23	0	69	2	0	2	5	.286	0	13	3.08
1991 California	AL	70	0	0	23	81.2	311	63	21	18	2	5	3	2	13	1	49	0	0	3	3	.500	0	1	1.98
7 ML YEARS		377	7	0	158	624	2596	565	232	209	39	39	20	28	193	41	473	13	9	34	31	.523	0	29	3.01

Dave Eiland

Pitches: Right **Bats:** Right **Pos:** SP/RP   **Ht:** 6' 3" **Wt:** 205 **Born:** 07/05/66 **Age:** 25

		HOW	MUCH	HE	PITCHED			WHAT	HE	GAVE	UP						THE	RESULTS		
Year Team	Lg	G	GS	CG	GF	IP	BFP	H	R	ER	HR	SH	SF	HB	TBB	IBB	SO	WP	Bk	W	L	Pct.	ShO	Sv	ERA
1988 New York	AL	3	3	0	0	12.2	57	15	9	9	6	0	0	2	4	0	7	0	0	0	0	.000	0	0	6.39
1989 New York	AL	6	6	0	0	34.1	152	44	25	22	5	1	2	2	13	3	11	0	0	1	3	.250	0	0	5.77
1990 New York	AL	5	5	0	0	30.1	127	31	14	12	2	0	0	0	5	0	16	0	0	2	1	.667	0	0	3.56
1991 New York	AL	18	13	0	4	72.2	317	87	51	43	10	0	3	3	23	1	18	0	0	2	5	.286	0	0	5.33
4 ML YEARS		32	27	0	4	150	653	177	99	86	23	1	5	7	45	4	52	0	0	5	9	.357	0	0	5.16

Jim Eisenreich

Bats: Left **Throws:** Left **Pos:** LF/1B/CF/RF   **Ht:** 5'11" **Wt:** 200 **Born:** 04/18/59 **Age:** 33

				BATTING														BASERUNNING				PERCENTAGES		
Year Team	Lg	G	AB	H	2B	3B	HR	(Hm	Rd)	TB	R	RBI	TBB	IBB	SO	HBP	SH	SF	SB	CS	SB%	GDP	Avg	OBP	SLG
1982 Minnesota	AL	34	99	30	6	0	2	(1	1)	42	10	9	11	0	13	1	0	0	0	0	.00	1	.303	.378	.424
1983 Minnesota	AL	2	7	2	1	0	0	(0	0)	3	1	0	1	0	1	0	0	0	0	0	.00	0	.286	.375	.429
1984 Minnesota	AL	12	32	7	1	0	0	(0	0)	8	1	3	2	1	4	0	0	0	2	0	1.00	1	.219	.250	.250
1987 Kansas City	AL	44	105	25	8	2	4	(3	1)	49	10	21	7	2	13	0	0	3	1	1	.50	2	.238	.278	.467
1988 Kansas City	AL	82	202	44	8	1	1	(0	1)	57	26	19	6	1	31	0	2	4	9	3	.75	2	.218	.236	.282
1989 Kansas City	AL	134	475	139	33	7	9	(4	5)	213	64	59	37	9	44	0	3	4	27	8	.77	8	.293	.341	.448
1990 Kansas City	AL	142	496	139	29	7	5	(2	3)	197	61	51	42	2	51	1	2	4	12	14	.46	7	.280	.335	.397
1991 Kansas City	AL	135	375	113	22	3	2	(2	0)	147	47	47	20	1	35	1	3	6	5	3	.63	11	.301	.333	.392
8 ML YEARS		585	1791	499	108	20	23	(12	11)	716	220	209	126	16	192	3	10	23	56	29	.66	32	.279	.323	.400

Cal Eldred

Pitches: Right **Bats:** Right **Pos:** SP   **Ht:** 6' 4" **Wt:** 215 **Born:** 11/24/67 **Age:** 24

		HOW	MUCH	HE	PITCHED			WHAT	HE	GAVE	UP						THE	RESULTS		
Year Team	Lg	G	GS	CG	GF	IP	BFP	H	R	ER	HR	SH	SF	HB	TBB	IBB	SO	WP	Bk	W	L	Pct.	ShO	Sv	ERA
1989 Beloit	A	5	5	0	0	31.1	127	23	10	8	0	1	0	1	11	1	32	2	2	2	1	.667	0	0	2.30
1990 Stockton	A	7	7	3	0	50	197	31	12	9	2	0	0	3	19	0	75	2	1	4	2	.667	1	0	1.62
El Paso	AA	19	19	0	0	110.1	485	126	61	55	9	3	3	2	47	0	93	4	1	5	4	.556	0	0	4.49
1991 Denver	AAA	29	29	3	0	185	784	161	82	77	13	4	8	12	84	2	168	8	2	13	9	.591	1	0	3.75
1991 Milwaukee	AL	3	3	0	0	16	73	20	9	8	2	0	0	0	6	0	10	0	0	2	0	1.000	0	0	4.50

Kevin Elster

Bats: Right **Throws:** Right **Pos:** SS   **Ht:** 6' 2" **Wt:** 200 **Born:** 08/03/64 **Age:** 27

				BATTING														BASERUNNING				PERCENTAGES		
Year Team	Lg	G	AB	H	2B	3B	HR	(Hm	Rd)	TB	R	RBI	TBB	IBB	SO	HBP	SH	SF	SB	CS	SB%	GDP	Avg	OBP	SLG
1986 New York	NL	19	30	5	1	0	0	(0	0)	6	3	0	3	1	8	0	0	0	0	0	.00	0	.167	.242	.200
1987 New York	NL	5	10	4	2	0	0	(0	0)	6	1	1	0	0	1	0	0	0	0	0	.00	1	.400	.400	.600

Year	Team	Lg	G	AB	H	2B	3B	HR	(Hm	Rd)	TB	R	RBI	TBB	IBB	SO	HBP	SH	SF	SB	CS	SB%	GDP	Avg	OBP	SLG
1988	New York	NL	149	406	87	11	1	9	(6	3)	127	41	37	35	12	47	3	6	0	2	0	1.00	5	.214	.282	.313
1989	New York	NL	151	458	106	25	2	10	(5	5)	165	52	55	34	11	77	2	6	8	4	3	.57	13	.231	.283	.360
1990	New York	NL	92	314	65	20	1	9	(2	7)	114	36	45	30	2	54	1	1	6	2	0	1.00	4	.207	.274	.363
1991	New York	NL	115	348	84	16	2	6	(3	3)	122	33	36	40	4	53	1	1	4	2	3	.40	7	.241	.318	.351
	6 ML YEARS		531	1566	351	75	6	34	(16	18)	540	166	174	142	32	240	7	14	18	10	6	.63	27	.224	.289	.345

Scott Erickson

Pitches: Right Bats: Right Pos: SP Ht: 6' 4" Wt: 225 Born: 02/02/68 Age: 24

			HOW MUCH HE PITCHED						WHAT HE GAVE UP											THE RESULTS					
Year	Team	Lg	G	GS	CG	GF	IP	BFP	H	R	ER	HR	SH	SF	HB	TBB	IBB	SO	WP	Bk	W	L	Pct.	ShO	Sv	ERA
1989	Visalia	A	12	12	2	0	78.2	320	79	29	26	3	0	0	3	22	0	59	3	4	3	4	.429	0	0	2.97
1990	Orlando	AA	15	15	3	0	101	397	75	38	34	3	1	2	5	24	0	69	4	1	8	3	.727	1	0	3.03
1990	Minnesota	AL	19	17	1	1	113	485	108	49	36	9	5	2	5	51	4	53	3	0	8	4	.667	0	0	2.87
1991	Minnesota	AL	32	32	5	0	204	851	189	80	72	13	5	7	6	71	3	108	4	0	20	8	.714	3	0	3.18
	2 ML YEARS		51	49	6	1	317	1336	297	129	108	22	10	9	11	122	7	161	7	0	28	12	.700	3	0	3.07

Jose Escobar

Bats: Right Throws: Right Pos: 2B Ht: 5'10" Wt: 140 Born: 10/30/60 Age: 31

									BATTING										BASERUNNING				PERCENTAGES		
Year	Team	Lg	G	AB	H	2B	3B	HR	(Hm	Rd)	TB	R	RBI	TBB	IBB	SO	HBP	SH	SF	SB	CS	SB%	GDP	Avg	OBP	SLG
1984	Knoxville	AA	96	340	80	13	4	1	--	--	104	40	45	14	0	56	2	2	4	6	2	.75	4	.235	.267	.306
1985	Reading	AA	40	122	31	4	0	1	--	--	38	17	8	11	1	17	0	1	1	3	2	.60	2	.254	.313	.311
	Portland	AAA	46	109	35	4	2	1	--	--	46	21	8	8	0	16	0	2	1	4	0	1.00	1	.321	.364	.422
1986	Knoxville	AA	19	66	16	1	1	0	--	--	19	9	5	5	1	6	1	4	1	1	1	.50	1	.242	.301	.288
	Syracuse	AAA	62	143	35	5	0	2	--	--	46	12	14	4	0	14	1	5	0	2	1	.67	4	.245	.270	.322
1987	Syracuse	AAA	37	68	24	2	2	0	--	--	30	12	14	0	0	8	0	0	0	0	0	.00	1	.353	.353	.441
	Knoxville	AA	26	92	13	3	0	0	--	--	16	4	4	4	0	11	1	1	0	2	1	.67	2	.141	.186	.174
1988	Knoxville	AA	11	24	7	1	0	0	--	--	8	1	2	2	0	3	0	0	0	0	1	.00	1	.292	.346	.333
	Syracuse	AAA	46	124	26	1	1	0	--	--	29	8	12	9	0	20	0	1	2	2	0	1.00	3	.210	.259	.234
1989	Omaha	AAA	23	76	6	0	0	0	--	--	6	3	1	2	0	19	0	0	1	0	0	.00	0	.079	.101	.079
	Syracuse	AAA	46	142	33	3	1	0	--	--	38	12	14	7	0	27	0	5	2	2	0	1.00	1	.232	.265	.268
1990	Syracuse	AAA	79	252	68	6	2	0	--	--	78	16	17	18	0	35	1	7	0	3	0	1.00	3	.270	.321	.310
1991	Cleveland	AL	10	15	3	0	0	0	(0	0)	3	0	1	1	0	4	0	1	0	0	0	.00	0	.200	.250	.200

Alvaro Espinoza

Bats: Right Throws: Right Pos: SS Ht: 6' 0" Wt: 189 Born: 02/19/62 Age: 30

									BATTING										BASERUNNING				PERCENTAGES		
Year	Team	Lg	G	AB	H	2B	3B	HR	(Hm	Rd)	TB	R	RBI	TBB	IBB	SO	HBP	SH	SF	SB	CS	SB%	GDP	Avg	OBP	SLG
1984	Minnesota	AL	1	0	0	0	0	0	(0	0)	0	0	0	0	0	0	0	0	0	0	0	.00	0	.000	.000	.000
1985	Minnesota	AL	32	57	15	2	0	0	(0	0)	17	5	9	1	0	9	1	3	0	0	1	.00	2	.263	.288	.298
1986	Minnesota	AL	37	42	9	1	0	0	(0	0)	10	4	1	1	0	10	0	2	0	0	1	.00	0	.214	.233	.238
1988	New York	AL	3	3	0	0	0	0	(0	0)	0	0	0	0	0	0	0	0	0	0	0	.00	0	.000	.000	.000
1989	New York	AL	146	503	142	23	1	0	(0	0)	167	51	41	14	1	60	1	23	3	3	3	.50	14	.282	.301	.332
1990	New York	AL	150	438	98	12	2	2	(0	2)	120	31	20	16	0	54	5	11	2	1	2	.33	13	.224	.258	.274
1991	New York	AL	148	480	123	23	2	5	(2	3)	165	51	33	16	0	57	2	9	2	4	1	.80	10	.256	.282	.344
	7 ML YEARS		517	1523	387	61	5	7	(2	5)	479	142	104	48	1	190	9	48	7	8	8	.50	39	.254	.280	.315

Cecil Espy

Bats: Both Throws: Right Pos: CF Ht: 6' 3" Wt: 195 Born: 01/20/63 Age: 29

									BATTING										BASERUNNING				PERCENTAGES		
Year	Team	Lg	G	AB	H	2B	3B	HR	(Hm	Rd)	TB	R	RBI	TBB	IBB	SO	HBP	SH	SF	SB	CS	SB%	GDP	Avg	OBP	SLG
1983	Los Angeles	NL	20	11	3	1	0	0	(0	0)	4	4	1	1	0	2	0	0	0	0	0	.00	0	.273	.333	.364
1987	Texas	AL	14	8	0	0	0	0	(0	0)	0	1	0	1	0	3	0	0	0	0	1	1.00	0	.000	.111	.000
1988	Texas	AL	123	347	86	17	6	2	(2	0)	121	46	39	20	1	83	1	5	3	33	10	.77	2	.248	.288	.349
1989	Texas	AL	142	475	122	12	7	3	(2	1)	157	65	31	38	2	99	2	10	2	45	20	.69	2	.257	.313	.331
1990	Texas	AL	52	71	9	0	0	0	(0	0)	9	10	1	10	0	20	0	1	0	11	5	.69	1	.127	.235	.127
1991	Pittsburgh	NL	43	82	20	4	0	1	(1	0)	27	7	11	5	0	17	0	3	2	4	0	1.00	0	.244	.281	.329
	6 ML YEARS		394	994	240	34	13	6	(5	1)	318	133	83	75	3	224	3	19	7	95	35	.73	6	.241	.295	.320

Tony Eusebio

Bats: Right Throws: Right Pos: C Ht: 6' 2" Wt: 180 Born: 04/27/67 Age: 25

									BATTING										BASERUNNING				PERCENTAGES		
Year	Team	Lg	G	AB	H	2B	3B	HR	(Hm	Rd)	TB	R	RBI	TBB	IBB	SO	HBP	SH	SF	SB	CS	SB%	GDP	Avg	OBP	SLG
1985	Astros	R	1	1	0	0	0	0	--	--	0	0	0	0	0	0	0	0	0	0	0	.00	0	.000	.000	.000
1987	Astros	R	42	125	26	1	2	1	--	--	34	26	15	18	0	19	7	0	0	8	2	.80	4	.208	.340	.272

Year	Team	Lg	G	AB	H	2B	3B	HR	(Hm	Rd)	TB	R	RBI	TBB	IBB	SO	HBP	SH	SF	SB	CS	SB%	GDP	Avg	OBP	SLG
1988	Osceola	A	118	392	96	6	3	0	--	--	108	45	40	40	2	69	6	1	3	20	13	.61	18	.245	.322	.276
1989	Columbus	AA	65	203	38	6	1	0	--	--	46	20	18	38	1	47	3	0	0	7	3	.70	7	.187	.324	.227
	Osceola	A	52	175	50	6	3	0	--	--	62	22	30	19	0	27	1	1	3	5	3	.63	10	.286	.354	.354
1990	Columbus	AA	92	318	90	18	0	4	--	--	120	36	37	21	0	80	4	1	1	6	2	.75	4	.283	.334	.377
1991	Tucson	AAA	5	20	8	1	0	0	--	--	9	5	2	3	0	3	0	0	0	1	1	.50	2	.400	.478	.450
	Jackson	AA	66	222	58	8	3	2	--	--	78	27	31	25	5	54	4	4	2	3	3	.50	7	.261	.344	.351
1991	Houston	NL	10	19	2	1	0	0	(0	0)	3	4	0	6	0	8	0	0	0	0	0	.00	1	.105	.320	.158

Dwight Evans

Bats: Right   **Throws:** Right   **Pos:** RF/DH   **Ht:** 6' 3"   **Wt:** 180   **Born:** 11/03/51   **Age:** 40

									BATTING											BASERUNNING				PERCENTAGES		
Year	Team	Lg	G	AB	H	2B	3B	HR	(Hm	Rd)	TB	R	RBI	TBB	IBB	SO	HBP	SH	SF	SB	CS	SB%	GDP	Avg	OBP	SLG
1972	Boston	AL	18	57	15	3	1	1	(1	0)	23	2	6	7	0	13	0	0	0	0	0	.00	2	.263	.344	.404
1973	Boston	AL	119	282	63	13	1	10	(6	4)	108	46	32	40	2	52	1	3	2	5	0	1.00	8	.223	.320	.383
1974	Boston	AL	133	463	130	19	8	10	(7	3)	195	60	70	38	2	77	2	6	5	4	4	.50	9	.281	.335	.421
1975	Boston	AL	128	412	113	24	6	13	(8	5)	188	61	56	47	3	60	4	5	2	3	4	.43	10	.274	.353	.456
1976	Boston	AL	146	501	121	34	5	17	(9	8)	216	61	62	57	4	92	6	3	4	6	7	.46	11	.242	.324	.431
1977	Boston	AL	73	230	66	9	2	14	(9	5)	121	39	36	28	0	58	0	6	1	4	2	.67	3	.287	.363	.526
1978	Boston	AL	147	497	123	24	2	24	(13	11)	223	75	63	65	2	119	2	6	2	8	5	.62	15	.247	.336	.449
1979	Boston	AL	152	489	134	24	1	21	(12	9)	223	69	58	69	7	76	1	3	1	6	9	.40	14	.274	.364	.456
1980	Boston	AL	148	463	123	37	5	18	(11	7)	224	72	60	64	6	98	5	6	4	3	1	.75	5	.266	.358	.484
1981	Boston	AL	108	412	122	19	4	22	(15	7)	215	84	71	85	1	85	1	3	3	3	2	.60	8	.296	.415	.522
1982	Boston	AL	162	609	178	37	7	32	(19	13)	325	122	98	112	1	125	1	3	2	3	2	.60	17	.292	.402	.534
1983	Boston	AL	126	470	112	19	4	22	(12	10)	205	74	58	70	5	97	2	0	2	3	0	1.00	12	.238	.338	.436
1984	Boston	AL	162	630	186	37	8	32	(15	17)	335	121	104	96	2	115	4	1	7	3	1	.75	19	.295	.388	.532
1985	Boston	AL	159	617	162	29	1	29	(14	15)	280	110	78	114	4	105	5	1	7	7	2	.78	16	.263	.378	.454
1986	Boston	AL	152	529	137	33	2	26	(8	18)	252	86	97	97	4	117	6	2	6	3	3	.50	11	.259	.376	.476
1987	Boston	AL	154	541	165	37	2	34	(14	20)	308	109	123	106	6	98	3	0	7	4	6	.40	10	.305	.417	.569
1988	Boston	AL	149	559	164	31	7	21	(11	10)	272	96	111	76	3	99	1	2	7	5	1	.83	16	.293	.375	.487
1989	Boston	AL	146	520	148	27	3	20	(8	12)	241	82	100	99	1	84	3	1	7	3	3	.50	16	.285	.397	.463
1990	Boston	AL	123	445	111	18	3	13	(7	6)	174	66	63	67	5	73	4	0	6	3	4	.43	18	.249	.349	.391
1991	Baltimore	AL	101	270	73	9	1	6	(4	2)	102	35	38	54	2	54	2	1	2	2	3	.40	7	.270	.393	.378
20	ML YEARS		2606	8996	2446	483	73	385	(203	182)	4230	1470	1384	1391	60	1697	53	52	77	78	59	.57	227	.272	.370	.470

Hector Fajardo

Pitches: Right   **Bats:** Right   **Pos:** SP   **Ht:** 6' 4"   **Wt:** 185   **Born:** 11/06/70   **Age:** 21

			HOW MUCH HE PITCHED						WHAT HE GAVE UP										THE RESULTS					
Year	Team	Lg	G	GS	CG	GF	IP	BFP	H	R	ER	HR	SH	SF	HB	TBB	IBB	SO	WP	Bk	W	L	Pct.	ShO	Sv	ERA
1989	Pirates	R	10	6	0	0	34.2	154	38	24	23	0	0	1	0	20	0	19	1	0	0	5	.000	0	0	5.97
1990	Pirates	R	5	4	0	0	21	92	23	10	9	0	0	1	3	8	0	17	1	1	1	1	.500	0	0	3.86
	Augusta	A	7	7	0	0	39.2	173	41	18	17	1	1	0	2	15	0	28	0	1	2	2	.500	0	0	3.86
1991	Augusta	A	11	11	1	0	60.1	250	44	26	18	1	1	2	2	24	0	79	3	1	4	3	.571	1	0	2.69
	Salem	A	1	1	1	0	7.2	30	4	3	2	1	1	0	0	1	1	7	0	0	0	1	.000	0	0	2.35
	Carolina	AA	10	10	1	0	61	258	55	32	28	4	2	3	0	24	0	53	3	2	3	4	.429	0	0	4.13
	Buffalo	AAA	8	0	0	4	9.1	36	6	1	1	0	0	0	0	3	0	12	0	0	1	0	1.000	0	1	0.96
1991	2 ML Teams		6	5	0	1	25.1	119	35	20	19	2	0	3	1	11	0	23	3	0	0	2	.000	0	0	6.75
1991	Pittsburgh	NL	2	2	0	0	6.1	35	10	7	7	0	0	0	0	7	0	8	3	0	0	0	.000	0	0	9.95
	Texas	AL	4	3	0	1	19	84	25	13	12	2	0	3	1	4	0	15	0	0	0	2	.000	0	0	5.68

Paul Faries

Bats: Right   **Throws:** Right   **Pos:** 2B   **Ht:** 5'10"   **Wt:** 165   **Born:** 02/20/65   **Age:** 27

									BATTING											BASERUNNING				PERCENTAGES		
Year	Team	Lg	G	AB	H	2B	3B	HR	(Hm	Rd)	TB	R	RBI	TBB	IBB	SO	HBP	SH	SF	SB	CS	SB%	GDP	Avg	OBP	SLG
1987	Spokane	A	74	280	86	9	3	0	--	--	101	67	27	36	0	25	5	4	5	30	9	.77	7	.307	.390	.361
1988	Riverside	A	141	579	183	39	4	2	--	--	236	108	77	72	1	79	8	7	7	65	30	.68	14	.316	.395	.408
1989	Wichita	AA	130	513	136	25	8	6	--	--	195	79	52	47	0	52	2	2	1	41	13	.76	13	.265	.329	.380
1990	Las Vegas	AAA	137	552	172	29	3	5	--	--	222	109	64	75	1	60	6	7	1	48	15	.76	16	.312	.399	.402
1991	High Desert	A	10	42	13	2	2	0	--	--	19	6	5	2	1	3	0	1	1	1	0	1.00	2	.310	.333	.452
	Las Vegas	AAA	20	75	23	2	1	1	--	--	30	16	12	12	0	5	0	2	1	7	3	.70	2	.307	.398	.400
1990	San Diego	NL	14	37	7	1	0	0	(0	0)	8	4	2	4	0	7	1	2	1	0	1	.00	0	.189	.279	.216
1991	San Diego	NL	57	130	23	3	1	0	(0	0)	28	13	7	14	0	21	1	4	0	3	1	.75	5	.177	.262	.215
	2 ML YEARS		71	167	30	4	1	0	(0	0)	36	17	9	18	0	28	2	6	1	3	2	.60	5	.180	.266	.216

Monty Fariss

Bats: Right **Throws:** Right **Pos:** LF **Ht:** 6' 4" **Wt:** 200 **Born:** 10/13/67 **Age:** 24

								BATTING											BASERUNNING				PERCENTAGES		
Year	Team	Lg	G	AB	H	2B	3B	HR	(Hm | Rd)	TB	R	RBI	TBB	IBB	SO	HBP	SH	SF	SB	CS	SB%	GDP	Avg	OBP	SLG
1988	Butte	R	17	53	21	1	0	4	--	--	34	16	22	20	2	7	2	0	2	2	0	1.00	1	.396	.558	.642
	Tulsa	AA	49	165	37	6	6	3	--	--	64	21	31	22	0	39	0	1	1	2	0	1.00	2	.224	.314	.388
1989	Tulsa	AA	132	497	135	27	2	5	--	--	181	72	52	64	0	112	0	8	6	12	6	.67	13	.272	.351	.364
1990	Tulsa	AA	71	244	73	15	6	7	--	--	121	45	34	36	0	60	1	1	0	8	5	.62	9	.299	.391	.496
	Okla City	AAA	62	225	68	12	3	4	--	--	98	30	31	34	0	48	0	0	2	1	1	.50	7	.302	.391	.436
1991	Okla City	AAA	137	494	134	31	9	13	--	--	222	84	73	91	1	143	0	3	2	4	7	.36	11	.271	.383	.449
1991	Texas	AL	19	31	8	1	0	1	(1 | 0)	12	6	6	7	0	11	0	0	0	0	0	.00	0	.258	.395	.387

Steve Farr

Pitches: Right **Bats:** Right **Pos:** RP **Ht:** 5'11" **Wt:** 200 **Born:** 12/12/56 **Age:** 35

			HOW MUCH HE PITCHED					WHAT HE GAVE UP										THE RESULTS					
Year	Team	Lg	G	GS	CG	GF	IP	BFP	H	R	ER	HR	SH	SF	HB	TBB	IBB	SO	WP	Bk	W	L	Pct.	ShO	Sv	ERA
1984	Cleveland	AL	31	16	0	4	116	488	106	61	59	14	2	3	5	46	3	83	2	2	3	11	.214	0	1	4.58
1985	Kansas City	AL	16	3	0	5	37.2	164	34	15	13	2	1	2	2	20	4	36	3	0	2	1	.667	0	1	3.11
1986	Kansas City	AL	56	0	0	33	109.1	443	90	39	38	10	3	2	4	39	8	83	4	1	8	4	.667	0	8	3.13
1987	Kansas City	AL	47	0	0	19	91	408	97	47	42	9	0	3	2	44	4	88	2	0	4	3	.571	0	1	4.15
1988	Kansas City	AL	62	1	0	49	82.2	344	74	25	23	5	1	3	2	30	6	72	4	2	5	4	.556	0	20	2.50
1989	Kansas City	AL	51	2	0	40	63.1	279	75	35	29	5	0	3	1	22	5	56	2	0	2	5	.286	0	18	4.12
1990	Kansas City	AL	57	6	1	20	127	515	99	32	28	6	10	1	5	48	9	94	2	0	13	7	.650	1	1	1.98
1991	New York	AL	60	0	0	48	70	285	57	19	17	4	0	0	5	20	3	60	2	0	5	5	.500	0	23	2.19
	8 ML YEARS		380	28	1	218	697	2926	632	273	249	55	17	17	26	269	42	572	21	5	42	40	.512	1	73	3.22

Jeff Fassero

Pitches: Left **Bats:** Left **Pos:** RP **Ht:** 6' 1" **Wt:** 180 **Born:** 01/05/63 **Age:** 29

			HOW MUCH HE PITCHED					WHAT HE GAVE UP										THE RESULTS					
Year	Team	Lg	G	GS	CG	GF	IP	BFP	H	R	ER	HR	SH	SF	HB	TBB	IBB	SO	WP	Bk	W	L	Pct.	ShO	Sv	ERA
1984	Johnson Cty	R	13	11	2	2	66.2	292	65	42	34	2	0	4	0	39	0	59	1	1	4	7	.364	0	1	4.59
1985	Springfield	A	29	15	1	2	119	533	125	78	53	11	4	3	3	45	3	65	4	3	4	8	.333	0	1	4.01
1986	St. Pete	A	26	26	6	0	176	720	156	63	48	5	7	3	0	56	4	112	5	3	13	7	.650	1	0	2.45
1987	Arkansas	AA	28	27	2	0	151.1	674	168	90	69	16	10	2	1	67	7	118	7	1	10	7	.588	1	0	4.10
1988	Arkansas	AA	70	1	0	36	78	375	97	48	31	1	7	2	3	41	13	72	5	2	5	5	.500	0	17	3.58
1989	Arkansas	AA	6	6	2	0	44	174	32	11	8	1	1	1	1	12	0	38	1	1	4	1	.800	1	0	1.64
	Louisville	AAA	22	19	0	0	112	511	136	79	65	13	8	3	2	47	1	73	8	4	3	10	.231	0	0	5.22
1990	Canton-Akrn	AA	61	0	0	30	64.1	281	66	24	20	5	5	0	1	24	6	61	2	0	5	4	.556	0	6	2.80
1991	Indianapols	AAA	18	0	0	11	18.1	71	11	3	3	1	1	0	1	7	3	12	1	0	3	0	1.000	0	4	1.47
1991	Montreal	NL	51	0	0	30	55.1	223	39	17	15	1	6	0	1	17	1	42	4	0	2	5	.286	0	8	2.44

Mike Felder

Bats: Both **Throws:** Right **Pos:** LF/CF/RF **Ht:** 5' 8" **Wt:** 160 **Born:** 11/18/62 **Age:** 29

								BATTING											BASERUNNING				PERCENTAGES		
Year	Team	Lg	G	AB	H	2B	3B	HR	(Hm	Rd)	TB	R	RBI	TBB	IBB	SO	HBP	SH	SF	SB	CS	SB%	GDP	Avg	OBP	SLG
1985	Milwaukee	AL	15	56	11	1	0	0	(0	0)	12	8	5	0	5	6	0	1	0	4	1	.80	2	.196	.262	.214
1986	Milwaukee	AL	44	155	37	2	4	1	(1	0)	50	24	13	13	1	16	0	1	5	16	2	.89	2	.239	.289	.323
1987	Milwaukee	AL	108	289	77	5	7	2	(1	1)	102	48	31	28	0	23	0	9	2	34	8	.81	3	.266	.329	.353
1988	Milwaukee	AL	50	81	14	1	0	0	(0	0)	15	14	5	0	0	11	1	3	0	8	2	.80	1	.173	.183	.185
1989	Milwaukee	AL	117	315	76	11	3	3	(1	2)	102	50	23	23	2	38	0	7	0	26	5	.84	4	.241	.293	.324
1990	Milwaukee	AL	121	237	65	7	2	3	(1	2)	85	38	27	22	0	17	0	8	5	20	9	.69	0	.274	.330	.359
1991	San Francisco	NL	132	348	92	10	6	0	(0	0)	114	51	18	30	2	31	1	4	0	21	6	.78	2	.264	.325	.328
	7 ML YEARS		587	1481	372	37	22	9	(4	5)	480	233	117	121	5	142	2	33	12	129	33	.80	14	.251	.306	.324

Junior Felix

Bats: Both **Throws:** Right **Pos:** CF **Ht:** 5'11" **Wt:** 165 **Born:** 10/03/67 **Age:** 24

								BATTING											BASERUNNING				PERCENTAGES		
Year	Team	Lg	G	AB	H	2B	3B	HR	(Hm	Rd)	TB	R	RBI	TBB	IBB	SO	HBP	SH	SF	SB	CS	SB%	GDP	Avg	OBP	SLG
1989	Toronto	AL	110	415	107	14	8	9	(4	5)	164	62	46	33	2	101	3	1	3	18	12	.60	5	.258	.315	.395
1990	Toronto	AL	127	463	122	23	7	15	(7	8)	204	73	65	45	0	99	2	2	5	13	8	.62	4	.263	.328	.441
1991	California	AL	66	230	65	10	2	2	(2	0)	85	32	26	11	0	55	3	0	2	7	5	.58	5	.283	.321	.370
	3 ML YEARS		303	1108	294	47	17	26	(13	13)	453	167	137	89	2	255	8	2	10	38	25	.60	14	.265	.322	.409

Felix Fermin

Bats: Right **Throws:** Right **Pos:** SS   **Ht:** 5'11" **Wt:** 170 **Born:** 10/09/63 **Age:** 28

							BATTING												BASERUNNING				PERCENTAGES		
Year	Team	Lg	G	AB	H	2B	3B	HR	(Hm | Rd)	TB	R	RBI	TBB	IBB	SO	HBP	SH	SF	SB	CS	SB%	GDP	Avg	OBP	SLG
1987	Pittsburgh	NL	23	68	17	0	0	0	(0 | 0)	17	6	4	4	1	9	1	2	0	0	0	.00	3	.250	.301	.250
1988	Pittsburgh	NL	43	87	24	0	2	0	(0 | 0)	28	9	2	8	1	10	3	1	1	3	1	.75	3	.276	.354	.322
1989	Cleveland	AL	156	484	115	9	1	0	(0 | 0)	126	50	21	41	0	27	4	32	1	6	4	.60	15	.238	.302	.260
1990	Cleveland	AL	148	414	106	13	2	1	(1 | 0)	126	47	40	26	0	22	0	13	5	3	3	.50	13	.256	.297	.304
1991	Cleveland	AL	129	424	111	13	2	0	(0 | 0)	128	30	31	26	0	27	3	13	3	5	4	.56	16	.262	.307	.302
	5 ML YEARS		499	1477	373	35	7	1	(1 | 0)	425	142	98	105	2	95	11	61	10	17	12	.59	50	.253	.305	.288

Alex Fernandez

Pitches: Right **Bats:** Right **Pos:** SP   **Ht:** 6' 1" **Wt:** 205 **Born:** 08/13/69 **Age:** 22

			HOW MUCH HE PITCHED						WHAT HE GAVE UP										THE RESULTS					
Year	Team	Lg	G	GS	CG	GF	IP	BFP	H	R	ER	HR	SH	SF	HB	TBB	IBB	SO	WP	Bk	W	L	Pct.	ShO	Sv	ERA
1990	White Sox	R	2	2	0	0	10	43	11	4	4	0	0	1	2	1	0	16	1	2	1	0	1.000	0	0	3.60
	Sarasota	A	2	2	0	0	14.2	59	8	4	3	0	0	1	0	3	0	23	0	1	1	1	.500	0	0	1.84
	Birmingham	AA	4	4	0	0	25	99	20	7	3	0	0	0	0	6	0	27	0	0	3	0	1.000	0	0	1.08
1990	Chicago	AL	13	13	3	0	87.2	378	89	40	37	6	5	0	3	34	0	61	1	0	5	5	.500	0	0	3.80
1991	Chicago	AL	34	32	2	1	191.2	827	186	100	96	16	7	11	2	88	2	145	4	1	9	13	.409	0	0	4.51
	2 ML YEARS		47	45	5	1	279.1	1205	275	140	133	22	12	11	5	122	2	206	5	1	14	18	.438	0	0	4.29

Sid Fernandez

Pitches: Left **Bats:** Left **Pos:** SP   **Ht:** 6' 1" **Wt:** 230 **Born:** 10/12/62 **Age:** 29

			HOW MUCH HE PITCHED						WHAT HE GAVE UP										THE RESULTS					
Year	Team	Lg	G	GS	CG	GF	IP	BFP	H	R	ER	HR	SH	SF	HB	TBB	IBB	SO	WP	Bk	W	L	Pct.	ShO	Sv	ERA
1983	Los Angeles	NL	2	1	0	0	6	33	7	4	4	0	0	0	1	7	0	9	0	0	0	1	.000	0	0	6.00
1984	New York	NL	15	15	0	0	90	371	74	40	35	8	5	5	0	34	3	62	1	4	6	6	.500	0	0	3.50
1985	New York	NL	26	26	3	0	170.1	685	108	56	53	14	4	3	2	80	3	180	3	2	9	9	.500	0	0	2.80
1986	New York	NL	32	31	2	1	204.1	855	161	82	80	13	9	7	2	91	1	200	6	0	16	6	.727	1	1	3.52
1987	New York	NL	28	27	3	0	156	665	130	75	66	16	3	6	8	67	8	134	2	0	12	8	.600	1	0	3.81
1988	New York	NL	31	31	1	0	187	751	127	69	63	15	2	7	6	70	1	189	4	9	12	10	.545	1	0	3.03
1989	New York	NL	35	32	6	0	219.1	883	157	73	69	21	4	4	6	75	3	198	1	3	14	5	.737	2	0	2.83
1990	New York	NL	30	30	2	0	179.1	735	130	79	69	18	7	6	5	67	4	181	1	0	9	14	.391	1	0	3.46
1991	New York	NL	8	8	0	0	44	177	36	18	14	4	5	1	0	9	0	31	0	0	1	3	.250	0	0	2.86
	9 ML YEARS		207	201	17	1	1256.1	5155	930	496	453	109	39	39	30	500	23	1184	18	18	79	62	.560	6	1	3.25

Tony Fernandez

Bats: Both **Throws:** Right **Pos:** SS   **Ht:** 6' 2" **Wt:** 175 **Born:** 06/30/62 **Age:** 30

							BATTING												BASERUNNING				PERCENTAGES		
Year	Team	Lg	G	AB	H	2B	3B	HR	(Hm	Rd)	TB	R	RBI	TBB	IBB	SO	HBP	SH	SF	SB	CS	SB%	GDP	Avg	OBP	SLG
1983	Toronto	AL	15	34	9	1	1	0	(0	0)	12	5	2	2	0	2	1	1	0	0	1	.00	1	.265	.324	.353
1984	Toronto	AL	88	233	63	5	3	3	(2	1)	83	29	19	17	0	15	0	2	2	5	7	.42	3	.270	.317	.356
1985	Toronto	AL	161	564	163	31	10	2	(1	1)	220	71	51	43	2	41	2	7	2	13	6	.68	12	.289	.340	.390
1986	Toronto	AL	163	687	213	33	9	10	(4	6)	294	91	65	27	0	52	4	5	4	25	12	.68	8	.310	.338	.428
1987	Toronto	AL	146	578	186	29	8	5	(1	4)	246	90	67	51	3	48	5	4	4	32	12	.73	14	.322	.379	.426
1988	Toronto	AL	154	648	186	41	4	5	(3	2)	250	76	70	45	3	65	4	3	4	15	5	.75	9	.287	.335	.386
1989	Toronto	AL	140	573	147	25	9	11	(2	9)	223	64	64	29	1	51	3	2	10	22	6	.79	9	.257	.291	.389
1990	Toronto	AL	161	635	175	27	17	4	(2	2)	248	84	66	71	4	70	7	2	6	26	13	.67	17	.276	.352	.391
1991	San Diego	NL	145	558	152	27	5	4	(1	3)	201	81	38	55	0	74	0	7	1	23	9	.72	11	.272	.337	.360
	9 ML YEARS		1173	4510	1294	219	66	44	(15	29)	1777	591	442	340	13	418	26	33	33	161	71	.69	84	.287	.338	.394

Mike Fetters

Pitches: Right **Bats:** Right **Pos:** RP/SP   **Ht:** 6' 4" **Wt:** 212 **Born:** 12/19/64 **Age:** 27

			HOW MUCH HE PITCHED						WHAT HE GAVE UP										THE RESULTS					
Year	Team	Lg	G	GS	CG	GF	IP	BFP	H	R	ER	HR	SH	SF	HB	TBB	IBB	SO	WP	Bk	W	L	Pct.	ShO	Sv	ERA
1989	California	AL	1	1	0	0	3.1	16	5	4	3	1	0	0	0	1	0	4	2	0	0	0	.000	0	0	8.10
1990	California	AL	26	2	0	10	67.2	291	77	33	31	9	1	0	2	20	0	35	3	0	1	1	.500	0	1	4.12
1991	California	AL	19	4	0	8	44.2	206	53	29	24	4	1	0	3	28	2	24	4	0	2	5	.286	0	0	4.84
	3 ML YEARS		46	6	0	18	115.2	513	135	66	58	14	2	0	5	49	2	63	9	0	3	6	.333	0	1	4.51

Cecil Fielder

Bats: Right **Throws:** Right **Pos:** 1B/DH   **Ht:** 6' 3" **Wt:** 230 **Born:** 09/21/63 **Age:** 28

							BATTING												BASERUNNING				PERCENTAGES		
Year	Team	Lg	G	AB	H	2B	3B	HR	(Hm	Rd)	TB	R	RBI	TBB	IBB	SO	HBP	SH	SF	SB	CS	SB%	GDP	Avg	OBP	SLG
1985	Toronto	AL	30	74	23	4	0	4	(2	2)	39	6	16	6	0	16	0	0	1	0	0	.00	2	.311	.358	.527
1986	Toronto	AL	34	83	13	2	0	4	(0	4)	27	7	13	6	0	27	1	0	0	0	0	.00	3	.157	.222	.325

63

Year Team	Lg	G	AB	H	2B	3B	HR	(Hm	Rd)	TB	R	RBI	TBB	IBB	SO	HBP	SH	SF	SB	CS	SB%	GDP	Avg	OBP	SLG
1987 Toronto	AL	82	175	47	7	1	14	(10	4)	98	30	32	20	2	48	1	0	1	0	1	.00	6	.269	.345	.560
1988 Toronto	AL	74	174	40	6	1	9	(6	3)	75	24	23	14	0	53	1	0	1	0	1	.00	6	.230	.289	.431
1990 Detroit	AL	159	573	159	25	1	51	(25	26)	339	104	132	90	11	182	5	0	5	0	1	.00	15	.277	.377	.592
1991 Detroit	AL	162	624	163	25	0	44	(27	17)	320	102	133	78	12	151	6	0	0	0	0	.00	17	.261	.347	.513
6 ML YEARS		541	1703	445	69	3	126	(70	56)	898	273	349	214	25	477	14	0	12	0	3	.00	49	.261	.346	.527

Chuck Finley

Pitches: Left **Bats:** Left **Pos:** SP   **Ht:** 6' 6" **Wt:** 214 **Born:** 11/26/62 **Age:** 29

Year Team	Lg	HOW MUCH HE PITCHED						WHAT HE GAVE UP												THE RESULTS					
		G	GS	CG	GF	IP	BFP	H	R	ER	HR	SH	SF	HB	TBB	IBB	SO	WP	Bk	W	L	Pct.	ShO	Sv	ERA
1986 California	AL	25	0	0	7	46.1	198	40	17	17	2	4	0	1	23	1	37	2	0	3	1	.750	0	0	3.30
1987 California	AL	35	3	0	17	90.2	405	102	54	47	7	2	2	3	43	3	63	4	3	2	7	.222	0	0	4.67
1988 California	AL	31	31	2	0	194.1	831	191	95	90	15	7	10	6	82	7	111	5	8	9	15	.375	0	0	4.17
1989 California	AL	29	29	9	0	199.2	827	171	64	57	13	7	3	2	82	0	156	4	2	16	9	.640	1	0	2.57
1990 California	AL	32	32	7	0	236	962	210	77	63	17	12	3	2	81	3	177	9	0	18	9	.667	2	0	2.40
1991 California	AL	34	34	4	0	227.1	955	205	102	96	23	4	3	8	101	1	171	6	3	18	9	.667	2	0	3.80
6 ML YEARS		186	129	22	24	994.1	4178	919	409	370	77	36	21	22	412	15	715	30	16	66	50	.569	5	0	3.35

Steve Finley

Bats: Left **Throws:** Left **Pos:** CF/RF   **Ht:** 6' 2" **Wt:** 180 **Born:** 03/12/65 **Age:** 27

Year Team	Lg	BATTING																	BASERUNNING				PERCENTAGES		
		G	AB	H	2B	3B	HR	(Hm	Rd)	TB	R	RBI	TBB	IBB	SO	HBP	SH	SF	SB	CS	SB%	GDP	Avg	OBP	SLG
1989 Baltimore	AL	81	217	54	5	2	2	(0	2)	69	35	25	15	1	30	1	6	2	17	3	.85	3	.249	.298	.318
1990 Baltimore	AL	142	464	119	16	4	3	(1	2)	152	46	37	32	3	53	2	10	5	22	9	.71	8	.256	.304	.328
1991 Houston	NL	159	596	170	28	10	8	(0	8)	242	84	54	42	5	65	2	10	6	34	18	.65	8	.285	.331	.406
3 ML YEARS		382	1277	343	49	16	13	(1	12)	463	165	116	89	9	148	5	26	13	73	30	.71	19	.269	.316	.363

Carlton Fisk

Bats: Right **Throws:** Right **Pos:** C/1B/DH   **Ht:** 6' 2" **Wt:** 223 **Born:** 12/26/47 **Age:** 44

Year Team	Lg	BATTING																	BASERUNNING				PERCENTAGES		
		G	AB	H	2B	3B	HR	(Hm	Rd)	TB	R	RBI	TBB	IBB	SO	HBP	SH	SF	SB	CS	SB%	GDP	Avg	OBP	SLG
1969 Boston	AL	2	5	0	0	0	0	(0	0)	0	0	0	0	0	2	0	0	0	0	0	.00	0	.000	.000	.000
1971 Boston	AL	14	48	15	2	1	2	(0	2)	25	7	6	1	0	10	0	0	0	0	0	.00	1	.313	.327	.521
1972 Boston	AL	131	457	134	28	9	22	(13	9)	246	74	61	52	6	83	4	1	0	5	2	.71	11	.293	.370	.538
1973 Boston	AL	135	508	125	21	0	26	(16	10)	224	65	71	37	2	99	10	1	2	7	2	.78	11	.246	.309	.441
1974 Boston	AL	52	187	56	12	1	11	(5	6)	103	36	26	24	2	23	2	2	1	5	1	.83	5	.299	.383	.551
1975 Boston	AL	79	263	87	14	4	10	(6	4)	139	47	52	27	4	32	2	0	2	4	3	.57	7	.331	.395	.529
1976 Boston	AL	134	487	124	17	5	17	(10	7)	202	76	58	56	3	71	6	3	5	12	5	.71	11	.255	.336	.415
1977 Boston	AL	152	536	169	26	3	26	(15	11)	279	106	102	75	3	85	9	2	10	7	6	.54	9	.315	.402	.521
1978 Boston	AL	157	571	162	39	5	20	(8	12)	271	94	88	71	6	83	7	3	6	7	2	.78	10	.284	.366	.475
1979 Boston	AL	91	320	87	23	2	10	(5	5)	144	49	42	10	0	38	6	1	3	3	0	1.00	9	.272	.304	.450
1980 Boston	AL	131	478	138	25	3	18	(12	6)	223	73	62	36	0	62	13	0	3	11	5	.69	12	.289	.353	.467
1981 Chicago	AL	96	338	89	12	0	7	(4	3)	122	44	45	38	3	37	12	1	5	3	2	.60	9	.263	.354	.361
1982 Chicago	AL	135	476	127	17	3	14	(7	7)	192	66	65	46	7	60	6	4	4	17	2	.89	12	.267	.336	.403
1983 Chicago	AL	138	488	141	26	4	26	(17	9)	253	85	86	46	3	88	6	2	3	9	6	.60	8	.289	.355	.518
1984 Chicago	AL	102	359	83	20	1	21	(11	10)	168	54	43	26	4	60	5	1	4	6	0	1.00	7	.231	.289	.468
1985 Chicago	AL	153	543	129	23	1	37	(20	17)	265	85	107	52	12	81	17	2	6	17	9	.65	9	.238	.320	.488
1986 Chicago	AL	125	457	101	11	0	14	(5	9)	154	42	63	22	2	92	6	0	6	2	4	.33	10	.221	.263	.337
1987 Chicago	AL	135	454	116	22	1	23	(5	18)	209	68	71	39	8	72	8	1	6	1	4	.20	9	.256	.321	.460
1988 Chicago	AL	76	253	70	8	1	19	(9	10)	137	37	50	37	9	40	5	1	2	0	0	.00	6	.277	.377	.542
1989 Chicago	AL	103	375	110	25	2	13	(4	9)	178	47	68	36	8	60	3	0	5	1	0	1.00	15	.293	.356	.475
1990 Chicago	AL	137	452	129	21	0	18	(5	13)	204	65	65	61	8	73	7	0	1	7	2	.78	12	.285	.378	.451
1991 Chicago	AL	134	460	111	25	0	18	(9	9)	190	42	74	32	4	86	7	0	2	1	2	.33	19	.241	.299	.413
22 ML YEARS		2412	8515	2303	417	46	372	(186	186)	3928	1262	1305	824	100	1337	141	25	76	125	57	.69	202	.270	.342	.461

Mike Fitzgerald

Bats: Right **Throws:** Right **Pos:** C   **Ht:** 5'11" **Wt:** 190 **Born:** 07/13/60 **Age:** 31

Year Team	Lg	BATTING																	BASERUNNING				PERCENTAGES		
		G	AB	H	2B	3B	HR	(Hm	Rd)	TB	R	RBI	TBB	IBB	SO	HBP	SH	SF	SB	CS	SB%	GDP	Avg	OBP	SLG
1983 New York	NL	8	20	2	0	0	1	(0	1)	5	1	2	3	1	6	0	0	0	0	0	.00	0	.100	.217	.250
1984 New York	NL	112	360	87	15	1	2	(2	0)	110	20	33	24	7	71	1	5	4	1	0	1.00	17	.242	.288	.306
1985 Montreal	NL	108	295	61	7	1	5	(3	2)	85	25	34	38	12	55	2	1	5	5	3	.63	8	.207	.297	.288
1986 Montreal	NL	73	209	59	13	1	6	(1	5)	92	20	37	27	6	34	1	4	2	3	2	.60	4	.282	.364	.440
1987 Montreal	NL	107	287	69	11	0	3	(1	2)	89	32	36	42	7	54	1	3	1	3	4	.43	10	.240	.338	.310
1988 Montreal	NL	63	155	42	6	1	5	(3	2)	65	17	23	19	0	22	0	4	2	2	2	.50	4	.271	.347	.419

Year	Team	Lg																								
1989	Montreal	NL	100	290	69	18	2	7	(3	4)	112	33	42	35	3	61	2	2	2	3	4	.43	8	.238	.322	.386
1990	Montreal	NL	111	313	76	18	1	9	(2	7)	123	36	41	60	2	60	2	5	3	8	1	.89	5	.243	.365	.393
1991	Montreal	NL	71	198	40	5	2	4	(1	3)	61	17	28	22	4	35	0	1	3	4	2	.67	5	.202	.278	.308
	9 ML YEARS		753	2127	505	93	9	42	(16	26)	742	201	276	270	42	398	9	25	22	29	18	.62	61	.237	.323	.349

Mike Flanagan

Pitches: Left **Bats:** Left **Pos:** RP **Ht:** 6' 0" **Wt:** 195 **Born:** 12/16/51 **Age:** 40

			HOW MUCH HE PITCHED					WHAT HE GAVE UP									THE RESULTS						
Year	Team	Lg	G	GS	CG	GF	IP	BFP	H	R	ER	HR	SH	SF	HB	TBB	IBB	SO	WP	Bk	W	L	Pct.	ShO	Sv	ERA
1975	Baltimore	AL	2	1	0	0	10	42	9	4	3	0	0	0	0	6	1	7	0	0	0	1	.000	0	0	2.70
1976	Baltimore	AL	20	10	4	7	85	358	83	41	39	7	2	4	0	33	0	56	2	1	3	5	.375	0	0	4.13
1977	Baltimore	AL	36	33	15	2	235	974	235	100	95	17	10	7	2	70	5	149	5	0	15	10	.600	2	1	3.64
1978	Baltimore	AL	40	40	17	0	281	1160	271	128	126	22	10	5	3	87	2	167	8	1	19	15	.559	2	0	4.04
1979	Baltimore	AL	39	38	16	0	266	1085	245	107	91	23	9	4	3	70	1	190	6	0	23	9	.719	5	0	3.08
1980	Baltimore	AL	37	37	12	0	251	1065	278	121	115	27	10	12	2	71	3	128	12	1	16	13	.552	2	0	4.12
1981	Baltimore	AL	20	20	3	0	116	482	108	55	54	11	0	0	2	37	1	72	6	0	9	6	.600	2	0	4.19
1982	Baltimore	AL	36	35	11	1	236	991	233	110	104	24	5	6	4	76	5	103	9	2	15	11	.577	1	0	3.97
1983	Baltimore	AL	20	20	3	0	125.1	528	135	53	46	10	4	6	2	31	2	50	1	0	12	4	.750	1	0	3.30
1984	Baltimore	AL	34	34	10	0	226.2	947	213	103	89	24	8	6	1	81	5	115	8	0	13	13	.500	2	0	3.53
1985	Baltimore	AL	15	15	1	0	86	379	101	49	49	14	7	2	2	28	0	42	3	0	4	5	.444	0	0	5.13
1986	Baltimore	AL	29	28	2	0	172	747	179	95	81	15	10	6	1	66	4	96	8	1	7	11	.389	0	0	4.24
1987	2 ML Teams		23	23	4	0	144	619	148	72	65	12	6	1	0	51	4	93	3	0	6	8	.429	0	0	4.06
1988	Toronto	AL	34	34	2	0	211	916	220	106	98	23	14	4	6	80	1	99	3	4	13	13	.500	1	0	4.18
1989	Toronto	AL	30	30	1	0	171.2	726	186	82	75	10	8	8	5	47	0	47	4	0	8	10	.444	1	0	3.93
1990	Toronto	AL	5	5	0	0	20.1	94	28	14	12	3	1	0	0	8	0	5	0	0	2	2	.500	0	0	5.31
1991	Baltimore	AL	64	1	0	24	98.1	391	84	27	26	6	4	3	3	25	6	55	2	2	2	7	.222	0	3	2.38
1987	Baltimore	AL	16	16	4	0	94.2	410	102	57	52	9	6	1	0	36	1	50	1	0	3	6	.333	0	0	4.94
	Toronto	AL	7	7	0	0	49.1	209	46	15	13	3	0	0	0	15	3	43	2	0	3	2	.600	0	0	2.37
	17 ML YEARS		484	404	101	34	2735.1	11504	2756	1267	1168	248	108	74	36	867	40	1474	80	12	167	143	.539	19	4	3.84

Dave Fleming

Pitches: Left **Bats:** Left **Pos:** RP/SP **Ht:** 6' 3" **Wt:** 200 **Born:** 11/07/69 **Age:** 22

			HOW MUCH HE PITCHED					WHAT HE GAVE UP									THE RESULTS						
Year	Team	Lg	G	GS	CG	GF	IP	BFP	H	R	ER	HR	SH	SF	HB	TBB	IBB	SO	WP	Bk	W	L	Pct.	ShO	Sv	ERA
1990	San Berndno	A	12	12	4	0	79.2	328	64	29	23	0	1	1	1	30	1	77	1	5	7	3	.700	0	0	2.60
1991	Jacksnville	AA	21	20	6	0	140	567	129	50	42	7	5	2	2	25	2	109	6	0	10	6	.625	1	0	2.70
1991	Calgary	AAA	3	2	1	0	16	60	10	2	2	1	0	1	0	3	0	16	0	0	2	0	1.000	0	0	1.13
1991	Seattle	AL	9	3	0	3	17.2	73	19	13	13	3	0	0	0	3	0	11	1	0	1	0	1.000	0	0	6.62

Darrin Fletcher

Bats: Left **Throws:** Right **Pos:** C **Ht:** 6' 1" **Wt:** 199 **Born:** 10/03/66 **Age:** 25

			BATTING															BASERUNNING				PERCENTAGES		
Year	Team	Lg	G	AB	H	2B	3B	HR	(Hm	Rd)	TB	R	RBI	TBB	IBB	SO	HBP	SH	SF	SB	CS	SB%	GDP	Avg	OBP	SLG
1987	Vero Beach	A	43	124	33	7	0	0	--	--	40	13	15	22	3	12	1	0	4	0	2	.00	6	.266	.371	.323
1988	San Antonio	AA	89	279	58	8	0	1	--	--	69	19	20	17	5	42	3	6	2	2	6	.25	6	.208	.259	.247
1989	Albuquerque	AAA	100	315	86	16	1	5	--	--	119	34	44	30	0	38	2	2	6	1	5	.17	12	.273	.334	.378
1990	Albuquerque	AAA	105	350	102	23	1	13	--	--	166	58	65	40	6	37	5	3	6	1	1	.50	11	.291	.367	.474
1991	Scranton-Wb	AAA	90	306	87	13	1	8	--	--	126	39	50	23	4	29	3	1	6	1	2	.33	7	.284	.334	.412
1989	Los Angeles	NL	5	8	4	0	0	1	(1	0)	7	1	2	1	0	1	0	0	0	0	0	.00	0	.500	.556	.875
1990	2 ML Teams		11	23	3	1	0	0	(0	0)	4	3	1	1	0	6	0	0	0	0	0	.00	0	.130	.167	.174
1991	Philadelphia	NL	46	136	31	8	0	1	(1	0)	42	5	12	5	0	15	0	1	0	0	1	.00	2	.228	.255	.309
1990	Los Angeles	NL	2	1	0	0	0	0	(0	0)	0	0	0	0	0	1	0	0	0	0	0	.00	0	.000	.000	.000
	Philadelphia	NL	9	22	3	1	0	0	(0	0)	4	3	1	1	0	5	0	0	0	0	0	.00	0	.136	.174	.182
	3 ML YEARS		62	167	38	9	0	2	(2	0)	53	9	15	7	0	21	0	1	0	0	1	.00	2	.228	.259	.317

Scott Fletcher

Bats: Right **Throws:** Right **Pos:** 2B **Ht:** 5'11" **Wt:** 173 **Born:** 07/30/58 **Age:** 33

			BATTING															BASERUNNING				PERCENTAGES		
Year	Team	Lg	G	AB	H	2B	3B	HR	(Hm | Rd)	TB	R	RBI	TBB	IBB	SO	HBP	SH	SF	SB	CS	SB%	GDP	Avg	OBP	SLG
1981	Chicago	NL	19	46	10	4	0	0	(0 | 0)	14	6	1	2	0	4	0	0	0	0	0	.00	0	.217	.250	.304
1982	Chicago	NL	11	24	4	0	0	0	(0 | 0)	4	4	1	4	0	5	0	0	0	1	0	1.00	0	.167	.286	.167
1983	Chicago	AL	114	262	62	16	5	3	(1 | 2)	97	42	31	29	0	22	2	7	2	5	1	.83	5	.237	.315	.370
1984	Chicago	AL	149	456	114	13	3	3	(2 | 1)	142	46	35	46	2	46	8	9	2	10	4	.71	5	.250	.328	.311
1985	Chicago	AL	119	301	77	8	1	2	(0 | 2)	93	38	31	35	0	47	0	11	1	5	5	.50	9	.256	.332	.309
1986	Texas	AL	147	530	159	34	5	3	(2 | 1)	212	82	50	47	0	59	4	10	3	12	11	.52	10	.300	.360	.400
1987	Texas	AL	156	588	169	28	4	5	(4 | 1)	220	82	63	61	3	66	5	12	2	13	12	.52	19	.287	.358	.374
1988	Texas	AL	140	515	142	19	4	0	(0 | 0)	169	59	47	62	1	34	12	15	5	8	5	.62	13	.276	.364	.328
1989	2 ML Teams		142	546	138	25	2	1	(0 | 1)	170	77	43	64	1	60	3	11	5	2	1	.67	12	.253	.332	.311

1990	Chicago	AL	151	509	123	18	3	4	(1	3)	159	54	56	45	3	63	3	11	5	1	3	.25	10	.242	.304	.312
1991	Chicago	AL	90	248	51	10	1	1	(0	1)	66	14	28	17	0	26	3	6	3	0	2	.00	3	.206	.262	.266
1989	Texas	AL	83	314	75	14	1	0	(0	0)	91	47	22	38	1	41	2	2	2	1	0	1.00	8	.239	.323	.290
	Chicago	AL	59	232	63	11	1	1	(0	1)	79	30	21	26	0	19	1	9	3	1	1	.50	4	.272	.344	.341
	11 ML YEARS		1238	4025	1049	175	28	22	(10	12)	1346	504	386	412	10	432	40	92	28	57	44	.56	84	.261	.333	.334

Kevin Flora

Bats: Right **Throws:** Right **Pos:** 2B **Ht:** 6' 0" **Wt:** 180 **Born:** 06/10/69 **Age:** 23

					BATTING															BASERUNNING				PERCENTAGES		
Year	Team	Lg	G	AB	H	2B	3B	HR	(Hm	Rd)	TB	R	RBI	TBB	IBB	SO	HBP	SH	SF	SB	CS	SB%	GDP	Avg	OBP	SLG
1987	Salem	A	35	88	24	5	1	0	--	--	31	17	12	21	0	14	0	3	0	8	4	.67	2	.273	.413	.352
1988	Quad City	A	48	152	33	3	4	0	--	--	44	19	15	18	4	33	0	1	0	5	3	.63	4	.217	.300	.289
1989	Quad City	A	120	372	81	8	4	1	--	--	100	46	21	57	2	107	6	5	3	30	10	.75	3	.218	.329	.269
1990	Midland	AA	71	232	53	16	5	5	--	--	94	35	32	23	0	53	0	3	1	11	5	.69	6	.228	.297	.405
1991	Midland	AA	124	484	138	14	15	12	--	--	218	97	67	37	0	92	3	3	3	40	8	.83	2	.285	.338	.450
1991	California	AL	3	8	1	0	0	0	(0	0)	1	1	0	0	0	5	0	1	0	1	0	1.00	1	.125	.222	.125

Tom Foley

Bats: Left **Throws:** Right **Pos:** SS/1B **Ht:** 6' 1" **Wt:** 180 **Born:** 09/09/59 **Age:** 32

					BATTING															BASERUNNING				PERCENTAGES		
Year	Team	Lg	G	AB	H	2B	3B	HR	(Hm	Rd)	TB	R	RBI	TBB	IBB	SO	HBP	SH	SF	SB	CS	SB%	GDP	Avg	OBP	SLG
1983	Cincinnati	NL	68	98	20	4	1	0	(0	0)	26	7	9	13	2	17	0	2	0	1	0	1.00	1	.204	.297	.265
1984	Cincinnati	NL	106	277	70	8	3	5	(2	3)	99	26	27	24	7	36	0	1	2	3	2	.60	2	.253	.310	.357
1985	2 ML Teams		89	250	60	13	1	3	(2	1)	84	24	23	19	8	34	0	0	0	2	3	.40	2	.240	.294	.336
1986	2 ML Teams		103	263	70	15	3	1	(1	0)	94	26	23	30	6	37	0	2	4	10	3	.77	4	.266	.337	.357
1987	Montreal	NL	106	280	82	18	3	5	(3	2)	121	35	28	11	0	40	1	1	0	6	10	.38	6	.293	.322	.432
1988	Montreal	NL	127	377	100	21	3	5	(3	2)	142	33	43	30	10	49	1	0	3	2	7	.22	11	.265	.319	.377
1989	Montreal	NL	122	375	86	19	2	7	(4	3)	130	34	39	45	4	53	3	4	4	2	3	.40	2	.229	.314	.347
1990	Montreal	NL	73	164	35	2	1	0	(0	0)	39	11	12	12	2	22	0	1	1	0	1	.00	4	.213	.266	.238
1991	Montreal	NL	86	168	35	11	1	0	(0	0)	48	12	15	14	4	30	1	1	3	2	0	1.00	4	.208	.269	.286
1985	Cincinnati	NL	43	92	18	5	1	0	(0	0)	25	7	6	6	1	16	0	0	0	1	0	1.00	1	.196	.245	.272
	Philadelphia	NL	46	158	42	8	0	3	(2	1)	59	17	17	13	7	18	0	0	0	1	3	.25	2	.266	.322	.373
1986	Philadelphia	NL	39	61	18	2	1	0	(0	0)	22	8	5	10	1	11	0	0	1	2	0	1.00	1	.295	.389	.361
	Montreal	NL	64	202	52	13	2	1	(1	0)	72	18	18	20	5	26	0	2	3	8	3	.73	3	.257	.320	.356
	9 ML YEARS		880	2252	558	111	18	26	(15	11)	783	208	219	198	43	318	6	12	17	28	29	.49	36	.248	.308	.348

Tony Fossas

Pitches: Left **Bats:** Left **Pos:** RP **Ht:** 6' 0" **Wt:** 190 **Born:** 09/23/57 **Age:** 34

			HOW MUCH HE PITCHED						WHAT HE GAVE UP									THE RESULTS					
Year	Team	Lg	G	GS	CG	GF	IP	BFP	H	R	ER	HR	SH	SF	HB	TBB	IBB	SO	WP	Bk	W	L	Pct.	ShO	Sv	ERA
1988	Texas	AL	5	0	0	1	5.2	28	11	3	3	0	0	0	0	2	0	0	1	0	0	0	.000	0	0	4.76
1989	Milwaukee	AL	51	0	0	16	61	256	57	27	24	3	7	3	1	22	7	42	1	3	2	2	.500	0	1	3.54
1990	Milwaukee	AL	32	0	0	9	29.1	146	44	23	21	5	2	1	0	10	2	24	0	0	2	3	.400	0	0	6.44
1991	Boston	AL	64	0	0	18	57	244	49	27	22	3	5	0	3	28	9	29	2	0	3	2	.600	0	1	3.47
	4 ML YEARS		152	0	0	44	153	674	161	80	70	11	14	4	4	62	18	95	4	3	7	7	.500	0	2	4.12

Steve Foster

Pitches: Right **Bats:** Right **Pos:** RP **Ht:** 6' 0" **Wt:** 180 **Born:** 08/16/66 **Age:** 25

			HOW MUCH HE PITCHED						WHAT HE GAVE UP									THE RESULTS					
Year	Team	Lg	G	GS	CG	GF	IP	BFP	H	R	ER	HR	SH	SF	HB	TBB	IBB	SO	WP	Bk	W	L	Pct.	ShO	Sv	ERA
1988	Billings	R	18	0	0	14	30.1	114	15	5	4	0	3	2	3	7	1	27	1	7	2	3	.400	0	7	1.19
1989	Cedar Rapds	A	51	0	0	47	59	245	46	16	14	2	2	1	5	19	6	55	5	5	0	0	.000	0	23	2.14
1990	Chattanooga	AA	50	0	0	42	59.1	277	69	38	35	6	3	8	4	33	4	51	2	2	5	10	.333	0	20	5.31
1991	Chattanooga	AA	17	0	0	16	15.2	64	14	4	2	0	1	0	3	4	0	18	2	1	0	2	.000	0	10	1.15
	Nashville	AAA	41	0	0	25	54.2	237	46	17	13	4	2	3	1	29	5	52	0	0	2	3	.400	0	12	2.14
1991	Cincinnati	NL	11	0	0	5	14	53	7	5	3	1	0	0	0	4	0	11	0	0	0	0	.000	0	0	1.93

John Franco

Pitches: Left **Bats:** Left **Pos:** RP **Ht:** 5'10" **Wt:** 185 **Born:** 09/17/60 **Age:** 31

			HOW MUCH HE PITCHED						WHAT HE GAVE UP									THE RESULTS					
Year	Team	Lg	G	GS	CG	GF	IP	BFP	H	R	ER	HR	SH	SF	HB	TBB	IBB	SO	WP	Bk	W	L	Pct.	ShO	Sv	ERA
1984	Cincinnati	NL	54	0	0	30	79.1	335	74	28	23	3	4	4	2	36	4	55	2	0	6	2	.750	0	4	2.61
1985	Cincinnati	NL	67	0	0	33	99	407	83	27	24	5	11	1	1	40	8	61	4	0	12	3	.800	0	12	2.18
1986	Cincinnati	NL	74	0	0	52	101	429	90	40	33	7	8	3	2	44	12	84	4	2	6	6	.500	0	29	2.94
1987	Cincinnati	NL	68	0	0	60	82	344	76	26	23	6	5	2	0	27	6	61	1	0	8	5	.615	0	32	2.52
1988	Cincinnati	NL	70	0	0	61	86	336	60	18	15	3	5	1	0	27	3	46	1	2	6	6	.500	0	39	1.57
1989	Cincinnati	NL	60	0	0	50	80.2	345	77	35	28	3	7	3	0	36	8	60	3	2	4	8	.333	0	32	3.12

Year	Team	Lg	G	GS	CG	GF	IP	BFP	H	R	ER	HR	SH	SF	HB	TBB	IBB	SO	WP	Bk	W	L	Pct.	ShO	Sv	ERA
1990	New York	NL	55	0	0	48	67.2	287	66	22	19	4	3	1	0	21	2	56	7	2	5	3	.625	0	33	2.53
1991	New York	NL	52	0	0	48	55.1	247	61	27	18	2	3	0	1	18	4	45	6	0	5	9	.357	0	30	2.93
	8 ML YEARS		500	0	0	382	651	2730	587	223	183	33	46	15	6	249	47	468	28	8	52	42	.553	0	211	2.53

Julio Franco

Bats: Right **Throws:** Right **Pos:** 2B   **Ht:** 6' 1" **Wt:** 188 **Born:** 08/23/61 **Age:** 30

						BATTING														BASERUNNING				PERCENTAGES		
Year	Team	Lg	G	AB	H	2B	3B	HR	(Hm	Rd)	TB	R	RBI	TBB	IBB	SO	HBP	SH	SF	SB	CS	SB%	GDP	Avg	OBP	SLG
1982	Philadelphia	NL	16	29	8	1	0	0	(0	0)	9	3	3	2	1	4	0	1	0	0	2	.00	1	.276	.323	.310
1983	Cleveland	AL	149	560	153	24	8	8	(6	2)	217	68	80	27	1	50	2	3	6	32	12	.73	21	.273	.306	.388
1984	Cleveland	AL	160	658	188	22	5	3	(1	2)	229	82	79	43	1	68	6	1	10	19	10	.66	23	.286	.331	.348
1985	Cleveland	AL	160	636	183	33	4	6	(3	3)	242	97	90	54	2	74	4	0	9	13	9	.59	26	.288	.343	.381
1986	Cleveland	AL	149	599	183	30	5	10	(4	6)	253	80	74	32	1	66	0	0	5	10	7	.59	28	.306	.338	.422
1987	Cleveland	AL	128	495	158	24	3	8	(5	3)	212	86	52	57	2	56	3	0	5	32	9	.78	23	.319	.389	.428
1988	Cleveland	AL	152	613	186	23	6	10	(3	7)	251	88	54	56	4	72	2	1	4	25	11	.69	17	.303	.361	.409
1989	Texas	AL	150	548	173	31	5	13	(9	4)	253	80	92	66	11	69	1	0	6	21	3	.88	27	.316	.386	.462
1990	Texas	AL	157	582	172	27	1	11	(4	7)	234	96	69	82	3	83	2	2	2	31	10	.76	12	.296	.383	.402
1991	Texas	AL	146	589	201	27	3	15	(7	8)	279	108	78	65	8	78	3	0	2	36	9	.80	13	.341	.408	.474
	10 ML YEARS		1367	5309	1605	242	40	84	(42	42)	2179	788	671	484	34	620	23	8	49	219	82	.73	191	.302	.360	.410

Willie Fraser

Pitches: Right **Bats:** Right **Pos:** RP   **Ht:** 6' 1" **Wt:** 206 **Born:** 05/26/64 **Age:** 28

			HOW MUCH HE PITCHED						WHAT HE GAVE UP											THE RESULTS					
Year	Team	Lg	G	GS	CG	GF	IP	BFP	H	R	ER	HR	SH	SF	HB	TBB	IBB	SO	WP	Bk	W	L	Pct.	ShO	Sv	ERA
1986	California	AL	1	1	0	0	4.1	20	6	4	4	0	1	1	0	1	0	2	0	0	0	0	.000	0	0	8.31
1987	California	AL	36	23	5	6	176.2	744	160	85	77	26	5	4	6	63	3	106	12	1	10	10	.500	1	1	3.92
1988	California	AL	34	32	2	0	194.2	861	203	129	117	33	2	9	9	80	7	86	12	6	12	13	.480	0	0	5.41
1989	California	AL	44	0	0	21	91.2	375	80	33	33	6	4	3	5	23	4	46	5	0	4	7	.364	0	2	3.24
1990	California	AL	45	0	0	20	76	315	69	29	26	4	2	3	0	24	3	32	1	0	5	4	.556	0	2	3.08
1991	2 ML Teams		48	1	0	22	75.2	333	77	48	45	13	1	3	6	32	5	37	6	0	3	5	.375	0	0	5.35
1991	Toronto	AL	13	1	0	6	26.1	123	33	20	18	4	0	0	3	11	2	12	2	0	0	2	.000	0	0	6.15
	St. Louis	NL	35	0	0	16	49.1	210	44	28	27	9	1	3	3	21	3	25	4	0	3	3	.500	0	0	4.93
	6 ML YEARS		208	57	7	69	619	2648	595	328	302	82	15	23	26	223	22	309	36	7	34	39	.466	1	5	4.39

Marvin Freeman

Pitches: Right **Bats:** Right **Pos:** RP   **Ht:** 6' 7" **Wt:** 222 **Born:** 04/10/63 **Age:** 29

			HOW MUCH HE PITCHED						WHAT HE GAVE UP											THE RESULTS					
Year	Team	Lg	G	GS	CG	GF	IP	BFP	H	R	ER	HR	SH	SF	HB	TBB	IBB	SO	WP	Bk	W	L	Pct.	ShO	Sv	ERA
1986	Philadelphia	NL	3	3	0	0	16	61	4	0	0	1	0	0	0	10	0	8	1	0	2	0	1.000	0	0	2.25
1988	Philadelphia	NL	11	11	0	0	51.2	249	55	36	35	2	5	1	1	43	2	37	3	1	2	3	.400	0	0	6.10
1989	Philadelphia	NL	1	1	0	0	3	16	2	2	2	0	0	0	0	5	0	0	0	1	0	0	.000	0	0	6.00
1990	2 ML Teams		25	3	0	5	48	207	41	24	23	5	2	0	5	17	2	38	4	0	1	2	.333	0	1	4.31
1991	Atlanta	NL	34	0	0	8	48	190	37	19	16	2	1	1	2	13	1	34	4	0	1	0	1.000	0	1	3.00
1990	Philadelphia	NL	16	3	0	4	32.1	147	34	21	20	5	1	0	3	14	2	26	4	0	0	2	.000	0	1	5.57
	Atlanta		9	0	0	1	15.2	60	7	3	3	0	1	0	2	3	0	12	0	0	1	0	1.000	0	0	1.72
	5 ML YEARS		74	18	0	11	166.2	723	141	85	80	9	8	3	8	88	5	117	12	2	6	5	.545	0	2	4.32

Steve Frey

Pitches: Left **Bats:** Right **Pos:** RP   **Ht:** 5' 9" **Wt:** 170 **Born:** 07/29/63 **Age:** 28

			HOW MUCH HE PITCHED						WHAT HE GAVE UP											THE RESULTS					
Year	Team	Lg	G	GS	CG	GF	IP	BFP	H	R	ER	HR	SH	SF	HB	TBB	IBB	SO	WP	Bk	W	L	Pct.	ShO	Sv	ERA
1989	Montreal	NL	20	0	0	11	21.1	103	29	15	13	4	0	2	1	11	1	15	1	1	3	2	.600	0	0	5.48
1990	Montreal	NL	51	0	0	21	55.2	236	44	15	13	4	3	2	1	29	6	29	0	0	8	2	.800	0	9	2.10
1991	Montreal	NL	31	0	0	5	39.2	182	43	31	22	3	3	2	1	23	4	21	3	1	0	1	.000	0	1	4.99
	3 ML YEARS		102	0	0	37	116.2	521	116	61	48	11	6	6	3	63	11	65	4	2	11	5	.688	0	10	3.70

Todd Frohwirth

Pitches: Right **Bats:** Right **Pos:** RP   **Ht:** 6' 4" **Wt:** 195 **Born:** 09/28/62 **Age:** 29

			HOW MUCH HE PITCHED						WHAT HE GAVE UP											THE RESULTS					
Year	Team	Lg	G	GS	CG	GF	IP	BFP	H	R	ER	HR	SH	SF	HB	TBB	IBB	SO	WP	Bk	W	L	Pct.	ShO	Sv	ERA
1987	Philadelphia	NL	10	0	0	2	11	43	12	0	0	0	0	0	0	2	0	9	0	0	1	0	1.000	0	0	0.00
1988	Philadelphia	NL	12	0	0	6	12	62	16	11	11	2	1	1	0	11	6	11	1	0	1	2	.333	0	0	8.25
1989	Philadelphia	NL	45	0	0	11	62.2	258	56	26	25	4	3	1	3	18	0	39	1	1	1	0	1.000	0	0	3.59
1990	Philadelphia	NL	5	0	0	0	1	12	3	2	2	0	0	0	0	6	2	1	1	0	0	1	.000	0	0	18.00
1991	Baltimore	AL	51	0	0	10	96.1	372	64	24	20	2	4	1	1	29	3	77	0	0	7	3	.700	0	3	1.87
	5 ML YEARS		123	0	0	29	183	747	151	63	58	8	8	3	4	66	11	137	3	1	10	6	.625	0	3	2.85

Travis Fryman

Bats: Right **Throws:** Right **Pos:** 3B/SS **Ht:** 6' 1" **Wt:** 194 **Born:** 03/25/69 **Age:** 23

Year Team	Lg	G	AB	H	2B	3B	HR	(Hm	Rd)	TB	R	RBI	TBB	IBB	SO	HBP	SH	SF	SB	CS	SB%	GDP	Avg	OBP	SLG
1987 Bristol	R	67	248	58	9	0	2	--	--	73	25	20	22	0	40	1	0	2	5	2	.71	12	.234	.297	.294
1988 Fayetteville	A	123	411	96	17	4	0	--	--	121	44	47	24	0	83	10	8	5	18	5	.78	6	.234	.289	.294
1989 London	AA	118	426	113	30	1	9	--	--	172	52	56	19	0	78	8	2	4	5	3	.63	5	.265	.306	.404
1990 Toledo	AAA	87	327	84	22	2	10	--	--	140	38	53	17	0	59	2	2	3	4	7	.36	7	.257	.295	.428
1990 Detroit	AL	66	232	69	11	1	9	(5	4)	109	32	27	17	0	51	1	1	0	3	3	.50	3	.297	.348	.470
1991 Detroit	AL	149	557	144	36	3	21	(8	13)	249	65	91	40	0	149	3	6	6	12	5	.71	13	.259	.309	.447
2 ML YEARS		215	789	213	47	4	30	(13	17)	358	97	118	57	0	200	4	7	6	15	8	.65	16	.270	.320	.454

Gary Gaetti

Bats: Right **Throws:** Right **Pos:** 3B **Ht:** 6' 0" **Wt:** 200 **Born:** 08/19/58 **Age:** 33

Year Team	Lg	G	AB	H	2B	3B	HR	(Hm	Rd)	TB	R	RBI	TBB	IBB	SO	HBP	SH	SF	SB	CS	SB%	GDP	Avg	OBP	SLG
1981 Minnesota	AL	9	26	5	0	0	2	(1	1)	11	4	3	0	0	6	0	0	0	0	0	.00	1	.192	.192	.423
1982 Minnesota	AL	145	508	117	25	4	25	(15	10)	225	59	84	37	2	107	3	4	13	0	4	.00	16	.230	.280	.443
1983 Minnesota	AL	157	584	143	30	3	21	(7	14)	242	81	78	54	2	121	4	0	8	7	1	.88	18	.245	.309	.414
1984 Minnesota	AL	162	588	154	29	4	5	(2	3)	206	55	65	44	1	81	4	3	5	11	5	.69	9	.262	.315	.350
1985 Minnesota	AL	160	560	138	31	0	20	(10	10)	229	71	63	37	3	89	7	3	1	13	5	.72	15	.246	.301	.409
1986 Minnesota	AL	157	596	171	34	1	34	(16	18)	309	91	108	52	4	108	6	1	6	14	15	.48	18	.287	.347	.518
1987 Minnesota	AL	154	584	150	36	2	31	(18	13)	283	95	109	37	7	92	3	1	3	10	7	.59	25	.257	.303	.485
1988 Minnesota	AL	133	468	141	29	2	28	(9	19)	258	66	88	36	5	85	5	1	6	7	4	.64	10	.301	.353	.551
1989 Minnesota	AL	130	498	125	11	4	19	(10	9)	201	63	75	25	5	87	3	1	9	6	2	.75	12	.251	.286	.404
1990 Minnesota	AL	154	577	132	27	5	16	(7	9)	217	61	85	36	1	101	3	1	8	6	1	.86	22	.229	.274	.376
1991 California	AL	152	586	144	22	1	18	(12	6)	222	58	66	33	3	104	8	2	5	5	5	.50	13	.246	.293	.379
11 ML YEARS		1513	5575	1420	274	26	219	(107	112)	2403	704	824	391	33	981	46	17	64	79	49	.62	159	.255	.306	.431

Greg Gagne

Bats: Right **Throws:** Right **Pos:** SS **Ht:** 5'11" **Wt:** 172 **Born:** 11/12/61 **Age:** 30

Year Team	Lg	G	AB	H	2B	3B	HR	(Hm	Rd)	TB	R	RBI	TBB	IBB	SO	HBP	SH	SF	SB	CS	SB%	GDP	Avg	OBP	SLG
1983 Minnesota	AL	10	27	3	1	0	0	(0	0)	4	2	3	0	0	6	0	0	2	0	0	.00	0	.111	.103	.148
1984 Minnesota	AL	2	1	0	0	0	0	(0	0)	0	0	0	0	0	0	0	0	0	0	0	.00	0	.000	.000	.000
1985 Minnesota	AL	114	293	66	15	3	2	(0	2)	93	37	23	20	0	57	3	3	3	10	4	.71	5	.225	.279	.317
1986 Minnesota	AL	156	472	118	22	6	12	(10	2)	188	63	54	30	0	108	6	13	3	12	10	.55	4	.250	.301	.398
1987 Minnesota	AL	137	437	116	28	7	10	(7	3)	188	68	40	25	0	84	4	10	2	6	6	.50	3	.265	.310	.430
1988 Minnesota	AL	149	461	109	20	6	14	(5	9)	183	70	48	27	2	110	7	11	1	15	7	.68	13	.236	.288	.397
1989 Minnesota	AL	149	460	125	29	7	9	(5	4)	195	69	48	17	0	80	2	7	5	11	4	.73	10	.272	.298	.424
1990 Minnesota	AL	138	388	91	22	3	7	(3	4)	140	38	38	24	0	76	1	8	2	8	8	.50	5	.235	.280	.361
1991 Minnesota	AL	139	408	108	23	3	8	(3	5)	161	52	42	26	0	72	3	5	5	11	9	.55	15	.265	.310	.395
9 ML YEARS		994	2947	736	160	35	62	(33	29)	1152	399	296	169	2	593	26	57	23	73	48	.60	55	.250	.294	.391

Dan Gakeler

Pitches: Right **Bats:** Right **Pos:** RP/SP **Ht:** 6' 6" **Wt:** 215 **Born:** 05/01/64 **Age:** 28

Year Team	Lg	G	GS	CG	GF	IP	BFP	H	R	ER	HR	SH	SF	HB	TBB	IBB	SO	WP	Bk	W	L	Pct.	ShO	Sv	ERA
1984 Elmira	A	14	13	0	1	76.2	341	67	47	35	9	5	2	7	41	3	54	2	2	4	6	.400	0	0	4.11
1985 Greensboro	A	23	16	3	2	108	509	135	86	66	8	2	3	3	54	0	51	4	0	7	5	.583	1	0	5.50
1986 Greensboro	A	24	23	5	1	154.1	679	158	73	57	6	4	4	4	69	1	154	11	2	7	6	.538	1	1	3.32
1987 New Britain	AA	30	25	5	3	173	769	188	112	89	14	2	7	7	63	5	90	7	3	8	13	.381	1	0	4.63
1988 New Britain	AA	26	25	5	0	153.2	660	157	74	63	4	3	1	5	54	1	110	9	3	6	13	.316	2	0	3.69
1989 Jacksnville	AA	14	14	2	0	86.2	365	70	31	23	1	1	1	3	39	1	76	6	1	5	4	.556	1	0	2.39
Indianapols	AAA	11	11	1	0	66.1	280	53	29	23	1	4	1	3	28	1	41	4	0	3	6	.333	0	0	3.12
1990 Indianapols	AAA	22	21	1	0	120	509	101	55	43	2	7	2	7	55	1	89	6	0	5	5	.500	1	0	3.22
1991 Toledo	AAA	23	2	0	12	43.2	187	44	22	17	0	2	1	1	13	1	32	3	0	2	3	.400	0	4	3.50
1991 Detroit	AL	31	7	0	11	73.2	331	73	52	47	5	3	3	1	39	1	43	7	0	1	4	.200	0	2	5.74

Andres Galarraga

Bats: Right **Throws:** Right **Pos:** 1B **Ht:** 6' 3" **Wt:** 235 **Born:** 06/18/61 **Age:** 31

Year Team	Lg	G	AB	H	2B	3B	HR	(Hm	Rd)	TB	R	RBI	TBB	IBB	SO	HBP	SH	SF	SB	CS	SB%	GDP	Avg	OBP	SLG
1985 Montreal	NL	24	75	14	1	0	2	(0	2)	21	9	4	3	0	18	1	0	0	1	2	.33	0	.187	.228	.280
1986 Montreal	NL	105	321	87	13	0	10	(4	6)	130	39	42	30	5	79	3	1	1	6	5	.55	8	.271	.338	.405
1987 Montreal	NL	147	551	168	40	3	13	(7	6)	253	72	90	41	13	127	10	0	4	7	10	.41	11	.305	.361	.459
1988 Montreal	NL	157	609	184	42	8	29	(14	15)	329	99	92	39	9	153	10	0	3	13	4	.76	12	.302	.352	.540

68

Year	Team	Lg	G	AB	H	2B	3B	HR	(Hm	Rd)	TB	R	RBI	TBB	IBB	SO	HBP	SH	SF	SB	CS	SB%	GDP	Avg	OBP	SLG
1989	Montreal	NL	152	572	147	30	1	23	(13	10)	248	76	85	48	10	158	13	0	3	12	5	.71	12	.257	.327	.434
1990	Montreal	NL	155	579	148	29	0	20	(6	14)	237	65	87	40	8	169	4	0	5	10	1	.91	14	.256	.306	.409
1991	Montreal	NL	107	375	82	13	2	9	(3	6)	126	34	33	23	5	86	2	0	0	5	6	.45	6	.219	.268	.336
	7 ML YEARS		847	3082	830	168	14	106	(47	59)	1344	394	433	224	50	790	43	1	16	54	33	.62	63	.269	.326	.436

Dave Gallagher

Bats: Right **Throws:** Right **Pos:** CF/RF   **Ht:** 6' 0" **Wt:** 184 **Born:** 09/20/60 **Age:** 31

			BATTING																	BASERUNNING				PERCENTAGES		
Year	Team	Lg	G	AB	H	2B	3B	HR	(Hm	Rd)	TB	R	RBI	TBB	IBB	SO	HBP	SH	SF	SB	CS	SB%	GDP	Avg	OBP	SLG
1987	Cleveland	AL	15	36	4	1	1	0	(0	0)	7	2	1	2	0	5	0	1	0	2	0	1.00	1	.111	.158	.194
1988	Chicago	AL	101	347	105	15	3	5	(1	4)	141	59	31	29	3	40	0	6	2	5	4	.56	8	.303	.354	.406
1989	Chicago	AL	161	601	160	22	2	1	(1	0)	189	74	46	46	1	79	2	16	2	5	6	.45	9	.266	.320	.314
1990	2 ML Teams		67	126	32	4	1	0	(0	0)	38	12	7	7	0	12	1	7	1	1	2	.33	3	.254	.296	.302
1991	California	AL	90	270	79	17	0	1	(0	1)	99	32	30	24	0	43	2	10	0	2	4	.33	6	.293	.355	.367
1990	Chicago	AL	44	75	21	3	1	0	(0	0)	26	5	5	3	0	9	1	5	0	0	1	.00	3	.280	.316	.347
	Baltimore	AL	23	51	11	1	0	0	(0	0)	12	7	2	4	0	3	0	2	1	1	1	.50	0	.216	.268	.235
	5 ML YEARS		434	1380	380	59	7	7	(2	5)	474	179	115	108	4	179	5	40	5	15	16	.48	27	.275	.329	.343

Mike Gallego

Bats: Right **Throws:** Right **Pos:** 2B/SS   **Ht:** 5' 8" **Wt:** 160 **Born:** 10/31/60 **Age:** 31

			BATTING																	BASERUNNING				PERCENTAGES		
Year	Team	Lg	G	AB	H	2B	3B	HR	(Hm	Rd)	TB	R	RBI	TBB	IBB	SO	HBP	SH	SF	SB	CS	SB%	GDP	Avg	OBP	SLG
1985	Oakland	AL	76	77	16	5	1	1	(0	1)	26	13	9	12	0	14	1	2	1	1	1	.50	2	.208	.319	.338
1986	Oakland	AL	20	37	10	2	0	0	(0	0)	12	2	4	1	0	6	0	2	0	0	2	.00	0	.270	.289	.324
1987	Oakland	AL	72	124	31	6	0	2	(0	2)	43	18	14	12	0	21	1	5	1	0	1	.00	5	.250	.319	.347
1988	Oakland	AL	129	277	58	8	0	2	(2	0)	72	38	20	34	0	53	1	8	0	2	3	.40	6	.209	.298	.260
1989	Oakland	AL	133	357	90	14	2	3	(2	1)	117	45	30	35	0	43	6	8	3	7	5	.58	10	.252	.327	.328
1990	Oakland	AL	140	389	80	13	2	3	(1	2)	106	36	34	35	0	50	4	17	2	5	5	.50	13	.206	.277	.272
1991	Oakland	AL	159	482	119	15	4	12	(6	6)	178	67	49	67	3	84	5	10	3	6	9	.40	8	.247	.343	.369
	7 ML YEARS		729	1743	404	63	9	23	(11	12)	554	219	160	196	3	271	18	52	10	21	26	.45	44	.232	.314	.318

Ron Gant

Bats: Right **Throws:** Right **Pos:** CF   **Ht:** 6' 0" **Wt:** 172 **Born:** 03/02/65 **Age:** 27

			BATTING																	BASERUNNING				PERCENTAGES		
Year	Team	Lg	G	AB	H	2B	3B	HR	(Hm	Rd)	TB	R	RBI	TBB	IBB	SO	HBP	SH	SF	SB	CS	SB%	GDP	Avg	OBP	SLG
1987	Atlanta	NL	21	83	22	4	0	2	(1	1)	32	9	9	1	0	11	0	1	1	4	2	.67	3	.265	.271	.386
1988	Atlanta	NL	146	563	146	28	8	19	(7	12)	247	85	60	46	4	118	3	2	4	19	10	.66	7	.259	.317	.439
1989	Atlanta	NL	75	260	46	8	3	9	(5	4)	87	26	25	20	0	63	1	2	2	9	6	.60	0	.177	.237	.335
1990	Atlanta	NL	152	575	174	34	3	32	(18	14)	310	107	84	50	0	86	1	1	4	33	16	.67	8	.303	.357	.539
1991	Atlanta	NL	154	561	141	35	3	32	(18	14)	278	101	105	71	8	104	5	0	5	34	15	.69	6	.251	.338	.496
	5 ML YEARS		548	2042	529	109	17	94	(49	45)	954	328	283	188	12	382	10	6	16	99	49	.67	24	.259	.322	.467

Jim Gantner

Bats: Left **Throws:** Right **Pos:** 3B/2B   **Ht:** 5'11" **Wt:** 175 **Born:** 01/05/54 **Age:** 38

			BATTING																	BASERUNNING				PERCENTAGES		
Year	Team	Lg	G	AB	H	2B	3B	HR	(Hm	Rd)	TB	R	RBI	TBB	IBB	SO	HBP	SH	SF	SB	CS	SB%	GDP	Avg	OBP	SLG
1976	Milwaukee	AL	26	69	17	1	0	0	(0	0)	18	6	7	6	0	11	1	3	0	1	0	1.00	1	.246	.316	.261
1977	Milwaukee	AL	14	47	14	1	0	1	(0	1)	18	4	2	2	0	5	0	0	0	2	1	.67	1	.298	.327	.383
1978	Milwaukee	AL	43	97	21	1	0	1	(0	1)	25	14	8	5	0	10	2	1	0	2	0	1.00	0	.216	.269	.258
1979	Milwaukee	AL	70	208	59	10	3	2	(0	2)	81	29	22	16	1	17	2	5	3	3	5	.38	3	.284	.336	.389
1980	Milwaukee	AL	132	415	117	21	3	4	(1	3)	156	47	40	30	5	29	1	8	3	11	10	.52	8	.282	.330	.376
1981	Milwaukee	AL	107	352	94	14	1	2	(0	2)	116	35	33	29	5	29	3	9	4	3	6	.33	6	.267	.325	.330
1982	Milwaukee	AL	132	447	132	17	2	4	(2	2)	165	48	43	26	3	36	2	7	3	6	3	.67	6	.295	.335	.369
1983	Milwaukee	AL	161	603	170	23	8	11	(5	6)	242	85	74	38	5	46	6	11	4	5	6	.45	10	.282	.329	.401
1984	Milwaukee	AL	153	613	173	27	1	3	(0	3)	211	61	56	30	0	51	3	2	10	6	5	.55	16	.282	.314	.344
1985	Milwaukee	AL	143	523	133	15	4	5	(4	1)	171	63	44	33	7	42	3	10	4	11	8	.58	13	.254	.300	.327
1986	Milwaukee	AL	139	497	136	25	1	7	(4	3)	184	58	38	26	2	50	6	6	7	13	7	.65	13	.274	.313	.370
1987	Milwaukee	AL	81	265	72	14	0	4	(0	4)	98	37	30	19	2	22	5	4	1	6	2	.75	7	.272	.331	.370
1988	Milwaukee	AL	155	539	149	28	2	0	(0	0)	181	67	47	34	1	50	3	18	2	20	8	.71	9	.276	.322	.336
1989	Milwaukee	AL	116	409	112	18	3	0	(0	0)	136	51	34	21	2	33	10	8	5	20	6	.77	10	.274	.321	.333
1990	Milwaukee	AL	88	323	85	8	5	0	(0	0)	103	36	25	29	0	19	2	4	0	18	3	.86	10	.263	.328	.319
1991	Milwaukee	AL	140	526	149	27	4	2	(1	1)	190	63	47	27	5	34	3	7	4	4	6	.40	13	.283	.320	.361
	16 ML YEARS		1700	5933	1633	250	37	46	(17	29)	2095	704	550	371	38	484	52	103	50	131	76	.63	126	.275	.321	.353

Carlos Garcia

Bats: Right **Throws:** Right **Pos:** SS **Ht:** 6' 1" **Wt:** 185 **Born:** 10/15/67 **Age:** 24

Year Team	Lg	G	AB	H	2B	3B	HR	(Hm	Rd)	TB	R	RBI	TBB	IBB	SO	HBP	SH	SF	SB	CS	SB%	GDP	Avg	OBP	SLG
1987 Macon	A	110	373	95	14	3	3	--	--	124	44	38	23	2	80	6	2	2	20	10	.67	6	.255	.307	.332
1988 Augusta	A	73	269	78	13	2	1	--	--	98	32	45	22	0	46	1	2	1	11	6	.65	5	.290	.345	.364
Salem	A	62	236	65	9	3	1	--	--	83	21	28	10	0	32	1	0	3	8	2	.80	9	.275	.304	.352
1989 Salem	A	81	304	86	12	4	7	--	--	127	45	49	18	0	51	4	1	5	19	6	.76	3	.283	.326	.418
Harrisburg	AA	54	188	53	5	5	3	--	--	77	28	25	8	0	36	0	0	1	6	4	.60	4	.282	.310	.410
1990 Harrisburg	AA	65	242	67	11	2	5	--	--	97	36	25	16	0	36	3	1	1	12	1	.92	6	.277	.328	.401
Buffalo	AAA	63	197	52	10	0	5	--	--	77	23	18	16	2	40	2	1	2	7	4	.64	5	.264	.323	.391
1991 Buffalo	AAA	127	463	123	21	6	7	--	--	177	62	60	33	5	78	7	6	3	30	7	.81	6	.266	.322	.382
1990 Pittsburgh	NL	4	4	2	0	0	0	(0	0)	2	1	0	0	0	2	0	0	0	0	0	.00	0	.500	.500	.500
1991 Pittsburgh	NL	12	24	6	0	2	0	(0	0)	10	2	1	1	0	8	0	0	1	0	0	.00	1	.250	.280	.417
2 ML YEARS		16	28	8	0	2	0	(0	0)	12	3	1	1	0	10	0	0	1	0	0	.00	1	.286	.310	.429

Ramon Garcia

Pitches: Right **Bats:** Right **Pos:** SP **Ht:** 6' 2" **Wt:** 200 **Born:** 12/09/69 **Age:** 22

Year Team	Lg	G	GS	CG	GF	IP	BFP	H	R	ER	HR	SH	SF	HB	TBB	IBB	SO	WP	Bk	W	L	Pct.	ShO	Sv	ERA
1989 White Sox	R	14	7	2	2	53	209	34	21	18	1	1	2		17	0	52	1	4	6	4	.600	1	0	3.06
1990 Sarasota	A	26	26	1	0	157.1	665	155	84	69	10	5	4	12	45	1	130	4	13	9	14	.391	0	0	3.95
Vancouver	AAA	1	0	0	1	1	5	2	0	0	0	0	0	0	0	0	1	0	0	0	0	.000	0	0	0.00
1991 Birmingham	AA	6	6	0	0	38.2	152	27	5	4	0	1	0	3	11	0	38	1	2	4	0	1.000	1	0	0.93
Vancouver	AAA	4	4	0	0	26.2	110	24	13	12	3	1	0	0	7	0	17	0	0	2	2	.500	0	0	4.05
1991 Chicago	AL	16	15	0	0	78.1	332	79	50	47	13	3	2	2	31	2	40	0	2	4	4	.500	0	0	5.40

Mike Gardiner

Pitches: Right **Bats:** Both **Pos:** SP **Ht:** 6' 0" **Wt:** 185 **Born:** 10/19/65 **Age:** 26

Year Team	Lg	G	GS	CG	GF	IP	BFP	H	R	ER	HR	SH	SF	HB	TBB	IBB	SO	WP	Bk	W	L	Pct.	ShO	Sv	ERA
1987 Bellingham	A	2	1	0	0	10	35	6	0	0	0	0	0	0	1	0	11	0	0	2	0	1.000	0	0	0.00
Wausau	A	13	13	2	0	81	368	91	54	47	9	2	5	3	33	2	80	3	1	3	5	.375	1	0	5.22
1988 Wausau	A	11	6	0	4	31.1	132	31	16	11	1	0	0	1	13	0	24	1	1	2	1	.667	0	1	3.16
1989 Wausau	A	15	1	0	11	30.1	120	21	5	2	0	2	0	1	11	0	48	0	0	4	0	1.000	0	7	0.59
Williamsprt	AA	30	3	1	14	63.1	274	54	25	20	6	1	3	1	32	6	60	4	1	4	6	.400	0	2	2.84
1990 Williamsprt	AA	26	26	5	0	179.2	697	136	47	38	8	4	3	1	29	1	149	4	1	12	8	.600	1	0	1.90
1991 Pawtucket	AAA	8	8	2	0	57.2	220	39	16	15	2	3	2	1	11	0	42	0	0	7	1	.875	1	0	2.34
1990 Seattle	AL	5	3	0	1	12.2	66	22	17	15	1	0	1	2	5	0	6	0	0	0	2	.000	0	0	10.66
1991 Boston	AL	22	22	0	0	130	562	140	79	70	18	1	3	0	47	2	91	1	0	9	10	.474	0	0	4.85
2 ML YEARS		27	25	0	1	142.2	628	162	96	85	19	1	4	2	52	2	97	1	0	9	12	.429	0	0	5.36

Chris Gardner

Pitches: Right **Bats:** Right **Pos:** SP **Ht:** 6' 0" **Wt:** 175 **Born:** 03/30/69 **Age:** 23

Year Team	Lg	G	GS	CG	GF	IP	BFP	H	R	ER	HR	SH	SF	HB	TBB	IBB	SO	WP	Bk	W	L	Pct.	ShO	Sv	ERA
1988 Astros	R	12	9	0	0	55.1	226	37	18	9	0	3	1	4	23	0	41	4	4	4	3	.571	0	0	1.46
1989 Asheville	A	15	15	2	0	77.1	360	76	53	33	5	1	3	1	58	0	49	8	10	3	8	.273	0	0	3.84
1990 Asheville	A	23	23	3	0	134	560	102	57	39	6	1	2	7	69	2	81	8	3	5	10	.333	1	0	2.62
1991 Jackson	AA	22	22	1	0	131.1	559	116	57	46	6	5	4	8	75	1	72	9	1	13	5	.722	1	0	3.15
1991 Houston	NL	5	4	0	0	24.2	103	19	12	11	5	2	0	0	14	1	12	0	0	1	2	.333	0	0	4.01

Jeff Gardner

Bats: Left **Throws:** Right **Pos:** SS **Ht:** 5'11" **Wt:** 165 **Born:** 02/04/64 **Age:** 28

Year Team	Lg	G	AB	H	2B	3B	HR	(Hm	Rd)	TB	R	RBI	TBB	IBB	SO	HBP	SH	SF	SB	CS	SB%	GDP	Avg	OBP	SLG
1985 Columbia	A	123	401	118	9	1	0	--	--	129	80	50	142	1	40	5	10	1	31	5	.86	9	.294	.483	.322
1986 Lynchburg	A	111	334	91	11	2	1	--	--	109	59	39	81	3	33	4	8	3	6	4	.60	10	.272	.417	.326
1987 Jackson	AA	119	399	109	10	3	0	--	--	125	55	30	58	1	55	3	5	2	1	5	.17	7	.273	.368	.313
1988 Jackson	AA	134	432	109	15	2	0	--	--	128	46	33	69	7	52	1	14	1	13	8	.62	6	.252	.356	.296
Tidewater	AAA	2	8	3	1	1	0	--	--	6	3	2	1	0	1	0	0	0	0	0	.00	0	.375	.444	.750
1989 Tidewater	AAA	101	269	75	11	0	0	--	--	86	28	24	25	1	27	0	4	3	0	0	.00	7	.279	.337	.320
1990 Tidewater	AAA	138	463	125	11	1	0	--	--	138	55	33	84	3	33	1	4	1	3	3	.50	12	.270	.383	.298
1991 Tidewater	AAA	136	504	147	23	4	1	--	--	181	73	56	84	4	48	3	7	5	6	5	.55	8	.292	.393	.359
1991 New York	NL	13	37	6	0	0	0	(0	0)	6	3	1	4	0	6	0	0	1	0	0	.00	0	.162	.238	.162

Mark Gardner

Pitches: Right   **Bats:** Right   **Pos:** SP   **Ht:** 6' 1"   **Wt:** 200   **Born:** 03/01/62   **Age:** 30

Year Team	Lg	HOW MUCH HE PITCHED						WHAT HE GAVE UP												THE RESULTS					
		G	GS	CG	GF	IP	BFP	H	R	ER	HR	SH	SF	HB	TBB	IBB	SO	WP	Bk	W	L	Pct.	ShO	Sv	ERA
1989 Montreal	NL	7	4	0	1	26.1	117	26	16	15	2	0	0	2	11	1	21	0	0	0	3	.000	0	0	5.13
1990 Montreal	NL	27	26	3	1	152.2	642	129	62	58	13	4	7	9	61	5	135	2	4	7	9	.438	3	0	3.42
1991 Montreal	NL	27	27	0	0	168.1	692	139	78	72	17	7	2	4	75	1	107	2	1	9	11	.450	0	0	3.85
3 ML YEARS		61	57	3	2	347.1	1451	294	156	145	32	11	9	15	147	7	263	4	5	16	23	.410	3	0	3.76

Wes Gardner

Pitches: Right   **Bats:** Right   **Pos:** RP   **Ht:** 6' 4"   **Wt:** 205   **Born:** 04/29/61   **Age:** 31

Year Team	Lg	HOW MUCH HE PITCHED						WHAT HE GAVE UP												THE RESULTS					
		G	GS	CG	GF	IP	BFP	H	R	ER	HR	SH	SF	HB	TBB	IBB	SO	WP	Bk	W	L	Pct.	ShO	Sv	ERA
1984 New York	NL	21	0	0	12	25.1	116	34	14	18	0	1	1	0	8	2	19	1	0	1	1	.500	0	1	6.39
1985 New York	NL	9	0	0	8	12	61	18	14	7	1	4	1	0	8	2	11	1	0	0	2	.000	0	0	5.25
1986 Boston	AL	1	0	0	0	1	4	1	1	1	0	0	1	0	0	0	1	0	0	0	0	.000	0	0	9.00
1987 Boston	AL	49	1	0	29	89.2	401	98	55	54	17	4	2	2	42	7	70	4	0	3	6	.333	0	10	5.42
1988 Boston	AL	36	18	1	12	149	620	119	61	58	17	5	6	3	64	2	106	5	0	8	6	.571	0	2	3.50
1989 Boston	AL	22	16	0	2	86	393	97	64	57	10	3	4	1	47	7	81	3	0	3	7	.300	0	0	5.97
1990 Boston	AL	34	9	0	9	77.1	340	77	43	42	6	4	2	2	35	0	58	2	1	3	7	.300	0	0	4.89
1991 2 ML Teams		17	0	0	4	26	125	32	20	17	1	0	0	0	14	1	12	1	0	0	1	.000	0	1	5.88
1991 San Diego	NL	14	0	0	2	20.1	99	27	16	16	1	0	0	0	12	1	9	1	0	0	1	.000	0	1	7.08
Kansas City	AL	3	0	0	2	5.2	26	5	4	1	0	0	0	0	2	0	3	0	0	0	0	.000	0	0	1.59
8 ML YEARS		189	44	1	76	466.1	2060	476	277	254	52	21	17	8	218	21	358	17	1	18	30	.375	0	14	4.90

Scott Garrelts

Pitches: Right   **Bats:** Right   **Pos:** RP/SP   **Ht:** 6' 4"   **Wt:** 210   **Born:** 10/30/61   **Age:** 30

Year Team	Lg	HOW MUCH HE PITCHED						WHAT HE GAVE UP												THE RESULTS					
		G	GS	CG	GF	IP	BFP	H	R	ER	HR	SH	SF	HB	TBB	IBB	SO	WP	Bk	W	L	Pct.	ShO	Sv	ERA
1982 San Francisco	NL	1	0	0	1	2	11	3	3	3	0	0	0	0	2	0	4	0	0	0	0	.000	0	0	13.50
1983 San Francisco	NL	5	5	1	0	35.2	154	33	11	10	4	3	0	2	19	4	16	4	1	2	2	.500	1	0	2.52
1984 San Francisco	NL	21	3	0	5	43	206	45	33	27	6	5	2	1	34	1	32	3	0	2	3	.400	0	0	5.65
1985 San Francisco	NL	74	0	0	44	105.2	454	76	37	27	2	6	3	3	58	12	106	7	1	9	6	.600	0	13	2.30
1986 San Francisco	NL	53	18	2	27	173.2	717	144	65	60	17	10	7	2	74	11	125	9	1	13	9	.591	0	10	3.11
1987 San Francisco	NL	64	0	0	43	106.1	428	70	41	38	10	7	2	0	55	4	127	5	1	11	7	.611	0	12	3.22
1988 San Francisco	NL	65	0	0	40	98	413	80	42	39	3	9	2	2	46	10	86	6	4	5	9	.357	0	13	3.58
1989 San Francisco	NL	30	29	2	0	193.1	766	149	58	49	11	9	7	0	46	3	119	7	2	14	5	.737	1	0	2.28
1990 San Francisco	NL	31	31	4	0	182	786	190	91	84	16	10	5	3	70	8	80	7	0	12	11	.522	2	0	4.15
1991 San Francisco	NL	8	3	0	2	19.2	90	25	14	14	5	0	1	0	9	0	8	0	0	1	1	.500	0	0	6.41
10 ML YEARS		352	89	9	162	959.1	4025	815	395	351	74	59	29	13	413	53	703	48	10	69	53	.566	4	48	3.29

Rich Gedman

Bats: Left   **Throws:** Right   **Pos:** C   **Ht:** 6' 0"   **Wt:** 212   **Born:** 09/26/59   **Age:** 32

Year Team	Lg	BATTING																			BASERUNNING				PERCENTAGES		
		G	AB	H	2B	3B	HR	(Hm	Rd)	TB	R	RBI	TBB	IBB	SO	HBP	SH	SF	SB	CS	SB%	GDP	Avg	OBP	SLG
1980 Boston	AL	9	24	5	0	0	0	(0	0)	5	2	1	0	0	5	0	0	0	0	0	.00	1	.208	.208	.208
1981 Boston	AL	62	205	59	15	0	5	(3	2)	89	22	26	9	1	31	1	1	3	0	0	.00	9	.288	.317	.434
1982 Boston	AL	92	289	72	17	2	4	(1	3)	105	30	26	10	2	37	2	4	0	0	1	.00	13	.249	.279	.363
1983 Boston	AL	81	204	60	16	1	2	(0	2)	84	21	18	15	6	37	1	3	0	0	1	.00	4	.294	.345	.412
1984 Boston	AL	133	449	121	26	4	24	(16	8)	227	54	72	29	8	72	1	2	5	0	0	.00	5	.269	.312	.506
1985 Boston	AL	144	498	147	30	5	18	(9	9)	241	66	80	50	11	79	3	3	2	2	0	1.00	12	.295	.362	.484
1986 Boston	AL	135	462	119	29	0	16	(2	14)	196	49	65	37	13	61	4	1	5	1	0	1.00	15	.258	.315	.424
1987 Boston	AL	52	151	31	8	0	1	(1	0)	42	11	13	10	2	24	0	1	3	0	0	.00	2	.205	.250	.278
1988 Boston	AL	95	260	55	14	0	9	(5	4)	110	33	39	18	2	49	3	9	3	0	0	.00	5	.231	.279	.368
1989 Boston	AL	93	260	55	9	0	4	(2	2)	76	24	16	23	1	47	0	3	3	0	1	.00	8	.212	.273	.292
1990 2 ML Teams		50	119	24	7	0	1	(0	1)	34	7	10	20	6	30	1	2	1	0	0	.00	3	.202	.319	.286
1991 St. Louis	NL	46	94	10	1	0	3	(1	2)	20	7	8	4	0	15	0	0	2	0	0	.00	2	.106	.140	.213
1990 Boston	AL	10	15	3	0	0	0	(0	0)	3	3	0	5	0	6	1	0	0	0	0	.00	1	.200	.429	.200
Houston	NL	40	104	21	7	0	1	(0	1)	31	4	10	15	6	24	0	2	1	0	0	.00	2	.202	.300	.298
12 ML YEARS		992	3054	772	172	12	87	(40	47)	1229	326	374	225	52	487	16	29	27	3	4	.43	80	.253	.305	.402

Chris George

Pitches: Right   **Bats:** Right   **Pos:** SP   **Ht:** 6' 2"   **Wt:** 200   **Born:** 09/24/66   **Age:** 25

Year Team	Lg	HOW MUCH HE PITCHED						WHAT HE GAVE UP												THE RESULTS					
		G	GS	CG	GF	IP	BFP	H	R	ER	HR	SH	SF	HB	TBB	IBB	SO	WP	Bk	W	L	Pct.	ShO	Sv	ERA
1988 Beloit	A	22	4	0	10	58	243	52	27	19	1	1	1	5	14	4	58	4	1	7	4	.636	0	6	2.95
1989 Stockton	A	55	0	0	52	79.2	345	61	30	19	1	6	5	1	37	8	85	8	2	7	7	.500	0	22	2.15

Year	Team	Lg	G	GS	CG	GF	IP	BFP	H	R	ER	HR	SH	SF	HB	TBB	IBB	SO	WP	Bk	W	L	Pct.	ShO	Sv	ERA
1990	Denver	AAA	7	0	0	1	5.1	36	17	11	11	1	0	0	0	4	0	4	1	0	1	1	.500	0	0	18.56
	El Paso	AA	39	0	0	30	55.2	226	41	16	11	1	7	1	3	20	7	38	7	1	8	3	.727	0	13	1.78
1991	Denver	AAA	43	1	0	16	85	350	74	31	22	6	6	7	0	26	5	65	4	0	4	5	.444	0	4	2.33
1991	Milwaukee	AL	2	1	0	1	6	25	8	2	2	0	0	1	0	0	0	2	0	0	0	0	.000	0	0	3.00

Bob Geren

Bats: Right **Throws:** Right **Pos:** C **Ht:** 6' 3" **Wt:** 228 **Born:** 09/22/61 **Age:** 30

							BATTING											BASERUNNING				PERCENTAGES		
Year	Team	Lg	G	AB	H	2B	3B	HR	(Hm | Rd)	TB	R	RBI	TBB	IBB	SO	HBP	SH	SF	SB	CS	SB%	GDP	Avg	OBP	SLG
1988	New York	AL	10	10	1	0	0	0	(0 | 0)	1	0	0	2	0	3	0	0	0	0	0	.00	0	.100	.250	.100
1989	New York	AL	65	205	59	5	1	9	(4 | 5)	93	26	27	12	0	44	1	6	1	0	0	.00	10	.288	.329	.454
1990	New York	AL	110	277	59	7	0	8	(4 | 4)	90	21	31	13	1	73	5	6	2	0	0	.00	7	.213	.259	.325
1991	New York	AL	64	128	28	3	0	2	(1 | 1)	37	7	12	9	0	31	0	3	0	0	1	.00	5	.219	.270	.289
	4 ML YEARS		249	620	147	15	1	19	(9 | 10)	221	54	70	36	1	151	6	15	3	0	1	.00	22	.237	.284	.356

Ray Giannelli

Bats: Left **Throws:** Right **Pos:** 3B **Ht:** 6' 0" **Wt:** 195 **Born:** 02/05/66 **Age:** 26

							BATTING											BASERUNNING				PERCENTAGES		
Year	Team	Lg	G	AB	H	2B	3B	HR	(Hm	Rd)	TB	R	RBI	TBB	IBB	SO	HBP	SH	SF	SB	CS	SB%	GDP	Avg	OBP	SLG
1988	Medicne Hat	R	47	123	30	8	3	4	--	--	56	17	28	19	2	22	0	1	3	0	0	.00	6	.244	.338	.455
1989	Myrtle Bch	A	127	458	138	17	1	18	--	--	211	76	84	78	4	53	5	1	8	2	6	.25	10	.301	.403	.461
1990	Dunedin	A	118	416	120	18	1	18	--	--	194	64	57	66	7	56	1	1	3	4	8	.33	12	.288	.385	.466
1991	Knoxville	AA	112	362	100	14	3	7	--	--	141	53	37	64	6	66	2	5	2	8	5	.62	6	.276	.386	.390
1991	Toronto	AL	9	24	4	1	0	0	(0	0)	5	2	0	5	0	9	0	0	0	1	0	1.00	0	.167	.310	.208

Kirk Gibson

Bats: Left **Throws:** Left **Pos:** LF/DH **Ht:** 6' 3" **Wt:** 225 **Born:** 05/28/57 **Age:** 35

							BATTING											BASERUNNING				PERCENTAGES		
Year	Team	Lg	G	AB	H	2B	3B	HR	(Hm | Rd)	TB	R	RBI	TBB	IBB	SO	HBP	SH	SF	SB	CS	SB%	GDP	Avg	OBP	SLG
1979	Detroit	AL	12	38	9	3	0	1	(0 | 1)	15	3	4	1	0	3	0	0	0	3	3	.50	0	.237	.256	.395
1980	Detroit	AL	51	175	46	2	1	9	(3 | 6)	77	23	16	10	0	45	1	1	2	4	7	.36	0	.263	.303	.440
1981	Detroit	AL	83	290	95	11	3	9	(4 | 5)	139	41	40	18	1	64	2	1	2	17	5	.77	9	.328	.369	.479
1982	Detroit	AL	69	266	74	16	2	8	(4 | 4)	118	34	35	25	2	41	1	1	1	9	7	.56	2	.278	.341	.444
1983	Detroit	AL	128	401	91	12	9	15	(5 | 10)	166	60	51	53	3	96	4	5	4	14	3	.82	2	.227	.320	.414
1984	Detroit	AL	149	531	150	23	10	27	(11 | 16)	274	92	91	63	6	103	8	3	6	29	9	.76	4	.282	.363	.516
1985	Detroit	AL	154	581	167	37	5	29	(18 | 11)	301	96	97	71	16	137	5	3	10	30	4	.88	5	.287	.364	.518
1986	Detroit	AL	119	441	118	11	2	28	(15 | 13)	217	84	86	68	4	107	7	1	4	34	6	.85	8	.268	.373	.492
1987	Detroit	AL	128	487	135	25	3	24	(14 | 10)	238	95	79	71	8	117	5	1	4	26	7	.79	5	.277	.372	.489
1988	Los Angeles	NL	150	542	157	28	1	25	(14 | 11)	262	106	76	73	14	120	7	3	7	31	4	.89	8	.290	.377	.483
1989	Los Angeles	NL	71	253	54	8	2	9	(4 | 5)	93	35	28	35	5	55	2	0	2	12	3	.80	5	.213	.312	.368
1990	Los Angeles	NL	89	315	82	20	0	8	(2 | 6)	126	59	38	39	0	65	3	0	2	26	2	.93	4	.260	.345	.400
1991	Kansas City	AL	132	462	109	17	6	16	(4 | 12)	186	81	55	69	3	103	6	1	2	18	4	.82	9	.236	.341	.403
	13 ML YEARS		1335	4782	1287	213	44	208	(98 | 110)	2212	809	696	596	62	1056	51	20	46	253	64	.80	61	.269	.353	.463

Paul Gibson

Pitches: Left **Bats:** Right **Pos:** RP **Ht:** 6' 1" **Wt:** 185 **Born:** 01/04/60 **Age:** 32

						HOW MUCH HE PITCHED			WHAT HE GAVE UP												THE RESULTS				
Year	Team	Lg	G	GS	CG	GF	IP	BFP	H	R	ER	HR	SH	SF	HB	TBB	IBB	SO	WP	Bk	W	L	Pct.	ShO	Sv	ERA
1988	Detroit	AL	40	1	0	18	92	390	83	33	30	6	3	5	2	34	8	50	3	1	4	2	.667	0	0	2.93
1989	Detroit	AL	45	13	0	16	132	573	129	71	68	11	7	5	6	57	12	77	4	1	4	8	.333	0	0	4.64
1990	Detroit	AL	61	0	0	17	97.1	422	99	36	33	10	4	5	1	44	12	56	1	1	5	4	.556	0	3	3.05
1991	Detroit	AL	68	0	0	28	96	432	112	51	49	10	2	2	3	48	8	52	4	0	5	7	.417	0	8	4.59
	4 ML YEARS		214	14	0	79	417.1	1817	423	191	180	37	16	17	12	183	40	235	12	3	18	21	.462	0	11	3.88

Bernard Gilkey

Bats: Right **Throws:** Right **Pos:** LF **Ht:** 6' 0" **Wt:** 170 **Born:** 09/24/66 **Age:** 25

							BATTING											BASERUNNING				PERCENTAGES		
Year	Team	Lg	G	AB	H	2B	3B	HR	(Hm	Rd)	TB	R	RBI	TBB	IBB	SO	HBP	SH	SF	SB	CS	SB%	GDP	Avg	OBP	SLG
1985	Erie	A	77	294	60	9	1	7	--	--	92	57	27	55	1	57	3	4	2	34	10	.77	4	.204	.333	.313
1986	Savannah	A	105	374	88	15	4	6	--	--	129	64	36	84	1	57	2	3	3	32	15	.68	6	.235	.376	.345
1987	Springfield	A	46	162	37	5	0	0	--	--	42	30	9	39	1	28	2	2	1	18	5	.78	3	.228	.380	.259
1988	Springfield	A	125	491	120	18	7	6	--	--	170	84	36	65	1	53	4	2	2	56	18	.76	10	.244	.336	.346
1989	Arkansas	AA	131	500	139	25	3	6	--	--	188	104	57	70	2	54	2	8	5	53	22	.71	9	.278	.366	.376
1990	Louisville	AAA	132	499	147	26	8	3	--	--	198	83	46	75	3	49	2	1	1	45	32	.58	11	.295	.388	.397
1991	Louisville	AAA	11	41	6	2	0	0	--	--	8	5	2	6	0	10	0	0	0	1	3	.25	0	.146	.255	.195

Year	Team	Lg	G	AB	H	2B	3B	HR	(Hm	Rd)	TB	R	RBI	TBB	IBB	SO	HBP	SH	SF	SB	CS	SB%	GDP	Avg	OBP	SLG
1990	St. Louis	NL	18	64	19	5	2	1	(0	1)	31	11	3	8	0	5	0	0	0	6	1	.86	1	.297	.375	.484
1991	St. Louis	NL	81	268	58	7	2	5	(2	3)	84	28	20	39	0	33	1	1	2	14	8	.64	14	.216	.316	.313
	2 ML YEARS		99	332	77	12	4	6	(2	4)	115	39	23	47	0	38	1	1	2	20	9	.69	15	.232	.327	.346

Joe Girardi

Bats: Right **Throws:** Right **Pos:** C **Ht:** 5'11" **Wt:** 195 **Born:** 10/14/64 **Age:** 27

									BATTING											BASERUNNING				PERCENTAGES		
Year	Team	Lg	G	AB	H	2B	3B	HR	(Hm	Rd)	TB	R	RBI	TBB	IBB	SO	HBP	SH	SF	SB	CS	SB%	GDP	Avg	OBP	SLG
1989	Chicago	NL	59	157	39	10	0	1	(0	1)	52	15	14	11	5	26	2	1	1	2	1	.67	4	.248	.304	.331
1990	Chicago	NL	133	419	113	24	2	1	(1	0)	144	36	38	17	11	50	3	4	4	8	3	.73	13	.270	.300	.344
1991	Chicago	NL	21	47	9	2	0	0	(0	0)	11	3	6	6	1	6	0	1	0	0	0	.00	0	.191	.283	.234
	3 ML YEARS		213	623	161	36	2	2	(1	1)	207	54	58	34	17	82	5	6	5	10	4	.71	17	.258	.300	.332

Dan Gladden

Bats: Right **Throws:** Right **Pos:** LF **Ht:** 5'11" **Wt:** 181 **Born:** 07/07/57 **Age:** 34

									BATTING											BASERUNNING				PERCENTAGES		
Year	Team	Lg	G	AB	H	2B	3B	HR	(Hm	Rd)	TB	R	RBI	TBB	IBB	SO	HBP	SH	SF	SB	CS	SB%	GDP	Avg	OBP	SLG
1983	San Francisco	NL	18	63	14	2	0	1	(1	0)	19	6	9	5	0	11	0	3	1	4	3	.57	3	.222	.275	.302
1984	San Francisco	NL	86	342	120	17	2	4	(4	0)	153	71	31	33	2	37	2	6	1	31	16	.66	3	.351	.410	.447
1985	San Francisco	NL	142	502	122	15	8	7	(6	1)	174	64	41	40	1	78	7	10	2	32	15	.68	10	.243	.307	.347
1986	San Francisco	NL	102	351	97	16	1	4	(1	3)	127	55	29	39	3	59	5	7	0	27	10	.73	5	.276	.357	.362
1987	Minnesota	AL	121	438	109	21	2	8	(4	4)	158	69	38	38	2	72	3	1	2	25	9	.74	8	.249	.312	.361
1988	Minnesota	AL	141	576	155	32	6	11	(8	3)	232	91	62	46	4	74	4	2	5	28	8	.78	9	.269	.325	.403
1989	Minnesota	AL	121	461	136	23	3	8	(1	7)	189	69	46	23	3	53	5	5	7	23	7	.77	6	.295	.331	.410
1990	Minnesota	AL	136	534	147	27	6	5	(2	3)	201	64	40	26	2	67	6	1	4	25	9	.74	17	.275	.314	.376
1991	Minnesota	AL	126	461	114	14	9	6	(3	3)	164	65	52	36	1	60	5	5	4	15	9	.63	13	.247	.306	.356
	9 ML YEARS		993	3728	1014	167	37	54	(30	24)	1417	554	348	286	18	511	37	40	26	210	86	.71	74	.272	.328	.380

Tom Glavine

Pitches: Left **Bats:** Left **Pos:** SP **Ht:** 6'1" **Wt:** 190 **Born:** 03/25/66 **Age:** 26

				HOW MUCH HE PITCHED						WHAT HE GAVE UP										THE RESULTS					
Year	Team	Lg	G	GS	CG	GF	IP	BFP	H	R	ER	HR	SH	SF	HB	TBB	IBB	SO	WP	Bk	W	L	Pct.	ShO	Sv	ERA
1987	Atlanta	NL	9	9	0	0	50.1	238	55	34	31	5	2	3	3	33	4	20	1	1	2	4	.333	0	0	5.54
1988	Atlanta	NL	34	34	1	0	195.1	844	201	111	99	12	17	11	8	63	7	84	2	2	7	17	.292	0	0	4.56
1989	Atlanta	NL	29	29	6	0	186	766	172	88	76	20	11	4	2	40	3	90	2	0	14	8	.636	4	0	3.68
1990	Atlanta	NL	33	33	1	0	214.1	929	232	111	102	18	21	2	1	78	10	129	8	1	10	12	.455	0	0	4.28
1991	Atlanta	NL	34	34	9	0	246.2	989	201	83	70	17	7	6	2	69	6	192	10	2	20	11	.645	1	0	2.55
	5 ML YEARS		139	139	17	0	892.2	3766	861	427	378	72	58	26	16	283	30	515	23	6	53	52	.505	5	0	3.81

Jerry Don Gleaton

Pitches: Left **Bats:** Left **Pos:** RP **Ht:** 6'3" **Wt:** 210 **Born:** 09/14/57 **Age:** 34

				HOW MUCH HE PITCHED						WHAT HE GAVE UP										THE RESULTS					
Year	Team	Lg	G	GS	CG	GF	IP	BFP	H	R	ER	HR	SH	SF	HB	TBB	IBB	SO	WP	Bk	W	L	Pct.	ShO	Sv	ERA
1979	Texas	AL	5	2	0	0	10	45	15	7	7	1	1	1	1	2	0	2	1	0	0	0	.000	0	0	6.30
1980	Texas	AL	5	0	0	2	7	30	5	2	2	0	0	2	0	4	0	2	0	0	0	0	.000	0	0	2.57
1981	Seattle	AL	20	13	1	3	85	369	88	50	45	10	3	4	2	38	2	31	3	0	4	7	.364	0	0	4.76
1982	Seattle	AL	3	0	0	1	4.2	24	7	7	7	3	0	0	1	2	0	1	0	0	0	0	.000	0	0	13.50
1984	Chicago	AL	11	1	0	4	18.1	81	20	12	7	2	0	4	1	6	0	4	4	0	1	2	.333	0	2	3.44
1985	Chicago	AL	31	0	0	9	29.2	135	37	19	19	3	4	1	0	13	3	22	3	0	1	0	1.000	0	1	5.76
1987	Kansas City	AL	48	0	0	22	50.2	210	38	28	24	4	3	3	0	28	3	44	4	1	4	4	.500	0	5	4.26
1988	Kansas City	AL	42	0	0	20	38	164	33	17	15	2	2	0	3	17	1	29	2	0	0	4	.000	0	3	3.55
1989	Kansas City	AL	15	0	0	5	14.1	66	20	10	9	0	0	2	0	6	0	9	0	1	0	0	.000	0	0	5.65
1990	Detroit	AL	57	0	0	34	82.2	325	62	27	27	5	2	4	3	25	2	56	2	1	1	3	.250	0	13	2.94
1991	Detroit	AL	47	0	0	16	75.1	319	74	37	34	7	1	4	0	39	8	47	1	1	3	2	.600	0	2	4.06
	11 ML YEARS		284	16	1	117	415.2	1768	399	216	196	36	16	25	11	180	19	247	20	4	14	23	.378	0	26	4.24

Leo Gomez

Bats: Right **Throws:** Right **Pos:** 3B **Ht:** 6'0" **Wt:** 202 **Born:** 03/02/67 **Age:** 25

									BATTING											BASERUNNING				PERCENTAGES		
Year	Team	Lg	G	AB	H	2B	3B	HR	(Hm	Rd)	TB	R	RBI	TBB	IBB	SO	HBP	SH	SF	SB	CS	SB%	GDP	Avg	OBP	SLG
1986	Bluefield	R	27	88	31	7	1	7	--	--	61	23	28	25	0	27	1	0	3	1	0	1.00	1	.352	.487	.693
1987	Hagerstown	A	131	466	152	38	2	19	--	--	251	94	110	95	3	85	2	1	10	6	2	.75	8	.326	.435	.539
1988	Charlotte	AA	24	89	26	5	0	1	--	--	34	6	10	10	0	17	0	0	0	1	2	.33	2	.292	.364	.382
1989	Hagerstown	AA	134	448	126	23	3	18	--	--	209	71	78	89	6	102	5	0	5	2	2	.50	8	.281	.402	.467
1990	Rochester	AAA	131	430	119	26	4	26	--	--	231	97	97	89	4	89	6	0	7	2	2	.50	11	.277	.402	.537
1991	Rochester	AAA	28	101	26	6	0	6	--	--	50	13	19	16	0	18	2	0	0	0	0	.00	1	.257	.370	.495

Year	Team	Lg	G	AB	H	2B	3B	HR	(Hm	Rd)	TB	R	RBI	TBB	IBB	SO	HBP	SH	SF	SB	CS	SB%	GDP	Avg	OBP	SLG
1990	Baltimore	AL	12	39	9	0	0	0	(0	0)	9	3	1	8	0	7	0	1	0	0	0	.00	2	.231	.362	.231
1991	Baltimore	AL	118	391	91	17	2	16	(7	9)	160	40	45	40	0	82	2	5	7	1	1	.50	11	.233	.302	.409
	2 ML YEARS		130	430	100	17	2	16	(7	9)	169	43	46	48	0	89	2	6	7	1	1	.50	13	.233	.308	.393

Rene Gonzales

Bats: Right **Throws:** Right **Pos:** SS/3B **Ht:** 6' 3" **Wt:** 195 **Born:** 09/03/61 **Age:** 30

Year	Team	Lg	G	AB	H	2B	3B	HR	(Hm	Rd)	TB	R	RBI	TBB	IBB	SO	HBP	SH	SF	SB	CS	SB%	GDP	Avg	OBP	SLG
1984	Montreal	NL	29	30	7	1	0	0	(0	0)	8	5	2	2	0	5	1	0	0	0	0	.00	0	.233	.303	.267
1986	Montreal	NL	11	26	3	0	0	0	(0	0)	3	1	0	2	0	7	0	0	0	0	2	.00	0	.115	.179	.115
1987	Baltimore	AL	37	60	16	2	1	1	(1	0)	23	14	7	3	0	11	0	2	0	1	0	1.00	0	.267	.302	.383
1988	Baltimore	AL	92	237	51	6	0	2	(1	1)	63	13	15	13	0	32	3	5	2	2	0	1.00	5	.215	.263	.266
1989	Baltimore	AL	71	166	36	4	0	1	(0	1)	43	16	11	12	0	30	0	6	1	5	3	.63	6	.217	.268	.259
1990	Baltimore	AL	67	103	22	3	1	1	(1	0)	30	13	12	12	0	14	0	6	0	1	2	.33	3	.214	.296	.291
1991	Toronto	AL	71	118	23	3	0	1	(1	0)	29	16	6	12	0	22	4	6	1	0	0	.00	5	.195	.289	.246
	7 ML YEARS		378	740	158	19	2	6	(4	2)	199	78	53	56	0	121	8	25	4	9	7	.56	21	.214	.275	.269

Jose Gonzalez

Bats: Right **Throws:** Right **Pos:** RF/CF **Ht:** 6' 2" **Wt:** 200 **Born:** 11/23/64 **Age:** 27

Year	Team	Lg	G	AB	H	2B	3B	HR	(Hm	Rd)	TB	R	RBI	TBB	IBB	SO	HBP	SH	SF	SB	CS	SB%	GDP	Avg	OBP	SLG
1985	Los Angeles	NL	23	11	3	2	0	0	(0	0)	5	6	0	1	0	3	0	0	0	1	1	.50	1	.273	.333	.455
1986	Los Angeles	NL	57	93	20	5	1	2	(1	1)	33	15	6	7	0	29	0	2	0	4	3	.57	0	.215	.270	.355
1987	Los Angeles	NL	19	16	3	2	0	0	(0	0)	5	2	1	1	0	2	0	0	1	5	0	1.00	0	.188	.222	.313
1988	Los Angeles	NL	37	24	2	1	0	0	(0	0)	3	7	0	2	0	10	0	0	0	3	0	1.00	0	.083	.154	.125
1989	Los Angeles	NL	95	261	70	11	2	3	(2	1)	94	31	18	23	5	53	0	1	1	9	3	.75	2	.268	.326	.360
1990	Los Angeles	NL	106	99	23	5	3	2	(2	0)	40	15	8	6	1	27	1	1	1	3	1	.75	1	.232	.280	.404
1991	3 ML Teams		91	117	13	2	1	2	(1	1)	23	15	7	13	0	42	1	2	1	8	0	1.00	2	.111	.205	.197
1991	Los Angeles	NL	42	28	0	0	0	0	(0	0)	0	3	0	2	0	9	0	0	0	0	0	.00	0	.000	.067	.000
	Pittsburgh	NL	16	20	2	0	0	1	(1	0)	5	2	3	0	0	6	0	2	1	0	0	.00	0	.100	.095	.250
	Cleveland	AL	33	69	11	2	1	1	(0	1)	18	10	4	11	0	27	1	0	0	8	0	1.00	2	.159	.284	.261
	7 ML YEARS		428	621	134	28	7	9	(6	3)	203	91	40	53	6	166	2	6	4	33	8	.80	6	.216	.278	.327

Juan Gonzalez

Bats: Right **Throws:** Right **Pos:** CF/LF **Ht:** 6' 3" **Wt:** 200 **Born:** 10/16/69 **Age:** 22

Year	Team	Lg	G	AB	H	2B	3B	HR	(Hm	Rd)	TB	R	RBI	TBB	IBB	SO	HBP	SH	SF	SB	CS	SB%	GDP	Avg	OBP	SLG
1989	Texas	AL	24	60	9	3	0	1	(1	0)	15	6	7	6	0	17	0	2	0	0	0	.00	4	.150	.227	.250
1990	Texas	AL	25	90	26	7	1	4	(3	1)	47	11	12	2	0	18	2	0	1	0	1	.00	2	.289	.316	.522
1991	Texas	AL	142	545	144	34	1	27	(7	20)	261	78	102	42	7	118	5	0	3	4	4	.50	10	.264	.321	.479
	3 ML YEARS		191	695	179	44	2	32	(11	21)	323	95	121	50	7	153	7	2	4	4	5	.44	16	.258	.312	.465

Luis Gonzalez

Bats: Left **Throws:** Right **Pos:** LF **Ht:** 6' 2" **Wt:** 180 **Born:** 09/03/67 **Age:** 24

Year	Team	Lg	G	AB	H	2B	3B	HR	(Hm	Rd)	TB	R	RBI	TBB	IBB	SO	HBP	SH	SF	SB	CS	SB%	GDP	Avg	OBP	SLG
1988	Auburn	A	39	157	49	10	3	5	--	--	80	32	27	12	1	19	1	1	5	2	0	1.00	1	.312	.354	.510
	Asheville	A	31	115	29	7	1	2	--	--	44	13	14	12	0	17	2	0	0	2	2	.50	4	.252	.333	.383
1989	Osceola	A	86	287	82	16	7	6	--	--	130	46	38	37	5	49	4	1	4	2	1	.67	3	.286	.370	.453
1990	Columbus	AA	138	495	131	30	6	24	--	--	245	86	89	54	9	100	6	1	12	27	9	.75	6	.265	.337	.495
1990	Houston	NL	12	21	4	2	0	0	(0	0)	6	1	0	2	1	5	0	0	0	0	0	.00	0	.190	.261	.286
1991	Houston	NL	137	473	120	28	9	13	(4	9)	205	51	69	40	4	101	8	1	4	10	7	.59	9	.254	.320	.433
	2 ML YEARS		149	494	124	30	9	13	(4	9)	211	52	69	42	5	106	8	1	4	10	7	.59	9	.251	.318	.427

Dwight Gooden

Pitches: Right **Bats:** Right **Pos:** SP **Ht:** 6' 3" **Wt:** 210 **Born:** 11/16/64 **Age:** 27

	HOW MUCH HE PITCHED								WHAT HE GAVE UP										THE RESULTS					
Year	Team	Lg	G	GS	CG	GF	IP	BFP	H	R	ER	HR	SH	SF	HB	TBB	IBB	SO	WP	Bk	W	L	Pct.	ShO	Sv	ERA
1984	New York	NL	31	31	7	0	218	879	161	72	63	7	3	2	2	73	2	276	3	7	17	9	.654	3	0	2.60
1985	New York	NL	35	35	16	0	276.2	1065	198	51	47	13	6	2	2	69	4	268	6	2	24	4	.857	8	0	1.53
1986	New York	NL	33	33	12	0	250	1020	197	92	79	17	10	8	4	80	3	200	4	4	17	6	.739	2	0	2.84
1987	New York	NL	25	25	7	0	179.2	730	162	68	64	11	5	5	2	53	2	148	1	1	15	7	.682	3	0	3.21
1988	New York	NL	34	34	10	0	248.1	1024	242	98	88	8	10	6	6	57	4	175	5	5	18	9	.667	3	0	3.19
1989	New York	NL	19	17	0	0	118.1	497	93	42	38	9	4	3	2	47	2	101	7	5	9	4	.692	0	1	2.89
1990	New York	NL	34	34	2	0	232.2	983	229	106	99	10	10	7	7	70	3	223	6	3	19	7	.731	1	0	3.83
1991	New York	NL	27	27	3	0	190	789	185	80	76	12	5	4	3	56	2	150	5	2	13	7	.650	1	0	3.60
	8 ML YEARS		238	236	57	1	1713.2	6987	1467	609	554	87	53	37	28	505	22	1541	37	29	132	53	.714	21	1	2.91

Tom Goodwin

Bats: Left **Throws:** Right **Pos:** CF **Ht:** 6' 1" **Wt:** 165 **Born:** 07/27/68 **Age:** 23

Year Team	Lg	G	AB	H	2B	3B	HR	(Hm	Rd)	TB	R	RBI	TBB	IBB	SO	HBP	SH	SF	SB	CS	SB%	GDP	Avg	OBP	SLG
1989 Great Falls	R	63	240	74	12	3	2	--	--	98	55	33	28	1	30	2	1	2	60	8	.88	3	.308	.382	.408
1990 Bakersfield	A	32	134	39	6	2	0	--	--	49	24	13	11	0	22	0	1	0	22	4	.85	0	.291	.345	.366
San Antonio	AA	102	428	119	14	4	0	--	--	141	76	28	38	2	72	1	8	3	60	11	.85	3	.278	.336	.329
1991 Albuquerque	AAA	132	509	139	19	4	1	--	--	169	84	45	59	0	83	2	10	3	48	22	.69	5	.273	.349	.332
1991 Los Angeles	NL	16	7	1	0	0	0	(0	0)	1	3	0	0	0	0	0	0	0	1	1	.50	0	.143	.143	.143

Tom Gordon

Pitches: Right **Bats:** Right **Pos:** RP/SP **Ht:** 5' 9" **Wt:** 180 **Born:** 11/18/67 **Age:** 24

		HOW MUCH HE PITCHED						WHAT HE GAVE UP									THE RESULTS					
Year Team	Lg	G	GS	CG	GF	IP	BFP	H	R	ER	HR	SH	SF	HB	TBB	IBB	SO	WP	Bk	W	L	Pct.	ShO	Sv	ERA
1988 Kansas City	AL	5	2	0	0	15.2	67	16	9	9	1	0	0	0	7	0	18	0	0	0	2	.000	0	0	5.17
1989 Kansas City	AL	49	16	1	16	163	677	122	67	66	10	4	4	1	86	4	153	12	0	17	9	.654	1	1	3.64
1990 Kansas City	AL	32	32	6	0	195.1	858	192	99	81	17	8	2	3	99	1	175	11	0	12	11	.522	1	0	3.73
1991 Kansas City	AL	45	14	1	11	158	684	129	76	68	16	5	3	4	87	6	167	5	0	9	14	.391	0	1	3.87
4 ML YEARS		131	64	8	27	532	2286	459	251	224	44	17	9	8	279	11	513	28	0	38	36	.514	2	2	3.79

Goose Gossage

Pitches: Right **Bats:** Right **Pos:** RP **Ht:** 6' 3" **Wt:** 225 **Born:** 07/05/51 **Age:** 40

		HOW MUCH HE PITCHED						WHAT HE GAVE UP									THE RESULTS					
Year Team	Lg	G	GS	CG	GF	IP	BFP	H	R	ER	HR	SH	SF	HB	TBB	IBB	SO	WP	Bk	W	L	Pct.	ShO	Sv	ERA
1972 Chicago	AL	36	1	0	7	80	352	72	44	38	2	10	2	4	44	3	57	7	0	7	1	.875	0	2	4.28
1973 Chicago	AL	20	4	1	4	50	232	57	44	41	9	5	4	3	37	2	33	6	0	0	4	.000	0	0	7.38
1974 Chicago	AL	39	3	0	19	89	397	92	45	41	4	6	4	2	47	7	64	2	1	4	6	.400	0	1	4.15
1975 Chicago	AL	62	0	0	49	142	582	99	32	29	3	15	0	5	70	15	130	3	0	9	8	.529	0	26	1.84
1976 Chicago	AL	31	29	15	1	224	956	214	104	98	16	8	7	9	90	3	135	6	0	9	17	.346	0	1	3.94
1977 Pittsburgh	NL	72	0	0	55	133	523	78	27	24	9	7	6	2	49	6	151	2	0	11	9	.550	0	26	1.62
1978 New York	AL	63	0	0	55	134	543	87	41	30	9	9	8	2	59	8	122	5	0	10	11	.476	0	27	2.01
1979 New York	AL	36	0	0	33	58	234	48	18	17	5	4	0	0	19	4	41	3	0	5	3	.625	0	18	2.64
1980 New York	AL	64	0	0	58	99	401	74	29	25	5	8	4	1	37	3	103	4	0	6	2	.750	0	33	2.27
1981 New York	AL	32	0	0	30	47	173	22	6	4	2	1	1	1	14	1	48	1	0	3	2	.600	0	20	0.77
1982 New York	AL	56	0	0	43	93	356	63	23	23	5	5	2	0	28	5	102	1	0	4	5	.444	0	30	2.23
1983 New York	AL	57	0	0	47	87.1	367	82	27	22	5	5	6	1	25	5	90	0	0	13	5	.722	0	22	2.27
1984 San Diego	NL	62	0	0	51	102.1	412	75	34	33	6	4	3	1	36	4	84	2	2	10	6	.625	0	25	2.90
1985 San Diego	NL	50	0	0	38	79	308	64	21	16	1	3	4	1	17	1	52	0	0	5	3	.625	0	26	1.82
1986 San Diego	NL	45	0	0	38	64.2	281	69	36	32	8	2	4	2	20	0	63	4	0	5	7	.417	0	21	4.45
1987 San Diego	NL	40	0	0	30	52	217	47	18	18	4	2	3	0	19	6	44	2	0	5	4	.556	0	11	3.12
1988 Chicago	NL	46	0	0	33	43.2	194	50	23	21	3	3	1	3	15	5	30	3	2	4	4	.500	0	13	4.33
1989 2 ML Teams		42	0	0	28	58	238	46	22	19	2	3	2	1	30	4	30	3	0	3	1	.750	0	5	2.95
1991 Texas	AL	44	0	0	16	40.1	167	33	16	16	4	3	0	3	16	1	28	3	0	2	1	.667	0	1	3.57
1989 San Francisco	NL	31	0	0	22	43.2	182	32	16	13	2	2	2	0	27	3	24	2	0	2	1	.667	0	4	2.68
New York	AL	11	0	0	6	14.1	56	14	6	6	0	1	0	1	3	1	6	1	0	1	0	1.000	0	1	3.77
19 ML YEARS		897	37	16	635	1676.1	6933	1372	610	547	102	103	61	41	672	83	1407	57	5	117	100	.539	0	308	2.94

Jim Gott

Pitches: Right **Bats:** Right **Pos:** RP **Ht:** 6' 4" **Wt:** 220 **Born:** 08/03/59 **Age:** 32

		HOW MUCH HE PITCHED						WHAT HE GAVE UP									THE RESULTS					
Year Team	Lg	G	GS	CG	GF	IP	BFP	H	R	ER	HR	SH	SF	HB	TBB	IBB	SO	WP	Bk	W	L	Pct.	ShO	Sv	ERA
1982 Toronto	AL	30	23	1	4	136	600	134	76	67	15	3	2	3	66	0	82	8	0	5	10	.333	1	0	4.43
1983 Toronto	AL	34	30	6	2	176.2	776	195	103	93	15	4	3	5	68	5	121	2	0	9	14	.391	1	0	4.74
1984 Toronto	AL	35	12	1	11	109.2	464	93	54	49	7	7	6	3	49	3	73	1	0	7	6	.538	1	2	4.02
1985 San Francisco	NL	26	26	2	0	148.1	629	144	73	64	10	6	4	1	51	3	78	3	2	7	10	.412	0	0	3.88
1986 San Francisco	NL	9	2	0	3	13	66	16	12	11	0	1	1	0	13	2	9	1	1	0	0	.000	0	1	7.62
1987 2 ML Teams		55	3	0	30	87	382	81	43	33	4	2	1	2	40	7	90	5	0	1	2	.333	0	13	3.41
1988 Pittsburgh	NL	67	0	0	59	77.1	314	68	30	30	9	7	3	2	22	5	76	1	6	6	6	.500	0	34	3.49
1989 Pittsburgh	NL	1	0	0	0	0.2	4	1	0	0	0	0	0	0	1	0	0	0	0	0	0	.000	0	0	0.00
1990 Los Angeles	NL	50	0	0	24	62	270	59	27	20	5	2	4	0	34	7	44	4	0	3	5	.375	0	3	2.90
1991 Los Angeles	NL	55	0	0	26	76	322	63	28	25	5	4	1	1	32	7	73	6	3	4	3	.571	0	2	2.96
1987 San Francisco	NL	30	3	0	8	56	253	53	32	28	4	1	1	2	32	5	63	3	0	1	0	1.000	0	0	4.50
Pittsburgh	NL	25	0	0	22	31	129	28	11	5	0	1	0	0	8	2	27	2	0	0	2	.000	0	13	1.45
10 ML YEARS		362	96	10	159	886.2	3827	854	446	392	70	38	25	17	376	39	647	31	12	42	56	.429	3	55	3.98

75

Mauro Gozzo

Pitches: Right **Bats:** Right **Pos:** SP   **Ht:** 6' 3" **Wt:** 212 **Born:** 03/07/66 **Age:** 26

				HOW MUCH HE PITCHED					WHAT HE GAVE UP									THE RESULTS					
Year Team	Lg	G	GS	CG	GF	IP	BFP	H	R	ER	HR	SH	SF	HB	TBB	IBB	SO	WP	Bk	W	L	Pct.	ShO	Sv	ERA
1984 Little Fls	A	24	0	0	8	38.1	176	40	27	24	3	0	2	0	28	4	30	7	1	4	3	.571	0	2	5.63
1985 Columbia	A	49	0	0	42	78	330	62	22	22	2	3	5	2	39	7	66	4	1	11	4	.733	0	14	2.54
1986 Lynchburg	A	60	0	0	46	78.1	341	80	30	27	3	5	2	2	35	3	50	4	1	9	4	.692	0	9	3.10
1987 Memphis	AA	19	14	1	2	91.1	400	95	58	46	13	1	2	4	36	2	56	3	3	6	5	.545	0	0	4.53
1988 Memphis	AA	33	12	0	9	92.2	430	127	64	59	9	2	7	1	36	1	48	14	3	4	9	.308	0	3	5.73
1989 Knoxville	AA	18	6	2	6	60.1	245	59	27	20	1	0	5	1	12	1	37	2	1	7	0	1.000	1	0	2.98
Syracuse	AAA	12	7	2	2	62	251	56	22	19	3	1	1	0	19	0	34	2	0	5	1	.833	1	2	2.76
1990 Syracuse	AAA	34	10	0	19	98	409	87	46	39	5	3	1	3	44	3	62	2	1	3	8	.273	0	7	3.58
1991 Colo Sprngs	AAA	25	20	3	4	130.1	588	143	86	76	9	3	7	6	68	3	81	7	4	10	6	.625	0	1	5.25
1989 Toronto	AL	9	3	0	2	31.2	133	35	19	17	1	0	2	1	9	1	10	0	0	4	1	.800	0	0	4.83
1990 Cleveland	AL	2	0	0	1	3	13	2	0	0	0	0	0	0	2	0	2	0	0	0	0	.000	0	0	0.00
1991 Cleveland	AL	2	2	0	0	4.2	28	9	10	10	0	0	1	0	7	0	3	2	0	0	0	.000	0	0	19.29
3 ML YEARS		13	5	0	3	39.1	174	46	29	27	1	0	3	1	18	1	15	2	0	4	1	.800	0	0	6.18

Mark Grace

Bats: Left **Throws:** Left **Pos:** 1B   **Ht:** 6' 2" **Wt:** 190 **Born:** 06/28/64 **Age:** 28

					BATTING														BASERUNNING				PERCENTAGES		
Year Team	Lg	G	AB	H	2B	3B	HR	(Hm	Rd)	TB	R	RBI	TBB	IBB	SO	HBP	SH	SF	SB	CS	SB%	GDP	Avg	OBP	SLG
1988 Chicago	NL	134	486	144	23	4	7	(0	7)	196	65	57	60	5	43	0	0	4	3	3	.50	12	.296	.371	.403
1989 Chicago	NL	142	510	160	28	3	13	(8	5)	233	74	79	80	13	42	0	3	3	14	7	.67	13	.314	.405	.457
1990 Chicago	NL	157	589	182	32	1	9	(4	5)	243	72	82	59	5	54	5	1	8	15	6	.71	10	.309	.372	.413
1991 Chicago	NL	160	619	169	28	5	8	(5	3)	231	87	58	70	7	53	3	4	7	3	4	.43	6	.273	.346	.373
4 ML YEARS		593	2204	655	111	13	37	(17	20)	903	298	276	269	30	192	8	8	22	35	20	.64	41	.297	.372	.410

Joe Grahe

Pitches: Right **Bats:** Right **Pos:** SP/RP   **Ht:** 6' 0" **Wt:** 200 **Born:** 08/14/67 **Age:** 24

				HOW MUCH HE PITCHED					WHAT HE GAVE UP									THE RESULTS					
Year Team	Lg	G	GS	CG	GF	IP	BFP	H	R	ER	HR	SH	SF	HB	TBB	IBB	SO	WP	Bk	W	L	Pct.	ShO	Sv	ERA
1990 Midland	AA	18	18	1	0	119	519	145	75	68	10	2	2	4	34	1	58	10	1	7	5	.583	0	0	5.14
Edmonton	AAA	5	5	2	0	40	159	35	10	6	4	0	0	0	11	0	21	0	0	3	0	1.000	0	0	1.35
1991 Edmonton	AAA	14	14	3	0	94.1	428	121	55	42	3	4	2	3	30	0	55	6	0	9	3	.750	1	0	4.01
1990 California	AL	8	8	0	0	43.1	200	51	30	24	3	0	0	3	23	1	25	1	0	3	4	.429	0	0	4.98
1991 California	AL	18	10	1	2	73	330	84	43	39	2	1	1	3	33	0	40	2	0	3	7	.300	0	0	4.81
2 ML YEARS		26	18	1	2	116.1	530	135	73	63	5	1	1	6	56	1	65	3	0	6	11	.353	0	0	4.87

Mark Grater

Pitches: Right **Bats:** Right **Pos:** RP   **Ht:** 5'10" **Wt:** 205 **Born:** 01/19/64 **Age:** 28

				HOW MUCH HE PITCHED					WHAT HE GAVE UP									THE RESULTS					
Year Team	Lg	G	GS	CG	GF	IP	BFP	H	R	ER	HR	SH	SF	HB	TBB	IBB	SO	WP	Bk	W	L	Pct.	ShO	Sv	ERA
1986 Johnson Cty	R	24	0	0	19	41.1	163	25	14	11	2	0	2	2	14	3	46	7	0	5	2	.714	0	8	2.40
1987 Savannah	A	50	0	0	28	74	319	54	35	25	4	5	1	6	48	9	59	11	1	6	10	.375	0	6	3.04
1988 Springfield	A	53	0	0	28	81	318	60	23	16	1	4	1	4	27	7	66	5	3	7	2	.778	0	11	1.78
1989 St.Pete	A	56	0	0	49	67.1	279	44	23	14	1	4	3	7	24	4	59	2	0	3	8	.273	0	32	1.87
1990 Louisville	AAA	24	0	0	15	28.1	124	24	13	10	0	3	2	0	15	4	18	0	0	0	2	.000	0	3	3.18
Arkansas	AA	29	0	0	22	44	182	31	18	14	1	2	1	4	18	0	43	6	0	2	0	1.000	0	17	2.86
1991 Louisville	AAA	58	0	0	41	80.1	329	68	20	18	1	6	0	3	33	7	53	4	0	3	5	.375	0	12	2.02
1991 St.Louis	NL	3	0	0	2	3	15	5	0	0	0	0	0	0	2	0	1	0	0	0	0	.000	0	0	0.00

Jeff Gray

Pitches: Right **Bats:** Right **Pos:** RP   **Ht:** 6' 1" **Wt:** 190 **Born:** 04/10/63 **Age:** 29

				HOW MUCH HE PITCHED					WHAT HE GAVE UP									THE RESULTS					
Year Team	Lg	G	GS	CG	GF	IP	BFP	H	R	ER	HR	SH	SF	HB	TBB	IBB	SO	WP	Bk	W	L	Pct.	ShO	Sv	ERA
1988 Cincinnati	NL	5	0	0	1	9.1	45	12	4	4	0	3	2	0	4	2	5	0	0	0	0	.000	0	0	3.86
1990 Boston	AL	41	0	0	28	50.2	217	53	27	25	3	2	1	1	15	3	50	2	0	2	4	.333	0	9	4.44
1991 Boston	AL	50	0	0	20	61.2	231	39	17	16	7	3	1	1	10	4	41	2	0	2	3	.400	0	1	2.34
3 ML YEARS		96	0	0	49	121.2	493	104	48	45	10	8	4	2	29	9	96	4	0	4	7	.364	0	10	3.33

Craig Grebeck

Bats: Right **Throws:** Right **Pos:** 3B/2B/SS   **Ht:** 5' 7" **Wt:** 160 **Born:** 12/29/64 **Age:** 27

					BATTING														BASERUNNING				PERCENTAGES		
Year Team	Lg	G	AB	H	2B	3B	HR	(Hm	Rd)	TB	R	RBI	TBB	IBB	SO	HBP	SH	SF	SB	CS	SB%	GDP	Avg	OBP	SLG
1987 Peninsula	A	104	378	106	22	3	15	--	--	179	63	67	37	0	62	1	2	4	3	6	.33	8	.280	.343	.474
1988 Birmingham	AA	133	450	126	21	1	9	--	--	176	57	53	65	3	72	2	7	3	5	7	.42	10	.280	.371	.391

Year	Team	Lg	G	AB	H	2B	3B	HR	(Hm	Rd)	TB	R	RBI	TBB	IBB	SO	HBP	SH	SF	SB	CS	SB%	GDP	Avg	OBP	SLG
1989	Birmingham	AA	143	533	153	25	4	5	--	--	201	85	80	63	4	77	4	11	7	14	15	.48	15	.287	.362	.377
1990	Vancouver	AAA	12	41	8	0	0	1	--	--	11	8	3	6	0	7	0	0	0	1	0	1.00	2	.195	.298	.268
1990	Chicago	AL	59	119	20	3	1	1	(1	0)	28	7	9	8	0	24	2	3	3	0	0	.00	2	.168	.227	.235
1991	Chicago	AL	107	224	63	16	3	6	(3	3)	103	37	31	38	0	40	1	4	1	1	3	.25	3	.281	.386	.460
	2 ML YEARS		166	343	83	19	4	7	(4	3)	131	44	40	46	0	64	3	7	4	1	3	.25	5	.242	.333	.382

Gary Green

Bats: Right **Throws:** Right **Pos:** SS   **Ht:** 6' 3" **Wt:** 175 **Born:** 01/14/62 **Age:** 30

			BATTING																BASERUNNING				PERCENTAGES		
Year	Team	Lg	G	AB	H	2B	3B	HR	(Hm	Rd)	TB	R	RBI	TBB	IBB	SO	HBP	SH	SF	SB	CS	SB%	GDP	Avg	OBP	SLG
1986	San Diego	NL	13	33	7	1	0	0	(0	0)	8	2	2	1	0	11	0	1	0	0	0	.00	0	.212	.235	.242
1989	San Diego	NL	15	27	7	3	0	0	(0	0)	10	4	0	1	0	1	0	0	0	0	1	.00	0	.259	.286	.370
1990	Texas	AL	62	88	19	3	0	0	(0	0)	22	10	8	6	0	18	0	4	1	1	1	.50	2	.216	.263	.250
1991	Texas	AL	8	20	3	1	0	0	(0	0)	4	0	1	1	0	6	0	2	0	0	0	.00	0	.150	.190	.200
	4 ML YEARS		98	168	36	8	0	0	(0	0)	44	16	11	9	0	36	0	7	1	1	2	.33	2	.214	.253	.262

Tommy Greene

Pitches: Right **Bats:** Right **Pos:** SP/RP   **Ht:** 6' 5" **Wt:** 227 **Born:** 04/06/67 **Age:** 25

			HOW MUCH HE PITCHED					WHAT HE GAVE UP									THE RESULTS					
Year	Team	Lg	G	GS	CG	GF	IP	BFP	H	R	ER	HR	SH	SF	HB	TBB	IBB	SO	WP	Bk	W	L	Pct.	ShO	Sv	ERA
1989	Atlanta	NL	4	4	1	0	26.1	103	22	12	12	5	1	2	0	6	1	17	1	0	1	2	.333	1	0	4.10
1990	2 ML Teams		15	9	0	1	51.1	227	50	31	29	8	5	0	1	26	1	21	1	0	3	3	.500	0	0	5.08
1991	Philadelphia	NL	36	27	3	3	207.2	857	177	85	78	19	9	11	3	66	4	154	9	1	13	7	.650	2	0	3.38
1990	Atlanta	NL	5	2	0	0	12.1	61	14	11	11	3	2	0	1	9	0	4	0	0	1	0	1.000	0	0	8.03
	Philadelphia	NL	10	7	0	1	39	166	36	20	18	5	3	0	0	17	1	17	1	0	2	3	.400	0	0	4.15
	3 ML YEARS		55	40	4	4	285.1	1187	249	128	119	32	15	13	4	98	6	192	11	1	17	12	.586	3	0	3.75

Mike Greenwell

Bats: Left **Throws:** Right **Pos:** LF   **Ht:** 6' 0" **Wt:** 200 **Born:** 07/18/63 **Age:** 28

			BATTING																BASERUNNING				PERCENTAGES		
Year	Team	Lg	G	AB	H	2B	3B	HR	(Hm	Rd)	TB	R	RBI	TBB	IBB	SO	HBP	SH	SF	SB	CS	SB%	GDP	Avg	OBP	SLG
1985	Boston	AL	17	31	10	1	0	4	(1	3)	23	7	8	3	1	4	0	0	0	1	0	1.00	0	.323	.382	.742
1986	Boston	AL	31	35	11	2	0	0	(0	0)	13	4	4	5	0	7	0	0	0	0	0	.00	1	.314	.400	.371
1987	Boston	AL	125	412	135	31	6	19	(8	11)	235	71	89	35	1	40	6	0	3	5	4	.56	1	.328	.386	.570
1988	Boston	AL	158	590	192	39	8	22	(12	10)	313	86	119	87	18	38	9	0	7	16	8	.67	11	.325	.416	.531
1989	Boston	AL	145	578	178	36	0	14	(6	8)	256	87	95	56	15	44	3	0	4	13	5	.72	21	.308	.370	.443
1990	Boston	AL	159	610	181	30	6	14	(6	8)	265	71	73	65	12	43	4	0	3	8	7	.53	19	.297	.367	.434
1991	Boston	AL	147	544	163	26	6	9	(5	4)	228	76	83	43	6	35	3	1	7	15	5	.75	11	.300	.350	.419
	7 ML YEARS		782	2800	870	165	26	82	(38	44)	1333	402	471	294	53	211	25	1	24	58	29	.67	70	.311	.378	.476

Tommy Gregg

Bats: Left **Throws:** Left **Pos:** 1B   **Ht:** 6' 1" **Wt:** 190 **Born:** 07/29/63 **Age:** 28

			BATTING																BASERUNNING				PERCENTAGES		
Year	Team	Lg	G	AB	H	2B	3B	HR	(Hm	Rd)	TB	R	RBI	TBB	IBB	SO	HBP	SH	SF	SB	CS	SB%	GDP	Avg	OBP	SLG
1987	Pittsburgh	NL	10	8	2	1	0	0	(0	0)	3	3	0	0	0	2	0	0	0	0	0	.00	2	.250	.250	.375
1988	2 ML Teams		25	44	13	4	0	1	(0	1)	20	5	7	3	1	6	0	0	1	0	1	.00	1	.295	.333	.455
1989	Atlanta	NL	102	276	67	8	0	6	(2	4)	93	24	23	18	2	45	0	3	1	3	4	.43	4	.243	.288	.337
1990	Atlanta	NL	124	239	63	13	1	5	(2	3)	93	18	32	20	4	39	1	0	1	4	3	.57	2	.264	.322	.389
1991	Atlanta	NL	72	107	20	8	1	1	(1	0)	33	13	4	12	2	24	1	0	0	2	2	.50	1	.187	.275	.308
1988	Pittsburgh	NL	14	15	3	1	0	1	(0	1)	7	4	3	1	0	4	0	0	1	0	1	.00	0	.200	.235	.467
	Atlanta	NL	11	29	10	3	0	0	(0	0)	13	1	4	2	1	2	0	0	0	0	0	.00	1	.345	.387	.448
	5 ML YEARS		333	674	165	34	2	13	(5	8)	242	63	66	53	9	116	2	3	3	9	10	.47	10	.245	.301	.359

Ken Griffey Jr

Bats: Left **Throws:** Left **Pos:** CF   **Ht:** 6' 3" **Wt:** 200 **Born:** 11/21/69 **Age:** 22

			BATTING																BASERUNNING				PERCENTAGES		
Year	Team	Lg	G	AB	H	2B	3B	HR	(Hm	Rd)	TB	R	RBI	TBB	IBB	SO	HBP	SH	SF	SB	CS	SB%	GDP	Avg	OBP	SLG
1989	Seattle	AL	127	455	120	23	0	16	(10	6)	191	61	61	44	8	83	2	1	4	16	7	.70	4	.264	.329	.420
1990	Seattle	AL	155	597	179	28	7	22	(8	14)	287	91	80	63	12	81	2	0	6	16	11	.59	12	.300	.366	.481
1991	Seattle	AL	154	548	179	42	1	22	(16	6)	289	76	100	71	21	82	1	4	9	18	6	.75	10	.327	.399	.527
	3 ML YEARS		436	1600	478	93	8	60	(34	26)	767	228	241	178	41	246	5	5	17	50	24	.68	26	.299	.367	.479

Ken Griffey Sr

Bats: Left **Throws:** Left **Pos:** LF   **Ht:** 6' 0" **Wt:** 210 **Born:** 04/10/50 **Age:** 42

			BATTING																BASERUNNING				PERCENTAGES		
Year	Team	Lg	G	AB	H	2B	3B	HR	(Hm	Rd)	TB	R	RBI	TBB	IBB	SO	HBP	SH	SF	SB	CS	SB%	GDP	Avg	OBP	SLG
1973	Cincinnati	NL	25	86	33	5	1	3	(2	1)	49	19	14	6	0	10	0	0	0	4	2	.67	0	.384	.424	.570

Year	Team	Lg	G	AB	H	2B	3B	HR	(Hm	Rd)	TB	R	RBI	TBB	IBB	SO	HBP	SH	SF	SB	CS	SB%	GDP	Avg	OBP	SLG
1974	Cincinnati	NL	88	227	57	9	5	2	(2	0)	82	24	19	27	2	43	1	1	0	9	4	.69	2	.251	.333	.361
1975	Cincinnati	NL	132	463	141	15	9	4	(1	3)	186	95	46	67	2	67	1	6	3	16	7	.70	10	.305	.391	.402
1976	Cincinnati	NL	148	562	189	28	9	6	(2	4)	253	111	74	62	0	65	1	0	3	34	11	.76	3	.336	.401	.450
1977	Cincinnati	NL	154	585	186	35	8	12	(4	8)	273	117	57	69	2	84	0	1	2	17	8	.68	12	.318	.389	.467
1978	Cincinnati	NL	158	614	177	33	8	10	(7	3)	256	90	63	54	1	70	0	9	3	23	5	.82	6	.288	.344	.417
1979	Cincinnati	NL	95	380	120	27	4	8	(3	5)	179	62	32	36	3	39	1	0	3	12	5	.71	7	.316	.374	.471
1980	Cincinnati	NL	146	544	160	28	10	13	(9	4)	247	89	85	62	4	77	1	3	5	23	1	.96	4	.294	.364	.454
1981	Cincinnati	NL	101	396	123	21	6	2	(0	2)	162	65	34	39	6	42	1	2	4	12	4	.75	9	.311	.370	.409
1982	New York	AL	127	484	134	23	2	12	(8	4)	197	70	54	39	1	58	0	1	3	10	4	.71	10	.277	.329	.407
1983	New York	AL	118	458	140	21	3	11	(8	3)	200	60	46	34	3	45	2	3	2	6	1	.86	3	.306	.355	.437
1984	New York	AL	120	399	109	20	1	7	(5	2)	152	44	56	29	2	32	1	3	4	2	2	.50	7	.273	.321	.381
1985	New York	AL	127	438	120	28	4	10	(6	4)	186	68	69	41	4	51	0	0	8	7	7	.50	2	.274	.331	.425
1986	2 ML Teams		139	490	150	22	3	21	(14	7)	241	69	58	35	4	67	1	1	5	14	9	.61	9	.306	.350	.492
1987	Atlanta	NL	122	399	114	24	1	14	(8	6)	182	65	64	46	11	54	1	1	4	4	7	.36	12	.286	.358	.456
1988	2 ML Teams		94	243	62	6	0	4	(3	1)	80	26	23	19	3	31	0	0	2	1	3	.25	5	.255	.307	.329
1989	Cincinnati	NL	106	236	62	8	3	8	(2	6)	100	26	30	29	3	42	1	0	0	4	2	.67	2	.263	.346	.424
1990	2 ML Teams		67	140	42	4	0	4	(2	2)	58	19	26	12	0	8	1	0	3	2	1	.67	1	.300	.353	.414
1991	Seattle	AL	30	85	24	7	0	1	(1	0)	34	10	9	13	0	13	1	0	1	0	0	.00	2	.282	.380	.400
1986	New York	AL	59	198	60	7	0	9	(5	4)	94	33	26	15	0	24	1	1	4	2	2	.50	7	.303	.349	.475
	Atlanta	NL	80	292	90	15	3	12	(9	3)	147	36	32	20	4	43	0	0	1	12	7	.63	2	.308	.351	.503
1988	Atlanta	NL	69	193	48	5	0	2	(2	0)	59	21	19	17	2	26	0	0	2	1	3	.25	5	.249	.307	.306
	Cincinnati	NL	25	50	14	1	0	2	(1	1)	21	5	4	2	1	5	0	0	0	0	0	.00	0	.280	.308	.420
1990	Cincinnati	NL	46	63	13	2	0	1	(1	0)	18	6	8	2	0	5	1	0	2	2	1	.67	0	.206	.235	.286
	Seattle	AL	21	77	29	2	0	3	(1	2)	40	13	18	10	0	3	0	0	1	0	0	.00	1	.377	.443	.519
19	ML YEARS		2097	7229	2143	364	77	152	(87	65)	3117	1129	859	719	51	898	14	31	55	200	83	.71	106	.296	.359	.431

Alfredo Griffin

Bats: Both **Throws:** Right **Pos:** SS **Ht:** 5'11" **Wt:** 166 **Born:** 03/06/57 **Age:** 35

			BATTING																	BASERUNNING				PERCENTAGES		
Year	Team	Lg	G	AB	H	2B	3B	HR	(Hm	Rd)	TB	R	RBI	TBB	IBB	SO	HBP	SH	SF	SB	CS	SB%	GDP	Avg	OBP	SLG
1976	Cleveland	AL	12	4	1	0	0	0	(0	0)	1	0	0	0	0	2	0	0	0	0	1	.00	0	.250	.250	.250
1977	Cleveland	AL	14	41	6	1	0	0	(0	0)	7	5	3	3	0	5	0	0	0	2	2	.50	1	.146	.205	.171
1978	Cleveland	AL	5	4	2	1	0	0	(0	0)	3	1	0	2	0	1	0	0	0	0	0	.00	0	.500	.667	.750
1979	Toronto	AL	153	624	179	22	10	2	(2	0)	227	81	31	40	0	59	5	16	4	21	16	.57	10	.287	.333	.364
1980	Toronto	AL	155	653	166	26	15	2	(1	1)	228	63	41	24	2	58	4	10	5	18	23	.44	8	.254	.283	.349
1981	Toronto	AL	101	388	81	19	6	0	(0	0)	112	30	21	17	1	38	1	6	2	8	12	.40	6	.209	.243	.289
1982	Toronto	AL	162	539	130	20	8	1	(0	1)	169	57	48	22	0	48	0	11	4	10	8	.56	7	.241	.269	.314
1983	Toronto	AL	162	528	132	22	9	4	(2	2)	184	62	47	27	0	44	3	11	3	8	11	.42	5	.250	.289	.348
1984	Toronto	AL	140	419	101	8	2	4	(1	3)	125	53	30	4	0	33	1	13	4	11	3	.79	5	.241	.248	.298
1985	Oakland	AL	162	614	166	18	7	2	(0	2)	204	75	64	20	1	50	0	5	7	24	9	.73	6	.270	.290	.332
1986	Oakland	AL	162	594	169	23	6	4	(1	3)	216	74	51	35	6	52	2	12	6	33	16	.67	5	.285	.323	.364
1987	Oakland	AL	144	494	130	23	5	3	(2	1)	172	69	60	28	2	41	4	10	3	26	13	.67	9	.263	.306	.348
1988	Los Angeles	NL	95	316	63	8	3	1	(0	0)	80	39	27	24	7	30	2	11	1	7	5	.58	3	.199	.259	.253
1989	Los Angeles	NL	136	506	125	27	2	0	(0	0)	156	49	29	29	2	57	0	11	1	10	7	.59	5	.247	.287	.308
1990	Los Angeles	NL	141	461	97	11	3	1	(0	1)	117	38	35	29	11	65	2	6	4	6	3	.67	5	.210	.258	.254
1991	Los Angeles	NL	109	350	85	6	2	0	(0	0)	95	27	27	22	5	49	1	7	5	5	4	.56	5	.243	.286	.271
16	ML YEARS		1853	6535	1633	235	78	24	(9	15)	2096	723	514	326	37	632	25	129	49	189	133	.59	80	.250	.286	.321

Jason Grimsley

Pitches: Right **Bats:** Right **Pos:** SP **Ht:** 6'3" **Wt:** 182 **Born:** 08/07/67 **Age:** 24

			HOW MUCH HE PITCHED						WHAT HE GAVE UP												THE RESULTS					
Year	Team	Lg	G	GS	CG	GF	IP	BFP	H	R	ER	HR	SH	SF	HB	TBB	IBB	SO	WP	Bk	W	L	Pct.	ShO	Sv	ERA
1989	Philadelphia	NL	4	4	0	0	18.1	91	19	13	12	2	0	2	1	19	1	7	2	0	1	3	.250	0	0	5.89
1990	Philadelphia	NL	11	11	0	0	57.1	255	47	21	21	1	2	1	2	43	0	41	6	1	3	2	.600	0	0	3.30
1991	Philadelphia	NL	12	12	0	0	61	272	54	34	33	4	3	2	3	41	3	42	14	0	1	7	.125	0	0	4.87
3	ML YEARS		27	27	0	0	136.2	618	120	68	66	7	6	3	5	103	4	90	22	1	5	12	.294	0	0	4.35

Marquis Grissom

Bats: Right **Throws:** Right **Pos:** CF **Ht:** 5'11" **Wt:** 190 **Born:** 04/17/67 **Age:** 25

			BATTING																	BASERUNNING				PERCENTAGES		
Year	Team	Lg	G	AB	H	2B	3B	HR	(Hm	Rd)	TB	R	RBI	TBB	IBB	SO	HBP	SH	SF	SB	CS	SB%	GDP	Avg	OBP	SLG
1989	Montreal	NL	26	74	19	2	0	1	(0	1)	24	16	2	12	0	21	0	1	0	1	0	1.00	0	.257	.360	.324
1990	Montreal	NL	98	288	74	14	2	3	(2	1)	101	42	29	27	2	40	0	4	1	22	2	.92	3	.257	.320	.351
1991	Montreal	NL	148	558	149	23	9	6	(3	3)	208	73	39	34	0	89	1	4	0	76	17	.82	8	.267	.310	.373
3	ML YEARS		272	920	242	39	11	10	(5	5)	333	131	70	73	2	150	1	9	1	99	19	.84	12	.263	.318	.362

Kevin Gross

Pitches: Right **Bats:** Right **Pos:** RP/SP **Ht:** 6' 5" **Wt:** 215 **Born:** 06/08/61 **Age:** 31

		HOW MUCH HE PITCHED					WHAT HE GAVE UP										THE RESULTS					
Year Team	Lg	G	GS	CG	GF	IP	BFP	H	R	ER	HR	SH	SF	HB	TBB	IBB	SO	WP	Bk	W	L	Pct.	ShO	Sv	ERA
1983 Philadelphia	NL	17	17	1	0	96	418	100	46	38	13	2	1	3	35	3	66	4	1	4	6	.400	1	0	3.56
1984 Philadelphia	NL	44	14	1	9	129	566	140	66	59	8	9	3	5	44	4	84	4	4	8	5	.615	0	1	4.12
1985 Philadelphia	NL	38	31	6	0	205.2	873	194	86	78	11	7	5	7	81	6	151	2	0	15	13	.536	2	0	3.41
1986 Philadelphia	NL	37	36	7	0	241.2	1040	240	115	108	28	8	5	8	94	2	154	2	1	12	12	.500	2	0	4.02
1987 Philadelphia	NL	34	33	3	1	200.2	878	205	107	97	26	8	6	10	87	7	110	3	7	9	16	.360	1	0	4.35
1988 Philadelphia	NL	33	33	5	0	231.2	989	209	101	95	18	9	4	11	89	5	162	5	7	12	14	.462	1	0	3.69
1989 Montreal	NL	31	31	4	0	201.1	867	188	105	98	20	10	3	6	88	6	158	5	5	11	12	.478	3	0	4.38
1990 Montreal	NL	31	26	2	3	163.1	712	171	86	83	9	6	9	4	65	7	111	4	1	9	12	.429	1	0	4.57
1991 Los Angeles	NL	46	10	0	16	115.2	509	123	55	46	10	6	4	2	50	6	95	3	0	10	11	.476	0	3	3.58
9 ML YEARS		311	231	29	29	1585	6852	1570	767	702	143	65	40	56	633	46	1091	32	26	90	101	.471	11	4	3.99

Kip Gross

Pitches: Right **Bats:** Right **Pos:** RP/SP **Ht:** 6' 2" **Wt:** 190 **Born:** 08/24/64 **Age:** 27

		HOW MUCH HE PITCHED					WHAT HE GAVE UP										THE RESULTS					
Year Team	Lg	G	GS	CG	GF	IP	BFP	H	R	ER	HR	SH	SF	HB	TBB	IBB	SO	WP	Bk	W	L	Pct.	ShO	Sv	ERA
1987 Lynchburg	A	16	15	2	0	89.1	379	92	37	27	1	2	3	6	22	1	39	1	1	7	4	.636	0	0	2.72
1988 St. Lucie	A	28	27	7	1	178.1	736	153	72	52	1	1	3	7	53	6	124	10	11	13	9	.591	3	0	2.62
1989 Jackson	AA	16	16	4	0	112	444	96	47	31	9	4	2	2	13	0	60	4	4	6	5	.545	0	0	2.49
Tidewater	AAA	12	12	0	0	70.1	289	72	33	31	3	5	2	1	17	0	39	1	1	4	4	.500	0	0	3.97
1990 Nashville	AAA	40	11	2	11	127	521	113	54	47	6	6	2	7	47	3	62	6	3	12	7	.632	1	3	3.33
1991 Nashville	AAA	14	6	1	3	47.2	195	39	13	11	3	2	1	4	16	0	28	3	1	5	3	.625	1	0	2.08
1990 Cincinnati	NL	5	0	0	2	6.1	25	6	3	3	0	0	1	0	2	0	3	0	0	0	0	.000	0	0	4.26
1991 Cincinnati	NL	29	9	1	6	85.2	381	93	43	33	8	6	2	0	40	2	40	5	1	6	4	.600	0	0	3.47
2 ML YEARS		34	9	1	8	92	406	99	46	36	8	6	3	0	42	2	43	5	1	6	4	.600	0	0	3.52

Kelly Gruber

Bats: Right **Throws:** Right **Pos:** 3B **Ht:** 6' 0" **Wt:** 185 **Born:** 02/26/62 **Age:** 30

		BATTING															BASERUNNING				PERCENTAGES		
Year Team	Lg	G	AB	H	2B	3B	HR	(Hm | Rd)	TB	R	RBI	TBB	IBB	SO	HBP	SH	SF	SB	CS	SB%	GDP	Avg	OBP	SLG
1984 Toronto	AL	15	16	1	0	0	1	(0 | 1)	4	1	2	0	0	5	0	0	0	0	0	.00	1	.063	.063	.250
1985 Toronto	AL	5	13	3	0	0	0	(0 | 0)	3	0	1	0	0	3	0	0	0	0	0	.00	0	.231	.231	.231
1986 Toronto	AL	87	143	28	4	1	5	(4 | 1)	49	20	15	5	0	27	0	2	2	2	5	.29	4	.196	.220	.343
1987 Toronto	AL	138	341	80	14	3	12	(5 | 7)	136	50	36	17	2	70	7	1	2	12	2	.86	11	.235	.283	.399
1988 Toronto	AL	158	569	158	33	5	16	(5 | 11)	249	75	81	38	1	92	7	5	4	23	5	.82	20	.278	.328	.438
1989 Toronto	AL	135	545	158	24	4	18	(8 | 10)	244	83	73	30	0	60	3	0	5	10	5	.67	13	.290	.328	.448
1990 Toronto	AL	150	592	162	36	6	31	(23 | 8)	303	92	118	48	2	94	8	1	13	14	2	.88	14	.274	.330	.512
1991 Toronto	AL	113	429	108	18	2	20	(8 | 12)	190	58	65	31	5	70	6	3	5	12	7	.63	7	.252	.308	.443
8 ML YEARS		801	2648	698	129	21	103	(53 | 50)	1178	379	391	169	10	421	31	12	31	73	26	.74	70	.264	.312	.445

Mark Gubicza

Pitches: Right **Bats:** Right **Pos:** SP **Ht:** 6' 5" **Wt:** 225 **Born:** 08/14/62 **Age:** 29

		HOW MUCH HE PITCHED					WHAT HE GAVE UP										THE RESULTS					
Year Team	Lg	G	GS	CG	GF	IP	BFP	H	R	ER	HR	SH	SF	HB	TBB	IBB	SO	WP	Bk	W	L	Pct.	ShO	Sv	ERA
1984 Kansas City	AL	29	29	4	0	189	800	172	90	85	13	4	9	5	75	0	111	3	1	10	14	.417	2	0	4.05
1985 Kansas City	AL	29	28	0	0	177.1	760	160	88	80	14	1	6	5	77	0	99	12	0	14	10	.583	0	0	4.06
1986 Kansas City	AL	35	24	3	2	180.2	765	155	77	73	8	4	8	5	84	2	118	15	0	12	6	.667	2	0	3.64
1987 Kansas City	AL	35	35	10	0	241.2	1036	231	114	107	18	6	11	6	120	3	166	14	1	13	18	.419	2	0	3.98
1988 Kansas City	AL	35	35	8	0	269.2	1111	237	94	81	11	3	6	6	83	3	183	12	4	20	8	.714	4	0	2.70
1989 Kansas City	AL	36	36	8	0	255	1060	252	100	86	10	11	8	5	63	8	173	9	0	15	11	.577	2	0	3.04
1990 Kansas City	AL	16	16	2	0	94	409	101	48	47	5	6	4	4	38	4	71	2	1	4	7	.364	0	0	4.50
1991 Kansas City	AL	26	26	0	0	133	601	168	90	84	10	3	5	6	42	1	89	5	0	9	12	.429	0	0	5.68
8 ML YEARS		241	229	35	2	1540.1	6542	1476	701	643	89	38	57	42	582	21	1010	72	7	97	86	.530	12	0	3.76

Pedro Guerrero

Bats: Right **Throws:** Right **Pos:** 1B **Ht:** 6' 0" **Wt:** 197 **Born:** 06/29/56 **Age:** 36

		BATTING															BASERUNNING				PERCENTAGES		
Year Team	Lg	G	AB	H	2B	3B	HR	(Hm | Rd)	TB	R	RBI	TBB	IBB	SO	HBP	SH	SF	SB	CS	SB%	GDP	Avg	OBP	SLG
1978 Los Angeles	NL	5	8	5	0	1	0	(0 | 0)	7	3	1	0	0	0	0	0	0	0	0	.00	0	.625	.625	.875
1979 Los Angeles	NL	25	62	15	2	0	2	(0 | 2)	23	7	9	1	1	14	0	0	0	1	0	1.00	1	.242	.250	.371
1980 Los Angeles	NL	75	183	59	9	1	7	(3 | 4)	91	27	31	12	3	31	0	1	3	2	1	.67	2	.322	.359	.497
1981 Los Angeles	NL	98	347	104	17	2	12	(5 | 7)	161	46	48	34	3	57	2	3	1	5	9	.36	12	.300	.365	.464
1982 Los Angeles	NL	150	575	175	27	5	32	(15 | 17)	308	87	100	65	16	89	5	4	3	22	5	.81	7	.304	.378	.536

79

1983 Los Angeles	NL	160	584	174	28	6	32	(13	19)	310	87	103	72	12	110	2	0	6	23	7	.77	11	.298	.373	.531
1984 Los Angeles	NL	144	535	162	29	4	16	(7	9)	247	85	72	49	7	105	1	1	8	9	8	.53	7	.303	.358	.462
1985 Los Angeles	NL	137	487	156	22	2	33	(13	20)	281	99	87	83	14	68	6	0	5	12	4	.75	13	.320	.422	.577
1986 Los Angeles	NL	31	61	15	3	0	5	(1	4)	33	7	10	2	0	19	1	0	0	0	0	.00	1	.246	.281	.541
1987 Los Angeles	NL	152	545	184	25	2	27	(12	15)	294	89	89	74	18	85	4	0	7	9	7	.56	16	.338	.416	.539
1988 2 ML Teams		103	364	104	14	2	10	(5	5)	152	40	65	46	9	59	5	0	7	4	1	.80	5	.286	.367	.418
1989 St. Louis	NL	162	570	177	42	1	17	(3	14)	272	60	117	79	13	84	4	0	12	2	0	1.00	17	.311	.391	.477
1990 St. Louis	NL	136	498	140	31	1	13	(8	5)	212	42	80	44	14	70	1	0	11	1	1	.50	14	.281	.334	.426
1991 St. Louis	NL	115	427	116	12	1	8	(4	4)	154	41	70	37	2	46	1	0	7	4	2	.67	12	.272	.326	.361
1988 Los Angeles	NL	59	215	64	7	1	5	(3	2)	88	24	35	25	2	33	3	0	3	2	1	.67	2	.298	.374	.409
St. Louis	NL	44	149	40	7	1	5	(2	3)	64	16	30	21	7	26	2	0	4	2	0	1.00	3	.268	.358	.430
14 ML YEARS		1493	5246	1586	261	28	214	(89	125)	2545	720	882	598	112	837	32	9	71	95	45	.68	118	.302	.373	.485

Lee Guetterman

Pitches: Left **Bats:** Left **Pos:** RP **Ht:** 6' 8" **Wt:** 235 **Born:** 11/22/58 **Age:** 33

			HOW	MUCH	HE	PITCHED			WHAT	HE	GAVE	UP							THE	RESULTS			
Year Team	Lg	G	GS	CG	GF	IP	BFP	H	R	ER	HR	SH	SF	HB	TBB	IBB	SO	WP	Bk	W	L	Pct.	ShO	Sv	ERA
1984 Seattle	AL	3	0	0	1	4.1	22	9	2	2	0	0	0	0	2	0	2	1	0	0	0	.000	0	0	4.15
1986 Seattle	AL	41	4	1	8	76	353	108	67	62	7	3	5	4	30	3	38	2	0	0	0	.000	0	0	7.34
1987 Seattle	AL	25	17	2	3	113.1	483	117	60	48	13	2	5	2	35	2	42	3	0	11	4	.733	1	0	3.81
1988 New York	AL	20	2	0	7	40.2	177	49	21	21	2	1	1	1	14	0	15	2	0	1	2	.333	0	0	4.65
1989 New York	AL	70	0	0	38	103	412	98	31	28	6	4	2	0	26	9	51	4	0	5	5	.500	0	13	2.45
1990 New York	AL	64	0	0	21	93	376	80	37	35	6	8	3	0	26	7	48	1	1	11	7	.611	0	2	3.39
1991 New York	AL	64	0	0	37	88	376	91	42	36	6	4	4	3	25	5	35	4	0	3	4	.429	0	6	3.68
7 ML YEARS		287	23	3	115	518.1	2199	552	260	232	40	22	20	10	158	26	231	17	1	31	26	.544	1	21	4.03

Ozzie Guillen

Bats: Left **Throws:** Right **Pos:** SS **Ht:** 5'11" **Wt:** 150 **Born:** 01/20/64 **Age:** 28

								BATTING											BASERUNNING			PERCENTAGES		
Year Team	Lg	G	AB	H	2B	3B	HR	(Hm	Rd)	TB	R	RBI	TBB	IBB	SO	HBP	SH	SF	SB	CS	SB%	GDP	Avg	OBP	SLG
1985 Chicago	AL	150	491	134	21	9	1	(1	0)	176	71	33	12	1	36	1	8	1	7	4	.64	5	.273	.291	.358
1986 Chicago	AL	159	547	137	19	4	2	(1	1)	170	58	47	12	1	52	1	12	5	8	4	.67	14	.250	.265	.311
1987 Chicago	AL	149	560	156	22	7	2	(2	0)	198	64	51	22	2	52	1	13	8	25	8	.76	10	.279	.303	.354
1988 Chicago	AL	156	566	148	16	7	0	(0	0)	178	58	39	25	3	40	2	10	3	25	13	.66	14	.261	.294	.314
1989 Chicago	AL	155	597	151	20	8	1	(0	1)	190	63	54	15	3	48	0	11	3	36	17	.68	8	.253	.270	.318
1990 Chicago	AL	160	516	144	21	4	1	(1	0)	176	61	58	26	8	37	1	15	5	13	17	.43	6	.279	.312	.341
1991 Chicago	AL	154	524	143	20	3	3	(1	2)	178	52	49	11	1	38	0	13	7	21	15	.58	7	.273	.284	.340
7 ML YEARS		1083	3801	1013	139	42	10	(6	4)	1266	427	331	123	19	303	6	82	32	135	78	.63	64	.267	.288	.333

Bill Gullickson

Pitches: Right **Bats:** Right **Pos:** SP **Ht:** 6' 3" **Wt:** 225 **Born:** 02/20/59 **Age:** 33

			HOW	MUCH	HE	PITCHED			WHAT	HE	GAVE	UP							THE	RESULTS			
Year Team	Lg	G	GS	CG	GF	IP	BFP	H	R	ER	HR	SH	SF	HB	TBB	IBB	SO	WP	Bk	W	L	Pct.	ShO	Sv	ERA
1979 Montreal	NL	1	0	0	1	1	4	2	0	0	0	0	0	0	0	0	0	0	0	0	0	.000	0	0	0.00
1980 Montreal	NL	24	19	5	1	141	593	127	53	47	6	3	4	2	50	2	120	5	0	10	5	.667	2	0	3.00
1981 Montreal	NL	22	22	3	0	157	640	142	54	49	3	5	2	4	34	4	115	4	0	7	9	.438	2	0	2.81
1982 Montreal	NL	34	34	6	0	236.2	990	231	101	94	25	9	6	4	61	2	155	11	3	12	14	.462	0	0	3.57
1983 Montreal	NL	34	34	10	0	242.1	990	230	108	101	19	4	7	4	59	4	120	4	1	17	12	.586	1	0	3.75
1984 Montreal	NL	32	32	3	0	226.2	919	230	100	91	27	8	4	1	37	7	100	5	0	12	9	.571	0	0	3.61
1985 Montreal	NL	29	29	4	0	181.1	759	187	78	71	8	12	8	1	47	9	68	1	1	14	12	.538	1	0	3.52
1986 Cincinnati	NL	37	37	6	0	244.2	1014	245	103	92	24	12	13	2	60	10	121	3	0	15	12	.556	2	0	3.38
1987 2 ML Teams		35	35	4	0	213	896	218	128	115	40	8	8	3	50	7	117	4	1	14	13	.519	1	0	4.86
1990 Houston	NL	32	32	2	0	193.1	846	221	100	82	21	6	8	2	61	14	73	3	2	10	14	.417	1	0	3.82
1991 Detroit	AL	35	35	4	0	226.1	954	256	109	98	22	8	8	4	44	13	91	4	0	20	9	.690	0	0	3.90
1987 Cincinnati	NL	27	27	3	0	165	698	172	99	89	33	6	6	2	39	6	89	4	1	10	11	.476	1	0	4.85
New York	AL	8	8	1	0	48	198	46	29	26	7	2	2	1	11	1	28	0	0	4	2	.667	0	0	4.88
11 ML YEARS		315	309	47	2	2063.1	8605	2089	934	840	195	75	68	27	503	72	1080	44	8	131	109	.546	10	0	3.66

Eric Gunderson

Pitches: Left **Bats:** Right **Pos:** RP **Ht:** 6' 0" **Wt:** 175 **Born:** 03/29/66 **Age:** 26

			HOW	MUCH	HE	PITCHED			WHAT	HE	GAVE	UP							THE	RESULTS			
Year Team	Lg	G	GS	CG	GF	IP	BFP	H	R	ER	HR	SH	SF	HB	TBB	IBB	SO	WP	Bk	W	L	Pct.	ShO	Sv	ERA
1987 Everett	A	15	15	5	0	98.2	406	80	34	27	4	2	2	3	34	1	99	4	3	8	4	.667	3	0	2.46
1988 San Jose	A	20	20	5	0	149.1	640	131	56	44	2	7	3	17	52	0	151	14	6	12	5	.706	4	0	2.65
Shreveport	AA	7	6	0	1	36.2	166	45	25	21	1	1	1	1	13	0	28	0	1	1	2	.333	0	0	5.15
1989 Shreveport	AA	11	11	2	0	72.2	298	68	24	22	1	1	3	1	23	0	61	1	1	8	2	.800	1	0	2.72
Phoenix	AAA	14	14	2	0	85.2	375	93	51	48	7	5	6	2	36	2	56	7	1	2	4	.333	0	0	5.04

Year Team	Lg	G	GS	CG	GF	IP	BFP	H	R	ER	HR	SH	SF	HB	TBB	IBB	SO	WP	Bk	W	L	Pct.	ShO	Sv	ERA
1990 Phoenix	AAA	16	16	0	0	82	418	137	87	75	11	5	3	3	46	1	41	4	2	5	7	.417	0	0	8.23
Shreveport	AA	8	8	1	0	52.2	225	51	24	19	7	1	3	2	17	1	44	1	0	2	2	.500	1	0	3.25
1991 Phoenix	AAA	40	14	0	8	107	511	153	85	73	10	3	4	3	44	4	53	3	0	7	6	.538	0	3	6.14
1990 San Francisco	NL	7	4	0	1	19.2	94	24	14	12	2	1	0	0	11	1	14	0	0	1	2	.333	0	0	5.49
1991 San Francisco	NL	2	0	0	1	3.1	18	6	4	2	0	0	0	0	1	0	2	0	0	0	0	.000	0	0	5.40
2 ML YEARS		9	4	0	2	23	112	30	18	14	2	1	0	0	12	1	16	0	0	1	2	.333	0	1	5.48

Mark Guthrie

Pitches: Left **Bats:** Both **Pos:** RP/SP   **Ht:** 6' 4" **Wt:** 196 **Born:** 09/22/65 **Age:** 26

		HOW MUCH HE PITCHED						WHAT HE GAVE UP												THE RESULTS				
Year Team	Lg	G	GS	CG	GF	IP	BFP	H	R	ER	HR	SH	SF	HB	TBB	IBB	SO	WP	Bk	W	L	Pct.	ShO	Sv	ERA
1989 Minnesota	AL	13	8	0	2	57.1	254	66	32	29	7	1	5	1	21	1	38	1	0	2	4	.333	0	0	4.55
1990 Minnesota	AL	24	21	3	0	144.2	603	154	65	61	8	6	0	1	39	3	101	9	0	7	9	.438	1	0	3.79
1991 Minnesota	AL	41	12	0	13	98	432	116	52	47	11	4	3	1	41	2	72	7	0	7	5	.583	0	2	4.32
3 ML YEARS		78	41	3	15	300	1289	336	149	137	26	11	8	3	101	6	211	17	0	16	18	.471	1	2	4.11

Johnny Guzman

Pitches: Left **Bats:** Right **Pos:** RP   **Ht:** 5'10" **Wt:** 155 **Born:** 01/21/71 **Age:** 21

		HOW MUCH HE PITCHED						WHAT HE GAVE UP												THE RESULTS				
Year Team	Lg	G	GS	CG	GF	IP	BFP	H	R	ER	HR	SH	SF	HB	TBB	IBB	SO	WP	Bk	W	L	Pct.	ShO	Sv	ERA
1988 Athletics	R	16	1	0	7	23	116	37	27	22	1	2	2	1	8	0	18	1	4	0	2	.000	0	1	8.61
1989 Modesto	A	5	3	0	1	16.2	81	23	11	9	0	0	0	0	13	0	12	2	1	0	2	.000	0	0	4.86
Madison	A	9	9	1	0	45.2	201	41	26	19	3	0	1	2	21	0	36	1	4	3	3	.500	0	0	3.74
1990 Modesto	A	13	13	1	0	84.2	337	67	25	18	3	4	2	4	23	2	58	2	1	7	4	.636	1	0	1.91
Huntsville	AA	16	16	0	0	105.2	458	89	52	42	9	4	1	7	54	1	63	6	2	5	6	.455	0	0	3.58
1991 Tacoma	AAA	17	13	0	2	79.2	394	113	74	60	8	3	4	2	51	0	40	4	6	2	5	.286	0	0	6.78
Huntsville	AA	7	7	0	0	44	194	46	17	17	3	2	1	1	25	0	23	4	5	2	1	.667	0	0	3.48
1991 Oakland	AL	5	0	0	1	5	24	11	5	5	0	0	0	0	2	0	3	0	0	1	0	1.000	0	0	9.00

Jose Guzman

Pitches: Right **Bats:** Right **Pos:** SP   **Ht:** 6' 3" **Wt:** 198 **Born:** 04/09/63 **Age:** 29

		HOW MUCH HE PITCHED						WHAT HE GAVE UP												THE RESULTS				
Year Team	Lg	G	GS	CG	GF	IP	BFP	H	R	ER	HR	SH	SF	HB	TBB	IBB	SO	WP	Bk	W	L	Pct.	ShO	Sv	ERA
1985 Texas	AL	5	5	0	0	32.2	140	27	13	10	3	0	0	0	14	1	24	1	0	3	2	.600	0	0	2.76
1986 Texas	AL	29	29	2	0	172.1	757	199	101	87	23	7	4	6	60	2	87	3	0	9	15	.375	0	0	4.54
1987 Texas	AL	37	30	6	1	208.1	880	196	115	108	30	6	8	3	82	0	143	6	5	14	14	.500	0	0	4.67
1988 Texas	AL	30	30	6	0	206.2	876	180	99	85	20	4	6	5	82	3	157	10	12	11	13	.458	2	0	3.70
1991 Texas	AL	25	25	5	0	169.2	730	152	67	58	10	2	3	4	84	1	125	8	1	13	7	.650	1	0	3.08
5 ML YEARS		126	119	19	1	789.2	3383	754	395	348	86	19	21	18	322	7	536	28	18	50	51	.495	3	0	3.97

Juan Guzman

Pitches: Right **Bats:** Right **Pos:** SP   **Ht:** 6' 0" **Wt:** 190 **Born:** 10/28/66 **Age:** 25

		HOW MUCH HE PITCHED						WHAT HE GAVE UP												THE RESULTS				
Year Team	Lg	G	GS	CG	GF	IP	BFP	H	R	ER	HR	SH	SF	HB	TBB	IBB	SO	WP	Bk	W	L	Pct.	ShO	Sv	ERA
1985 Dodgers	R	21	3	0	12	42	189	39	26	18	2	3	2	1	25	3	43	15	3	5	1	.833	0	4	3.86
1986 Vero Beach	A	26	24	3	0	131.1	594	114	69	51	3	4	3	4	90	4	96	16	2	10	9	.526	0	0	3.49
1987 Bakersfield	A	22	21	0	0	110	508	106	71	58	4	0	1	1	84	0	113	19	1	5	6	.455	0	0	4.75
1988 Knoxville	AA	46	2	0	23	84	363	52	29	22	1	4	4	1	61	5	90	6	6	4	5	.444	0	6	2.36
1989 Syracuse	AAA	14	0	0	4	20.1	99	13	9	9	0	0	1	0	30	0	28	5	0	1	1	.500	0	0	3.98
Knoxville	AA	22	8	0	7	47.2	232	34	36	33	2	2	1	2	60	0	50	8	5	1	4	.200	0	0	6.23
1990 Knoxville	AA	37	21	2	7	157	685	145	84	74	10	6	11	3	80	6	138	21	8	11	9	.550	0	1	4.24
1991 Syracuse	AAA	12	11	0	0	67	287	46	39	30	4	1	3	2	42	0	67	7	2	4	5	.444	0	0	4.03
1991 Toronto	AL	23	23	1	0	138.2	574	98	53	46	6	2	5	4	66	0	123	10	0	10	3	.769	0	0	2.99

Chris Gwynn

Bats: Left **Throws:** Left **Pos:** LF/RF   **Ht:** 6' 0" **Wt:** 210 **Born:** 10/13/64 **Age:** 27

		BATTING																BASERUNNING				PERCENTAGES		
Year Team	Lg	G	AB	H	2B	3B	HR	(Hm	Rd)	TB	R	RBI	TBB	IBB	SO	HBP	SH	SF	SB	CS	SB%	GDP	Avg	OBP	SLG
1987 Los Angeles	NL	17	32	7	1	0	0	(0	0)	8	2	2	1	0	7	0	1	0	0	0	.00	0	.219	.242	.250
1988 Los Angeles	NL	12	11	2	0	0	0	(0	0)	2	1	0	1	0	2	0	0	0	0	0	.00	0	.182	.250	.182
1989 Los Angeles	NL	32	68	16	4	1	0	(0	0)	22	8	7	2	0	9	0	2	1	1	0	1.00	0	.235	.254	.324
1990 Los Angeles	NL	101	141	40	2	1	5	(0	5)	59	19	22	7	2	28	0	1	3	1	0	1.00	2	.284	.311	.418
1991 Los Angeles	NL	94	139	35	5	1	5	(3	2)	57	18	22	10	1	23	1	1	3	1	0	1.00	5	.252	.301	.410
5 ML YEARS		256	391	100	12	3	10	(3	7)	148	48	53	21	3	69	1	4	7	2	1	.67	8	.256	.290	.379

Tony Gwynn

Bats: Left **Throws:** Left **Pos:** RF **Ht:** 5'11" **Wt:** 210 **Born:** 05/09/60 **Age:** 32

Year Team	Lg	BATTING G	AB	H	2B	3B	HR	(Hm	Rd)	TB	R	RBI	TBB	IBB	SO	HBP	SH	SF	BASERUNNING SB	CS	SB%	GDP	PERCENTAGES Avg	OBP	SLG
1982 San Diego	NL	54	190	55	12	2	1	(0	1)	74	33	17	14	0	16	0	4	1	8	3	.73	5	.289	.337	.389
1983 San Diego	NL	86	304	94	12	2	1	(0	1)	113	34	37	23	5	21	0	4	3	7	4	.64	9	.309	.355	.372
1984 San Diego	NL	158	606	213	21	10	5	(3	2)	269	88	71	59	13	23	2	6	2	33	18	.65	15	.351	.410	.444
1985 San Diego	NL	154	622	197	29	5	6	(3	3)	254	90	46	45	4	33	2	1	1	14	11	.56	17	.317	.364	.408
1986 San Diego	NL	160	642	211	33	7	14	(8	6)	300	107	59	52	11	35	3	2	2	37	9	.80	20	.329	.381	.467
1987 San Diego	NL	157	589	218	36	13	7	(5	2)	301	119	54	82	26	35	3	2	4	56	12	.82	13	.370	.447	.511
1988 San Diego	NL	133	521	163	22	5	7	(3	4)	216	64	70	51	13	40	0	4	2	26	11	.70	11	.313	.373	.415
1989 San Diego	NL	158	604	203	27	7	4	(3	1)	256	82	62	56	16	30	1	11	7	40	16	.71	12	.336	.389	.424
1990 San Diego	NL	141	573	177	29	10	4	(2	2)	238	79	72	44	20	23	1	7	4	17	8	.68	14	.309	.357	.415
1991 San Diego	NL	134	530	168	27	11	4	(1	3)	229	69	62	34	8	19	0	0	5	8	8	.50	11	.317	.355	.432
10 ML YEARS		1335	5181	1699	248	72	53	(28	25)	2250	765	550	460	116	275	12	41	31	246	100	.71	126	.328	.382	.434

Dave Haas

Pitches: Right **Bats:** Right **Pos:** RP **Ht:** 6'1" **Wt:** 200 **Born:** 10/19/65 **Age:** 26

Year Team	Lg	HOW MUCH HE PITCHED G	GS	CG	GF	IP	BFP	WHAT HE GAVE UP H	R	ER	HR	SH	SF	HB	TBB	IBB	SO	WP	Bk	THE RESULTS W	L	Pct.	ShO	Sv	ERA
1988 Fayetteville	A	11	11	0	0	54.2	243	59	20	11	0	1	1	6	19	1	46	2	4	4	3	.571	0	0	1.81
1989 Lakeland	A	10	10	1	0	62	247	50	16	14	1	0	1	6	16	0	46	1	4	4	1	.800	1	0	2.03
London	AA	18	18	2	0	103.2	460	107	69	65	13	5	2	11	51	1	75	5	1	3	11	.214	1	0	5.64
1990 London	AA	27	27	3	0	177.2	740	151	64	59	10	4	3	10	74	1	116	14	1	13	8	.619	1	0	2.99
1991 Toledo	AAA	28	28	1	0	158.1	718	187	103	92	11	8	3	8	77	3	133	8	1	8	10	.444	0	0	5.23
1991 Detroit	AL	11	0	0	0	10.2	50	8	8	8	1	2	2	1	12	3	6	1	0	1	0	1.000	0	0	6.75

John Habyan

Pitches: Right **Bats:** Right **Pos:** RP **Ht:** 6'2" **Wt:** 195 **Born:** 01/29/64 **Age:** 28

Year Team	Lg	HOW MUCH HE PITCHED G	GS	CG	GF	IP	BFP	WHAT HE GAVE UP H	R	ER	HR	SH	SF	HB	TBB	IBB	SO	WP	Bk	THE RESULTS W	L	Pct.	ShO	Sv	ERA
1985 Baltimore	AL	2	0	0	1	2.2	12	3	1	0	0	0	0	0	0	0	2	0	0	1	0	1.000	0	0	0.00
1986 Baltimore	AL	6	5	0	1	26.1	117	24	17	13	3	2	1	0	18	2	14	1	0	1	3	.250	0	0	4.44
1987 Baltimore	AL	27	13	0	4	116.1	493	110	67	62	20	4	4	2	40	1	64	3	0	6	7	.462	0	1	4.80
1988 Baltimore	AL	7	0	0	1	14.2	68	22	10	7	2	0	2	0	4	0	4	1	1	1	0	1.000	0	0	4.30
1990 New York	AL	6	0	0	1	8.2	37	10	2	2	0	0	0	1	2	0	4	1	0	0	0	.000	0	0	2.08
1991 New York	AL	66	0	0	16	90	349	73	28	23	2	2	1	2	20	2	70	1	2	4	2	.667	0	2	2.30
6 ML YEARS		114	18	0	24	258.2	1076	242	125	107	27	8	8	5	84	5	158	7	3	13	12	.520	0	3	3.72

Mel Hall

Bats: Left **Throws:** Left **Pos:** RF/LF/DH **Ht:** 6'1" **Wt:** 218 **Born:** 09/16/60 **Age:** 31

Year Team	Lg	BATTING G	AB	H	2B	3B	HR	(Hm	Rd)	TB	R	RBI	TBB	IBB	SO	HBP	SH	SF	BASERUNNING SB	CS	SB%	GDP	PERCENTAGES Avg	OBP	SLG
1981 Chicago	NL	10	11	1	0	0	1	(1	0)	4	1	2	1	0	4	0	0	0	0	0	.00	0	.091	.167	.364
1982 Chicago	NL	24	80	21	3	2	0	(0	0)	28	6	4	5	1	17	2	0	1	0	1	.00	0	.263	.318	.350
1983 Chicago	NL	112	410	116	23	5	17	(6	11)	200	60	56	42	6	101	3	1	2	6	6	.50	4	.283	.352	.488
1984 2 ML Teams		131	407	108	24	4	11	(7	4)	173	68	52	47	8	78	2	0	7	3	2	.60	5	.265	.339	.425
1985 Cleveland	AL	23	66	21	6	0	0	(0	0)	27	7	12	8	0	12	0	0	1	0	1	.00	2	.318	.387	.409
1986 Cleveland	AL	140	442	131	29	2	18	(8	10)	218	68	77	33	8	65	2	0	3	6	2	.75	8	.296	.346	.493
1987 Cleveland	AL	142	485	136	21	1	18	(8	10)	213	57	76	20	6	68	1	0	2	5	4	.56	7	.280	.309	.439
1988 Cleveland	AL	150	515	144	32	4	6	(3	3)	202	69	71	28	12	50	0	2	8	7	3	.70	8	.280	.312	.392
1989 New York	AL	113	361	94	9	0	17	(11	6)	154	54	58	21	4	37	0	1	8	0	0	.00	9	.260	.295	.427
1990 New York	AL	113	360	93	23	2	12	(3	9)	156	41	46	6	2	46	2	0	3	0	0	.00	7	.258	.272	.433
1991 New York	AL	141	492	140	23	2	19	(13	6)	224	67	80	26	6	40	3	0	6	0	1	.00	6	.285	.321	.455
1984 Chicago	NL	48	150	42	11	3	4	(3	1)	71	25	22	12	3	23	0	0	2	2	1	.67	2	.280	.329	.473
Cleveland	AL	83	257	66	13	1	7	(4	3)	102	43	30	35	5	55	2	0	5	1	1	.50	3	.257	.344	.397
11 ML YEARS		1099	3629	1005	193	22	119	(60	59)	1599	498	534	237	53	518	15	4	41	27	20	.57	56	.277	.320	.441

Daryl Hamilton

Bats: Left **Throws:** Right **Pos:** CF/LF/RF **Ht:** 6'1" **Wt:** 180 **Born:** 12/03/64 **Age:** 27

Year Team	Lg	BATTING G	AB	H	2B	3B	HR	(Hm	Rd)	TB	R	RBI	TBB	IBB	SO	HBP	SH	SF	BASERUNNING SB	CS	SB%	GDP	PERCENTAGES Avg	OBP	SLG
1988 Milwaukee	AL	44	103	19	4	0	1	(1	0)	26	14	11	12	0	9	1	0	1	7	3	.70	2	.184	.274	.252
1990 Milwaukee	AL	89	156	46	5	0	1	(1	0)	54	27	18	9	0	12	0	3	0	10	3	.77	2	.295	.333	.346
1991 Milwaukee	AL	122	405	126	15	6	1	(0	1)	156	64	57	33	2	38	0	7	3	16	6	.73	9	.311	.361	.385
3 ML YEARS		255	664	191	24	6	3	(2	1)	236	105	86	54	2	59	1	10	4	33	12	.73	13	.288	.340	.355

Jeff Hamilton

Bats: Right **Throws:** Right **Pos:** 3B **Ht:** 6' 3" **Wt:** 207 **Born:** 03/19/64 **Age:** 28

| | | | | | | | | BATTING | | | | | | | | | | | BASERUNNING | | | | PERCENTAGES | | |
Year Team	Lg	G	AB	H	2B	3B	HR	(Hm Rd)	TB	R	RBI	TBB	IBB	SO	HBP	SH	SF	SB	CS	SB%	GDP	Avg	OBP	SLG
1986 Los Angeles	NL	71	147	33	5	0	5	(2 3)	53	22	19	2	1	43	0	0	2	0	0	.00	3	.224	.232	.361
1987 Los Angeles	NL	35	83	18	3	0	0	(0 0)	21	5	1	7	2	22	1	0	0	0	1	.00	0	.217	.286	.253
1988 Los Angeles	NL	111	309	73	14	2	6	(4 2)	109	34	33	10	1	51	4	2	2	0	2	.00	8	.236	.268	.353
1989 Los Angeles	NL	151	548	134	35	1	12	(8 4)	207	45	56	20	5	71	3	4	6	0	0	.00	10	.245	.272	.378
1990 Los Angeles	NL	7	24	3	0	0	0	(0 0)	3	1	1	0	0	3	0	0	0	0	0	.00	1	.125	.125	.125
1991 Los Angeles	NL	41	94	21	4	0	1	(1 0)	28	4	14	4	0	21	0	1	0	0	0	.00	2	.223	.255	.298
6 ML YEARS		416	1205	282	61	3	24	(15 9)	421	111	124	43	9	211	8	7	10	0	3	.00	24	.234	.263	.349

Atlee Hammaker

Pitches: Left **Bats:** Both **Pos:** SP **Ht:** 6' 2" **Wt:** 204 **Born:** 01/24/58 **Age:** 34

| | | HOW MUCH HE PITCHED | | | | | | WHAT HE GAVE UP | | | | | | | | | | | | THE RESULTS | | | | | |
Year Team	Lg	G	GS	CG	GF	IP	BFP	H	R	ER	HR	SH	SF	HB	TBB	IBB	SO	WP	Bk	W	L	Pct.	ShO	Sv	ERA
1981 Kansas City	AL	10	6	0	2	39	169	44	24	24	2	2	1	0	12	1	11	0	1	1	3	.250	0	0	5.54
1982 San Francisco	NL	29	27	4	0	175	725	189	86	80	16	12	4	2	28	8	102	2	4	12	8	.600	1	0	4.11
1983 San Francisco	NL	23	23	8	0	172.1	695	147	57	43	9	10	4	3	32	12	127	6	2	10	9	.526	3	0	2.25
1984 San Francisco	NL	6	6	0	0	33	139	32	10	8	2	3	2	0	9	1	24	0	2	2	0	1.000	0	0	2.18
1985 San Francisco	NL	29	29	1	0	170.2	713	161	81	71	17	8	6	0	47	5	100	4	4	5	12	.294	1	0	3.74
1987 San Francisco	NL	31	27	2	1	168.1	706	159	73	67	22	3	3	3	57	10	107	8	7	10	10	.500	0	0	3.58
1988 San Francisco	NL	43	17	3	11	144.2	607	136	68	60	11	10	4	3	41	9	65	1	2	9	9	.500	1	5	3.73
1989 San Francisco	NL	28	9	0	5	76.2	322	78	34	32	5	6	4	1	23	2	30	1	2	6	6	.500	0	0	3.76
1990 2 ML Teams		34	7	0	8	86.2	363	85	44	42	8	4	4	0	27	5	44	4	2	4	9	.308	0	0	4.36
1991 San Diego	NL	1	1	0	0	4.2	27	8	7	3	0	2	0	0	3	0	1	1	0	0	1	.000	0	0	5.79
1990 San Francisco	NL	25	6	0	5	67.1	282	69	33	32	7	4	4	0	21	4	28	3	1	4	5	.444	0	0	4.28
San Diego	NL	9	1	0	3	19.1	81	16	11	10	1	0	0	0	6	1	16	1	1	0	4	.000	0	0	4.66
10 ML YEARS		234	152	18	27	1071	4466	1039	484	430	92	60	32	12	279	53	611	27	26	59	67	.468	6	5	3.61

Chris Hammond

Pitches: Left **Bats:** Left **Pos:** SP **Ht:** 6' 1" **Wt:** 190 **Born:** 01/21/66 **Age:** 26

| | | HOW MUCH HE PITCHED | | | | | | WHAT HE GAVE UP | | | | | | | | | | | | THE RESULTS | | | | | |
Year Team	Lg	G	GS	CG	GF	IP	BFP	H	R	ER	HR	SH	SF	HB	TBB	IBB	SO	WP	Bk	W	L	Pct.	ShO	Sv	ERA
1986 Reds	R	7	7	1	0	41.2	176	27	21	13	0	1	0	0	17	1	53	5	0	3	2	.600	0	0	2.81
Tampa	A	5	5	0	0	21.2	100	25	8	8	0	0	0	1	13	1	5	1	0	0	2	.000	0	0	3.32
1987 Tampa	A	25	24	6	1	170	745	174	81	67	10	4	4	3	60	1	126	6	3	11	11	.500	0	0	3.55
1988 Chattanooga	AA	26	26	4	0	182.2	743	127	48	35	2	1	3	3	77	3	127	5	4	16	5	.762	2	0	1.72
1989 Nashville	AAA	24	24	3	0	157.1	697	144	69	59	7	6	4	3	96	1	142	9	2	11	7	.611	1	0	3.38
1990 Nashville	AAA	24	24	5	0	149	611	118	43	36	7	1	3	5	63	1	149	8	7	15	1	.938	3	0	2.17
1990 Cincinnati	NL	3	3	0	0	11.1	56	13	9	8	2	1	0	0	12	1	4	1	3	0	2	.000	0	0	6.35
1991 Cincinnati	NL	20	18	0	0	99.2	425	92	51	45	4	6	1	2	48	3	50	3	0	7	7	.500	0	0	4.06
2 ML YEARS		23	21	0	0	111	481	105	60	53	6	7	1	2	60	4	54	4	3	7	9	.438	0	0	4.30

Chris Haney

Pitches: Left **Bats:** Left **Pos:** SP **Ht:** 6' 3" **Wt:** 185 **Born:** 11/16/68 **Age:** 23

| | | HOW MUCH HE PITCHED | | | | | | WHAT HE GAVE UP | | | | | | | | | | | | THE RESULTS | | | | | |
Year Team	Lg	G	GS	CG	GF	IP	BFP	H	R	ER	HR	SH	SF	HB	TBB	IBB	SO	WP	Bk	W	L	Pct.	ShO	Sv	ERA
1990 Jamestown	A	6	5	0	1	28	109	17	3	3	1	1	0	4	11	0	26	0	1	3	0	1.000	0	1	0.96
Rockford	A	8	8	3	0	53	204	40	15	13	1	3	2	1	6	0	45	0	0	2	4	.333	0	0	2.21
Jacksnville	AA	1	1	0	0	6	25	6	0	0	0	0	0	0	3	0	6	0	0	1	0	1.000	0	0	0.00
1991 Harrisburg	AA	12	12	3	0	83.1	334	65	21	20	4	8	2	3	31	1	68	3	1	5	3	.625	0	0	2.16
Indianapols	AAA	2	2	0	0	10.1	50	14	10	5	2	0	0	0	6	0	8	2	0	1	1	.500	0	0	4.35
1991 Montreal	NL	16	16	0	0	84.2	387	94	49	38	6	6	1	1	43	1	51	9	0	3	7	.300	0	0	4.04

Dave Hansen

Bats: Left **Throws:** Right **Pos:** 3B **Ht:** 6' 0" **Wt:** 180 **Born:** 11/24/68 **Age:** 23

| | | | | | | | | BATTING | | | | | | | | | | | BASERUNNING | | | | PERCENTAGES | | |
Year Team	Lg	G	AB	H	2B	3B	HR	(Hm Rd)	TB	R	RBI	TBB	IBB	SO	HBP	SH	SF	SB	CS	SB%	GDP	Avg	OBP	SLG
1986 Great Falls	R	61	204	61	7	3	1	-- --	77	39	36	27	0	28	0	1	0	9	3	.75	6	.299	.381	.377
1987 Bakersfield	A	132	432	113	22	1	3	-- --	146	68	38	65	1	61	4	6	1	4	2	.67	11	.262	.363	.338
1988 Vero Beach	A	135	512	149	28	6	7	-- --	210	68	81	56	6	46	4	1	9	2	2	.50	9	.291	.360	.410
1989 San Antonio	AA	121	464	138	21	4	6	-- --	185	72	52	50	5	44	2	0	5	3	2	.60	18	.297	.365	.399
Albuquerque	AAA	6	30	8	1	0	2	-- --	15	6	10	2	0	3	0	0	0	0	0	.00	1	.267	.313	.500
1990 Albuquerque	AAA	135	487	154	20	3	11	-- --	213	90	92	90	4	54	3	0	9	9	4	.69	12	.316	.419	.437
1991 Albuquerque	AAA	68	254	77	11	1	5	-- --	105	42	40	49	3	33	0	0	7	4	3	.57	7	.303	.406	.413

Year Team	Lg	G	AB	H	2B	3B	HR	(Hm	Rd)	TB	R	RBI	TBB	IBB	SO	HBP	SH	SF	SB	CS	SB%	GDP	Avg	OBP	SLG
1990 Los Angeles	NL	5	7	1	0	0	0	(0	0)	1	0	1	0	0	3	0	0	0	0	0	.00	0	.143	.143	.143
1991 Los Angeles	NL	53	56	15	4	0	1	(0	1)	22	3	5	2	0	12	0	0	0	1	0	1.00	2	.268	.293	.393
2 ML YEARS		58	63	16	4	0	1	(0	1)	23	3	6	2	0	15	0	0	0	1	0	1.00	2	.254	.277	.365

Erik Hanson

Pitches: Right **Bats:** Right **Pos:** SP — **Ht:** 6' 6" **Wt:** 210 **Born:** 05/18/65 **Age:** 27

Year Team	Lg	G	GS	CG	GF	IP	BFP	H	R	ER	HR	SH	SF	HB	TBB	IBB	SO	WP	Bk	W	L	Pct.	ShO	Sv	ERA
1988 Seattle	AL	6	6	0	0	41.2	168	35	17	15	4	3	0	1	12	1	36	2	2	2	3	.400	0	0	3.24
1989 Seattle	AL	17	17	1	0	113.1	465	103	44	40	7	4	1	5	32	1	75	3	0	9	5	.643	0	0	3.18
1990 Seattle	AL	33	33	5	0	236	964	205	88	85	15	5	6	2	68	6	211	10	1	18	9	.667	1	0	3.24
1991 Seattle	AL	27	27	2	0	174.2	744	182	82	74	16	2	8	2	56	2	143	14	1	8	8	.500	1	0	3.81
4 ML YEARS		83	83	8	0	565.2	2341	525	231	214	42	14	15	10	168	10	465	29	4	37	25	.597	2	0	3.40

Shawn Hare

Bats: Left **Throws:** Left **Pos:** RF — **Ht:** 6' 2" **Wt:** 190 **Born:** 03/26/67 **Age:** 25

Year Team	Lg	G	AB	H	2B	3B	HR	(Hm	Rd)	TB	R	RBI	TBB	IBB	SO	HBP	SH	SF	SB	CS	SB%	GDP	Avg	OBP	SLG
1989 Lakeland	A	93	290	94	16	4	2	--	--	124	32	36	41	4	32	2	2	1	11	5	.69	7	.324	.410	.428
1990 Toledo	AAA	127	429	109	25	4	9	--	--	169	53	55	49	9	77	4	0	3	9	6	.60	10	.254	.334	.394
1991 London	AA	31	125	34	12	0	4	--	--	58	20	28	12	1	23	1	0	0	2	2	.50	5	.272	.341	.464
Toledo	AAA	80	252	78	18	2	9	--	--	127	44	42	30	1	53	2	1	5	1	2	.33	6	.310	.381	.504
1991 Detroit	AL	9	19	1	1	0	0	(0	0)	2	0	0	2	0	1	0	0	0	0	0	.00	3	.053	.143	.105

Mike Harkey

Pitches: Right **Bats:** Right **Pos:** SP — **Ht:** 6' 5" **Wt:** 220 **Born:** 10/25/66 **Age:** 25

Year Team	Lg	G	GS	CG	GF	IP	BFP	H	R	ER	HR	SH	SF	HB	TBB	IBB	SO	WP	Bk	W	L	Pct.	ShO	Sv	ERA
1988 Chicago	NL	5	5	0	0	34.2	155	33	14	10	0	5	0	2	15	3	18	2	1	0	3	.000	0	0	2.60
1990 Chicago	NL	27	27	2	0	173.2	728	153	71	63	14	5	4	7	59	8	94	8	1	12	6	.667	1	0	3.26
1991 Chicago	NL	4	4	0	0	18.2	84	21	11	11	3	0	1	0	6	1	15	1	0	0	2	.000	0	0	5.30
3 ML YEARS		36	36	2	0	227	967	207	96	84	17	10	5	9	80	12	127	11	2	12	11	.522	1	0	3.33

Pete Harnisch

Pitches: Right **Bats:** Right **Pos:** SP — **Ht:** 6' 0" **Wt:** 207 **Born:** 09/23/66 **Age:** 25

Year Team	Lg	G	GS	CG	GF	IP	BFP	H	R	ER	HR	SH	SF	HB	TBB	IBB	SO	WP	Bk	W	L	Pct.	ShO	Sv	ERA
1988 Baltimore	AL	2	2	0	0	13	61	13	8	8	1	2	0	0	9	1	10	1	0	0	2	.000	0	0	5.54
1989 Baltimore	AL	18	18	2	0	103.1	468	97	55	53	10	4	5	5	64	3	70	5	1	5	9	.357	0	0	4.62
1990 Baltimore	AL	31	31	3	0	188.2	821	189	96	91	17	6	5	5	86	4	122	2	2	11	11	.500	0	0	4.34
1991 Houston	NL	33	33	4	0	216.2	900	169	71	65	14	9	7	5	83	3	172	5	2	12	9	.571	2	0	2.70
4 ML YEARS		84	83	9	1	521.2	2250	468	230	217	42	21	17	11	242	12	374	13	5	28	31	.475	2	0	3.74

Brian Harper

Bats: Right **Throws:** Right **Pos:** C — **Ht:** 6' 2" **Wt:** 205 **Born:** 10/16/59 **Age:** 32

Year Team	Lg	G	AB	H	2B	3B	HR	(Hm	Rd)	TB	R	RBI	TBB	IBB	SO	HBP	SH	SF	SB	CS	SB%	GDP	Avg	OBP	SLG
1979 California	AL	1	2	0	0	0	0	(0	0)	0	0	0	0	0	1	0	0	0	0	0	.00	0	.000	.000	.000
1981 California	AL	4	11	3	0	0	0	(0	0)	3	1	1	0	0	0	0	0	1	0	0	1.00	0	.273	.250	.273
1982 Pittsburgh	NL	20	29	8	1	0	2	(0	2)	15	4	4	1	1	4	0	1	0	0	0	.00	1	.276	.300	.517
1983 Pittsburgh	NL	61	131	29	4	1	7	(5	2)	56	16	20	2	0	15	1	2	4	0	0	.00	3	.221	.232	.427
1984 Pittsburgh	NL	46	112	29	4	0	2	(1	1)	39	4	11	5	0	11	2	1	1	0	0	.00	4	.259	.300	.348
1985 St. Louis	NL	43	52	13	4	0	0	(0	0)	17	5	8	2	0	3	0	0	1	0	0	.00	1	.250	.273	.327
1986 Detroit	AL	19	36	5	1	0	0	(0	0)	6	2	3	3	0	3	0	0	1	0	0	.00	1	.139	.200	.167
1987 Oakland	AL	11	17	4	1	0	0	(0	0)	5	1	3	0	0	4	0	1	1	0	0	.00	0	.235	.222	.294
1988 Minnesota	AL	60	166	49	11	1	3	(0	3)	71	15	20	10	1	12	3	2	1	0	3	.00	1	.295	.344	.428
1989 Minnesota	AL	126	385	125	24	0	8	(4	4)	173	43	57	13	3	16	6	4	4	2	4	.33	11	.325	.353	.449
1990 Minnesota	AL	134	479	141	42	3	6	(1	5)	207	61	54	19	2	27	7	0	4	3	2	.60	20	.294	.328	.432
1991 Minnesota	AL	123	441	137	28	1	10	(4	6)	197	54	69	14	3	22	6	2	6	1	2	.33	14	.311	.336	.447
12 ML YEARS		648	1861	543	120	6	38	(15	23)	789	206	250	69	10	118	25	14	24	7	11	.39	69	.292	.322	.424

Donald Harris

Bats: Right **Throws:** Right **Pos:** CF — **Ht:** 6' 1" **Wt:** 185 **Born:** 11/12/67 **Age:** 24

Year Team	Lg	G	AB	H	2B	3B	HR	(Hm	Rd)	TB	R	RBI	TBB	IBB	SO	HBP	SH	SF	SB	CS	SB%	GDP	Avg	OBP	SLG
1989 Butte	R	65	264	75	7	8	6	--	--	116	50	37	12	0	54	6	0	3	14	4	.78	6	.284	.326	.439

Year	Team	Lg	G	AB	H	2B	3B	HR	(Hm	Rd)	TB	R	RBI	TBB	IBB	SO	HBP	SH	SF	SB	CS	SB%	GDP	Avg	OBP	SLG
1990	Tulsa	AA	64	213	34	5	1	1	--	--	44	16	15	7	0	69	3	3	0	7	3	.70	0	.160	.197	.207
	Gastonia	A	58	221	46	10	0	3	--	--	65	27	13	14	0	63	2	4	0	15	8	.65	2	.208	.262	.294
1991	Tulsa	AA	130	450	102	17	8	11	--	--	168	47	53	26	1	118	7	7	2	9	6	.60	11	.227	.278	.373
1991	Texas	AL	18	8	3	0	0	1	(0	1)	6	4	2	1	0	3	0	0	0	1	0	1.00	0	.375	.444	.750

Gene Harris

Pitches: Right **Bats:** Right **Pos:** RP   **Ht:** 5'11" **Wt:** 190 **Born:** 12/05/64 **Age:** 27

			HOW MUCH HE PITCHED						WHAT HE GAVE UP									THE RESULTS					
Year	Team	Lg	G	GS	CG	GF	IP	BFP	H	R	ER	HR	SH	SF	HB	TBB	IBB	SO	WP	Bk	W	L	Pct.	ShO	Sv	ERA
1989	2 ML Teams		21	6	0	9	53.1	236	63	38	35	4	7	4	1	25	1	25	3	0	2	5	.286	0	1	5.91
1990	Seattle	AL	25	0	0	8	38	176	31	25	20	5	0	2	1	30	5	43	2	0	1	2	.333	0	0	4.74
1991	Seattle	AL	8	0	0	3	13.1	66	15	8	6	1	1	0	0	10	3	6	1	0	0	0	.000	0	1	4.05
1989	Montreal	NL	11	0	0	7	20	84	16	11	11	1	7	1	0	10	0	11	3	0	1	1	.500	0	0	4.95
	Seattle	AL	10	6	0	2	33.1	152	47	27	24	3	0	3	1	15	1	14	0	0	1	4	.200	0	1	6.48
	3 ML YEARS		54	6	0	24	104.2	478	109	71	61	10	8	6	2	65	6	74	6	0	3	7	.300	0	2	5.25

Greg Harris

Pitches: Right **Bats:** Both **Pos:** RP/SP   **Ht:** 6' 0" **Wt:** 175 **Born:** 11/02/55 **Age:** 36

			HOW MUCH HE PITCHED						WHAT HE GAVE UP									THE RESULTS					
Year	Team	Lg	G	GS	CG	GF	IP	BFP	H	R	ER	HR	SH	SF	HB	TBB	IBB	SO	WP	Bk	W	L	Pct.	ShO	Sv	ERA
1981	New York	NL	16	14	0	2	69	300	65	36	34	8	4	1	2	28	2	54	3	2	3	5	.375	0	1	4.43
1982	New York	NL	34	10	1	9	91.1	398	96	56	49	12	5	3	2	37	1	67	2	2	2	6	.250	0	1	4.83
1983	San Diego	NL	1	0	0	1	1	9	2	3	3	0	1	0	1	3	2	1	0	0	0	0	.000	0	0	27.00
1984	2 ML Teams		34	1	0	14	54.1	226	38	18	15	3	2	3	4	25	1	45	3	0	2	2	.500	0	3	2.48
1985	Texas	AL	58	0	0	35	113	450	74	35	31	7	3	2	5	43	3	111	2	1	5	4	.556	0	11	2.47
1986	Texas	AL	73	0	0	63	111.1	462	103	40	35	12	3	6	1	42	6	95	2	1	10	8	.556	0	20	2.83
1987	Texas	AL	42	19	0	14	140.2	629	157	92	76	18	7	3	4	56	3	106	4	2	5	10	.333	0	0	4.86
1988	Philadelphia	NL	66	1	0	19	107	446	80	34	28	7	6	2	4	52	14	71	8	2	4	6	.400	0	1	2.36
1989	2 ML Teams		59	0	0	24	103.1	442	85	46	38	8	4	3	2	58	9	76	12	0	4	4	.500	0	1	3.31
1990	Boston	AL	34	30	1	3	184.1	803	186	90	82	13	8	9	6	77	7	117	7	1	13	9	.591	0	4	4.00
1991	Boston	AL	53	21	1	15	173	733	157	79	74	13	4	8	5	69	5	127	6	1	11	12	.478	0	2	3.85
1984	Montreal	NL	15	0	0	4	17.2	68	10	4	4	0	1	0	2	7	1	15	0	0	0	1	.000	0	2	2.04
	San Diego	NL	19	1	0	10	36.2	158	28	14	11	3	1	3	2	18	0	30	3	0	2	1	.667	0	1	2.70
1989	Philadelphia	NL	44	0	0	17	75.1	324	64	34	30	7	3	2	2	43	7	51	10	0	2	2	.500	0	1	3.58
	Boston	AL	15	0	0	7	28	118	21	12	8	1	1	1	0	15	2	25	2	0	2	2	.500	0	0	2.57
	11 ML YEARS		470	96	3	198	1148.1	4896	1043	529	465	101	47	40	36	490	53	870	49	12	59	66	.472	0	40	3.64

Greg W. Harris

Pitches: Right **Bats:** Right **Pos:** SP   **Ht:** 6' 2" **Wt:** 187 **Born:** 12/01/63 **Age:** 28

			HOW MUCH HE PITCHED						WHAT HE GAVE UP									THE RESULTS					
Year	Team	Lg	G	GS	CG	GF	IP	BFP	H	R	ER	HR	SH	SF	HB	TBB	IBB	SO	WP	Bk	W	L	Pct.	ShO	Sv	ERA
1988	San Diego	NL	3	1	1	2	18	68	13	3	3	0	0	0	0	3	0	15	0	0	2	0	1.000	0	0	1.50
1989	San Diego	NL	56	8	0	25	135	554	106	43	39	8	5	2	2	52	9	106	3	3	8	9	.471	0	6	2.60
1990	San Diego	NL	73	0	0	33	117.1	488	92	35	30	6	9	7	4	49	13	97	2	3	8	8	.500	0	9	2.30
1991	San Diego	NL	20	20	3	0	133	537	116	42	33	16	9	2	1	27	6	95	2	0	9	5	.643	2	0	2.23
	4 ML YEARS		152	29	4	60	403.1	1647	327	123	105	30	23	11	7	131	28	313	7	6	27	22	.551	2	15	2.34

Lenny Harris

Bats: Left **Throws:** Right **Pos:** 3B/2B/SS   **Ht:** 5'10" **Wt:** 205 **Born:** 10/28/64 **Age:** 27

			BATTING																BASERUNNING				PERCENTAGES		
Year	Team	Lg	G	AB	H	2B	3B	HR	(Hm	Rd)	TB	R	RBI	TBB	IBB	SO	HBP	SH	SF	SB	CS	SB%	GDP	Avg	OBP	SLG
1988	Cincinnati	NL	16	43	16	1	0	0	(0	0)	17	7	8	5	0	4	0	1	2	4	1	.80	0	.372	.420	.395
1989	2 ML Teams		115	335	79	10	1	3	(1	2)	100	36	26	20	0	33	2	1	0	14	9	.61	14	.236	.283	.299
1990	Los Angeles	NL	137	431	131	16	4	2	(0	2)	161	61	29	29	2	31	1	3	1	15	10	.60	8	.304	.348	.374
1991	Los Angeles	NL	145	429	123	16	1	3	(1	2)	150	59	38	37	5	32	5	12	2	12	3	.80	17	.287	.349	.350
1989	Cincinnati	NL	61	188	42	4	0	2	(0	2)	52	17	11	9	0	20	1	1	0	10	6	.63	5	.223	.263	.277
	Los Angeles	NL	54	147	37	6	1	1	(1	0)	48	19	15	11	0	13	1	0	0	4	3	.57	9	.252	.308	.327
	4 ML YEARS		413	1238	349	43	6	8	(2	6)	428	163	101	91	7	100	8	17	5	45	23	.66	39	.282	.334	.346

Reggie Harris

Pitches: Right **Bats:** Right **Pos:** RP   **Ht:** 6' 1" **Wt:** 190 **Born:** 08/12/68 **Age:** 23

			HOW MUCH HE PITCHED						WHAT HE GAVE UP									THE RESULTS					
Year	Team	Lg	G	GS	CG	GF	IP	BFP	H	R	ER	HR	SH	SF	HB	TBB	IBB	SO	WP	Bk	W	L	Pct.	ShO	Sv	ERA
1987	Elmira	A	9	8	1	0	46.2	212	50	29	26	3	1	1	6	22	0	25	3	0	2	3	.400	1	0	5.01
1988	Lynchburg	A	17	11	0	2	64	310	86	60	53	8	0	3	4	34	5	48	5	7	1	8	.111	0	0	7.45
	Elmira	A	10	10	0	0	54.1	237	56	37	32	5	1	3	2	28	0	46	1	2	3	6	.333	0	0	5.30
1989	Winter Havn	A	29	26	1	2	153.1	670	144	81	68	6	5	11	7	77	2	85	7	4	10	13	.435	0	0	3.99
1990	Huntsville	AA	5	5	0	0	29.2	131	26	12	10	3	1	1	4	16	0	34	4	0	0	2	.000	0	0	3.03

Year Team	Lg	G	GS	CG	GF	IP	BFP	H	R	ER	HR	SH	SF	HB	TBB	IBB	SO	WP	Bk	W	L	Pct.	ShO	Sv	ERA
1991 Tacoma	AAA	16	15	0	0	83	380	83	55	46	11	0	4	3	58	0	72	5	0	5	4	.556	0	0	4.99
1990 Oakland	AL	16	1	0	9	41.1	168	25	16	16	5	1	2	2	21	1	31	2	0	1	0	1.000	0	0	3.48
1991 Oakland	AL	2	0	0	1	3	15	5	4	4	0	0	1	0	3	1	2	2	0	0	0	.000	0	0	12.00
2 ML YEARS		18	1	0	10	44.1	183	30	20	20	5	1	3	2	24	2	33	4	0	1	0	1.000	0	0	4.06

Mike Hartley

Pitches: Right **Bats:** Right **Pos:** RP   **Ht:** 6' 1" **Wt:** 197 **Born:** 08/31/61 **Age:** 30

		HOW MUCH HE PITCHED						WHAT HE GAVE UP												THE RESULTS					
Year Team	Lg	G	GS	CG	GF	IP	BFP	H	R	ER	HR	SH	SF	HB	TBB	IBB	SO	WP	Bk	W	L	Pct.	ShO	Sv	ERA
1989 Los Angeles	NL	5	0	0	3	6	20	2	1	1	0	0	0	0	0	0	4	0	0	0	1	.000	0	0	1.50
1990 Los Angeles	NL	32	6	1	8	79.1	325	58	32	26	7	2	1	2	30	2	76	3	0	6	3	.667	0	1	2.95
1991 2 ML Teams		58	0	0	16	83.1	368	74	40	39	11	2	1	6	47	8	63	10	2	4	1	.800	0	2	4.21
1991 Los Angeles	NL	40	0	0	11	57	258	53	29	28	7	1	1	3	37	7	44	8	1	2	0	1.000	0	1	4.42
Philadelphia	NL	18	0	0	5	26.1	110	21	11	11	4	1	0	3	10	1	19	2	1	2	1	.667	0	1	3.76
3 ML YEARS		95	6	1	27	168.2	713	134	73	66	18	4	2	8	77	10	143	13	2	10	5	.667	1	3	3.52

Bryan Harvey

Pitches: Right **Bats:** Right **Pos:** RP   **Ht:** 6' 2" **Wt:** 219 **Born:** 06/02/63 **Age:** 29

		HOW MUCH HE PITCHED						WHAT HE GAVE UP												THE RESULTS					
Year Team	Lg	G	GS	CG	GF	IP	BFP	H	R	ER	HR	SH	SF	HB	TBB	IBB	SO	WP	Bk	W	L	Pct.	ShO	Sv	ERA
1987 California	AL	3	0	0	2	5	22	6	0	0	0	0	0	0	2	0	3	3	0	0	0	.000	0	0	0.00
1988 California	AL	50	0	0	38	76	303	59	22	18	4	3	3	1	20	6	67	4	1	7	5	.583	0	17	2.13
1989 California	AL	51	0	0	42	55	245	36	21	21	6	5	2	0	41	1	78	5	0	3	3	.500	0	25	3.44
1990 California	AL	54	0	0	47	64.1	267	45	24	23	4	4	4	0	35	6	82	7	1	4	4	.500	0	25	3.22
1991 California	AL	67	0	0	63	78.2	309	51	20	14	6	3	2	1	17	3	101	2	2	2	4	.333	0	46	1.60
5 ML YEARS		225	0	0	192	279	1146	197	87	76	20	15	11	2	115	16	331	21	4	16	16	.500	0	113	2.45

Ron Hassey

Bats: Left **Throws:** Right **Pos:** C   **Ht:** 6' 2" **Wt:** 195 **Born:** 02/27/53 **Age:** 39

		BATTING																		BASERUNNING				PERCENTAGES		
Year Team	Lg	G	AB	H	2B	3B	HR	(Hm	Rd)	TB	R	RBI	TBB	IBB	SO	HBP	SH	SF	SB	CS	SB%	GDP	Avg	OBP	SLG
1978 Cleveland	AL	25	74	15	0	0	2	(1	1)	21	5	9	5	0	7	1	1	2	2	0	1.00	1	.203	.256	.284
1979 Cleveland	AL	75	223	64	14	0	4	(2	2)	90	20	32	19	2	19	0	4	3	1	0	1.00	8	.287	.339	.404
1980 Cleveland	AL	130	390	124	18	4	8	(5	3)	174	43	65	49	3	51	1	1	6	0	2	.00	13	.318	.390	.446
1981 Cleveland	AL	61	190	44	4	0	1	(0	1)	51	8	25	17	0	11	2	3	3	1	0	.00	5	.232	.297	.268
1982 Cleveland	AL	113	323	81	18	0	5	(2	3)	114	33	34	53	5	32	1	3	2	3	2	.60	10	.251	.356	.353
1983 Cleveland	AL	117	341	92	21	0	6	(4	2)	131	48	42	38	2	35	2	2	5	2	2	.50	11	.270	.342	.384
1984 2 ML Teams		67	182	49	5	1	2	(1	1)	62	16	24	19	3	32	0	0	1	1	1	.50	5	.269	.337	.341
1985 New York	AL	92	267	79	16	1	13	(3	10)	136	31	42	28	4	21	3	0	0	0	0	.00	7	.296	.369	.509
1986 2 ML Teams		113	341	110	25	1	9	(5	4)	164	45	49	46	3	27	3	1	2	1	1	.50	15	.323	.406	.481
1987 Chicago	AL	49	145	31	9	0	3	(1	2)	49	15	12	17	2	11	2	0	1	0	0	.00	9	.214	.303	.338
1988 Oakland	AL	107	323	83	15	0	7	(3	4)	119	32	45	30	1	42	4	3	5	2	0	1.00	9	.257	.323	.368
1989 Oakland	AL	97	268	61	12	0	5	(3	2)	88	29	23	24	2	45	1	1	4	1	1	1.00	5	.228	.290	.328
1990 Oakland	AL	94	254	54	7	0	5	(2	3)	76	18	22	27	3	29	1	1	3	0	0	.00	3	.213	.288	.299
1991 Montreal	NL	52	119	27	8	0	1	(0	1)	38	5	14	13	1	16	0	2	1	1	1	.50	5	.227	.301	.319
1984 Cleveland	AL	48	149	38	5	1	0	(0	0)	45	11	19	15	2	26	0	0	1	1	0	1.00	4	.255	.321	.302
Chicago	NL	19	33	11	0	0	2	(1	1)	17	5	5	4	1	6	0	0	0	0	1	.00	1	.333	.405	.515
1986 New York	AL	64	191	57	14	0	6	(2	4)	89	23	29	24	1	16	2	1	1	1	0	.50	8	.298	.381	.466
Chicago	AL	49	150	53	11	1	3	(3	0)	75	22	20	22	2	11	1	0	1	0	0	.00	7	.353	.437	.500
14 ML YEARS		1192	3440	914	172	7	71	(32	39)	1313	348	438	385	31	378	21	22	38	14	10	.58	110	.266	.340	.382

Billy Hatcher

Bats: Right **Throws:** Right **Pos:** LF/CF   **Ht:** 5'10" **Wt:** 190 **Born:** 10/04/60 **Age:** 31

		BATTING																		BASERUNNING				PERCENTAGES		
Year Team	Lg	G	AB	H	2B	3B	HR	(Hm	Rd)	TB	R	RBI	TBB	IBB	SO	HBP	SH	SF	SB	CS	SB%	GDP	Avg	OBP	SLG
1984 Chicago	NL	8	9	1	0	0	0	(0	0)	1	1	0	1	1	0	0	0	0	2	0	1.00	0	.111	.200	.111
1985 Chicago	NL	53	163	40	12	1	2	(2	0)	60	24	10	8	0	12	3	2	2	2	4	.33	9	.245	.290	.368
1986 Houston	NL	127	419	108	15	4	6	(2	4)	149	55	36	22	1	52	5	6	1	38	14	.73	3	.258	.302	.356
1987 Houston	NL	141	564	167	28	3	11	(3	8)	234	96	63	42	1	70	9	7	5	53	9	.85	11	.296	.352	.415
1988 Houston	NL	145	530	142	25	4	7	(3	4)	196	79	52	37	4	52	6	8	8	32	13	.71	6	.268	.321	.370
1989 2 ML Teams		135	481	111	19	3	4	(0	4)	148	59	51	30	2	62	2	3	4	24	7	.77	4	.231	.277	.308
1990 Cincinnati	NL	139	504	139	28	5	5	(2	3)	192	68	25	33	5	42	6	1	1	30	10	.75	4	.276	.327	.381
1991 Cincinnati	NL	138	442	116	25	3	4	(2	2)	159	45	41	26	4	55	7	4	3	11	9	.55	9	.262	.312	.360
1989 Houston	NL	108	395	90	15	3	3	(0	3)	120	49	44	30	2	53	1	3	4	22	6	.79	3	.228	.281	.304
Pittsburgh	NL	27	86	21	4	0	1	(0	1)	28	10	7	0	0	9	1	0	0	2	1	.67	1	.244	.253	.326
8 ML YEARS		886	3112	824	152	23	39	(14	25)	1139	427	278	199	18	349	40	31	24	192	66	.74	46	.265	.315	.366

Andy Hawkins

Pitches: Right **Bats:** Right **Pos:** SP **Ht:** 6' 3" **Wt:** 223 **Born:** 01/21/60 **Age:** 32

		HOW MUCH HE PITCHED						WHAT HE GAVE UP									THE RESULTS				
Year Team	Lg	G	GS	CG	GF	IP	BFP	H	R	ER	HR	SH	SF	HB	TBB	IBB	SO	WP	Bk	W	L	Pct.	ShO	Sv	ERA
1982 San Diego	NL	15	10	1	2	63.2	281	66	33	29	4	6	5	2	27	3	25	2	3	2	5	.286	0	0	4.10
1983 San Diego	NL	21	19	4	1	119.2	501	106	50	39	8	10	4	5	48	4	59	4	1	5	7	.417	1	0	2.93
1984 San Diego	NL	36	22	2	9	146	650	143	90	76	13	10	4	2	72	2	77	1	2	8	9	.471	1	0	4.68
1985 San Diego	NL	33	33	5	0	228.2	953	229	88	80	18	13	12	4	65	8	69	3	3	18	8	.692	2	0	3.15
1986 San Diego	NL	37	35	3	0	209.1	905	218	111	100	24	7	6	5	75	7	117	6	2	10	8	.556	1	0	4.30
1987 San Diego	NL	24	20	0	2	117.2	516	131	71	66	16	5	3	2	49	2	51	2	3	3	10	.231	0	0	5.05
1988 San Diego	NL	33	33	4	0	217.2	906	196	88	81	16	14	6	6	76	4	91	1	3	14	11	.560	2	0	3.35
1989 New York	AL	34	34	5	0	208.1	908	238	127	111	23	3	3	6	76	6	98	1	2	15	15	.500	2	0	4.80
1990 New York	AL	28	26	2	1	157.2	692	156	101	94	20	4	5	2	82	3	74	2	1	5	12	.294	1	0	5.37
1991 2 ML Teams		19	17	1	2	89.2	399	91	56	55	10	2	3	5	42	0	45	1	1	4	6	.400	0	0	5.52
1991 New York	AL	4	3	0	1	12.2	66	23	15	14	5	0	0	0	6	0	5	1	0	0	2	.000	0	0	9.95
Oakland	AL	15	14	1	1	77	333	68	41	41	5	2	3	5	36	0	40	0	1	4	4	.500	0	0	4.79
10 ML YEARS		280	249	27	17	1558.1	6711	1574	815	731	152	74	51	39	612	39	706	23	21	84	91	.480	10	0	4.22

Charlie Hayes

Bats: Right **Throws:** Right **Pos:** 3B **Ht:** 6' 0" **Wt:** 210 **Born:** 05/29/65 **Age:** 27

		BATTING															BASERUNNING				PERCENTAGES		
Year Team	Lg	G	AB	H	2B	3B	HR	(Hm | Rd)	TB	R	RBI	TBB	IBB	SO	HBP	SH	SF	SB	CS	SB%	GDP	Avg	OBP	SLG
1988 San Francisco	NL	7	11	1	0	0	0	(0 | 0)	1	0	0	0	0	3	0	0	0	0	0	.00	0	.091	.091	.091
1989 2 ML Teams		87	304	78	15	1	8	(3 | 5)	119	26	43	11	1	50	0	2	3	3	1	.75	6	.257	.280	.391
1990 Philadelphia	NL	152	561	145	20	0	10	(3 | 7)	195	56	57	28	3	91	2	0	6	4	4	.50	12	.258	.293	.348
1991 Philadelphia	NL	142	460	106	23	1	12	(6 | 6)	167	34	53	16	3	75	1	2	1	3	3	.50	13	.230	.257	.363
1989 San Francisco	NL	3	5	1	0	0	0	(0 | 0)	1	0	0	0	0	1	0	0	0	0	0	.00	0	.200	.200	.200
Philadelphia	NL	84	299	77	15	1	8	(3 | 5)	118	26	43	11	1	49	0	2	3	3	1	.75	6	.258	.281	.395
4 ML YEARS		388	1336	330	58	2	30	(12 | 18)	482	116	153	55	7	219	3	4	10	10	8	.56	31	.247	.276	.361

Von Hayes

Bats: Left **Throws:** Right **Pos:** CF/LF **Ht:** 6' 5" **Wt:** 188 **Born:** 08/31/58 **Age:** 33

		BATTING															BASERUNNING				PERCENTAGES		
Year Team	Lg	G	AB	H	2B	3B	HR	(Hm | Rd)	TB	R	RBI	TBB	IBB	SO	HBP	SH	SF	SB	CS	SB%	GDP	Avg	OBP	SLG
1981 Cleveland	AL	43	109	28	8	2	1	(0 | 1)	43	21	17	14	1	10	2	4	2	8	1	.89	2	.257	.346	.394
1982 Cleveland	AL	150	527	132	25	3	14	(3 | 11)	205	65	82	42	3	63	4	8	2	32	13	.71	10	.250	.310	.389
1983 Philadelphia	NL	124	351	93	9	5	6	(3 | 3)	130	45	32	36	7	55	3	0	2	20	12	.63	11	.265	.337	.370
1984 Philadelphia	NL	152	561	164	27	6	16	(10 | 6)	251	85	67	59	4	84	0	0	2	48	13	.79	10	.292	.359	.447
1985 Philadelphia	NL	152	570	150	30	4	13	(12 | 1)	227	76	70	61	6	99	0	2	4	21	8	.72	6	.263	.332	.398
1986 Philadelphia	NL	158	610	186	46	2	19	(11 | 8)	293	107	98	74	9	77	1	1	4	24	12	.67	14	.305	.379	.480
1987 Philadelphia	NL	158	556	154	36	5	21	(14 | 7)	263	84	84	121	12	77	0	0	4	16	7	.70	12	.277	.404	.473
1988 Philadelphia	NL	104	367	100	28	2	6	(2 | 4)	150	43	45	49	5	59	1	1	5	20	9	.69	3	.272	.355	.409
1989 Philadelphia	NL	154	540	140	27	2	26	(15 | 11)	249	93	78	101	14	103	4	0	7	28	7	.80	7	.259	.376	.461
1990 Philadelphia	NL	129	467	122	14	3	17	(10 | 7)	193	70	73	87	16	81	4	0	10	16	7	.70	10	.261	.375	.413
1991 Philadelphia	NL	77	284	64	15	1	0	(0 | 0)	81	43	21	31	1	42	3	0	5	9	2	.82	6	.225	.303	.285
11 ML YEARS		1401	4942	1333	265	35	139	(80 | 59)	2085	732	667	675	78	750	22	16	47	242	91	.73	91	.270	.357	.422

Mike Heath

Bats: Right **Throws:** Right **Pos:** C **Ht:** 5'11" **Wt:** 180 **Born:** 02/05/55 **Age:** 37

		BATTING															BASERUNNING				PERCENTAGES		
Year Team	Lg	G	AB	H	2B	3B	HR	(Hm | Rd)	TB	R	RBI	TBB	IBB	SO	HBP	SH	SF	SB	CS	SB%	GDP	Avg	OBP	SLG
1978 New York	AL	33	92	21	3	1	0	(0 | 0)	26	6	8	4	0	9	1	1	1	1	0	.00	1	.228	.265	.283
1979 Oakland	AL	74	258	66	8	0	3	(2 | 1)	83	19	27	17	1	18	3	3	5	1	0	1.00	14	.256	.304	.322
1980 Oakland	AL	92	305	74	10	2	1	(1 | 0)	91	27	33	16	2	28	0	7	1	3	3	.50	7	.243	.280	.298
1981 Oakland	AL	84	301	71	7	1	8	(4 | 4)	104	26	30	13	1	36	1	5	1	3	3	.50	9	.236	.269	.346
1982 Oakland	AL	101	318	77	18	4	3	(3 | 0)	112	43	39	27	3	36	0	2	4	8	3	.73	3	.242	.298	.352
1983 Oakland	AL	96	345	97	17	0	6	(5 | 1)	132	45	33	18	4	59	1	1	1	3	4	.43	9	.281	.318	.383
1984 Oakland	AL	140	475	118	21	5	13	(8 | 5)	188	49	64	26	2	72	1	2	4	7	4	.64	14	.248	.287	.396
1985 Oakland	AL	138	436	109	18	6	13	(8 | 5)	178	71	55	41	0	63	1	10	4	7	7	.50	13	.250	.313	.408
1986 2 ML Teams		95	288	65	11	1	8	(4 | 4)	102	30	36	27	4	53	1	1	2	6	4	.60	6	.226	.292	.354
1987 Detroit	AL	93	270	76	16	0	8	(8 | 0)	116	34	33	21	0	42	3	1	1	1	5	.17	5	.281	.339	.430
1988 Detroit	AL	86	219	54	7	2	5	(4 | 1)	80	24	18	18	0	32	1	3	0	1	0	1.00	6	.247	.307	.365
1989 Detroit	AL	122	396	104	16	2	10	(5 | 5)	154	38	43	24	2	71	4	1	4	7	1	.88	18	.263	.308	.389
1990 Detroit	AL	122	370	100	18	2	7	(3 | 4)	143	46	38	19	0	71	4	2	3	7	6	.54	12	.270	.311	.386
1991 Atlanta	NL	49	139	29	3	1	1	(1 | 0)	37	14	12	7	5	26	1	2	1	0	0	.00	4	.209	.250	.266
1986 St. Louis	NL	65	190	39	8	1	4	(1 | 3)	61	19	25	23	4	36	1	1	1	2	3	.40	5	.205	.293	.321

		G	GS	CG	GF	IP	BFP	H	R	ER	HR	SH	SF	HB	TBB	IBB	SO	WP	Bk	W	L	Pct.	ShO	Sv	ERA
Detroit	AL	30	98	26	3	0	4	(3	1)	41	11	11	4	0	17	0	0	1		4	1	.80	1		.265 .291 .418
14 ML YEARS		1325	4212	1061	173	27	86	(56	30)	1546	462	469	278	24	616	22	41	32		54	40	.57	121		.252 .300 .367

Neal Heaton

Pitches: Left **Bats:** Left **Pos:** RP **Ht:** 6' 1" **Wt:** 205 **Born:** 03/03/60 **Age:** 32

		HOW MUCH HE PITCHED						WHAT HE GAVE UP												THE RESULTS					
Year Team	Lg	G	GS	CG	GF	IP	BFP	H	R	ER	HR	SH	SF	HB	TBB	IBB	SO	WP	Bk	W	L	Pct.	ShO	Sv	ERA
1982 Cleveland	AL	8	4	0	0	31	142	32	21	18	1	1	2	0	16	0	14	4	0	0	2	.000	0	0	5.23
1983 Cleveland	AL	39	16	4	19	149.1	637	157	79	69	11	3	5	1	44	10	75	1	0	11	7	.611	3	7	4.16
1984 Cleveland	AL	38	34	4	2	198.2	880	231	128	115	21	6	10	0	75	5	75	3	1	12	15	.444	1	0	5.21
1985 Cleveland	AL	36	33	5	2	207.2	921	244	119	113	19	7	8	7	80	2	82	2	2	9	17	.346	1	0	4.90
1986 2 ML Teams		33	29	5	2	198.2	850	201	102	90	26	6	5	2	81	8	90	4	0	7	15	.318	0	1	4.08
1987 Montreal	NL	32	32	3	0	193.1	807	207	103	97	25	5	5	3	37	3	105	2	5	13	10	.565	1	0	4.52
1988 Montreal	NL	32	11	0	7	97.1	415	98	54	54	14	5	3	3	43	5	43	1	5	3	10	.231	0	2	4.99
1989 Pittsburgh	NL	42	18	1	5	147.1	620	127	55	50	12	12	3	6	55	12	67	4	5	6	7	.462	0	0	3.05
1990 Pittsburgh	NL	30	24	0	2	146	599	143	66	56	17	10	6	2	38	1	68	4	1	12	9	.571	0	0	3.45
1991 Pittsburgh	NL	42	1	0	5	68.2	293	72	37	33	6	3	3	4	21	2	34	0	1	3	3	.500	0	0	4.33
1986 Cleveland	AL	12	12	2	0	74.1	324	73	42	35	8	2	0	1	34	4	24	2	0	3	6	.333	0	0	4.24
Minnesota	AL	21	17	3	2	124.1	526	128	60	55	18	4	5	1	47	4	66	2	0	4	9	.308	0	1	3.98
10 ML YEARS		332	202	22	44	1438	6164	1512	764	695	152	58	50	28	490	48	653	25	20	76	95	.444	6	10	4.35

Danny Heep

Bats: Left **Throws:** Left **Pos:** PH **Ht:** 5'11" **Wt:** 177 **Born:** 07/03/57 **Age:** 34

		BATTING															BASERUNNING				PERCENTAGES		
Year Team	Lg	G	AB	H	2B	3B	HR	(Hm | Rd)	TB	R	RBI	TBB	IBB	SO	HBP	SH	SF	SB	CS	SB%	GDP	Avg	OBP	SLG
1979 Houston	NL	14	14	2	0	0	0	(0 | 0)	2	0	2	1	1	4	0	0	2	0	0	.00	0	.143	.176	.143
1980 Houston	NL	33	87	24	8	0	0	(0 | 0)	32	6	6	8	0	9	1	0	1	0	0	.00	0	.276	.340	.368
1981 Houston	NL	33	96	24	3	0	0	(0 | 0)	27	6	11	10	2	11	0	0	0	0	0	.00	0	.250	.321	.281
1982 Houston	NL	85	198	47	14	1	4	(1 | 3)	75	16	22	21	3	31	1	0	2	0	2	.00	5	.237	.311	.379
1983 New York	NL	115	253	64	12	0	8	(6 | 2)	100	30	21	29	6	40	1	1	5	3	3	.50	5	.253	.326	.395
1984 New York	NL	99	199	46	9	2	1	(1 | 0)	62	36	12	27	3	22	1	1	5	3	1	.75	9	.231	.319	.312
1985 New York	NL	95	271	76	17	0	7	(2 | 5)	114	26	42	27	1	27	1	0	6	2	2	.50	12	.280	.341	.421
1986 New York	NL	86	195	55	8	2	5	(3 | 2)	82	24	33	30	5	31	1	0	1	1	4	.20	3	.282	.379	.421
1987 Los Angeles	NL	60	98	16	4	0	0	(0 | 0)	20	7	9	8	0	10	0	1	0	1	0	1.00	6	.163	.226	.204
1988 Los Angeles	NL	95	149	36	2	0	0	(0 | 0)	38	14	11	22	0	13	1	0	1	2	0	1.00	4	.242	.341	.255
1989 Boston	AL	113	320	96	17	0	5	(1 | 4)	128	36	49	29	4	26	1	1	4	0	1	.00	13	.300	.356	.400
1990 Boston	AL	41	69	12	1	1	0	(0 | 0)	15	3	8	7	0	14	1	0	1	0	0	.00	0	.174	.256	.217
1991 Atlanta	NL	14	12	5	1	0	0	(0 | 0)	6	4	3	1	0	4	0	0	0	0	1	.00	0	.417	.462	.500
13 ML YEARS		883	1961	503	96	6	30	(14 | 16)	701	208	229	220	25	242	9	4	28	12	14	.46	60	.257	.330	.357

Scott Hemond

Bats: Right **Throws:** Right **Pos:** C **Ht:** 6' 0" **Wt:** 205 **Born:** 11/18/65 **Age:** 26

		BATTING															BASERUNNING				PERCENTAGES		
Year Team	Lg	G	AB	H	2B	3B	HR	(Hm	Rd)	TB	R	RBI	TBB	IBB	SO	HBP	SH	SF	SB	CS	SB%	GDP	Avg	OBP	SLG
1986 Madison	A	22	85	26	2	0	2	--	--	34	9	13	5	0	19	0	0	1	2	1	.67	0	.306	.341	.400
1987 Madison	A	90	343	99	21	4	8	--	--	152	60	52	40	1	79	1	0	2	27	12	.69	10	.289	.363	.443
Huntsville	AA	33	110	20	3	1	1	--	--	28	10	8	4	0	30	0	1	0	5	1	.83	3	.182	.211	.255
1988 Huntsville	AA	133	482	106	22	4	9	--	--	163	51	53	48	1	114	3	1	7	29	8	.78	7	.220	.291	.338
1989 Huntsville	AA	132	490	130	26	6	5	--	--	183	89	62	62	0	77	7	13	6	45	17	.73	11	.265	.352	.373
1990 Tacoma	AAA	72	218	53	11	0	8	--	--	88	32	35	24	3	52	1	3	3	10	5	.67	7	.243	.317	.404
1991 Tacoma	AAA	92	327	89	19	5	3	--	--	127	50	31	39	1	69	7	5	1	11	8	.58	11	.272	.361	.388
1989 Oakland	AL	4	0	0	0	0	0	(0	0)	0	2	0	0	0	0	0	0	0	0	0	.00	0	.000	.000	.000
1990 Oakland	AL	7	13	2	0	0	0	(0	0)	2	0	1	0	0	5	0	0	0	0	0	.00	0	.154	.154	.154
1991 Oakland	AL	23	23	5	0	0	0	(0	0)	5	4	0	1	0	7	0	0	0	1	2	.33	0	.217	.250	.217
3 ML YEARS		34	36	7	0	0	0	(0	0)	7	6	1	1	0	12	0	0	0	1	2	.33	0	.194	.216	.194

Dave Henderson

Bats: Right **Throws:** Right **Pos:** CF **Ht:** 6' 2" **Wt:** 220 **Born:** 07/21/58 **Age:** 33

		BATTING															BASERUNNING				PERCENTAGES		
Year Team	Lg	G	AB	H	2B	3B	HR	(Hm | Rd)	TB	R	RBI	TBB	IBB	SO	HBP	SH	SF	SB	CS	SB%	GDP	Avg	OBP	SLG
1981 Seattle	AL	59	126	21	3	0	6	(5 | 1)	42	17	13	16	1	24	1	1	1	2	1	.67	4	.167	.264	.333
1982 Seattle	AL	104	324	82	17	1	14	(8 | 6)	143	47	48	36	2	67	0	1	1	2	5	.29	5	.253	.327	.441
1983 Seattle	AL	137	484	130	24	5	17	(9 | 8)	215	50	55	28	3	93	1	2	6	9	3	.75	5	.269	.306	.444
1984 Seattle	AL	112	350	98	23	0	14	(8 | 6)	163	42	43	19	0	56	2	2	1	5	5	.50	4	.280	.320	.466
1985 Seattle	AL	139	502	121	28	2	14	(8 | 6)	195	70	68	48	2	104	3	1	2	6	1	.86	11	.241	.310	.388
1986 2 ML Teams		139	388	103	22	4	15	(10 | 5)	178	59	47	39	4	110	2	2	1	2	3	.40	6	.265	.335	.459
1987 2 ML Teams		90	205	48	12	0	8	(4 | 4)	84	32	26	30	0	53	0	1	2	3	1	.75	3	.234	.329	.410

88

Year	Team	Lg	G	AB	H	2B	3B	HR	(Hm	Rd)	TB	R	RBI	TBB	IBB	SO	HBP	SH	SF	SB	CS	SB%	GDP	Avg	OBP	SLG
1988	Oakland	AL	146	507	154	38	1	24	(12	12)	266	100	94	47	1	92	4	5	7	2	4	.33	14	.304	.363	.525
1989	Oakland	AL	152	579	145	24	3	15	(10	5)	220	77	80	54	1	131	3	1	6	8	5	.62	13	.250	.315	.380
1990	Oakland	AL	127	450	122	28	0	20	(11	9)	210	65	63	40	1	105	1	1	2	3	1	.75	5	.271	.331	.467
1991	Oakland	AL	150	572	158	33	0	25	(15	10)	266	86	85	58	3	113	4	1	2	6	6	.50	8	.276	.346	.465
1986	Seattle	AL	103	337	93	19	4	14	(10	4)	162	51	44	37	4	95	2	1	1	1	3	.25	5	.276	.350	.481
	Boston		36	51	10	3	0	1	(0	1)	16	8	3	2	0	15	0	1	0	1	0	1.00	1	.196	.226	.314
1987	Boston	AL	75	184	43	10	0	8	(4	4)	77	30	25	22	0	48	0	1	2	1	1	.50	3	.234	.313	.418
	San Francisco	NL	15	21	5	2	0	0	(0	0)	7	2	1	8	0	5	0	0	0	2	0	1.00	0	.238	.448	.333
11 ML YEARS			1355	4487	1182	252	16	172	(100	72)	1982	645	622	415	18	948	21	18	31	48	35	.58	78	.263	.327	.442

Rickey Henderson

Bats: Right Throws: Left Pos: LF Ht: 5'10" Wt: 190 Born: 12/25/58 Age: 33

					BATTING														BASERUNNING				PERCENTAGES		
Year	Team	Lg	G	AB	H	2B	3B	HR	(Hm	Rd)	TB	R	RBI	TBB	IBB	SO	HBP	SH	SF	SB	CS	SB%	GDP	Avg	OBP	SLG
1979	Oakland	AL	89	351	96	13	3	1	(1	0)	118	49	26	34	0	39	2	8	3	33	11	.75	4	.274	.338	.336
1980	Oakland	AL	158	591	179	22	4	9	(3	6)	236	111	53	117	7	54	5	6	3	100	26	.79	6	.303	.420	.399
1981	Oakland	AL	108	423	135	18	7	6	(5	1)	185	89	35	64	4	68	2	0	4	56	22	.72	7	.319	.408	.437
1982	Oakland	AL	149	536	143	24	4	10	(5	5)	205	119	51	116	1	94	2	0	2	130	42	.76	5	.267	.398	.382
1983	Oakland	AL	145	513	150	25	7	9	(5	4)	216	105	48	103	8	80	4	1	1	108	19	.85	11	.292	.414	.421
1984	Oakland	AL	142	502	147	27	4	16	(7	9)	230	113	58	86	1	81	5	1	3	66	18	.79	7	.293	.399	.458
1985	New York	AL	143	547	172	28	5	24	(8	16)	282	146	72	99	1	65	3	0	5	80	10	.89	8	.314	.419	.516
1986	New York	AL	153	608	160	31	5	28	(13	15)	285	130	74	89	2	81	2	0	2	87	18	.83	12	.263	.358	.469
1987	New York	AL	95	358	104	17	3	17	(10	7)	178	78	37	80	1	52	2	0	0	41	8	.84	10	.291	.423	.497
1988	New York	AL	140	554	169	30	2	6	(2	4)	221	118	50	82	1	54	3	2	6	93	13	.88	6	.305	.394	.399
1989	2 ML Teams		150	541	148	26	3	12	(7	5)	216	113	57	126	5	68	3	0	4	77	14	.85	8	.274	.411	.399
1990	Oakland	AL	136	489	159	33	3	28	(8	20)	282	119	61	97	2	60	4	2	2	65	10	.87	13	.325	.439	.577
1991	Oakland	AL	134	470	126	17	1	18	(8	10)	199	105	57	98	7	73	7	0	3	58	18	.76	7	.268	.400	.423
1989	New York	AL	65	235	58	13	1	3	(1	2)	82	41	22	56	0	29	1	0	1	25	8	.76	0	.247	.392	.349
	Oakland	AL	85	306	90	13	2	9	(6	3)	134	72	35	70	5	39	2	0	3	52	6	.90	8	.294	.425	.438
13 ML YEARS			1742	6483	1888	311	51	184	(82	102)	2853	1395	679	1191	40	869	44	20	38	994	229	.81	104	.291	.403	.440

Tom Henke

Pitches: Right Bats: Right Pos: RP Ht: 6'5" Wt: 225 Born: 12/21/57 Age: 34

			HOW	MUCH	HE	PITCHED			WHAT	HE	GAVE	UP					THE	RESULTS			
Year	Team	Lg	G	GS	CG	GF	IP	BFP	H	R	ER	HR	SH	SF	HB	TBB	IBB	SO	WP	Bk	W	L	Pct.	ShO	Sv	ERA
1982	Texas	AL	8	0	0	6	15.2	67	14	2	2	0	1	0	1	8	2	9	0	0	1	0	1.000	0	0	1.15
1983	Texas	AL	8	0	0	5	16	65	16	6	6	1	0	0	0	4	0	17	0	0	1	0	1.000	0	1	3.38
1984	Texas	AL	25	0	0	13	28.1	141	36	21	20	0	1	4	1	20	2	25	2	2	1	1	.500	0	2	6.35
1985	Toronto	AL	28	0	0	22	40	153	29	12	9	4	2	2	0	8	2	42	0	0	3	3	.500	0	13	2.03
1986	Toronto	AL	63	0	0	51	91.1	370	63	39	34	6	2	6	1	32	4	118	3	1	9	5	.643	0	27	3.35
1987	Toronto	AL	72	0	0	62	94	363	62	27	26	10	3	5	0	25	3	128	5	0	0	6	.000	0	34	2.49
1988	Toronto	AL	52	0	0	44	68	285	60	23	22	6	4	2	2	24	3	66	0	0	4	4	.500	0	25	2.91
1989	Toronto	AL	64	0	0	56	89	356	66	20	19	5	4	3	2	25	4	116	2	0	8	3	.727	0	20	1.92
1990	Toronto	AL	61	0	0	58	74.2	297	58	18	18	8	4	1	1	19	2	75	6	0	2	4	.333	0	32	2.17
1991	Toronto	AL	49	0	0	43	50.1	190	33	13	13	4	0	0	0	11	2	53	1	0	0	2	.000	0	32	2.32
10 ML YEARS			430	0	0	360	567.1	2287	437	181	169	44	21	23	8	176	24	649	19	3	29	28	.509	0	186	2.68

Mike Henneman

Pitches: Right Bats: Right Pos: RP Ht: 6'4" Wt: 205 Born: 12/11/61 Age: 30

			HOW	MUCH	HE	PITCHED			WHAT	HE	GAVE	UP					THE	RESULTS			
Year	Team	Lg	G	GS	CG	GF	IP	BFP	H	R	ER	HR	SH	SF	HB	TBB	IBB	SO	WP	Bk	W	L	Pct.	ShO	Sv	ERA
1987	Detroit	AL	55	0	0	28	96.2	399	86	36	32	8	2	2	3	30	5	75	7	0	11	3	.786	0	7	2.98
1988	Detroit	AL	65	0	0	51	91.1	364	72	23	19	7	5	2	2	24	10	58	8	1	9	6	.600	0	22	1.87
1989	Detroit	AL	60	0	0	35	90	401	84	46	37	4	7	3	5	51	15	69	0	1	11	4	.733	0	8	3.70
1990	Detroit	AL	69	0	0	53	94.1	399	90	36	32	4	5	2	3	33	12	50	3	0	8	6	.571	0	22	3.05
1991	Detroit	AL	60	0	0	50	84.1	358	81	29	27	2	5	5	0	34	8	61	5	0	10	2	.833	0	21	2.88
5 ML YEARS			309	0	0	217	456.2	1921	413	170	147	25	24	14	13	172	50	313	23	2	49	21	.700	0	80	2.90

Doug Henry

Pitches: Right Bats: Right Pos: RP Ht: 6'4" Wt: 185 Born: 12/10/63 Age: 28

			HOW	MUCH	HE	PITCHED			WHAT	HE	GAVE	UP					THE	RESULTS			
Year	Team	Lg	G	GS	CG	GF	IP	BFP	H	R	ER	HR	SH	SF	HB	TBB	IBB	SO	WP	Bk	W	L	Pct.	ShO	Sv	ERA
1986	Beloit	A	27	24	4	1	143.1	639	153	95	74	16	3	5	6	60	4	115	9	4	7	8	.467	1	1	4.65
1987	Beloit	A	31	15	1	5	132.2	593	145	83	72	6	2	4	5	51	5	106	7	0	8	9	.471	0	2	4.88
1988	Stockton	A	23	1	1	14	70.2	280	46	19	14	1	1	1	1	31	1	71	5	4	7	1	.875	0	7	1.78
	El Paso	AA	14	3	3	1	45.2	182	33	16	16	4	0	1	1	19	0	50	3	3	4	0	1.000	1	0	3.15
1989	El Paso	AA	1	1	0	0	2	11	3	3	3	1	0	0	0	3	0	2	0	0	0	0	.000	0	0	13.50

89

							IP	BFP	H	R	ER	HR	SH	SF	HB	TBB	IBB	SO	WP	Bk	W	L	Pct.	ShO	Sv	ERA
	Stockton	A	4	3	0	0	11	43	9	4	0	0	0	0	0	3	0	9	0	0	0	1	.000	0	0	0.00
1990	Stockton	A	4	0	0	3	8	35	4	1	1	0	0	1	2	3	0	13	1	0	1	0	1.000	0	1	1.13
	El Paso	AA	15	0	0	12	30.2	131	31	13	10	1	0	1	0	11	0	25	0	2	1	0	1.000	0	9	2.93
	Denver	AAA	27	0	0	15	50.2	219	46	26	25	4	3	1	0	27	2	54	3	0	2	3	.400	0	8	4.44
1991	Denver	AAA	32	0	0	27	57.2	234	47	16	14	4	4	2	3	20	3	47	4	2	3	2	.600	0	14	2.18
1991	Milwaukee	AL	32	0	0	25	36	137	16	4	4	1	1	2	0	14	1	28	0	0	2	1	.667	0	15	1.00

Dwayne Henry

Pitches: Right **Bats:** Right **Pos:** RP   **Ht:** 6' 3" **Wt:** 205 **Born:** 02/16/62 **Age:** 30

			HOW MUCH HE PITCHED						WHAT HE GAVE UP												THE RESULTS					
Year	Team	Lg	G	GS	CG	GF	IP	BFP	H	R	ER	HR	SH	SF	HB	TBB	IBB	SO	WP	Bk	W	L	Pct.	ShO	Sv	ERA
1984	Texas	AL	3	0	0	1	4.1	25	5	4	4	0	1	0	0	7	0	2	0	0	0	1	.000	0	0	8.31
1985	Texas	AL	16	0	0	10	21	86	16	7	6	0	2	1	0	7	0	20	1	0	2	2	.500	0	3	2.57
1986	Texas	AL	19	0	0	4	19.1	93	14	11	10	1	1	2	1	22	0	17	7	1	1	0	1.000	0	0	4.66
1987	Texas	AL	5	0	0	1	10	50	12	10	10	2	0	0	0	9	0	7	1	0	0	0	.000	0	0	9.00
1988	Texas	AL	11	0	0	5	10.1	59	15	10	10	1	0	1	3	9	1	10	3	1	0	1	.000	0	1	8.71
1989	Atlanta	NL	12	0	0	6	12.2	55	12	6	6	2	2	0	0	5	1	16	1	0	0	2	.000	0	1	4.26
1990	Atlanta	NL	34	0	0	14	38.1	176	41	26	24	3	0	1	0	25	0	34	2	1	2	2	.500	0	0	5.63
1991	Houston	NL	52	0	0	25	67.2	282	51	25	24	7	6	2	2	39	7	51	5	0	3	2	.600	0	2	3.19
	8 ML YEARS		152	0	0	66	183.2	826	166	99	94	16	12	7	6	123	9	157	20	3	8	10	.444	0	7	4.61

Pat Hentgen

Pitches: Right **Bats:** Right **Pos:** RP   **Ht:** 6' 2" **Wt:** 200 **Born:** 11/13/68 **Age:** 23

			HOW MUCH HE PITCHED						WHAT HE GAVE UP												THE RESULTS					
Year	Team	Lg	G	GS	CG	GF	IP	BFP	H	R	ER	HR	SH	SF	HB	TBB	IBB	SO	WP	Bk	W	L	Pct.	ShO	Sv	ERA
1986	St.Cathrnes	A	13	11	0	2	40	191	38	27	20	3	2	1	2	30	1	30	3	0	0	4	.000	0	1	4.50
1987	Myrtle Bch	A	32	31	2	0	188	753	145	62	49	5	4	2	8	60	0	131	14	3	11	5	.688	2	0	2.35
1988	Dunedin	A	31	30	0	1	151.1	651	139	80	58	10	4	6	4	65	1	125	14	2	3	12	.200	0	0	3.45
1989	Dunedin	A	29	28	0	0	151.1	633	123	53	45	5	6	7	2	71	1	148	16	4	9	8	.529	0	0	2.68
1990	Knoxville	AA	28	26	0	0	153.1	633	121	57	52	10	3	5	3	68	0	142	8	2	9	5	.643	0	0	3.05
1991	Syracuse	AAA	31	28	1	2	171	729	146	91	85	17	5	6	2	90	1	155	11	2	8	9	.471	0	0	4.47
1991	Toronto	AL	3	1	0	1	7.1	30	5	2	2	1	0	2	1	3	0	3	1	0	0	0	.000	0	0	2.45

Gil Heredia

Pitches: Right **Bats:** Right **Pos:** SP   **Ht:** 6' 1" **Wt:** 190 **Born:** 10/26/65 **Age:** 26

			HOW MUCH HE PITCHED						WHAT HE GAVE UP												THE RESULTS					
Year	Team	Lg	G	GS	CG	GF	IP	BFP	H	R	ER	HR	SH	SF	HB	TBB	IBB	SO	WP	Bk	W	L	Pct.	ShO	Sv	ERA
1987	Everett	A	3	3	1	0	20	80	24	8	8	2	0	0	0	1	0	14	1	0	2	0	1.000	0	0	3.60
	Fresno	A	11	11	5	0	80.2	321	62	28	26	8	2	5	0	23	1	60	2	2	5	3	.625	2	0	2.90
1988	San Jose	A	27	27	9	0	206.1	863	216	107	80	9	9	7	4	46	0	121	9	0	13	12	.520	0	0	3.49
1989	Shreveport	AA	7	2	1	1	24.2	104	28	10	7	1	1	0	1	4	0	8	2	0	1	0	1.000	0	0	2.55
1990	Phoenix	AAA	29	19	0	2	147	626	159	81	67	7	6	6	3	37	0	75	4	1	9	7	.563	0	1	4.10
1991	Phoenix	AAA	33	15	5	7	140.1	592	155	60	44	3	9	2	2	28	5	75	4	0	9	11	.450	1	1	2.82
1991	San Francisco	NL	7	4	0	1	33	126	27	14	14	4	2	1	0	7	2	13	1	0	0	2	.000	0	0	3.82

Carlos Hernandez

Bats: Right **Throws:** Right **Pos:** C   **Ht:** 5'11" **Wt:** 185 **Born:** 05/24/67 **Age:** 25

			BATTING															BASERUNNING				PERCENTAGES		
Year	Team	Lg	G	AB	H	2B	3B	HR	(Hm | Rd)	TB	R	RBI	TBB	IBB	SO	HBP	SH	SF	SB	CS	SB%	GDP	Avg	OBP	SLG
1985	Dodgers	R	22	49	12	1	0	0	--	--	13	3	6	3	0	8	0	0	0	0	0	.00	4	.245	.288	.265
1986	Dodgers	R	57	205	64	7	0	1	--	--	74	19	31	5	2	18	2	1	1	1	2	.33	7	.312	.333	.361
1987	Bakersfield	A	48	162	37	6	1	3	--	--	54	22	22	14	0	23	3	1	2	8	4	.67	6	.228	.298	.333
1988	Bakersfield	A	92	333	103	15	2	5	--	--	137	37	52	16	2	39	1	3	4	3	2	.60	18	.309	.339	.411
	Albuquerque	AAA	3	8	1	0	0	0	--	--	1	0	1	0	0	0	0	0	0	0	0	.00	1	.125	.125	.125
1989	San Antonio	AA	99	370	111	16	3	8	--	--	157	37	41	12	0	46	7	1	3	2	3	.40	12	.300	.332	.424
	Albuquerque	AAA	4	14	3	0	0	0	--	--	3	1	1	2	1	1	0	0	0	0	0	.00	0	.214	.313	.214
1990	Albuquerque	AAA	52	143	45	8	1	0	--	--	55	11	16	8	1	25	1	0	3	2	2	.50	5	.315	.348	.385
1991	Albuquerque	AAA	95	345	119	24	2	8	--	--	171	60	44	24	5	36	1	0	2	5	5	.50	10	.345	.387	.496
1990	Los Angeles	NL	10	20	4	1	0	0	(0 | 0)	5	2	1	0	0	2	0	0	0	0	0	.00	0	.200	.200	.250
1991	Los Angeles	NL	15	14	3	1	0	0	(0 | 0)	4	1	1	0	0	5	1	0	1	1	0	1.00	2	.214	.250	.286
	2 ML YEARS		25	34	7	2	0	0	(0 | 0)	9	3	2	0	0	7	1	0	1	1	0	1.00	2	.206	.222	.265

Jeremy Hernandez

Pitches: Right **Bats:** Right **Pos:** RP **Ht:** 6' 5" **Wt:** 195 **Born:** 07/07/66 **Age:** 25

			HOW MUCH HE PITCHED						WHAT HE GAVE UP									THE RESULTS					
Year Team	Lg	G	GS	CG	GF	IP	BFP	H	R	ER	HR	SH	SF	HB	TBB	IBB	SO	WP	Bk	W	L	Pct.	ShO	Sv	ERA
1987 Erie	A	16	16	1	0	99.1	412	87	36	31	7	2	3	2	41	3	62	7	1	5	4	.556	0	0	2.81
1988 Springfield	A	24	24	3	0	147.1	615	133	73	58	8	0	3	7	34	2	97	4	8	12	6	.667	1	0	3.54
1989 St.Pete	A	3	3	0	0	14	63	17	14	12	0	2	1	0	5	0	5	2	0	0	2	.000	0	0	7.71
Chston-Sc	A	10	10	2	0	58.2	260	65	37	23	2	2	0	3	16	1	39	1	3	3	5	.375	1	0	3.53
Riverside	A	9	9	4	0	67	264	55	17	13	2	0	0	4	11	0	65	2	0	5	2	.714	1	0	1.75
Wichita	AA	4	3	0	0	19	91	30	18	18	6	1	1	0	8	0	9	4	0	2	1	.667	0	0	8.53
1990 Wichita	AA	26	26	1	0	155	675	163	92	78	18	7	7	7	50	0	101	6	1	7	6	.538	0	0	4.53
1991 Las Vegas	AAA	56	0	0	45	68.1	309	76	36	36	1	5	2	4	25	10	67	2	0	4	8	.333	0	13	4.74
1991 San Diego	NL	9	0	0	7	14.1	56	8	1	0	0	0	0	0	5	0	9	2	0	0	0	.000	0	2	0.00

Jose Hernandez

Bats: Right **Throws:** Right **Pos:** SS **Ht:** 6' 1" **Wt:** 180 **Born:** 07/14/69 **Age:** 22

					BATTING													BASERUNNING				PERCENTAGES		
Year Team	Lg	G	AB	H	2B	3B	HR	(Hm	Rd)	TB	R	RBI	TBB	IBB	SO	HBP	SH	SF	SB	CS	SB%	GDP	Avg	OBP	SLG
1987 Rangers	R	24	52	9	1	1	0	--	--	12	5	2	9	0	25	1	1	0	2	1	.67	1	.173	.306	.231
1988 Rangers	R	55	162	26	1	4	1	--	--	38	19	13	12	0	36	0	0	1	4	1	.80	5	.160	.217	.235
1989 Gastonia	A	91	215	47	7	6	1	--	--	69	35	16	33	0	67	0	8	0	9	2	.82	3	.219	.323	.321
1990 Charlotte	A	121	388	99	14	7	1	--	--	130	43	44	50	4	122	4	11	2	11	8	.58	8	.255	.345	.335
1991 Okla City	AAA	14	46	14	1	1	1	--	--	20	6	3	4	0	10	0	3	1	0	0	.00	1	.304	.353	.435
Tulsa	AA	91	301	72	17	4	1	--	--	100	36	20	26	0	75	1	5	4	4	3	.57	6	.239	.298	.332
1991 Texas	AL	45	98	18	2	1	0	(0	0)	22	8	4	3	0	31	0	6	0	0	1	.00	2	.184	.208	.224

Roberto Hernandez

Pitches: Right **Bats:** Right **Pos:** RP/SP **Ht:** 6' 4" **Wt:** 220 **Born:** 11/11/64 **Age:** 27

				HOW MUCH HE PITCHED						WHAT HE GAVE UP									THE RESULTS					
Year Team	Lg	G	GS	CG	GF	IP	BFP	H	R	ER	HR	SH	SF	HB	TBB	IBB	SO	WP	Bk	W	L	Pct.	ShO	Sv	ERA
1986 Salem	A	10	10	0	0	55	0	57	37	28	3	0	0	1	42	1	38	6	0	2	2	.500	0	0	4.58
1987 Quad City	A	7	6	0	1	21	102	24	21	16	2	0	0	2	12	0	21	5	0	2	3	.400	0	1	6.86
1988 Quad City	A	24	24	6	0	164.2	699	157	70	58	8	6	4	6	48	0	114	7	5	9	10	.474	1	0	3.17
Midland	AA	3	3	0	0	12.1	59	16	13	9	0	0	0	1	8	0	7	1	0	0	2	.000	0	0	6.57
1989 Midland	AA	12	12	0	0	64	305	94	57	49	4	1	5	2	30	0	42	4	1	2	7	.222	0	0	6.89
Palm Sprngs	A	7	7	0	0	42.2	188	49	27	22	2	3	1	2	16	0	33	4	0	1	4	.200	0	0	4.64
South Bend	A	4	4	0	0	24.1	95	19	9	9	1	2	0	0	7	0	17	0	0	1	1	.500	0	0	3.33
1990 Birmingham	AA	17	17	1	0	108	469	103	57	44	6	5	5	6	43	2	62	3	1	8	5	.615	0	0	3.67
Vancouver	AAA	11	11	3	0	79.1	329	73	33	25	4	3	3	2	26	0	49	3	0	3	5	.375	1	0	2.84
1991 Vancouver	AAA	7	7	0	0	44.2	195	41	17	16	2	1	1	0	23	0	40	1	0	4	1	.800	0	0	3.22
White Sox	R	1	1	0	0	6	18	2	0	0	0	0	0	0	0	0	7	0	0	0	0	.000	0	0	0.00
Birmingham	AA	4	4	0	0	22.2	85	11	5	5	2	0	1	2	6	0	25	2	0	2	1	.667	0	0	1.99
1991 Chicago	AL	9	3	0	1	15	69	18	15	13	1	0	0	0	7	0	6	1	0	1	0	1.000	0	0	7.80

Xavier Hernandez

Pitches: Right **Bats:** Left **Pos:** RP/SP **Ht:** 6' 2" **Wt:** 185 **Born:** 08/16/65 **Age:** 26

				HOW MUCH HE PITCHED						WHAT HE GAVE UP									THE RESULTS					
Year Team	Lg	G	GS	CG	GF	IP	BFP	H	R	ER	HR	SH	SF	HB	TBB	IBB	SO	WP	Bk	W	L	Pct.	ShO	Sv	ERA
1989 Toronto	AL	7	1	0	0	22.2	101	25	15	12	2	0	2	1	8	0	7	1	0	1	0	1.000	0	0	4.76
1990 Houston	NL	34	1	0	10	62.1	268	60	34	32	8	2	4	4	24	5	24	6	0	2	1	.667	0	0	4.62
1991 Houston	NL	32	6	0	8	63	285	66	34	33	6	1	1	0	32	7	55	0	0	2	7	.222	0	3	4.71
3 ML YEARS		73	7	0	20	148	654	151	83	77	16	3	7	5	64	12	86	7	0	5	8	.385	0	3	4.68

Tommy Herr

Bats: Both **Throws:** Right **Pos:** 2B **Ht:** 6' 0" **Wt:** 196 **Born:** 04/04/56 **Age:** 36

					BATTING													BASERUNNING				PERCENTAGES		
Year Team	Lg	G	AB	H	2B	3B	HR	(Hm	Rd)	TB	R	RBI	TBB	IBB	SO	HBP	SH	SF	SB	CS	SB%	GDP	Avg	OBP	SLG
1979 St. Louis	NL	14	10	2	0	0	0	(0	0)	2	4	1	2	0	2	0	0	0	1	0	1.00	0	.200	.333	.200
1980 St. Louis	NL	76	222	55	12	5	0	(0	0)	77	29	15	16	5	21	1	1	2	23	2	.82	8	.248	.299	.347
1981 St. Louis	NL	103	411	110	14	9	0	(0	0)	142	50	46	39	3	30	1	6	5	23	7	.77	9	.268	.329	.345
1982 St. Louis	NL	135	493	131	19	4	0	(0	0)	158	83	36	57	2	56	2	3	5	25	12	.68	5	.266	.341	.320
1983 St. Louis	NL	89	313	101	14	4	2	(1	1)	129	43	31	43	2	27	1	8	3	6	8	.43	7	.323	.403	.412

Year	Team	Lg	G	AB	H	2B	3B	HR	(SH	SF)	TB	R	RBI	BB			IBB	SO		SB	CS	Pct.		Avg	OBP	SLG
1984	St. Louis	NL	145	558	154	23	2	4	(1 | 3)	193	67	49	49	2		56	2	10	3	13	7	.65	11	.276	.335	.346
1985	St. Louis	NL	159	596	180	38	3	8	(4 | 4)	248	97	110	80	5		55	2	5	13	31	3	.91	6	.302	.379	.416
1986	St. Louis	NL	152	559	141	30	4	2	(1 | 1)	185	48	61	73	10		75	5	6	4	22	8	.73	8	.252	.342	.331
1987	St. Louis	NL	141	510	134	29	0	2	(1 | 1)	169	73	83	68	3		62	3	4	12	19	4	.83	12	.263	.346	.331
1988	2 ML Teams		101	354	93	16	0	2	(1 | 1)	115	46	24	51	4		51	0	3	0	13	3	.81	10	.263	.356	.325
1989	Philadelphia	NL	151	561	161	25	6	2	(0 | 2)	204	65	37	54	2		63	3	6	2	10	7	.59	9	.287	.352	.364
1990	2 ML Teams		146	547	143	26	3	5	(4 | 1)	190	48	60	50	4		58	2	6	2	7	1	.88	11	.261	.324	.347
1991	2 ML Teams		102	215	45	8	1	1	(0 | 1)	58	23	21	45	5		28	0	2	2	9	2	.82	4	.209	.344	.270
1988	St. Louis	NL	15	50	13	0	0	1	(1 | 0)	16	4	3	11	3		4	0	2	0	3	0	1.00	1	.260	.393	.320
	Minnesota	AL	86	304	80	16	0	1	(0 | 1)	99	42	21	40	1		47	0	1	0	10	3	.77	9	.263	.349	.326
1990	Philadelphia	NL	119	447	118	21	3	4	(3 | 1)	157	39	50	36	4		47	2	6	2	7	1	.88	10	.264	.320	.351
	New York	NL	27	100	25	5	0	1	(1 | 0)	33	9	10	14	0		11	0	0	0	0	0	.00	1	.250	.342	.330
1991	New York	NL	70	155	30	7	0	1	(0 | 1)	40	17	14	32	4		21	0	2	2	7	2	.78	1	.194	.328	.258
	San Francisco	NL	32	60	15	1	1	0	(0 | 0)	18	6	7	13	1		7	0	0	0	2	0	1.00	3	.250	.384	.300
13 ML YEARS			1514	5349	1450	254	41	28	(13 | 15)	1870	676	574	627	47		584	22	60	53	188	64	.75	100	.271	.347	.350

Orel Hershiser

Pitches: Right Bats: Right Pos: SP **Ht: 6' 3" Wt: 192 Born: 09/16/58 Age: 33**

			HOW MUCH HE PITCHED						WHAT HE GAVE UP												THE RESULTS					
Year	Team	Lg	G	GS	CG	GF	IP	BFP	H	R	ER	HR	SH	SF	HB	TBB	IBB	SO	WP	Bk	W	L	Pct.	ShO	Sv	ERA
1983	Los Angeles	NL	8	0	0	4	8	37	7	6	3	1	1	0	0	6	0	5	1	0	0	0	.000	0	1	3.38
1984	Los Angeles	NL	45	20	8	10	189.2	771	160	65	56	9	2	3	4	50	8	150	8	1	11	8	.579	4	2	2.66
1985	Los Angeles	NL	36	34	9	1	239.2	953	179	72	54	8	5	4	6	68	5	157	5	0	19	3	.864	5	0	2.03
1986	Los Angeles	NL	35	35	8	0	231.1	988	213	112	99	13	14	6	5	86	11	153	12	3	14	14	.500	1	0	3.85
1987	Los Angeles	NL	37	35	10	2	264.2	1093	247	105	90	17	8	2	9	74	5	190	11	2	16	16	.500	1	1	3.06
1988	Los Angeles	NL	35	34	15	1	267	1068	208	73	67	18	9	6	4	73	10	178	6	5	23	8	.742	8	1	2.26
1989	Los Angeles	NL	35	33	8	0	256.2	1047	226	75	66	9	19	6	3	77	14	178	8	4	15	15	.500	4	0	2.31
1990	Los Angeles	NL	4	4	0	0	25.1	106	26	12	12	1	1	0	1	4	0	16	0	1	1	1	.500	0	0	4.26
1991	Los Angeles	NL	21	21	0	0	112	473	112	43	43	3	2	1	5	32	6	73	2	4	7	2	.778	0	0	3.46
9 ML YEARS			256	216	58	18	1594.1	6536	1378	563	490	79	61	28	37	470	59	1100	53	20	106	67	.613	23	5	2.77

Joe Hesketh

Pitches: Left Bats: Left Pos: RP/SP **Ht: 6' 2" Wt: 170 Born: 02/15/59 Age: 33**

			HOW MUCH HE PITCHED						WHAT HE GAVE UP												THE RESULTS					
Year	Team	Lg	G	GS	CG	GF	IP	BFP	H	R	ER	HR	SH	SF	HB	TBB	IBB	SO	WP	Bk	W	L	Pct.	ShO	Sv	ERA
1984	Montreal	NL	11	5	1	2	45	182	38	12	9	2	2	2	0	15	3	32	1	3	2	2	.500	1	1	1.80
1985	Montreal	NL	25	25	2	0	155.1	618	125	52	43	10	8	2	0	45	2	113	3	3	10	5	.667	1	0	2.49
1986	Montreal	NL	15	15	0	0	82.2	362	92	46	46	11	2	2	2	31	4	67	4	3	6	5	.545	0	0	5.01
1987	Montreal	NL	18	0	0	3	28.2	128	23	12	10	2	2	0	2	15	3	31	1	0	0	0	.000	0	1	3.14
1988	Montreal	NL	60	0	0	23	72.2	304	63	30	23	1	5	4	0	35	9	64	5	1	4	3	.571	0	9	2.85
1989	Montreal	NL	43	0	0	17	48.1	219	54	34	31	5	6	2	0	26	6	44	1	3	6	4	.600	0	3	5.77
1990	3 ML Teams		45	2	0	19	59.2	269	69	35	30	7	0	1	1	25	2	50	8	0	1	6	.143	0	5	4.53
1991	Boston	AL	39	17	0	5	153.1	631	142	59	56	19	7	3	0	53	3	104	8	0	12	4	.750	0	0	3.29
1990	Montreal	NL	2	0	0	0	3	12	2	0	0	0	0	0	0	2	1	3	0	0	1	0	1.000	0	0	0.00
	Atlanta	NL	31	0	0	15	31	135	30	23	20	5	0	1	1	12	0	21	5	0	0	2	.000	0	5	5.81
	Boston	AL	12	2	0	4	25.2	122	37	12	10	2	0	0	0	11	1	26	3	0	0	4	.000	0	0	3.51
8 ML YEARS			256	64	3	69	645.2	2713	606	280	248	57	32	16	5	245	32	505	31	13	41	29	.586	2	19	3.46

Greg Hibbard

Pitches: Left Bats: Left Pos: SP **Ht: 6' 0" Wt: 190 Born: 09/13/64 Age: 27**

			HOW MUCH HE PITCHED						WHAT HE GAVE UP												THE RESULTS					
Year	Team	Lg	G	GS	CG	GF	IP	BFP	H	R	ER	HR	SH	SF	HB	TBB	IBB	SO	WP	Bk	W	L	Pct.	ShO	Sv	ERA
1989	Chicago	AL	23	23	2	0	137.1	581	142	58	49	5	5	4	2	41	0	55	4	0	6	7	.462	0	0	3.21
1990	Chicago	AL	33	33	3	0	211	871	202	80	74	11	8	10	6	55	2	92	2	1	14	9	.609	1	0	3.16
1991	Chicago	AL	32	29	5	1	194	806	196	107	93	23	8	2	2	57	1	71	1	0	11	11	.500	0	0	4.31
3 ML YEARS			88	85	10	1	542.1	2258	540	245	216	39	21	16	10	153	3	218	7	1	31	27	.534	1	0	3.58

Bryan Hickerson

Pitches: Left Bats: Left Pos: RP/SP **Ht: 6' 2" Wt: 195 Born: 10/13/63 Age: 28**

			HOW MUCH HE PITCHED						WHAT HE GAVE UP												THE RESULTS					
Year	Team	Lg	G	GS	CG	GF	IP	BFP	H	R	ER	HR	SH	SF	HB	TBB	IBB	SO	WP	Bk	W	L	Pct.	ShO	Sv	ERA
1986	Visalia	A	11	11	3	0	72.1	302	72	37	34	3	9	3	1	25	1	69	2	0	4	3	.571	0	0	4.23
1987	Clinton	A	17	10	2	3	94	371	60	17	13	1	3	1	1	37	0	103	5	0	11	0	1.000	1	1	1.24
	Shreveport	AA	4	3	0	0	16	70	20	7	7	0	1	1	0	4	0	23	1	0	1	2	.333	0	0	3.94
1989	San Jose	A	21	21	1	0	134	561	111	52	38	1	6	5	1	57	0	110	3	2	11	6	.647	1	0	2.55
1990	Shreveport	AA	27	6	0	7	66	294	71	37	31	2	4	2	1	26	2	63	2	2	3	6	.333	0	0	4.23
	Phoenix	AAA	12	4	0	3	34.1	162	48	25	21	2	2	2	0	16	2	26	0	1	0	4	.000	0	0	5.50
1991	Shreveport	AA	23	0	0	6	39	165	36	15	13	2	6	0	0	14	3	41	2	1	3	4	.429	0	2	3.00

Year Team	Lg	G	GS	CG	GF	IP	BFP	H	R	ER	HR	SH	SF	HB	TBB	IBB	SO	WP	Bk	W	L	Pct.	ShO	Sv	ERA
Phoenix	AAA	12	0	0	7	21.1	97	29	10	9	1	1	1	0	5	1	21	1	0	1	1	.500	0	2	3.80
1991 San Francisco	NL	17	6	0	4	50	212	53	20	20	3	2	0	0	17	3	43	2	0	2	2	.500	0	0	3.60

Kevin Hickey

Pitches: Left **Bats:** Left **Pos:** RP   **Ht:** 6' 1" **Wt:** 201 **Born:** 02/25/56 **Age:** 36

		HOW MUCH HE PITCHED						WHAT HE GAVE UP												THE RESULTS					
Year Team	Lg	G	GS	CG	GF	IP	BFP	H	R	ER	HR	SH	SF	HB	TBB	IBB	SO	WP	Bk	W	L	Pct.	ShO	Sv	ERA
1981 Chicago	AL	41	0	0	14	44	188	38	22	18	3	3	2	1	18	5	17	1	0	0	2	.000	0	3	3.68
1982 Chicago	AL	60	0	0	20	78	327	73	32	26	4	6	4	2	30	6	38	0	0	4	4	.500	0	6	3.00
1983 Chicago	AL	23	0	0	13	20.2	98	23	14	12	5	0	0	0	11	2	8	1	0	1	2	.333	0	5	5.23
1989 Baltimore	AL	51	0	0	17	49.1	199	38	16	16	3	2	0	1	23	4	28	3	2	2	3	.400	0	2	2.92
1990 Baltimore	AL	37	0	0	9	26.1	113	26	16	15	3	1	1	0	13	2	17	1	0	1	3	.250	0	1	5.13
1991 Baltimore	AL	19	0	0	6	14	62	15	14	14	3	0	2	0	6	0	10	0	0	1	0	1.000	0	0	9.00
6 ML YEARS		231	0	0	79	232.1	987	213	114	101	21	12	9	4	101	19	118	6	2	9	14	.391	0	17	3.91

Teddy Higuera

Pitches: Left **Bats:** Both **Pos:** SP   **Ht:** 5'10" **Wt:** 178 **Born:** 11/09/58 **Age:** 33

		HOW MUCH HE PITCHED						WHAT HE GAVE UP												THE RESULTS					
Year Team	Lg	G	GS	CG	GF	IP	BFP	H	R	ER	HR	SH	SF	HB	TBB	IBB	SO	WP	Bk	W	L	Pct.	ShO	Sv	ERA
1985 Milwaukee	AL	32	30	7	2	212.1	874	186	105	92	22	5	10	3	63	0	127	4	3	15	8	.652	2	0	3.90
1986 Milwaukee	AL	34	34	15	0	248.1	1031	226	84	77	26	7	11	3	74	5	207	3	0	20	11	.645	4	0	2.79
1987 Milwaukee	AL	35	35	14	0	261.2	1084	236	120	112	24	6	9	2	87	2	240	4	2	18	10	.643	3	0	3.85
1988 Milwaukee	AL	31	31	8	0	227.1	895	168	66	62	15	10	7	6	59	4	192	0	6	16	9	.640	1	0	2.45
1989 Milwaukee	AL	22	22	2	0	135.1	567	125	56	52	9	6	5	4	48	2	91	0	1	9	6	.600	1	0	3.46
1990 Milwaukee	AL	27	27	4	0	170	720	167	90	71	16	10	4	3	50	2	129	2	1	11	10	.524	1	0	3.76
1991 Milwaukee	AL	7	6	0	1	36.1	153	37	18	18	2	0	1	1	10	0	33	0	0	3	2	.600	0	0	4.46
7 ML YEARS		188	185	50	3	1291.1	5324	1145	529	484	114	44	47	22	391	15	1019	13	13	92	56	.622	12	0	3.37

Donnie Hill

Bats: Both **Throws:** Right **Pos:** 2B/SS   **Ht:** 5'10" **Wt:** 161 **Born:** 11/12/60 **Age:** 31

		BATTING															BASERUNNING				PERCENTAGES		
Year Team	Lg	G	AB	H	2B	3B	HR	(Hm | Rd)	TB	R	RBI	TBB	IBB	SO	HBP	SH	SF	SB	CS	SB%	GDP	Avg	OBP	SLG
1983 Oakland	AL	53	158	42	7	0	2	(1 | 1)	55	20	15	4	0	21	0	5	2	1	1	.50	3	.266	.280	.348
1984 Oakland	AL	73	174	40	6	0	2	(0 | 2)	52	21	16	5	0	12	0	4	2	1	1	.50	3	.230	.249	.299
1985 Oakland	AL	123	393	112	13	2	3	(0 | 3)	138	45	48	23	2	33	0	16	4	9	4	.69	7	.285	.321	.351
1986 Oakland	AL	108	339	96	16	2	4	(0 | 4)	128	37	29	23	1	38	0	4	0	5	2	.71	9	.283	.329	.378
1987 Chicago	AL	111	410	98	14	6	9	(1 | 8)	151	57	46	30	1	35	1	4	4	1	0	1.00	11	.239	.290	.368
1988 Chicago	AL	83	221	48	6	1	2	(1 | 1)	62	17	20	26	1	32	0	3	3	3	1	.75	3	.217	.296	.281
1990 California	AL	102	352	93	18	2	3	(0 | 3)	124	36	32	29	1	27	1	6	4	1	2	.33	10	.264	.319	.352
1991 California	AL	77	209	50	8	1	1	(1 | 0)	63	36	20	30	1	21	0	3	0	1	0	1.00	1	.239	.335	.301
8 ML YEARS		730	2256	579	88	14	26	(4 | 22)	773	269	226	170	7	219	2	45	19	22	11	.67	47	.257	.307	.343

Glenallen Hill

Bats: Right **Throws:** Right **Pos:** CF/LF/DH   **Ht:** 6' 2" **Wt:** 210 **Born:** 03/22/65 **Age:** 27

		BATTING															BASERUNNING				PERCENTAGES		
Year Team	Lg	G	AB	H	2B	3B	HR	(Hm | Rd)	TB	R	RBI	TBB	IBB	SO	HBP	SH	SF	SB	CS	SB%	GDP	Avg	OBP	SLG
1989 Toronto	AL	19	52	15	0	0	1	(1 | 0)	18	4	7	3	0	12	0	0	0	2	1	.67	0	.288	.327	.346
1990 Toronto	AL	84	260	60	11	3	12	(7 | 5)	113	47	32	18	0	62	0	0	0	8	3	.73	5	.231	.281	.435
1991 2 ML Teams		72	221	57	8	2	8	(3 | 5)	93	29	25	23	0	54	0	1	3	6	4	.60	7	.258	.324	.421
1991 Toronto	AL	35	99	25	5	2	3	(2 | 1)	43	14	11	7	0	24	0	0	2	2	2	.50	2	.253	.296	.434
Cleveland	AL	37	122	32	3	0	5	(1 | 4)	50	15	14	16	0	30	0	1	1	4	2	.67	5	.262	.345	.410
3 ML YEARS		175	533	132	19	5	21	(11 | 10)	224	80	64	44	0	128	0	1	3	16	8	.67	12	.248	.303	.420

Ken Hill

Pitches: Right **Bats:** Right **Pos:** SP   **Ht:** 6' 2" **Wt:** 175 **Born:** 12/14/65 **Age:** 26

		HOW MUCH HE PITCHED						WHAT HE GAVE UP												THE RESULTS					
Year Team	Lg	G	GS	CG	GF	IP	BFP	H	R	ER	HR	SH	SF	HB	TBB	IBB	SO	WP	Bk	W	L	Pct.	ShO	Sv	ERA
1988 St. Louis	NL	4	1	0	0	14	62	16	9	8	0	0	0	0	6	0	6	1	0	0	1	.000	0	0	5.14
1989 St. Louis	NL	33	33	2	0	196.2	862	186	92	83	9	14	5	5	99	6	112	11	2	7	15	.318	1	0	3.80
1990 St. Louis	NL	17	14	1	1	78.2	343	79	49	48	7	5	5	1	33	1	58	5	0	5	6	.455	0	0	5.49
1991 St. Louis	NL	30	30	0	0	181.1	743	147	76	72	15	7	7	6	67	4	121	7	1	11	10	.524	0	0	3.57
4 ML YEARS		84	78	3	1	470.2	2010	428	226	211	31	26	17	12	205	11	297	24	3	23	32	.418	1	0	4.03

Milt Hill

Pitches: Right **Bats:** Right **Pos:** RP **Ht:** 6' 0" **Wt:** 180 **Born:** 08/22/65 **Age:** 26

Year	Team	Lg	G	GS	CG	GF	IP	BFP	H	R	ER	HR	SH	SF	HB	TBB	IBB	SO	WP	Bk	W	L	Pct.	ShO	Sv	ERA
1987	Billings	R	21	0	0	19	32.2	125	25	10	6	1	1	0	0	4	2	40	5	0	3	1	.750	0	7	1.65
1988	Cedar Rapids	A	44	0	0	38	78.1	300	52	21	18	3	3	1	1	17	7	69	4	8	9	4	.692	0	13	2.07
1989	Chattanooga	AA	51	0	0	42	70	281	49	19	16	4	1	5	0	28	6	63	1	4	6	5	.545	0	13	2.06
1990	Nashville	AAA	48	0	0	11	71.1	276	51	20	18	4	1	5	2	18	1	58	1	4	4	4	.500	0	3	2.27
1991	Nashville	AAA	37	0	0	16	67.1	269	59	26	22	3	3	3	0	15	1	62	3	3	3	3	.500	0	3	2.94
1991	Cincinnati	NL	22	0	0	8	33.1	137	36	14	14	1	4	3	0	8	2	20	1	0	1	1	.500	0	0	3.78

Shawn Hillegas

Pitches: Right **Bats:** Right **Pos:** RP/SP **Ht:** 6' 2" **Wt:** 223 **Born:** 08/21/64 **Age:** 27

Year	Team	Lg	G	GS	CG	GF	IP	BFP	H	R	ER	HR	SH	SF	HB	TBB	IBB	SO	WP	Bk	W	L	Pct.	ShO	Sv	ERA
1987	Los Angeles	NL	12	10	0	1	58	252	52	27	23	5	4	1	0	31	0	51	4	0	4	3	.571	0	0	3.57
1988	2 ML Teams		17	16	0	0	96.2	405	84	42	40	9	1	4	4	35	1	56	3	0	6	6	.500	0	0	3.72
1989	Chicago	AL	50	13	0	12	119.2	533	132	67	63	12	4	2	3	51	4	76	4	1	7	11	.389	0	3	4.74
1990	Chicago	AL	7	0	0	3	11.1	43	4	1	1	0	1	0	0	5	1	5	2	0	0	0	.000	0	0	0.79
1991	Cleveland	AL	51	3	0	31	83	359	67	42	40	7	4	7	2	46	7	66	5	0	3	4	.429	0	7	4.34
1988	Los Angeles	NL	11	10	0	0	56.2	239	54	26	26	5	1	2	3	17	1	30	3	0	3	4	.429	0	0	4.13
	Chicago	AL	6	6	0	0	40	166	30	16	14	4	0	2	1	18	0	26	0	0	3	2	.600	0	0	3.15
	5 ML YEARS		137	42	0	47	368.2	1592	339	179	167	33	14	15	9	168	13	254	18	1	20	24	.455	0	10	4.08

Chris Hoiles

Bats: Right **Throws:** Right **Pos:** C/DH **Ht:** 6' 0" **Wt:** 213 **Born:** 03/20/65 **Age:** 27

Year	Team	Lg	G	AB	H	2B	3B	HR	(Hm	Rd)	TB	R	RBI	TBB	IBB	SO	HBP	SH	SF	SB	CS	SB%	GDP	Avg	OBP	SLG
1989	Baltimore	AL	6	9	1	1	0	0	(0	0)	2	0	1	1	0	3	0	0	0	0	0	.00	0	.111	.200	.222
1990	Baltimore	AL	23	63	12	3	0	1	(1	0)	18	7	6	5	1	12	0	0	0	0	0	.00	0	.190	.250	.286
1991	Baltimore	AL	107	341	83	15	0	11	(5	6)	131	36	31	29	1	61	0	1	1	0	2	.00	11	.243	.304	.384
	3 ML YEARS		136	413	96	19	0	12	(6	6)	151	43	38	35	2	76	1	1	1	0	2	.00	11	.232	.293	.366

Dave Hollins

Bats: Both **Throws:** Right **Pos:** 3B **Ht:** 6' 1" **Wt:** 207 **Born:** 05/25/66 **Age:** 26

Year	Team	Lg	G	AB	H	2B	3B	HR	(Hm	Rd)	TB	R	RBI	TBB	IBB	SO	HBP	SH	SF	SB	CS	SB%	GDP	Avg	OBP	SLG
1987	Spokane	A	75	278	86	14	4	2	--	--	114	52	44	53	7	36	2	3	4	20	5	.80	3	.309	.418	.410
1988	Riverside	A	139	516	157	32	1	9	--	--	218	90	92	82	2	67	1	0	9	13	11	.54	15	.304	.395	.422
1989	Wichita	AA	131	459	126	29	4	9	--	--	190	69	79	63	4	88	5	1	10	8	3	.73	4	.275	.361	.414
1991	Scranton-Wb	AAA	72	229	61	11	6	8	--	--	108	37	35	43	3	42	4	0	2	4	1	.80	7	.266	.388	.472
1990	Philadelphia	NL	72	114	21	0	0	5	(2	3)	36	14	15	10	3	28	1	0	2	0	0	.00	1	.184	.252	.316
1991	Philadelphia	NL	56	151	45	10	2	6	(3	3)	77	18	21	17	1	26	3	0	1	1	1	.50	2	.298	.378	.510
	2 ML YEARS		128	265	66	10	2	11	(5	6)	113	32	36	27	4	54	4	0	3	1	1	.50	3	.249	.324	.426

Brian Holman

Pitches: Right **Bats:** Right **Pos:** SP **Ht:** 6' 4" **Wt:** 185 **Born:** 01/25/65 **Age:** 27

Year	Team	Lg	G	GS	CG	GF	IP	BFP	H	R	ER	HR	SH	SF	HB	TBB	IBB	SO	WP	Bk	W	L	Pct.	ShO	Sv	ERA
1988	Montreal	NL	18	16	1	1	100.1	422	101	39	36	3	4	1	0	34	2	58	2	0	4	8	.333	1	0	3.23
1989	2 ML Teams		33	25	6	1	191.1	833	194	86	78	11	6	4	7	77	6	105	8	1	9	12	.429	2	0	3.67
1990	Seattle	AL	28	28	3	0	189.2	804	188	92	85	17	1	7	6	66	2	121	8	2	11	11	.500	2	0	4.03
1991	Seattle	AL	30	30	5	0	195.1	839	199	86	80	16	6	3	10	77	0	108	8	1	13	14	.481	3	0	3.69
1989	Montreal	NL	10	3	0	0	31.2	145	34	18	17	2	2	1	1	15	0	23	3	1	1	2	.333	0	0	4.83
	Seattle	AL	23	22	6	1	159.2	688	160	68	61	9	4	3	6	62	6	82	5	0	8	10	.444	2	0	3.44
	4 ML YEARS		109	99	15	2	676.2	2898	682	303	279	47	17	15	23	254	10	392	26	4	37	45	.451	6	0	3.71

Darren Holmes

Pitches: Right **Bats:** Right **Pos:** RP **Ht:** 6' 0" **Wt:** 199 **Born:** 04/25/66 **Age:** 26

Year	Team	Lg	G	GS	CG	GF	IP	BFP	H	R	ER	HR	SH	SF	HB	TBB	IBB	SO	WP	Bk	W	L	Pct.	ShO	Sv	ERA
1984	Great Falls	R	18	6	1	4	44.2		53	41	33	5	0	0	2	30	1	29	3	3	2	5	.286	0	0	6.65
1985	Vero Beach	A	33	0	0	20	63.2	277	57	31	22	0	4	5	0	35	2	46	6	1	4	3	.571	0	2	3.11
1986	Vero Beach	A	11	10	0	1	64.2	288	55	30	21	0	3	0	3	39	2	59	5	0	3	6	.333	0	0	2.92
1987	Vero Beach	A	19	19	1	0	99.2	455	111	60	50	4	4	6	1	53	0	46	5	1	6	4	.600	1	0	4.52
1988	Albuquerque	AAA	2	1	0	0	5.1	22	6	3	3	0	0	0	0	1	0	1	0	0	0	1	.000	0	0	5.06

Year	Team	Lg	G	GS	CG	GF	IP	BFP	H	R	ER	HR	SH	SF	HB	TBB	IBB	SO	WP	Bk	W	L	Pct.	ShO	Sv	ERA
1989	San Antonio	AA	17	16	3	1	110.1	471	102	59	47	5	2	4	3	44	2	81	8	6	5	8	.385	2	1	3.83
	Albuquerque	AAA	9	8	0	1	38.2	177	50	32	32	8	0	2	0	18	1	31	2	0	1	4	.200	0	0	7.45
1990	Albuquerque	AAA	56	0	0	30	92.2	389	78	34	32	3	0	4	4	39	2	99	5	2	12	2	.857	0	13	3.11
1991	Denver	AAA	1	0	0	1	1	6	1	1	1	0	0	0	0	2	0	2	0	0	0	0	.000	0	0	9.00
	Beloit	A	2	0	0	2	2	6	0	0	0	0	0	0	0	0	0	3	0	0	0	0	.000	0	2	0.00
1990	Los Angeles	NL	14	0	0	1	17.1	77	15	10	10	1	1	2	0	11	3	19	1	0	0	1	.000	0	0	5.19
1991	Milwaukee	AL	40	0	0	9	76.1	344	90	43	40	6	8	3	1	27	1	59	6	0	1	4	.200	0	3	4.72
	2 ML YEARS		54	0	0	10	93.2	421	105	53	50	7	9	5	1	38	4	78	7	0	1	5	.167	0	3	4.80

Rick Honeycutt

Pitches: Left **Bats:** Left **Pos:** RP **Ht:** 6' 1" **Wt:** 191 **Born:** 06/29/54 **Age:** 38

			HOW MUCH HE PITCHED						WHAT HE GAVE UP												THE RESULTS					
Year	Team	Lg	G	GS	CG	GF	IP	BFP	H	R	ER	HR	SH	SF	HB	TBB	IBB	SO	WP	Bk	W	L	Pct.	ShO	Sv	ERA
1977	Seattle	AL	10	3	0	3	29	125	26	16	14	7	0	2	3	11	2	17	2	1	0	1	.000	0	0	4.34
1978	Seattle	AL	26	24	4	0	134	594	150	81	73	12	9	7	3	49	5	50	3	0	5	11	.313	1	0	4.90
1979	Seattle	AL	33	28	8	2	194	839	201	103	89	22	11	6	6	67	7	83	5	1	11	12	.478	1	0	4.04
1980	Seattle	AL	30	30	9	0	203	871	221	99	89	22	11	7	3	60	7	79	4	0	10	17	.370	1	0	3.95
1981	Texas	AL	20	20	8	0	128	509	120	49	47	12	5	0	0	17	1	40	1	0	11	6	.647	2	0	3.30
1982	Texas	AL	30	26	4	3	164	728	201	103	96	20	4	8	3	54	4	64	3	1	5	17	.227	1	0	5.27
1983	2 ML Teams		34	32	6	0	213.2	865	214	85	72	15	5	6	8	50	6	74	1	3	16	11	.593	2	0	3.03
1984	Los Angeles	NL	29	28	6	0	183.2	762	180	72	58	11	6	5	2	51	11	75	1	2	10	9	.526	2	0	2.84
1985	Los Angeles	NL	31	25	1	2	142	600	141	71	54	9	5	4	1	49	7	67	2	0	8	12	.400	0	1	3.42
1986	Los Angeles	NL	32	28	0	2	171	713	164	71	63	9	6	1	3	45	4	100	4	1	11	9	.550	0	0	3.32
1987	2 ML Teams		34	24	1	1	139.1	631	158	91	73	13	1	3	4	54	4	102	5	1	3	16	.158	1	0	4.72
1988	Oakland	AL	55	0	0	17	79.2	330	74	36	31	6	3	6	3	25	2	47	3	8	3	2	.600	0	7	3.50
1989	Oakland	AL	64	0	0	24	76.2	305	56	26	20	5	5	2	1	26	3	52	6	1	2	2	.500	0	12	2.35
1990	Oakland	AL	63	0	0	13	63.1	256	46	23	19	2	2	6	1	22	2	38	1	1	2	2	.500	0	7	2.70
1991	Oakland	AL	43	0	0	7	37.2	167	37	16	15	3	2	1	2	20	3	26	0	0	2	4	.333	0	0	3.58
1983	Texas	AL	25	25	5	0	174.2	693	168	59	47	9	3	6	6	37	2	56	1	2	14	8	.636	2	0	2.42
	Los Angeles	NL	9	7	1	0	39	172	46	26	25	6	2	0	2	13	4	18	0	1	2	3	.400	0	0	5.77
1987	Los Angeles	NL	27	20	1	0	115.2	525	133	74	59	10	0	0	2	45	4	92	4	0	2	12	.143	1	0	4.59
	Oakland		7	4	0	1	23.2	106	25	17	14	3	1	3	2	9	0	10	1	1	1	4	.200	0	0	5.32
	15 ML YEARS		534	268	47	74	1959	8295	1989	942	811	168	75	64	43	600	68	914	41	20	99	131	.430	11	27	3.73

Sam Horn

Bats: Left **Throws:** Left **Pos:** DH **Ht:** 6' 5" **Wt:** 250 **Born:** 11/02/63 **Age:** 28

			BATTING																BASERUNNING				PERCENTAGES		
Year	Team	Lg	G	AB	H	2B	3B	HR	(Hm	Rd)	TB	R	RBI	TBB	IBB	SO	HBP	SH	SF	SB	CS	SB%	GDP	Avg	OBP	SLG
1987	Boston	AL	46	158	44	7	0	14	(6	8)	93	31	34	17	0	55	2	0	0	0	1	.00	5	.278	.356	.589
1988	Boston	AL	24	61	9	0	0	2	(2	0)	15	4	8	11	3	20	0	0	1	0	0	.00	1	.148	.274	.246
1989	Boston	AL	33	54	8	2	0	0	(0	0)	10	1	4	8	1	16	0	0	0	0	0	.00	4	.148	.258	.185
1990	Baltimore	AL	79	246	61	13	0	14	(8	6)	116	30	45	32	1	62	0	0	2	0	0	.00	10	.248	.332	.472
1991	Baltimore	AL	121	317	74	16	0	23	(12	11)	159	45	61	41	4	99	3	0	1	0	0	.00	10	.233	.326	.502
	5 ML YEARS		303	836	196	38	0	53	(28	25)	393	111	152	109	9	252	5	0	4	0	1	.00	28	.234	.325	.470

Vince Horsman

Pitches: Left **Bats:** Right **Pos:** RP **Ht:** 6' 2" **Wt:** 175 **Born:** 03/09/67 **Age:** 25

			HOW MUCH HE PITCHED						WHAT HE GAVE UP												THE RESULTS					
Year	Team	Lg	G	GS	CG	GF	IP	BFP	H	R	ER	HR	SH	SF	HB	TBB	IBB	SO	WP	Bk	W	L	Pct.	ShO	Sv	ERA
1985	Medicne Hat	R	18	1	0	2	40.1	0	56	31	28	1	0	0	0	23	3	30	1	0	0	3	.000	0	1	6.25
1986	Florence	A	29	9	1	10	90.2	419	93	56	41	8	1	6	1	49	0	64	5	4	4	3	.571	1	1	4.07
1987	Myrtle Bch	A	30	28	0	1	149	621	144	74	55	20	6	5	2	37	2	109	5	2	7	7	.500	0	0	3.32
1988	Knoxville	AA	20	6	1	6	58.1	260	57	34	30	5	4	4	3	28	3	40	4	1	3	2	.600	0	0	4.63
	Dunedin	A	14	2	0	3	39.2	159	28	7	6	1	1	1	1	13	2	34	4	1	3	1	.750	0	1	1.36
1989	Dunedin	A	35	1	0	23	79	330	72	24	22	3	5	1	1	27	3	60	3	4	5	6	.455	0	8	2.51
	Knoxville	AA	4	0	0	3	5	19	3	1	1	0	0	0	0	2	1	3	0	0	0	0	.000	0	1	1.80
1990	Dunedin	A	28	0	0	14	50	209	53	21	18	0	2	2	1	15	2	41	2	0	4	7	.364	0	3	3.24
	Knoxville	AA	8	0	0	2	11.2	51	11	7	6	1	1	0	0	5	2	10	1	0	2	1	.667	0	0	4.63
1991	Knoxville	AA	42	2	0	17	80.2	335	80	23	21	2	3	1	0	19	5	80	3	1	4	1	.800	0	3	2.34
1991	Toronto	AL	4	0	0	2	4	16	2	0	0	0	1	0	0	3	1	2	0	0	0	0	.000	0	0	0.00

Charlie Hough

Pitches: Right **Bats:** Right **Pos:** SP **Ht:** 6' 2" **Wt:** 190 **Born:** 01/05/48 **Age:** 44

			HOW MUCH HE PITCHED						WHAT HE GAVE UP												THE RESULTS					
Year	Team	Lg	G	GS	CG	GF	IP	BFP	H	R	ER	HR	SH	SF	HB	TBB	IBB	SO	WP	Bk	W	L	Pct.	ShO	Sv	ERA
1970	Los Angeles	NL	8	0	0	5	17	79	18	11	10	7	0	0	0	11	0	8	0	0	0	0	.000	0	2	5.29
1971	Los Angeles	NL	4	0	0	3	4	19	3	3	2	1	1	0	0	3	0	4	0	0	0	0	.000	0	0	4.50
1972	Los Angeles	NL	2	0	0	2	3	13	2	1	1	0	0	0	1	2	0	4	0	0	0	0	.000	0	0	3.00
1973	Los Angeles	NL	37	0	0	18	72	309	52	24	22	3	4	3	6	45	2	70	2	0	4	2	.667	0	5	2.75

Year	Team	Lg	G	GS	CG	GF	IP	BFP	H	R	ER	HR	SH	SF	HB	BB	IBB	SO	WP	BK	W	L	Pct	ShO	Sv	ERA
1974	Los Angeles	NL	49	0	0	16	96	389	65	45	40	12	6	8	4	40	2	63	4	0	9	4	.692	0	1	3.75
1975	Los Angeles	NL	38	0	0	24	61	266	43	25	20	3	3	0	8	34	0	34	4	1	3	7	.300	0	4	2.95
1976	Los Angeles	NL	77	0	0	55	143	600	102	43	35	6	4	1	8	77	3	81	9	0	12	8	.600	0	18	2.20
1977	Los Angeles	NL	70	1	0	53	127	551	98	53	47	10	10	4	7	70	6	105	8	0	6	12	.333	0	22	3.33
1978	Los Angeles	NL	55	0	0	31	93	390	69	38	34	6	0	0	5	48	4	66	6	0	5	5	.500	0	7	3.29
1979	Los Angeles	NL	42	14	0	10	151	662	152	88	80	16	9	4	8	66	2	76	9	1	7	5	.583	0	0	4.77
1980	2 ML Teams		35	3	2	12	93	426	91	51	47	6	7	4	5	58	2	72	11	0	3	5	.375	1	1	4.55
1981	Texas	AL	21	5	2	9	82	330	61	30	27	4	1	1	3	31	1	69	4	0	4	1	.800	0	1	2.96
1982	Texas	AL	34	34	12	0	228	954	217	111	100	21	7	4	7	72	5	128	9	0	16	13	.552	2	0	3.95
1983	Texas	AL	34	33	11	1	252	1030	219	96	89	22	5	5	3	95	0	152	6	1	15	13	.536	3	0	3.18
1984	Texas	AL	36	36	17	0	266	1133	260	127	111	26	5	7	9	94	3	164	12	2	16	14	.533	1	0	3.76
1985	Texas	AL	34	34	14	0	250.1	1018	198	102	92	23	1	7	7	83	1	141	11	3	14	16	.467	1	0	3.31
1986	Texas	AL	33	33	7	0	230.1	958	188	115	97	32	9	1	9	89	2	146	16	0	17	10	.630	2	0	3.79
1987	Texas	AL	40	40	13	0	285.1	1231	238	159	120	36	5	14	19	124	1	223	12	9	18	13	.581	0	0	3.79
1988	Texas	AL	34	34	10	0	252	1067	202	111	93	20	8	8	12	126	1	174	10	10	15	16	.484	0	0	3.32
1989	Texas	AL	30	30	5	0	182	795	168	97	88	28	3	6	6	95	2	94	7	5	10	13	.435	1	0	4.35
1990	Texas	AL	32	32	5	0	218.2	950	190	108	99	24	2	11	11	119	2	114	4	0	12	12	.500	0	0	4.07
1991	Chicago	AL	31	29	4	1	199.1	858	167	98	89	21	8	16	11	94	0	107	5	1	9	10	.474	1	0	4.02
1980	Los Angeles	NL	19	1	0	5	32	156	37	21	20	4	3	3	2	21	0	25	3	0	1	3	.250	0	1	5.63
	Texas	AL	16	2	2	7	61	270	54	30	27	2	4	1	3	37	2	47	8	0	2	2	.500	1	0	3.98
22 ML YEARS			776	358	102	240	3306	14028	2803	1536	1343	327	98	104	149	1476	39	2095	149	33	195	179	.521	12	61	3.66

Wayne Housie

Bats: Both **Throws:** Right **Pos:** CF **Ht:** 5' 9" **Wt:** 165 **Born:** 05/20/65 **Age:** 27

Year	Team	Lg	G	AB	H	2B	3B	HR	(Hm	Rd)	TB	R	RBI	TBB	IBB	SO	HBP	SH	SF	SB	CS	SB%	GDP	Avg	OBP	SLG
1986	Gastonia	A	90	336	87	10	6	2	--	--	115	55	29	43	0	85	4	4	1	38	13	.75	4	.259	.349	.342
1987	Lakeland	A	125	458	118	12	7	1	--	--	147	58	45	39	2	74	3	6	6	26	11	.70	7	.258	.316	.321
1988	Glens Falls	AA	63	202	38	4	2	1	--	--	49	26	16	28	1	34	3	5	2	9	5	.64	2	.188	.294	.243
	Lakeland	A	55	212	57	11	3	0	--	--	74	31	23	13	0	40	3	2	1	24	6	.80	1	.269	.319	.349
1989	London	AA	127	434	103	17	2	5	--	--	139	56	28	52	3	90	4	3	3	23	14	.62	5	.237	.323	.320
1990	Salinas	A	92	367	99	20	6	5	--	--	146	51	49	22	1	72	4	5	3	27	11	.71	5	.270	.316	.398
	New Britain	AA	30	113	31	8	3	1	--	--	48	13	12	6	0	33	1	5	0	7	2	.78	0	.274	.317	.425
1991	New Britain	AA	113	444	123	24	2	6	--	--	169	58	26	55	2	86	3	6	0	43	14	.75	5	.277	.361	.381
	Pawtucket	AAA	21	79	26	9	2	2	--	--	41	14	8	6	0	20	1	0	0	2	2	.50	1	.329	.384	.519
1991	Boston	AL	11	8	2	1	0	0	(0	0)	3	2	0	1	0	3	0	1	0	1	0	1.00	1	.250	.333	.375

Chris Howard

Bats: Right **Throws:** Right **Pos:** C **Ht:** 6' 2" **Wt:** 200 **Born:** 02/27/66 **Age:** 26

Year	Team	Lg	G	AB	H	2B	3B	HR	(Hm	Rd)	TB	R	RBI	TBB	IBB	SO	HBP	SH	SF	SB	CS	SB%	GDP	Avg	OBP	SLG
1988	Bellingham	A	2	9	3	0	0	1	--	--	6	3	3	1	0	2	0	0	0	0	0	.00	0	.333	.400	.667
	Wausau	A	61	187	45	10	1	7	--	--	78	20	20	18	0	60	3	0	1	1	3	.25	4	.241	.316	.417
1989	Wausau	A	36	125	30	8	0	4	--	--	50	13	32	13	1	35	1	0	1	0	0	.00	0	.240	.314	.400
	Williamsprt	AA	86	296	75	13	0	9	--	--	115	30	36	28	0	79	5	2	0	0	1	.00	10	.253	.328	.389
1990	Williamsprt	AA	118	401	95	19	1	5	--	--	131	48	49	37	1	91	3	4	4	3	1	.75	16	.237	.303	.327
1991	Calgary	AAA	82	293	72	12	1	8	--	--	110	32	36	16	1	56	2	3	1	1	1	.50	10	.246	.288	.375
1991	Seattle	AL	9	6	1	1	0	0	(0	0)	2	1	1	1	0	2	0	0	0	0	0	.00	0	.167	.286	.333

Dave Howard

Bats: Both **Throws:** Right **Pos:** SS/2B **Ht:** 6' 0" **Wt:** 165 **Born:** 02/26/67 **Age:** 25

Year	Team	Lg	G	AB	H	2B	3B	HR	(Hm	Rd)	TB	R	RBI	TBB	IBB	SO	HBP	SH	SF	SB	CS	SB%	GDP	Avg	OBP	SLG
1987	Ft. Myers	A	89	289	56	9	4	1	--	--	76	26	19	30	0	68	0	7	0	11	10	.52	3	.194	.270	.263
1988	Appleton	A	110	368	82	9	4	1	--	--	102	48	22	25	0	80	2	4	3	7	5	.58	3	.223	.274	.277
1989	Baseball Cy	A	83	267	63	7	3	3	--	--	85	36	30	23	1	44	1	3	2	12	2	.86	1	.236	.297	.318
1990	Memphis	AA	116	384	96	10	4	5	--	--	129	41	44	39	0	73	1	10	6	15	4	.79	8	.250	.316	.336
1991	Omaha	AAA	14	41	5	0	0	0	--	--	5	2	2	7	0	11	1	2	0	1	1	.50	0	.122	.265	.122
1991	Kansas City	AL	94	236	51	7	0	1	(0	1)	61	20	17	16	0	45	1	9	2	3	2	.60	1	.216	.267	.258

Thomas Howard

Bats: Both **Throws:** Right **Pos:** CF/LF/RF **Ht:** 6' 2" **Wt:** 198 **Born:** 12/11/64 **Age:** 27

Year	Team	Lg	G	AB	H	2B	3B	HR	(Hm	Rd)	TB	R	RBI	TBB	IBB	SO	HBP	SH	SF	SB	CS	SB%	GDP	Avg	OBP	SLG
1986	Spokane	A	13	55	23	3	3	3	--	--	38	16	17	3	0	9	1	0	0	2	1	.67	0	.418	.458	.691
	Reno	A	61	223	57	7	3	10	--	--	100	35	39	34	1	49	0	1	3	10	2	.83	3	.256	.350	.448

Year	Team	Lg	G	AB	H	2B	3B	HR	(Hm	Rd)	TB	R	RBI	TBB	IBB	SO	HBP	SH	SF	SB	CS	SB%	GDP	Avg	OBP	SLG
1987	Wichita	AA	113	401	133	27	4	14	--	--	210	72	60	36	9	72	1	8	1	26	8	.76	8	.332	.387	.524
1988	Las Vegas	AAA	44	167	42	9	1	0	--	--	53	29	15	12	2	31	1	1	0	3	4	.43	5	.251	.306	.317
	Wichita	AA	29	103	31	9	2	0	--	--	44	15	16	13	0	14	0	0	0	6	3	.67	3	.301	.379	.427
1989	Las Vegas	AAA	80	303	91	18	3	3	--	--	124	45	31	30	1	56	0	3	1	22	11	.67	6	.300	.362	.409
1990	Las Vegas	AAA	89	341	112	26	8	5	--	--	169	58	51	44	5	63	0	4	4	27	5	.84	5	.328	.401	.496
1991	Las Vegas	AAA	25	94	29	3	1	2	--	--	40	22	16	10	3	16	0	1	2	11	5	.69	1	.309	.368	.426
1990	San Diego	NL	20	44	12	2	0	0	(0	0)	14	4	0	0	0	11	0	1	0	0	1	1.00	1	.273	.273	.318
1991	San Diego	NL	106	281	70	12	3	4	(4	0)	100	30	22	24	4	57	1	2	1	10	7	.59	4	.249	.309	.356
	2 ML YEARS		126	325	82	14	3	4	(4	0)	114	34	22	24	4	68	1	3	1	10	8	.56	5	.252	.305	.351

Steve Howe

Pitches: Left **Bats:** Left **Pos:** RP   **Ht:** 6' 1" **Wt:** 180 **Born:** 03/10/58 **Age:** 34

			HOW MUCH HE PITCHED						WHAT HE GAVE UP										THE RESULTS					
Year	Team	Lg	G	GS	CG	GF	IP	BFP	H	R	ER	HR	SH	SF	HB	TBB	IBB	SO	WP	Bk	W	L	Pct.	ShO	Sv	ERA
1980	Los Angeles	NL	59	0	0	36	85	359	83	33	25	1	8	3	2	22	10	39	1	0	7	9	.438	0	17	2.65
1981	Los Angeles	NL	41	0	0	25	54	227	51	17	15	2	4	4	0	18	7	32	0	0	5	3	.625	0	8	2.50
1982	Los Angeles	NL	66	0	0	41	99.1	393	87	27	23	3	10	3	0	17	11	49	1	0	7	5	.583	0	13	2.08
1983	Los Angeles	NL	46	0	0	33	68.2	274	55	15	11	2	5	3	1	12	7	52	3	0	4	7	.364	0	18	1.44
1985	2 ML Teams		32	0	0	19	41	198	58	33	25	3	2	5	1	12	4	21	3	0	3	4	.429	0	3	5.49
1987	Texas	AL	24	0	0	15	31.1	131	33	15	15	2	2	0	3	8	1	19	2	1	3	3	.500	0	1	4.31
1991	New York	AL	37	0	0	10	48.1	189	39	12	9	1	2	1	3	7	2	34	2	0	3	1	.750	0	3	1.68
1985	Los Angeles	NL	19	0	0	14	22	104	30	17	12	2	2	2	1	5	2	11	2	0	1	1	.500	0	3	4.91
	Minnesota	AL	13	0	0	5	19	94	28	16	13	1	0	3	0	7	2	10	1	0	2	3	.400	0	0	6.16
	7 ML YEARS		305	0	0	179	427.2	1771	406	152	123	14	33	19	10	96	42	246	12	1	32	32	.500	0	63	2.59

Jack Howell

Bats: Left **Throws:** Right **Pos:** 3B/2B   **Ht:** 6' 0" **Wt:** 190 **Born:** 08/18/61 **Age:** 30

			BATTING																BASERUNNING				PERCENTAGES		
Year	Team	Lg	G	AB	H	2B	3B	HR	(Hm	Rd)	TB	R	RBI	TBB	IBB	SO	HBP	SH	SF	SB	CS	SB%	GDP	Avg	OBP	SLG
1985	California	AL	43	137	27	4	0	5	(2	3)	46	19	18	16	2	33	0	4	1	1	1	.50	1	.197	.279	.336
1986	California	AL	63	151	41	14	2	4	(1	3)	71	26	21	19	0	28	0	3	2	2	0	1.00	1	.272	.349	.470
1987	California	AL	138	449	110	18	5	23	(15	8)	207	64	64	57	4	118	2	1	2	4	3	.57	7	.245	.331	.461
1988	California	AL	154	500	127	32	2	16	(9	7)	211	59	63	46	8	130	6	4	2	2	4	.25	8	.254	.323	.422
1989	California	AL	144	474	108	19	4	20	(9	11)	195	56	52	52	9	125	3	3	1	0	3	.00	8	.228	.308	.411
1990	California	AL	105	316	72	19	1	8	(3	5)	117	35	33	46	5	61	1	1	2	3	0	1.00	3	.228	.326	.370
1991	2 ML Teams		90	241	50	5	1	8	(3	5)	81	35	23	29	1	44	0	1	0	1	1	.50	2	.207	.293	.336
1991	California	AL	32	81	17	2	0	2	(0	2)	25	11	7	11	0	11	0	0	0	1	1	.50	1	.210	.304	.309
	San Diego	NL	58	160	33	3	1	6	(3	3)	56	24	16	18	1	33	0	1	0	0	0	.00	1	.206	.287	.350
	7 ML YEARS		737	2268	535	111	15	84	(42	42)	928	294	274	265	29	539	12	17	10	13	14	.48	30	.236	.318	.409

Jay Howell

Pitches: Right **Bats:** Right **Pos:** RP   **Ht:** 6' 3" **Wt:** 220 **Born:** 11/26/55 **Age:** 36

			HOW MUCH HE PITCHED						WHAT HE GAVE UP										THE RESULTS					
Year	Team	Lg	G	GS	CG	GF	IP	BFP	H	R	ER	HR	SH	SF	HB	TBB	IBB	SO	WP	Bk	W	L	Pct.	ShO	Sv	ERA
1980	Cincinnati	NL	5	0	0	1	3	19	8	5	5	0	0	1	1	0	0	1	0	0	0	0	.000	0	0	15.00
1981	Chicago	NL	10	2	0	1	22	97	23	13	12	3	1	1	2	10	2	10	0	0	2	0	1.000	0	0	4.91
1982	New York	AL	6	6	0	0	28	138	42	25	24	1	0	2	0	13	0	21	1	0	2	3	.400	0	0	7.71
1983	New York	AL	19	12	2	3	82	368	89	53	49	7	1	5	3	35	0	61	2	1	1	5	.167	0	1	5.38
1984	New York	AL	61	1	0	23	103.2	426	86	33	31	5	3	3	0	34	3	109	4	0	9	4	.692	0	7	2.69
1985	Oakland	AL	63	0	0	58	98	414	98	32	31	5	3	4	1	31	3	68	4	1	9	8	.529	0	29	2.85
1986	Oakland	AL	38	0	0	33	53.1	230	53	23	20	3	3	1	1	23	4	42	4	0	3	6	.333	0	16	3.38
1987	Oakland	AL	36	0	0	27	44.1	200	48	30	29	6	3	2	1	21	1	35	4	0	3	4	.429	0	16	5.89
1988	Los Angeles	NL	50	0	0	38	65	262	44	16	15	1	3	3	1	21	2	70	2	2	5	3	.625	0	21	2.08
1989	Los Angeles	NL	56	0	0	41	79.2	312	60	15	14	3	4	2	0	22	6	55	1	0	5	3	.625	0	28	1.58
1990	Los Angeles	NL	45	0	0	35	66	271	59	17	16	5	1	0	6	20	3	59	4	1	5	5	.500	0	16	2.18
1991	Los Angeles	NL	44	0	0	35	51	202	39	19	18	3	5	2	1	11	3	40	0	0	6	5	.545	0	16	3.18
	12 ML YEARS		433	21	2	295	696	2939	649	281	264	42	27	26	17	241	27	571	26	5	50	46	.521	0	149	3.41

Dann Howitt

Bats: Left **Throws:** Right **Pos:** CF   **Ht:** 6' 5" **Wt:** 205 **Born:** 02/13/64 **Age:** 28

			BATTING																BASERUNNING				PERCENTAGES		
Year	Team	Lg	G	AB	H	2B	3B	HR	(Hm	Rd)	TB	R	RBI	TBB	IBB	SO	HBP	SH	SF	SB	CS	SB%	GDP	Avg	OBP	SLG
1986	Medford	A	66	208	66	9	2	6	--	--	97	36	37	49	3	37	1	1	1	5	1	.83	7	.317	.448	.466
1987	Modesto	A	109	336	70	11	2	8	--	--	109	44	42	59	1	110	4	3	3	7	9	.44	8	.208	.331	.324
1988	Modesto	A	132	480	121	20	2	18	--	--	199	75	76	81	3	106	2	0	2	11	5	.69	9	.252	.361	.415
	Tacoma	AAA	4	15	2	1	0	0	--	--	3	1	0	0	0	4	0	0	0	0	0	.00	0	.133	.133	.200
1989	Huntsville	AA	138	509	143	28	2	26	--	--	253	78	111	68	7	107	3	2	6	2	1	.67	6	.281	.365	.497

Year	Team	Lg	G	AB	H	2B	3B	HR	(Hm	Rd)	TB	R	RBI	TBB	IBB	SO	HBP	SH	SF	SB	CS	SB%	GDP	Avg	OBP	SLG
1990	Tacoma	AAA	118	437	116	30	1	11	--	--	181	58	69	38	3	95	2	0	4	4	4	.50	16	.265	.324	.414
1991	Tacoma	AAA	122	449	120	28	6	14	--	--	202	58	73	49	2	92	2	1	5	5	2	.71	14	.267	.339	.450
1989	Oakland	AL	3	3	0	0	0	0	(0	0)	0	0	0	0	0	2	0	0	0	0	0	.00	0	.000	.000	.000
1990	Oakland	AL	14	22	3	0	1	0	(0	0)	5	3	1	3	0	12	0	0	0	0	0	.00	0	.136	.240	.227
1991	Oakland	AL	21	42	7	1	0	1	(0	1)	11	5	3	1	0	12	0	0	1	0	0	.00	1	.167	.182	.262
	3 ML YEARS		38	67	10	1	1	1	(0	1)	16	8	4	4	0	26	0	0	1	0	0	.00	1	.149	.194	.239

Kent Hrbek

Bats: Left   **Throws:** Right   **Pos:** 1B   **Ht:** 6' 4"   **Wt:** 253   **Born:** 05/21/60   **Age:** 32

									BATTING											BASERUNNING				PERCENTAGES		
Year	Team	Lg	G	AB	H	2B	3B	HR	(Hm	Rd)	TB	R	RBI	TBB	IBB	SO	HBP	SH	SF	SB	CS	SB%	GDP	Avg	OBP	SLG
1981	Minnesota	AL	24	67	16	5	0	1	(0	1)	24	5	7	5	1	9	1	0	0	0	0	.00	0	.239	.301	.358
1982	Minnesota	AL	140	532	160	21	4	23	(11	12)	258	82	92	54	12	80	0	1	4	3	1	.75	17	.301	.363	.485
1983	Minnesota	AL	141	515	153	41	5	16	(7	9)	252	75	84	57	5	71	3	0	7	4	6	.40	12	.297	.366	.489
1984	Minnesota	AL	149	559	174	31	3	27	(15	12)	292	80	107	65	15	87	4	1	6	1	1	.50	17	.311	.383	.522
1985	Minnesota	AL	158	593	165	31	2	21	(10	11)	263	78	93	67	12	87	2	0	4	1	1	.50	12	.278	.351	.444
1986	Minnesota	AL	149	550	147	27	1	29	(18	11)	263	85	91	71	9	81	6	0	9	2	2	.50	15	.267	.353	.478
1987	Minnesota	AL	143	477	136	20	1	34	(20	14)	260	85	90	84	12	60	0	0	5	5	2	.71	13	.285	.389	.545
1988	Minnesota	AL	143	510	159	31	0	25	(13	12)	265	75	76	67	7	54	0	2	7	0	3	.00	9	.312	.387	.520
1989	Minnesota	AL	109	375	102	17	0	25	(17	8)	194	59	84	53	4	35	1	1	4	3	0	1.00	6	.272	.360	.517
1990	Minnesota	AL	143	492	141	26	0	22	(8	14)	233	61	79	69	8	45	7	2	8	5	2	.71	17	.287	.377	.474
1991	Minnesota	AL	132	462	131	20	1	20	(11	9)	213	72	89	67	4	48	0	3	2	4	4	.50	15	.284	.373	.461
	11 ML YEARS		1431	5132	1484	270	17	243	(130	113)	2517	757	892	659	89	657	24	10	54	28	22	.56	133	.289	.369	.490

Rex Hudler

Bats: Right   **Throws:** Right   **Pos:** LF/CF   **Ht:** 6' 0"   **Wt:** 180   **Born:** 09/02/60   **Age:** 31

									BATTING											BASERUNNING				PERCENTAGES		
Year	Team	Lg	G	AB	H	2B	3B	HR	(Hm	Rd)	TB	R	RBI	TBB	IBB	SO	HBP	SH	SF	SB	CS	SB%	GDP	Avg	OBP	SLG
1984	New York	AL	9	7	1	1	0	0	(0	0)	2	2	0	1	0	5	1	0	0	0	0	.00	0	.143	.333	.286
1985	New York	AL	20	51	8	0	1	0	(0	0)	10	4	1	1	0	9	0	5	0	1	1	.50	0	.157	.173	.196
1986	Baltimore	AL	14	1	0	0	0	0	(0	0)	0	1	0	0	0	0	0	0	0	1	0	1.00	0	.000	.000	.000
1988	Montreal	NL	77	216	59	14	2	4	(1	3)	89	38	14	10	6	34	0	1	2	29	7	.81	2	.273	.303	.412
1989	Montreal	NL	92	155	38	7	0	6	(3	3)	63	21	13	6	2	23	1	0	0	15	4	.79	2	.245	.278	.406
1990	2 ML Teams		93	220	62	11	2	7	(2	5)	98	31	22	12	1	32	2	2	1	18	10	.64	3	.282	.323	.445
1991	St. Louis	NL	101	207	47	10	2	1	(1	0)	64	21	15	10	1	29	0	2	2	12	8	.60	1	.227	.260	.309
1990	Montreal	NL	4	3	1	0	0	0	(0	0)	1	1	0	0	0	1	0	0	0	0	0	.00	0	.333	.333	.333
	St. Louis	NL	89	217	61	11	2	7	(2	5)	97	30	22	12	1	31	2	2	1	18	10	.64	3	.281	.323	.447
	7 ML YEARS		406	857	215	43	7	18	(7	11)	326	118	65	40	10	132	4	10	5	75	30	.71	8	.251	.286	.380

Mike Huff

Bats: Right   **Throws:** Right   **Pos:** CF/RF   **Ht:** 6' 1"   **Wt:** 180   **Born:** 08/11/63   **Age:** 28

									BATTING											BASERUNNING				PERCENTAGES		
Year	Team	Lg	G	AB	H	2B	3B	HR	(Hm	Rd)	TB	R	RBI	TBB	IBB	SO	HBP	SH	SF	SB	CS	SB%	GDP	Avg	OBP	SLG
1989	Los Angeles	NL	12	25	5	1	0	0	(0	0)	6	4	2	3	0	6	1	1	0	0	1	.00	0	.200	.310	.360
1991	2 ML Teams		102	243	61	10	2	3	(1	2)	84	42	25	37	2	48	6	6	2	14	4	.78	7	.251	.361	.346
1991	Cleveland	AL	51	146	35	6	1	2	(1	1)	49	28	10	25	0	30	4	3	1	11	2	.85	2	.240	.364	.336
	Chicago	AL	51	97	26	4	1	1	(0	1)	35	14	15	12	2	18	2	3	1	3	2	.60	5	.268	.357	.361
	2 ML YEARS		114	268	66	11	2	4	(1	3)	93	46	27	40	2	54	7	7	2	14	5	.74	7	.246	.356	.347

Mark Huismann

Pitches: Right   **Bats:** Right   **Pos:** RP   **Ht:** 6' 3"   **Wt:** 205   **Born:** 05/11/58   **Age:** 34

						HOW MUCH HE PITCHED				WHAT HE GAVE UP									THE RESULTS					
Year	Team	Lg	G	GS	CG	GF	IP	BFP	H	R	ER	HR	SH	SF	HB	TBB	IBB	SO	WP	Bk	W	L	Pct.	ShO	Sv	ERA
1983	Kansas City	AL	13	0	0	5	30.2	135	29	20	19	1	1	1	0	17	3	20	4	1	2	1	.667	0	0	5.58
1984	Kansas City	AL	38	0	0	23	75	324	84	38	35	7	3	5	1	21	3	54	3	0	3	3	.500	0	3	4.20
1985	Kansas City	AL	9	0	0	6	18.2	70	14	4	4	1	1	2	0	3	0	9	0	0	1	0	1.000	0	0	1.93
1986	2 ML Teams		46	1	0	19	97.1	408	98	47	41	19	0	3	1	25	0	72	5	0	3	4	.429	0	5	3.79
1987	2 ML Teams		26	0	0	11	50	212	48	32	28	7	4	3	2	12	0	38	3	0	2	3	.400	0	2	5.04
1988	Detroit	AL	5	0	0	2	5.1	23	6	3	3	0	0	0	0	2	1	6	0	0	1	0	1.000	0	0	5.06
1989	Baltimore	AL	8	0	0	4	11.1	48	13	8	8	0	0	1	0	0	0	13	1	0	0	0	.000	0	1	6.35
1990	Pittsburgh	NL	2	0	0	0	3	15	6	5	3	2	0	0	1	1	0	2	1	0	1	0	1.000	0	0	9.00
1991	Pittsburgh	NL	5	0	0	0	5	25	7	4	4	1	1	0	0	2	1	5	0	0	0	0	.000	0	0	7.20
1986	Kansas City	AL	10	0	0	5	17.1	74	18	8	8	1	0	1	0	6	0	13	1	0	0	1	.000	0	1	4.15
	Seattle	AL	36	1	0	14	80	334	80	39	33	18	0	2	1	19	0	59	4	0	3	3	.500	0	4	3.71
1987	Seattle	AL	6	0	0	1	14.2	61	10	10	8	1	3	1	2	4	0	15	0	0	0	0	.000	0	0	4.91
	Cleveland	AL	20	0	0	10	35.1	151	38	22	20	6	1	2	0	8	0	23	3	0	2	3	.400	0	2	5.09
	9 ML YEARS		152	1	0	67	296.1	1260	305	163	145	37	9	15	5	83	8	219	17	1	13	11	.542	0	11	4.40

Tim Hulett

Bats: Right **Throws:** Right **Pos:** 3B/2B/DH   **Ht:** 6' 0" **Wt:** 197 **Born:** 01/12/60 **Age:** 32

								BATTING										BASERUNNING				PERCENTAGES		
Year	Team	Lg	G	AB	H	2B	3B	HR	(Hm | Rd)	TB	R	RBI	TBB	IBB	SO	HBP	SH	SF	SB	CS	SB%	GDP	Avg	OBP	SLG
1983	Chicago	AL	6	5	1	0	0	0	(0 | 0)	1	0	0	0	0	0	0	0	0	1	0	1.00	0	.200	.200	.200
1984	Chicago	AL	8	7	0	0	0	0	(0 | 0)	0	1	0	1	0	4	0	0	0	1	0	1.00	0	.000	.125	.000
1985	Chicago	AL	141	395	106	19	4	5	(2 | 3)	148	52	37	30	1	81	4	4	3	6	4	.60	8	.268	.324	.375
1986	Chicago	AL	150	520	120	16	5	17	(7 | 10)	197	53	44	21	0	91	1	6	4	4	1	.80	11	.231	.260	.379
1987	Chicago	AL	68	240	52	10	0	7	(3 | 4)	83	20	28	10	1	41	0	5	2	0	2	.00	6	.217	.246	.346
1989	Baltimore	AL	33	97	27	5	0	3	(2 | 1)	41	12	18	10	0	17	0	1	1	0	0	.00	3	.278	.343	.423
1990	Baltimore	AL	53	153	39	7	1	3	(2 | 1)	57	16	16	15	0	41	0	1	0	1	0	1.00	2	.255	.321	.373
1991	Baltimore	AL	79	206	42	9	0	7	(1 | 6)	72	29	18	13	0	49	1	1	0	0	1	.00	3	.204	.255	.350
	8 ML YEARS		538	1623	387	66	10	42	(17 | 25)	599	183	161	100	2	324	6	18	10	13	8	.62	33	.238	.283	.369

Mike Humphreys

Bats: Right **Throws:** Right **Pos:** 3B   **Ht:** 6' 0" **Wt:** 185 **Born:** 04/10/67 **Age:** 25

								BATTING										BASERUNNING				PERCENTAGES		
Year	Team	Lg	G	AB	H	2B	3B	HR	(Hm | Rd)	TB	R	RBI	TBB	IBB	SO	HBP	SH	SF	SB	CS	SB%	GDP	Avg	OBP	SLG
1988	Spokane	A	76	303	93	16	5	6	--	--	137	67	59	46	1	57	0	0	4	21	4	.84	9	.307	.394	.452
1989	Riverside	A	117	420	121	26	1	13	--	--	188	77	66	72	4	79	7	3	5	23	10	.70	9	.288	.397	.448
1990	Wichita	AA	116	421	116	21	4	17	--	--	196	92	79	67	4	79	5	2	4	37	9	.80	6	.276	.378	.466
	Las Vegas	AAA	12	42	10	1	0	2	--	--	17	7	6	4	0	11	1	2	0	1	0	1.00	4	.238	.319	.405
1991	Columbus	AAA	117	413	117	23	5	9	--	--	177	71	53	63	3	61	3	1	6	34	9	.79	10	.283	.377	.429
1991	New York	AL	25	40	8	0	0	0	(0 | 0)	8	9	3	9	0	7	0	1	0	2	0	1.00	0	.200	.347	.200

Todd Hundley

Bats: Both **Throws:** Right **Pos:** C   **Ht:** 5'11" **Wt:** 185 **Born:** 05/27/69 **Age:** 23

								BATTING										BASERUNNING				PERCENTAGES		
Year	Team	Lg	G	AB	H	2B	3B	HR	(Hm | Rd)	TB	R	RBI	TBB	IBB	SO	HBP	SH	SF	SB	CS	SB%	GDP	Avg	OBP	SLG
1987	Little Fls	A	34	103	15	4	0	1	--	--	22	12	10	12	2	27	3	0	0	0	0	.00	2	.146	.254	.214
1988	Little Fls	A	52	176	33	8	0	2	--	--	47	23	18	16	1	31	4	2	1	1	1	.50	2	.188	.269	.267
	St. Lucie	A	1	1	0	0	0	0	--	--	0	0	0	2	0	1	0	0	0	0	0	.00	0	.000	.667	.000
1989	Columbia	A	125	439	118	23	4	11	--	--	182	67	66	54	10	67	8	1	5	6	3	.67	20	.269	.356	.415
1990	Jackson	AA	81	279	74	12	2	1	--	--	93	27	35	34	3	44	1	0	3	5	3	.63	5	.265	.344	.333
1991	Tidewater	AAA	125	454	124	24	4	14	--	--	198	62	66	51	2	95	2	4	8	1	2	.33	12	.273	.344	.436
1990	New York	NL	36	67	14	6	0	0	(0 | 0)	20	8	2	6	0	18	0	1	0	0	0	.00	1	.209	.274	.299
1991	New York	NL	21	60	8	0	1	1	(1 | 0)	13	5	7	6	0	14	1	1	1	0	0	.00	3	.133	.221	.217
	2 ML YEARS		57	127	22	6	1	1	(1 | 0)	33	13	9	12	0	32	1	2	1	0	0	.00	4	.173	.248	.260

Brian Hunter

Bats: Right **Throws:** Left **Pos:** 1B   **Ht:** 6' 0" **Wt:** 195 **Born:** 03/04/68 **Age:** 24

								BATTING										BASERUNNING				PERCENTAGES		
Year	Team	Lg	G	AB	H	2B	3B	HR	(Hm | Rd)	TB	R	RBI	TBB	IBB	SO	HBP	SH	SF	SB	CS	SB%	GDP	Avg	OBP	SLG
1987	Pulaski	R	65	251	58	10	2	8	--	--	96	38	30	18	0	47	5	0	1	3	2	.60	7	.231	.295	.382
1988	Burlington	A	117	417	108	17	0	22	--	--	191	58	71	45	2	90	8	1	7	7	2	.78	7	.259	.338	.458
	Durham	A	13	49	17	3	0	3	--	--	29	13	9	7	0	8	0	0	0	2	0	1.00	0	.347	.429	.592
1989	Greenville	AA	124	451	114	19	2	19	--	--	194	57	82	33	2	61	7	1	9	5	4	.56	4	.253	.308	.430
1990	Richmond	AAA	43	137	27	4	0	5	--	--	46	13	16	18	0	37	0	1	1	2	1	.67	0	.197	.288	.336
	Greenville	AA	88	320	77	13	1	14	--	--	134	45	55	43	1	62	3	0	4	3	4	.43	6	.241	.332	.419
1991	Richmond	AAA	48	181	47	7	0	10	--	--	84	28	30	11	1	24	1	2	3	3	2	.60	6	.260	.301	.464
1991	Atlanta	NL	97	271	68	16	1	12	(7 | 5)	122	32	50	17	0	48	1	0	2	0	2	.00	6	.251	.296	.450

Jim Hunter

Pitches: Right **Bats:** Right **Pos:** SP   **Ht:** 6' 3" **Wt:** 205 **Born:** 06/22/64 **Age:** 28

				HOW MUCH HE PITCHED				WHAT HE GAVE UP										THE RESULTS					
Year	Team	Lg	G	GS	CG	GF	IP	BFP	H	R	ER	HR	SH	SF	HB	TBB	IBB	SO	WP	Bk	W	L	Pct.	ShO	Sv	ERA
1985	Jamestown	A	14	13	1	1	70.2	310	65	30	22	1	2	1	1	34	1	41	3	0	3	3	.500	0	0	2.80
1986	Burlington	A	9	9	1	0	45	210	52	28	23	1	0	1	2	25	0	28	2	1	2	3	.400	0	0	4.60
	Beloit	A	15	15	2	0	89.1	382	91	47	37	4	2	1	5	22	3	52	5	1	4	5	.444	0	0	3.73
1987	Stockton	A	8	8	0	0	51.1	214	39	16	14	1	1	2	5	20	0	44	2	0	6	1	.857	0	0	2.45
	El Paso	AA	16	15	1	0	95.2	421	117	60	49	14	1	2	2	33	1	62	4	0	5	5	.500	0	0	4.61
1988	El Paso	AA	26	26	2	0	147.2	666	163	107	93	15	3	4	8	77	2	103	4	3	8	11	.421	0	0	5.67
1989	El Paso	AA	19	19	4	0	124.2	547	149	70	58	9	3	4	4	45	1	68	5	0	7	10	.412	0	0	4.19
1990	El Paso	AA	9	9	2	0	62	258	64	31	27	9	0	1	1	15	0	37	0	0	6	3	.667	0	0	3.92

Year Team	Lg	G	GS	CG	GF	IP	BFP	H	R	ER	HR	SH	SF	HB	TBB	IBB	SO	WP	Bk	W	L	Pct.	ShO	Sv	ERA
Denver	AAA	20	20	2	0	117	512	138	76	61	5	4	8	5	45	1	57	1	0	6	8	.429	0	0	4.69
1991 Denver	AAA	14	14	0	0	87.1	374	94	38	32	6	4	1	5	27	0	43	2	0	7	4	.636	0	0	3.30
1991 Milwaukee	AL	8	6	0	0	31	152	45	26	25	3	1	1	4	17	0	14	3	0	0	5	.000	0	0	7.26

Bruce Hurst

Pitches: Left Bats: Left Pos: SP Ht: 6' 3" Wt: 219 Born: 03/24/58 Age: 34

		HOW MUCH HE PITCHED						WHAT HE GAVE UP												THE RESULTS					
Year Team	Lg	G	GS	CG	GF	IP	BFP	H	R	ER	HR	SH	SF	HB	TBB	IBB	SO	WP	Bk	W	L	Pct.	ShO	Sv	ERA
1980 Boston	AL	12	7	0	2	31	147	39	33	31	4	0	2	2	16	0	16	4	2	2	2	.500	0	0	9.00
1981 Boston	AL	5	5	0	0	23	104	23	11	11	1	0	2	1	12	2	11	2	0	2	0	1.000	0	0	4.30
1982 Boston	AL	28	19	0	3	117	535	161	87	75	16	2	7	3	40	2	53	5	0	3	7	.300	0	0	5.77
1983 Boston	AL	33	32	6	0	211.1	903	241	102	96	22	3	4	3	62	5	115	1	2	12	12	.500	2	0	4.09
1984 Boston	AL	33	33	9	0	218	958	232	106	95	25	3	4	6	88	3	136	1	1	12	12	.500	2	0	3.92
1985 Boston	AL	35	31	6	0	229.1	973	243	123	115	31	6	4	3	70	4	189	3	4	11	13	.458	1	0	4.51
1986 Boston	AL	25	25	11	0	174.1	721	169	63	58	18	5	3	3	50	2	167	6	0	13	8	.619	4	0	2.99
1987 Boston	AL	33	33	15	0	238.2	1001	239	124	117	35	5	8	1	76	5	190	3	1	15	13	.536	3	0	4.41
1988 Boston	AL	33	32	7	0	216.2	922	222	98	88	21	8	5	2	65	1	166	5	3	18	6	.750	1	0	3.66
1989 San Diego	NL	33	33	10	0	244.2	990	214	84	73	16	18	3	0	66	7	179	8	0	15	11	.577	2	0	2.69
1990 San Diego	NL	33	33	9	0	223.2	903	188	85	78	21	15	1	1	63	5	162	7	1	11	9	.550	4	0	3.14
1991 San Diego	NL	31	31	4	0	221.2	909	201	89	81	17	8	4	3	59	3	141	5	1	15	8	.652	0	0	3.29
12 ML YEARS		334	314	77	5	2149.1	9066	2172	1005	918	227	73	47	28	667	39	1525	50	15	129	101	.561	19	0	3.84

Jeff Huson

Bats: Left Throws: Right Pos: SS Ht: 6' 3" Wt: 180 Born: 08/15/64 Age: 27

					BATTING												BASERUNNING				PERCENTAGES		
Year Team	Lg	G	AB	H	2B	3B	HR	(Hm | Rd)	TB	R	RBI	TBB	IBB	SO	HBP	SH	SF	SB	CS	SB%	GDP	Avg	OBP	SLG
1988 Montreal	NL	20	42	13	2	0	0	(0 | 0)	15	7	3	4	2	3	0	0	0	2	1	.67	3	.310	.370	.357
1989 Montreal	NL	32	74	12	5	0	0	(0 | 0)	17	1	2	6	3	6	0	3	0	3	0	1.00	6	.162	.225	.230
1990 Texas	AL	145	396	95	12	2	0	(0 | 0)	111	57	28	46	0	54	2	7	3	12	4	.75	8	.240	.320	.280
1991 Texas	AL	119	268	57	8	3	2	(1 | 1)	77	36	26	39	0	32	0	9	1	8	3	.73	6	.213	.312	.287
4 ML YEARS		316	780	177	27	5	2	(1 | 1)	220	101	59	95	5	95	2	19	4	25	8	.76	22	.227	.311	.282

Mike Ignasiak

Pitches: Right Bats: Both Pos: RP Ht: 5'11" Wt: 175 Born: 03/12/66 Age: 26

		HOW MUCH HE PITCHED						WHAT HE GAVE UP												THE RESULTS					
Year Team	Lg	G	GS	CG	GF	IP	BFP	H	R	ER	HR	SH	SF	HB	TBB	IBB	SO	WP	Bk	W	L	Pct.	ShO	Sv	ERA
1988 Helena	R	7	0	0	7	11.2	53	10	5	4	1	0	0	1	7	0	18	2	0	2	0	1.000	0	1	3.09
Beloit	A	9	9	1	0	56.1	232	52	21	17	4	3	2	2	12	1	66	1	1	2	4	.333	0	0	2.72
1989 Stockton	A	28	28	4	0	179	763	140	67	54	4	4	5	5	97	0	142	12	1	11	6	.647	4	0	2.72
1990 Stockton	A	6	6	1	0	32	130	18	14	14	3	0	0	2	17	0	23	2	1	3	1	.750	1	0	3.94
El Paso	AA	15	15	1	0	82.2	368	96	45	40	5	2	3	1	34	1	39	4	3	6	3	.667	0	0	4.35
1991 Denver	AAA	24	22	1	1	137.2	587	119	68	65	14	1	1	6	57	2	103	4	1	9	5	.643	0	1	4.25
1991 Milwaukee	AL	4	1	0	0	12.2	51	7	8	8	2	0	0	0	8	0	10	0	0	2	1	.667	0	0	5.68

Pete Incaviglia

Bats: Right Throws: Right Pos: LF/DH Ht: 6' 1" Wt: 230 Born: 04/02/64 Age: 28

					BATTING												BASERUNNING				PERCENTAGES		
Year Team	Lg	G	AB	H	2B	3B	HR	(Hm | Rd)	TB	R	RBI	TBB	IBB	SO	HBP	SH	SF	SB	CS	SB%	GDP	Avg	OBP	SLG
1986 Texas	AL	153	540	135	21	2	30	(17 | 13)	250	82	88	55	2	185	4	0	7	3	2	.60	9	.250	.320	.463
1987 Texas	AL	139	509	138	26	4	27	(11 | 16)	253	85	80	48	1	168	1	0	5	9	3	.75	8	.271	.332	.497
1988 Texas	AL	116	418	104	19	3	22	(10 | 12)	195	59	54	39	3	153	7	0	3	6	4	.60	6	.249	.321	.467
1989 Texas	AL	133	453	107	27	4	21	(13 | 8)	205	48	81	32	0	136	6	0	4	5	7	.42	12	.236	.293	.453
1990 Texas	AL	153	529	123	27	0	24	(15 | 9)	222	59	85	45	5	146	9	0	4	3	4	.43	18	.233	.302	.420
1991 Detroit	AL	97	337	72	12	1	11	(6 | 5)	119	38	38	36	0	92	1	1	2	1	3	.25	6	.214	.290	.353
6 ML YEARS		791	2786	679	132	14	135	(74 | 61)	1244	371	426	255	11	880	28	1	25	27	23	.54	59	.244	.311	.447

Jeff Innis

Pitches: Right Bats: Right Pos: RP Ht: 6' 1" Wt: 180 Born: 07/05/62 Age: 29

		HOW MUCH HE PITCHED						WHAT HE GAVE UP												THE RESULTS					
Year Team	Lg	G	GS	CG	GF	IP	BFP	H	R	ER	HR	SH	SF	HB	TBB	IBB	SO	WP	Bk	W	L	Pct.	ShO	Sv	ERA
1987 New York	NL	17	0	0	8	25.2	109	29	9	9	5	0	0	1	4	1	28	1	1	0	1	.000	0	0	3.16
1988 New York	NL	12	0	0	7	19	80	19	6	4	1	1	0	1	2	1	14	0	0	1	1	.500	0	0	1.89
1989 New York	NL	29	0	0	12	39.2	160	38	16	14	2	1	1	1	8	0	16	0	0	0	1	.000	0	0	3.18
1990 New York	NL	18	0	0	12	26.1	104	19	9	7	4	2	1	0	10	3	12	1	1	1	3	.250	0	1	2.39
1991 New York	NL	69	0	0	29	84.2	336	66	30	25	2	6	5	0	23	6	47	4	0	0	2	.000	0	0	2.66
5 ML YEARS		145	1	0	68	195.1	789	171	70	59	13	8	9	3	47	11	117	6	2	2	8	.200	0	1	2.72

100

Daryl Irvine

Pitches: Right **Bats:** Right **Pos:** RP **Ht:** 6' 3" **Wt:** 195 **Born:** 11/15/64 **Age:** 27

Year Team	Lg	G	GS	CG	GF	IP	BFP	H	R	ER	HR	SH	SF	HB	TBB	IBB	SO	WP	Bk	W	L	Pct.	ShO	Sv	ERA
1985 Greensboro	A	8	7	0	0	37	173	46	26	18	3	1	0	1	17	0	19	3	1	4	2	.667	0	0	4.38
1986 Winter Havn	A	26	24	3	0	161	702	162	73	57	2	9	3	7	67	3	73	13	1	9	8	.529	0	0	3.19
1987 New Britain	AA	37	16	3	8	127	588	156	101	75	7	9	6	2	59	4	70	16	9	4	13	.235	0	0	5.31
1988 New Britain	AA	39	14	4	13	125.1	536	113	62	43	4	5	2	5	57	4	82	8	7	5	11	.313	1	0	3.09
1989 New Britain	AA	54	1	0	45	91.1	366	74	24	13	0	5	0	3	23	2	50	9	0	4	6	.400	0	16	1.28
1990 Pawtucket	AAA	42	0	0	30	50	216	47	24	18	1	6	1	3	19	5	35	1	1	2	5	.286	0	12	3.24
1991 Pawtucket	AAA	27	0	0	25	33	132	27	11	11	2	1	0	0	13	1	19	9	0	1	1	.500	0	17	3.00
1990 Boston	AL	11	0	0	6	17.1	75	15	10	9	0	1	3	0	10	3	9	1	1	1	1	.500	0	0	4.67
1991 Boston	AL	9	0	0	5	18	90	25	13	12	2	1	0	2	9	1	8	1	0	0	0	.000	0	0	6.00
2 ML YEARS		20	0	0	11	35.1	165	40	23	21	2	2	3	2	19	4	17	2	1	1	1	.500	0	0	5.35

Bo Jackson

Bats: Right **Throws:** Right **Pos:** DH **Ht:** 6' 1" **Wt:** 235 **Born:** 11/30/62 **Age:** 29

Year Team	Lg	G	AB	H	2B	3B	HR	(Hm	Rd)	TB	R	RBI	TBB	IBB	SO	HBP	SH	SF	SB	CS	SB%	GDP	Avg	OBP	SLG
1986 Kansas City	AL	25	82	17	2	1	2	(1	1)	27	9	9	7	0	34	2	0	0	3	1	.75	1	.207	.286	.329
1987 Kansas City	AL	116	396	93	17	2	22	(14	8)	180	46	53	30	0	158	5	1	2	10	4	.71	3	.235	.296	.455
1988 Kansas City	AL	124	439	108	16	4	25	(10	15)	207	63	68	25	6	146	1	1	2	27	6	.82	6	.246	.287	.472
1989 Kansas City	AL	135	515	132	15	6	32	(11	21)	255	86	105	39	8	172	3	0	4	26	9	.74	10	.256	.310	.495
1990 Kansas City	AL	111	405	110	16	1	28	(12	16)	212	74	78	44	2	128	2	0	5	15	9	.63	10	.272	.342	.523
1991 Chicago	AL	23	71	16	4	0	3	(3	0)	29	8	14	12	1	25	0	0	1	0	1	.00	3	.225	.333	.408
6 ML YEARS		534	1908	476	70	14	112	(51	61)	910	286	327	157	17	663	13	2	14	81	30	.73	33	.249	.309	.477

Danny Jackson

Pitches: Left **Bats:** Right **Pos:** SP **Ht:** 6' 0" **Wt:** 205 **Born:** 01/05/62 **Age:** 30

Year Team	Lg	G	GS	CG	GF	IP	BFP	H	R	ER	HR	SH	SF	HB	TBB	IBB	SO	WP	Bk	W	L	Pct.	ShO	Sv	ERA
1983 Kansas City	AL	4	3	0	0	19	87	26	12	11	1	1	0	0	6	0	9	0	0	1	1	.500	0	0	5.21
1984 Kansas City	AL	15	11	1	3	76	338	84	41	36	4	3	0	5	35	0	40	3	2	2	6	.250	0	0	4.26
1985 Kansas City	AL	32	32	4	0	208	893	209	94	79	7	5	4	6	76	2	114	4	2	14	12	.538	3	0	3.42
1986 Kansas City	AL	32	27	4	3	185.2	789	177	83	66	13	10	4	4	79	1	115	7	0	11	12	.478	1	1	3.20
1987 Kansas City	AL	36	34	11	1	224	981	219	115	100	11	8	7	7	109	1	152	5	0	9	18	.333	2	0	4.02
1988 Cincinnati	NL	35	35	15	0	260.2	1034	206	86	79	13	13	5	2	71	6	161	5	2	23	8	.742	6	0	2.73
1989 Cincinnati	NL	20	20	1	0	115.2	519	122	78	72	10	6	4	1	57	7	70	3	2	6	11	.353	0	0	5.60
1990 Cincinnati	NL	22	21	0	1	117.1	499	119	54	47	11	4	5	2	40	4	76	3	1	6	6	.500	0	0	3.61
1991 Chicago	NL	17	14	0	0	70.2	347	89	59	53	8	8	2	1	48	4	31	1	1	1	5	.167	0	0	6.75
9 ML YEARS		213	197	36	8	1277	5487	1251	622	543	78	58	31	28	521	25	768	31	10	73	79	.480	12	1	3.83

Darrin Jackson

Bats: Right **Throws:** Right **Pos:** CF/LF **Ht:** 6' 0" **Wt:** 186 **Born:** 08/22/63 **Age:** 28

Year Team	Lg	G	AB	H	2B	3B	HR	(Hm	Rd)	TB	R	RBI	TBB	IBB	SO	HBP	SH	SF	SB	CS	SB%	GDP	Avg	OBP	SLG
1985 Chicago	NL	5	11	1	0	0	0	(0	0)	1	0	0	0	0	3	0	0	0	0	0	.00	0	.091	.091	.091
1987 Chicago	NL	7	5	4	1	0	0	(0	0)	5	2	0	0	0	0	0	0	0	0	0	.00	0	.800	.800	1.000
1988 Chicago	NL	100	188	50	11	3	6	(3	3)	85	29	20	5	1	28	1	2	1	4	1	.80	3	.266	.287	.452
1989 2 ML Teams		70	170	37	7	0	4	(1	3)	56	17	20	13	5	34	0	0	2	1	4	.20	2	.218	.270	.329
1990 San Diego	NL	58	113	29	3	0	3	(1	2)	41	10	9	5	1	24	0	1	1	3	0	1.00	1	.257	.286	.363
1991 San Diego	NL	122	359	94	1	1	21	(12	9)	171	51	49	27	2	66	2	3	3	5	3	.63	5	.262	.315	.476
1989 Chicago	NL	45	83	19	4	0	1	(0	1)	26	7	8	6	1	17	0	0	0	1	2	.33	1	.229	.281	.313
San Diego	NL	25	87	18	3	0	3	(1	2)	30	10	12	7	4	17	0	0	0	0	2	.00	1	.207	.260	.345
6 ML YEARS		362	846	215	34	4	34	(17	17)	359	109	98	50	9	155	3	6	7	13	8	.62	11	.254	.296	.424

Mike Jackson

Pitches: Right **Bats:** Right **Pos:** RP **Ht:** 6' 0" **Wt:** 200 **Born:** 12/22/64 **Age:** 27

Year Team	Lg	G	GS	CG	GF	IP	BFP	H	R	ER	HR	SH	SF	HB	TBB	IBB	SO	WP	Bk	W	L	Pct.	ShO	Sv	ERA
1986 Philadelphia	NL	9	0	0	4	13.1	54	12	5	5	2	0	0	2	4	1	3	0	0	0	0	.000	0	0	3.38
1987 Philadelphia	NL	55	7	0	8	109.1	468	88	55	51	16	3	4	3	56	6	93	6	8	3	10	.231	0	1	4.20
1988 Seattle	AL	62	0	0	29	99.1	412	74	37	29	10	3	10	2	43	10	76	6	6	6	5	.545	0	4	2.63
1989 Seattle	AL	65	0	0	27	99.1	431	81	43	35	8	6	2	6	54	6	94	1	2	4	6	.400	0	7	3.17
1990 Seattle	AL	63	0	0	28	77.1	338	64	42	39	8	8	5	2	44	12	69	9	2	5	7	.417	0	3	4.54

Year Team	Lg	G	GS	CG	GF	IP	BFP	H	R	ER	HR	SH	SF	HB	TBB	IBB	SO	WP	Bk	W	L	Pct.	ShO	Sv	ERA
1991 Seattle	AL	72	0	0	35	88.2	363	64	35	32	5	4	0	6	34	11	74	3	0	7	7	.500	0	14	3.25
6 ML YEARS		326	7	0	131	487.1	2066	383	217	191	49	24	21	21	235	46	409	25	18	25	35	.417	0	29	3.53

Brook Jacoby

Bats: Right **Throws:** Right **Pos:** 3B/1B   **Ht:** 5'11" **Wt:** 195 **Born:** 11/23/59 **Age:** 32

				BATTING															BASERUNNING				PERCENTAGES		
Year Team	Lg	G	AB	H	2B	3B	HR	(Hm	Rd)	TB	R	RBI	TBB	IBB	SO	HBP	SH	SF	SB	CS	SB%	GDP	Avg	OBP	SLG
1981 Atlanta	NL	11	10	2	0	0	0	(0	0)	2	0	1	0	0	3	0	1	0	0	0	.00	1	.200	.200	.200
1983 Atlanta	NL	4	8	0	0	0	0	(0	0)	0	0	0	0	0	1	0	1	0	0	0	.00	0	.000	.000	.000
1984 Cleveland	AL	126	439	116	19	3	7	(2	5)	162	64	40	32	0	73	3	2	7	3	2	.60	13	.264	.314	.369
1985 Cleveland	AL	161	606	166	26	3	20	(9	11)	258	72	87	48	3	120	0	1	7	2	3	.40	17	.274	.324	.426
1986 Cleveland	AL	158	583	168	30	4	17	(10	7)	257	83	80	56	5	137	0	1	1	2	1	.67	15	.288	.350	.441
1987 Cleveland	AL	155	540	162	26	4	32	(21	11)	292	73	69	75	2	73	3	0	2	2	3	.40	19	.300	.387	.541
1988 Cleveland	AL	152	552	133	25	0	9	(3	6)	185	59	49	48	2	101	1	0	5	2	3	.40	12	.241	.300	.335
1989 Cleveland	AL	147	519	141	26	5	13	(7	6)	216	49	64	62	3	90	3	0	8	2	5	.29	15	.272	.348	.416
1990 Cleveland	AL	155	553	162	24	4	14	(10	4)	236	77	75	63	6	58	2	2	4	1	4	.20	20	.293	.365	.427
1991 2 ML Teams		122	419	94	21	1	4	(2	2)	129	28	44	27	3	54	3	0	4	2	1	.67	13	.224	.274	.308
1991 Cleveland	AL	66	231	54	9	1	4	(2	2)	77	14	24	16	2	32	2	0	0	1	1	.00	7	.234	.289	.333
Oakland	AL	56	188	40	12	0	0	(0	0)	52	14	20	11	1	22	1	0	4	1	0	1.00	6	.213	.255	.277
10 ML YEARS		1191	4229	1144	197	24	116	(64	52)	1737	505	509	411	24	710	15	7	38	16	22	.42	125	.271	.335	.411

Chris James

Bats: Right **Throws:** Right **Pos:** DH/1B/LF/RF   **Ht:** 6' 1" **Wt:** 190 **Born:** 10/04/62 **Age:** 29

				BATTING															BASERUNNING				PERCENTAGES		
Year Team	Lg	G	AB	H	2B	3B	HR	(Hm	Rd)	TB	R	RBI	TBB	IBB	SO	HBP	SH	SF	SB	CS	SB%	GDP	Avg	OBP	SLG
1986 Philadelphia	NL	16	46	13	3	0	1	(0	1)	19	5	5	1	0	13	0	1	0	0	0	.00	1	.283	.298	.413
1987 Philadelphia	NL	115	358	105	20	6	17	(9	8)	188	48	54	27	0	67	2	1	3	3	1	.75	4	.293	.344	.525
1988 Philadelphia	NL	150	566	137	24	1	19	(10	9)	220	57	66	31	2	73	3	0	5	7	4	.64	15	.242	.283	.389
1989 2 ML Teams		132	482	117	17	2	13	(7	6)	177	55	65	26	2	68	1	4	3	5	2	.71	20	.243	.281	.367
1990 Cleveland	AL	140	528	158	32	4	12	(6	6)	234	62	70	31	4	71	4	3	3	4	3	.57	11	.299	.341	.443
1991 Cleveland	AL	115	437	104	16	2	5	(1	4)	139	31	41	18	2	61	4	2	2	3	4	.43	9	.238	.273	.318
1989 Philadelphia	NL	45	179	37	4	0	2	(1	1)	47	14	19	4	0	23	0	1	1	3	1	.75	9	.207	.223	.263
San Diego	NL	87	303	80	13	2	11	(6	5)	130	41	46	22	2	45	1	3	2	2	1	.67	11	.264	.314	.429
6 ML YEARS		668	2417	634	112	15	67	(33	34)	977	258	301	134	10	353	14	11	16	22	14	.61	60	.262	.303	.404

Stan Javier

Bats: Both **Throws:** Right **Pos:** LF/RF   **Ht:** 6' 0" **Wt:** 185 **Born:** 01/09/64 **Age:** 28

				BATTING															BASERUNNING				PERCENTAGES		
Year Team	Lg	G	AB	H	2B	3B	HR	(Hm	Rd)	TB	R	RBI	TBB	IBB	SO	HBP	SH	SF	SB	CS	SB%	GDP	Avg	OBP	SLG
1984 New York	AL	7	7	1	0	0	0	(0	0)	1	1	0	0	0	1	0	0	0	0	0	.00	0	.143	.143	.143
1986 Oakland	AL	59	114	23	8	0	0	(0	0)	31	13	8	16	0	27	1	0	0	8	0	1.00	2	.202	.305	.272
1987 Oakland	AL	81	151	28	3	1	2	(1	1)	39	22	9	19	3	33	0	6	0	3	2	.60	2	.185	.276	.258
1988 Oakland	AL	125	397	102	13	3	2	(1	1)	127	49	35	32	1	63	2	6	3	20	1	.95	13	.257	.313	.320
1989 Oakland	AL	112	310	77	12	3	1	(1	0)	98	42	28	31	1	45	1	4	2	12	2	.86	6	.248	.317	.316
1990 2 ML Teams		123	309	92	9	6	3	(1	2)	122	60	27	40	2	50	0	6	4	15	7	.68	6	.298	.376	.395
1991 Los Angeles	NL	121	176	36	5	3	1	(0	1)	50	21	11	16	0	36	0	3	2	7	1	.88	4	.205	.268	.284
1990 Oakland	AL	19	33	8	0	2	0	(0	0)	12	4	3	3	0	6	0	0	0	0	0	.00	0	.242	.306	.364
Los Angeles	NL	104	276	84	9	4	3	(1	2)	110	56	24	37	2	44	0	6	4	15	7	.68	6	.304	.384	.399
7 ML YEARS		628	1464	359	50	16	9	(3	6)	468	208	118	154	7	255	4	25	9	65	13	.83	33	.245	.317	.320

Mike Jeffcoat

Pitches: Left **Bats:** Left **Pos:** RP   **Ht:** 6' 2" **Wt:** 190 **Born:** 08/03/59 **Age:** 32

		HOW MUCH HE PITCHED						WHAT HE GAVE UP											THE RESULTS					
Year Team	Lg	G	GS	CG	GF	IP	BFP	H	R	ER	HR	SH	SF	HB	TBB	IBB	SO	WP	Bk	W	L	Pct.	ShO	Sv	ERA
1983 Cleveland	AL	11	2	0	1	32.2	140	32	13	12	1	1	0	1	13	1	9	1	1	1	3	.250	0	0	3.31
1984 Cleveland	AL	63	1	0	12	75.1	327	82	28	25	7	3	7	1	24	7	41	8	1	5	2	.714	0	1	2.99
1985 2 ML Teams		28	1	0	10	31.2	143	35	18	16	5	4	3	2	12	4	14	1	0	0	2	.000	0	0	4.55
1987 Texas	AL	2	2	0	0	7	35	11	10	10	4	0	0	0	4	0	1	0	0	0	1	.000	0	0	12.86
1988 Texas	AL	5	2	0	2	10	52	19	13	13	1	1	0	2	5	1	5	0	0	0	2	.000	0	0	11.70
1989 Texas	AL	22	22	0	0	130.2	559	139	65	52	7	3	5	4	33	0	64	0	1	9	6	.600	2	0	3.58
1990 Texas	AL	44	12	1	11	110.2	466	122	57	55	12	3	2	2	28	5	58	1	0	5	6	.455	0	1	4.47
1991 Texas	AL	70	0	0	21	79.2	363	104	46	41	8	5	4	4	25	3	43	3	0	5	3	.625	0	1	4.63
1985 Cleveland	AL	9	0	0	3	9.2	44	8	5	3	1	2	2	0	6	1	4	0	0	0	0	.000	0	0	2.79
San Francisco	NL	19	1	0	7	22	99	27	13	13	4	2	1	2	6	3	10	1	0	0	2	.000	0	0	5.32
8 ML YEARS		245	42	3	57	477.2	2085	544	250	224	45	20	21	16	144	21	235	14	3	25	25	.500	2	7	4.22

Gregg Jefferies

Bats: Both **Throws:** Right **Pos:** 2B/3B   **Ht:** 5'10" **Wt:** 185 **Born:** 08/01/67 **Age:** 24

			BATTING																BASERUNNING				PERCENTAGES		
Year Team	Lg	G	AB	H	2B	3B	HR	(Hm	Rd)	TB	R	RBI	TBB	IBB	SO	HBP	SH	SF	SB	CS	SB%	GDP	Avg	OBP	SLG
1987 New York	NL	6	6	3	1	0	0	(0	0)	4	0	2	0	0	0	0	0	0	0	0	.00	0	.500	.500	.667
1988 New York	NL	29	109	35	8	2	6	(3	3)	65	19	17	8	0	10	0	0	1	5	1	.83	1	.321	.364	.596
1989 New York	NL	141	508	131	28	2	12	(7	5)	199	72	56	39	8	46	5	2	5	21	6	.78	16	.258	.314	.392
1990 New York	NL	153	604	171	40	3	15	(9	6)	262	96	68	46	2	40	5	0	4	11	2	.85	13	.283	.337	.434
1991 New York	NL	136	486	132	19	2	9	(5	4)	182	59	62	47	2	38	2	1	3	26	5	.84	12	.272	.336	.374
5 ML YEARS		465	1713	472	96	9	42	(24	18)	712	246	205	140	12	134	12	3	13	63	14	.82	42	.276	.332	.416

Reggie Jefferson

Bats: Both **Throws:** Left **Pos:** 1B   **Ht:** 6'4" **Wt:** 210 **Born:** 09/25/68 **Age:** 23

			BATTING																BASERUNNING				PERCENTAGES		
Year Team	Lg	G	AB	H	2B	3B	HR	(Hm	Rd)	TB	R	RBI	TBB	IBB	SO	HBP	SH	SF	SB	CS	SB%	GDP	Avg	OBP	SLG
1986 Reds	R	59	208	54	4	5	3	--	--	77	28	33	24	1	40	2	1	2	10	9	.53	3	.260	.339	.370
1987 Cedar Rapds	A	15	54	12	5	0	3	--	--	26	9	11	1	0	12	3	0	0	1	1	.50	2	.222	.276	.481
Billings	R	8	22	8	1	0	1	--	--	12	10	9	4	1	2	1	0	0	1	0	1.00	1	.364	.481	.545
1988 Cedar Rapds	A	135	517	149	26	2	18	--	--	233	76	90	40	6	89	13	0	5	2	1	.67	12	.288	.351	.451
1989 Chattanooga	AA	135	487	140	19	3	17	--	--	216	66	80	43	5	73	7	0	4	2	3	.40	11	.287	.351	.444
1990 Nashville	AAA	37	126	34	11	2	5	--	--	64	24	23	14	1	30	1	0	0	1	0	1.00	3	.270	.348	.508
1991 Nashville	AAA	28	103	33	3	1	3	--	--	47	15	20	10	1	22	4	0	0	3	1	.75	3	.320	.402	.456
Canton-Akrn	AA	6	25	7	1	0	0	--	--	8	2	4	1	0	5	0	0	0	0	0	.00	1	.280	.308	.320
Colo Sprngs	AAA	39	136	42	11	0	3	--	--	62	29	21	16	1	28	1	0	2	0	0	.00	1	.309	.381	.456
1991 2 ML Teams		31	108	21	3	0	3	(2	1)	33	11	13	4	0	24	0	0	1	0	0	.00	2	.194	.221	.306
1991 Cincinnati	NL	5	7	1	0	0	1	(1	0)	4	1	1	1	0	2	0	0	0	0	0	.00	0	.143	.250	.571
Cleveland	AL	26	101	20	3	0	2	(1	1)	29	10	12	3	0	22	0	0	1	0	0	.00	1	.198	.219	.287

Stan Jefferson

Bats: Both **Throws:** Right **Pos:** LF   **Ht:** 5'11" **Wt:** 180 **Born:** 12/04/62 **Age:** 29

			BATTING																BASERUNNING				PERCENTAGES		
Year Team	Lg	G	AB	H	2B	3B	HR	(Hm	Rd)	TB	R	RBI	TBB	IBB	SO	HBP	SH	SF	SB	CS	SB%	GDP	Avg	OBP	SLG
1986 New York	NL	14	24	5	1	0	1	(1	0)	9	6	3	2	0	8	1	0	0	0	0	.00	1	.208	.296	.375
1987 San Diego	NL	116	422	97	8	7	8	(5	3)	143	59	29	39	2	92	2	3	3	34	11	.76	6	.230	.296	.339
1988 San Diego	NL	49	111	16	1	2	1	(1	0)	24	16	4	9	0	22	1	2	2	5	1	.83	3	.144	.211	.216
1989 2 ML Teams		45	139	34	7	0	4	(3	1)	53	20	21	4	0	26	1	0	2	10	4	.71	1	.245	.267	.381
1990 2 ML Teams		59	117	27	8	0	2	(1	1)	41	22	10	10	0	26	2	1	3	9	4	.69	2	.231	.295	.350
1991 Cincinnati	NL	13	19	1	0	0	0	(0	0)	1	2	0	1	0	3	0	0	0	2	0	1.00	0	.053	.100	.053
1989 New York	AL	10	12	1	0	0	0	(0	0)	1	1	1	0	0	4	0	0	0	1	1	.50	0	.083	.083	.083
Baltimore	AL	35	127	33	7	0	4	(3	1)	52	19	20	4	0	22	1	0	2	9	3	.75	1	.260	.284	.409
1990 Baltimore	AL	10	19	0	0	0	0	(0	0)	0	1	0	2	0	8	0	0	0	1	0	1.00	0	.000	.095	.000
Cleveland	AL	49	98	27	8	0	2	(1	1)	41	21	10	8	0	18	2	1	3	8	4	.67	2	.276	.333	.418
6 ML YEARS		296	832	180	25	9	16	(11	5)	271	125	67	65	2	177	7	6	10	60	20	.75	13	.216	.276	.326

Doug Jennings

Bats: Left **Throws:** Left **Pos:** LF   **Ht:** 5'10" **Wt:** 175 **Born:** 09/30/64 **Age:** 27

			BATTING																BASERUNNING				PERCENTAGES		
Year Team	Lg	G	AB	H	2B	3B	HR	(Hm	Rd)	TB	R	RBI	TBB	IBB	SO	HBP	SH	SF	SB	CS	SB%	GDP	Avg	OBP	SLG
1988 Oakland	AL	71	101	21	6	0	1	(0	1)	30	9	15	21	1	28	2	1	3	0	1	.00	1	.208	.346	.297
1989 Oakland	AL	4	4	0	0	0	0	(0	0)	0	0	0	0	0	2	0	0	0	0	0	.00	0	.000	.000	.000
1990 Oakland	AL	64	156	30	7	2	2	(1	1)	47	19	14	17	0	48	2	2	3	0	3	.00	1	.192	.275	.301
1991 Oakland	AL	8	9	1	0	0	0	(0	0)	1	0	0	2	0	2	0	0	0	0	1	.00	1	.111	.273	.111
4 ML YEARS		147	270	52	13	2	3	(1	2)	78	28	29	40	1	80	4	3	6	0	5	.00	3	.193	.300	.289

Dave Johnson

Pitches: Right **Bats:** Right **Pos:** SP/RP   **Ht:** 5'11" **Wt:** 181 **Born:** 10/24/59 **Age:** 32

		HOW MUCH HE PITCHED						WHAT HE GAVE UP										THE RESULTS					
Year Team	Lg	G	GS	CG	GF	IP	BFP	H	R	ER	HR	SH	SF	HB	TBB	IBB	SO	WP	Bk	W	L	Pct.	ShO	Sv	ERA
1987 Pittsburgh	NL	5	0	0	3	6.1	31	13	7	7	1	0	0	0	2	0	4	0	0	0	0	.000	0	0	9.95
1989 Baltimore	AL	14	14	4	0	89.1	378	90	44	42	11	3	3	4	28	1	26	0	2	4	7	.364	0	0	4.23
1990 Baltimore	AL	30	29	3	0	180	758	196	83	82	30	5	7	3	43	2	68	1	2	13	9	.591	0	0	4.10
1991 Baltimore	AL	22	14	0	4	84	393	127	68	66	18	0	1	4	24	3	38	0	0	4	8	.333	0	0	7.07
4 ML YEARS		71	57	7	7	359.2	1560	426	202	197	60	8	11	11	97	6	136	1	4	21	24	.467	0	0	4.93

Howard Johnson

Bats: Both **Throws:** Right **Pos:** 3B/SS/RF · **Ht:** 5'10" **Wt:** 195 **Born:** 11/29/60 **Age:** 31

Year Team	Lg	G	AB	H	2B	3B	HR	(Hm	Rd)	TB	R	RBI	TBB	IBB	SO	HBP	SH	SF	SB	CS	SB%	GDP	Avg	OBP	SLG
1982 Detroit	AL	54	155	49	5	0	4	(1	3)	66	23	14	16	1	30	1	1	0	7	4	.64	3	.316	.384	.426
1983 Detroit	AL	27	66	14	0	0	3	(2	1)	23	11	5	7	0	10	1	0	0	0	0	.00	1	.212	.297	.348
1984 Detroit	AL	116	355	88	14	1	12	(4	8)	140	43	50	40	1	67	1	4	2	10	6	.63	6	.248	.324	.394
1985 New York	NL	126	389	94	18	4	11	(5	6)	153	38	46	34	10	78	0	1	4	6	4	.60	6	.242	.324	.393
1986 New York	NL	88	220	54	14	0	10	(5	5)	98	30	39	31	8	64	1	1	0	8	1	.89	2	.245	.341	.445
1987 New York	NL	157	554	147	22	1	36	(13	23)	279	93	99	83	18	113	5	0	3	32	10	.76	8	.265	.364	.504
1988 New York	NL	148	495	114	21	1	24	(9	15)	209	85	68	86	25	104	3	2	8	23	7	.77	6	.230	.343	.422
1989 New York	NL	153	571	164	41	3	36	(19	17)	319	104	101	77	8	126	1	0	6	41	8	.84	4	.287	.369	.559
1990 New York	NL	154	590	144	37	3	23	(13	10)	256	89	90	69	12	100	0	0	9	34	8	.81	7	.244	.319	.434
1991 New York	NL	156	564	146	34	4	38	(21	17)	302	108	117	78	12	120	1	0	15	30	16	.65	4	.259	.342	.535
10 ML YEARS		1179	3959	1014	206	17	197	(92	105)	1845	624	629	521	95	812	14	9	47	191	64	.75	47	.256	.341	.466

Jeff Johnson

Pitches: Left **Bats:** Right **Pos:** SP · **Ht:** 6'3" **Wt:** 200 **Born:** 08/04/66 **Age:** 25

Year Team	Lg	G	GS	CG	GF	IP	BFP	H	R	ER	HR	SH	SF	HB	TBB	IBB	SO	WP	Bk	W	L	Pct.	ShO	Sv	ERA
1988 Oneonta	A	14	14	0	0	87.2	371	67	35	29	2	3	3	2	39	0	91	3	2	6	1	.857	0	0	2.98
1989 Pr William	A	25	24	0	0	138.2	578	125	59	45	7	8	2	0	55	1	99	14	2	4	10	.286	0	0	2.92
1990 Ft.Laurdrle	A	17	17	1	0	103.2	439	101	55	42	2	5	2	3	25	0	84	5	2	6	8	.429	0	0	3.65
Albany	AA	9	9	3	0	60.2	239	44	14	11	0	2	0	2	15	0	41	1	0	4	3	.571	1	0	1.63
1991 Columbus	AAA	10	10	0	0	62	261	58	27	18	1	4	1	1	25	0	40	1	3	4	0	1.000	0	0	2.61
1991 New York	AL	23	23	0	0	127	562	156	89	83	15	7	4	6	33	1	62	5	1	6	11	.353	0	0	5.88

Lance Johnson

Bats: Left **Throws:** Left **Pos:** CF · **Ht:** 5'11" **Wt:** 160 **Born:** 07/06/63 **Age:** 28

Year Team	Lg	G	AB	H	2B	3B	HR	(Hm	Rd)	TB	R	RBI	TBB	IBB	SO	HBP	SH	SF	SB	CS	SB%	GDP	Avg	OBP	SLG
1987 St. Louis	NL	33	59	13	1	1	0	(0	0)	17	4	7	4	1	6	0	0	0	6	1	.86	2	.220	.270	.288
1988 Chicago	AL	33	124	23	4	1	0	(0	0)	29	11	6	6	0	11	0	2	0	6	2	.75	1	.185	.223	.234
1989 Chicago	AL	50	180	54	8	2	0	(0	0)	66	28	16	17	0	24	0	2	0	16	3	.84	1	.300	.360	.367
1990 Chicago	AL	151	541	154	18	9	1	(0	1)	193	76	51	33	2	45	1	8	4	36	22	.62	12	.285	.325	.357
1991 Chicago	AL	160	588	161	14	13	0	(0	0)	201	72	49	26	2	58	1	6	3	26	11	.70	13	.274	.304	.342
5 ML YEARS		427	1492	405	46	26	1	(0	1)	506	191	129	86	5	144	2	18	7	90	39	.70	29	.271	.311	.339

Randy Johnson

Pitches: Left **Bats:** Right **Pos:** SP · **Ht:** 6'10" **Wt:** 225 **Born:** 09/10/63 **Age:** 28

Year Team	Lg	G	GS	CG	GF	IP	BFP	H	R	ER	HR	SH	SF	HB	TBB	IBB	SO	WP	Bk	W	L	Pct.	ShO	Sv	ERA
1988 Montreal	NL	4	4	1	0	26	109	23	8	7	3	0	0	0	7	0	25	3	0	3	0	1.000	0	0	2.42
1989 2 ML Teams		29	28	2	1	160.2	715	147	100	86	13	10	13	3	96	2	130	7	7	7	13	.350	0	0	4.82
1990 Seattle	AL	33	33	5	0	219.2	944	174	103	89	26	7	6	5	120	2	194	4	2	14	11	.560	2	0	3.65
1991 Seattle	AL	33	33	2	0	201.1	889	151	96	89	15	9	8	12	152	0	228	12	2	13	10	.565	1	0	3.98
1989 Montreal	NL	7	6	0	1	29.2	143	29	25	22	2	3	4	0	26	1	26	2	2	0	4	.000	0	0	6.67
Seattle	AL	22	22	2	0	131	572	118	75	64	11	7	9	3	70	1	104	5	5	7	9	.438	0	0	4.40
4 ML YEARS		99	98	10	1	607.2	2657	495	307	271	57	26	27	20	375	4	577	26	11	37	34	.521	3	0	4.01

Joel Johnston

Pitches: Right **Bats:** Right **Pos:** RP · **Ht:** 6'4" **Wt:** 220 **Born:** 03/08/67 **Age:** 25

Year Team	Lg	G	GS	CG	GF	IP	BFP	H	R	ER	HR	SH	SF	HB	TBB	IBB	SO	WP	Bk	W	L	Pct.	ShO	Sv	ERA
1988 Eugene	A	14	14	0	0	64	295	64	49	37	1	4	3	7	34	0	64	7	6	4	7	.364	0	0	5.20
1989 Baseball Cy	A	26	26	0	0	131.2	586	135	84	72	6	2	6	11	63	2	76	8	5	9	4	.692	0	0	4.92
1990 Memphis	AA	4	3	0	1	6.2	40	5	9	5	1	0	0	0	16	0	6	3	0	0	0	.000	0	0	6.75
Baseball Cy	A	31	7	1	18	55.1	251	36	37	30	2	6	3	3	49	0	60	6	1	2	4	.333	0	7	4.88
Omaha	AAA	2	0	0	0	3	9	1	0	0	0	0	0	0	1	0	3	0	0	0	0	.000	0	0	0.00
1991 Omaha	AAA	47	0	0	27	74.1	318	60	43	43	12	4	0	1	42	2	63	6	0	4	7	.364	0	8	5.21
1991 Kansas City	AL	13	0	0	1	22.1	85	9	1	1	0	1	0	0	9	3	21	0	0	1	0	1.000	0	0	0.40

Barry Jones

Pitches: Right Bats: Right Pos: RP Ht: 6' 4" Wt: 225 Born: 02/15/63 Age: 29

				HOW MUCH HE PITCHED				WHAT HE GAVE UP									THE RESULTS					
Year Team	Lg	G	GS	CG	GF	IP	BFP	H	R	ER	HR	SH	SF	HB	TBB	IBB	SO	WP	Bk	W	L	Pct.	ShO	Sv	ERA
1986 Pittsburgh	NL	26	0	0	10	37.1	159	29	16	12	3	2	1	0	21	2	29	2	0	3	4	.429	0	3	2.89
1987 Pittsburgh	NL	32	0	0	10	43.1	203	55	34	27	6	3	2	0	23	6	28	3	0	2	4	.333	0	1	5.61
1988 2 ML Teams		59	0	0	25	82.1	347	72	28	26	6	5	5	1	38	7	48	13	2	3	3	.500	0	3	2.84
1989 Chicago	AL	22	0	0	8	30.1	121	22	12	8	2	4	2	1	8	0	17	1	0	3	2	.600	0	1	2.37
1990 Chicago	AL	65	0	0	9	74	310	62	20	19	2	7	5	1	33	7	45	0	1	11	4	.733	0	1	2.31
1991 Montreal	NL	77	0	0	46	88.2	353	76	35	33	8	7	3	1	33	8	46	1	1	4	9	.308	0	13	3.35
1988 Pittsburgh	NL	42	0	0	15	56.1	241	57	21	19	3	5	4	1	21	6	31	7	1	1	1	.500	0	2	3.04
Chicago	AL	17	0	0	10	26	106	15	7	7	3	0	1	0	17	1	17	6	1	2	2	.500	0	1	2.42
6 ML YEARS		281	0	0	108	356	1493	316	145	125	27	28	18	4	156	30	213	20	4	26	26	.500	0	22	3.16

Calvin Jones

Pitches: Right Bats: Right Pos: RP Ht: 6' 3" Wt: 185 Born: 09/26/63 Age: 28

				HOW MUCH HE PITCHED				WHAT HE GAVE UP									THE RESULTS					
Year Team	Lg	G	GS	CG	GF	IP	BFP	H	R	ER	HR	SH	SF	HB	TBB	IBB	SO	WP	Bk	W	L	Pct.	ShO	Sv	ERA
1984 Bellingham	A	10	9	0	0	59.2	0	29	23	16	0	0	0	7	36	0	59	8	1	5	0	1.000	0	0	2.41
1985 Wausau	A	20	19	1	0	106	473	96	59	46	10	0	2	5	65	1	71	9	2	4	11	.267	0	0	3.91
1986 Salinas	A	26	25	2	0	157.1	680	141	76	63	9	4	4	4	90	2	137	15	2	11	8	.579	0	0	3.60
1987 Chattanooga	AA	26	10	0	12	81.1	372	90	58	45	5	5	1	2	38	0	77	4	0	2	9	.182	0	2	4.98
1988 Vermont	AA	24	4	0	6	74.2	312	52	26	22	1	0	2	0	47	2	58	4	3	7	5	.583	0	0	2.65
1989 San Berndno	A	5	0	0	4	12.1	49	8	1	1	0	0	1	0	7	0	15	0	2	2	0	1.000	0	1	0.73
Williamsprt	AA	5	0	0	3	6.2	34	13	9	9	1	0	0	0	4	0	5	1	0	0	0	.000	0	0	12.15
1990 San Berndno	A	53	0	0	27	67	298	43	32	22	4	1	3	4	54	2	94	6	0	5	3	.625	0	9	2.96
1991 Calgary	AAA	20	0	0	15	23	109	19	12	10	1	0	0	2	19	1	25	6	2	1	1	.500	0	7	3.91
1991 Seattle	AL	27	0	0	6	46.1	194	33	14	13	0	6	0	1	29	5	42	6	0	2	2	.500	0	2	2.53

Chris Jones

Bats: Right Throws: Right Pos: LF Ht: 6' 2" Wt: 205 Born: 12/16/65 Age: 26

							BATTING												BASERUNNING				PERCENTAGES		
Year Team	Lg	G	AB	H	2B	3B	HR	(Hm	Rd)	TB	R	RBI	TBB	IBB	SO	HBP	SH	SF	SB	CS	SB%	GDP	Avg	OBP	SLG
1984 Billings	R	21	73	11	2	0	2	--	--	19	8	13	2	0	24	0	1	0	4	0	1.00	0	.151	.171	.260
1985 Billings	R	63	240	62	12	5	4	--	--	96	43	33	19	0	72	1	1	1	13	0	1.00	3	.258	.314	.400
1986 Cedar Rapds	A	128	473	117	13	9	20	--	--	208	65	78	20	1	126	3	0	4	23	17	.58	7	.247	.280	.440
1987 Vermont	AA	113	383	88	11	4	10	--	--	137	50	39	23	4	99	4	2	3	13	10	.57	12	.230	.278	.358
1988 Chattanooga	AA	116	410	111	20	7	4	--	--	157	50	61	29	1	102	2	0	7	11	9	.55	4	.271	.317	.383
1989 Nashville	AAA	21	49	8	1	0	2	--	--	15	8	5	0	0	16	0	0	1	2	0	1.00	0	.163	.163	.306
Chattanooga	AA	103	378	95	18	2	10	--	--	147	47	54	23	1	68	3	0	1	10	2	.83	13	.251	.299	.389
1990 Nashville	AAA	134	436	114	23	3	10	--	--	173	53	52	23	3	86	2	5	1	12	8	.60	18	.261	.301	.397
1991 Nashville	AAA	73	267	65	5	4	9	--	--	105	29	33	19	1	65	2	0	1	10	5	.67	6	.243	.298	.393
1991 Cincinnati	NL	52	89	26	1	2	2	(0	2)	37	14	6	2	0	31	0	0	1	2	1	.67	2	.292	.304	.416

Doug Jones

Pitches: Right Bats: Right Pos: RP/SP Ht: 6' 2" Wt: 195 Born: 06/24/57 Age: 35

				HOW MUCH HE PITCHED				WHAT HE GAVE UP									THE RESULTS					
Year Team	Lg	G	GS	CG	GF	IP	BFP	H	R	ER	HR	SH	SF	HB	TBB	IBB	SO	WP	Bk	W	L	Pct.	ShO	Sv	ERA
1982 Milwaukee	AL	4	0	0	2	2.2	14	5	3	3	1	0	0	0	1	0	1	0	0	0	0	.000	0	0	10.13
1986 Cleveland	AL	11	0	0	5	18	79	18	5	5	0	1	1	1	6	1	12	0	0	1	0	1.000	0	1	2.50
1987 Cleveland	AL	49	0	0	29	91.1	400	101	45	32	4	5	5	6	24	5	87	0	0	6	5	.545	0	8	3.15
1988 Cleveland	AL	51	0	0	46	83.1	338	69	26	21	1	3	0	2	16	3	72	2	3	3	4	.429	0	37	2.27
1989 Cleveland	AL	59	0	0	53	80.2	331	76	25	21	4	8	6	1	13	4	65	1	1	7	10	.412	0	32	2.34
1990 Cleveland	AL	66	0	0	64	84.1	331	66	26	24	5	2	2	2	22	4	55	2	0	5	5	.500	0	43	2.56
1991 Cleveland	AL	36	4	0	29	63.1	293	87	42	39	7	2	2	0	17	5	48	1	0	4	8	.333	0	7	5.54
7 ML YEARS		276	4	0	228	423.2	1786	422	172	145	22	21	16	12	99	22	340	6	4	26	32	.448	0	128	3.08

Jimmy Jones

Pitches: Right Bats: Right Pos: SP Ht: 6' 2" Wt: 190 Born: 04/20/64 Age: 28

				HOW MUCH HE PITCHED				WHAT HE GAVE UP									THE RESULTS					
Year Team	Lg	G	GS	CG	GF	IP	BFP	H	R	ER	HR	SH	SF	HB	TBB	IBB	SO	WP	Bk	W	L	Pct.	ShO	Sv	ERA
1986 San Diego	NL	3	3	1	0	18	65	10	6	5	1	1	0	0	3	0	15	0	0	2	0	1.000	1	0	2.50
1987 San Diego	NL	30	22	2	4	145.2	639	154	85	67	14	5	5	5	54	2	51	3	2	9	7	.563	1	0	4.14
1988 San Diego	NL	29	29	3	0	179	760	192	98	82	14	11	9	3	44	3	82	4	1	9	14	.391	0	0	4.12
1989 New York	AL	11	6	0	3	48	211	56	29	28	7	1	1	2	16	1	25	1	0	2	1	.667	0	0	5.25

Year	Team	Lg	G	GS	CG	GF	IP	BFP	H	R	ER	HR	SH	SF	HB	TBB	IBB	SO	WP	Bk	W	L	Pct.	ShO	Sv	ERA
1990	New York	AL	17	7	0	9	50	238	72	42	35	8	1	4	1	23	0	25	3	0	1	2	.333	0	0	6.30
1991	Houston	NL	26	22	1	0	135.1	593	143	73	66	9	7	2	3	51	3	88	4	0	6	8	.429	1	0	4.39
	6 ML YEARS		116	89	7	16	576	2506	627	333	283	53	26	21	14	191	9	286	15	3	29	32	.475	3	0	4.42

Ron Jones

Bats: Left   Throws: Right   Pos: PH   **Ht: 5'10"   Wt: 208   Born: 06/11/64   Age: 28**

						BATTING														BASERUNNING				PERCENTAGES		
Year	Team	Lg	G	AB	H	2B	3B	HR	(Hm	Rd)	TB	R	RBI	TBB	IBB	SO	HBP	SH	SF	SB	CS	SB%	GDP	Avg	OBP	SLG
1988	Philadelphia	NL	33	124	36	6	1	8	(5	3)	68	15	26	2	0	14	0	0	3	0	0	.00	2	.290	.295	.548
1989	Philadelphia	NL	12	31	9	0	0	2	(1	1)	15	7	4	9	1	1	0	0	0	0	1	1.00	2	.290	.450	.484
1990	Philadelphia	NL	24	58	16	2	0	3	(2	1)	27	5	7	9	0	9	0	0	0	0	1	.00	2	.276	.373	.466
1991	Philadelphia	NL	28	26	4	2	0	0	(0	0)	6	0	3	2	0	9	0	0	0	0	0	.00	1	.154	.214	.231
	4 ML YEARS		97	239	65	10	1	13	(8	5)	116	27	40	22	1	33	0	0	3	1	1	.50	6	.272	.330	.485

Stacy Jones

Pitches: Right   Bats: Right   Pos: RP   **Ht: 6' 6"   Wt: 225   Born: 05/26/67   Age: 25**

			HOW MUCH HE PITCHED						WHAT HE GAVE UP								THE RESULTS						
Year	Team	Lg	G	GS	CG	GF	IP	BFP	H	R	ER	HR	SH	SF	HB	TBB	IBB	SO	WP	Bk	W	L	Pct.	ShO	Sv	ERA
1988	Erie	A	7	7	3	0	54.1	218	51	12	8	1	1	0	0	15	2	40	2	0	3	3	.500	2	0	1.33
	Hagerstown	A	6	6	3	0	37.2	156	35	14	12	2	1	4	1	12	0	23	2	0	3	1	.750	2	0	2.87
1989	Frederick	A	15	15	3	0	82.2	374	93	57	45	11	1	3	2	35	0	58	3	4	5	6	.455	1	0	4.90
1990	Frederick	A	15	0	0	11	26.2	119	31	13	10	0	0	1	1	7	1	24	1	0	1	2	.333	0	2	3.38
	Hagerstown	AA	19	0	0	11	40.1	176	46	27	23	1	4	1	1	11	1	41	2	0	1	6	.143	0	2	5.13
1991	Hagerstown	AA	12	0	0	4	30.1	130	24	6	6	1	2	0	1	15	1	26	1	0	0	1	.000	0	1	1.78
	Rochester	AAA	33	1	0	21	50.2	221	53	22	19	4	7	2	0	20	2	47	2	1	4	4	.500	0	8	3.38
1991	Baltimore	AL	4	1	0	0	11	49	11	6	5	1	0	1	0	5	0	10	0	0	0	0	.000	0	0	4.09

Tim Jones

Bats: Left   Throws: Right   Pos: SS   **Ht: 5'10"   Wt: 175   Born: 12/01/62   Age: 29**

						BATTING														BASERUNNING				PERCENTAGES		
Year	Team	Lg	G	AB	H	2B	3B	HR	(Hm	Rd)	TB	R	RBI	TBB	IBB	SO	HBP	SH	SF	SB	CS	SB%	GDP	Avg	OBP	SLG
1988	St. Louis	NL	31	52	14	0	0	0	(0	0)	14	2	3	4	0	10	0	0	0	4	1	.80	1	.269	.321	.269
1989	St. Louis	NL	42	75	22	6	0	0	(0	0)	28	11	7	7	1	8	1	1	2	1	0	1.00	2	.293	.353	.373
1990	St. Louis	NL	67	128	28	7	1	1	(1	0)	40	9	12	12	1	20	1	4	0	3	4	.43	1	.219	.291	.313
1991	St. Louis	NL	16	24	4	2	0	0	(0	0)	6	1	2	2	1	6	0	0	1	0	1	.00	0	.167	.222	.250
	4 ML YEARS		156	279	68	15	1	1	(1	0)	88	23	24	25	3	44	2	5	3	8	6	.57	4	.244	.307	.315

Tracy Jones

Bats: Right   Throws: Right   Pos: LF/DH   **Ht: 6' 3"   Wt: 220   Born: 03/31/61   Age: 31**

						BATTING														BASERUNNING				PERCENTAGES		
Year	Team	Lg	G	AB	H	2B	3B	HR	(Hm	Rd)	TB	R	RBI	TBB	IBB	SO	HBP	SH	SF	SB	CS	SB%	GDP	Avg	OBP	SLG
1986	Cincinnati	NL	46	86	30	3	0	2	(1	1)	39	16	10	9	1	5	0	0	1	7	1	.88	2	.349	.406	.453
1987	Cincinnati	NL	117	359	104	17	3	10	(4	6)	157	53	44	23	0	40	3	0	5	31	8	.79	10	.290	.333	.437
1988	2 ML Teams		90	224	66	6	1	3	(3	0)	83	29	24	20	3	18	2	3	0	18	6	.75	5	.295	.358	.371
1989	2 ML Teams		86	255	59	14	0	3	(3	0)	82	22	38	21	4	30	2	1	3	3	2	.60	5	.231	.292	.322
1990	2 ML Teams		75	204	53	8	1	6	(3	3)	81	23	24	9	0	25	5	2	0	1	2	.33	7	.260	.307	.397
1991	Seattle	AL	79	175	44	8	1	3	(1	2)	63	30	24	18	2	22	1	1	2	2	0	1.00	8	.251	.321	.360
1988	Cincinnati	NL	37	83	19	1	0	1	(0	1)	23	9	9	8	2	6	1	0	1	9	0	1.00	4	.229	.304	.277
	Montreal	NL	53	141	47	5	1	2	(0	2)	60	20	15	12	1	12	1	3	0	9	6	.60	1	.333	.390	.426
1989	San Francisco	NL	40	97	18	4	0	0	(0	0)	22	5	12	5	3	14	1	0	0	2	1	.67	4	.186	.233	.227
	Detroit	AL	46	158	41	10	0	3	(3	0)	60	17	26	16	1	16	1	1	3	1	1	.50	1	.259	.326	.380
1990	Detroit	AL	50	118	27	4	1	4	(2	2)	45	15	9	6	0	13	3	1	0	1	1	.50	3	.229	.283	.381
	Seattle	AL	25	86	26	4	0	2	(1	1)	36	8	15	3	0	12	2	1	0	0	1	.00	4	.302	.341	.419
	6 ML YEARS		493	1303	356	56	6	27	(12	15)	505	173	164	100	10	140	13	7	11	62	19	.77	37	.273	.329	.388

Ricky Jordan

Bats: Right   Throws: Right   Pos: 1B   **Ht: 6' 3"   Wt: 209   Born: 05/26/65   Age: 27**

						BATTING														BASERUNNING				PERCENTAGES		
Year	Team	Lg	G	AB	H	2B	3B	HR	(Hm	Rd)	TB	R	RBI	TBB	IBB	SO	HBP	SH	SF	SB	CS	SB%	GDP	Avg	OBP	SLG
1988	Philadelphia	NL	69	273	84	15	1	11	(6	5)	134	41	43	7	2	39	0	0	1	1	1	.50	5	.308	.324	.491
1989	Philadelphia	NL	144	523	149	22	3	12	(7	5)	213	63	75	23	5	62	5	0	8	4	3	.57	19	.285	.317	.407
1990	Philadelphia	NL	92	324	78	21	0	5	(2	3)	114	32	44	13	6	39	5	0	4	2	0	1.00	9	.241	.277	.352
1991	Philadelphia	NL	101	301	82	21	3	9	(5	4)	136	38	49	14	2	49	2	0	5	0	2	.00	11	.272	.304	.452
	4 ML YEARS		406	1421	393	79	7	37	(20	17)	597	174	211	57	15	189	12	0	18	7	6	.54	44	.277	.306	.420

Felix Jose

Bats: Both **Throws:** Right **Pos:** RF **Ht:** 6' 1" **Wt:** 190 **Born:** 05/08/65 **Age:** 27

		BATTING																	BASERUNNING				PERCENTAGES		
Year Team	Lg	G	AB	H	2B	3B	HR	(Hm Rd)	TB	R	RBI	TBB	IBB	SO	HBP	SH	SF	SB	CS	SB%	GDP	Avg	OBP	SLG
1988 Oakland	AL	8	6	2	1	0	0	(0 0)	3	2	1	0	0	1	0	0	0	1	0	1.00	0	.333	.333	.500
1989 Oakland	AL	20	57	11	2	0	0	(0 0)	13	3	5	4	0	13	0	0	0	0	1	.00	2	.193	.246	.228
1990 2 ML Teams		126	426	113	16	1	11	(5 6)	164	54	52	24	0	81	5	2	1	12	6	.67	9	.265	.311	.385
1991 St. Louis	NL	154	568	173	40	6	8	(3 5)	249	69	77	50	8	113	2	0	5	20	12	.63	12	.305	.360	.438
1990 Oakland	AL	101	341	90	12	0	8	(3 5)	126	42	39	16	0	65	5	2	1	8	2	.80	8	.264	.306	.370
St. Louis	NL	25	85	23	4	1	3	(2 1)	38	12	13	8	0	16	0	0	0	4	4	.50	1	.271	.333	.447
4 ML YEARS		308	1057	299	59	7	19	(8 11)	429	128	135	78	8	208	7	2	6	33	19	.63	23	.283	.334	.406

Wally Joyner

Bats: Left **Throws:** Left **Pos:** 1B **Ht:** 6' 2" **Wt:** 203 **Born:** 06/16/62 **Age:** 30

		BATTING																	BASERUNNING				PERCENTAGES		
Year Team	Lg	G	AB	H	2B	3B	HR	(Hm Rd)	TB	R	RBI	TBB	IBB	SO	HBP	SH	SF	SB	CS	SB%	GDP	Avg	OBP	SLG
1986 California	AL	154	593	172	27	3	22	(11 11)	271	82	100	57	8	58	2	10	12	5	2	.71	11	.290	.348	.457
1987 California	AL	149	564	161	33	1	34	(19 15)	298	100	117	72	12	64	5	2	10	8	2	.80	14	.285	.366	.528
1988 California	AL	158	597	176	31	2	13	(6 7)	250	81	85	55	14	51	5	0	6	8	2	.80	16	.295	.356	.419
1989 California	AL	159	593	167	30	2	16	(8 8)	249	78	79	46	7	58	6	1	8	3	2	.60	15	.282	.335	.420
1990 California	AL	83	310	83	15	0	8	(5 3)	122	35	41	41	4	34	1	1	5	2	1	.67	10	.268	.350	.394
1991 California	AL	143	551	166	34	3	21	(10 11)	269	79	96	52	4	66	1	2	5	2	0	1.00	11	.301	.360	.488
6 ML YEARS		846	3208	925	170	11	114	(59 55)	1459	455	518	323	49	331	20	16	46	28	9	.76	77	.288	.353	.455

Jeff Juden

Pitches: Right **Bats:** Right **Pos:** SP **Ht:** 6' 7" **Wt:** 245 **Born:** 01/19/71 **Age:** 21

		HOW MUCH HE PITCHED						WHAT HE GAVE UP											THE RESULTS					
Year Team	Lg	G	GS	CG	GF	IP	BFP	H	R	ER	HR	SH	SF	HB	TBB	IBB	SO	WP	Bk	W	L	Pct.	ShO	Sv	ERA
1989 Astros	R	9	8	0	0	39.2	177	33	21	15	0	1	3	3	17	0	49	7	2	1	4	.200	0	0	3.40
1990 Osceola	A	15	15	2	0	91	390	72	37	23	2	3	1	5	42	0	85	7	4	10	1	.909	0	0	2.27
Columbus	AA	11	11	0	0	52	250	55	36	31	2	2	1	4	42	2	40	9	2	1	3	.250	0	0	5.37
1991 Jackson	AA	16	16	0	0	95.2	408	84	43	33	4	8	4	3	44	0	75	5	2	6	3	.667	0	0	3.10
Tucson	AAA	10	10	0	0	56.2	245	56	28	20	2	4	3	0	25	0	51	7	0	3	2	.600	0	0	3.18
1991 Houston	NL	4	3	0	0	18	81	19	14	12	3	2	3	0	7	1	11	0	1	0	2	.000	0	0	6.00

Dave Justice

Bats: Left **Throws:** Left **Pos:** RF **Ht:** 6' 3" **Wt:** 200 **Born:** 04/14/66 **Age:** 26

		BATTING																	BASERUNNING				PERCENTAGES		
Year Team	Lg	G	AB	H	2B	3B	HR	(Hm Rd)	TB	R	RBI	TBB	IBB	SO	HBP	SH	SF	SB	CS	SB%	GDP	Avg	OBP	SLG
1989 Atlanta	NL	16	51	12	3	0	1	(1 0)	18	7	3	3	1	9	1	1	0	2	1	.67	1	.235	.291	.353
1990 Atlanta	NL	127	439	124	23	2	28	(19 9)	235	76	78	64	4	92	0	0	1	11	6	.65	2	.282	.373	.535
1991 Atlanta	NL	109	396	109	25	1	21	(11 10)	199	67	87	65	9	81	3	0	5	8	8	.50	4	.275	.377	.503
3 ML YEARS		252	886	245	51	3	50	(31 19)	452	150	168	132	14	182	4	1	6	21	15	.58	7	.277	.371	.510

Jeff Kaiser

Pitches: Left **Bats:** Right **Pos:** RP **Ht:** 6' 3" **Wt:** 195 **Born:** 07/24/60 **Age:** 31

		HOW MUCH HE PITCHED						WHAT HE GAVE UP											THE RESULTS					
Year Team	Lg	G	GS	CG	GF	IP	BFP	H	R	ER	HR	SH	SF	HB	TBB	IBB	SO	WP	Bk	W	L	Pct.	ShO	Sv	ERA
1985 Oakland	AL	15	0	0	4	16.2	97	25	32	27	6	1	2	1	20	2	10	2	0	0	0	.000	0	0	14.58
1987 Cleveland	AL	2	0	0	0	3.1	18	4	6	6	1	0	0	1	3	0	2	0	0	0	0	.000	0	0	16.20
1988 Cleveland	AL	3	0	0	1	2.2	11	2	0	0	0	2	1	0	1	0	0	0	0	0	0	.000	0	0	0.00
1989 Cleveland	AL	6	0	0	1	3.2	22	5	5	3	1	0	1	0	5	0	4	1	0	0	1	.000	0	0	7.36
1990 Cleveland	AL	5	0	0	0	12.2	60	16	5	5	2	0	1	0	7	1	9	0	0	0	0	.000	0	0	3.55
1991 Detroit	AL	10	0	0	4	5	26	6	5	5	1	0	0	0	5	2	4	0	0	0	1	.000	0	2	9.00
6 ML YEARS		41	0	0	10	44	234	58	53	46	11	3	5	2	41	5	29	3	0	0	2	.000	0	2	9.41

Scott Kamieniecki

Pitches: Right **Bats:** Right **Pos:** SP **Ht:** 6' 0" **Wt:** 195 **Born:** 04/19/64 **Age:** 28

		HOW MUCH HE PITCHED						WHAT HE GAVE UP											THE RESULTS					
Year Team	Lg	G	GS	CG	GF	IP	BFP	H	R	ER	HR	SH	SF	HB	TBB	IBB	SO	WP	Bk	W	L	Pct.	ShO	Sv	ERA
1987 Pr William	A	19	19	1	0	112.1	499	91	61	52	7	1	2	5	78	3	84	9	2	9	5	.643	0	0	4.17
Albany	AA	10	7	0	1	37	176	41	25	22	0	5	0	1	33	3	19	3	1	1	3	.250	0	0	5.35
1988 Pr William	A	15	15	7	0	100.1	451	115	62	49	3	2	0	2	50	1	72	10	1	6	7	.462	2	0	4.40
Ft.Lauderdle	A	12	11	0	0	77	329	71	36	31	2	1	2	1	40	1	51	7	0	3	6	.333	1	0	3.62
1989 Albany	AA	24	23	6	1	151	636	142	67	62	13	1	3	2	57	1	140	5	0	10	9	.526	3	1	3.70
1990 Albany	AA	22	21	3	1	132	562	113	55	47	5	6	6	0	61	2	99	4	1	10	9	.526	1	0	3.20

Year	Team	Lg					IP																		ERA
1991	Columbus	AAA	11	11	3	0	76.1	308	61	25	20	2	3	2	3	20	0	58	2	3	6	3	.667	1	0	2.36
1991	New York	AL	9	9	0	0	55.1	239	54	24	24	8	2	1	3	22	1	34	1	0	4	4	.500	0	0	3.90

Ron Karkovice

Bats: Right **Throws:** Right **Pos:** C **Ht:** 6' 1" **Wt:** 215 **Born:** 08/08/63 **Age:** 28

Year	Team	Lg	G	AB	H	2B	3B	HR	(Hm	Rd)	TB	R	RBI	TBB	IBB	SO	HBP	SH	SF	SB	CS	SB%	GDP	Avg	OBP	SLG
1986	Chicago	AL	37	97	24	7	0	4	(1	3)	43	13	13	9	0	37	1	1	1	0	1	1.00	3	.247	.315	.443
1987	Chicago	AL	39	85	6	0	0	2	(1	1)	12	7	7	7	0	40	2	1	0	3	0	1.00	2	.071	.160	.141
1988	Chicago	AL	46	115	20	4	0	3	(1	2)	33	10	9	7	0	30	1	3	0	4	2	.67	1	.174	.228	.287
1989	Chicago	AL	71	182	48	9	2	3	(0	3)	70	21	24	10	0	56	2	7	2	2	0	.00	0	.264	.306	.385
1990	Chicago	AL	68	183	45	10	0	6	(0	6)	73	30	20	16	1	52	1	7	1	2	0	1.00	1	.246	.308	.399
1991	Chicago	AL	75	167	41	13	0	5	(0	5)	69	25	22	15	1	42	1	9	1	0	0	.00	2	.246	.310	.413
	6 ML YEARS		336	829	184	43	2	23	(3	20)	300	106	95	64	2	257	8	28	5	10	2	.83	9	.222	.283	.362

Eric Karros

Bats: Right **Throws:** Right **Pos:** 1B **Ht:** 6' 4" **Wt:** 205 **Born:** 11/04/67 **Age:** 24

Year	Team	Lg	G	AB	H	2B	3B	HR	(Hm	Rd)	TB	R	RBI	TBB	IBB	SO	HBP	SH	SF	SB	CS	SB%	GDP	Avg	OBP	SLG
1988	Great Falls	R	66	268	98	12	1	12	--	--	148	68	55	32	0	35	3	0	4	9	2	.82	7	.366	.433	.552
1989	Bakersfield	A	142	545	165	40	1	15	--	--	252	86	86	63	3	99	2	0	4	18	7	.72	15	.303	.375	.462
1990	San Antonio	AA	131	509	179	45	2	18	--	--	282	90	78	57	5	80	6	1	6	8	10	.44	18	.352	.419	.554
1991	Albuquerque	AAA	132	488	154	33	8	22	--	--	269	88	101	58	8	80	6	0	5	3	2	.60	6	.316	.391	.551
1991	Los Angeles	NL	14	14	1	1	0	0	(0	0)	2	0	1	1	0	6	0	0	0	0	0	.00	0	.071	.133	.143

Pat Kelly

Bats: Right **Throws:** Right **Pos:** 3B/2B **Ht:** 6' 0" **Wt:** 180 **Born:** 10/14/67 **Age:** 24

Year	Team	Lg	G	AB	H	2B	3B	HR	(Hm	Rd)	TB	R	RBI	TBB	IBB	SO	HBP	SH	SF	SB	CS	SB%	GDP	Avg	OBP	SLG
1988	Oneonta	A	71	280	92	11	6	2	--	--	121	49	34	16	0	45	5	5	1	25	6	.81	0	.329	.374	.432
1989	Pr William	A	124	436	116	21	7	3	--	--	160	61	45	32	1	79	8	4	7	31	9	.78	3	.266	.323	.367
1990	Albany	AA	126	418	113	19	6	8	--	--	168	67	44	37	1	79	6	5	4	31	14	.69	7	.270	.335	.402
1991	Columbus	AAA	31	116	39	9	2	3	--	--	61	27	19	9	1	16	0	1	0	8	2	.80	1	.336	.384	.526
1991	New York	AL	96	298	72	12	4	3	(3	0)	101	35	23	15	0	52	5	2	2	12	1	.92	5	.242	.288	.339

Roberto Kelly

Bats: Right **Throws:** Right **Pos:** CF/LF **Ht:** 6' 2" **Wt:** 192 **Born:** 10/01/64 **Age:** 27

Year	Team	Lg	G	AB	H	2B	3B	HR	(Hm	Rd)	TB	R	RBI	TBB	IBB	SO	HBP	SH	SF	SB	CS	SB%	GDP	Avg	OBP	SLG
1987	New York	AL	23	52	14	3	0	1	(0	1)	20	12	7	5	0	15	0	1	1	9	3	.75	0	.269	.328	.385
1988	New York	AL	38	77	19	4	1	1	(0	1)	28	9	7	3	0	15	0	3	1	5	2	.71	0	.247	.272	.364
1989	New York	AL	137	441	133	18	3	9	(2	7)	184	65	48	41	3	89	6	8	0	35	12	.74	9	.302	.369	.417
1990	New York	AL	162	641	183	32	4	15	(5	10)	268	85	61	33	0	148	4	4	4	42	17	.71	7	.285	.323	.418
1991	New York	AL	126	486	130	22	2	20	(11	9)	216	68	69	45	2	77	5	2	5	32	9	.78	14	.267	.333	.444
	5 ML YEARS		486	1697	479	79	10	46	(19	27)	716	239	192	127	5	344	15	18	11	123	43	.74	30	.282	.336	.422

Terry Kennedy

Bats: Left **Throws:** Right **Pos:** C **Ht:** 6' 4" **Wt:** 220 **Born:** 06/04/56 **Age:** 36

Year	Team	Lg	G	AB	H	2B	3B	HR	(Hm	Rd)	TB	R	RBI	TBB	IBB	SO	HBP	SH	SF	SB	CS	SB%	GDP	Avg	OBP	SLG
1978	St. Louis	NL	10	29	5	0	0	0	(0	0)	5	0	2	4	2	3	0	0	0	0	0	.00	2	.172	.273	.172
1979	St. Louis	NL	33	109	31	7	0	2	(2	0)	44	11	17	6	2	20	0	0	1	0	0	.00	2	.284	.319	.404
1980	St. Louis	NL	84	248	63	12	3	4	(1	3)	93	28	34	28	3	34	0	1	4	0	0	.00	9	.254	.325	.375
1981	San Diego	NL	101	382	115	24	1	2	(1	1)	147	32	41	22	6	53	2	4	2	0	2	.00	7	.301	.341	.385
1982	San Diego	NL	153	562	166	42	1	21	(10	11)	273	75	97	26	9	91	5	3	8	1	0	1.00	7	.295	.328	.486
1983	San Diego	NL	149	549	156	27	2	17	(7	10)	238	47	98	51	15	89	2	1	9	1	3	.25	10	.284	.342	.434
1984	San Diego	NL	148	530	127	16	1	14	(8	6)	187	54	57	33	8	99	2	0	5	1	2	.33	16	.240	.284	.353
1985	San Diego	NL	143	532	139	27	1	10	(7	3)	198	54	74	31	10	102	0	0	2	0	0	.00	19	.261	.301	.372
1986	San Diego	NL	143	432	114	22	1	12	(7	5)	174	46	57	37	7	74	2	4	1	0	3	.00	10	.264	.324	.403
1987	Baltimore	AL	143	512	128	13	1	18	(11	7)	197	51	62	35	6	112	1	1	0	1	0	1.00	13	.250	.299	.385
1988	Baltimore	AL	85	265	60	10	0	3	(2	1)	79	20	16	15	0	53	1	2	2	0	0	.00	13	.226	.269	.298
1989	San Francisco	NL	125	355	85	15	0	5	(1	4)	115	19	34	35	7	56	0	3	2	1	3	.25	6	.239	.306	.324
1990	San Francisco	NL	107	303	84	22	0	2	(2	0)	112	25	26	31	7	38	0	3	2	1	2	.33	7	.277	.342	.370
1991	San Francisco	NL	69	171	40	7	1	3	(2	1)	58	12	13	11	4	31	0	1	0	0	0	.00	4	.234	.283	.339
	14 ML YEARS		1491	4979	1313	244	12	113	(61	52)	1920	474	628	365	86	855	16	22	39	6	15	.29	125	.264	.314	.386

Jimmy Key

Pitches: Left   **Bats:** Right   **Pos:** SP   **Ht:** 6' 1"   **Wt:** 190   **Born:** 04/22/61   **Age:** 31

		HOW MUCH HE PITCHED						WHAT HE GAVE UP									THE RESULTS				
Year Team	Lg	G	GS	CG	GF	IP	BFP	H	R	ER	HR	SH	SF	HB	TBB	IBB	SO	WP	Bk	W	L	Pct.	ShO	Sv	ERA
1984 Toronto	AL	63	0	0	24	62	285	70	37	32	8	6	1	1	32	8	44	3	1	4	5	.444	0	10	4.65
1985 Toronto	AL	35	32	3	0	212.2	856	188	77	71	22	5	5	2	50	1	85	6	1	14	6	.700	0	0	3.00
1986 Toronto	AL	36	35	4	0	232	959	222	98	92	24	10	6	3	74	1	141	3	0	14	11	.560	2	0	3.57
1987 Toronto	AL	36	36	8	0	261	1033	210	93	80	24	11	3	2	66	6	161	8	5	17	8	.680	1	0	2.76
1988 Toronto	AL	21	21	2	0	131.1	551	127	55	48	13	4	3	5	30	2	65	1	0	12	5	.706	2	0	3.29
1989 Toronto	AL	33	33	5	0	216	886	226	99	93	18	9	9	3	27	2	118	4	1	13	14	.481	1	0	3.88
1990 Toronto	AL	27	27	0	0	154.2	636	169	79	73	20	5	6	1	22	2	88	0	1	13	7	.650	0	0	4.25
1991 Toronto	AL	33	33	2	0	209.1	877	207	84	71	12	10	5	3	44	3	125	1	0	16	12	.571	2	0	3.05
8 ML YEARS		284	217	24	24	1479	6083	1419	622	560	141	60	38	20	345	25	827	26	9	103	68	.602	8	10	3.41

Dana Kiecker

Pitches: Right   **Bats:** Right   **Pos:** RP/SP   **Ht:** 6' 3"   **Wt:** 195   **Born:** 02/25/61   **Age:** 31

		HOW MUCH HE PITCHED						WHAT HE GAVE UP									THE RESULTS				
Year Team	Lg	G	GS	CG	GF	IP	BFP	H	R	ER	HR	SH	SF	HB	TBB	IBB	SO	WP	Bk	W	L	Pct.	ShO	Sv	ERA
1984 Winston-Sal	A	29	19	5	8	137.2	615	142	86	67	12	2	3	1	55	2	82	12	2	6	11	.353	1	1	4.38
1985 Winter Havn	A	29	29	9	0	193.2	789	176	72	56	4	7	10	2	59	2	60	7	0	12	12	.500	2	0	2.60
1986 New Britain	AA	24	24	7	0	156.1	675	171	88	72	8	5	8	4	48	3	71	10	5	7	12	.368	0	0	4.14
1987 New Britain	AA	39	17	2	18	153	691	164	76	65	6	5	6	10	66	5	66	9	1	7	10	.412	0	6	3.82
1988 New Britain	AA	1	1	0	0	6	22	3	0	0	0	0	0	1	0	0	1	0	0	1	0	1.000	0	0	0.00
Pawtucket	AAA	23	22	4	1	132.1	556	120	65	54	7	2	2	6	46	2	74	5	7	7	7	.500	1	0	3.67
1989 Pawtucket	AAA	28	19	3	3	147.1	644	163	83	60	12	0	6	4	36	2	87	6	2	8	9	.471	0	0	3.67
1991 Pawtucket	AAA	8	7	0	0	38	175	42	24	16	4	3	0	3	19	2	23	2	0	2	3	.400	0	0	3.79
1990 Boston	AL	32	25	0	3	152	641	145	74	67	7	1	5	9	54	2	93	9	1	8	9	.471	0	0	3.97
1991 Boston	AL	18	5	0	3	40.1	194	56	34	33	6	5	1	2	23	4	21	3	2	2	3	.400	0	0	7.36
2 ML YEARS		50	30	0	6	192.1	835	201	108	100	13	6	6	11	77	6	114	12	3	10	12	.455	0	0	4.68

John Kiely

Pitches: Right   **Bats:** Right   **Pos:** RP   **Ht:** 6' 3"   **Wt:** 210   **Born:** 10/04/64   **Age:** 27

		HOW MUCH HE PITCHED						WHAT HE GAVE UP									THE RESULTS				
Year Team	Lg	G	GS	CG	GF	IP	BFP	H	R	ER	HR	SH	SF	HB	TBB	IBB	SO	WP	Bk	W	L	Pct.	ShO	Sv	ERA
1988 Bristol	R	8	0	0	6	11.2	53	9	9	8	0	2	0	0	7	0	14	2	0	2	2	.500	0	1	6.17
1989 Lakeland	A	36	0	0	22	63.2	267	52	26	17	2	4	3	0	27	4	56	1	2	4	3	.571	0	8	2.40
1990 London	AA	46	0	0	25	76.2	321	63	17	15	2	2	4	2	42	6	52	2	0	3	0	1.000	0	12	1.76
1991 Toledo	AAA	42	0	0	27	72	301	57	25	17	3	4	2	3	35	3	60	2	0	4	2	.667	0	6	2.13
1991 Detroit	AL	7	0	0	3	6.2	42	13	11	11	0	2	1	1	9	2	1	1	0	0	1	.000	0	0	14.85

Darryl Kile

Pitches: Right   **Bats:** Right   **Pos:** SP/RP   **Ht:** 6' 5"   **Wt:** 185   **Born:** 12/02/68   **Age:** 23

		HOW MUCH HE PITCHED						WHAT HE GAVE UP									THE RESULTS				
Year Team	Lg	G	GS	CG	GF	IP	BFP	H	R	ER	HR	SH	SF	HB	TBB	IBB	SO	WP	Bk	W	L	Pct.	ShO	Sv	ERA
1988 Astros	R	12	12	0	0	59.2	263	48	34	21	1	3	1	3	33	0	54	9	8	5	3	.625	0	0	3.17
1989 Columbus	AA	20	20	6	0	125.2	508	74	47	36	5	3	4	6	68	1	108	5	6	11	6	.647	2	0	2.58
Tucson	AAA	6	6	1	0	25.2	122	33	20	17	1	0	0	1	13	0	18	1	1	2	1	.667	1	0	5.96
1990 Tucson	AAA	26	23	1	1	123.1	575	147	97	91	16	2	5	6	68	1	77	13	4	5	10	.333	0	0	6.64
1991 Houston	NL	37	22	0	5	153.2	689	144	81	63	16	9	5	6	84	4	100	5	4	7	11	.389	0	0	3.69

Paul Kilgus

Pitches: Left   **Bats:** Left   **Pos:** RP   **Ht:** 6' 1"   **Wt:** 185   **Born:** 02/02/62   **Age:** 30

		HOW MUCH HE PITCHED						WHAT HE GAVE UP									THE RESULTS				
Year Team	Lg	G	GS	CG	GF	IP	BFP	H	R	ER	HR	SH	SF	HB	TBB	IBB	SO	WP	Bk	W	L	Pct.	ShO	Sv	ERA
1987 Texas	AL	25	12	0	2	89.1	385	95	45	41	14	2	0	2	31	2	42	0	0	2	7	.222	0	0	4.13
1988 Texas	AL	32	32	5	0	203.1	871	190	105	94	18	4	4	10	71	2	88	6	4	12	15	.444	3	0	4.16
1989 Chicago	NL	35	23	0	5	145.2	642	164	90	71	9	5	4	5	49	6	61	3	2	6	10	.375	0	2	4.39
1990 Toronto	AL	11	0	0	4	16.1	74	19	11	11	2	1	3	1	7	1	7	0	0	0	0	.000	0	0	6.06
1991 Baltimore	AL	38	0	0	14	62	267	60	38	35	8	2	4	3	24	2	32	2	0	0	2	.000	0	1	5.08
5 ML YEARS		141	67	5	25	516.2	2239	528	289	252	51	14	15	21	182	13	230	11	6	20	34	.370	3	3	4.39

Eric King

Pitches: Right   **Bats:** Right   **Pos:** SP   **Ht:** 6' 2"   **Wt:** 218   **Born:** 04/10/64   **Age:** 28

		HOW MUCH HE PITCHED						WHAT HE GAVE UP									THE RESULTS				
Year Team	Lg	G	GS	CG	GF	IP	BFP	H	R	ER	HR	SH	SF	HB	TBB	IBB	SO	WP	Bk	W	L	Pct.	ShO	Sv	ERA
1986 Detroit	AL	33	16	3	9	138.1	579	108	54	54	11	6	1	8	63	3	79	4	3	11	4	.733	1	3	3.51
1987 Detroit	AL	55	4	0	26	116	513	111	67	63	15	3	3	4	60	10	89	5	1	6	9	.400	0	9	4.89

109

Year	Team	Lg	G	GS	CG	GF	IP	BFP	H	R	ER	HR	SH	SF	HB	TBB	IBB	SO	WP	Bk	W	L	Pct.	ShO	Sv	ERA
1988	Detroit	AL	23	5	0	8	68.2	303	60	28	26	5	5	2	5	34	2	45	4	2	4	1	.800	0	3	3.41
1989	Chicago	AL	25	25	1	0	159.1	666	144	69	60	13	3	4	4	64	1	72	5	4	9	10	.474	1	0	3.39
1990	Chicago	AL	25	25	2	0	151	623	135	59	55	10	6	1	6	40	0	70	2	3	12	4	.750	2	0	3.28
1991	Cleveland	AL	25	24	2	0	150.2	656	166	83	77	7	7	8	3	44	4	59	2	2	6	11	.353	1	0	4.60
6 ML YEARS			186	99	8	43	784	3340	724	360	335	61	30	19	30	305	20	414	22	15	48	39	.552	5	15	3.85

Jeff King

Bats: Right **Throws:** Right **Pos:** 3B **Ht:** 6' 1" **Wt:** 185 **Born:** 12/26/64 **Age:** 27

							BATTING												BASERUNNING				PERCENTAGES		
Year	Team	Lg	G	AB	H	2B	3B	HR	(Hm | Rd)	TB	R	RBI	TBB	IBB	SO	HBP	SH	SF	SB	CS	SB%	GDP	Avg	OBP	SLG
1989	Pittsburgh	NL	75	215	42	13	3	5	(3 | 2)	76	31	19	20	1	34	2	2	4	4	2	.67	3	.195	.266	.353
1990	Pittsburgh	NL	127	371	91	17	1	14	(9 | 5)	152	46	53	21	1	50	1	2	7	3	3	.50	12	.245	.283	.410
1991	Pittsburgh	NL	33	109	26	1	1	4	(3 | 1)	41	16	18	14	3	15	1	0	1	3	1	.75	3	.239	.328	.376
3 ML YEARS			235	695	159	31	5	23	(15 | 8)	269	93	90	55	5	99	4	4	12	10	6	.63	18	.229	.285	.387

Mike Kingery

Bats: Left **Throws:** Left **Pos:** RF **Ht:** 6' 0" **Wt:** 185 **Born:** 03/29/61 **Age:** 31

							BATTING												BASERUNNING				PERCENTAGES		
Year	Team	Lg	G	AB	H	2B	3B	HR	(Hm	Rd)	TB	R	RBI	TBB	IBB	SO	HBP	SH	SF	SB	CS	SB%	GDP	Avg	OBP	SLG
1986	Kansas City	AL	62	209	54	8	5	3	(1	2)	81	25	14	12	2	30	0	0	2	7	3	.70	4	.258	.296	.388
1987	Seattle	AL	120	354	99	25	4	9	(5	4)	159	38	52	27	0	43	2	1	6	7	9	.44	4	.280	.329	.449
1988	Seattle	AL	57	123	25	6	0	1	(1	0)	34	21	9	19	1	23	1	1	1	3	1	.75	1	.203	.313	.276
1989	Seattle	AL	31	76	17	3	0	2	(2	0)	26	14	6	7	0	14	0	0	1	1	1	.50	2	.224	.286	.342
1990	San Francisco	NL	105	207	61	7	1	0	(0	0)	70	24	24	12	0	19	1	5	1	6	1	.86	1	.295	.335	.338
1991	San Francisco	NL	91	110	20	2	2	0	(0	0)	26	13	8	15	1	21	0	0	0	1	0	1.00	3	.182	.280	.236
6 ML YEARS			466	1079	276	51	12	15	(9	6)	396	135	113	92	4	150	4	7	11	25	15	.63	15	.256	.314	.367

Bob Kipper

Pitches: Left **Bats:** Right **Pos:** RP **Ht:** 6' 2" **Wt:** 185 **Born:** 07/08/64 **Age:** 27

			HOW MUCH HE PITCHED						WHAT HE GAVE UP										THE RESULTS					
Year	Team	Lg	G	GS	CG	GF	IP	BFP	H	R	ER	HR	SH	SF	HB	TBB	IBB	SO	WP	Bk	W	L	Pct.	ShO	Sv	ERA
1985	2 ML Teams		7	5	0	1	28	124	28	24	22	5	1	3	0	10	0	13	0	0	1	3	.250	0	0	7.07
1986	Pittsburgh	NL	20	19	0	1	114	496	123	60	51	17	3	3	0	34	3	81	3	3	6	8	.429	0	0	4.03
1987	Pittsburgh	NL	24	20	1	0	110.2	493	117	74	73	25	4	3	2	52	4	83	5	0	5	9	.357	1	0	5.94
1988	Pittsburgh	NL	50	0	0	15	65	267	54	33	27	7	5	3	2	26	4	39	1	1	2	6	.250	0	0	3.74
1989	Pittsburgh	NL	52	0	0	15	83	334	55	29	27	5	5	3	0	33	6	58	5	2	3	4	.429	0	4	2.93
1990	Pittsburgh	NL	41	1	0	7	62.2	260	44	24	21	7	2	3	3	26	1	35	1	5	5	2	.714	0	0	3.02
1991	Pittsburgh	NL	52	0	0	18	60	264	66	34	31	7	1	2	0	22	3	38	0	1	2	2	.500	0	4	4.65
1985	California	AL	2	1	0	0	3.1	20	7	8	8	1	0	2	0	3	0	0	0	0	0	1	.000	0	0	21.60
	Pittsburgh	NL	5	4	0	1	24.2	104	21	16	14	4	1	1	0	7	0	13	0	0	1	2	.333	0	0	5.11
7 ML YEARS			246	45	1	57	523.1	2238	487	278	252	73	21	20	9	203	21	347	15	12	24	34	.414	1	11	4.33

Wayne Kirby

Bats: Left **Throws:** Right **Pos:** RF **Ht:** 5'10" **Wt:** 185 **Born:** 01/22/64 **Age:** 28

							BATTING												BASERUNNING				PERCENTAGES		
Year	Team	Lg	G	AB	H	2B	3B	HR	(Hm	Rd)	TB	R	RBI	TBB	IBB	SO	HBP	SH	SF	SB	CS	SB%	GDP	Avg	OBP	SLG
1984	Vero Beach	A	76	224	61	6	3	0	--	--	73	39	21	21	2	30	6	5	2	11	9	.55	3	.272	.348	.326
	Great Falls	R	20	84	26	2	1	0	--	--	35	19	11	12	2	9	0	1	1	19	3	.86	2	.310	.392	.417
	Bakersfield	A	23	84	23	3	0	0	--	--	26	14	10	4	0	5	0	2	1	8	3	.73	0	.274	.303	.310
1985	Vero Beach	A	122	437	123	9	3	0	--	--	138	70	28	41	1	41	3	4	3	31	14	.69	3	.281	.345	.316
1986	Vero Beach	A	114	387	101	9	4	2	--	--	124	60	31	37	3	30	1	2	2	28	17	.62	5	.261	.326	.320
1987	San Antonio	AA	24	80	19	1	2	1	--	--	27	7	9	4	0	7	0	3	0	6	4	.60	0	.238	.274	.338
	Bakersfield	A	105	416	112	14	3	0	--	--	132	77	34	49	1	41	3	5	2	56	21	.73	3	.269	.349	.317
1988	Bakersfield	A	12	47	13	0	1	0	--	--	15	12	4	11	0	4	0	0	0	9	2	.82	0	.277	.414	.319
	San Antonio	AA	100	334	80	9	2	0	--	--	93	50	21	21	2	42	3	10	1	26	10	.72	5	.240	.290	.278
1989	San Antonio	AA	44	140	30	3	1	0	--	--	35	14	7	18	0	17	1	2	1	11	6	.65	4	.214	.306	.250
	Albuquerque	AAA	78	310	106	18	8	0	--	--	140	62	30	26	1	27	1	5	1	29	14	.67	2	.342	.393	.452
1990	Albuquerque	AAA	119	342	95	14	5	0	--	--	119	56	30	28	1	36	3	4	3	29	7	.81	2	.278	.335	.348
1991	Colo Sprngs	AAA	118	385	113	14	4	1	--	--	138	66	39	34	2	36	2	5	3	29	14	.67	3	.294	.351	.358
1991	Cleveland	AL	21	43	9	2	0	0	(0	0)	11	4	5	2	0	6	0	1	1	1	2	.33	2	.209	.239	.256

Garland Kiser

Pitches: Left   **Bats:** Left   **Pos:** RP   **Ht:** 6' 3"   **Wt:** 190   **Born:** 07/08/68   **Age:** 23

		HOW MUCH HE PITCHED						WHAT HE GAVE UP										THE RESULTS				
Year Team	Lg	G	GS	CG	GF	IP	BFP	H	R	ER	HR	SH	SF	HB	TBB	IBB	SO	WP	Bk	W	L	Pct.	ShO	Sv	ERA
1986 Bend	A	14	12	0	2	70.2	0	79	58	43	4	0	0	2	48	2	46	6	1	4	5	.444	0	0	5.48
1987 Spartanburg	A	21	5	0	6	43	204	49	37	31	2	4	1	4	24	2	27	6	0	0	5	.000	0	1	6.49
1988 Indians	R	7	7	2	1	56	221	31	12	8	0	0	0	2	17	0	45	0	2	5	1	.833	0	0	1.29
Burlington	R	7	5	1	1	31	123	22	11	7	0	0	0	0	9	0	29	1	2	2	2	.500	0	0	2.03
1989 Kinston	A	6	0	0	1	12.2	60	14	10	10	1	1	1	2	7	0	7	0	0	0	1	.000	0	0	7.11
Watertown	A	12	9	2	2	74	304	66	36	28	4	4	0	2	18	0	74	5	2	7	1	.875	0	0	3.41
1990 Kinston	A	55	0	0	24	94.2	388	81	35	18	3	5	3	3	27	1	82	5	0	5	3	.625	0	9	1.71
1991 Kinston	A	31	0	0	12	48.1	197	35	11	8	2	3	0	1	14	2	52	3	0	6	1	.857	0	5	1.49
Canton-Akrn	AA	17	4	0	6	44.1	170	35	13	10	1	1	0	1	11	2	34	3	0	2	3	.400	0	0	2.03
1991 Cleveland	AL	7	0	0	1	4.2	25	7	5	5	0	1	0	1	4	0	3	0	0	0	0	.000	0	0	9.64

Ron Kittle

Bats: Right   **Throws:** Right   **Pos:** 1B   **Ht:** 6' 4"   **Wt:** 220   **Born:** 01/05/58   **Age:** 34

		BATTING																BASERUNNING				PERCENTAGES		
Year Team	Lg	G	AB	H	2B	3B	HR	(Hm	Rd)	TB	R	RBI	TBB	IBB	SO	HBP	SH	SF	SB	CS	SB%	GDP	Avg	OBP	SLG
1982 Chicago	AL	20	29	7	2	0	1	(0	1)	12	3	7	3	0	12	0	0	0	0	0	.00	0	.241	.313	.414
1983 Chicago	AL	145	520	132	19	3	35	(18	17)	262	75	100	39	3	150	8	0	3	8	3	.73	10	.254	.314	.504
1984 Chicago	AL	139	466	100	15	0	32	(17	15)	211	67	74	49	5	137	6	0	4	3	6	.33	7	.215	.295	.453
1985 Chicago	AL	116	379	87	12	0	26	(12	14)	177	51	58	31	1	92	5	0	2	1	4	.20	12	.230	.295	.467
1986 2 ML Teams		116	376	82	13	0	21	(6	15)	158	42	60	35	1	110	3	0	8	4	1	.80	10	.218	.284	.420
1987 New York	AL	59	159	44	5	0	12	(7	5)	85	21	28	10	1	36	1	0	3	0	1	.00	4	.277	.318	.535
1988 Cleveland	AL	75	225	58	8	0	18	(7	11)	120	31	43	16	1	65	8	0	5	0	0	.00	0	.258	.323	.533
1989 Chicago	AL	51	169	51	10	0	11	(6	5)	94	26	37	22	1	42	1	0	4	0	1	.00	2	.302	.378	.556
1990 2 ML Teams		105	338	78	16	0	18	(8	10)	148	33	46	26	2	91	4	0	1	0	0	.00	6	.231	.293	.438
1991 Chicago	AL	17	47	9	0	0	2	(0	2)	15	7	7	5	0	9	2	0	1	0	0	.00	2	.191	.264	.319
1986 Chicago	AL	86	296	63	11	0	17	(5	12)	125	34	48	28	0	87	3	0	6	2	1	.67	10	.213	.282	.422
New York	AL	30	80	19	2	0	4	(1	3)	33	8	12	7	1	23	0	0	2	2	0	1.00	0	.238	.292	.413
1990 Chicago	AL	83	277	68	14	0	16	(7	9)	130	29	43	24	2	77	3	0	1	0	0	.00	3	.245	.311	.469
Baltimore	AL	22	61	10	2	0	2	(1	1)	18	4	3	2	0	14	1	0	0	0	0	.00	3	.164	.203	.295
10 ML YEARS		843	2708	648	100	3	176	(81	95)	1282	356	460	236	20	744	38	0	31	16	16	.50	53	.239	.306	.473

Joe Klink

Pitches: Left   **Bats:** Left   **Pos:** RP   **Ht:** 5'11"   **Wt:** 175   **Born:** 02/03/62   **Age:** 30

		HOW MUCH HE PITCHED						WHAT HE GAVE UP										THE RESULTS				
Year Team	Lg	G	GS	CG	GF	IP	BFP	H	R	ER	HR	SH	SF	HB	TBB	IBB	SO	WP	Bk	W	L	Pct.	ShO	Sv	ERA
1987 Minnesota	AL	12	0	0	5	23	116	37	18	17	4	1	1	0	11	0	17	1	0	0	1	.000	0	0	6.65
1990 Oakland	AL	40	0	0	19	39.2	165	34	9	9	1	0	0	0	18	0	19	3	1	0	0	.000	0	1	2.04
1991 Oakland	AL	62	0	0	10	62	266	60	30	30	4	8	0	5	21	5	34	4	0	10	3	.769	0	4	4.35
3 ML YEARS		114	0	0	34	124.2	547	131	57	56	9	10	1	5	50	5	70	8	1	10	4	.714	0	3	4.04

Chuck Knoblauch

Bats: Right   **Throws:** Right   **Pos:** 2B   **Ht:** 5' 9"   **Wt:** 175   **Born:** 07/07/68   **Age:** 23

		BATTING																BASERUNNING				PERCENTAGES		
Year Team	Lg	G	AB	H	2B	3B	HR	(Hm	Rd)	TB	R	RBI	TBB	IBB	SO	HBP	SH	SF	SB	CS	SB%	GDP	Avg	OBP	SLG
1989 Kenosha	A	51	196	56	13	1	2	--	--	77	29	19	32	0	23	1	1	1	9	7	.56	5	.286	.387	.393
Visalia	A	18	77	28	10	0	0	--	--	38	20	21	6	0	11	1	1	1	4	0	1.00	1	.364	.412	.494
1990 Orlando	AA	118	432	125	24	6	2	--	--	167	74	53	63	0	31	2	2	3	23	7	.77	13	.289	.389	.387
1991 Minnesota	AL	151	565	159	24	6	1	(1	0)	198	78	50	59	0	40	4	1	5	25	5	.83	8	.281	.351	.350

Randy Knorr

Bats: Right   **Throws:** Right   **Pos:** C   **Ht:** 6' 2"   **Wt:** 205   **Born:** 11/12/68   **Age:** 23

		BATTING																BASERUNNING				PERCENTAGES		
Year Team	Lg	G	AB	H	2B	3B	HR	(Hm	Rd)	TB	R	RBI	TBB	IBB	SO	HBP	SH	SF	SB	CS	SB%	GDP	Avg	OBP	SLG
1986 Medicne Hat	R	55	215	58	13	0	4	--	--	83	21	32	17	0	53	0	3	3	0	0	.00	6	.270	.319	.386
1987 Medicne Hat	R	26	106	31	7	0	10	--	--	68	21	21	6	5	26	1	0	3	0	0	.00	1	.292	.322	.642
Myrtle Bch	A	46	129	34	4	0	6	--	--	56	17	21	6	0	48	0	0	2	0	0	.00	1	.264	.292	.434
1988 Myrtle Bch	A	117	364	85	13	0	9	--	--	125	43	42	41	0	91	0	9	2	0	1	.00	7	.234	.310	.343
1989 Dunedin	A	33	122	32	6	0	6	--	--	56	13	23	6	0	21	0	0	3	0	2	.00	0	.262	.292	.459
1990 Knoxville	AA	116	392	108	12	1	13	--	--	161	51	64	31	2	83	2	4	6	0	3	.00	7	.276	.327	.411

Year Team	Lg	G	AB	H	2B	3B	HR	(Hm	Rd)	TB	R	RBI	TBB	IBB	SO	HBP	SH	SF	SB	CS	SB%	GDP	Avg	OBP	SLG
1991 Knoxville	AA	24	74	13	4	0	0	(--	--)	17	7	4	10	1	18	1	0	1	2	0	1.00	0	.176	.279	.230
Syracuse	AAA	91	342	89	20	0	5	(--	--)	124	29	44	23	3	58	3	0	4	1	0	1.00	17	.260	.309	.363
1991 Toronto	AL	3	3	0	0	0	0	(0	0)	0	0	0	1	0	1	0	0	0	0	0	.00	0	.000	.500	.000

Mark Knudson

Pitches: Right **Bats:** Right **Pos:** SP/RP   **Ht:** 6' 5" **Wt:** 200 **Born:** 10/28/60 **Age:** 31

Year Team	Lg	G	GS	CG	GF	IP	BFP	H	R	ER	HR	SH	SF	HB	TBB	IBB	SO	WP	Bk	W	L	Pct.	ShO	Sv	ERA
1985 Houston	NL	2	2	0	0	11	53	21	11	11	0	1	0	0	3	0	4	0	0	0	2	.000	0	0	9.00
1986 2 ML Teams		13	8	0	2	60.1	273	70	38	35	12	3	0	1	20	6	29	2	0	1	6	.143	0	0	5.22
1987 Milwaukee	AL	15	8	1	3	62	288	88	46	37	7	3	5	0	14	1	26	1	0	4	4	.500	0	0	5.37
1988 Milwaukee	AL	5	0	0	3	16	63	17	3	2	1	0	0	0	2	0	7	1	0	0	0	.000	0	0	1.13
1989 Milwaukee	AL	40	7	1	16	123.2	499	110	50	46	15	2	1	3	29	2	47	2	0	8	5	.615	0	0	3.35
1990 Milwaukee	AL	30	27	4	0	168.1	719	187	84	77	14	3	9	3	40	1	56	6	0	10	9	.526	2	0	4.12
1991 Milwaukee	AL	12	7	0	3	35	174	54	33	31	8	3	3	1	15	0	23	1	0	1	3	.250	0	0	7.97
1986 Houston	NL	9	7	0	1	42.2	191	48	23	20	5	3	0	1	15	5	20	1	0	1	5	.167	0	0	4.22
Milwaukee	AL	4	1	0	1	17.2	82	22	15	15	7	0	0	0	5	1	9	1	0	0	1	.000	0	0	7.64
7 ML YEARS		117	59	6	27	476.1	2069	547	265	239	57	15	18	8	123	10	192	13	0	24	29	.453	2	0	4.52

Brad Komminsk

Bats: Right **Throws:** Right **Pos:** LF   **Ht:** 6' 2" **Wt:** 205 **Born:** 04/04/61 **Age:** 31

Year Team	Lg	G	AB	H	2B	3B	HR	(Hm	Rd)	TB	R	RBI	TBB	IBB	SO	HBP	SH	SF	SB	CS	SB%	GDP	Avg	OBP	SLG
1983 Atlanta	NL	19	36	8	2	0	0	(0	0)	10	2	4	5	0	7	0	0	0	0	0	.00	1	.222	.317	.278
1984 Atlanta	NL	90	301	61	10	0	8	(3	5)	95	37	36	29	0	77	2	1	1	18	8	.69	5	.203	.276	.316
1985 Atlanta	NL	106	300	68	12	3	4	(1	3)	98	52	21	38	1	71	1	2	2	10	8	.56	4	.227	.314	.327
1986 Atlanta	NL	5	5	2	0	0	0	(0	0)	2	1	1	0	0	1	0	0	0	0	1	.00	0	.400	.400	.400
1987 Milwaukee	AL	7	15	1	0	0	0	(0	0)	1	0	0	1	0	7	0	1	0	1	0	1.00	0	.067	.125	.067
1989 Cleveland	AL	71	198	47	8	2	8	(6	2)	83	27	33	24	0	55	1	1	3	8	2	.80	4	.237	.319	.419
1990 2 ML Teams		54	106	25	4	0	3	(3	0)	38	20	8	15	1	31	2	2	0	1	1	.50	2	.236	.341	.358
1991 Oakland	AL	24	25	3	1	0	0	(0	0)	4	1	2	2	0	9	0	0	0	1	0	1.00	0	.120	.185	.160
1990 San Francisco	NL	8	5	1	0	0	0	(0	0)	1	2	0	1	0	2	0	0	0	0	0	.00	0	.200	.333	.200
Baltimore	AL	46	101	24	4	0	3	(3	0)	37	18	8	14	1	29	2	2	0	1	1	.50	2	.238	.342	.366
8 ML YEARS		376	986	215	37	5	23	(13	10)	331	140	105	114	2	258	6	7	6	39	20	.66	16	.218	.301	.336

Tom Kramer

Pitches: Right **Bats:** Both **Pos:** RP   **Ht:** 6' 0" **Wt:** 185 **Born:** 01/09/68 **Age:** 24

Year Team	Lg	G	GS	CG	GF	IP	BFP	H	R	ER	HR	SH	SF	HB	TBB	IBB	SO	WP	Bk	W	L	Pct.	ShO	Sv	ERA
1987 Burlington	R	12	11	2	1	71.2	292	57	31	24	2	0	1	1	26	0	71	0	0	7	3	.700	1	1	3.01
1988 Waterloo	A	27	27	10	0	198.2	814	173	70	56	9	10	3	3	60	3	152	5	3	14	7	.667	2	0	2.54
1989 Kinston	A	18	17	5	1	131.2	527	97	44	38	7	5	3	4	42	3	89	4	1	9	5	.643	1	0	2.60
Canton-Akrn	AA	10	8	1	0	43.1	202	58	34	30	6	3	4	0	20	0	26	3	0	1	6	.143	0	0	6.23
1990 Kinston	A	16	16	2	0	98	402	82	34	31	5	1	2	2	29	0	96	2	1	7	4	.636	1	0	2.85
Canton-Akrn	AA	12	10	2	0	72	287	67	25	24	3	2	1	0	14	1	46	1	0	6	3	.667	0	0	3.00
1991 Canton-Akrn	AA	35	5	0	13	79.1	320	61	23	21	5	6	1	1	34	3	61	3	0	7	3	.700	0	6	2.38
Colo Sprngs	AAA	10	1	0	6	11.1	43	5	1	1	1	0	0	0	5	0	18	1	0	1	0	1.000	0	4	0.79
1991 Cleveland	AL	4	0	0	1	4.2	30	10	9	9	2	0	3	0	6	0	4	0	0	0	0	.000	0	0	17.36

Chad Kreuter

Bats: Both **Throws:** Right **Pos:** C   **Ht:** 6' 2" **Wt:** 190 **Born:** 08/26/64 **Age:** 27

Year Team	Lg	G	AB	H	2B	3B	HR	(Hm	Rd)	TB	R	RBI	TBB	IBB	SO	HBP	SH	SF	SB	CS	SB%	GDP	Avg	OBP	SLG
1988 Texas	AL	16	51	14	2	1	1	(0	1)	21	3	5	7	0	13	0	0	0	0	0	.00	1	.275	.362	.412
1989 Texas	AL	87	158	24	3	0	5	(2	3)	42	16	9	27	0	40	0	6	1	0	1	.00	0	.152	.274	.266
1990 Texas	AL	22	22	1	1	0	0	(0	0)	2	2	2	8	0	9	0	1	1	0	0	.00	0	.045	.290	.091
1991 Texas	AL	3	4	0	0	0	0	(0	0)	0	0	0	0	0	1	0	0	0	0	0	.00	0	.000	.000	.000
4 ML YEARS		128	235	39	6	1	6	(2	4)	65	21	16	42	0	63	0	7	2	0	1	.00	5	.166	.290	.277

Bill Krueger

Pitches: Left **Bats:** Left **Pos:** SP/RP   **Ht:** 6' 5" **Wt:** 205 **Born:** 04/24/58 **Age:** 34

Year Team	Lg	G	GS	CG	GF	IP	BFP	H	R	ER	HR	SH	SF	HB	TBB	IBB	SO	WP	Bk	W	L	Pct.	ShO	Sv	ERA
1983 Oakland	AL	17	16	2	0	109.2	473	104	54	44	7	0	5	2	53	1	58	1	1	7	6	.538	0	0	3.61
1984 Oakland	AL	26	24	1	0	142	602	156	95	75	9	4	8	2	85	2	61	5	1	10	10	.500	0	0	4.75
1985 Oakland	AL	32	23	2	4	151.1	674	165	95	76	13	4	5	2	69	1	56	6	3	9	10	.474	0	0	4.52
1986 Oakland	AL	11	3	0	4	34.1	149	40	25	23	4	1	2	0	13	0	10	3	1	1	2	.333	0	1	6.03

Year Team	Lg	G	GS	CG	GF	IP	BFP	H	R	ER	HR	SH	SF	HB	TBB	IBB	SO	WP	Bk	W	L	Pct.	ShO	Sv	ERA
1987 2 ML Teams		11	0	0	1	8	46	12	9	6	0	0	0	0	9	3	4	0	1	0	3	.000	0	0	6.75
1988 Los Angeles	NL	1	1	0	0	2.1	14	4	3	3	0	0	0	1	2	1	1	0	0	0	0	.000	0	0	11.57
1989 Milwaukee	AL	34	5	0	8	93.2	403	96	43	40	9	5	1	0	33	3	72	10	1	3	2	.600	0	3	3.84
1990 Milwaukee	AL	30	17	0	4	129	566	137	70	57	10	3	10	3	54	6	64	8	0	6	8	.429	0	0	3.98
1991 Seattle	AL	35	25	1	2	175	751	194	82	70	15	6	9	4	60	4	91	10	1	11	8	.579	0	0	3.60
1987 Oakland	AL	9	0	0	1	5.2	33	9	7	6	0	0	0	0	8	3	2	0	1	0	3	.000	0	0	9.53
Los Angeles	NL	2	0	0	0	2.1	13	3	2	0	0	0	0	0	1	0	2	0	0	0	0	.000	0	0	0.00
9 ML YEARS		197	114	6	23	845.1	3723	908	476	394	67	20	40	14	378	21	417	43	9	47	49	.490	0	4	4.19

John Kruk

Bats: Left   **Throws:** Left   **Pos:** 1B/LF/CF   **Ht:** 5'10"   **Wt:** 200   **Born:** 02/09/61   **Age:** 31

						BATTING														BASERUNNING				PERCENTAGES		
Year Team	Lg	G	AB	H	2B	3B	HR	(Hm	Rd)	TB	R	RBI	TBB	IBB	SO	HBP	SH	SF	SB	CS	SB%	GDP	Avg	OBP	SLG
1986 San Diego	NL	122	278	86	16	2	4	(1	3)	118	33	38	45	0	58	0	2	2	2	4	.33	11	.309	.403	.424
1987 San Diego	NL	138	447	140	14	2	20	(8	12)	218	72	91	73	15	93	0	3	4	18	10	.64	6	.313	.406	.488
1988 San Diego	NL	120	378	91	17	1	9	(8	1)	137	54	44	80	12	68	0	3	5	5	3	.63	7	.241	.369	.362
1989 2 ML Teams		112	357	107	13	6	8	(6	2)	156	53	44	44	2	53	0	2	3	3	0	1.00	10	.300	.374	.437
1990 Philadelphia	NL	142	443	129	25	8	7	(2	5)	191	52	67	69	16	70	0	2	1	10	5	.67	11	.291	.386	.431
1991 Philadelphia	NL	152	538	158	27	6	21	(8	13)	260	84	92	67	16	100	1	0	9	7	0	1.00	10	.294	.367	.483
1989 San Diego	NL	31	76	14	0	0	3	(2	1)	23	7	6	17	0	14	0	1	0	0	0	.00	5	.184	.333	.303
Philadelphia	NL	81	281	93	13	6	5	(4	1)	133	46	38	27	2	39	0	1	3	3	0	1.00	5	.331	.386	.473
6 ML YEARS		786	2441	711	112	25	69	(33	36)	1080	348	376	378	61	442	1	12	24	45	22	.67	55	.291	.383	.442

Mike LaCoss

Pitches: Right   **Bats:** Right   **Pos:** RP/SP   **Ht:** 6' 6"   **Wt:** 200   **Born:** 05/30/56   **Age:** 36

			HOW MUCH HE PITCHED					WHAT HE GAVE UP												THE RESULTS					
Year Team	Lg	G	GS	CG	GF	IP	BFP	H	R	ER	HR	SH	SF	HB	TBB	IBB	SO	WP	Bk	W	L	Pct.	ShO	Sv	ERA
1978 Cincinnati	NL	16	15	2	0	96	420	104	56	48	5	6	6	1	46	9	31	2	1	4	8	.333	1	0	4.50
1979 Cincinnati	NL	35	32	6	0	206	868	202	92	80	13	12	6	2	79	8	73	3	3	14	8	.636	1	0	3.50
1980 Cincinnati	NL	34	29	4	1	169	762	207	101	87	9	7	3	2	68	8	59	3	2	10	12	.455	2	0	4.63
1981 Cincinnati	NL	20	13	1	3	78	354	102	55	53	7	4	5	1	30	4	22	1	0	4	7	.364	1	1	6.12
1982 Houston	NL	41	8	0	11	115	488	107	41	37	3	5	0	4	54	6	51	5	1	6	6	.500	2	0	2.90
1983 Houston	NL	38	17	2	6	138	590	142	81	68	10	6	6	2	56	11	53	9	1	5	7	.417	0	1	4.43
1984 Houston	NL	39	18	2	6	132	565	132	64	59	3	3	2	0	55	5	86	9	1	7	5	.583	1	3	4.02
1985 Kansas City	AL	21	0	0	7	40.2	193	49	25	23	2	3	0	0	29	6	26	2	0	1	1	.500	0	1	5.09
1986 San Francisco	NL	37	31	4	1	204.1	842	179	99	81	14	16	3	6	70	8	86	5	5	10	13	.435	1	0	3.57
1987 San Francisco	NL	39	26	2	4	171	728	184	78	70	16	9	3	2	63	12	79	6	1	13	10	.565	1	0	3.68
1988 San Francisco	NL	19	19	1	0	114.1	477	99	55	46	5	5	1	1	47	3	70	6	2	7	7	.500	1	0	3.62
1989 San Francisco	NL	45	18	1	16	150.1	647	143	62	53	3	8	7	7	65	4	78	1	5	10	10	.500	0	6	3.17
1990 San Francisco	NL	13	12	1	0	77.2	337	75	37	34	5	4	4	0	39	2	39	1	1	6	4	.600	0	0	3.94
1991 San Francisco	NL	18	5	0	6	47.1	225	61	39	38	4	3	2	2	24	0	30	2	0	1	5	.167	0	0	7.23
14 ML YEARS		415	243	26	61	1739.2	7496	1786	885	777	99	91	48	29	725	86	783	55	23	98	103	.488	9	12	4.02

Steve Lake

Bats: Right   **Throws:** Right   **Pos:** C   **Ht:** 6' 1"   **Wt:** 202   **Born:** 03/14/57   **Age:** 35

						BATTING														BASERUNNING				PERCENTAGES		
Year Team	Lg	G	AB	H	2B	3B	HR	(Hm	Rd)	TB	R	RBI	TBB	IBB	SO	HBP	SH	SF	SB	CS	SB%	GDP	Avg	OBP	SLG
1983 Chicago	NL	38	85	22	4	1	1	(1	0)	31	9	7	2	2	6	1	0	0	0	0	.00	4	.259	.284	.365
1984 Chicago	NL	25	54	12	4	0	2	(1	1)	22	4	7	0	0	7	1	1	1	0	0	.00	0	.222	.232	.407
1985 Chicago	NL	58	119	18	2	0	1	(1	0)	23	5	11	3	1	21	1	4	1	1	0	1.00	3	.151	.177	.193
1986 2 ML Teams		36	68	20	2	0	2	(0	2)	28	8	14	3	1	7	0	1	0	0	0	.00	3	.294	.324	.412
1987 St. Louis	NL	74	179	45	7	2	2	(1	1)	62	19	19	10	4	18	0	5	1	0	0	.00	2	.251	.289	.346
1988 St. Louis	NL	36	54	15	3	0	1	(1	0)	21	5	4	3	0	15	2	0	0	0	0	.00	0	.278	.339	.389
1989 Philadelphia	NL	58	155	39	5	1	2	(1	1)	52	9	14	12	4	20	0	1	1	0	0	.00	6	.252	.304	.335
1990 Philadelphia	NL	29	80	20	2	0	0	(0	0)	22	4	6	3	1	12	1	0	1	0	0	.00	1	.250	.286	.275
1991 Philadelphia	NL	58	158	36	4	1	1	(0	1)	45	12	11	2	1	26	0	4	0	0	0	.00	2	.228	.238	.285
1986 Chicago	NL	10	19	8	1	0	0	(0	0)	9	4	4	1	1	2	0	1	0	0	0	.00	1	.421	.450	.474
St. Louis	NL	26	49	12	1	0	2	(0	2)	19	4	10	2	0	5	0	0	0	0	0	.00	2	.245	.275	.388
9 ML YEARS		412	952	227	33	5	12	(6	6)	306	75	93	38	14	132	6	16	4	1	0	1.00	24	.238	.271	.321

Dennis Lamp

Pitches: Right   **Bats:** Right   **Pos:** RP   **Ht:** 6' 3"   **Wt:** 215   **Born:** 09/23/52   **Age:** 39

			HOW MUCH HE PITCHED					WHAT HE GAVE UP												THE RESULTS					
Year Team	Lg	G	GS	CG	GF	IP	BFP	H	R	ER	HR	SH	SF	HB	TBB	IBB	SO	WP	Bk	W	L	Pct.	ShO	Sv	ERA
1977 Chicago	NL	11	3	0	4	30	137	43	21	21	3	1	1	2	8	4	12	0	1	0	2	.000	0	0	6.30
1978 Chicago	NL	37	36	6	0	224	928	221	96	82	16	10	3	4	56	8	73	2	2	7	15	.318	3	0	3.29
1979 Chicago	NL	38	32	6	3	200	843	223	96	78	14	9	5	5	46	9	86	1	0	11	10	.524	1	0	3.51

Year	Team	Lg	G	AB	H	2B	3B	HR	IP	BFP	R	RBI	TBB	IBB	SO	HBP	SH	SF	SB	CS	SB%	GDP	Avg	OBP	SLG
1980	Chicago	NL	41	37	2	3	203	921	259	123	117	16	17	4	1	82	7	83	10	0	10	14	.417	1	0	5.19
1981	Chicago	AL	27	10	3	5	127	514	103	41	34	4	5	0	1	43	1	71	4	1	7	6	.538	0	0	2.41
1982	Chicago	AL	44	27	3	11	189.2	817	206	96	84	9	12	2	6	59	3	78	5	0	11	8	.579	2	5	3.99
1983	Chicago	AL	49	5	1	31	116.1	483	123	52	48	6	2	1	4	29	7	44	0	0	7	7	.500	0	15	3.71
1984	Toronto	AL	56	4	0	37	85	387	97	53	43	9	7	1	1	38	7	45	2	0	8	8	.500	0	9	4.55
1985	Toronto	AL	53	1	0	11	105.2	426	96	42	39	7	5	6	0	27	3	68	5	0	11	0	1.000	0	2	3.32
1986	Toronto	AL	40	2	0	11	73	329	93	50	41	5	4	1	0	23	6	30	2	0	2	6	.250	0	2	5.05
1987	Oakland	AL	36	5	0	10	56.2	262	76	38	32	5	3	3	1	22	3	36	4	0	1	3	.250	0	0	5.08
1988	Boston	AL	46	0	0	14	82.2	350	92	39	32	3	3	2	2	19	3	49	5	8	7	6	.538	0	0	3.48
1989	Boston	AL	42	0	0	14	112.1	445	96	37	29	4	5	5	0	27	6	61	1	1	4	2	.667	0	2	2.32
1990	Boston	AL	47	1	0	5	105.2	453	114	61	55	10	8	4	3	30	8	49	2	0	3	5	.375	0	0	4.68
1991	Boston	AL	51	0	0	12	92	403	100	54	48	8	3	2	3	31	7	57	1	0	6	3	.667	0	0	4.70
15 ML YEARS			618	163	21	171	1803	7698	1942	899	783	119	94	40	33	540	82	842	44	13	95	95	.500	7	35	3.91

Tom Lampkin

Bats: Left   **Throws:** Right   **Pos:** C   **Ht:** 5'11" **Wt:** 183 **Born:** 03/04/64 **Age:** 28

									BATTING												BASERUNNING				PERCENTAGES		
Year	Team	Lg	G	AB	H	2B	3B	HR	(Hm	Rd)	TB	R	RBI	TBB	IBB	SO	HBP	SH	SF	SB	CS	SB%	GDP	Avg	OBP	SLG
1986	Batavia	A	63	190	49	5	1	1	--	--	59	24	20	31	3	14	0	1	1	4	3	.57	4	.258	.360	.311
1987	Waterloo	A	118	398	106	19	2	7	--	--	150	49	55	34	2	41	2	1	6	5	0	1.00	1	.266	.323	.377
1988	Williamsprt	AA	80	263	71	10	0	3	--	--	90	38	23	25	3	20	3	0	0	1	2	.33	6	.270	.340	.342
	Colo Sprngs	AAA	34	107	30	5	0	0	--	--	35	14	7	9	1	12	2	1	0	0	0	.00	3	.280	.347	.327
1989	Colo Sprngs	AAA	63	209	67	10	3	4	--	--	95	26	32	10	1	18	2	2	1	4	2	.67	5	.321	.356	.455
1990	Colo Sprngs	AAA	69	199	44	7	5	1	--	--	64	32	18	19	0	19	2	0	1	7	2	.78	2	.221	.294	.322
	Las Vegas	AAA	1	2	1	0	0	0	--	--	1	0	0	0	0	1	0	0	0	0	0	.00	0	.500	.500	.500
1991	Las Vegas	AAA	45	164	52	11	1	2	--	--	71	25	29	10	1	20	2	0	1	2	1	.67	4	.317	.362	.433
1988	Cleveland	AL	4	4	0	0	0	0	(0	0)	0	0	0	1	0	0	0	0	0	0	0	.00	1	.000	.000	.000
1990	San Diego	NL	26	63	14	0	1	1	(1	0)	19	4	4	4	1	9	0	0	0	0	1	.00	2	.222	.269	.302
1991	San Diego	NL	38	58	11	3	1	0	(0	0)	16	4	3	3	0	9	0	0	0	1	0	.00	0	.190	.230	.276
3 ML YEARS			68	125	25	3	2	1	(1	0)	35	8	7	8	1	18	0	0	0	1	1	.00	3	.200	.248	.280

Les Lancaster

Pitches: Right   **Bats:** Right   **Pos:** RP/SP   **Ht:** 6' 2" **Wt:** 200 **Born:** 04/21/62 **Age:** 30

			HOW MUCH HE PITCHED					WHAT HE GAVE UP										THE RESULTS					
Year	Team	Lg	G	GS	CG	GF	IP	BFP	H	R	ER	HR	SH	SF	HB	TBB	IBB	SO	WP	Bk	W	L	Pct.	ShO	Sv	ERA
1987	Chicago	NL	27	18	0	4	132.1	578	138	76	72	14	5	6	1	51	5	78	7	8	8	3	.727	0	0	4.90
1988	Chicago	NL	44	3	1	15	85.2	371	89	42	36	4	3	7	1	34	7	36	3	3	4	6	.400	0	5	3.78
1989	Chicago	NL	42	0	0	15	72.2	288	60	12	11	2	3	4	0	15	1	56	2	1	4	2	.667	0	8	1.36
1990	Chicago	NL	55	6	1	26	109	479	121	57	56	11	6	5	1	40	8	65	7	0	9	5	.643	1	6	4.62
1991	Chicago	NL	64	11	0	21	156	653	150	68	61	13	9	4	4	49	7	102	2	2	9	7	.563	0	3	3.52
5 ML YEARS			232	38	3	81	555.2	2369	558	255	236	44	26	26	7	189	28	337	21	14	34	23	.596	1	22	3.82

Bill Landrum

Pitches: Right   **Bats:** Right   **Pos:** RP   **Ht:** 6' 2" **Wt:** 205 **Born:** 08/17/58 **Age:** 33

			HOW MUCH HE PITCHED					WHAT HE GAVE UP										THE RESULTS					
Year	Team	Lg	G	GS	CG	GF	IP	BFP	H	R	ER	HR	SH	SF	HB	TBB	IBB	SO	WP	Bk	W	L	Pct.	ShO	Sv	ERA
1986	Cincinnati	NL	10	0	0	4	13.1	65	23	11	10	0	1	1	0	4	0	14	0	0	0	0	.000	0	0	6.75
1987	Cincinnati	NL	44	2	0	14	65	276	68	35	34	3	7	2	0	34	6	42	4	1	3	2	.600	0	2	4.71
1988	Chicago	NL	7	0	0	5	12.1	55	19	8	8	1	0	0	0	3	0	6	1	1	1	0	1.000	0	0	5.84
1989	Pittsburgh	NL	56	0	0	40	81	325	60	18	15	2	3	2	0	28	8	51	2	0	2	3	.400	0	26	1.67
1990	Pittsburgh	NL	54	0	0	41	71.2	292	69	22	17	4	5	3	0	21	5	39	1	1	7	3	.700	0	13	2.13
1991	Pittsburgh	NL	61	0	0	43	76.1	322	76	32	27	4	1	1	0	19	5	45	3	2	4	4	.500	0	17	3.18
6 ML YEARS			232	2	0	147	319.2	1335	315	126	111	14	17	9	0	109	24	197	11	5	17	12	.586	0	58	3.13

Ced Landrum

Bats: Left   **Throws:** Right   **Pos:** CF/LF   **Ht:** 5' 7" **Wt:** 167 **Born:** 09/03/63 **Age:** 28

									BATTING												BASERUNNING				PERCENTAGES		
Year	Team	Lg	G	AB	H	2B	3B	HR	(Hm	Rd)	TB	R	RBI	TBB	IBB	SO	HBP	SH	SF	SB	CS	SB%	GDP	Avg	OBP	SLG
1986	Geneva	A	64	213	67	6	2	3	--	--	86	51	16	40	1	33	3	4	3	49	10	.83	1	.315	.425	.404
1987	Winston-Sal	A	126	458	129	13	7	4	--	--	168	82	49	78	3	50	6	1	4	79	18	.81	6	.282	.390	.367
1988	Pittsfield	AA	128	445	109	15	8	1	--	--	143	82	39	55	2	63	8	10	4	69	17	.80	4	.245	.336	.321
1989	Charlotte	AA	123	361	92	11	2	6	--	--	125	72	37	48	0	54	5	5	2	45	9	.83	4	.255	.349	.346
1990	Iowa	AAA	123	372	110	10	4	0	--	--	128	71	24	43	1	63	1	5	3	46	16	.74	4	.296	.368	.344
1991	Iowa	AAA	38	131	44	8	2	1	--	--	59	14	11	5	0	21	0	2	0	13	4	.76	2	.336	.360	.450
1991	Chicago	NL	56	86	20	2	1	0	(0	0)	24	28	6	10	0	18	0	3	0	27	5	.84	2	.233	.313	.279

Mark Langston

Pitches: Left   Bats: Right   Pos: SP   Ht: 6' 2"   Wt: 184   Born: 08/20/60   Age: 31

Year	Team	Lg	G	GS	CG	GF	IP	BFP	H	R	ER	HR	SH	SF	HB	TBB	IBB	SO	WP	Bk	W	L	Pct.	ShO	Sv	ERA
1984	Seattle	AL	35	33	5	0	225	965	188	99	85	16	13	7	8	118	5	204	4	2	17	10	.630	2	0	3.40
1985	Seattle	AL	24	24	2	0	126.2	577	122	85	77	22	3	2	2	91	2	72	3	3	7	14	.333	0	0	5.47
1986	Seattle	AL	37	36	9	1	239.1	1057	234	142	129	30	5	8	4	123	1	245	10	3	12	14	.462	0	0	4.85
1987	Seattle	AL	35	35	14	0	272	1152	242	132	116	30	12	6	5	114	0	262	9	2	19	13	.594	3	0	3.84
1988	Seattle	AL	35	35	9	0	261.1	1078	222	108	97	32	6	5	3	110	2	235	7	4	15	11	.577	3	0	3.34
1989	2 ML Teams		34	34	8	0	250	1037	198	87	76	16	9	7	4	112	6	235	6	4	16	14	.533	5	0	2.74
1990	California	AL	33	33	5	0	223	950	215	120	109	13	6	6	5	104	1	195	8	0	10	17	.370	1	0	4.40
1991	California	AL	34	34	7	0	246.1	992	190	89	82	30	4	6	2	96	3	183	6	0	19	8	.704	0	0	3.00
1989	Seattle	AL	10	10	2	0	73.1	297	60	30	29	3	0	3	4	19	0	60	1	2	4	5	.444	1	0	3.56
	Montreal	NL	24	24	6	0	176.2	740	138	57	47	13	9	4	0	93	6	175	5	2	12	9	.571	4	0	2.39
8 ML YEARS			267	264	59	1	1843.2	7808	1611	862	771	189	58	47	33	868	20	1631	53	18	115	101	.532	14	0	3.76

Ray Lankford

Bats: Left   Throws: Left   Pos: CF   Ht: 5'11"   Wt: 180   Born: 06/05/67   Age: 25

Year	Team	Lg	G	AB	H	2B	3B	HR	(Hm	Rd)	TB	R	RBI	TBB	IBB	SO	HBP	SH	SF	SB	CS	SB%	GDP	Avg	OBP	SLG
1987	Johnson Cty	R	66	253	78	17	4	3	--	--	112	45	32	19	0	43	5	0	1	14	11	.56	5	.308	.367	.443
1988	Springfield	A	135	532	151	26	16	11	--	--	242	90	66	60	2	92	10	1	2	33	17	.66	4	.284	.366	.455
1989	Arkansas	AA	134	498	158	28	12	11	--	--	243	98	98	65	6	57	4	0	7	38	10	.79	7	.317	.395	.488
1990	Louisville	AAA	132	473	123	25	8	10	--	--	194	61	72	72	9	81	5	0	2	29	7	.81	6	.260	.362	.410
1990	St. Louis	NL	39	126	36	10	1	3	(2	1)	57	12	12	13	0	27	0	0	0	8	2	.80	1	.286	.353	.452
1991	St. Louis	NL	151	566	142	23	15	9	(4	5)	222	83	69	41	1	114	1	4	3	44	20	.69	4	.251	.301	.392
2 ML YEARS			190	692	178	33	16	12	(6	6)	279	95	81	54	1	141	1	4	3	52	22	.70	5	.257	.311	.403

Carney Lansford

Bats: Right   Throws: Right   Pos: 3B   Ht: 6' 2"   Wt: 195   Born: 02/07/57   Age: 35

Year	Team	Lg	G	AB	H	2B	3B	HR	(Hm	Rd)	TB	R	RBI	TBB	IBB	SO	HBP	SH	SF	SB	CS	SB%	GDP	Avg	OBP	SLG
1978	California	AL	121	453	133	23	2	8	(4	4)	184	63	52	31	2	67	4	5	7	20	9	.69	4	.294	.339	.406
1979	California	AL	157	654	188	30	5	19	(5	14)	285	114	79	39	2	115	3	12	4	20	8	.71	16	.287	.329	.436
1980	California	AL	151	602	157	27	3	15	(8	7)	235	87	80	50	2	93	0	7	11	14	5	.74	12	.261	.312	.390
1981	Boston	AL	102	399	134	23	3	4	(1	3)	175	61	52	34	3	28	2	1	2	15	10	.60	6	.336	.389	.439
1982	Boston	AL	128	482	145	28	4	11	(4	7)	214	65	63	46	2	48	2	1	8	9	4	.69	15	.301	.359	.444
1983	Oakland	AL	80	299	92	16	2	10	(4	6)	142	43	45	22	4	33	3	0	4	3	8	.27	8	.308	.357	.475
1984	Oakland	AL	151	597	179	31	5	14	(7	7)	262	70	74	40	6	62	3	2	9	9	3	.75	12	.300	.342	.439
1985	Oakland	AL	98	401	111	18	2	13	(7	6)	172	51	46	18	1	27	4	4	5	2	3	.40	6	.277	.311	.429
1986	Oakland	AL	151	591	168	16	4	19	(10	9)	249	80	72	39	2	51	5	1	4	16	7	.70	16	.284	.332	.421
1987	Oakland	AL	151	554	160	27	4	19	(9	10)	252	89	76	60	11	44	9	5	3	27	8	.77	9	.289	.366	.455
1988	Oakland	AL	150	556	155	20	2	7	(1	6)	200	80	57	35	4	35	7	5	4	29	8	.78	17	.279	.327	.360
1989	Oakland	AL	148	551	185	28	2	2	(1	1)	223	81	52	51	2	25	9	1	4	37	15	.71	21	.336	.398	.405
1990	Oakland	AL	134	507	136	15	1	3	(1	2)	162	58	50	45	4	50	6	2	4	16	14	.53	10	.268	.333	.320
1991	Oakland	AL	5	16	1	0	0	0	(0	0)	1	0	1	0	0	2	0	0	0	0	0	.00	0	.063	.063	.063
14 ML YEARS			1727	6662	1944	302	39	144	(62	82)	2756	942	799	510	45	680	57	46	69	217	102	.68	152	.292	.344	.414

Dave LaPoint

Pitches: Left   Bats: Left   Pos: SP   Ht: 6' 3"   Wt: 231   Born: 07/29/59   Age: 32

Year	Team	Lg	G	GS	CG	GF	IP	BFP	H	R	ER	HR	SH	SF	HB	TBB	IBB	SO	WP	Bk	W	L	Pct.	ShO	Sv	ERA
1980	Milwaukee	AL	5	3	0	0	15	75	17	14	10	2	2	2	0	13	1	5	0	1	1	0	1.000	0	1	6.00
1981	St. Louis	NL	3	2	0	0	11	45	12	5	5	1	1	0	1	2	0	4	0	0	1	0	1.000	0	0	4.09
1982	St. Louis	NL	42	21	0	6	152.2	656	170	63	58	8	9	5	3	52	8	81	4	2	9	3	.750	0	0	3.42
1983	St. Louis	NL	37	29	1	1	191.1	832	191	92	84	12	17	11	4	84	7	113	11	4	12	9	.571	0	0	3.95
1984	St. Louis	NL	33	33	2	0	193	827	205	94	85	9	8	3	1	77	8	130	15	3	12	10	.545	1	0	3.96
1985	San Francisco	NL	31	31	2	0	206.2	886	215	99	82	18	7	5	0	74	6	122	10	0	7	17	.292	1	0	3.57
1986	2 ML Teams		40	12	0	6	129	588	152	86	72	19	9	2	1	56	7	77	3	5	4	10	.286	0	0	5.02
1987	2 ML Teams		20	14	2	3	98.2	420	95	41	39	11	1	0	1	36	0	51	4	1	7	4	.636	1	0	3.56
1988	2 ML Teams		33	33	2	0	213.1	892	205	87	77	14	13	4	2	57	3	98	1	7	14	13	.519	1	0	3.25
1989	New York	AL	20	20	0	0	113.2	524	146	73	71	12	2	4	2	45	4	51	1	2	6	9	.400	0	0	5.62
1990	New York	AL	28	27	2	0	157.2	694	180	84	72	11	8	11	1	57	3	67	4	0	7	10	.412	0	0	4.11
1991	Philadelphia	NL	2	2	0	0	5	32	10	10	9	0	1	1	1	6	0	3	0	0	0	0	.000	0	0	16.20
1986	Detroit	AL	16	8	0	2	67.2	314	85	49	43	11	4	1	0	32	3	36	2	1	3	6	.333	0	0	5.72
	San Diego	NL	24	4	0	4	61.1	274	67	37	29	8	5	1	1	24	4	41	1	0	1	4	.200	0	0	4.26
1987	St. Louis	NL	6	2	0	3	16	79	26	12	12	0	0	0	0	5	0	8	1	1	1	0	.500	0	0	6.75

Team	Lg	G	GS	CG	GF	IP	BFP	H	R	ER	HR	SH	SF	HB	TBB	IBB	SO	WP	Bk	W	L	Pct.	ShO	Sv	ERA
Chicago	AL	14	12	2	0	82.2	341	69	29	27	7	1	0	1	31	0	43	3	0	6	3	.667	1	0	2.94
1988 Chicago	AL	25	25	1	0	161.1	677	151	69	61	10	8	3	2	47	1	79	1	5	10	11	.476	1	0	3.40
Pittsburgh	NL	8	8	1	0	52	215	54	18	16	4	5	1	0	10	2	19	0	2	4	2	.667	0	0	2.77
12 ML YEARS		294	227	11	17	1487	6471	1598	748	664	117	78	48	17	559	47	802	53	25	80	86	.482	4	1	4.02

Barry Larkin

Bats: Right **Throws:** Right **Pos:** SS   **Ht:** 6' 0" **Wt:** 190 **Born:** 04/28/64 **Age:** 28

Year Team	Lg	G	AB	H	2B	3B	HR	(Hm	Rd)	TB	R	RBI	TBB	IBB	SO	HBP	SH	SF	SB	CS	SB%	GDP	Avg	OBP	SLG
1986 Cincinnati	NL	41	159	45	4	3	3	(3	0)	64	27	19	9	1	21	0	0	1	8	0	1.00	2	.283	.320	.403
1987 Cincinnati	NL	125	439	107	16	2	12	(6	6)	163	64	43	36	3	52	5	5	3	21	6	.78	8	.244	.306	.371
1988 Cincinnati	NL	151	588	174	32	5	12	(9	3)	252	91	56	41	3	24	8	10	5	40	7	.85	7	.296	.347	.429
1989 Cincinnati	NL	97	325	111	14	4	4	(1	3)	145	47	36	20	5	23	2	2	8	10	5	.67	7	.342	.375	.446
1990 Cincinnati	NL	158	614	185	25	6	7	(4	3)	243	85	67	49	3	49	7	7	4	30	5	.86	14	.301	.358	.396
1991 Cincinnati	NL	123	464	140	27	4	20	(16	4)	235	88	69	55	1	64	3	3	2	24	6	.80	7	.302	.378	.506
6 ML YEARS		695	2589	762	118	24	58	(39	19)	1102	402	290	210	16	233	25	27	23	133	29	.82	45	.294	.350	.426

Gene Larkin

Bats: Both **Throws:** Right **Pos:** RF/1B   **Ht:** 6' 3" **Wt:** 205 **Born:** 10/24/62 **Age:** 29

Year Team	Lg	G	AB	H	2B	3B	HR	(Hm	Rd)	TB	R	RBI	TBB	IBB	SO	HBP	SH	SF	SB	CS	SB%	GDP	Avg	OBP	SLG
1987 Minnesota	AL	85	233	62	11	2	4	(0	4)	89	23	28	25	3	31	2	0	2	1	4	.20	4	.266	.340	.382
1988 Minnesota	AL	149	505	135	30	2	8	(5	3)	193	56	70	68	8	55	15	1	5	3	2	.60	12	.267	.368	.382
1989 Minnesota	AL	136	446	119	25	1	6	(3	3)	164	61	46	54	6	57	9	5	6	5	2	.71	13	.267	.353	.368
1990 Minnesota	AL	119	401	108	26	4	5	(5	0)	157	46	42	42	2	55	5	5	4	5	3	.63	7	.269	.343	.392
1991 Minnesota	AL	98	255	73	14	1	2	(0	2)	95	34	19	30	3	21	1	3	2	2	3	.40	9	.286	.361	.373
5 ML YEARS		587	1840	497	106	10	25	(13	12)	698	220	205	219	22	219	32	14	19	16	14	.53	45	.270	.355	.379

Mike LaValliere

Bats: Left **Throws:** Right **Pos:** C   **Ht:** 5'10" **Wt:** 210 **Born:** 08/18/60 **Age:** 31

Year Team	Lg	G	AB	H	2B	3B	HR	(Hm	Rd)	TB	R	RBI	TBB	IBB	SO	HBP	SH	SF	SB	CS	SB%	GDP	Avg	OBP	SLG
1984 Philadelphia	NL	6	7	0	0	0	0	(0	0)	0	0	0	2	0	2	0	0	0	0	0	.00	0	.000	.222	.000
1985 St. Louis	NL	12	34	5	1	0	0	(0	0)	6	2	6	7	0	3	0	0	3	0	0	.00	2	.147	.273	.176
1986 St. Louis	NL	110	303	71	10	2	3	(1	2)	94	18	30	36	5	37	1	10	0	0	1	.00	7	.234	.318	.310
1987 Pittsburgh	NL	121	340	102	19	0	1	(1	0)	124	33	36	43	9	32	1	3	3	0	0	.00	4	.300	.377	.365
1988 Pittsburgh	NL	120	352	92	18	0	2	(1	2)	116	24	47	50	10	34	2	1	4	3	2	.60	4	.261	.353	.330
1989 Pittsburgh	NL	68	190	60	10	0	2	(2	0)	76	15	23	29	7	24	0	4	0	0	2	.00	4	.316	.406	.400
1990 Pittsburgh	NL	96	279	72	15	0	3	(2	1)	96	27	31	44	8	20	2	4	1	0	3	.00	6	.258	.362	.344
1991 Pittsburgh	NL	108	336	97	11	2	3	(1	2)	121	25	41	33	4	27	2	1	5	2	1	.67	10	.289	.351	.360
8 ML YEARS		641	1841	499	84	4	14	(7	7)	633	144	214	244	43	179	8	23	16	5	9	.36	41	.271	.356	.344

Vance Law

Bats: Right **Throws:** Right **Pos:** 3B   **Ht:** 6' 1" **Wt:** 190 **Born:** 10/01/56 **Age:** 35

Year Team	Lg	G	AB	H	2B	3B	HR	(Hm	Rd)	TB	R	RBI	TBB	IBB	SO	HBP	SH	SF	SB	CS	SB%	GDP	Avg	OBP	SLG
1980 Pittsburgh	NL	25	74	17	2	2	0	(0	0)	23	11	3	3	0	7	0	1	0	2	0	1.00	2	.230	.260	.311
1981 Pittsburgh	NL	30	67	9	0	1	0	(0	0)	11	1	3	2	0	15	0	1	1	1	1	.50	2	.134	.157	.164
1982 Chicago	AL	114	359	101	20	1	5	(2	3)	138	40	54	26	1	46	1	7	5	4	2	.67	10	.281	.327	.384
1983 Chicago	AL	145	408	99	21	5	4	(1	3)	142	55	42	51	1	56	1	6	5	3	1	.75	7	.243	.325	.348
1984 Chicago	AL	151	481	121	18	2	17	(11	6)	194	60	59	41	2	75	1	6	4	4	1	.80	13	.252	.309	.403
1985 Montreal	NL	147	519	138	30	6	10	(5	5)	210	75	52	86	0	96	2	8	6	6	5	.55	11	.266	.369	.405
1986 Montreal	NL	112	360	81	17	2	5	(3	2)	117	37	44	37	1	66	1	2	2	3	5	.38	9	.225	.298	.325
1987 Montreal	NL	133	436	119	27	1	12	(9	3)	184	52	56	51	5	62	0	2	3	8	5	.62	8	.273	.347	.422
1988 Chicago	NL	151	556	163	29	2	11	(5	6)	229	73	78	55	4	79	3	4	3	1	4	.20	15	.293	.358	.412
1989 Chicago	NL	130	408	96	22	3	7	(4	3)	145	38	42	38	0	73	0	1	7	2	2	.50	11	.235	.296	.355
1991 Oakland	AL	74	134	28	7	1	0	(0	0)	37	11	9	18	0	27	0	5	0	0	0	.00	4	.209	.303	.276
11 ML YEARS		1212	3802	972	193	26	71	(34	37)	1430	453	442	408	14	602	9	43	36	34	26	.57	92	.256	.326	.376

Tim Layana

Pitches: Right **Bats:** Right **Pos:** RP   **Ht:** 6' 2" **Wt:** 190 **Born:** 03/02/64 **Age:** 28

Year Team	Lg	G	GS	CG	GF	IP	BFP	H	R	ER	HR	SH	SF	HB	TBB	IBB	SO	WP	Bk	W	L	Pct.	ShO	Sv	ERA
1986 Oneonta	A	3	3	0	0	19	71	10	5	5	1	1	0	1	5	0	24	1	0	2	0	1.000	0	0	2.37
Ft.Laudrdle	A	11	10	3	1	68.1	276	59	19	17	1	2	0	4	19	1	52	5	1	5	4	.556	1	1	2.24
1987 Albany	AA	8	7	1	1	46.1	195	51	28	26	4	2	1	2	18	0	19	1	1	2	4	.333	0	0	5.05

Year Team	Lg	G	GS	CG	GF	IP	BFP	H	R	ER	HR	SH	SF	HB	TBB	IBB	SO	WP	Bk	W	L	Pct.	ShO	Sv	ERA
Pr William	A	7	3	0	2	22.2	111	29	22	16	3	1	2	1	11	0	17	5	2	2	1	.667	0	0	6.35
Columbus	AAA	13	13	0	0	70	310	77	37	37	6	3	1	1	37	2	36	3	0	4	5	.444	0	0	4.76
1988 Albany	AA	14	14	1	0	87	378	90	52	42	3	3	3	6	30	2	42	2	8	5	7	.417	0	0	4.34
Columbus	AAA	11	9	0	0	47.2	216	54	34	32	2	0	1	6	25	0	25	2	4	1	7	.125	0	0	6.04
1989 Albany	AA	40	1	0	37	67.2	261	53	17	13	2	5	1	3	15	3	48	2	4	7	4	.636	0	17	1.73
1991 Nashville	AAA	26	2	0	4	47.1	210	41	17	17	3	3	0	2	28	0	43	5	1	3	1	.750	0	1	3.23
1990 Cincinnati	NL	55	0	0	17	80	344	71	33	31	7	4	3	2	44	6	53	5	4	5	3	.625	0	2	3.49
1991 Cincinnati	NL	22	0	0	9	20.2	95	23	18	16	1	1	0	0	11	0	14	3	0	0	2	.000	0	0	6.97
2 ML YEARS		77	0	0	26	100.2	439	94	51	47	8	5	3	2	55	6	67	8	4	5	5	.500	0	2	4.20

Terry Leach

Pitches: Right Bats: Right Pos: RP   **Ht: 6' 0" Wt: 190 Born: 03/13/54 Age: 38**

		HOW MUCH HE PITCHED						WHAT HE GAVE UP												THE RESULTS					
Year Team	Lg	G	GS	CG	GF	IP	BFP	H	R	ER	HR	SH	SF	HB	TBB	IBB	SO	WP	Bk	W	L	Pct.	ShO	Sv	ERA
1981 New York	NL	21	1	0	3	35	139	26	11	10	2	0	0	0	12	1	16	0	0	1	1	.500	0	0	2.57
1982 New York	NL	21	1	1	12	45.1	194	46	22	21	2	5	1	0	18	5	30	0	0	2	1	.667	1	3	4.17
1985 New York	NL	22	4	1	4	55.2	226	48	19	18	3	5	2	1	14	3	30	0	0	3	4	.429	1	1	2.91
1986 New York	NL	6	0	0	1	6.2	30	6	3	2	0	0	0	0	3	0	4	0	0	0	0	.000	0	0	2.70
1987 New York	NL	44	12	1	7	131.1	542	132	54	47	14	8	1	1	29	5	61	0	1	11	1	.917	1	0	3.22
1988 New York	NL	52	0	0	21	92	392	95	32	26	5	8	3	3	24	4	51	0	0	7	2	.778	0	3	2.54
1989 2 ML Teams		40	3	0	10	95	413	97	57	44	5	6	6	2	40	9	36	1	1	5	6	.455	0	4	4.17
1990 Minnesota	AL	55	0	0	29	81.2	344	84	31	29	2	7	2	1	21	10	46	1	1	2	5	.286	0	2	3.20
1991 Minnesota	AL	50	0	0	22	67.1	292	82	28	27	3	3	1	0	14	5	32	1	0	1	2	.333	0	1	3.61
1989 New York	AL	10	0	0	4	21.1	85	19	11	10	1	0	2	1	4	0	2	0	0	0	0	.000	0	0	4.22
Kansas City	AL	30	3	0	6	73.2	328	78	46	34	4	6	4	1	36	9	34	1	1	5	6	.455	0	0	4.15
9 ML YEARS		311	21	3	109	610	2572	616	257	224	36	42	16	8	175	42	306	3	3	32	22	.593	3	9	3.30

Tim Leary

Pitches: Right Bats: Right Pos: SP/RP   **Ht: 6' 3" Wt: 212 Born: 12/23/58 Age: 33**

		HOW MUCH HE PITCHED						WHAT HE GAVE UP												THE RESULTS					
Year Team	Lg	G	GS	CG	GF	IP	BFP	H	R	ER	HR	SH	SF	HB	TBB	IBB	SO	WP	Bk	W	L	Pct.	ShO	Sv	ERA
1981 New York	NL	1	1	0	0	2	7	0	0	0	0	0	0	0	1	0	3	0	0	0	0	.000	0	0	0.00
1983 New York	NL	2	2	1	0	10.2	53	15	10	4	0	1	1	0	4	0	9	0	1	1	1	.500	0	0	3.38
1984 New York	NL	20	7	0	3	53.2	237	61	28	24	2	1	2	2	18	3	29	2	3	3	3	.500	0	0	4.02
1985 Milwaukee	AL	5	5	0	0	33.1	146	40	18	15	5	2	0	1	8	0	29	1	0	1	4	.200	0	0	4.05
1986 Milwaukee	AL	33	30	3	2	188.1	817	216	97	88	20	4	6	7	53	4	110	7	0	12	12	.500	2	0	4.21
1987 Los Angeles	NL	39	12	0	11	107.2	469	121	62	57	15	6	1	2	36	5	61	3	1	3	11	.214	0	1	4.76
1988 Los Angeles	NL	35	34	9	0	228.2	932	201	87	74	13	7	3	6	56	4	180	9	6	17	11	.607	6	0	2.91
1989 2 ML Teams		33	31	2	0	207	874	205	84	81	17	7	8	5	68	15	123	10	0	8	14	.364	0	0	3.52
1990 New York	AL	31	31	6	0	208	881	202	105	95	18	7	4	7	78	1	138	23	0	9	19	.321	1	0	4.11
1991 New York	AL	28	18	1	4	120.2	551	150	89	87	20	7	2	4	57	1	83	10	0	4	10	.286	0	0	6.49
1989 Los Angeles	NL	19	17	2	0	117.1	481	107	45	44	9	4	4	2	37	7	59	4	0	6	7	.462	0	0	3.38
Cincinnati	NL	14	14	0	0	89.2	393	98	39	37	8	3	4	3	31	8	64	6	0	2	7	.222	0	0	3.71
10 ML YEARS		227	171	22	20	1160	4967	1211	580	525	110	42	27	34	379	33	765	66	11	58	85	.406	9	1	4.07

Manuel Lee

Bats: Both Throws: Right Pos: SS   **Ht: 5' 9" Wt: 161 Born: 06/17/65 Age: 27**

		BATTING																BASERUNNING				PERCENTAGES		
Year Team	Lg	G	AB	H	2B	3B	HR	(Hm	Rd)	TB	R	RBI	TBB	IBB	SO	HBP	SH	SF	SB	CS	SB%	GDP	Avg	OBP	SLG
1985 Toronto	AL	64	40	8	0	0	0	(0	0)	8	9	0	2	0	9	0	1	0	1	4	.20	2	.200	.238	.200
1986 Toronto	AL	35	78	16	0	1	1	(1	0)	21	8	7	4	0	10	0	2	1	0	1	.00	5	.205	.241	.269
1987 Toronto	AL	56	121	31	2	3	1	(0	1)	42	14	11	6	0	13	0	1	1	2	0	1.00	1	.256	.289	.347
1988 Toronto	AL	116	381	111	16	3	2	(2	0)	139	38	38	26	1	64	0	4	4	3	3	.50	13	.291	.338	.365
1989 Toronto	AL	99	300	78	9	2	3	(1	2)	100	27	34	20	1	60	0	1	1	4	2	.67	8	.260	.305	.333
1990 Toronto	AL	117	391	95	12	4	6	(2	4)	133	45	41	26	0	90	0	1	3	3	1	.75	9	.243	.288	.340
1991 Toronto	AL	138	445	104	18	3	0	(0	0)	128	41	29	24	0	107	2	10	4	7	2	.78	10	.234	.274	.288
7 ML YEARS		625	1756	443	57	16	13	(6	7)	571	182	160	108	2	353	2	20	14	20	13	.61	48	.252	.294	.325

Mark Lee

Pitches: Left Bats: Left Pos: RP   **Ht: 6' 3" Wt: 200 Born: 07/20/64 Age: 27**

		HOW MUCH HE PITCHED						WHAT HE GAVE UP												THE RESULTS					
Year Team	Lg	G	GS	CG	GF	IP	BFP	H	R	ER	HR	SH	SF	HB	TBB	IBB	SO	WP	Bk	W	L	Pct.	ShO	Sv	ERA
1985 Bristol	R	15	1	0	11	33	127	18	5	4	1	1	0	0	12	0	40	2	0	3	0	1.000	0	5	1.09
1986 Lakeland	A	41	0	0	31	62.2	281	73	44	36	4	4	1	2	21	8	39	5	0	2	5	.286	0	10	5.17
1987 Glens Falls	AA	7	0	0	4	8.1	38	13	9	8	1	1	1	0	1	0	3	0	0	0	0	.000	0	0	8.64
Lakeland	A	30	0	0	15	53	223	48	17	15	1	0	1	1	18	3	42	1	0	3	2	.600	0	4	2.55
1988 Lakeland	A	10	0	0	2	19	73	16	7	3	0	2	3	0	4	1	15	0	1	1	0	1.000	0	1	1.42

	Lg	G	GS	CG	GF	IP	BFP	H	R	ER	HR	SH	SF	HB	TBB	IBB	SO	WP	Bk	W	L	Pct.	ShO	Sv	ERA
Glens Falls	AA	14	0	0	6	26	106	27	10	7	0	2	1	0	4	2	25	0	0	3	0	1.000	0	1	2.42
Toledo	AAA	22	0	0	6	19.1	79	18	7	6	0	0	2	0	7	2	13	0	0	0	1	.000	0	0	2.79
1989 Memphis	AA	25	24	0	1	122.2	558	149	84	71	13	4	4	3	44	2	79	6	8	5	11	.313	0	0	5.21
1990 Stockton	A	5	0	0	2	7.2	32	5	2	2	0	1	0	0	3	0	7	0	0	1	0	1.000	0	1	2.35
Denver	AAA	20	0	0	6	28	110	25	7	7	2	1	0	0	6	1	35	1	1	3	1	.750	0	4	2.25
1988 Kansas City	AL	4	0	0	4	5	21	6	2	2	0	0	0	0	1	0	0	0	0	0	0	.000	0	0	3.60
1990 Milwaukee	AL	11	0	0	1	21.1	85	20	5	5	1	1	2	0	4	0	14	0	0	1	0	1.000	0	0	2.11
1991 Milwaukee	AL	62	0	0	9	67.2	291	72	33	29	10	4	1	1	31	7	43	0	0	2	5	.286	0	0	3.86
3 ML YEARS		77	0	0	14	94	397	98	40	36	11	5	3	1	36	7	57	0	0	3	5	.375	0	1	3.45

Terry Lee

Bats: Right Throws: Right Pos: 1B　　　　　　**Ht: 6' 5" Wt: 220 Born: 03/13/62 Age: 30**

							BATTING													BASERUNNING				PERCENTAGES		
Year Team	Lg	G	AB	H	2B	3B	HR	(Hm	Rd)	TB	R	RBI	TBB	IBB	SO	HBP	SH	SF	SB	CS	SB%	GDP	Avg	OBP	SLG
1984 Vermont	AA	134	422	102	10	2	11	--	--	149	56	47	44	1	94	3	2	4	2	4	.33	13	.242	.315	.353
1985 Vermont	AA	121	409	118	20	2	12	--	--	178	56	62	48	2	51	3	0	4	4	0	1.00	9	.289	.364	.435
1986 Denver	AAA	34	104	25	2	1	2	--	--	35	10	10	4	0	24	0	0	2	0	1	.00	3	.240	.264	.337
1988 Greensboro	A	25	56	18	5	0	2	--	--	29	8	9	11	2	11	0	0	0	0	0	.00	2	.321	.433	.518
1989 Chattanooga	AA	51	177	46	13	0	5	--	--	74	23	27	13	0	32	1	1	4	0	0	.00	10	.260	.308	.418
Nashville	AAA	13	47	11	4	0	0	--	--	15	5	3	3	0	8	1	1	0	0	0	.00	2	.234	.294	.319
1990 Chattanooga	AA	43	156	51	8	1	8	--	--	85	25	20	20	1	27	2	1	2	4	1	.80	5	.327	.406	.545
Nashville	AAA	72	260	79	18	1	15	--	--	144	38	67	31	1	47	4	1	7	3	1	.75	10	.304	.377	.554
1991 Nashville	AAA	126	437	133	21	4	15	--	--	207	70	67	62	1	80	5	0	4	12	6	.67	9	.304	.394	.474
1990 Cincinnati	NL	12	19	4	1	0	0	(0	0)	5	1	3	2	0	2	0	0	1	0	0	.00	1	.211	.273	.263
1991 Cincinnati	NL	3	6	0	0	0	0	(0	0)	0	0	0	0	0	2	0	0	0	0	0	.00	0	.000	.000	.000
2 ML YEARS		15	25	4	1	0	0	(0	0)	5	1	3	2	0	4	0	0	1	0	0	.00	1	.160	.214	.200

Craig Lefferts

Pitches: Left Bats: Left Pos: RP　　　　　　**Ht: 6' 1" Wt: 209 Born: 09/29/57 Age: 34**

			HOW MUCH HE PITCHED					WHAT HE GAVE UP										THE RESULTS						
Year Team	Lg	G	GS	CG	GF	IP	BFP	H	R	ER	HR	SH	SF	HB	TBB	IBB	SO	WP	Bk	W	L	Pct.	ShO	Sv	ERA
1983 Chicago	NL	56	5	0	10	89	367	80	35	31	13	7	0	2	29	3	60	2	0	3	4	.429	0	1	3.13
1984 San Diego	NL	62	0	0	29	105.2	420	88	29	25	4	4	6	1	24	1	56	2	2	3	4	.429	0	10	2.13
1985 San Diego	NL	60	0	0	24	83.1	345	75	34	31	7	7	1	0	30	4	48	2	0	7	6	.538	0	2	3.35
1986 San Diego	NL	83	0	0	36	107.2	446	98	41	37	7	9	5	1	44	11	72	1	1	9	8	.529	0	4	3.09
1987 2 ML Teams		77	0	0	22	98.2	416	92	47	42	13	6	2	2	33	11	57	6	3	5	5	.500	0	6	3.83
1988 San Francisco	NL	64	0	0	30	92.1	362	74	33	30	7	6	3	1	23	5	58	4	0	3	8	.273	0	11	2.92
1989 San Francisco	NL	70	0	0	32	107	430	93	38	32	11	4	4	1	22	5	71	4	1	2	4	.333	0	20	2.69
1990 San Diego	NL	56	0	0	44	78.2	327	86	26	22	10	5	1	1	22	4	60	1	0	7	5	.583	0	23	2.52
1991 San Diego	NL	54	0	0	40	69	290	74	35	30	5	10	5	1	14	3	48	3	1	1	6	.143	0	23	3.91
1987 San Diego	NL	33	0	0	8	51.1	225	56	29	25	9	2	0	2	15	5	39	5	2	2	2	.500	0	2	4.38
San Francisco	NL	44	0	0	14	47.1	191	36	18	17	4	4	2	0	18	6	18	1	1	3	3	.500	0	4	3.23
9 ML YEARS		582	5	0	267	831.1	3403	742	318	280	77	58	27	10	241	47	530	25	8	40	50	.444	0	100	3.03

Charlie Leibrandt

Pitches: Left Bats: Right Pos: SP　　　　　　**Ht: 6' 3" Wt: 200 Born: 10/04/56 Age: 35**

			HOW MUCH HE PITCHED					WHAT HE GAVE UP										THE RESULTS						
Year Team	Lg	G	GS	CG	GF	IP	BFP	H	R	ER	HR	SH	SF	HB	TBB	IBB	SO	WP	Bk	W	L	Pct.	ShO	Sv	ERA
1979 Cincinnati	NL	3	0	0	1	4	16	2	2	0	0	1	0	0	2	0	1	0	0	0	0	.000	0	0	0.00
1980 Cincinnati	NL	36	27	5	3	174	754	200	84	82	15	12	2	2	54	4	62	1	6	10	9	.526	2	0	4.24
1981 Cincinnati	NL	7	4	1	0	30	128	28	12	12	0	4	2	0	15	2	9	0	0	1	1	.500	1	0	3.60
1982 Cincinnati	NL	36	11	0	10	107.2	484	130	68	61	4	10	2	2	48	9	34	6	1	5	7	.417	0	2	5.10
1984 Kansas City	AL	23	23	0	0	143.2	621	158	65	58	11	3	7	3	38	2	53	5	1	11	7	.611	0	0	3.63
1985 Kansas City	AL	33	33	8	0	237.2	983	223	86	71	17	8	5	2	68	3	108	4	3	17	9	.654	3	0	2.69
1986 Kansas City	AL	35	34	8	0	231.1	975	238	112	105	18	14	5	4	63	0	108	2	1	14	11	.560	1	0	4.09
1987 Kansas City	AL	35	35	8	0	240.1	1015	235	104	91	23	5	5	1	74	2	151	9	3	16	11	.593	3	0	3.41
1988 Kansas City	AL	35	35	7	0	243	1002	244	98	86	20	5	7	4	62	3	125	10	4	13	12	.520	2	0	3.19
1989 Kansas City	AL	33	27	3	3	161	712	196	98	92	13	8	4	2	54	4	73	9	2	5	11	.313	1	0	5.14
1990 Atlanta	NL	24	24	5	0	162.1	680	164	72	57	9	7	6	4	35	3	76	4	3	9	11	.450	2	0	3.16
1991 Atlanta	NL	36	36	1	0	229.2	949	212	105	89	18	19	6	4	56	3	128	5	3	15	13	.536	1	0	3.49
12 ML YEARS		336	289	46	17	1964.2	8319	2030	906	804	148	95	52	28	569	35	928	55	27	116	102	.532	16	2	3.68

Al Leiter

Pitches: Left Bats: Left Pos: RP　　　　　　**Ht: 6' 3" Wt: 215 Born: 10/23/65 Age: 26**

			HOW MUCH HE PITCHED					WHAT HE GAVE UP										THE RESULTS						
Year Team	Lg	G	GS	CG	GF	IP	BFP	H	R	ER	HR	SH	SF	HB	TBB	IBB	SO	WP	Bk	W	L	Pct.	ShO	Sv	ERA
1987 New York	AL	4	4	0	0	22.2	104	24	16	16	2	1	0	0	15	0	28	4	0	2	2	.500	0	0	6.35
1988 New York	AL	14	14	0	0	57.1	251	49	27	25	7	1	0	5	33	0	60	1	4	4	4	.500	0	0	3.92

Year Team	Lg	G	GS	CG	GF	IP	BFP	H	R	ER	HR	SH	SF	HB	TBB	IBB	SO	WP	Bk	W	L	Pct.	ShO	Sv	ERA
1989 2 ML Teams		5	5	0	0	33.1	154	32	23	21	2	1	1	2	23	0	26	2	1	1	2	.333	0	0	5.67
1990 Toronto	AL	4	0	0	2	6.1	22	1	0	0	0	0	0	0	2	0	5	0	0	0	0	.000	0	0	0.00
1991 Toronto	AL	3	0	0	1	1.2	13	3	5	5	0	1	0	0	5	0	1	0	0	0	0	.000	0	0	27.00
1989 New York	AL	4	4	0	0	26.2	123	23	20	18	1	1	1	2	21	0	22	1	1	1	2	.333	0	0	6.08
Toronto	AL	1	1	0	0	6.2	31	9	3	3	1	0	0	0	2	0	4	1	0	0	0	.000	0	0	4.05
5 ML YEARS		30	23	0	3	121.1	544	109	71	67	11	4	1	7	78	0	120	7	5	7	8	.467	0	0	4.97

Mark Leiter

Pitches: Right **Bats:** Right **Pos:** RP/SP   **Ht:** 6' 3" **Wt:** 210 **Born:** 04/13/63 **Age:** 29

		HOW MUCH HE PITCHED						WHAT HE GAVE UP												THE RESULTS					
Year Team	Lg	G	GS	CG	GF	IP	BFP	H	R	ER	HR	SH	SF	HB	TBB	IBB	SO	WP	Bk	W	L	Pct.	ShO	Sv	ERA
1984 Hagerstown	A	27	24	5	2	139.1	643	132	96	87	13	6	4	8	108	2	105	13	1	8	13	.381	1	0	5.62
1985 Hagerstown	A	34	6	1	22	83.1	351	77	44	32	2	4	4	7	29	3	82	3	0	2	8	.200	0	8	3.46
Charlotte	AA	5	0	0	2	6.1	23	3	1	1	1	0	0	0	2	0	8	0	0	0	1	.000	0	1	1.42
1989 Ft.Laudrdle	A	6	4	1	1	35.1	143	27	9	6	1	0	1	2	5	0	22	0	1	2	2	.500	0	1	1.53
Columbus	AAA	22	12	0	2	90	404	102	50	50	5	2	3	5	34	2	70	3	5	9	6	.600	0	0	5.00
1990 Columbus	AAA	30	14	2	6	122.2	508	114	56	49	5	2	3	1	27	0	115	7	0	9	4	.692	1	1	3.60
1991 Toledo	AAA	5	0	0	3	6.2	29	6	0	0	0	0	0	0	3	0	7	0	0	1	0	1.000	0	1	0.00
1990 New York	AL	8	3	0	2	26.1	119	33	20	20	5	2	1	2	9	0	21	0	0	1	1	.500	0	1	6.84
1991 Detroit	AL	38	15	1	7	134.2	578	125	66	63	16	5	6	6	50	4	103	2	0	9	7	.563	0	1	4.21
2 ML YEARS		46	18	1	9	161	697	158	86	83	21	7	7	8	59	4	124	2	0	10	8	.556	0	1	4.64

Scott Leius

Bats: Right **Throws:** Right **Pos:** 3B/SS   **Ht:** 6' 3" **Wt:** 185 **Born:** 09/24/65 **Age:** 26

		BATTING									BASERUNNING				PERCENTAGES		
Year Team	Lg	G	AB	H	2B	3B	HR	(Hm Rd)	TB	R	RBI	TBB	IBB	SO	HBP	SH	SF	SB	CS	SB%	GDP	Avg	OBP	SLG
1986 Elizabethtn	R	61	237	66	14	1	4	-- --	94	37	23	26	0	45	3	2	1	5	0	1.00	6	.278	.356	.397
1987 Kenosha	A	126	414	99	16	4	8	-- --	147	65	51	50	0	88	3	5	4	6	4	.60	2	.239	.323	.355
1988 Visalia	A	93	308	73	14	4	3	-- --	104	44	46	42	0	50	3	8	1	3	1	.75	11	.237	.333	.338
1989 Orlando	AA	99	346	105	22	2	4	-- --	143	49	45	38	0	74	0	3	2	5	2	.60	4	.303	.370	.413
1990 Portland	AAA	103	353	81	13	5	2	-- --	110	34	23	35	0	66	0	4	0	5	3	.63	8	.229	.299	.312
1990 Minnesota	AL	14	25	6	1	0	1	(0 1)	10	4	4	2	0	2	0	1	0	0	0	.00	2	.240	.296	.400
1991 Minnesota	AL	109	199	57	7	2	5	(2 3)	83	35	20	30	1	35	0	5	1	5	5	.50	4	.286	.378	.417
2 ML YEARS		123	224	63	8	2	6	(2 4)	93	39	24	32	1	37	0	6	1	5	5	.50	6	.281	.370	.415

Mark Lemke

Bats: Both **Throws:** Right **Pos:** 2B/3B   **Ht:** 5' 9" **Wt:** 167 **Born:** 08/13/65 **Age:** 26

		BATTING									BASERUNNING				PERCENTAGES		
Year Team	Lg	G	AB	H	2B	3B	HR	(Hm Rd)	TB	R	RBI	TBB	IBB	SO	HBP	SH	SF	SB	CS	SB%	GDP	Avg	OBP	SLG
1988 Atlanta	NL	16	58	13	4	0	0	(0 0)	17	8	2	4	0	5	0	2	0	0	2	.00	1	.224	.274	.293
1989 Atlanta	NL	14	55	10	2	1	2	(1 1)	20	4	10	5	0	7	0	0	0	0	1	.00	1	.182	.250	.364
1990 Atlanta	NL	102	239	54	13	0	0	(0 0)	67	22	21	21	3	22	0	4	2	0	1	.00	6	.226	.286	.280
1991 Atlanta	NL	136	269	63	11	2	2	(2 0)	84	36	23	29	2	27	0	6	4	1	2	.33	9	.234	.305	.312
4 ML YEARS		268	621	140	30	3	4	(3 1)	188	70	56	59	5	61	0	12	6	1	6	.14	17	.225	.290	.303

Patrick Lennon

Bats: Right **Throws:** Right **Pos:** DH   **Ht:** 6' 2" **Wt:** 200 **Born:** 04/27/68 **Age:** 24

		BATTING									BASERUNNING				PERCENTAGES		
Year Team	Lg	G	AB	H	2B	3B	HR	(Hm Rd)	TB	R	RBI	TBB	IBB	SO	HBP	SH	SF	SB	CS	SB%	GDP	Avg	OBP	SLG
1986 Bellingham	A	51	169	41	5	2	3	-- --	59	35	27	36	0	50	0	1	1	8	6	.57	3	.243	.374	.349
1987 Wausau	A	98	319	80	21	3	7	-- --	128	54	34	46	1	82	1	1	2	25	8	.76	10	.251	.345	.401
1988 Vermont	AA	95	321	83	9	3	9	-- --	125	44	40	21	1	87	3	3	4	15	6	.71	9	.259	.307	.389
1989 Williamsprt	AA	66	248	65	14	2	3	-- --	92	32	31	23	2	53	0	0	5	7	4	.64	9	.262	.319	.371
1990 San Berndno	A	44	163	47	6	2	8	-- --	81	29	30	15	1	51	0	0	1	6	0	1.00	4	.288	.346	.497
Williamsprt	AA	49	167	49	6	4	5	-- --	78	24	22	10	0	37	2	0	3	10	4	.71	2	.293	.335	.467
1991 Calgary	AAA	112	416	137	29	5	15	-- --	221	75	74	46	4	68	4	1	1	12	5	.71	9	.329	.400	.531
1991 Seattle	AL	9	8	1	1	0	0	(0 0)	2	2	1	3	0	1	0	0	0	0	0	.00	0	.125	.364	.250

Mark Leonard

Bats: Left **Throws:** Right **Pos:** LF/RF   **Ht:** 6' 1" **Wt:** 195 **Born:** 08/14/64 **Age:** 27

		BATTING									BASERUNNING				PERCENTAGES		
Year Team	Lg	G	AB	H	2B	3B	HR	(Hm Rd)	TB	R	RBI	TBB	IBB	SO	HBP	SH	SF	SB	CS	SB%	GDP	Avg	OBP	SLG
1986 Everett	A	2	8	1	0	0	0	-- --	1	0	2	2	0	2	0	0	1	0	0	.00	0	.125	.273	.125
Tri-Cities	A	36	120	32	6	0	4	-- --	50	21	15	25	0	19	1	0	0	4	2	.67	7	.267	.397	.417
1987 Clinton	A	128	413	132	31	2	15	-- --	212	57	80	71	3	61	5	0	3	5	8	.38	7	.320	.423	.513
1988 San Jose	A	142	510	176	50	6	15	-- --	283	102	118	118	13	82	5	0	11	11	6	.65	10	.345	.464	.555
1989 Shreveport	AA	63	219	68	15	3	10	-- --	119	29	52	33	8	40	3	0	3	1	5	.17	7	.311	.403	.543

Team	Lg	G	AB	H	2B	3B	HR	(Hm	Rd)	TB	R	RBI	TBB	IBB	SO	HBP	SH	SF	SB	CS	SB%	GDP	Avg	OBP	SLG
Phoenix	AAA	27	78	21	4	0	0	--	--	25	7	6	9	1	15	0	0	1	1	1	.50	3	.269	.341	.321
1990 Phoenix	AAA	109	390	130	22	2	19	--	--	213	76	82	76	1	81	4	0	4	6	3	.67	7	.333	.443	.546
1991 Phoenix	AAA	41	146	37	7	0	8	--	--	68	27	25	21	1	29	0	0	2	1	0	1.00	5	.253	.343	.466
1990 San Francisco	NL	11	17	3	1	0	1	(0	1)	7	3	2	3	0	8	0	0	0	0	0	.00	0	.176	.300	.412
1991 San Francisco	NL	64	129	31	7	1	2	(0	2)	46	14	14	12	1	25	1	1	2	0	1	.00	3	.240	.306	.357
2 ML YEARS		75	146	34	8	1	3	(0	3)	53	17	16	15	1	33	1	1	2	0	1	.00	3	.233	.305	.363

Darren Lewis

Bats: Right **Throws:** Right **Pos:** CF   **Ht:** 6' 0" **Wt:** 175 **Born:** 08/28/67 **Age:** 24

								BATTING												BASERUNNING				PERCENTAGES		
Year Team	Lg	G	AB	H	2B	3B	HR	(Hm	Rd)	TB	R	RBI	TBB	IBB	SO	HBP	SH	SF	SB	CS	SB%	GDP	Avg	OBP	SLG
1988 Athletics	R	5	15	5	3	0	0	--	--	8	8	4	6	0	5	1	1	1	4	0	1.00	1	.333	.522	.533
Madison	A	60	199	49	4	1	0	--	--	55	38	19	46	0	37	4	4	3	21	10	.68	3	.246	.393	.276
1989 Modesto	A	129	503	150	23	5	4	--	--	195	74	39	59	0	84	11	2	4	27	22	.55	4	.298	.381	.388
Huntsville	AA	9	31	10	1	1	1	--	--	16	7	7	2	0	6	1	2	0	0	1	.00	1	.323	.382	.516
1990 Huntsville	AA	71	284	84	11	3	3	--	--	110	52	23	36	3	28	7	0	3	21	7	.75	8	.296	.385	.387
Tacoma	AAA	60	247	72	5	2	2	--	--	87	32	26	16	0	35	1	4	2	16	6	.73	2	.291	.335	.352
1991 Phoenix	AAA	81	315	107	12	10	2	--	--	145	63	52	41	1	36	2	4	5	32	11	.76	11	.340	.413	.460
1990 Oakland	AL	25	35	8	0	0	0	(0	0)	8	4	1	7	0	4	1	3	0	2	0	1.00	1	.229	.372	.229
1991 San Francisco	NL	72	222	55	5	3	1	(0	1)	69	41	15	36	0	30	2	7	0	13	7	.65	1	.248	.358	.311
2 ML YEARS		97	257	63	5	3	1	(0	1)	77	45	16	43	0	34	3	10	0	15	7	.68	3	.245	.360	.300

Jim Lewis

Pitches: Right **Bats:** Right **Pos:** RP   **Ht:** 6' 2" **Wt:** 200 **Born:** 07/20/64 **Age:** 27

			HOW MUCH HE PITCHED						WHAT HE GAVE UP									THE RESULTS				
Year Team	Lg	G	GS	CG	GF	IP	BFP	H	R	ER	HR	SH	SF	HB	TBB	IBB	SO	WP	Bk	W	L	Pct.	ShO	Sv	ERA
1985 Spokane	A	20	6	1	0	67.1	0	60	34	29	4	0	0	2	21	0	54	6	0	4	4	.500	0	0	3.88
1986 Charleston	A	51	1	1	25	84	366	87	48	32	4	6	3	0	32	4	61	4	1	4	8	.333	1	4	3.43
1987 Reno	A	13	2	1	3	29.1	135	34	26	20	3	0	1	1	21	0	28	2	0	2	2	.500	1	0	6.14
1988 Riverside	A	44	1	0	18	98.1	444	99	57	39	7	9	1	1	54	4	80	9	0	7	7	.500	0	7	3.57
1989 Wichita	AA	63	0	0	50	83.1	359	83	28	25	3	5	2	3	33	5	53	2	0	8	4	.667	0	18	2.70
1990 Las Vegas	AAA	59	1	0	18	93	424	109	60	47	6	3	7	2	46	3	54	7	0	5	6	.455	0	5	4.55
1991 Wichita	AA	2	0	0	1	2.2	15	4	2	0	0	0	0	0	4	0	3	0	0	0	0	.000	0	1	0.00
Las Vegas	AAA	48	0	0	15	85.1	381	93	41	32	4	3	6	3	34	4	76	2	0	6	3	.667	0	3	3.38
1991 San Diego	NL	12	0	0	2	13	64	14	7	6	2	2	0	0	11	2	10	1	0	0	0	.000	0	0	4.15

Mark Lewis

Bats: Right **Throws:** Right **Pos:** 2B/SS   **Ht:** 6' 1" **Wt:** 190 **Born:** 11/30/69 **Age:** 22

								BATTING												BASERUNNING				PERCENTAGES		
Year Team	Lg	G	AB	H	2B	3B	HR	(Hm	Rd)	TB	R	RBI	TBB	IBB	SO	HBP	SH	SF	SB	CS	SB%	GDP	Avg	OBP	SLG
1988 Burlington	R	61	227	60	13	1	7	--	--	96	39	43	25	0	44	5	0	5	14	6	.70	2	.264	.344	.423
1989 Kinston	A	93	349	94	16	3	1	--	--	119	50	32	34	4	50	2	3	5	17	9	.65	7	.269	.333	.341
Canton-Akrn	AA	7	25	5	1	0	0	--	--	6	4	1	1	0	3	0	0	0	0	0	.00	1	.200	.231	.240
1990 Canton-Akrn	AA	102	390	106	19	3	10	--	--	161	55	60	23	3	49	4	2	5	8	7	.53	10	.272	.315	.413
Colo Sprngs	AAA	34	124	38	8	1	1	--	--	51	16	21	9	0	13	0	1	1	2	3	.40	4	.306	.351	.411
1991 Colo Sprngs	AAA	46	179	50	10	3	2	--	--	72	29	31	18	0	23	0	0	6	2	1	.67	4	.279	.335	.402
1991 Cleveland	AL	84	314	83	15	1	0	(0	0)	100	29	30	15	0	45	0	2	5	2	2	.50	12	.264	.293	.318

Scott Lewis

Pitches: Right **Bats:** Right **Pos:** SP/RP   **Ht:** 6' 3" **Wt:** 178 **Born:** 12/05/65 **Age:** 26

			HOW MUCH HE PITCHED						WHAT HE GAVE UP									THE RESULTS				
Year Team	Lg	G	GS	CG	GF	IP	BFP	H	R	ER	HR	SH	SF	HB	TBB	IBB	SO	WP	Bk	W	L	Pct.	ShO	Sv	ERA
1988 Bend	A	9	9	2	0	61.2	262	63	33	24	3	1	3	5	12	0	53	3	2	5	3	.625	0	0	3.50
Quad City	A	3	3	1	0	21.1	85	19	12	11	0	1	0	0	5	0	20	1	2	1	2	.333	0	0	4.64
Palm Sprngs	A	2	1	0	0	8	37	12	5	5	3	0	0	0	2	0	7	0	0	0	1	.000	0	0	5.63
1989 Midland	AA	25	25	4	0	162.1	729	195	121	89	15	2	3	8	55	9	104	12	9	11	12	.478	1	0	4.93
1990 Edmonton	AAA	27	27	6	0	177.2	749	198	90	77	16	4	3	7	35	1	124	2	0	13	11	.542	0	0	3.90
1991 Edmonton	AAA	17	17	4	0	110	489	132	71	55	7	4	4	8	26	2	87	5	3	3	9	.250	0	0	4.50
1990 California	AL	2	2	1	0	16.1	60	10	4	4	2	0	0	0	2	0	9	0	0	1	1	.500	0	0	2.20
1991 California	AL	16	11	0	0	60.1	281	81	43	42	9	2	0	2	21	0	37	3	0	3	5	.375	0	0	6.27
2 ML YEARS		18	13	1	0	76.2	341	91	47	46	11	2	0	2	23	0	46	3	0	4	6	.400	0	0	5.40

Jim Leyritz

Bats: Right **Throws:** Right **Pos:** 3B   **Ht:** 6' 0" **Wt:** 190 **Born:** 12/27/63 **Age:** 28

					BATTING													BASERUNNING				PERCENTAGES		
Year Team	Lg	G	AB	H	2B	3B	HR	(Hm | Rd)	TB	R	RBI	TBB	IBB	SO	HBP	SH	SF	SB	CS	SB%	GDP	Avg	OBP	SLG
1986 Ft.Laudrdle	A	12	34	10	1	1	0	--	--	13	3	1	4	1	5	1	0	0	0	0	.00	1	.294	.385	.382
Oneonta	A	23	91	33	3	1	4	--	--	50	12	15	5	1	10	0	2	3	1	0	1.00	0	.363	.384	.549
1987 Ft.Laudrdle	A	102	374	115	22	0	6	--	--	155	48	51	38	1	54	6	7	4	2	1	.67	8	.307	.377	.414
1988 Albany	AA	112	382	92	18	3	5	--	--	131	40	50	43	5	60	6	3	2	3	3	.50	8	.241	.326	.343
1989 Albany	AA	114	375	118	18	2	10	--	--	170	53	66	65	5	51	9	2	5	2	1	.67	8	.315	.423	.453
1990 Columbus	AAA	59	204	59	11	1	8	--	--	96	36	32	37	1	33	3	2	1	4	2	.67	6	.289	.404	.471
1991 Columbus	AAA	79	270	72	24	1	11	--	--	131	50	48	38	1	49	8	1	3	1	2	.33	5	.267	.370	.485
1990 New York	AL	92	303	78	13	1	5	(1 | 4)	108	28	25	27	1	51	7	1	1	2	3	.40	11	.257	.331	.356
1991 New York	AL	32	77	14	3	0	0	(0 | 0)	17	8	4	13	0	15	0	1	0	0	1	.00	0	.182	.300	.221
2 ML YEARS		124	380	92	16	1	5	(1 | 4)	125	36	29	40	1	66	7	2	1	2	4	.33	11	.242	.325	.329

Derek Lilliquist

Pitches: Left **Bats:** Left **Pos:** RP   **Ht:** 6' 0" **Wt:** 214 **Born:** 02/20/66 **Age:** 26

		HOW MUCH HE PITCHED						WHAT HE GAVE UP									THE RESULTS					
Year Team	Lg	G	GS	CG	GF	IP	BFP	H	R	ER	HR	SH	SF	HB	TBB	IBB	SO	WP	Bk	W	L	Pct.	ShO	Sv	ERA
1989 Atlanta	NL	32	30	0	0	165.2	718	202	87	73	16	8	3	2	34	5	79	4	3	8	10	.444	0	0	3.97
1990 2 ML Teams		28	18	1	3	122	537	136	74	72	16	9	5	3	42	5	63	2	3	5	11	.313	1	0	5.31
1991 San Diego	NL	6	2	0	1	14.1	70	25	14	14	3	0	0	0	4	1	7	0	0	0	2	.000	0	0	8.79
1990 Atlanta	NL	12	11	0	1	61.2	279	75	45	43	10	6	4	1	19	4	34	0	2	2	8	.200	0	0	6.28
San Diego	NL	16	7	1	2	60.1	258	61	29	29	6	3	1	2	23	1	29	2	1	3	3	.500	1	0	4.33
3 ML YEARS		66	50	1	4	302	1325	363	175	159	35	17	8	5	80	11	149	6	6	13	23	.361	1	0	4.74

Jose Lind

Bats: Right **Throws:** Right **Pos:** 2B   **Ht:** 5'11" **Wt:** 175 **Born:** 05/01/64 **Age:** 28

					BATTING													BASERUNNING				PERCENTAGES		
Year Team	Lg	G	AB	H	2B	3B	HR	(Hm	Rd)	TB	R	RBI	TBB	IBB	SO	HBP	SH	SF	SB	CS	SB%	GDP	Avg	OBP	SLG
1987 Pittsburgh	NL	35	143	46	8	4	0	(0	0)	62	21	11	8	1	12	0	6	0	2	1	.67	5	.322	.358	.434
1988 Pittsburgh	NL	154	611	160	24	4	2	(1	1)	198	82	49	42	0	75	0	12	3	15	4	.79	11	.262	.308	.324
1989 Pittsburgh	NL	153	578	134	21	3	2	(2	0)	167	52	48	39	7	64	2	13	5	15	1	.94	13	.232	.280	.289
1990 Pittsburgh	NL	152	514	134	28	5	1	(1	0)	175	46	48	35	19	52	1	4	7	8	0	1.00	20	.261	.305	.340
1991 Pittsburgh	NL	150	502	133	16	6	3	(2	1)	170	53	54	30	10	56	2	5	6	7	4	.64	19	.265	.306	.339
5 ML YEARS		644	2348	607	97	22	8	(6	2)	772	254	210	154	37	259	5	40	21	47	10	.82	68	.259	.303	.329

Jim Lindeman

Bats: Right **Throws:** Right **Pos:** LF   **Ht:** 6' 1" **Wt:** 200 **Born:** 01/10/62 **Age:** 30

					BATTING													BASERUNNING				PERCENTAGES		
Year Team	Lg	G	AB	H	2B	3B	HR	(Hm	Rd)	TB	R	RBI	TBB	IBB	SO	HBP	SH	SF	SB	CS	SB%	GDP	Avg	OBP	SLG
1986 St. Louis	NL	19	55	14	1	0	1	(0	1)	18	7	6	2	0	10	0	0	1	1	1	.50	2	.255	.276	.327
1987 St. Louis	NL	75	207	43	13	0	8	(2	6)	80	20	28	11	0	56	3	2	4	3	1	.75	4	.208	.253	.386
1988 St. Louis	NL	17	43	9	1	0	2	(0	2)	16	3	7	2	0	9	0	1	0	0	0	.00	0	.209	.244	.372
1989 St. Louis	NL	73	45	5	1	0	0	(0	0)	6	8	2	3	0	18	0	1	1	0	0	.00	2	.111	.163	.133
1990 Detroit	AL	12	32	7	1	0	2	(2	0)	14	5	8	2	0	13	0	0	0	0	0	.00	0	.219	.265	.438
1991 Philadelphia	NL	65	95	32	5	0	0	(0	0)	37	13	12	13	1	14	0	2	1	0	1	.00	1	.337	.413	.389
6 ML YEARS		261	477	110	22	0	13	(4	9)	171	56	63	33	1	120	3	6	7	4	3	.57	10	.231	.281	.358

Doug Lindsey

Bats: Right **Throws:** Right **Pos:** C   **Ht:** 6' 2" **Wt:** 200 **Born:** 09/22/67 **Age:** 24

					BATTING													BASERUNNING				PERCENTAGES		
Year Team	Lg	G	AB	H	2B	3B	HR	(Hm	Rd)	TB	R	RBI	TBB	IBB	SO	HBP	SH	SF	SB	CS	SB%	GDP	Avg	OBP	SLG
1987 Utica	A	52	169	41	7	0	1	--	--	51	23	25	22	0	34	1	0	3	1	3	.25	2	.243	.328	.302
1988 Spartanburg	A	90	324	76	19	0	4	--	--	107	29	46	29	1	68	4	2	3	4	2	.67	5	.235	.303	.330
1989 Spartanburg	A	39	136	31	7	0	3	--	--	47	14	17	23	2	31	0	1	1	2	2	.50	7	.228	.338	.346
Clearwater	A	36	118	23	3	0	0	--	--	26	8	9	5	0	18	0	0	2	0	0	.00	4	.195	.224	.220
1990 Reading	AA	107	323	56	11	0	1	--	--	70	16	32	26	1	78	1	6	3	2	1	.67	10	.173	.235	.217
1991 Reading	AA	94	313	81	13	0	1	--	--	97	26	34	21	0	49	2	4	4	1	0	1.00	12	.259	.306	.310
1991 Philadelphia	NL	1	3	0	0	0	0	(0	0)	0	0	0	0	0	3	0	0	0	0	0	.00	0	.000	.000	.000

Nelson Liriano

Bats: Both **Throws:** Right **Pos:** 2B **Ht:** 5'10" **Wt:** 172 **Born:** 06/03/64 **Age:** 28

Year Team	Lg	G	AB	H	2B	3B	HR	(Hm	Rd)	TB	R	RBI	TBB	IBB	SO	HBP	SH	SF	SB	CS	SB%	GDP	Avg	OBP	SLG
1987 Toronto	AL	37	158	38	6	2	2	(1	1)	54	29	10	16	2	22	0	2	0	13	2	.87	3	.241	.310	.342
1988 Toronto	AL	99	276	73	6	2	3	(0	3)	92	36	23	11	0	40	2	5	1	12	5	.71	4	.264	.297	.333
1989 Toronto	AL	132	418	110	26	3	5	(3	2)	157	51	53	43	0	51	2	10	5	16	7	.70	10	.263	.331	.376
1990 2 ML Teams		103	355	83	12	9	1	(1	0)	116	46	28	38	0	44	1	4	2	8	7	.53	8	.234	.308	.327
1991 Kansas City	AL	10	22	9	0	0	0	(0	0)	9	5	1	0	0	2	0	1	0	0	1	.00	0	.409	.409	.409
1990 Toronto	AL	50	170	36	7	2	1	(1	0)	50	16	15	16	0	20	1	1	1	3	5	.38	5	.212	.282	.294
Minnesota	AL	53	185	47	5	7	0	(0	0)	66	30	13	22	0	24	0	3	1	5	2	.71	3	.254	.332	.357
5 ML YEARS		381	1229	313	50	16	11	(5	6)	428	167	115	108	2	159	5	22	8	49	22	.69	25	.255	.316	.348

Greg Litton

Bats: Right **Throws:** Right **Pos:** 2B/1B **Ht:** 6' 0" **Wt:** 190 **Born:** 07/13/64 **Age:** 27

Year Team	Lg	G	AB	H	2B	3B	HR	(Hm	Rd)	TB	R	RBI	TBB	IBB	SO	HBP	SH	SF	SB	CS	SB%	GDP	Avg	OBP	SLG
1989 San Francisco	NL	71	143	36	5	3	4	(3	1)	59	12	17	7	0	29	1	4	0	0	2	.00	3	.252	.291	.413
1990 San Francisco	NL	93	204	50	9	1	1	(0	1)	64	17	24	11	0	45	1	2	2	1	0	1.00	5	.245	.284	.314
1991 San Francisco	NL	59	127	23	7	1	1	(0	1)	35	13	15	11	0	25	1	3	1	0	2	.00	2	.181	.250	.276
3 ML YEARS		223	474	109	21	5	6	(3	3)	158	42	56	29	0	99	3	9	3	1	4	.20	10	.230	.277	.333

Scott Livingstone

Bats: Left **Throws:** Right **Pos:** 3B **Ht:** 6' 0" **Wt:** 190 **Born:** 07/15/65 **Age:** 26

Year Team	Lg	G	AB	H	2B	3B	HR	(Hm	Rd)	TB	R	RBI	TBB	IBB	SO	HBP	SH	SF	SB	CS	SB%	GDP	Avg	OBP	SLG
1988 Lakeland	A	53	180	51	8	1	2	--	--	67	28	25	11	3	25	3	2	2	1	1	.50	3	.283	.332	.372
1989 London	AA	124	452	98	18	1	14	--	--	160	46	71	52	4	67	2	0	6	1	1	.50	4	.217	.297	.354
1990 Toledo	AAA	103	345	94	19	0	6	--	--	131	44	36	21	0	40	1	0	1	1	5	.17	7	.272	.315	.380
1991 Toledo	AAA	92	331	100	13	3	3	--	--	128	48	62	40	3	52	2	3	6	2	1	.67	9	.302	.375	.387
1991 Detroit	AL	44	127	37	5	0	2	(1	1)	48	19	11	10	0	25	0	1	1	2	1	.67	0	.291	.341	.378

Kenny Lofton

Bats: Left **Throws:** Left **Pos:** CF **Ht:** 6' 0" **Wt:** 180 **Born:** 05/31/67 **Age:** 25

Year Team	Lg	G	AB	H	2B	3B	HR	(Hm	Rd)	TB	R	RBI	TBB	IBB	SO	HBP	SH	SF	SB	CS	SB%	GDP	Avg	OBP	SLG
1988 Auburn	A	48	187	40	6	1	1	--	--	51	23	14	19	0	51	0	1	0	26	4	.87	3	.214	.286	.273
1989 Auburn	A	34	110	29	3	1	0	--	--	34	21	8	14	0	30	0	1	4	26	5	.84	1	.264	.336	.309
Asheville	A	22	82	27	2	0	1	--	--	32	14	9	12	0	10	1	2	0	14	6	.70	1	.329	.421	.390
1990 Osceola	A	124	481	159	15	5	2	--	--	190	98	35	61	2	77	3	8	3	62	16	.79	4	.331	.407	.395
1991 Tucson	AAA	130	545	168	19	17	2	--	--	227	93	50	52	5	95	0	8	2	40	23	.63	2	.308	.367	.417
1991 Houston	NL	20	74	15	1	0	0	(0	0)	16	9	0	5	0	19	0	0	0	2	1	.67	0	.203	.253	.216

Bill Long

Pitches: Right **Bats:** Right **Pos:** RP **Ht:** 6' 0" **Wt:** 190 **Born:** 02/29/60 **Age:** 32

Year Team	Lg	G	GS	CG	GF	IP	BFP	H	R	ER	HR	SH	SF	HB	TBB	IBB	SO	WP	Bk	W	L	Pct.	ShO	Sv	ERA
1985 Chicago	AL	4	3	0	1	14	71	25	17	16	4	1	1	0	5	2	13	1	0	0	0	.000	0	0	10.29
1987 Chicago	AL	29	23	5	2	169	699	179	85	82	20	6	3	3	28	1	72	0	1	8	8	.500	2	1	4.37
1988 Chicago	AL	47	18	3	14	174	732	187	89	78	21	8	8	4	43	4	77	2	0	8	11	.421	0	2	4.03
1989 Chicago	AL	30	8	0	3	98.2	432	101	49	43	8	4	6	4	37	0	51	3	0	5	5	.500	1	3	3.92
1990 2 ML Teams		46	0	0	21	61.1	270	72	34	31	10	4	0	1	23	4	34	1	0	6	2	.750	0	5	4.55
1991 Montreal	NL	3	0	0	1	1.2	12	4	2	2	0	0	0	0	4	0	0	0	0	0	0	.000	0	0	10.80
1990 Chicago	AL	4	0	0	0	5.2	26	6	5	4	2	1	0	0	2	0	2	0	0	0	1	.000	0	0	6.35
Chicago	NL	42	0	0	21	55.2	244	66	29	27	8	3	0	1	21	4	32	1	0	6	1	.857	0	5	4.37
6 ML YEARS		159	52	8	42	518.2	2216	568	276	252	63	23	18	12	140	11	247	7	1	27	27	.500	2	9	4.37

Luis Lopez

Bats: Right **Throws:** Right **Pos:** C **Ht:** 6' 1" **Wt:** 190 **Born:** 09/01/64 **Age:** 27

Year Team	Lg	G	AB	H	2B	3B	HR	(Hm	Rd)	TB	R	RBI	TBB	IBB	SO	HBP	SH	SF	SB	CS	SB%	GDP	Avg	OBP	SLG
1984 Great Falls	R	68	275	90	15	5	1	--	--	133	60	61	27	1	15	5	1	2	4	4	.50	10	.327	.395	.484
1985 Vero Beach	A	120	382	106	18	2	1	--	--	131	47	43	25	3	41	6	3	3	2	2	.50	19	.277	.329	.343
1986 Vero Beach	A	122	434	124	21	3	1	--	--	154	52	60	33	3	25	2	2	4	5	7	.42	21	.286	.336	.355
1987 Bakersfield	A	142	550	181	43	2	16	--	--	276	89	96	38	3	49	9	5	6	6	6	.50	9	.329	.378	.502
1988 San Antonio	AA	124	470	116	16	3	7	--	--	159	56	65	32	5	33	13	5	7	3	4	.43	12	.247	.308	.338

1989 San Antonio	AA	99	327	87	17	0	10	--	--	134	46	51	38	4	39	5	0	2	1	0	1.00	14	.266	.349	.410
Albuquerque	AAA	19	75	37	7	0	2	--	--	50	17	16	6	0	7	1	0	2	1	0	1.00	1	.493	.524	.667
1990 Albuquerque	AAA	128	448	158	23	2	11	--	--	218	65	81	47	4	49	4	0	2	3	3	.50	12	.353	.417	.487
1991 Colo Sprngs	AAA	41	176	61	11	4	1	--	--	83	29	31	9	0	10	3	0	0	0	0	.00	4	.347	.388	.472
1990 Los Angeles	NL	6	6	0	0	0	0	(0	0)	0	0	0	0	0	2	0	0	0	0	0	.00	0	.000	.000	.000
1991 Cleveland	AL	35	82	18	4	1	0	(0	0)	24	7	7	4	1	7	1	1	1	0	0	.00	0	.220	.261	.293
2 ML YEARS		41	88	18	4	1	0	(0	0)	24	7	7	4	1	9	1	1	1	0	0	.00	0	.205	.245	.273

Torey Lovullo

Bats: Both **Throws:** Right **Pos:** 3B **Ht:** 6' 0" **Wt:** 185 **Born:** 07/25/65 **Age:** 26

		BATTING																	BASERUNNING				PERCENTAGES		
Year Team	Lg	G	AB	H	2B	3B	HR	(Hm	Rd)	TB	R	RBI	TBB	IBB	SO	HBP	SH	SF	SB	CS	SB%	GDP	Avg	OBP	SLG
1987 Fayettevlle	A	55	191	49	13	0	8	--	--	86	34	32	37	4	30	2	2	1	6	0	1.00	3	.257	.381	.450
Lakeland	A	18	60	16	3	0	1	--	--	22	11	16	10	0	8	0	0	3	0	0	.00	0	.267	.356	.367
1988 Glens Falls	AA	78	270	74	17	1	9	--	--	120	37	50	36	3	44	1	0	6	2	0	1.00	5	.274	.355	.444
Toledo	AAA	57	177	41	8	1	5	--	--	66	18	20	9	0	24	0	7	1	2	1	.67	1	.232	.267	.373
1989 Toledo	AAA	112	409	94	23	2	10	--	--	151	48	52	44	10	57	1	7	4	2	1	.67	10	.230	.303	.369
1990 Toledo	AAA	141	486	131	38	1	14	--	--	213	71	58	61	6	74	4	2	4	4	1	.80	12	.270	.353	.438
1991 Columbus	AAA	106	395	107	24	5	10	--	--	171	74	75	59	4	56	0	2	6	4	4	.50	10	.271	.361	.433
1988 Detroit	AL	12	21	8	1	1	1	(0	1)	14	2	2	1	0	2	0	1	0	0	0	.00	1	.381	.409	.667
1989 Detroit	AL	29	87	10	2	0	1	(0	1)	15	8	4	14	0	20	0	1	2	0	0	.00	3	.115	.233	.172
1991 New York	AL	22	51	9	2	0	0	(0	0)	11	0	2	5	1	7	0	3	0	0	0	.00	0	.176	.250	.216
3 ML YEARS		63	159	27	5	1	2	(0	2)	40	10	8	20	1	29	0	5	2	0	0	.00	4	.170	.260	.252

Scott Lusader

Bats: Left **Throws:** Left **Pos:** CF **Ht:** 5'10" **Wt:** 170 **Born:** 09/30/64 **Age:** 27

		BATTING																	BASERUNNING				PERCENTAGES		
Year Team	Lg	G	AB	H	2B	3B	HR	(Hm	Rd)	TB	R	RBI	TBB	IBB	SO	HBP	SH	SF	SB	CS	SB%	GDP	Avg	OBP	SLG
1987 Detroit	AL	23	47	15	3	1	1	(1	0)	23	8	8	5	1	7	0	1	1	1	0	1.00	0	.319	.377	.489
1988 Detroit	AL	16	16	1	0	0	1	(0	1)	4	3	3	1	0	4	0	0	1	0	0	.00	1	.063	.111	.250
1989 Detroit	AL	40	103	26	4	0	1	(1	0)	33	15	8	9	0	21	0	0	1	3	0	1.00	2	.252	.310	.320
1990 Detroit	AL	45	87	21	2	0	2	(1	1)	29	13	16	12	0	8	0	0	3	0	0	.00	2	.241	.324	.333
1991 New York	AL	11	7	1	0	0	0	(0	0)	1	2	1	1	0	3	0	0	0	0	1	.00	0	.143	.250	.143
5 ML YEARS		135	260	64	9	1	5	(3	2)	90	41	36	28	1	43	0	1	6	4	1	.80	5	.246	.313	.346

Barry Lyons

Bats: Right **Throws:** Right **Pos:** C **Ht:** 6' 1" **Wt:** 200 **Born:** 06/03/60 **Age:** 32

		BATTING																	BASERUNNING				PERCENTAGES		
Year Team	Lg	G	AB	H	2B	3B	HR	(Hm	Rd)	TB	R	RBI	TBB	IBB	SO	HBP	SH	SF	SB	CS	SB%	GDP	Avg	OBP	SLG
1986 New York	NL	6	9	0	0	0	0	(0	0)	0	1	2	1	1	2	0	0	0	0	0	.00	0	.000	.100	.000
1987 New York	NL	53	130	33	4	1	4	(4	0)	51	15	24	8	1	24	2	0	3	0	0	.00	1	.254	.301	.392
1988 New York	NL	50	91	21	7	1	0	(0	0)	30	5	11	3	0	12	0	3	1	0	0	.00	3	.231	.253	.330
1989 New York	NL	79	235	58	13	0	3	(1	2)	80	15	27	11	1	28	2	1	3	0	1	.00	7	.247	.283	.340
1990 2 ML Teams		27	85	20	0	0	3	(1	2)	29	9	9	2	0	10	1	0	0	0	0	.00	2	.235	.261	.341
1991 2 ML Teams		11	14	1	0	0	0	(0	0)	1	0	0	0	0	2	0	0	0	0	0	.00	0	.071	.071	.071
1990 New York	NL	24	80	19	0	0	2	(1	1)	25	8	7	2	0	9	1	0	0	0	0	.00	2	.238	.265	.313
Los Angeles	NL	3	5	1	0	0	1	(0	1)	4	1	2	0	0	1	0	0	0	0	0	.00	0	.200	.200	.800
1991 Los Angeles	NL	9	9	0	0	0	0	(0	0)	0	0	0	0	0	2	0	0	0	0	0	.00	0	.000	.000	.000
California	AL	2	5	1	0	0	0	(0	0)	1	0	0	0	0	0	0	0	0	0	0	.00	0	.200	.200	.200
6 ML YEARS		226	564	133	24	2	10	(6	4)	191	45	73	25	3	78	5	4	7	0	1	.00	13	.236	.271	.339

Steve Lyons

Bats: Left **Throws:** Right **Pos:** CF/2B **Ht:** 6' 3" **Wt:** 192 **Born:** 06/03/60 **Age:** 32

		BATTING																	BASERUNNING				PERCENTAGES		
Year Team	Lg	G	AB	H	2B	3B	HR	(Hm	Rd)	TB	R	RBI	TBB	IBB	SO	HBP	SH	SF	SB	CS	SB%	GDP	Avg	OBP	SLG
1985 Boston	AL	133	371	98	14	3	5	(4	1)	133	52	30	32	0	64	1	2	3	12	9	.57	2	.264	.322	.358
1986 2 ML Teams		101	247	56	9	3	1	(1	0)	74	30	20	19	2	47	1	4	4	4	6	.40	4	.227	.280	.300
1987 Chicago	AL	76	193	54	11	1	1	(0	1)	70	26	19	12	0	37	0	4	1	3	1	.75	4	.280	.320	.363
1988 Chicago	AL	146	472	127	28	3	5	(1	4)	176	59	45	32	1	59	1	15	6	1	2	.33	6	.269	.313	.373
1989 Chicago	AL	140	443	117	21	3	2	(0	2)	150	51	50	35	3	68	1	12	3	9	6	.60	3	.264	.317	.339
1990 Chicago	AL	93	146	28	6	1	1	(0	1)	39	22	11	10	1	41	1	4	2	1	0	1.00	1	.192	.245	.267
1991 Boston	AL	87	212	51	10	1	4	(2	2)	75	15	17	11	2	35	0	3	1	10	3	.77	1	.241	.277	.354
1986 Boston	AL	59	124	31	7	2	1	(1	0)	45	20	14	12	2	23	0	1	2	2	3	.40	3	.250	.312	.363
Chicago	AL	42	123	25	2	1	0	(0	0)	29	10	6	7	0	24	1	3	2	2	3	.40	1	.203	.248	.236
7 ML YEARS		776	2084	531	99	15	19	(8	11)	717	255	192	151	9	351	5	44	20	40	27	.60	21	.255	.304	.344

Kevin Maas

Bats: Left   **Throws:** Left   **Pos:** DH/1B   **Ht:** 6' 3"   **Wt:** 206   **Born:** 01/20/65   **Age:** 27

								BATTING												BASERUNNING				PERCENTAGES		
Year Team	Lg	G	AB	H	2B	3B	HR	(Hm	Rd)	TB	R	RBI	TBB	IBB	SO	HBP	SH	SF	SB	CS	SB%	GDP	Avg	OBP	SLG
1986 Oneonta	A	28	101	36	10	0	0	--	--	46	14	18	7	1	9	0	0	1	5	1	.83	1	.356	.394	.455
1987 Ft.Laudrdle	A	116	439	122	28	4	11	--	--	191	77	73	53	4	108	2	0	8	14	4	.78	5	.278	.353	.435
1988 Pr William	A	29	108	32	7	0	12	--	--	75	24	35	17	1	28	4	0	4	3	1	.75	0	.296	.398	.694
Albany	AA	109	372	98	14	3	16	--	--	166	66	55	64	4	103	4	3	2	5	1	.83	5	.263	.376	.446
1989 Columbus	AAA	83	291	93	23	2	6	--	--	138	42	45	40	0	73	1	0	4	2	3	.40	3	.320	.399	.474
1990 Columbus	AAA	57	194	55	15	2	13	--	--	113	37	38	34	1	45	0	0	0	2	2	.50	5	.284	.390	.582
1990 New York	AL	79	254	64	9	0	21	(12	9)	136	42	41	43	10	76	3	0	0	1	2	.33	2	.252	.367	.535
1991 New York	AL	148	500	110	14	1	23	(8	15)	195	69	63	83	3	128	4	0	5	5	1	.83	4	.220	.333	.390
2 ML YEARS		227	754	174	23	1	44	(20	24)	331	111	104	126	13	204	7	0	5	6	3	.67	6	.231	.344	.439

Bob MacDonald

Pitches: Left   **Bats:** Left   **Pos:** RP   **Ht:** 6' 2"   **Wt:** 180   **Born:** 04/27/65   **Age:** 27

		HOW MUCH HE PITCHED						WHAT HE GAVE UP												THE RESULTS					
Year Team	Lg	G	GS	CG	GF	IP	BFP	H	R	ER	HR	SH	SF	HB	TBB	IBB	SO	WP	Bk	W	L	Pct.	ShO	Sv	ERA
1987 St.Cathrnes	A	1	1	0	0	4	20	8	4	2	0	0	0	0	0	0	4	0	0	0	0	.000	0	0	4.50
Medicne Hat	R	13	0	0	9	24.2	109	22	13	8	0	1	0	1	12	1	26	5	0	3	1	.750	0	2	2.92
Myrtle Bch	A	10	0	0	4	20.2	94	24	18	13	1	2	1	0	7	1	12	2	0	2	1	.667	0	1	5.66
1988 Myrtle Bch	A	52	0	0	48	53.1	222	42	13	10	2	3	1	0	18	3	43	2	0	3	4	.429	0	15	1.69
1989 Knoxville	AA	43	0	0	27	63	264	52	27	23	0	5	0	2	23	2	58	0	1	3	5	.375	0	9	3.29
Syracuse	AAA	12	0	0	4	16	75	16	10	10	0	3	1	1	6	0	12	0	0	1	0	1.000	0	0	5.63
1990 Knoxville	AA	36	0	0	29	57	237	37	17	12	2	9	1	0	29	4	54	3	0	1	2	.333	0	15	1.89
Syracuse	AAA	9	0	0	5	8.1	35	4	5	5	1	0	0	0	9	0	6	0	0	0	2	.000	0	2	5.40
1991 Syracuse	AAA	7	0	0	5	6	29	5	3	3	1	0	0	0	5	0	8	3	0	1	0	1.000	0	1	4.50
1990 Toronto	AL	4	0	0	1	2.1	8	0	0	0	0	0	0	0	2	0	0	0	0	0	0	.000	0	0	0.00
1991 Toronto	AL	45	0	0	10	53.2	231	51	19	17	5	2	2	0	25	4	24	1	1	3	3	.500	0	0	2.85
2 ML YEARS		49	0	0	11	56	239	51	19	17	5	2	2	0	27	4	24	1	1	3	3	.500	0	0	2.73

Mike Macfarlane

Bats: Right   **Throws:** Right   **Pos:** C   **Ht:** 6' 1"   **Wt:** 205   **Born:** 04/12/64   **Age:** 28

								BATTING												BASERUNNING				PERCENTAGES		
Year Team	Lg	G	AB	H	2B	3B	HR	(Hm	Rd)	TB	R	RBI	TBB	IBB	SO	HBP	SH	SF	SB	CS	SB%	GDP	Avg	OBP	SLG
1987 Kansas City	AL	8	19	4	1	0	0	(0	0)	5	0	3	2	0	2	0	0	0	0	0	.00	1	.211	.286	.263
1988 Kansas City	AL	70	211	56	15	0	4	(2	2)	83	25	26	21	2	37	1	1	2	0	0	.00	5	.265	.332	.393
1989 Kansas City	AL	69	157	35	6	0	2	(0	2)	47	13	19	7	0	27	2	0	1	0	0	.00	8	.223	.263	.299
1990 Kansas City	AL	124	400	102	24	4	6	(1	5)	152	37	58	25	2	69	7	1	6	1	0	1.00	9	.255	.306	.380
1991 Kansas City	AL	84	267	74	18	2	13	(6	7)	135	34	41	17	0	52	6	1	4	1	0	1.00	4	.277	.330	.506
5 ML YEARS		355	1054	271	64	6	25	(9	16)	422	109	147	72	4	187	16	3	13	2	0	1.00	27	.257	.311	.400

Julio Machado

Pitches: Right   **Bats:** Right   **Pos:** RP   **Ht:** 5' 9"   **Wt:** 165   **Born:** 12/01/65   **Age:** 26

		HOW MUCH HE PITCHED						WHAT HE GAVE UP												THE RESULTS					
Year Team	Lg	G	GS	CG	GF	IP	BFP	H	R	ER	HR	SH	SF	HB	TBB	IBB	SO	WP	Bk	W	L	Pct.	ShO	Sv	ERA
1989 New York	NL	10	0	0	9	11	45	9	4	4	0	0	0	0	3	0	14	0	0	0	1	.000	0	0	3.27
1990 2 ML Teams		37	0	0	21	47.1	207	41	14	13	4	1	3	2	25	6	39	3	0	4	1	.800	0	3	2.47
1991 Milwaukee	AL	54	0	0	13	88.2	371	65	36	34	12	3	2	3	55	1	98	5	0	3	3	.500	0	3	3.45
1990 New York	NL	27	0	0	14	34.1	151	32	13	12	4	1	2	2	17	4	27	3	0	4	1	.800	0	0	3.15
Milwaukee	AL	10	0	0	7	13	56	9	1	1	0	0	1	0	8	2	12	0	0	0	0	.000	0	0	0.69
3 ML YEARS		101	0	0	43	147	623	115	54	51	16	4	5	5	83	7	151	8	0	7	5	.583	0	6	3.12

Shane Mack

Bats: Right   **Throws:** Right   **Pos:** RF/LF/CF   **Ht:** 6' 0"   **Wt:** 190   **Born:** 12/07/63   **Age:** 28

								BATTING												BASERUNNING				PERCENTAGES		
Year Team	Lg	G	AB	H	2B	3B	HR	(Hm	Rd)	TB	R	RBI	TBB	IBB	SO	HBP	SH	SF	SB	CS	SB%	GDP	Avg	OBP	SLG
1987 San Diego	NL	105	238	57	11	3	4	(2	2)	86	28	25	18	0	47	3	6	2	4	6	.40	11	.239	.299	.361
1988 San Diego	NL	56	119	29	3	0	0	(0	0)	32	13	12	14	0	21	3	3	1	5	1	.83	2	.244	.336	.269
1990 Minnesota	AL	125	313	102	10	4	8	(5	3)	144	50	44	29	1	69	5	6	0	13	4	.76	1	.326	.392	.460
1991 Minnesota	AL	143	442	137	27	8	18	(4	14)	234	79	74	34	1	79	6	2	5	13	9	.59	11	.310	.363	.529
4 ML YEARS		429	1112	325	51	15	30	(11	19)	496	170	155	95	2	216	17	17	8	35	20	.64	31	.292	.355	.446

Greg Maddux

Pitches: Right **Bats:** Right **Pos:** SP   **Ht:** 6' 0" **Wt:** 170 **Born:** 04/14/66 **Age:** 26

		HOW MUCH HE PITCHED						WHAT HE GAVE UP								THE RESULTS					
Year Team	Lg	G	GS	CG	GF	IP	BFP	H	R	ER	HR	SH	SF	HB	TBB	IBB	SO	WP	Bk	W	L	Pct.	ShO	Sv	ERA
1986 Chicago	NL	6	5	1	1	31	144	44	20	19	3	1	0	1	11	2	20	2	0	2	4	.333	0	0	5.52
1987 Chicago	NL	30	27	1	2	155.2	701	181	111	97	17	7	1	4	74	13	101	4	7	6	14	.300	1	0	5.61
1988 Chicago	NL	34	34	9	0	249	1047	230	97	88	13	11	2	9	81	16	140	3	6	18	8	.692	3	0	3.18
1989 Chicago	NL	35	35	7	0	238.1	1002	222	90	78	13	18	6	6	82	13	135	5	3	19	12	.613	1	0	2.95
1990 Chicago	NL	35	35	8	0	237	1011	242	116	91	11	18	5	4	71	10	144	3	3	15	15	.500	2	0	3.46
1991 Chicago	NL	37	37	7	0	263	1070	232	113	98	18	16	3	6	66	9	198	6	3	15	11	.577	2	0	3.35
6 ML YEARS		177	173	33	3	1174	4975	1151	547	471	75	71	17	30	385	63	738	23	22	75	64	.540	9	0	3.61

Mike Maddux

Pitches: Right **Bats:** Left **Pos:** RP   **Ht:** 6' 2" **Wt:** 180 **Born:** 08/27/61 **Age:** 30

		HOW MUCH HE PITCHED						WHAT HE GAVE UP								THE RESULTS					
Year Team	Lg	G	GS	CG	GF	IP	BFP	H	R	ER	HR	SH	SF	HB	TBB	IBB	SO	WP	Bk	W	L	Pct.	ShO	Sv	ERA
1986 Philadelphia	NL	16	16	0	0	78	351	88	56	47	6	3	3	3	34	4	44	4	2	3	7	.300	0	0	5.42
1987 Philadelphia	NL	7	2	0	0	17	72	17	5	5	0	0	0	0	5	0	15	1	0	2	0	1.000	0	0	2.65
1988 Philadelphia	NL	25	11	0	4	88.2	380	91	41	37	6	7	3	5	34	4	59	4	2	4	3	.571	0	0	3.76
1989 Philadelphia	NL	16	4	2	1	43.2	191	52	29	25	3	3	1	2	14	3	26	3	1	1	3	.250	1	1	5.15
1990 Los Angeles	NL	11	2	0	3	20.2	88	24	15	15	3	0	1	1	4	0	11	2	0	0	1	.000	0	0	6.53
1991 San Diego	NL	64	1	0	27	98.2	388	78	30	27	4	5	2	1	27	3	57	5	0	7	2	.778	0	5	2.46
6 ML YEARS		139	36	2	35	346.2	1470	350	176	156	22	18	10	12	118	14	212	19	5	17	16	.515	1	6	4.05

Dave Magadan

Bats: Left **Throws:** Right **Pos:** 1B   **Ht:** 6' 3" **Wt:** 200 **Born:** 09/30/62 **Age:** 29

		BATTING																	BASERUNNING				PERCENTAGES		
Year Team	Lg	G	AB	H	2B	3B	HR	(Hm	Rd)	TB	R	RBI	TBB	IBB	SO	HBP	SH	SF	SB	CS	SB%	GDP	Avg	OBP	SLG
1986 New York	NL	10	18	8	0	0	0	(0	0)	8	3	3	3	0	1	0	0	0	0	0	.00	0	.444	.524	.444
1987 New York	NL	85	192	61	13	1	3	(2	1)	85	21	24	22	2	22	0	1	1	0	0	.00	5	.318	.386	.443
1988 New York	NL	112	314	87	15	0	1	(1	0)	105	39	35	60	4	39	2	1	3	0	1	.00	9	.277	.393	.334
1989 New York	NL	127	374	107	22	3	4	(3	1)	147	47	41	49	6	37	1	1	4	1	0	1.00	2	.286	.367	.393
1990 New York	NL	144	451	148	28	6	6	(2	4)	206	74	72	74	4	55	2	4	10	2	1	.67	10	.328	.417	.457
1991 New York	NL	124	418	108	23	0	4	(2	2)	143	58	51	83	3	50	2	7	7	1	1	.50	5	.258	.378	.342
6 ML YEARS		602	1767	519	101	10	18	(10	8)	694	242	226	291	19	204	7	14	25	4	3	.57	32	.294	.391	.393

Ever Magallanes

Bats: Left **Throws:** Right **Pos:** SS   **Ht:** 5'10" **Wt:** 165 **Born:** 11/06/65 **Age:** 26

		BATTING																	BASERUNNING				PERCENTAGES		
Year Team	Lg	G	AB	H	2B	3B	HR	(Hm	Rd)	TB	R	RBI	TBB	IBB	SO	HBP	SH	SF	SB	CS	SB%	GDP	Avg	OBP	SLG
1987 Kinston	A	58	205	50	4	3	2	--	--	66	20	23	16	0	18	1	2	0	2	0	1.00	7	.244	.302	.322
1988 Kinston	A	119	396	104	13	3	1	--	--	126	67	45	76	3	48	2	3	3	12	6	.67	16	.263	.382	.318
1989 Canton-Akrn	AA	74	241	67	5	0	0	--	--	72	26	18	37	0	24	1	4	3	1	6	.14	5	.278	.372	.299
Colo Sprngs	AAA	12	44	11	1	0	1	--	--	15	2	3	4	0	3	0	1	0	1	0	1.00	2	.250	.313	.341
1990 Colo Sprngs	AAA	125	377	116	17	3	1	--	--	142	60	63	43	0	49	1	5	6	3	2	.60	13	.308	.375	.377
1991 Colo Sprngs	AAA	94	305	87	13	1	1	--	--	105	37	33	23	1	36	2	1	1	1	2	.33	9	.285	.338	.344
1991 Cleveland	AL	3	2	0	0	0	0	(0	0)	0	0	0	1	0	1	0	0	0	0	0	.00	0	.000	.333	.000

Mike Magnante

Pitches: Left **Bats:** Left **Pos:** RP   **Ht:** 6' 1" **Wt:** 180 **Born:** 06/17/65 **Age:** 27

		HOW MUCH HE PITCHED						WHAT HE GAVE UP								THE RESULTS					
Year Team	Lg	G	GS	CG	GF	IP	BFP	H	R	ER	HR	SH	SF	HB	TBB	IBB	SO	WP	Bk	W	L	Pct.	ShO	Sv	ERA
1988 Eugene	A	3	3	0	0	16	59	10	6	1	0	0	0	0	2	0	26	0	0	1	1	.500	0	0	0.56
Appleton	A	9	8	0	0	47.2	199	48	20	17	3	4	1	0	15	0	40	3	0	3	2	.600	0	0	3.21
Baseball Cy	A	4	4	1	0	24	95	19	12	11	1	1	0	0	8	0	19	0	0	1	1	.500	0	0	4.13
1989 Memphis	AA	26	26	4	0	157.1	659	137	70	64	10	6	2	9	53	3	118	8	0	8	9	.471	1	0	3.66
1990 Omaha	AAA	13	13	2	0	76.2	320	72	39	35	6	3	0	2	25	0	56	3	1	2	5	.286	0	0	4.11
1991 Omaha	AAA	10	10	2	1	65.2	264	53	23	22	2	2	2	1	23	0	50	0	0	6	1	.857	0	0	3.02
1991 Kansas City	AL	38	0	0	10	55	236	55	19	15	3	2	1	0	23	3	42	1	0	0	1	.000	0	0	2.45

Rick Mahler

Pitches: Right **Bats:** Right **Pos:** RP/SP   **Ht:** 6' 1" **Wt:** 202 **Born:** 08/05/53 **Age:** 38

			HOW MUCH HE PITCHED						WHAT HE GAVE UP											THE RESULTS					
Year	Team	Lg	G	GS	CG	GF	IP	BFP	H	R	ER	HR	SH	SF	HB	TBB	IBB	SO	WP	Bk	W	L	Pct.	ShO	Sv	ERA
1979	Atlanta	NL	15	0	0	5	22	101	28	16	15	4	0	0	0	11	2	12	1	1	0	0	.000	0	0	6.14
1980	Atlanta	NL	2	0	0	0	4	13	2	1	1	0	0	0	0	0	0	1	0	0	0	0	.000	0	0	2.25
1981	Atlanta	NL	34	14	1	10	112	478	109	41	35	5	8	3	1	43	5	54	3	1	8	6	.571	0	2	2.81
1982	Atlanta	NL	39	33	5	0	205.1	857	213	105	96	18	6	6	1	62	5	105	8	2	9	10	.474	2	0	4.21
1983	Atlanta	NL	10	0	0	1	14.1	66	16	8	8	0	1	2	0	9	1	7	0	0	0	0	.000	0	0	5.02
1984	Atlanta	NL	38	29	9	1	222	918	209	86	77	13	13	8	3	62	7	106	3	1	13	10	.565	1	0	3.12
1985	Atlanta	NL	39	39	6	0	266.2	1110	272	116	103	24	10	5	2	79	8	107	3	1	17	15	.531	1	0	3.48
1986	Atlanta	NL	39	39	7	0	237.2	1056	283	139	129	25	10	8	3	95	10	137	5	1	14	18	.438	1	0	4.88
1987	Atlanta	NL	39	28	3	1	197	849	212	118	109	24	9	3	2	85	8	95	5	2	8	13	.381	1	0	4.98
1988	Atlanta	NL	39	34	5	2	249	1063	279	125	102	17	19	5	8	42	6	131	5	8	9	16	.360	0	0	3.69
1989	Cincinnati	NL	40	31	5	1	220.2	940	242	113	94	15	15	5	10	51	13	102	4	4	9	13	.409	2	0	3.83
1990	Cincinnati	NL	35	16	2	9	134.2	564	134	67	64	16	4	4	3	39	4	68	3	2	7	6	.538	1	4	4.28
1991	2 ML Teams		23	8	0	2	66	291	70	37	33	4	5	1	2	28	1	27	1	0	2	4	.333	0	0	4.50
1991	Montreal	NL	10	6	0	1	37.1	158	37	17	15	2	4	1	0	15	0	17	0	0	1	3	.250	0	0	3.62
	Atlanta	NL	13	2	0	1	28.2	133	33	20	18	2	1	0	2	13	1	10	1	0	1	1	.500	0	0	5.65
	13 ML YEARS		392	271	43	32	1951.1	8306	2069	972	866	165	100	50	35	606	70	952	41	23	96	111	.464	9	6	3.99

Candy Maldonado

Bats: Right **Throws:** Right **Pos:** LF/RF   **Ht:** 6' 0" **Wt:** 195 **Born:** 09/05/60 **Age:** 31

Year	Team	Lg	G	AB	H	2B	3B	HR	(Hm	Rd)	TB	R	RBI	TBB	IBB	SO	HBP	SH	SF	SB	CS	SB%	GDP	Avg	OBP	SLG
1981	Los Angeles	NL	11	12	1	0	0	0	(0	0)	1	0	0	0	0	5	0	0	0	0	0	.00	0	.083	.083	.083
1982	Los Angeles	NL	6	4	0	0	0	0	(0	0)	0	0	0	1	1	2	0	0	0	0	0	.00	0	.000	.200	.000
1983	Los Angeles	NL	42	62	12	1	1	1	(1	0)	18	5	6	5	0	14	0	1	0	0	0	.00	1	.194	.254	.290
1984	Los Angeles	NL	116	254	68	14	0	5	(1	4)	97	25	28	19	0	29	1	1	3	0	3	.00	6	.268	.318	.382
1985	Los Angeles	NL	121	213	48	7	1	5	(2	3)	72	20	19	19	4	40	0	2	1	1	1	.50	3	.225	.288	.338
1986	San Francisco	NL	133	405	102	31	3	18	(6	12)	193	49	85	20	4	77	3	0	4	4	4	.50	12	.252	.289	.477
1987	San Francisco	NL	118	442	129	28	4	20	(14	6)	225	69	85	34	4	78	6	0	7	8	8	.50	9	.292	.346	.509
1988	San Francisco	NL	142	499	127	23	1	12	(5	7)	188	53	68	37	1	89	7	3	6	6	5	.55	13	.255	.311	.377
1989	San Francisco	NL	129	345	75	23	0	9	(1	8)	125	39	41	37	4	69	3	1	3	4	1	.80	8	.217	.296	.362
1990	Cleveland	AL	155	590	161	32	2	22	(12	10)	263	76	95	49	4	134	5	0	7	3	5	.38	13	.273	.330	.446
1991	2 ML Teams		86	288	72	15	0	12	(7	5)	123	37	48	36	4	76	6	0	3	4	0	1.00	8	.250	.342	.427
1991	Milwaukee	AL	34	111	23	6	0	5	(3	2)	44	11	20	13	0	23	0	0	1	1	0	1.00	4	.207	.288	.396
	Toronto	AL	52	177	49	9	0	7	(4	3)	79	26	28	23	4	53	6	0	2	3	0	1.00	4	.277	.375	.446
	11 ML YEARS		1059	3114	795	174	12	104	(49	55)	1305	373	475	257	26	613	31	8	34	30	27	.53	73	.255	.315	.419

Carlos Maldonado

Pitches: Right **Bats:** Right **Pos:** RP   **Ht:** 6' 2" **Wt:** 215 **Born:** 10/18/66 **Age:** 25

Year	Team	Lg	G	GS	CG	GF	IP	BFP	H	R	ER	HR	SH	SF	HB	TBB	IBB	SO	WP	Bk	W	L	Pct.	ShO	Sv	ERA
1986	Royals	R	10	4	0	2	34.1	136	29	10	7	1	1	1	1	10	1	16	3	0	0	2	.000	0	1	1.83
1987	Appleton	A	2	0	0	1	2.1	13	4	3	3	0	0	1	0	3	0	4	1	0	0	0	.000	0	0	11.57
	Royals	R	20	0	0	8	58	223	32	18	16	2	2	0	2	19	2	56	2	1	5	1	.833	0	4	2.48
1988	Baseball Cy	A	16	7	0	2	52.2	242	46	35	31	5	2	1	7	39	0	44	3	0	1	5	.167	0	0	5.30
1989	Baseball Cy	A	28	0	0	19	76.2	300	47	14	10	3	3	1	1	24	4	66	2	0	11	3	.786	0	9	1.17
1990	Memphis	AA	55	0	0	48	77.1	325	61	29	25	5	3	4	1	39	0	77	6	0	4	5	.444	0	20	2.91
1991	Omaha	AAA	41	1	0	31	61	282	67	31	29	6	3	2	2	42	1	46	6	0	1	1	.500	0	9	4.28
1990	Kansas City	AL	4	0	0	1	6	31	9	6	6	0	0	1	0	4	0	9	1	0	0	0	.000	0	0	9.00
1991	Kansas City	AL	5	0	0	2	7.2	43	11	9	7	0	1	0	1	9	1	1	4	0	0	0	.000	0	0	8.22
	2 ML YEARS		9	0	0	3	13.2	74	20	15	13	0	1	1	1	13	1	10	5	0	0	0	.000	0	0	8.56

Rob Mallicoat

Pitches: Left **Bats:** Left **Pos:** RP   **Ht:** 6' 3" **Wt:** 180 **Born:** 11/16/64 **Age:** 27

Year	Team	Lg	G	GS	CG	GF	IP	BFP	H	R	ER	HR	SH	SF	HB	TBB	IBB	SO	WP	Bk	W	L	Pct.	ShO	Sv	ERA
1984	Auburn	A	1	1	0	0	5	25	8	3	3	1	0	0	0	3	0	6	2	0	0	0	.000	0	0	5.40
	Asheville	A	11	11	2	0	64.1	276	49	30	28	5	1	1	4	36	0	57	7	2	3	4	.429	0	0	3.92
1985	Osceola	A	26	25	5	0	178.2	717	119	41	27	2	6	5	3	74	3	158	14	2	16	6	.727	2	0	1.36
1986	Tucson	AAA	3	3	0	0	14	68	18	14	10	1	1	0	0	8	0	9	0	1	0	2	.000	0	0	6.43
	Columbus	AA	10	10	1	0	58	281	61	38	31	2	0	4	3	45	1	52	2	0	0	6	.000	0	0	4.81
1987	Columbus	AA	24	24	3	0	152.1	656	132	68	49	13	8	4	5	78	2	141	8	0	10	7	.588	0	0	2.89
	Tucson	AAA	2	2	0	0	9.2	45	9	5	4	0	1	0	0	7	0	8	2	1	0	0	.000	0	0	3.72

Year	Team	Lg	G	GS	CG	GF	IP	BFP	H	R	ER	HR	SH	SF	HB	TBB	IBB	SO	WP	Bk	W	L	Pct.	ShO	Sv	ERA
1990	Astros	R	7	4	0	0	16.1	78	15	15	9	0	3	1	2	15	0	21	4	1	0	1	.000	0	0	4.96
	Osceola	A	3	3	0	0	12	51	8	2	0	0	0	0	0	9	0	10	1	1	0	0	.000	0	0	0.00
1991	Jackson	AA	18	0	0	6	31	121	20	15	13	1	0	3	2	11	1	34	2	1	4	1	.800	0	1	3.77
	Tucson	AAA	19	6	0	4	47.2	221	43	32	29	3	4	3	2	38	4	32	2	0	4	4	.500	0	1	5.48
1987	Houston	NL	4	1	0	0	6.2	31	8	5	5	0	0	0	0	6	0	4	0	0	0	0	.000	0	0	6.75
1991	Houston	NL	24	0	0	4	23.1	103	22	10	10	2	1	2	2	13	1	18	1	0	0	2	.000	0	1	3.86
	2 ML YEARS		28	1	0	4	30	134	30	15	15	2	1	2	2	19	1	22	1	0	0	2	.000	0	1	4.50

Fred Manrique

Bats: Right **Throws:** Right **Pos:** SS **Ht:** 6' 1" **Wt:** 175 **Born:** 11/05/61 **Age:** 30

Year	Team	Lg	G	AB	H	2B	3B	HR	(Hm	Rd)	TB	R	RBI	TBB	IBB	SO	HBP	SH	SF	SB	CS	SB%	GDP	Avg	OBP	SLG
1981	Toronto	AL	14	14	2	0	0	0	(0	0)	4	1	1	0	0	12	1	0	0	0	1	.00	1	.143	.172	.143
1984	Toronto	AL	10	9	3	0	0	0	(0	0)	3	0	1	0	0	1	0	0	0	0	0	.00	1	.333	.333	.333
1985	Montreal	NL	9	13	4	1	1	1	(1	0)	10	5	1	1	0	3	0	0	0	0	0	.00	0	.308	.357	.769
1986	St. Louis	NL	13	17	3	0	0	1	(0	1)	6	2	1	1	0	1	0	0	0	1	0	1.00	1	.176	.222	.353
1987	Chicago	AL	115	298	77	13	3	4	(2	2)	108	30	29	19	1	69	1	9	3	5	3	.63	4	.258	.302	.362
1988	Chicago	AL	140	345	81	10	6	5	(3	2)	118	43	37	21	1	54	3	16	2	6	5	.55	7	.235	.283	.342
1989	2 ML Teams		119	378	111	25	1	4	(1	3)	150	46	52	17	1	63	2	13	2	4	5	.44	9	.294	.326	.397
1990	Minnesota	AL	69	228	54	10	0	5	(3	2)	79	22	29	4	0	35	2	1	2	2	0	1.00	8	.237	.254	.346
1991	Oakland	AL	9	21	3	0	0	0	(0	0)	3	2	0	2	0	1	0	0	0	0	0	.00	1	.143	.217	.143
1989	Chicago	AL	65	187	56	13	1	2	(1	1)	77	23	30	8	1	30	2	4	1	0	4	.00	6	.299	.333	.412
	Texas	AL	54	191	55	12	0	2	(0	2)	73	23	22	9	0	33	0	9	1	4	1	.80	3	.288	.318	.382
	9 ML YEARS		498	1337	340	59	11	20	(10	10)	481	151	151	65	3	239	9	39	9	18	14	.56	31	.254	.292	.360

Jeff Manto

Bats: Right **Throws:** Right **Pos:** 3B **Ht:** 6' 3" **Wt:** 210 **Born:** 08/23/64 **Age:** 27

Year	Team	Lg	G	AB	H	2B	3B	HR	(Hm	Rd)	TB	R	RBI	TBB	IBB	SO	HBP	SH	SF	SB	CS	SB%	GDP	Avg	OBP	SLG
1985	Quad City	A	74	233	46	5	2	11	--	--	88	34	34	40	0	74	5	1	3	3	1	.75	7	.197	.324	.378
1986	Quad City	A	73	239	59	13	0	8	--	--	96	31	49	37	0	70	4	1	2	2	1	.67	2	.247	.355	.402
1987	Palm Sprngs	A	112	375	96	21	4	7	--	--	146	61	63	102	1	85	8	5	7	8	2	.80	7	.256	.419	.389
1988	Midland	AA	120	408	123	23	3	24	--	--	224	88	101	62	5	76	8	3	4	7	5	.58	17	.301	.400	.549
1989	Edmonton	AAA	127	408	113	25	3	23	--	--	213	89	67	91	5	81	9	3	4	4	4	.50	12	.277	.416	.522
1990	Colo Sprngs	AAA	96	316	94	27	1	18	--	--	177	73	82	78	2	65	9	1	3	10	3	.77	9	.297	.446	.560
1991	Colo Sprngs	AAA	43	153	49	16	0	6	--	--	83	36	36	33	2	24	3	0	3	1	0	1.00	3	.320	.443	.542
1990	Cleveland	AL	30	76	17	5	1	2	(1	1)	30	12	14	21	1	18	0	0	0	0	1	.00	0	.224	.392	.395
1991	Cleveland	AL	47	128	27	7	0	2	(0	2)	40	15	13	14	0	22	4	1	1	2	0	1.00	3	.211	.306	.313
	2 ML YEARS		77	204	44	12	1	4	(1	3)	70	27	27	35	1	40	4	1	1	2	1	.67	3	.216	.340	.343

Barry Manuel

Pitches: Right **Bats:** Right **Pos:** RP **Ht:** 5'11" **Wt:** 180 **Born:** 08/12/65 **Age:** 26

Year	Team	Lg	G	GS	CG	GF	IP	BFP	H	R	ER	HR	SH	SF	HB	TBB	IBB	SO	WP	Bk	W	L	Pct.	ShO	Sv	ERA
1987	Rangers	R	1	0	0	0	1	7	3	2	2	0	0	0	0	1	0	1	2	0	0	0	.000	0	0	18.00
	Charlotte	A	13	5	0	3	30	138	33	24	22	2	1	2	3	18	0	19	4	0	1	2	.333	0	0	6.60
1988	Charlotte	A	37	0	0	22	60.1	259	47	24	17	4	6	1	4	32	0	55	8	3	4	3	.571	0	4	2.54
1989	Tulsa	AA	11	11	0	0	49.1	237	49	44	41	5	3	6	9	39	0	40	3	3	3	4	.429	0	0	7.48
	Charlotte	A	15	14	0	0	76.1	330	77	43	40	6	4	3	8	30	0	51	6	1	4	7	.364	0	0	4.72
1990	Charlotte	A	57	0	0	56	56.1	238	39	23	18	2	4	2	3	30	2	60	1	0	1	5	.167	0	36	2.88
1991	Tulsa	AA	56	0	0	48	68.1	300	63	29	25	5	4	2	5	34	1	45	0	1	2	7	.222	0	25	3.29
1991	Texas	AL	8	0	0	5	16	58	7	2	2	0	0	3	0	6	0	5	2	0	1	0	1.000	0	0	1.13

Kirt Manwaring

Bats: Right **Throws:** Right **Pos:** C **Ht:** 5'11" **Wt:** 190 **Born:** 07/15/65 **Age:** 26

Year	Team	Lg	G	AB	H	2B	3B	HR	(Hm	Rd)	TB	R	RBI	TBB	IBB	SO	HBP	SH	SF	SB	CS	SB%	GDP	Avg	OBP	SLG
1987	San Francisco	NL	6	7	1	0	0	0	(0	0)	1	0	0	0	0	1	1	0	0	0	0	.00	1	.143	.250	.143
1988	San Francisco	NL	40	116	29	7	0	1	(0	1)	39	12	15	2	0	21	3	1	1	0	1	.00	1	.250	.279	.336
1989	San Francisco	NL	85	200	42	4	2	0	(0	0)	50	14	18	11	1	28	4	7	1	2	1	.67	5	.210	.264	.250
1990	San Francisco	NL	8	13	2	1	0	0	(0	0)	4	0	1	1	0	3	0	0	0	0	0	.00	0	.154	.154	.308
1991	San Francisco	NL	67	178	40	9	0	0	(0	0)	49	16	19	9	0	22	3	7	2	1	1	.50	2	.225	.271	.275
	5 ML YEARS		206	514	114	20	3	1	(0	1)	143	42	53	22	1	75	11	15	4	3	3	.50	9	.222	.267	.278

Josias Manzanillo

Pitches: Right **Bats:** Right **Pos:** RP   **Ht:** 6' 0" **Wt:** 190 **Born:** 10/16/67 **Age:** 24

			HOW MUCH HE PITCHED						WHAT HE GAVE UP												THE RESULTS					
Year	Team	Lg	G	GS	CG	GF	IP	BFP	H	R	ER	HR	SH	SF	HB	TBB	IBB	SO	WP	Bk	W	L	Pct.	ShO	Sv	ERA
1984	Elmira	A	14	0	0	7	25.2	128	27	24	15	1	1	1	1	26	1	15	9	0	2	3	.400	0	1	5.26
1985	Greensboro	A	7	0	0	2	12	62	12	13	13	1	0	0	0	18	0	10	2	0	1	1	.500	0	0	9.75
	Elmira	A	19	4	0	10	39.2	181	36	19	17	1	0	1	2	36	4	43	12	0	2	4	.333	0	1	3.86
1986	Winter Havn	A	23	21	3	2	142.2	601	110	51	36	3	6	4	3	81	0	102	9	0	13	5	.722	0	0	2.27
1987	New Britain	AA	2	2	0	0	10	45	8	5	5	1	0	0	0	8	0	12	0	0	2	0	1.000	0	0	4.50
1989	New Britain	AA	26	26	3	0	147.2	657	129	78	60	11	4	5	5	85	7	93	16	2	9	10	.474	1	0	3.66
1990	New Britain	AA	12	12	2	0	74	317	66	34	28	3	1	0	2	37	1	51	7	3	4	4	.500	1	0	3.41
	Pawtucket	AAA	15	15	5	0	82.2	368	75	57	51	9	1	2	2	45	0	77	8	0	4	7	.364	0	0	5.55
1991	New Britain	AA	7	7	0	0	49.2	212	37	25	16	0	5	0	1	28	1	35	2	1	2	2	.500	0	0	2.90
	Pawtucket	AAA	20	16	0	0	102.2	459	109	69	64	12	2	4	4	53	0	65	9	1	5	5	.500	0	0	5.61
1991	Boston	AL	1	0	0	1	1	8	2	2	2	0	0	0	0	3	0	1	0	0	0	0	.000	0	0	18.00

Mike Marshall

Bats: Right **Throws:** Right **Pos:** DH   **Ht:** 6' 5" **Wt:** 215 **Born:** 01/12/60 **Age:** 32

					BATTING														BASERUNNING				PERCENTAGES		
Year	Team	Lg	G	AB	H	2B	3B	HR	(Hm	Rd)	TB	R	RBI	TBB	IBB	SO	HBP	SH	SF	SB	CS	SB%	GDP	Avg	OBP	SLG
1981	Los Angeles	NL	14	25	5	3	0	0	(0	0)	8	2	1	1	0	4	1	0	0	0	0	.00	1	.200	.259	.320
1982	Los Angeles	NL	49	95	23	3	0	5	(2	3)	41	10	9	13	1	23	1	0	1	2	0	1.00	1	.242	.336	.432
1983	Los Angeles	NL	140	465	132	17	1	17	(6	11)	202	47	65	43	4	127	5	0	5	7	3	.70	8	.284	.347	.434
1984	Los Angeles	NL	134	495	127	27	0	21	(11	10)	217	68	65	40	6	93	3	1	2	4	3	.57	12	.257	.315	.438
1985	Los Angeles	NL	135	518	152	27	2	28	(15	13)	267	72	95	37	6	137	3	2	4	3	10	.23	8	.293	.342	.515
1986	Los Angeles	NL	103	330	77	11	0	19	(13	6)	145	47	53	27	3	90	4	0	1	4	4	.50	5	.233	.298	.439
1987	Los Angeles	NL	104	402	118	19	0	16	(5	11)	185	45	72	18	2	79	4	0	4	0	5	.00	13	.294	.327	.460
1988	Los Angeles	NL	144	542	150	27	2	20	(9	11)	241	63	82	24	7	93	7	0	4	4	1	.80	17	.277	.314	.445
1989	Los Angeles	NL	105	377	98	21	1	11	(6	5)	154	41	42	33	4	78	5	0	4	2	5	.29	8	.260	.325	.408
1990	2 ML Teams		83	275	71	14	2	10	(7	3)	119	34	39	11	0	66	4	0	3	0	2	.00	4	.258	.294	.433
1991	2 ML Teams		24	69	18	4	0	1	(1	0)	25	4	7	0	0	20	0	0	2	0	0	.00	2	.261	.261	.362
1990	New York	NL	53	163	39	8	1	6	(4	2)	67	24	27	7	0	40	3	0	3	0	2	.00	2	.239	.278	.411
	Boston	AL	30	112	32	6	1	4	(3	1)	52	10	12	4	0	26	1	0	0	0	0	.00	2	.286	.316	.464
1991	Boston	AL	22	62	18	4	0	1	(1	0)	25	4	7	0	0	19	0	0	2	0	0	.00	2	.290	.290	.403
	California	AL	2	7	0	0	0	0	(0	0)	0	0	0	0	0	1	0	0	0	0	0	.00	0	.000	.000	.000
11 ML YEARS			1035	3593	971	173	8	148	(78	70)	1604	433	530	247	33	810	37	3	28	26	33	.44	79	.270	.321	.446

Carlos Martinez

Bats: Right **Throws:** Right **Pos:** DH/1B   **Ht:** 6' 5" **Wt:** 175 **Born:** 08/11/65 **Age:** 26

					BATTING														BASERUNNING				PERCENTAGES		
Year	Team	Lg	G	AB	H	2B	3B	HR	(Hm	Rd)	TB	R	RBI	TBB	IBB	SO	HBP	SH	SF	SB	CS	SB%	GDP	Avg	OBP	SLG
1988	Chicago	AL	17	55	9	1	0	0	(0	0)	10	5	0	0	0	12	0	0	0	1	0	1.00	0	.164	.164	.182
1989	Chicago	AL	109	350	105	22	0	5	(2	3)	142	44	32	21	2	57	1	6	1	4	1	.80	14	.300	.340	.406
1990	Chicago	AL	92	272	61	6	5	4	(2	2)	89	18	24	10	2	40	0	1	0	0	4	.00	8	.224	.252	.327
1991	Cleveland	AL	72	257	73	14	0	5	(3	2)	102	22	30	10	2	43	2	1	5	3	2	.60	10	.284	.310	.397
4 ML YEARS			290	934	248	43	5	14	(7	7)	343	89	86	41	6	152	3	8	6	8	7	.53	33	.266	.297	.367

Carmelo Martinez

Bats: Right **Throws:** Right **Pos:** 1B/LF   **Ht:** 6' 2" **Wt:** 225 **Born:** 07/28/60 **Age:** 31

					BATTING														BASERUNNING				PERCENTAGES		
Year	Team	Lg	G	AB	H	2B	3B	HR	(Hm	Rd)	TB	R	RBI	TBB	IBB	SO	HBP	SH	SF	SB	CS	SB%	GDP	Avg	OBP	SLG
1983	Chicago	NL	29	89	23	3	0	6	(2	4)	44	8	16	4	0	19	0	0	1	0	0	.00	3	.258	.287	.494
1984	San Diego	NL	149	488	122	28	2	13	(6	7)	193	64	66	68	4	82	4	0	10	1	3	.25	7	.250	.340	.395
1985	San Diego	NL	150	514	130	28	1	21	(15	6)	223	64	72	87	4	82	3	2	4	4	4	.00	10	.253	.362	.434
1986	San Diego	NL	113	244	58	10	0	9	(6	3)	95	28	25	35	2	46	1	1	2	1	1	.50	9	.238	.333	.389
1987	San Diego	NL	139	447	122	21	2	15	(10	5)	192	59	70	70	5	82	3	1	4	5	5	.50	11	.273	.372	.430
1988	San Diego	NL	121	365	86	12	0	18	(11	7)	152	48	65	35	3	57	0	3	2	1	1	.50	10	.236	.301	.416
1989	San Diego	NL	111	267	59	12	2	6	(2	4)	93	23	39	32	3	54	0	0	2	0	0	.00	12	.221	.302	.348
1990	2 ML Teams		83	217	52	9	0	10	(6	4)	91	26	35	30	0	42	0	0	0	2	1	.67	3	.240	.332	.419
1991	3 ML Teams		108	275	61	11	0	10	(5	5)	102	30	36	43	4	64	0	0	3	0	1	.00	7	.222	.324	.371
1990	Philadelphia	NL	71	198	48	8	0	8	(4	4)	80	23	31	29	0	37	0	0	0	2	1	.67	3	.242	.339	.404
	Pittsburgh	NL	12	19	4	1	0	2	(2	0)	11	3	4	1	0	5	0	0	0	0	0	.00	0	.211	.250	.579
1991	Pittsburgh	NL	11	16	4	0	0	0	(0	0)	4	1	0	1	0	2	0	0	0	0	0	.00	2	.250	.294	.250
	Kansas City	AL	44	121	25	6	0	4	(3	1)	43	17	17	27	3	25	0	0	0	0	0	.00	4	.207	.351	.355
	Cincinnati	NL	53	138	32	5	0	6	(2	4)	55	12	19	15	1	37	0	0	3	0	1	.00	1	.232	.301	.399
9 ML YEARS			1003	2906	713	134	7	108	(63	45)	1185	350	424	404	25	528	11	7	28	10	16	.38	72	.245	.337	.408

128

Chito Martinez

Bats: Left **Throws:** Left **Pos:** RF **Ht:** 5'10" **Wt:** 180 **Born:** 12/19/65 **Age:** 26

Year	Team	Lg	G	AB	H	2B	3B	HR	(Hm	Rd)	TB	R	RBI	TBB	IBB	SO	HBP	SH	SF	SB	CS	SB%	GDP	Avg	OBP	SLG
1984	Eugene	A	59	176	53	12	3	0	--	--	71	18	26	24	2	38	0	1	0	4	4	.50	3	.301	.385	.403
1985	Ft. Myers	A	76	248	65	9	5	0	--	--	84	35	29	31	3	42	1	1	3	11	5	.69	8	.262	.343	.339
1986	Memphis	AA	93	283	86	16	5	11	--	--	145	48	44	42	4	58	2	2	1	4	4	.50	2	.304	.396	.512
1987	Omaha	AAA	35	121	26	10	1	2	--	--	44	14	14	11	0	43	0	0	0	0	0	.00	0	.215	.280	.364
	Memphis	AA	78	283	74	10	3	9	--	--	117	34	43	33	0	94	1	0	2	5	3	.63	4	.261	.339	.413
1988	Memphis	AA	141	485	110	16	4	13	--	--	173	67	65	66	4	130	1	2	6	20	3	.87	6	.227	.317	.357
1989	Memphis	AA	127	399	97	20	2	23	--	--	190	55	62	63	7	137	1	4	4	3	3	.50	8	.243	.345	.476
1990	Omaha	AAA	122	364	96	12	8	21	--	--	187	64	67	54	5	129	3	0	3	6	6	.50	3	.264	.361	.514
1991	Rochester	AAA	60	211	68	8	1	20	--	--	138	42	50	26	3	69	0	0	2	2	2	.50	3	.322	.393	.654
1991	Baltimore	AL	67	216	58	12	1	13	(8	5)	111	32	33	11	0	51	0	0	1	1	1	.50	1	.269	.303	.514

Dave Martinez

Bats: Left **Throws:** Left **Pos:** RF/LF/CF **Ht:** 5'10" **Wt:** 175 **Born:** 09/26/64 **Age:** 27

Year	Team	Lg	G	AB	H	2B	3B	HR	(Hm	Rd)	TB	R	RBI	TBB	IBB	SO	HBP	SH	SF	SB	CS	SB%	GDP	Avg	OBP	SLG
1986	Chicago	NL	53	108	15	1	1	1	(1	0)	21	13	7	6	0	22	1	0	1	4	2	.67	1	.139	.190	.194
1987	Chicago	NL	142	459	134	18	8	8	(5	3)	192	70	36	57	4	96	2	1	4	16	8	.67	4	.292	.372	.418
1988	2 ML Teams		138	447	114	13	6	6	(2	4)	157	51	46	38	8	94	2	2	5	23	9	.72	3	.255	.313	.351
1989	Montreal	NL	126	361	99	16	7	3	(1	2)	138	41	27	27	2	57	0	7	1	23	4	.85	1	.274	.324	.382
1990	Montreal	NL	118	391	109	13	5	11	(5	6)	165	60	39	24	2	48	1	3	2	13	11	.54	8	.279	.321	.422
1991	Montreal	NL	124	396	117	18	5	7	(3	4)	166	47	42	20	3	54	1	3	3	16	7	.70	3	.295	.332	.419
1988	Chicago	NL	75	256	65	10	1	4	(2	2)	89	27	34	21	5	46	2	0	4	7	3	.70	2	.254	.311	.348
	Montreal	NL	63	191	49	3	5	2	(0	2)	68	24	12	17	3	48	0	2	1	16	6	.73	1	.257	.316	.356
	6 ML YEARS		701	2162	588	79	32	36	(17	19)	839	282	197	172	19	371	9	18	13	95	41	.70	20	.272	.326	.388

Dennis Martinez

Pitches: Right **Bats:** Right **Pos:** SP **Ht:** 6' 1" **Wt:** 180 **Born:** 05/14/55 **Age:** 37

Year	Team	Lg	G	GS	CG	GF	IP	BFP	H	R	ER	HR	SH	SF	HB	TBB	IBB	SO	WP	Bk	W	L	Pct.	ShO	Sv	ERA
1976	Baltimore	AL	4	2	1	1	28	106	23	8	8	1	1	0	0	8	0	18	1	0	1	2	.333	0	0	2.57
1977	Baltimore	AL	42	13	5	19	167	709	157	86	76	10	8	8	8	64	5	107	5	0	14	7	.667	0	4	4.10
1978	Baltimore	AL	40	38	15	0	276	1140	257	121	108	20	8	7	3	93	4	142	8	0	16	11	.593	2	0	3.52
1979	Baltimore	AL	40	39	18	0	292	1206	279	129	119	28	12	12	1	78	1	132	9	2	15	16	.484	3	0	3.67
1980	Baltimore	AL	25	12	2	8	100	428	103	44	44	12	1	3	2	44	6	42	0	1	6	4	.600	0	1	3.96
1981	Baltimore	AL	25	24	9	0	179	753	173	84	66	10	2	5	2	62	1	88	6	1	14	5	.737	2	0	3.32
1982	Baltimore	AL	40	39	10	0	252	1093	262	123	118	30	11	7	7	87	2	111	7	1	16	12	.571	2	0	4.21
1983	Baltimore	AL	32	25	4	3	153	688	209	108	94	21	3	5	2	45	0	71	2	0	7	16	.304	0	0	5.53
1984	Baltimore	AL	34	20	2	4	141.2	599	145	81	79	26	0	5	3	37	2	77	13	0	6	9	.400	0	0	5.02
1985	Baltimore	AL	33	31	3	1	180	789	203	110	103	29	0	11	9	63	3	68	4	1	13	11	.542	1	0	5.15
1986	2 ML Teams		23	15	1	2	104.2	449	114	57	55	11	8	2	3	30	4	65	3	2	3	6	.333	1	0	4.73
1987	Montreal	NL	22	22	2	0	144.2	599	133	59	53	9	4	3	6	40	2	84	4	2	11	4	.733	1	0	3.30
1988	Montreal	NL	34	34	9	0	235.1	968	215	94	71	21	2	6	6	55	3	120	5	10	15	13	.536	2	0	2.72
1989	Montreal	NL	34	33	5	1	232	950	227	88	82	21	8	2	7	49	4	142	5	0	16	7	.696	2	0	3.18
1990	Montreal	NL	32	32	7	0	226	908	191	80	74	16	11	3	6	49	9	156	1	1	10	11	.476	2	0	2.95
1991	Montreal	NL	31	31	9	0	222	905	187	70	59	9	7	3	4	62	3	123	3	0	14	11	.560	5	0	2.39
1986	Baltimore	AL	4	0	0	1	6.2	33	11	5	5	0	0	1	0	2	0	2	1	0	0	0	.000	0	0	6.75
	Montreal	NL	19	15	1	1	98	416	103	52	50	11	8	1	3	28	4	63	2	2	3	6	.333	1	0	4.59
	16 ML YEARS		491	410	102	39	2933.1	12290	2878	1342	1209	274	86	82	71	866	49	1546	76	23	177	145	.550	23	5	3.71

Edgar Martinez

Bats: Right **Throws:** Right **Pos:** 3B **Ht:** 5'11" **Wt:** 175 **Born:** 01/02/63 **Age:** 29

Year	Team	Lg	G	AB	H	2B	3B	HR	(Hm	Rd)	TB	R	RBI	TBB	IBB	SO	HBP	SH	SF	SB	CS	SB%	GDP	Avg	OBP	SLG
1987	Seattle	AL	13	43	16	5	2	0	(0	0)	25	6	5	2	0	5	1	0	0	0	0	.00	0	.372	.413	.581
1988	Seattle	AL	14	32	9	4	0	0	(0	0)	13	0	5	4	0	7	0	1	1	0	0	.00	0	.281	.351	.406
1989	Seattle	AL	65	171	41	5	0	2	(0	2)	52	20	20	17	1	26	3	2	3	2	1	.67	3	.240	.314	.304
1990	Seattle	AL	144	487	147	27	2	11	(3	8)	211	71	49	74	3	62	5	1	3	1	4	.20	13	.302	.397	.433
1991	Seattle	AL	150	544	167	35	1	14	(8	6)	246	98	52	84	9	72	8	2	4	0	3	.00	19	.307	.405	.452
	5 ML YEARS		386	1277	380	76	5	27	(11	16)	547	195	131	181	13	172	17	6	11	3	8	.27	35	.298	.389	.428

Ramon Martinez

Pitches: Right **Bats:** Left **Pos:** SP **Ht:** 6' 4" **Wt:** 173 **Born:** 03/22/68 **Age:** 24

Year Team	Lg	G	GS	CG	GF	IP	BFP	H	R	ER	HR	SH	SF	HB	TBB	IBB	SO	WP	Bk	W	L	Pct.	ShO	Sv	ERA
1988 Los Angeles	NL	9	6	0	0	35.2	151	27	17	15	0	4	0	0	22	1	23	1	0	1	3	.250	0	0	3.79
1989 Los Angeles	NL	15	15	2	0	98.2	410	79	39	35	11	4	0	5	41	1	89	1	0	6	4	.600	2	0	3.19
1990 Los Angeles	NL	33	33	12	0	234.1	950	191	89	76	22	7	5	4	67	5	223	3	3	20	6	.769	3	0	2.92
1991 Los Angeles	NL	33	33	6	0	220.1	916	190	89	80	18	8	4	7	69	4	150	6	0	17	13	.567	4	0	3.27
4 ML YEARS		90	87	20	0	589	2427	487	234	206	51	23	9	16	199	11	485	11	3	44	26	.629	9	0	3.15

Tino Martinez

Bats: Left **Throws:** Right **Pos:** 1B **Ht:** 6' 2" **Wt:** 205 **Born:** 12/07/67 **Age:** 24

Year Team	Lg	G	AB	H	2B	3B	HR	(Hm	Rd)	TB	R	RBI	TBB	IBB	SO	HBP	SH	SF	SB	CS	SB%	GDP	Avg	OBP	SLG
1989 Williamsprt	AA	137	509	131	29	2	13	--	--	203	62	64	59	13	54	0	1	8	7	1	.88	11	.257	.330	.399
1990 Calgary	AAA	128	453	145	28	1	17	--	--	226	83	93	74	11	37	3	2	8	8	5	.62	9	.320	.413	.499
1991 Calgary	AAA	122	442	144	34	5	18	--	--	242	94	86	82	7	44	3	0	8	3	3	.50	5	.326	.428	.548
1990 Seattle	AL	24	68	15	4	0	0	(0	0)	19	4	5	9	0	9	0	0	1	0	0	.00	0	.221	.308	.279
1991 Seattle	AL	36	112	23	2	0	4	(3	1)	37	11	9	11	0	24	0	0	2	0	0	.00	2	.205	.272	.330
2 ML YEARS		60	180	38	6	0	4	(3	1)	56	15	14	20	0	33	0	0	3	0	0	.00	2	.211	.286	.311

John Marzano

Bats: Right **Throws:** Right **Pos:** C **Ht:** 5'11" **Wt:** 197 **Born:** 02/14/63 **Age:** 29

Year Team	Lg	G	AB	H	2B	3B	HR	(Hm	Rd)	TB	R	RBI	TBB	IBB	SO	HBP	SH	SF	SB	CS	SB%	GDP	Avg	OBP	SLG
1987 Boston	AL	52	168	41	11	0	5	(4	1)	67	20	24	7	0	41	3	2	2	0	1	.00	3	.244	.283	.399
1988 Boston	AL	10	29	4	1	0	0	(0	0)	5	3	1	1	0	3	0	0	0	0	0	.00	1	.138	.167	.172
1989 Boston	AL	7	18	8	3	0	1	(1	0)	14	5	3	0	0	2	0	1	1	0	0	.00	0	.444	.421	.778
1990 Boston	AL	32	83	20	4	0	0	(0	0)	24	8	6	5	0	10	0	2	1	0	1	.00	0	.241	.281	.289
1991 Boston	AL	49	114	30	8	0	0	(0	0)	38	10	9	1	0	16	1	1	2	0	0	.00	5	.263	.271	.333
5 ML YEARS		150	412	103	27	0	6	(5	1)	148	46	43	14	0	72	4	6	6	0	2	.00	10	.250	.278	.359

Roger Mason

Pitches: Right **Bats:** Right **Pos:** RP **Ht:** 6' 6" **Wt:** 215 **Born:** 09/18/58 **Age:** 33

Year Team	Lg	G	GS	CG	GF	IP	BFP	H	R	ER	HR	SH	SF	HB	TBB	IBB	SO	WP	Bk	W	L	Pct.	ShO	Sv	ERA
1984 Detroit	AL	5	2	0	2	22	97	23	11	11	1	0	2	0	10	0	15	2	0	1	1	.500	0	1	4.50
1985 San Francisco	NL	5	5	1	0	29.2	128	28	13	7	1	2	0	0	11	1	26	0	0	1	3	.250	1	0	2.12
1986 San Francisco	NL	11	11	1	0	60	262	56	35	32	5	2	3	3	30	3	43	1	0	3	4	.429	0	0	4.80
1987 San Francisco	NL	5	5	0	0	26	110	30	15	13	4	1	0	0	10	0	18	1	1	1	1	.500	0	0	4.50
1989 Houston	NL	2	0	0	1	1.1	8	2	3	3	0	0	0	0	2	0	3	0	0	0	0	.000	0	0	20.25
1991 Pittsburgh	NL	24	0	0	6	29.2	114	21	11	10	2	1	1	1	6	1	21	2	0	3	2	.600	0	3	3.03
6 ML YEARS		52	23	2	9	168.2	719	160	88	76	13	6	6	4	69	5	126	6	1	9	11	.450	1	4	4.06

Terry Mathews

Pitches: Right **Bats:** Left **Pos:** RP **Ht:** 6' 2" **Wt:** 200 **Born:** 10/05/64 **Age:** 27

Year Team	Lg	G	GS	CG	GF	IP	BFP	H	R	ER	HR	SH	SF	HB	TBB	IBB	SO	WP	Bk	W	L	Pct.	ShO	Sv	ERA
1987 Gastonia	A	34	1	0	13	48.1	234	53	35	30	5	4	5	2	32	4	46	7	1	3	3	.500	0	0	5.59
1988 Charlotte	A	27	26	2	0	163.2	672	141	68	51	6	3	3	4	49	2	94	11	3	13	6	.684	1	0	2.80
1989 Tulsa	AA	10	10	1	0	45.1	211	53	40	31	3	2	6	2	24	1	32	6	3	2	5	.286	0	0	6.15
Charlotte	A	10	10	0	0	59.1	241	55	28	24	2	1	3	2	17	0	30	2	0	4	2	.667	0	0	3.64
1990 Tulsa	AA	14	14	4	0	86.1	375	88	50	41	1	1	6	2	36	2	48	9	0	5	7	.417	2	0	4.27
Okla City	AAA	12	11	1	0	70.2	307	81	39	29	4	3	4	3	15	0	36	2	0	2	7	.222	1	0	3.69
1991 Okla City	AAA	18	13	1	2	95.1	410	98	39	37	2	3	3	2	34	3	63	4	1	5	6	.455	0	1	3.49
1991 Texas	AL	34	2	0	8	57.1	236	54	24	23	5	2	0	1	18	3	51	5	0	4	0	1.000	0	1	3.61

Don Mattingly

Bats: Left **Throws:** Left **Pos:** 1B/DH **Ht:** 6' 0" **Wt:** 193 **Born:** 04/20/61 **Age:** 31

Year Team	Lg	G	AB	H	2B	3B	HR	(Hm	Rd)	TB	R	RBI	TBB	IBB	SO	HBP	SH	SF	SB	CS	SB%	GDP	Avg	OBP	SLG
1982 New York	AL	7	12	2	0	0	0	(0	0)	2	0	1	0	0	1	0	0	1	0	0	.00	2	.167	.154	.167
1983 New York	AL	91	279	79	15	4	4	(0	4)	114	34	32	21	5	31	1	2	2	0	0	.00	8	.283	.333	.409
1984 New York	AL	153	603	207	44	2	23	(12	11)	324	91	110	41	8	33	1	8	9	1	1	.50	15	.343	.381	.537
1985 New York	AL	159	652	211	48	3	35	(22	13)	370	107	145	56	13	41	2	2	15	2	2	.50	15	.324	.371	.567

Year	Team	Lg	G	AB	H	2B	3B	HR	(Hm	Rd)	TB	R	RBI	TBB	IBB	SO	HBP	SH	SF	SB	CS	SB%	GDP	Avg	OBP	SLG
1986	New York	AL	162	677	238	53	2	31	(17	14)	388	117	113	53	11	35	1	1	10	0	0	.00	17	.352	.394	.573
1987	New York	AL	141	569	186	38	2	30	(17	13)	318	93	115	51	13	38	1	0	8	1	4	.20	16	.327	.378	.559
1988	New York	AL	144	599	186	37	0	18	(11	7)	277	94	88	41	14	29	3	0	8	1	0	1.00	13	.311	.353	.462
1989	New York	AL	158	631	191	37	2	23	(19	4)	301	79	113	51	18	30	1	0	10	3	0	1.00	15	.303	.351	.477
1990	New York	AL	102	394	101	16	0	5	(4	1)	132	40	42	28	13	20	3	0	3	1	0	1.00	13	.256	.308	.335
1991	New York	AL	152	587	169	35	0	9	(7	2)	231	64	68	46	11	42	4	0	9	2	0	1.00	21	.288	.339	.394
	10 ML YEARS		1269	5003	1570	323	15	178	(109	69)	2457	719	827	388	106	300	17	13	75	11	7	.61	135	.314	.360	.491

Rob Maurer

Bats: Left **Throws:** Left **Pos:** 1B **Ht:** 6' 3" **Wt:** 210 **Born:** 01/07/67 **Age:** 25

			BATTING																BASERUNNING				PERCENTAGES		
Year	Team	Lg	G	AB	H	2B	3B	HR	(Hm | Rd)	TB	R	RBI	TBB	IBB	SO	HBP	SH	SF	SB	CS	SB%	GDP	Avg	OBP	SLG
1988	Butte	R	63	233	91	18	3	8	--	--	139	65	60	35	3	33	3	0	2	0	0	.00	2	.391	.473	.597
1989	Charlotte	A	132	456	126	18	9	6	--	--	180	69	51	86	6	109	8	0	4	3	4	.43	9	.276	.397	.395
1990	Tulsa	AA	104	367	110	31	4	21	--	--	212	55	78	54	6	112	6	0	2	4	2	.67	5	.300	.396	.578
1991	Okla City	AAA	132	459	138	41	3	20	--	--	245	76	77	96	8	134	3	0	6	2	3	.40	5	.301	.420	.534
1991	Texas	AL	13	16	1	1	0	0	(0 | 0)	2	2	2	0	1	6	1	0	0	0	0	.00	0	.063	.211	.125

Tim Mauser

Pitches: Right **Bats:** Right **Pos:** RP **Ht:** 6' 0" **Wt:** 185 **Born:** 10/04/66 **Age:** 25

			HOW MUCH HE PITCHED					WHAT HE GAVE UP											THE RESULTS					
Year	Team	Lg	G	GS	CG	GF	IP	BFP	H	R	ER	HR	SH	SF	HB	TBB	IBB	SO	WP	Bk	W	L	Pct.	ShO	Sv	ERA
1988	Spartanburg	A	4	3	0	0	23	88	15	6	5	0	2	2	0	5	0	18	1	0	2	1	.667	0	0	1.96
	Reading	AA	5	5	0	0	28.1	120	27	14	11	4	2	0	2	6	0	17	0	0	2	3	.400	0	0	3.49
1989	Clearwater	A	16	16	5	0	107	457	105	40	32	4	2	0	5	40	0	73	2	1	6	7	.462	0	0	2.69
	Reading	AA	11	11	4	0	72	302	62	36	29	5	0	2	1	33	0	54	3	1	7	4	.636	2	0	3.63
1990	Reading	AA	8	8	1	0	46.1	194	35	20	17	2	0	2	3	15	0	40	4	0	3	4	.429	0	0	3.30
	Scr Wil-Bar	AAA	16	16	4	0	98.1	396	75	48	40	10	1	3	3	34	1	54	4	0	5	7	.417	1	0	3.66
1991	Scranton-Wb	AAA	26	18	1	3	128.1	544	119	66	53	11	4	4	2	55	3	75	3	0	6	11	.353	0	1	3.72
1991	Philadelphia	NL	3	0	0	1	10.2	53	18	10	9	3	1	0	0	3	0	6	2	0	0	0	.000	0	0	7.59

Derrick May

Bats: Left **Throws:** Right **Pos:** LF **Ht:** 6' 4" **Wt:** 205 **Born:** 07/14/68 **Age:** 23

			BATTING																BASERUNNING				PERCENTAGES		
Year	Team	Lg	G	AB	H	2B	3B	HR	(Hm	Rd)	TB	R	RBI	TBB	IBB	SO	HBP	SH	SF	SB	CS	SB%	GDP	Avg	OBP	SLG
1986	Wytheville	R	54	178	57	6	1	0	--	--	65	25	23	16	1	15	2	0	1	17	4	.81	3	.320	.381	.365
1987	Peoria	A	128	439	131	19	8	9	--	--	193	60	52	42	4	106	1	0	5	5	7	.42	5	.298	.357	.440
1988	Winston-Sal	A	130	485	148	29	9	8	--	--	219	76	65	37	4	82	5	0	5	13	8	.62	3	.305	.357	.452
1989	Charlotte	AA	136	491	145	26	5	9	--	--	208	72	70	33	4	76	5	1	0	19	7	.73	8	.295	.346	.424
1990	Iowa	AAA	119	459	136	27	1	8	--	--	189	55	69	23	4	50	0	1	6	5	6	.45	11	.296	.326	.412
1991	Iowa	AAA	82	310	92	18	4	3	--	--	127	47	49	19	4	38	4	1	3	7	9	.44	9	.297	.342	.410
1990	Chicago	NL	17	61	15	3	0	1	(1	0)	21	8	11	2	0	7	0	0	0	1	0	1.00	1	.246	.270	.344
1991	Chicago	NL	15	22	5	2	0	1	(1	0)	10	4	3	2	0	1	0	0	1	0	0	.00	1	.227	.280	.455
	2 ML YEARS		32	83	20	5	0	2	(2	0)	31	12	14	4	0	8	0	0	1	1	0	1.00	2	.241	.273	.373

Scott May

Pitches: Right **Bats:** Right **Pos:** RP **Ht:** 6' 1" **Wt:** 190 **Born:** 11/11/61 **Age:** 30

			HOW MUCH HE PITCHED					WHAT HE GAVE UP											THE RESULTS					
Year	Team	Lg	G	GS	CG	GF	IP	BFP	H	R	ER	HR	SH	SF	HB	TBB	IBB	SO	WP	Bk	W	L	Pct.	ShO	Sv	ERA
1984	Bakersfield	A	25	23	7	2	152.2	0	128	78	65	7	0	0	2	81	1	107	6	3	8	10	.444	1	0	3.83
1985	San Antonio	AA	26	26	9	0	191.2	829	181	85	74	15	6	8	1	99	3	125	10	4	10	6	.625	2	0	3.47
1986	Albuquerque	AAA	27	8	0	12	65	320	97	59	50	6	4	2	2	39	2	57	4	1	0	0	.000	0	1	6.92
	San Antonio	AA	4	4	1	0	24	106	31	15	14	3	1	1	1	7	0	12	1	0	2	0	1.000	0	0	5.25
1987	San Antonio	AA	30	16	2	4	111.1	516	136	83	74	19	2	3	1	52	1	108	11	1	8	8	.500	1	0	5.98
1988	Okla City	AAA	36	17	4	6	151.2	628	132	56	50	11	4	1	5	57	0	103	5	6	8	7	.533	1	0	2.97
1989	Okla City	AAA	17	16	4	0	111	471	100	61	46	6	2	1	4	41	4	77	4	4	6	7	.462	2	0	3.73
	Denver	AAA	12	12	1	0	69.1	319	80	46	43	4	5	2	3	38	3	52	5	0	3	6	.333	0	0	5.58
1990	Denver	AAA	7	5	0	0	28	143	45	26	25	3	1	4	2	13	0	20	4	0	1	1	.500	0	0	8.04
	El Paso	AA	22	13	2	3	99.2	437	113	48	42	7	4	3	1	38	3	85	4	0	6	4	.600	0	0	3.79
1991	Iowa	AAA	57	0	0	26	94	404	75	38	31	7	5	0	2	54	3	93	6	0	4	4	.500	0	10	2.97
1988	Texas	AL	3	1	0	0	7.1	33	8	7	7	3	0	2	0	4	1	4	0	0	0	0	.000	0	0	8.59
1991	Chicago	NL	2	0	0	1	2	12	6	4	4	0	0	0	0	1	0	1	1	0	0	0	.000	0	0	18.00
	2 ML YEARS		5	1	0	1	9.1	45	14	11	11	3	0	2	0	5	1	5	1	0	0	0	.000	0	0	10.61

Brent Mayne

Bats: Left **Throws:** Right **Pos:** C **Ht:** 6' 1" **Wt:** 190 **Born:** 04/19/68 **Age:** 24

					BATTING														BASERUNNING				PERCENTAGES		
Year	Team	Lg	G	AB	H	2B	3B	HR	(Hm	Rd)	TB	R	RBI	TBB	IBB	SO	HBP	SH	SF	SB	CS	SB%	GDP	Avg	OBP	SLG
1989	Baseball Cy	A	7	24	13	3	1	0	--	--	18	5	8	0	0	3	0	0	0	0	1	.00	0	.542	.542	.750
1990	Memphis	AA	115	412	110	16	3	2	--	--	138	48	61	52	1	51	2	7	8	5	2	.71	13	.267	.346	.335
1990	Kansas City	AL	5	13	3	0	0	0	(0	0)	3	2	1	3	0	3	0	0	0	0	1	.00	0	.231	.375	.231
1991	Kansas City	AL	85	231	58	8	0	3	(2	1)	75	22	31	23	4	42	0	2	3	2	4	.33	6	.251	.315	.325
	2 ML YEARS		90	244	61	8	0	3	(2	1)	78	24	32	26	4	45	0	2	3	2	5	.29	6	.250	.319	.320

Kirk McCaskill

Pitches: Right **Bats:** Right **Pos:** SP **Ht:** 6' 1" **Wt:** 205 **Born:** 04/09/61 **Age:** 31

				HOW MUCH HE PITCHED					WHAT HE GAVE UP									THE RESULTS					
Year	Team	Lg	G	GS	CG	GF	IP	BFP	H	R	ER	HR	SH	SF	HB	TBB	IBB	SO	WP	Bk	W	L	Pct.	ShO	Sv	ERA
1985	California	AL	30	29	6	0	189.2	807	189	105	99	23	2	5	4	64	1	102	5	0	12	12	.500	1	0	4.70
1986	California	AL	34	33	10	1	246.1	1013	207	98	92	19	6	5	5	92	1	202	10	2	17	10	.630	2	0	3.36
1987	California	AL	14	13	1	0	74.2	334	84	52	47	14	3	1	2	34	0	56	1	0	4	6	.400	1	0	5.67
1988	California	AL	23	23	4	0	146.1	635	155	78	70	9	1	6	1	61	3	98	13	2	8	6	.571	2	0	4.31
1989	California	AL	32	32	6	0	212	864	202	73	69	16	3	4	3	59	1	107	7	2	15	10	.600	4	0	2.93
1990	California	AL	29	29	2	0	174.1	738	161	77	63	9	3	1	2	72	1	78	6	1	12	11	.522	1	0	3.25
1991	California	AL	30	30	1	0	177.2	762	193	93	84	19	6	6	3	66	1	71	6	0	10	19	.345	0	0	4.26
	7 ML YEARS		192	189	30	1	1221	5153	1191	576	524	109	24	28	20	448	8	714	48	7	78	74	.513	11	0	3.86

Paul McClellan

Pitches: Right **Bats:** Right **Pos:** SP **Ht:** 6' 2" **Wt:** 180 **Born:** 02/08/66 **Age:** 26

				HOW MUCH HE PITCHED					WHAT HE GAVE UP									THE RESULTS					
Year	Team	Lg	G	GS	CG	GF	IP	BFP	H	R	ER	HR	SH	SF	HB	TBB	IBB	SO	WP	Bk	W	L	Pct.	ShO	Sv	ERA
1986	Everett	A	13	13	2	0	86.1	0	71	39	32	2	0	0	0	46	0	74	8	0	5	4	.556	0	0	3.34
1987	Clinton	A	28	27	5	0	177.1	756	141	86	64	18	10	1	6	100	2	209	10	2	12	10	.545	2	0	3.25
1988	Shreveport	AA	27	27	4	0	167	701	146	89	75	11	7	5	4	62	4	128	3	22	10	12	.455	1	0	4.04
1989	Shreveport	AA	12	12	2	0	84.1	339	56	26	21	4	3	3	1	35	0	56	5	3	8	3	.727	0	0	2.24
	Phoenix	AAA	9	9	0	0	56.2	248	56	34	31	6	0	4	4	29	1	25	4	2	3	4	.429	0	0	4.92
1990	Phoenix	AAA	28	27	1	0	172.1	770	192	112	99	17	9	10	5	78	3	102	7	6	7	16	.304	0	0	5.17
1991	Shreveport	AA	14	14	1	0	95.2	384	75	33	30	4	1	2	2	30	0	63	8	2	11	1	.917	1	0	2.82
	Phoenix	AAA	5	5	2	0	38.1	160	27	12	12	2	3	1	0	21	2	18	2	1	2	2	.500	0	0	2.82
1990	San Francisco	NL	4	1	0	2	7.2	44	14	10	10	3	1	0	1	6	0	2	0	0	0	1	.000	0	0	11.74
1991	San Francisco	NL	13	12	1	1	71	300	68	41	36	12	3	1	1	25	1	44	5	0	3	6	.333	0	0	4.56
	2 ML YEARS		17	13	1	3	78.2	344	82	51	46	15	4	1	2	31	1	46	5	0	3	7	.300	0	0	5.26

Lloyd McClendon

Bats: Right **Throws:** Right **Pos:** 1B/RF **Ht:** 5'11" **Wt:** 210 **Born:** 01/11/59 **Age:** 33

					BATTING														BASERUNNING				PERCENTAGES		
Year	Team	Lg	G	AB	H	2B	3B	HR	(Hm	Rd)	TB	R	RBI	TBB	IBB	SO	HBP	SH	SF	SB	CS	SB%	GDP	Avg	OBP	SLG
1987	Cincinnati	NL	45	72	15	5	0	2	(0	2)	26	8	13	4	0	15	0	0	1	1	0	1.00	1	.208	.247	.361
1988	Cincinnati	NL	72	137	30	4	0	3	(0	3)	43	9	14	15	1	22	2	1	2	4	0	1.00	6	.219	.301	.314
1989	Chicago	NL	92	259	74	12	1	12	(9	3)	124	47	40	37	3	31	1	1	7	6	4	.60	3	.286	.368	.479
1990	2 ML Teams		53	110	18	3	0	2	(0	2)	27	6	12	14	2	22	0	0	1	1	0	1.00	2	.164	.256	.245
1991	Pittsburgh	NL	85	163	47	7	0	7	(2	5)	75	24	24	18	0	23	2	0	0	2	1	.67	2	.288	.366	.460
1990	Chicago	NL	49	107	17	3	0	1	(0	1)	23	5	10	14	2	21	0	0	1	1	0	1.00	2	.159	.254	.215
	Pittsburgh	NL	4	3	1	0	0	1	(0	1)	4	1	2	0	0	1	0	0	0	0	0	.00	0	.333	.333	1.333
	5 ML YEARS		347	741	184	31	1	26	(11	15)	295	94	103	88	6	113	5	2	11	14	5	.74	14	.248	.328	.398

Bob McClure

Pitches: Left **Bats:** Right **Pos:** RP **Ht:** 5'11" **Wt:** 188 **Born:** 04/29/53 **Age:** 39

				HOW MUCH HE PITCHED					WHAT HE GAVE UP									THE RESULTS					
Year	Team	Lg	G	GS	CG	GF	IP	BFP	H	R	ER	HR	SH	SF	HB	TBB	IBB	SO	WP	Bk	W	L	Pct.	ShO	Sv	ERA
1975	Kansas City	AL	12	0	0	4	15	66	4	0	0	0	0	0	0	14	2	15	0	2	1	0	1.000	0	1	0.00
1976	Kansas City	AL	8	0	0	4	4	22	3	4	4	0	0	0	0	8	0	3	0	0	0	0	.000	0	0	9.00
1977	Milwaukee	AL	68	0	0	31	71	302	64	25	20	2	5	5	1	34	5	57	1	2	2	1	.667	0	6	2.54
1978	Milwaukee	AL	44	0	0	29	65	283	53	30	27	8	7	2	6	30	4	47	1	1	2	6	.250	0	9	3.74
1979	Milwaukee	AL	36	0	0	16	51	229	53	29	22	6	2	3	3	24	0	37	5	0	5	2	.714	0	5	3.88
1980	Milwaukee	AL	52	5	2	23	91	390	83	34	31	6	1	5	2	37	2	47	0	2	5	8	.385	1	10	3.07
1981	Milwaukee	AL	4	0	0	1	8	34	7	3	3	1	0	0	0	4	1	6	0	0	0	0	.000	0	0	3.38
1982	Milwaukee	AL	34	26	5	5	172.2	734	160	90	81	21	6	4	4	74	4	99	5	5	12	7	.632	0	0	4.22
1983	Milwaukee	AL	24	23	4	0	142	625	152	75	71	11	0	4	5	68	1	68	4	6	9	9	.500	0	0	4.50
1984	Milwaukee	AL	39	18	1	5	139.2	616	154	76	68	9	8	8	2	52	4	68	1	3	4	8	.333	0	1	4.38

132

1985	Milwaukee	AL	38	1	0	12	85.2	370	91	43	41	10	3	2	3	30	2	57	5	0	4	1	.800	0	3	4.31
1986	2 ML Teams		65	0	0	22	79	332	71	29	28	4	4	3	1	33	3	53	1	1	4	6	.400	0	6	3.19
1987	Montreal	NL	52	0	0	16	52.1	222	47	30	20	8	5	2	0	20	3	33	0	1	6	1	.857	0	5	3.44
1988	2 ML Teams		33	0	0	13	30	133	35	18	18	4	3	2	2	8	0	19	1	3	2	3	.400	0	5	5.40
1989	California	AL	48	0	0	27	52.1	205	39	14	9	2	1	4	1	15	1	36	2	2	6	1	.857	0	3	1.55
1990	California	AL	11	0	0	1	7	30	7	6	5	0	1	0	0	3	0	6	0	1	2	0	1.000	0	0	6.43
1991	2 ML Teams		45	0	0	11	32.2	146	37	19	18	4	1	4	2	13	2	20	2	1	1	1	.500	0	0	4.96
1986	Milwaukee	AL	13	0	0	7	16.1	75	18	7	7	2	1	1	0	10	1	11	0	0	2	1	.667	0	0	3.86
	Montreal	NL	52	0	0	15	62.2	257	53	22	21	2	3	2	1	23	2	42	1	1	2	5	.286	0	6	3.02
1988	Montreal	NL	19	0	0	8	19	87	23	13	13	3	3	2	1	6	0	12	0	3	1	3	.250	0	2	6.16
	New York	NL	14	0	0	5	11	46	12	5	5	1	0	0	1	2	0	7	1	0	1	0	1.000	0	1	4.09
1991	California	AL	13	0	0	2	9.2	48	13	11	10	3	0	1	1	5	0	5	2	1	0	0	.000	0	0	9.31
	St. Louis	NL	32	0	0	9	23	98	24	8	8	1	1	3	1	8	2	15	0	0	1	1	.500	0	0	3.13
	17 ML YEARS		613	73	12	216	1098.1	4739	1060	525	466	96	47	48	32	467	34	671	28	30	65	54	.546	1	52	3.82

Rodney McCray

Bats: Right **Throws:** Right **Pos:** CF **Ht:** 5'10" **Wt:** 175 **Born:** 09/13/63 **Age:** 28

							BATTING													BASERUNNING				PERCENTAGES		
Year	Team	Lg	G	AB	H	2B	3B	HR	(Hm	Rd)	TB	R	RBI	TBB	IBB	SO	HBP	SH	SF	SB	CS	SB%	GDP	Avg	OBP	SLG
1984	Spokane	A	71	244	50	6	1	1	--	--	61	40	20	65	0	50	2	0	4	25	5	.83	8	.205	.371	.250
1985	Charleston	A	117	373	77	8	1	1	--	--	90	81	27	80	2	88	6	5	1	49	7	.88	6	.206	.354	.241
1986	Charleston	A	123	417	107	13	3	4	--	--	138	88	33	108	2	80	5	6	2	81	32	.72	3	.257	.414	.331
1987	Reno	A	117	413	87	11	5	0	--	--	108	69	26	69	3	96	10	9	3	65	16	.80	4	.211	.335	.262
1988	South Bend	A	107	306	65	10	2	1	--	--	82	48	24	56	0	72	10	7	2	55	12	.82	5	.212	.350	.268
1989	Sarasota	A	124	422	112	19	4	1	--	--	142	81	34	96	3	81	9	4	2	44	22	.67	6	.265	.410	.336
1990	Birmingham	AA	60	188	37	2	2	1	--	--	46	36	16	36	0	42	5	6	2	25	10	.71	2	.197	.338	.245
	Vancouver	AAA	19	53	12	4	2	0	--	--	20	7	6	10	0	20	2	1	0	4	3	.57	0	.226	.369	.377
1991	Vancouver	AAA	83	222	51	9	5	0	--	--	70	37	13	26	0	48	8	2	2	14	10	.58	4	.230	.329	.315
1990	Chicago	AL	32	6	0	0	0	0	(0	0)	0	8	0	1	0	4	0	0	0	6	0	1.00	0	.000	.143	.000
1991	Chicago	AL	17	7	2	0	0	0	(0	0)	2	2	0	0	0	2	0	0	0	1	1	.50	0	.286	.286	.286
	2 ML YEARS		49	13	2	0	0	0	(0	0)	2	10	0	1	0	6	0	0	0	7	1	.88	0	.154	.214	.154

Terry McDaniel

Bats: Both **Throws:** Right **Pos:** CF **Ht:** 5'9" **Wt:** 205 **Born:** 12/06/66 **Age:** 25

							BATTING													BASERUNNING				PERCENTAGES		
Year	Team	Lg	G	AB	H	2B	3B	HR	(Hm	Rd)	TB	R	RBI	TBB	IBB	SO	HBP	SH	SF	SB	CS	SB%	GDP	Avg	OBP	SLG
1986	Kingsport	R	41	114	28	5	1	6	--	--	53	24	21	32	0	29	1	1	3	14	3	.82	1	.246	.407	.465
1987	Little Fls	A	70	237	57	4	2	5	--	--	80	51	31	52	0	82	1	3	1	20	10	.67	1	.241	.378	.338
1988	Columbia	A	127	449	111	16	6	5	--	--	154	76	43	74	5	173	7	3	3	41	10	.80	4	.247	.360	.343
	St. Lucie	A	4	12	3	0	0	0	--	--	3	1	0	1	0	3	1	0	0	0	0	.00	0	.250	.357	.250
1989	St.Lucie	A	105	351	81	17	11	7	--	--	141	70	43	71	1	106	8	0	5	43	19	.69	3	.231	.368	.402
1990	Jackson	AA	67	234	67	15	2	5	--	--	101	34	37	31	3	70	7	0	3	18	9	.67	4	.286	.382	.432
1991	Tidewater	AAA	118	399	99	23	6	9	--	--	161	63	42	50	4	117	5	2	0	17	4	.81	8	.248	.339	.404
1991	New York	NL	23	29	6	1	0	0	(0	0)	7	3	2	1	0	11	0	0	0	2	0	1.00	0	.207	.233	.241

Ben McDonald

Pitches: Right **Bats:** Right **Pos:** SP **Ht:** 6'7" **Wt:** 212 **Born:** 11/24/67 **Age:** 24

			HOW MUCH HE PITCHED						WHAT HE GAVE UP										THE RESULTS					
Year	Team	Lg	G	GS	CG	GF	IP	BFP	H	R	ER	HR	SH	SF	HB	TBB	IBB	SO	WP	Bk	W	L	Pct.	ShO	Sv	ERA
1989	Baltimore	AL	6	0	0	2	7.1	33	8	7	7	2	0	1	0	4	0	3	1	1	1	0	1.000	0	0	8.59
1990	Baltimore	AL	21	15	3	2	118.2	472	88	36	32	9	3	5	0	35	0	65	5	0	8	5	.615	2	0	2.43
1991	Baltimore	AL	21	21	1	0	126.1	532	126	71	68	16	2	3	1	43	2	85	3	0	6	8	.429	0	0	4.84
	3 ML YEARS		48	36	4	4	252.1	1037	222	114	107	27	5	9	1	82	2	153	9	1	15	13	.536	2	0	3.82

Jack McDowell

Pitches: Right **Bats:** Right **Pos:** SP **Ht:** 6'5" **Wt:** 180 **Born:** 01/16/66 **Age:** 26

			HOW MUCH HE PITCHED						WHAT HE GAVE UP										THE RESULTS					
Year	Team	Lg	G	GS	CG	GF	IP	BFP	H	R	ER	HR	SH	SF	HB	TBB	IBB	SO	WP	Bk	W	L	Pct.	ShO	Sv	ERA
1987	Chicago	AL	4	4	0	0	28	103	16	6	6	1	0	0	2	6	0	15	0	0	3	0	1.000	0	0	1.93
1988	Chicago	AL	26	26	1	0	158.2	687	147	85	70	12	6	7	7	68	5	84	11	1	5	10	.333	0	0	3.97
1990	Chicago	AL	33	33	4	0	205	866	189	93	87	20	1	5	7	77	0	165	7	1	14	9	.609	0	0	3.82
1991	Chicago	AL	35	35	15	0	253.2	1028	212	97	96	19	8	4	4	82	2	191	10	1	17	10	.630	3	0	3.41
	4 ML YEARS		98	98	20	0	645.1	2684	564	281	259	52	15	16	20	233	7	455	28	3	39	29	.574	3	0	3.61

Roger McDowell

Pitches: Right **Bats:** Right **Pos:** RP **Ht:** 6' 1" **Wt:** 186 **Born:** 12/21/60 **Age:** 31

Year Team	Lg	G	GS	CG	GF	IP	BFP	H	R	ER	HR	SH	SF	HB	TBB	IBB	SO	WP	Bk	W	L	Pct.	ShO	Sv	ERA
1985 New York	NL	62	2	0	36	127.1	516	108	43	40	9	6	2	1	37	8	70	6	2	6	5	.545	0	17	2.83
1986 New York	NL	75	0	0	52	128	524	107	48	43	4	7	3	3	42	5	65	3	3	14	9	.609	0	22	3.02
1987 New York	NL	56	0	0	45	88.2	384	95	41	41	7	5	5	2	28	4	32	3	1	7	5	.583	0	25	4.16
1988 New York	NL	62	0	0	41	89	378	80	31	26	1	3	5	3	31	7	46	6	1	5	5	.500	0	16	2.63
1989 2 ML Teams		69	0	0	56	92	387	79	36	20	3	6	1	3	38	8	47	3	1	4	8	.333	0	23	1.96
1990 Philadelphia	NL	72	0	0	60	86.1	373	92	41	37	2	10	4	2	35	9	39	1	1	6	8	.429	0	22	3.86
1991 2 ML Teams		71	0	0	34	101.1	445	100	40	33	4	11	3	2	48	20	50	2	0	9	9	.500	0	10	2.93
1989 New York	NL	25	0	0	15	35.1	156	34	21	13	1	3	1	2	16	3	15	3	1	1	5	.167	0	4	3.31
Philadelphia	NL	44	0	0	41	56.2	231	45	15	7	2	3	0	1	22	5	32	0	0	3	3	.500	0	19	1.11
1991 Philadelphia	NL	38	0	0	16	59	271	61	28	21	1	7	1	2	32	12	28	1	0	3	6	.333	0	3	3.20
Los Angeles	NL	33	0	0	18	42.1	174	39	12	12	3	4	2	0	16	8	22	1	0	6	3	.667	0	7	2.55
7 ML YEARS		467	2	0	324	712.2	3007	661	280	240	30	48	23	16	259	61	349	24	9	51	49	.510	0	135	3.03

Chuck McElroy

Pitches: Left **Bats:** Left **Pos:** RP **Ht:** 6' 0" **Wt:** 160 **Born:** 10/01/67 **Age:** 24

Year Team	Lg	G	GS	CG	GF	IP	BFP	H	R	ER	HR	SH	SF	HB	TBB	IBB	SO	WP	Bk	W	L	Pct.	ShO	Sv	ERA
1986 Utica	A	14	14	5	0	94.2	386	85	40	31	4	8	2	2	28	0	91	2	0	4	6	.400	1	0	2.95
1987 Spartanburg	A	24	21	5	0	130.1	535	117	51	45	6	4	1	0	48	2	115	7	1	14	4	.778	2	0	3.11
Clearwater	A	2	2	0	0	7.1	27	1	1	0	0	0	1	0	4	0	7	0	0	1	0	1.000	0	0	0.00
1988 Reading	AA	28	26	4	0	160	698	173	89	80	9	2	6	2	70	2	92	4	1	9	12	.429	2	0	4.50
1989 Reading	AA	32	0	0	24	47	188	39	14	14	0	3	2	3	14	2	39	3	0	3	1	.750	0	12	2.68
Scr Wil-Bar	AAA	14	0	0	9	15.1	68	13	6	5	1	1	1		11	1	12	0	0	1	2	.333	0	3	2.93
1990 Scr Wil-Bar	AAA	57	1	0	26	76	324	62	24	23	6	7	2	5	34	4	78	2	0	6	8	.429	0	7	2.72
1989 Philadelphia	NL	11	0	0	4	10.1	46	12	2	2	1	0	0	0	4	1	8	0	0	0	0	.000	0	0	1.74
1990 Philadelphia	NL	16	0	0	8	14	76	24	13	12	0	0	1	0	10	2	16	0	0	0	1	.000	0	0	7.71
1991 Chicago	NL	71	0	0	12	101.1	419	73	33	22	7	9	6	0	57	7	92	1	0	6	2	.750	0	3	1.95
3 ML YEARS		98	0	0	24	125.2	541	109	48	36	8	9	7	0	71	10	116	1	0	6	3	.667	0	3	2.58

Andy McGaffigan

Pitches: Right **Bats:** Right **Pos:** RP **Ht:** 6' 3" **Wt:** 200 **Born:** 10/25/56 **Age:** 35

Year Team	Lg	G	GS	CG	GF	IP	BFP	H	R	ER	HR	SH	SF	HB	TBB	IBB	SO	WP	Bk	W	L	Pct.	ShO	Sv	ERA
1981 New York	AL	2	0	0	0	7	31	5	3	2	1	1	2	0	3	0	2	0	1	0	0	.000	0	0	2.57
1982 San Francisco	NL	4	0	0	2	8	30	5	1	0	0	0	0	1	1	0	4	0	1	1	0	1.000	0	0	0.00
1983 San Francisco	NL	43	16	0	11	134.1	560	131	64	47	17	5	2	1	39	5	93	8	7	3	9	.250	0	2	4.29
1984 2 ML Teams		30	6	0	10	69	282	60	28	27	4	2	1	0	23	2	57	1	2	3	6	.333	0	1	3.52
1985 Cincinnati	NL	15	15	2	0	94.1	392	88	40	39	4	4	0	2	30	4	83	2	0	3	3	.500	0	0	3.72
1986 Montreal	NL	48	14	1	8	142.2	583	114	49	42	9	10	5	2	55	8	104	5	4	10	5	.667	1	2	2.65
1987 Montreal	NL	69	0	0	30	120.1	500	105	38	32	5	5	3	3	42	7	100	6	0	5	2	.714	0	12	2.39
1988 Montreal	NL	63	0	0	24	91.1	392	81	31	28	4	4	2	2	37	7	71	2	2	6	0	1.000	0	4	2.76
1989 Montreal	NL	57	0	0	23	75	333	85	40	39	3	6	4	3	30	4	40	3	0	3	5	.375	0	2	4.68
1990 2 ML Teams		28	11	0	3	83.1	363	85	49	36	8	2	2	2	32	1	53	3	0	4	3	.571	0	1	3.89
1991 Kansas City	AL	4	0	0	1	8	39	14	5	4	0	0	1	0	2	0	3	0	0	0	0	.000	0	0	4.50
1984 Montreal	NL	21	3	0	8	46	182	37	14	13	2	0	1	0	15	2	39	1	2	3	4	.429	0	1	2.54
Cincinnati	NL	9	3	0	2	23	98	23	14	14	2	2	0	0	8	0	18	0	0	0	2	.000	0	0	5.48
1990 San Francisco	NL	4	0	0	1	4.2	27	10	9	9	2	1	0	0	4	0	4	0	0	0	0	.000	0	0	17.36
Kansas City	AL	24	11	0	2	78.2	336	75	40	27	6	1	2	2	28	1	49	3	0	4	3	.571	0	1	3.09
11 ML YEARS		363	62	3	112	833.1	3505	773	351	313	55	39	22	16	294	38	610	30	16	38	33	.535	1	24	3.38

Willie McGee

Bats: Both **Throws:** Right **Pos:** CF/RF **Ht:** 6' 1" **Wt:** 195 **Born:** 11/02/58 **Age:** 33

Year Team	Lg	G	AB	H	2B	3B	HR	(Hm	Rd)	TB	R	RBI	TBB	IBB	SO	HBP	SH	SF	SB	CS	SB%	GDP	Avg	OBP	SLG
1982 St. Louis	NL	123	422	125	12	8	4	(2	2)	165	43	56	12	2	58	1	2	1	24	12	.67	9	.296	.318	.391
1983 St. Louis	NL	147	601	172	22	8	5	(4	1)	225	75	75	26	2	98	0	1	3	39	8	.83	8	.286	.314	.374
1984 St. Louis	NL	145	571	166	19	11	6	(2	4)	225	82	50	29	2	80	1	0	3	43	10	.81	12	.291	.325	.394
1985 St. Louis	NL	152	612	216	26	18	10	(3	7)	308	114	82	34	2	86	0	1	5	56	16	.78	9	.353	.384	.503
1986 St. Louis	NL	124	497	127	22	7	7	(7	0)	184	65	48	37	7	82	1	0	4	19	16	.54	8	.256	.306	.370
1987 St. Louis	NL	153	620	177	37	11	11	(6	5)	269	76	105	24	5	90	2	1	5	16	4	.80	24	.285	.312	.434
1988 St. Louis	NL	137	562	164	24	6	3	(1	2)	209	73	50	32	5	84	1	2	3	41	6	.87	10	.292	.329	.372
1989 St. Louis	NL	58	199	47	10	2	3	(1	2)	70	23	17	10	0	34	1	0	1	8	6	.57	2	.236	.275	.352

Year Team	Lg	G	AB	H	2B	3B	HR	(Hm	Rd)	TB	R	RBI	TBB	IBB	SO	HBP	SH	SF	SB	CS	SB%	GDP	Avg	OBP	SLG
1990 2 ML Teams		154	614	199	35	7	3	(1	2)	257	99	77	48	6	104	1	0	2	31	9	.78	13	.324	.373	.419
1991 San Francisco	NL	131	497	155	30	3	4	(2	2)	203	67	43	34	3	74	2	8	2	17	9	.65	11	.312	.357	.408
1990 St. Louis	NL	125	501	168	32	5	3	(1	2)	219	76	62	38	6	86	1	0	2	28	9	.76	9	.335	.382	.437
Oakland	AL	29	113	31	3	2	0	(0	0)	38	23	15	10	0	18	0	0	0	3	0	1.00	4	.274	.333	.336
10 ML YEARS		1324	5195	1548	237	81	56	(29	27)	2115	717	603	286	34	790	11	15	29	294	96	.75	100	.298	.334	.407

Fred McGriff

Bats: Left   **Throws:** Left   **Pos:** 1B   **Ht:** 6' 3"   **Wt:** 215   **Born:** 10/31/63   **Age:** 28

							BATTING												BASERUNNING				PERCENTAGES		
Year Team	Lg	G	AB	H	2B	3B	HR	(Hm	Rd)	TB	R	RBI	TBB	IBB	SO	HBP	SH	SF	SB	CS	SB%	GDP	Avg	OBP	SLG
1986 Toronto	AL	3	5	1	0	0	0	(0	0)	1	1	0	0	0	2	0	0	0	0	0	.00	0	.200	.200	.200
1987 Toronto	AL	107	295	73	16	0	20	(7	13)	149	58	43	60	4	104	1	0	0	3	2	.60	3	.247	.376	.505
1988 Toronto	AL	154	536	151	35	4	34	(18	16)	296	100	82	79	3	149	4	0	4	6	1	.86	15	.282	.376	.552
1989 Toronto	AL	161	551	148	27	3	36	(18	18)	289	98	92	119	12	132	4	1	5	7	4	.64	14	.269	.399	.525
1990 Toronto	AL	153	557	167	21	1	35	(14	21)	295	91	88	94	12	108	2	1	4	5	3	.63	7	.300	.400	.530
1991 San Diego	NL	153	528	147	19	1	31	(18	13)	261	84	106	105	26	135	2	0	7	4	1	.80	14	.278	.396	.494
6 ML YEARS		731	2472	687	118	9	156	(75	81)	1291	432	411	457	57	630	13	2	20	25	11	.69	53	.278	.391	.522

Mark McGwire

Bats: Right   **Throws:** Right   **Pos:** 1B   **Ht:** 6' 5"   **Wt:** 225   **Born:** 10/01/63   **Age:** 28

							BATTING												BASERUNNING				PERCENTAGES		
Year Team	Lg	G	AB	H	2B	3B	HR	(Hm	Rd)	TB	R	RBI	TBB	IBB	SO	HBP	SH	SF	SB	CS	SB%	GDP	Avg	OBP	SLG
1986 Oakland	AL	18	53	10	1	0	3	(1	2)	20	10	9	4	0	18	1	0	0	0	1	.00	0	.189	.259	.377
1987 Oakland	AL	151	557	161	28	4	49	(21	28)	344	97	118	71	8	131	5	0	8	1	1	.50	6	.289	.370	.618
1988 Oakland	AL	155	550	143	22	1	32	(12	20)	263	87	99	76	4	117	4	1	4	0	0	.00	15	.260	.352	.478
1989 Oakland	AL	143	490	113	17	0	33	(12	21)	229	74	95	83	5	94	3	0	11	1	1	.50	23	.231	.339	.467
1990 Oakland	AL	156	523	123	16	0	39	(14	25)	256	87	108	110	9	116	7	1	9	2	1	.67	13	.235	.370	.489
1991 Oakland	AL	154	483	97	22	0	22	(15	7)	185	62	75	93	3	116	3	1	5	2	1	.67	13	.201	.330	.383
6 ML YEARS		777	2656	647	106	5	178	(75	103)	1297	417	504	437	29	592	23	3	37	6	5	.55	70	.244	.351	.488

Tim McIntosh

Bats: Right   **Throws:** Right   **Pos:** DH   **Ht:** 5'11"   **Wt:** 195   **Born:** 03/21/65   **Age:** 27

							BATTING												BASERUNNING				PERCENTAGES		
Year Team	Lg	G	AB	H	2B	3B	HR	(Hm	Rd)	TB	R	RBI	TBB	IBB	SO	HBP	SH	SF	SB	CS	SB%	GDP	Avg	OBP	SLG
1986 Beloit	A	49	173	45	3	2	4	--	--	64	26	21	18	0	33	2	0	3	0	0	.00	3	.260	.332	.370
1987 Beloit	A	130	461	139	30	3	20	--	--	235	83	85	49	2	96	7	1	3	7	4	.64	4	.302	.373	.510
1988 Stockton	A	138	519	147	32	6	15	--	--	236	81	92	57	1	96	11	6	5	10	5	.67	6	.283	.363	.455
1989 El Paso	AA	120	463	139	30	3	17	--	--	226	72	93	29	3	72	8	2	9	5	4	.56	8	.300	.346	.488
1990 Denver	AAA	116	416	120	20	3	18	--	--	200	72	74	26	0	58	14	3	7	6	2	.75	9	.288	.346	.481
1991 Denver	AAA	122	462	135	19	9	18	--	--	226	69	91	37	4	59	11	0	7	2	5	.29	13	.292	.354	.489
1990 Milwaukee	AL	5	5	1	0	0	1	(1	0)	4	1	1	0	0	2	0	0	0	0	0	.00	0	.200	.200	.800
1991 Milwaukee	AL	7	11	4	1	0	1	(1	0)	8	2	1	0	0	4	0	0	0	0	0	.00	0	.364	.364	.727
2 ML YEARS		12	16	5	1	0	2	(2	0)	12	3	2	0	0	6	0	0	0	0	0	.00	0	.313	.313	.750

Jeff McKnight

Bats: Both   **Throws:** Right   **Pos:** LF   **Ht:** 6' 0"   **Wt:** 188   **Born:** 02/18/63   **Age:** 29

							BATTING												BASERUNNING				PERCENTAGES		
Year Team	Lg	G	AB	H	2B	3B	HR	(Hm	Rd)	TB	R	RBI	TBB	IBB	SO	HBP	SH	SF	SB	CS	SB%	GDP	Avg	OBP	SLG
1984 Columbia	A	95	251	64	10	1	1	--	--	79	31	27	26	2	17	1	1	1	9	1	.90	5	.255	.326	.315
1985 Columbia	A	67	159	42	6	1	1	--	--	53	26	24	21	2	18	1	0	2	6	2	.75	2	.264	.350	.333
Lynchburg	A	49	150	33	6	1	0	--	--	41	19	21	29	0	19	0	4	3	0	0	.00	1	.220	.341	.273
1986 Jackson	AA	132	469	118	24	3	4	--	--	160	71	55	76	3	58	3	5	9	5	2	.71	10	.252	.354	.341
1987 Jackson	AA	16	59	12	3	0	2	--	--	21	5	8	4	0	12	1	0	0	1	1	.50	3	.203	.266	.356
Tidewater	AAA	87	184	47	7	3	2	--	--	66	21	25	24	1	22	1	1	4	0	0	.00	6	.255	.338	.359
1988 Tidewater	AAA	113	345	88	14	0	2	--	--	108	36	25	36	5	32	0	1	3	0	4	.00	3	.255	.323	.313
1989 Tidewater	AAA	116	425	106	19	2	9	--	--	156	84	48	79	1	56	1	3	1	3	0	1.00	13	.249	.368	.367
1990 Rochester	AAA	100	339	95	21	3	7	--	--	143	56	45	41	3	58	0	4	6	7	5	.58	4	.280	.352	.422
1991 Rochester	AAA	22	81	31	7	2	1	--	--	45	19	18	14	0	10	0	0	1	1	2	.33	3	.383	.469	.556
1989 New York	NL	6	12	3	0	0	0	(0	0)	3	2	0	2	0	1	0	0	0	0	0	.00	1	.250	.357	.250
1990 Baltimore	AL	29	75	15	2	0	1	(1	0)	20	11	4	5	0	17	1	3	0	0	0	.00	0	.200	.259	.267
1991 Baltimore	AL	16	41	7	1	0	0	(0	0)	8	2	2	2	0	7	0	0	0	1	0	1.00	2	.171	.209	.195
3 ML YEARS		51	128	25	3	0	1	(1	0)	31	15	6	9	0	25	1	3	0	1	0	1.00	3	.195	.254	.242

Mark McLemore

Bats: Both **Throws:** Right **Pos:** 2B **Ht:** 5'11" **Wt:** 195 **Born:** 10/04/64 **Age:** 27

Year	Team	Lg	G	AB	H	2B	3B	HR	(Hm	Rd)	TB	R	RBI	TBB	IBB	SO	HBP	SH	SF	SB	CS	SB%	GDP	Avg	OBP	SLG
1986	California	AL	5	4	0	0	0	0	(0	0)	0	0	0	2	0	1	0	0	0	0	1	.00	0	.000	.200	.000
1987	California	AL	138	433	102	13	3	3	(3	0)	130	61	41	48	0	72	0	15	3	25	8	.76	7	.236	.310	.300
1988	California	AL	77	233	56	11	2	2	(1	1)	77	38	16	25	0	28	0	5	2	13	7	.65	6	.240	.312	.330
1989	California	AL	32	103	25	3	1	0	(0	0)	30	12	14	7	0	19	1	3	1	6	1	.86	2	.243	.295	.291
1990	2 ML Teams		28	60	9	2	0	0	(0	0)	11	6	2	4	0	15	0	1	0	1	0	1.00	1	.150	.203	.183
1991	Houston	NL	21	61	9	1	0	0	(0	0)	10	6	2	6	0	13	0	0	1	0	1	.00	1	.148	.221	.164
1990	California	AL	20	48	7	2	0	0	(0	0)	9	4	2	4	0	9	0	1	0	1	0	1.00	1	.146	.212	.188
	Cleveland	AL	8	12	2	0	0	0	(0	0)	2	2	0	0	0	6	0	0	0	0	0	.00	0	.167	.167	.167
	6 ML YEARS		301	894	201	30	6	5	(4	1)	258	123	75	91	0	149	1	25	7	45	18	.71	17	.225	.295	.289

Brian McRae

Bats: Both **Throws:** Right **Pos:** CF **Ht:** 6' 0" **Wt:** 185 **Born:** 08/27/67 **Age:** 24

Year	Team	Lg	G	AB	H	2B	3B	HR	(Hm	Rd)	TB	R	RBI	TBB	IBB	SO	HBP	SH	SF	SB	CS	SB%	GDP	Avg	OBP	SLG
1985	Royals	R	60	217	58	6	5	0	--	--	74	40	23	28	0	34	2	4	2	27	12	.69	7	.267	.353	.341
1986	Eugene	A	72	306	82	10	3	1	--	--	101	66	29	41	1	49	5	1	2	28	4	.88	6	.268	.362	.330
1987	Ft. Myers	A	131	481	121	14	1	1	--	--	140	62	31	22	1	70	6	0	0	33	18	.65	4	.252	.293	.291
1988	Baseball Cy	A	30	107	33	2	0	1	--	--	38	18	11	9	0	11	3	2	0	8	4	.67	2	.308	.378	.355
	Memphis	AA	91	288	58	13	1	4	--	--	85	33	15	16	0	60	2	10	0	13	5	.72	8	.201	.248	.295
1989	Memphis	AA	138	533	121	18	8	5	--	--	170	72	42	43	1	94	8	7	1	23	8	.74	5	.227	.294	.319
1990	Memphis	AA	116	470	126	24	6	10	--	--	192	78	64	44	1	66	3	14	1	21	10	.68	9	.268	.334	.409
1990	Kansas City	AL	46	168	48	8	3	2	(1	1)	68	21	23	9	0	29	0	3	2	4	3	.57	5	.286	.318	.405
1991	Kansas City	AL	152	629	164	28	9	8	(3	5)	234	86	64	24	1	99	2	3	5	20	11	.65	12	.261	.288	.372
	2 ML YEARS		198	797	212	36	12	10	(4	6)	302	107	87	33	1	128	2	6	7	24	14	.63	17	.266	.294	.379

Kevin McReynolds

Bats: Right **Throws:** Right **Pos:** LF/CF **Ht:** 6' 1" **Wt:** 215 **Born:** 10/16/59 **Age:** 32

Year	Team	Lg	G	AB	H	2B	3B	HR	(Hm	Rd)	TB	R	RBI	TBB	IBB	SO	HBP	SH	SF	SB	CS	SB%	GDP	Avg	OBP	SLG
1983	San Diego	NL	39	140	31	3	1	4	(3	1)	48	15	14	12	1	29	0	0	3	2	1	.67	1	.221	.277	.343
1984	San Diego	NL	147	525	146	26	6	20	(10	10)	244	68	75	34	8	69	0	3	9	3	6	.33	14	.278	.317	.465
1985	San Diego	NL	152	564	132	24	4	15	(6	9)	209	61	75	43	6	81	3	2	4	4	0	1.00	17	.234	.290	.371
1986	San Diego	NL	158	560	161	31	6	26	(14	12)	282	89	96	66	6	83	1	5	9	8	6	.57	9	.288	.358	.504
1987	New York	NL	151	590	163	32	5	29	(18	11)	292	86	95	39	5	70	1	1	8	14	1	.93	13	.276	.318	.495
1988	New York	NL	147	552	159	30	2	27	(13	14)	274	82	99	38	3	56	4	1	5	21	0	1.00	6	.288	.336	.496
1989	New York	NL	148	545	148	25	3	22	(12	10)	245	74	85	46	10	74	1	0	7	15	7	.68	8	.272	.326	.450
1990	New York	NL	147	521	140	23	1	24	(11	13)	237	75	82	71	11	61	1	0	8	9	2	.82	8	.269	.353	.455
1991	New York	NL	143	522	135	32	1	16	(7	9)	217	65	74	49	7	46	2	1	4	6	6	.50	8	.259	.322	.416
	9 ML YEARS		1232	4519	1215	226	29	183	(94	89)	2048	615	695	398	57	569	13	13	57	82	29	.74	84	.269	.326	.453

Rusty Meacham

Pitches: Right **Bats:** Right **Pos:** RP/SP **Ht:** 6' 2" **Wt:** 166 **Born:** 01/27/68 **Age:** 24

			HOW MUCH HE PITCHED						WHAT HE GAVE UP									THE RESULTS				
Year	Team	Lg	G	GS	CG	GF	IP	BFP	H	R	ER	HR	SH	SF	HB	TBB	IBB	SO	WP	Bk	W	L	Pct.	ShO	Sv	ERA
1988	Fayetteville	A	6	5	0	0	24.2	117	37	19	17	3	0	1	2	6	1	16	2	5	0	3	.000	0	0	6.20
	Bristol	R	13	9	2	1	75.1	303	55	14	12	2	1	1	7	22	0	85	5	1	9	1	.900	2	0	1.43
1989	Fayetteville	A	16	15	2	1	102	413	103	33	26	4	1	4	1	23	0	74	2	3	10	3	.769	0	0	2.29
	Lakeland	A	11	9	1	1	64.2	259	59	15	14	3	3	0	2	12	2	39	0	0	5	4	.556	2	0	1.95
1990	London	AA	26	26	9	0	178	722	160	70	62	11	3	7	4	36	0	123	5	1	15	9	.625	3	0	3.13
1991	Toledo	AAA	26	17	3	4	125.1	517	117	53	43	8	2	5	1	40	3	70	6	0	9	7	.563	1	2	3.09
1991	Detroit	AL	10	4	0	1	27.2	126	35	17	16	4	1	3	0	11	0	14	0	1	2	1	.667	0	0	5.20

Luis Medina

Bats: Right **Throws:** Left **Pos:** DH **Ht:** 6' 3" **Wt:** 195 **Born:** 03/26/63 **Age:** 29

Year	Team	Lg	G	AB	H	2B	3B	HR	(Hm	Rd)	TB	R	RBI	TBB	IBB	SO	HBP	SH	SF	SB	CS	SB%	GDP	Avg	OBP	SLG
1988	Cleveland	AL	16	51	13	0	0	6	(4	2)	31	10	8	2	0	18	2	1	0	0	0	.00	0	.255	.309	.608
1989	Cleveland	AL	30	83	17	1	0	4	(1	3)	30	8	8	6	0	35	0	0	0	0	1	.00	3	.205	.258	.361

Year Team	Lg	G	AB	H	2B	3B	HR	(Hm	Rd)	TB	R	RBI	TBB	IBB	SO	HBP	SH	SF	SB	CS	SB%	GDP	Avg	OBP	SLG
1991 Cleveland	AL	5	16	1	0	0	0	(0	0)	1	0	0	1	0	7	0	1	0	0	0	.00	0	.063	.118	.063
3 ML YEARS		51	150	31	1	0	10	(5	5)	62	18	16	9	0	60	2	2	0	0	1	.00	3	.207	.261	.413

Jose Melendez

Pitches: Right **Bats:** Right **Pos:** RP/SP **Ht:** 6' 2" **Wt:** 175 **Born:** 09/02/65 **Age:** 26

		HOW MUCH HE PITCHED						WHAT HE GAVE UP									THE RESULTS					
Year Team	Lg	G	GS	CG	GF	IP	BFP	H	R	ER	HR	SH	SF	HB	TBB	IBB	SO	WP	Bk	W	L	Pct.	ShO	Sv	ERA
1984 Watertown	A	15	15	3	0	91	372	61	37	28	6	1	2	6	40	0	68	4	2	5	7	.417	1	0	2.77
1985 Pr William	A	9	8	1	1	44.1	180	25	17	12	2	0	3	0	26	0	41	2	0	3	2	.600	0	1	2.44
1986 Pr William	A	28	27	6	0	186.1	768	141	75	54	9	7	5	2	81	1	146	6	5	13	10	.565	1	0	2.61
1987 Harrisburg	AA	6	6	0	0	18.1	91	28	24	22	4	1	0	0	11	0	13	0	1	1	3	.250	0	0	10.80
Salem	A	20	20	1	0	116.1	493	96	62	59	17	0	5	8	56	0	86	4	0	9	6	.600	1	0	4.56
1988 Salem	A	8	8	2	0	53.2	233	55	26	24	10	0	0	1	19	0	50	2	1	4	2	.667	1	0	4.02
Harrisburg	AA	22	4	2	6	71.1	274	46	20	18	2	2	3	1	19	1	38	3	4	5	3	.625	2	1	2.27
1989 Williamsprt	AA	11	11	0	0	73.1	295	54	23	20	7	1	2	2	22	1	56	0	6	3	4	.429	0	0	2.45
Calgary	AAA	17	2	0	4	40.2	184	42	27	26	6	2	3	3	19	2	24	1	0	1	2	.333	0	0	5.75
1990 Calgary	AAA	45	10	1	14	124.2	525	119	61	54	11	2	5	6	44	2	95	2	1	11	4	.733	0	2	3.90
1991 Las Vegas	AAA	9	8	1	1	58.2	238	54	27	26	8	1	4	3	11	0	45	0	0	7	0	1.000	0	0	3.99
1990 Seattle	AL	3	0	0	1	5.1	28	8	8	7	2	0	0	1	3	0	7	1	0	0	0	.000	0	0	11.81
1991 San Diego	NL	31	9	0	10	93.2	381	77	35	34	11	2	6	1	24	3	60	3	2	8	5	.615	0	3	3.27
2 ML YEARS		34	9	0	11	99	409	85	43	41	13	2	6	2	27	3	67	4	2	8	5	.615	0	3	3.73

Bob Melvin

Bats: Right **Throws:** Right **Pos:** C **Ht:** 6' 4" **Wt:** 206 **Born:** 10/28/61 **Age:** 30

		BATTING																	BASERUNNING				PERCENTAGES		
Year Team	Lg	G	AB	H	2B	3B	HR	(Hm	Rd)	TB	R	RBI	TBB	IBB	SO	HBP	SH	SF	SB	CS	SB%	GDP	Avg	OBP	SLG
1985 Detroit	AL	41	82	18	4	1	0	(0	0)	24	10	4	3	0	21	0	2	0	0	0	.00	1	.220	.247	.293
1986 San Francisco	NL	89	268	60	14	2	5	(2	3)	93	24	25	15	1	69	0	3	3	3	2	.60	7	.224	.262	.347
1987 San Francisco	NL	84	246	49	8	0	11	(6	5)	90	31	31	17	3	44	0	0	2	0	4	.00	7	.199	.249	.366
1988 San Francisco	NL	92	273	64	13	1	8	(4	4)	103	23	27	13	0	46	0	1	1	0	2	.00	5	.234	.268	.377
1989 Baltimore	AL	85	278	67	10	1	1	(0	1)	82	22	32	15	3	53	0	7	1	1	4	.20	10	.241	.279	.295
1990 Baltimore	AL	93	301	73	14	1	5	(3	2)	104	30	37	11	1	53	0	3	3	0	1	.00	8	.243	.267	.346
1991 Baltimore	AL	79	228	57	10	0	1	(0	1)	70	11	23	11	2	46	0	1	5	0	0	.00	5	.250	.279	.307
7 ML YEARS		563	1676	388	73	6	31	(15	16)	566	151	179	85	10	332	0	17	15	4	13	.24	43	.232	.266	.338

Orlando Merced

Bats: Both **Throws:** Right **Pos:** 1B **Ht:** 5'11" **Wt:** 175 **Born:** 11/02/66 **Age:** 25

		BATTING																	BASERUNNING				PERCENTAGES		
Year Team	Lg	G	AB	H	2B	3B	HR	(Hm	Rd)	TB	R	RBI	TBB	IBB	SO	HBP	SH	SF	SB	CS	SB%	GDP	Avg	OBP	SLG
1985 Pirates	R	40	136	31	6	0	0	--	--	40	16	13	9	0	9	1	0	0	3	1	.75	3	.228	.281	.294
1986 Macon	A	65	173	34	4	1	2	--	--	46	20	24	12	0	38	1	0	2	5	3	.63	3	.197	.250	.266
Watertown	A	27	89	16	0	1	3	--	--	27	12	9	14	2	21	0	2	1	6	2	.75	2	.180	.302	.303
1987 Macon	A	4	4	0	0	0	0	--	--	0	1	0	1	0	3	0	0	0	0	0	.00	0	.000	.200	.000
Watertown	A	4	12	5	0	1	0	--	--	7	4	3	1	0	1	1	0	0	1	0	1.00	0	.417	.500	.583
1988 Augusta	A	37	136	36	6	3	1	--	--	51	19	17	7	1	20	2	0	1	2	0	1.00	2	.265	.308	.375
Salem	A	80	298	87	12	7	7	--	--	134	47	42	27	1	64	1	1	5	13	3	.81	7	.292	.347	.450
1989 Harrisburg	AA	95	341	82	16	4	6	--	--	124	43	48	32	6	65	2	1	4	13	3	.81	6	.240	.306	.364
Buffalo	AAA	35	129	44	5	3	1	--	--	58	18	16	7	1	26	0	2	1	0	1	.00	2	.341	.372	.450
1990 Buffalo	AAA	101	378	99	12	6	9	--	--	150	52	55	46	3	63	0	1	1	14	5	.74	8	.262	.341	.397
1991 Buffalo	AAA	3	12	2	0	0	0	--	--	2	1	0	0	0	4	0	0	0	1	1	.50	0	.167	.231	.167
1990 Pittsburgh	NL	25	24	5	1	0	0	(0	0)	6	3	0	1	0	9	0	0	0	0	0	.00	1	.208	.240	.250
1991 Pittsburgh	NL	120	411	113	17	2	10	(5	5)	164	83	50	64	4	81	1	1	1	8	4	.67	6	.275	.373	.399
2 ML YEARS		145	435	118	18	2	10	(5	5)	170	86	50	65	4	90	1	1	1	8	4	.67	7	.271	.367	.391

Luis Mercedes

Bats: Right **Throws:** Right **Pos:** LF **Ht:** 6' 0" **Wt:** 180 **Born:** 02/20/68 **Age:** 24

		BATTING																	BASERUNNING				PERCENTAGES		
Year Team	Lg	G	AB	H	2B	3B	HR	(Hm	Rd)	TB	R	RBI	TBB	IBB	SO	HBP	SH	SF	SB	CS	SB%	GDP	Avg	OBP	SLG
1988 Bluefield	R	59	215	59	8	4	0	--	--	75	36	20	32	0	39	2	3	1	16	11	.59	6	.274	.372	.349
1989 Frederick	A	108	401	124	12	5	3	--	--	155	62	36	30	2	62	3	2	2	29	11	.73	7	.309	.360	.387
1990 Hagerstown	AA	108	416	139	12	4	3	--	--	168	71	37	34	2	70	6	6	2	38	14	.73	13	.334	.391	.404
1991 Rochester	AAA	102	374	125	14	5	2	--	--	155	68	36	65	0	63	5	6	4	23	14	.62	10	.334	.435	.414
1991 Baltimore	AL	19	54	11	2	0	0	(0	0)	13	10	2	4	0	9	1	0	0	0	0	.00	1	.204	.259	.241

Kent Mercker

Pitches: Left　Bats: Left　Pos: RP/SP　　Ht: 6' 2"　Wt: 195　Born: 02/01/68　Age: 24

		HOW MUCH HE PITCHED						WHAT HE GAVE UP									THE RESULTS				
Year Team	Lg	G	GS	CG	GF	IP	BFP	H	R	ER	HR	SH	SF	HB	TBB	IBB	SO	WP	Bk	W	L	Pct.	ShO	Sv	ERA
1989 Atlanta	NL	2	1	0	1	4.1	26	8	6	6	0	0	0	0	6	0	4	0	0	0	0	.000	0	0	12.46
1990 Atlanta	NL	36	0	0	28	48.1	211	43	22	17	6	1	2	2	24	3	39	2	0	4	7	.364	0	7	3.17
1991 Atlanta	NL	50	4	0	28	73.1	306	56	23	21	5	2	2	1	35	3	62	4	1	5	3	.625	0	6	2.58
3 ML YEARS		88	5	0	57	126	543	107	51	44	11	3	4	3	65	6	105	6	1	9	10	.474	0	13	3.14

Matt Merullo

Bats: Left　Throws: Right　Pos: C/1B　　Ht: 6' 2"　Wt: 200　Born: 08/04/65　Age: 26

					BATTING														BASERUNNING				PERCENTAGES		
Year Team	Lg	G	AB	H	2B	3B	HR	(Hm	Rd)	TB	R	RBI	TBB	IBB	SO	HBP	SH	SF	SB	CS	SB%	GDP	Avg	OBP	SLG
1989 Chicago	AL	31	81	18	1	0	1	(1	0)	22	5	8	6	0	14	0	2	1	0	1	.00	2	.222	.273	.272
1991 Chicago	AL	80	140	32	1	0	5	(1	4)	48	8	21	9	1	18	0	1	4	0	0	.00	1	.229	.268	.343
2 ML YEARS		111	221	50	2	0	6	(2	4)	70	13	29	15	1	32	0	3	5	0	1	.00	3	.226	.270	.317

Jose Mesa

Pitches: Right　Bats: Right　Pos: SP　　Ht: 6' 3"　Wt: 219　Born: 05/22/66　Age: 26

				HOW MUCH HE PITCHED						WHAT HE GAVE UP										THE RESULTS				
Year Team	Lg	G	GS	CG	GF	IP	BFP	H	R	ER	HR	SH	SF	HB	TBB	IBB	SO	WP	Bk	W	L	Pct.	ShO	Sv	ERA
1987 Baltimore	AL	6	5	0	0	31.1	143	38	23	21	7	0	0	0	15	0	17	4	0	1	3	.250	0	0	6.03
1990 Baltimore	AL	7	7	0	0	46.2	202	37	20	20	2	2	2	1	27	2	24	1	1	3	2	.600	0	0	3.86
1991 Baltimore	AL	23	23	2	0	123.2	566	151	86	82	11	5	4	3	62	2	64	3	0	6	11	.353	1	0	5.97
3 ML YEARS		36	35	2	0	201.2	911	226	129	123	20	7	6	4	104	4	105	8	1	10	16	.385	1	0	5.49

Hensley Meulens

Bats: Right　Throws: Right　Pos: LF/RF/DH　　Ht: 6' 3"　Wt: 212　Born: 06/23/67　Age: 25

					BATTING														BASERUNNING				PERCENTAGES		
Year Team	Lg	G	AB	H	2B	3B	HR	(Hm	Rd)	TB	R	RBI	TBB	IBB	SO	HBP	SH	SF	SB	CS	SB%	GDP	Avg	OBP	SLG
1986 Yankees	R	59	219	51	10	4	4	--	--	81	36	31	28	0	66	4	1	1	4	2	.67	7	.233	.329	.370
1987 Pr William	A	116	430	129	23	2	28	--	--	240	76	103	53	3	124	9	0	6	14	3	.82	7	.300	.384	.558
Ft.Laudrdle	A	17	58	10	3	0	0	--	--	13	2	2	7	0	25	0	0	0	0	0	.00	0	.172	.262	.224
1988 Albany	AA	79	278	68	9	1	13	--	--	118	50	40	37	2	97	1	0	0	3	3	.50	7	.245	.335	.424
Columbus	AAA	55	209	48	9	1	6	--	--	77	27	22	14	0	61	0	0	1	2	0	1.00	5	.230	.277	.368
1989 Albany	AA	104	335	86	8	2	11	--	--	131	55	45	61	0	108	9	0	1	3	2	.60	6	.257	.384	.391
Columbus	AAA	14	45	13	4	0	1	--	--	20	8	3	8	0	13	0	0	0	2	0	.00	2	.289	.396	.444
1990 Columbus	AAA	136	480	137	20	5	26	--	--	245	81	96	66	4	132	7	1	5	6	4	.60	12	.285	.376	.510
1989 New York	AL	8	28	5	0	0	0	(0	0)	5	2	1	2	0	8	0	0	0	0	1	.00	2	.179	.233	.179
1990 New York	AL	23	83	20	7	0	3	(2	1)	36	12	10	9	0	25	3	0	0	1	0	1.00	3	.241	.337	.434
1991 New York	AL	96	288	64	8	1	6	(4	2)	92	37	29	18	1	97	4	1	2	3	0	1.00	7	.222	.276	.319
3 ML YEARS		127	399	89	15	1	9	(6	3)	133	51	40	29	1	130	7	1	2	4	1	.80	12	.223	.286	.333

Bob Milacki

Pitches: Right　Bats: Right　Pos: SP/RP　　Ht: 6' 4"　Wt: 234　Born: 07/28/64　Age: 27

				HOW MUCH HE PITCHED						WHAT HE GAVE UP										THE RESULTS				
Year Team	Lg	G	GS	CG	GF	IP	BFP	H	R	ER	HR	SH	SF	HB	TBB	IBB	SO	WP	Bk	W	L	Pct.	ShO	Sv	ERA
1988 Baltimore	AL	3	3	1	0	25	91	9	2	2	1	0	0	0	9	0	18	0	0	2	0	1.000	1	0	0.72
1989 Baltimore	AL	37	36	3	1	243	1022	233	105	101	21	7	6	2	88	4	113	1	1	14	12	.538	2	0	3.74
1990 Baltimore	AL	27	24	1	0	135.1	594	143	73	67	18	5	5	0	61	2	60	2	1	5	8	.385	1	0	4.46
1991 Baltimore	AL	31	26	3	1	184	758	175	86	82	17	7	5	1	53	3	108	1	2	10	9	.526	1	0	4.01
4 ML YEARS		98	89	8	2	587.1	2465	560	266	252	57	19	16	3	211	9	299	4	4	31	29	.517	5	0	3.86

Keith Miller

Bats: Right　Throws: Right　Pos: 2B/RF　　Ht: 5'11"　Wt: 185　Born: 06/12/63　Age: 29

					BATTING														BASERUNNING				PERCENTAGES		
Year Team	Lg	G	AB	H	2B	3B	HR	(Hm	Rd)	TB	R	RBI	TBB	IBB	SO	HBP	SH	SF	SB	CS	SB%	GDP	Avg	OBP	SLG
1987 New York	NL	25	51	19	2	2	0	(0	0)	25	14	1	2	0	6	1	3	0	8	1	.89	1	.373	.407	.490
1988 New York	NL	40	70	15	1	1	1	(1	0)	21	9	5	6	0	10	0	3	0	5	5	.00	1	.214	.276	.300
1989 New York	NL	57	143	33	7	0	1	(0	1)	43	15	7	5	0	27	1	3	0	6	0	1.00	3	.231	.262	.301
1990 New York	NL	88	233	60	8	0	1	(0	1)	71	42	12	23	1	46	2	2	2	16	3	.84	2	.258	.327	.305
1991 New York	NL	98	275	77	22	1	4	(2	2)	113	41	23	23	0	44	5	0	1	14	4	.78	2	.280	.345	.411
5 ML YEARS		308	772	204	40	4	7	(4	3)	273	121	48	59	1	133	9	11	3	44	13	.77	9	.264	.323	.354

Paul Miller

Pitches: Right   **Bats:** Right   **Pos:** SP   **Ht:** 6' 5"   **Wt:** 215   **Born:** 04/27/65   **Age:** 27

			HOW	MUCH	HE	PITCHED			WHAT	HE	GAVE	UP							THE	RESULTS			
Year	Team	Lg	G	GS	CG	GF	IP	BFP	H	R	ER	HR	SH	SF	HB	TBB	IBB	SO	WP	Bk	W	L	Pct.	ShO	Sv	ERA
1987	Pirates	R	12	12	1	0	70.1	292	55	34	25	3	4	1	2	26	0	62	3	0	3	6	.333	1	0	3.20
1988	Augusta	A	15	15	2	0	90.1	374	80	34	29	3	3	5	4	28	1	51	8	5	6	5	.545	2	0	2.89
1989	Salem	A	26	20	2	0	133.2	599	138	86	62	17	2	4	8	64	0	82	8	1	6	12	.333	1	0	4.17
1990	Salem	A	22	22	5	0	150.2	628	145	58	41	6	3	6	7	33	1	83	5	1	8	6	.571	1	0	2.45
	Harrisburg	AA	5	5	2	0	37	148	27	9	9	1	1	2	2	10	0	11	0	0	2	1	.667	1	0	2.19
1991	Carolina	AA	15	15	1	0	89.1	369	69	29	24	4	7	1	3	35	4	69	5	1	7	2	.778	0	0	2.42
	Buffalo	AAA	10	10	2	0	67	272	41	17	11	2	4	0	5	29	0	30	1	1	5	2	.714	0	0	1.48
1991	Pittsburgh	NL	1	1	0	0	5	21	4	3	3	0	0	0	0	3	0	2	0	0	0	0	.000	0	0	5.40

Randy Milligan

Bats: Right   **Throws:** Right   **Pos:** 1B/DH   **Ht:** 6' 1"   **Wt:** 235   **Born:** 11/27/61   **Age:** 30

									BATTING										BASERUNNING				PERCENTAGES		
Year	Team	Lg	G	AB	H	2B	3B	HR	(Hm	Rd)	TB	R	RBI	TBB	IBB	SO	HBP	SH	SF	SB	CS	SB%	GDP	Avg	OBP	SLG
1987	New York	NL	3	1	0	0	0	0	(0	0)	0	0	0	1	0	1	0	0	0	0	0	.00	0	.000	.500	.000
1988	Pittsburgh	NL	40	82	18	5	0	3	(1	2)	32	10	8	20	0	24	1	0	0	1	2	.33	2	.220	.379	.390
1989	Baltimore	AL	124	365	98	23	5	12	(6	6)	167	56	45	74	2	75	3	0	2	9	5	.64	12	.268	.394	.458
1990	Baltimore	AL	109	362	96	20	1	20	(11	9)	178	64	60	88	3	68	2	0	4	6	3	.67	11	.265	.408	.492
1991	Baltimore	AL	141	483	127	17	2	16	(8	8)	196	57	70	84	4	108	2	0	0	0	5	.00	23	.263	.373	.406
	5 ML YEARS		417	1293	339	65	8	51	(26	25)	573	187	183	267	9	276	8	0	8	16	15	.52	48	.262	.390	.443

Alan Mills

Pitches: Right   **Bats:** Both   **Pos:** RP   **Ht:** 6' 1"   **Wt:** 190   **Born:** 10/18/66   **Age:** 25

				HOW	MUCH	HE	PITCHED			WHAT	HE	GAVE	UP							THE	RESULTS			
Year	Team	Lg	G	GS	CG	GF	IP	BFP	H	R	ER	HR	SH	SF	HB	TBB	IBB	SO	WP	Bk	W	L	Pct.	ShO	Sv	ERA
1986	Pirates	A	14	14	1	0	83.2		77	58	43	1	0	0	5	60	0	50	5	0	6	6	.500	0	0	4.63
1987	Pr William	A	35	8	0	11	85.2	424	102	75	58	7	7	0	4	64	3	53	9	0	2	11	.154	0	1	6.09
1988	Pr William	A	42	5	0	19	93.2	416	93	56	43	4	5	5	5	43	2	59	6	1	3	8	.273	0	4	4.13
1989	Ft.Laudrdle	A	22	0	0	15	31	140	40	15	13	0	3	3	4	9	1	25	3	2	1	4	.200	0	6	3.77
	Pr William	A	26	0	0	26	39.2	155	22	5	4	0	1	2	5	13	1	44	6	0	6	1	.857	0	7	0.91
1990	Columbus	AAA	17	0	0	13	29.1	123	22	11	11	0	1	1	2	14	0	30	2	0	3	3	.500	0	6	3.38
1991	Columbus	AAA	38	15	0	18	113.2	522	109	65	56	3	5	6	6	75	1	77	12	1	7	5	.583	0	8	4.43
1990	New York	AL	36	0	0	18	41.2	200	48	21	19	4	4	1	1	33	6	24	3	0	1	5	.167	0	0	4.10
1991	New York	AL	6	2	0	3	16.1	72	16	9	8	1	0	1	0	8	0	11	2	0	1	1	.500	0	0	4.41
	2 ML YEARS		42	2	0	21	58	272	64	30	27	5	4	2	1	41	6	35	5	0	2	6	.250	0	0	4.19

Gino Minutelli

Pitches: Left   **Bats:** Left   **Pos:** RP/SP   **Ht:** 6' 0"   **Wt:** 185   **Born:** 05/23/64   **Age:** 28

				HOW	MUCH	HE	PITCHED			WHAT	HE	GAVE	UP							THE	RESULTS			
Year	Team	Lg	G	GS	CG	GF	IP	BFP	H	R	ER	HR	SH	SF	HB	TBB	IBB	SO	WP	Bk	W	L	Pct.	ShO	Sv	ERA
1985	Tri-Cities	A	20	10	0	7	57	0	61	57	51	3	0	0	0	57	0	79	6	0	4	8	.333	0	0	8.05
1986	Cedar Rapds	A	27	27	3	0	152.2	671	133	73	62	14	4	6	5	76	1	149	16	2	15	5	.750	2	0	3.66
1987	Tampa	A	17	15	5	1	104.1	461	98	51	44	4	10	3	5	48	4	70	13	1	7	6	.538	1	0	3.80
	Vermont	AA	6	6	0	0	39.2	168	34	15	14	3	0	0	2	16	0	39	2	1	4	1	.800	0	0	3.18
1988	Chattanooga	AA	2	2	0	0	5.2	27	6	2	1	0	0	0	1	4	0	3	0	2	0	1	.000	0	0	1.59
1989	Reds	R	1	1	0	0	1	4	0	0	0	0	0	0	0	1	0	0	0	1	0	0	.000	0	0	0.00
	Chattanooga	AA	6	6	1	0	29	140	28	19	17	1	0	1	6	23	0	20	8	4	1	1	.500	0	0	5.28
1990	Chattanooga	AA	17	17	5	0	108.1	467	106	52	48	9	5	2	2	46	1	75	5	13	9	5	.643	0	0	3.99
	Nashville	AAA	11	11	3	0	78.1	315	65	34	28	5	1	1	1	31	0	61	1	0	5	2	.714	0	0	3.22
1991	Chston-Wv	A	2	2	0	0	8	28	2	0	0	0	0	0	0	4	0	8	0	0	1	0	1.000	0	0	0.00
	Nashville	AAA	13	13	1	0	80.1	325	57	25	17	3	6	2	1	35	2	64	6	1	4	7	.364	1	0	1.90
1990	Cincinnati	NL	2	0	0	0	1	6	0	1	1	0	0	0	1	2	0	0	1	0	0	0	.000	0	0	9.00
1991	Cincinnati	NL	16	3	0	2	25.1	124	30	17	17	5	0	0	0	18	1	21	3	0	0	2	.000	0	0	6.04
	2 ML YEARS		18	3	0	2	26.1	130	30	18	18	5	0	0	1	20	1	21	4	0	0	2	.000	0	0	6.15

Keith Mitchell

Bats: Right   **Throws:** Right   **Pos:** LF   **Ht:** 5'10"   **Wt:** 180   **Born:** 08/06/69   **Age:** 22

									BATTING										BASERUNNING				PERCENTAGES		
Year	Team	Lg	G	AB	H	2B	3B	HR	(Hm	Rd)	TB	R	RBI	TBB	IBB	SO	HBP	SH	SF	SB	CS	SB%	GDP	Avg	OBP	SLG
1987	Braves	R	57	208	50	12	1	2	--	--	70	24	21	29	0	50	2	0	2	7	2	.78	4	.240	.336	.337
1988	Sumter	A	98	341	85	16	1	5	--	--	118	35	33	41	0	50	4	3	2	9	6	.60	8	.249	.335	.346
1989	Burlington	A	127	448	117	23	0	10	--	--	170	64	49	70	1	65	5	0	4	12	7	.63	9	.261	.364	.379

139

Year	Team	Lg	G	AB	H	2B	3B	HR	(Hm	Rd)	TB	R	RBI	TBB	IBB	SO	HBP	SH	SF	SB	CS	SB%	GDP	Avg	OBP	SLG
1990	Durham	A	129	456	134	24	3	6	--	--	182	81	48	92	2	48	4	1	7	18	17	.51	16	.294	.411	.399
1991	Greenville	AA	60	214	70	15	3	10	--	--	121	46	47	29	0	29	1	3	5	12	8	.60	5	.327	.402	.565
	Richmond	AAA	25	95	31	6	1	2	--	--	45	16	17	9	0	13	1	2	3	0	2	.00	3	.326	.380	.474
1991	Atlanta	NL	48	66	21	0	0	2	(1	1)	27	11	5	8	0	12	0	0	0	3	1	.75	1	.318	.392	.409

Kevin Mitchell

Bats: Right **Throws:** Right **Pos:** LF **Ht:** 5'11" **Wt:** 210 **Born:** 01/13/62 **Age:** 30

			BATTING																	BASERUNNING				PERCENTAGES		
Year	Team	Lg	G	AB	H	2B	3B	HR	(Hm	Rd)	TB	R	RBI	TBB	IBB	SO	HBP	SH	SF	SB	CS	SB%	GDP	Avg	OBP	SLG
1984	New York	NL	7	14	3	0	0	0	(0	0)	3	0	1	0	0	3	0	0	0	0	1	.00	0	.214	.214	.214
1986	New York	NL	108	328	91	22	2	12	(4	8)	153	51	43	33	0	61	1	1	1	3	3	.50	6	.277	.344	.466
1987	2 ML Teams		131	464	130	20	2	22	(9	13)	220	68	70	48	4	88	2	0	1	9	6	.60	10	.280	.350	.474
1988	San Francisco	NL	148	505	127	25	7	19	(10	9)	223	60	80	48	7	85	5	1	7	5	5	.50	9	.251	.319	.442
1989	San Francisco	NL	154	543	158	34	6	47	(22	25)	345	100	125	87	32	115	3	0	7	3	4	.43	6	.291	.388	.635
1990	San Francisco	NL	140	524	152	24	2	35	(15	20)	285	90	93	58	9	87	2	0	5	4	7	.36	9	.290	.360	.544
1991	San Francisco	NL	113	371	95	13	1	27	(9	18)	191	52	69	43	8	57	5	0	4	2	3	.40	6	.256	.338	.515
1987	San Diego	NL	62	196	48	7	1	7	(2	5)	78	19	26	20	3	38	0	0	1	0	0	.00	5	.245	.313	.398
	San Francisco	NL	69	268	82	13	1	15	(7	8)	142	49	44	28	1	50	2	0	0	9	6	.60	5	.306	.376	.530
	7 ML YEARS		801	2749	756	138	20	162	(69	93)	1420	421	481	317	60	496	18	2	25	26	29	.47	46	.275	.351	.517

Paul Molitor

Bats: Right **Throws:** Right **Pos:** DH/1B **Ht:** 6' 0" **Wt:** 185 **Born:** 08/22/56 **Age:** 35

			BATTING																	BASERUNNING				PERCENTAGES		
Year	Team	Lg	G	AB	H	2B	3B	HR	(Hm	Rd)	TB	R	RBI	TBB	IBB	SO	HBP	SH	SF	SB	CS	SB%	GDP	Avg	OBP	SLG
1978	Milwaukee	AL	125	521	142	26	4	6	(4	2)	194	73	45	19	2	54	4	7	5	30	12	.71	6	.273	.301	.372
1979	Milwaukee	AL	140	584	188	27	16	9	(3	6)	274	88	62	48	5	48	2	6	5	33	13	.72	9	.322	.372	.469
1980	Milwaukee	AL	111	450	137	29	2	9	(2	7)	197	81	37	48	4	48	3	6	5	34	7	.83	9	.304	.372	.438
1981	Milwaukee	AL	64	251	67	11	0	2	(1	1)	84	45	19	25	1	29	3	5	0	10	6	.63	3	.267	.341	.335
1982	Milwaukee	AL	160	666	201	26	8	19	(9	10)	300	136	71	69	1	93	1	10	5	41	9	.82	9	.302	.366	.450
1983	Milwaukee	AL	152	608	164	28	6	15	(9	6)	249	95	47	59	4	74	2	7	6	41	8	.84	12	.270	.333	.410
1984	Milwaukee	AL	13	46	10	1	0	0	(0	0)	11	3	6	2	0	8	0	0	1	1	0	1.00	0	.217	.245	.239
1985	Milwaukee	AL	140	576	171	28	3	10	(6	4)	235	93	48	54	6	80	1	7	4	21	7	.75	12	.297	.356	.408
1986	Milwaukee	AL	105	437	123	24	6	9	(5	4)	186	62	55	40	0	81	0	2	3	20	5	.80	9	.281	.340	.426
1987	Milwaukee	AL	118	465	164	41	5	16	(7	9)	263	114	75	69	2	67	2	5	1	45	10	.82	4	.353	.438	.566
1988	Milwaukee	AL	154	609	190	34	6	13	(9	4)	275	115	60	71	8	54	2	5	3	41	10	.80	10	.312	.384	.452
1989	Milwaukee	AL	155	615	194	35	4	11	(6	5)	270	84	56	64	4	67	4	4	9	27	11	.71	11	.315	.379	.439
1990	Milwaukee	AL	103	418	119	27	6	12	(6	6)	194	64	45	37	4	51	1	0	2	18	3	.86	7	.285	.343	.464
1991	Milwaukee	AL	158	665	216	32	13	17	(7	10)	325	133	75	77	16	62	6	0	1	19	8	.70	11	.325	.399	.489
	14 ML YEARS		1698	6911	2086	369	79	148	(74	74)	3057	1186	701	682	57	816	31	64	50	381	109	.78	112	.302	.365	.442

Rich Monteleone

Pitches: Right **Bats:** Right **Pos:** RP **Ht:** 6' 2" **Wt:** 234 **Born:** 03/22/63 **Age:** 29

			HOW MUCH HE PITCHED					WHAT HE GAVE UP									THE RESULTS					
Year	Team	Lg	G	GS	CG	GF	IP	BFP	H	R	ER	HR	SH	SF	HB	TBB	IBB	SO	WP	Bk	W	L	Pct.	ShO	Sv	ERA
1987	Seattle	AL	3	0	0	1	7	34	10	5	5	2	0	1	0	4	0	2	0	0	0	0	.000	0	0	6.43
1988	California	AL	3	0	0	2	4.1	20	4	0	0	0	0	0	1	1	1	3	0	1	0	0	.000	0	0	0.00
1989	California	AL	24	0	0	8	39.2	170	39	15	14	3	1	2	1	13	1	27	2	0	2	2	.500	0	0	3.18
1990	New York	AL	5	0	0	2	7.1	31	8	5	5	0	0	0	0	2	0	8	0	0	0	1	.000	0	0	6.14
1991	New York	AL	26	0	0	10	47	201	42	27	19	5	2	2	0	19	3	34	1	1	3	1	.750	0	0	3.64
	5 ML YEARS		61	0	0	23	105.1	456	103	52	43	10	3	4	3	39	5	74	3	2	5	4	.556	0	0	3.67

Jeff Montgomery

Pitches: Right **Bats:** Right **Pos:** RP **Ht:** 5'11" **Wt:** 180 **Born:** 01/07/62 **Age:** 30

			HOW MUCH HE PITCHED					WHAT HE GAVE UP									THE RESULTS					
Year	Team	Lg	G	GS	CG	GF	IP	BFP	H	R	ER	HR	SH	SF	HB	TBB	IBB	SO	WP	Bk	W	L	Pct.	ShO	Sv	ERA
1987	Cincinnati	NL	14	0	0	6	19.1	89	25	15	14	2	0	0	0	9	1	13	1	1	2	2	.500	0	0	6.52
1988	Kansas City	AL	45	0	0	13	62.2	271	54	25	24	6	3	2	2	30	1	47	3	6	7	2	.778	0	1	3.45
1989	Kansas City	AL	63	0	0	39	92	363	66	16	14	3	1	1	2	25	4	94	6	1	7	3	.700	0	18	1.37
1990	Kansas City	AL	73	0	0	59	94.1	400	81	36	25	6	2	2	5	34	8	94	3	0	6	5	.545	0	24	2.39
1991	Kansas City	AL	67	0	0	55	90	376	83	32	29	6	6	2	2	28	2	77	6	0	4	4	.500	0	33	2.90
	5 ML YEARS		262	1	0	172	358.1	1499	309	124	106	23	12	7	11	126	16	325	19	8	26	16	.619	0	76	2.66

Bobby Moore

Bats: Right **Throws:** Right **Pos:** CF   **Ht:** 5' 9" **Wt:** 165 **Born:** 10/27/65 **Age:** 26

								BATTING										BASERUNNING				PERCENTAGES		
Year	Team	Lg	G	AB	H	2B	3B	HR	(Hm	Rd)	TB	R	RBI	TBB	IBB	SO	HBP	SH	SF	SB	CS	SB%	GDP	Avg	OBP	SLG
1987	Eugene	A	57	235	88	13	4	1	--	--	112	40	25	14	2	22	1	2	1	23	1	.96	5	.374	.410	.477
1988	Baseball Cy	A	60	224	52	4	2	0	--	--	60	25	10	17	0	20	2	4	0	12	7	.63	4	.232	.292	.268
1989	Baseball Cy	A	131	483	131	21	5	0	--	--	162	85	42	51	1	35	6	6	3	34	19	.64	6	.271	.346	.335
1990	Memphis	AA	112	422	128	20	6	2	--	--	166	93	36	56	0	32	2	8	4	27	7	.79	5	.303	.384	.393
1991	Omaha	AAA	130	494	120	13	3	0	--	--	139	65	34	37	0	41	3	13	2	35	15	.70	10	.243	.299	.281
1991	Kansas City	AL	18	14	5	1	0	0	(0	0)	6	3	0	1	0	2	0	0	0	3	2	.60	0	.357	.400	.429

Mike Moore

Pitches: Right **Bats:** Right **Pos:** SP   **Ht:** 6' 4" **Wt:** 205 **Born:** 11/26/59 **Age:** 32

			HOW MUCH HE PITCHED					WHAT HE GAVE UP										THE RESULTS					
Year	Team	Lg	G	GS	CG	GF	IP	BFP	H	R	ER	HR	SH	SF	HB	TBB	IBB	SO	WP	Bk	W	L	Pct.	ShO	Sv	ERA
1982	Seattle	AL	28	27	1	0	144.1	651	159	91	86	21	8	4	2	79	0	73	6	0	7	14	.333	1	0	5.36
1983	Seattle	AL	22	21	3	1	128	556	130	75	67	10	1	6	3	60	4	108	7	0	6	8	.429	2	0	4.71
1984	Seattle	AL	34	33	6	0	212	937	236	127	117	16	5	6	5	85	10	158	7	2	7	17	.292	0	0	4.97
1985	Seattle	AL	35	34	14	1	247	1016	230	100	95	18	2	7	4	70	2	155	10	3	17	10	.630	2	0	3.46
1986	Seattle	AL	38	37	11	1	266	1145	279	141	127	28	10	6	12	94	6	146	4	1	11	13	.458	1	1	4.30
1987	Seattle	AL	33	33	12	0	231	1020	268	145	121	29	9	8	0	84	3	115	4	2	9	19	.321	0	0	4.71
1988	Seattle	AL	37	32	9	3	228.2	918	196	104	96	24	3	3	3	63	6	182	4	3	9	15	.375	3	1	3.78
1989	Oakland	AL	35	35	6	0	241.2	976	193	82	70	14	5	6	2	83	1	172	17	0	19	11	.633	3	0	2.61
1990	Oakland	AL	33	33	3	0	199.1	862	204	113	103	14	4	7	3	84	2	73	13	0	13	15	.464	0	0	4.65
1991	Oakland	AL	33	33	3	0	210	887	176	75	69	11	5	4	5	105	1	153	14	0	17	8	.680	1	0	2.96
	10 ML YEARS		328	318	68	6	2108	8968	2071	1053	951	185	52	57	39	807	35	1335	86	11	115	130	.469	13	2	4.06

Mickey Morandini

Bats: Left **Throws:** Right **Pos:** 2B   **Ht:** 5'11" **Wt:** 167 **Born:** 04/22/66 **Age:** 26

								BATTING										BASERUNNING				PERCENTAGES		
Year	Team	Lg	G	AB	H	2B	3B	HR	(Hm	Rd)	TB	R	RBI	TBB	IBB	SO	HBP	SH	SF	SB	CS	SB%	GDP	Avg	OBP	SLG
1989	Spartanburg	A	63	231	78	19	1	1	--	--	102	43	30	35	0	45	3	4	2	18	9	.67	3	.338	.428	.442
	Clearwater	A	17	63	19	4	1	0	--	--	25	14	4	7	1	8	1	0	1	3	1	.75	0	.302	.375	.397
	Reading	AA	48	188	66	12	1	5	--	--	95	39	29	23	4	32	1	1	0	5	5	.50	2	.351	.425	.505
1990	Scr Wil-Bar	AAA	138	502	131	24	10	1	--	--	178	77	31	60	0	90	5	10	0	16	6	.73	11	.261	.346	.355
1991	Scranton-Wb	AAA	12	46	12	4	0	1	--	--	19	7	9	5	0	6	0	0	1	2	0	1.00	0	.261	.327	.413
1990	Philadelphia	NL	25	79	19	4	0	1	(1	0)	26	9	3	6	0	19	0	2	0	3	0	1.00	1	.241	.294	.329
1991	Philadelphia	NL	98	325	81	11	4	1	(1	0)	103	38	20	29	0	45	2	6	2	13	2	.87	7	.249	.313	.317
	2 ML YEARS		123	404	100	15	4	2	(2	0)	129	47	23	35	0	64	2	8	2	16	2	.89	8	.248	.309	.319

Mike Morgan

Pitches: Right **Bats:** Right **Pos:** SP   **Ht:** 6' 2" **Wt:** 222 **Born:** 10/08/59 **Age:** 32

			HOW MUCH HE PITCHED					WHAT HE GAVE UP										THE RESULTS					
Year	Team	Lg	G	GS	CG	GF	IP	BFP	H	R	ER	HR	SH	SF	HB	TBB	IBB	SO	WP	Bk	W	L	Pct.	ShO	Sv	ERA
1978	Oakland	AL	3	3	1	0	12	60	19	12	10	1	1	0	0	8	0	0	0	0	0	3	.000	0	0	7.50
1979	Oakland	AL	13	13	2	0	77	368	102	57	51	7	4	4	3	50	0	17	7	0	2	10	.167	0	0	5.96
1982	New York	AL	30	23	2	2	150.1	661	167	77	73	15	2	4	2	67	5	71	6	0	7	11	.389	0	0	4.37
1983	Toronto	AL	16	4	0	2	45.1	198	48	26	26	6	0	1	0	21	0	22	3	0	0	3	.000	0	0	5.16
1985	Seattle	AL	2	2	0	0	6	33	11	8	8	2	0	0	0	5	0	2	1	0	1	1	.500	0	0	12.00
1986	Seattle	AL	37	33	9	2	216.1	951	243	122	109	24	7	3	4	86	3	116	8	1	11	17	.393	1	1	4.53
1987	Seattle	AL	34	31	8	2	207	898	245	117	107	25	8	5	5	53	3	85	11	0	12	17	.414	2	0	4.65
1988	Baltimore	AL	22	10	2	6	71.1	299	70	45	43	6	1	0	1	23	1	29	5	0	1	6	.143	0	1	5.43
1989	Los Angeles	NL	40	19	0	7	152.2	604	130	51	43	6	8	6	2	33	8	72	6	0	8	11	.421	0	0	2.53
1990	Los Angeles	NL	33	33	6	0	211	891	216	100	88	19	11	4	5	60	5	106	4	1	11	15	.423	4	0	3.75
1991	Los Angeles	NL	34	33	5	1	236.1	949	197	85	73	12	10	4	3	61	10	140	6	0	14	10	.583	1	1	2.78
	11 ML YEARS		264	204	35	22	1385.1	5912	1448	700	631	123	52	31	25	467	35	660	57	2	67	104	.392	8	3	4.10

Russ Morman

Bats: Right **Throws:** Right **Pos:** 1B   **Ht:** 6' 4" **Wt:** 220 **Born:** 04/28/62 **Age:** 30

								BATTING										BASERUNNING				PERCENTAGES		
Year	Team	Lg	G	AB	H	2B	3B	HR	(Hm | Rd)	TB	R	RBI	TBB	IBB	SO	HBP	SH	SF	SB	CS	SB%	GDP	Avg	OBP	SLG
1986	Chicago	AL	49	159	40	5	0	4	(1 | 3)	57	18	17	16	0	36	2	1	2	1	0	1.00	5	.252	.324	.358
1988	Chicago	AL	40	75	18	2	0	0	(0 | 0)	20	8	3	3	0	17	0	2	0	0	0	.00	0	.240	.269	.267
1989	Chicago	AL	37	58	13	2	0	0	(0 | 0)	15	5	8	6	1	16	0	0	1	0	1	1.00	1	.224	.292	.259

141

Year	Team	Lg	G	AB	H	2B	3B	HR	(Hm	Rd)	TB	R	RBI	TBB	IBB	SO	HBP	SH	SF	SB	CS	SB%	GDP	Avg	OBP	SLG
1990	Kansas City	AL	12	37	10	4	2	1	(0	1)	21	5	3	3	0	3	0	0	1	0	0	.00	0	.270	.317	.568
1991	Kansas City	AL	12	23	6	0	0	0	(0	0)	6	1	1	1	1	5	0	0	0	0	0	.00	0	.261	.292	.261
	5 ML YEARS		150	352	87	13	2	5	(1	4)	119	37	32	29	2	77	2	5	4	2	0	1.00	11	.247	.305	.338

Hal Morris

Bats: Left **Throws: Left** **Pos: 1B**   Ht: 6' 4" Wt: 215 Born: 04/09/65 **Age: 27**

									BATTING												BASERUNNING				PERCENTAGES		
Year	Team	Lg	G	AB	H	2B	3B	HR	(Hm	Rd)	TB	R	RBI	TBB	IBB	SO	HBP	SH	SF	SB	CS	SB%	GDP	Avg	OBP	SLG
1988	New York	AL	15	20	2	0	0	0	(0	0)	2	1	0	0	0	9	0	0	0	0	0	.00	0	.100	.100	.100
1989	New York	AL	15	18	5	0	0	0	(0	0)	5	2	4	1	0	4	0	0	0	0	0	.00	2	.278	.316	.278
1990	Cincinnati	NL	107	309	105	22	3	7	(3	4)	154	50	36	21	4	32	1	3	2	9	3	.75	12	.340	.381	.498
1991	Cincinnati	NL	136	478	152	33	1	14	(9	5)	229	72	59	46	7	61	1	5	7	10	4	.71	4	.318	.374	.479
	4 ML YEARS		273	825	264	55	4	21	(12	9)	390	125	99	68	11	106	2	8	9	19	7	.73	18	.320	.369	.473

Jack Morris

Pitches: Right **Bats: Right** **Pos: SP**   Ht: 6' 3" Wt: 200 Born: 05/16/55 **Age: 37**

				HOW MUCH HE PITCHED					WHAT HE GAVE UP									THE RESULTS					
Year	Team	Lg	G	GS	CG	GF	IP	BFP	H	R	ER	HR	SH	SF	HB	TBB	IBB	SO	WP	Bk	W	L	Pct.	ShO	Sv	ERA
1977	Detroit	AL	7	6	1	0	46	189	38	20	19	4	3	1	0	23	0	28	2	0	1	1	.500	0	0	3.72
1978	Detroit	AL	28	7	0	10	106	469	107	57	51	8	8	9	3	49	5	48	4	0	3	5	.375	0	0	4.33
1979	Detroit	AL	27	27	9	0	198	806	179	76	72	19	3	6	4	59	4	113	9	1	17	7	.708	1	0	3.27
1980	Detroit	AL	36	36	11	0	250	1074	252	125	116	20	10	13	4	87	5	112	6	2	16	15	.516	2	0	4.18
1981	Detroit	AL	25	25	15	0	198	798	153	69	67	14	8	9	2	78	11	97	2	2	14	7	.667	1	0	3.05
1982	Detroit	AL	37	37	17	0	266.1	1107	247	131	120	37	4	5	0	96	7	135	10	0	17	16	.515	3	0	4.06
1983	Detroit	AL	37	37	20	0	293.2	1204	257	117	109	30	8	9	3	83	5	232	18	0	20	13	.606	1	0	3.34
1984	Detroit	AL	35	35	9	0	240.1	1015	221	108	96	20	5	3	2	87	7	148	14	0	19	11	.633	1	0	3.60
1985	Detroit	AL	35	35	13	0	257	1077	212	102	95	21	11	7	5	110	7	191	15	3	16	11	.593	4	0	3.33
1986	Detroit	AL	35	35	15	0	267	1092	229	105	97	40	7	3	0	82	7	223	12	0	21	8	.724	6	0	3.27
1987	Detroit	AL	34	34	13	0	266	1101	227	111	100	39	6	5	1	93	7	208	24	1	18	11	.621	0	0	3.38
1988	Detroit	AL	34	34	10	0	235	997	225	115	103	20	12	3	4	83	7	168	11	11	15	13	.536	2	0	3.94
1989	Detroit	AL	24	24	10	0	170.1	743	189	102	92	23	6	7	2	59	3	115	12	1	6	14	.300	0	0	4.86
1990	Detroit	AL	36	36	11	0	249.2	1073	231	144	125	26	7	10	6	97	13	162	16	2	15	18	.455	3	0	4.51
1991	Minnesota	AL	35	35	10	0	246.2	1032	226	107	94	18	5	8	3	92	5	163	15	1	18	12	.600	2	0	3.43
	15 ML YEARS		465	443	164	10	3290	13777	2993	1489	1356	339	103	98	41	1178	93	2143	170	24	216	162	.571	26	0	3.71

John Morris

Bats: Left **Throws: Left** **Pos: CF/RF**   Ht: 6' 1" Wt: 185 Born: 02/23/61 **Age: 31**

									BATTING												BASERUNNING				PERCENTAGES		
Year	Team	Lg	G	AB	H	2B	3B	HR	(Hm	Rd)	TB	R	RBI	TBB	IBB	SO	HBP	SH	SF	SB	CS	SB%	GDP	Avg	OBP	SLG
1986	St. Louis	NL	39	100	24	0	1	1	(1	0)	29	8	14	7	2	15	0	0	1	6	2	.75	2	.240	.287	.290
1987	St. Louis	NL	101	157	41	6	4	3	(1	2)	64	22	23	11	4	22	1	1	0	5	2	.71	2	.261	.314	.408
1988	St. Louis	NL	20	38	11	2	1	0	(0	0)	15	3	3	1	0	7	0	0	0	0	0	.00	0	.289	.308	.395
1989	St. Louis	NL	96	117	28	4	1	2	(2	0)	40	8	14	4	0	22	0	3	0	1	0	1.00	4	.239	.264	.342
1990	St. Louis	NL	18	18	2	0	0	0	(0	0)	2	0	0	3	0	6	0	0	0	0	0	.00	0	.111	.238	.111
1991	Philadelphia	NL	85	127	28	2	1	1	(1	0)	35	15	6	12	4	25	1	0	0	2	0	1.00	1	.220	.293	.276
	6 ML YEARS		359	557	134	14	8	7	(5	2)	185	56	60	38	10	97	2	4	1	14	4	.78	9	.241	.291	.332

Kevin Morton

Pitches: Left **Bats: Right** **Pos: SP**   Ht: 6' 2" Wt: 185 Born: 08/03/68 **Age: 23**

				HOW MUCH HE PITCHED					WHAT HE GAVE UP									THE RESULTS					
Year	Team	Lg	G	GS	CG	GF	IP	BFP	H	R	ER	HR	SH	SF	HB	TBB	IBB	SO	WP	Bk	W	L	Pct.	ShO	Sv	ERA
1989	Red Sox	R	2	1	0	1	6	22	2	0	0	0	0	0	0	1	0	11	0	0	1	0	1.000	0	1	0.00
	Elmira	A	3	3	2	0	24	90	11	6	5	0	2	2	1	6	0	32	1	0	1	1	.500	0	0	1.88
	Lynchburg	A	9	9	4	0	65	253	42	20	17	2	0	2	2	17	0	68	3	0	4	5	.444	2	0	2.35
1990	New Britain	AA	26	26	7	0	163	685	151	86	69	10	4	3	14	48	0	131	6	5	8	14	.364	2	0	3.81
1991	Pawtucket	AAA	16	15	1	0	98	412	91	41	38	8	2	2	2	30	1	80	3	2	7	3	.700	1	0	3.49
1991	Boston	AL	16	15	1	0	86.1	379	93	49	44	9	3	7	1	40	2	45	1	1	6	5	.545	0	0	4.59

Lloyd Moseby

Bats: Left **Throws: Right** **Pos: LF**   Ht: 6' 2" Wt: 205 Born: 11/05/59 **Age: 32**

									BATTING												BASERUNNING				PERCENTAGES		
Year	Team	Lg	G	AB	H	2B	3B	HR	(Hm	Rd)	TB	R	RBI	TBB	IBB	SO	HBP	SH	SF	SB	CS	SB%	GDP	Avg	OBP	SLG
1980	Toronto	AL	114	389	89	24	1	9	(4	5)	142	44	46	25	4	85	4	10	2	4	6	.40	11	.229	.281	.365
1981	Toronto	AL	100	378	88	16	2	9	(3	6)	135	36	43	24	3	86	1	5	4	11	8	.58	4	.233	.278	.357
1982	Toronto	AL	147	487	115	20	9	9	(4	5)	180	51	52	33	3	106	8	3	2	11	7	.61	10	.236	.294	.370
1983	Toronto	AL	151	539	170	31	7	18	(13	5)	269	104	81	51	4	85	5	3	6	27	8	.77	10	.315	.376	.499
1984	Toronto	AL	158	592	166	28	15	18	(10	8)	278	97	92	78	9	122	8	3	7	39	9	.81	8	.280	.368	.470

142

Year	Team	Lg	G	AB	H	2B	3B	HR	(Hm	Rd)	TB	R	RBI	TBB	IBB	SO	HBP	SH	SF	SB	CS	SB%	GDP	Avg	OBP	SLG
1985	Toronto	AL	152	584	151	30	7	18	(11	7)	249	92	70	76	4	91	4	1	5	37	15	.71	12	.259	.345	.426
1986	Toronto	AL	152	589	149	24	5	21	(11	10)	246	89	86	64	3	122	6	2	7	32	11	.74	7	.253	.329	.418
1987	Toronto	AL	155	592	167	27	4	26	(15	11)	280	106	96	70	4	124	2	3	3	39	7	.85	11	.282	.358	.473
1988	Toronto	AL	128	472	113	17	7	10	(2	8)	174	77	42	70	6	93	6	1	3	31	8	.79	8	.239	.343	.369
1989	Toronto	AL	135	502	111	25	3	11	(4	7)	175	72	43	56	1	101	6	7	1	24	7	.77	7	.221	.306	.349
1990	Detroit	AL	122	431	107	16	5	14	(8	6)	175	64	51	48	3	77	5	1	2	17	5	.77	15	.248	.329	.406
1991	Detroit	AL	74	260	68	15	1	6	(4	2)	103	37	35	21	2	43	3	1	3	8	1	.89	3	.262	.321	.396
12 ML YEARS			1588	5815	1494	273	66	169	(89	80)	2406	869	737	616	46	1135	58	40	45	280	92	.75	106	.257	.332	.414

John Moses

Bats: Both **Throws:** Left **Pos:** LF **Ht:** 5'10" **Wt:** 170 **Born:** 08/09/57 **Age:** 34

Year	Team	Lg	G	AB	H	2B	3B	HR	(Hm	Rd)	TB	R	RBI	TBB	IBB	SO	HBP	SH	SF	SB	CS	SB%	GDP	Avg	OBP	SLG
1982	Seattle	AL	22	44	14	5	1	1	(1	0)	24	7	3	4	0	5	0	0	0	5	1	.83	0	.318	.375	.545
1983	Seattle	AL	93	130	27	4	1	0	(0	0)	33	19	6	12	0	20	1	0	0	11	5	.69	4	.208	.280	.254
1984	Seattle	AL	19	35	12	1	1	0	(0	0)	15	3	2	2	0	5	1	1	0	1	0	1.00	0	.343	.395	.429
1985	Seattle	AL	33	62	12	0	0	0	(0	0)	12	4	3	2	0	8	0	1	0	5	2	.71	3	.194	.219	.194
1986	Seattle	AL	103	399	102	16	3	3	(2	1)	133	56	34	34	3	65	0	5	4	25	18	.58	7	.256	.311	.333
1987	Seattle	AL	116	390	96	16	4	3	(2	1)	129	58	38	29	2	49	3	8	3	23	15	.61	6	.246	.301	.331
1988	Minnesota	AL	105	206	65	10	3	2	(0	2)	87	33	12	15	2	21	2	1	1	11	6	.65	4	.316	.366	.422
1989	Minnesota	AL	129	242	68	12	3	1	(0	1)	89	33	31	19	1	23	1	3	2	14	7	.67	5	.281	.333	.368
1990	Minnesota	AL	115	172	38	3	1	1	(0	1)	46	26	14	19	1	19	2	0	2	2	3	.40	4	.221	.303	.267
1991	Detroit	AL	13	21	1	1	0	0	(0	0)	2	5	1	2	0	7	0	1	0	4	0	1.00	0	.048	.130	.095
10 ML YEARS			748	1701	435	68	17	11	(5	6)	570	244	144	138	9	222	10	20	12	101	57	.64	33	.256	.313	.335

Andy Mota

Bats: Right **Throws:** Right **Pos:** 2B **Ht:** 5'10" **Wt:** 180 **Born:** 03/04/66 **Age:** 26

Year	Team	Lg	G	AB	H	2B	3B	HR	(Hm	Rd)	TB	R	RBI	TBB	IBB	SO	HBP	SH	SF	SB	CS	SB%	GDP	Avg	OBP	SLG
1987	Auburn	A	70	255	67	9	1	4	--	--	90	26	14	16	0	42	5	5	1	6	5	.55	7	.263	.318	.353
1988	Auburn	A	72	271	95	15	3	3	--	--	125	56	47	38	2	34	5	0	4	31	6	.84	4	.351	.434	.461
1989	Osceola	A	131	505	161	21	4	4	--	--	202	68	69	42	3	61	11	3	10	28	9	.76	9	.319	.377	.400
1990	Columbus	A	111	413	118	21	1	11	--	--	174	59	62	28	2	81	10	9	6	17	7	.71	5	.286	.341	.421
1991	Tucson	AAA	123	462	138	19	4	2	--	--	171	65	46	22	3	76	7	4	2	14	9	.61	6	.299	.339	.370
1991	Houston	NL	27	90	17	2	0	1	(0	1)	22	4	6	1	0	17	0	0	0	2	0	1.00	0	.189	.198	.244

Jose Mota

Bats: Both **Throws:** Right **Pos:** 2B **Ht:** 5' 9" **Wt:** 155 **Born:** 03/16/65 **Age:** 27

Year	Team	Lg	G	AB	H	2B	3B	HR	(Hm	Rd)	TB	R	RBI	TBB	IBB	SO	HBP	SH	SF	SB	CS	SB%	GDP	Avg	OBP	SLG
1985	Buffalo	AAA	6	18	5	0	0	0	--	--	5	3	1	2	0	0	0	0	0	0	0	.00	1	.278	.350	.278
	Niagara Fls	A	65	254	77	9	2	0	--	--	90	35	27	28	3	29	2	5	2	8	5	.62	1	.303	.374	.354
1986	Tulsa	AA	41	158	51	7	3	1	--	--	67	26	11	22	0	13	0	3	1	14	8	.64	0	.323	.403	.424
	Okla City	AAA	71	255	71	9	1	0	--	--	82	38	20	24	1	43	3	5	0	7	5	.58	7	.278	.348	.322
1987	Tulsa	AA	21	71	15	2	0	0	--	--	17	11	4	13	0	12	0	0	1	2	2	.50	0	.211	.329	.239
	San Antonio	AA	54	190	50	4	3	0	--	--	60	23	11	21	1	34	2	5	0	3	4	.43	3	.263	.343	.316
1988	Albuquerque	AAA	6	15	5	0	0	0	--	--	5	4	1	3	0	3	0	1	0	1	0	1.00	1	.333	.444	.333
	San Antonio	AA	82	214	56	11	1	1	--	--	72	32	18	27	1	35	0	3	1	10	4	.71	7	.262	.343	.336
1989	Huntsville	AA	27	81	11	1	0	0	--	--	12	15	6	30	0	15	1	5	1	3	2	.60	0	.136	.372	.148
	Wichita	AA	41	109	35	5	1	1	--	--	45	17	9	17	0	21	0	4	0	3	2	.60	1	.321	.413	.413
1990	Las Vegas	AAA	92	247	74	4	4	4	--	--	98	44	21	42	2	35	3	3	1	2	1	.67	0	.300	.406	.397
1991	Las Vegas	AAA	107	377	109	10	2	1	--	--	126	56	37	54	2	48	2	6	3	15	10	.60	10	.289	.378	.334
1991	San Diego	NL	17	36	8	0	0	0	(0	0)	8	4	2	2	0	7	1	2	0	0	0	.00	0	.222	.282	.222

Jamie Moyer

Pitches: Left **Bats:** Left **Pos:** SP **Ht:** 6' 0" **Wt:** 170 **Born:** 11/18/62 **Age:** 29

			HOW MUCH HE PITCHED					WHAT HE GAVE UP										THE RESULTS					
Year	Team	Lg	G	GS	CG	GF	IP	BFP	H	R	ER	HR	SH	SF	HB	TBB	IBB	SO	WP	Bk	W	L	Pct.	ShO	Sv	ERA
1986	Chicago	NL	16	16	1	0	87.1	395	107	52	49	10	3	3	3	42	1	45	3	3	7	4	.636	1	0	5.05
1987	Chicago	NL	35	33	1	1	201	899	210	127	114	28	14	7	5	97	9	147	11	2	12	15	.444	0	0	5.10
1988	Chicago	NL	34	30	3	1	202	855	212	84	78	20	14	4	4	55	7	121	4	0	9	15	.375	1	0	3.48
1989	Texas	AL	15	15	1	0	76	337	84	51	41	10	1	4	2	33	0	44	1	0	4	9	.308	0	0	4.86
1990	Texas	AL	33	10	1	6	102.1	447	115	59	53	6	1	7	4	39	4	58	1	0	2	6	.250	0	0	4.66
1991	St. Louis	NL	8	7	0	1	31.1	142	38	21	20	5	4	2	1	16	0	20	2	1	0	5	.000	0	0	5.74
6 ML YEARS			141	111	7	9	700	3075	766	394	355	79	37	27	19	282	21	435	22	6	34	54	.386	2	0	4.56

Terry Mulholland

Pitches: Left **Bats:** Right **Pos:** SP **Ht:** 6' 3" **Wt:** 208 **Born:** 03/09/63 **Age:** 29

			HOW MUCH HE PITCHED						WHAT HE GAVE UP												THE RESULTS					
Year	Team	Lg	G	GS	CG	GF	IP	BFP	H	R	ER	HR	SH	SF	HB	TBB	IBB	SO	WP	Bk	W	L	Pct.	ShO	Sv	ERA
1986	San Francisco	NL	15	10	0	1	54.2	245	51	33	30	3	5	1	1	35	2	27	6	0	1	7	.125	0	0	4.94
1988	San Francisco	NL	9	6	2	1	46	191	50	20	19	3	5	0	1	7	0	18	1	0	2	1	.667	1	0	3.72
1989	2 ML Teams		25	18	2	4	115.1	513	137	66	63	8	7	1	4	36	3	66	3	0	4	7	.364	1	0	4.92
1990	Philadelphia	NL	33	26	6	2	180.2	746	172	78	67	15	7	12	2	42	7	75	7	2	9	10	.474	1	0	3.34
1991	Philadelphia	NL	34	34	8	0	232	956	231	100	93	15	11	6	3	49	2	142	3	0	16	13	.552	3	0	3.61
1989	San Francisco	NL	5	1	0	2	11	51	15	5	5	0	0	0	0	4	0	6	0	0	0	0	.000	0	0	4.09
	Philadelphia	NL	20	17	2	2	104.1	462	122	61	58	8	7	1	4	32	3	60	3	0	4	7	.364	1	0	5.00
	5 ML YEARS		116	94	18	8	628.2	2651	641	297	272	44	35	20	11	169	14	328	20	2	32	38	.457	6	0	3.89

Rance Mulliniks

Bats: Left **Throws:** Right **Pos:** DH **Ht:** 6' 0" **Wt:** 175 **Born:** 01/15/56 **Age:** 36

									BATTING											BASERUNNING				PERCENTAGES		
Year	Team	Lg	G	AB	H	2B	3B	HR	(Hm	Rd)	TB	R	RBI	TBB	IBB	SO	HBP	SH	SF	SB	CS	SB%	GDP	Avg	OBP	SLG
1977	California	AL	78	271	73	13	2	3	(2	1)	99	36	21	23	2	36	1	8	0	1	1	.50	2	.269	.329	.365
1978	California	AL	50	119	22	3	1	1	(1	0)	30	6	6	8	0	23	1	0	2	2	0	1.00	3	.185	.238	.252
1979	California	AL	22	68	10	0	0	1	(0	1)	13	7	8	4	0	14	1	0	5	0	0	.00	2	.147	.192	.191
1980	Kansas City	AL	36	54	14	3	0	0	(0	0)	17	8	6	7	0	10	0	0	1	0	0	.00	2	.259	.339	.315
1981	Kansas City	AL	24	44	10	3	0	0	(0	0)	13	6	5	2	0	7	0	0	0	0	1	.00	2	.227	.261	.295
1982	Toronto	AL	112	311	76	25	0	4	(2	2)	113	32	35	37	1	49	1	3	1	3	2	.60	10	.244	.326	.363
1983	Toronto	AL	129	364	100	34	3	10	(4	6)	170	54	49	57	5	43	1	3	2	0	2	.00	14	.275	.373	.467
1984	Toronto	AL	125	343	111	21	5	3	(1	2)	151	41	42	33	3	44	1	0	2	2	3	.40	5	.324	.383	.440
1985	Toronto	AL	129	366	108	26	1	10	(4	6)	166	55	57	55	2	54	0	1	5	2	0	1.00	10	.295	.383	.454
1986	Toronto	AL	117	348	90	22	0	11	(5	6)	145	50	45	43	1	60	1	1	2	1	1	.50	12	.259	.340	.417
1987	Toronto	AL	124	332	103	28	1	11	(6	5)	166	37	44	34	1	55	0	3	3	1	1	.50	10	.310	.371	.500
1988	Toronto	AL	119	337	101	21	1	12	(7	5)	160	49	48	56	3	57	0	2	4	1	0	1.00	10	.300	.395	.475
1989	Toronto	AL	103	273	65	11	2	3	(1	2)	89	25	29	34	6	40	0	0	2	0	0	.00	12	.238	.320	.326
1990	Toronto	AL	57	97	28	4	0	2	(1	1)	38	11	16	22	2	19	0	0	1	2	1	.67	2	.289	.417	.392
1991	Toronto	AL	97	240	60	12	1	2	(1	1)	80	27	24	44	2	44	0	0	2	0	0	.00	9	.250	.364	.333
	15 ML YEARS		1322	3567	971	226	17	73	(35	38)	1450	444	435	459	28	555	7	21	32	15	12	.56	105	.272	.354	.407

Mike Munoz

Pitches: Left **Bats:** Left **Pos:** RP **Ht:** 6' 3" **Wt:** 195 **Born:** 07/12/65 **Age:** 26

			HOW MUCH HE PITCHED						WHAT HE GAVE UP												THE RESULTS					
Year	Team	Lg	G	GS	CG	GF	IP	BFP	H	R	ER	HR	SH	SF	HB	TBB	IBB	SO	WP	Bk	W	L	Pct.	ShO	Sv	ERA
1986	Great Falls	R	14	14	2	0	81.1	0	85	44	29	4	0	0	1	38	0	49	3	0	4	4	.500	2	0	3.21
1987	Bakersfield	A	52	12	2	23	118	524	125	68	49	5	11	2	0	43	3	80	6	1	8	7	.533	0	8	3.74
1988	San Antonio	AA	56	0	0	35	71.2	302	63	18	8	0	5	1	1	24	1	71	6	0	7	2	.778	0	14	1.00
1989	Albuquerque	AAA	60	0	0	27	79	345	72	32	27	2	6	3	0	40	8	81	6	0	6	4	.600	0	6	3.08
1990	Albuquerque	AAA	49	0	0	14	59.1	258	65	33	28	8	4	2	0	19	3	40	3	1	4	1	.800	0	6	4.25
1991	Toledo	AAA	38	0	0	19	54	235	44	30	23	4	2	1	0	35	4	38	2	0	2	3	.400	0	8	3.83
1989	Los Angeles	NL	3	0	0	1	2.2	14	5	5	5	1	0	0	0	2	0	3	0	0	0	0	.000	0	0	16.88
1990	Los Angeles	NL	8	0	0	3	5.2	24	6	2	2	0	1	0	0	3	0	2	0	0	0	1	.000	0	0	3.18
1991	Detroit	AL	6	0	0	4	9.1	46	14	10	10	0	0	1	0	5	0	3	1	0	0	0	.000	0	0	9.64
	3 ML YEARS		17	0	0	8	17.2	84	25	17	17	1	1	1	0	10	0	8	1	0	0	1	.000	0	0	8.66

Pedro Munoz

Bats: Right **Throws:** Right **Pos:** RF **Ht:** 5'10" **Wt:** 200 **Born:** 09/19/68 **Age:** 23

									BATTING											BASERUNNING				PERCENTAGES		
Year	Team	Lg	G	AB	H	2B	3B	HR	(Hm	Rd)	TB	R	RBI	TBB	IBB	SO	HBP	SH	SF	SB	CS	SB%	GDP	Avg	OBP	SLG
1985	Blue Jays	R	40	145	38	3	0	2	--	--	47	14	17	9	0	20	4	1	1	4	1	.80	4	.262	.321	.324
1986	Florence	A	122	445	131	16	5	14	--	--	199	69	82	54	4	100	5	2	2	9	5	.64	12	.294	.375	.447
1987	Dunedin	A	92	341	80	11	5	8	--	--	125	55	44	34	0	74	2	1	4	13	4	.76	7	.235	.304	.367
1988	Dunedin	A	133	481	141	21	7	8	--	--	200	59	73	52	5	87	4	0	7	15	4	.79	23	.293	.362	.416
1989	Knoxville	AA	122	442	118	15	4	19	--	--	198	54	65	20	2	85	2	0	4	10	4	.71	11	.267	.299	.448
1990	Syracuse	AAA	86	317	101	22	3	7	--	--	150	41	56	24	3	64	1	0	3	16	7	.70	12	.319	.365	.473
	Portland	AAA	30	110	35	4	0	5	--	--	54	19	21	15	1	18	4	0	0	8	4	.67	1	.318	.419	.491
1991	Portland	AAA	56	212	67	19	2	5	--	--	105	33	28	19	3	42	1	0	1	9	5	.64	6	.316	.373	.495
1990	Minnesota	AL	22	85	23	4	1	0	(0	0)	29	13	5	2	0	16	0	1	2	3	0	1.00	3	.271	.281	.341
1991	Minnesota	AL	51	138	39	7	1	7	(4	3)	69	15	26	9	0	31	1	1	2	3	0	1.00	2	.283	.327	.500
	2 ML YEARS		73	223	62	11	2	7	(4	3)	98	28	31	11	0	47	1	2	4	6	0	1.00	5	.278	.310	.439

Dale Murphy

Bats: Right **Throws:** Right **Pos:** RF **Ht:** 6' 4" **Wt:** 221 **Born:** 03/12/56 **Age:** 36

					BATTING															BASERUNNING				PERCENTAGES		
Year	Team	Lg	G	AB	H	2B	3B	HR	(Hm	Rd)	TB	R	RBI	TBB	IBB	SO	HBP	SH	SF	SB	CS	SB%	GDP	Avg	OBP	SLG
1976	Atlanta	NL	19	65	17	6	0	0	(0	0)	23	3	9	7	0	9	0	0	0	0	0	.00	0	.262	.333	.354
1977	Atlanta	NL	18	76	24	8	1	2	(0	2)	40	5	14	0	0	8	0	0	0	0	1	.00	3	.316	.316	.526
1978	Atlanta	NL	151	530	120	14	3	23	(17	6)	209	66	79	42	3	145	3	3	5	11	7	.61	15	.226	.284	.394
1979	Atlanta	NL	104	384	106	7	2	21	(12	9)	180	53	57	38	5	67	2	0	5	6	1	.86	12	.276	.340	.469
1980	Atlanta	NL	156	569	160	27	2	33	(17	16)	290	98	89	59	9	133	1	2	2	9	6	.60	8	.281	.349	.510
1981	Atlanta	NL	104	369	91	12	1	13	(8	5)	144	43	50	44	8	72	0	1	2	14	5	.74	10	.247	.325	.390
1982	Atlanta	NL	162	598	168	23	2	36	(24	12)	303	113	109	93	9	134	3	0	4	23	11	.68	10	.281	.378	.507
1983	Atlanta	NL	162	589	178	24	4	36	(17	19)	318	131	121	90	12	110	2	0	6	30	4	.88	15	.302	.393	.540
1984	Atlanta	NL	162	607	176	32	8	36	(18	18)	332	94	100	79	20	134	2	0	3	19	7	.73	13	.290	.372	.547
1985	Atlanta	NL	162	616	185	32	2	37	(19	18)	332	118	111	90	15	141	1	0	5	10	3	.77	14	.300	.388	.539
1986	Atlanta	NL	160	614	163	29	7	29	(17	12)	293	89	83	75	5	141	2	0	1	7	7	.50	10	.265	.347	.477
1987	Atlanta	NL	159	566	167	27	1	44	(25	19)	328	115	105	115	29	136	7	0	5	16	6	.73	11	.295	.417	.580
1988	Atlanta	NL	156	592	134	35	4	24	(14	10)	249	77	77	74	16	125	2	0	3	3	5	.38	24	.226	.313	.421
1989	Atlanta	NL	154	574	131	16	0	20	(9	11)	207	60	84	65	10	142	2	0	6	3	2	.60	14	.228	.306	.361
1990	2 ML Teams		154	563	138	23	1	24	(9	15)	235	60	83	61	14	130	1	0	4	9	3	.75	22	.245	.318	.417
1991	Philadelphia	NL	153	544	137	33	1	18	(9	9)	226	66	81	48	3	93	0	0	7	1	0	1.00	20	.252	.309	.415
1990	Atlanta	NL	97	349	81	14	0	17	(8	9)	146	38	55	41	11	84	1	0	3	9	2	.82	11	.232	.312	.418
	Philadelphia	NL	57	214	57	9	1	7	(1	6)	89	22	28	20	3	46	0	0	1	0	1	.00	11	.266	.328	.416
16 ML YEARS			2136	7856	2095	348	39	396	(215	181)	3709	1191	1252	980	158	1720	28	6	58	161	68	.70	201	.267	.348	.472

Rob Murphy

Pitches: Left **Bats:** Left **Pos:** RP **Ht:** 6' 2" **Wt:** 215 **Born:** 05/26/60 **Age:** 32

			HOW MUCH HE PITCHED						WHAT HE GAVE UP									THE RESULTS					
Year	Team	Lg	G	GS	CG	GF	IP	BFP	H	R	ER	HR	SH	SF	HB	TBB	IBB	SO	WP	Bk	W	L	Pct.	ShO	Sv	ERA
1985	Cincinnati	NL	2	0	0	2	3	12	2	2	2	1	0	0	0	2	0	1	0	0	0	0	.000	0	0	6.00
1986	Cincinnati	NL	34	0	0	12	50.1	195	26	4	4	0	3	0	0	21	2	36	5	0	6	0	1.000	0	1	0.72
1987	Cincinnati	NL	87	0	0	21	100.2	415	91	37	34	7	1	2	0	32	5	99	1	0	8	5	.615	0	3	3.04
1988	Cincinnati	NL	76	0	0	28	84.2	350	69	34	29	3	9	1	1	38	6	74	5	1	0	6	.000	0	3	3.08
1989	Boston	AL	74	0	0	27	105	438	97	38	32	7	7	3	1	41	8	107	6	0	5	7	.417	0	9	2.74
1990	Boston	AL	68	0	0	20	57	285	85	46	40	10	4	4	1	32	3	54	4	0	0	6	.000	0	7	6.32
1991	Seattle	AL	57	0	0	26	48	211	47	17	16	4	3	0	1	19	4	34	4	0	0	1	.000	0	4	3.00
7 ML YEARS			398	0	0	136	448.2	1906	417	175	157	32	27	13	4	185	28	405	25	1	19	25	.432	0	27	3.15

Eddie Murray

Bats: Both **Throws:** Right **Pos:** 1B **Ht:** 6' 2" **Wt:** 222 **Born:** 02/24/56 **Age:** 36

					BATTING															BASERUNNING				PERCENTAGES		
Year	Team	Lg	G	AB	H	2B	3B	HR	(Hm	Rd)	TB	R	RBI	TBB	IBB	SO	HBP	SH	SF	SB	CS	SB%	GDP	Avg	OBP	SLG
1977	Baltimore	AL	160	611	173	29	2	27	(14	13)	287	81	88	48	6	104	1	0	6	0	1	.00	22	.283	.333	.470
1978	Baltimore	AL	161	610	174	32	3	27	(10	17)	293	85	95	70	7	97	1	1	8	6	5	.55	15	.285	.356	.480
1979	Baltimore	AL	159	606	179	30	2	25	(10	15)	288	90	99	72	9	78	2	1	6	10	2	.83	16	.295	.369	.475
1980	Baltimore	AL	158	621	186	36	2	32	(10	22)	322	100	116	54	10	71	2	0	6	7	2	.78	18	.300	.354	.519
1981	Baltimore	AL	99	378	111	21	2	22	(12	10)	202	57	78	40	10	43	1	0	3	2	3	.40	10	.294	.360	.534
1982	Baltimore	AL	151	550	174	30	1	32	(18	14)	302	87	110	70	18	82	1	0	6	7	2	.78	17	.316	.391	.549
1983	Baltimore	AL	156	582	178	30	3	33	(16	17)	313	115	111	86	13	90	3	0	9	5	1	.83	13	.306	.393	.538
1984	Baltimore	AL	162	588	180	26	3	29	(18	11)	299	97	110	107	25	87	2	0	8	10	2	.83	9	.306	.410	.509
1985	Baltimore	AL	156	583	173	37	1	31	(15	16)	305	111	124	84	12	68	2	0	8	5	2	.71	8	.297	.383	.523
1986	Baltimore	AL	137	495	151	25	1	17	(9	8)	229	61	84	78	7	49	0	0	5	3	0	1.00	11	.305	.396	.463
1987	Baltimore	AL	160	618	171	28	3	30	(14	16)	295	89	91	73	6	80	0	0	3	1	2	.33	15	.277	.352	.477
1988	Baltimore	AL	161	603	171	27	2	28	(14	14)	286	75	84	75	8	78	0	0	3	5	2	.71	20	.284	.361	.474
1989	Los Angeles	NL	160	594	147	29	1	20	(4	16)	238	66	88	87	24	85	2	0	7	7	2	.78	12	.247	.342	.401
1990	Los Angeles	NL	155	558	184	22	3	26	(12	14)	290	96	95	82	21	64	1	0	4	8	5	.62	19	.330	.414	.520
1991	Los Angeles	NL	153	576	150	23	1	19	(11	8)	232	69	96	55	17	74	0	0	8	10	3	.77	17	.260	.321	.403
15 ML YEARS			2288	8573	2502	425	30	398	(187	211)	4181	1279	1469	1081	193	1150	18	2	90	86	34	.72	228	.292	.369	.488

Mike Mussina

Pitches: Right **Bats:** Right **Pos:** SP **Ht:** 6' 2" **Wt:** 185 **Born:** 12/08/68 **Age:** 23

			HOW MUCH HE PITCHED						WHAT HE GAVE UP									THE RESULTS					
Year	Team	Lg	G	GS	CG	GF	IP	BFP	H	R	ER	HR	SH	SF	HB	TBB	IBB	SO	WP	Bk	W	L	Pct.	ShO	Sv	ERA
1990	Hagerstown	AA	7	7	2	0	42.1	168	34	10	7	1	1	1	0	7	0	40	3	1	3	0	1.000	1	0	1.49

Year Team	Lg	G	GS	CG	GF	IP	BFP	H	R	ER	HR	SH	SF	HB	TBB	IBB	SO	WP	Bk	W	L	Pct.	ShO	Sv	ERA
Rochester	AAA	2	2	0	0	13.1	50	8	2	2	2	0	0	0	4	0	15	0	0	0	0	.000	0	0	1.35
1991 Rochester	AAA	19	19	3	0	122.1	497	108	42	39	9	3	1	2	31	0	107	6	1	10	4	.714	1	0	2.87
1991 Baltimore	AL	12	12	2	0	87.2	349	77	31	28	7	3	2	1	21	0	52	3	1	4	5	.444	0	0	2.87

Jeff Mutis

Pitches: Left **Bats:** Left **Pos:** SP   **Ht:** 6' 2" **Wt:** 185 **Born:** 12/20/66 **Age:** 25

		HOW MUCH HE PITCHED						WHAT HE GAVE UP												THE RESULTS					
Year Team	Lg	G	GS	CG	GF	IP	BFP	H	R	ER	HR	SH	SF	HB	TBB	IBB	SO	WP	Bk	W	L	Pct.	ShO	Sv	ERA
1988 Burlington	R	3	3	0	0	22	79	8	1	1	0	0	0	0	6	0	20	1	2	3	0	1.000	0	0	0.41
Kinston	A	1	1	0	0	5.2	24	6	1	1	0	1	0	0	3	0	2	1	0	1	0	1.000	0	0	1.59
1989 Kinston	A	16	15	5	1	99.2	406	87	42	29	6	1	4	2	20	0	68	3	2	7	3	.700	2	0	2.62
1990 Canton-Akrn	AA	26	26	7	0	165	702	178	73	58	6	3	2	3	44	2	94	5	1	11	10	.524	3	0	3.16
1991 Canton-Akrn	AA	25	24	7	0	169.2	682	138	42	34	0	8	4	6	51	2	89	3	1	11	5	.688	4	0	1.80
1991 Cleveland	AL	3	3	0	0	12.1	68	23	16	16	1	2	1	0	7	1	6	1	0	0	3	.000	0	0	11.68

Greg Myers

Bats: Left **Throws:** Right **Pos:** C   **Ht:** 6' 2" **Wt:** 206 **Born:** 04/14/66 **Age:** 26

		BATTING															BASERUNNING			PERCENTAGES		
Year Team	Lg	G	AB	H	2B	3B	HR	(Hm | Rd)	TB	R	RBI	TBB	IBB	SO	HBP	SH	SF	SB	CS	SB%	GDP	Avg	OBP	SLG
1987 Toronto	AL	7	9	1	0	0	0	(0 | 0)	1	1	0	0	0	3	0	0	0	0	0	.00	2	.111	.111	.111
1989 Toronto	AL	17	44	5	2	0	0	(0 | 0)	7	0	1	2	0	9	0	0	0	0	1	.00	2	.114	.152	.159
1990 Toronto	AL	87	250	59	7	1	5	(3 | 2)	83	33	22	22	0	33	0	1	4	0	1	.00	12	.236	.293	.332
1991 Toronto	AL	107	309	81	22	0	8	(5 | 3)	127	25	36	21	4	45	0	0	3	0	0	.00	13	.262	.306	.411
4 ML YEARS		218	612	146	31	1	13	(8 | 5)	218	59	59	45	4	90	0	1	7	0	2	.00	29	.239	.288	.356

Randy Myers

Pitches: Left **Bats:** Left **Pos:** RP/SP   **Ht:** 6' 1" **Wt:** 215 **Born:** 09/19/62 **Age:** 29

		HOW MUCH HE PITCHED						WHAT HE GAVE UP												THE RESULTS					
Year Team	Lg	G	GS	CG	GF	IP	BFP	H	R	ER	HR	SH	SF	HB	TBB	IBB	SO	WP	Bk	W	L	Pct.	ShO	Sv	ERA
1985 New York	NL	1	0	0	1	2	7	0	0	0	0	0	0	0	1	0	2	0	0	0	0	.000	0	0	0.00
1986 New York	NL	10	0	0	5	10.2	53	11	5	5	1	0	0	0	9	1	13	0	0	0	0	.000	0	0	4.22
1987 New York	NL	54	0	0	18	75	314	61	36	33	6	7	6	0	30	5	92	3	0	3	6	.333	0	6	3.96
1988 New York	NL	55	0	0	44	68	261	45	15	13	5	3	2	2	17	2	69	2	0	7	3	.700	0	26	1.72
1989 New York	NL	65	0	0	47	84.1	349	62	23	22	4	6	2	0	40	4	88	3	0	7	4	.636	0	24	2.35
1990 Cincinnati	NL	66	0	0	59	86.2	353	59	24	20	6	4	2	3	38	8	98	2	1	4	6	.400	0	31	2.08
1991 Cincinnati	NL	58	12	1	18	132	575	116	61	52	8	8	6	1	80	5	108	2	1	6	13	.316	0	6	3.55
7 ML YEARS		309	12	1	192	458.2	1912	354	164	145	30	28	18	7	215	25	470	12	2	27	32	.458	0	93	2.85

Chris Nabholz

Pitches: Left **Bats:** Left **Pos:** SP   **Ht:** 6' 5" **Wt:** 210 **Born:** 01/05/67 **Age:** 25

		HOW MUCH HE PITCHED						WHAT HE GAVE UP												THE RESULTS					
Year Team	Lg	G	GS	CG	GF	IP	BFP	H	R	ER	HR	SH	SF	HB	TBB	IBB	SO	WP	Bk	W	L	Pct.	ShO	Sv	ERA
1989 Rockford	A	24	23	3	0	161.1	654	132	54	39	6	5	4	0	41	0	149	11	2	13	5	.722	3	0	2.18
1990 Jacksnville	AA	11	11	0	0	74.1	304	62	28	25	6	1	1	0	27	0	77	6	1	7	2	.778	0	0	3.03
Indianapols	AAA	10	10	0	0	63.1	274	66	38	34	7	1	6	1	28	0	44	3	0	0	6	.000	0	0	4.83
1991 Indianapols	AAA	4	4	0	0	19.1	74	13	5	4	2	1	0	0	5	0	16	0	0	2	2	.500	0	0	1.86
1990 Montreal	NL	11	11	1	0	70	282	43	23	22	6	1	2	2	32	1	53	1	1	6	2	.750	1	0	2.83
1991 Montreal	NL	24	24	1	0	153.2	631	134	66	62	5	2	4	2	57	4	99	3	1	8	7	.533	0	0	3.63
2 ML YEARS		35	35	2	0	223.2	913	177	89	84	11	3	6	4	89	5	152	4	2	14	9	.609	1	0	3.38

Tim Naehring

Bats: Right **Throws:** Right **Pos:** SS   **Ht:** 6' 2" **Wt:** 190 **Born:** 02/01/67 **Age:** 25

		BATTING															BASERUNNING			PERCENTAGES		
Year Team	Lg	G	AB	H	2B	3B	HR	(Hm	Rd)	TB	R	RBI	TBB	IBB	SO	HBP	SH	SF	SB	CS	SB%	GDP	Avg	OBP	SLG
1988 Elmira	A	19	59	18	3	0	1	--	--	24	6	13	8	0	11	1	1	4	0	0	.00	1	.305	.375	.407
Winter Havn	A	42	141	32	7	0	0	--	--	39	17	10	19	1	24	3	0	1	1	1	.50	1	.227	.329	.277
1989 Lynchburg	A	56	209	63	7	1	4	--	--	84	24	37	23	0	30	0	1	3	2	0	1.00	3	.301	.366	.402
Pawtucket	AAA	79	273	75	16	1	3	--	--	102	32	31	27	1	41	3	2	7	2	3	.40	6	.275	.339	.374
1990 Pawtucket	AAA	82	290	78	16	1	15	--	--	141	45	47	37	2	56	3	2	0	0	1	.00	6	.269	.354	.486
1990 Boston	AL	24	85	23	6	0	2	(2	0)	35	10	12	8	1	15	0	0	0	0	0	.00	2	.271	.333	.412
1991 Boston	AL	20	55	6	1	0	0	(0	0)	7	1	3	6	0	15	0	4	0	0	0	.00	0	.109	.197	.127
2 ML YEARS		44	140	29	7	0	2	(2	0)	42	11	15	14	1	30	0	4	0	0	0	.00	2	.207	.279	.300

Charles Nagy

Pitches: Right Bats: Left Pos: SP   Ht: 6' 3" Wt: 200 Born: 05/05/67 Age: 25

Year Team	Lg	G	GS	CG	GF	IP	BFP	H	R	ER	HR	SH	SF	HB	TBB	IBB	SO	WP	Bk	W	L	Pct.	ShO	Sv	ERA
1989 Kinston	A	13	13	6	0	95.1	373	69	22	16	0	1	3	4	24	0	99	3	0	8	4	.667	4	0	1.51
Canton-Akrn	AA	15	14	2	0	94	400	102	44	35	4	3	2	2	32	0	65	7	0	4	5	.444	0	0	3.35
1990 Canton-Akrn	AA	23	23	9	0	175	694	132	62	49	9	4	4	6	39	0	99	3	3	13	8	.619	0	0	2.52
1990 Cleveland	AL	9	8	0	1	45.2	208	58	31	30	7	1	1	1	21	1	26	1	1	2	4	.333	0	0	5.91
1991 Cleveland	AL	33	33	6	0	211.1	914	228	103	97	15	5	9	6	66	7	109	6	2	10	15	.400	1	0	4.13
2 ML YEARS		42	41	6	1	257	1122	286	134	127	22	6	10	7	87	8	135	7	3	12	19	.387	1	0	4.45

Jaime Navarro

Pitches: Right Bats: Right Pos: SP   Ht: 6' 4" Wt: 210 Born: 03/27/67 Age: 25

Year Team	Lg	G	GS	CG	GF	IP	BFP	H	R	ER	HR	SH	SF	HB	TBB	IBB	SO	WP	Bk	W	L	Pct.	ShO	Sv	ERA
1989 Milwaukee	AL	19	17	1	1	109.2	470	119	47	38	6	5	2	1	32	3	56	3	0	7	8	.467	0	0	3.12
1990 Milwaukee	AL	32	22	3	2	149.1	654	176	83	74	11	4	5	4	41	3	75	6	5	8	7	.533	0	1	4.46
1991 Milwaukee	AL	34	34	10	0	234	1002	237	117	102	18	7	8	6	73	3	114	10	0	15	12	.556	2	0	3.92
3 ML YEARS		85	73	14	3	493	2126	532	247	214	35	16	15	11	146	9	245	19	5	30	27	.526	2	1	3.91

Denny Neagle

Pitches: Left Bats: Left Pos: RP/SP   Ht: 6' 4" Wt: 200 Born: 09/13/68 Age: 23

Year Team	Lg	G	GS	CG	GF	IP	BFP	H	R	ER	HR	SH	SF	HB	TBB	IBB	SO	WP	Bk	W	L	Pct.	ShO	Sv	ERA
1989 Elizabethtn	R	6	3	0	3	22	91	20	11	11	1	1	1	1	8	0	32	1	1	1	2	.333	0	1	4.50
Kenosha	A	6	6	1	0	43.2	166	25	9	8	3	5	1	1	16	0	40	1	0	2	1	.667	1	0	1.65
1990 Visalia	A	10	10	0	0	63	241	39	13	10	2	1	1	0	16	0	92	0	2	8	0	1.000	0	0	1.43
Orlando	AA	17	17	4	0	121.1	486	94	40	33	11	4	2	5	31	0	94	2	0	12	3	.800	1	0	2.45
1991 Portland	AAA	19	17	1	1	104.2	438	101	41	38	6	4	2	2	32	1	94	4	0	9	4	.692	1	0	3.27
1991 Minnesota	AL	7	3	0	2	20	92	28	9	9	3	0	0	0	7	2	14	1	0	0	1	.000	0	0	4.05

Gene Nelson

Pitches: Right Bats: Right Pos: RP   Ht: 6' 0" Wt: 174 Born: 12/03/60 Age: 31

Year Team	Lg	G	GS	CG	GF	IP	BFP	H	R	ER	HR	SH	SF	HB	TBB	IBB	SO	WP	Bk	W	L	Pct.	ShO	Sv	ERA
1981 New York	AL	8	7	0	0	39	179	40	24	21	5	0	2	1	23	1	16	2	0	3	1	.750	0	0	4.85
1982 Seattle	AL	22	19	2	2	122.2	545	133	70	63	16	4	2	2	60	1	71	4	2	6	9	.400	1	0	4.62
1983 Seattle	AL	10	5	1	2	32	153	38	29	28	6	2	0	1	21	2	11	1	0	0	3	.000	0	0	7.88
1984 Chicago	AL	20	9	2	4	74.2	304	72	38	37	9	1	2	1	17	0	36	4	1	3	5	.375	0	0	4.46
1985 Chicago	AL	46	18	1	11	145.2	643	144	74	69	23	9	2	7	67	4	101	11	1	10	10	.500	0	2	4.26
1986 Chicago	AL	54	1	0	26	114.2	488	118	52	49	7	7	1	3	41	5	70	3	0	6	6	.500	0	6	3.85
1987 Oakland	AL	54	6	0	15	123.2	530	120	58	54	12	3	5	5	35	0	94	7	0	6	5	.545	0	3	3.93
1988 Oakland	AL	54	1	0	20	111.2	456	93	42	38	9	3	4	3	38	4	67	4	6	9	6	.600	0	3	3.06
1989 Oakland	AL	50	0	0	15	80	335	60	33	29	5	3	4	2	30	3	70	5	0	3	5	.375	0	3	3.26
1990 Oakland	AL	51	0	0	17	74.2	291	55	14	13	5	1	5	3	17	1	38	1	0	3	3	.500	0	5	1.57
1991 Oakland	AL	44	0	0	11	48.2	229	60	38	37	12	3	4	3	23	1	23	0	0	1	5	.167	0	0	6.84
11 ML YEARS		413	66	6	123	967.1	4153	933	472	438	109	36	31	31	372	22	597	42	10	50	58	.463	1	23	4.08

Al Newman

Bats: Both Throws: Right Pos: SS/2B/3B   Ht: 5' 9" Wt: 198 Born: 06/30/60 Age: 32

Year Team	Lg	G	AB	H	2B	3B	HR	(Hm	Rd)	TB	R	RBI	TBB	IBB	SO	HBP	SH	SF	SB	CS	SB%	GDP	Avg	OBP	SLG
1985 Montreal	NL	25	29	5	1	0	0	(0	0)	6	7	1	3	0	4	0	0	0	2	1	.67	0	.172	.250	.207
1986 Montreal	NL	95	185	37	3	0	1	(0	1)	43	23	8	21	2	20	0	4	2	11	11	.50	4	.200	.279	.232
1987 Minnesota	AL	110	307	68	15	5	0	(0	0)	93	44	29	34	0	27	0	7	1	15	11	.58	5	.221	.298	.303
1988 Minnesota	AL	105	260	58	7	0	0	(0	0)	65	35	19	29	0	34	0	6	0	12	3	.80	4	.223	.250	.250
1989 Minnesota	AL	141	446	113	18	2	0	(0	0)	135	62	38	59	0	46	2	10	4	25	12	.68	3	.253	.341	.303
1990 Minnesota	AL	144	388	94	14	0	0	(0	0)	108	43	30	33	0	34	2	8	2	13	6	.68	7	.242	.304	.278
1991 Minnesota	AL	118	246	47	5	0	0	(0	0)	52	25	19	23	0	21	1	5	3	4	5	.44	5	.191	.260	.211
7 ML YEARS		738	1861	422	63	7	1	(0	1)	502	239	144	202	2	186	5	40	12	82	49	.63	28	.227	.302	.270

Warren Newson

Bats: Left **Throws:** Left **Pos:** RF/LF **Ht:** 5' 7" **Wt:** 190 **Born:** 07/03/64 **Age:** 27

						BATTING													BASERUNNING				PERCENTAGES		
Year	Team	Lg	G	AB	H	2B	3B	HR	(Hm | Rd)	TB	R	RBI	TBB	IBB	SO	HBP	SH	SF	SB	CS	SB%	GDP	Avg	OBP	SLG
1986	Spokane	A	54	159	37	8	1	2	--	--	53	29	31	47	1	37	0	1	1	3	1	.75	5	.233	.406	.333
1987	Chston-Sc	A	58	191	66	12	2	7	--	--	103	50	32	52	1	35	0	2	1	13	7	.65	5	.346	.484	.539
	Reno	A	51	165	51	7	2	6	--	--	80	44	28	39	0	34	0	2	1	2	6	.25	1	.309	.439	.485
1988	Riverside	A	130	438	130	23	7	22	--	--	233	99	91	107	3	102	0	0	3	36	19	.65	11	.297	.432	.532
1989	Wichita	AA	128	427	130	20	6	18	--	--	216	94	70	103	10	99	0	1	5	20	9	.69	9	.304	.436	.506
1990	Las Vegas	AAA	123	404	123	20	3	13	--	--	188	80	58	83	3	110	0	1	4	13	5	.72	10	.304	.420	.465
1991	Vancouver	AAA	33	111	41	12	1	2	--	--	61	19	19	30	1	26	0	0	2	5	4	.56	2	.369	.497	.550
1991	Chicago	AL	71	132	39	5	0	4	(1 | 3)	56	20	25	28	1	34	0	0	0	2	2	.50	4	.295	.419	.424

Carl Nichols

Bats: Right **Throws:** Right **Pos:** C **Ht:** 6' 0" **Wt:** 192 **Born:** 10/14/62 **Age:** 29

						BATTING													BASERUNNING				PERCENTAGES		
Year	Team	Lg	G	AB	H	2B	3B	HR	(Hm	Rd)	TB	R	RBI	TBB	IBB	SO	HBP	SH	SF	SB	CS	SB%	GDP	Avg	OBP	SLG
1986	Baltimore	AL	5	5	0	0	0	0	(0	0)	0	0	0	1	1	4	0	0	0	0	0	.00	0	.000	.167	.000
1987	Baltimore	AL	13	21	8	1	0	0	(0	0)	9	4	3	1	0	4	0	1	0	0	0	.00	0	.381	.409	.429
1988	Baltimore	AL	18	47	9	1	0	0	(0	0)	10	2	1	3	0	10	0	1	1	0	0	.00	3	.191	.235	.213
1989	Houston	NL	8	13	1	0	0	0	(0	0)	1	0	2	0	0	3	0	0	0	0	0	.00	0	.077	.077	.077
1990	Houston	NL	32	49	10	3	0	0	(0	0)	13	7	11	8	1	11	1	1	2	0	0	.00	1	.204	.317	.265
1991	Houston	NL	20	51	10	3	0	0	(0	0)	13	3	1	5	1	17	0	0	0	0	0	.00	0	.196	.268	.255
	6 ML YEARS		96	186	38	8	0	0	(0	0)	46	16	18	18	3	49	1	3	3	0	0	.00	4	.204	.274	.247

Rod Nichols

Pitches: Right **Bats:** Right **Pos:** SP/RP **Ht:** 6' 2" **Wt:** 190 **Born:** 12/29/64 **Age:** 27

			HOW MUCH HE PITCHED					WHAT HE GAVE UP										THE RESULTS						
Year	Team	Lg	G	GS	CG	GF	IP	BFP	H	R	ER	HR	SH	SF	HB	TBB	IBB	SO	WP	Bk	W	L	Pct.	ShO	Sv	ERA
1988	Cleveland	AL	11	10	3	1	69.1	297	73	41	39	5	2	2	2	23	1	31	2	3	1	7	.125	0	0	5.06
1989	Cleveland	AL	15	11	0	2	71.2	315	81	42	35	9	3	2	2	24	0	42	0	0	4	6	.400	0	0	4.40
1990	Cleveland	AL	4	2	0	0	16	79	24	14	14	5	1	0	2	6	0	3	0	0	0	3	.000	0	0	7.88
1991	Cleveland	AL	31	16	3	4	137.1	578	145	63	54	6	6	4	6	30	3	76	3	0	2	11	.154	1	1	3.54
	4 ML YEARS		61	39	6	7	294.1	1269	323	160	142	25	12	8	12	83	4	152	5	3	7	27	.206	1	1	4.34

Otis Nixon

Bats: Both **Throws:** Right **Pos:** LF/CF/RF **Ht:** 6' 2" **Wt:** 180 **Born:** 01/09/59 **Age:** 33

						BATTING													BASERUNNING				PERCENTAGES		
Year	Team	Lg	G	AB	H	2B	3B	HR	(Hm	Rd)	TB	R	RBI	TBB	IBB	SO	HBP	SH	SF	SB	CS	SB%	GDP	Avg	OBP	SLG
1983	New York	AL	13	14	2	0	0	0	(0	0)	2	2	0	1	0	5	0	0	0	2	0	1.00	0	.143	.200	.143
1984	Cleveland	AL	49	91	14	0	0	0	(0	0)	14	16	1	8	0	11	0	3	1	12	6	.67	2	.154	.220	.154
1985	Cleveland	AL	104	162	38	4	0	3	(1	2)	51	34	9	8	0	27	0	4	0	20	11	.65	2	.235	.271	.315
1986	Cleveland	AL	105	95	25	4	1	0	(0	0)	31	33	8	13	0	12	0	2	0	23	6	.79	1	.263	.352	.326
1987	Cleveland	AL	19	17	1	0	0	0	(0	0)	1	2	1	3	0	4	0	0	0	2	3	.40	0	.059	.200	.059
1988	Montreal	NL	90	271	66	8	2	0	(0	0)	78	47	15	28	0	42	0	4	2	46	13	.78	0	.244	.312	.288
1989	Montreal	NL	126	258	56	7	2	0	(0	0)	67	41	21	33	1	36	0	2	0	37	12	.76	4	.217	.306	.260
1990	Montreal	NL	119	231	58	6	2	1	(0	1)	71	46	20	28	0	33	0	3	1	50	13	.79	2	.251	.331	.307
1991	Atlanta	NL	124	401	119	10	1	0	(0	0)	131	81	26	47	3	40	2	7	3	72	21	.77	5	.297	.371	.327
	9 ML YEARS		749	1540	379	39	8	4	(1	3)	446	302	101	169	4	210	2	25	7	264	85	.76	16	.246	.320	.290

Junior Noboa

Bats: Right **Throws:** Right **Pos:** 2B **Ht:** 5'10" **Wt:** 165 **Born:** 11/10/64 **Age:** 27

						BATTING													BASERUNNING				PERCENTAGES		
Year	Team	Lg	G	AB	H	2B	3B	HR	(Hm	Rd)	TB	R	RBI	TBB	IBB	SO	HBP	SH	SF	SB	CS	SB%	GDP	Avg	OBP	SLG
1984	Cleveland	AL	23	11	4	0	0	0	(0	0)	4	3	0	0	0	2	0	1	0	1	0	1.00	1	.364	.364	.364
1987	Cleveland	AL	39	80	18	2	1	0	(0	0)	22	7	7	3	1	6	0	5	0	1	0	1.00	1	.225	.253	.275
1988	California	AL	21	16	1	0	0	0	(0	0)	1	4	0	0	0	1	0	0	0	0	0	.00	2	.063	.063	.063
1989	Montreal	NL	21	44	10	0	0	0	(0	0)	10	3	1	1	0	3	0	0	0	0	0	.00	0	.227	.244	.227
1990	Montreal	NL	81	158	42	7	2	0	(0	0)	53	15	14	7	2	14	1	3	4	4	1	.80	2	.266	.294	.335
1991	Montreal	NL	67	95	23	3	0	1	(0	1)	29	5	2	1	1	8	0	0	0	2	3	.40	1	.242	.250	.305
	6 ML YEARS		252	404	98	12	3	1	(0	1)	119	37	24	12	4	34	1	9	4	8	4	.67	7	.243	.264	.295

Matt Nokes

Bats: Left   **Throws:** Right   **Pos:** C   **Ht:** 6' 1" **Wt:** 191 **Born:** 10/31/63 **Age:** 28

				BATTING														BASERUNNING				PERCENTAGES		
Year Team	Lg	G	AB	H	2B	3B	HR	(Hm	Rd)	TB	R	RBI	TBB	IBB	SO	HBP	SH	SF	SB	CS	SB%	GDP	Avg	OBP	SLG
1985 San Francisco	NL	19	53	11	2	0	2	(1	1)	19	3	5	1	0	9	1	0	0	0	0	.00	2	.208	.236	.358
1986 Detroit	AL	7	24	8	1	0	1	(0	1)	12	2	2	1	1	1	0	0	0	0	0	.00	1	.333	.360	.500
1987 Detroit	AL	135	461	133	14	2	32	(14	18)	247	69	87	35	2	70	6	3	3	2	1	.67	13	.289	.345	.536
1988 Detroit	AL	122	382	96	18	0	16	(9	7)	162	53	53	34	3	58	1	6	2	0	1	.00	11	.251	.313	.424
1989 Detroit	AL	87	268	67	10	0	9	(7	2)	104	15	39	17	1	37	2	1	2	1	0	1.00	7	.250	.298	.388
1990 2 ML Teams		136	351	87	9	1	11	(4	7)	131	33	40	24	6	47	6	0	1	2	2	.50	11	.248	.306	.373
1991 New York	AL	135	456	122	20	0	24	(13	11)	214	52	77	25	5	49	5	0	7	3	2	.60	6	.268	.308	.469
1990 Detroit	AL	44	111	30	5	1	3	(1	2)	46	12	8	4	3	14	2	0	1	0	0	.00	5	.270	.305	.414
New York	AL	92	240	57	4	0	8	(3	5)	85	21	32	20	3	33	4	0	0	2	2	.50	6	.238	.307	.354
7 ML YEARS		641	1995	524	74	3	95	(48	47)	889	227	303	137	18	271	21	10	15	8	6	.57	51	.263	.315	.446

Eric Nolte

Pitches: Left   **Bats:** Left   **Pos:** SP   **Ht:** 6' 3" **Wt:** 200 **Born:** 04/28/64 **Age:** 28

		HOW MUCH HE PITCHED						WHAT HE GAVE UP										THE RESULTS					
Year Team	Lg	G	GS	CG	GF	IP	BFP	H	R	ER	HR	SH	SF	HB	TBB	IBB	SO	WP	Bk	W	L	Pct.	ShO	Sv	ERA
1987 San Diego	NL	12	12	1	0	67.1	293	57	28	24	6	2	1	2	36	2	44	3	1	2	6	.250	0	0	3.21
1988 San Diego	NL	2	0	0	1	3	14	3	2	2	1	1	0	0	2	0	1	0	1	0	0	.000	0	0	6.00
1989 San Diego	NL	3	1	0	1	9	49	15	12	11	1	1	1	0	7	1	8	3	0	0	0	.000	0	0	11.00
1991 2 ML Teams		9	6	0	2	24.2	125	40	28	28	6	0	3	0	13	0	16	1	1	3	2	.600	0	0	10.22
1991 San Diego	NL	6	6	0	0	22	111	37	27	27	6	0	3	0	10	0	15	1	1	3	2	.600	0	0	11.05
Texas	AL	3	0	0	2	2.2	14	3	1	1	0	0	0	0	3	0	1	0	0	0	0	.000	0	0	3.38
4 ML YEARS		26	19	1	4	104	481	115	70	65	14	4	5	2	58	3	69	7	3	5	8	.385	0	0	5.63

Edwin Nunez

Pitches: Right   **Bats:** Right   **Pos:** RP   **Ht:** 6' 5" **Wt:** 240 **Born:** 05/27/63 **Age:** 29

		HOW MUCH HE PITCHED						WHAT HE GAVE UP										THE RESULTS					
Year Team	Lg	G	GS	CG	GF	IP	BFP	H	R	ER	HR	SH	SF	HB	TBB	IBB	SO	WP	Bk	W	L	Pct.	ShO	Sv	ERA
1982 Seattle	AL	8	5	0	0	35.1	153	36	18	18	7	3	0	0	16	0	27	0	2	1	2	.333	0	0	4.58
1983 Seattle	AL	14	5	0	4	37	170	40	21	18	3	1	0	3	22	1	35	0	2	0	4	.000	0	0	4.38
1984 Seattle	AL	37	0	0	23	67.2	280	55	26	24	8	1	3	3	21	2	57	1	0	2	2	.500	0	7	3.19
1985 Seattle	AL	70	0	0	53	90.1	378	79	36	31	13	4	3	0	34	5	58	2	1	7	3	.700	0	16	3.09
1986 Seattle	AL	14	1	0	6	21.2	93	25	15	14	5	0	0	0	5	1	17	0	1	1	2	.333	0	0	5.82
1987 Seattle	AL	48	0	0	40	47.1	198	45	20	20	7	3	4	1	18	3	34	2	0	3	4	.429	0	12	3.80
1988 2 ML Teams		24	3	0	6	43.1	210	66	40	33	5	2	4	2	17	3	27	1	1	2	4	.333	0	0	6.85
1989 Detroit	AL	27	0	0	12	54	238	49	33	25	6	6	3	0	36	13	41	2	1	3	4	.429	0	1	4.17
1990 Detroit	AL	42	0	0	15	80.1	343	65	26	20	4	5	1	2	37	6	66	4	0	3	1	.750	0	6	2.24
1991 Milwaukee	AL	23	0	0	18	25.1	119	28	20	17	6	3	2	0	13	2	24	0	1	2	1	.667	0	8	6.04
1988 Seattle	AL	14	3	0	2	29.1	145	45	33	26	4	2	4	2	14	3	19	0	1	1	4	.200	0	0	7.98
New York	NL	10	0	0	4	14	65	21	7	7	1	0	0	0	3	0	8	1	0	1	0	1.000	0	0	4.50
10 ML YEARS		307	14	0	177	502.1	2182	488	255	220	64	28	20	11	219	36	386	12	8	24	27	.471	0	50	3.94

Charlie O'Brien

Bats: Right   **Throws:** Right   **Pos:** C   **Ht:** 6' 2" **Wt:** 190 **Born:** 05/01/61 **Age:** 31

				BATTING														BASERUNNING				PERCENTAGES		
Year Team	Lg	G	AB	H	2B	3B	HR	(Hm	Rd)	TB	R	RBI	TBB	IBB	SO	HBP	SH	SF	SB	CS	SB%	GDP	Avg	OBP	SLG
1985 Oakland	AL	16	11	3	1	0	0	(0	0)	4	3	1	3	0	3	0	0	0	0	0	.00	0	.273	.429	.364
1987 Milwaukee	AL	10	35	7	3	1	0	(0	0)	12	2	0	4	0	4	0	1	0	0	1	.00	0	.200	.282	.343
1988 Milwaukee	AL	40	118	26	6	0	2	(2	0)	38	12	9	5	0	16	0	4	0	0	1	.00	3	.220	.252	.322
1989 Milwaukee	AL	62	188	44	10	0	6	(4	2)	72	22	35	21	1	11	9	8	0	0	0	.00	11	.234	.339	.383
1990 2 ML Teams		74	213	38	10	2	0	(0	0)	52	17	20	21	3	34	3	10	2	0	0	.00	4	.178	.259	.244
1991 New York	NL	69	168	31	6	0	2	(1	1)	43	16	14	17	1	25	4	0	2	0	2	.00	5	.185	.272	.256
1990 Milwaukee	AL	46	145	27	7	2	0	(0	0)	38	11	11	11	1	26	2	8	0	0	0	.00	3	.186	.253	.262
New York	NL	28	68	11	3	0	0	(0	0)	14	6	9	10	2	8	1	2	2	0	0	.00	1	.162	.272	.206
6 ML YEARS		271	733	149	36	3	10	(7	3)	221	72	79	71	5	93	16	23	4	0	4	.00	23	.203	.286	.302

Pete O'Brien

Bats: Left   **Throws:** Left   **Pos:** 1B/LF/DH   **Ht:** 6' 2" **Wt:** 195 **Born:** 02/09/58 **Age:** 34

				BATTING														BASERUNNING				PERCENTAGES		
Year Team	Lg	G	AB	H	2B	3B	HR	(Hm	Rd)	TB	R	RBI	TBB	IBB	SO	HBP	SH	SF	SB	CS	SB%	GDP	Avg	OBP	SLG
1982 Texas	AL	20	67	16	4	1	4	(2	2)	34	13	13	6	0	8	0	0	1	1	0	1.00	0	.239	.297	.507

1983	Texas	AL	154	524	124	24	5	8	(4	4)	182	53	53	58	2	62	1	3	2	5	4	.56	12	.237	.313	.347
1984	Texas	AL	142	520	149	26	2	18	(7	11)	233	57	80	53	8	50	0	1	7	3	5	.38	11	.287	.348	.448
1985	Texas	AL	159	573	153	34	3	22	(12	10)	259	69	92	69	4	53	1	3	9	5	10	.33	18	.267	.342	.452
1986	Texas	AL	156	551	160	23	3	23	(11	12)	258	86	90	87	11	66	0	0	3	4	4	.50	19	.290	.385	.468
1987	Texas	AL	159	569	163	26	1	23	(9	14)	260	84	88	59	6	61	0	0	10	0	4	.00	9	.286	.348	.457
1988	Texas	AL	156	547	149	24	1	16	(6	10)	223	57	71	72	9	73	0	1	8	1	4	.20	12	.272	.352	.408
1989	Cleveland	AL	155	554	144	24	1	12	(5	7)	206	75	55	83	17	48	2	2	5	3	1	.75	10	.260	.356	.372
1990	Seattle	AL	108	366	82	18	0	5	(3	2)	115	32	27	44	1	33	2	1	4	0	0	.00	12	.224	.308	.314
1991	Seattle	AL	152	560	139	29	3	17	(12	5)	225	58	88	44	7	61	1	3	9	0	1	.00	14	.248	.300	.402
	10 ML YEARS		1361	4831	1279	232	20	148	(71	77)	1995	584	657	575	65	515	7	14	58	22	33	.40	117	.265	.340	.413

Paul O'Neill

Bats: Left   **Throws:** Left   **Pos:** RF   **Ht:** 6' 4"   **Wt:** 215   **Born:** 02/25/63   **Age:** 29

							BATTING												BASERUNNING				PERCENTAGES		
Year	Team	Lg	G	AB	H	2B	3B	HR	(Hm	Rd)	TB	R	RBI	TBB	IBB	SO	HBP	SH	SF	SB	CS	SB%	GDP	Avg	OBP	SLG
1985	Cincinnati	NL	5	12	4	1	0	0	(0	0)	5	1	1	0	0	2	0	0	0	0	0	.00	0	.333	.333	.417
1986	Cincinnati	NL	3	2	0	0	0	0	(0	0)	0	0	0	1	0	1	0	0	0	0	0	.00	0	.000	.333	.000
1987	Cincinnati	NL	84	160	41	14	1	7	(4	3)	78	24	28	18	1	29	0	0	0	2	1	.67	3	.256	.331	.488
1988	Cincinnati	NL	145	485	122	25	3	16	(12	4)	201	58	73	38	5	65	2	3	5	8	6	.57	7	.252	.306	.414
1989	Cincinnati	NL	117	428	118	24	2	15	(11	4)	191	49	74	46	8	64	2	0	4	20	5	.80	7	.276	.346	.446
1990	Cincinnati	NL	145	503	136	28	0	16	(10	6)	212	59	78	53	13	103	2	1	5	13	11	.54	12	.270	.339	.421
1991	Cincinnati	NL	152	532	136	36	0	28	(20	8)	256	71	91	73	14	107	1	0	1	12	7	.63	8	.256	.346	.481
	7 ML YEARS		651	2122	557	128	6	82	(57	25)	943	262	345	229	41	371	7	4	15	55	30	.65	37	.262	.334	.444

Ken Oberkfell

Bats: Left   **Throws:** Right   **Pos:** 1B   **Ht:** 6' 1"   **Wt:** 210   **Born:** 05/04/56   **Age:** 36

							BATTING												BASERUNNING				PERCENTAGES		
Year	Team	Lg	G	AB	H	2B	3B	HR	(Hm	Rd)	TB	R	RBI	TBB	IBB	SO	HBP	SH	SF	SB	CS	SB%	GDP	Avg	OBP	SLG
1977	St. Louis	NL	9	9	1	0	0	0	(0	0)	1	0	1	0	0	3	0	0	0	0	0	.00	0	.111	.111	.111
1978	St. Louis	NL	24	50	6	1	0	0	(0	0)	7	7	0	3	0	1	0	1	0	0	0	.00	1	.120	.170	.140
1979	St. Louis	NL	135	369	111	19	5	1	(1	0)	143	53	35	57	9	35	4	1	4	4	1	.80	9	.301	.396	.388
1980	St. Louis	NL	116	422	128	27	6	3	(0	3)	176	58	46	51	8	23	1	9	3	4	4	.50	11	.303	.377	.417
1981	St. Louis	NL	102	376	110	12	6	2	(0	2)	140	43	45	37	6	28	0	3	4	13	5	.72	11	.293	.353	.372
1982	St. Louis	NL	137	470	136	22	5	2	(1	1)	174	55	34	40	6	31	1	3	2	11	9	.55	11	.289	.345	.370
1983	St. Louis	NL	151	488	143	26	5	3	(0	3)	188	62	38	61	5	27	1	4	3	12	6	.67	12	.293	.371	.385
1984	2 ML Teams		100	324	87	19	2	1	(1	0)	113	38	21	31	3	27	1	3	3	2	5	.29	7	.269	.331	.349
1985	Atlanta	NL	134	412	112	19	4	3	(2	1)	148	30	35	51	6	38	6	1	2	1	2	.33	10	.272	.359	.359
1986	Atlanta	NL	151	503	136	24	3	5	(2	3)	181	62	48	83	6	40	2	4	4	7	4	.64	11	.270	.373	.360
1987	Atlanta	NL	135	508	142	29	2	3	(2	1)	184	59	48	48	5	29	2	5	3	3	3	.50	13	.280	.342	.362
1988	2 ML Teams		140	476	129	22	4	3	(1	2)	168	49	42	37	7	34	2	6	8	4	5	.44	8	.271	.321	.353
1989	2 ML Teams		97	156	42	6	1	2	(1	1)	56	19	17	10	0	10	2	2	3	1	0	.00	4	.269	.316	.359
1990	Houston	NL	77	150	31	6	1	1	(0	1)	42	10	12	15	1	17	1	1	1	1	1	.50	3	.207	.281	.280
1991	Houston	NL	53	70	16	4	0	0	(0	0)	20	7	14	14	4	8	0	0	0	0	0	.00	0	.229	.357	.286
1984	St. Louis	NL	50	152	47	11	1	0	(0	0)	60	17	11	16	2	10	1	0	0	1	2	.33	3	.309	.379	.395
	Atlanta	NL	50	172	40	8	1	1	(1	0)	53	21	10	15	1	17	0	3	3	1	3	.25	4	.233	.289	.308
1988	Atlanta	NL	120	422	117	20	4	3	(1	2)	154	42	40	32	6	28	2	5	8	4	5	.44	6	.277	.325	.365
	Pittsburgh	NL	20	54	12	2	0	0	(0	0)	14	7	2	5	1	6	0	1	0	0	0	.00	2	.222	.288	.259
1989	Pittsburgh	NL	14	40	5	1	0	0	(0	0)	6	2	2	2	0	2	0	1	1	0	0	.00	0	.125	.163	.150
	San Francisco	NL	83	116	37	5	1	2	(1	1)	50	17	15	8	0	8	2	1	2	1	0	.00	4	.319	.367	.431
	15 ML YEARS		1561	4783	1330	236	44	29	(11	18)	1741	552	436	538	66	351	23	43	40	62	46	.57	111	.278	.351	.364

Jose Offerman

Bats: Both   **Throws:** Right   **Pos:** SS   **Ht:** 6' 0"   **Wt:** 160   **Born:** 11/08/68   **Age:** 23

							BATTING												BASERUNNING				PERCENTAGES		
Year	Team	Lg	G	AB	H	2B	3B	HR	(Hm	Rd)	TB	R	RBI	TBB	IBB	SO	HBP	SH	SF	SB	CS	SB%	GDP	Avg	OBP	SLG
1988	Vero Beach	A	4	14	4	2	0	0	--	--	6	4	2	2	0	0	0	0	0	0	0	.00	0	.286	.375	.429
	Great Falls	R	60	251	83	11	5	2	--	--	110	75	28	38	1	42	2	1	1	57	10	.85	3	.331	.421	.438
1989	Bakersfield	A	62	245	75	9	4	2	--	--	98	53	22	35	2	48	2	0	1	37	13	.74	0	.306	.396	.400
	San Antonio	AA	68	278	80	6	3	2	--	--	98	47	22	40	4	39	1	3	0	32	13	.71	1	.288	.379	.353
1990	Albuquerque	AAA	117	454	148	16	11	0	--	--	186	104	56	71	2	81	2	4	4	60	19	.76	7	.326	.416	.410
1991	Albuquerque	AAA	79	289	86	8	4	0	--	--	102	58	29	47	3	58	0	4	0	32	15	.68	5	.298	.396	.353
1990	Los Angeles	NL	29	58	9	0	0	1	(1	0)	12	7	7	4	1	14	0	1	0	1	0	1.00	0	.155	.210	.207
1991	Los Angeles	NL	52	113	22	2	0	0	(0	0)	24	10	3	25	2	32	1	1	0	3	2	.60	5	.195	.345	.212
	2 ML YEARS		81	171	31	2	0	1	(1	0)	36	17	10	29	3	46	1	2	0	4	2	.67	5	.181	.303	.211

Bobby Ojeda

Pitches: Left **Bats:** Left **Pos:** SP   **Ht:** 6' 1" **Wt:** 195 **Born:** 12/17/57 **Age:** 34

| | | | HOW MUCH | HE | PITCHED | | | WHAT | HE | GAVE | UP | | | | | | | | | | THE | RESULTS | | | |
Year Team	Lg	G	GS	CG	GF	IP	BFP	H	R	ER	HR	SH	SF	HB	TBB	IBB	SO	WP	Bk	W	L	Pct.	ShO	Sv	ERA
1980 Boston	AL	7	7	0	0	26	122	39	20	20	2	0	0	0	14	1	12	1	0	1	1	.500	0	0	6.92
1981 Boston	AL	10	10	2	0	66	267	50	25	23	6	3	1	2	25	2	28	0	0	6	2	.750	0	0	3.14
1982 Boston	AL	22	14	0	6	78.1	352	95	53	49	13	0	1	1	29	0	52	5	0	4	6	.400	0	0	5.63
1983 Boston	AL	29	28	5	0	173.2	746	173	85	78	15	6	11	3	73	2	94	2	0	12	7	.632	0	0	4.04
1984 Boston	AL	33	32	8	0	216.2	928	211	106	96	17	8	6	2	96	2	137	0	1	12	12	.500	5	0	3.99
1985 Boston	AL	39	22	5	10	157.2	671	166	74	70	11	10	3	2	48	9	102	3	3	9	11	.450	0	1	4.00
1986 New York	NL	32	30	7	1	217.1	871	185	72	62	15	10	3	2	52	3	148	2	1	18	5	.783	2	0	2.57
1987 New York	NL	10	7	0	0	46.1	192	45	23	20	5	3	1	0	10	1	21	1	0	3	5	.375	0	0	3.88
1988 New York	NL	29	29	5	0	190.1	752	158	74	61	6	6	6	4	33	2	133	4	7	10	13	.435	5	0	2.88
1989 New York	NL	31	31	5	0	192	824	179	83	74	16	6	7	2	78	5	95	0	2	13	11	.542	2	0	3.47
1990 New York	NL	38	12	0	9	118	500	123	53	48	10	3	3	2	40	4	62	2	3	7	6	.538	0	0	3.66
1991 Los Angeles	NL	31	31	2	0	189.1	802	181	78	67	15	15	9	3	70	9	120	4	2	12	9	.571	1	0	3.18
12 ML YEARS		311	253	39	26	1671.2	7027	1605	746	668	131	70	51	23	568	40	1004	24	19	107	88	.549	15	1	3.60

Jim Olander

Bats: Right **Throws:** Right **Pos:** CF   **Ht:** 6' 2" **Wt:** 175 **Born:** 02/21/63 **Age:** 29

| | | | | | | | | BATTING | | | | | | | | | | | BASERUNNING | | | | PERCENTAGES | | |
Year Team	Lg	G	AB	H	2B	3B	HR	(Hm	Rd)	TB	R	RBI	TBB	IBB	SO	HBP	SH	SF	SB	CS	SB%	GDP	Avg	OBP	SLG
1981 Helena	R	61	222	72	10	3	6	--	--	106	37	37	17	0	59	0	0	0	5	0	1.00	0	.324	.372	.477
1982 Spartanburg	A	121	423	129	25	6	12	--	--	202	77	63	61	0	86	0	0	0	12	0	1.00	0	.305	.393	.478
1983 Peninsula	A	126	503	125	21	3	15	--	--	197	62	79	43	0	146	0	0	0	12	0	1.00	0	.249	.308	.392
1984 Reading	AA	117	362	95	12	2	8	--	--	135	44	47	29	0	62	2	1	5	10	10	.50	10	.262	.317	.373
1985 Portland	AAA	44	72	16	2	0	0	--	--	18	6	6	2	0	17	0	0	2	3	0	1.00	3	.222	.237	.250
Reading	AA	64	208	67	15	2	4	--	--	98	30	39	29	1	45	3	2	1	2	2	.50	4	.322	.411	.471
1986 Reading	AA	129	464	151	33	4	8	--	--	216	77	68	56	3	84	2	3	5	10	15	.40	5	.325	.397	.466
1987 Maine	AAA	43	145	31	7	0	1	--	--	41	17	8	13	1	30	0	1	0	2	2	.50	5	.214	.278	.283
1988 Maine	AAA	25	71	15	3	0	0	--	--	18	5	4	4	1	18	1	1	0	0	2	.00	1	.211	.263	.254
1989 Scr Wil-Bar	AAA	111	274	69	17	4	3	--	--	103	35	29	27	1	69	3	8	2	5	7	.42	3	.252	.324	.376
1990 Tucson	AAA	33	98	23	8	2	1	--	--	38	12	12	14	1	24	1	1	0	0	3	.00	3	.235	.336	.388
Denver	AAA	74	233	67	12	4	3	--	--	96	33	36	20	1	47	4	9	6	2	5	.29	3	.288	.346	.412
1991 Denver	AAA	134	498	162	32	10	9	--	--	241	89	78	64	5	83	4	3	2	14	2	.88	10	.325	.405	.484
1991 Milwaukee	AL	12	9	0	0	0	0	(0	0)	0	2	0	2	0	5	0	0	0	0	0	.00	0	.000	.182	.000

John Olerud

Bats: Left **Throws:** Left **Pos:** 1B   **Ht:** 6' 5" **Wt:** 218 **Born:** 08/05/68 **Age:** 23

| | | | | | | | | BATTING | | | | | | | | | | | BASERUNNING | | | | PERCENTAGES | | |
Year Team	Lg	G	AB	H	2B	3B	HR	(Hm	Rd)	TB	R	RBI	TBB	IBB	SO	HBP	SH	SF	SB	CS	SB%	GDP	Avg	OBP	SLG
1989 Toronto	AL	6	8	3	0	0	0	(0	0)	3	2	0	0	0	1	0	0	0	0	0	.00	0	.375	.375	.375
1990 Toronto	AL	111	358	95	15	1	14	(11	3)	154	43	48	57	6	75	1	1	4	0	2	.00	5	.265	.364	.430
1991 Toronto	AL	139	454	116	30	1	17	(7	10)	199	64	68	68	9	84	6	3	10	0	2	.00	12	.256	.353	.438
3 ML YEARS		256	820	214	45	2	31	(18	13)	356	109	116	125	15	160	7	4	14	0	4	.00	17	.261	.358	.434

Steve Olin

Pitches: Right **Bats:** Right **Pos:** RP   **Ht:** 6' 2" **Wt:** 190 **Born:** 10/04/65 **Age:** 26

| | | | HOW MUCH | HE | PITCHED | | | WHAT | HE | GAVE | UP | | | | | | | | | | THE | RESULTS | | | |
Year Team	Lg	G	GS	CG	GF	IP	BFP	H	R	ER	HR	SH	SF	HB	TBB	IBB	SO	WP	Bk	W	L	Pct.	ShO	Sv	ERA
1989 Cleveland	AL	25	0	0	8	36	152	35	16	15	1	1	0	0	14	2	24	2	0	1	4	.200	0	1	3.75
1990 Cleveland	AL	50	1	0	16	92.1	394	96	41	35	3	5	2	6	26	2	64	0	0	4	4	.500	0	1	3.41
1991 Cleveland	AL	48	0	0	32	56.1	249	61	26	21	2	2	0	1	23	7	38	0	0	3	6	.333	0	17	3.36
3 ML YEARS		123	1	0	56	184.2	795	192	83	71	6	8	2	7	63	11	126	2	0	8	14	.364	0	19	3.46

Omar Olivares

Pitches: Right **Bats:** Right **Pos:** SP   **Ht:** 6' 1" **Wt:** 185 **Born:** 07/06/67 **Age:** 24

| | | | HOW MUCH | HE | PITCHED | | | WHAT | HE | GAVE | UP | | | | | | | | | | THE | RESULTS | | | |
Year Team	Lg	G	GS	CG	GF	IP	BFP	H	R	ER	HR	SH	SF	HB	TBB	IBB	SO	WP	Bk	W	L	Pct.	ShO	Sv	ERA
1987 Chston-Sc	A	31	24	5	3	170.1	744	182	107	87	9	6	10	7	57	4	86	3	1	4	14	.222	0	0	4.60
1988 Chston-Sc	A	24	24	10	0	185.1	746	166	63	46	3	5	7	3	43	2	94	9	7	13	6	.684	3	0	2.23
Riverside	A	4	3	1	0	23.1	96	18	9	3	2	1	0	2	9	0	16	1	1	3	0	1.000	0	0	1.16
1989 Wichita	AA	26	26	6	0	185.2	771	175	87	70	10	3	8	10	61	6	79	10	1	12	11	.522	1	0	3.39
1990 Louisville	AAA	23	23	5	0	159.1	643	127	58	50	6	4	2	9	59	1	88	6	2	10	11	.476	2	0	2.82

Year Team	Lg	G	GS	CG	GF	IP	BFP	H	R	ER	HR	SH	SF	HB	TBB	IBB	SO	WP	Bk	W	L	Pct.	ShO	Sv	ERA
1991 Louisville	AAA	6	6	0	0	36.1	158	39	15	14	1	1	1	1	16	1	27	2	1	1	2	.333	0	0	3.47
1990 St. Louis	NL	9	6	0	0	49.1	201	45	17	16	2	1	0	2	17	0	20	1	1	1	1	.500	0	0	2.92
1991 St. Louis	NL	28	24	0	2	167.1	688	148	72	69	13	11	2	5	61	1	91	3	1	11	7	.611	0	1	3.71
2 ML YEARS		37	30	0	2	216.2	889	193	89	85	15	12	2	7	78	1	111	4	2	12	8	.600	0	1	3.53

Joe Oliver

Bats: Right **Throws:** Right **Pos:** C   **Ht:** 6' 3" **Wt:** 210 **Born:** 07/24/65 **Age:** 26

								BATTING												BASERUNNING				PERCENTAGES		
Year Team	Lg	G	AB	H	2B	3B	HR	(Hm	Rd)	TB	R	RBI	TBB	IBB	SO	HBP	SH	SF	SB	CS	SB%	GDP	Avg	OBP	SLG
1989 Cincinnati	NL	49	151	41	8	0	3	(1	2)	58	13	23	6	1	28	1	1	2	0	0	.00	3	.272	.300	.384
1990 Cincinnati	NL	121	364	84	23	0	8	(3	5)	131	34	52	37	15	75	2	5	1	1	1	.50	6	.231	.304	.360
1991 Cincinnati	NL	94	269	58	11	0	11	(7	4)	102	21	41	18	5	53	0	4	0	0	0	.00	14	.216	.265	.379
3 ML YEARS		264	784	183	42	0	22	(11	11)	291	68	116	61	21	156	3	10	3	1	1	.50	23	.233	.290	.371

Francisco Oliveras

Pitches: Right **Bats:** Right **Pos:** RP   **Ht:** 5'10" **Wt:** 180 **Born:** 01/31/63 **Age:** 29

									HOW MUCH HE PITCHED			WHAT HE GAVE UP									THE RESULTS					
Year Team	Lg	G	GS	CG	GF	IP	BFP	H	R	ER	HR	SH	SF	HB	TBB	IBB	SO	WP	Bk	W	L	Pct.	ShO	Sv	ERA
1989 Minnesota	AL	12	8	1	1	55.2	239	64	28	28	8	0	1	1	15	0	24	0	2	3	4	.429	0	0	4.53
1990 San Francisco	NL	33	2	0	9	55.1	231	47	22	17	5	1	3	2	21	6	41	2	1	2	2	.500	0	2	2.77
1991 San Francisco	NL	55	1	0	17	79.1	316	69	36	34	12	5	3	1	22	4	48	2	2	6	6	.500	0	3	3.86
3 ML YEARS		100	11	1	27	190.1	786	180	86	79	25	6	7	4	58	10	113	4	5	11	12	.478	0	5	3.74

Greg Olson

Bats: Right **Throws:** Right **Pos:** C   **Ht:** 6' 0" **Wt:** 200 **Born:** 09/06/60 **Age:** 31

								BATTING												BASERUNNING				PERCENTAGES		
Year Team	Lg	G	AB	H	2B	3B	HR	(Hm	Rd)	TB	R	RBI	TBB	IBB	SO	HBP	SH	SF	SB	CS	SB%	GDP	Avg	OBP	SLG
1989 Minnesota	AL	3	2	1	0	0	0	(0	0)	1	0	0	0	0	0	0	0	0	0	0	.00	0	.500	.500	.500
1990 Atlanta	NL	100	298	78	12	1	7	(4	3)	113	36	36	30	4	51	2	1	1	1	1	.50	8	.262	.332	.379
1991 Atlanta	NL	133	411	99	25	0	6	(6	0)	142	46	44	44	3	48	3	2	4	1	1	.50	13	.241	.316	.345
3 ML YEARS		236	711	178	37	1	13	(10	3)	256	82	80	74	7	99	5	3	5	2	2	.50	21	.250	.323	.360

Gregg Olson

Pitches: Right **Bats:** Right **Pos:** RP   **Ht:** 6' 4" **Wt:** 209 **Born:** 10/11/66 **Age:** 25

									HOW MUCH HE PITCHED			WHAT HE GAVE UP									THE RESULTS					
Year Team	Lg	G	GS	CG	GF	IP	BFP	H	R	ER	HR	SH	SF	HB	TBB	IBB	SO	WP	Bk	W	L	Pct.	ShO	Sv	ERA
1988 Baltimore	AL	10	0	0	4	11	51	10	4	4	1	0	0	0	10	1	9	0	1	1	1	.500	0	0	3.27
1989 Baltimore	AL	64	0	0	52	85	356	57	17	16	1	4	1	1	46	10	90	9	3	5	2	.714	0	27	1.69
1990 Baltimore	AL	64	0	0	58	74.1	305	57	20	20	3	1	2	3	31	3	74	5	0	6	5	.545	0	37	2.42
1991 Baltimore	AL	72	0	0	62	73.2	319	74	28	26	1	5	1	1	29	5	72	8	1	4	6	.400	0	31	3.18
4 ML YEARS		210	0	0	176	244	1031	198	69	66	6	10	4	5	116	19	245	22	5	16	14	.533	0	95	2.43

Jose Oquendo

Bats: Both **Throws:** Right **Pos:** 2B/SS   **Ht:** 5'10" **Wt:** 160 **Born:** 07/04/63 **Age:** 28

								BATTING												BASERUNNING				PERCENTAGES		
Year Team	Lg	G	AB	H	2B	3B	HR	(Hm	Rd)	TB	R	RBI	TBB	IBB	SO	HBP	SH	SF	SB	CS	SB%	GDP	Avg	OBP	SLG
1983 New York	NL	120	328	70	7	0	1	(0	1)	80	29	17	19	2	60	2	3	1	8	9	.47	10	.213	.260	.244
1984 New York	NL	81	189	42	5	0	0	(0	0)	47	23	10	15	2	26	2	3	2	10	1	.91	2	.222	.284	.249
1986 St. Louis	NL	76	138	41	4	1	0	(0	0)	47	20	13	15	4	20	0	2	3	2	3	.40	3	.297	.359	.341
1987 St. Louis	NL	116	248	71	9	0	1	(0	1)	83	43	24	54	6	29	0	6	4	4	4	.50	6	.286	.408	.335
1988 St. Louis	NL	148	451	125	10	1	7	(4	3)	158	36	46	52	7	40	0	12	3	4	6	.40	8	.277	.350	.350
1989 St. Louis	NL	163	556	162	28	7	1	(0	1)	207	59	48	79	7	59	0	7	8	3	5	.38	12	.291	.375	.372
1990 St. Louis	NL	156	469	118	17	5	1	(1	0)	148	38	37	74	8	46	0	5	5	1	1	.50	7	.252	.350	.316
1991 St. Louis	NL	127	366	88	11	4	1	(0	1)	110	37	26	67	13	48	1	4	3	1	2	.33	5	.240	.357	.301
8 ML YEARS		987	2745	717	91	18	12	(5	7)	880	285	221	375	49	328	5	42	29	33	31	.52	53	.261	.348	.321

Jesse Orosco

Pitches: Left **Bats:** Right **Pos:** RP   **Ht:** 6' 2" **Wt:** 185 **Born:** 04/21/57 **Age:** 35

									HOW MUCH HE PITCHED			WHAT HE GAVE UP									THE RESULTS					
Year Team	Lg	G	GS	CG	GF	IP	BFP	H	R	ER	HR	SH	SF	HB	TBB	IBB	SO	WP	Bk	W	L	Pct.	ShO	Sv	ERA
1979 New York	NL	18	2	0	6	35	154	33	20	19	4	3	0	2	22	0	22	0	0	1	2	.333	0	0	4.89
1981 New York	NL	8	0	0	4	17	69	13	4	3	2	2	0	0	6	2	18	0	1	0	1	.000	0	1	1.59
1982 New York	NL	54	2	0	22	109.1	451	92	37	33	7	5	4	2	40	2	89	3	2	4	10	.286	0	4	2.72
1983 New York	NL	62	0	0	42	110	432	76	27	18	4	3	1	1	38	7	84	1	2	13	7	.650	0	17	1.47
1984 New York	NL	60	0	0	52	87	355	58	29	25	7	3	3	2	34	6	85	1	1	10	6	.625	0	31	2.59
1985 New York	NL	54	0	0	39	79	331	66	26	24	6	1	1	0	34	7	68	4	0	8	6	.571	0	17	2.73

1986 New York	NL	58	0	0	40	81	338	64	23	21	6	2	3	3	35	3	62	2	0	8	6	.571	0	21	2.33
1987 New York	NL	58	0	0	41	77	335	78	41	38	5	5	4	2	31	9	78	2	0	3	9	.250	0	16	4.44
1988 Los Angeles	NL	55	0	0	21	53	229	41	18	16	4	3	3	2	30	3	43	1	0	3	2	.600	0	9	2.72
1989 Cleveland	AL	69	0	0	29	78	312	54	20	18	7	8	3	2	26	4	79	0	0	3	4	.429	0	3	2.08
1990 Cleveland	AL	55	0	0	28	64.2	289	58	35	28	9	5	3	0	38	7	55	1	0	5	4	.556	0	2	3.90
1991 Cleveland	AL	47	0	0	20	45.2	202	52	20	19	4	1	3	1	15	8	36	1	1	2	0	1.000	0	0	3.74
12 ML YEARS		598	4	0	344	836.2	3497	685	300	262	64	42	30	17	349	58	719	16	7	60	57	.513	0	121	2.82

Joe Orsulak

Bats: Left   **Throws:** Left   **Pos:** LF/RF   **Ht:** 6' 1" **Wt:** 203 **Born:** 05/31/62 **Age:** 30

							BATTING												BASERUNNING				PERCENTAGES		
Year Team	Lg	G	AB	H	2B	3B	HR	(Hm	Rd)	TB	R	RBI	TBB	IBB	SO	HBP	SH	SF	SB	CS	SB%	GDP	Avg	OBP	SLG
1983 Pittsburgh	NL	7	11	2	0	0	0	(0	0)	2	0	1	0	0	2	0	0	1	0	1	.00	0	.182	.167	.182
1984 Pittsburgh	NL	32	67	17	1	2	0	(0	0)	22	12	3	1	0	7	1	3	1	3	1	.75	0	.254	.271	.328
1985 Pittsburgh	NL	121	397	119	14	6	0	(0	0)	145	54	21	26	3	27	1	9	3	24	11	.69	5	.300	.342	.365
1986 Pittsburgh	NL	138	401	100	19	6	2	(0	2)	137	60	19	28	2	38	1	6	1	24	11	.69	4	.249	.299	.342
1988 Baltimore	AL	125	379	109	21	3	8	(3	5)	160	48	27	23	2	30	3	8	3	9	8	.53	7	.288	.331	.422
1989 Baltimore	AL	123	390	111	22	5	7	(0	7)	164	59	55	41	6	35	2	7	6	5	3	.63	8	.285	.351	.421
1990 Baltimore	AL	124	413	111	14	3	11	(9	2)	164	49	57	46	9	48	1	4	1	6	8	.43	7	.269	.343	.397
1991 Baltimore	AL	143	486	135	22	1	5	(3	2)	174	57	43	28	1	45	4	0	3	6	2	.75	9	.278	.321	.358
8 ML YEARS		813	2544	704	113	26	33	(15	18)	968	339	226	193	23	232	13	37	19	77	45	.63	40	.277	.329	.381

Javier Ortiz

Bats: Right   **Throws:** Right   **Pos:** LF   **Ht:** 6' 4" **Wt:** 220 **Born:** 01/22/63 **Age:** 29

							BATTING												BASERUNNING				PERCENTAGES		
Year Team	Lg	G	AB	H	2B	3B	HR	(Hm	Rd)	TB	R	RBI	TBB	IBB	SO	HBP	SH	SF	SB	CS	SB%	GDP	Avg	OBP	SLG
1983 Burlington	A	101	378	133	23	4	16	--	--	212	72	79	42	3	94	2	2	3	10	6	.63	14	.352	.416	.561
1984 Tulsa	AA	94	325	97	21	3	8	--	--	148	42	53	47	2	67	5	4	4	4	5	.44	8	.298	.391	.455
1985 Tulsa	AA	86	304	75	12	3	5	--	--	108	47	31	52	2	75	4	0	1	11	3	.79	10	.247	.363	.355
1986 Tulsa	AA	110	378	114	29	3	14	--	--	191	52	65	54	2	94	7	3	1	15	10	.60	7	.302	.398	.505
1987 Okla City	AAA	119	381	105	23	7	15	--	--	187	58	69	58	2	99	4	1	10	5	2	.71	6	.276	.369	.491
1988 San Antonio	AA	51	182	53	13	2	8	--	--	94	35	33	22	0	38	5	0	5	6	3	.67	5	.291	.374	.516
1989 Albuquerque	AAA	70	220	59	10	0	11	--	--	102	42	36	34	1	54	4	1	0	2	2	.50	4	.268	.376	.464
Tucson	AAA	11	40	7	0	0	0	--	--	7	5	0	2	0	9	0	0	0	0	0	.00	1	.175	.214	.175
1990 Tucson	AAA	49	179	63	16	2	5	--	--	98	36	39	22	1	36	1	0	3	2	3	.40	6	.352	.420	.547
1991 Tucson	AAA	34	127	41	13	0	3	--	--	63	20	22	10	0	22	0	0	0	0	3	.00	4	.323	.367	.496
1990 Houston	NL	30	77	21	5	1	1	(1	0)	31	7	10	12	0	11	0	0	1	1	1	.50	1	.273	.367	.403
1991 Houston	NL	47	83	23	4	1	1	(0	1)	32	7	5	14	0	14	0	0	0	0	0	.00	3	.277	.381	.386
2 ML YEARS		77	160	44	9	2	2	(1	1)	63	14	15	26	0	25	0	0	1	1	1	.50	4	.275	.374	.394

Junior Ortiz

Bats: Right   **Throws:** Right   **Pos:** C   **Ht:** 5'11" **Wt:** 181 **Born:** 10/24/59 **Age:** 32

							BATTING												BASERUNNING				PERCENTAGES		
Year Team	Lg	G	AB	H	2B	3B	HR	(Hm	Rd)	TB	R	RBI	TBB	IBB	SO	HBP	SH	SF	SB	CS	SB%	GDP	Avg	OBP	SLG
1982 Pittsburgh	NL	7	15	3	1	0	0	(0	0)	4	1	0	1	0	3	0	0	0	0	0	.00	1	.200	.250	.267
1983 2 ML Teams		73	193	48	5	0	0	(0	0)	53	11	12	4	0	34	1	2	0	1	0	1.00	1	.249	.268	.275
1984 New York	NL	40	91	18	3	0	0	(0	0)	21	6	11	5	0	15	0	0	2	1	0	1.00	2	.198	.235	.231
1985 Pittsburgh	NL	23	72	21	2	0	1	(0	1)	26	4	5	3	1	17	0	1	0	1	0	1.00	1	.292	.320	.361
1986 Pittsburgh	NL	49	110	37	6	0	0	(0	0)	43	11	14	9	0	13	0	1	2	0	1	.00	4	.336	.380	.391
1987 Pittsburgh	NL	75	192	52	8	1	1	(0	1)	65	16	22	15	1	23	0	5	1	0	2	.00	6	.271	.322	.339
1988 Pittsburgh	NL	49	118	33	6	0	2	(1	1)	45	8	18	9	0	9	2	1	2	1	4	.20	6	.280	.336	.381
1989 Pittsburgh	NL	91	230	50	6	1	1	(0	1)	61	16	22	20	4	20	2	3	3	2	2	.50	9	.217	.282	.265
1990 Minnesota	AL	71	170	57	7	1	0	(0	0)	66	18	18	12	0	16	2	2	1	0	4	.00	4	.335	.384	.388
1991 Minnesota	AL	61	134	28	5	1	0	(0	0)	35	9	11	6	1	12	1	1	0	0	1	.00	6	.209	.293	.261
1983 Pittsburgh	NL	5	8	1	0	0	0	(0	0)	1	1	0	1	0	0	0	1	0	0	0	.00	0	.125	.222	.125
New York	NL	68	185	47	5	0	0	(0	0)	52	10	12	3	0	34	1	1	0	1	0	1.00	1	.254	.270	.281
10 ML YEARS		539	1325	347	49	4	5	(1	4)	419	100	133	93	6	162	8	16	11	6	14	.30	40	.262	.312	.316

John Orton

Bats: Right   **Throws:** Right   **Pos:** C   **Ht:** 6' 1" **Wt:** 192 **Born:** 12/08/65 **Age:** 26

							BATTING												BASERUNNING				PERCENTAGES		
Year Team	Lg	G	AB	H	2B	3B	HR	(Hm	Rd)	TB	R	RBI	TBB	IBB	SO	HBP	SH	SF	SB	CS	SB%	GDP	Avg	OBP	SLG
1989 California	AL	16	39	7	1	0	0	(0	0)	8	4	4	2	0	17	0	1	0	0	0	.00	0	.179	.220	.205
1990 California	AL	31	84	16	5	0	1	(0	1)	24	8	6	5	0	31	1	2	0	0	1	.00	2	.190	.244	.286
1991 California	AL	29	69	14	4	0	0	(0	0)	18	7	3	10	0	17	1	4	0	0	1	.00	2	.203	.313	.261
3 ML YEARS		76	192	37	10	0	1	(0	1)	50	19	13	17	0	65	2	7	0	0	2	.00	4	.193	.265	.260

Al Osuna

Pitches: Left **Bats:** Right **Pos:** RP | **Ht:** 6' 3" **Wt:** 200 **Born:** 08/10/65 **Age:** 26

		HOW MUCH HE PITCHED						WHAT HE GAVE UP									THE RESULTS				
Year Team	Lg	G	GS	CG	GF	IP	BFP	H	R	ER	HR	SH	SF	HB	TBB	IBB	SO	WP	Bk	W	L	Pct.	ShO	Sv	ERA
1987 Auburn	A	8	0	0	3	15.2	75	16	16	10	1	0	0	0	14	2	20	0	2	1	0	1.000	0	0	5.74
Asheville	A	14	0	0	7	19.2	81	20	6	6	1	0	0	0	6	0	20	0	3	2	0	1.000	0	2	2.75
1988 Osceola	A	8	0	0	2	11.2	58	12	9	9	1	0	1	0	9	1	5	0	0	0	1	.000	0	0	6.94
Asheville	A	31	0	0	19	50	212	41	19	11	1	1	0	2	25	2	41	4	9	6	1	.857	0	3	1.98
1989 Osceola	A	46	0	0	26	67.2	283	50	27	20	2	7	2	2	27	4	62	5	5	3	4	.429	0	7	2.66
1990 Columbus	AA	60	0	0	26	69.1	289	57	30	26	4	3	1	3	33	2	82	4	1	7	5	.583	0	6	3.37
1990 Houston	NL	12	0	0	2	11.1	48	10	6	6	1	0	2	3	6	1	6	3	0	2	0	1.000	0	0	4.76
1991 Houston	NL	71	0	0	32	81.2	353	59	39	31	5	6	5	3	46	5	68	3	1	7	6	.538	0	12	3.42
2 ML YEARS		83	0	0	34	93	401	69	45	37	6	6	7	6	52	6	74	6	1	9	6	.600	0	12	3.58

Dave Otto

Pitches: Left **Bats:** Left **Pos:** SP | **Ht:** 6' 7" **Wt:** 210 **Born:** 11/12/64 **Age:** 27

		HOW MUCH HE PITCHED						WHAT HE GAVE UP									THE RESULTS				
Year Team	Lg	G	GS	CG	GF	IP	BFP	H	R	ER	HR	SH	SF	HB	TBB	IBB	SO	WP	Bk	W	L	Pct.	ShO	Sv	ERA
1985 Medford	A	11	11	0	0	42.1	0	42	27	19	1	0	0	2	22	0	27	5	0	2	2	.500	0	0	4.04
1986 Madison	A	26	26	6	0	169	724	154	72	50	9	10	5	2	71	0	125	6	1	13	7	.650	1	0	2.66
1987 Madison	A	1	1	0	0	3	11	2	0	0	0	0	0	0	0	0	2	0	0	0	0	.000	0	0	0.00
Huntsville	AA	9	8	1	0	50	192	36	14	13	1	0	1	0	11	0	25	4	0	4	1	.800	0	0	2.34
1988 Tacoma	AAA	21	21	2	0	127.2	564	124	71	50	7	1	4	0	63	3	80	7	4	4	9	.308	0	0	3.52
1989 Tacoma	AAA	29	28	2	0	169	714	164	84	69	6	3	4	1	61	3	122	18	2	10	13	.435	1	0	3.67
1990 Tacoma	AAA	2	0	0	2	10	0	3	1	1	0	0	0	0	1	0	2	1	0	0	0	.000	0	0	4.50
1991 Colo Sprngs	AAA	17	15	1	1	94.2	418	110	56	50	7	3	3	1	43	2	62	7	3	5	6	.455	0	0	4.75
1987 Oakland	AL	3	0	0	3	6	24	7	6	6	1	0	0	0	1	0	3	0	0	0	0	.000	0	0	9.00
1988 Oakland	AL	3	2	0	1	10	43	9	2	2	0	0	0	0	6	0	7	0	1	0	0	.000	0	0	1.80
1989 Oakland	AL	1	1	0	0	6.2	26	6	2	2	0	1	0	0	2	0	4	0	0	0	0	.000	0	0	2.70
1990 Oakland	AL	2	0	0	2	2.1	13	3	3	2	0	0	0	0	3	0	2	0	0	0	0	.000	0	0	7.71
1991 Cleveland	AL	18	14	1	0	100	425	108	52	47	7	8	4	4	27	6	47	3	0	2	8	.200	0	0	4.23
5 ML YEARS		27	17	1	6	125	531	133	65	59	8	9	4	4	39	6	63	3	1	2	8	.200	0	0	4.25

Spike Owen

Bats: Both **Throws:** Right **Pos:** SS | **Ht:** 5'10" **Wt:** 170 **Born:** 04/19/61 **Age:** 31

		BATTING																		BASERUNNING				PERCENTAGES		
Year Team	Lg	G	AB	H	2B	3B	HR	(Hm	Rd)	TB	R	RBI	TBB	IBB	SO	HBP	SH	SF	SB	CS	SB%	GDP	Avg	OBP	SLG
1983 Seattle	AL	80	306	60	11	3	2	(1	1)	83	36	21	24	0	44	2	5	3	10	6	.63	2	.196	.257	.271
1984 Seattle	AL	152	530	130	18	8	3	(2	1)	173	67	43	46	0	63	3	9	2	16	8	.67	5	.245	.308	.326
1985 Seattle	AL	118	352	91	10	6	6	(3	3)	131	41	37	34	0	27	0	5	2	11	5	.69	5	.259	.322	.372
1986 2 ML Teams		154	528	122	24	7	1	(0	1)	163	67	45	51	1	51	2	9	3	4	4	.50	13	.231	.300	.309
1987 Boston	AL	132	437	113	17	7	2	(2	0)	150	50	48	53	2	43	1	9	4	11	8	.58	9	.259	.337	.343
1988 Boston	AL	89	257	64	14	1	5	(2	3)	95	40	18	27	0	27	2	7	1	0	1	.00	7	.249	.324	.370
1989 Montreal	NL	142	437	102	17	4	6	(5	1)	145	52	41	76	25	44	3	3	3	3	2	.60	11	.233	.349	.332
1990 Montreal	NL	149	453	106	24	5	5	(2	3)	155	55	35	70	12	60	0	5	5	8	6	.57	6	.234	.333	.342
1991 Montreal	NL	139	424	108	22	8	3	(1	2)	155	39	26	42	11	61	1	4	4	2	6	.25	11	.255	.321	.366
1986 Seattle	AL	112	402	99	22	6	0	(0	0)	133	46	35	34	1	42	1	7	2	1	3	.25	11	.246	.305	.331
Boston	AL	42	126	23	2	1	1	(0	1)	30	21	10	17	0	9	1	2	1	3	1	.75	2	.183	.283	.238
9 ML YEARS		1155	3724	896	157	49	33	(18	15)	1250	447	314	423	51	420	14	56	27	65	46	.59	69	.241	.318	.336

Mike Pagliarulo

Bats: Left **Throws:** Right **Pos:** 3B | **Ht:** 6' 2" **Wt:** 195 **Born:** 03/15/60 **Age:** 32

		BATTING																		BASERUNNING				PERCENTAGES		
Year Team	Lg	G	AB	H	2B	3B	HR	(Hm	Rd)	TB	R	RBI	TBB	IBB	SO	HBP	SH	SF	SB	CS	SB%	GDP	Avg	OBP	SLG
1984 New York	AL	67	201	48	15	3	7	(4	3)	90	24	34	15	0	46	0	0	3	0	0	.00	5	.239	.288	.448
1985 New York	AL	138	380	91	16	2	19	(8	11)	168	55	62	45	4	86	4	3	3	0	0	.00	6	.239	.324	.442
1986 New York	AL	149	504	120	24	3	28	(14	14)	234	71	71	54	10	120	4	1	2	4	1	.80	10	.238	.316	.464
1987 New York	AL	150	522	122	26	3	32	(17	15)	250	76	87	53	9	111	2	2	3	1	3	.25	9	.234	.305	.479
1988 New York	AL	125	444	96	20	1	15	(8	7)	163	46	67	37	9	104	2	1	6	1	0	1.00	5	.216	.276	.367
1989 2 ML Teams		124	371	73	17	0	7	(5	2)	111	31	30	37	4	82	3	1	1	3	1	.75	5	.197	.275	.299
1990 San Diego	NL	128	398	101	23	2	7	(1	6)	149	29	38	39	3	66	3	2	4	1	3	.25	12	.254	.322	.374
1991 Minnesota	AL	121	365	102	20	0	6	(4	2)	140	38	36	21	3	55	3	2	2	1	2	.33	9	.279	.322	.384
1989 New York	AL	74	223	44	10	0	4	(3	1)	66	19	16	19	0	43	2	0	0	1	1	.50	2	.197	.266	.296
San Diego	NL	50	148	29	7	0	3	(2	1)	45	12	14	18	4	39	1	1	0	2	0	1.00	3	.196	.287	.304
8 ML YEARS		1002	3185	753	161	14	121	(61	60)	1305	370	425	301	42	670	21	12	23	11	10	.52	61	.236	.305	.410

Tom Pagnozzi

Bats: Right   **Throws:** Right   **Pos:** C   **Ht:** 6' 1"   **Wt:** 190   **Born:** 07/30/62   **Age:** 29

						BATTING												BASERUNNING				PERCENTAGES		
Year Team	Lg	G	AB	H	2B	3B	HR	(Hm	Rd)	TB	R	RBI	TBB	IBB	SO	HBP	SH	SF	SB	CS	SB%	GDP	Avg	OBP	SLG
1987 St. Louis	NL	27	48	9	1	0	2	(2	0)	16	8	9	4	2	13	0	1	0	1	0	1.00	0	.188	.250	.333
1988 St. Louis	NL	81	195	55	9	0	0	(0	0)	64	17	15	11	1	32	0	2	1	0	0	.00	5	.282	.319	.328
1989 St. Louis	NL	52	80	12	2	0	0	(0	0)	14	3	3	6	2	19	1	0	1	0	0	.00	7	.150	.216	.175
1990 St. Louis	NL	69	220	61	15	0	2	(2	0)	82	20	23	14	1	37	1	0	2	1	1	.50	0	.277	.321	.373
1991 St. Louis	NL	140	459	121	24	5	2	(2	0)	161	38	57	36	6	63	4	6	5	9	13	.41	10	.264	.319	.351
5 ML YEARS		369	1002	258	51	5	6	(6	0)	337	86	107	71	12	164	6	9	9	11	14	.44	22	.257	.308	.336

Vince Palacios

Pitches: Right   **Bats:** Right   **Pos:** RP/SP   **Ht:** 6' 3"   **Wt:** 195   **Born:** 07/19/63   **Age:** 28

		HOW MUCH HE PITCHED						WHAT HE GAVE UP									THE RESULTS					
Year Team	Lg	G	GS	CG	GF	IP	BFP	H	R	ER	HR	SH	SF	HB	TBB	IBB	SO	WP	Bk	W	L	Pct.	ShO	Sv	ERA
1987 Pittsburgh	NL	6	4	0	0	29.1	120	27	14	14	1	2	0	1	9	1	13	0	2	2	1	.667	0	0	4.30
1988 Pittsburgh	NL	7	3	0	0	24.1	113	28	18	18	3	2	1	0	15	1	15	2	3	1	2	.333	0	0	6.66
1990 Pittsburgh	NL	7	0	0	4	15	50	4	0	0	0	0	0	0	2	0	8	2	0	0	0	.000	0	3	0.00
1991 Pittsburgh	NL	36	7	1	8	81.2	347	69	34	34	12	4	1	1	38	2	64	6	2	6	3	.667	1	3	3.75
4 ML YEARS		56	14	1	12	150.1	630	128	66	66	16	8	2	2	64	4	100	10	7	9	6	.600	1	6	3.95

Donn Pall

Pitches: Right   **Bats:** Right   **Pos:** RP   **Ht:** 6' 1"   **Wt:** 183   **Born:** 01/11/62   **Age:** 30

		HOW MUCH HE PITCHED						WHAT HE GAVE UP									THE RESULTS					
Year Team	Lg	G	GS	CG	GF	IP	BFP	H	R	ER	HR	SH	SF	HB	TBB	IBB	SO	WP	Bk	W	L	Pct.	ShO	Sv	ERA
1988 Chicago	AL	17	0	0	6	28.2	130	39	11	11	1	2	1	0	8	1	16	1	0	0	2	.000	0	0	3.45
1989 Chicago	AL	53	0	0	27	87	366	90	35	32	9	8	2	8	19	3	58	4	1	4	5	.444	0	6	3.31
1990 Chicago	AL	56	0	0	11	76	306	63	33	28	7	4	2	4	24	8	39	2	0	3	5	.375	0	2	3.32
1991 Chicago	AL	51	0	0	7	71	282	59	22	19	7	4	0	3	20	3	40	2	0	7	2	.778	0	0	2.41
4 ML YEARS		177	0	0	51	262.2	1088	251	101	90	24	18	5	15	71	15	153	9	1	14	14	.500	0	8	3.08

Rafael Palmeiro

Bats: Left   **Throws:** Left   **Pos:** 1B   **Ht:** 6' 0"   **Wt:** 188   **Born:** 09/24/64   **Age:** 27

						BATTING												BASERUNNING				PERCENTAGES		
Year Team	Lg	G	AB	H	2B	3B	HR	(Hm	Rd)	TB	R	RBI	TBB	IBB	SO	HBP	SH	SF	SB	CS	SB%	GDP	Avg	OBP	SLG
1986 Chicago	NL	22	73	18	4	0	3	(1	2)	31	9	12	4	0	6	1	0	0	1	1	.50	4	.247	.295	.425
1987 Chicago	NL	84	221	61	15	1	14	(5	9)	120	32	30	20	1	26	1	0	2	2	2	.50	4	.276	.336	.543
1988 Chicago	NL	152	580	178	41	5	8	(8	0)	253	75	53	38	6	34	3	2	6	12	2	.86	11	.307	.349	.436
1989 Texas	AL	156	559	154	23	4	8	(4	4)	209	76	64	63	3	48	6	2	4	4	3	.57	18	.275	.354	.374
1990 Texas	AL	154	598	191	35	6	14	(9	5)	280	72	89	40	6	59	3	2	8	3	3	.50	24	.319	.361	.468
1991 Texas	AL	159	631	203	49	3	26	(12	14)	336	115	88	68	10	72	6	2	7	4	3	.57	18	.322	.389	.532
6 ML YEARS		727	2662	805	167	19	73	(39	34)	1229	379	336	233	26	245	20	8	25	26	14	.65	79	.302	.360	.462

Dean Palmer

Bats: Right   **Throws:** Right   **Pos:** 3B/LF   **Ht:** 6' 1"   **Wt:** 190   **Born:** 12/27/68   **Age:** 23

						BATTING												BASERUNNING				PERCENTAGES		
Year Team	Lg	G	AB	H	2B	3B	HR	(Hm	Rd)	TB	R	RBI	TBB	IBB	SO	HBP	SH	SF	SB	CS	SB%	GDP	Avg	OBP	SLG
1986 Rangers	R	50	163	34	7	1	0	--	--	43	19	12	22	0	34	5	0	2	6	3	.67	3	.209	.318	.264
1987 Gastonia	A	128	484	104	16	0	9	--	--	147	51	54	36	1	126	6	0	1	4	4	.50	16	.215	.277	.304
1988 Charlotte	A	74	305	81	12	1	4	--	--	107	38	35	15	1	69	1	0	3	0	0	.00	12	.266	.299	.351
1989 Tulsa	AA	133	498	125	32	5	25	--	--	242	82	90	41	4	152	4	3	4	15	5	.75	6	.251	.311	.486
1990 Tulsa	AA	7	24	7	0	1	3	--	--	18	4	9	4	1	10	1	0	0	0	1	.00	0	.292	.414	.750
Okla City	AAA	88	316	69	17	4	12	--	--	130	33	39	20	0	106	4	0	3	1	1	.50	2	.218	.271	.411
1991 Okla City	AAA	60	234	70	11	2	22	--	--	151	45	59	20	2	61	2	1	2	4	5	.44	2	.299	.357	.645
1989 Texas	AL	16	19	2	2	0	0	(0	0)	4	0	1	0	0	12	0	0	1	0	0	.00	0	.105	.100	.211
1991 Texas	AL	81	268	50	9	2	15	(6	9)	108	38	37	32	0	98	3	1	0	0	2	.00	4	.187	.281	.403
2 ML YEARS		97	287	52	11	2	15	(6	9)	112	38	38	32	0	110	3	1	1	0	2	.00	4	.181	.269	.390

Erik Pappas

Bats: Right   **Throws:** Right   **Pos:** C   **Ht:** 6' 0"   **Wt:** 190   **Born:** 04/25/66   **Age:** 26

						BATTING												BASERUNNING				PERCENTAGES		
Year Team	Lg	G	AB	H	2B	3B	HR	(Hm	Rd)	TB	R	RBI	TBB	IBB	SO	HBP	SH	SF	SB	CS	SB%	GDP	Avg	OBP	SLG
1984 Salem	A	56	177	43	3	3	1	--	--	55	24	15	31	0	26	3	3	1	10	5	.67	1	.243	.363	.311
1985 Quad City	A	100	317	76	8	4	2	--	--	98	53	29	61	1	56	3	3	1	16	6	.73	3	.240	.366	.309
1986 Palm Sprngs	A	74	248	61	16	2	5	--	--	96	40	38	56	1	58	1	1	4	9	5	.64	7	.246	.382	.387
1987 Palm Sprngs	A	119	395	96	20	3	3	--	--	131	50	64	66	0	77	0	3	7	16	6	.73	8	.243	.346	.332
1988 Midland	AA	83	275	76	17	2	4	--	--	109	40	38	29	0	53	2	4	4	16	3	.84	6	.276	.345	.396

Year Team	Lg	G	AB	H	2B	3B	HR	(Hm	Rd)	TB	R	RBI	TBB	IBB	SO	HBP	SH	SF	SB	CS	SB%	GDP	Avg	OBP	SLG
1989 Charlotte	AA	119	354	106	31	1	16	--	--	187	69	49	66	1	50	8	4	2	7	8	.47	8	.299	.419	.528
1990 Iowa	AAA	131	405	101	19	2	16	--	--	172	56	55	65	1	84	8	6	3	6	5	.55	13	.249	.362	.425
1991 Iowa	AAA	88	284	78	19	1	7	--	--	120	41	48	45	4	47	4	4	3	5	3	.63	12	.275	.378	.423
1991 Chicago	NL	7	17	3	0	0	0	(0	0)	3	1	2	1	0	5	0	0	0	0	0	.00	0	.176	.222	.176

Johnny Paredes

Bats: Right **Throws:** Right **Pos:** 2B **Ht:** 5'11" **Wt:** 175 **Born:** 09/02/62 **Age:** 29

							BATTING												BASERUNNING				PERCENTAGES		
Year Team	Lg	G	AB	H	2B	3B	HR	(Hm	Rd)	TB	R	RBI	TBB	IBB	SO	HBP	SH	SF	SB	CS	SB%	GDP	Avg	OBP	SLG
1988 Montreal	NL	35	91	17	2	0	1	(0	1)	22	6	10	9	0	17	3	1	0	5	2	.71	1	.187	.282	.242
1990 2 ML Teams		9	14	3	1	0	0	(0	0)	4	2	1	2	1	0	0	0	0	0	0	.00	0	.214	.313	.286
1991 Detroit	AL	16	18	6	0	0	0	(0	0)	6	4	0	0	0	1	0	0	0	1	1	.50	0	.333	.333	.333
1990 Detroit	AL	6	8	1	0	0	0	(0	0)	1	2	0	1	0	0	0	0	0	0	0	.00	0	.125	.222	.125
Montreal	NL	3	6	2	1	0	0	(0	0)	3	0	1	1	1	0	0	0	0	0	0	.00	0	.333	.429	.500
3 ML YEARS		60	123	26	3	0	1	(0	1)	32	12	11	11	1	18	3	1	0	6	3	.67	1	.211	.292	.260

Mark Parent

Bats: Right **Throws:** Right **Pos:** C **Ht:** 6'5" **Wt:** 225 **Born:** 09/16/61 **Age:** 30

							BATTING												BASERUNNING				PERCENTAGES		
Year Team	Lg	G	AB	H	2B	3B	HR	(Hm	Rd)	TB	R	RBI	TBB	IBB	SO	HBP	SH	SF	SB	CS	SB%	GDP	Avg	OBP	SLG
1986 San Diego	NL	8	14	2	0	0	0	(0	0)	2	1	0	1	0	3	0	0	0	0	0	.00	1	.143	.200	.143
1987 San Diego	NL	12	25	2	0	0	0	(0	0)	2	0	2	0	0	9	0	0	0	0	0	.00	0	.080	.080	.080
1988 San Diego	NL	41	118	23	3	0	6	(4	2)	44	9	15	6	0	23	0	0	1	0	0	.00	0	.195	.232	.373
1989 San Diego	NL	52	141	27	4	0	7	(6	1)	52	12	21	8	2	34	0	1	4	1	0	1.00	5	.191	.229	.369
1990 San Diego	NL	65	189	42	11	0	3	(1	2)	62	13	16	16	3	29	0	3	0	1	0	1.00	2	.222	.283	.328
1991 Texas	AL	3	1	0	0	0	0	(0	0)	0	0	0	0	0	1	0	0	0	0	0	.00	0	.000	.000	.000
6 ML YEARS		181	488	96	18	0	16	(11	5)	162	35	54	31	5	99	0	4	5	2	0	1.00	9	.197	.242	.332

Dave Parker

Bats: Left **Throws:** Right **Pos:** DH **Ht:** 6'5" **Wt:** 250 **Born:** 06/09/51 **Age:** 41

							BATTING												BASERUNNING				PERCENTAGES		
Year Team	Lg	G	AB	H	2B	3B	HR	(Hm	Rd)	TB	R	RBI	TBB	IBB	SO	HBP	SH	SF	SB	CS	SB%	GDP	Avg	OBP	SLG
1973 Pittsburgh	NL	54	139	40	9	1	4	(2	2)	63	17	14	2	1	27	2	1	0	1	1	.50	2	.288	.308	.453
1974 Pittsburgh	NL	73	220	62	10	3	4	(3	1)	90	27	29	10	1	53	3	0	0	3	3	.50	2	.282	.322	.409
1975 Pittsburgh	NL	148	558	172	35	10	25	(10	15)	302	75	101	38	4	89	5	0	1	8	6	.57	18	.308	.357	.541
1976 Pittsburgh	NL	138	537	168	28	10	13	(5	8)	255	82	90	30	6	80	2	0	4	19	7	.73	16	.313	.349	.475
1977 Pittsburgh	NL	159	637	215	44	8	21	(10	11)	338	107	88	58	13	107	7	0	4	17	19	.47	7	.338	.397	.531
1978 Pittsburgh	NL	148	581	194	32	12	30	(14	16)	340	102	117	57	23	92	2	0	2	20	7	.74	8	.334	.394	.585
1979 Pittsburgh	NL	158	622	193	45	7	25	(14	11)	327	109	94	67	14	101	9	0	9	20	4	.83	7	.310	.380	.526
1980 Pittsburgh	NL	139	518	153	31	1	17	(10	7)	237	71	79	25	5	69	2	0	5	10	7	.59	8	.295	.327	.458
1981 Pittsburgh	NL	67	240	62	14	3	9	(4	5)	109	29	48	9	3	25	2	0	3	6	2	.75	5	.258	.287	.454
1982 Pittsburgh	NL	73	244	66	19	3	6	(4	2)	109	41	29	22	2	45	1	0	3	7	5	.58	7	.270	.330	.447
1983 Pittsburgh	NL	144	552	154	29	4	12	(6	6)	227	68	69	28	6	89	0	0	6	12	9	.57	11	.279	.311	.411
1984 Cincinnati	NL	156	607	173	28	0	16	(10	6)	249	73	94	41	10	89	1	0	6	11	10	.52	8	.285	.328	.410
1985 Cincinnati	NL	160	635	198	42	4	34	(18	16)	350	88	125	52	24	80	3	0	4	5	13	.28	26	.312	.365	.551
1986 Cincinnati	NL	162	637	174	31	3	31	(17	14)	304	89	116	56	16	126	1	0	6	1	6	.14	18	.273	.330	.477
1987 Cincinnati	NL	153	589	149	28	0	26	(14	12)	255	77	97	44	13	104	1	0	6	7	3	.70	14	.253	.311	.433
1988 Oakland	AL	101	377	97	18	1	12	(6	6)	153	43	55	32	2	70	0	0	2	0	1	.00	3	.257	.314	.406
1989 Oakland	AL	144	553	146	27	0	22	(10	12)	239	56	97	38	13	91	1	0	8	0	0	.00	21	.264	.308	.432
1990 Milwaukee	AL	157	610	176	30	3	21	(9	12)	275	71	92	41	11	102	4	0	14	4	7	.36	18	.289	.330	.451
1991 2 ML Teams		132	502	120	26	2	11	(6	5)	183	47	59	33	3	98	3	0	3	3	3	.50	9	.239	.288	.365
1991 California	AL	119	466	108	22	2	11	(6	5)	167	45	56	29	3	91	3	0	3	3	2	.60	9	.232	.279	.358
Toronto	AL	13	36	12	4	0	0	(0	0)	16	2	3	4	0	7	0	0	0	0	1	.00	0	.333	.400	.444
19 ML YEARS		2466	9358	2712	526	75	339	(170	169)	4405	1272	1493	683	170	1537	56	1	86	154	113	.58	209	.290	.339	.471

Rick Parker

Bats: Right **Throws:** Right **Pos:** LF **Ht:** 6'0" **Wt:** 185 **Born:** 03/20/63 **Age:** 29

							BATTING												BASERUNNING				PERCENTAGES		
Year Team	Lg	G	AB	H	2B	3B	HR	(Hm	Rd)	TB	R	RBI	TBB	IBB	SO	HBP	SH	SF	SB	CS	SB%	GDP	Avg	OBP	SLG
1985 Bend	A	55	205	51	9	1	2	--	--	68	45	20	40	0	42	4	0	3	14	7	.67	2	.249	.377	.332
1986 Spartanburg	A	62	233	69	7	3	5	--	--	97	39	28	36	0	39	2	2	0	14	9	.61	7	.296	.395	.416
Clearwater	A	63	218	51	10	2	0	--	--	65	24	15	21	1	29	2	3	2	8	9	.47	2	.234	.305	.298
1987 Clearwater	A	101	330	83	13	3	3	--	--	111	56	34	31	3	36	3	2	3	6	4	.60	4	.252	.319	.336
1988 Reading	AA	116	362	93	13	3	3	--	--	121	50	47	26	2	50	1	1	6	24	6	.80	6	.257	.324	.334
1989 Reading	AA	103	388	92	7	9	3	--	--	126	59	32	42	0	62	5	2	3	17	13	.57	8	.237	.317	.325
Phoenix	AAA	18	68	18	2	2	0	--	--	24	5	11	2	0	14	1	1	0	1	2	.33	1	.265	.296	.353

		G			GF	IP	BFP	H	R	ER	HR	SH	SF	HB	TBB	IBB	SO		Bk	W	L	Pct.	ShO	Sv	ERA
1990 Phoenix	AAA	44	173	58	7	4	1	--	--	76	38	18	22	0	25	0	0	0	18	10	.64	1	.335	.410	.439
1991 Phoenix	AAA	85	297	89	10	9	6	--	--	135	41	41	26	1	35	2	0	6	16	3	.84	7	.300	.353	.455
1990 San Francisco	NL	54	107	26	5	0	2	(0	2)	37	19	14	10	0	15	1	3	0	6	1	.86	1	.243	.314	.346
1991 San Francisco	NL	13	14	1	0	0	0	(0	0)	1	0	1	1	0	5	0	0	0	0	0	.00	0	.071	.133	.071
2 ML YEARS		67	121	27	5	0	2	(0	2)	38	19	15	11	0	20	1	3	0	6	1	.86	1	.223	.293	.314

Jeff Parrett

Pitches: Right **Bats:** Right **Pos:** RP **Ht:** 6' 3" **Wt:** 193 **Born:** 08/26/61 **Age:** 30

		HOW MUCH HE PITCHED						WHAT HE GAVE UP										THE RESULTS					
Year Team	Lg	G	GS	CG	GF	IP	BFP	H	R	ER	HR	SH	SF	HB	TBB	IBB	SO	WP	Bk	W	L	Pct.	ShO	Sv	ERA
1986 Montreal	NL	12	0	0	6	20.1	91	19	11	11	3	0	1	0	13	0	21	2	0	0	1	.000	0	0	4.87
1987 Montreal	NL	45	0	0	26	62	267	53	33	29	8	5	1	0	30	4	56	6	1	7	6	.538	0	6	4.21
1988 Montreal	NL	61	0	0	34	91.2	369	66	29	27	8	9	6	1	45	9	62	4	1	12	4	.750	0	6	2.65
1989 Philadelphia	NL	72	0	0	34	105.2	444	90	43	35	6	7	5	0	44	13	98	7	3	12	6	.667	0	6	2.98
1990 2 ML Teams		67	5	0	19	108.2	479	119	62	56	11	7	5	2	55	10	86	5	1	5	10	.333	0	2	4.64
1991 Atlanta	NL	18	0	0	9	21.1	109	31	18	15	2	2	0	0	12	2	14	4	0	1	2	.333	0	1	6.33
1990 Philadelphia	NL	47	5	0	14	81.2	355	92	51	47	10	3	1	1	36	8	69	3	1	4	9	.308	0	1	5.18
Atlanta	NL	20	0	0	5	27	124	27	11	9	1	4	4	1	19	2	17	2	0	1	1	.500	0	1	3.00
6 ML YEARS		275	5	0	128	409.2	1759	378	196	173	38	30	18	3	199	38	337	28	6	37	29	.561	0	21	3.80

Lance Parrish

Bats: Right **Throws:** Right **Pos:** C **Ht:** 6' 3" **Wt:** 224 **Born:** 06/15/56 **Age:** 36

		BATTING																	BASERUNNING				PERCENTAGES		
Year Team	Lg	G	AB	H	2B	3B	HR	(Hm	Rd)	TB	R	RBI	TBB	IBB	SO	HBP	SH	SF	SB	CS	SB%	GDP	Avg	OBP	SLG
1977 Detroit	AL	12	46	9	2	0	3	(2	1)	20	10	7	5	0	12	0	0	0	0	0	.00	2	.196	.275	.435
1978 Detroit	AL	85	288	63	11	3	14	(7	7)	122	37	41	11	0	71	3	1	1	0	0	.00	8	.219	.254	.424
1979 Detroit	AL	143	493	136	26	3	19	(8	11)	225	65	65	49	2	105	2	3	1	6	7	.46	15	.276	.343	.456
1980 Detroit	AL	144	553	158	34	6	24	(7	17)	276	79	82	31	3	109	3	2	3	6	4	.60	24	.286	.325	.499
1981 Detroit	AL	96	348	85	18	2	10	(8	2)	137	39	46	34	6	52	0	1	1	2	3	.40	16	.244	.311	.394
1982 Detroit	AL	133	486	138	19	2	32	(22	10)	257	75	87	40	5	99	1	0	2	3	4	.43	5	.284	.338	.529
1983 Detroit	AL	155	605	163	42	3	27	(12	15)	292	80	114	44	7	106	1	0	13	1	3	.25	21	.269	.314	.483
1984 Detroit	AL	147	578	137	16	2	33	(13	20)	256	75	98	41	6	120	2	2	6	2	3	.40	12	.237	.287	.443
1985 Detroit	AL	140	549	150	27	1	28	(11	17)	263	64	98	41	5	90	2	3	5	2	6	.25	10	.273	.323	.479
1986 Detroit	AL	91	327	84	6	1	22	(8	14)	158	53	62	38	3	83	5	1	3	0	0	.00	3	.257	.340	.483
1987 Philadelphia	NL	130	466	114	21	0	17	(5	12)	186	42	67	47	2	104	1	1	3	0	1	.00	23	.245	.313	.399
1988 Philadelphia	NL	123	424	91	17	2	15	(11	4)	157	44	60	47	7	93	2	0	5	0	0	.00	11	.215	.293	.370
1989 California	AL	124	433	103	12	1	17	(8	9)	168	48	50	42	6	104	2	1	4	1	1	.50	10	.238	.308	.388
1990 California	AL	133	470	126	14	0	24	(14	10)	212	54	70	46	4	107	5	0	2	2	2	.50	13	.268	.338	.451
1991 California	AL	119	402	87	12	0	19	(9	10)	156	38	51	35	2	117	5	0	7	0	1	.00	7	.216	.285	.388
15 ML YEARS		1775	6468	1644	277	26	304	(145	159)	2885	803	998	551	58	1372	34	15	52	25	35	.42	180	.254	.314	.446

Dan Pasqua

Bats: Left **Throws:** Left **Pos:** 1B/RF **Ht:** 6' 0" **Wt:** 203 **Born:** 10/17/61 **Age:** 30

		BATTING																	BASERUNNING				PERCENTAGES		
Year Team	Lg	G	AB	H	2B	3B	HR	(Hm	Rd)	TB	R	RBI	TBB	IBB	SO	HBP	SH	SF	SB	CS	SB%	GDP	Avg	OBP	SLG
1985 New York	AL	60	148	31	3	1	9	(7	2)	63	17	25	16	4	38	1	0	1	0	0	.00	1	.209	.289	.426
1986 New York	AL	102	280	82	17	0	16	(9	7)	147	44	45	47	3	78	3	1	1	2	0	1.00	4	.293	.399	.525
1987 New York	AL	113	318	74	7	1	17	(6	11)	134	42	42	40	3	99	1	2	1	0	2	.00	7	.233	.319	.421
1988 Chicago	AL	129	422	96	16	2	20	(11	9)	176	48	50	46	5	100	3	2	2	1	0	1.00	10	.227	.307	.417
1989 Chicago	AL	73	246	61	9	1	11	(5	6)	105	26	47	25	1	58	1	1	4	1	2	.33	6	.248	.315	.427
1990 Chicago	AL	112	325	89	27	3	13	(10	8)	161	43	58	37	1	66	2	0	5	1	1	.50	4	.274	.347	.495
1991 Chicago	AL	134	417	108	22	5	18	(10	8)	194	71	66	62	4	86	3	1	1	0	2	.00	9	.259	.358	.465
7 ML YEARS		723	2156	541	101	13	104	(52	52)	980	291	333	273	27	525	14	7	15	5	7	.42	35	.251	.337	.455

Bob Patterson

Pitches: Left **Bats:** Right **Pos:** RP **Ht:** 6' 2" **Wt:** 192 **Born:** 05/16/59 **Age:** 33

		HOW MUCH HE PITCHED						WHAT HE GAVE UP										THE RESULTS					
Year Team	Lg	G	GS	CG	GF	IP	BFP	H	R	ER	HR	SH	SF	HB	TBB	IBB	SO	WP	Bk	W	L	Pct.	ShO	Sv	ERA
1985 San Diego	NL	3	0	0	2	4	26	13	11	11	2	0	0	0	3	0	1	0	1	0	0	.000	0	0	24.75
1986 Pittsburgh	NL	11	5	0	2	36.1	159	49	20	20	0	1	1	0	5	2	20	0	1	2	3	.400	0	0	4.95
1987 Pittsburgh	NL	15	7	0	2	43	201	49	34	32	5	6	3	1	22	4	27	1	0	1	4	.200	0	0	6.70
1989 Pittsburgh	NL	12	3	0	2	26.2	109	23	13	12	3	1	1	0	8	2	20	0	0	4	3	.571	0	1	4.05
1990 Pittsburgh	NL	55	5	0	19	94.2	386	88	33	31	9	5	3	3	21	7	70	1	2	8	5	.615	0	5	2.95
1991 Pittsburgh	NL	54	1	0	19	65.2	270	67	32	30	7	2	2	0	15	1	57	0	0	4	3	.571	0	2	4.11
6 ML YEARS		150	21	0	46	270.1	1151	289	143	136	26	15	10	4	74	16	195	2	4	19	18	.514	0	8	4.53

Ken Patterson

Pitches: Left **Bats:** Left **Pos:** RP **Ht:** 6' 4" **Wt:** 210 **Born:** 07/08/64 **Age:** 27

Year Team	Lg	G	GS	CG	GF	IP	BFP	H	R	ER	HR	SH	SF	HB	TBB	IBB	SO	WP	Bk	W	L	Pct.	ShO	Sv	ERA
1988 Chicago	AL	9	2	0	3	20.2	92	25	11	11	2	0	0	0	7	0	8	1	1	0	2	.000	0	1	4.79
1989 Chicago	AL	50	1	0	18	65.2	284	64	37	33	11	1	4	2	28	3	43	3	1	6	1	.857	0	0	4.52
1990 Chicago	AL	43	0	0	15	66.1	283	58	27	25	6	2	5	2	34	1	40	2	0	2	1	.667	0	2	3.39
1991 Chicago	AL	43	0	0	13	63.2	265	48	22	20	5	3	2	1	35	1	32	2	0	3	0	1.000	0	0	2.83
4 ML YEARS		145	3	0	49	216.1	924	195	97	89	24	6	11	5	104	5	123	8	2	11	4	.733	0	4	3.70

Dave Pavlas

Pitches: Right **Bats:** Right **Pos:** RP **Ht:** 6' 7" **Wt:** 195 **Born:** 08/12/62 **Age:** 29

Year Team	Lg	G	GS	CG	GF	IP	BFP	H	R	ER	HR	SH	SF	HB	TBB	IBB	SO	WP	Bk	W	L	Pct.	ShO	Sv	ERA
1985 Peoria	A	17	15	3	2	110	452	90	40	32	7	3	1	3	32	0	86	6	1	8	3	.727	1	1	2.62
1986 Winston-Sal	A	28	26	5	0	173.1	739	172	91	74	8	6	4	6	57	2	143	11	1	14	6	.700	2	0	3.84
1987 Pittsfield	AA	7	7	0	0	45	199	49	25	19	6	0	3	3	17	0	27	1	1	6	1	.857	0	0	3.80
Tulsa	AA	13	12	0	1	59.2	280	79	51	51	9	1	0	3	27	0	46	7	0	1	6	.143	0	0	7.69
1988 Tulsa	AA	26	5	1	9	77.1	299	52	26	17	3	6	2	5	18	1	69	4	6	5	2	.714	0	2	1.98
Okla City	AAA	13	8	0	2	52.1	237	59	29	26	1	1	2	3	28	0	40	2	1	3	1	.750	0	0	4.47
1989 Okla City	AAA	29	21	4	4	143.2	652	175	89	75	7	6	7	7	67	4	94	8	1	2	14	.125	0	0	4.70
1990 Iowa	AAA	53	3	0	22	99.1	421	84	38	36	4	4	3	10	48	6	96	8	1	8	3	.727	0	8	3.26
1991 Iowa	AAA	61	0	0	29	97.1	418	92	49	43	5	10	5	5	43	9	54	13	0	5	6	.455	0	7	3.98
1990 Chicago	NL	13	0	0	3	21.1	93	23	7	5	2	0	2	0	6	2	12	3	0	2	0	1.000	0	0	2.11
1991 Chicago	NL	1	0	0	1	1	5	3	2	2	1	1	0	0	0	0	0	0	0	0	0	.000	0	0	18.00
2 ML YEARS		14	0	0	4	22.1	98	26	9	7	3	1	2	0	6	2	12	3	0	2	0	1.000	0	0	2.82

Bill Pecota

Bats: Right **Throws:** Right **Pos:** 3B/2B **Ht:** 6' 2" **Wt:** 190 **Born:** 02/16/60 **Age:** 32

Year Team	Lg	G	AB	H	2B	3B	HR	(Hm	Rd)	TB	R	RBI	TBB	IBB	SO	HBP	SH	SF	SB	CS	SB%	GDP	Avg	OBP	SLG
1986 Kansas City	AL	12	29	6	2	0	0	(0	0)	8	3	2	3	0	3	1	0	1	0	2	.00	1	.207	.294	.276
1987 Kansas City	AL	66	156	43	5	1	3	(0	3)	59	22	14	15	0	25	1	0	0	5	0	1.00	3	.276	.343	.378
1988 Kansas City	AL	90	178	37	3	3	1	(0	1)	49	25	15	18	0	34	2	7	1	7	2	.78	1	.208	.286	.275
1989 Kansas City	AL	65	83	17	4	2	3	(0	3)	34	21	5	7	1	9	1	1	0	5	0	1.00	1	.205	.275	.410
1990 Kansas City	AL	87	240	58	15	2	5	(3	2)	92	43	20	33	0	39	1	6	0	8	5	.62	5	.242	.336	.383
1991 Kansas City	AL	125	398	114	23	2	6	(4	2)	159	53	45	41	6	45	2	7	0	16	7	.70	12	.286	.356	.399
6 ML YEARS		445	1084	275	52	10	18	(7	11)	401	167	101	117	7	155	8	21	2	41	16	.72	26	.254	.330	.370

Jorge Pedre

Bats: Right **Throws:** Right **Pos:** C **Ht:** 5'11" **Wt:** 210 **Born:** 10/12/66 **Age:** 25

Year Team	Lg	G	AB	H	2B	3B	HR	(Hm	Rd)	TB	R	RBI	TBB	IBB	SO	HBP	SH	SF	SB	CS	SB%	GDP	Avg	OBP	SLG
1987 Eugene	A	64	233	63	15	0	13	(--	--)	117	28	66	16	2	48	12	0	1	2	1	.67	10	.270	.347	.502
1988 Appleton	A	111	412	112	20	2	6	(--	--)	154	44	54	23	1	76	4	0	6	4	2	.67	7	.272	.312	.374
1989 Baseball Cy	A	55	208	68	17	2	5	(--	--)	104	39	40	13	1	31	4	0	3	1	2	.33	2	.327	.373	.500
Memphis	AA	38	141	33	5	0	2	(--	--)	44	17	16	9	0	18	0	1	2	0	0	.00	4	.234	.276	.312
1990 Memphis	AA	99	360	93	14	1	9	(--	--)	136	55	54	27	1	47	6	0	7	6	1	.86	17	.258	.315	.378
1991 Memphis	AA	100	363	92	28	1	9	(--	--)	149	43	59	24	4	72	7	1	3	1	2	.33	7	.253	.310	.410
Omaha	AAA	31	116	25	4	0	1	(--	--)	32	12	4	4	0	18	0	0	0	2	1	.67	1	.216	.242	.276
1991 Kansas City	AL	10	19	5	1	1	0	(0	0)	8	2	3	3	0	5	0	0	0	0	0	.00	0	.263	.364	.421

Alejandro Pena

Pitches: Right **Bats:** Right **Pos:** RP **Ht:** 6' 1" **Wt:** 203 **Born:** 06/25/59 **Age:** 33

Year Team	Lg	G	GS	CG	GF	IP	BFP	H	R	ER	HR	SH	SF	HB	TBB	IBB	SO	WP	Bk	W	L	Pct.	ShO	Sv	ERA
1981 Los Angeles	NL	14	0	0	7	25	104	18	8	8	2	0	0	0	11	1	14	0	0	1	1	.500	0	2	2.88
1982 Los Angeles	NL	29	0	0	11	35.2	160	37	24	19	2	2	0	1	21	7	20	1	1	0	2	.000	0	0	4.79
1983 Los Angeles	NL	34	26	4	4	177	730	152	67	54	7	8	5	1	51	7	120	2	1	12	9	.571	3	1	2.75
1984 Los Angeles	NL	28	28	8	0	199.1	813	186	67	55	7	6	2	3	46	7	135	5	1	12	6	.667	4	0	2.48
1985 Los Angeles	NL	2	1	0	0	4.1	23	7	5	4	1	0	0	0	3	1	2	0	0	0	1	.000	0	0	8.31
1986 Los Angeles	NL	24	10	0	6	70	309	74	40	38	6	3	1	1	30	5	46	1	1	1	2	.333	0	1	4.89
1987 Los Angeles	NL	37	7	0	17	87.1	377	82	41	34	9	5	6	2	37	5	76	0	1	2	7	.222	0	11	3.50
1988 Los Angeles	NL	60	0	0	31	94.1	378	75	29	20	4	3	3	1	27	6	83	3	2	6	7	.462	0	12	1.91
1989 Los Angeles	NL	53	0	0	28	76	306	62	20	18	6	3	1	2	18	4	75	1	1	4	3	.571	0	5	2.13
1990 New York	NL	52	0	0	32	76	320	71	31	27	4	1	6	1	22	5	76	0	0	3	3	.500	0	5	3.20

Geronimo Pena

Bats: Both   **Throws:** Right   **Pos:** 2B   **Ht:** 6' 1"   **Wt:** 170   **Born:** 03/29/67   **Age:** 25

						BATTING													BASERUNNING				PERCENTAGES		
Year	Team	Lg	G	AB	H	2B	3B	HR	(Hm | Rd)	TB	R	RBI	TBB	IBB	SO	HBP	SH	SF	SB	CS	SB%	GDP	Avg	OBP	SLG
1986	Johnson Cty	R	56	202	60	7	4	3	--	--	84	55	20	46	4	33	7	1	3	27	3	.90	1	.297	.438	.416
1987	Savannah	A	134	505	136	28	3	9	--	--	197	95	51	73	6	98	8	1	3	80	21	.79	6	.269	.368	.390
1988	St. Pete	A	130	484	125	25	10	4	--	--	182	82	35	88	3	103	8	8	5	35	18	.66	5	.258	.378	.376
1989	St.Pete	A	6	21	4	1	0	0	--	--	5	2	2	3	0	6	3	0	0	2	3	.40	0	.190	.370	.238
	Arkansas	AA	77	267	79	16	8	9	--	--	138	61	44	38	3	68	8	3	4	14	6	.70	0	.296	.394	.517
1990	Louisville	AAA	118	390	97	24	6	6	--	--	151	65	35	69	0	116	18	3	4	24	12	.67	3	.249	.383	.387
1990	St. Louis	NL	18	45	11	2	0	0	(0 | 0)	13	5	2	4	0	14	1	0	1	1	1	.50	0	.244	.314	.289
1991	St. Louis	NL	104	185	45	8	3	5	(1 | 4)	74	38	17	18	1	45	5	1	3	15	5	.75	0	.243	.322	.400
	2 ML YEARS		122	230	56	10	3	5	(1 | 4)	87	43	19	22	1	59	6	1	4	16	6	.73	0	.243	.321	.378

Tony Pena

Bats: Right   **Throws:** Right   **Pos:** C   **Ht:** 6' 0"   **Wt:** 184   **Born:** 06/04/57   **Age:** 35

						BATTING													BASERUNNING				PERCENTAGES		
Year	Team	Lg	G	AB	H	2B	3B	HR	(Hm	Rd)	TB	R	RBI	TBB	IBB	SO	HBP	SH	SF	SB	CS	SB%	GDP	Avg	OBP	SLG
1980	Pittsburgh	NL	8	21	9	1	1	0	(0	0)	12	1	1	0	0	4	0	0	0	0	1	.00	1	.429	.429	.571
1981	Pittsburgh	NL	66	210	63	9	1	2	(1	1)	80	16	17	8	2	23	1	2	2	1	2	.33	4	.300	.326	.381
1982	Pittsburgh	NL	138	497	147	28	4	11	(5	6)	216	53	63	17	3	57	4	3	2	2	5	.29	17	.296	.323	.435
1983	Pittsburgh	NL	151	542	163	22	3	15	(8	7)	236	51	70	31	8	73	0	6	1	6	7	.46	13	.301	.338	.435
1984	Pittsburgh	NL	147	546	156	27	2	15	(7	8)	232	77	78	36	5	79	4	4	2	12	8	.60	14	.286	.333	.425
1985	Pittsburgh	NL	147	546	136	27	2	10	(2	8)	197	53	59	29	4	67	0	7	5	12	8	.60	19	.249	.284	.361
1986	Pittsburgh	NL	144	510	147	26	2	10	(5	5)	207	56	52	53	6	69	1	0	1	9	10	.47	21	.288	.356	.406
1987	St. Louis	NL	116	384	82	13	4	5	(1	4)	118	40	44	36	9	54	1	2	2	6	1	.86	19	.214	.281	.307
1988	St. Louis	NL	149	505	133	23	1	10	(4	6)	188	55	51	33	11	60	1	3	4	6	2	.75	12	.263	.308	.372
1989	St. Louis	NL	141	424	110	17	2	4	(3	1)	143	36	37	35	19	33	2	2	1	5	3	.63	19	.259	.318	.337
1990	Boston	AL	143	491	129	19	1	7	(3	4)	171	62	56	43	3	71	1	2	3	8	6	.57	23	.263	.322	.348
1991	Boston	AL	141	464	107	23	2	5	(2	3)	149	45	48	37	1	53	4	4	3	8	3	.73	23	.231	.291	.321
	12 ML YEARS		1491	5140	1382	235	25	94	(41	53)	1949	545	576	358	71	643	19	35	26	75	56	.57	185	.269	.317	.379

Terry Pendleton

Bats: Both   **Throws:** Right   **Pos:** 3B   **Ht:** 5' 9"   **Wt:** 195   **Born:** 07/16/60   **Age:** 31

						BATTING													BASERUNNING				PERCENTAGES		
Year	Team	Lg	G	AB	H	2B	3B	HR	(Hm	Rd)	TB	R	RBI	TBB	IBB	SO	HBP	SH	SF	SB	CS	SB%	GDP	Avg	OBP	SLG
1984	St. Louis	NL	67	262	85	16	3	1	(0	1)	110	37	33	16	3	32	0	0	5	20	5	.80	7	.324	.357	.420
1985	St. Louis	NL	149	559	134	16	3	5	(3	2)	171	56	69	37	4	75	0	3	3	17	12	.59	18	.240	.285	.306
1986	St. Louis	NL	159	578	138	26	5	1	(0	1)	177	56	59	34	10	59	1	6	7	24	6	.80	12	.239	.279	.306
1987	St. Louis	NL	159	583	167	29	4	12	(5	7)	240	82	96	70	6	74	2	3	9	19	12	.61	18	.286	.360	.412
1988	St. Louis	NL	110	391	99	20	2	6	(3	3)	141	44	53	21	4	51	2	4	3	3	3	.50	9	.253	.293	.361
1989	St. Louis	NL	162	613	162	28	5	13	(8	5)	239	83	74	44	3	81	0	2	2	9	5	.64	16	.264	.313	.390
1990	St. Louis	NL	121	447	103	20	2	6	(6	0)	145	46	58	30	8	58	1	0	6	7	5	.58	12	.230	.277	.324
1991	Atlanta	NL	153	586	187	34	8	22	(13	9)	303	94	86	43	8	70	1	7	7	10	2	.83	16	.319	.363	.517
	8 ML YEARS		1080	4019	1075	189	32	66	(38	28)	1526	498	528	295	46	500	7	25	42	109	50	.69	108	.267	.316	.380

Melido Perez

Pitches: Right   **Bats:** Right   **Pos:** RP/SP   **Ht:** 6' 4"   **Wt:** 180   **Born:** 02/15/66   **Age:** 26

						HOW MUCH HE PITCHED				WHAT HE GAVE UP											THE RESULTS			
Year	Team	Lg	G	GS	CG	GF	IP	BFP	H	R	ER	HR	SH	SF	HB	TBB	IBB	SO	WP	Bk	W	L	Pct.	ShO	Sv	ERA
1987	Kansas City	AL	3	3	0	0	10.1	53	18	12	9	2	0	0	0	5	0	5	0	0	1	1	.500	0	0	7.84
1988	Chicago	AL	32	32	3	0	197	836	186	105	83	26	5	8	2	72	0	138	13	3	12	10	.545	1	0	3.79
1989	Chicago	AL	31	31	2	0	183.1	810	187	106	102	23	5	4	3	90	3	141	12	5	11	14	.440	0	0	5.01
1990	Chicago	AL	35	35	3	0	197	833	177	111	101	14	4	6	2	86	1	161	8	4	13	14	.481	3	0	4.61
1991	Chicago	AL	49	8	0	16	135.2	553	111	49	47	15	4	1	1	52	0	128	11	1	8	7	.533	0	1	3.12
	5 ML YEARS		150	109	8	16	723.1	3085	679	383	342	80	18	19	8	305	4	573	44	13	45	46	.495	4	1	4.26

Mike Perez

Pitches: Right **Bats:** Right **Pos:** RP **Ht:** 6' 0" **Wt:** 187 **Born:** 10/19/64 **Age:** 27

Year Team	Lg	G	GS	CG	GF	IP	BFP	H	R	ER	HR	SH	SF	HB	TBB	IBB	SO	WP	Bk	W	L	Pct.	ShO	Sv	ERA
1986 Johnson Cty	R	18	8	2	6	72.2	314	69	35	24	3	1	2	5	22	0	72	1	0	3	5	.375	0	3	2.97
1987 Springfield	A	58	0	0	51	84.1	321	47	12	8	2	3	2	2	21	3	119	2	0	6	2	.750	0	41	0.85
1988 Arkansas	AA	11	0	0	6	14.1	75	18	18	18	2	1	2	1	13	2	17	2	3	1	3	.250	0	0	11.30
St. Pete	A	35	0	0	28	43.1	173	24	12	10	0	2	3	4	16	1	45	2	4	2	2	.500	0	17	2.08
1989 Arkansas	AA	57	0	0	51	76.2	329	68	34	31	5	0	2	2	32	2	74	3	1	4	6	.400	0	33	3.64
1990 Louisville	AAA	57	0	0	50	67.1	298	64	34	32	9	4	1	2	33	4	69	3	0	7	7	.500	0	31	4.28
1991 Louisville	AAA	37	0	0	23	47	225	54	38	32	5	5	2	2	25	6	38	5	0	3	5	.375	0	4	6.13
1990 St. Louis	NL	13	0	0	7	13.2	55	12	6	6	0	0	2	0	3	0	5	0	0	1	0	1.000	0	1	3.95
1991 St. Louis	NL	14	0	0	2	17	75	19	11	11	1	1	0	1	7	2	7	0	1	0	2	.000	0	0	5.82
2 ML YEARS		27	0	0	9	30.2	130	31	17	17	1	1	2	1	10	2	12	0	1	1	2	.333	0	1	4.99

Pascual Perez

Pitches: Right **Bats:** Right **Pos:** SP **Ht:** 6' 3" **Wt:** 183 **Born:** 05/17/57 **Age:** 35

Year Team	Lg	G	GS	CG	GF	IP	BFP	H	R	ER	HR	SH	SF	HB	TBB	IBB	SO	WP	Bk	W	L	Pct.	ShO	Sv	ERA
1980 Pittsburgh	NL	2	2	0	0	12	51	15	6	5	0	1	2	2	2	0	7	0	0	0	1	.000	0	0	3.75
1981 Pittsburgh	NL	17	13	2	1	86	380	92	50	38	5	6	0	3	34	9	46	5	1	2	7	.222	0	0	3.98
1982 Atlanta	NL	16	11	0	2	79.1	333	85	35	27	4	5	3	0	17	3	29	2	1	4	4	.500	0	0	3.06
1983 Atlanta	NL	33	33	7	0	215.1	889	213	88	82	20	12	4	4	51	5	144	7	0	15	8	.652	1	0	3.43
1984 Atlanta	NL	30	30	4	0	211.2	864	208	96	88	26	6	4	3	51	5	145	4	5	14	8	.636	1	0	3.74
1985 Atlanta	NL	22	22	0	0	95.1	453	115	72	65	10	5	3	1	57	10	57	2	2	1	13	.071	0	0	6.14
1987 Montreal	NL	10	10	2	0	70.1	273	52	21	18	5	3	1	1	16	1	58	1	1	7	0	1.000	0	0	2.30
1988 Montreal	NL	27	27	4	0	188	741	133	59	51	15	10	3	7	44	6	131	5	10	12	8	.600	2	0	2.44
1989 Montreal	NL	33	28	2	3	198.1	811	178	85	73	15	6	4	4	45	13	152	6	1	9	13	.409	0	0	3.31
1990 New York	AL	3	3	0	0	14	52	8	3	2	0	0	0	0	3	0	12	1	0	1	2	.333	0	0	1.29
1991 New York	AL	14	14	0	0	73.2	299	68	26	26	7	3	0	0	24	1	41	3	2	2	4	.333	0	0	3.18
11 ML YEARS		207	193	21	6	1244	5146	1167	541	475	107	57	24	25	344	53	822	36	23	67	68	.496	4	0	3.44

Yorkis Perez

Pitches: Left **Bats:** Left **Pos:** RP **Ht:** 6' 0" **Wt:** 180 **Born:** 09/30/67 **Age:** 24

Year Team	Lg	G	GS	CG	GF	IP	BFP	H	R	ER	HR	SH	SF	HB	TBB	IBB	SO	WP	Bk	W	L	Pct.	ShO	Sv	ERA
1984 Elizabethtn	R	1	0	0	0	1.1	6	1	0	0	0	0	0	0	1	0	1	1	0	0	0	.000	0	0	0.00
1986 Kenosha	A	31	18	3	9	131	591	120	81	75	9	4	4	3	88	1	144	13	1	4	11	.267	0	0	5.15
1987 Jacksnville	AA	12	10	1	1	60	263	61	34	27	4	0	5	1	30	0	60	4	0	2	7	.222	1	1	4.05
Wst Plm Bch	A	15	15	3	0	100	413	78	36	26	4	2	3	0	46	0	111	8	1	6	2	.750	0	0	2.34
1988 Jacksnville	AA	27	25	2	1	130	618	142	96	84	11	2	6	4	94	0	105	13	9	8	12	.400	1	0	5.82
1989 Wst Plm Bch	A	18	12	0	3	94.2	385	62	34	29	2	1	2	3	54	0	85	5	4	7	6	.538	0	1	2.76
Jacksnville	AA	20	0	0	3	35	164	25	16	14	0	1	0	0	34	1	50	1	2	4	3	.571	0	1	3.60
1990 Jacksnville	AA	28	2	0	8	42	200	36	34	28	5	2	1	1	34	2	39	4	0	2	2	.500	0	1	6.00
Indianapols	AAA	9	0	0	2	11.2	49	8	5	3	1	2	0	0	6	0	8	0	0	1	1	.500	0	1	2.31
1991 Richmond	AAA	36	10	0	5	107	459	99	47	45	7	3	7	2	53	1	102	7	2	12	3	.800	0	1	3.79
1991 Chicago	NL	3	0	0	0	4.1	16	2	1	1	0	0	2	0	2	0	3	2	0	1	0	1.000	0	0	2.08

Tony Perezchica

Bats: Right **Throws:** Right **Pos:** SS **Ht:** 5'11" **Wt:** 165 **Born:** 04/20/66 **Age:** 26

Year Team	Lg	G	AB	H	2B	3B	HR	(Hm	Rd)	TB	R	RBI	TBB	IBB	SO	HBP	SH	SF	SB	CS	SB%	GDP	Avg	OBP	SLG
1984 Everett	A	33	119	23	6	1	0	--	--	31	10	10	6	0	24	1	1	2	0	0	.00	4	.193	.234	.261
1985 Clinton	A	127	452	109	21	8	4	--	--	158	54	40	28	0	77	9	6	5	23	7	.77	9	.241	.296	.350
1986 Fresno	A	126	452	126	30	8	9	--	--	199	65	54	35	0	91	14	10	2	18	6	.75	11	.279	.348	.440
1987 Shreveport	AA	89	332	106	24	1	11	--	--	165	44	47	19	4	74	4	3	3	3	3	.50	10	.319	.360	.497
1988 Phoenix	AAA	134	517	158	18	10	9	--	--	223	79	64	44	1	125	3	7	3	10	13	.43	16	.306	.362	.431
1989 Phoenix	AAA	94	307	71	11	3	8	--	--	112	40	33	15	0	65	5	2	7	5	4	.56	8	.231	.272	.365
1990 Phoenix	AAA	105	392	105	22	6	9	--	--	166	55	49	34	3	76	7	0	4	8	5	.62	8	.268	.334	.423
1991 Phoenix	AAA	51	191	56	10	4	8	--	--	98	41	34	18	0	43	6	1	3	1	0	1.00	4	.293	.367	.513
1988 San Francisco	NL	7	8	1	0	0	0	(0	0)	1	1	1	2	0	1	0	0	1	0	0	.00	0	.125	.273	.125
1990 San Francisco	NL	4	3	1	0	0	0	(0	0)	1	1	0	1	0	2	0	0	0	0	0	.00	0	.333	.500	.333
1991 2 ML Teams		40	70	19	6	1	0	(0	0)	27	6	3	5	0	17	0	0	0	0	0	.00	4	.271	.320	.386
1991 San Francisco	NL	23	48	11	4	1	0	(0	0)	17	2	3	2	0	12	0	0	0	0	0	.00	0	.229	.260	.354

Year Team	Lg	G	AB	H	2B	3B	HR	(Hm Rd)	TB	R	RBI	TBB	IBB	SO	HBP	SH	SF	SB	CS	SB%	GDP	Avg	OBP	SLG
Cleveland	AL	17	22	8	2	0	0	(0 0)	10	4	0	3	0	5	0	0	0	0	0	.00	0	.364	.440	.455
3 ML YEARS		51	81	21	6	1	0	(0 0)	29	8	4	8	0	20	0	0	1	0	1	.00	0	.259	.322	.358

Gerald Perry

Bats: Left   **Throws:** Right   **Pos:** 1B   **Ht:** 6' 0"   **Wt:** 190   **Born:** 10/30/60   **Age:** 31

		BATTING																BASERUNNING				PERCENTAGES		
Year Team	Lg	G	AB	H	2B	3B	HR	(Hm Rd)	TB	R	RBI	TBB	IBB	SO	HBP	SH	SF	SB	CS	SB%	GDP	Avg	OBP	SLG
1983 Atlanta	NL	27	39	14	2	0	1	(0 1)	19	5	6	5	0	4	0	0	1	0	1	.00	1	.359	.422	.487
1984 Atlanta	NL	122	347	92	12	2	7	(3 4)	129	52	47	61	5	38	2	2	7	15	12	.56	9	.265	.372	.372
1985 Atlanta	NL	110	238	51	5	0	3	(3 0)	65	22	13	23	1	28	0	0	1	9	5	.64	7	.214	.282	.273
1986 Atlanta	NL	29	70	19	2	0	2	(2 0)	27	6	11	8	1	4	0	1	1	0	0	.00	4	.271	.342	.386
1987 Atlanta	NL	142	533	144	35	2	12	(2 10)	219	77	74	48	1	63	1	3	5	42	16	.72	18	.270	.329	.411
1988 Atlanta	NL	141	547	164	29	1	8	(4 4)	219	61	74	36	9	41	1	1	10	29	14	.67	18	.300	.338	.400
1989 Atlanta	NL	72	266	67	11	0	4	(2 2)	90	24	21	32	5	28	3	0	2	10	6	.63	5	.252	.337	.338
1990 Kansas City	AL	133	465	118	22	2	8	(3 5)	168	57	57	39	4	56	3	0	5	17	4	.81	15	.254	.313	.361
1991 St. Louis	NL	109	242	58	8	4	6	(1 5)	92	29	36	22	1	34	0	0	3	15	8	.65	2	.240	.300	.380
9 ML YEARS		885	2747	727	126	11	51	(20 31)	1028	333	339	274	27	304	10	7	35	137	67	.67	79	.265	.330	.374

Adam Peterson

Pitches: Right   **Bats:** Right   **Pos:** SP   **Ht:** 6' 3"   **Wt:** 190   **Born:** 12/11/65   **Age:** 26

		HOW MUCH HE PITCHED						WHAT HE GAVE UP										THE RESULTS					
Year Team	Lg	G	GS	CG	GF	IP	BFP	H	R	ER	HR	SH	SF	HB	TBB	IBB	SO	WP	Bk	W	L	Pct.	ShO	Sv	ERA
1987 Chicago	AL	1	1	0	0	4	22	8	6	6	1	0	1	0	3	0	1	0	0	0	0	.000	0	0	13.50
1988 Chicago	AL	2	2	0	0	6	31	6	9	9	0	0	0	0	6	1	5	1	0	0	1	.000	0	0	13.50
1989 Chicago	AL	3	2	0	0	5.1	31	13	9	9	1	1	0	0	2	0	3	0	0	0	1	.000	0	0	15.19
1990 Chicago	AL	20	11	2	4	85	357	90	46	43	12	2	3	2	26	0	29	3	0	2	5	.286	0	0	4.55
1991 San Diego	NL	13	11	0	0	54.2	241	50	33	27	10	4	2	0	28	2	37	7	1	3	4	.429	0	0	4.45
5 ML YEARS		39	27	2	4	155	682	167	103	94	24	7	6	2	65	3	75	11	1	5	11	.313	0	0	5.46

Mark Petkovsek

Pitches: Right   **Bats:** Right   **Pos:** RP   **Ht:** 6' 0"   **Wt:** 185   **Born:** 11/18/65   **Age:** 26

		HOW MUCH HE PITCHED						WHAT HE GAVE UP										THE RESULTS					
Year Team	Lg	G	GS	CG	GF	IP	BFP	H	R	ER	HR	SH	SF	HB	TBB	IBB	SO	WP	Bk	W	L	Pct.	ShO	Sv	ERA
1987 Rangers	R	3	1	0	0	5.2	26	4	2	2	0	0	2	2	0	7	0	0	0	0	.000	0	0	3.18
Charlotte	A	11	10	0	1	56	249	67	36	25	2	3	3	0	17	0	23	5	1	3	4	.429	0	0	4.02
1988 Charlotte	A	28	28	7	0	175.2	708	156	71	58	5	6	7	3	42	2	95	11	4	10	11	.476	5	0	2.97
1989 Okla City	AAA	6	6	0	0	30.2	147	39	27	25	3	1	1	3	18	1	8	2	0	4	0	.000	0	0	7.34
Tulsa	AA	21	21	1	0	140	585	144	63	54	7	6	7	3	35	0	66	5	0	8	5	.615	0	0	3.47
1990 Okla City	AAA	28	28	2	0	151	669	187	103	88	9	3	2	4	42	1	81	8	0	7	14	.333	1	0	5.25
1991 Okla City	AAA	25	24	3	0	149.2	646	162	89	82	9	5	9	7	38	2	67	10	1	9	8	.529	1	0	4.93
1991 Texas	AL	4	1	0	1	9.1	53	21	16	15	4	0	1	0	4	0	6	2	0	0	1	.000	0	0	14.46

Geno Petralli

Bats: Left   **Throws:** Right   **Pos:** C   **Ht:** 6' 1"   **Wt:** 190   **Born:** 09/25/59   **Age:** 32

		BATTING																BASERUNNING				PERCENTAGES		
Year Team	Lg	G	AB	H	2B	3B	HR	(Hm Rd)	TB	R	RBI	TBB	IBB	SO	HBP	SH	SF	SB	CS	SB%	GDP	Avg	OBP	SLG
1982 Toronto	AL	16	44	16	2	0	0	(0 0)	18	3	1	4	0	6	0	1	0	0	0	.00	1	.364	.417	.409
1983 Toronto	AL	6	4	0	0	0	0	(0 0)	0	0	0	1	0	1	0	0	0	0	0	.00	0	.000	.200	.000
1984 Toronto	AL	3	3	0	0	0	0	(0 0)	0	0	0	0	0	0	0	0	0	0	0	.00	0	.000	.000	.000
1985 Texas	AL	42	100	27	2	0	0	(0 0)	29	7	11	8	0	12	1	3	4	1	0	1.00	4	.270	.319	.290
1986 Texas	AL	69	137	35	9	3	2	(1 1)	56	17	18	5	0	14	0	0	0	3	0	1.00	7	.255	.282	.409
1987 Texas	AL	101	202	61	11	2	7	(4 3)	97	28	31	27	2	29	2	0	1	0	2	.00	4	.302	.388	.480
1988 Texas	AL	129	351	99	14	2	7	(1 6)	138	35	36	41	5	52	2	1	5	0	1	.00	12	.282	.356	.393
1989 Texas	AL	70	184	56	7	0	4	(1 3)	75	18	23	17	1	24	2	1	1	0	0	.00	5	.304	.368	.408
1990 Texas	AL	133	325	83	13	1	0	(0 0)	98	28	21	50	3	49	3	1	3	0	2	.00	12	.255	.357	.302
1991 Texas	AL	87	199	54	8	1	2	(0 2)	70	21	20	21	1	25	0	7	1	2	1	.67	4	.271	.339	.352
10 ML YEARS		656	1549	431	66	9	22	(7 15)	581	157	161	174	12	212	10	14	15	6	6	.50	49	.278	.352	.375

Dan Petry

Pitches: Right   **Bats:** Right   **Pos:** RP/SP   **Ht:** 6' 4"   **Wt:** 215   **Born:** 11/13/58   **Age:** 33

		HOW MUCH HE PITCHED						WHAT HE GAVE UP										THE RESULTS					
Year Team	Lg	G	GS	CG	GF	IP	BFP	H	R	ER	HR	SH	SF	HB	TBB	IBB	SO	WP	Bk	W	L	Pct.	ShO	Sv	ERA
1979 Detroit	AL	15	15	2	0	98	401	90	46	44	11	5	5	4	33	1	43	3	1	6	5	.545	0	0	3.95
1980 Detroit	AL	27	25	4	1	165	716	156	82	72	9	10	5	1	83	14	88	5	2	10	9	.526	3	0	3.93
1981 Detroit	AL	23	22	7	1	141	583	115	53	47	10	9	2	1	57	4	79	3	1	10	9	.526	2	0	3.00
1982 Detroit	AL	35	35	8	0	246	1031	220	98	88	15	8	8	4	100	5	132	9	0	15	9	.625	1	0	3.22
1983 Detroit	AL	38	38	9	0	266.1	1115	256	126	116	37	5	5	6	99	7	122	12	0	19	11	.633	2	0	3.92

161

Year	Team	Lg	G	GS	CG	GF	IP	BFP	H	R	ER	HR	SH	SF	HB	TBB	IBB	SO	WP	Bk	W	L	Pct.	ShO	Sv	ERA
1984	Detroit	AL	35	35	7	0	233.1	968	231	94	84	21	5	2	3	66	4	144	7	0	18	8	.692	2	0	3.24
1985	Detroit	AL	34	34	8	0	238.2	962	190	98	89	24	0	2	3	81	9	109	6	0	15	13	.536	0	0	3.36
1986	Detroit	AL	20	20	2	0	116	520	122	78	60	15	3	3	5	53	3	56	5	0	5	10	.333	0	0	4.66
1987	Detroit	AL	30	21	0	3	134.2	628	148	101	84	22	4	7	10	76	5	93	8	1	9	7	.563	0	0	5.61
1988	California	AL	22	22	4	0	139.2	604	139	70	68	18	5	6	6	59	5	64	5	2	3	9	.250	1	0	4.38
1989	California	AL	19	4	0	3	51	223	53	32	31	8	1	5	1	23	0	21	2	0	3	2	.600	0	0	5.47
1990	Detroit	AL	32	23	1	2	149.2	655	148	78	74	14	8	6	1	77	7	73	10	0	10	9	.526	0	0	4.45
1991	3 ML Teams	AL	40	6	0	12	101.1	454	116	69	55	14	4	1	2	45	6	39	2	0	2	3	.400	0	1	4.88
1991	Detroit	AL	17	6	0	1	54.2	240	66	35	30	9	1	0	0	19	3	18	0	0	2	3	.400	0	0	4.94
	Atlanta	NL	10	0	0	4	24.1	116	29	17	15	2	3	0	1	14	1	9	2	0	0	0	.000	0	0	5.55
	Boston	AL	13	0	0	7	22.1	98	21	17	10	3	0	1	1	12	2	12	0	0	0	0	.000	0	1	4.03
13 ML YEARS			370	300	52	22	2080.2	8860	1984	1025	911	218	67	57	47	852	74	1063	77	7	125	104	.546	11	1	3.94

Gary Pettis

Bats: Both **Throws:** Right **Pos:** CF **Ht:** 6' 1" **Wt:** 160 **Born:** 04/03/58 **Age:** 34

								BATTING												BASERUNNING				PERCENTAGES		
Year	Team	Lg	G	AB	H	2B	3B	HR	(Hm	Rd)	TB	R	RBI	TBB	IBB	SO	HBP	SH	SF	SB	CS	SB%	GDP	Avg	OBP	SLG
1982	California	AL	10	5	1	0	0	1	(1	0)	4	5	1	0	0	2	0	0	0	0	0	.00	0	.200	.200	.800
1983	California	AL	22	85	25	2	3	3	(3	0)	42	19	6	7	0	15	0	1	0	8	3	.73	1	.294	.348	.494
1984	California	AL	140	397	90	11	6	2	(1	1)	119	63	29	60	1	115	3	5	1	48	17	.74	4	.227	.332	.300
1985	California	AL	125	443	114	10	8	1	(0	1)	143	67	32	62	0	125	0	9	2	56	9	.86	5	.257	.347	.323
1986	California	AL	154	539	139	23	4	5	(1	4)	185	93	58	69	2	132	0	15	5	50	13	.79	7	.258	.338	.343
1987	California	AL	133	394	82	13	2	1	(1	0)	102	49	17	52	0	124	1	1	0	24	5	.83	8	.208	.302	.259
1988	Detroit	AL	129	458	96	14	4	3	(0	3)	127	65	36	47	0	85	1	6	0	44	10	.81	3	.210	.285	.277
1989	Detroit	AL	119	444	114	8	6	1	(1	0)	137	77	18	84	0	106	0	8	0	43	15	.74	14	.257	.375	.309
1990	Texas	AL	136	423	101	16	8	3	(3	0)	142	66	31	57	0	118	4	11	3	38	15	.72	6	.239	.333	.336
1991	Texas	AL	137	282	61	7	5	0	(0	0)	78	37	19	54	0	91	0	6	1	29	13	.69	4	.216	.341	.277
10 ML YEARS			1105	3470	823	104	46	20	(11	9)	1079	541	247	492	3	913	9	62	12	340	100	.77	52	.237	.332	.311

Tony Phillips

Bats: Both **Throws:** Right **Pos:** 3B/2B/SS/LF/RF/DH **Ht:** 5'10" **Wt:** 175 **Born:** 04/25/59 **Age:** 33

								BATTING												BASERUNNING				PERCENTAGES		
Year	Team	Lg	G	AB	H	2B	3B	HR	(Hm	Rd)	TB	R	RBI	TBB	IBB	SO	HBP	SH	SF	SB	CS	SB%	GDP	Avg	OBP	SLG
1982	Oakland	AL	40	81	17	2	2	0	(0	0)	23	11	8	12	0	26	2	5	0	2	3	.40	0	.210	.326	.284
1983	Oakland	AL	148	412	102	12	3	4	(1	3)	132	54	35	48	1	70	2	11	3	16	5	.76	5	.248	.327	.320
1984	Oakland	AL	154	451	120	24	3	4	(2	2)	162	62	37	42	1	86	0	7	5	10	6	.63	5	.266	.325	.359
1985	Oakland	AL	42	161	45	12	2	4	(2	2)	73	23	17	13	0	34	0	3	1	3	2	.60	1	.280	.331	.453
1986	Oakland	AL	118	441	113	14	5	5	(3	2)	152	76	52	76	0	82	3	9	3	15	10	.60	2	.256	.367	.345
1987	Oakland	AL	111	379	91	20	0	10	(5	5)	141	48	46	57	1	76	0	2	3	7	6	.54	9	.240	.337	.372
1988	Oakland	AL	79	212	43	8	4	2	(2	0)	65	32	17	36	0	50	1	1	1	0	2	.00	6	.203	.320	.307
1989	Oakland	AL	143	451	118	15	6	4	(2	2)	157	48	47	58	2	66	3	5	7	3	8	.27	17	.262	.345	.348
1990	Detroit	AL	152	573	144	23	5	8	(4	4)	201	97	55	99	0	85	4	9	2	19	9	.68	10	.251	.364	.351
1991	Detroit	AL	146	564	160	28	4	17	(9	8)	247	87	72	79	5	95	3	4	2	10	5	.67	8	.284	.371	.438
10 ML YEARS			1133	3725	953	158	34	58	(30	28)	1353	538	386	520	10	670	18	55	31	85	56	.60	63	.256	.347	.363

Doug Piatt

Pitches: Right **Bats:** Left **Pos:** RP **Ht:** 6' 1" **Wt:** 185 **Born:** 09/26/65 **Age:** 26

						HOW MUCH HE PITCHED			WHAT HE GAVE UP											THE RESULTS					
Year	Team	Lg	G	GS	CG	GF	IP	BFP	H	R	ER	HR	SH	SF	HB	TBB	IBB	SO	WP	Bk	W	L	Pct.	ShO	Sv	ERA
1988	Burlington	R	2	0	0	1	1.1	9	4	2	2	0	0	0	0	1	0	1	0	0	0	0	.000	0	1	13.50
	Waterloo	A	26	0	0	22	36.2	153	33	18	9	2	1	1	0	11	1	40	1	1	2	1	.667	0	12	2.21
1989	Kinston	A	20	0	0	12	28.2	115	24	8	8	1	3	0	3	8	0	31	0	1	2	0	1.000	0	1	2.51
	Watertown	A	15	0	0	15	35	137	21	5	2	0	1	0	0	9	4	43	2	0	4	2	.667	0	6	0.51
	Rockford	A	11	0	0	6	19.2	86	19	7	7	1	1	0	0	11	1	24	2	0	2	2	.500	0	2	3.20
1990	Wst Plm Bch	A	21	0	0	13	27.1	111	12	6	3	0	2	0	1	16	0	41	0	2	4	1	.800	0	9	0.99
	Jacksnville	AA	35	0	0	22	49	206	30	17	12	1	2	1	3	29	2	51	1	0	5	1	.833	0	6	2.20
1991	Indianapolis	AAA	44	0	0	32	47	210	40	24	18	2	3	3	3	27	1	61	5	1	6	4	.600	0	13	3.45
1991	Montreal	NL	21	0	0	3	34.2	145	29	11	10	2	0	0	0	17	0	29	1	0	0	0	.000	0	0	2.60

Phil Plantier

Bats: Left **Throws:** Right **Pos:** RF/LF **Ht:** 6' 0" **Wt:** 175 **Born:** 01/27/69 **Age:** 23

								BATTING												BASERUNNING				PERCENTAGES		
Year	Team	Lg	G	AB	H	2B	3B	HR	(Hm	Rd)	TB	R	RBI	TBB	IBB	SO	HBP	SH	SF	SB	CS	SB%	GDP	Avg	OBP	SLG
1987	Elmira	A	28	80	14	0	0	2	--	--	22	9	9	9	0	21	1	1	0	0	0	.00	4	.175	.256	.275
1988	Winter Havn	A	111	337	81	13	1	4	--	--	108	29	32	51	6	62	5	3	3	0	2	.00	4	.240	.346	.320
1989	Lynchburg	A	131	443	133	26	1	27	--	--	242	73	105	74	7	122	7	0	4	4	5	.44	2	.300	.405	.546
1990	Pawtucket	AAA	123	430	109	22	3	33	--	--	236	83	79	62	3	148	9	3	3	1	8	.11	4	.253	.357	.549

162

Year	Team		G	AB	H	2B	3B	HR	(Hm	Rd)	TB	R	RBI	TBB	IBB	SO	HBP	SH	SF	SB	CS	SB%	GDP	Avg	OBP	SLG
1991	Pawtucket	AAA	84	298	91	19	4	16	--	--	166	69	61	65	2	64	5	0	0	6	1	.86	4	.305	.438	.557
1990	Boston	AL	14	15	2	1	0	0	(0	0)	3	1	3	4	0	6	1	0	1	0	0	.00	1	.133	.333	.200
1991	Boston	AL	53	148	49	7	1	11	(6	5)	91	27	35	23	2	38	1	0	2	1	0	1.00	3	.331	.420	.615
	2 ML YEARS		67	163	51	8	1	11	(6	5)	94	28	38	27	2	44	2	0	3	1	0	1.00	4	.313	.410	.577

Dan Plesac

Pitches: Left **Bats:** Left **Pos:** RP/SP **Ht:** 6' 5" **Wt:** 215 **Born:** 02/04/62 **Age:** 30

			HOW MUCH HE PITCHED						WHAT HE GAVE UP											THE RESULTS					
Year	Team	Lg	G	GS	CG	GF	IP	BFP	H	R	ER	HR	SH	SF	HB	TBB	IBB	SO	WP	Bk	W	L	Pct.	ShO	Sv	ERA
1986	Milwaukee	AL	51	0	0	33	91	377	81	34	30	5	6	5	0	29	1	75	4	0	10	7	.588	0	14	2.97
1987	Milwaukee	AL	57	0	0	47	79.1	325	63	30	23	8	1	2	3	23	1	89	6	0	5	6	.455	0	23	2.61
1988	Milwaukee	AL	50	0	0	48	52.1	211	46	14	14	2	2	0	0	12	2	52	4	6	1	2	.333	0	30	2.41
1989	Milwaukee	AL	52	0	0	51	61.1	242	47	16	16	6	0	4	0	17	1	52	0	0	3	4	.429	0	33	2.35
1990	Milwaukee	AL	66	0	0	52	69	299	67	36	34	5	2	2	3	31	6	65	2	0	3	7	.300	0	24	4.43
1991	Milwaukee	AL	45	10	0	25	92.1	402	92	49	44	12	3	7	3	39	1	61	2	1	2	7	.222	0	8	4.29
	6 ML YEARS		321	10	0	256	445.1	1856	396	179	161	38	14	20	9	151	12	394	18	7	24	33	.421	0	132	3.25

Eric Plunk

Pitches: Right **Bats:** Right **Pos:** RP/SP **Ht:** 6' 5" **Wt:** 217 **Born:** 09/03/63 **Age:** 28

			HOW MUCH HE PITCHED						WHAT HE GAVE UP											THE RESULTS					
Year	Team	Lg	G	GS	CG	GF	IP	BFP	H	R	ER	HR	SH	SF	HB	TBB	IBB	SO	WP	Bk	W	L	Pct.	ShO	Sv	ERA
1986	Oakland	AL	26	15	0	2	120.1	537	91	75	71	14	2	3	5	102	2	98	9	6	4	7	.364	0	0	5.31
1987	Oakland	AL	32	11	0	11	95	432	91	53	50	8	3	5	2	62	3	90	5	2	4	6	.400	0	2	4.74
1988	Oakland	AL	49	0	0	22	78	331	62	27	26	6	3	2	1	39	4	79	4	7	7	2	.778	0	5	3.00
1989	2 ML Teams		50	7	0	17	104.1	445	82	43	38	10	3	4	1	64	2	85	10	3	8	6	.571	0	1	3.28
1990	New York	AL	47	0	0	16	72.2	310	58	27	22	6	7	0	2	43	4	67	4	2	6	3	.667	0	0	2.72
1991	New York	AL	43	8	0	6	111.2	521	128	69	59	18	6	4	1	62	1	103	6	2	2	5	.286	0	0	4.76
1989	New York	AL	23	0	0	12	28.2	113	17	7	7	1	1	0	1	12	0	24	4	0	1	1	.500	0	1	2.20
	New York	AL	27	7	0	5	75.2	332	65	36	31	9	2	4	0	52	2	61	6	3	7	5	.583	0	0	3.69
	6 ML YEARS		247	41	0	74	582	2576	512	294	266	62	24	18	12	372	16	522	38	22	31	29	.517	0	8	4.11

Jeff Plympton

Pitches: Right **Bats:** Right **Pos:** RP **Ht:** 6' 2" **Wt:** 205 **Born:** 11/24/65 **Age:** 26

			HOW MUCH HE PITCHED						WHAT HE GAVE UP											THE RESULTS					
Year	Team	Lg	G	GS	CG	GF	IP	BFP	H	R	ER	HR	SH	SF	HB	TBB	IBB	SO	WP	Bk	W	L	Pct.	ShO	Sv	ERA
1987	New Britain	AA	23	6	1	7	63.2	281	61	35	27	2	1	3	2	34	2	60	4	3	4	1	.800	0	1	3.82
1988	Lynchburg	A	41	0	0	22	83	360	69	30	24	5	7	2	2	45	8	105	6	1	5	4	.556	0	12	2.60
1989	New Britain	AA	38	6	0	17	72.2	332	72	36	30	3	2	6	5	39	5	63	4	0	4	4	.500	0	5	3.72
1990	New Britain	AA	37	0	0	30	64	265	62	31	19	1	0	5	1	16	5	55	0	2	3	4	.429	0	13	2.67
	Pawtucket	AAA	11	0	0	8	17.1	71	10	0	0	0	1	1	1	11	4	11	0	0	1	0	1.000	0	3	0.00
1991	Pawtucket	AAA	41	1	0	26	69.1	299	65	31	24	11	1	1	6	29	2	58	1	1	2	6	.250	0	7	3.12
1991	Boston	AL	4	0	0	3	5.1	24	5	0	0	0	0	1	0	4	0	2	1	0	0	0	.000	0	0	0.00

Luis Polonia

Bats: Left **Throws:** Left **Pos:** LF **Ht:** 5' 8" **Wt:** 150 **Born:** 10/12/64 **Age:** 27

			BATTING																BASERUNNING				PERCENTAGES		
Year	Team	Lg	G	AB	H	2B	3B	HR	(Hm	Rd)	TB	R	RBI	TBB	IBB	SO	HBP	SH	SF	SB	CS	SB%	GDP	Avg	OBP	SLG
1987	Oakland	AL	125	435	125	16	10	4	(1	3)	173	78	49	32	1	64	0	1	1	29	7	.81	4	.287	.335	.398
1988	Oakland	AL	84	288	84	11	4	2	(1	1)	109	51	27	21	0	40	0	2	2	24	9	.73	3	.292	.338	.378
1989	2 ML Teams		125	433	130	17	6	3	(1	2)	168	70	46	25	1	44	2	2	4	22	8	.73	13	.300	.338	.388
1990	2 ML Teams		120	403	135	7	9	2	(2	0)	166	52	35	25	1	43	1	3	4	21	14	.60	9	.335	.372	.412
1991	California	AL	150	604	179	28	8	2	(1	1)	229	92	50	52	4	74	1	2	3	48	23	.68	11	.296	.352	.379
1989	New York	AL	59	206	59	6	4	1	(0	1)	76	31	17	9	0	15	0	2	1	13	4	.76	5	.286	.315	.369
	New York	AL	66	227	71	11	2	2	(1	1)	92	39	29	16	1	29	2	0	3	9	4	.69	8	.313	.359	.405
1990	New York	AL	11	22	7	0	0	0	(0	0)	7	2	3	0	0	1	0	0	1	1	0	1.00	1	.318	.304	.318
	California	AL	109	381	128	7	9	2	(2	0)	159	50	32	25	1	42	1	3	3	20	14	.59	8	.336	.376	.417
	5 ML YEARS		604	2163	653	79	37	13	(6	7)	845	343	207	155	7	265	4	10	14	144	61	.70	40	.302	.348	.391

Jim Poole

Pitches: Left **Bats:** Left **Pos:** RP **Ht:** 6' 2" **Wt:** 190 **Born:** 04/28/66 **Age:** 26

			HOW MUCH HE PITCHED						WHAT HE GAVE UP											THE RESULTS					
Year	Team	Lg	G	GS	CG	GF	IP	BFP	H	R	ER	HR	SH	SF	HB	TBB	IBB	SO	WP	Bk	W	L	Pct.	ShO	Sv	ERA
1988	Vero Beach	A	10	0	0	6	14.1	63	13	7	6	0	1	1	1	9	1	12	1	1	1	1	.500	0	0	3.77
1989	Vero Beach	A	60	0	0	50	78.1	306	57	16	14	0	5	0	2	24	7	93	3	0	11	4	.733	0	19	1.61
	Bakersfield	A	1	0	0	1	1.2	7	2	1	0	0	0	0	0	0	0	1	0	0	0	0	.000	0	0	0.00
1990	San Antonio	AA	54	0	0	35	63.2	278	55	31	17	3	8	0	2	27	5	77	6	0	6	7	.462	0	16	2.40
1991	Okla City	AAA	10	0	0	7	12.1	41	4	0	0	0	0	2	0	1	0	14	0	0	0	0	.000	0	3	0.00

Year Team	Lg	G	GS	CG	GF	IP	BFP	H	R	ER	HR	SH	SF	HB	TBB	IBB	SO	WP	Bk	W	L	Pct.	ShO	Sv	ERA
Rochester	AAA	27	0	0	19	29	123	29	11	9	1	0	1	0	9	0	25	3	0	3	2	.600	0	9	2.79
1990 Los Angeles	NL	16	0	0	4	10.2	46	7	5	5	1	0	0	0	8	4	6	1	0	0	0	.000	0	0	4.22
1991 2 ML Teams		29	0	0	5	42	166	29	14	11	3	3	3	0	12	2	38	2	0	3	2	.600	0	1	2.36
1991 Texas	AL	5	0	0	2	6	31	10	4	3	0	0	1	0	3	0	4	0	0	0	0	.000	0	1	4.50
Baltimore	AL	24	0	0	3	36	135	19	10	8	3	3	2	0	9	2	34	2	0	3	2	.600	0	0	2.00
2 ML YEARS		45	0	0	9	52.2	212	36	19	16	4	3	3	0	20	6	44	3	0	3	2	.600	0	1	2.73

Mark Portugal

Pitches: Right Bats: Right Pos: SP/RP **Ht: 6' 0" Wt: 190 Born: 10/30/62 Age: 29**

Year Team	Lg	G	GS	CG	GF	IP	BFP	H	R	ER	HR	SH	SF	HB	TBB	IBB	SO	WP	Bk	W	L	Pct.	ShO	Sv	ERA
1985 Minnesota	AL	6	4	0	0	24.1	105	24	16	15	3	0	2	0	14	0	12	1	1	1	3	.250	0	0	5.55
1986 Minnesota	AL	27	15	3	7	112.2	481	112	56	54	10	5	3	1	50	1	67	5	0	6	10	.375	0	1	4.31
1987 Minnesota	AL	13	7	0	3	44	204	58	40	38	13	0	1	1	24	1	28	2	0	1	3	.250	0	0	7.77
1988 Minnesota	AL	26	0	0	7	57.2	242	60	30	29	11	2	3	1	17	1	31	2	2	3	3	.500	0	3	4.53
1989 Houston	NL	20	15	2	1	108	440	91	34	33	7	8	1	2	37	0	86	3	0	7	1	.875	1	0	2.75
1990 Houston	NL	32	32	1	0	196.2	831	187	90	79	21	7	6	4	67	4	136	6	0	11	10	.524	0	0	3.62
1991 Houston	NL	32	27	1	3	168.1	710	163	91	84	19	6	6	2	59	5	120	4	1	10	12	.455	0	1	4.49
7 ML YEARS		156	100	7	23	711.2	3013	695	357	332	84	28	22	11	268	12	480	23	4	39	42	.481	1	5	4.20

Alonzo Powell

Bats: Right Throws: Right Pos: LF/RF **Ht: 6' 2" Wt: 190 Born: 12/12/64 Age: 27**

Year Team	Lg	G	AB	H	2B	3B	HR	(Hm	Rd)	TB	R	RBI	TBB	IBB	SO	HBP	SH	SF	SB	CS	SB%	GDP	Avg	OBP	SLG
1984 Everett	A	6	17	3	1	0	1	--	--	7	2	4	1	0	3	0	0	2	0	0	.00	1	.176	.200	.412
Clinton	A	47	149	37	3	2	1	--	--	47	22	10	19	0	31	0	2	0	0	0	.00	3	.248	.333	.315
1985 San Jose	A	136	473	122	27	6	9	--	--	188	79	62	71	0	118	3	3	6	34	11	.76	11	.258	.354	.397
1986 Wst Plm Bch	A	23	76	25	7	1	4	--	--	46	20	18	22	0	16	0	0	1	5	1	.83	2	.329	.475	.605
Jacksnville	AA	105	402	121	21	5	15	--	--	197	67	80	49	3	78	4	2	3	15	11	.58	10	.301	.380	.490
1987 Indianapols	AAA	90	331	99	14	10	19	--	--	190	64	74	32	1	68	1	3	3	12	8	.60	7	.299	.360	.574
1988 Indianapols	AAA	88	282	74	18	3	4	--	--	110	31	39	28	0	72	0	2	3	10	8	.56	7	.262	.326	.390
1989 Wst Plm Bch	A	12	41	13	4	3	1	--	--	26	7	8	7	2	3	0	0	1	1	1	.50	1	.317	.408	.634
Indianapols	AAA	121	423	98	26	5	13	--	--	173	50	59	38	2	106	2	1	3	9	6	.60	6	.232	.296	.409
1990 Portland	AAA	107	376	121	25	3	8	--	--	176	56	62	40	1	79	4	0	3	23	11	.68	9	.322	.390	.468
1991 Calgary	AAA	53	192	72	18	7	7	--	--	125	45	43	31	2	33	0	0	5	2	6	.25	3	.375	.452	.651
1987 Montreal	NL	14	41	8	3	0	0	(0	0)	11	3	4	5	0	17	0	0	0	0	0	.00	0	.195	.283	.268
1991 Seattle	AL	57	111	24	6	1	3	(1	2)	41	16	12	11	0	24	1	0	2	0	2	.00	1	.216	.288	.369
2 ML YEARS		71	152	32	9	1	3	(1	2)	52	19	16	16	0	41	1	0	2	0	2	.00	1	.211	.287	.342

Ted Power

Pitches: Right Bats: Right Pos: RP **Ht: 6' 4" Wt: 220 Born: 01/31/55 Age: 37**

Year Team	Lg	G	GS	CG	GF	IP	BFP	H	R	ER	HR	SH	SF	HB	TBB	IBB	SO	WP	Bk	W	L	Pct.	ShO	Sv	ERA
1981 Los Angeles	NL	5	2	0	1	14	66	16	6	5	0	0	2	1	7	2	7	0	0	1	3	.250	0	0	3.21
1982 Los Angeles	NL	12	4	0	4	33.2	160	38	27	25	4	4	1	0	23	1	15	3	3	1	1	.500	0	0	6.68
1983 Cincinnati	NL	49	6	1	14	111	480	120	62	56	10	4	6	1	49	3	57	1	0	5	6	.455	0	2	4.54
1984 Cincinnati	NL	78	0	0	42	108.2	456	93	37	34	4	9	8	0	46	8	81	3	0	9	7	.563	0	11	2.82
1985 Cincinnati	NL	64	0	0	50	80	342	65	27	24	2	6	4	1	45	8	42	1	0	8	6	.571	0	27	2.70
1986 Cincinnati	NL	56	10	0	30	129	537	115	59	53	13	6	6	1	52	10	95	5	1	10	6	.625	0	1	3.70
1987 Cincinnati	NL	34	34	2	0	204	887	213	115	102	28	8	7	3	71	7	133	3	2	10	13	.435	1	0	4.50
1988 2 ML Teams		26	14	2	3	99	443	121	67	65	8	2	4	3	38	7	57	4	2	6	7	.462	2	0	5.91
1989 St. Louis	NL	23	15	0	2	97	407	96	47	40	7	5	3	1	21	3	43	1	0	7	7	.500	0	0	3.71
1990 Pittsburgh	NL	40	0	0	25	51.2	218	50	23	21	5	3	2	0	17	6	42	1	0	1	3	.250	0	7	3.66
1991 Cincinnati	NL	68	0	0	22	87	371	87	37	35	6	6	4	2	31	5	51	6	1	5	3	.625	0	3	3.62
1988 Kansas City	AL	22	12	2	3	80.1	360	98	54	53	7	2	4	3	30	3	44	3	2	6	7	.455	2	0	5.94
Detroit	AL	4	2	0	0	18.2	83	23	13	12	1	0	0	0	8	4	13	1	0	1	1	.500	0	0	5.79
11 ML YEARS		455	85	5	193	1015	4367	1014	507	460	87	56	47	13	400	60	623	28	9	63	62	.504	3	51	4.08

Jim Presley

Bats: Right Throws: Right Pos: 3B **Ht: 6' 1" Wt: 200 Born: 10/23/61 Age: 30**

Year Team	Lg	G	AB	H	2B	3B	HR	(Hm	Rd)	TB	R	RBI	TBB	IBB	SO	HBP	SH	SF	SB	CS	SB%	GDP	Avg	OBP	SLG
1984 Seattle	AL	70	251	57	12	1	10	(5	5)	101	27	36	6	1	63	1	0	1	1	1	.50	4	.227	.247	.402
1985 Seattle	AL	155	570	157	33	1	28	(12	16)	276	71	84	44	9	100	1	1	9	2	2	.50	29	.275	.324	.484
1986 Seattle	AL	155	616	163	33	4	27	(16	11)	285	83	107	32	3	172	4	3	5	0	4	.00	18	.265	.303	.463
1987 Seattle	AL	152	575	142	23	6	24	(11	13)	249	78	88	38	1	157	4	1	4	2	0	1.00	15	.247	.296	.433

Year	Team	Lg	G	AB	H	2B	3B	HR	(Hm	Rd)	TB	R	RBI	TBB	IBB	SO	HBP	SH	SF	SB	CS	SB%	GDP	Avg	OBP	SLG
1988	Seattle	AL	150	544	125	26	0	14	(7	7)	193	50	62	36	1	114	4	3	5	3	5	.38	14	.230	.280	.355
1989	Seattle	AL	117	390	92	20	1	12	(7	5)	150	42	41	21	2	107	1	3	2	0	0	.00	12	.236	.275	.385
1990	Atlanta	NL	140	541	131	34	1	19	(10	9)	224	59	72	29	0	130	3	0	4	1	1	.50	10	.242	.282	.414
1991	San Diego	NL	20	59	8	0	0	1	(0	1)	11	3	5	4	1	16	1	1	1	0	1	.00	2	.136	.200	.186
8 ML YEARS			959	3546	875	181	14	135	(68	67)	1489	413	495	210	18	859	19	12	31	9	14	.39	104	.247	.290	.420

Tom Prince

Bats: Right **Throws:** Right **Pos:** C   **Ht:** 5'11" **Wt:** 185 **Born:** 08/13/64 **Age:** 27

									BATTING											BASERUNNING				PERCENTAGES		
Year	Team	Lg	G	AB	H	2B	3B	HR	(Hm	Rd)	TB	R	RBI	TBB	IBB	SO	HBP	SH	SF	SB	CS	SB%	GDP	Avg	OBP	SLG
1987	Pittsburgh	NL	4	9	2	1	0	1	(0	1)	6	1	2	0	0	2	0	0	0	0	0	.00	0	.222	.222	.667
1988	Pittsburgh	NL	29	74	13	2	0	0	(0	0)	15	3	6	4	0	15	0	2	0	0	0	.00	5	.176	.218	.203
1989	Pittsburgh	NL	21	52	7	4	0	0	(0	0)	11	1	5	6	1	12	0	0	1	1	1	.50	1	.135	.220	.212
1990	Pittsburgh	NL	4	10	1	0	0	0	(0	0)	1	1	0	1	0	2	0	0	0	0	1	.00	0	.100	.182	.100
1991	Pittsburgh	NL	26	34	9	3	0	1	(0	1)	15	4	2	7	0	3	1	0	0	0	0	.00	3	.265	.405	.441
5 ML YEARS			84	179	32	10	0	2	(0	2)	48	10	15	18	1	34	1	2	1	1	2	.33	9	.179	.256	.268

Kirby Puckett

Bats: Right **Throws:** Right **Pos:** CF/RF   **Ht:** 5' 8" **Wt:** 216 **Born:** 03/14/61 **Age:** 31

									BATTING											BASERUNNING				PERCENTAGES		
Year	Team	Lg	G	AB	H	2B	3B	HR	(Hm	Rd)	TB	R	RBI	TBB	IBB	SO	HBP	SH	SF	SB	CS	SB%	GDP	Avg	OBP	SLG
1984	Minnesota	AL	128	557	165	12	5	0	(0	0)	187	63	31	16	1	69	4	4	2	14	7	.67	11	.296	.320	.336
1985	Minnesota	AL	161	691	199	29	13	4	(2	2)	266	80	74	41	0	87	4	5	3	21	12	.64	9	.288	.330	.385
1986	Minnesota	AL	161	680	223	37	6	31	(14	17)	365	119	96	34	4	99	7	2	0	20	12	.63	14	.328	.366	.537
1987	Minnesota	AL	157	624	207	32	5	28	(18	10)	333	96	99	32	7	91	6	0	6	12	7	.63	16	.332	.367	.534
1988	Minnesota	AL	158	657	234	42	5	24	(13	11)	358	109	121	23	4	83	2	0	9	6	7	.46	17	.356	.375	.545
1989	Minnesota	AL	159	635	215	45	4	9	(7	2)	295	75	85	41	9	59	3	0	5	11	4	.73	21	.339	.379	.465
1990	Minnesota	AL	146	551	164	40	3	12	(6	6)	246	82	80	57	11	73	3	1	3	5	4	.56	15	.298	.365	.446
1991	Minnesota	AL	152	611	195	29	6	15	(7	8)	281	92	89	31	4	78	4	8	7	11	5	.69	27	.319	.352	.460
8 ML YEARS			1222	5006	1602	266	47	123	(67	56)	2331	716	675	275	40	639	33	20	35	100	58	.63	130	.320	.357	.466

Terry Puhl

Bats: Left **Throws:** Right **Pos:** DH   **Ht:** 6' 2" **Wt:** 200 **Born:** 07/08/56 **Age:** 35

									BATTING											BASERUNNING				PERCENTAGES		
Year	Team	Lg	G	AB	H	2B	3B	HR	(Hm	Rd)	TB	R	RBI	TBB	IBB	SO	HBP	SH	SF	SB	CS	SB%	GDP	Avg	OBP	SLG
1977	Houston	NL	60	229	69	13	5	0	(0	0)	92	40	10	30	0	31	1	5	0	10	1	.91	3	.301	.385	.402
1978	Houston	NL	149	585	169	25	6	3	(1	2)	215	87	35	48	5	46	4	3	7	32	14	.70	11	.289	.343	.368
1979	Houston	NL	157	600	172	22	4	8	(2	6)	226	87	49	58	8	46	4	8	2	30	22	.58	7	.287	.352	.377
1980	Houston	NL	141	535	151	24	5	13	(4	9)	224	75	55	60	3	52	4	6	3	27	11	.71	3	.282	.357	.419
1981	Houston	NL	96	350	88	19	4	3	(1	2)	124	43	28	31	5	49	4	4	5	22	4	.85	3	.251	.315	.354
1982	Houston	NL	145	507	133	17	9	8	(5	3)	192	64	50	51	2	49	2	5	2	17	9	.65	6	.262	.331	.379
1983	Houston	NL	137	465	136	25	7	8	(1	7)	199	66	44	36	2	48	2	5	4	24	11	.69	4	.292	.343	.428
1984	Houston	NL	132	449	135	19	7	9	(2	7)	195	66	55	59	12	45	1	6	4	13	8	.62	5	.301	.380	.434
1985	Houston	NL	57	194	55	14	3	2	(1	1)	81	34	23	18	4	23	1	4	3	6	2	.75	0	.284	.343	.418
1986	Houston	NL	81	172	42	10	0	3	(1	2)	61	17	14	15	1	24	0	4	2	3	2	.60	6	.244	.302	.355
1987	Houston	NL	90	122	28	5	0	2	(1	1)	39	9	15	11	0	16	0	1	0	1	1	.50	3	.230	.293	.320
1988	Houston	NL	113	234	71	7	2	3	(2	1)	91	42	19	35	3	30	1	1	1	22	4	.85	0	.303	.395	.389
1989	Houston	NL	121	354	96	25	4	0	(0	0)	129	41	27	45	3	39	1	4	2	9	8	.53	7	.271	.353	.364
1990	Houston	NL	37	41	12	1	0	0	(0	0)	13	5	8	5	0	7	1	1	1	1	2	.33	0	.293	.375	.317
1991	Kansas City	AL	15	18	4	0	0	0	(0	0)	4	0	3	3	1	2	0	0	0	0	0	.00	1	.222	.333	.222
15 ML YEARS			1531	4855	1361	226	56	62	(21	41)	1885	676	435	505	49	507	26	57	36	217	99	.69	59	.280	.349	.388

Harvey Pulliam

Bats: Right **Throws:** Right **Pos:** LF   **Ht:** 6' 0" **Wt:** 210 **Born:** 10/20/67 **Age:** 24

									BATTING											BASERUNNING				PERCENTAGES		
Year	Team	Lg	G	AB	H	2B	3B	HR	(Hm	Rd)	TB	R	RBI	TBB	IBB	SO	HBP	SH	SF	SB	CS	SB%	GDP	Avg	OBP	SLG
1986	Royals	R	48	168	35	3	0	4	--	--	50	14	23	8	1	33	3	2	3	3	2	.60	9	.208	.253	.298
1987	Appleton	A	110	395	109	20	1	9	--	--	158	54	55	26	0	79	3	1	3	21	7	.75	10	.276	.323	.400
1988	Baseball Cy	A	132	457	111	19	4	4	--	--	150	56	42	34	3	87	5	2	3	21	16	.63	13	.243	.301	.328
1989	Omaha	AAA	7	22	4	2	0	0	--	--	6	3	2	3	0	6	0	0	0	0	0	.00	0	.182	.280	.273
	Memphis	AA	116	417	121	28	8	10	--	--	195	67	67	44	4	65	5	0	3	5	5	.50	12	.290	.362	.468
1990	Omaha	AAA	123	436	117	18	5	16	--	--	193	72	72	49	0	82	3	2	4	9	3	.75	14	.268	.343	.443
1991	Omaha	AAA	104	346	89	18	2	6	--	--	129	35	39	31	0	62	1	1	3	2	4	.33	4	.257	.318	.373
1991	Kansas City	AL	18	33	9	1	0	3	(2	1)	19	4	4	3	1	9	0	1	0	0	0	.00	1	.273	.333	.576

Luis Quinones

Bats: Both   Throws: Right   Pos: 2B/3B   Ht: 5'11"   Wt: 185   Born: 04/28/62   Age: 30

					BATTING													BASERUNNING				PERCENTAGES		
Year	Team	Lg	G	AB	H	2B	3B	HR	(Hm | Rd)	TB	R	RBI	TBB	IBB	SO	HBP	SH	SF	SB	CS	SB%	GDP	Avg	OBP	SLG
1983	Oakland	AL	19	42	8	2	1	0	(0 | 0)	12	5	4	1	0	4	0	1	1	1	1	.50	0	.190	.205	.286
1986	San Francisco	NL	71	106	19	1	3	0	(0 | 0)	26	13	11	3	1	17	1	4	1	3	1	.75	1	.179	.207	.245
1987	Chicago	NL	49	101	22	6	0	0	(0 | 0)	28	12	8	10	0	16	0	0	0	0	0	.00	0	.218	.288	.277
1988	Cincinnati	NL	23	52	12	3	0	1	(0 | 1)	18	4	11	2	1	11	0	2	1	1	1	.50	0	.231	.255	.346
1989	Cincinnati	NL	97	340	83	13	4	12	(5 | 7)	140	43	34	25	0	46	3	8	2	2	4	.33	3	.244	.300	.412
1990	Cincinnati	NL	83	145	35	7	0	2	(1 | 1)	48	10	17	13	3	29	1	1	4	1	0	1.00	3	.241	.301	.331
1991	Cincinnati	NL	97	212	47	4	3	4	(2 | 2)	69	15	20	21	3	31	2	1	1	1	2	.33	2	.222	.297	.325
	7 ML YEARS		439	998	226	36	11	19	(8 | 11)	341	102	105	75	8	154	7	17	10	9	9	.50	9	.226	.283	.342

Carlos Quintana

Bats: Right   Throws: Right   Pos: 1B/RF   Ht: 6' 2"   Wt: 195   Born: 08/26/65   Age: 26

					BATTING													BASERUNNING				PERCENTAGES		
Year	Team	Lg	G	AB	H	2B	3B	HR	(Hm | Rd)	TB	R	RBI	TBB	IBB	SO	HBP	SH	SF	SB	CS	SB%	GDP	Avg	OBP	SLG
1988	Boston	AL	5	6	2	0	0	0	(0 | 0)	2	1	2	2	0	3	0	0	0	0	0	.00	0	.333	.500	.333
1989	Boston	AL	34	77	16	5	0	0	(0 | 0)	21	6	6	7	0	12	0	0	0	0	0	.00	5	.208	.274	.273
1990	Boston	AL	149	512	147	28	0	7	(3 | 4)	196	56	67	52	0	74	2	4	2	1	2	.33	19	.287	.354	.383
1991	Boston	AL	149	478	141	21	1	11	(2 | 9)	197	69	71	61	2	66	2	6	3	1	0	1.00	17	.295	.375	.412
	4 ML YEARS		337	1073	306	54	1	18	(5 | 13)	416	132	146	122	2	155	4	10	5	2	2	.50	41	.285	.359	.388

Jamie Quirk

Bats: Left   Throws: Right   Pos: C   Ht: 6' 4"   Wt: 200   Born: 10/22/54   Age: 37

					BATTING													BASERUNNING				PERCENTAGES		
Year	Team	Lg	G	AB	H	2B	3B	HR	(Hm | Rd)	TB	R	RBI	TBB	IBB	SO	HBP	SH	SF	SB	CS	SB%	GDP	Avg	OBP	SLG
1975	Kansas City	AL	14	39	10	0	0	1	(1 | 0)	13	2	5	2	1	7	0	0	0	0	0	.00	1	.256	.293	.333
1976	Kansas City	AL	64	114	28	6	0	1	(1 | 0)	37	11	15	2	0	22	0	0	3	0	0	.00	5	.246	.252	.325
1977	Milwaukee	AL	93	221	48	14	1	3	(2 | 1)	73	16	13	8	2	47	2	2	0	0	1	.00	4	.217	.251	.330
1978	Kansas City	AL	17	29	6	2	0	0	(0 | 0)	8	3	2	5	0	4	0	0	0	0	0	.00	0	.207	.324	.276
1979	Kansas City	AL	51	79	24	6	1	1	(0 | 1)	35	8	11	5	0	13	1	0	0	0	0	.00	0	.304	.353	.443
1980	Kansas City	AL	62	163	45	5	0	5	(3 | 2)	65	13	21	7	2	24	1	3	3	3	2	.60	7	.276	.305	.399
1981	Kansas City	AL	46	100	25	7	0	0	(0 | 0)	32	8	10	6	1	17	1	0	0	0	2	.00	5	.250	.299	.320
1982	Kansas City	AL	36	78	18	3	0	1	(1 | 0)	24	8	5	3	0	15	0	1	0	0	0	.00	2	.231	.256	.308
1983	St. Louis	NL	48	86	18	2	1	2	(0 | 2)	28	3	11	6	0	27	1	0	0	0	0	.00	2	.209	.269	.326
1984	2 ML Teams		4	3	1	0	0	1	(1 | 0)	4	1	2	0	0	2	0	0	1	0	0	.00	0	.333	.250	1.333
1985	Kansas City	AL	19	57	16	3	1	0	(0 | 0)	21	3	4	2	0	9	0	0	0	0	0	.00	1	.281	.305	.368
1986	Kansas City	AL	80	219	47	10	0	8	(5 | 3)	81	24	26	17	3	41	1	0	1	0	1	.00	4	.215	.273	.370
1987	Kansas City	AL	109	296	70	17	0	5	(0 | 5)	102	24	33	28	1	56	4	2	4	1	0	1.00	8	.236	.307	.345
1988	Kansas City	AL	84	196	47	7	1	8	(2 | 6)	80	22	25	28	2	41	1	4	3	1	5	.17	2	.240	.333	.408
1989	3 ML Teams		47	85	15	2	0	1	(0 | 1)	20	6	10	12	0	20	0	1	1	0	2	.00	4	.176	.276	.235
1990	Oakland	AL	56	121	34	5	1	3	(1 | 2)	50	12	26	14	1	34	1	5	3	0	0	.00	1	.281	.353	.413
1991	Oakland	AL	76	203	53	4	0	1	(0 | 1)	60	16	17	16	1	28	2	3	0	0	3	.00	7	.261	.321	.296
1984	Chicago	AL	3	2	0	0	0	0	(0 | 0)	0	0	1	0	0	2	0	0	1	0	0	.00	0	.000	.000	.000
	Cleveland	AL	1	1	1	0	0	1	(1 | 0)	4	1	1	0	0	0	0	0	0	0	0	.00	0	1.000	1.000	4.000
1989	New York	AL	13	24	2	0	0	0	(0 | 0)	2	0	0	3	0	5	0	0	0	0	1	.00	1	.083	.185	.083
	Oakland	AL	9	10	2	0	0	1	(0 | 1)	5	1	1	0	0	4	0	0	0	0	0	.00	0	.200	.200	.500
	Baltimore	AL	25	51	11	2	0	0	(0 | 0)	13	5	9	9	0	11	0	1	1	0	1	.00	3	.216	.328	.255
	17 ML YEARS		906	2089	505	93	6	41	(18 | 23)	733	180	236	161	14	407	15	20	20	5	16	.24	53	.242	.298	.351

Scott Radinsky

Pitches: Left   Bats: Left   Pos: RP   Ht: 6' 3"   Wt: 190   Born: 03/03/68   Age: 24

				HOW MUCH HE PITCHED					WHAT HE GAVE UP											THE RESULTS					
Year	Team	Lg	G	GS	CG	GF	IP	BFP	H	R	ER	HR	SH	SF	HB	TBB	IBB	SO	WP	Bk	W	L	Pct.	ShO	Sv	ERA
1986	White Sox	R	7	7	0	0	26.2	122	24	20	10	0	1	3	0	17	0	18	2	1	1	0	1.000	0	0	3.38
1987	Peninsula	A	12	8	0	2	39	187	43	30	25	2	2	2	3	32	0	37	3	1	1	7	.125	0	0	5.77
	White Sox	R	11	10	0	0	58.1	249	43	23	15	1	0	2	4	39	0	41	5	1	3	3	.500	0	0	2.31
1988	White Sox	R	5	0	0	2	3.1	17	2	2	2	0	0	0	0	4	0	7	1	2	0	0	.000	0	0	5.40
1989	South Bend	A	53	0	0	49	61.2	248	39	21	12	1	4	2	5	19	2	83	2	2	7	5	.583	0	31	1.75
1990	Chicago	AL	62	0	0	18	52.1	237	47	29	28	1	2	2	2	36	1	46	2	1	6	1	.857	0	4	4.82
1991	Chicago	AL	67	0	0	19	71.1	289	53	18	16	4	4	4	1	23	2	49	0	0	5	5	.500	0	8	2.02
	2 ML YEARS		129	0	0	37	123.2	526	100	47	44	5	6	6	3	59	3	95	2	1	11	6	.647	0	12	3.20

Tim Raines

Bats: Both **Throws:** Right **Pos:** LF/DH   **Ht:** 5' 8" **Wt:** 185 **Born:** 09/16/59 **Age:** 32

						BATTING												BASERUNNING				PERCENTAGES		
Year	Team	Lg	G	AB	H	2B	3B	HR	(Hm | Rd)	TB	R	RBI	TBB	IBB	SO	HBP	SH	SF	SB	CS	SB%	GDP	Avg	OBP	SLG
1979	Montreal	NL	6	0	0	0	0	0	(0 | 0)	0	3	0	0	0	0	0	0	0	2	0	1.00	0	.000	.000	.000
1980	Montreal	NL	15	20	1	0	0	0	(0 | 0)	1	5	0	6	0	3	0	1	0	5	0	1.00	0	.050	.269	.050
1981	Montreal	NL	88	313	95	13	7	5	(3 | 2)	137	61	37	45	5	31	2	0	3	71	11	.87	7	.304	.391	.438
1982	Montreal	NL	156	647	179	32	8	4	(1 | 3)	239	90	43	75	9	83	2	6	1	78	16	.83	6	.277	.353	.369
1983	Montreal	NL	156	615	183	32	8	11	(5 | 6)	264	133	71	97	9	70	2	2	4	90	14	.87	12	.298	.393	.429
1984	Montreal	NL	160	622	192	38	9	8	(2 | 6)	272	106	60	87	7	69	2	3	4	75	10	.88	7	.309	.393	.437
1985	Montreal	NL	150	575	184	30	13	11	(4 | 7)	273	115	41	81	13	60	3	3	3	70	9	.89	9	.320	.405	.475
1986	Montreal	NL	151	580	194	35	10	9	(4 | 5)	276	91	62	78	9	60	2	1	3	70	9	.89	6	.334	.413	.476
1987	Montreal	NL	139	530	175	34	8	18	(9 | 9)	279	123	68	90	26	52	4	0	3	50	5	.91	9	.330	.429	.526
1988	Montreal	NL	109	429	116	19	7	12	(5 | 7)	185	66	48	53	14	44	2	0	4	33	7	.83	8	.270	.350	.431
1989	Montreal	NL	145	517	148	29	6	9	(6 | 3)	216	76	60	93	18	48	3	0	5	41	9	.82	8	.286	.395	.418
1990	Montreal	NL	130	457	131	11	5	9	(6 | 3)	179	65	62	70	8	43	3	0	8	49	16	.75	9	.287	.379	.392
1991	Chicago	AL	155	609	163	20	6	5	(1 | 4)	210	102	50	83	9	68	5	9	3	51	15	.77	7	.268	.359	.345
	13 ML YEARS		1560	5914	1761	293	87	101	(46 | 55)	2531	1036	602	858	127	631	30	25	41	685	121	.85	88	.298	.387	.428

Rafael Ramirez

Bats: Right **Throws:** Right **Pos:** SS/2B   **Ht:** 5'11" **Wt:** 190 **Born:** 02/18/59 **Age:** 33

						BATTING												BASERUNNING				PERCENTAGES		
Year	Team	Lg	G	AB	H	2B	3B	HR	(Hm | Rd)	TB	R	RBI	TBB	IBB	SO	HBP	SH	SF	SB	CS	SB%	GDP	Avg	OBP	SLG
1980	Atlanta	NL	50	165	44	6	1	2	(2 | 0)	58	17	11	2	0	33	4	3	0	2	1	.67	2	.267	.292	.352
1981	Atlanta	NL	95	307	67	16	2	2	(1 | 1)	93	30	20	24	3	47	1	9	1	7	3	.70	3	.218	.276	.303
1982	Atlanta	NL	157	609	169	24	4	10	(7 | 3)	231	74	52	36	7	49	3	16	5	27	14	.66	10	.278	.319	.379
1983	Atlanta	NL	152	622	185	13	5	7	(2 | 5)	229	82	58	36	4	48	2	6	2	16	12	.57	8	.297	.337	.368
1984	Atlanta	NL	145	591	157	22	4	2	(1 | 1)	193	51	48	26	1	70	1	5	6	14	17	.45	9	.266	.295	.327
1985	Atlanta	NL	138	568	141	25	4	5	(4 | 1)	189	54	58	20	1	63	0	2	5	2	6	.25	21	.248	.272	.333
1986	Atlanta	NL	134	496	119	21	1	8	(1 | 7)	166	57	33	21	1	60	3	7	3	19	8	.70	16	.240	.273	.335
1987	Atlanta	NL	56	179	47	12	0	1	(0 | 1)	62	22	21	8	0	16	2	4	1	6	3	.67	3	.263	.300	.346
1988	Houston	NL	155	566	156	30	5	6	(2 | 4)	214	51	59	18	6	61	3	4	6	3	2	.60	16	.276	.298	.378
1989	Houston	NL	151	537	132	20	2	6	(3 | 3)	174	46	54	29	3	64	0	6	3	3	1	.75	8	.246	.283	.324
1990	Houston	NL	132	445	116	19	3	2	(1 | 1)	147	44	37	24	9	46	1	9	1	10	5	.67	9	.261	.299	.330
1991	Houston	NL	101	233	55	10	0	1	(0 | 1)	68	17	20	13	1	40	0	1	2	3	3	.50	3	.236	.274	.292
	12 ML YEARS		1466	5318	1388	218	31	52	(24 | 28)	1824	545	471	257	36	597	20	72	35	112	75	.60	108	.261	.296	.343

John Ramos

Bats: Right **Throws:** Right **Pos:** C   **Ht:** 6' 0" **Wt:** 190 **Born:** 08/06/65 **Age:** 26

						BATTING												BASERUNNING				PERCENTAGES		
Year	Team	Lg	G	AB	H	2B	3B	HR	(Hm | Rd)	TB	R	RBI	TBB	IBB	SO	HBP	SH	SF	SB	CS	SB%	GDP	Avg	OBP	SLG
1986	Ft.Laudrdle	A	54	184	49	10	1	2	--	--	67	25	28	26	0	23	1	4	2	8	3	.73	5	.266	.357	.364
	Oneonta	A	3	8	4	2	1	0	--	--	8	3	1	2	0	1	0	0	0	0	0	.00	0	.500	.600	1.000
1987	Pr William	A	76	235	51	6	1	2	--	--	65	26	27	28	3	30	2	3	3	8	5	.62	10	.217	.302	.277
1988	Pr William	A	109	391	119	18	2	8	--	--	165	47	57	49	1	34	7	2	5	8	2	.80	7	.304	.387	.422
	Albany	AA	21	72	16	1	3	1	--	--	26	11	13	12	0	9	1	0	2	2	1	.67	1	.222	.333	.361
1989	Albany	AA	105	359	98	21	0	9	--	--	146	55	60	40	2	65	7	2	2	7	5	.58	14	.273	.355	.407
1990	Columbus	AAA	2	6	0	0	0	0	--	--	0	0	1	0	0	0	0	0	0	0	0	.00	0	.000	.000	.000
	Albany	AA	84	287	90	20	1	4	--	--	124	38	45	36	0	39	3	0	5	1	0	1.00	10	.314	.390	.432
1991	Columbus	AAA	104	377	116	18	3	10	--	--	170	52	63	56	3	54	3	1	9	1	5	.17	15	.308	.393	.451
1991	New York	AL	10	26	8	1	0	0	(0 | 0)	9	4	3	1	0	3	0	0	2	0	0	.00	1	.308	.310	.346

Willie Randolph

Bats: Right **Throws:** Right **Pos:** 2B   **Ht:** 5'11" **Wt:** 171 **Born:** 07/06/54 **Age:** 37

						BATTING												BASERUNNING				PERCENTAGES		
Year	Team	Lg	G	AB	H	2B	3B	HR	(Hm | Rd)	TB	R	RBI	TBB	IBB	SO	HBP	SH	SF	SB	CS	SB%	GDP	Avg	OBP	SLG
1975	Pittsburgh	NL	30	61	10	1	0	0	(0 | 0)	11	9	3	7	1	6	0	1	1	1	0	1.00	3	.164	.246	.180
1976	New York	AL	125	430	115	15	4	1	(0 | 1)	141	59	40	58	5	39	3	6	3	37	12	.76	10	.267	.356	.328
1977	New York	AL	147	551	151	28	11	4	(2 | 2)	213	91	40	64	1	53	1	2	6	13	6	.68	11	.274	.347	.387
1978	New York	AL	134	499	139	18	6	3	(2 | 1)	178	87	42	82	1	51	4	6	5	36	7	.84	12	.279	.381	.357
1979	New York	AL	153	574	155	15	13	5	(2 | 3)	211	98	61	95	5	39	3	5	5	33	12	.73	23	.270	.374	.368
1980	New York	AL	138	513	151	23	7	7	(2 | 5)	209	99	46	119	4	45	2	5	3	30	5	.86	6	.294	.427	.407
1981	New York	AL	93	357	83	14	3	2	(1 | 1)	109	59	24	57	0	24	0	5	3	14	5	.74	10	.232	.336	.305

167

1982 New York	AL	144	553	155	21	4	3	(1	2)	193	85	36	75	3	35	3	10	2	16	9	.64	13	.280	.368	.349
1983 New York	AL	104	420	117	21	1	2	(1	1)	146	73	38	53	0	32	1	3	0	12	4	.75	11	.279	.361	.348
1984 New York	AL	142	564	162	24	2	2	(1	1)	196	86	31	86	4	42	0	7	7	10	6	.63	15	.287	.377	.348
1985 New York	AL	143	497	137	21	2	5	(3	2)	177	75	40	85	3	39	4	5	6	16	9	.64	24	.276	.382	.356
1986 New York	AL	141	492	136	15	2	5	(2	3)	170	76	50	94	0	49	3	8	4	15	2	.88	11	.276	.393	.346
1987 New York	AL	120	449	137	24	2	7	(3	4)	186	96	67	82	1	25	2	5	5	11	1	.92	15	.305	.411	.414
1988 New York	AL	110	404	93	20	1	2	(1	1)	121	43	34	55	2	39	2	8	5	8	4	.67	10	.230	.322	.300
1989 Los Angeles	NL	145	549	155	18	0	2	(0	2)	179	62	36	71	2	51	4	4	5	7	6	.54	10	.282	.366	.326
1990 2 ML Teams		119	388	101	13	3	2	(1	1)	126	52	30	45	1	34	2	10	1	7	1	.88	14	.260	.339	.325
1991 Milwaukee		124	431	141	14	3	0	(0	0)	161	60	54	75	3	38	0	3	3	4	2	.67	14	.327	.424	.374
1990 Los Angeles	NL	26	96	26	4	0	1	(0	1)	33	15	9	13	0	9	1	3	0	1	0	1.00	3	.271	.364	.344
Oakland	AL	93	292	75	9	3	1	(1	0)	93	37	21	32	1	25	1	7	1	6	1	.86	11	.257	.331	.318
17 ML YEARS		2112	7732	2138	305	64	52	(22	30)	2727	1210	672	1203	36	641	34	93	64	270	91	.75	212	.277	.374	.353

Dennis Rasmussen

Pitches: Left **Bats:** Left **Pos:** SP   **Ht:** 6' 7" **Wt:** 233 **Born:** 04/18/59 **Age:** 33

		HOW MUCH HE PITCHED						WHAT HE GAVE UP											THE RESULTS					
Year Team	Lg	G	GS	CG	GF	IP	BFP	H	R	ER	HR	SH	SF	HB	TBB	IBB	SO	WP	Bk	W	L	Pct.	ShO	Sv	ERA
1983 San Diego	NL	4	1	0	1	13.2	58	10	5	3	1	0	0	0	8	0	13	1	0	0	0	.000	0	0	1.98
1984 New York	AL	24	24	1	0	147.2	616	127	79	75	16	3	7	4	60	0	110	8	2	9	6	.600	0	0	4.57
1985 New York	AL	22	16	2	1	101.2	429	97	56	45	10	1	5	1	42	1	63	3	1	3	5	.375	0	0	3.98
1986 New York	AL	31	31	3	0	202	819	160	91	87	28	1	5	2	74	0	131	5	0	18	6	.750	1	0	3.88
1987 2 ML Teams		33	32	2	0	191.1	814	184	100	97	36	8	6	5	67	1	128	7	2	13	8	.619	0	0	4.56
1988 2 ML Teams		31	31	7	0	204.2	854	199	84	78	17	10	4	4	58	4	112	7	5	16	10	.615	1	0	3.43
1989 San Diego	NL	33	33	1	0	183.2	799	190	100	87	18	9	11	3	72	6	87	4	2	10	10	.500	1	0	4.26
1990 San Diego	NL	32	32	3	0	187.2	825	217	110	94	28	14	4	3	62	4	86	9	1	11	15	.423	1	0	4.51
1991 San Diego	NL	24	24	1	0	146.2	633	155	74	61	12	4	6	2	49	3	75	1	1	6	13	.316	1	0	3.74
1987 New York	AL	26	25	2	0	146	627	145	78	77	31	5	5	4	55	1	89	6	0	9	7	.563	0	0	4.75
Cincinnati		7	7	0	0	45.1	187	39	22	20	5	3	1	1	12	0	39	1	2	4	1	.800	0	0	3.97
1988 Cincinnati	NL	11	11	1	0	56.1	255	68	36	36	8	2	2	2	22	4	27	1	5	2	6	.250	0	0	5.75
San Diego	NL	20	20	6	0	148.1	599	131	48	42	9	8	2	2	36	0	85	6	0	14	4	.778	0	0	2.55
9 ML YEARS		234	224	20	2	1379	5847	1339	699	627	166	50	48	24	492	19	805	45	14	86	73	.541	4	0	4.09

Randy Ready

Bats: Right **Throws:** Right **Pos:** 2B   **Ht:** 5'11" **Wt:** 182 **Born:** 01/08/60 **Age:** 32

		BATTING																	BASERUNNING				PERCENTAGES		
Year Team	Lg	G	AB	H	2B	3B	HR	(Hm	Rd)	TB	R	RBI	TBB	IBB	SO	HBP	SH	SF	SB	CS	SB%	GDP	Avg	OBP	SLG
1983 Milwaukee	AL	12	37	15	3	2	1	(1	0)	25	8	6	6	1	3	0	1	0	0	1	.00	0	.405	.488	.676
1984 Milwaukee	AL	37	123	23	6	1	3	(3	0)	40	13	13	14	0	18	0	3	0	0	0	.00	2	.187	.270	.325
1985 Milwaukee	AL	48	181	48	9	5	1	(0	1)	70	29	21	14	0	23	1	2	2	0	0	.00	6	.265	.318	.387
1986 2 ML Teams		24	82	15	4	0	1	(0	1)	22	8	4	9	0	10	0	1	0	2	0	1.00	3	.183	.264	.268
1987 San Diego	NL	124	350	108	26	6	12	(7	5)	182	69	54	67	2	44	3	2	1	7	3	.70	7	.309	.423	.520
1988 San Diego	NL	114	331	88	16	2	7	(3	4)	129	43	39	39	1	38	3	4	3	6	2	.75	3	.266	.346	.390
1989 2 ML Teams		100	254	67	13	2	8	(3	5)	108	37	26	42	0	37	2	1	4	4	3	.57	4	.264	.368	.425
1990 Philadelphia	NL	101	217	53	9	1	1	(0	1)	67	26	26	29	0	35	1	3	3	3	2	.60	3	.244	.332	.309
1991 Philadelphia	NL	76	205	51	10	1	1	(1	0)	66	32	20	47	3	25	1	1	1	2	1	.67	1	.249	.385	.322
1986 Milwaukee	AL	23	79	15	4	0	1	(0	1)	22	8	4	9	0	9	0	1	0	2	0	1.00	3	.190	.273	.278
San Diego	NL	1	3	0	0	0	0	(0	0)	0	0	0	0	0	1	0	0	0	0	0	.00	0	.000	.000	.000
1989 San Diego	NL	28	67	17	2	1	0	(0	0)	21	4	5	11	0	6	0	1	1	0	0	.00	0	.254	.354	.313
Philadelphia	NL	72	187	50	11	1	8	(3	5)	87	33	21	31	0	31	2	0	3	4	3	.57	2	.267	.372	.465
9 ML YEARS		636	1780	468	96	20	35	(17	18)	709	265	209	267	7	233	11	17	17	24	12	.67	33	.263	.360	.398

Jeff Reardon

Pitches: Right **Bats:** Right **Pos:** RP   **Ht:** 6' 0" **Wt:** 200 **Born:** 10/01/55 **Age:** 36

		HOW MUCH HE PITCHED						WHAT HE GAVE UP											THE RESULTS					
Year Team	Lg	G	GS	CG	GF	IP	BFP	H	R	ER	HR	SH	SF	HB	TBB	IBB	SO	WP	Bk	W	L	Pct.	ShO	Sv	ERA
1979 New York	NL	18	0	0	10	21	81	12	7	4	2	2	1	0	9	3	10	2	0	1	2	.333	0	2	1.71
1980 New York	NL	61	0	0	35	110	475	96	36	32	10	8	5	0	47	15	101	2	0	8	7	.533	0	6	2.62
1981 2 ML Teams		43	0	0	33	70.1	279	48	17	17	5	3	1	2	21	4	49	1	0	3	0	1.000	0	8	2.18
1982 Montreal	NL	75	0	0	53	109	444	87	28	25	6	8	4	2	36	4	86	2	0	7	4	.636	0	26	2.06
1983 Montreal	NL	66	0	0	53	92	403	87	34	31	7	8	2	1	44	9	78	2	0	7	9	.438	0	21	3.03
1984 Montreal	NL	68	0	0	58	87	363	70	31	28	5	3	2	3	37	7	79	4	0	7	7	.500	0	23	2.90
1985 Montreal	NL	63	0	0	50	87.2	356	68	31	31	7	3	1	1	26	4	67	2	0	2	8	.200	0	41	3.18
1986 Montreal	NL	62	0	0	48	89	368	83	46	39	12	9	1	1	26	2	67	0	0	7	9	.438	0	35	3.94
1987 Minnesota	AL	63	0	0	58	80.1	337	70	41	40	14	1	3	3	28	4	83	2	0	8	8	.500	0	31	4.48
1988 Minnesota	AL	63	0	0	58	73	299	68	21	20	6	4	1	2	15	2	56	0	3	2	4	.333	0	42	2.47
1989 Minnesota	AL	65	0	0	61	73	297	68	33	33	8	1	5	3	12	3	46	1	1	5	4	.556	0	31	4.07
1990 Boston	AL	47	0	0	37	51.1	210	39	19	18	5	1	0	1	19	4	33	0	0	5	3	.625	0	21	3.16

Year	Team	Lg	G																							
1991	Boston	AL	57	0	0	51	59.1	248	54	21	20	9	0	2	1	16	3	44	0	0	1	4	.200	0	40	3.03
1981	New York	NL	18	0	0	14	28.2	124	27	11	11	2	0	1	1	12	4	28	0	0	1	0	1.000	0	2	3.45
	Montreal	NL	25	0	0	19	41.2	155	21	6	6	3	3	0	1	9	0	21	1	0	2	0	1.000	0	6	1.30
	13 ML YEARS		751	0	0	605	1003	4160	850	361	338	96	51	28	20	336	64	799	18	4	63	69	.477	0	327	3.03

Joe Redfield

Bats: Right **Throws:** Right **Pos:** 3B   **Ht:** 6' 2" **Wt:** 185 **Born:** 01/14/61 **Age:** 31

							BATTING													BASERUNNING				PERCENTAGES		
Year	Team	Lg	G	AB	H	2B	3B	HR	(Hm	Rd)	TB	R	RBI	TBB	IBB	SO	HBP	SH	SF	SB	CS	SB%	GDP	Avg	OBP	SLG
1982	Little Fls	A	54	206	59	14	5	8	--	--	107	44	57	31	0	46	0	0	0	11	0	1.00	0	.286	.380	.519
1983	Jackson	AA	36	127	25	4	1	2	--	--	37	16	12	17	0	43	0	0	0	0	0	.00	0	.197	.292	.291
	Lynchburg	A	62	192	39	4	7	4	--	--	69	32	27	25	0	44	0	0	0	5	0	1.00	0	.203	.295	.359
1984	Lynchburg	A	122	428	115	18	7	11	--	--	180	80	58	64	1	81	4	2	3	14	7	.67	12	.269	.367	.421
1985	Tidewater	AAA	4	10	3	1	0	0	--	--	4	0	0	1	0	1	0	0	0	0	0	.00	0	.300	.364	.400
	Jackson	AA	39	73	10	4	0	1	--	--	17	12	5	15	0	23	0	2	0	0	0	.00	3	.137	.284	.233
	Lynchburg	A	41	132	32	8	0	3	--	--	49	22	18	33	0	29	4	0	0	10	3	.77	5	.242	.408	.371
1986	Jackson	AA	15	60	17	1	2	0	--	--	22	8	3	4	0	10	0	0	0	2	0	1.00	0	.283	.328	.367
	Charlotte	AA	95	344	102	16	4	14	--	--	168	65	49	38	1	62	7	1	1	8	4	.67	4	.297	.377	.488
1987	Midland	AA	128	498	160	31	7	30	--	--	295	108	108	67	2	83	6	4	4	17	4	.81	11	.321	.405	.592
1988	Edmonton	AAA	118	417	121	38	1	3	--	--	170	67	52	36	0	83	6	4	3	11	4	.73	9	.290	.353	.408
1989	Scr Wil-Bar	AAA	123	428	103	13	6	9	--	--	155	45	49	40	0	74	6	4	4	21	8	.72	11	.241	.312	.362
1990	Denver	AAA	137	525	144	23	10	17	--	--	238	87	71	57	0	76	10	5	5	34	18	.65	8	.274	.353	.453
1991	Buffalo	AAA	105	356	98	20	6	7	--	--	151	60	50	54	2	50	15	10	1	21	4	.84	12	.275	.392	.424
1988	California	AL	2	2	0	0	0	0	(0	0)	0	0	0	0	0	0	0	0	0	0	0	.00	0	.000	.000	.000
1991	Pittsburgh	NL	11	18	2	0	0	0	(0	0)	2	1	0	4	0	1	0	0	1	0	1	.00	0	.111	.273	.111
	2 ML YEARS		13	20	2	0	0	0	(0	0)	2	1	0	4	0	1	0	0	1	0	1	.00	0	.100	.250	.100

Gary Redus

Bats: Right **Throws:** Right **Pos:** 1B   **Ht:** 6' 1" **Wt:** 195 **Born:** 11/01/56 **Age:** 35

							BATTING													BASERUNNING				PERCENTAGES		
Year	Team	Lg	G	AB	H	2B	3B	HR	(Hm	Rd)	TB	R	RBI	TBB	IBB	SO	HBP	SH	SF	SB	CS	SB%	GDP	Avg	OBP	SLG
1982	Cincinnati	NL	20	83	18	3	2	1	(1	0)	28	12	7	5	0	21	0	0	1	11	2	.85	0	.217	.258	.337
1983	Cincinnati	NL	125	453	112	20	9	17	(6	11)	201	90	51	71	4	111	3	2	2	39	14	.74	6	.247	.352	.444
1984	Cincinnati	NL	123	394	100	21	3	7	(4	3)	148	69	22	52	3	71	1	3	5	48	11	.81	4	.254	.338	.376
1985	Cincinnati	NL	101	246	62	14	4	6	(4	2)	102	51	28	44	2	52	1	2	1	48	12	.80	0	.252	.366	.415
1986	Philadelphia	NL	90	340	84	22	4	11	(8	3)	147	62	33	47	4	78	3	1	1	25	7	.78	2	.247	.343	.432
1987	Chicago	AL	130	475	112	26	6	12	(4	8)	186	78	48	69	0	90	0	3	7	52	11	.83	7	.236	.328	.392
1988	2 ML Teams		107	333	83	12	4	8	(3	5)	127	54	38	48	1	71	3	0	8	31	4	.89	6	.249	.342	.381
1989	Pittsburgh	NL	98	279	79	18	7	6	(3	3)	129	42	33	40	3	51	1	1	3	25	6	.81	5	.283	.372	.462
1990	Pittsburgh	NL	96	227	56	15	3	6	(2	4)	95	32	23	33	0	38	2	1	5	11	5	.69	1	.247	.341	.419
1991	Pittsburgh	NL	98	252	62	12	2	7	(3	4)	99	45	24	28	2	39	3	1	4	17	3	.85	0	.246	.324	.393
1988	Chicago	AL	77	262	69	10	4	6	(1	5)	105	42	34	33	1	52	2	0	7	26	2	.93	5	.263	.342	.401
	Pittsburgh	NL	30	71	14	2	0	2	(2	0)	22	12	4	15	0	19	1	0	1	5	2	.71	1	.197	.341	.310
	10 ML YEARS		988	3082	768	163	44	81	(38	43)	1262	535	307	437	19	622	17	14	37	307	75	.80	31	.249	.342	.409

Jeff Reed

Bats: Left **Throws:** Right **Pos:** C   **Ht:** 6' 2" **Wt:** 190 **Born:** 11/12/62 **Age:** 29

							BATTING													BASERUNNING				PERCENTAGES		
Year	Team	Lg	G	AB	H	2B	3B	HR	(Hm	Rd)	TB	R	RBI	TBB	IBB	SO	HBP	SH	SF	SB	CS	SB%	GDP	Avg	OBP	SLG
1984	Minnesota	AL	18	21	3	3	0	0	(0	0)	6	3	1	2	0	6	0	1	0	0	0	.00	0	.143	.217	.286
1985	Minnesota	AL	7	10	2	0	0	0	(0	0)	2	2	0	0	0	3	0	0	0	0	0	.00	0	.200	.200	.200
1986	Minnesota	AL	68	165	39	6	1	2	(1	1)	53	13	9	16	0	19	1	3	0	1	0	1.00	2	.236	.308	.321
1987	Montreal	NL	75	207	44	11	0	1	(1	0)	58	15	21	12	1	20	1	4	4	0	1	.00	8	.213	.254	.280
1988	2 ML Teams		92	265	60	9	2	1	(1	0)	76	20	16	28	1	41	0	1	1	1	0	1.00	5	.226	.299	.287
1989	Cincinnati	NL	102	287	64	11	0	3	(1	2)	84	16	23	34	5	46	2	3	4	0	0	.00	6	.223	.306	.293
1990	Cincinnati	NL	72	175	44	8	1	3	(2	1)	63	12	16	24	5	26	0	5	1	0	0	.00	4	.251	.340	.360
1991	Cincinnati	NL	91	270	72	15	2	3	(1	2)	100	20	31	23	3	38	1	1	5	0	0	.00	6	.267	.321	.370
1988	Montreal	NL	43	123	27	3	2	0	(0	0)	34	10	9	13	1	22	0	1	1	0	1	1.00	3	.220	.292	.276
	Cincinnati	NL	49	142	33	6	0	1	(1	0)	42	10	7	15	0	19	0	0	0	0	0	.00	2	.232	.306	.296
	8 ML YEARS		525	1400	328	63	6	13	(	6)	442	101	117	139	15	199	5	18	15	2	2	.50	31	.234	.303	.316

Jody Reed

Bats: Right **Throws:** Right **Pos:** 2B   **Ht:** 5' 9" **Wt:** 165 **Born:** 07/26/62 **Age:** 29

							BATTING													BASERUNNING				PERCENTAGES		
Year	Team	Lg	G	AB	H	2B	3B	HR	(Hm	Rd)	TB	R	RBI	TBB	IBB	SO	HBP	SH	SF	SB	CS	SB%	GDP	Avg	OBP	SLG
1987	Boston	AL	9	30	9	1	1	0	(0	0)	12	4	8	4	0	0	0	1	0	1	1	.50	0	.300	.382	.400
1988	Boston	AL	109	338	99	23	1	1	(1	0)	127	60	28	45	1	21	4	11	2	1	3	.25	5	.293	.380	.376
1989	Boston	AL	146	524	151	42	2	3	(2	1)	206	76	40	73	0	44	4	13	5	4	5	.44	12	.288	.376	.393

Year Team	Lg	G	AB	H	2B	3B	HR	(Hm	Rd)	TB	R	RBI	TBB	IBB	SO	HBP	SH	SF	SB	CS	SB%	GDP	Avg	OBP	SLG
1990 Boston	AL	155	598	173	45	0	5	(3	2)	233	70	51	75	4	65	4	11	3	4	4	.50	19	.289	.371	.390
1991 Boston	AL	153	618	175	42	2	5	(3	2)	236	87	60	60	2	53	4	11	3	6	5	.55	15	.283	.349	.382
5 ML YEARS		572	2108	607	153	6	14	(9	5)	814	297	187	257	7	183	16	47	13	16	18	.47	51	.288	.368	.386

Rick Reed

Pitches: Right **Bats:** Right **Pos:** SP   **Ht:** 6' 0" **Wt:** 195 **Born:** 08/16/64 **Age:** 27

	HOW MUCH HE PITCHED						WHAT HE GAVE UP											THE RESULTS					
Year Team	Lg	G	GS	CG	GF	IP	BFP	H	R	ER	HR	SH	SF	HB	TBB	IBB	SO	WP	Bk	W	L	Pct.	ShO	Sv	ERA
1988 Pittsburgh	NL	2	0	0	0	12	47	10	4	4	1	2	0	0	2	0	6	0	0	1	0	1.000	0	0	3.00
1989 Pittsburgh	NL	15	7	0	2	54.2	232	62	35	34	5	2	3	2	11	3	34	0	3	1	4	.200	0	0	5.60
1990 Pittsburgh	NL	13	8	1	2	53.2	238	62	32	26	6	2	1	1	12	6	27	0	0	2	3	.400	1	1	4.36
1991 Pittsburgh	NL	1	1	0	0	4.1	21	8	6	5	1	0	0	0	1	0	2	0	0	0	0	.000	0	0	10.38
4 ML YEARS		31	18	1	4	124.2	538	142	77	69	13	6	4	3	26	9	69	0	3	4	7	.364	1	1	4.98

Kevin Reimer

Bats: Left **Throws:** Right **Pos:** LF/DH   **Ht:** 6' 2" **Wt:** 225 **Born:** 06/28/64 **Age:** 28

	BATTING																	BASERUNNING				PERCENTAGES		
Year Team	Lg	G	AB	H	2B	3B	HR	(Hm | Rd)	TB	R	RBI	TBB	IBB	SO	HBP	SH	SF	SB	CS	SB%	GDP	Avg	OBP	SLG
1988 Texas	AL	12	25	3	0	0	1	(0 | 1)	6	2	2	0	0	6	0	0	1	0	0	.00	0	.120	.115	.240
1989 Texas	AL	3	5	0	0	0	0	(0 | 0)	0	0	0	0	0	1	0	0	0	0	0	.00	1	.000	.000	.000
1990 Texas	AL	64	100	26	9	1	2	(0 | 2)	43	5	15	10	0	22	1	0	0	0	1	.00	3	.260	.333	.430
1991 Texas	AL	136	394	106	22	0	20	(13 | 7)	188	46	69	33	6	93	7	0	6	0	3	.00	10	.269	.332	.477
4 ML YEARS		215	524	135	31	1	23	(13 | 10)	237	53	86	43	6	122	8	0	7	0	4	.00	14	.258	.320	.452

Mike Remlinger

Pitches: Left **Bats:** Left **Pos:** SP   **Ht:** 6' 0" **Wt:** 195 **Born:** 03/23/66 **Age:** 26

	HOW MUCH HE PITCHED						WHAT HE GAVE UP											THE RESULTS					
Year Team	Lg	G	GS	CG	GF	IP	BFP	H	R	ER	HR	SH	SF	HB	TBB	IBB	SO	WP	Bk	W	L	Pct.	ShO	Sv	ERA
1987 Everett	A	2	1	0	0	5	19	1	2	2	0	0	0	0	5	0	11	1	0	0	0	.000	0	0	3.60
Clinton	A	6	5	0	0	30	124	21	12	11	2	1	1	1	14	0	43	3	1	2	1	.667	0	0	3.30
Shreveport	AA	6	6	0	0	34.1	142	14	11	9	2	0	0	3	22	0	51	2	0	4	2	.667	0	0	2.36
1988 Shreveport	AA	3	3	0	0	13	50	7	4	1	0	0	0	3	4	0	18	1	3	1	0	1.000	0	0	0.69
1989 Shreveport	AA	16	16	0	0	90.2	399	68	43	30	2	1	1	3	73	0	92	16	2	4	6	.400	0	0	2.98
Phoenix	AAA	11	10	0	0	43	233	51	47	44	8	1	2	2	52	0	28	5	0	1	6	.143	0	0	9.21
1990 Shreveport	AA	25	25	2	0	147.2	644	149	82	64	9	8	4	8	72	1	75	16	0	9	11	.450	1	0	3.90
1991 Phoenix	AAA	19	19	1	0	108.2	508	134	86	77	15	4	5	1	59	0	68	6	1	5	5	.500	1	0	6.38
1991 San Francisco	NL	8	6	1	1	35	155	36	17	17	5	1	1	0	20	1	19	2	1	2	1	.667	1	0	4.37

Laddie Renfroe

Pitches: Right **Bats:** Both **Pos:** RP   **Ht:** 5'11" **Wt:** 200 **Born:** 05/09/62 **Age:** 30

	HOW MUCH HE PITCHED						WHAT HE GAVE UP											THE RESULTS					
Year Team	Lg	G	GS	CG	GF	IP	BFP	H	R	ER	HR	SH	SF	HB	TBB	IBB	SO	WP	Bk	W	L	Pct.	ShO	Sv	ERA
1984 Geneva	A	24	0	0	18	39	170	34	10	6	1	4	1	3	10	5	33	1	0	3	3	.500	0	10	1.38
1985 Peoria	A	57	0	0	37	95.2	396	79	36	34	2	4	3	5	39	2	56	1	0	10	6	.625	0	8	3.20
1986 Winston-Sal	A	65	0	0	54	83	356	84	37	27	2	3	5	2	27	5	51	6	1	6	6	.500	0	21	2.93
1987 Pittsfield	AA	40	0	0	37	46.1	205	56	22	21	2	3	0	0	15	8	27	3	0	4	5	.444	0	16	4.08
Iowa	AAA	8	0	0	1	14.1	56	8	9	8	1	0	0	0	5	0	9	1	0	0	1	.000	0	0	5.02
1988 Iowa	AAA	16	0	0	5	24	109	28	13	13	2	1	0	0	11	1	12	0	2	1	3	.250	0	0	4.88
Pittsfield	AA	29	7	1	11	110.1	441	102	32	24	4	10	1	4	24	5	57	3	1	9	4	.692	0	1	1.96
1989 Charlotte	AA	78	2	1	58	132	554	127	52	46	12	11	1	4	34	10	85	2	1	19	7	.731	0	15	3.14
1990 Iowa	AAA	44	14	1	22	118	517	146	68	65	12	4	1	1	30	7	56	0	1	7	3	.700	0	9	4.96
1991 Iowa	AAA	63	1	0	40	98.1	422	101	52	46	10	5	6	3	32	5	52	2	0	8	5	.615	0	18	4.21
1991 Chicago	NL	4	0	0	2	4.2	27	11	7	7	1	0	0	0	2	1	4	1	0	0	1	.000	0	0	13.50

Rick Reuschel

Pitches: Right **Bats:** Right **Pos:** RP   **Ht:** 6' 3" **Wt:** 250 **Born:** 05/16/49 **Age:** 43

	HOW MUCH HE PITCHED						WHAT HE GAVE UP											THE RESULTS					
Year Team	Lg	G	GS	CG	GF	IP	BFP	H	R	ER	HR	SH	SF	HB	TBB	IBB	SO	WP	Bk	W	L	Pct.	ShO	Sv	ERA
1972 Chicago	NL	21	18	5	1	129	527	127	46	42	3	4	2	3	29	6	87	1	2	10	8	.556	4	0	2.93
1973 Chicago	NL	36	36	7	0	237	1003	244	95	79	15	5	2	5	62	6	168	10	1	14	15	.483	3	0	3.00
1974 Chicago	NL	41	38	8	2	241	1061	262	130	115	18	14	8	6	83	12	160	7	1	13	12	.520	2	0	4.29
1975 Chicago	NL	38	37	6	1	234	1007	244	116	97	17	20	4	7	67	8	155	4	1	11	17	.393	0	1	3.73
1976 Chicago	NL	38	37	9	1	260	1078	260	117	100	17	11	13	8	64	8	146	7	1	14	12	.538	2	1	3.46
1977 Chicago	NL	39	37	8	2	252	1030	233	84	78	13	3	4	5	74	11	166	9	1	20	10	.667	4	1	2.79
1978 Chicago	NL	35	35	9	0	243	1007	235	98	92	16	16	8	5	54	8	115	13	1	14	15	.483	1	0	3.41
1979 Chicago	NL	36	36	5	0	239	1021	251	104	96	16	13	6	10	75	8	125	5	0	18	12	.600	1	0	3.62
1980 Chicago	NL	38	38	6	0	257	1094	281	111	97	13	19	14	4	76	10	140	3	1	11	13	.458	0	0	3.40

Year Team	Lg	G	GS	CG	GF	IP	BFP	H	R	ER	HR	SH	SF	HB	TBB	IBB	SO	WP	Bk	W	L	Pct.	ShO	Sv	ERA
1981 2 ML Teams		25	24	4	1	157	640	162	64	54	8	6	2	5	33	4	75	5	0	8	11	.421	0	0	3.10
1983 Chicago	NL	4	4	0	0	20.2	88	18	9	9	1	0	1	0	10	2	9	0	0	1	1	.500	0	0	3.92
1984 Chicago	NL	19	14	1	2	92.1	405	123	57	53	7	7	9	3	23	0	43	2	0	5	5	.500	0	0	5.17
1985 Pittsburgh	NL	31	26	9	4	194	773	153	58	49	7	5	3	3	52	10	138	4	0	14	8	.636	1	1	2.27
1986 Pittsburgh	NL	35	34	4	0	215.2	930	232	106	95	20	9	10	8	57	2	125	6	1	9	16	.360	2	0	3.96
1987 2 ML Teams		34	33	12	0	227	920	207	91	78	13	8	8	8	42	3	107	7	0	13	9	.591	4	0	3.09
1988 San Francisco	NL	36	36	7	0	245	1000	242	88	85	11	9	14	6	42	8	92	4	0	19	11	.633	2	0	3.12
1989 San Francisco	NL	32	32	2	0	208.1	860	195	75	68	18	7	7	2	54	4	111	1	0	17	8	.680	0	0	2.94
1990 San Francisco	NL	15	13	0	1	87	390	102	40	38	8	10	5	1	31	9	49	1	0	3	6	.333	0	1	3.93
1991 San Francisco	NL	4	1	0	1	10.2	54	17	5	5	0	1	0	0	7	1	4	0	0	0	2	.000	0	0	4.22
1981 Chicago	NL	13	13	1	0	86	358	87	40	33	4	5	0	4	23	4	53	5	0	4	7	.364	0	0	3.45
New York	AL	12	11	3	1	71	282	75	24	21	4	1	2	1	10	0	22	0	0	4	4	.500	0	0	2.66
1987 Pittsburgh	NL	25	25	9	0	177	715	163	63	54	12	4	7	6	35	1	80	5	0	8	6	.571	3	0	2.75
San Francisco	NL	9	8	3	0	50	205	44	28	24	1	4	1	2	7	2	27	2	0	5	3	.625	1	0	4.32
19 ML YEARS		557	529	102	16	3549.2	14888	3588	1494	1330	221	167	120	88	935	117	2015	89	10	214	191	.528	26	5	3.37

Gil Reyes

Bats: Right **Throws:** Right **Pos:** C   **Ht:** 6' 2" **Wt:** 200 **Born:** 12/10/63 **Age:** 28

								BATTING											BASERUNNING				PERCENTAGES		
Year Team	Lg	G	AB	H	2B	3B	HR	(Hm	Rd)	TB	R	RBI	TBB	IBB	SO	HBP	SH	SF	SB	CS	SB%	GDP	Avg	OBP	SLG
1983 Los Angeles	NL	19	31	5	2	0	0	(0	0)	7	1	0	0	0	5	1	0	0	0	0	.00	3	.161	.188	.226
1984 Los Angeles	NL	4	5	0	0	0	0	(0	0)	0	0	0	0	0	3	0	0	0	0	0	.00	0	.000	.000	.000
1985 Los Angeles	NL	6	1	0	0	0	0	(0	0)	0	0	0	1	0	1	1	0	0	0	0	.00	0	.000	.667	.000
1987 Los Angeles	NL	1	0	0	0	0	0	(0	0)	0	0	0	0	0	0	0	0	0	0	0	.00	0	.000	.000	.000
1988 Los Angeles	NL	5	9	1	0	0	0	(0	0)	1	1	0	0	0	3	0	0	0	0	0	.00	0	.111	.111	.111
1989 Montreal	NL	4	5	1	0	0	0	(0	0)	1	0	1	0	0	1	0	0	0	0	0	.00	0	.200	.200	.200
1991 Montreal	NL	83	207	45	9	0	0	(0	0)	54	11	13	19	2	51	1	1	1	2	4	.33	3	.217	.285	.261
7 ML YEARS		122	258	52	11	0	0	(0	0)	63	13	14	20	2	64	3	1	1	2	4	.33	6	.202	.266	.244

Harold Reynolds

Bats: Both **Throws:** Right **Pos:** 2B   **Ht:** 5'11" **Wt:** 165 **Born:** 11/26/60 **Age:** 31

								BATTING											BASERUNNING				PERCENTAGES		
Year Team	Lg	G	AB	H	2B	3B	HR	(Hm	Rd)	TB	R	RBI	TBB	IBB	SO	HBP	SH	SF	SB	CS	SB%	GDP	Avg	OBP	SLG
1983 Seattle	AL	20	59	12	4	1	0	(0	0)	18	8	1	2	0	9	0	1	1	0	2	.00	1	.203	.226	.305
1984 Seattle	AL	10	10	3	0	0	0	(0	0)	3	3	0	0	0	1	0	1	0	1	1	.50	0	.300	.364	.300
1985 Seattle	AL	67	104	15	3	1	0	(0	0)	20	15	6	17	0	14	0	1	0	3	2	.60	0	.144	.264	.192
1986 Seattle	AL	126	445	99	19	4	1	(1	0)	129	46	24	29	0	42	3	9	0	30	12	.71	6	.222	.275	.290
1987 Seattle	AL	160	530	146	31	8	1	(1	0)	196	73	35	39	0	34	2	8	5	60	20	.75	7	.275	.325	.370
1988 Seattle	AL	158	598	169	26	11	4	(4	0)	229	61	41	51	1	51	2	10	2	35	29	.55	9	.283	.340	.383
1989 Seattle	AL	153	613	184	24	9	0	(0	0)	226	87	43	55	1	45	3	3	3	25	18	.58	4	.300	.359	.369
1990 Seattle	AL	160	642	162	36	5	5	(0	5)	223	100	55	81	3	52	3	5	6	31	16	.66	9	.252	.336	.347
1991 Seattle	AL	161	631	160	34	6	3	(1	2)	215	95	57	72	2	63	5	14	6	28	8	.78	11	.254	.332	.341
9 ML YEARS		1015	3632	950	177	45	14	(7	7)	1259	488	262	346	7	311	19	52	23	213	108	.66	47	.262	.327	.347

Armando Reynoso

Pitches: Right **Bats:** Right **Pos:** SP   **Ht:** 6' 0" **Wt:** 186 **Born:** 05/01/66 **Age:** 26

				HOW MUCH HE PITCHED				WHAT HE GAVE UP											THE RESULTS					
Year Team	Lg	G	GS	CG	GF	IP	BFP	H	R	ER	HR	SH	SF	HB	TBB	IBB	SO	WP	Bk	W	L	Pct.	ShO	Sv	ERA
1990 Richmond	AAA	4	3	0	0	24	102	26	7	6	3	1	1	0	7	0	15	0	3	3	1	.750	0	0	2.25
1991 Richmond	AAA	22	19	3	1	131	544	117	44	38	9	7	3	10	39	1	97	8	6	10	6	.625	3	0	2.61
1991 Atlanta	NL	6	5	0	1	23.1	103	26	18	16	4	3	0	3	10	1	10	2	0	2	1	.667	0	0	6.17

Arthur Rhodes

Pitches: Left **Bats:** Left **Pos:** SP   **Ht:** 6' 2" **Wt:** 190 **Born:** 10/24/69 **Age:** 22

				HOW MUCH HE PITCHED				WHAT HE GAVE UP											THE RESULTS					
Year Team	Lg	G	GS	CG	GF	IP	BFP	H	R	ER	HR	SH	SF	HB	TBB	IBB	SO	WP	Bk	W	L	Pct.	ShO	Sv	ERA
1988 Bluefield	R	11	7	0	3	35.1	155	29	17	13	1	0	1	1	15	0	44	0	3	3	4	.429	0	0	3.31
1989 Erie	A	5	5	1	0	31	115	13	7	4	1	0	0	0	10	0	45	2	1	2	0	1.000	0	0	1.16
Frederick	A	7	6	0	0	24.1	109	19	16	14	2	0	1	0	19	0	28	4	1	2	2	.500	0	0	5.18
1990 Frederick	A	13	13	4	0	80.2	322	62	25	19	6	0	1	1	21	0	103	3	1	4	6	.400	0	0	2.12
Hagerstown	AA	12	12	0	0	72.1	303	62	32	30	3	1	3	0	39	0	60	5	0	3	4	.429	0	0	3.73
1991 Hagerstown	AA	19	19	2	0	106.2	428	73	37	32	2	1	3	0	47	1	115	10	0	7	4	.636	2	0	2.70
1991 Baltimore	AL	8	8	0	0	36	174	47	35	32	4	1	3	0	23	0	23	2	0	0	3	.000	0	0	8.00

Karl Rhodes

Bats: Left **Throws:** Left **Pos:** RF **Ht:** 5'11" **Wt:** 170 **Born:** 08/21/68 **Age:** 23

Year Team	Lg	G	AB	H	2B	3B	HR	(Hm	Rd)	TB	R	RBI	TBB	IBB	SO	HBP	SH	SF	SB	CS	SB%	GDP	Avg	OBP	SLG
1986 Astros	R	62	222	65	10	3	0	--	--	81	36	22	32	3	33	0	5	2	14	6	.70	1	.293	.379	.365
1987 Asheville	A	129	413	104	16	4	3	--	--	137	62	50	77	6	82	0	3	8	43	14	.75	4	.252	.363	.332
1988 Osceola	A	132	452	128	4	2	1	--	--	139	69	34	81	4	58	2	6	5	65	23	.74	7	.283	.391	.308
1989 Columbus	AA	143	520	134	25	5	4	--	--	181	81	63	93	3	105	3	0	3	18	12	.60	13	.258	.372	.348
1990 Tucson	AAA	107	385	106	24	11	3	--	--	161	68	59	47	2	75	0	3	5	24	4	.86	9	.275	.350	.418
1991 Tucson	AAA	84	308	80	17	1	1	--	--	102	45	46	38	1	48	0	5	4	5	8	.38	10	.260	.337	.331
1990 Houston	NL	38	86	21	6	1	1	(0	1)	32	12	3	13	3	12	0	1	1	4	1	.80	1	.244	.340	.372
1991 Houston	NL	44	136	29	3	1	1	(0	1)	37	7	12	14	3	26	1	0	1	2	2	.50	3	.213	.289	.272
2 ML YEARS		82	222	50	9	2	2	(0	2)	69	19	15	27	6	38	1	1	2	6	3	.67	4	.225	.310	.311

Pat Rice

Pitches: Right **Bats:** Right **Pos:** RP **Ht:** 6'2" **Wt:** 200 **Born:** 11/02/63 **Age:** 28

Year Team	Lg	G	GS	CG	GF	IP	BFP	H	R	ER	HR	SH	SF	HB	TBB	IBB	SO	WP	Bk	W	L	Pct.	ShO	Sv	ERA
1986 Salt Lk Cty	R	18	6	0	7	59.1	0	67	33	22	1	0	0	1	15	0	39	5	0	1	3	.250	0	0	3.34
1987 Wausau	A	28	27	4	0	166.1	732	192	100	71	13	4	6	7	43	2	127	15	1	12	11	.522	1	0	3.84
1988 San Berndno	A	33	12	3	8	121	518	120	56	46	10	4	3	8	32	1	114	5	3	7	7	.500	1	3	3.42
Vermont	AA	6	3	0	1	26	111	22	7	3	2	1	0	1	7	1	16	1	3	3	0	1.000	0	0	1.04
1989 Williamsprt	AA	13	5	2	3	47.1	190	39	13	12	0	1	0	0	12	2	40	2	0	4	1	.800	1	0	2.28
Calgary	AAA	17	5	0	3	55.2	247	63	32	30	8	1	1	0	21	1	35	1	0	6	3	.667	0	1	4.85
1990 Calgary	AAA	15	2	0	2	28.1	129	34	21	20	2	1	1	1	13	2	27	4	0	1	1	.500	0	2	6.35
Williamsprt	AA	25	8	0	4	72.1	313	77	36	32	4	1	3	1	24	1	58	5	0	4	4	.500	0	0	3.98
1991 Calgary	AAA	21	21	1	1	121.2	520	138	70	68	18	2	5	2	37	0	59	5	0	13	4	.765	0	0	5.03
1991 Seattle	AL	7	2	0	0	21	91	18	10	7	3	0	3	1	10	1	12	0	0	1	1	.500	0	0	3.00

Jeff Richardson

Bats: Right **Throws:** Right **Pos:** SS **Ht:** 6'2" **Wt:** 180 **Born:** 08/26/65 **Age:** 26

Year Team	Lg	G	AB	H	2B	3B	HR	(Hm	Rd)	TB	R	RBI	TBB	IBB	SO	HBP	SH	SF	SB	CS	SB%	GDP	Avg	OBP	SLG
1989 Cincinnati	NL	53	125	21	4	0	2	(1	1)	31	10	11	10	0	23	1	3	1	1	0	1.00	3	.168	.234	.248
1991 Pittsburgh	NL	6	4	1	0	0	0	(0	0)	1	0	0	0	0	3	0	0	0	0	0	.00	0	.250	.250	.250
2 ML YEARS		59	129	22	4	0	2	(1	1)	32	10	11	10	0	26	1	3	1	1	0	1.00	3	.171	.234	.248

Nikco Riesgo

Bats: Right **Throws:** Right **Pos:** RF **Ht:** 6'2" **Wt:** 185 **Born:** 01/11/67 **Age:** 25

Year Team	Lg	G	AB	H	2B	3B	HR	(Hm	Rd)	TB	R	RBI	TBB	IBB	SO	HBP	SH	SF	SB	CS	SB%	GDP	Avg	OBP	SLG
1988 Spokane	A	65	219	55	8	3	7	--	--	90	45	51	44	1	59	6	0	3	24	4	.86	5	.251	.386	.411
1989 Chston-Sc	A	119	402	96	25	1	13	--	--	162	74	53	73	3	81	10	3	3	34	13	.72	5	.239	.367	.403
1990 St. Lucie	A	131	456	136	35	3	14	--	--	219	93	94	74	10	77	8	0	5	46	14	.77	16	.298	.440	.480
1991 Wst Plm Bch	A	5	18	5	1	0	1	--	--	9	4	1	4	1	5	0	0	0	0	1	.00	0	.278	.409	.500
Reading	AA	98	356	92	18	2	14	--	--	156	61	66	48	1	71	0	0	4	8	6	.57	10	.258	.343	.438
1991 Montreal	NL	4	7	1	0	0	0	(0	0)	1	1	0	3	0	1	0	0	0	0	0	.00	1	.143	.400	.143

Dave Righetti

Pitches: Left **Bats:** Left **Pos:** RP **Ht:** 6'4" **Wt:** 212 **Born:** 11/28/58 **Age:** 33

Year Team	Lg	G	GS	CG	GF	IP	BFP	H	R	ER	HR	SH	SF	HB	TBB	IBB	SO	WP	Bk	W	L	Pct.	ShO	Sv	ERA
1979 New York	AL	3	3	0	0	17	67	10	7	7	2	1	1	0	10	0	13	0	0	0	1	.000	0	0	3.71
1981 New York	AL	15	15	2	0	105	422	75	25	24	1	0	2	0	38	0	89	1	1	8	4	.667	0	0	2.06
1982 New York	AL	33	27	4	3	183	804	155	88	77	11	8	5	6	108	4	163	9	5	11	10	.524	0	1	3.79
1983 New York	AL	31	31	7	0	217	900	194	96	83	12	10	4	2	67	2	169	10	1	14	8	.636	2	0	3.44
1984 New York	AL	64	0	0	53	96.1	400	79	29	25	5	4	4	0	37	7	90	0	2	5	6	.455	0	31	2.34
1985 New York	AL	74	0	0	60	107	452	96	36	33	5	6	3	0	45	3	92	7	0	12	7	.632	0	29	2.78
1986 New York	AL	74	0	0	68	106.2	435	88	31	29	4	5	4	2	35	7	83	1	0	8	8	.500	0	46	2.45
1987 New York	AL	60	0	0	54	95	419	95	45	37	9	6	5	2	44	4	77	1	3	8	6	.571	0	31	3.51
1988 New York	AL	60	0	0	41	87	377	86	35	34	5	4	0	1	37	2	70	2	4	5	4	.556	0	25	3.52
1989 New York	AL	55	0	0	53	69	300	73	32	23	3	7	2	1	26	6	51	0	0	2	6	.250	0	25	3.00
1990 New York	AL	53	0	0	47	53	235	48	24	21	8	1	1	2	26	2	43	2	0	1	1	.500	0	36	3.57
1991 San Francisco	NL	61	0	0	49	71.2	304	64	29	27	4	4	2	3	28	6	51	1	1	2	7	.222	0	24	3.39
12 ML YEARS		583	76	13	428	1207.2	5115	1063	477	420	69	56	33	19	501	43	991	34	17	76	68	.528	2	248	3.13

Jose Rijo

Pitches: Right **Bats:** Right **Pos:** SP   **Ht:** 6' 2" **Wt:** 210 **Born:** 05/13/65 **Age:** 27

		HOW	MUCH	HE	PITCHED			WHAT	HE	GAVE	UP							THE	RESULTS			
Year Team	Lg	G	GS	CG	GF	IP	BFP	H	R	ER	HR	SH	SF	HB	TBB	IBB	SO	WP	Bk	W	L	Pct.	ShO	Sv	ERA
1984 New York	AL	24	5	0	8	62.1	289	74	40	33	5	6	1	1	33	1	47	2	1	2	8	.200	0	2	4.76
1985 Oakland	AL	12	9	0	1	63.2	272	57	26	25	6	5	0	1	28	2	65	0	0	6	4	.600	0	0	3.53
1986 Oakland	AL	39	26	4	9	193.2	856	172	116	100	24	10	9	4	108	7	176	6	4	9	11	.450	0	1	4.65
1987 Oakland	AL	21	14	1	3	82.1	394	106	67	54	10	0	3	2	41	1	67	5	2	2	7	.222	0	0	5.90
1988 Cincinnati	NL	49	19	0	12	162	653	120	47	43	7	8	5	3	63	7	160	1	4	13	8	.619	0	0	2.39
1989 Cincinnati	NL	19	19	1	0	111	464	101	39	35	6	3	6	2	48	3	86	4	3	7	6	.538	1	0	2.84
1990 Cincinnati	NL	29	29	7	0	197	801	151	65	59	10	8	1	2	78	1	152	2	5	14	8	.636	1	0	2.70
1991 Cincinnati	NL	30	30	3	0	204.1	825	165	69	57	8	4	8	3	55	4	172	2	4	15	6	.714	1	0	2.51
8 ML YEARS		223	151	16	33	1076.1	4554	946	469	406	76	44	33	18	454	26	925	22	23	68	58	.540	3	3	3.39

Ernest Riles

Bats: Left **Throws:** Right **Pos:** 3B/SS   **Ht:** 6' 1" **Wt:** 180 **Born:** 10/02/60 **Age:** 31

								BATTING										BASERUNNING				PERCENTAGES		
Year Team	Lg	G	AB	H	2B	3B	HR	(Hm	Rd)	TB	R	RBI	TBB	IBB	SO	HBP	SH	SF	SB	CS	SB%	GDP	Avg	OBP	SLG
1985 Milwaukee	AL	116	448	128	12	7	5	(2	3)	169	54	45	36	0	54	2	6	3	2	2	.50	16	.286	.339	.377
1986 Milwaukee	AL	145	524	132	24	2	9	(2	7)	187	69	47	54	0	80	1	6	3	7	7	.50	14	.252	.321	.357
1987 Milwaukee	AL	83	276	72	11	1	4	(1	3)	97	38	38	30	1	47	1	3	6	3	4	.43	6	.261	.329	.351
1988 2 ML Teams		120	314	87	13	3	4	(4	0)	118	33	37	17	2	59	0	1	4	3	4	.43	8	.277	.310	.376
1989 San Francisco	NL	122	302	84	13	2	7	(5	2)	122	43	40	28	3	50	2	1	4	0	6	.00	7	.278	.339	.404
1990 San Francisco	NL	92	155	31	2	1	8	(7	1)	59	22	21	26	3	26	0	2	1	0	0	.00	2	.200	.313	.381
1991 Oakland	AL	108	281	60	8	4	5	(3	2)	91	30	32	31	3	42	1	4	4	3	2	.60	8	.214	.290	.324
1988 Milwaukee	AL	41	127	32	6	1	1	(1	0)	43	7	9	7	0	26	0	1	0	2	2	.50	3	.252	.291	.339
San Francisco	NL	79	187	55	7	2	3	(3	0)	75	26	28	10	2	33	0	0	4	1	2	.33	5	.294	.323	.401
7 ML YEARS		786	2300	594	83	20	42	(24	18)	843	289	260	222	12	358	7	23	25	18	25	.42	61	.258	.322	.367

Billy Ripken

Bats: Right **Throws:** Right **Pos:** 2B   **Ht:** 6' 1" **Wt:** 182 **Born:** 12/16/64 **Age:** 27

								BATTING										BASERUNNING				PERCENTAGES		
Year Team	Lg	G	AB	H	2B	3B	HR	(Hm	Rd)	TB	R	RBI	TBB	IBB	SO	HBP	SH	SF	SB	CS	SB%	GDP	Avg	OBP	SLG
1987 Baltimore	AL	58	234	72	9	0	2	(0	2)	87	27	20	21	0	23	0	1	1	4	1	.80	3	.308	.363	.372
1988 Baltimore	AL	150	512	106	18	1	2	(0	2)	132	52	34	33	0	63	5	6	3	8	2	.80	14	.207	.260	.258
1989 Baltimore	AL	115	318	76	11	2	2	(0	2)	97	31	26	22	0	53	0	19	5	1	2	.33	12	.239	.284	.305
1990 Baltimore	AL	129	406	118	28	1	3	(2	1)	157	48	38	28	2	43	4	17	1	5	2	.71	7	.291	.342	.387
1991 Baltimore	AL	104	287	62	11	1	0	(0	0)	75	24	14	15	0	31	0	11	2	0	1	.00	14	.216	.253	.261
5 ML YEARS		556	1757	434	77	5	9	(2	7)	548	182	132	119	2	213	9	54	12	18	8	.69	50	.247	.296	.312

Cal Ripken

Bats: Right **Throws:** Right **Pos:** SS   **Ht:** 6' 4" **Wt:** 225 **Born:** 08/24/60 **Age:** 31

								BATTING										BASERUNNING				PERCENTAGES		
Year Team	Lg	G	AB	H	2B	3B	HR	(Hm	Rd)	TB	R	RBI	TBB	IBB	SO	HBP	SH	SF	SB	CS	SB%	GDP	Avg	OBP	SLG
1981 Baltimore	AL	23	39	5	0	0	0	(0	0)	5	1	0	1	0	8	0	0	0	0	0	.00	4	.128	.150	.128
1982 Baltimore	AL	160	598	158	32	5	28	(11	17)	284	90	93	46	3	95	3	2	6	3	3	.50	16	.264	.317	.475
1983 Baltimore	AL	162	663	211	47	2	27	(12	15)	343	121	102	58	0	97	0	0	5	0	4	.00	24	.318	.371	.517
1984 Baltimore	AL	162	641	195	37	7	27	(16	11)	327	103	86	71	1	89	2	0	2	2	1	.67	16	.304	.374	.510
1985 Baltimore	AL	161	642	181	32	5	26	(15	11)	301	116	110	67	1	68	1	0	8	2	3	.40	32	.282	.347	.469
1986 Baltimore	AL	162	627	177	35	1	25	(10	15)	289	98	81	70	5	60	4	0	6	4	2	.67	19	.282	.355	.461
1987 Baltimore	AL	162	624	157	28	3	27	(17	10)	272	97	98	81	2	77	1	0	11	3	5	.38	19	.252	.333	.436
1988 Baltimore	AL	161	575	152	25	1	23	(11	12)	248	87	81	102	7	69	2	0	10	2	2	.50	14	.264	.372	.431
1989 Baltimore	AL	162	646	166	30	0	21	(13	8)	259	80	93	57	5	72	3	0	6	3	2	.60	22	.257	.317	.401
1990 Baltimore	AL	161	600	150	28	4	21	(8	13)	249	78	84	82	18	66	5	1	7	3	1	.75	12	.250	.341	.415
1991 Baltimore	AL	162	650	210	46	5	34	(16	18)	368	99	114	53	15	46	5	0	9	6	1	.86	19	.323	.374	.566
11 ML YEARS		1638	6305	1762	340	33	259	(129	130)	2945	970	942	688	55	747	26	3	70	28	24	.54	193	.279	.349	.467

Wally Ritchie

Pitches: Left **Bats:** Left **Pos:** RP   **Ht:** 6' 2" **Wt:** 180 **Born:** 07/12/65 **Age:** 26

			HOW	MUCH	HE	PITCHED			WHAT	HE	GAVE	UP							THE	RESULTS			
Year Team	Lg	G	GS	CG	GF	IP	BFP	H	R	ER	HR	SH	SF	HB	TBB	IBB	SO	WP	Bk	W	L	Pct.	ShO	Sv	ERA
1987 Philadelphia	NL	49	0	0	13	62.1	273	60	27	26	8	5	2	1	29	11	45	2	3	3	2	.600	0	3	3.75
1988 Philadelphia	NL	19	0	0	8	26	115	19	14	9	1	2	3	1	17	2	8	2	0	0	0	.000	0	0	3.12
1991 Philadelphia	NL	39	0	0	13	50.1	213	44	17	14	4	2	4	2	17	5	26	1	0	1	2	.333	0	0	2.50
3 ML YEARS		107	0	0	34	138.2	601	123	58	49	13	9	9	4	63	18	79	5	3	4	4	.500	0	3	3.18

173

Kevin Ritz

Pitches: Right **Bats:** Right **Pos:** RP/SP **Ht:** 6' 4" **Wt:** 210 **Born:** 06/08/65 **Age:** 27

			HOW MUCH HE PITCHED					WHAT HE GAVE UP								THE RESULTS				
Year Team	Lg	G	GS	CG	GF	IP	BFP	H	R	ER	HR	SH	SF	HB	TBB	IBB	SO	WP	Bk	W	L	Pct.	ShO	Sv	ERA
1989 Detroit	AL	12	12	1	0	74	334	75	41	36	2	1	5	1	44	5	56	6	0	4	6	.400	0	0	4.38
1990 Detroit	AL	4	4	0	0	7.1	52	14	12	9	0	3	0	0	14	2	3	3	0	0	4	.000	0	0	11.05
1991 Detroit	AL	11	5	0	3	15.1	86	17	22	20	1	1	2	2	22	1	9	0	0	0	3	.000	0	0	11.74
3 ML YEARS		27	21	1	3	96.2	472	106	75	65	3	5	7	3	80	8	68	9	0	4	13	.235	0	0	6.05

Luis Rivera

Bats: Right **Throws:** Right **Pos:** SS **Ht:** 5'10" **Wt:** 170 **Born:** 01/03/64 **Age:** 28

					BATTING														BASERUNNING				PERCENTAGES		
Year Team	Lg	G	AB	H	2B	3B	HR	(Hm	Rd)	TB	R	RBI	TBB	IBB	SO	HBP	SH	SF	SB	CS	SB%	GDP	Avg	OBP	SLG
1986 Montreal	NL	55	166	34	11	1	0	(0	0)	47	20	13	17	0	33	2	1	1	1	1	.50	1	.205	.285	.283
1987 Montreal	NL	18	32	5	2	0	0	(0	0)	7	0	1	1	0	8	0	0	0	0	0	.00	0	.156	.182	.219
1988 Montreal	NL	123	371	83	17	3	4	(2	2)	118	35	30	24	4	69	1	3	3	3	4	.43	9	.224	.271	.318
1989 Boston	AL	93	323	83	17	1	5	(4	1)	117	35	29	20	1	60	1	4	1	2	3	.40	7	.257	.301	.362
1990 Boston	AL	118	346	78	20	0	7	(4	3)	119	38	45	25	0	58	1	12	1	4	3	.57	10	.225	.279	.344
1991 Boston	AL	129	414	107	22	3	8	(4	4)	159	64	40	35	0	86	3	12	4	3	4	.50	10	.258	.318	.384
6 ML YEARS		536	1652	390	89	8	24	(14	10)	567	192	158	122	5	314	8	32	10	14	15	.48	37	.236	.290	.343

Bip Roberts

Bats: Both **Throws:** Right **Pos:** 2B/LF/CF **Ht:** 5' 7" **Wt:** 160 **Born:** 10/27/63 **Age:** 28

					BATTING														BASERUNNING				PERCENTAGES		
Year Team	Lg	G	AB	H	2B	3B	HR	(Hm	Rd)	TB	R	RBI	TBB	IBB	SO	HBP	SH	SF	SB	CS	SB%	GDP	Avg	OBP	SLG
1986 San Diego	NL	101	241	61	5	2	1	(0	1)	73	34	12	14	1	29	0	2	1	14	12	.54	0	.253	.293	.303
1988 San Diego	NL	5	9	3	0	0	0	(0	0)	3	1	0	1	0	2	0	0	0	0	2	.00	0	.333	.400	.333
1989 San Diego	NL	117	329	99	15	8	3	(2	1)	139	81	25	49	0	45	1	6	2	21	11	.66	3	.301	.391	.422
1990 San Diego	NL	149	556	172	36	3	9	(4	5)	241	104	44	55	1	65	6	8	4	46	12	.79	8	.309	.375	.433
1991 San Diego	NL	117	424	119	13	3	3	(3	0)	147	66	32	37	0	71	4	4	3	26	11	.70	6	.281	.342	.347
5 ML YEARS		489	1559	454	69	16	16	(9	7)	603	286	113	156	2	212	11	20	10	107	48	.69	19	.291	.358	.387

Don Robinson

Pitches: Right **Bats:** Right **Pos:** RP/SP **Ht:** 6' 4" **Wt:** 240 **Born:** 06/08/57 **Age:** 35

			HOW MUCH HE PITCHED					WHAT HE GAVE UP								THE RESULTS				
Year Team	Lg	G	GS	CG	GF	IP	BFP	H	R	ER	HR	SH	SF	HB	TBB	IBB	SO	WP	Bk	W	L	Pct.	ShO	Sv	ERA
1978 Pittsburgh	NL	35	32	9	1	228	937	203	98	88	20	8	8	3	57	4	135	6	4	14	6	.700	1	1	3.47
1979 Pittsburgh	NL	29	25	4	1	161	684	171	74	69	12	6	5	4	52	5	96	6	1	8	8	.500	0	0	3.86
1980 Pittsburgh	NL	29	24	3	1	160	671	157	74	71	14	8	3	5	45	5	103	7	2	7	10	.412	2	1	3.99
1981 Pittsburgh	NL	16	2	0	4	38	182	47	27	25	4	7	2	0	23	4	17	3	0	0	3	.000	0	2	5.92
1982 Pittsburgh	NL	38	30	6	3	227	977	213	123	108	26	12	8	3	103	11	165	17	0	15	13	.536	0	0	4.28
1983 Pittsburgh	NL	9	6	0	2	36.1	168	43	21	18	5	2	0	0	21	3	28	2	0	2	2	.500	0	0	4.46
1984 Pittsburgh	NL	51	1	0	28	122	500	99	45	41	6	4	9	0	49	4	110	5	0	5	6	.455	0	10	3.02
1985 Pittsburgh	NL	44	6	0	22	95.1	418	95	49	41	6	2	0	2	42	11	65	2	0	5	11	.313	0	3	3.87
1986 Pittsburgh	NL	50	0	0	41	69.1	295	61	27	26	5	5	4	2	27	3	53	4	1	3	4	.429	0	14	3.37
1987 2 ML Teams		67	0	0	54	108	460	105	42	41	7	7	3	0	40	6	79	7	1	11	7	.611	0	19	3.42
1988 San Francisco	NL	51	19	3	19	176.2	725	152	63	48	11	7	8	3	49	12	122	4	2	10	5	.667	2	6	2.45
1989 San Francisco	NL	34	32	5	2	197	793	184	80	75	22	6	5	2	37	6	96	4	4	12	11	.522	1	0	3.43
1990 San Francisco	NL	26	25	4	0	157.2	667	173	84	80	18	4	3	1	41	8	78	2	0	10	7	.588	0	0	4.57
1991 San Francisco	NL	34	16	0	7	121.1	525	123	64	59	12	4	5	1	50	7	78	1	0	5	9	.357	0	1	4.38
1987 Pittsburgh	NL	42	0	0	37	65.1	276	66	29	28	6	6	1	0	22	3	53	6	1	6	6	.500	0	12	3.86
San Francisco		25	0	0	17	42.2	184	39	13	13	1	1	2	0	18	3	26	1	0	5	1	.833	0	7	2.74
14 ML YEARS		513	218	34	185	1897.2	8002	1826	871	790	168	82	63	26	636	89	1225	73	15	107	102	.512	6	57	3.75

Jeff Robinson

Pitches: Right **Bats:** Right **Pos:** RP **Ht:** 6' 4" **Wt:** 200 **Born:** 12/13/60 **Age:** 31

			HOW MUCH HE PITCHED					WHAT HE GAVE UP								THE RESULTS				
Year Team	Lg	G	GS	CG	GF	IP	BFP	H	R	ER	HR	SH	SF	HB	TBB	IBB	SO	WP	Bk	W	L	Pct.	ShO	Sv	ERA
1984 San Francisco	NL	34	33	1	0	171.2	749	195	99	87	12	5	8	7	52	4	102	7	2	7	15	.318	1	0	4.56
1985 San Francisco	NL	8	0	0	3	12.1	59	16	11	7	2	0	1	0	10	1	8	1	0	0	0	.000	0	0	5.11
1986 San Francisco	NL	64	1	0	22	104.1	431	92	46	39	8	1	3	1	32	7	90	11	0	6	3	.667	0	8	3.36
1987 2 ML Teams		81	0	0	40	123.1	495	89	43	39	11	10	4	1	54	11	101	5	2	8	9	.471	0	14	2.85
1988 Pittsburgh	NL	75	0	0	35	124.2	513	113	44	42	6	2	6	3	39	5	87	11	0	11	5	.688	0	9	3.03
1989 Pittsburgh	NL	50	19	0	18	141.1	643	161	92	72	14	7	7	1	59	11	95	14	2	7	13	.350	0	4	4.58
1990 New York	AL	54	4	1	12	88.2	372	82	35	34	8	5	1	1	34	3	43	2	0	3	6	.333	0	3	3.45
1991 California	AL	39	0	0	16	57	252	56	34	34	9	3	2	2	29	4	57	10	0	0	0	.000	0	3	5.37

1987	San Francisco	NL	63	0	0	33	96.2	395	69	34	30	10	9	4	1	48	10	82	3	2	6	8	.429	0	10	2.79
	Pittsburgh	NL	18	0	0	7	26.2	100	20	9	9	1	1	0	0	6	1	19	2	0	2	1	.667	0	4	3.04
	8 ML YEARS		405	57	2	143	823.1	3514	804	404	354	70	33	32	16	309	46	583	61	6	42	54	.438	1	38	3.87

Jeff M. Robinson

Pitches: Right Bats: Right Pos: SP Ht: 6' 6" Wt: 235 Born: 12/14/61 Age: 30

			HOW MUCH HE PITCHED						WHAT HE GAVE UP											THE RESULTS					
Year	Team	Lg	G	GS	CG	GF	IP	BFP	H	R	ER	HR	SH	SF	HB	TBB	IBB	SO	WP	Bk	W	L	Pct.	ShO	Sv	ERA
1987	Detroit	AL	29	21	2	2	127.1	569	132	86	76	16	2	2	7	54	3	98	4	3	9	6	.600	1	0	5.37
1988	Detroit	AL	24	23	6	0	172	698	121	61	57	19	2	6	3	72	5	114	8	1	13	6	.684	2	0	2.98
1989	Detroit	AL	16	16	1	0	78	347	76	47	41	10	3	3	1	46	1	40	5	0	4	5	.444	1	0	4.73
1990	Detroit	AL	27	27	1	0	145	654	141	101	96	23	3	5	6	88	9	76	16	1	10	9	.526	1	0	5.96
1991	Baltimore	AL	21	19	0	0	104.1	472	119	62	60	12	3	0	6	51	2	65	8	0	4	9	.308	0	0	5.18
	5 ML YEARS		117	106	10	2	626.2	2740	589	357	330	80	13	16	23	311	20	393	41	5	40	35	.533	5	0	4.74

Ron Robinson

Pitches: Right Bats: Right Pos: SP Ht: 6' 4" Wt: 235 Born: 03/24/62 Age: 30

			HOW MUCH HE PITCHED						WHAT HE GAVE UP											THE RESULTS					
Year	Team	Lg	G	GS	CG	GF	IP	BFP	H	R	ER	HR	SH	SF	HB	TBB	IBB	SO	WP	Bk	W	L	Pct.	ShO	Sv	ERA
1984	Cincinnati	NL	12	5	1	2	39.2	166	35	18	12	3	1	1	0	13	3	24	0	2	1	2	.333	0	0	2.72
1985	Cincinnati	NL	33	12	0	9	108.1	453	107	53	48	11	3	4	1	32	3	76	3	0	7	7	.500	0	1	3.99
1986	Cincinnati	NL	70	0	0	32	116.2	487	110	44	42	10	4	3	2	43	8	117	3	0	10	3	.769	0	14	3.24
1987	Cincinnati	NL	48	18	0	14	154	638	148	71	63	14	8	7	1	43	8	99	2	0	7	5	.583	0	4	3.68
1988	Cincinnati	NL	17	16	0	0	78.2	347	88	47	36	5	5	5	2	26	4	38	3	0	3	7	.300	0	0	4.12
1989	Cincinnati	NL	15	15	0	0	83.1	353	80	36	31	8	5	1	2	28	2	36	2	0	5	3	.625	0	0	3.35
1990	2 ML Teams		28	27	7	0	179.2	764	194	78	65	7	4	7	6	51	1	71	3	0	14	7	.667	2	0	3.26
1991	Milwaukee	AL	1	1	0	0	4.1	21	6	3	3	0	0	0	1	3	1	0	0	0	0	1	.000	0	0	6.23
1990	Cincinnati	NL	6	5	0	0	31.1	137	36	18	17	2	1	0	0	14	0	14	1	0	2	2	.500	0	0	4.88
	Milwaukee	AL	22	22	7	0	148.1	627	158	60	48	5	3	7	6	37	1	57	2	0	12	5	.706	2	0	2.91
	8 ML YEARS		224	94	8	57	764.2	3229	768	350	300	58	30	28	15	239	30	461	16	2	47	35	.573	2	19	3.53

Carlos Rodriguez

Bats: Both Throws: Right Pos: SS Ht: 5' 9" Wt: 160 Born: 11/01/67 Age: 24

			BATTING																BASERUNNING				PERCENTAGES		
Year	Team	Lg	G	AB	H	2B	3B	HR	(Hm	Rd)	TB	R	RBI	TBB	IBB	SO	HBP	SH	SF	SB	CS	SB%	GDP	Avg	OBP	SLG
1987	Yankees	R	50	115	18	0	0	0	--	--	18	15	11	23	0	8	1	6	1	2	1	.67	1	.157	.300	.157
1988	Ft.Lauderdle	A	124	461	110	15	1	0	--	--	127	39	36	23	2	30	2	20	4	3	2	.60	16	.239	.276	.275
1989	Ft.Lauderdle	A	102	353	85	15	1	0	--	--	102	48	26	49	1	25	3	21	3	9	8	.53	7	.241	.336	.289
	Albany	AA	36	107	27	4	2	0	--	--	35	15	8	13	0	4	0	3	1	1	1	.50	3	.252	.331	.327
1990	Albany	AA	18	75	21	4	0	0	--	--	25	10	7	2	0	2	1	0	0	1	1	.50	2	.280	.308	.333
	Columbus	AAA	71	220	60	12	0	0	--	--	72	31	16	30	2	8	2	2	2	3	1	.75	5	.273	.362	.327
1991	Columbus	AAA	73	212	54	9	3	0	--	--	69	32	21	42	1	13	1	5	5	1	4	.20	10	.255	.373	.325
1991	New York	AL	15	37	7	0	0	0	(0	0)	7	1	2	1	0	2	0	1	0	0	0	.00	3	.189	.211	.189

Ivan Rodriguez

Bats: Right Throws: Right Pos: C Ht: 5' 9" Wt: 165 Born: 11/30/71 Age: 20

			BATTING																BASERUNNING				PERCENTAGES		
Year	Team	Lg	G	AB	H	2B	3B	HR	(Hm	Rd)	TB	R	RBI	TBB	IBB	SO	HBP	SH	SF	SB	CS	SB%	GDP	Avg	OBP	SLG
1989	Gastonia	A	112	386	92	22	1	7	--	--	137	38	42	21	0	58	2	5	4	2	5	.29	6	.238	.278	.355
1990	Charlotte	A	109	408	117	17	7	2	--	--	154	48	55	12	2	50	7	1	4	1	0	1.00	6	.287	.316	.377
1991	Tulsa	AA	50	175	48	7	2	3	--	--	68	16	28	6	0	27	1	1	5	1	2	.33	5	.274	.294	.389
1991	Texas	AL	88	280	74	16	0	3	(3	0)	99	24	27	5	0	42	0	2	1	0	1	.00	10	.264	.276	.354

Rich Rodriguez

Pitches: Left Bats: Right Pos: RP Ht: 5'11" Wt: 200 Born: 03/01/63 Age: 29

			HOW MUCH HE PITCHED						WHAT HE GAVE UP											THE RESULTS					
Year	Team	Lg	G	GS	CG	GF	IP	BFP	H	R	ER	HR	SH	SF	HB	TBB	IBB	SO	WP	Bk	W	L	Pct.	ShO	Sv	ERA
1984	Little Fls	A	25	1	0	6	35.1	171	28	21	11	0	4	2	1	36	7	27	3	0	2	1	.667	0	0	2.80
1985	Columbia	A	49	3	0	19	80.1	365	89	41	36	4	6	1	1	36	2	71	7	1	6	3	.667	0	6	4.03
1986	Jackson	AA	13	5	1	2	33	161	51	35	33	5	2	2	0	15	2	15	2	0	3	4	.429	0	0	9.00
	Lynchburg	A	36	0	0	16	45.1	184	37	20	18	2	1	1	1	19	0	38	4	1	2	1	.667	0	3	3.57
1987	Lynchburg	A	69	0	0	30	68	291	69	23	21	3	1	2	0	26	6	59	8	0	3	1	.750	0	5	2.78
1988	Jackson	AA	47	1	0	25	78.1	335	66	35	25	3	9	4	1	42	6	68	6	5	2	7	.222	0	6	2.87
1989	Wichita	AA	54	0	0	38	74.1	319	74	30	30	3	3	1	2	37	11	40	4	1	8	3	.727	0	6	3.63
1990	Las Vegas	AAA	27	2	0	13	59	243	50	24	23	5	1	3	1	22	1	46	3	1	3	4	.429	0	8	3.51

Year	Team	Lg	G	GS	CG	GF	IP	BFP	H	R	ER	HR	SH	SF	HB	TBB	IBB	SO	WP	Bk	W	L	Pct.	ShO	Sv	ERA
1990	San Diego	NL	32	0	0	15	47.2	201	52	17	15	2	2	1	1	16	4	22	1	1	1	1	.500	0	1	2.83
1991	San Diego	NL	64	1	0	19	80	335	66	31	29	8	7	2	0	44	8	40	4	1	3	1	.750	0	0	3.26
	2 ML YEARS		96	1	0	34	127.2	536	118	48	44	10	9	3	1	60	12	62	5	2	4	2	.667	0	1	3.10

Rosario Rodriguez

Pitches: Left **Bats:** Right **Pos:** RP **Ht:** 6' 0" **Wt:** 185 **Born:** 07/08/69 **Age:** 22

			HOW MUCH HE PITCHED						WHAT HE GAVE UP								THE RESULTS					
Year	Team	Lg	G	GS	CG	GF	IP	BFP	H	R	ER	HR	SH	SF	HB	TBB	IBB	SO	WP	Bk	W	L	Pct.	ShO	Sv	ERA
1987	Reds	R	17	10	0	4	64.1	271	64	32	22	2	2	2	2	21	5	33	1	3	1	5	.167	0	1	3.08
1988	Greensboro	A	23	3	1	13	65.1	267	49	15	11	2	5	1	3	24	3	53	4	8	6	4	.600	1	2	1.52
	Cedar Rapds	A	13	11	0	0	70	314	73	41	31	4	2	4	5	25	2	47	3	11	3	4	.429	0	0	3.99
1989	Chattanooga	AA	28	0	0	11	44.1	195	48	24	22	6	3	2	4	18	2	36	6	3	3	0	1.000	0	2	4.47
1990	Nashville	AAA	5	0	0	1	4.1	19	4	5	5	1	0	1	0	3	0	1	0	1	0	1	.000	0	0	10.38
	Chattanooga	AA	36	2	1	22	53.2	256	52	29	26	5	11	0	6	48	5	39	7	3	2	2	.500	0	7	4.36
1991	Buffalo	AAA	48	0	0	21	51	218	38	22	17	1	7	1	2	31	1	43	3	1	4	3	.571	0	8	3.00
1989	Cincinnati	NL	7	0	0	4	4.1	19	3	2	2	0	0	0	0	3	1	0	1	0	1	1	.500	0	0	4.15
1990	Cincinnati	NL	9	0	0	4	10.1	47	15	7	7	3	1	1	1	2	0	8	0	0	0	0	.000	0	0	6.10
1991	Pittsburgh	NL	18	0	0	8	15.1	67	14	7	7	1	1	0	1	8	0	10	2	0	1	1	.500	0	6	4.11
	3 ML YEARS		34	0	0	16	30	133	32	16	16	4	2	1	2	13	1	18	3	0	2	2	.500	0	6	4.80

Kenny Rogers

Pitches: Left **Bats:** Left **Pos:** RP/SP **Ht:** 6' 1" **Wt:** 205 **Born:** 11/10/64 **Age:** 27

			HOW MUCH HE PITCHED						WHAT HE GAVE UP								THE RESULTS					
Year	Team	Lg	G	GS	CG	GF	IP	BFP	H	R	ER	HR	SH	SF	HB	TBB	IBB	SO	WP	Bk	W	L	Pct.	ShO	Sv	ERA
1989	Texas	AL	73	0	0	24	73.2	316	60	28	24	2	6	3	4	42	9	63	6	0	3	4	.429	0	2	2.93
1990	Texas	AL	69	3	0	46	97.2	428	93	40	34	6	7	4	1	42	5	74	5	0	10	6	.625	0	15	3.13
1991	Texas	AL	63	9	0	20	109.2	511	121	80	66	14	9	5	6	61	7	73	3	1	10	10	.500	0	5	5.42
	3 ML YEARS		205	12	0	90	281	1253	274	148	124	22	22	12	11	145	21	210	14	1	23	20	.535	0	22	3.97

David Rohde

Bats: Both **Throws:** Right **Pos:** 2B **Ht:** 6' 2" **Wt:** 182 **Born:** 05/08/64 **Age:** 28

			BATTING																BASERUNNING				PERCENTAGES		
Year	Team	Lg	G	AB	H	2B	3B	HR	(Hm	Rd)	TB	R	RBI	TBB	IBB	SO	HBP	SH	SF	SB	CS	SB%	GDP	Avg	OBP	SLG
1986	Auburn	A	61	207	54	6	4	2	--	--	74	41	22	37	1	37	0	1	2	28	9	.76	2	.261	.370	.357
1987	Osceola	A	103	377	108	15	1	5	--	--	140	57	42	50	1	58	4	10	0	12	6	.67	4	.286	.376	.371
1988	Columbus	AA	142	486	130	20	2	4	--	--	166	76	53	81	1	62	5	4	7	36	4	.90	14	.267	.373	.342
1989	Columbus	AA	67	254	71	5	2	2	--	--	86	40	27	41	0	25	1	5	2	15	5	.75	6	.280	.379	.339
	Tucson	AAA	75	234	68	7	3	1	--	--	84	35	30	32	1	30	1	7	5	11	5	.69	4	.291	.371	.359
1990	Tucson	AAA	47	170	60	10	2	0	--	--	74	42	20	40	0	20	1	1	0	5	2	.71	7	.353	.479	.435
1991	Tucson	AAA	73	253	94	10	4	1	--	--	115	36	40	52	3	34	5	2	5	15	6	.71	4	.372	.479	.455
1990	Houston	NL	59	98	18	4	0	0	(0	0)	22	8	5	9	2	20	5	4	1	0	0	.00	3	.184	.283	.224
1991	Houston	NL	29	41	5	0	0	0	(0	0)	5	3	0	5	0	8	0	2	0	0	0	.00	1	.122	.217	.122
	2 ML YEARS		88	139	23	4	0	0	(0	0)	27	11	5	14	2	28	5	6	1	0	0	.00	4	.165	.264	.194

Mel Rojas

Pitches: Right **Bats:** Right **Pos:** RP **Ht:** 5'11" **Wt:** 175 **Born:** 12/10/66 **Age:** 25

			HOW MUCH HE PITCHED						WHAT HE GAVE UP								THE RESULTS					
Year	Team	Lg	G	GS	CG	GF	IP	BFP	H	R	ER	HR	SH	SF	HB	TBB	IBB	SO	WP	Bk	W	L	Pct.	ShO	Sv	ERA
1986	Expos	R	13	12	1	1	55.1	261	63	39	30	0	3	3	2	37	0	34	4	0	4	5	.444	0	0	4.88
1987	Burlington	A	25	25	4	0	158.2	686	146	84	67	10	4	6	3	67	1	100	8	0	8	9	.471	1	0	3.80
1988	Rockford	A	12	12	3	0	73.1	302	52	30	20	3	3	1	2	29	0	72	3	2	6	4	.600	0	0	2.45
	Wst Plm Bch	A	2	2	0	0	5	19	4	2	2	1	0	0	0	1	0	4	0	0	1	0	1.000	0	0	3.60
1989	Jacksnville	AA	34	12	1	17	112	447	62	39	31	1	7	4	5	57	0	104	8	1	10	7	.588	1	5	2.49
1990	Indianapols	AAA	17	17	0	0	97.2	412	84	42	34	9	5	2	1	47	3	64	3	1	2	4	.333	0	0	3.13
1991	Indianapols	AAA	14	10	0	2	52.2	221	50	29	24	4	5	1	1	14	1	55	2	1	4	2	.667	0	1	4.10
1990	Montreal	NL	23	0	0	5	40	173	34	17	16	5	2	0	2	24	4	26	2	0	3	1	.750	0	1	3.60
1991	Montreal	NL	37	0	0	13	48	200	42	21	20	4	0	2	1	13	1	37	3	0	3	3	.500	0	6	3.75
	2 ML YEARS		60	0	0	18	88	373	76	38	36	9	2	2	3	37	5	63	5	0	6	4	.600	0	7	3.68

Kevin Romine

Bats: Right **Throws:** Right **Pos:** LF **Ht:** 5'11" **Wt:** 204 **Born:** 05/23/61 **Age:** 31

			BATTING																BASERUNNING				PERCENTAGES		
Year	Team	Lg	G	AB	H	2B	3B	HR	(Hm	Rd)	TB	R	RBI	TBB	IBB	SO	HBP	SH	SF	SB	CS	SB%	GDP	Avg	OBP	SLG
1985	Boston	AL	24	28	6	2	0	0	(0 | 0)	8	3	1	0	4	0	2	0	1	0	1	0	1.00	1	.214	.241	.286
1986	Boston	AL	35	35	9	2	0	0	(0	0)	11	6	2	3	0	9	0	1	0	2	0	1.00	1	.257	.316	.314
1987	Boston	AL	9	24	7	2	0	0	(0	0)	9	5	2	2	0	6	0	0	0	0	0	.00	0	.292	.346	.375
1988	Boston	AL	57	78	15	2	1	1	(1	0)	22	17	5	7	0	15	0	0	0	2	0	1.00	3	.192	.259	.282

Year	Team	Lg	G	AB	H	2B	3B	HR	(Hm	Rd)	TB	R	RBI	TBB	IBB	SO	HBP	SH	SF	SB	CS	SB%	GDP	Avg	OBP	SLG
1989	Boston	AL	92	274	75	13	0	1	(1	0)	91	30	23	21	1	53	2	3	3	1	1	.50	11	.274	.327	.332
1990	Boston	AL	70	136	37	7	0	2	(2	0)	50	21	14	12	0	27	1	0	2	4	0	1.00	7	.272	.331	.368
1991	Boston	AL	44	55	9	2	0	1	(0	1)	14	7	7	3	0	10	0	0	0	1	1	.50	1	.164	.207	.255
	7 ML YEARS		331	630	158	30	1	5	(4	1)	205	89	55	49	1	124	3	6	5	11	2	.85	24	.251	.306	.325

Bobby Rose

Bats: Right **Throws:** Right **Pos:** 2B   **Ht:** 5'11" **Wt:** 185 **Born:** 03/15/67 **Age:** 25

Year	Team	Lg	G	AB	H	2B	3B	HR	(Hm	Rd)	TB	R	RBI	TBB	IBB	SO	HBP	SH	SF	SB	CS	SB%	GDP	Avg	OBP	SLG
1985	Salem	A	50	167	37	6	2	0	--	--	47	15	16	14	0	43	0	1	0	8	2	.80	3	.222	.282	.281
1986	Quad City	A	129	467	118	21	5	7	--	--	170	67	56	66	2	116	0	2	4	13	9	.59	11	.253	.343	.364
1988	Quad City	A	135	483	137	23	3	13	--	--	205	75	78	78	3	92	7	3	3	14	7	.67	9	.284	.389	.424
	Palm Sprngs	A	1	3	1	0	0	0	--	--	1	0	1	0	0	1	0	0	0	0	0	.00	0	.333	.333	.333
1989	Midland	AA	99	351	126	21	5	11	--	--	190	64	73	50	3	62	6	3	8	3	2	.60	6	.359	.439	.541
1990	Edmonton	AAA	134	502	142	27	10	9	--	--	216	84	68	56	0	83	4	7	6	6	2	.75	14	.283	.356	.430
1991	Edmonton	AAA	62	242	72	14	5	6	--	--	114	35	56	21	1	41	5	1	8	3	0	1.00	7	.298	.355	.471
1989	California	AL	14	38	8	1	2	1	(1	0)	16	4	3	2	0	10	1	1	0	0	0	.00	2	.211	.268	.421
1990	California	AL	7	13	5	0	0	1	(1	0)	8	5	2	2	0	1	0	1	0	0	0	.00	0	.385	.467	.615
1991	California	AL	22	65	18	5	1	1	(0	1)	28	5	8	3	0	13	0	0	1	0	0	.00	1	.277	.304	.431
	3 ML YEARS		43	116	31	6	3	3	(2	1)	52	14	13	7	0	24	1	2	1	0	0	.00	3	.267	.312	.448

Steve Rosenberg

Pitches: Left **Bats:** Left **Pos:** RP   **Ht:** 6' 0" **Wt:** 185 **Born:** 10/31/64 **Age:** 27

Year	Team	Lg	G	GS	CG	GF	IP	BFP	H	R	ER	HR	SH	SF	HB	TBB	IBB	SO	WP	Bk	W	L	Pct.	ShO	Sv	ERA
1988	Chicago	AL	33	0	0	18	46	203	53	22	22	5	3	3	0	19	0	28	1	0	0	1	.000	0	1	4.30
1989	Chicago	AL	38	21	2	2	142	617	148	92	78	14	7	9	1	58	1	77	7	2	4	13	.235	0	0	4.94
1990	Chicago	AL	6	0	0	3	10	44	10	6	6	2	0	0	0	5	0	4	0	0	1	0	1.000	0	0	5.40
1991	San Diego	NL	10	0	0	5	11.2	49	11	9	9	3	0	0	0	5	1	6	2	0	1	1	.500	0	0	6.94
	4 ML YEARS		87	21	2	28	209.2	913	222	129	115	24	10	12	1	87	2	115	10	2	6	15	.286	0	1	4.94

Wayne Rosenthal

Pitches: Right **Bats:** Right **Pos:** RP   **Ht:** 6' 5" **Wt:** 220 **Born:** 02/19/65 **Age:** 27

Year	Team	Lg	G	GS	CG	GF	IP	BFP	H	R	ER	HR	SH	SF	HB	TBB	IBB	SO	WP	Bk	W	L	Pct.	ShO	Sv	ERA
1986	Rangers	R	23	3	1	16	61.2	234	36	9	5	0	1	0	0	11	0	73	4	0	4	2	.667	1	9	0.73
1987	Gastonia	A	56	0	0	55	68.2	273	44	19	13	6	5	3	0	25	5	101	10	0	1	5	.167	0	30	1.70
1988	Charlotte	A	23	0	0	19	26.1	98	20	6	6	1	1	0	0	4	0	21	1	1	1	2	.333	0	7	2.05
1989	Charlotte	A	20	0	0	16	24.1	95	13	8	6	1	4	1	0	8	1	26	1	1	2	1	.667	0	10	2.22
	Tulsa	AA	31	0	0	22	50	209	40	20	17	2	1	3	0	21	3	47	0	0	2	4	.333	0	10	3.06
1990	Tulsa	AA	12	0	0	10	15	62	9	6	4	1	1	1	0	9	1	18	3	1	2	2	.500	0	4	2.40
	Okla City	AAA	42	0	0	33	48	200	40	24	16	1	2	1	2	18	3	39	5	1	3	4	.429	0	14	3.00
1991	Okla City	AAA	32	0	0	16	51.2	226	52	24	23	2	3	3	3	22	2	59	3	1	3	2	.600	0	5	4.01
1991	Texas	AL	36	0	0	8	70.1	321	72	43	41	9	3	1	1	36	1	61	8	1	1	4	.200	0	1	5.25

Rico Rossy

Bats: Right **Throws:** Right **Pos:** PH   **Ht:** 5'10" **Wt:** 175 **Born:** 02/16/64 **Age:** 28

Year	Team	Lg	G	AB	H	2B	3B	HR	(Hm	Rd)	TB	R	RBI	TBB	IBB	SO	HBP	SH	SF	SB	CS	SB%	GDP	Avg	OBP	SLG
1985	Newark	A	73	246	53	14	2	3	--	--	80	38	25	32	1	22	1	3	1	17	7	.71	13	.215	.307	.325
1986	Miami	A	38	134	34	7	1	1	--	--	46	26	9	24	0	8	1	6	1	10	6	.63	4	.254	.369	.343
	Charlotte	AA	77	232	68	16	2	3	--	--	97	40	25	26	0	19	2	8	1	13	5	.72	2	.293	.368	.418
1987	Charlotte	AA	127	471	135	22	3	4	--	--	175	69	50	43	0	38	3	3	1	20	9	.69	20	.287	.349	.372
1988	Buffalo	AAA	68	187	46	4	0	1	--	--	53	12	20	13	0	17	0	1	0	1	5	.17	4	.246	.294	.283
1989	Harrisburg	AA	78	238	60	16	1	2	--	--	84	20	25	27	0	19	3	0	2	2	4	.33	5	.252	.333	.353
	Buffalo	AAA	38	109	21	5	0	0	--	--	26	11	10	18	1	11	1	1	2	4	0	1.00	4	.193	.308	.239
1990	Buffalo	AAA	8	17	3	0	1	0	--	--	5	3	2	4	0	2	0	1	1	1	1	1.00	0	.176	.318	.294
	Greenville	AA	5	21	4	1	0	0	--	--	5	4	0	1	0	2	0	0	0	0	2	.00	1	.190	.227	.238
	Richmond	AAA	107	380	88	13	0	4	--	--	113	58	32	69	1	43	3	7	2	11	6	.65	12	.232	.352	.297
1991	Richmond	AAA	139	482	124	25	1	2	--	--	157	58	48	67	1	46	5	13	3	4	8	.33	12	.257	.352	.326
1991	Atlanta	NL	5	1	0	0	0	0	(0	0)	0	0	0	0	0	1	0	0	0	0	0	.00	0	.000	.000	.000

Rich Rowland

Bats: Right   **Throws:** Right   **Pos:** C   **Ht:** 6' 1"   **Wt:** 210   **Born:** 02/25/67   **Age:** 25

								BATTING												BASERUNNING				PERCENTAGES		
Year Team	Lg	G	AB	H	2B	3B	HR	(Hm	Rd)	TB	R	RBI	TBB	IBB	SO	HBP	SH	SF	SB	CS	SB%	GDP	Avg	OBP	SLG
1988 Bristol	R	56	186	51	10	1	4	--	--	75	29	41	27	1	39	1	0	3	1	2	.33	2	.274	.364	.403
1989 Fayettevlle	A	108	375	102	17	1	9	--	--	148	43	59	54	2	98	3	3	3	4	1	.80	2	.272	.366	.395
1990 London	AA	47	161	46	10	0	8	--	--	80	22	30	20	3	33	3	0	1	1	1	.50	7	.286	.373	.497
Toledo	AAA	62	192	50	12	0	7	--	--	83	28	22	15	0	33	1	3	2	2	3	.40	3	.260	.314	.432
1991 Toledo	AAA	109	383	104	25	0	13	--	--	168	56	68	60	3	77	3	0	1	4	2	.67	8	.272	.374	.439
1990 Detroit	AL	7	19	3	1	0	0	(0	0)	4	3	0	2	1	4	0	0	0	0	0	.00	1	.158	.238	.211
1991 Detroit	AL	4	4	1	0	0	0	(0	0)	1	0	1	1	0	2	0	0	1	0	0	.00	0	.250	.333	.250
2 ML YEARS		11	23	4	1	0	0	(0	0)	5	3	1	3	1	6	0	0	1	0	0	.00	1	.174	.259	.217

Stan Royer

Bats: Right   **Throws:** Right   **Pos:** 3B   **Ht:** 6' 3"   **Wt:** 195   **Born:** 08/31/67   **Age:** 24

								BATTING												BASERUNNING				PERCENTAGES		
Year Team	Lg	G	AB	H	2B	3B	HR	(Hm	Rd)	TB	R	RBI	TBB	IBB	SO	HBP	SH	SF	SB	CS	SB%	GDP	Avg	OBP	SLG
1988 Sou Oregon	A	73	286	91	19	3	6	--	--	134	47	48	33	1	71	2	1	4	1	0	1.00	6	.318	.388	.469
1989 Tacoma	AAA	6	19	5	1	0	0	--	--	6	2	2	2	0	6	0	0	0	0	0	.00	1	.263	.333	.316
Modesto	A	127	476	120	28	1	11	--	--	183	54	69	58	3	132	1	2	2	3	2	.60	11	.252	.333	.384
1990 Huntsville	AA	137	527	136	29	3	14	--	--	213	69	89	43	3	113	3	8	4	4	1	.80	13	.258	.315	.404
Louisville	AAA	4	15	4	1	1	0	--	--	7	1	4	2	0	5	0	0	0	0	0	.00	0	.267	.353	.467
1991 Louisville	AAA	138	523	133	29	6	14	--	--	216	48	74	43	1	126	3	0	6	1	2	.33	13	.254	.311	.413
1991 St. Louis	NL	9	21	6	1	0	0	(0	0)	7	1	1	1	0	2	0	0	0	0	0	.00	0	.286	.318	.333

Bruce Ruffin

Pitches: Left   **Bats:** Both   **Pos:** RP/SP   **Ht:** 6' 2"   **Wt:** 213   **Born:** 10/04/63   **Age:** 28

				HOW MUCH HE PITCHED					WHAT HE GAVE UP										THE RESULTS				
Year Team	Lg	G	GS	CG	GF	IP	BFP	H	R	ER	HR	SH	SF	HB	TBB	IBB	SO	WP	Bk	W	L	Pct.	ShO	Sv	ERA
1986 Philadelphia	NL	21	21	6	0	146.1	600	138	53	40	6	2	4	1	44	6	70	0	1	9	4	.692	0	0	2.46
1987 Philadelphia	NL	35	35	3	0	204.2	884	236	118	99	17	8	10	2	73	4	93	6	0	11	14	.440	1	0	4.35
1988 Philadelphia	NL	55	15	3	14	144.1	646	151	86	71	7	10	3	3	80	6	82	12	0	6	10	.375	0	3	4.43
1989 Philadelphia	NL	24	23	1	0	125.2	576	152	69	62	10	8	1	0	62	6	70	8	0	6	10	.375	0	0	4.44
1990 Philadelphia	NL	32	25	2	1	149	678	178	99	89	14	10	6	1	62	7	79	3	2	6	13	.316	1	0	5.38
1991 Philadelphia	NL	31	15	1	2	119	508	125	52	50	6	6	4	1	38	3	85	4	0	4	7	.364	1	0	3.78
6 ML YEARS		198	134	16	17	889	3892	980	477	411	60	44	28	8	359	32	479	33	3	42	58	.420	3	3	4.16

Scott Ruskin

Pitches: Left   **Bats:** Right   **Pos:** RP   **Ht:** 6' 1"   **Wt:** 185   **Born:** 06/06/63   **Age:** 29

				HOW MUCH HE PITCHED					WHAT HE GAVE UP										THE RESULTS				
Year Team	Lg	G	GS	CG	GF	IP	BFP	H	R	ER	HR	SH	SF	HB	TBB	IBB	SO	WP	Bk	W	L	Pct.	ShO	Sv	ERA
1989 Salem	A	14	13	3	1	84.2	359	71	35	21	5	1	1	4	33	0	92	6	4	4	5	.444	0	1	2.23
Harrisburg	AA	12	10	2	0	63	278	64	38	34	5	2	3	1	32	0	56	2	2	2	3	.400	0	0	4.86
1990 2 ML Teams		67	0	0	12	75.1	336	75	28	23	4	5	2	2	38	6	57	3	1	3	2	.600	0	2	2.75
1991 Montreal	NL	64	0	0	24	63.2	275	57	31	30	4	5	0	2	30	2	46	5	0	4	4	.500	0	6	4.24
1990 Pittsburgh	NL	44	0	0	8	47.2	221	50	21	16	2	3	2	2	28	3	34	3	1	2	2	.500	0	2	3.02
Montreal	NL	23	0	0	4	27.2	115	25	7	7	2	2	0	0	10	3	23	0	0	1	0	1.000	0	0	2.28
2 ML YEARS		131	0	0	36	139	611	132	59	53	8	10	2	5	68	8	103	8	1	7	6	.538	0	8	3.43

Jeff Russell

Pitches: Right   **Bats:** Right   **Pos:** RP   **Ht:** 6' 3"   **Wt:** 205   **Born:** 09/02/61   **Age:** 30

				HOW MUCH HE PITCHED					WHAT HE GAVE UP										THE RESULTS				
Year Team	Lg	G	GS	CG	GF	IP	BFP	H	R	ER	HR	SH	SF	HB	TBB	IBB	SO	WP	Bk	W	L	Pct.	ShO	Sv	ERA
1983 Cincinnati	NL	10	10	2	0	68.1	282	58	30	23	7	6	5	0	22	3	40	1	1	4	5	.444	0	0	3.03
1984 Cincinnati	NL	33	30	4	1	181.2	787	186	97	86	15	8	3	4	65	8	101	3	3	6	18	.250	2	0	4.26
1985 Texas	AL	13	13	0	0	62	295	85	55	52	10	1	3	2	27	1	44	2	0	3	6	.333	0	0	7.55
1986 Texas	AL	37	0	0	9	82	338	74	40	31	11	1	2	1	31	2	54	5	0	5	2	.714	0	2	3.40
1987 Texas	AL	52	2	0	12	97.1	442	109	56	48	9	0	5	2	52	5	56	6	1	5	4	.556	0	3	4.44
1988 Texas	AL	34	24	5	1	188.2	793	183	86	80	15	4	3	7	66	3	88	5	7	10	9	.526	0	0	3.82
1989 Texas	AL	71	0	0	66	72.2	278	45	21	16	4	1	3	3	24	5	77	6	0	6	4	.600	0	38	1.98
1990 Texas	AL	27	0	0	22	25.1	111	23	15	12	1	3	1	0	16	5	16	2	0	1	5	.167	0	10	4.26
1991 Texas	AL	68	0	0	56	79.1	336	71	36	29	11	3	4	1	26	1	52	6	0	6	4	.600	0	30	3.29
9 ML YEARS		345	79	11	167	857.1	3662	834	436	377	83	27	29	20	329	33	528	36	12	46	57	.447	2	83	3.96

John Russell

Bats: Right **Throws:** Right **Pos:** C **Ht:** 6' 0" **Wt:** 195 **Born:** 01/05/61 **Age:** 31

Year	Team	Lg	G	AB	H	2B	3B	HR	(Hm	Rd)	TB	R	RBI	TBB	IBB	SO	HBP	SH	SF	SB	CS	SB%	GDP	Avg	OBP	SLG
1984	Philadelphia	NL	39	99	28	8	1	2	(1	1)	44	11	11	12	2	33	0	0	3	0	1	.00	2	.283	.351	.444
1985	Philadelphia	NL	81	216	47	12	0	9	(6	3)	86	22	23	18	0	72	0	0	0	2	0	1.00	5	.218	.278	.398
1986	Philadelphia	NL	93	315	76	21	2	13	(8	5)	140	35	60	25	2	103	3	1	4	0	1	.00	6	.241	.300	.444
1987	Philadelphia	NL	24	62	9	1	0	3	(1	2)	19	5	8	3	0	17	0	0	0	0	1	.00	4	.145	.185	.306
1988	Philadelphia	NL	22	49	12	1	0	2	(1	1)	19	5	4	3	0	15	1	0	0	0	0	.00	2	.245	.302	.388
1989	Atlanta	NL	74	159	29	2	0	2	(1	1)	37	14	9	8	1	53	1	0	1	0	0	.00	4	.182	.225	.233
1990	Texas	AL	68	128	35	4	0	2	(0	2)	45	16	8	11	2	41	0	1	0	1	0	1.00	3	.273	.331	.352
1991	Texas	AL	22	27	3	0	0	0	(0	0)	3	3	1	1	0	7	0	0	1	0	0	.00	0	.111	.138	.111
8 ML YEARS			423	1055	239	49	3	33	(18	15)	393	111	124	81	7	341	5	2	9	3	3	.50	26	.227	.283	.373

Nolan Ryan

Pitches: Right **Bats:** Right **Pos:** SP **Ht:** 6' 2" **Wt:** 212 **Born:** 01/31/47 **Age:** 45

Year	Team	Lg	G	GS	CG	GF	IP	BFP	H	R	ER	HR	SH	SF	HB	TBB	IBB	SO	WP	Bk	W	L	Pct.	ShO	Sv	ERA
1966	New York	NL	2	1	0	0	3	17	5	5	5	1	0	0	0	3	1	6	1	0	0	1	.000	0	0	15.00
1968	New York	NL	21	18	3	1	134	559	93	50	46	12	12	4	4	75	4	133	7	0	6	9	.400	0	0	3.09
1969	New York	NL	25	10	2	4	89	375	60	38	35	3	2	2	1	53	3	92	1	3	6	3	.667	0	1	3.54
1970	New York	NL	27	19	5	4	132	570	86	59	50	10	8	4	4	97	2	125	8	0	7	11	.389	2	1	3.41
1971	New York	NL	30	26	3	1	152	705	125	78	67	8	3	0	15	116	4	137	6	1	10	14	.417	0	0	3.97
1972	California	AL	39	39	20	0	284	1154	166	80	72	14	11	3	10	157	4	329	18	0	19	16	.543	9	0	2.28
1973	California	AL	41	39	26	2	326	1355	238	113	104	18	7	7	7	162	2	383	15	0	21	16	.568	4	1	2.87
1974	California	AL	42	41	26	1	333	1392	221	127	107	18	12	4	9	202	3	367	9	0	22	16	.579	3	0	2.89
1975	California	AL	28	28	10	0	198	864	152	90	76	13	6	7	7	132	0	186	12	0	14	12	.538	5	0	3.45
1976	California	AL	39	39	21	0	284	1196	193	117	106	13	13	4	5	183	2	327	5	2	17	18	.486	7	0	3.36
1977	California	AL	37	37	22	0	299	1272	198	110	92	12	22	10	9	204	7	341	21	3	19	16	.543	4	0	2.77
1978	California	AL	31	31	14	0	235	1008	183	106	97	12	11	14	3	148	7	260	13	2	10	13	.435	3	0	3.71
1979	California	AL	34	34	17	0	223	937	169	104	89	15	8	10	6	114	3	223	9	0	16	14	.533	5	0	3.59
1980	Houston	NL	35	35	4	0	234	982	205	100	87	10	7	7	3	98	1	200	10	1	11	10	.524	2	0	3.35
1981	Houston	NL	21	21	5	0	149	605	99	34	28	2	5	3	1	68	1	140	16	2	11	5	.688	3	0	1.69
1982	Houston	NL	35	35	10	0	250.1	1050	196	100	88	20	9	3	8	109	3	245	18	2	16	12	.571	3	0	3.16
1983	Houston	NL	29	29	5	0	196.1	804	134	74	65	9	7	5	4	101	3	183	5	1	14	9	.609	2	0	2.98
1984	Houston	NL	30	30	5	0	183.2	760	143	78	62	12	4	6	4	69	2	197	6	3	12	11	.522	2	0	3.04
1985	Houston	NL	35	35	4	0	232	983	205	108	98	12	11	12	9	95	8	209	14	2	10	12	.455	0	0	3.80
1986	Houston	NL	30	30	1	0	178	729	119	72	66	14	5	4	4	82	5	194	15	0	12	8	.600	0	0	3.34
1987	Houston	NL	34	34	0	0	211.2	873	154	75	65	14	9	1	4	87	2	270	10	2	8	16	.333	0	0	2.76
1988	Houston	NL	33	33	4	0	220	930	186	98	86	18	10	8	7	87	6	228	10	7	12	11	.522	1	0	3.52
1989	Texas	AL	32	32	6	0	239.1	988	162	96	85	17	9	5	9	98	3	301	19	1	16	10	.615	2	0	3.20
1990	Texas	AL	30	30	5	0	204	818	137	86	78	18	3	5	9	74	2	232	9	1	13	9	.591	2	0	3.44
1991	Texas	AL	27	27	2	0	173	683	102	58	56	12	3	9	5	72	0	203	8	0	12	6	.667	2	0	2.91
25 ML YEARS			767	733	220	13	5163.1	21609	3731	2056	1810	307	197	137	145	2686	78	5511	265	33	314	278	.530	61	3	3.15

Bret Saberhagen

Pitches: Right **Bats:** Right **Pos:** SP **Ht:** 6' 1" **Wt:** 200 **Born:** 04/11/64 **Age:** 28

Year	Team	Lg	G	GS	CG	GF	IP	BFP	H	R	ER	HR	SH	SF	HB	TBB	IBB	SO	WP	Bk	W	L	Pct.	ShO	Sv	ERA
1984	Kansas City	AL	38	18	2	9	157.2	634	138	71	61	13	8	5	2	36	4	73	7	1	10	11	.476	1	1	3.48
1985	Kansas City	AL	32	32	10	0	235.1	931	211	79	75	19	9	7	1	38	1	158	1	3	20	6	.769	1	0	2.87
1986	Kansas City	AL	30	25	4	4	156	652	165	77	72	15	3	3	2	29	1	112	1	1	7	12	.368	2	0	4.15
1987	Kansas City	AL	33	33	15	0	257	1048	246	99	96	27	8	5	6	53	2	163	6	1	18	10	.643	4	0	3.36
1988	Kansas City	AL	35	35	9	0	260.2	1089	271	122	110	18	8	10	4	59	5	171	9	0	14	16	.467	0	0	3.80
1989	Kansas City	AL	36	35	12	0	262.1	1021	209	74	63	13	9	6	2	43	6	193	8	1	23	6	.793	4	0	2.16
1990	Kansas City	AL	20	20	5	0	135	561	146	52	49	9	4	4	1	28	1	87	1	0	5	9	.357	0	0	3.27
1991	Kansas City	AL	28	28	7	0	196.1	789	165	76	67	12	8	3	9	45	5	136	8	1	13	8	.619	2	0	3.07
8 ML YEARS			252	226	64	13	1660.1	6725	1551	650	593	126	57	43	27	331	25	1093	41	8	110	78	.585	14	1	3.21

Chris Sabo

Bats: Right **Throws:** Right **Pos:** 3B **Ht:** 6' 0" **Wt:** 185 **Born:** 01/19/62 **Age:** 30

Year	Team	Lg	G	AB	H	2B	3B	HR	(Hm	Rd)	TB	R	RBI	TBB	IBB	SO	HBP	SH	SF	SB	CS	SB%	GDP	Avg	OBP	SLG
1988	Cincinnati	NL	137	538	146	40	2	11	(8	3)	223	74	44	29	1	52	6	5	4	46	14	.77	12	.271	.314	.414
1989	Cincinnati	NL	82	304	79	21	1	6	(3	3)	120	40	29	25	2	33	1	4	2	14	9	.61	2	.260	.316	.395
1990	Cincinnati	NL	148	567	153	38	2	25	(15	10)	270	95	71	61	7	58	4	1	3	25	10	.71	8	.270	.343	.476

179

Year	Team	Lg	G	AB	H	2B	3B	HR	(Hm	Rd)	TB	R	RBI	TBB	IBB	SO	HBP	SH	SF	SB	CS	SB%	GDP	Avg	OBP	SLG
1991	Cincinnati	NL	153	582	175	35	3	26	(15	11)	294	91	88	44	3	79	6	5	3	19	6	.76	13	.301	.354	.505
	4 ML YEARS		520	1991	553	134	8	68	(41	27)	907	300	232	159	13	222	17	15	12	104	39	.73	35	.278	.335	.456

Mark Salas

Bats: Left **Throws:** Right **Pos:** C   **Ht:** 6' 0" **Wt:** 205 **Born:** 03/08/61 **Age:** 31

Year	Team	Lg	G	AB	H	2B	3B	HR	(Hm	Rd)	TB	R	RBI	TBB	IBB	SO	HBP	SH	SF	SB	CS	SB%	GDP	Avg	OBP	SLG
1984	St. Louis	NL	14	20	2	1	0	0	(0	0)	3	1	1	0	0	3	0	1	0	0	0	.00	0	.100	.100	.150
1985	Minnesota	AL	120	360	108	20	5	9	(6	3)	165	51	41	18	5	37	1	0	3	0	1	.00	0	.300	.332	.458
1986	Minnesota	AL	91	258	60	7	4	8	(5	3)	99	28	33	18	2	32	1	5	3	3	1	.75	8	.233	.282	.384
1987	2 ML Teams		72	160	40	6	0	6	(3	3)	64	21	21	15	1	23	3	1	2	0	1	.00	2	.250	.322	.400
1988	Chicago	AL	75	196	49	7	0	3	(2	1)	65	17	9	12	2	17	3	0	0	0	0	.00	3	.250	.303	.332
1989	Cleveland	AL	30	77	17	4	1	2	(1	1)	29	4	7	5	1	13	1	0	0	0	0	.00	0	.221	.277	.377
1990	Detroit	AL	74	164	38	3	0	9	(8	1)	68	18	24	21	2	28	1	1	0	0	0	.00	3	.232	.323	.415
1991	Detroit	AL	33	57	5	1	0	1	(0	1)	9	2	7	0	0	10	2	0	1	0	0	.00	0	.088	.117	.158
1987	Minnesota	AL	22	45	17	2	0	3	(1	2)	28	8	9	5	1	6	0	0	1	0	1	.00	0	.378	.431	.622
	New York	AL	50	115	23	4	0	3	(2	1)	36	13	12	10	0	17	3	1	1	0	0	.00	2	.200	.279	.313
	8 ML YEARS		509	1292	319	49	10	38	(25	13)	502	142	143	89	13	163	12	8	9	3	3	.50	25	.247	.300	.389

Luis Salazar

Bats: Right **Throws:** Right **Pos:** 3B   **Ht:** 5' 9" **Wt:** 180 **Born:** 05/19/56 **Age:** 36

Year	Team	Lg	G	AB	H	2B	3B	HR	(Hm	Rd)	TB	R	RBI	TBB	IBB	SO	HBP	SH	SF	SB	CS	SB%	GDP	Avg	OBP	SLG
1980	San Diego	NL	44	169	57	4	7	1	(0	1)	78	28	25	9	1	25	1	3	1	11	2	.85	4	.337	.372	.462
1981	San Diego	NL	109	400	121	19	6	3	(2	1)	161	37	38	16	2	72	1	5	2	11	8	.58	7	.303	.329	.403
1982	San Diego	NL	145	524	127	15	5	8	(6	2)	176	55	62	23	10	80	2	5	5	32	9	.78	10	.242	.274	.336
1983	San Diego	NL	134	481	124	16	2	14	(10	4)	186	52	45	17	8	80	2	8	2	24	9	.73	4	.258	.285	.387
1984	San Diego	NL	93	228	55	7	2	3	(1	2)	75	20	17	6	1	38	0	2	0	11	7	.61	5	.241	.261	.329
1985	Chicago	AL	122	327	80	18	2	10	(4	6)	132	39	45	12	2	60	0	9	5	14	4	.78	5	.245	.267	.404
1986	Chicago	AL	4	7	1	0	0	0	(0	0)	1	1	0	1	0	3	0	0	0	0	0	.00	0	.143	.250	.143
1987	San Diego	NL	84	189	48	5	0	3	(1	2)	62	13	17	14	2	30	0	1	2	3	3	.50	2	.254	.302	.328
1988	Detroit	AL	130	452	122	14	1	12	(5	7)	174	61	62	21	2	70	3	10	3	6	0	1.00	13	.270	.305	.385
1989	2 ML Teams		121	326	92	12	2	9	(6	3)	135	34	34	15	3	57	1	7	0	1	4	.20	6	.282	.316	.414
1990	Chicago	NL	115	410	104	13	3	12	(7	5)	159	44	47	19	3	59	4	0	1	3	1	.75	4	.254	.293	.388
1991	Chicago	NL	103	333	86	14	1	14	(8	6)	144	34	38	15	1	45	1	2	0	0	3	.00	8	.258	.292	.432
1989	San Diego	NL	95	246	66	7	2	8	(5	3)	101	27	22	11	3	44	1	7	0	1	3	.25	4	.268	.302	.411
	Chicago	NL	26	80	26	5	0	1	(1	0)	34	7	12	4	0	13	0	0	0	0	1	.00	2	.325	.357	.425
	12 ML YEARS		1204	3846	1017	137	31	89	(50	39)	1483	418	430	168	35	619	15	52	21	116	50	.70	68	.264	.296	.386

Bill Sampen

Pitches: Right **Bats:** Right **Pos:** RP/SP   **Ht:** 6' 2" **Wt:** 190 **Born:** 01/18/63 **Age:** 29

Year	Team	Lg	G	GS	CG	GF	IP	BFP	H	R	ER	HR	SH	SF	HB	TBB	IBB	SO	WP	Bk	W	L	Pct.	ShO	Sv	ERA
1985	Watertown	A	5	0	0	2	10	48	9	3	2	0	1	1	1	7	0	11	2	0	0	0	.000	0	1	1.80
1986	Watertown	A	9	5	0	3	29.2	130	27	18	14	0	1	2	1	13	0	29	3	0	0	3	.000	0	2	4.25
1987	Salem	A	26	26	2	0	152.1	650	126	77	65	16	5	5	7	72	1	137	3	2	9	8	.529	1	0	3.84
1988	Salem	A	8	8	1	0	51.1	217	47	22	19	4	1	1	5	14	0	59	1	2	3	3	.500	0	0	3.33
	Harrisburg	AA	13	12	3	0	82.2	349	72	38	34	3	1	2	2	27	1	65	2	2	6	3	.667	0	0	3.70
1989	Harrisburg	AA	26	26	6	0	165.2	691	148	75	59	8	7	8	5	40	3	134	6	0	11	9	.550	0	0	3.21
1991	Indianapolis	AAA	7	7	1	0	39.2	170	33	13	9	1	1	1	1	19	0	41	2	0	4	0	1.000	0	0	2.04
1990	Montreal	NL	59	4	0	26	90.1	394	94	34	30	7	5	3	2	33	6	69	4	0	12	7	.632	0	0	2.99
1991	Montreal	NL	43	8	0	8	92.1	409	96	49	41	13	4	4	3	46	7	52	3	1	9	5	.643	0	0	4.00
	2 ML YEARS		102	12	0	34	182.2	803	190	83	71	20	9	7	5	79	13	121	7	1	21	12	.636	0	2	3.50

Juan Samuel

Bats: Right **Throws:** Right **Pos:** 2B   **Ht:** 5'11" **Wt:** 170 **Born:** 12/09/60 **Age:** 31

Year	Team	Lg	G	AB	H	2B	3B	HR	(Hm	Rd)	TB	R	RBI	TBB	IBB	SO	HBP	SH	SF	SB	CS	SB%	GDP	Avg	OBP	SLG
1983	Philadelphia	NL	18	65	18	1	2	2	(1	1)	29	14	5	4	1	16	1	0	1	3	2	.60	1	.277	.324	.446
1984	Philadelphia	NL	160	701	191	36	19	15	(8	7)	310	105	69	28	2	168	7	0	1	72	15	.83	6	.272	.307	.442
1985	Philadelphia	NL	161	663	175	31	13	19	(8	11)	289	101	74	33	2	141	6	2	5	53	19	.74	8	.264	.303	.436
1986	Philadelphia	NL	145	591	157	36	12	16	(10	6)	265	90	78	26	3	142	8	1	7	42	14	.75	8	.266	.302	.448
1987	Philadelphia	NL	160	655	178	37	15	28	(15	13)	329	113	100	60	5	162	5	0	6	35	15	.70	12	.272	.335	.502
1988	Philadelphia	NL	157	629	153	32	9	12	(7	5)	239	68	67	39	6	151	12	0	5	33	10	.77	8	.243	.298	.380
1989	2 ML Teams		137	532	125	16	2	11	(5	6)	178	69	48	42	2	120	11	2	4	42	12	.78	7	.235	.303	.335
1990	Los Angeles	NL	143	492	119	24	3	13	(6	7)	188	62	52	51	5	126	5	5	5	38	20	.66	8	.242	.316	.382
1991	Los Angeles	NL	153	594	161	22	6	12	(4	8)	231	74	58	49	4	133	3	10	3	23	8	.74	8	.271	.328	.389

1989 Philadelphia	NL	51	199	49	3	1	8	(3	5)	78	32	20	18	1	45	1	0	1	11	3	.79	2	.246	.311	.392
New York	NL	86	333	76	13	1	3	(2	1)	100	37	28	24	1	75	10	2	1	31	9	.78	5	.228	.299	.300
9 ML YEARS		1234	4922	1277	235	81	128	(64	64)	2058	696	551	332	30	1159	58	20	35	341	115	.75	66	.259	.312	.418

Rey Sanchez

Bats: Right **Throws:** Right **Pos:** SS   **Ht:** 5'10" **Wt:** 180 **Born:** 10/05/67 **Age:** 24

					BATTING														BASERUNNING				PERCENTAGES		
Year Team	Lg	G	AB	H	2B	3B	HR	(Hm	Rd)	TB	R	RBI	TBB	IBB	SO	HBP	SH	SF	SB	CS	SB%	GDP	Avg	OBP	SLG
1986 Rangers	R	52	169	49	3	1	0	--	--	54	27	23	41	0	18	3	3	1	10	10	.50	3	.290	.435	.320
1987 Gastonia	A	50	160	35	1	2	1	--	--	43	19	10	22	0	17	2	3	0	6	3	.67	9	.219	.321	.269
Butte	R	49	189	69	10	6	0	--	--	91	36	25	21	1	11	2	3	2	22	6	.79	6	.365	.430	.481
1988 Charlotte	A	128	418	128	6	5	0	--	--	144	60	38	35	4	24	5	1	3	29	11	.73	14	.306	.364	.344
1989 Okla City	AAA	134	464	104	10	4	1	--	--	125	38	39	21	0	50	2	5	3	4	4	.50	14	.224	.259	.269
1991 Iowa	AAA	126	417	121	16	5	2	--	--	153	60	46	37	1	27	7	11	2	13	7	.65	11	.290	.356	.367
1991 Chicago	NL	13	23	6	0	0	0	(0	0)	6	1	2	4	0	3	0	0	0	0	0	.00	0	.261	.370	.261

Ryne Sandberg

Bats: Right **Throws:** Right **Pos:** 2B   **Ht:** 6'2" **Wt:** 180 **Born:** 09/18/59 **Age:** 32

					BATTING														BASERUNNING				PERCENTAGES		
Year Team	Lg	G	AB	H	2B	3B	HR	(Hm	Rd)	TB	R	RBI	TBB	IBB	SO	HBP	SH	SF	SB	CS	SB%	GDP	Avg	OBP	SLG
1981 Philadelphia	NL	13	6	1	0	0	0	(0	0)	1	2	0	0	0	1	0	0	0	0	0	.00	0	.167	.167	.167
1982 Chicago	NL	156	635	172	33	5	7	(5	2)	236	103	54	36	3	90	4	7	5	32	12	.73	7	.271	.312	.372
1983 Chicago	NL	158	633	165	25	4	8	(4	4)	222	94	48	51	3	79	3	7	5	37	11	.77	8	.261	.316	.351
1984 Chicago	NL	156	636	200	36	19	19	(11	8)	331	114	84	52	3	101	3	5	4	32	7	.82	7	.314	.367	.520
1985 Chicago	NL	153	609	186	31	6	26	(17	9)	307	113	83	57	5	97	1	2	4	54	11	.83	10	.305	.364	.504
1986 Chicago	NL	154	627	178	28	5	14	(8	6)	258	68	76	46	6	79	0	3	6	34	11	.76	11	.284	.330	.411
1987 Chicago	NL	132	523	154	25	2	16	(8	8)	231	81	59	59	4	79	2	1	2	21	2	.91	11	.294	.367	.442
1988 Chicago	NL	155	618	163	23	8	19	(10	9)	259	77	69	54	3	91	1	1	5	25	10	.71	14	.264	.322	.419
1989 Chicago	NL	157	606	176	25	5	30	(16	14)	301	104	76	59	8	85	4	1	2	15	5	.75	9	.290	.356	.497
1990 Chicago	NL	155	615	188	30	3	40	(25	15)	344	116	100	50	8	84	1	0	9	25	7	.78	8	.306	.354	.559
1991 Chicago	NL	158	585	170	32	2	26	(15	11)	284	104	100	87	4	89	2	1	9	22	8	.73	9	.291	.379	.485
11 ML YEARS		1547	6093	1753	288	59	205	(119	86)	2774	976	749	551	47	875	21	28	51	297	84	.78	94	.288	.346	.455

Deion Sanders

Bats: Left **Throws:** Left **Pos:** LF   **Ht:** 6'1" **Wt:** 195 **Born:** 08/09/67 **Age:** 24

					BATTING														BASERUNNING				PERCENTAGES		
Year Team	Lg	G	AB	H	2B	3B	HR	(Hm	Rd)	TB	R	RBI	TBB	IBB	SO	HBP	SH	SF	SB	CS	SB%	GDP	Avg	OBP	SLG
1989 New York	AL	14	47	11	2	0	2	(0	2)	19	7	7	3	1	8	0	0	0	1	0	1.00	0	.234	.280	.404
1990 New York	AL	57	133	21	2	2	3	(1	2)	36	24	9	13	0	27	1	1	1	8	2	.80	2	.158	.236	.271
1991 Atlanta	NL	54	110	21	1	2	4	(2	2)	38	16	13	12	0	23	0	0	0	11	3	.79	1	.191	.270	.345
3 ML YEARS		125	290	53	5	4	9	(3	6)	93	47	29	28	1	58	1	1	1	20	5	.80	3	.183	.256	.321

Reggie Sanders

Bats: Right **Throws:** Right **Pos:** CF   **Ht:** 6'1" **Wt:** 180 **Born:** 12/01/67 **Age:** 24

					BATTING														BASERUNNING				PERCENTAGES		
Year Team	Lg	G	AB	H	2B	3B	HR	(Hm	Rd)	TB	R	RBI	TBB	IBB	SO	HBP	SH	SF	SB	CS	SB%	GDP	Avg	OBP	SLG
1988 Billings	R	17	64	15	1	1	0	--	--	18	11	3	6	0	4	0	1	1	10	2	.83	1	.234	.296	.281
1989 Greensboro	A	81	315	91	18	5	9	--	--	146	53	53	29	2	63	3	1	5	21	7	.75	3	.289	.353	.463
1990 Cedar Rapds	A	127	466	133	21	4	17	--	--	213	89	63	59	2	95	4	2	1	40	15	.73	8	.285	.370	.457
1991 Chattanooga	AA	86	302	95	15	8	8	--	--	150	50	49	41	5	67	1	1	4	15	2	.88	5	.315	.394	.497
1991 Cincinnati	NL	9	40	8	0	0	1	(0	1)	11	6	3	0	0	9	0	0	0	1	1	.50	1	.200	.200	.275

Scott Sanderson

Pitches: Right **Bats:** Right **Pos:** SP   **Ht:** 6'5" **Wt:** 200 **Born:** 07/22/56 **Age:** 35

			HOW MUCH HE PITCHED					WHAT HE GAVE UP										THE RESULTS					
Year Team	Lg	G	GS	CG	GF	IP	BFP	H	R	ER	HR	SH	SF	HB	TBB	IBB	SO	WP	Bk	W	L	Pct.	ShO	Sv	ERA
1978 Montreal	NL	10	9	1	1	61	251	52	20	17	3	3	2	1	21	0	50	2	0	4	2	.667	1	0	2.51
1979 Montreal	NL	34	24	5	3	168	696	148	69	64	16	5	7	3	54	4	138	2	3	9	8	.529	3	1	3.43
1980 Montreal	NL	33	33	7	0	211	875	206	76	73	18	11	5	3	56	3	125	6	0	16	11	.593	3	0	3.11
1981 Montreal	NL	22	22	4	0	137	560	122	50	45	10	7	4	1	31	2	77	2	0	9	7	.563	1	0	2.96
1982 Montreal	NL	32	32	7	0	224	922	212	98	86	24	9	6	3	58	5	158	2	1	12	12	.500	0	0	3.46
1983 Montreal	NL	18	16	0	1	81.1	346	98	50	42	12	2	1	0	20	0	55	0	0	6	7	.462	0	0	4.65
1984 Chicago	NL	24	24	3	0	140.2	571	140	54	49	5	6	8	2	24	3	76	3	2	8	5	.615	0	0	3.14
1985 Chicago	NL	19	19	2	0	121	480	100	49	42	13	7	7	0	27	4	80	1	0	5	6	.455	0	0	3.12
1986 Chicago	NL	37	28	1	2	169.2	697	165	85	79	21	6	5	2	37	2	124	3	1	9	11	.450	1	1	4.19
1987 Chicago	NL	32	22	0	5	144.2	631	156	72	69	23	4	5	3	50	5	106	1	0	8	9	.471	0	2	4.29

181

Year	Team	Lg	G	GS	CG	GF	IP	BFP	H	R	ER	HR	SH	SF	HB	TBB	IBB	SO	WP	Bk	W	L	Pct.	ShO	Sv	ERA
1988	Chicago	NL	11	0	0	3	15.1	62	13	9	9	1	0	3	0	3	1	6	0	0	1	2	.333	0	0	5.28
1989	Chicago	NL	37	23	2	2	146.1	611	155	69	64	16	8	3	2	31	6	86	1	3	11	9	.550	0	0	3.94
1990	Oakland	AL	34	34	2	0	206.1	885	205	99	89	27	4	8	4	66	2	128	7	1	17	11	.607	1	0	3.88
1991	New York	AL	34	34	2	0	208	837	200	95	88	22	5	5	3	29	0	130	4	1	16	10	.615	2	0	3.81
	14 ML YEARS		377	320	36	17	2034.1	8424	1972	895	816	211	77	69	27	507	37	1339	34	12	131	110	.544	12	5	3.61

Mo Sanford

Pitches: Right **Bats:** Right **Pos:** SP   **Ht:** 6' 6" **Wt:** 220 **Born:** 12/24/66 **Age:** 25

			HOW MUCH HE PITCHED						WHAT HE GAVE UP								THE RESULTS				
Year	Team	Lg	G	GS	CG	GF	IP	BFP	H	R	ER	HR	SH	SF	HB	TBB	IBB	SO	WP	W	L	Pct.	ShO	Sv	ERA
1988	Reds	R	14	11	0	1	53	217	34	24	19	6	0	1	0	25	1	64	3	4	3	4	.429	0	1	3.23
1989	Greensboro	A	25	25	3	0	153.2	629	112	52	48	8	4	2	2	64	0	160	6	3	12	6	.667	1	0	2.81
1990	Cedar Rapds	A	25	25	2	0	157.2	628	112	50	48	15	3	2	4	55	1	180	8	1	13	4	.765	1	0	2.74
1991	Chattanooga	AA	16	16	1	0	95.1	395	69	37	29	7	4	3	1	55	2	124	1		7	4	.636	1	0	2.74
	Nashville	AAA	5	5	2	0	33.2	140	19	7	6	0	0	0	1	22	0	38	3		3	0	1.000	2	0	1.60
1991	Cincinnati	NL	5	5	0	0	28	118	19	14	12	3	0	0	1	15	1	31	4	0	1	2	.333	0	0	3.86

Benito Santiago

Bats: Right **Throws:** Right **Pos:** C   **Ht:** 6' 1" **Wt:** 182 **Born:** 03/09/65 **Age:** 27

						BATTING												BASERUNNING				PERCENTAGES		
Year	Team	Lg	G	AB	H	2B	3B	HR	(Hm | Rd)	TB	R	RBI	TBB	IBB	SO	HBP	SH	SF	SB	CS	SB%	GDP	Avg	OBP	SLG
1986	San Diego	NL	17	62	18	2	0	3	(2 | 1)	29	10	6	2	0	12	0	0	1	0	1	.00	0	.290	.308	.468
1987	San Diego	NL	146	546	164	33	2	18	(11 | 7)	255	64	79	16	2	112	5	1	4	21	12	.64	12	.300	.324	.467
1988	San Diego	NL	139	492	122	22	2	10	(3 | 7)	178	49	46	24	2	82	1	5	5	15	7	.68	18	.248	.282	.362
1989	San Diego	NL	129	462	109	16	3	16	(8 | 8)	179	50	62	26	6	89	1	3	2	11	6	.65	9	.236	.277	.387
1990	San Diego	NL	100	344	93	8	5	11	(5 | 6)	144	42	53	27	2	55	3	1	7	5	5	.50	4	.270	.323	.419
1991	San Diego	NL	152	580	155	22	3	17	(6 | 11)	234	60	87	23	5	114	4	0	7	8	10	.44	21	.267	.296	.403
	6 ML YEARS		683	2486	661	103	15	75	(35 | 40)	1019	275	333	118	17	464	14	10	26	60	41	.59	64	.266	.300	.410

Nelson Santovenia

Bats: Right **Throws:** Right **Pos:** C   **Ht:** 6' 3" **Wt:** 210 **Born:** 07/27/61 **Age:** 30

						BATTING												BASERUNNING				PERCENTAGES		
Year	Team	Lg	G	AB	H	2B	3B	HR	(Hm | Rd)	TB	R	RBI	TBB	IBB	SO	HBP	SH	SF	SB	CS	SB%	GDP	Avg	OBP	SLG
1987	Montreal	NL	2	1	0	0	0	0	(0 | 0)	0	0	0	0	0	0	0	0	0	0	0	.00	0	.000	.000	.000
1988	Montreal	NL	92	309	73	20	2	8	(6 | 2)	121	26	41	24	3	77	3	4	4	2	3	.40	4	.236	.294	.392
1989	Montreal	NL	97	304	76	14	1	5	(4 | 1)	107	30	31	24	2	37	3	2	4	2	1	.67	12	.250	.307	.352
1990	Montreal	NL	59	163	31	3	1	6	(4 | 2)	54	13	28	8	0	31	0	0	5	0	3	.00	5	.190	.222	.331
1991	Montreal	NL	41	96	24	5	0	2	(1 | 1)	35	7	14	2	2	18	0	0	0	0	0	.00	4	.250	.255	.365
	5 ML YEARS		291	873	204	42	4	21	(15 | 6)	317	76	114	58	7	163	6	6	17	4	7	.36	25	.234	.281	.363

Mackey Sasser

Bats: Left **Throws:** Right **Pos:** C/RF   **Ht:** 6' 1" **Wt:** 210 **Born:** 08/03/62 **Age:** 29

						BATTING												BASERUNNING				PERCENTAGES		
Year	Team	Lg	G	AB	H	2B	3B	HR	(Hm | Rd)	TB	R	RBI	TBB	IBB	SO	HBP	SH	SF	SB	CS	SB%	GDP	Avg	OBP	SLG
1987	2 ML Teams		14	27	5	0	0	0	(0 | 0)	5	2	2	0	0	2	0	0	0	0	0	.00	1	.185	.185	.185
1988	New York	NL	60	123	35	10	1	1	(0 | 1)	50	9	17	6	4	9	0	0	2	0	0	.00	4	.285	.313	.407
1989	New York	NL	72	182	53	14	2	1	(1 | 0)	74	17	22	7	4	15	0	1	1	0	1	.00	5	.291	.316	.407
1990	New York	NL	100	270	83	14	0	6	(3 | 3)	115	31	41	15	9	19	1	0	2	0	0	.00	7	.307	.344	.426
1991	New York	NL	96	228	62	14	2	5	(3 | 2)	95	18	35	9	2	19	1	1	4	0	2	.00	6	.272	.298	.417
1987	San Francisco	NL	2	4	0	0	0	0	(0 | 0)	0	0	0	0	0	0	0	0	0	0	0	.00	0	.000	.000	.000
	Pittsburgh	NL	12	23	5	0	0	0	(0 | 0)	5	2	2	0	0	2	0	0	0	0	0	.00	1	.217	.217	.217
	5 ML YEARS		342	830	238	52	5	13	(7 | 6)	339	77	117	37	19	64	2	2	9	0	3	.00	21	.287	.315	.408

Richard Sauveur

Pitches: Left **Bats:** Left **Pos:** RP   **Ht:** 6' 4" **Wt:** 170 **Born:** 11/23/63 **Age:** 28

			HOW MUCH HE PITCHED						WHAT HE GAVE UP								THE RESULTS				
Year	Team	Lg	G	GS	CG	GF	IP	BFP	H	R	ER	HR	SH	SF	HB	TBB	IBB	SO	WP	Bk	W	L	Pct.	ShO	Sv	ERA
1984	Pr William	A	10	10	0	0	54.2	240	43	22	19	5	2	1	1	31	0	54	3	0	3	3	.500	0	0	3.13
	Nashua	AA	10	10	2	0	70.2	291	54	27	23	4	4	1	3	34	1	48	2	4	5	3	.625	2	0	2.93
1985	Nashua	AA	25	25	4	0	157.1	666	146	73	62	7	9	6	3	78	2	85	7	4	9	10	.474	2	0	3.55
1986	Nashua	AA	5	5	2	0	38	141	21	5	5	1	1	0	1	16	0	28	1	1	3	1	.750	1	0	1.18
	Hawaii	AAA	14	14	6	0	92	391	73	40	31	3	2	0	6	45	1	68	4	8	7	6	.538	1	0	3.03
1987	Harrisburg	AA	30	27	7	0	195	825	174	71	62	9	7	9	9	96	3	160	9	7	13	6	.684	1	0	2.86
1988	Jacksnville	AA	8	0	0	4	6.2	32	7	5	3	0	0	0	0	5	0	8	0	0	0	2	.000	0	1	4.05
	Indianapols	AAA	43	0	0	18	81.1	318	60	26	22	8	5	1	1	28	5	58	3	3	7	4	.636	0	10	2.43
1989	Indianapols	AAA	8	0	0	4	9.2	44	10	8	8	1	0	1	0	6	0	8	0	0	1	0	1.000	0	1	7.45
1990	Miami	A	11	6	1	2	40.2	178	41	16	15	2	2	0	4	17	0	34	0	0	0	4	.000	0	0	3.32

Team	Lg	G				IP	BFP																		ERA
Indianapols	AAA	14	7	0	0	56	232	45	14	12	1	2	2	3	25	0	24	1	3	2	2	.500	0	0	1.93
1991 Tidewater	AAA	42	0	0	21	45.1	188	31	14	12	0	4	0	0	23	5	49	3	3	2	2	.500	0	6	2.38
1986 Pittsburgh	NL	3	3	0	0	12	57	17	8	8	3	1	0	2	6	0	6	0	2	0	0	.000	0	0	6.00
1988 Montreal	NL	4	0	0	0	3	14	3	2	2	1	0	0	0	2	0	3	0	0	0	0	.000	0	0	6.00
1991 New York	NL	6	0	0	0	3.1	19	7	4	4	1	2	0	0	2	0	4	0	0	0	0	.000	0	0	10.80
3 ML YEARS		13	3	0	0	18.1	90	27	14	14	5	3	0	2	10	0	13	0	2	0	0	.000	0	0	6.87

Steve Sax

Bats: Right **Throws:** Right **Pos:** 2B   **Ht:** 6' 0" **Wt:** 183 **Born:** 01/29/60 **Age:** 32

							BATTING												BASERUNNING				PERCENTAGES		
Year Team	Lg	G	AB	H	2B	3B	HR	(Hm	Rd)	TB	R	RBI	TBB	IBB	SO	HBP	SH	SF	SB	CS	SB%	GDP	Avg	OBP	SLG
1981 Los Angeles	NL	31	119	33	2	0	2	(0	2)	41	15	9	7	1	14	0	1	0	5	7	.42	0	.277	.317	.345
1982 Los Angeles	NL	150	638	180	23	7	4	(2	2)	229	88	47	49	1	53	2	10	0	49	19	.72	10	.282	.335	.359
1983 Los Angeles	NL	155	623	175	18	5	5	(3	2)	218	94	41	58	3	73	1	8	2	56	30	.65	8	.281	.342	.350
1984 Los Angeles	NL	145	569	138	24	4	1	(1	0)	173	70	35	47	3	53	1	2	3	34	19	.64	12	.243	.300	.304
1985 Los Angeles	NL	136	488	136	8	4	1	(1	0)	155	62	42	54	12	43	3	3	3	27	11	.71	15	.279	.352	.318
1986 Los Angeles	NL	157	633	210	43	4	6	(1	5)	279	91	56	59	5	58	3	6	3	40	17	.70	12	.332	.390	.441
1987 Los Angeles	NL	157	610	171	22	7	6	(2	4)	225	84	46	44	5	61	3	5	1	37	11	.77	13	.280	.331	.369
1988 Los Angeles	NL	160	632	175	19	4	5	(2	3)	217	70	57	45	6	51	1	7	2	42	12	.78	11	.277	.325	.343
1989 New York	AL	158	651	205	26	3	5	(2	3)	252	88	63	52	2	44	1	8	5	43	17	.72	19	.315	.364	.387
1990 New York	AL	155	615	160	24	2	4	(3	1)	200	70	42	49	3	46	4	6	6	43	9	.83	13	.260	.316	.325
1991 New York	AL	158	652	198	38	2	10	(6	4)	270	85	56	41	2	38	3	5	6	31	11	.74	16	.304	.345	.414
11 ML YEARS		1562	6230	1781	247	42	49	(23	26)	2259	817	494	505	43	534	22	61	31	407	163	.71	129	.286	.340	.363

Bob Scanlan

Pitches: Right **Bats:** Right **Pos:** RP/SP   **Ht:** 6' 7" **Wt:** 215 **Born:** 08/09/66 **Age:** 25

		HOW MUCH HE PITCHED						WHAT HE GAVE UP								THE RESULTS					
Year Team	Lg	G	GS	CG	GF	IP	BFP	H	R	ER	HR	SH	SF	HB	TBB	IBB	SO	WP	Bk	W	L	Pct.	ShO	Sv	ERA
1984 Phillies	R	13	6	0	2	33.1	173	43	31	24	0	3	2	0	30	0	17	4	1	0	2	.000	0	0	6.48
1985 Spartanburg	A	26	25	4	0	152.1	669	160	95	70	7	3	6	4	53	0	108	8	0	8	12	.400	1	0	4.14
1986 Clearwater	A	24	22	5	0	125.2	559	146	73	58	1	6	4	5	45	4	51	4	1	8	12	.400	0	0	4.15
1987 Reading	AA	27	26	3	0	164	718	187	98	93	12	9	9	11	55	3	91	4	1	15	5	.750	1	0	5.10
1988 Maine	AAA	28	27	4	0	161	713	181	110	100	10	13	7	8	50	7	79	17	8	5	18	.217	1	0	5.59
1989 Reading	AA	31	17	4	8	118.1	531	124	88	76	9	3	5	5	58	1	63	12	1	6	10	.375	1	0	5.78
1990 Scr Wil-Bar	AAA	23	23	1	0	130	565	128	79	70	11	3	4	7	59	3	74	3	0	8	11	.421	0	0	4.85
1991 Iowa	AAA	4	3	0	1	18.1	79	14	8	6	0	2	0	0	10	1	15	3	0	1	0	1.000	0	0	2.95
1991 Chicago	NL	40	13	0	16	111	482	114	60	48	5	8	6	3	40	3	44	5	1	7	8	.467	0	1	3.89

Jeff Schaefer

Bats: Right **Throws:** Right **Pos:** SS/3B   **Ht:** 5'10" **Wt:** 170 **Born:** 05/31/60 **Age:** 32

							BATTING												BASERUNNING				PERCENTAGES		
Year Team	Lg	G	AB	H	2B	3B	HR	(Hm	Rd)	TB	R	RBI	TBB	IBB	SO	HBP	SH	SF	SB	CS	SB%	GDP	Avg	OBP	SLG
1989 Chicago	AL	15	10	1	0	0	0	(0	0)	1	2	0	0	0	2	0	1	0	1	1	.50	0	.100	.100	.100
1990 Seattle	AL	55	108	22	3	0	0	(0	0)	25	11	6	3	0	11	2	2	1	4	1	.80	1	.206	.239	.234
1991 Seattle	AL	84	164	41	7	1	1	(0	1)	53	19	11	5	0	25	0	6	0	3	1	.75	7	.250	.272	.323
3 ML YEARS		154	281	64	10	1	1	(0	1)	79	32	17	8	0	38	2	9	1	8	3	.73	8	.228	.253	.281

Dan Schatzeder

Pitches: Left **Bats:** Left **Pos:** RP   **Ht:** 6' 0" **Wt:** 195 **Born:** 12/01/54 **Age:** 37

		HOW MUCH HE PITCHED						WHAT HE GAVE UP								THE RESULTS					
Year Team	Lg	G	GS	CG	GF	IP	BFP	H	R	ER	HR	SH	SF	HB	TBB	IBB	SO	WP	Bk	W	L	Pct.	ShO	Sv	ERA
1977 Montreal	NL	6	3	1	0	22	93	16	6	6	0	0	1	0	13	0	14	1	0	2	1	.667	1	0	2.45
1978 Montreal	NL	29	18	2	1	144	586	108	54	49	10	5	4	2	68	5	69	4	3	7	7	.500	0	0	3.06
1979 Montreal	NL	32	21	3	4	162	677	136	57	51	17	10	3	1	59	2	106	6	0	10	5	.667	0	0	2.83
1980 Detroit	AL	32	26	9	2	193	794	178	88	86	23	6	3	3	58	9	94	8	0	11	13	.458	2	0	4.01
1981 Detroit	AL	17	14	1	1	71	318	74	49	48	13	4	4	2	29	1	20	3	0	6	8	.429	0	0	6.08
1982 2 ML Teams		39	4	0	11	69.1	307	84	46	41	4	3	3	2	24	9	33	4	0	1	6	.143	0	0	5.32
1983 Montreal	NL	58	2	0	23	87	369	88	34	31	3	5	2	5	25	6	48	5	0	5	2	.714	0	2	3.21
1984 Montreal	NL	36	14	1	6	136	547	112	44	41	13	4	4	2	36	1	89	3	1	7	7	.500	1	1	2.71
1985 Montreal	NL	24	15	1	2	104.1	431	101	52	44	13	7	3	0	31	0	64	4	0	3	5	.375	0	0	3.80
1986 2 ML Teams		55	1	0	19	88.1	375	81	43	32	9	5	3	0	35	9	47	1	0	6	5	.545	0	2	3.26
1987 2 ML Teams		56	1	0	13	81.1	372	104	58	48	12	2	6	1	32	10	58	8	0	6	2	.750	0	3	5.31
1988 2 ML Teams		25	0	0	10	26.1	121	34	21	19	7	1	0	2	7	1	17	0	0	0	3	.000	0	3	6.49
1989 Houston	NL	36	0	0	7	56.2	259	64	33	28	2	5	0	3	28	6	46	7	1	4	1	.800	0	1	4.45
1990 2 ML Teams		51	2	0	16	69.2	283	66	23	17	2	2	5	0	23	4	39	2	0	1	3	.250	0	0	2.20
1991 Kansas City	AL	8	0	0	2	6.2	37	11	9	7	0	0	0	0	7	1	4	0	0	0	0	.000	0	0	9.45

Year Team	Lg	G	GS	CG	GF	IP	BFP	H	R	ER	HR	SH	SF	HB	TBB	IBB	SO	WP	Bk	W	L	Pct.	ShO	Sv	ERA
1982 San Francisco	NL	13	3	0	1	33.1	155	47	30	27	3	1	1	0	12	4	18	2	0	1	4	.200	0	0	7.29
Montreal	NL	26	1	0	10	36	152	37	16	14	1	2	2	2	12	5	15	2	0	0	2	.000	0	0	3.50
1986 Montreal	NL	30	1	0	9	59	244	53	29	21	6	2	2	0	19	2	33	1	0	3	2	.600	0	1	3.20
Philadelphia	NL	25	0	0	10	29.1	131	28	14	11	3	3	1	0	16	7	14	0	0	3	3	.500	0	1	3.38
1987 Philadelphia	NL	26	0	0	8	37.2	164	40	21	17	4	2	4	0	14	7	28	0	0	3	1	.750	0	4	4.06
Minnesota	AL	30	1	0	5	43.2	208	64	37	31	8	0	2	1	18	3	30	8	0	3	1	.750	0	0	6.39
1988 Cleveland	AL	15	0	0	8	16	77	26	19	17	6	0	0	1	2	0	10	0	0	0	0	.000	0	3	9.56
Minnesota	AL	10	0	0	2	10.1	44	8	2	2	1	1	0	1	5	1	7	0	0	0	1	.000	0	0	1.74
1990 Houston	NL	45	2	0	13	64	264	61	23	17	2	2	5	0	23	4	37	2	0	1	3	.250	0	0	2.39
New York	NL	6	0	0	3	5.2	19	5	0	0	0	0	0	0	0	0	2	0	0	0	0	.000	0	0	0.00
15 ML YEARS		504	121	18	117	1317.2	5569	1257	617	548	128	59	41	23	475	64	748	56	5	69	68	.504	4	10	3.74

Curt Schilling

Pitches: Right Bats: Right Pos: RP **Ht: 6' 4" Wt: 215 Born: 11/14/66 Age: 25**

		HOW MUCH HE PITCHED						WHAT HE GAVE UP												THE RESULTS					
Year Team	Lg	G	GS	CG	GF	IP	BFP	H	R	ER	HR	SH	SF	HB	TBB	IBB	SO	WP	Bk	W	L	Pct.	ShO	Sv	ERA
1988 Baltimore	AL	4	4	0	0	14.2	76	22	19	16	3	0	3	1	10	1	4	2	0	0	3	.000	0	0	9.82
1989 Baltimore	AL	5	1	0	0	8.2	38	10	6	6	2	0	0	0	3	0	6	1	0	0	1	.000	0	0	6.23
1990 Baltimore	AL	35	0	0	16	46	191	38	13	13	1	2	4	0	19	0	32	0	0	1	2	.333	0	3	2.54
1991 Houston	NL	56	0	0	34	75.2	336	79	35	32	2	5	1	0	39	7	71	4	1	3	5	.375	0	8	3.81
4 ML YEARS		100	5	0	50	145	641	149	73	67	8	7	8	1	71	8	113	7	1	4	11	.267	0	11	4.16

Calvin Schiraldi

Pitches: Right Bats: Right Pos: RP **Ht: 6' 5" Wt: 215 Born: 06/16/62 Age: 30**

		HOW MUCH HE PITCHED						WHAT HE GAVE UP												THE RESULTS					
Year Team	Lg	G	GS	CG	GF	IP	BFP	H	R	ER	HR	SH	SF	HB	TBB	IBB	SO	WP	Bk	W	L	Pct.	ShO	Sv	ERA
1984 New York	NL	5	3	0	0	17.1	80	20	13	11	3	0	0	0	10	0	16	0	0	0	2	.000	0	0	5.71
1985 New York	NL	10	4	0	2	26.1	131	43	27	26	4	0	0	3	11	0	21	2	1	2	1	.667	0	0	8.89
1986 Boston	AL	25	0	0	21	51	198	36	8	8	5	2	1	1	15	2	55	1	0	4	2	.667	0	9	1.41
1987 Boston	AL	62	1	0	52	83.2	361	75	45	41	15	5	2	1	40	5	93	5	2	8	5	.615	0	6	4.41
1988 Chicago	NL	29	27	2	2	166.1	717	166	87	81	13	2	4	2	63	7	140	6	3	9	13	.409	1	1	4.38
1989 2 ML Teams		59	4	0	25	100	429	72	40	39	8	2	2	1	63	2	71	4	1	6	7	.462	0	4	3.51
1990 San Diego	NL	42	8	0	14	104	468	105	59	51	11	7	3	1	60	6	74	3	1	3	8	.273	0	1	4.41
1991 Texas	AL	3	0	0	1	4.2	25	5	6	6	3	1	0	0	5	0	1	0	0	0	0	.000	0	0	11.57
1989 Chicago	NL	54	0	0	24	78.2	342	60	34	33	7	2	2	1	50	2	54	3	0	3	6	.333	0	4	3.78
San Diego	NL	5	4	0	1	21.1	87	12	6	6	1	0	0	0	13	0	17	1	1	3	1	.750	0	0	2.53
8 ML YEARS		235	47	2	117	553.1	2409	522	285	263	62	19	12	9	267	22	471	21	8	32	39	.451	1	21	4.28

Dave Schmidt

Pitches: Right Bats: Right Pos: RP **Ht: 6' 1" Wt: 194 Born: 04/22/57 Age: 35**

		HOW MUCH HE PITCHED						WHAT HE GAVE UP												THE RESULTS					
Year Team	Lg	G	GS	CG	GF	IP	BFP	H	R	ER	HR	SH	SF	HB	TBB	IBB	SO	WP	Bk	W	L	Pct.	ShO	Sv	ERA
1981 Texas	AL	14	1	0	8	32	132	31	11	11	1	0	0	1	11	3	13	3	1	0	1	.000	0	1	3.09
1982 Texas	AL	33	8	0	14	109.2	462	118	45	39	5	6	3	5	25	5	69	2	0	4	6	.400	0	6	3.20
1983 Texas	AL	31	0	0	20	46.1	191	42	20	20	3	1	1	1	14	1	29	2	0	3	3	.500	0	2	3.88
1984 Texas	AL	43	0	0	37	70.1	293	69	30	20	3	7	3	0	20	9	46	4	0	6	6	.500	0	12	2.56
1985 Texas	AL	51	4	1	35	85.2	356	81	36	30	6	3	2	0	22	8	46	2	1	7	6	.538	1	5	3.15
1986 Chicago	AL	49	1	0	21	92.1	394	94	37	34	10	3	3	0	27	7	67	5	0	3	6	.333	0	8	3.31
1987 Baltimore	AL	35	14	2	7	124	515	128	57	52	13	0	1	1	26	2	70	2	0	10	5	.667	2	1	3.77
1988 Baltimore	AL	41	9	0	11	129.2	541	129	58	49	14	5	3	3	38	5	67	3	0	8	5	.615	0	2	3.40
1989 Baltimore	AL	38	26	2	5	156.2	686	196	102	99	24	9	7	2	36	2	46	3	1	10	13	.435	0	0	5.69
1990 Montreal	NL	34	0	0	20	48	213	58	26	23	3	4	1	0	13	5	22	1	0	3	3	.500	0	13	4.31
1991 Montreal	NL	4	0	0	1	4.1	24	9	5	5	2	1	0	0	2	0	3	0	0	0	1	.000	0	0	10.38
11 ML YEARS		373	63	5	179	899	3807	955	427	382	84	39	24	18	234	47	478	27	3	54	55	.495	3	50	3.82

Dick Schofield

Bats: Right Throws: Right Pos: SS **Ht: 5'10" Wt: 179 Born: 11/21/62 Age: 29**

		BATTING																BASERUNNING				PERCENTAGES		
Year Team	Lg	G	AB	H	2B	3B	HR	(Hm	Rd)	TB	R	RBI	TBB	IBB	SO	HBP	SH	SF	SB	CS	SB%	GDP	Avg	OBP	SLG
1983 California	AL	21	54	11	2	0	3	(2	1)	22	4	4	6	0	8	1	1	0	0	0	.00	2	.204	.295	.407
1984 California	AL	140	400	77	10	3	4	(0	4)	105	39	21	33	0	79	6	13	0	5	2	.71	7	.193	.264	.263
1985 California	AL	147	438	96	19	3	8	(5	3)	145	50	41	35	0	70	8	12	3	11	4	.73	8	.219	.287	.331
1986 California	AL	139	458	114	17	6	13	(7	6)	182	67	57	48	2	55	5	9	5	23	5	.82	8	.249	.321	.397
1987 California	AL	134	479	120	17	3	9	(4	5)	170	52	46	37	0	63	2	10	3	19	3	.86	4	.251	.305	.355
1988 California	AL	155	527	126	11	6	6	(3	3)	167	61	34	40	0	57	9	11	2	20	5	.80	5	.239	.303	.317
1989 California	AL	91	302	69	11	2	4	(1	3)	96	42	26	28	0	47	3	11	2	9	3	.75	4	.228	.299	.318

Year Team	Lg	G	AB	H	2B	3B	HR	(Hm	Rd)	TB	R	RBI	TBB	IBB	SO	HBP	SH	SF	SB	CS	SB%	GDP	Avg	OBP	SLG
1990 California	AL	99	310	79	8	1	1	(1	0)	92	41	18	52	3	61	2	13	2	3	4	.43	3	.255	.363	.297
1991 California	AL	134	427	96	9	3	0	(0	0)	111	44	31	50	2	69	3	7	0	8	4	.67	3	.225	.310	.260
9 ML YEARS		1060	3395	788	104	27	48	(23	25)	1090	400	278	329	7	509	39	87	21	98	30	.77	44	.232	.305	.321

Mike Schooler

Pitches: Right **Bats:** Right **Pos:** RP **Ht:** 6' 3" **Wt:** 220 **Born:** 08/10/62 **Age:** 29

		HOW MUCH HE PITCHED						WHAT HE GAVE UP												THE RESULTS					
Year Team	Lg	G	GS	CG	GF	IP	BFP	H	R	ER	HR	SH	SF	HB	TBB	IBB	SO	WP	Bk	W	L	Pct.	ShO	Sv	ERA
1988 Seattle	AL	40	0	0	33	48.1	214	45	21	19	4	2	3	1	24	4	54	4	1	5	8	.385	0	15	3.54
1989 Seattle	AL	67	0	0	60	77	329	81	27	24	2	3	1	2	19	3	69	6	1	1	7	.125	0	33	2.81
1990 Seattle	AL	49	0	0	45	56	229	47	18	14	5	3	2	1	16	5	45	1	0	1	4	.200	0	30	2.25
1991 Seattle	AL	34	0	0	23	34.1	138	25	14	14	2	1	1	0	10	0	31	2	1	3	3	.500	0	7	3.67
4 ML YEARS		190	0	0	161	215.2	910	198	80	71	13	9	7	4	69	12	199	13	3	10	22	.313	0	85	2.96

Pete Schourek

Pitches: Left **Bats:** Left **Pos:** RP/SP **Ht:** 6' 5" **Wt:** 195 **Born:** 05/10/69 **Age:** 23

		HOW MUCH HE PITCHED						WHAT HE GAVE UP												THE RESULTS					
Year Team	Lg	G	GS	CG	GF	IP	BFP	H	R	ER	HR	SH	SF	HB	TBB	IBB	SO	WP	Bk	W	L	Pct.	ShO	Sv	ERA
1987 Kingsport	R	12	12	2	0	78.1	336	70	37	32	7	4	1	2	34	0	57	2	1	4	5	.444	0	0	3.68
1989 Columbia	A	27	19	5	3	136	593	120	66	43	11	7	4	2	66	2	131	5	3	5	9	.357	1	1	2.85
St.Lucie	A	2	1	0	1	4	16	3	1	1	0	0	0	0	2	0	4	0	0	0	0	.000	0	0	2.25
1990 Tidewater	AAA	2	2	1	0	14	54	9	4	4	0	2	0	1	5	0	14	0	0	1	0	1.000	1	0	2.57
St. Lucie	A	5	5	2	0	37	143	29	4	4	1	0	0	2	8	0	28	0	0	4	1	.800	2	0	0.97
Jackson	AA	19	19	1	0	124.1	518	109	53	42	8	5	7	8	39	2	94	5	1	11	4	.733	0	0	3.04
1991 Tidewater	AAA	4	4	0	0	25	100	18	7	7	3	1	0	0	10	0	17	0	0	1	1	.500	0	0	2.52
1991 New York	NL	35	8	1	7	86.1	385	82	49	41	7	5	4	2	43	4	67	1	0	5	4	.556	1	2	4.27

Rick Schu

Bats: Right **Throws:** Right **Pos:** 3B **Ht:** 6' 0" **Wt:** 185 **Born:** 01/26/62 **Age:** 30

		BATTING																	BASERUNNING				PERCENTAGES		
Year Team	Lg	G	AB	H	2B	3B	HR	(Hm	Rd)	TB	R	RBI	TBB	IBB	SO	HBP	SH	SF	SB	CS	SB%	GDP	Avg	OBP	SLG
1984 Philadelphia	NL	17	29	8	2	1	2	(1	1)	18	12	5	6	0	6	0	0	1	0	0	.00	0	.276	.389	.621
1985 Philadelphia	NL	112	416	105	21	4	7	(2	5)	155	54	24	38	3	78	2	1	0	8	6	.57	1	.252	.318	.373
1986 Philadelphia	NL	92	208	57	10	1	8	(1	7)	93	32	25	18	1	44	2	3	2	2	2	.50	1	.274	.335	.447
1987 Philadelphia	NL	92	196	46	6	3	7	(5	2)	79	24	23	20	1	36	2	0	1	0	2	.00	1	.235	.311	.403
1988 Baltimore	AL	89	270	69	9	4	4	(2	2)	98	22	20	21	0	49	3	0	0	6	4	.60	7	.256	.316	.363
1989 2 ML Teams		99	266	57	11	0	7	(3	4)	89	25	21	24	0	37	0	2	1	1	2	.33	6	.214	.278	.335
1990 California	AL	61	157	42	8	0	6	(3	3)	68	19	14	11	0	25	0	0	1	0	0	.00	4	.268	.314	.433
1991 Philadelphia	NL	17	22	2	0	0	0	(0	0)	2	1	2	1	0	7	0	0	1	0	0	.00	1	.091	.125	.091
1989 Baltimore	AL	1	0	0	0	0	0	(0	0)	0	0	0	0	0	0	0	0	0	0	0	.00	0	.000	.000	.000
Detroit	AL	98	266	57	11	0	7	(3	4)	89	25	21	24	0	37	0	2	1	1	2	.33	6	.214	.278	.335
8 ML YEARS		579	1564	386	67	13	41	(17	24)	602	189	134	139	5	282	9	6	7	17	16	.52	27	.247	.311	.385

Jeff Schulz

Bats: Left **Throws:** Right **Pos:** PH **Ht:** 6' 1" **Wt:** 190 **Born:** 06/02/61 **Age:** 31

		BATTING																	BASERUNNING				PERCENTAGES		
Year Team	Lg	G	AB	H	2B	3B	HR	(Hm	Rd)	TB	R	RBI	TBB	IBB	SO	HBP	SH	SF	SB	CS	SB%	GDP	Avg	OBP	SLG
1984 Charleston	A	69	265	89	14	3	5	--	--	124	52	54	34	3	20	1	0	2	4	2	.67	1	.336	.411	.468
Ft. Myers	A	59	204	64	10	0	0	--	--	74	23	26	18	0	23	1	2	2	8	5	.62	7	.314	.369	.363
1985 Memphis	AA	136	488	149	15	5	4	--	--	186	73	53	59	5	42	0	4	8	8	4	.67	15	.305	.375	.381
1986 Omaha	AAA	123	400	121	19	4	2	--	--	154	40	61	37	9	51	2	2	8	0	2	.00	15	.303	.358	.385
1987 Omaha	AAA	99	316	81	12	7	4	--	--	119	25	36	24	1	56	2	1	2	1	0	1.00	12	.256	.311	.377
1988 Omaha	AAA	101	359	103	20	3	5	--	--	144	37	41	17	7	47	0	0	3	1	3	.25	8	.287	.317	.401
1989 Omaha	AAA	95	331	92	19	5	2	--	--	127	31	37	28	6	47	2	1	1	2	0	1.00	10	.278	.337	.384
1990 Omaha	AAA	69	231	69	16	1	4	--	--	99	35	27	16	4	46	1	1	3	2	0	1.00	4	.299	.343	.429
1991 Buffalo	AAA	122	437	131	20	4	2	--	--	165	55	54	42	8	41	1	2	8	7	2	.78	14	.300	.357	.378
1989 Kansas City	AL	7	9	2	0	0	0	(0	0)	2	0	1	0	0	2	0	0	0	0	0	.00	0	.222	.222	.222
1990 Kansas City	AL	30	66	17	5	1	0	(0	0)	24	5	6	6	2	13	0	1	0	0	0	.00	2	.258	.319	.364
1991 Pittsburgh	NL	3	3	0	0	0	0	(0	0)	0	0	0	0	0	2	0	0	0	0	0	.00	0	.000	.000	.000
3 ML YEARS		40	78	19	5	1	0	(0	0)	26	5	7	6	2	17	0	1	0	0	0	.00	2	.244	.298	.333

Mike Scioscia

Bats: Left **Throws:** Right **Pos:** C **Ht:** 6' 2" **Wt:** 229 **Born:** 11/27/58 **Age:** 33

		BATTING																	BASERUNNING				PERCENTAGES		
Year Team	Lg	G	AB	H	2B	3B	HR	(Hm	Rd)	TB	R	RBI	TBB	IBB	SO	HBP	SH	SF	SB	CS	SB%	GDP	Avg	OBP	SLG
1980 Los Angeles	NL	54	134	34	5	1	1	(1	0)	44	8	8	12	2	9	0	5	1	1	0	1.00	2	.254	.313	.328
1981 Los Angeles	NL	93	290	80	10	0	2	(0	2)	96	27	29	36	8	18	1	4	4	0	2	.00	8	.276	.353	.331

Year	Team	Lg	G	AB	H	2B	3B	HR	(Hm	Rd)	TB	R	RBI	TBB	IBB	SO	HBP	SH	SF	SB	CS	SB%	GDP	Avg	OBP	SLG
1982	Los Angeles	NL	129	365	80	11	1	5	(2	3)	108	31	38	44	11	31	1	5	4	2	0	1.00	8	.219	.302	.296
1983	Los Angeles	NL	12	35	11	3	0	1	(0	1)	17	3	7	5	1	2	0	0	0	0	0	.00	1	.314	.400	.486
1984	Los Angeles	NL	114	341	93	18	0	5	(0	5)	126	29	38	52	10	26	1	1	4	2	1	.67	10	.273	.367	.370
1985	Los Angeles	NL	141	429	127	26	3	7	(1	6)	180	47	53	77	9	21	5	11	3	3	3	.50	10	.296	.407	.420
1986	Los Angeles	NL	122	374	94	18	1	5	(2	3)	129	36	26	62	4	23	3	6	4	3	3	.50	11	.251	.359	.345
1987	Los Angeles	NL	142	461	122	26	1	6	(2	4)	168	44	38	55	9	23	1	4	2	7	4	.64	13	.265	.343	.364
1988	Los Angeles	NL	130	408	105	18	0	3	(1	2)	132	29	35	38	12	31	0	3	3	0	3	.00	4	.257	.318	.324
1989	Los Angeles	NL	133	408	102	16	0	10	(4	6)	148	40	44	52	14	29	3	7	1	0	2	.00	4	.250	.338	.363
1990	Los Angeles	NL	135	435	115	25	0	12	(5	7)	176	46	66	55	14	31	3	1	4	4	1	.80	11	.264	.348	.405
1991	Los Angeles	NL	119	345	91	16	2	8	(3	5)	135	39	40	47	3	32	3	5	4	4	3	.57	5	.264	.353	.391
	12 ML YEARS		1324	4025	1054	192	9	65	(21	44)	1459	379	422	535	97	276	21	52	34	26	22	.54	97	.262	.349	.362

Donnie Scott

Bats: Both   **Throws:** Right   **Pos:** C   **Ht:** 5'11"   **Wt:** 200   **Born:** 08/16/61   **Age:** 30

						BATTING														BASERUNNING				PERCENTAGES		
Year	Team	Lg	G	AB	H	2B	3B	HR	(Hm	Rd)	TB	R	RBI	TBB	IBB	SO	HBP	SH	SF	SB	CS	SB%	GDP	Avg	OBP	SLG
1983	Texas	AL	2	4	0	0	0	0	(0	0)	0	0	0	0	0	0	0	0	0	0	0	.00	0	.000	.000	.000
1984	Texas	AL	81	235	52	9	0	3	(0	3)	70	16	20	20	1	44	0	6	2	0	1	.00	5	.221	.280	.298
1985	Seattle	AL	80	185	41	13	0	4	(3	1)	66	18	23	15	0	41	0	1	4	1	1	.50	3	.222	.275	.357
1991	Cincinnati	NL	10	19	3	0	0	0	(0	0)	3	0	0	0	0	2	0	0	0	0	0	.00	0	.158	.158	.158
	4 ML YEARS		173	443	96	22	0	7	(3	4)	139	34	43	35	1	87	0	7	6	1	2	.33	8	.217	.271	.314

Gary Scott

Bats: Right   **Throws:** Right   **Pos:** 3B   **Ht:** 6'0"   **Wt:** 175   **Born:** 08/22/68   **Age:** 23

						BATTING														BASERUNNING				PERCENTAGES		
Year	Team	Lg	G	AB	H	2B	3B	HR	(Hm	Rd)	TB	R	RBI	TBB	IBB	SO	HBP	SH	SF	SB	CS	SB%	GDP	Avg	OBP	SLG
1989	Geneva	A	48	175	49	10	1	10	--	--	91	33	42	22	2	23	9	0	2	4	1	.80	2	.280	.385	.520
1990	Winston-Sal	A	102	380	112	22	0	12	--	--	170	63	70	29	4	66	14	5	6	17	3	.85	7	.295	.361	.447
	Charlotte	AA	35	143	44	9	0	4	--	--	65	21	17	7	1	17	0	0	3	3	4	.43	3	.308	.333	.455
1991	Iowa	AAA	63	231	48	10	2	3	--	--	71	21	34	20	2	45	6	3	2	0	6	.00	11	.208	.286	.307
1991	Chicago	NL	31	79	13	3	0	1	(1	0)	19	8	5	13	4	14	3	1	0	0	1	.00	2	.165	.305	.241

Mike Scott

Pitches: Right   **Bats:** Right   **Pos:** SP   **Ht:** 6'3"   **Wt:** 215   **Born:** 04/26/55   **Age:** 37

			HOW MUCH HE PITCHED					WHAT HE GAVE UP												THE RESULTS					
Year	Team	Lg	G	GS	CG	GF	IP	BFP	H	R	ER	HR	SH	SF	HB	TBB	IBB	SO	WP	Bk	W	L	Pct.	ShO	Sv	ERA
1979	New York	NL	18	9	0	0	52	229	59	35	31	4	4	1	0	20	3	21	1	1	1	3	.250	0	0	5.37
1980	New York	NL	6	6	1	0	29	132	40	14	14	1	2	1	0	8	1	13	1	0	1	1	.500	1	0	4.34
1981	New York	NL	23	23	1	0	136	551	130	65	59	11	12	5	1	34	1	54	1	2	5	10	.333	0	0	3.90
1982	New York	NL	37	22	1	10	147	670	185	100	84	13	21	11	2	60	3	63	1	2	7	13	.350	0	3	5.14
1983	Houston	NL	24	24	2	0	145	612	143	67	60	8	1	5	5	46	0	73	4	4	10	6	.625	2	0	3.72
1984	Houston	NL	31	29	0	1	154	675	179	96	80	7	8	11	3	43	4	83	2	2	5	11	.313	0	0	4.68
1985	Houston	NL	36	35	4	1	221.2	922	194	91	81	20	6	6	3	80	4	137	7	2	18	8	.692	2	0	3.29
1986	Houston	NL	37	37	7	0	275.1	1065	182	73	68	17	8	6	2	72	6	306	0	3	18	10	.643	5	0	2.22
1987	Houston	NL	36	36	8	0	247.2	1010	199	94	89	21	8	3	4	79	6	233	10	2	16	13	.552	3	0	3.23
1988	Houston	NL	32	32	8	0	218.2	875	162	74	71	19	16	4	8	53	6	190	1	1	14	8	.636	5	0	2.92
1989	Houston	NL	33	32	9	1	229	924	180	87	79	23	7	4	3	62	12	172	7	0	20	10	.667	2	0	3.10
1990	Houston	NL	32	32	4	0	205.2	871	194	102	87	27	7	8	1	66	6	121	1	3	9	13	.409	2	0	3.81
1991	Houston	NL	2	2	0	0	7	35	11	10	10	2	0	0	1	4	1	3	0	0	0	2	.000	0	0	12.86
	13 ML YEARS		347	319	45	13	2068	8571	1858	908	813	173	100	65	33	627	53	1469	39	19	124	108	.534	22	3	3.54

Tim Scott

Pitches: Right   **Bats:** Right   **Pos:** RP   **Ht:** 6'2"   **Wt:** 185   **Born:** 11/16/66   **Age:** 25

			HOW MUCH HE PITCHED					WHAT HE GAVE UP												THE RESULTS					
Year	Team	Lg	G	GS	CG	GF	IP	BFP	H	R	ER	HR	SH	SF	HB	TBB	IBB	SO	WP	Bk	W	L	Pct.	ShO	Sv	ERA
1984	Great Falls	R	13	13	3	0	78	0	90	58	38	4	0	0	2	38	1	44	5	2	5	4	.556	2	0	4.38
1985	Bakersfield	A	12	10	2	1	63.2	0	84	46	41	4	0	0	1	28	0	31	2	4	3	4	.429	0	0	5.80
1986	Vero Beach	A	20	13	3	2	95.1	418	113	44	36	2	4	9	2	34	2	37	5	5	5	4	.556	1	0	3.40
1987	San Antonio	AA	2	2	0	0	5.1	33	14	10	10	2	0	0	1	2	0	6	1	0	0	1	.000	0	0	16.88
	Bakersfield	A	7	5	1	1	32.1	137	33	19	16	2	0	1	1	10	1	29	2	0	2	3	.400	0	0	4.45
1988	Bakersfield	A	36	2	0	25	64.1	272	52	34	26	3	4	4	2	26	5	59	2	0	4	7	.364	0	7	3.64
1989	San Antonio	AA	48	0	0	28	68	308	71	30	28	3	5	3	0	36	5	64	1	4	4	2	.667	0	4	3.71
1990	Albuquerque	AAA	17	0	0	8	15	73	14	9	7	1	0	0	0	14	2	15	0	0	2	1	.667	0	3	4.20
	San Antonio	AA	30	0	0	20	47.1	186	35	17	15	5	0	1	1	14	0	52	0	0	3	3	.500	0	7	2.85
1991	Las Vegas	AAA	41	11	0	9	111	497	133	78	64	8	5	2	1	39	8	74	1	0	8	8	.500	0	0	5.19
1991	San Diego	NL	2	0	0	0	1	5	2	1	1	0	0	0	0	0	0	0	0	0	0	0	.000	0	0	9.00

Tony Scruggs

Bats: Right **Throws:** Right **Pos:** LF   **Ht:** 6' 1" **Wt:** 210 **Born:** 03/19/66 **Age:** 26

							BATTING												BASERUNNING				PERCENTAGES		
Year	Team	Lg	G	AB	H	2B	3B	HR	(Hm	Rd)	TB	R	RBI	TBB	IBB	SO	HBP	SH	SF	SB	CS	SB%	GDP	Avg	OBP	SLG
1987	Rangers	R	30	119	41	5	0	6	--	--	64	24	24	12	3	22	2	0	0	12	5	.71	3	.345	.414	.538
	Charlotte	A	23	86	28	4	0	3	--	--	41	14	11	4	0	17	2	1	0	4	2	.67	2	.326	.370	.477
1988	Rangers	R	5	12	1	0	0	0	--	--	1	1	0	3	0	4	1	0	0	1	0	1.00	1	.083	.313	.083
	Charlotte	A	67	240	70	11	4	6	--	--	107	35	42	23	0	52	3	1	3	6	3	.67	3	.292	.357	.446
1989	Tulsa	AA	60	195	38	3	3	1	--	--	50	19	21	22	0	60	2	2	1	3	1	.75	6	.195	.282	.256
	Charlotte	A	60	197	58	9	4	3	--	--	84	29	34	38	1	50	2	2	4	15	5	.75	9	.294	.407	.426
1990	Gastonia	A	75	274	84	16	0	8	--	--	124	50	48	26	1	57	7	1	1	20	2	.91	4	.307	.380	.453
	Tulsa	AA	53	195	67	5	6	4	--	--	96	28	38	15	1	50	2	2	1	4	5	.44	2	.344	.394	.492
1991	Okla City	AAA	53	182	37	4	0	3	--	--	50	19	21	20	0	41	4	3	3	4	4	.50	6	.203	.292	.275
1991	Texas	AL	5	6	0	0	0	0	(0	0)	0	1	0	0	0	1	0	0	0	0	0	.00	1	.000	.000	.000

Scott Scudder

Pitches: Right **Bats:** Right **Pos:** SP/RP   **Ht:** 6' 2" **Wt:** 185 **Born:** 02/14/68 **Age:** 24

			HOW MUCH HE PITCHED						WHAT HE GAVE UP											THE RESULTS					
Year	Team	Lg	G	GS	CG	GF	IP	BFP	H	R	ER	HR	SH	SF	HB	TBB	IBB	SO	WP	Bk	W	L	Pct.	ShO	Sv	ERA
1989	Cincinnati	NL	23	17	0	3	100.1	451	91	54	50	14	7	2	1	61	11	66	0	1	4	9	.308	0	0	4.49
1990	Cincinnati	NL	21	10	0	3	71.2	316	74	41	39	12	3	1	3	30	4	42	2	2	5	5	.500	0	0	4.90
1991	Cincinnati	NL	27	14	0	4	101.1	443	91	52	49	6	8	3	6	56	4	51	7	0	6	9	.400	0	1	4.35
	3 ML YEARS		71	41	0	10	273.1	1210	256	147	138	32	18	6	10	147	19	159	9	3	15	23	.395	0	1	4.54

Rudy Seanez

Pitches: Right **Bats:** Right **Pos:** RP   **Ht:** 5'10" **Wt:** 185 **Born:** 10/20/68 **Age:** 23

			HOW MUCH HE PITCHED						WHAT HE GAVE UP											THE RESULTS					
Year	Team	Lg	G	GS	CG	GF	IP	BFP	H	R	ER	HR	SH	SF	HB	TBB	IBB	SO	WP	Bk	W	L	Pct.	ShO	Sv	ERA
1989	Cleveland	AL	5	0	0	2	5	20	1	2	2	0	0	2	0	4	1	7	1	1	0	0	.000	0	0	3.60
1990	Cleveland	AL	24	0	0	12	27.1	127	22	17	17	2	0	1	1	25	1	24	5	0	2	1	.667	0	0	5.60
1991	Cleveland	AL	5	0	0	5	33	10	12	9	2	0	0	0	7	0	7	2	0	0	0	.000	0	0	16.20
	3 ML YEARS		34	0	0	14	37.1	180	33	31	28	4	0	3	1	36	2	38	8	1	2	1	.667	0	0	6.75

Steve Searcy

Pitches: Left **Bats:** Left **Pos:** RP/SP   **Ht:** 6' 1" **Wt:** 195 **Born:** 06/04/64 **Age:** 28

			HOW MUCH HE PITCHED						WHAT HE GAVE UP											THE RESULTS					
Year	Team	Lg	G	GS	CG	GF	IP	BFP	H	R	ER	HR	SH	SF	HB	TBB	IBB	SO	WP	Bk	W	L	Pct.	ShO	Sv	ERA
1988	Detroit	AL	2	2	0	0	8	37	8	6	5	3	0	0	0	4	0	5	0	0	0	2	.000	0	0	5.63
1989	Detroit	AL	8	2	0	3	22.1	100	27	16	15	3	0	0	0	12	1	11	0	0	1	1	.500	0	0	6.04
1990	Detroit	AL	16	12	1	2	75.1	341	76	44	39	9	2	6	0	51	3	66	3	0	2	7	.222	0	0	4.66
1991	2 ML Teams		34	5	0	8	71	335	81	56	52	10	5	5	0	44	1	53	5	1	3	3	.500	0	0	6.59
1991	Detroit	AL	16	5	0	4	40.2	201	52	40	38	8	2	3	0	30	0	32	4	0	1	2	.333	0	0	8.41
	Philadelphia	NL	18	0	0	4	30.1	134	29	16	14	2	3	2	0	14	1	21	1	1	2	1	.667	0	0	4.15
	4 ML YEARS		60	21	1	13	176.2	813	192	122	111	25	7	11	0	111	5	135	8	1	6	13	.316	0	0	5.65

David Segui

Bats: Both **Throws:** Left **Pos:** LF/1B   **Ht:** 6' 1" **Wt:** 195 **Born:** 07/19/66 **Age:** 25

							BATTING												BASERUNNING				PERCENTAGES		
Year	Team	Lg	G	AB	H	2B	3B	HR	(Hm	Rd)	TB	R	RBI	TBB	IBB	SO	HBP	SH	SF	SB	CS	SB%	GDP	Avg	OBP	SLG
1988	Hagerstown	A	60	190	51	12	4	3	--	--	80	35	31	22	3	23	3	0	4	0	0	.00	7	.268	.347	.421
1989	Frederick	A	83	284	90	19	0	10	--	--	139	43	50	41	3	32	4	0	3	2	1	.67	4	.317	.407	.489
	Hagerstown	AA	44	173	56	14	1	1	--	--	75	22	27	16	0	16	2	1	2	0	0	.00	6	.324	.383	.434
1990	Rochester	AAA	86	307	103	28	0	2	--	--	137	55	51	45	4	28	0	0	5	5	4	.56	15	.336	.415	.446
1991	Rochester	AAA	28	96	26	2	0	1	--	--	31	9	10	15	1	6	1	0	3	1	1	.50	6	.271	.369	.323
1990	Baltimore	AL	40	123	30	7	0	2	(1	1)	43	14	15	11	2	15	1	1	0	0	0	.00	12	.244	.311	.350
1991	Baltimore	AL	86	212	59	7	0	2	(1	1)	72	15	22	12	2	19	0	3	1	1	1	.50	7	.278	.316	.340
	2 ML YEARS		126	335	89	14	0	4	(2	2)	115	29	37	23	4	34	1	4	1	1	1	.50	19	.266	.314	.343

Jose Segura

Pitches: Right **Bats:** Right **Pos:** RP   **Ht:** 5'11" **Wt:** 180 **Born:** 01/26/63 **Age:** 29

			HOW MUCH HE PITCHED						WHAT HE GAVE UP											THE RESULTS					
Year	Team	Lg	G	GS	CG	GF	IP	BFP	H	R	ER	HR	SH	SF	HB	TBB	IBB	SO	WP	Bk	W	L	Pct.	ShO	Sv	ERA
1984	Kinston	A	16	14	2	1	97.1	402	88	48	43	7	2	1	2	35	1	55	7	0	7	4	.636	2	0	3.98
	Knoxville	AA	12	12	1	0	69	322	75	47	34	4	2	1	0	47	1	26	8	1	4	6	.400	0	0	4.43
1985	Kinston	A	34	15	1	10	110.1	499	109	66	51	9	1	3	7	69	4	73	7	1	4	13	.235	1	1	4.16
1986	Knoxville	AA	24	17	1	3	106.2	491	101	72	50	7	0	7	6	72	1	55	11	1	4	7	.364	0	2	4.22
1987	Syracuse	AAA	43	12	0	12	107	499	136	90	78	13	2	10	1	59	2	54	14	1	5	8	.385	0	0	6.56

Year Team	Lg	G	GS	CG	GF	IP	BFP	H	R	ER	HR	SH	SF	HB	TBB	IBB	SO	WP	Bk	W	L	Pct.	ShO	Sv	ERA
1988 Vancouver	AAA	20	19	0	0	111	507	127	69	56	4	5	7	0	60	0	39	3	6	6	6	.500	0	0	4.54
1989 Vancouver	AAA	44	0	0	32	66.2	263	50	21	17	0	1	3	0	19	2	52	1	3	1	2	.333	0	17	2.30
1990 Vancouver	AAA	40	0	0	27	54.2	246	49	34	31	0	2	5	1	35	1	47	6	0	1	3	.250	0	8	5.10
1991 Phoenix	AAA	32	0	0	27	39.1	177	46	15	15	4	3	3	1	17	2	21	3	0	5	5	.500	0	4	3.43
1988 Chicago	AL	4	0	0	1	8.2	52	19	17	13	1	0	0	0	8	0	2	2	3	0	0	.000	0	0	13.50
1989 Chicago	AL	7	0	0	2	6	34	13	11	10	2	2	1	0	3	1	4	0	0	0	1	.000	0	0	15.00
1991 San Francisco	NL	11	0	0	2	16.1	72	20	11	8	1	1	0	0	5	0	10	2	0	0	1	.000	0	0	4.41
3 ML YEARS		22	0	0	5	31	158	52	39	31	4	3	1	0	16	1	16	4	3	0	2	.000	0	0	9.00

Kevin Seitzer

Bats: Right **Throws:** Right **Pos:** 3B　　　　　　　　**Ht:** 5'11" **Wt:** 190 **Born:** 03/26/62 **Age:** 30

							BATTING												BASERUNNING				PERCENTAGES		
Year Team	Lg	G	AB	H	2B	3B	HR	(Hm	Rd)	TB	R	RBI	TBB	IBB	SO	HBP	SH	SF	SB	CS	SB%	GDP	Avg	OBP	SLG
1986 Kansas City	AL	28	96	31	4	1	2	(1	1)	43	16	11	19	0	14	1	0	0	0	0	.00	0	.323	.440	.448
1987 Kansas City	AL	161	641	207	33	8	15	(7	8)	301	105	83	80	0	85	2	1	1	12	7	.63	18	.323	.399	.470
1988 Kansas City	AL	149	559	170	32	5	5	(4	1)	227	90	60	72	4	64	6	3	3	10	8	.56	15	.304	.388	.406
1989 Kansas City	AL	160	597	168	17	2	4	(2	2)	201	78	48	102	7	76	5	4	7	17	8	.68	16	.281	.387	.337
1990 Kansas City	AL	158	622	171	31	5	6	(5	1)	230	91	38	67	2	66	2	4	2	7	5	.58	11	.275	.346	.370
1991 Kansas City	AL	85	234	62	11	3	1	(0	1)	82	28	25	29	3	21	2	1	1	4	1	.80	4	.265	.350	.350
6 ML YEARS		741	2749	809	128	24	33	(19	14)	1084	408	265	369	16	326	18	13	14	50	29	.63	64	.294	.380	.394

Scott Servais

Bats: Right **Throws:** Right **Pos:** C　　　　　　　　**Ht:** 6'2" **Wt:** 195 **Born:** 06/04/67 **Age:** 25

							BATTING												BASERUNNING				PERCENTAGES		
Year Team	Lg	G	AB	H	2B	3B	HR	(Hm	Rd)	TB	R	RBI	TBB	IBB	SO	HBP	SH	SF	SB	CS	SB%	GDP	Avg	OBP	SLG
1989 Osceola	A	46	153	41	9	0	2	--	--	56	16	23	16	2	35	2	0	5	0	2	.00	1	.268	.335	.366
Columbus	AA	63	199	47	5	0	1	--	--	55	20	22	19	0	42	3	1	4	0	3	.00	5	.236	.307	.276
1990 Tucson	AAA	89	303	66	11	3	5	--	--	98	37	37	18	1	61	4	3	4	0	0	.00	5	.218	.267	.323
1991 Tucson	AAA	60	219	71	12	0	2	--	--	89	34	27	13	2	19	6	3	1	0	4	.00	9	.324	.377	.406
1991 Houston	NL	16	37	6	3	0	0	(0	0)	9	0	6	4	0	8	0	1	0	0	0	.00	0	.162	.244	.243

Mike Sharperson

Bats: Right **Throws:** Right **Pos:** 3B　　　　　　　　**Ht:** 6'3" **Wt:** 190 **Born:** 10/04/61 **Age:** 30

							BATTING												BASERUNNING				PERCENTAGES		
Year Team	Lg	G	AB	H	2B	3B	HR	(Hm	Rd)	TB	R	RBI	TBB	IBB	SO	HBP	SH	SF	SB	CS	SB%	GDP	Avg	OBP	SLG
1987 2 ML Teams		42	129	29	6	1	0	(0	0)	37	11	10	11	1	20	1	1	0	2	1	.67	3	.225	.291	.287
1988 Los Angeles	NL	46	59	16	1	0	0	(0	0)	17	8	4	1	0	12	1	2	1	0	1	.00	1	.271	.290	.288
1989 Los Angeles	NL	27	28	7	3	0	0	(0	0)	10	2	5	4	1	7	0	1	1	0	1	.00	0	.250	.333	.357
1990 Los Angeles	NL	129	357	106	14	2	3	(1	2)	133	42	36	46	6	39	1	8	3	15	6	.71	6	.297	.376	.373
1991 Los Angeles	NL	105	216	60	11	2	2	(1	1)	81	24	20	25	0	24	1	10	0	1	3	.25	2	.278	.355	.375
1987 Toronto	AL	32	96	20	4	1	0	(0	0)	26	4	9	7	0	15	1	1	0	2	1	.67	2	.208	.269	.271
Los Angeles	NL	10	33	9	2	0	0	(0	0)	11	7	1	4	1	5	0	0	0	0	0	.00	1	.273	.351	.333
5 ML YEARS		349	789	218	35	5	5	(2	3)	278	87	75	87	8	102	4	22	5	18	12	.60	12	.276	.349	.352

Jeff Shaw

Pitches: Right **Bats:** Right **Pos:** RP　　　　　　　　**Ht:** 6'2" **Wt:** 185 **Born:** 07/07/66 **Age:** 25

			HOW MUCH HE PITCHED					WHAT HE GAVE UP										THE RESULTS					
Year Team	Lg	G	GS	CG	GF	IP	BFP	H	R	ER	HR	SH	SF	HB	TBB	IBB	SO	WP	Bk	W	L	Pct.	ShO	Sv	ERA
1986 Batavia	A	14	12	3	1	88.2	367	79	32	24	5	3	4	5	35	0	71	10	0	8	4	.667	1	0	2.44
1987 Waterloo	A	28	28	6	0	184.1	788	192	89	72	15	4	6	6	56	0	117	8	5	11	11	.500	4	0	3.52
1988 Williamsprt	AA	27	27	6	0	163.2	718	173	94	66	11	10	10	4	75	1	61	12	4	5	19	.208	1	0	3.63
1989 Canton-Akrn	AA	30	22	6	3	154.1	661	134	84	62	9	5	7	14	67	3	95	7	0	7	10	.412	3	0	3.62
1990 Colo Sprngs	AAA	17	16	4	0	98.2	438	98	54	47	7	4	5	3	52	0	55	5	0	10	3	.769	0	0	4.29
1991 Colo Sprngs	AAA	12	12	0	0	75.2	329	77	47	39	9	0	2	4	25	0	55	1	1	6	3	.667	0	0	4.64
1990 Cleveland	AL	12	9	0	0	48.2	229	73	38	36	11	1	3	0	20	0	25	3	0	3	4	.429	0	0	6.66
1991 Cleveland	AL	29	1	0	9	72.1	311	72	34	27	6	1	4	4	27	5	31	6	0	0	5	.000	0	1	3.36
2 ML YEARS		41	10	0	9	121	540	145	72	63	17	2	7	4	47	5	56	9	0	3	9	.250	0	1	4.69

Gary Sheffield

Bats: Right **Throws:** Right **Pos:** 3B　　　　　　　　**Ht:** 5'11" **Wt:** 190 **Born:** 11/18/68 **Age:** 23

							BATTING												BASERUNNING				PERCENTAGES		
Year Team	Lg	G	AB	H	2B	3B	HR	(Hm	Rd)	TB	R	RBI	TBB	IBB	SO	HBP	SH	SF	SB	CS	SB%	GDP	Avg	OBP	SLG
1988 Milwaukee	AL	24	80	19	1	0	4	(1	3)	32	12	12	7	0	7	0	1	0	3	1	.75	5	.238	.295	.400
1989 Milwaukee	AL	95	368	91	18	0	5	(2	3)	124	34	32	27	0	33	4	3	3	10	6	.63	9	.247	.303	.337
1990 Milwaukee	AL	125	487	143	30	1	10	(3	7)	205	67	67	44	1	41	3	4	9	25	10	.71	11	.294	.350	.421
1991 Milwaukee	AL	50	175	34	12	2	2	(2	0)	56	25	22	19	1	15	3	1	5	5	5	.50	3	.194	.277	.320
4 ML YEARS		294	1110	287	61	3	21	(8	13)	417	138	133	97	2	96	10	9	18	43	22	.66	23	.259	.319	.376

John Shelby

Bats: Both **Throws:** Right **Pos:** LF/CF **Ht:** 6' 1" **Wt:** 175 **Born:** 02/23/58 **Age:** 34

				BATTING														BASERUNNING				PERCENTAGES		
Year	Team	Lg	G	AB	H	2B	3B	HR	(Hm | Rd)	TB	R	RBI	TBB	IBB	SO	HBP	SH	SF	SB	CS	SB%	GDP	Avg	OBP	SLG
1981	Baltimore	AL	7	2	0	0	0	0	(0 | 0)	0	2	0	0	0	1	0	0	0	2	0	1.00	0	.000	.000	.000
1982	Baltimore	AL	26	35	11	3	0	1	(1 | 0)	17	8	2	0	0	5	0	0	0	0	1	.00	0	.314	.314	.486
1983	Baltimore	AL	126	325	84	15	2	5	(0 | 5)	118	52	27	18	2	64	0	6	0	15	2	.88	2	.258	.297	.363
1984	Baltimore	AL	128	383	80	12	5	6	(2 | 4)	120	44	30	20	0	71	0	12	0	12	4	.75	4	.209	.248	.313
1985	Baltimore	AL	69	205	58	6	2	7	(4 | 3)	89	28	27	7	0	44	0	2	0	5	1	.83	4	.283	.307	.434
1986	Baltimore	AL	135	404	92	14	4	11	(5 | 6)	147	54	49	18	0	75	2	2	2	18	6	.75	3	.228	.263	.364
1987	2 ML Teams		141	508	138	26	0	22	(8 | 14)	230	65	72	32	2	110	1	2	9	16	7	.70	9	.272	.311	.453
1988	Los Angeles	NL	140	494	130	23	6	10	(5 | 5)	195	65	64	44	5	128	0	1	6	16	5	.76	13	.263	.320	.395
1989	Los Angeles	NL	108	345	63	11	1	1	(0 | 1)	79	28	12	25	5	92	0	0	1	10	7	.59	6	.183	.237	.229
1990	2 ML Teams		103	246	61	10	3	4	(3 | 1)	89	24	22	10	0	58	0	6	0	4	5	.44	7	.248	.277	.362
1991	Detroit	AL	53	143	22	8	1	3	(2 | 1)	41	19	8	8	1	23	1	1	0	0	2	.00	3	.154	.204	.287
1987	Detroit	AL	21	32	6	0	0	1	(0 | 1)	9	4	3	1	0	13	0	1	0	0	1	.00	0	.188	.212	.281
	Los Angeles	NL	120	476	132	26	0	21	(8 | 13)	221	61	69	31	2	97	1	1	9	16	6	.73	9	.277	.317	.464
1990	Los Angeles	NL	25	24	6	1	0	0	(0 | 0)	7	2	2	0	0	7	0	0	0	1	0	1.00	1	.250	.250	.292
	Detroit	AL	78	222	55	9	3	4	(3 | 1)	82	22	20	10	0	51	0	6	0	3	5	.38	6	.248	.280	.369
	11 ML YEARS		1036	3090	739	128	24	70	(30 | 40)	1125	389	313	182	15	671	4	32	18	98	40	.71	51	.239	.281	.364

Pat Sheridan

Bats: Left **Throws:** Right **Pos:** RF **Ht:** 6' 3" **Wt:** 195 **Born:** 12/04/57 **Age:** 34

				BATTING														BASERUNNING				PERCENTAGES		
Year	Team	Lg	G	AB	H	2B	3B	HR	(Hm | Rd)	TB	R	RBI	TBB	IBB	SO	HBP	SH	SF	SB	CS	SB%	GDP	Avg	OBP	SLG
1981	Kansas City	AL	3	1	0	0	0	0	(0 | 0)	0	0	0	0	0	1	0	0	0	0	0	.00	0	.000	.000	.000
1983	Kansas City	AL	109	333	90	12	2	7	(4 | 3)	127	43	36	20	0	64	0	4	0	12	3	.80	3	.270	.312	.381
1984	Kansas City	AL	138	481	136	24	4	8	(3 | 5)	192	64	53	41	3	91	1	5	3	19	6	.76	6	.283	.338	.399
1985	Kansas City	AL	78	206	47	9	2	3	(2 | 1)	69	18	17	23	2	38	1	3	1	11	3	.79	4	.228	.307	.335
1986	Detroit	AL	98	236	56	9	1	6	(3 | 3)	85	41	19	21	4	57	1	2	2	9	2	.82	3	.237	.300	.360
1987	Detroit	AL	141	421	109	19	3	6	(3 | 3)	152	57	49	44	4	90	1	2	5	18	13	.58	7	.259	.327	.361
1988	Detroit	AL	127	347	88	9	5	11	(7 | 4)	140	47	47	44	4	64	2	7	2	8	6	.57	6	.254	.339	.403
1989	2 ML Teams		120	281	62	6	4	6	(2 | 4)	94	36	29	30	1	66	0	1	1	8	1	.89	3	.221	.295	.335
1991	New York	AL	62	113	23	3	0	4	(2 | 2)	38	13	7	13	1	30	0	1	0	1	1	.50	6	.204	.286	.336
1989	Detroit	AL	50	120	29	3	0	3	(2 | 1)	41	16	15	17	0	21	0	1	1	4	0	1.00	2	.242	.333	.342
	San Francisco	NL	70	161	33	3	4	3	(0 | 3)	53	20	14	13	1	45	0	0	0	4	1	.80	1	.205	.264	.329
	9 ML YEARS		876	2419	611	91	21	51	(26 | 25)	897	319	257	236	19	501	6	25	14	86	35	.71	38	.253	.319	.371

Tim Sherrill

Pitches: Left **Bats:** Left **Pos:** RP **Ht:** 5'11" **Wt:** 170 **Born:** 09/10/65 **Age:** 26

			HOW MUCH HE PITCHED						WHAT HE GAVE UP								THE RESULTS					
Year	Team	Lg	G	GS	CG	GF	IP	BFP	H	R	ER	HR	SH	SF	HB	TBB	IBB	SO	WP	Bk	W	L	Pct.	ShO	Sv	ERA
1987	Johnson Cty	R	25	0	0	18	42	172	25	18	14	1	1	0	2	18	2	62	0	0	3	4	.429	0	8	3.00
1988	Savannah	A	31	0	0	29	45.1	173	26	12	9	2	5	2	1	13	2	62	0	1	3	2	.600	0	16	1.79
	St. Pete	A	16	0	0	11	23.1	87	14	4	4	0	0	3	1	8	1	25	0	2	2	0	1.000	0	6	1.54
1989	Savannah	A	3	0	0	3	3.2	16	3	0	0	0	0	1	0	2	0	6	0	0	0	0	.000	0	2	0.00
	St.Pete	A	52	0	0	21	68	269	52	19	16	3	7	2	0	23	3	48	2	0	4	0	1.000	0	6	2.12
1990	Louisville	AAA	52	0	0	20	61.1	253	49	17	17	4	4	1	1	21	2	57	4	0	4	3	.571	0	2	2.49
1991	Louisville	AAA	42	0	0	29	60.1	257	56	21	21	5	3	0	0	26	3	38	2	0	5	5	.500	0	10	3.13
1990	St. Louis	NL	8	0	0	2	4.1	25	10	5	3	0	1	0	0	3	0	3	1	0	0	0	.000	0	0	6.23
1991	St. Louis	NL	10	0	0	3	14.1	67	20	13	13	2	1	2	2	3	1	4	1	0	0	0	.000	0	0	8.16
	2 ML YEARS		18	0	0	5	18.2	92	30	18	16	2	2	2	2	6	1	7	2	0	0	0	.000	0	0	7.71

Craig Shipley

Bats: Right **Throws:** Right **Pos:** SS/2B **Ht:** 6' 0" **Wt:** 170 **Born:** 01/07/63 **Age:** 29

				BATTING														BASERUNNING				PERCENTAGES		
Year	Team	Lg	G	AB	H	2B	3B	HR	(Hm	Rd)	TB	R	RBI	TBB	IBB	SO	HBP	SH	SF	SB	CS	SB%	GDP	Avg	OBP	SLG
1984	Vero Beach	A	85	293	82	11	2	0	--	--	97	56	28	52	6	44	4	1	1	18	7	.72	9	.280	.394	.331
1985	Albuquerque	AAA	124	414	100	9	2	0	--	--	113	50	30	22	3	43	1	3	3	24	6	.80	12	.242	.280	.273
1986	Albuquerque	AAA	61	203	59	8	2	0	--	--	71	33	16	11	0	23	2	3	1	6	7	.46	3	.291	.332	.350
1987	Albuquerque	AAA	49	139	31	6	1	1	--	--	42	17	15	13	0	19	1	1	0	6	2	.75	3	.223	.294	.302
	San Antonio	AA	33	127	30	5	3	2	--	--	47	14	9	5	0	17	1	0	1	2	1	.67	0	.236	.269	.370
1988	Jackson	AA	89	335	88	14	3	6	--	--	126	41	41	24	2	40	3	0	1	6	5	.55	9	.263	.317	.376
	Tidewater	AAA	40	151	41	5	0	1	--	--	49	12	13	4	0	15	0	2	2	0	0	.00	3	.272	.287	.325
1989	Tidewater	AAA	44	131	27	1	0	2	--	--	34	6	9	7	0	22	0	2	2	0	0	.00	6	.206	.243	.260
1990	Tidewater	AAA	4	3	0	0	0	0	--	--	0	1	0	0	0	1	0	0	0	0	0	.00	0	.000	.000	.000
1991	Las Vegas	AAA	65	230	69	9	5	5	--	--	103	27	34	10	1	32	4	4	0	2	2	.50	7	.300	.340	.448

Year	Team	Lg	G																								
1986	Los Angeles	NL	12	27	3	1	0	0	(0	0)	4	3	4	2	1	5	1	1	0	0	0	.00	1	.111	.200	.148
1987	Los Angeles	NL	26	35	9	1	0	0	(0	0)	10	3	2	0	0	6	0	0	0	0	0	.00	2	.257	.257	.286
1989	New York	NL	4	7	1	0	0	0	(0	0)	1	3	0	0	0	1	0	0	0	0	0	.00		.143	.143	.143
1991	San Diego	NL	37	91	25	3	0	1	(0	1)	31	6	6	2	0	14	1	1	0	0	0	.00	1	.275	.298	.341
	4 ML YEARS		79	160	38	5	0	1	(0	1)	46	15	12	4	1	26	2	2	0	0	0	.00	4	.238	.265	.288

Eric Show

Pitches: Right **Bats:** Right **Pos:** RP/SP   **Ht:** 6' 1" **Wt:** 185 **Born:** 05/19/56 **Age:** 36

			HOW MUCH HE PITCHED						WHAT HE GAVE UP										THE RESULTS					
Year	Team	Lg	G	GS	CG	GF	IP	BFP	H	R	ER	HR	SH	SF	HB	TBB	IBB	SO	WP	Bk	W	L	Pct.	ShO	Sv	ERA
1981	San Diego	NL	15	0	0	4	23	92	17	9	8	2	2	0	1	9	3	22	0	0	1	3	.250	0	3	3.13
1982	San Diego	NL	47	14	2	12	150	611	117	49	44	10	13	6	5	48	3	88	2	0	10	6	.625	2	3	2.64
1983	San Diego	NL	35	33	4	0	200.2	857	201	97	93	25	9	4	6	74	3	120	4	2	15	12	.556	2	0	4.17
1984	San Diego	NL	32	32	3	0	206.2	862	175	88	78	18	17	4	4	88	4	104	6	2	15	9	.625	1	0	3.40
1985	San Diego	NL	35	35	5	0	233	977	212	95	80	27	9	5	5	87	7	141	4	0	12	11	.522	2	0	3.09
1986	San Diego	NL	24	22	2	1	136.1	569	109	47	45	11	10	1	4	69	4	94	3	2	9	5	.643	0	0	2.97
1987	San Diego	NL	34	34	5	0	206.1	887	188	99	88	26	9	5	9	85	7	117	6	5	8	16	.333	3	0	3.84
1988	San Diego	NL	32	32	13	0	234.2	936	201	86	85	22	3	5	6	53	5	144	4	5	16	11	.593	1	0	3.26
1989	San Diego	NL	16	16	1	0	106.1	464	113	59	50	9	6	5	2	39	3	66	2	2	8	6	.571	0	0	4.23
1990	San Diego	NL	39	12	0	14	106.1	482	131	74	68	16	5	4	4	41	9	55	3	3	6	8	.429	0	1	5.76
1991	Oakland	AL	23	5	0	6	51.2	231	62	36	34	5	2	4	0	17	1	20	2	1	1	2	.333	0	0	5.92
	11 ML YEARS		332	235	35	37	1655	6968	1526	739	673	171	85	43	46	610	49	971	36	22	101	89	.532	11	7	3.66

Terry Shumpert

Bats: Right **Throws:** Right **Pos:** 2B   **Ht:** 5'11" **Wt:** 190 **Born:** 08/16/66 **Age:** 25

			BATTING														BASERUNNING				PERCENTAGES		
Year	Team	Lg	G	AB	H	2B	3B	HR	(Hm	Rd)	TB	R	RBI	TBB	IBB	SO	HBP	SH	SF	SB	CS	SB%	GDP	Avg	OBP	SLG
1987	Eugene	A	48	186	54	16	1	4	--	--	84	38	21	27	0	41	3	0	1	16	4	.80	0	.290	.385	.452
1988	Appleton	A	114	422	102	37	2	7	--	--	164	64	38	56	1	90	3	0	5	36	3	.92	1	.242	.331	.389
1989	Omaha	AAA	113	355	88	29	2	4	--	--	133	54	22	25	0	63	10	7	1	23	7	.77	5	.248	.315	.375
1990	Omaha	AAA	39	153	39	6	4	2	--	--	59	24	12	14	0	28	3	4	1	18	0	1.00	3	.255	.327	.386
1990	Kansas City	AL	32	91	25	6	1	0	(0	0)	33	7	8	2	0	17	1	0	2	3	3	.50	4	.275	.292	.363
1991	Kansas City	AL	144	369	80	16	4	5	(1	4)	119	45	34	30	0	75	5	10	3	17	11	.61	10	.217	.283	.322
	2 ML YEARS		176	460	105	22	5	5	(1	4)	152	52	42	32	0	92	6	10	5	20	14	.59	14	.228	.284	.330

Ruben Sierra

Bats: Both **Throws:** Right **Pos:** RF   **Ht:** 6' 1" **Wt:** 200 **Born:** 10/06/65 **Age:** 26

			BATTING														BASERUNNING				PERCENTAGES		
Year	Team	Lg	G	AB	H	2B	3B	HR	(Hm | Rd)	TB	R	RBI	TBB	IBB	SO	HBP	SH	SF	SB	CS	SB%	GDP	Avg	OBP	SLG
1986	Texas	AL	113	382	101	13	10	16	(8 | 8)	182	50	55	22	3	65	1	1	5	7	8	.47	8	.264	.302	.476
1987	Texas	AL	158	643	169	35	4	30	(15 | 15)	302	97	109	39	4	114	2	0	12	16	11	.59	18	.263	.302	.470
1988	Texas	AL	156	615	156	32	2	23	(15 | 8)	261	77	91	44	10	91	1	0	8	18	4	.82	15	.254	.301	.424
1989	Texas	AL	162	634	194	35	14	29	(21 | 8)	344	101	119	43	2	82	2	0	10	8	2	.80	7	.306	.347	.543
1990	Texas	AL	159	608	170	37	2	16	(10 | 6)	259	70	96	49	13	86	1	0	8	9	0	1.00	15	.280	.330	.426
1991	Texas	AL	161	661	203	44	5	25	(12 | 13)	332	110	116	56	7	91	0	0	9	16	4	.80	17	.307	.357	.502
	6 ML YEARS		909	3543	993	196	37	139	(81 | 58)	1680	505	586	253	39	529	7	1	52	74	29	.72	80	.280	.325	.474

Mike Simms

Bats: Right **Throws:** Right **Pos:** RF   **Ht:** 6' 4" **Wt:** 185 **Born:** 01/12/67 **Age:** 25

			BATTING														BASERUNNING				PERCENTAGES		
Year	Team	Lg	G	AB	H	2B	3B	HR	(Hm	Rd)	TB	R	RBI	TBB	IBB	SO	HBP	SH	SF	SB	CS	SB%	GDP	Avg	OBP	SLG
1985	Astros	R	21	70	19	2	1	3	--	--	32	10	18	6	0	26	4	0	3	0	0	.00	1	.271	.349	.457
1986	Astros	R	54	181	47	14	1	4	--	--	75	33	37	22	1	48	4	0	4	2	1	.67	4	.260	.346	.414
1987	Asheville	A	133	469	128	19	0	39	--	--	264	93	100	73	5	167	9	0	3	7	0	1.00	4	.273	.379	.563
1988	Osceola	A	123	428	104	19	1	16	--	--	173	63	73	76	3	130	1	0	6	9	6	.60	6	.243	.354	.404
1989	Columbus	AA	109	378	97	21	3	20	--	--	184	64	81	66	4	110	2	0	6	12	6	.67	2	.257	.365	.487
1990	Tucson	AAA	124	421	115	34	5	13	--	--	198	75	72	74	3	135	8	1	8	3	6	.33	5	.273	.386	.470
1991	Tucson	AAA	85	297	73	20	2	15	--	--	142	53	59	36	0	94	4	1	7	2	2	.50	3	.246	.328	.478
1990	Houston	NL	12	13	4	1	0	1	(0	1)	8	3	2	0	0	4	0	0	0	0	0	.00		.308	.308	.615
1991	Houston	NL	49	123	25	5	0	3	(1	2)	39	18	16	18	0	38	0	0	2	1	0	1.00	2	.203	.301	.317
	2 ML YEARS		61	136	29	6	0	4	(1	3)	47	21	18	18	0	42	0	0	2	1	0	1.00	3	.213	.301	.346

190

Doug Simons

Pitches: Left **Bats:** Left **Pos:** RP **Ht:** 6' 0" **Wt:** 170 **Born:** 09/15/66 **Age:** 25

			HOW MUCH HE PITCHED					WHAT HE GAVE UP												THE RESULTS					
Year Team	Lg	G	GS	CG	GF	IP	BFP	H	R	ER	HR	SH	SF	HB	TBB	IBB	SO	WP	Bk	W	L	Pct.	ShO	Sv	ERA
1988 Visalia	A	17	16	5	1	107.1	467	100	59	47	10	4	3	5	46	0	123	6	1	6	5	.545	2	0	3.94
1989 Visalia	A	14	14	1	0	90.2	372	77	33	15	4	1	4	5	33	1	79	4	1	6	2	.750	0	0	1.49
Orlando	AA	14	14	3	0	87.1	374	83	39	37	7	2	2	2	37	0	58	1	2	7	3	.700	0	0	3.81
1990 Orlando	AA	29	28	5	0	188	765	160	76	53	13	9	4	6	43	2	109	7	1	15	12	.556	0	0	2.54
1991 New York	NL	42	1	0	11	60.2	258	55	40	35	5	9	4	2	19	5	38	3	0	2	3	.400	0	1	5.19

Matt Sinatro

Bats: Right **Throws:** Right **Pos:** C **Ht:** 5' 9" **Wt:** 175 **Born:** 03/22/60 **Age:** 32

								BATTING											BASERUNNING				PERCENTAGES		
Year Team	Lg	G	AB	H	2B	3B	HR	(Hm Rd)	TB	R	RBI	TBB	IBB	SO	HBP	SH	SF	SB	CS	SB%	GDP	Avg	OBP	SLG
1981 Atlanta	NL	12	32	9	1	1	0	(0 0)	12	4	4	5	1	4	0	0	0	1	0	.00	0	.281	.378	.375
1982 Atlanta	NL	37	81	11	2	0	1	(0 1)	16	10	4	4	0	9	0	2	0	0	1	.00	3	.136	.176	.198
1983 Atlanta	NL	7	12	2	0	0	0	(0 0)	2	0	2	2	0	1	0	0	0	0	0	.00	0	.167	.286	.167
1984 Atlanta	NL	2	4	0	0	0	0	(0 0)	0	0	0	0	0	0	0	0	0	0	0	.00	0	.000	.000	.000
1987 Oakland	AL	6	3	0	0	0	0	(0 0)	0	0	0	0	0	1	0	0	0	0	0	.00	0	.000	.000	.000
1988 Oakland	AL	10	9	3	2	0	0	(0 0)	5	1	5	0	0	1	0	0	1	0	0	.00	2	.333	.300	.556
1989 Detroit	AL	13	25	3	0	0	0	(0 0)	3	2	1	1	0	3	1	0	0	0	0	.00	1	.120	.185	.120
1990 Seattle	AL	30	50	15	1	0	0	(0 0)	16	2	4	4	0	10	0	3	0	1	0	1.00	3	.300	.352	.320
1991 Seattle	AL	5	8	2	0	0	0	(0 0)	2	1	1	1	0	1	0	0	0	0	0	.00	0	.250	.333	.250
9 ML YEARS		122	224	45	6	1	1	(0 1)	56	20	21	17	1	30	1	5	1	2	1	.67	10	.201	.259	.250

Doug Sisk

Pitches: Right **Bats:** Right **Pos:** RP **Ht:** 6' 2" **Wt:** 210 **Born:** 09/26/57 **Age:** 34

			HOW MUCH HE PITCHED					WHAT HE GAVE UP												THE RESULTS					
Year Team	Lg	G	GS	CG	GF	IP	BFP	H	R	ER	HR	SH	SF	HB	TBB	IBB	SO	WP	Bk	W	L	Pct.	ShO	Sv	ERA
1982 New York	NL	8	0	0	4	8.2	34	5	1	1	1	0	0	1	4	2	4	0	0	0	1	.000	0	1	1.04
1983 New York	NL	67	0	0	39	104.1	447	88	38	26	1	6	4	4	59	7	33	5	1	5	4	.556	0	11	2.24
1984 New York	NL	50	0	0	31	77.2	329	57	24	18	1	7	0	3	54	5	32	1	0	1	3	.250	0	15	2.09
1985 New York	NL	42	0	0	22	73	341	86	48	43	3	3	0	2	40	2	26	1	1	4	5	.444	0	2	5.30
1986 New York	NL	41	0	0	15	70.2	312	77	31	24	0	3	0	5	31	5	31	2	1	4	2	.667	0	1	3.06
1987 New York	NL	55	0	0	17	78	339	83	38	30	5	5	2	3	22	4	37	2	0	3	1	.750	0	3	3.46
1988 Baltimore	AL	52	0	0	29	94.1	410	109	43	39	3	5	2	2	45	6	26	3	0	3	3	.500	0	0	3.72
1990 Atlanta	NL	3	0	0	2	2.1	13	1	1	1	0	0	2	0	4	0	1	1	0	0	0	.000	0	0	3.86
1991 Atlanta	NL	14	0	0	2	14.1	73	21	14	8	1	1	1	0	8	2	5	0	0	2	1	.667	0	0	5.02
9 ML YEARS		332	0	0	161	523.1	2298	527	238	190	15	30	11	20	267	33	195	15	3	22	20	.524	0	33	3.27

Joel Skinner

Bats: Right **Throws:** Right **Pos:** C **Ht:** 6' 4" **Wt:** 200 **Born:** 02/21/61 **Age:** 31

								BATTING											BASERUNNING				PERCENTAGES		
Year Team	Lg	G	AB	H	2B	3B	HR	(Hm Rd)	TB	R	RBI	TBB	IBB	SO	HBP	SH	SF	SB	CS	SB%	GDP	Avg	OBP	SLG
1983 Chicago	AL	6	11	3	0	0	0	(0 0)	3	2	1	0	0	1	0	0	0	0	0	.00	2	.273	.273	.273
1984 Chicago	AL	43	80	17	2	0	0	(0 0)	19	4	3	7	0	19	0	0	1	1	0	1.00	2	.213	.273	.238
1985 Chicago	AL	22	44	15	4	1	1	(1 0)	24	5	5	5	0	13	0	1	0	0	0	.00	2	.341	.408	.545
1986 2 ML Teams		114	315	73	9	1	5	(1 4)	99	23	37	16	0	83	1	2	2	1	4	.20	6	.232	.269	.314
1987 New York	AL	64	139	19	4	0	3	(1 2)	32	9	14	8	0	46	1	4	2	0	0	.00	9	.137	.187	.230
1988 New York	AL	88	251	57	15	0	4	(1 3)	84	23	23	14	0	72	0	6	1	0	0	.00	6	.227	.267	.335
1989 Cleveland	AL	79	178	41	10	0	1	(0 1)	54	10	13	9	0	42	1	1	0	1	1	.50	3	.230	.271	.303
1990 Cleveland	AL	49	139	35	4	1	2	(1 1)	47	16	16	7	0	44	0	0	0	0	0	.00	3	.252	.288	.338
1991 Cleveland	AL	99	284	69	14	0	1	(1 0)	86	23	24	14	1	67	1	4	2	2	0	.00	8	.243	.279	.303
1986 Chicago	AL	60	149	30	5	1	4	(1 3)	49	17	20	9	0	43	1	2	1	1	0	1.00	2	.201	.250	.329
New York	AL	54	166	43	4	0	1	(0 1)	50	6	17	7	0	40	0	0	1	0	0	.00	4	.259	.287	.301
9 ML YEARS		564	1441	329	62	3	17	(5 12)	448	119	136	80	1	387	4	18	8	3	7	.30	41	.228	.269	.311

Don Slaught

Bats: Right **Throws:** Right **Pos:** C **Ht:** 6' 1" **Wt:** 190 **Born:** 09/11/58 **Age:** 33

								BATTING											BASERUNNING				PERCENTAGES		
Year Team	Lg	G	AB	H	2B	3B	HR	(Hm Rd)	TB	R	RBI	TBB	IBB	SO	HBP	SH	SF	SB	CS	SB%	GDP	Avg	OBP	SLG
1982 Kansas City	AL	43	115	32	6	0	3	(0 3)	47	14	8	9	0	12	0	2	0	0	0	.00	3	.278	.331	.409
1983 Kansas City	AL	83	276	86	13	4	0	(0 0)	107	21	28	11	0	27	0	1	2	3	1	.75	8	.312	.336	.388
1984 Kansas City	AL	124	409	108	27	4	4	(1 3)	155	48	42	20	4	55	2	8	7	0	0	.00	8	.264	.297	.379

Year	Team	Lg	G	AB	H	2B	3B	HR	(GW	RBI)	TB	R	RBI	BB	IBB	SO	HBP	SH	SF	SB	CS	SB%	GDP	AVG	OBP	SLG
1985	Texas	AL	102	343	96	17	4	8	(4	4)	145	34	35	20	1	41	6	1	0	5	4	.56	8	.280	.331	.423
1986	Texas	AL	95	314	83	17	1	13	(5	8)	141	39	46	16	0	59	5	3	3	3	2	.60	8	.264	.308	.449
1987	Texas	AL	95	237	53	15	2	8	(5	3)	96	25	16	24	3	51	1	4	0	0	3	.00	7	.224	.298	.405
1988	New York	AL	97	322	91	25	1	9	(7	2)	145	33	43	24	3	54	1	5	4	1	0	1.00	10	.283	.334	.450
1989	New York	AL	117	350	88	21	3	5	(3	2)	130	34	38	30	3	57	5	2	5	1	1	.50	9	.251	.315	.371
1990	Pittsburgh	NL	84	230	69	18	3	4	(1	3)	105	27	29	27	2	27	3	3	4	0	1	.00	2	.300	.375	.457
1991	Pittsburgh	NL	77	220	65	17	1	1	(0	1)	87	19	29	21	1	32	3	5	1	0	1	1.00	6	.295	.363	.395
10 ML YEARS			917	2816	771	176	23	55	(26	29)	1158	294	314	202	17	415	28	34	26	14	12	.54	69	.274	.326	.411

Heathcliff Slocumb

Pitches: Right   Bats: Right   Pos: RP   **Ht: 6' 3"   Wt: 210   Born: 06/07/66   Age: 26**

			HOW MUCH HE PITCHED						WHAT HE GAVE UP												THE RESULTS					
Year	Team	Lg	G	GS	CG	GF	IP	BFP	H	R	ER	HR	SH	SF	HB	TBB	IBB	SO	WP	Bk	W	L	Pct.	ShO	Sv	ERA
1984	Kingsport	R	1	0	0	0	0.1	3	0	1	0	0	1	0	0	1	0	0	0	0	0	0	.000	0	0	0.00
	Little Fls	A	4	1	0	0	9	51	8	11	11	0	0	0	1	16	0	10	4	0	0	0	.000	0	0	11.00
1985	Kingsport	R	11	9	1	0	52.1	232	47	32	22	0	2	1	1	31	0	29	15	0	3	2	.600	0	0	3.78
1986	Little Fls	A	25	0	0	13	43.2	186	24	17	8	3	1	0	0	36	1	41	8	0	3	1	.750	0	1	1.65
1987	Winston-Sal	A	9	4	0	1	27.1	135	26	25	19	1	2	3	0	26	0	27	0	1	1	2	.333	0	0	6.26
	Peoria	A	16	16	3	0	103.2	455	97	44	30	2	0	2	3	42	3	81	15	0	10	4	.714	1	0	2.60
1988	Winston-Sal	A	25	19	2	3	119.2	567	122	76	66	5	2	5	3	90	1	78	19	2	6	6	.500	1	1	4.96
1989	Peoria	A	49	0	0	43	55.2	233	31	16	11	0	5	3	1	33	4	52	6	0	5	3	.625	0	22	1.78
1990	Charlotte	AA	43	0	0	37	50.1	232	50	20	12	0	6	2	3	32	5	37	4	0	3	1	.750	0	12	2.15
	Iowa	AAA	20	0	0	10	27	115	16	10	6	1	2	1	2	18	2	21	3	0	3	2	.600	0	1	2.00
1991	Iowa	AAA	12	0	0	6	13.1	59	10	8	6	0	1	0	1	6	0	9	1	0	1	0	1.000	0	1	4.05
1991	Chicago	NL	52	0	0	21	62.2	274	53	29	24	3	6	6	3	30	6	34	9	0	2	1	.667	0	1	3.45

Joe Slusarski

Pitches: Right   Bats: Right   Pos: SP   **Ht: 6' 4"   Wt: 195   Born: 12/19/66   Age: 25**

			HOW MUCH HE PITCHED						WHAT HE GAVE UP												THE RESULTS					
Year	Team	Lg	G	GS	CG	GF	IP	BFP	H	R	ER	HR	SH	SF	HB	TBB	IBB	SO	WP	Bk	W	L	Pct.	ShO	Sv	ERA
1989	Modesto	A	27	27	4	0	184	753	155	78	65	15	5	3	8	50	0	160	13	1	13	10	.565	1	0	3.18
1990	Huntsville	AA	17	17	2	0	108.2	471	114	65	54	9	2	9	3	35	0	75	5	0	6	8	.429	0	0	4.47
	Tacoma	AAA	9	9	0	0	55.2	241	54	24	21	3	1	3	2	22	0	37	1	1	4	2	.667	0	0	3.40
1991	Tacoma	AAA	7	7	0	0	46.1	182	42	20	14	4	0	0	0	10	0	25	0	0	4	2	.667	0	0	2.72
1991	Oakland	AL	20	19	1	0	109.1	486	121	69	64	14	0	3	4	52	1	60	4	0	5	7	.417	0	0	5.27

John Smiley

Pitches: Left   Bats: Left   Pos: SP   **Ht: 6' 4"   Wt: 200   Born: 03/17/65   Age: 27**

			HOW MUCH HE PITCHED						WHAT HE GAVE UP												THE RESULTS					
Year	Team	Lg	G	GS	CG	GF	IP	BFP	H	R	ER	HR	SH	SF	HB	TBB	IBB	SO	WP	Bk	W	L	Pct.	ShO	Sv	ERA
1986	Pittsburgh	NL	12	0	0	2	11.2	42	4	6	5	2	0	0	0	4	0	9	0	0	1	0	1.000	0	0	3.86
1987	Pittsburgh	NL	63	0	0	19	75	336	69	49	48	7	0	3	0	50	8	58	5	1	5	5	.500	0	4	5.76
1988	Pittsburgh	NL	34	32	0	0	205	835	185	81	74	15	11	8	3	46	4	129	6	6	13	11	.542	1	0	3.25
1989	Pittsburgh	NL	28	28	8	0	205.1	835	174	78	64	22	5	7	4	49	5	123	5	2	12	8	.600	1	0	2.81
1990	Pittsburgh	NL	26	25	2	0	149.1	632	161	83	77	15	5	4	2	36	1	86	2	2	9	10	.474	0	0	4.64
1991	Pittsburgh	NL	33	32	2	0	207.2	836	194	78	71	17	11	4	3	44	0	129	3	1	20	8	.714	1	0	3.08
6 ML YEARS			196	117	17	21	854	3516	787	375	339	78	32	26	12	229	18	534	21	12	60	42	.588	3	4	3.57

Bryn Smith

Pitches: Right   Bats: Right   Pos: SP   **Ht: 6' 2"   Wt: 205   Born: 08/11/55   Age: 36**

			HOW MUCH HE PITCHED						WHAT HE GAVE UP												THE RESULTS					
Year	Team	Lg	G	GS	CG	GF	IP	BFP	H	R	ER	HR	SH	SF	HB	TBB	IBB	SO	WP	Bk	W	L	Pct.	ShO	Sv	ERA
1981	Montreal	NL	7	0	0	1	13	53	14	4	4	1	0	0	0	3	0	9	2	0	1	0	1.000	0	0	2.77
1982	Montreal	NL	47	1	0	16	79.1	335	81	43	37	5	1	4	0	23	5	50	5	1	2	4	.333	0	3	4.20
1983	Montreal	NL	49	12	5	17	155.1	636	142	51	43	13	14	2	5	43	6	101	5	3	6	11	.353	3	3	2.49
1984	Montreal	NL	28	28	4	0	179	751	178	72	66	15	7	2	3	51	7	101	2	2	12	13	.480	2	0	3.32
1985	Montreal	NL	32	32	4	0	222.1	890	193	85	72	12	13	4	1	41	3	127	1	1	18	5	.783	2	0	2.91
1986	Montreal	NL	30	30	1	0	187.1	807	182	101	82	15	10	3	6	63	6	105	4	2	10	8	.556	0	0	3.94
1987	Montreal	NL	26	26	2	0	150.1	643	164	81	73	16	7	5	2	31	4	94	2	0	10	9	.526	0	0	4.37
1988	Montreal	NL	32	32	1	0	198	791	179	79	66	15	7	6	10	32	2	122	2	5	12	10	.545	0	0	3.00
1989	Montreal	NL	33	32	3	0	215.2	864	177	76	68	16	7	5	4	54	4	129	3	1	10	11	.476	1	0	2.84
1990	St. Louis	NL	26	25	0	0	141.1	605	160	81	67	11	7	5	4	30	1	78	2	0	9	8	.529	0	0	4.27
1991	St. Louis	NL	31	31	3	0	198.2	818	188	95	85	16	10	7	7	45	3	94	3	1	12	9	.571	0	0	3.85
11 ML YEARS			341	249	23	34	1740.1	7193	1658	768	663	135	83	43	42	416	41	1010	31	16	102	88	.537	8	6	3.43

Dave Smith

Pitches: Right **Bats:** Right **Pos:** RP **Ht:** 6' 1" **Wt:** 195 **Born:** 01/21/55 **Age:** 37

			HOW MUCH HE PITCHED					WHAT HE GAVE UP												THE RESULTS					
Year Team	Lg	G	GS	CG	GF	IP	BFP	H	R	ER	HR	SH	SF	HB	TBB	IBB	SO	WP	Bk	W	L	Pct.	ShO	Sv	ERA
1980 Houston	NL	57	0	0	35	103	422	90	24	22	1	6	1	4	32	7	85	3	1	7	5	.583	0	10	1.92
1981 Houston	NL	42	0	0	22	75	305	54	26	23	2	6	1	2	23	4	52	4	0	5	3	.625	0	8	2.76
1982 Houston	NL	49	1	0	29	63.1	286	69	30	27	4	9	4	0	31	4	28	2	4	5	4	.556	0	11	3.84
1983 Houston	NL	42	0	0	24	72.2	323	72	32	25	2	3	5	0	36	4	41	1	1	3	1	.750	0	6	3.10
1984 Houston	NL	53	0	0	24	77.1	304	60	22	19	5	2	1	1	20	3	45	1	1	5	4	.556	0	5	2.21
1985 Houston	NL	64	0	0	46	79.1	315	69	26	20	3	3	1	1	17	5	40	4	1	9	5	.643	0	27	2.27
1986 Houston	NL	54	0	0	51	56	223	39	17	17	5	4	1	1	22	3	46	2	0	4	7	.364	0	33	2.73
1987 Houston	NL	50	0	0	44	60	240	39	13	11	0	3	1	1	21	8	73	2	2	2	3	.400	0	24	1.65
1988 Houston	NL	51	0	0	39	57.1	249	60	26	17	1	4	1	1	19	8	38	1	3	4	5	.444	0	27	2.67
1989 Houston	NL	52	0	0	44	58	239	49	20	17	1	8	1	1	19	7	31	2	2	3	4	.429	0	25	2.64
1990 Houston	NL	49	0	0	42	60.1	239	45	18	16	4	4	1	0	20	4	50	5	5	6	6	.500	0	23	2.39
1991 Chicago	NL	35	0	0	28	33	151	39	22	22	6	2	0	1	19	5	16	1	1	0	6	.000	0	17	6.00
12 ML YEARS		598	1	0	428	795.1	3296	685	276	236	34	54	18	13	279	62	545	28	21	53	53	.500	0	216	2.67

Dwight Smith

Bats: Left **Throws:** Right **Pos:** RF/CF **Ht:** 5'11" **Wt:** 175 **Born:** 11/08/63 **Age:** 28

					BATTING											BASERUNNING				PERCENTAGES		
Year Team	Lg	G	AB	H	2B	3B	HR	(Hm | Rd)	TB	R	RBI	TBB	IBB	SO	HBP	SH	SF	SB	CS	SB%	GDP	Avg	OBP	SLG
1989 Chicago	NL	109	343	111	19	6	9	(5 | 4)	169	52	52	31	0	51	2	4	1	9	4	.69	4	.324	.382	.493
1990 Chicago	NL	117	290	76	15	0	6	(3 | 3)	109	34	27	28	2	46	2	0	2	11	6	.65	7	.262	.329	.376
1991 Chicago	NL	90	167	38	7	2	3	(2 | 1)	58	16	21	11	2	32	1	1	0	2	3	.40	2	.228	.279	.347
3 ML YEARS		316	800	225	41	8	18	(10 | 8)	336	102	100	70	4	129	5	5	3	22	13	.63	13	.281	.342	.420

Greg Smith

Bats: Both **Throws:** Right **Pos:** PH **Ht:** 5'11" **Wt:** 170 **Born:** 04/05/67 **Age:** 25

					BATTING											BASERUNNING				PERCENTAGES		
Year Team	Lg	G	AB	H	2B	3B	HR	(Hm	Rd)	TB	R	RBI	TBB	IBB	SO	HBP	SH	SF	SB	CS	SB%	GDP	Avg	OBP	SLG
1985 Wytheville	R	51	179	42	6	2	0	--	--	52	28	15	20	1	27	2	3	1	8	1	.89	1	.235	.317	.291
1986 Peoria	A	53	170	43	6	3	2	--	--	61	24	26	19	1	45	1	2	0	9	2	.82	2	.253	.332	.359
1987 Peoria	A	124	444	120	23	5	6	--	--	171	69	56	62	5	96	4	7	5	26	9	.74	11	.270	.361	.385
1988 Winston-Sal	A	95	361	101	12	2	4	--	--	129	62	29	46	2	50	2	6	3	52	12	.81	5	.280	.362	.357
1989 Charlotte	AA	126	467	138	23	6	5	--	--	188	59	64	42	1	52	6	9	4	38	13	.75	8	.296	.358	.403
1990 Iowa	AAA	105	398	116	19	1	5	--	--	152	54	44	37	1	57	2	4	1	26	14	.65	8	.291	.354	.382
1991 Albuquerque	AAA	48	161	35	3	2	0	--	--	42	25	17	10	1	30	0	1	1	11	0	1.00	7	.217	.262	.261
1989 Chicago	NL	4	5	2	0	0	0	(0	0)	2	1	2	0	0	0	1	0	0	0	0	.00	0	.400	.500	.400
1990 Chicago	NL	18	44	9	2	1	0	(0	0)	13	4	5	2	0	5	0	1	1	1	0	1.00	1	.205	.234	.295
1991 Los Angeles	NL	5	3	0	0	0	0	(0	0)	0	1	0	0	0	2	0	1	0	0	0	.00	0	.000	.000	.000
3 ML YEARS		27	52	11	2	1	0	(0	0)	15	6	7	2	0	7	1	2	1	1	0	1.00	1	.212	.250	.288

Lee Smith

Pitches: Right **Bats:** Right **Pos:** RP **Ht:** 6' 6" **Wt:** 250 **Born:** 12/04/57 **Age:** 34

			HOW MUCH HE PITCHED					WHAT HE GAVE UP												THE RESULTS					
Year Team	Lg	G	GS	CG	GF	IP	BFP	H	R	ER	HR	SH	SF	HB	TBB	IBB	SO	WP	Bk	W	L	Pct.	ShO	Sv	ERA
1980 Chicago	NL	18	0	0	6	22	97	21	9	7	0	1	1	0	14	5	17	0	0	2	0	1.000	0	0	2.86
1981 Chicago	NL	40	1	0	12	67	280	57	31	26	2	8	2	1	31	8	50	7	1	3	6	.333	0	1	3.49
1982 Chicago	NL	72	5	0	38	117	480	105	38	35	5	6	5	3	37	5	99	6	1	2	5	.286	0	17	2.69
1983 Chicago	NL	66	0	0	56	103.1	413	70	23	19	5	9	2	1	41	14	91	5	2	4	10	.286	0	29	1.65
1984 Chicago	NL	69	0	0	59	101	428	98	42	41	6	4	5	0	35	7	86	6	0	9	7	.563	0	33	3.65
1985 Chicago	NL	65	0	0	57	97.2	397	87	35	33	9	3	1	1	32	6	112	4	0	7	4	.636	0	33	3.04
1986 Chicago	NL	66	0	0	59	90.1	372	69	32	31	7	6	3	0	42	11	93	2	0	9	9	.500	0	31	3.09
1987 Chicago	NL	62	0	0	55	83.2	360	84	30	29	4	4	0	0	32	5	96	4	0	4	10	.286	0	36	3.12
1988 Boston	AL	64	0	0	57	83.2	363	72	34	26	7	3	2	1	37	6	96	2	0	4	5	.444	0	29	2.80
1989 Boston	AL	64	0	0	50	70.2	290	53	30	28	6	2	2	0	33	6	96	1	0	6	1	.857	0	25	3.57
1990 2 ML Teams		64	0	0	53	83	344	71	24	19	3	2	3	0	29	7	87	2	0	5	5	.500	0	31	2.06
1991 St. Louis	NL	67	0	0	61	73	300	70	19	19	5	5	1	0	13	5	67	1	0	6	3	.667	0	47	2.34
1990 Boston	AL	11	0	0	8	14.1	64	13	4	3	0	0	0	0	9	2	17	1	0	2	1	.667	0	4	1.88
St. Louis	NL	53	0	0	45	68.2	280	58	20	16	3	2	3	0	20	5	70	1	0	3	4	.429	0	27	2.10
12 ML YEARS		717	6	0	563	992.1	4124	857	347	313	59	53	27	7	376	85	990	40	4	61	65	.484	0	312	2.84

193

Lonnie Smith

Bats: Right **Throws:** Right **Pos:** LF **Ht:** 5' 9" **Wt:** 190 **Born:** 12/22/55 **Age:** 36

Year	Team	Lg	G	AB	H	2B	3B	HR	(Hm	Rd)	TB	R	RBI	TBB	IBB	SO	HBP	SH	SF	SB	CS	SB%	GDP	Avg	OBP	SLG
1978	Philadelphia	NL	17	4	0	0	0	0	(0	0)	0	6	0	4	0	3	0	0	0	4	0	1.00	0	.000	.500	.000
1979	Philadelphia	NL	17	30	5	2	0	0	(0	0)	7	4	3	1	0	7	0	0	0	2	1	.67	0	.167	.194	.233
1980	Philadelphia	NL	100	298	101	14	4	3	(2	1)	132	69	20	26	2	48	4	1	2	33	13	.72	5	.339	.397	.443
1981	Philadelphia	NL	62	176	57	14	3	2	(1	1)	83	40	11	18	1	14	5	3	0	21	10	.68	1	.324	.402	.472
1982	St. Louis	NL	156	592	182	35	8	8	(3	5)	257	120	69	64	2	74	9	3	4	68	26	.72	11	.307	.381	.434
1983	St. Louis	NL	130	492	158	31	5	8	(4	4)	223	83	45	41	2	55	9	1	4	43	18	.70	11	.321	.381	.453
1984	St. Louis	NL	145	504	126	20	4	6	(3	3)	172	77	49	70	0	90	9	3	4	50	13	.79	7	.250	.349	.341
1985	2 ML Teams		148	544	140	25	6	6	(2	4)	195	92	48	56	0	89	7	1	5	52	13	.80	7	.257	.332	.358
1986	Kansas City	AL	134	508	146	25	7	8	(2	6)	209	80	44	46	0	78	10	2	2	26	9	.74	10	.287	.357	.411
1987	Kansas City	AL	48	167	42	7	1	3	(1	2)	60	26	8	24	0	31	4	0	2	9	4	.69	1	.251	.355	.359
1988	Atlanta	NL	43	114	27	3	0	3	(2	1)	39	14	9	10	0	25	0	0	1	4	2	.67	0	.237	.296	.342
1989	Atlanta	NL	134	482	152	34	4	21	(10	11)	257	89	79	76	3	95	11	1	7	25	12	.68	7	.315	.415	.533
1990	Atlanta	NL	135	466	142	27	9	9	(2	7)	214	72	42	58	3	69	6	1	6	10	10	.50	2	.305	.384	.459
1991	Atlanta	NL	122	353	97	19	1	7	(6	1)	139	58	44	50	3	64	9	2	2	9	5	.64	4	.275	.377	.394
1985	St. Louis	NL	28	96	25	2	2	0	(0	0)	31	15	7	15	0	20	3	1	0	12	6	.67	2	.260	.377	.323
	Kansas City	AL	120	448	115	23	4	6	(2	4)	164	77	41	41	0	69	4	0	5	40	7	.85	2	.257	.321	.366
14 ML YEARS			1391	4730	1375	256	52	84	(38	46)	1987	830	471	544	16	742	83	18	39	356	136	.72	63	.291	.371	.420

Ozzie Smith

Bats: Both **Throws:** Right **Pos:** SS **Ht:** 5'10" **Wt:** 160 **Born:** 12/26/54 **Age:** 37

Year	Team	Lg	G	AB	H	2B	3B	HR	(Hm	Rd)	TB	R	RBI	TBB	IBB	SO	HBP	SH	SF	SB	CS	SB%	GDP	Avg	OBP	SLG
1978	San Diego	NL	159	590	152	17	6	1	(0	1)	184	69	46	47	0	43	0	28	3	40	12	.77	11	.258	.311	.312
1979	San Diego	NL	156	587	124	18	6	0	(0	0)	154	77	27	37	5	37	2	22	1	28	7	.80	11	.211	.260	.262
1980	San Diego	NL	158	609	140	18	5	0	(0	0)	168	67	35	71	1	49	5	23	4	57	15	.79	9	.230	.313	.276
1981	San Diego	NL	110	450	100	11	2	0	(0	0)	115	53	21	41	1	37	5	10	1	22	12	.65	8	.222	.294	.256
1982	St. Louis	NL	140	488	121	24	1	2	(0	2)	153	58	43	68	12	32	2	4	5	25	5	.83	10	.248	.339	.314
1983	St. Louis	NL	159	552	134	30	6	3	(1	2)	185	69	50	64	9	36	1	7	2	34	7	.83	10	.243	.321	.335
1984	St. Louis	NL	124	412	106	20	5	1	(1	0)	139	53	44	56	5	17	2	11	3	35	7	.83	8	.257	.347	.337
1985	St. Louis	NL	158	537	148	22	3	6	(2	4)	194	70	54	65	11	27	2	9	2	31	8	.79	13	.276	.355	.361
1986	St. Louis	NL	153	514	144	19	4	0	(0	0)	171	67	54	79	13	27	2	11	3	31	7	.82	9	.280	.376	.333
1987	St. Louis	NL	158	600	182	40	4	0	(0	0)	230	104	75	89	3	36	1	12	4	43	9	.83	9	.303	.392	.383
1988	St. Louis	NL	153	575	155	27	1	3	(2	1)	193	80	51	74	2	43	1	12	7	57	9	.86	7	.270	.350	.336
1989	St. Louis	NL	155	593	162	30	8	2	(1	1)	214	82	50	55	3	37	2	11	3	29	7	.81	10	.273	.335	.361
1990	St. Louis	NL	143	512	130	21	1	1	(0	1)	156	61	50	61	0	33	2	7	10	32	6	.84	8	.254	.330	.305
1991	St. Louis	NL	150	550	157	30	3	3	(2	1)	202	96	50	83	2	36	1	6	1	35	9	.80	8	.285	.380	.367
14 ML YEARS			2076	7569	1955	327	55	22	(9	13)	2458	1006	650	890	71	490	28	173	49	499	120	.81	131	.258	.337	.325

Pete Smith

Pitches: Right **Bats:** Right **Pos:** SP **Ht:** 6' 2" **Wt:** 200 **Born:** 02/27/66 **Age:** 26

Year	Team	Lg	G	GS	CG	GF	IP	BFP	H	R	ER	HR	SH	SF	HB	TBB	IBB	SO	WP	Bk	W	L	Pct.	ShO	Sv	ERA
1987	Atlanta	NL	6	6	0	0	31.2	143	39	21	17	3	0	2	0	14	0	11	3	1	1	2	.333	0	0	4.83
1988	Atlanta	NL	32	32	5	0	195.1	837	183	89	80	15	12	4	1	88	3	124	5	7	7	15	.318	3	0	3.69
1989	Atlanta	NL	28	27	1	0	142	613	144	83	75	13	4	5	0	57	2	115	3	5	5	14	.263	0	0	4.75
1990	Atlanta	NL	13	13	3	0	77	327	77	45	41	11	4	3	0	24	2	56	2	1	5	6	.455	0	0	4.79
1991	Atlanta	NL	14	10	0	2	48	211	48	33	27	5	2	4	0	22	3	29	1	4	1	3	.250	0	0	5.06
5 ML YEARS			93	88	9	2	494	2131	491	271	240	47	22	18	1	205	10	335	14	20	19	40	.322	3	0	4.37

Roy Smith

Pitches: Right **Bats:** Right **Pos:** SP **Ht:** 6' 3" **Wt:** 217 **Born:** 09/06/61 **Age:** 30

Year	Team	Lg	G	GS	CG	GF	IP	BFP	H	R	ER	HR	SH	SF	HB	TBB	IBB	SO	WP	Bk	W	L	Pct.	ShO	Sv	ERA
1984	Cleveland	AL	22	14	0	1	86.1	382	91	49	44	14	1	3	1	40	5	55	3	2	5	5	.500	0	0	4.59
1985	Cleveland	AL	12	11	1	0	62.1	285	84	40	37	8	1	4	1	17	0	28	1	0	1	4	.200	0	0	5.34
1986	Minnesota	AL	5	0	0	2	10.1	50	13	8	8	1	0	1	1	5	1	8	0	0	0	0	.000	0	0	6.97
1987	Minnesota	AL	7	1	0	1	16.1	78	20	10	9	3	0	1	2	6	0	8	0	0	0	2	.000	0	0	4.96
1988	Minnesota	AL	9	4	0	1	37	152	29	12	11	3	0	1	1	12	1	17	1	4	3	0	1.000	0	0	2.68
1989	Minnesota	AL	32	26	2	1	172.1	733	180	82	75	22	5	3	5	51	5	92	5	1	10	6	.625	0	1	3.92
1990	Minnesota	AL	32	23	0	2	153.1	671	191	91	82	20	2	11	0	47	4	87	10	0	5	10	.333	1	0	4.81

						IP	BFP	H	R	ER	HR	SH	SF	HB	TBB	IBB	SO	WP	Bk	W	L	Pct.	ShO	Sv	ERA
1991 Baltimore	AL	17	14	0	0	80.1	348	99	52	50	9	2	3	1	24	0	25	3	1	5	4	.556	0	0	5.60
8 ML YEARS		136	93	4	7	618.1	2699	707	344	316	80	11	26	12	202	16	320	23	8	30	31	.492	1	1	4.60

Zane Smith

Pitches: Left **Bats:** Left **Pos:** SP **Ht:** 6' 2" **Wt:** 200 **Born:** 12/28/60 **Age:** 31

			HOW MUCH HE PITCHED					WHAT HE GAVE UP												THE RESULTS					
Year Team	Lg	G	GS	CG	GF	IP	BFP	H	R	ER	HR	SH	SF	HB	TBB	IBB	SO	WP	Bk	W	L	Pct.	ShO	Sv	ERA
1984 Atlanta	NL	3	3	0	0	20	87	16	7	5	1	1	0	0	13	2	16	0	0	1	0	1.000	0	0	2.25
1985 Atlanta	NL	42	18	2	3	147	631	135	70	62	4	16	1	3	80	5	85	2	0	9	10	.474	2	0	3.80
1986 Atlanta	NL	38	32	3	2	204.2	889	209	109	92	8	13	6	5	105	6	139	8	0	8	16	.333	1	1	4.05
1987 Atlanta	NL	36	36	9	0	242	1035	245	130	110	19	12	5	5	91	6	130	5	1	15	10	.600	3	0	4.09
1988 Atlanta	NL	23	22	3	0	140.1	609	159	72	67	8	15	2	3	44	4	59	2	2	5	10	.333	0	0	4.30
1989 2 ML Teams		48	17	0	10	147	634	141	76	57	7	15	5	3	52	7	93	4	0	1	13	.071	0	2	3.49
1990 2 ML Teams		33	31	4	1	215.1	860	196	77	61	15	3	3	3	50	4	130	2	0	12	9	.571	2	0	2.55
1991 Pittsburgh	NL	35	35	6	0	228	916	234	95	81	15	7	5	2	29	3	120	1	0	16	10	.615	3	0	3.20
1989 Atlanta	NL	17	17	0	0	99	432	102	65	49	5	10	5	2	33	3	58	3	0	1	12	.077	0	0	4.45
Montreal	NL	31	0	0	10	48	202	39	11	8	2	5	0	1	19	4	35	1	0	0	1	.000	0	2	1.50
1990 Montreal	NL	22	21	1	0	139.1	578	141	57	50	11	2	2	3	41	3	80	1	0	6	7	.462	0	0	3.23
Pittsburgh	NL	11	10	3	1	76	282	55	20	11	4	1	1	0	9	1	50	1	0	6	2	.750	2	0	1.30
8 ML YEARS		258	194	27	16	1344.1	5661	1335	636	535	77	82	27	24	464	37	772	24	3	67	78	.462	11	3	3.58

John Smoltz

Pitches: Right **Bats:** Right **Pos:** SP **Ht:** 6' 3" **Wt:** 185 **Born:** 05/15/67 **Age:** 25

			HOW MUCH HE PITCHED					WHAT HE GAVE UP												THE RESULTS					
Year Team	Lg	G	GS	CG	GF	IP	BFP	H	R	ER	HR	SH	SF	HB	TBB	IBB	SO	WP	Bk	W	L	Pct.	ShO	Sv	ERA
1988 Atlanta	NL	12	12	0	0	64	297	74	40	39	10	2	0	2	33	4	37	2	1	2	7	.222	0	0	5.48
1989 Atlanta	NL	29	29	5	0	208	847	160	79	68	15	10	7	2	72	2	168	8	3	12	11	.522	0	0	2.94
1990 Atlanta	NL	34	34	6	0	231.1	966	206	109	99	20	9	8	1	90	3	170	14	3	14	11	.560	2	0	3.85
1991 Atlanta	NL	36	36	5	0	229.2	947	206	101	97	16	9	9	3	77	1	148	20	2	14	13	.519	0	0	3.80
4 ML YEARS		111	111	16	0	733	3057	646	329	303	61	30	24	8	272	10	523	44	9	42	42	.500	2	0	3.72

Cory Snyder

Bats: Right **Throws:** Right **Pos:** RF/1B **Ht:** 6' 3" **Wt:** 185 **Born:** 11/11/62 **Age:** 29

			BATTING														BASERUNNING				PERCENTAGES		
Year Team	Lg	G	AB	H	2B	3B	HR	(Hm | Rd)	TB	R	RBI	TBB	IBB	SO	HBP	SH	SF	SB	CS	SB%	GDP	Avg	OBP	SLG
1986 Cleveland	AL	103	416	113	21	1	24	(12 | 12)	208	58	69	16	0	123	0	1	0	2	3	.40	8	.272	.299	.500
1987 Cleveland	AL	157	577	136	24	2	33	(17 | 16)	263	74	82	31	4	166	1	0	6	5	1	.83	3	.236	.273	.456
1988 Cleveland	AL	142	511	139	24	3	26	(11 | 15)	247	71	75	42	7	101	1	0	4	5	1	.83	12	.272	.326	.483
1989 Cleveland	AL	132	489	105	17	0	18	(6 | 12)	176	49	59	23	1	134	2	0	4	6	5	.55	11	.215	.251	.360
1990 Cleveland	AL	123	438	102	27	3	14	(3 | 11)	177	46	55	21	3	118	2	1	6	1	4	.20	11	.233	.268	.404
1991 2 ML Teams		71	166	29	4	1	3	(2 | 1)	44	14	17	9	1	60	0	4	1	0	0	.00	6	.175	.216	.265
1991 Chicago	AL	50	117	22	4	0	3	(2 | 1)	35	10	11	6	1	41	0	3	1	0	0	.00	5	.188	.228	.299
Toronto	AL	21	49	7	0	1	0	(0 | 0)	9	4	6	3	0	19	0	1	0	0	0	.00	1	.143	.189	.184
6 ML YEARS		728	2597	624	117	10	118	(51 | 67)	1115	312	357	142	16	702	6	6	21	19	14	.58	51	.240	.279	.429

Luis Sojo

Bats: Right **Throws:** Right **Pos:** 2B **Ht:** 5'11" **Wt:** 175 **Born:** 01/03/66 **Age:** 26

			BATTING														BASERUNNING				PERCENTAGES		
Year Team	Lg	G	AB	H	2B	3B	HR	(Hm | Rd)	TB	R	RBI	TBB	IBB	SO	HBP	SH	SF	SB	CS	SB%	GDP	Avg	OBP	SLG
1987 Myrtle Bch	A	72	223	47	5	4	2	--	--	66	23	15	17	0	18	0	4	1	5	1	.83	9	.211	.266	.296
1988 Myrtle Bch	A	135	536	155	22	5	5	--	--	202	83	56	35	1	35	2	7	6	14	9	.61	18	.289	.332	.377
1989 Syracuse	AAA	121	482	133	20	5	3	--	--	172	54	54	21	0	42	1	4	5	9	14	.39	9	.276	.305	.357
1990 Syracuse	AAA	75	297	88	12	3	6	--	--	124	39	25	14	0	23	1	3	9	10	2	.83	8	.296	.321	.418
1990 Toronto	AL	33	80	18	3	0	1	(0 | 1)	24	14	9	5	0	5	0	0	0	1	1	.50	1	.225	.271	.300
1991 California	AL	113	364	94	14	1	3	(1 | 2)	119	38	20	14	0	26	5	5	19	4	2	.67	12	.258	.295	.327
2 ML YEARS		146	444	112	17	1	4	(1 | 3)	143	52	29	19	0	31	5	5	19	5	3	.63	13	.252	.291	.322

Paul Sorrento

Bats: Left **Throws:** Right **Pos:** 1B **Ht:** 6' 2" **Wt:** 217 **Born:** 11/17/65 **Age:** 26

			BATTING														BASERUNNING				PERCENTAGES		
Year Team	Lg	G	AB	H	2B	3B	HR	(Hm | Rd)	TB	R	RBI	TBB	IBB	SO	HBP	SH	SF	SB	CS	SB%	GDP	Avg	OBP	SLG
1989 Minnesota	AL	14	21	5	0	0	0	(0 | 0)	5	2	1	5	1	4	0	0	1	0	0	.00	0	.238	.370	.238
1990 Minnesota	AL	41	121	25	4	1	5	(2 | 3)	46	11	13	12	0	31	1	0	1	1	1	.50	3	.207	.281	.380
1991 Minnesota	AL	26	47	12	2	0	4	(2 | 2)	26	6	13	4	2	11	0	0	0	0	0	.00	3	.255	.314	.553
3 ML YEARS		81	189	42	6	1	9	(4 | 5)	77	19	27	21	3	46	1	0	2	1	1	.50	6	.222	.300	.407

Sammy Sosa

Bats: Right **Throws:** Right **Pos:** RF/CF **Ht:** 6' 0" **Wt:** 175 **Born:** 11/12/68 **Age:** 23

Year Team	Lg	G	AB	H	2B	3B	HR	(Hm	Rd)	TB	R	RBI	TBB	IBB	SO	HBP	SH	SF	SB	CS	SB%	GDP	Avg	OBP	SLG
1989 2 ML Teams		58	183	47	8	0	4	(1	3)	67	27	13	11	2	47	2	5	2	7	5	.58	6	.257	.303	.366
1990 Chicago	AL	153	532	124	26	10	15	(10	5)	215	72	70	33	4	150	6	2	6	32	16	.67	10	.233	.282	.404
1991 Chicago	AL	116	316	64	10	1	10	(3	7)	106	39	33	14	2	98	2	5	1	13	6	.68	5	.203	.240	.335
1989 Texas	AL	25	84	20	3	0	1	(0	1)	26	8	3	0	0	20	0	4	0	0	2	.00	3	.238	.238	.310
Chicago	AL	33	99	27	5	0	3	(1	2)	41	19	10	11	2	27	2	1	2	7	3	.70	3	.273	.351	.414
3 ML YEARS		327	1031	235	44	11	29	(14	15)	388	138	116	58	8	295	10	12	9	52	27	.66	21	.228	.273	.376

Tim Spehr

Bats: Right **Throws:** Right **Pos:** C **Ht:** 6' 2" **Wt:** 205 **Born:** 07/02/66 **Age:** 25

Year Team	Lg	G	AB	H	2B	3B	HR	(Hm	Rd)	TB	R	RBI	TBB	IBB	SO	HBP	SH	SF	SB	CS	SB%	GDP	Avg	OBP	SLG
1988 Appleton	A	31	110	29	3	0	5	--	--	47	15	22	10	0	28	4	0	2	3	0	1.00	1	.264	.341	.427
1989 Baseball Cy	A	18	64	16	5	0	1	--	--	24	8	7	5	0	17	0	2	0	1	0	1.00	1	.250	.304	.375
Memphis	AA	61	216	42	9	0	8	--	--	75	22	23	16	0	59	2	1	1	1	3	.25	2	.194	.255	.347
1990 Omaha	AAA	102	307	69	10	2	6	--	--	101	42	34	41	0	88	10	6	2	5	5	.50	4	.225	.333	.329
1991 Omaha	AAA	72	215	59	14	2	6	--	--	95	27	26	25	1	48	4	3	3	3	2	.60	0	.274	.356	.442
1991 Kansas City	AL	37	74	14	5	0	3	(1	2)	28	7	14	9	0	18	1	3	1	1	0	1.00	2	.189	.282	.378

Bill Spiers

Bats: Left **Throws:** Right **Pos:** SS **Ht:** 6' 2" **Wt:** 190 **Born:** 06/05/66 **Age:** 26

Year Team	Lg	G	AB	H	2B	3B	HR	(Hm	Rd)	TB	R	RBI	TBB	IBB	SO	HBP	SH	SF	SB	CS	SB%	GDP	Avg	OBP	SLG
1989 Milwaukee	AL	114	345	88	9	3	4	(1	3)	115	44	33	21	1	63	1	4	2	10	2	.83	2	.255	.298	.333
1990 Milwaukee	AL	112	363	88	15	3	2	(2	0)	115	44	36	16	0	45	1	6	3	11	6	.65	12	.242	.274	.317
1991 Milwaukee	AL	133	414	117	13	6	8	(1	7)	166	71	54	34	0	55	2	10	4	14	8	.64	9	.283	.337	.401
3 ML YEARS		359	1122	293	37	12	14	(4	10)	396	159	123	71	1	163	4	20	9	35	16	.69	23	.261	.305	.353

Ed Sprague

Bats: Right **Throws:** Right **Pos:** 3B/1B **Ht:** 6' 2" **Wt:** 215 **Born:** 07/25/67 **Age:** 24

Year Team	Lg	G	AB	H	2B	3B	HR	(Hm	Rd)	TB	R	RBI	TBB	IBB	SO	HBP	SH	SF	SB	CS	SB%	GDP	Avg	OBP	SLG
1989 Dunedin	A	52	192	42	9	2	7	--	--	76	21	23	16	2	40	7	0	2	1	1	.50	1	.219	.300	.396
Syracuse	AAA	86	288	60	14	1	5	--	--	91	23	33	18	2	73	5	1	3	0	0	.00	1	.208	.264	.316
1990 Syracuse	AAA	142	519	124	23	5	20	--	--	217	60	75	31	1	100	10	3	4	4	2	.67	9	.239	.293	.418
1991 Syracuse	AAA	23	88	32	8	5	0	--	--	55	24	13	10	0	21	2	0	2	2	0	1.00	1	.364	.431	.625
1991 Toronto	AL	61	160	44	7	0	4	(3	1)	63	17	20	19	2	43	3	0	1	0	3	.00	2	.275	.361	.394

Randy St. Claire

Pitches: Right **Bats:** Right **Pos:** RP **Ht:** 6' 2" **Wt:** 190 **Born:** 08/23/60 **Age:** 31

Year Team	Lg	G	GS	CG	GF	IP	BFP	H	R	ER	HR	SH	SF	HB	TBB	IBB	SO	WP	Bk	W	L	Pct.	ShO	Sv	ERA
1984 Montreal	NL	4	0	0	4	8	38	11	4	4	0	1	2	1	2	1	4	0	0	0	0	.000	0	0	4.50
1985 Montreal	NL	42	0	0	14	68.2	294	69	32	30	3	6	1	1	26	7	25	1	0	5	3	.625	0	0	3.93
1986 Montreal	NL	11	0	0	2	19	76	13	5	5	2	0	0	1	6	1	21	1	0	2	0	1.000	0	1	2.37
1987 Montreal	NL	44	0	0	24	67	282	64	31	30	9	1	3	1	20	4	43	4	0	3	3	.500	0	7	4.03
1988 2 ML Teams		16	0	0	9	21	98	24	13	9	5	0	2	0	10	3	14	0	1	1	0	1.000	0	0	3.86
1989 Minnesota	AL	14	0	0	8	22.1	98	19	13	13	4	1	1	2	10	2	14	1	0	1	0	1.000	0	1	5.24
1991 Atlanta	NL	19	0	0	5	28.2	123	31	17	13	4	3	1	0	9	3	30	4	0	0	0	.000	0	0	4.08
1988 Montreal	NL	6	0	0	3	7.1	38	11	5	5	2	0	1	0	5	1	6	0	1	0	0	.000	0	0	6.14
Cincinnati	NL	10	0	0	6	13.2	60	13	8	4	3	0	1	0	5	2	8	0	0	1	0	1.000	0	0	2.63
7 ML YEARS		150	0	0	66	234.2	1009	231	115	104	27	12	10	5	83	21	151	11	1	12	6	.667	0	9	3.99

Mike Stanley

Bats: Right **Throws:** Right **Pos:** C **Ht:** 6' 0" **Wt:** 190 **Born:** 06/25/63 **Age:** 29

Year Team	Lg	G	AB	H	2B	3B	HR	(Hm	Rd)	TB	R	RBI	TBB	IBB	SO	HBP	SH	SF	SB	CS	SB%	GDP	Avg	OBP	SLG
1986 Texas	AL	15	30	10	3	0	1	(0	1)	16	4	1	3	0	7	0	0	0	1	0	1.00	2	.333	.394	.533
1987 Texas	AL	78	216	59	8	1	6	(3	3)	87	34	37	31	0	48	1	1	4	3	0	1.00	6	.273	.361	.403
1988 Texas	AL	94	249	57	8	0	3	(1	2)	74	21	27	37	0	62	0	1	5	0	0	.00	6	.229	.323	.297
1989 Texas	AL	67	122	30	3	1	1	(1	0)	38	9	11	12	1	29	2	1	0	1	0	1.00	5	.246	.324	.311
1990 Texas	AL	103	189	47	8	1	2	(1	1)	63	21	19	30	2	25	0	6	1	1	0	1.00	4	.249	.350	.333
1991 Texas	AL	95	181	45	13	1	3	(1	2)	69	25	25	34	0	44	2	5	1	0	0	.00	2	.249	.372	.381
6 ML YEARS		452	987	248	43	4	16	(7	9)	347	114	120	147	3	215	5	14	11	6	0	1.00	23	.251	.348	.352

Mike Stanton

Pitches: Left Bats: Left Pos: RP Ht: 6' 1" Wt: 190 Born: 06/02/67 Age: 25

		HOW MUCH HE PITCHED						WHAT HE GAVE UP												THE RESULTS					
Year Team	Lg	G	GS	CG	GF	IP	BFP	H	R	ER	HR	SH	SF	HB	TBB	IBB	SO	WP	Bk	W	L	Pct.	ShO	Sv	ERA
1987 Pulaski	R	15	13	3	1	83.1	354	64	37	30	7	3	4	3	42	0	82	2	0	4	8	.333	2	0	3.24
1988 Burlington	A	30	23	1	3	154	675	154	86	62	7	4	3	1	69	2	160	16	1	11	5	.688	1	0	3.62
Durham	A	2	2	1	0	12.1	55	14	3	2	0	0	0	0	5	0	14	1	1	1	0	1.000	1	0	1.46
1989 Greenville	AA	47	0	0	36	51.1	207	32	10	9	1	5	2	0	31	3	58	4	0	4	1	.800	0	19	1.58
Richmond	AAA	13	0	0	11	20	77	6	0	0	0	1	0	1	13	2	20	0	0	2	0	1.000	0	8	0.00
1990 Greenville	AA	4	4	0	0	5.2	27	7	1	1	1	0	0	0	3	0	4	0	0	0	1	.000	0	0	1.59
1989 Atlanta	NL	20	0	0	10	24	94	17	4	4	0	4	0	0	8	1	27	1	0	1	0	1.000	0	7	1.50
1990 Atlanta	NL	7	0	0	4	7	42	16	16	14	1	1	0	1	4	2	7	1	0	0	3	.000	0	2	18.00
1991 Atlanta	NL	74	0	0	20	78	314	62	27	25	6	6	0	1	21	6	54	0	0	5	5	.500	0	7	2.88
3 ML YEARS		101	0	0	34	109	450	95	47	43	7	11	0	2	33	9	88	2	0	5	9	.357	0	16	3.55

Terry Steinbach

Bats: Right Throws: Right Pos: C Ht: 6' 1" Wt: 195 Born: 03/02/62 Age: 30

		BATTING																		BASERUNNING				PERCENTAGES		
Year Team	Lg	G	AB	H	2B	3B	HR	(Hm	Rd)	TB	R	RBI	TBB	IBB	SO	HBP	SH	SF		SB	CS	SB%	GDP	Avg	OBP	SLG
1986 Oakland	AL	6	15	5	0	0	2	(0	2)	11	3	4	1	0	0	0	0	0		0	0	.00	0	.333	.375	.733
1987 Oakland	AL	122	391	111	16	3	16	(6	10)	181	66	56	32	2	66	9	3	3		1	2	.33	10	.284	.349	.463
1988 Oakland	AL	104	351	93	19	1	9	(6	3)	141	42	51	33	2	47	6	3	5		3	0	1.00	13	.265	.334	.402
1989 Oakland	AL	130	454	124	13	1	7	(5	2)	160	37	42	30	2	66	2	2	3		1	2	.33	14	.273	.319	.352
1990 Oakland	AL	114	379	95	15	2	9	(3	6)	141	32	57	19	1	66	4	5	3		0	1	.00	11	.251	.291	.372
1991 Oakland	AL	129	456	125	31	1	6	(1	5)	176	50	67	22	4	70	7	0	9		2	2	.50	15	.274	.312	.386
6 ML YEARS		605	2046	553	94	8	49	(21	28)	810	230	277	137	11	315	28	13	23		7	7	.50	63	.270	.321	.396

Ray Stephens

Bats: Right Throws: Right Pos: C Ht: 6' 0" Wt: 190 Born: 09/22/62 Age: 29

		BATTING																		BASERUNNING				PERCENTAGES		
Year Team	Lg	G	AB	H	2B	3B	HR	(Hm	Rd)	TB	R	RBI	TBB	IBB	SO	HBP	SH	SF		SB	CS	SB%	GDP	Avg	OBP	SLG
1985 Erie	A	9	31	9	1	1	1	--	--	15	3	5	7	0	6	0	0	0		0	0	.00	1	.290	.421	.484
Savannah	A	39	127	26	6	0	0	--	--	32	11	6	14	0	32	1	1	1		1	1	.50	3	.205	.287	.252
1986 Savannah	A	95	325	71	10	0	13	--	--	120	52	56	57	1	76	3	1	2		2	4	.33	6	.218	.339	.369
Louisville	AAA	12	31	6	1	0	1	--	--	10	2	2	1	0	13	1	0	1		0	0	.00	0	.194	.235	.323
1987 Arkansas	AA	100	307	77	20	0	8	--	--	121	35	42	37	4	68	3	2	2		6	2	.75	10	.251	.335	.394
Louisville	AAA	9	30	4	0	0	0	--	--	4	1	2	5	1	9	0	0	1		0	1	.00	3	.133	.250	.133
1988 Louisville	AAA	115	355	67	13	2	3	--	--	93	26	25	45	3	78	1	0	3		2	0	1.00	6	.189	.280	.262
1989 Arkansas	AA	112	363	95	14	0	7	--	--	130	49	44	44	2	61	4	4	3		2	1	.67	11	.262	.345	.358
1990 Louisville	AAA	98	294	65	8	1	3	--	--	84	20	27	27	3	74	4	9	1		1	0	.00	12	.221	.294	.286
1991 Louisville	AAA	60	165	46	7	0	7	--	--	74	16	28	24	1	39	4	2	0		0	3	.00	4	.279	.383	.448
1990 St. Louis	NL	5	15	2	1	0	1	(1	0)	6	2	1	0	0	3	0	0	0		0	0	.00	0	.133	.133	.400
1991 St. Louis	NL	6	7	2	0	0	0	(0	0)	2	0	0	1	0	3	0	0	0		0	0	.00	2	.286	.375	.286
2 ML YEARS		11	22	4	1	0	1	(1	0)	8	2	1	1	0	6	0	0	0		0	0	.00	2	.182	.217	.364

Phil Stephenson

Bats: Left Throws: Left Pos: PH Ht: 6' 1" Wt: 201 Born: 09/19/60 Age: 31

		BATTING																		BASERUNNING				PERCENTAGES		
Year Team	Lg	G	AB	H	2B	3B	HR	(Hm	Rd)	TB	R	RBI	TBB	IBB	SO	HBP	SH	SF		SB	CS	SB%	GDP	Avg	OBP	SLG
1989 2 ML Teams		27	38	9	0	0	2	(2	0)	15	4	2	5	0	5	0	2	0		1	0	1.00	0	.237	.326	.395
1990 San Diego	NL	103	182	38	9	1	4	(2	2)	61	26	19	30	1	43	0	0	1		2	1	.67	2	.209	.319	.335
1991 San Diego	NL	11	7	2	0	0	0	(0	0)	2	0	0	2	0	3	0	0	0		0	0	.00	0	.286	.444	.286
1989 Chicago	NL	17	21	3	0	0	0	(0	0)	3	0	0	2	0	3	0	0	0		1	0	1.00	0	.143	.217	.143
San Diego	NL	10	17	6	0	0	2	(2	0)	12	4	2	3	0	2	0	2	0		0	0	.00	0	.353	.450	.706
3 ML YEARS		141	227	49	9	1	6	(4	2)	78	30	21	37	1	51	0	2	1		3	1	.75	2	.216	.325	.344

Lee Stevens

Bats: Left Throws: Left Pos: 1B Ht: 6' 4" Wt: 219 Born: 07/10/67 Age: 24

		BATTING																		BASERUNNING				PERCENTAGES		
Year Team	Lg	G	AB	H	2B	3B	HR	(Hm	Rd)	TB	R	RBI	TBB	IBB	SO	HBP	SH	SF		SB	CS	SB%	GDP	Avg	OBP	SLG
1986 Salem	A	72	267	75	18	2	6	--	--	115	45	47	45	3	49	2	0	1		13	6	.68	6	.281	.387	.431
1987 Palm Sprngs	A	140	532	130	29	2	19	--	--	220	82	97	61	5	117	4	0	4		1	9	.10	18	.244	.324	.414
1988 Midland	AA	116	414	123	26	2	23	--	--	222	79	76	58	4	108	5	2	3		0	5	.00	16	.297	.388	.536
1989 Edmonton	AAA	127	446	110	29	9	14	--	--	199	72	74	61	3	115	4	0	2		5	3	.63	14	.247	.341	.446
1990 Edmonton	AAA	90	338	99	31	2	16	--	--	182	57	66	55	11	83	1	0	3		1	2	.33	10	.293	.390	.538
1991 Edmonton	AAA	123	481	151	29	3	19	--	--	243	75	96	37	4	78	2	0	4		4	1	.80	12	.314	.363	.505

Year	Team	Lg	G	AB	H	2B	3B	HR	(Hm	Rd)	TB	R	RBI	TBB	IBB	SO	HBP	SH	SF	SB	CS	SB%	GDP	Avg	OBP	SLG
1990	California	AL	67	248	53	10	0	7	(4	3)	84	28	32	22	3	75	0	2	3	1	1	.50	8	.214	.275	.339
1991	California	AL	18	58	17	7	0	0	(0	0)	24	8	9	6	2	12	0	1	1	2	2	.33	0	.293	.354	.414
	2 ML YEARS		85	306	70	17	0	7	(4	3)	108	36	41	28	5	87	0	3	4	2	3	.40	8	.229	.290	.353

Dave Stewart

Pitches: Right **Bats:** Right **Pos:** SP **Ht:** 6' 2" **Wt:** 200 **Born:** 02/19/57 **Age:** 35

			HOW MUCH HE PITCHED						WHAT HE GAVE UP												THE RESULTS					
Year	Team	Lg	G	GS	CG	GF	IP	BFP	H	R	ER	HR	SH	SF	HB	TBB	IBB	SO	WP	Bk	W	L	Pct.	ShO	Sv	ERA
1978	Los Angeles	NL	1	0	0	1	2	6	1	0	0	0	0	0	0	0	0	1	0	0	0	0	.000	0	0	0.00
1981	Los Angeles	NL	32	0	0	14	43	184	40	13	12	3	7	3	0	14	5	29	4	0	4	3	.571	0	6	2.51
1982	Los Angeles	NL	45	14	0	9	146.1	616	137	72	62	14	10	5	2	49	11	80	3	0	9	8	.529	0	1	3.81
1983	2 ML Teams		54	9	2	25	135	565	117	43	39	6	9	4	4	50	7	78	3	0	10	4	.714	0	8	2.60
1984	Texas	AL	32	27	3	2	192.1	847	193	106	101	26	4	5	4	87	3	119	12	0	7	14	.333	0	0	4.73
1985	2 ML Teams		46	5	0	32	85.2	383	91	57	52	13	5	2	2	41	5	66	7	1	0	6	.000	0	4	5.46
1986	2 ML Teams		37	17	4	4	161.2	700	152	76	71	16	4	7	3	69	0	111	10	3	9	5	.643	1	0	3.95
1987	Oakland	AL	37	37	8	0	261.1	1103	224	121	107	24	7	5	6	105	2	205	11	0	20	13	.606	1	0	3.68
1988	Oakland	AL	37	37	14	0	275.2	1156	240	111	99	14	7	9	3	110	5	192	14	16	21	12	.636	2	0	3.23
1989	Oakland	AL	36	36	8	0	257.2	1081	260	105	95	23	9	10	6	69	0	155	13	0	21	9	.700	0	0	3.32
1990	Oakland	AL	36	36	11	0	267	1088	226	84	76	16	10	10	5	83	1	166	8	0	22	11	.667	4	0	2.56
1991	Oakland	AL	35	35	2	0	226	1014	245	135	130	24	5	15	9	105	1	144	12	0	11	11	.500	1	0	5.18
1983	Los Angeles	NL	46	1	0	25	76	328	67	28	25	4	7	3	2	33	7	54	2	0	5	2	.714	0	8	2.96
	Texas	AL	8	8	2	0	59	237	50	15	14	2	2	1	2	17	0	24	1	0	5	2	.714	0	0	2.14
1985	Texas	AL	42	5	0	29	81.1	361	86	53	49	13	5	2	2	37	5	64	5	1	0	6	.000	0	4	5.42
	Philadelphia	NL	4	0	0	3	4.1	22	5	4	3	0	0	0	0	4	0	2	2	0	0	0	.000	0	0	6.23
1986	Philadelphia	NL	8	0	0	2	12.1	56	15	9	9	1	0	3	0	4	0	9	1	3	0	0	.000	0	0	6.57
	Oakland	AL	29	17	4	2	149.1	644	137	67	62	15	4	4	3	65	0	102	9	0	9	5	.643	1	0	3.74
	12 ML YEARS		428	253	52	87	2053.2	8743	1926	923	844	179	77	75	44	782	40	1346	97	20	134	96	.583	9	19	3.70

Dave Stieb

Pitches: Right **Bats:** Right **Pos:** SP **Ht:** 6' 1" **Wt:** 195 **Born:** 07/22/57 **Age:** 34

			HOW MUCH HE PITCHED						WHAT HE GAVE UP												THE RESULTS					
Year	Team	Lg	G	GS	CG	GF	IP	BFP	H	R	ER	HR	SH	SF	HB	TBB	IBB	SO	WP	Bk	W	L	Pct.	ShO	Sv	ERA
1979	Toronto	AL	18	18	7	0	129	563	139	70	62	11	4	4	4	48	3	52	3	1	8	8	.500	1	0	4.33
1980	Toronto	AL	34	32	14	0	243	1004	232	108	100	12	12	9	6	83	6	108	6	2	12	15	.444	4	0	3.70
1981	Toronto	AL	25	25	11	0	184	748	148	70	65	10	5	7	11	61	6	89	1	2	11	10	.524	2	0	3.18
1982	Toronto	AL	38	38	19	0	288.1	1187	271	116	104	27	10	3	5	75	4	141	3	1	17	14	.548	5	0	3.25
1983	Toronto	AL	36	36	14	0	278	1141	223	105	94	21	6	9	4	93	6	187	5	1	17	12	.586	4	0	3.04
1984	Toronto	AL	35	35	11	0	267	1085	215	87	84	19	8	6	11	88	1	198	2	0	16	8	.667	2	0	2.83
1985	Toronto	AL	36	36	8	0	265	1087	206	89	73	22	14	2	9	96	3	167	4	1	14	13	.519	2	0	2.48
1986	Toronto	AL	37	34	1	2	205	919	239	108	108	29	6	6	15	87	1	127	7	0	7	12	.368	1	1	4.74
1987	Toronto	AL	33	31	3	1	185	789	164	92	84	16	5	5	7	87	4	115	4	0	13	9	.591	1	0	4.09
1988	Toronto	AL	32	31	8	1	207.1	844	157	76	70	15	0	4	13	79	0	147	4	5	16	8	.667	4	0	3.04
1989	Toronto	AL	33	33	3	0	206.2	850	164	83	77	12	10	3	13	76	2	101	3	1	17	8	.680	2	0	3.35
1990	Toronto	AL	33	33	2	0	208.2	861	179	73	68	11	6	3	10	64	0	125	5	0	18	6	.750	2	0	2.93
1991	Toronto	AL	9	9	1	0	59.2	244	52	29	21	4	4	1	2	23	0	29	0	0	4	3	.571	0	0	3.17
	13 ML YEARS		399	391	102	4	2726.2	11322	2389	1119	1010	209	90	62	120	960	32	1586	47	14	170	126	.574	30	1	3.33

Kurt Stillwell

Bats: Both **Throws:** Right **Pos:** SS **Ht:** 5'11" **Wt:** 185 **Born:** 06/04/65 **Age:** 27

			BATTING																	BASERUNNING				PERCENTAGES		
Year	Team	Lg	G	AB	H	2B	3B	HR	(Hm	Rd)	TB	R	RBI	TBB	IBB	SO	HBP	SH	SF	SB	CS	SB%	GDP	Avg	OBP	SLG
1986	Cincinnati	NL	104	279	64	6	1	0	(0	0)	72	31	26	30	1	47	2	4	0	6	2	.75	5	.229	.309	.258
1987	Cincinnati	NL	131	395	102	20	7	4	(3	1)	148	54	33	32	2	50	2	2	2	4	6	.40	5	.258	.316	.375
1988	Kansas City	AL	128	459	115	28	5	10	(4	6)	183	63	53	47	0	76	3	6	3	6	5	.55	7	.251	.322	.399
1989	Kansas City	AL	130	463	121	20	5	7	(2	5)	176	52	54	42	2	64	3	5	3	6	4	.60	3	.261	.325	.380
1990	Kansas City	AL	144	506	126	35	4	3	(3	0)	178	60	51	39	1	60	4	4	7	0	2	.00	11	.249	.304	.352
1991	Kansas City	AL	122	385	102	17	1	6	(1	5)	139	44	51	33	5	56	1	5	4	3	4	.43	8	.265	.322	.361
	6 ML YEARS		759	2487	630	126	25	30	(13	17)	896	304	268	223	11	353	15	26	19	28	25	.53	39	.253	.316	.360

Todd Stottlemyre

Pitches: Right **Bats:** Left **Pos:** SP **Ht:** 6' 3" **Wt:** 195 **Born:** 05/20/65 **Age:** 27

			HOW MUCH HE PITCHED						WHAT HE GAVE UP												THE RESULTS					
Year	Team	Lg	G	GS	CG	GF	IP	BFP	H	R	ER	HR	SH	SF	HB	TBB	IBB	SO	WP	Bk	W	L	Pct.	ShO	Sv	ERA
1988	Toronto	AL	28	16	0	2	98	443	109	70	62	15	5	3	4	46	5	67	2	3	4	8	.333	0	0	5.69
1989	Toronto	AL	27	18	0	4	127.2	545	137	56	55	11	3	7	5	44	4	63	4	1	7	7	.500	0	0	3.88

Year	Team	Lg	G	GS	CG	GF	IP	BFP	H	R	ER	HR	SH	SF	HB	TBB	IBB	SO	WP	Bk	W	L	Pct.	ShO	Sv	ERA
1990	Toronto	AL	33	33	4	0	203	866	214	101	98	18	3	5	8	69	4	115	6	1	13	17	.433	0	0	4.34
1991	Toronto	AL	34	34	1	0	219	921	194	97	92	21	0	8	12	75	3	116	4	0	15	8	.652	0	0	3.78
	4 ML YEARS		122	101	5	6	647.2	2775	654	324	307	65	11	23	29	234	16	361	16	5	39	40	.494	0	0	4.27

Doug Strange

Bats: Both **Throws:** Right **Pos:** 3B **Ht:** 6' 2" **Wt:** 170 **Born:** 04/13/64 **Age:** 28

						BATTING												BASERUNNING				PERCENTAGES		
Year	Team	Lg	G	AB	H	2B	3B	HR	(Hm | Rd)	TB	R	RBI	TBB	IBB	SO	HBP	SH	SF	SB	CS	SB%	GDP	Avg	OBP	SLG
1989	Detroit	AL	64	196	42	4	1	1	(1 | 0)	51	16	14	17	0	36	1	3	0	3	3	.50	6	.214	.280	.260
1991	Chicago	NL	3	9	4	1	0	0	(0 | 0)	5	0	1	0	0	1	1	0	1	1	0	1.00	0	.444	.455	.556
	2 ML YEARS		67	205	46	5	1	1	(1 | 0)	56	16	15	17	0	37	2	3	1	4	3	.57	6	.224	.289	.273

Darryl Strawberry

Bats: Left **Throws:** Left **Pos:** RF **Ht:** 6' 6" **Wt:** 200 **Born:** 03/12/62 **Age:** 30

Year	Team	Lg	G	AB	H	2B	3B	HR	(Hm	Rd)	TB	R	RBI	TBB	IBB	SO	HBP	SH	SF	SB	CS	SB%	GDP	Avg	OBP	SLG
1983	New York	NL	122	420	108	15	7	26	(10	16)	215	63	74	47	4	128	4	0	2	19	6	.76	5	.257	.336	.512
1984	New York	NL	147	522	131	27	4	26	(8	18)	244	75	97	75	15	131	0	1	4	27	8	.77	8	.251	.343	.467
1985	New York	NL	111	393	109	15	4	29	(14	15)	219	78	79	73	13	96	1	0	3	26	11	.70	9	.277	.389	.557
1986	New York	NL	136	475	123	27	5	27	(11	16)	241	76	93	72	9	141	6	0	9	28	12	.70	4	.259	.358	.507
1987	New York	NL	154	532	151	32	5	39	(20	19)	310	108	104	97	13	122	7	0	4	36	12	.75	4	.284	.398	.583
1988	New York	NL	153	543	146	27	3	39	(21	18)	296	101	101	85	21	127	3	0	9	29	14	.67	6	.269	.366	.545
1989	New York	NL	134	476	107	26	1	29	(15	14)	222	69	77	61	13	105	1	0	3	11	4	.73	4	.225	.312	.466
1990	New York	NL	152	542	150	18	1	37	(24	13)	281	92	108	70	15	110	4	0	5	15	8	.65	5	.277	.361	.518
1991	Los Angeles	NL	139	505	134	22	4	28	(14	14)	248	86	99	75	4	125	3	0	5	10	8	.56	8	.265	.361	.491
	9 ML YEARS		1248	4408	1159	209	34	280	(137	143)	2276	748	832	655	112	1085	29	1	44	201	83	.71	53	.263	.359	.516

Franklin Stubbs

Bats: Left **Throws:** Left **Pos:** 1B **Ht:** 6' 2" **Wt:** 208 **Born:** 10/21/60 **Age:** 31

Year	Team	Lg	G	AB	H	2B	3B	HR	(Hm	Rd)	TB	R	RBI	TBB	IBB	SO	HBP	SH	SF	SB	CS	SB%	GDP	Avg	OBP	SLG
1984	Los Angeles	NL	87	217	42	2	3	8	(4	4)	74	22	17	24	3	63	0	3	1	2	2	.50	0	.194	.273	.341
1985	Los Angeles	NL	10	9	2	0	0	0	(0	0)	2	0	2	0	0	3	0	0	0	0	0	.00	0	.222	.222	.222
1986	Los Angeles	NL	132	420	95	11	1	23	(12	11)	177	55	58	37	11	107	2	4	2	7	1	.88	9	.226	.291	.421
1987	Los Angeles	NL	129	386	90	16	3	16	(6	10)	160	48	52	31	9	85	1	3	2	8	1	.89	7	.233	.290	.415
1988	Los Angeles	NL	115	242	54	13	0	8	(3	5)	91	30	34	23	3	61	1	2	5	11	3	.79	4	.223	.288	.376
1989	Los Angeles	NL	69	103	30	6	0	4	(1	3)	48	11	15	16	2	27	0	1	0	3	2	.60	3	.291	.387	.466
1990	Houston	NL	146	448	117	23	2	23	(9	14)	213	59	71	48	3	114	2	1	2	19	6	.76	4	.261	.334	.475
1991	Milwaukee	AL	103	362	77	16	2	11	(8	3)	130	48	38	35	3	71	2	0	5	13	4	.76	4	.213	.282	.359
	8 ML YEARS		791	2187	507	87	11	93	(43	50)	895	273	287	214	34	531	8	14	17	63	19	.77	31	.232	.300	.409

B.J. Surhoff

Bats: Left **Throws:** Right **Pos:** C **Ht:** 6' 1" **Wt:** 200 **Born:** 08/04/64 **Age:** 27

Year	Team	Lg	G	AB	H	2B	3B	HR	(Hm	Rd)	TB	R	RBI	TBB	IBB	SO	HBP	SH	SF	SB	CS	SB%	GDP	Avg	OBP	SLG
1987	Milwaukee	AL	115	395	118	22	3	7	(5	2)	167	50	68	36	1	30	0	5	9	11	10	.52	13	.299	.350	.423
1988	Milwaukee	AL	139	493	121	21	0	5	(2	3)	157	47	38	31	9	49	3	11	3	21	6	.78	12	.245	.292	.318
1989	Milwaukee	AL	126	436	108	17	4	5	(3	2)	148	42	55	25	1	29	3	3	10	14	12	.54	8	.248	.287	.339
1990	Milwaukee	AL	135	474	131	21	4	6	(4	2)	178	55	59	41	5	37	1	7	7	18	7	.72	8	.276	.331	.376
1991	Milwaukee	AL	143	505	146	19	4	5	(3	2)	188	57	68	26	2	33	0	13	9	5	8	.38	21	.289	.319	.372
	5 ML YEARS		658	2303	624	100	15	28	(17	11)	838	251	288	159	18	178	7	39	38	69	43	.62	62	.271	.315	.364

Rick Sutcliffe

Pitches: Right **Bats:** Left **Pos:** SP **Ht:** 6' 7" **Wt:** 215 **Born:** 06/21/56 **Age:** 36

			HOW MUCH HE PITCHED						WHAT HE GAVE UP												THE RESULTS				
Year	Team	Lg	G	GS	CG	GF	IP	BFP	H	R	ER	HR	SH	SF	HB	TBB	IBB	SO	WP	Bk	W	L	Pct.	ShO	Sv	ERA
1976	Los Angeles	NL	1	1	0	0	5	17	2	0	0	0	0	0	0	1	0	3	0	0	0	0	.000	0	0	0.00
1978	Los Angeles	NL	2	0	0	0	2	9	2	0	0	0	0	0	1	1	0	0	0	0	0	0	.000	0	0	0.00
1979	Los Angeles	NL	39	30	5	2	242	1016	217	104	93	16	16	9	2	97	6	117	8	6	17	10	.630	1	0	3.46
1980	Los Angeles	NL	42	10	1	19	110	491	122	73	68	10	4	3	1	55	2	59	4	5	3	9	.250	1	5	5.56
1981	Los Angeles	NL	14	6	0	5	47	197	41	24	21	5	1	2	2	20	2	16	0	0	2	2	.500	0	0	4.02
1982	Cleveland	AL	34	27	6	3	216	887	174	81	71	16	7	8	4	98	2	142	6	1	14	8	.636	1	1	2.96
1983	Cleveland	AL	36	35	10	0	243.1	1061	251	131	116	23	8	9	6	102	5	160	7	3	17	11	.607	2	0	4.29
1984	2 ML Teams		35	35	9	0	244.2	1030	234	113	99	16	5	4	3	85	3	213	6	3	20	6	.769	3	0	3.64
1985	Chicago	NL	20	20	6	0	130	549	119	51	46	12	3	4	3	44	3	102	6	0	8	8	.500	3	0	3.18
1986	Chicago	NL	28	27	4	0	176.2	764	166	92	91	18	6	2	1	96	8	122	13	1	5	14	.263	1	0	4.64

199

Year Team	Lg	G	GS	CG	GF	IP	BFP	H	R	ER	HR	SH	SF	HB	TBB	IBB	SO	WP	Bk	W	L	Pct.	ShO	Sv	ERA
1987 Chicago	NL	34	34	6	0	237.1	1012	223	106	97	24	9	8	4	106	14	174	9	4	18	10	.643	1	0	3.68
1988 Chicago	NL	32	32	12	0	226	958	232	97	97	18	17	5	2	70	9	144	11	4	13	14	.481	2	0	3.86
1989 Chicago	NL	35	34	5	0	229	938	202	98	93	18	15	10	2	69	8	153	12	6	16	11	.593	1	0	3.66
1990 Chicago	NL	5	5	0	0	21.1	97	25	14	14	2	1	2	0	12	0	7	4	0	0	2	.000	0	0	5.91
1991 Chicago	NL	19	18	0	0	96.2	422	96	52	44	4	5	8	0	45	2	52	2	2	6	5	.545	0	0	4.10
1984 Cleveland	AL	15	15	2	0	94.1	428	111	60	54	7	4	3	2	46	3	58	3	1	4	5	.444	0	0	5.15
Chicago	NL	20	20	7	0	150.1	602	123	53	45	9	1	1	1	39	0	155	3	2	16	1	.941	3	0	2.69
15 ML YEARS		376	314	64	29	2227	9448	2106	1036	950	182	97	74	31	901	64	1464	88	35	139	110	.558	16	6	3.84

Glenn Sutko

Bats: Right **Throws:** Right **Pos:** C **Ht:** 6' 3" **Wt:** 225 **Born:** 05/09/68 **Age:** 24

								BATTING												BASERUNNING				PERCENTAGES		
Year Team	Lg	G	AB	H	2B	3B	HR	(Hm	Rd)	TB	R	RBI	TBB	IBB	SO	HBP	SH	SF	SB	CS	SB%	GDP	Avg	OBP	SLG
1988 Billings	R	30	84	13	2	1	1	--	--	20	3	8	14	0	38	1	3	2	3	1	.75	2	.155	.277	.238
1989 Greensboro	A	109	333	78	21	0	7	--	--	120	44	41	47	1	105	4	0	3	1	3	.25	5	.234	.333	.360
1990 Cedar Rapds	A	4	10	3	0	0	0	--	--	3	0	0	0	0	2	1	0	0	0	0	.00	1	.300	.364	.300
Chattanooga	AA	53	174	29	7	1	2	--	--	44	12	11	8	1	66	1	0	0	1	1	.50	2	.167	.208	.253
1991 Chattanooga	AA	23	63	18	3	0	3	--	--	30	12	11	9	2	20	0	2	0	0	0	.00	1	.286	.375	.476
Nashville	AAA	45	134	28	2	1	3	--	--	41	9	15	22	3	67	0	0	0	1	0	1.00	3	.209	.321	.306
1990 Cincinnati	NL	1	1	0	0	0	0	(0	0)	0	0	0	0	0	0	0	0	0	0	0	.00	0	.000	.000	.000
1991 Cincinnati	NL	10	10	1	0	0	0	(0	0)	1	0	1	2	0	6	0	0	0	0	0	.00	0	.100	.250	.100
2 ML YEARS		11	11	1	0	0	0	(0	0)	1	0	1	2	0	7	0	0	0	0	0	.00	0	.091	.231	.091

Dale Sveum

Bats: Both **Throws:** Right **Pos:** SS/3B **Ht:** 6' 3" **Wt:** 185 **Born:** 11/23/63 **Age:** 28

								BATTING												BASERUNNING				PERCENTAGES		
Year Team	Lg	G	AB	H	2B	3B	HR	(Hm	Rd)	TB	R	RBI	TBB	IBB	SO	HBP	SH	SF	SB	CS	SB%	GDP	Avg	OBP	SLG
1986 Milwaukee	AL	91	317	78	13	2	7	(4	3)	116	35	35	32	0	63	1	5	1	4	3	.57	7	.246	.316	.366
1987 Milwaukee	AL	153	535	135	27	3	25	(9	16)	243	86	95	40	4	133	1	5	5	2	6	.25	11	.252	.303	.454
1988 Milwaukee	AL	129	467	113	14	4	9	(2	7)	162	41	51	21	0	122	1	3	3	1	0	1.00	6	.242	.274	.347
1990 Milwaukee	AL	48	117	23	7	0	1	(1	0)	33	15	12	12	0	30	2	0	2	0	1	.00	2	.197	.278	.282
1991 Milwaukee	AL	90	266	64	19	1	4	(3	1)	97	33	43	32	0	78	1	1	4	2	4	.33	8	.241	.320	.365
5 ML YEARS		511	1702	413	80	10	46	(19	27)	651	210	236	137	4	426	6	18	15	9	14	.39	34	.243	.299	.382

Russ Swan

Pitches: Left **Bats:** Left **Pos:** RP **Ht:** 6' 4" **Wt:** 215 **Born:** 01/03/64 **Age:** 28

				HOW MUCH HE PITCHED					WHAT HE GAVE UP											THE RESULTS					
Year Team	Lg	G	GS	CG	GF	IP	BFP	H	R	ER	HR	SH	SF	HB	TBB	IBB	SO	WP	Bk	W	L	Pct.	ShO	Sv	ERA
1989 San Francisco	NL	2	2	0	0	6.2	34	11	10	8	4	2	0	0	4	0	2	0	0	0	2	.000	0	0	10.80
1990 2 ML Teams		13	9	0	0	49.1	213	48	26	20	3	2	3	0	22	2	16	1	1	2	4	.333	0	0	3.65
1991 Seattle	AL	63	0	0	11	78.2	336	81	35	30	8	6	1	0	28	7	33	8	0	6	2	.750	0	2	3.43
1990 San Francisco	NL	2	1	0	0	2.1	18	6	4	1	0	0	0	0	4	0	1	1	0	0	1	.000	0	0	3.86
Seattle	AL	11	8	0	0	47	195	42	22	19	3	2	3	0	18	2	15	0	1	2	3	.400	0	0	3.64
3 ML YEARS		78	11	0	11	134.2	583	140	71	58	15	10	4	0	54	9	51	9	1	8	8	.500	0	2	3.88

Bill Swift

Pitches: Right **Bats:** Right **Pos:** RP **Ht:** 6' 0" **Wt:** 180 **Born:** 10/27/61 **Age:** 30

				HOW MUCH HE PITCHED					WHAT HE GAVE UP											THE RESULTS					
Year Team	Lg	G	GS	CG	GF	IP	BFP	H	R	ER	HR	SH	SF	HB	TBB	IBB	SO	WP	Bk	W	L	Pct.	ShO	Sv	ERA
1985 Seattle	AL	23	21	0	0	120.2	532	131	71	64	8	6	3	5	48	5	55	5	3	6	10	.375	0	0	4.77
1986 Seattle	AL	29	17	1	3	115.1	534	148	85	70	5	5	3	7	55	2	55	2	1	2	9	.182	0	0	5.46
1988 Seattle	AL	38	24	6	4	174.2	757	199	99	89	10	5	3	8	65	4	47	6	2	8	12	.400	1	0	4.59
1989 Seattle	AL	37	16	0	7	130	551	140	72	64	7	4	3	2	38	4	45	4	1	7	3	.700	0	1	4.43
1990 Seattle	AL	55	8	0	18	128	533	135	46	34	4	5	4	7	21	6	42	8	3	6	4	.600	0	6	2.39
1991 Seattle	AL	71	0	0	30	90.1	359	74	22	20	3	2	0	1	26	4	48	2	1	1	2	.333	0	17	1.99
6 ML YEARS		253	86	7	62	759	3266	827	395	341	37	27	16	30	253	24	292	27	11	30	40	.429	1	24	4.04

Greg Swindell

Pitches: Left **Bats:** Both **Pos:** SP **Ht:** 6' 3" **Wt:** 225 **Born:** 01/02/65 **Age:** 27

				HOW MUCH HE PITCHED					WHAT HE GAVE UP											THE RESULTS					
Year Team	Lg	G	GS	CG	GF	IP	BFP	H	R	ER	HR	SH	SF	HB	TBB	IBB	SO	WP	Bk	W	L	Pct.	ShO	Sv	ERA
1986 Cleveland	AL	9	9	1	0	61.2	255	57	35	29	9	3	1	1	15	0	46	3	2	5	2	.714	0	0	4.23
1987 Cleveland	AL	16	15	4	0	102.1	441	112	62	58	18	4	3	1	37	1	97	0	1	3	8	.273	1	0	5.10
1988 Cleveland	AL	33	33	12	0	242	988	234	97	86	18	9	5	1	45	3	180	5	0	18	14	.563	4	0	3.20
1989 Cleveland	AL	28	28	5	0	184.1	749	170	71	69	16	4	4	0	51	1	129	3	1	13	6	.684	2	0	3.37
1990 Cleveland	AL	34	34	3	0	214.2	912	245	110	105	27	8	6	1	47	2	135	3	2	12	9	.571	0	0	4.40

1991 Cleveland	AL	33	33	7	0	238	971	241	112	92	21	13	8	3	31	1	169	3	1	9	16	.360	0	0	3.48
6 ML YEARS		153	152	32	0	1043	4316	1059	487	439	109	41	27	7	226	8	756	17	7	60	55	.522	7	0	3.79

Pat Tabler

Bats: Right **Throws:** Right **Pos:** DH/1B **Ht:** 6' 2" **Wt:** 200 **Born:** 02/02/58 **Age:** 34

			BATTING																BASERUNNING				PERCENTAGES		
Year Team	Lg	G	AB	H	2B	3B	HR	(Hm	Rd)	TB	R	RBI	TBB	IBB	SO	HBP	SH	SF	SB	CS	SB%	GDP	Avg	OBP	SLG
1981 Chicago	NL	35	101	19	3	1	1	(1	0)	27	11	5	13	0	26	0	3	0	0	1	.00	4	.188	.281	.267
1982 Chicago	NL	25	85	20	4	2	1	(0	1)	31	9	7	6	0	20	1	0	2	0	0	.00	3	.235	.287	.365
1983 Cleveland	AL	124	430	125	23	5	6	(3	3)	176	56	65	56	1	63	1	0	5	2	4	.33	18	.291	.370	.409
1984 Cleveland	AL	144	473	137	21	3	10	(5	5)	194	66	68	47	2	62	3	0	5	3	1	.75	16	.290	.354	.410
1985 Cleveland	AL	117	404	111	18	3	5	(5	0)	150	47	59	27	2	55	2	2	3	0	6	.00	15	.275	.321	.371
1986 Cleveland	AL	130	473	154	29	2	6	(5	1)	205	61	48	29	3	75	3	2	1	3	1	.75	11	.326	.368	.433
1987 Cleveland	AL	151	553	170	34	3	11	(5	6)	243	66	86	51	6	84	6	3	5	5	2	.71	6	.307	.369	.439
1988 2 ML Teams		130	444	125	22	3	2	(0	2)	159	53	66	46	1	68	3	0	5	3	3	.50	9	.282	.349	.358
1989 Kansas City	AL	123	390	101	11	1	2	(2	0)	120	36	42	37	0	42	2	3	2	0	0	.00	14	.259	.325	.308
1990 2 ML Teams		92	238	65	15	1	2	(1	1)	88	18	29	23	2	29	2	0	3	0	2	.00	8	.273	.338	.370
1991 Toronto	AL	82	185	40	5	1	1	(1	0)	50	20	21	29	5	21	1	2	5	0	0	.00	3	.216	.318	.270
1988 Cleveland	AL	41	143	32	5	1	1	(0	1)	42	16	17	23	1	27	1	0	1	1	0	1.00	3	.224	.333	.294
Kansas City	AL	89	301	93	17	2	1	(0	1)	117	37	49	23	0	41	2	0	4	2	3	.40	6	.309	.358	.389
1990 Kansas City	AL	75	195	53	14	0	1	(0	1)	70	12	19	20	2	21	1	0	3	0	2	.00	8	.272	.338	.359
New York	NL	17	43	12	1	1	1	(1	0)	18	6	10	3	0	8	1	0	0	0	0	.00	0	.279	.340	.419
11 ML YEARS		1153	3776	1067	185	25	47	(28	19)	1443	443	496	364	22	545	24	15	36	16	20	.44	107	.283	.346	.382

Jeff Tackett

Bats: Right **Throws:** Right **Pos:** C **Ht:** 6' 2" **Wt:** 200 **Born:** 12/01/65 **Age:** 26

			BATTING																BASERUNNING				PERCENTAGES		
Year Team	Lg	G	AB	H	2B	3B	HR	(Hm	Rd)	TB	R	RBI	TBB	IBB	SO	HBP	SH	SF	SB	CS	SB%	GDP	Avg	OBP	SLG
1984 Bluefield	R	34	98	16	2	0	0	--	--	18	9	12	23	0	28	0	0	1	1	1	.50	1	.163	.317	.184
1985 Daytona Bch	A	40	103	20	5	2	0	--	--	29	8	10	13	0	16	1	0	1	1	3	.25	6	.194	.288	.282
Newark	A	62	187	39	6	0	0	--	--	45	21	22	22	0	33	2	3	1	2	2	.50	4	.209	.297	.241
1986 Hagerstown	A	83	246	70	15	1	0	--	--	87	53	21	36	0	36	5	0	1	16	5	.76	2	.285	.385	.354
1987 Charlotte	AA	61	205	46	6	1	0	--	--	54	18	13	12	0	34	2	1	1	5	5	.50	2	.224	.273	.263
1988 Charlotte	AA	81	272	56	9	0	0	--	--	65	24	18	42	0	46	2	0	1	6	4	.60	7	.206	.315	.239
1989 Rochester	AAA	67	199	36	3	1	2	--	--	47	13	17	19	0	45	1	2	2	3	1	.75	3	.181	.253	.236
1990 Rochester	AAA	108	306	73	8	3	4	--	--	99	37	33	47	0	50	7	3	0	4	8	.33	3	.239	.353	.324
1991 Rochester	AAA	126	433	102	18	2	6	--	--	142	64	50	54	0	60	2	4	3	3	3	.50	15	.236	.321	.328
1991 Baltimore	AL	6	8	1	0	0	0	(0	0)	1	1	0	2	0	2	0	1	0	0	0	.00	0	.125	.300	.125

Frank Tanana

Pitches: Left **Bats:** Left **Pos:** SP **Ht:** 6' 3" **Wt:** 195 **Born:** 07/03/53 **Age:** 38

		HOW MUCH HE PITCHED						WHAT HE GAVE UP											THE RESULTS					
Year Team	Lg	G	GS	CG	GF	IP	BFP	H	R	ER	HR	SH	SF	HB	TBB	IBB	SO	WP	Bk	W	L	Pct.	ShO	Sv	ERA
1973 California	AL	4	4	2	0	26	108	20	11	9	2	0	0	0	8	0	22	2	0	2	2	.500	1	0	3.12
1974 California	AL	39	35	12	2	269	1127	262	104	93	27	10	4	8	77	4	180	4	2	14	19	.424	4	0	3.11
1975 California	AL	34	33	16	1	257	1029	211	80	75	21	13	4	7	73	6	269	8	1	16	9	.640	5	0	2.63
1976 California	AL	34	34	23	0	288	1142	212	88	78	24	14	3	9	73	5	261	5	0	19	10	.655	2	0	2.44
1977 California	AL	31	31	20	0	241	973	201	72	68	19	8	7	12	61	2	205	8	1	15	9	.625	7	0	2.54
1978 California	AL	33	33	10	0	239	1014	239	108	97	26	8	10	9	60	7	137	5	8	18	12	.600	4	0	3.65
1979 California	AL	18	17	2	0	90	382	93	44	39	9	1	2	2	25	0	46	6	1	7	5	.583	1	0	3.90
1980 California	AL	32	31	7	1	204	870	223	107	94	18	8	4	8	45	0	113	3	1	11	12	.478	0	0	4.15
1981 Boston	AL	24	23	5	0	141	596	142	70	63	17	9	4	4	43	4	78	2	0	4	10	.286	2	0	4.02
1982 Texas	AL	30	30	7	0	194.1	832	199	102	91	16	13	4	7	55	10	87	0	1	7	18	.280	0	0	4.21
1983 Texas	AL	29	22	3	1	159.1	667	144	70	56	14	7	3	7	49	5	108	6	1	7	9	.438	0	0	3.16
1984 Texas	AL	35	35	9	0	246.1	1054	234	117	89	30	6	5	6	81	3	141	12	4	15	15	.500	1	0	3.25
1985 2 ML Teams		33	33	4	0	215	907	220	112	102	28	5	8	3	57	8	159	5	1	12	14	.462	0	0	4.27
1986 Detroit	AL	32	31	3	1	188.1	812	196	104	87	27	8	5	3	65	9	119	7	1	12	9	.571	1	0	4.16
1987 Detroit	AL	34	34	5	0	218.2	924	216	106	95	27	8	11	5	56	5	146	6	0	15	10	.600	3	0	3.91
1988 Detroit	AL	32	32	2	0	203	876	213	105	95	25	6	3	4	64	7	127	6	0	14	11	.560	0	0	4.21
1989 Detroit	AL	33	33	6	0	223.2	955	227	105	89	21	7	10	8	74	8	147	8	0	10	14	.417	1	0	3.58
1990 Detroit	AL	34	29	1	4	176.1	763	190	104	104	25	3	7	9	66	7	114	5	1	9	8	.529	0	1	5.31
1991 Detroit	AL	33	33	3	0	217.1	920	217	98	89	26	12	9	2	78	9	107	3	1	13	12	.520	2	0	3.69
1985 Texas	AL	13	13	0	0	77.2	340	89	53	51	15	2	4	1	23	2	52	3	0	2	7	.222	0	0	5.91
Detroit	AL	20	20	4	0	137.1	567	131	59	51	13	3	4	2	34	6	107	2	1	10	7	.588	0	0	3.34
19 ML YEARS		574	553	140	10	3797.1	15951	3659	1698	1513	398	146	103	113	1110	99	2566	101	24	220	208	.514	34	1	3.59

201

Kevin Tapani

Pitches: Right **Bats:** Right **Pos:** SP **Ht:** 6' 0" **Wt:** 187 **Born:** 02/18/64 **Age:** 28

			HOW MUCH HE PITCHED					WHAT HE GAVE UP									THE RESULTS					
Year Team	Lg	G	GS	CG	GF	IP	BFP	H	R	ER	HR	SH	SF	HB	TBB	IBB	SO	WP	Bk	W	L	Pct.	ShO	Sv	ERA
1989 2 ML Teams		8	5	0	1	40	169	39	18	17	3	1	2	0	12	1	23	0	1	2	2	.500	0	0	3.83
1990 Minnesota	AL	28	28	1	0	159.1	659	164	75	72	12	3	4	2	29	2	101	1	0	12	8	.600	1	0	4.07
1991 Minnesota	AL	34	34	4	0	244	974	225	84	81	23	9	6	2	40	0	135	3	3	16	9	.640	1	0	2.99
1989 New York	NL	3	0	0	1	7.1	31	5	3	3	1	0	1	0	4	0	2	0	1	0	0	.000	0	0	3.68
Minnesota	AL	5	5	0	0	32.2	138	34	15	14	2	1	1	0	8	1	21	0	0	2	2	.500	0	0	3.86
3 ML YEARS		70	67	5	1	443.1	1802	428	177	170	38	13	12	4	81	3	259	4	4	30	19	.612	2	0	3.45

Danny Tartabull

Bats: Right **Throws:** Right **Pos:** RF **Ht:** 6' 1" **Wt:** 210 **Born:** 10/30/62 **Age:** 29

					BATTING														BASERUNNING				PERCENTAGES		
Year Team	Lg	G	AB	H	2B	3B	HR	(Hm	Rd)	TB	R	RBI	TBB	IBB	SO	HBP	SH	SF	SB	CS	SB%	GDP	Avg	OBP	SLG
1984 Seattle	AL	10	20	6	1	0	2	(1	1)	13	3	7	2	0	3	1	0	1	0	0	.00	0	.300	.375	.650
1985 Seattle	AL	19	61	20	7	1	1	(0	1)	32	8	7	8	0	14	0	0	0	1	0	1.00	1	.328	.406	.525
1986 Seattle	AL	137	511	138	25	6	25	(13	12)	250	76	96	61	2	157	1	2	3	4	8	.33	10	.270	.347	.489
1987 Kansas City	AL	158	582	180	27	3	34	(15	19)	315	95	101	79	2	136	1	0	5	9	4	.69	14	.309	.390	.541
1988 Kansas City	AL	146	507	139	38	3	26	(15	11)	261	80	102	76	4	119	4	0	6	8	5	.62	10	.274	.369	.515
1989 Kansas City	AL	133	441	118	22	0	18	(9	9)	194	54	62	69	2	123	3	0	2	4	2	.67	12	.268	.369	.440
1990 Kansas City	AL	88	313	84	19	0	15	(5	10)	148	41	60	36	0	93	0	0	3	1	1	.50	9	.268	.341	.473
1991 Kansas City	AL	132	484	153	35	3	31	(13	18)	287	78	100	65	6	121	3	0	5	6	3	.67	9	.316	.397	.593
8 ML YEARS		823	2919	838	174	16	152	(71	81)	1500	435	535	396	16	766	13	2	25	33	23	.59	65	.287	.372	.514

Eddie Taubensee

Bats: Left **Throws:** Right **Pos:** C **Ht:** 6' 4" **Wt:** 205 **Born:** 10/31/68 **Age:** 23

					BATTING														BASERUNNING				PERCENTAGES		
Year Team	Lg	G	AB	H	2B	3B	HR	(Hm	Rd)	TB	R	RBI	TBB	IBB	SO	HBP	SH	SF	SB	CS	SB%	GDP	Avg	OBP	SLG
1986 Reds	R	35	107	21	3	0	1	--	--	27	8	11	11	0	33	0	0	0	0	1	.00	2	.196	.271	.252
1987 Billings	R	55	162	43	7	0	5	--	--	65	24	28	25	5	47	1	0	2	2	2	.50	2	.265	.363	.401
1988 Chattanooga	AA	5	12	2	0	0	1	--	--	5	2	1	3	0	4	0	0	0	0	0	.00	0	.167	.333	.417
Greensboro	A	103	330	85	16	1	10	--	--	133	36	41	44	5	93	4	1	1	8	4	.67	2	.258	.351	.403
1989 Cedar Rapds	A	59	196	39	5	0	8	--	--	68	25	22	25	4	55	2	0	0	4	1	.80	3	.199	.296	.347
Chattanooga	AA	45	127	24	2	0	3	--	--	35	11	13	11	2	28	0	1	3	0	0	.00	3	.189	.248	.276
1990 Cedar Rapds	A	122	417	108	22	1	16	--	--	180	57	62	51	5	98	4	1	4	11	4	.73	8	.259	.342	.432
1991 Colo Spngs	AAA	91	287	89	23	3	13	--	--	157	53	39	31	5	61	0	0	0	0	0	.00	6	.310	.377	.547
1991 Cleveland	AL	26	66	16	2	1	0	(0	0)	20	5	8	5	1	16	0	0	2	0	0	.00	1	.242	.288	.303

Wade Taylor

Pitches: Right **Bats:** Right **Pos:** SP **Ht:** 6' 1" **Wt:** 185 **Born:** 10/19/65 **Age:** 26

				HOW MUCH HE PITCHED					WHAT HE GAVE UP									THE RESULTS					
Year Team	Lg	G	GS	CG	GF	IP	BFP	H	R	ER	HR	SH	SF	HB	TBB	IBB	SO	WP	Bk	W	L	Pct.	ShO	Sv	ERA
1987 Bellingham	A	12	10	0	2	58.1	259	58	31	29	4	1	2	13	22	0	53	4	1	3	5	.375	0	1	4.47
1988 Ft.Lauderdle	A	24	17	7	4	122.2	532	109	53	47	3	6	3	7	57	6	90	7	3	4	11	.267	1	0	3.45
1989 Pr William	A	25	25	4	0	142.2	603	131	63	53	9	4	3	5	56	2	104	9	5	9	8	.529	2	0	3.34
1990 Albany	AA	12	12	1	0	84.1	332	71	30	27	3	3	4	2	18	0	44	2	2	6	4	.600	0	0	2.88
Columbus	AAA	14	14	4	0	98.2	402	91	25	24	3	3	3	3	30	0	57	0	3	6	4	.600	3	0	2.19
1991 Columbus	AAA	9	9	3	0	61	259	59	27	24	4	3	3	3	22	1	36	0	0	4	1	.800	1	0	3.54
1991 New York	AL	23	22	0	0	116.1	528	144	85	81	13	2	7	7	53	0	72	3	3	7	12	.368	0	0	6.27

Anthony Telford

Pitches: Right **Bats:** Right **Pos:** RP **Ht:** 6' 0" **Wt:** 184 **Born:** 03/06/66 **Age:** 26

				HOW MUCH HE PITCHED					WHAT HE GAVE UP									THE RESULTS					
Year Team	Lg	G	GS	CG	GF	IP	BFP	H	R	ER	HR	SH	SF	HB	TBB	IBB	SO	WP	Bk	W	L	Pct.	ShO	Sv	ERA
1987 Newark	A	6	2	0	3	17.2	72	16	2	2	0	0	0	0	3	0	27	0	0	1	0	1.000	0	0	1.02
Hagerstown	A	2	2	0	0	11.1	46	9	2	2	0	0	0	1	5	0	10	0	0	1	0	1.000	0	0	1.59
Rochester	AAA	1	0	0	0	2	9	0	0	0	0	0	0	0	0	0	3	1	0	0	0	.000	0	0	0.00
1988 Hagerstown	A	1	1	0	0	7	24	3	0	0	0	0	0	0	0	0	10	0	0	1	0	1.000	0	0	0.00
1989 Frederick	A	9	5	0	2	25.2	116	25	15	12	1	1	2	2	12	0	19	2	0	2	1	.667	0	1	4.21
1990 Frederick	A	8	8	1	0	53.2	207	35	15	10	1	0	0	4	11	1	49	4	0	4	2	.667	0	0	1.68
Hagerstown	AA	14	13	3	1	96	384	80	26	21	3	5	3	3	25	1	73	4	0	10	2	.833	1	0	1.97
1991 Rochester	AAA	27	25	3	0	157.1	666	166	82	69	18	5	3	4	48	2	115	7	1	12	9	.571	0	0	3.95
1990 Baltimore	AL	8	8	0	0	36.1	168	43	22	20	4	0	2	1	19	0	20	1	0	3	3	.500	0	0	4.95
1991 Baltimore	AL	9	1	0	4	26.2	109	27	12	12	3	0	1	0	6	1	24	1	0	0	0	.000	0	0	4.05
2 ML YEARS		17	9	0	4	63	277	70	34	32	7	0	3	1	25	1	44	2	0	3	3	.500	0	0	4.57

Garry Templeton

Bats: Both　**Throws:** Right　**Pos:** SS/1B/3B　　　　　**Ht:** 6' 0"　**Wt:** 205　**Born:** 03/24/56　**Age:** 36

Year Team	Lg	G	AB	H	2B	3B	HR	(Hm	Rd)	TB	R	RBI	TBB	IBB	SO	HBP	SH	SF	SB	CS	SB%	GDP	Avg	OBP	SLG
1976 St. Louis	NL	53	213	62	8	2	1	(1	0)	77	32	17	7	0	33	1	2	2	11	7	.61	1	.291	.314	.362
1977 St. Louis	NL	153	621	200	19	18	8	(2	6)	279	94	79	15	3	70	1	2	5	28	24	.54	9	.322	.336	.449
1978 St. Louis	NL	155	647	181	31	13	2	(1	1)	244	82	47	22	3	87	1	2	3	34	11	.76	7	.280	.303	.377
1979 St. Louis	NL	154	672	211	32	19	9	(2	7)	308	105	62	18	4	91	1	2	3	26	10	.72	8	.314	.331	.458
1980 St. Louis	NL	118	504	161	19	9	4	(1	3)	210	83	43	18	6	43	0	1	1	31	15	.67	13	.319	.342	.417
1981 St. Louis	NL	80	333	96	16	8	1	(1	0)	131	47	33	14	3	55	0	1	2	8	12	.40	4	.288	.315	.393
1982 San Diego	NL	141	563	139	25	8	6	(2	4)	198	76	64	26	7	82	1	6	5	27	16	.63	19	.247	.279	.352
1983 San Diego	NL	126	460	121	20	2	3	(1	2)	154	39	40	21	7	57	0	7	2	16	6	.73	16	.263	.294	.335
1984 San Diego	NL	148	493	127	19	3	2	(2	0)	158	40	35	39	23	81	1	0	2	8	3	.73	10	.258	.312	.320
1985 San Diego	NL	148	546	154	30	2	6	(4	2)	206	63	55	41	24	88	1	5	3	16	6	.73	5	.282	.332	.377
1986 San Diego	NL	147	510	126	21	2	2	(1	1)	157	42	44	35	21	86	1	1	2	10	5	.67	12	.247	.296	.308
1987 San Diego	NL	148	510	113	13	5	5	(2	3)	151	42	48	42	11	92	1	5	3	14	3	.82	15	.222	.281	.296
1988 San Diego	NL	110	362	90	15	7	3	(3	0)	128	35	36	20	10	50	0	7	3	8	2	.80	6	.249	.286	.354
1989 San Diego	NL	142	506	129	26	3	6	(5	1)	179	43	40	23	12	80	0	4	3	1	3	.25	15	.255	.286	.354
1990 San Diego	NL	144	505	125	25	3	9	(6	3)	183	45	59	24	7	59	0	8	4	1	4	.20	17	.248	.280	.362
1991 2 ML Teams		112	276	61	10	2	3	(2	1)	84	25	26	10	3	38	0	4	3	3	2	.60	10	.221	.246	.304
1991 San Diego	NL	32	57	11	1	1	1	(1	0)	17	5	6	1	0	9	0	0	1	0	1	.00	3	.193	.203	.298
New York	NL	80	219	50	9	1	2	(1	1)	67	20	20	9	3	29	0	4	2	3	1	.75	7	.228	.257	.306
16 ML YEARS		2079	7721	2096	329	106	70	(36	34)	2847	893	728	375	144	1092	9	57	46	242	129	.65	167	.271	.304	.369

Walt Terrell

Pitches: Right　**Bats:** Left　**Pos:** SP　　　　　**Ht:** 6' 2"　**Wt:** 205　**Born:** 05/11/58　**Age:** 34

Year Team	Lg	G	GS	CG	GF	IP	BFP	H	R	ER	HR	SH	SF	HB	TBB	IBB	SO	WP	Bk	W	L	Pct.	ShO	Sv	ERA
1982 New York	NL	3	3	0	0	21	97	22	12	8	2	1	0	0	14	2	8	1	1	0	3	.000	0	0	3.43
1983 New York	NL	21	20	4	1	133.2	561	123	57	53	7	9	5	2	55	7	59	5	0	8	8	.500	2	0	3.57
1984 New York	NL	33	33	3	0	215	926	232	99	84	16	11	8	4	80	1	114	6	0	11	12	.478	1	0	3.52
1985 Detroit	AL	34	34	5	0	229	983	221	107	98	9	11	7	4	95	5	130	5	0	15	10	.600	3	0	3.85
1986 Detroit	AL	34	33	9	1	217.1	918	199	116	110	30	2	3	3	98	5	93	5	0	15	12	.556	2	0	4.56
1987 Detroit	AL	35	35	10	0	244.2	1057	254	123	110	30	3	10	3	94	7	143	8	0	17	10	.630	1	0	4.05
1988 Detroit	AL	29	29	11	0	206.1	870	199	101	91	20	13	6	2	78	8	84	7	2	7	16	.304	1	0	3.97
1989 2 ML Teams		32	32	5	0	206.1	882	236	117	103	23	10	4	2	50	1	93	6	0	11	18	.379	2	0	4.49
1990 2 ML Teams		29	28	0	0	158	710	184	98	92	20	9	3	12	57	4	64	7	2	8	11	.421	0	0	5.24
1991 Detroit	AL	35	33	8	1	218.2	954	257	115	103	16	10	9	2	79	10	80	8	0	12	14	.462	1	0	4.24
1989 San Diego	NL	19	19	4	0	123.1	520	134	65	55	14	8	2	0	26	1	63	4	0	5	13	.278	1	0	4.01
New York	AL	13	13	1	0	83	362	102	52	48	9	2	2	2	24	0	30	2	0	6	5	.545	1	0	5.20
1990 Pittsburgh	NL	16	16	0	0	82.2	377	98	59	54	13	6	2	4	33	1	34	7	2	2	7	.222	0	0	5.88
Detroit	AL	13	12	0	0	75.1	333	86	39	38	7	3	1	8	24	3	30	0	0	6	4	.600	0	0	4.54
10 ML YEARS		285	280	55	3	1850	7958	1927	945	852	173	79	55	34	700	50	868	58	5	104	114	.477	14	0	4.14

Scott Terry

Pitches: Right　**Bats:** Right　**Pos:** RP　　　　　**Ht:** 5'11"　**Wt:** 195　**Born:** 11/21/59　**Age:** 32

Year Team	Lg	G	GS	CG	GF	IP	BFP	H	R	ER	HR	SH	SF	HB	TBB	IBB	SO	WP	Bk	W	L	Pct.	ShO	Sv	ERA
1986 Cincinnati	NL	28	3	0	7	55.2	258	66	40	38	8	5	1	0	32	3	32	2	0	1	2	.333	0	0	6.14
1987 St. Louis	NL	11	0	0	2	13.1	59	13	5	5	0	1	0	0	8	2	9	0	0	0	0	.000	0	0	3.38
1988 St. Louis	NL	51	11	1	14	129.1	524	119	48	42	5	6	3	0	34	6	65	1	2	9	6	.600	0	3	2.92
1989 St. Louis	NL	31	24	1	5	148.2	619	142	65	59	14	8	4	3	43	6	69	2	2	8	10	.444	0	2	3.57
1990 St. Louis	NL	50	2	0	26	72	323	75	45	38	7	3	5	4	27	5	35	2	0	2	6	.250	0	2	4.75
1991 St. Louis	NL	65	0	0	13	80.1	339	76	31	25	1	2	0	0	32	14	52	0	0	4	4	.500	0	1	2.80
6 ML YEARS		236	40	2	67	499.1	2122	491	234	207	35	25	13	7	176	36	262	7	4	24	28	.462	0	8	3.73

Mickey Tettleton

Bats: Both　**Throws:** Right　**Pos:** C/DH　　　　　**Ht:** 6' 2"　**Wt:** 212　**Born:** 09/16/60　**Age:** 31

Year Team	Lg	G	AB	H	2B	3B	HR	(Hm	Rd)	TB	R	RBI	TBB	IBB	SO	HBP	SH	SF	SB	CS	SB%	GDP	Avg	OBP	SLG
1984 Oakland	AL	33	76	20	2	1	1	(1	0)	27	10	5	11	0	21	0	0	1	0	0	.00	3	.263	.352	.355
1985 Oakland	AL	78	211	53	12	0	3	(1	2)	74	23	15	28	0	59	2	5	0	2	2	.50	6	.251	.344	.351
1986 Oakland	AL	90	211	43	9	0	10	(4	6)	82	26	35	39	0	51	1	7	4	7	1	.88	3	.204	.325	.389
1987 Oakland	AL	82	211	41	3	0	8	(5	3)	68	19	26	30	0	65	0	5	2	1	1	.50	3	.194	.292	.322
1988 Baltimore	AL	86	283	74	11	1	11	(7	4)	120	31	37	28	2	70	2	1	2	0	1	.00	9	.261	.330	.424

Year	Team	Lg	G	AB	H	2B	3B	HR	(Hm	Rd)	TB	R	RBI	TBB	IBB	SO	HBP	SH	SF	SB	CS	SB%	GDP	Avg	OBP	SLG
1989	Baltimore	AL	117	411	106	21	2	26	(15	11)	209	72	65	73	4	117	1	1	3	3	2	.60	8	.258	.369	.509
1990	Baltimore	AL	135	444	99	21	2	15	(8	7)	169	68	51	106	3	160	5	0	4	2	4	.33	7	.223	.376	.381
1991	Detroit	AL	154	501	132	17	2	31	(15	16)	246	85	89	101	9	131	2	0	4	3	3	.50	12	.263	.387	.491
8 ML YEARS			775	2348	568	96	8	105	(56	49)	995	334	323	416	18	674	13	19	20	18	14	.56	51	.242	.356	.424

Tim Teufel

Bats: Right **Throws:** Right **Pos:** 2B/3B   **Ht:** 6' 0" **Wt:** 175 **Born:** 07/07/58 **Age:** 33

						BATTING														BASERUNNING				PERCENTAGES		
Year	Team	Lg	G	AB	H	2B	3B	HR	(Hm	Rd)	TB	R	RBI	TBB	IBB	SO	HBP	SH	SF	SB	CS	SB%	GDP	Avg	OBP	SLG
1983	Minnesota	AL	21	78	24	7	1	3	(3	0)	42	11	6	2	0	8	0	2	0	0	0	.00	1	.308	.325	.538
1984	Minnesota	AL	157	568	149	30	3	14	(9	5)	227	76	61	76	8	73	2	2	4	1	3	.25	18	.262	.349	.400
1985	Minnesota	AL	138	434	113	24	3	10	(6	4)	173	58	50	48	2	70	3	7	4	4	2	.67	14	.260	.335	.399
1986	New York	NL	93	279	69	20	1	4	(2	2)	103	35	31	32	1	42	1	3	3	1	2	.33	6	.247	.324	.369
1987	New York	NL	97	299	92	29	0	14	(4	10)	163	55	61	44	2	53	2	3	2	3	2	.60	7	.308	.398	.545
1988	New York	NL	90	273	64	20	0	4	(1	3)	96	35	31	29	1	41	1	2	4	0	1	.00	6	.234	.306	.352
1989	New York	NL	83	219	56	7	2	2	(1	1)	73	27	15	32	1	50	1	0	2	1	3	.25	4	.256	.350	.333
1990	New York	NL	80	175	43	11	0	10	(4	6)	84	28	24	15	1	33	0	1	1	0	0	.00	5	.246	.304	.480
1991	2 ML Teams		117	341	74	16	0	12	(6	6)	126	41	44	51	4	77	1	1	4	9	3	.75	8	.217	.319	.370
1991	New York	NL	20	34	4	0	0	1	(1	0)	7	2	2	2	0	8	0	0	0	1	1	.50	0	.118	.167	.206
	San Diego	NL	97	307	70	16	0	11	(5	6)	119	39	42	49	4	69	1	1	4	8	2	.80	8	.228	.334	.388
9 ML YEARS			876	2666	684	164	10	73	(36	37)	1087	366	323	329	20	447	11	24	22	19	16	.54	69	.257	.338	.408

Bob Tewksbury

Pitches: Right **Bats:** Right **Pos:** SP   **Ht:** 6' 4" **Wt:** 200 **Born:** 11/30/60 **Age:** 31

			HOW MUCH HE PITCHED						WHAT HE GAVE UP										THE RESULTS					
Year	Team	Lg	G	GS	CG	GF	IP	BFP	H	R	ER	HR	SH	SF	HB	TBB	IBB	SO	WP	Bk	W	L	Pct.	ShO	Sv	ERA
1986	New York	AL	23	20	2	0	130.1	558	144	58	48	8	4	7	5	31	0	49	3	2	9	5	.643	0	0	3.31
1987	2 ML Teams		15	9	0	4	51.1	242	79	41	38	6	5	1	1	20	3	22	1	2	1	8	.111	0	0	6.66
1988	Chicago	NL	1	1	0	0	3.1	18	6	5	3	1	0	1	0	2	0	1	0	0	0	0	.000	0	0	8.10
1989	St. Louis	NL	7	4	1	2	30	125	25	12	11	2	1	1	2	10	3	17	0	0	1	0	1.000	1	0	3.30
1990	St. Louis	NL	28	20	3	1	145.1	595	151	67	56	7	5	7	3	15	3	50	2	0	10	9	.526	2	1	3.47
1991	St. Louis	NL	30	30	3	0	191	798	206	86	69	13	12	10	5	38	2	75	0	0	11	12	.478	0	0	3.25
1987	New York	AL	8	6	0	1	33.1	149	47	26	25	5	2	0	1	7	0	12	0	0	1	4	.200	0	0	6.75
	Chicago	NL	7	3	0	3	18	93	32	15	13	1	3	1	0	13	3	10	1	2	0	4	.000	0	0	6.50
6 ML YEARS			104	84	9	7	551.1	2336	611	269	225	37	27	27	16	116	11	214	6	4	32	34	.485	3	1	3.67

Bobby Thigpen

Pitches: Right **Bats:** Right **Pos:** RP   **Ht:** 6' 3" **Wt:** 195 **Born:** 07/17/63 **Age:** 28

			HOW MUCH HE PITCHED						WHAT HE GAVE UP										THE RESULTS					
Year	Team	Lg	G	GS	CG	GF	IP	BFP	H	R	ER	HR	SH	SF	HB	TBB	IBB	SO	WP	Bk	W	L	Pct.	ShO	Sv	ERA
1986	Chicago	AL	20	0	0	14	35.2	142	26	7	7	1	1	1	1	12	0	20	0	0	2	0	1.000	0	7	1.77
1987	Chicago	AL	51	0	0	37	89	369	86	30	27	10	6	0	3	24	5	52	0	0	7	5	.583	0	16	2.73
1988	Chicago	AL	68	0	0	59	90	398	96	38	33	6	4	5	4	33	3	62	6	2	5	8	.385	0	34	3.30
1989	Chicago	AL	61	0	0	56	79	336	62	34	33	10	5	5	1	40	3	47	2	1	2	6	.250	0	34	3.76
1990	Chicago	AL	77	0	0	73	88.2	347	60	20	18	5	4	3	1	32	3	70	2	0	4	6	.400	0	57	1.83
1991	Chicago	AL	67	0	0	58	69.2	309	63	32	27	10	7	3	4	38	8	47	2	0	7	5	.583	0	30	3.49
6 ML YEARS			344	0	0	297	452	1901	393	161	145	42	27	17	14	179	22	298	12	3	27	30	.474	0	178	2.89

Frank Thomas

Bats: Right **Throws:** Right **Pos:** DH/1B   **Ht:** 6' 5" **Wt:** 240 **Born:** 05/27/68 **Age:** 24

						BATTING														BASERUNNING				PERCENTAGES		
Year	Team	Lg	G	AB	H	2B	3B	HR	(Hm	Rd)	TB	R	RBI	TBB	IBB	SO	HBP	SH	SF	SB	CS	SB%	GDP	Avg	OBP	SLG
1989	White Sox	R	17	52	19	5	0	1	--	--	27	8	11	11	0	3	1	0	2	1	0	1.00	0	.365	.470	.519
	Sarasota	A	55	188	52	9	1	4	--	--	75	27	30	31	0	33	3	0	1	0	1	.00	6	.277	.386	.399
1990	Birmingham	AA	109	353	114	27	5	18	--	--	205	85	71	112	2	74	5	0	4	7	5	.58	13	.323	.487	.581
1990	Chicago	AL	60	191	63	11	3	7	(2	5)	101	39	31	44	0	54	2	0	3	0	1	.00	5	.330	.454	.529
1991	Chicago	AL	158	559	178	31	2	32	(24	8)	309	104	109	138	13	112	1	0	2	1	2	.33	20	.318	.453	.553
2 ML YEARS			218	750	241	42	5	39	(26	13)	410	143	140	182	13	166	3	0	5	1	3	.25	25	.321	.453	.547

Jim Thome

Bats: Left **Throws:** Right **Pos:** 3B   **Ht:** 6' 3" **Wt:** 200 **Born:** 08/27/70 **Age:** 21

						BATTING														BASERUNNING				PERCENTAGES		
Year	Team	Lg	G	AB	H	2B	3B	HR	(Hm	Rd)	TB	R	RBI	TBB	IBB	SO	HBP	SH	SF	SB	CS	SB%	GDP	Avg	OBP	SLG
1989	Indians	R	55	186	44	8	3	0	--	--	55	22	22	21	1	33	1	3	2	6	4	.60	5	.237	.314	.296
1990	Burlington	R	34	118	44	7	1	12	--	--	89	31	34	27	3	18	4	0	4	6	3	.67	2	.373	.503	.754
	Kinston	A	33	117	36	4	1	4	--	--	54	19	16	24	0	26	1	0	1	4	1	.80	4	.308	.427	.462
1991	Canton-Akrn	AA	84	294	99	20	2	5	--	--	138	47	45	44	4	58	4	0	3	8	2	.80	7	.337	.426	.469

204

Team	Lg	G	AB	H	2B	3B	HR	(Hm	Rd)	TB	R	RBI	TBB	IBB	SO	HBP	SH	SF	SB	CS	SB%	GDP	Avg	OBP	SLG
Colo Sprngs	AAA	41	151	43	7	3	2	--	--	62	20	28	12	0	29	0	0	3	0	0	.00	4	.285	.331	.411
1991 Cleveland	AL	27	98	25	4	2	1	(0	1)	36	7	9	5	1	16	1	0	0	1	1	.50	4	.255	.298	.367

Milt Thompson

Bats: Left **Throws:** Right **Pos:** LF **Ht:** 5'11" **Wt:** 170 **Born:** 01/05/59 **Age:** 33

								BATTING											BASERUNNING				PERCENTAGES		
Year Team	Lg	G	AB	H	2B	3B	HR	(Hm	Rd)	TB	R	RBI	TBB	IBB	SO	HBP	SH	SF	SB	CS	SB%	GDP	Avg	OBP	SLG
1984 Atlanta	NL	25	99	30	1	0	2	(0	2)	37	16	4	11	1	11	0	1	0	14	2	.88	1	.303	.373	.374
1985 Atlanta	NL	73	182	55	7	2	0	(0	0)	66	17	6	7	0	36	3	1	0	9	4	.69	1	.302	.339	.363
1986 Philadelphia	NL	96	299	75	7	1	6	(4	2)	102	38	23	26	1	62	1	4	2	19	4	.83	4	.251	.311	.341
1987 Philadelphia	NL	150	527	159	26	9	7	(3	4)	224	86	43	42	2	87	0	3	3	46	10	.82	5	.302	.351	.425
1988 Philadelphia	NL	122	378	109	16	2	2	(1	1)	135	53	33	39	6	59	1	2	3	17	9	.65	8	.288	.354	.357
1989 St. Louis	NL	155	545	158	28	8	4	(2	2)	214	60	68	39	5	91	4	0	3	27	8	.77	12	.290	.340	.393
1990 St. Louis	NL	135	418	91	14	7	6	(3	3)	137	42	30	39	5	60	5	1	0	25	5	.83	4	.218	.292	.328
1991 St. Louis	NL	115	326	100	16	5	1	(4	2)	144	55	34	32	7	53	0	2	1	16	9	.64	4	.307	.368	.442
8 ML YEARS		871	2774	777	115	34	33	(17	16)	1059	367	241	235	27	459	14	14	12	173	51	.77	39	.280	.338	.382

Robby Thompson

Bats: Right **Throws:** Right **Pos:** 2B **Ht:** 5'11" **Wt:** 170 **Born:** 05/10/62 **Age:** 30

								BATTING											BASERUNNING				PERCENTAGES		
Year Team	Lg	G	AB	H	2B	3B	HR	(Hm	Rd)	TB	R	RBI	TBB	IBB	SO	HBP	SH	SF	SB	CS	SB%	GDP	Avg	OBP	SLG
1986 San Francisco	NL	149	549	149	27	3	7	(0	7)	203	73	47	42	0	112	5	18	1	12	15	.44	11	.271	.328	.370
1987 San Francisco	NL	132	420	110	26	5	10	(7	3)	176	62	44	40	3	91	8	6	0	16	11	.59	8	.262	.338	.419
1988 San Francisco	NL	138	477	126	24	6	7	(3	4)	183	66	48	40	0	111	4	14	5	14	5	.74	7	.264	.323	.384
1989 San Francisco	NL	148	547	132	26	11	13	(7	6)	219	91	50	51	0	133	13	9	0	12	2	.86	6	.241	.321	.400
1990 San Francisco	NL	144	498	122	22	3	15	(8	7)	195	67	56	34	1	96	6	8	3	14	4	.78	9	.245	.299	.392
1991 San Francisco	NL	144	492	129	24	5	19	(11	8)	220	74	48	63	2	95	6	11	1	14	7	.67	5	.262	.352	.447
6 ML YEARS		855	2983	768	149	33	71	(36	35)	1196	433	293	270	6	638	42	66	10	82	44	.65	46	.257	.327	.401

Dickie Thon

Bats: Right **Throws:** Right **Pos:** SS **Ht:** 5'11" **Wt:** 176 **Born:** 06/20/58 **Age:** 34

								BATTING											BASERUNNING				PERCENTAGES		
Year Team	Lg	G	AB	H	2B	3B	HR	(Hm	Rd)	TB	R	RBI	TBB	IBB	SO	HBP	SH	SF	SB	CS	SB%	GDP	Avg	OBP	SLG
1979 California	AL	35	56	19	3	0	0	(0	0)	22	6	8	5	0	10	0	1	0	0	0	.00	2	.339	.393	.393
1980 California	AL	80	267	68	12	2	0	(0	0)	84	32	15	10	0	28	1	5	2	7	5	.58	5	.255	.282	.315
1981 Houston	NL	49	95	26	6	0	0	(0	0)	32	13	3	9	1	13	0	1	0	6	1	.86	3	.274	.337	.337
1982 Houston	NL	136	496	137	31	10	3	(1	2)	197	73	36	37	2	48	1	5	1	37	8	.82	4	.276	.327	.397
1983 Houston	NL	154	619	177	28	9	20	(4	16)	283	81	79	54	10	73	2	3	8	34	16	.68	12	.286	.341	.457
1984 Houston	NL	5	17	6	0	1	0	(0	0)	8	3	1	0	0	4	1	0	0	0	1	.00	1	.353	.389	.471
1985 Houston	NL	84	251	63	6	1	6	(3	3)	89	26	29	18	4	50	0	1	2	8	3	.73	2	.251	.299	.355
1986 Houston	NL	106	278	69	13	1	3	(0	3)	93	24	21	29	5	49	0	1	1	6	5	.55	8	.248	.318	.335
1987 Houston	NL	32	66	14	1	0	1	(0	1)	18	6	3	16	3	13	0	1	0	3	0	1.00	1	.212	.366	.273
1988 San Diego	NL	95	258	68	12	2	1	(0	1)	87	36	18	33	0	49	1	2	2	19	4	.83	4	.264	.347	.337
1989 Philadelphia	NL	136	435	118	18	4	15	(8	7)	189	45	60	33	6	81	0	1	3	6	3	.67	6	.271	.321	.434
1990 Philadelphia	NL	149	552	141	20	4	8	(3	5)	193	54	48	37	10	77	3	1	2	12	5	.71	14	.255	.305	.350
1991 Philadelphia	NL	146	539	136	18	4	9	(4	5)	189	44	44	25	6	84	0	2	4	11	5	.69	9	.252	.283	.351
13 ML YEARS		1207	3929	1042	168	38	66	(23	43)	1484	443	365	306	47	579	9	24	25	149	56	.73	71	.265	.318	.378

Gary Thurman

Bats: Right **Throws:** Right **Pos:** LF/RF **Ht:** 5'10" **Wt:** 175 **Born:** 11/12/64 **Age:** 27

								BATTING											BASERUNNING				PERCENTAGES		
Year Team	Lg	G	AB	H	2B	3B	HR	(Hm	Rd)	TB	R	RBI	TBB	IBB	SO	HBP	SH	SF	SB	CS	SB%	GDP	Avg	OBP	SLG
1987 Kansas City	AL	27	81	24	2	0	0	(0	0)	26	12	5	8	0	20	0	1	0	7	2	.78	1	.296	.360	.321
1988 Kansas City	AL	35	66	11	1	0	0	(0	0)	12	6	2	4	0	20	0	0	0	5	1	.83	0	.167	.214	.182
1989 Kansas City	AL	72	87	17	2	1	0	(0	0)	21	24	5	15	0	26	0	2	1	16	0	1.00	0	.195	.311	.241
1990 Kansas City	AL	23	60	14	3	0	0	(0	0)	17	5	3	2	0	12	0	1	0	1	1	.50	2	.233	.258	.283
1991 Kansas City	AL	80	184	51	9	0	2	(1	1)	66	24	13	11	0	42	1	3	1	15	5	.75	4	.277	.320	.359
5 ML YEARS		237	478	117	17	1	2	(1	1)	142	71	28	40	0	120	1	7	2	44	9	.83	7	.245	.303	.297

Mike Timlin

Pitches: Right **Bats:** Right **Pos:** RP/SP **Ht:** 6'4" **Wt:** 205 **Born:** 03/10/66 **Age:** 26

						HOW MUCH HE PITCHED				WHAT HE GAVE UP									THE RESULTS				
Year Team	Lg	G	GS	CG	GF	IP	BFP	H	R	ER	HR	SH	SF	HB	TBB	IBB	SO	WP	Bk	W	L	Pct.	ShO	Sv	ERA
1987 Medicne Hat	R	13	12	2	0	75.1	326	79	50	43	4	1	2	5	26	0	66	9	5	4	8	.333	0	0	5.14
1988 Myrtle Bch	A	35	22	0	1	151	653	119	68	48	4	2	2	19	77	2	106	8	4	10	6	.625	0	0	2.86
1989 Dunedin	A	33	7	1	16	88.2	397	90	44	32	2	9	3	5	36	2	64	10	3	5	8	.385	0	7	3.25

205

1990	Dunedin	A	42	0	0	40	50.1	203	36	11	8	0	3	0	1	16	2	46	3	0	7	2	.778	0	22	1.43
	Knoxville	AA	17	0	0	15	26	105	20	6	5	0	0	0	1	7	1	21	0	0	1	2	.333	0	8	1.73
1991	Toronto	AL	63	3	0	17	108.1	463	94	43	38	6	6	2	1	50	11	85	5	0	11	6	.647	0	3	3.16

Ron Tingley

Bats: Right   **Throws:** Right   **Pos:** C   **Ht:** 6' 2"   **Wt:** 194   **Born:** 05/27/59   **Age:** 33

							BATTING													BASERUNNING				PERCENTAGES		
Year	Team	Lg	G	AB	H	2B	3B	HR	(Hm	Rd)	TB	R	RBI	TBB	IBB	SO	HBP	SH	SF	SB	CS	SB%	GDP	Avg	OBP	SLG
1985	Calgary	AAA	83	277	70	11	3	11	--	--	120	36	47	30	1	74	2	2	0	3	3	.50	11	.253	.330	.433
1986	Richmond	AAA	9	23	4	0	0	0	--	--	4	1	1	0	0	9	0	1	0	1	0	1.00	0	.174	.174	.174
	Maine	AAA	49	151	31	2	1	3	--	--	44	12	12	12	0	27	0	2	1	1	0	1.00	7	.205	.262	.291
1987	Buffalo	AAA	57	167	45	8	5	5	--	--	78	27	30	25	1	42	4	0	1	1	2	.33	3	.269	.376	.467
1988	Colo Sprngs	AAA	44	130	37	5	1	3	--	--	53	11	20	12	0	23	2	1	3	1	0	1.00	4	.285	.347	.408
1989	Colo Sprngs	AAA	66	207	54	8	2	6	--	--	84	28	39	19	1	49	1	1	6	2	1	.67	6	.261	.318	.406
1990	Edmonton	AAA	54	172	46	9	2	5	--	--	74	27	23	21	0	39	2	1	2	1	1	.50	6	.267	.350	.430
1991	Edmonton	AAA	17	55	16	5	0	3	--	--	30	11	15	8	0	14	1	0	1	1	0	1.00	0	.291	.391	.545
1982	San Diego	NL	8	20	2	0	0	0	(0	0)	2	0	0	0	0	7	0	1	0	0	0	.00	0	.100	.100	.100
1988	Cleveland	AL	4	24	4	0	0	1	(0	1)	7	1	2	2	0	8	0	0	0	0	0	.00	1	.167	.231	.292
1989	California	AL	4	3	1	0	0	0	(0	0)	1	0	0	1	0	0	0	0	0	0	0	.00	0	.333	.500	.333
1990	California	AL	5	3	0	0	0	0	(0	0)	0	0	0	1	0	1	0	0	0	0	0	.00	1	.000	.250	.000
1991	California	AL	45	115	23	7	0	1	(1	0)	33	11	13	8	0	34	1	4	0	1	1	.50	1	.200	.258	.287
	5 ML YEARS		71	165	30	7	0	2	(1	1)	43	12	15	12	0	50	1	5	0	1	1	.50	3	.182	.242	.261

Jose Tolentino

Bats: Left   **Throws:** Left   **Pos:** 1B   **Ht:** 6' 1"   **Wt:** 195   **Born:** 06/03/61   **Age:** 31

							BATTING													BASERUNNING				PERCENTAGES		
Year	Team	Lg	G	AB	H	2B	3B	HR	(Hm	Rd)	TB	R	RBI	TBB	IBB	SO	HBP	SH	SF	SB	CS	SB%	GDP	Avg	OBP	SLG
1984	Modesto	A	66	251	71	17	1	14	--	--	132	40	54	29	7	34	5	2	0	4	4	.50	5	.283	.368	.526
	Albany	AA	71	257	73	13	1	5	--	--	103	32	43	16	0	35	0	2	3	2	1	.67	5	.284	.322	.401
1985	Tacoma	AAA	106	339	87	24	1	6	--	--	131	38	41	38	5	53	3	1	4	1	3	.25	9	.257	.333	.386
1986	Huntsville	AA	137	540	170	28	0	16	--	--	246	80	105	53	6	57	4	2	7	7	2	.78	10	.315	.376	.456
1987	Tacoma	AAA	59	202	46	8	0	3	--	--	63	16	26	21	0	29	0	2	0	0	0	.00	9	.228	.300	.312
	Huntsville	AA	49	173	41	6	0	6	--	--	65	20	25	21	2	28	1	1	1	1	0	1.00	4	.237	.321	.376
1988	Okla City	AAA	48	131	28	4	0	0	--	--	32	6	8	20	3	20	0	4	0	1	0	1.00	5	.214	.318	.244
	Columbus	AA	72	259	79	10	3	9	--	--	122	33	53	36	6	32	6	0	5	1	3	.25	7	.305	.395	.471
1989	Tucson	AAA	128	408	111	27	1	9	--	--	167	61	64	62	6	72	3	3	10	2	4	.33	11	.272	.364	.409
1990	Tucson	AAA	116	377	116	32	3	21	--	--	217	69	78	48	2	44	5	2	4	0	1	.00	12	.308	.389	.576
1991	Tucson	AAA	90	303	88	24	5	6	--	--	140	44	51	44	8	44	2	0	1	2	3	.40	10	.290	.383	.462
1991	Houston	NL	44	54	14	4	0	1	(1	0)	21	6	6	4	0	9	0	0	1	0	0	.00	2	.259	.305	.389

Randy Tomlin

Pitches: Left   **Bats:** Left   **Pos:** SP   **Ht:** 5'11"   **Wt:** 179   **Born:** 06/14/66   **Age:** 26

			HOW MUCH HE PITCHED						WHAT HE GAVE UP										THE RESULTS					
Year	Team	Lg	G	GS	CG	GF	IP	BFP	H	R	ER	HR	SH	SF	HB	TBB	IBB	SO	WP	Bk	W	L	Pct.	ShO	Sv	ERA
1988	Watertown	A	15	15	5	0	103.1	407	75	31	25	4	3	3	6	25	1	87	4	2	7	5	.583	2	0	2.18
1989	Salem	A	21	21	3	0	138.2	582	131	60	50	11	2	2	3	43	0	99	7	0	12	6	.667	2	0	3.25
	Harrisburg	AA	5	5	1	0	32	119	18	6	3	0	1	3	1	6	0	31	0	0	2	2	.500	0	0	0.84
1990	Buffalo	AAA	3	1	0	1	8	33	12	3	3	1	0	1	0	1	0	3	0	0	0	0	.000	0	0	3.38
	Harrisburg	AA	19	18	4	1	126.1	521	101	43	32	3	2	4	6	34	6	92	2	1	9	6	.600	3	0	2.28
1990	Pittsburgh	NL	12	12	2	0	77.2	297	62	24	22	5	2	2	1	12	1	42	1	3	4	4	.500	2	0	2.55
1991	Pittsburgh	NL	31	27	4	0	175	736	170	75	58	9	5	2	6	54	4	104	2	3	8	7	.533	2	0	2.98
	2 ML YEARS		43	39	6	0	252.2	1033	232	99	80	14	7	4	7	66	5	146	3	6	12	11	.522	2	0	2.85

Kelvin Torve

Bats: Left   **Throws:** Right   **Pos:** PH   **Ht:** 6' 3"   **Wt:** 190   **Born:** 01/10/60   **Age:** 32

							BATTING													BASERUNNING				PERCENTAGES		
Year	Team	Lg	G	AB	H	2B	3B	HR	(Hm	Rd)	TB	R	RBI	TBB	IBB	SO	HBP	SH	SF	SB	CS	SB%	GDP	Avg	OBP	SLG
1981	Clinton	A	57	211	55	10	0	1	--	--	68	27	27	26	2	26	0	0	2	7	4	.64	7	.261	.339	.322
1982	Shreveport	AA	127	449	137	29	7	15	--	--	225	66	84	43	11	47	2	3	9	9	1	.90	6	.305	.362	.501
1983	Phoenix	AAA	115	392	102	21	5	4	--	--	145	58	54	34	2	33	1	4	7	6	4	.60	7	.260	.316	.370
1984	Shreveport	AA	114	316	94	21	5	16	--	--	173	59	62	43	3	42	2	0	6	2	0	1.00	8	.297	.379	.547
1985	Charlotte	AA	134	482	140	34	1	15	--	--	221	85	77	75	9	53	2	4	7	5	2	.71	16	.290	.383	.459
1986	Rochester	AAA	109	356	86	16	1	4	--	--	116	39	41	37	0	43	0	0	4	5	2	.71	8	.242	.310	.326
1987	Rochester	AAA	86	252	66	10	0	9	--	--	103	27	32	38	6	36	0	5	1	1	0	.91	3	.262	.357	.409
1988	Portland	AAA	103	385	116	28	2	9	--	--	175	58	47	40	3	36	1	2	1	5	1	.83	7	.301	.368	.455
1989	Portland	AAA	137	499	145	41	2	8	--	--	214	62	62	52	7	59	4	3	5	10	7	.59	11	.291	.359	.429
1990	Tidewater	AAA	115	402	122	25	1	11	--	--	182	62	76	56	6	43	6	0	5	9	2	.82	13	.303	.392	.453

1991	Tidewater	AAA	103	336	92	20	2	9	--	--	143	57	49	62	2	58	1	1	6	4	4	.50	14	.274	.383	.426
1988	Minnesota	AL	12	16	3	0	0	1	(0	1)	6	1	2	1	0	2	0	0	0	0	1	.00	0	.188	.235	.375
1990	New York	NL	20	38	11	4	0	0	(0	0)	15	0	2	4	0	9	2	0	0	0	0	.00	1	.289	.386	.395
1991	New York	NL	10	8	0	0	0	0	(0	0)	0	0	0	0	0	0	1	0	0	0	0	.00	1	.000	.000	.000
3 ML YEARS			42	62	14	4	0	1	(0	1)	21	1	4	5	0	12	2	0	0	0	1	.00	2	.226	.304	.339

Alan Trammell

Bats: Right **Throws:** Right **Pos:** SS   **Ht:** 6' 0" **Wt:** 180 **Born:** 02/21/58 **Age:** 34

								BATTING											BASERUNNING				PERCENTAGES		
Year	Team	Lg	G	AB	H	2B	3B	HR	(Hm	Rd)	TB	R	RBI	TBB	IBB	SO	HBP	SH	SF	SB	CS	SB%	GDP	Avg	OBP	SLG
1977	Detroit	AL	19	43	8	0	0	0	(0	0)	8	6	0	4	0	12	0	1	0	0	0	.00	1	.186	.255	.186
1978	Detroit	AL	139	448	120	14	6	2	(0	2)	152	49	34	45	0	56	2	6	3	3	1	.75	12	.268	.335	.339
1979	Detroit	AL	142	460	127	11	4	6	(4	2)	164	68	50	43	0	55	0	12	5	17	14	.55	6	.276	.335	.357
1980	Detroit	AL	146	560	168	21	5	9	(5	4)	226	107	65	69	2	63	3	13	7	12	12	.50	10	.300	.376	.404
1981	Detroit	AL	105	392	101	15	3	2	(2	0)	128	52	31	49	2	31	3	16	3	10	3	.77	10	.258	.342	.327
1982	Detroit	AL	157	489	126	34	3	9	(5	4)	193	66	57	52	0	47	0	9	6	19	8	.70	5	.258	.325	.395
1983	Detroit	AL	142	505	161	31	2	14	(8	6)	238	83	66	57	2	64	0	15	4	30	10	.75	7	.319	.385	.471
1984	Detroit	AL	139	555	174	34	5	14	(7	7)	260	85	69	60	2	63	3	6	2	19	13	.59	8	.314	.382	.468
1985	Detroit	AL	149	605	156	21	7	13	(7	6)	230	79	57	50	4	71	2	11	9	14	5	.74	6	.258	.312	.380
1986	Detroit	AL	151	574	159	33	7	21	(8	13)	269	107	75	59	4	57	5	11	4	25	12	.68	7	.277	.347	.469
1987	Detroit	AL	151	597	205	34	3	28	(13	15)	329	109	105	60	8	47	3	2	6	21	2	.91	11	.343	.402	.551
1988	Detroit	AL	128	466	145	24	1	15	(7	8)	216	73	69	46	8	46	4	0	7	7	4	.64	14	.311	.373	.464
1989	Detroit	AL	121	449	109	20	3	5	(2	3)	150	54	43	45	1	45	4	3	5	10	2	.83	9	.243	.314	.334
1990	Detroit	AL	146	559	170	37	1	14	(9	5)	251	71	89	68	7	55	1	3	6	12	10	.55	11	.304	.377	.449
1991	Detroit	AL	101	375	93	20	0	9	(6	3)	140	57	55	37	1	39	3	5	1	11	2	.85	7	.248	.320	.373
15 ML YEARS			1936	7077	2022	349	50	161	(83	78)	2954	1066	865	744	41	751	33	113	68	210	98	.68	124	.286	.353	.417

Jeff Treadway

Bats: Left **Throws:** Right **Pos:** 2B   **Ht:** 5'11" **Wt:** 170 **Born:** 01/22/63 **Age:** 29

								BATTING											BASERUNNING				PERCENTAGES		
Year	Team	Lg	G	AB	H	2B	3B	HR	(Hm	Rd)	TB	R	RBI	TBB	IBB	SO	HBP	SH	SF	SB	CS	SB%	GDP	Avg	OBP	SLG
1987	Cincinnati	NL	23	84	28	4	0	2	(2	0)	38	9	4	2	0	6	1	3	0	1	0	1.00	1	.333	.356	.452
1988	Cincinnati	NL	103	301	76	19	4	2	(2	0)	109	30	23	27	7	30	3	4	6	2	0	1.00	4	.252	.315	.362
1989	Atlanta	NL	134	473	131	18	3	8	(2	6)	179	58	40	30	3	38	0	6	5	3	2	.60	9	.277	.317	.378
1990	Atlanta	NL	128	474	134	20	2	11	(5	6)	191	56	59	25	1	42	3	5	4	3	4	.43	10	.283	.320	.403
1991	Atlanta	NL	106	306	98	17	2	3	(1	2)	128	41	32	23	1	19	2	2	3	2	2	.50	8	.320	.368	.418
5 ML YEARS			494	1638	467	78	11	26	(12	14)	645	194	158	107	12	135	9	20	18	11	8	.58	32	.285	.329	.394

Shane Turner

Bats: Left **Throws:** Right **Pos:** PH   **Ht:** 5'10" **Wt:** 180 **Born:** 01/08/63 **Age:** 29

								BATTING											BASERUNNING				PERCENTAGES		
Year	Team	Lg	G	AB	H	2B	3B	HR	(Hm	Rd)	TB	R	RBI	TBB	IBB	SO	HBP	SH	SF	SB	CS	SB%	GDP	Avg	OBP	SLG
1985	Oneonta	A	64	228	56	7	3	0	--	--	69	35	26	35	2	44	3	1	2	12	0	1.00	1	.246	.351	.303
1986	Ft.Laurdrle	A	66	222	71	12	2	2	--	--	93	48	36	51	1	35	3	4	3	12	8	.60	6	.320	.448	.419
1987	Columbus	AAA	25	76	17	0	2	0	--	--	21	10	7	5	0	16	0	1	0	2	1	.67	2	.224	.272	.276
	Albany	AA	20	73	23	3	1	1	--	--	31	19	8	12	0	3	1	1	1	2	1	.67	3	.315	.414	.425
	Reading	AA	74	283	96	16	6	3	--	--	133	50	47	21	1	35	3	1	1	3	6	.33	5	.339	.390	.470
1988	Maine	AAA	38	117	21	3	1	0	--	--	26	10	9	7	0	21	1	3	2	2	2	.50	1	.179	.228	.222
	Reading	AA	78	295	88	11	6	3	--	--	120	52	21	26	3	53	7	6	2	14	2	.88	3	.298	.367	.407
1989	Reading	AA	46	141	28	5	1	1	--	--	38	18	11	27	1	27	2	0	0	13	3	.81	2	.199	.335	.270
	Rochester	AAA	59	194	43	6	1	2	--	--	57	31	19	19	1	33	1	4	1	6	4	.60	5	.222	.293	.294
1990	Hagerstown	AA	10	38	9	1	0	0	--	--	10	5	1	0	0	10	0	0	0	1	0	1.00	1	.237	.237	.263
	Rochester	AAA	86	209	59	7	0	1	--	--	69	29	19	25	2	41	0	7	2	3	5	.38	4	.282	.356	.330
1991	Rochester	AAA	110	404	114	13	2	1	--	--	134	49	57	47	1	75	3	1	2	6	7	.46	13	.282	.360	.332
1988	Philadelphia	NL	18	35	6	0	0	0	(0	0)	6	1	1	5	0	9	0	0	0	0	0	.00	1	.171	.275	.171
1991	Baltimore	AL	4	1	0	0	0	0	(0	0)	0	0	0	0	0	0	0	0	0	0	0	.00	0	.000	.000	.000
2 ML YEARS			22	36	6	0	0	0	(0	0)	6	1	1	5	0	9	0	0	0	0	0	.00	1	.167	.268	.167

Jose Uribe

Bats: Both **Throws:** Right **Pos:** SS   **Ht:** 5'10" **Wt:** 165 **Born:** 01/21/60 **Age:** 32

								BATTING											BASERUNNING				PERCENTAGES		
Year	Team	Lg	G	AB	H	2B	3B	HR	(Hm	Rd)	TB	R	RBI	TBB	IBB	SO	HBP	SH	SF	SB	CS	SB%	GDP	Avg	OBP	SLG
1984	St. Louis	NL	8	19	4	0	0	0	(0	0)	4	4	3	0	0	2	0	1	0	1	0	1.00	1	.211	.211	.211
1985	San Francisco	NL	147	476	113	20	4	3	(2	1)	150	46	26	30	8	57	2	5	0	8	2	.80	5	.237	.285	.315
1986	San Francisco	NL	157	453	101	15	1	3	(1	2)	127	46	43	61	19	76	0	3	0	22	11	.67	2	.223	.315	.280
1987	San Francisco	NL	95	309	90	16	5	5	(4	1)	131	44	30	24	9	35	1	5	1	12	2	.86	1	.291	.343	.424
1988	San Francisco	NL	141	493	124	10	7	3	(1	2)	157	47	35	36	10	69	0	4	2	14	10	.58	3	.252	.301	.318

Year	Team	Lg	G	AB	H	2B	3B	HR	(SH	SF)	TB	R	RBI	BB	SO	SB	CS	GDP					Avg	OBP	SLG
1989	San Francisco	NL	151	453	100	12	6	1	(0 | 1)	127	34	30	34	12	74	0	6	4	6	6	.50	7	.221	.273	.280
1990	San Francisco	NL	138	415	103	8	6	1	(0 | 1)	126	35	24	29	13	49	0	4	0	5	9	.36	8	.248	.297	.304
1991	San Francisco	NL	90	231	51	8	4	1	(0 | 1)	70	23	12	20	6	33	0	1	0	3	4	.43	2	.221	.283	.303
	8 ML YEARS		927	2849	686	89	33	17	(8 | 9)	892	279	203	234	77	395	3	29	7	71	44	62	29	.241	.298	.313

Efrain Valdez

Pitches: Left **Bats:** Left **Pos:** RP **Ht:** 5'11" **Wt:** 170 **Born:** 07/11/66 **Age:** 25

Year	Team	Lg	G	GS	CG	GF	IP	BFP	H	R	ER	HR	SH	SF	HB	TBB	IBB	SO	WP	Bk	W	L	Pct.	ShO	Sv	ERA
1984	Spokane	A	13	1	0	6	16.2	0	26	18	14	1	0	0	0	8	0	15	0	0	0	1	.333	0	0	7.56
1986	Tulsa	AA	4	2	0	1	12.1	52	12	8	8	1	1	0	1	6	0	4	0	1	0	1	.000	0	0	5.84
1987	Tulsa	AA	11	8	1	1	49.1	235	62	44	39	9	1	3	2	24	3	38	3	0	1	4	.200	1	0	7.11
	Charlotte	A	17	8	0	2	70.1	301	67	32	29	6	2	3	1	28	2	45	3	2	3	6	.333	0	0	3.71
1988	Tulsa	AA	43	3	0	21	63.1	276	63	37	32	6	3	2	4	24	2	52	3	1	6	5	.545	0	6	4.55
1989	Canton-Akrn	AA	44	2	0	18	75.1	318	60	26	18	1	6	3	4	33	3	55	4	0	2	4	.333	0	1	2.15
1990	Colo Sprngs	AAA	46	1	0	17	75.2	330	72	38	32	6	4	5	4	30	8	52	4	2	4	2	.667	0	6	3.81
1991	Colo Sprngs	AAA	14	1	0	5	30.2	133	26	15	13	1	3	1	0	13	3	25	1	2	3	1	.750	0	1	3.82
	Syracuse	AAA	21	1	0	4	43.2	201	50	27	26	7	2	2	0	25	0	30	3	0	3	2	.600	0	0	5.36
1990	Cleveland	AL	13	0	0	4	23.2	104	20	10	8	2	1	3	0	14	3	13	1	0	1	1	.500	0	0	3.04
1991	Cleveland	AL	7	0	0	0	6	27	5	1	1	0	1	1	1	3	1	1	0	0	0	0	.000	0	0	1.50
	2 ML YEARS		20	0	0	4	29.2	131	25	11	9	2	2	4	1	17	4	14	1	0	1	1	.500	0	0	2.73

Sergio Valdez

Pitches: Right **Bats:** Right **Pos:** RP **Ht:** 6'1" **Wt:** 190 **Born:** 09/07/65 **Age:** 26

Year	Team	Lg	G	GS	CG	GF	IP	BFP	H	R	ER	HR	SH	SF	HB	TBB	IBB	SO	WP	Bk	W	L	Pct.	ShO	Sv	ERA
1986	Montreal	NL	5	5	0	0	25	120	39	20	19	2	0	0	1	11	0	20	2	0	0	4	.000	0	0	6.84
1989	Atlanta	NL	19	1	0	8	32.2	145	31	24	22	5	2	0	0	17	3	26	2	0	1	2	.333	0	0	6.06
1990	2 ML Teams		30	13	0	7	107.2	466	115	66	58	17	5	5	1	38	2	66	4	0	6	6	.500	0	0	4.85
1991	Cleveland	AL	6	0	0	1	16.1	70	15	11	10	3	1	1	0	5	1	11	1	0	1	0	1.000	0	0	5.51
1990	Atlanta	NL	6	0	0	3	5.1	26	6	4	4	0	1	0	0	3	0	3	1	0	0	0	.000	0	0	6.75
	Cleveland	AL	24	13	0	4	102.1	440	109	62	54	17	4	5	1	35	2	63	3	0	6	6	.500	0	0	4.75
	4 ML YEARS		60	19	0	16	181.2	801	200	121	109	27	8	6	2	71	6	123	9	0	8	12	.400	0	0	5.40

Fernando Valenzuela

Pitches: Left **Bats:** Left **Pos:** SP **Ht:** 5'11" **Wt:** 202 **Born:** 11/01/60 **Age:** 31

Year	Team	Lg	G	GS	CG	GF	IP	BFP	H	R	ER	HR	SH	SF	HB	TBB	IBB	SO	WP	Bk	W	L	Pct.	ShO	Sv	ERA
1980	Los Angeles	NL	10	0	0	4	18	66	8	2	0	0	1	1	0	5	0	16	0	1	2	0	1.000	0	1	0.00
1981	Los Angeles	NL	25	25	11	0	192	758	140	55	53	11	9	3	1	61	4	180	4	0	13	7	.650	8	0	2.48
1982	Los Angeles	NL	37	37	18	0	285	1156	247	105	91	13	19	6	2	83	4	199	4	0	19	13	.594	4	0	2.87
1983	Los Angeles	NL	35	35	9	0	257	1094	245	122	107	16	27	5	3	99	10	189	12	1	15	10	.600	4	0	3.75
1984	Los Angeles	NL	34	34	12	0	261	1078	218	109	88	14	11	7	2	106	4	240	11	1	12	17	.414	2	0	3.03
1985	Los Angeles	NL	35	35	14	0	272.1	1109	211	92	74	14	13	8	1	101	5	208	10	1	17	10	.630	5	0	2.45
1986	Los Angeles	NL	34	34	20	0	269.1	1102	226	104	94	18	15	3	1	85	5	242	13	0	21	11	.656	3	0	3.14
1987	Los Angeles	NL	34	34	12	0	251	1116	254	120	111	25	18	2	4	124	4	190	14	1	14	14	.500	1	0	3.98
1988	Los Angeles	NL	23	22	3	1	142.1	626	142	71	67	11	15	5	0	76	4	64	7	1	5	8	.385	0	1	4.24
1989	Los Angeles	NL	31	31	3	0	196.2	852	185	89	75	11	7	7	2	98	6	116	6	4	10	13	.435	0	0	3.43
1990	Los Angeles	NL	33	33	5	0	204	900	223	112	104	19	11	4	0	77	4	115	13	1	13	13	.500	2	0	4.59
1991	California	AL	2	2	0	0	6.2	36	14	10	9	3	1	1	0	3	0	5	1	0	0	2	.000	0	0	12.15
	12 ML YEARS		333	322	107	5	2355.1	9893	2113	991	873	155	147	52	16	918	58	1764	95	11	141	118	.544	29	2	3.34

Julio Valera

Pitches: Right **Bats:** Right **Pos:** RP **Ht:** 6'2" **Wt:** 215 **Born:** 10/13/68 **Age:** 23

Year	Team	Lg	G	GS	CG	GF	IP	BFP	H	R	ER	HR	SH	SF	HB	TBB	IBB	SO	WP	Bk	W	L	Pct.	ShO	Sv	ERA
1986	Kingsport	R	13	13	2	0	76.1	356	91	58	44	5	4	0	0	29	2	64	4	1	3	10	.231	1	0	5.19
1987	Columbia	A	22	22	2	0	125.1	522	114	53	39	7	2	1	4	31	0	97	6	0	8	7	.533	2	0	2.80
1988	Columbia	A	30	27	8	3	191	775	171	77	68	8	5	7	4	51	3	144	9	6	15	11	.577	2	0	3.20
1989	St.Lucie	A	6	6	3	0	45	173	34	5	5	1	2	0	0	6	1	45	0	0	4	2	.667	2	0	1.00
	Jackson	AA	19	19	6	0	137.1	566	123	47	38	4	7	3	8	36	2	107	10	0	10	6	.625	2	0	2.49
	Tidewater	AAA	2	2	0	0	13	52	8	3	3	1	0	0	1	5	0	10	1	0	0	0	.500	0	0	2.08
1990	Tidewater	AAA	24	24	9	0	158	648	146	66	53	12	6	5	5	39	3	133	7	5	10	10	.500	2	0	3.02
1991	Tidewater	AAA	26	26	3	0	176.1	739	152	79	75	12	8	6	6	70	4	117	8	3	10	10	.500	1	0	3.83
1990	New York	NL	3	3	0	0	13	64	20	11	10	1	0	0	0	7	0	4	0	0	1	1	.500	0	0	6.92
1991	New York	NL	2	0	0	1	2	11	1	0	0	0	0	0	0	4	1	3	0	0	0	0	.000	0	0	0.00
	2 ML YEARS		5	3	0	1	15	75	21	11	10	1	0	0	0	11	1	7	0	0	1	1	.500	0	0	6.00

Dave Valle

Bats: Right **Throws:** Right **Pos:** C   **Ht:** 6' 2" **Wt:** 200 **Born:** 10/30/60 **Age:** 31

Year Team	Lg	G	AB	H	2B	3B	HR	(Hm	Rd)	TB	R	RBI	TBB	IBB	SO	HBP	SH	SF	SB	CS	SB%	GDP	Avg	OBP	SLG
1984 Seattle	AL	13	27	8	1	0	1	(1	0)	12	4	4	1	0	5	0	0	0	0	0	.00	0	.296	.321	.444
1985 Seattle	AL	31	70	11	1	0	0	(0	0)	12	2	4	1	0	17	1	1	0	0	0	.00	1	.157	.181	.171
1986 Seattle	AL	22	53	18	3	0	5	(4	1)	36	10	15	7	0	7	0	0	0	0	0	.00	2	.340	.417	.679
1987 Seattle	AL	95	324	83	16	3	12	(8	4)	141	40	53	15	2	46	3	0	4	2	1	1.00	13	.256	.292	.435
1988 Seattle	AL	92	290	67	15	2	10	(5	5)	116	29	50	18	0	38	9	3	2	0	1	.00	13	.231	.295	.400
1989 Seattle	AL	94	316	75	10	3	7	(1	6)	112	32	34	29	2	32	6	1	3	0	0	.00	13	.237	.311	.354
1990 Seattle	AL	107	308	66	15	0	7	(1	6)	102	37	33	45	0	48	7	4	0	1	2	.33	11	.214	.328	.331
1991 Seattle	AL	132	324	63	8	1	8	(0	8)	97	38	32	34	0	49	9	6	3	0	2	.00	19	.194	.286	.299
8 ML YEARS		586	1712	391	69	9	50	(20	30)	628	192	225	150	4	242	35	15	12	3	5	.38	72	.228	.302	.367

Todd Van Poppel

Pitches: Right **Bats:** Right **Pos:** SP   **Ht:** 6' 5" **Wt:** 210 **Born:** 12/09/71 **Age:** 20

Year Team	Lg	G	GS	CG	GF	IP	BFP	H	R	ER	HR	SH	SF	HB	TBB	IBB	SO	WP	Bk	W	L	Pct.	ShO	Sv	ERA
1990 Sou Oregon	A	5	5	0	0	24	92	10	5	3	1	0	1	2	9	0	32	0	0	1	1	.500	0	0	1.13
Madison	A	3	3	0	0	13.2	61	8	11	6	0	0	1	1	10	0	17	0	0	2	1	.667	0	0	3.95
1991 Huntsville	AA	24	24	1	0	132.1	607	118	69	51	2	4	6	6	90	0	115	12	1	6	13	.316	1	0	3.47
1991 Oakland	AL	1	1	0	0	4.2	21	7	5	5	1	0	0	0	2	0	6	0	0	0	0	.000	0	0	9.64

Andy Van Slyke

Bats: Left **Throws:** Right **Pos:** CF   **Ht:** 6' 2" **Wt:** 195 **Born:** 12/21/60 **Age:** 31

Year Team	Lg	G	AB	H	2B	3B	HR	(Hm	Rd)	TB	R	RBI	TBB	IBB	SO	HBP	SH	SF	SB	CS	SB%	GDP	Avg	OBP	SLG
1983 St. Louis	NL	101	309	81	15	5	8	(3	5)	130	51	38	46	5	64	1	2	3	21	7	.75	4	.262	.357	.421
1984 St. Louis	NL	137	361	88	16	4	7	(3	4)	133	45	50	63	9	71	0	0	2	28	5	.85	5	.244	.354	.368
1985 St. Louis	NL	146	424	110	25	6	13	(5	8)	186	61	55	47	6	54	2	1	1	34	6	.85	7	.259	.335	.439
1986 St. Louis	NL	137	418	113	23	7	13	(6	7)	189	48	61	47	5	85	1	1	3	21	8	.72	2	.270	.343	.452
1987 Pittsburgh	NL	157	564	165	36	11	21	(11	10)	286	93	82	56	4	122	4	3	3	34	8	.81	6	.293	.359	.507
1988 Pittsburgh	NL	154	587	169	23	15	25	(16	9)	297	101	100	57	2	126	1	1	13	30	9	.77	8	.288	.345	.506
1989 Pittsburgh	NL	130	476	113	18	9	9	(4	5)	176	64	53	47	3	100	3	1	4	16	4	.80	13	.237	.308	.370
1990 Pittsburgh	NL	136	493	140	26	6	17	(6	11)	229	67	77	66	2	89	1	3	4	14	4	.78	6	.284	.367	.465
1991 Pittsburgh	NL	138	491	130	24	7	17	(9	8)	219	87	83	71	1	85	4	0	11	10	3	.77	5	.265	.355	.446
9 ML YEARS		1236	4123	1109	206	70	130	(63	67)	1845	617	599	500	37	796	17	12	44	208	54	.79	56	.269	.347	.447

John VanderWal

Bats: Left **Throws:** Left **Pos:** LF   **Ht:** 6' 1" **Wt:** 180 **Born:** 04/29/66 **Age:** 26

Year Team	Lg	G	AB	H	2B	3B	HR	(Hm	Rd)	TB	R	RBI	TBB	IBB	SO	HBP	SH	SF	SB	CS	SB%	GDP	Avg	OBP	SLG
1987 Jamestown	A	18	69	33	12	3	3	--	--	60	24	15	3	0	14	0	0	1	3	2	.60	2	.478	.493	.870
Wst Plm Bch	A	50	189	54	11	2	2	--	--	75	29	22	30	0	25	0	1	3	8	3	.73	2	.286	.378	.397
1988 Wst Plm Bch	A	62	231	64	15	2	10	--	--	113	50	33	32	2	40	3	3	3	11	4	.73	0	.277	.368	.489
Jacksnville	AA	58	208	54	14	0	3	--	--	77	22	14	17	1	49	1	0	1	3	4	.43	3	.260	.317	.370
1989 Jacksnville	AA	71	217	55	9	2	6	--	--	86	30	24	22	1	51	1	0	2	2	3	.40	5	.253	.322	.396
1990 Jacksnville	AA	77	277	84	25	3	8	--	--	139	45	40	39	2	46	3	0	2	6	3	.67	7	.303	.393	.502
Indianapols	AAA	51	135	40	6	0	2	--	--	52	16	14	13	0	28	0	0	0	0	1	.00	3	.296	.358	.385
1991 Indianapols	AAA	133	478	140	36	8	15	--	--	237	84	71	79	4	118	2	1	4	8	1	.89	10	.293	.393	.496
1991 Montreal	NL	21	61	13	4	1	1	(0	1)	22	4	8	1	0	18	0	0	1	0	0	.00	2	.213	.222	.361

Gary Varsho

Bats: Left **Throws:** Right **Pos:** RF   **Ht:** 5'11" **Wt:** 190 **Born:** 06/20/61 **Age:** 31

Year Team	Lg	G	AB	H	2B	3B	HR	(Hm	Rd)	TB	R	RBI	TBB	IBB	SO	HBP	SH	SF	SB	CS	SB%	GDP	Avg	OBP	SLG
1988 Chicago	NL	46	73	20	3	0	0	(0	0)	23	6	5	1	0	6	0	0	1	5	0	1.00	0	.274	.280	.315
1989 Chicago	NL	61	87	16	4	2	0	(0	0)	24	10	6	4	1	13	0	0	0	3	0	1.00	0	.184	.220	.276
1990 Chicago	NL	46	48	12	4	0	0	(0	0)	16	10	1	1	1	6	0	0	0	2	0	1.00	1	.250	.265	.333
1991 Pittsburgh	NL	99	187	51	11	2	4	(1	3)	78	23	23	19	2	34	2	1	1	9	2	.82	2	.273	.344	.417
4 ML YEARS		252	395	99	22	4	4	(1	3)	141	49	35	25	4	59	2	1	2	19	2	.90	3	.251	.297	.357

Jim Vatcher

Bats: Right **Throws:** Right **Pos:** RF **Ht:** 5' 9" **Wt:** 165 **Born:** 05/27/66 **Age:** 26

Year	Team	Lg	G	AB	H	2B	3B	HR	(Hm	Rd)	TB	R	RBI	TBB	IBB	SO	HBP	SH	SF	SB	CS	SB%	GDP	Avg	OBP	SLG
1987	Utica	A	67	249	67	15	2	3	--	--	95	44	21	28	0	31	2	2	1	10	5	.67	5	.269	.346	.382
1988	Spartanburg	A	137	496	150	32	2	12	--	--	222	90	72	89	1	73	8	9	3	26	13	.67	10	.302	.414	.448
1989	Clearwater	A	92	349	105	30	5	4	--	--	157	51	46	41	0	49	2	0	2	7	3	.70	11	.301	.376	.450
	Reading	AA	48	171	56	11	3	4	--	--	85	27	32	26	1	29	1	0	4	2	0	1.00	4	.327	.411	.497
1990	Scr Wil-Bar	AAA	55	181	46	12	4	5	--	--	81	30	22	32	1	33	0	1	2	1	4	.20	8	.254	.363	.448
1991	Las Vegas	AAA	117	395	105	28	6	17	--	--	196	67	67	53	3	76	3	3	2	4	12	.25	14	.266	.355	.496
1990	2 ML Teams		57	73	19	2	1	1	(1	0)	26	7	7	5	0	15	0	0	0	0	0	.00	1	.260	.308	.356
1991	San Diego	NL	17	20	4	0	0	0	(0	0)	4	3	2	4	0	6	0	0	0	1	0	1.00	0	.200	.333	.200
1990	Philadelphia	NL	36	46	12	1	0	1	(1	0)	16	5	4	4	0	6	0	0	0	0	0	.00	1	.261	.320	.348
	Atlanta	NL	21	27	7	1	1	0	(0	0)	10	2	3	1	0	9	0	0	0	0	0	.00	0	.259	.286	.370
	2 ML YEARS		74	93	23	2	1	1	(1	0)	30	10	9	9	0	21	0	0	0	1	0	1.00	1	.247	.314	.323

Greg Vaughn

Bats: Right **Throws:** Right **Pos:** LF **Ht:** 6' 0" **Wt:** 193 **Born:** 07/03/65 **Age:** 26

Year	Team	Lg	G	AB	H	2B	3B	HR	(Hm	Rd)	TB	R	RBI	TBB	IBB	SO	HBP	SH	SF	SB	CS	SB%	GDP	Avg	OBP	SLG
1989	Milwaukee	AL	38	113	30	3	0	5	(1	4)	48	18	23	10	1	23	0	0	2	4	1	.80	0	.265	.336	.425
1990	Milwaukee	AL	120	382	84	26	2	17	(9	8)	165	51	61	33	1	91	1	7	6	7	4	.64	11	.220	.280	.432
1991	Milwaukee	AL	145	542	132	24	5	27	(16	11)	247	81	98	62	2	125	1	2	7	2	2	.50	5	.244	.319	.456
	3 ML YEARS		303	1037	246	53	7	49	(26	23)	460	150	182	108	3	239	2	9	15	13	7	.65	16	.237	.306	.444

Mo Vaughn

Bats: Left **Throws:** Right **Pos:** 1B/DH **Ht:** 6' 1" **Wt:** 225 **Born:** 12/15/67 **Age:** 24

Year	Team	Lg	G	AB	H	2B	3B	HR	(Hm	Rd)	TB	R	RBI	TBB	IBB	SO	HBP	SH	SF	SB	CS	SB%	GDP	Avg	OBP	SLG
1989	New Britain	AA	73	245	68	15	0	8	--	--	107	28	38	25	3	47	3	1	1	1	3	.25	7	.278	.350	.437
1990	Pawtucket	AAA	108	386	114	26	1	22	--	--	208	62	72	44	2	87	6	0	2	3	2	.60	10	.295	.374	.539
1991	Pawtucket	AAA	69	234	64	10	0	14	--	--	116	35	50	60	7	44	3	0	4	2	1	.67	6	.274	.422	.496
1991	Boston	AL	74	219	57	12	0	4	(1	3)	81	21	32	26	2	43	2	0	4	2	1	.67	7	.260	.339	.370

Randy Velarde

Bats: Right **Throws:** Right **Pos:** 3B/SS **Ht:** 6' 0" **Wt:** 190 **Born:** 11/24/62 **Age:** 29

Year	Team	Lg	G	AB	H	2B	3B	HR	(Hm	Rd)	TB	R	RBI	TBB	IBB	SO	HBP	SH	SF	SB	CS	SB%	GDP	Avg	OBP	SLG
1987	New York	AL	8	22	4	0	0	0	(0	0)	4	1	1	0	0	6	0	0	0	0	0	.00	1	.182	.182	.182
1988	New York	AL	48	115	20	6	0	5	(2	3)	41	18	12	8	0	24	2	0	0	1	1	.50	3	.174	.240	.357
1989	New York	AL	33	100	34	4	2	2	(1	1)	48	12	11	7	0	14	1	3	0	0	3	.00	0	.340	.389	.480
1990	New York	AL	95	229	48	6	2	5	(1	4)	73	21	19	20	0	53	1	2	1	0	3	.00	6	.210	.275	.319
1991	New York	AL	80	184	45	11	1	1	(0	1)	61	19	15	18	0	43	3	5	0	3	1	.75	6	.245	.322	.332
	5 ML YEARS		264	650	151	27	5	13	(4	9)	227	71	58	53	0	140	7	10	2	4	8	.33	16	.232	.297	.349

Max Venable

Bats: Left **Throws:** Right **Pos:** CF/RF **Ht:** 5'10" **Wt:** 193 **Born:** 06/06/57 **Age:** 35

Year	Team	Lg	G	AB	H	2B	3B	HR	(Hm	Rd)	TB	R	RBI	TBB	IBB	SO	HBP	SH	SF	SB	CS	SB%	GDP	Avg	OBP	SLG
1979	San Francisco	NL	55	85	14	1	1	0	(0	0)	17	12	3	10	1	18	1	1	0	3	3	.50	0	.165	.260	.200
1980	San Francisco	NL	64	138	37	5	0	0	(0	0)	42	13	10	15	0	22	0	1	3	8	2	.80	3	.268	.333	.304
1981	San Francisco	NL	18	32	6	0	2	0	(0	0)	10	2	1	4	0	3	0	0	0	3	1	.75	0	.188	.278	.313
1982	San Francisco	NL	71	125	28	2	1	1	(1	0)	35	17	7	7	0	16	0	0	0	9	3	.75	2	.224	.265	.280
1983	San Francisco	NL	94	228	50	7	4	6	(3	3)	83	28	27	22	1	34	3	2	1	15	2	.88	3	.219	.295	.364
1984	Montreal	NL	38	71	17	2	0	2	(0	2)	25	7	7	3	1	7	1	0	1	1	0	1.00	0	.239	.276	.352
1985	Cincinnati	NL	77	135	39	12	3	0	(0	0)	57	21	10	6	0	17	0	3	2	11	3	.79	2	.289	.315	.422
1986	Cincinnati	NL	108	147	31	7	1	2	(1	1)	46	17	15	17	2	24	0	2	2	7	2	.78	0	.211	.289	.313
1987	Cincinnati	NL	7	7	1	0	0	0	(0	0)	1	2	2	0	0	0	0	0	0	0	0	.00	0	.143	.143	.143
1989	California	AL	20	53	19	4	0	0	(0	0)	23	7	4	1	0	16	0	3	0	0	0	.00	0	.358	.370	.434
1990	California	AL	93	189	49	9	3	4	(3	1)	76	26	21	24	2	31	0	7	3	5	1	.83	3	.259	.340	.402
1991	California	AL	82	187	46	8	2	3	(2	1)	67	24	21	11	2	30	2	4	2	2	1	.67	5	.246	.292	.358
	12 ML YEARS		727	1397	337	57	17	18	(10	8)	482	176	128	120	9	218	7	23	13	64	18	.78	18	.241	.302	.345

210

Robin Ventura

Bats: Left   Throws: Right   Pos: 3B/1B   Ht: 6' 1"   Wt: 192   Born: 07/14/67   Age: 24

								BATTING											BASERUNNING				PERCENTAGES		
Year Team	Lg	G	AB	H	2B	3B	HR	(Hm Rd)	TB	R	RBI	TBB	IBB	SO	HBP	SH	SF	SB	CS	SB%	GDP	Avg	OBP	SLG
1989 Chicago	AL	16	45	8	3	0	0	(0 0)	11	5	7	8	0	6	1	1	3	0	0	.00	1	.178	.298	.244
1990 Chicago	AL	150	493	123	17	1	5	(2 3)	157	48	54	55	2	53	1	13	3	1	4	.20	5	.249	.324	.318
1991 Chicago	AL	157	606	172	25	1	23	(16 7)	268	92	100	80	3	67	4	8	7	2	4	.33	22	.284	.367	.442
3 ML YEARS		323	1144	303	45	2	28	(18 10)	436	145	161	143	5	126	6	22	13	3	8	.27	28	.265	.346	.381

Hector Villanueva

Bats: Right   Throws: Right   Pos: C   Ht: 6' 1"   Wt: 220   Born: 10/02/64   Age: 27

								BATTING											BASERUNNING				PERCENTAGES		
Year Team	Lg	G	AB	H	2B	3B	HR	(Hm Rd)	TB	R	RBI	TBB	IBB	SO	HBP	SH	SF	SB	CS	SB%	GDP	Avg	OBP	SLG
1985 Peoria	A	65	193	45	7	0	1	-- --	55	22	19	27	0	36	3	2	1	0	2	.00	7	.233	.335	.285
1986 Winston-Sal	A	125	412	131	20	2	13	-- --	194	58	100	81	3	42	2	2	12	6	4	.60	12	.318	.422	.471
1987 Pittsfield	AA	109	391	107	31	0	14	-- --	180	59	70	43	1	38	1	2	3	3	4	.43	8	.274	.345	.460
1988 Pittsfield	AA	127	436	137	24	3	10	-- --	197	50	75	71	6	58	4	2	8	5	4	.56	9	.314	.408	.452
1989 Iowa	AAA	120	444	112	25	1	12	-- --	175	46	57	32	2	95	1	1	2	1	1	.50	6	.252	.303	.394
1990 Iowa	AAA	52	177	47	7	1	8	-- --	80	20	34	19	2	36	1	1	0	0	1	.00	4	.266	.340	.452
1991 Iowa	AAA	6	25	9	3	0	2	-- --	18	2	9	1	1	6	0	0	0	0	0	.00	0	.360	.370	.720
1990 Chicago	NL	52	114	31	4	1	7	(2 5)	58	14	18	4	2	27	2	0	0	1	0	1.00	3	.272	.308	.509
1991 Chicago	NL	71	192	53	10	1	13	(11 2)	104	23	32	21	1	30	0	0	1	0	0	.00	3	.276	.346	.542
2 ML YEARS		123	306	84	14	2	20	(13 7)	162	37	50	25	3	57	2	0	1	1	0	1.00	6	.275	.332	.529

Frank Viola

Pitches: Left   Bats: Left   Pos: SP   Ht: 6' 4"   Wt: 210   Born: 04/19/60   Age: 32

			HOW MUCH HE PITCHED						WHAT HE GAVE UP									THE RESULTS					
Year Team	Lg	G	GS	CG	GF	IP	BFP	H	R	ER	HR	SH	SF	HB	TBB	IBB	SO	WP	Bk	W	L	Pct.	ShO	Sv	ERA
1982 Minnesota	AL	22	22	3	0	126	543	152	77	73	22	2	0	0	38	2	84	4	1	4	10	.286	1	0	5.21
1983 Minnesota	AL	35	34	4	0	210	949	242	141	128	34	5	2	8	92	7	127	6	2	7	15	.318	0	0	5.49
1984 Minnesota	AL	35	35	10	0	257.2	1047	225	101	92	28	1	5	4	73	1	149	6	1	18	12	.600	4	0	3.21
1985 Minnesota	AL	36	36	9	0	250.2	1059	262	136	114	26	5	5	2	68	3	135	6	2	18	14	.563	0	0	4.09
1986 Minnesota	AL	37	37	7	0	245.2	1053	257	136	123	37	4	5	3	83	0	191	12	0	16	13	.552	1	0	4.51
1987 Minnesota	AL	36	36	7	0	251.2	1037	230	91	81	29	7	3	6	66	1	197	1	1	17	10	.630	1	0	2.90
1988 Minnesota	AL	35	35	7	0	255.1	1031	236	80	75	20	6	6	3	54	2	193	5	1	24	7	.774	2	0	2.64
1989 2 ML Teams		36	36	9	0	261	1082	246	115	106	22	12	6	4	74	4	211	8	1	13	17	.433	2	0	3.66
1990 New York	NL	35	35	7	0	249.2	1016	227	83	74	15	13	3	2	60	2	182	11	0	20	12	.625	3	0	2.67
1991 New York	NL	35	35	3	0	231.1	980	259	112	102	25	15	5	1	54	4	132	6	1	13	15	.464	0	0	3.97
1989 Minnesota	AL	24	24	7	0	175.2	731	171	80	74	17	9	4	3	47	1	138	5	1	8	12	.400	1	0	3.79
New York	NL	12	12	2	0	85.1	351	75	35	32	5	3	2	1	27	3	73	3	0	5	5	.500	1	0	3.38
10 ML YEARS		342	341	66	0	2339	9797	2336	1072	968	258	70	40	33	662	26	1601	65	10	150	125	.545	14	0	3.72

Jose Vizcaino

Bats: Both   Throws: Right   Pos: SS/3B   Ht: 6' 1"   Wt: 180   Born: 03/26/68   Age: 24

								BATTING											BASERUNNING				PERCENTAGES		
Year Team	Lg	G	AB	H	2B	3B	HR	(Hm Rd)	TB	R	RBI	TBB	IBB	SO	HBP	SH	SF	SB	CS	SB%	GDP	Avg	OBP	SLG
1989 Los Angeles	NL	7	10	2	0	0	0	(0 0)	2	2	0	0	0	1	0	1	0	0	0	.00	0	.200	.200	.200
1990 Los Angeles	NL	37	51	14	1	1	0	(0 0)	17	3	2	4	1	8	0	0	0	1	1	.50	1	.275	.327	.333
1991 Chicago	NL	93	145	38	5	0	0	(0 0)	43	7	10	5	0	18	0	2	2	2	1	.67	1	.262	.283	.297
3 ML YEARS		137	206	54	6	1	0	(0 0)	62	12	12	9	1	27	0	3	2	3	2	.60	2	.262	.290	.301

Omar Vizquel

Bats: Both   Throws: Right   Pos: SS   Ht: 5' 9"   Wt: 165   Born: 04/24/67   Age: 25

								BATTING											BASERUNNING				PERCENTAGES		
Year Team	Lg	G	AB	H	2B	3B	HR	(Hm Rd)	TB	R	RBI	TBB	IBB	SO	HBP	SH	SF	SB	CS	SB%	GDP	Avg	OBP	SLG
1989 Seattle	AL	143	387	85	7	3	1	(1 0)	101	45	20	28	0	40	1	13	2	1	4	.20	6	.220	.273	.261
1990 Seattle	AL	81	255	63	3	2	2	(0 2)	76	19	18	18	0	22	0	10	2	4	1	.80	7	.247	.295	.298
1991 Seattle	AL	142	426	98	16	4	1	(1 0)	125	42	41	45	0	37	0	8	3	7	2	.78	8	.230	.302	.293
3 ML YEARS		366	1068	246	26	9	4	(2 2)	302	106	79	91	0	99	1	31	7	12	7	.63	21	.230	.290	.283

Hector Wagner

Pitches: Right   Bats: Right   Pos: SP   Ht: 6' 3"   Wt: 200   Born: 11/26/68   Age: 23

			HOW MUCH HE PITCHED						WHAT HE GAVE UP									THE RESULTS					
Year Team	Lg	G	GS	CG	GF	IP	BFP	H	R	ER	HR	SH	SF	HB	TBB	IBB	SO	WP	Bk	W	L	Pct.	ShO	Sv	ERA
1987 Royals	R	13	12	0	0	53	226	63	26	18	0	2	2	2	12	0	28	0	0	1	3	.250	0	0	3.06
1988 Eugene	A	15	15	0	0	85.2	365	76	46	35	3	0	1	4	28	0	67	3	0	4	9	.308	0	0	3.68
1989 Appleton	A	24	23	3	1	130.1	557	149	79	66	9	5	1	6	29	1	71	6	1	6	11	.353	0	0	4.56

1990 Memphis	AA	40	11	1	8	133.1	538	114	37	30	7	5	1	2	41	0	63	3	0	12	4	.750	1	1	2.03
1991 Omaha	AAA	17	14	1	0	86.1	380	88	45	33	4	4	0	5	38	0	36	0	0	5	6	.455	0	0	3.44
1990 Kansas City	AL	5	5	0	0	23.1	112	32	24	21	4	0	2	0	11	1	14	3	0	0	2	.000	0	0	8.10
1991 Kansas City	AL	2	2	0	0	10	49	16	10	8	2	0	0	0	3	0	5	0	0	1	1	.500	0	0	7.20
2 ML YEARS		7	7	0	0	33.1	161	48	34	29	6	0	2	0	14	1	19	3	0	1	3	.250	0	0	7.83

David Wainhouse

Pitches: Right **Bats:** Left **Pos:** RP **Ht:** 6' 2" **Wt:** 190 **Born:** 11/07/67 **Age:** 24

		HOW MUCH HE PITCHED						WHAT HE GAVE UP												THE RESULTS					
Year Team	Lg	G	GS	CG	GF	IP	BFP	H	R	ER	HR	SH	SF	HB	TBB	IBB	SO	WP	Bk	W	L	Pct.	ShO	Sv	ERA
1989 Wst Plm Bch	A	13	13	0	0	66.1	286	75	35	30	4	3	2	8	19	0	26	6	3	1	5	.167	0	0	4.07
1990 Wst Plm Bch	A	12	12	2	0	76.2	327	68	28	18	1	0	3	5	34	0	58	2	3	6	3	.667	1	0	2.11
Jacksnville	AA	17	16	2	0	95.2	428	97	59	46	8	2	3	7	47	2	59	2	0	7	7	.500	0	0	4.33
1991 Harrisburg	AA	33	0	0	27	52	224	49	17	15	1	2	0	4	17	2	46	3	0	2	2	.500	0	11	2.60
Indianapols	AAA	14	0	0	8	28.2	127	28	14	13	1	2	1	3	15	1	13	3	0	2	0	1.000	0	1	4.08
1991 Montreal	NL	2	0	0	1	2.2	14	2	2	2	0	0	1	0	4	0	1	2	0	0	1	.000	0	0	6.75

Don Wakamatsu

Bats: Right **Throws:** Right **Pos:** C **Ht:** 6' 2" **Wt:** 200 **Born:** 02/22/63 **Age:** 29

		BATTING																BASERUNNING				PERCENTAGES		
Year Team	Lg	G	AB	H	2B	3B	HR	(Hm | Rd)	TB	R	RBI	TBB	IBB	SO	HBP	SH	SF	SB	CS	SB%	GDP	Avg	OBP	SLG
1985 Billings	R	58	196	49	7	0	0	--	--	56	22	24	36	2	36	0	5	2	1	0	1.00	7	.250	.332	.286
1986 Tampa	A	112	361	100	18	2	1	--	--	125	41	66	53	2	66	5	0	8	6	1	.86	11	.277	.370	.346
1987 Cedar Rapds	A	103	365	79	13	1	7	--	--	115	33	41	30	1	71	3	2	3	3	3	.50	9	.216	.279	.315
1988 Chattanooga	AA	79	235	56	9	1	1	--	--	70	22	26	37	0	41	0	1	2	0	1	.00	5	.238	.339	.298
1989 Birmingham	AA	92	287	73	15	0	2	--	--	94	45	45	32	0	54	7	5	5	7	6	.54	4	.254	.338	.328
1990 Vancouver	AAA	62	187	49	10	0	0	--	--	59	20	13	13	1	35	7	1	1	2	2	.50	2	.262	.332	.316
1991 Vancouver	AAA	55	172	34	8	0	4	--	--	54	20	19	12	0	39	1	4	2	0	0	.00	3	.198	.251	.314
1991 Chicago	AL	18	31	7	0	0	0	(0 | 0)	7	2	0	1	0	6	0	0	0	0	0	.00	0	.226	.250	.226

Bob Walk

Pitches: Right **Bats:** Right **Pos:** SP/RP **Ht:** 6' 4" **Wt:** 217 **Born:** 11/26/56 **Age:** 35

		HOW MUCH HE PITCHED						WHAT HE GAVE UP												THE RESULTS					
Year Team	Lg	G	GS	CG	GF	IP	BFP	H	R	ER	HR	SH	SF	HB	TBB	IBB	SO	WP	Bk	W	L	Pct.	ShO	Sv	ERA
1980 Philadelphia	NL	27	27	2	0	152	673	163	82	77	8	5	5	2	71	2	94	6	3	11	7	.611	0	0	4.56
1981 Atlanta	NL	12	8	0	1	43	189	41	25	22	6	2	0	0	23	0	16	1	0	1	4	.200	0	0	4.60
1982 Atlanta	NL	32	27	3	1	164.1	717	179	101	89	19	8	5	6	59	2	84	7	0	11	9	.550	1	0	4.87
1983 Atlanta	NL	1	1	0	0	3.2	20	7	3	3	0	1	0	0	2	0	4	0	0	0	0	.000	0	0	7.36
1984 Pittsburgh	NL	2	2	0	0	10.1	44	8	5	3	1	0	0	0	4	1	10	0	0	1	1	.500	0	0	2.61
1985 Pittsburgh	NL	9	9	1	0	58.2	248	60	27	24	3	3	1	0	18	2	40	2	3	2	3	.400	1	0	3.68
1986 Pittsburgh	NL	44	15	1	7	141.2	592	129	66	59	14	6	5	3	64	7	78	12	1	7	8	.467	1	2	3.75
1987 Pittsburgh	NL	39	12	1	6	117	498	107	52	43	11	6	2	3	51	2	78	7	3	8	2	.800	1	0	3.31
1988 Pittsburgh	NL	32	32	1	0	212.2	881	183	75	64	6	14	5	2	65	5	81	13	9	12	10	.545	1	0	2.71
1989 Pittsburgh	NL	33	31	2	1	196	843	208	106	96	15	4	2	4	65	1	83	7	4	13	10	.565	0	0	4.41
1990 Pittsburgh	NL	26	24	1	1	129.2	549	136	59	54	17	3	3	4	36	2	73	5	3	7	5	.583	1	1	3.75
1991 Pittsburgh	NL	25	20	0	0	115	484	104	53	46	10	7	4	5	35	2	67	11	2	9	2	.818	0	0	3.60
12 ML YEARS		282	208	12	17	1344	5738	1325	654	580	110	59	32	29	493	26	708	71	28	82	61	.573	6	3	3.88

Chico Walker

Bats: Both **Throws:** Right **Pos:** 3B/CF **Ht:** 5' 9" **Wt:** 170 **Born:** 11/25/57 **Age:** 34

		BATTING																BASERUNNING				PERCENTAGES		
Year Team	Lg	G	AB	H	2B	3B	HR	(Hm | Rd)	TB	R	RBI	TBB	IBB	SO	HBP	SH	SF	SB	CS	SB%	GDP	Avg	OBP	SLG
1980 Boston	AL	19	57	12	0	0	1	(1 | 0)	15	3	5	6	1	10	1	1	1	3	2	.60	1	.211	.292	.263
1981 Boston	AL	6	17	6	0	0	0	(0 | 0)	6	3	2	1	0	2	0	0	0	0	2	.00	0	.353	.389	.353
1983 Boston	AL	4	5	2	0	2	0	(0 | 0)	6	2	1	0	0	0	0	0	0	0	0	.00	0	.400	.400	1.200
1984 Boston	AL	3	2	0	0	0	0	(0 | 0)	0	0	1	0	0	1	0	0	1	0	0	.00	0	.000	.000	.000
1985 Chicago	NL	21	12	1	0	0	0	(0 | 0)	1	3	0	0	0	5	0	0	0	1	0	1.00	0	.083	.083	.083
1986 Chicago	NL	28	101	28	3	2	1	(0 | 1)	38	21	7	10	0	20	0	0	1	15	4	.79	3	.277	.339	.376
1987 Chicago	NL	47	105	21	4	0	0	(0 | 0)	25	15	7	12	1	23	0	2	2	11	4	.73	1	.200	.277	.238
1988 California	AL	33	78	12	1	0	0	(0 | 0)	13	8	2	6	0	15	0	2	0	2	1	.67	2	.154	.214	.167
1991 Chicago	NL	124	374	96	10	1	6	(4 | 2)	126	51	34	33	2	57	0	1	3	13	5	.72	3	.257	.315	.337
9 ML YEARS		285	751	178	18	5	8	(5 | 3)	230	106	59	68	4	133	1	6	8	45	18	.71	10	.237	.298	.306

Larry Walker

Bats: Left Throws: Right Pos: RF/1B   Ht: 6' 3" Wt: 210 Born: 12/01/66 Age: 25

Year Team	Lg	G	AB	H	2B	3B	HR	(Hm	Rd)	TB	R	RBI	TBB	IBB	SO	HBP	SH	SF	SB	CS	SB%	GDP	Avg	OBP	SLG
1989 Montreal	NL	20	47	8	0	0	0	(0	0)	8	4	4	5	0	13	1	3	0	1	1	.50	0	.170	.264	.170
1990 Montreal	NL	133	419	101	18	3	19	(9	10)	182	59	51	49	5	112	5	3	2	21	7	.75	8	.241	.326	.434
1991 Montreal	NL	137	487	141	30	2	16	(5	11)	223	59	64	42	2	102	5	1	4	14	9	.61	7	.290	.349	.458
3 ML YEARS		290	953	250	48	5	35	(14	21)	413	122	119	96	7	227	11	7	6	36	17	.68	15	.262	.335	.433

Mike Walker

Pitches: Right Bats: Right Pos: RP   Ht: 6' 1" Wt: 195 Born: 10/04/66 Age: 25

Year Team	Lg	G	GS	CG	GF	IP	BFP	H	R	ER	HR	SH	SF	HB	TBB	IBB	SO	WP	Bk	W	L	Pct.	ShO	Sv	ERA
1988 Cleveland	AL	3	1	0	0	8.2	42	8	7	7	0	1	0	0	10	0	7	0	0	0	1	.000	0	0	7.27
1990 Cleveland	AL	18	11	0	2	75.2	350	82	49	41	6	4	2	6	42	4	34	3	1	2	6	.250	0	0	4.88
1991 Cleveland	AL	5	0	0	3	4.1	22	6	1	1	0	0	0	1	2	1	2	0	0	0	1	.000	0	0	2.08
3 ML YEARS		26	12	0	5	88.2	414	96	57	49	6	5	2	7	54	5	43	3	1	2	8	.200	0	0	4.97

Tim Wallach

Bats: Right Throws: Right Pos: 3B   Ht: 6' 3" Wt: 200 Born: 09/14/57 Age: 34

Year Team	Lg	G	AB	H	2B	3B	HR	(Hm	Rd)	TB	R	RBI	TBB	IBB	SO	HBP	SH	SF	SB	CS	SB%	GDP	Avg	OBP	SLG
1980 Montreal	NL	5	11	2	0	0	1	(0	1)	5	1	2	1	0	5	0	0	0	0	0	.00	0	.182	.250	.455
1981 Montreal	NL	71	212	50	9	1	4	(1	3)	73	19	13	15	2	37	4	0	0	0	1	.00	3	.236	.299	.344
1982 Montreal	NL	158	596	160	31	3	28	(11	17)	281	89	97	36	4	81	4	5	4	6	4	.60	15	.268	.313	.471
1983 Montreal	NL	156	581	156	33	3	19	(9	10)	252	54	70	55	8	97	6	0	5	0	3	.00	9	.269	.335	.434
1984 Montreal	NL	160	582	143	25	4	18	(4	14)	230	55	72	50	6	101	7	0	4	3	7	.30	12	.246	.311	.395
1985 Montreal	NL	155	569	148	36	3	22	(9	13)	256	70	81	38	8	79	5	0	5	9	9	.50	17	.260	.310	.450
1986 Montreal	NL	134	480	112	22	1	18	(6	12)	190	50	71	44	8	72	10	0	5	8	4	.67	16	.233	.308	.396
1987 Montreal	NL	153	593	177	42	4	26	(13	13)	305	89	123	37	5	98	7	0	7	9	5	.64	6	.298	.343	.514
1988 Montreal	NL	159	592	152	32	5	12	(3	9)	230	52	69	38	7	88	3	0	7	2	6	.25	19	.257	.302	.389
1989 Montreal	NL	154	573	159	42	0	13	(6	7)	240	76	77	58	10	81	1	0	7	3	7	.30	21	.277	.341	.419
1990 Montreal	NL	161	626	185	37	5	21	(9	12)	295	69	98	42	11	80	3	0	7	6	9	.40	12	.296	.339	.471
1991 Montreal	NL	151	577	130	22	1	13	(5	8)	193	60	73	50	8	100	6	0	4	2	4	.33	12	.225	.292	.334
12 ML YEARS		1617	5992	1574	331	30	195	(76	119)	2550	684	846	464	77	919	56	5	55	48	59	.45	142	.263	.319	.426

Denny Walling

Bats: Left Throws: Right Pos: 3B   Ht: 6' 1" Wt: 185 Born: 04/17/54 Age: 38

Year Team	Lg	G	AB	H	2B	3B	HR	(Hm	Rd)	TB	R	RBI	TBB	IBB	SO	HBP	SH	SF	SB	CS	SB%	GDP	Avg	OBP	SLG
1975 Oakland	AL	6	8	1	1	0	0	(0	0)	2	0	2	0	0	4	0	0	0	0	0	.00	0	.125	.125	.250
1976 Oakland	AL	3	11	3	0	0	0	(0	0)	3	1	0	0	0	3	0	0	0	0	0	.00	0	.273	.273	.273
1977 Houston	NL	6	21	6	0	1	0	(0	0)	8	1	6	2	0	4	0	0	0	1	0	1.00	0	.286	.348	.381
1978 Houston	NL	120	247	62	11	3	3	(2	1)	88	30	36	30	3	24	1	0	2	9	2	.82	2	.251	.332	.356
1979 Houston	NL	82	147	48	8	4	3	(3	0)	73	21	31	17	2	21	0	0	1	3	2	.60	2	.327	.394	.497
1980 Houston	NL	100	284	85	6	5	3	(1	2)	110	30	29	35	4	26	0	0	2	4	3	.57	2	.299	.374	.387
1981 Houston	NL	65	158	37	6	0	5	(2	3)	58	23	23	28	1	17	0	1	2	2	1	.67	3	.234	.346	.367
1982 Houston	NL	85	146	30	4	1	1	(1	0)	39	22	14	23	3	19	0	0	1	4	2	.67	6	.205	.312	.267
1983 Houston	NL	100	135	40	5	3	3	(1	2)	60	24	19	15	1	16	0	1	2	2	2	.50	1	.296	.364	.444
1984 Houston	NL	87	249	70	11	5	3	(0	3)	100	37	31	16	2	28	1	0	1	7	1	.88	4	.281	.325	.402
1985 Houston	NL	119	345	93	20	1	7	(2	5)	136	44	45	25	2	26	0	0	4	5	2	.71	8	.270	.316	.394
1986 Houston	NL	130	382	119	23	1	6	(5	8)	183	54	58	36	5	31	0	0	4	1	1	.50	8	.312	.367	.479
1987 Houston	NL	110	325	92	21	4	5	(2	3)	136	45	33	39	1	37	0	2	4	5	1	.83	9	.283	.356	.418
1988 2 ML Teams		84	234	56	13	2	1	(0	1)	76	22	21	17	3	25	0	1	0	2	0	1.00	3	.239	.291	.325
1989 St. Louis	NL	69	79	24	7	0	1	(0	1)	34	9	11	14	2	12	0	0	0	0	0	.00	0	.304	.409	.430
1990 St. Louis	NL	78	127	28	5	0	1	(1	0)	36	7	19	8	0	15	0	1	1	0	0	.00	5	.220	.265	.283
1991 Texas	AL	24	44	4	1	0	0	(0	0)	5	1	2	3	0	8	2	0	0	0	0	.00	3	.091	.184	.114
1988 Houston	NL	65	176	43	10	2	1	(0	1)	60	19	20	15	3	18	0	1	0	1	0	1.00	2	.244	.304	.341
St. Louis	NL	19	58	13	3	0	0	(0	0)	16	3	1	2	0	7	0	0	0	1	0	1.00	1	.224	.250	.276
17 ML YEARS		1268	2942	798	142	30	49	(20	29)	1147	371	380	308	29	316	4	6	24	44	18	.71	57	.271	.339	.390

Bruce Walton

Pitches: Right **Bats:** Right **Pos:** RP   **Ht:** 6' 2" **Wt:** 195 **Born:** 12/25/62 **Age:** 29

			HOW MUCH HE PITCHED					WHAT HE GAVE UP								THE RESULTS					
Year Team	Lg	G	GS	CG	GF	IP	BFP	H	R	ER	HR	SH	SF	HB	TBB	IBB	SO	WP	Bk	W	L	Pct.	ShO	Sv	ERA
1985 Pocatello	R	18	9	2	6	76.2	0	89	46	35	2	0	0	1	27	3	69	2	0	3	7	.300	0	3	4.11
1986 Modesto	A	27	27	4	0	176	778	204	96	80	16	10	5	9	41	1	107	7	1	13	7	.650	0	0	4.09
Madison	A	1	1	0	0	5	21	5	3	3	0	0	0	0	1	0	1	0	0	0	0	.000	0	0	5.40
1987 Modesto	A	16	16	3	0	106.1	437	97	44	34	6	1	3	4	27	0	84	2	0	8	6	.571	1	0	2.88
Huntsville	AA	18	2	0	6	58	248	61	24	20	4	2	3	1	13	1	40	4	2	2	2	.500	0	2	3.10
1988 Huntsville	AA	42	3	0	17	116.1	502	126	64	59	10	5	3	5	23	7	82	2	6	4	5	.444	0	3	4.56
1989 Tacoma	AAA	32	14	1	7	107.2	461	118	59	45	7	4	4	1	27	1	76	3	2	8	6	.571	1	0	3.76
1990 Tacoma	AAA	46	5	0	21	98.1	403	103	42	34	12	4	7	2	23	5	67	1	5	5	5	.500	0	3	3.11
1991 Tacoma	AAA	38	0	0	38	46.2	184	39	11	7	0	2	0	0	5	1	49	2	0	1	1	.500	0	20	1.35
1991 Oakland	AL	12	0	0	5	13	56	11	9	9	3	0	1	1	6	0	10	3	0	1	0	1.000	0	0	6.23

Jerome Walton

Bats: Right **Throws:** Right **Pos:** CF   **Ht:** 6' 1" **Wt:** 175 **Born:** 07/08/65 **Age:** 26

				BATTING													BASERUNNING				PERCENTAGES		
Year Team	Lg	G	AB	H	2B	3B	HR	(Hm | Rd)	TB	R	RBI	TBB	IBB	SO	HBP	SH	SF	SB	CS	SB%	GDP	Avg	OBP	SLG
1989 Chicago	NL	116	475	139	23	3	5	(3 | 2)	183	64	46	27	1	77	6	2	5	24	7	.77	6	.293	.335	.385
1990 Chicago	NL	101	392	103	16	2	2	(2 | 0)	129	63	21	50	1	70	4	1	2	14	7	.67	4	.263	.350	.329
1991 Chicago	NL	123	270	59	13	1	5	(3 | 2)	89	42	17	19	0	55	3	3	3	7	3	.70	7	.219	.275	.330
3 ML YEARS		340	1137	301	52	6	12	(8 | 4)	401	169	84	96	2	202	13	6	10	45	17	.73	17	.265	.326	.353

Steve Wapnick

Pitches: Right **Bats:** Right **Pos:** RP   **Ht:** 6' 2" **Wt:** 196 **Born:** 09/25/65 **Age:** 26

				HOW MUCH HE PITCHED					WHAT HE GAVE UP								THE RESULTS					
Year Team	Lg	G	GS	CG	GF	IP	BFP	H	R	ER	HR	SH	SF	HB	TBB	IBB	SO	WP	Bk	W	L	Pct.	ShO	Sv	ERA
1987 St.Cathrnes	A	20	6	0	4	65.2	272	53	28	22	5	1	1	2	21	0	63	3	1	3	4	.429	0	1	3.02
1988 Myrtle Bch	A	54	0	0	27	60.1	252	44	18	15	2	2	2	0	31	5	69	3	3	4	3	.571	0	12	2.24
1989 Dunedin	A	24	1	0	11	66	262	48	19	15	2	0	1	3	22	1	59	9	1	4	0	1.000	0	7	2.05
Knoxville	AA	12	0	0	9	18.1	73	12	1	1	1	1	0	0	7	0	20	0	1	1	0	1.000	0	2	0.49
Syracuse	AAA	6	1	0	4	13	51	9	1	1	0	1	0	1	5	0	10	0	0	1	0	1.000	0	0	0.69
1990 Syracuse	AAA	11	1	0	6	16	70	16	9	9	2	1	1	1	6	0	19	1	0	0	1	.000	0	2	5.06
1991 Syracuse	AAA	53	0	0	42	71.2	302	68	23	22	4	7	2	2	25	4	58	4	1	6	3	.667	0	20	2.76
1990 Detroit	AL	4	0	0	1	7	37	8	5	5	0	0	0	0	10	0	6	0	0	0	0	.000	0	0	6.43
1991 Chicago	AL	6	0	0	4	5	22	2	1	1	0	0	0	0	4	0	1	0	0	0	0	.000	0	0	1.80
2 ML YEARS		10	0	0	5	12	59	10	6	6	0	0	0	0	14	0	7	0	0	0	0	.000	0	0	4.50

Duane Ward

Pitches: Right **Bats:** Right **Pos:** RP   **Ht:** 6' 4" **Wt:** 215 **Born:** 05/28/64 **Age:** 28

				HOW MUCH HE PITCHED					WHAT HE GAVE UP								THE RESULTS					
Year Team	Lg	G	GS	CG	GF	IP	BFP	H	R	ER	HR	SH	SF	HB	TBB	IBB	SO	WP	Bk	W	L	Pct.	ShO	Sv	ERA
1986 2 ML Teams		12	1	0	7	18	88	25	17	16	2	2	0	1	12	0	9	1	1	0	2	.000	0	0	8.00
1987 Toronto	AL	12	1	0	4	11.2	57	14	9	9	0	1	1	0	12	2	10	0	0	1	0	1.000	0	0	6.94
1988 Toronto	AL	64	0	0	32	111.2	487	101	46	41	5	4	5	5	60	8	91	10	3	9	3	.750	0	15	3.30
1989 Toronto	AL	66	0	0	39	114.2	494	94	55	48	4	12	11	5	58	11	122	13	0	4	10	.286	0	15	3.77
1990 Toronto	AL	73	0	0	39	127.2	508	101	51	49	9	6	2	1	42	10	112	5	0	2	8	.200	0	11	3.45
1991 Toronto	AL	81	0	0	46	107.1	428	80	36	33	3	3	4	2	33	3	132	6	0	7	6	.538	0	23	2.77
1986 Atlanta	NL	10	0	0	6	16	73	22	13	13	2	2	0	0	8	0	8	0	1	0	0	.000	0	0	7.31
Toronto	AL	2	1	0	1	2	15	3	4	3	0	0	0	1	4	0	1	1	0	0	1	.000	0	0	13.50
6 ML YEARS		308	2	0	167	491	2062	415	214	196	23	28	23	14	217	34	476	35	4	23	29	.442	0	64	3.59

Kevin Ward

Bats: Right **Throws:** Right **Pos:** LF   **Ht:** 6' 1" **Wt:** 195 **Born:** 09/28/61 **Age:** 30

				BATTING													BASERUNNING				PERCENTAGES		
Year Team	Lg	G	AB	H	2B	3B	HR	(Hm | Rd)	TB	R	RBI	TBB	IBB	SO	HBP	SH	SF	SB	CS	SB%	GDP	Avg	OBP	SLG
1984 Peninsula	A	130	456	119	18	5	13	--	--	186	84	69	53	3	90	6	4	7	21	3	.88	11	.261	.341	.408
1985 Reading	AA	42	132	40	9	6	1	--	--	64	23	21	23	1	19	5	0	2	7	5	.58	2	.303	.420	.485
1986 Reading	AA	119	398	109	27	6	7	--	--	169	79	59	66	1	66	6	1	7	28	14	.67	9	.274	.379	.425
1987 Reading	AA	16	56	14	5	1	0	--	--	21	9	6	6	0	12	1	0	1	5	2	.71	0	.250	.328	.375
Maine	AAA	106	326	68	13	3	13	--	--	126	48	37	30	0	68	5	1	2	14	8	.64	9	.209	.284	.387
1988 Maine	AAA	134	456	105	22	8	11	--	--	176	60	63	62	1	118	7	9	3	17	11	.61	9	.230	.330	.386
1989 Huntsville	AA	27	84	26	4	4	3	--	--	47	20	18	29	0	18	1	0	3	15	0	1.00	1	.310	.479	.560
1990 Tacoma	AAA	123	421	125	30	14	10	--	--	213	83	60	44	1	72	14	4	4	24	10	.71	8	.297	.379	.506

Year Team	Lg	G	AB	H	2B	3B	HR	(Hm	Rd)	TB	R	RBI	TBB	IBB	SO	HBP	SH	SF	SB	CS	SB%	GDP	Avg	OBP	SLG
1991 Las Vegas	AAA	83	276	89	17	6	6	--	--	136	51	43	58	2	53	7	1	5	10	4	.71	4	.322	.445	.493
1991 San Diego	NL	44	107	26	7	2	2	(0	2)	43	13	8	9	0	27	1	1	0	1	4	.20	3	.243	.308	.402

Turner Ward

Bats: Both **Throws:** Right **Pos:** RF **Ht:** 6' 2" **Wt:** 200 **Born:** 04/11/65 **Age:** 27

								BATTING												BASERUNNING				PERCENTAGES		
Year Team	Lg	G	AB	H	2B	3B	HR	(Hm	Rd)	TB	R	RBI	TBB	IBB	SO	HBP	SH	SF	SB	CS	SB%	GDP	Avg	OBP	SLG
1986 Oneonta	A	63	221	62	4	1	1	--	--	71	42	19	31	1	39	2	2	3	6	6	.50	4	.281	.370	.321
1987 Ft.Laudrdle	A	130	493	145	15	2	7	--	--	185	83	55	64	4	83	6	7	3	25	3	.89	8	.294	.380	.375
1988 Columbus	AAA	134	490	123	24	1	7	--	--	170	55	50	48	5	100	3	8	2	28	5	.85	7	.251	.320	.347
1989 Indians	R	4	15	3	0	0	0	--	--	3	2	1	2	0	2	0	0	0	1	0	1.00	0	.200	.294	.200
Canton-Akrn	AA	30	93	28	5	1	0	--	--	35	19	3	15	0	16	0	0	0	1	2	.33	2	.301	.398	.376
1990 Colo Sprngs	AAA	133	495	148	24	9	6	--	--	208	89	65	72	1	70	4	5	9	22	15	.59	16	.299	.386	.420
1991 Colo Sprngs	AAA	14	51	10	1	1	1	--	--	16	5	3	6	0	9	0	1	0	2	1	.67	1	.196	.281	.314
Syracuse	AAA	59	218	72	11	3	7	--	--	110	40	32	47	1	22	0	1	0	9	6	.60	5	.330	.449	.505
1990 Cleveland	AL	14	46	16	2	1	1	(0	1)	23	10	10	3	0	8	0	0	1	3	0	1.00	1	.348	.388	.500
1991 2 ML Teams		48	113	27	7	0	0	(0	0)	34	12	7	11	0	18	0	4	0	0	0	.00	2	.239	.306	.301
1991 Cleveland	AL	40	100	23	7	0	0	(0	0)	30	11	5	10	0	16	0	4	0	0	0	.00	1	.230	.300	.300
Toronto	AL	8	13	4	0	0	0	(0	0)	4	1	2	1	0	2	0	0	0	0	0	.00	1	.308	.357	.308
2 ML YEARS		62	159	43	9	1	1	(0	1)	57	22	17	14	0	26	0	4	0	3	0	1.00	3	.270	.329	.358

Gary Wayne

Pitches: Left **Bats:** Left **Pos:** RP **Ht:** 6' 3" **Wt:** 192 **Born:** 11/30/62 **Age:** 29

			HOW	MUCH	HE	PITCHED				WHAT	HE	GAVE	UP							THE	RESULTS			
Year Team	Lg	G	GS	CG	GF	IP	BFP	H	R	ER	HR	SH	SF	HB	TBB	IBB	SO	WP	Bk	W	L	Pct.	ShO	Sv	ERA
1989 Minnesota	AL	60	0	0	21	71	302	55	28	26	4	4	2	1	36	4	41	7	0	3	4	.429	0	1	3.30
1990 Minnesota	AL	38	0	0	12	38.2	166	38	19	18	5	1	2	1	13	0	28	4	0	1	1	.500	0	1	4.19
1991 Minnesota	AL	8	0	0	2	12.1	52	11	7	7	1	1	1	1	4	0	7	0	0	1	0	1.000	0	1	5.11
3 ML YEARS		106	0	0	35	122	520	104	54	51	10	6	5	3	53	4	76	11	0	5	5	.500	0	3	3.76

Dave Weathers

Pitches: Right **Bats:** Right **Pos:** RP **Ht:** 6' 3" **Wt:** 205 **Born:** 09/25/69 **Age:** 22

			HOW	MUCH	HE	PITCHED				WHAT	HE	GAVE	UP							THE	RESULTS			
Year Team	Lg	G	GS	CG	GF	IP	BFP	H	R	ER	HR	SH	SF	HB	TBB	IBB	SO	WP	Bk	W	L	Pct.	ShO	Sv	ERA
1988 St.Cathrnes	A	15	12	0	2	62.2	267	58	30	21	3	2	0	2	26	0	36	5	4	4	4	.500	0	0	3.02
1989 Myrtle Bch	A	31	31	2	0	172.2	759	163	99	74	3	5	2	7	86	2	111	12	1	11	13	.458	0	0	3.86
1990 Dunedin	A	27	27	2	0	158	675	158	82	65	2	4	7	9	59	0	96	10	9	10	7	.588	0	0	3.70
1991 Knoxville	AA	24	22	5	0	139.1	575	121	51	38	3	1	3	8	49	1	114	7	2	10	7	.588	2	0	2.45
1991 Toronto	AL	15	0	0	4	14.2	79	15	9	8	1	2	1	2	17	3	13	0	0	1	0	1.000	0	0	4.91

Lenny Webster

Bats: Right **Throws:** Right **Pos:** C **Ht:** 5' 9" **Wt:** 192 **Born:** 02/10/65 **Age:** 27

								BATTING												BASERUNNING				PERCENTAGES		
Year Team	Lg	G	AB	H	2B	3B	HR	(Hm	Rd)	TB	R	RBI	TBB	IBB	SO	HBP	SH	SF	SB	CS	SB%	GDP	Avg	OBP	SLG
1986 Kenosha	A	22	65	10	2	0	0	--	--	12	2	8	10	0	12	0	1	0	0	0	.00	3	.154	.267	.185
Elizabethtn	R	48	152	35	4	0	3	--	--	48	29	14	22	0	21	2	0	0	1	0	1.00	6	.230	.335	.316
1987 Kenosha	A	52	140	35	7	0	3	--	--	51	17	17	17	0	20	0	0	3	2	0	1.00	8	.250	.325	.364
1988 Kenosha	A	129	465	134	23	2	11	--	--	194	82	87	71	5	47	1	2	7	3	2	.60	13	.288	.379	.417
1989 Visalia	A	63	231	62	7	0	5	--	--	84	36	39	27	1	27	1	0	5	2	1	.67	9	.268	.341	.364
Orlando	AA	59	191	45	7	0	2	--	--	58	29	17	44	1	20	3	2	2	2	0	1.00	3	.236	.383	.304
1990 Orlando	AA	126	455	119	31	0	8	--	--	174	69	71	68	5	57	0	0	3	0	0	.00	11	.262	.356	.382
1991 Portland	AAA	87	325	82	18	0	7	--	--	121	43	34	24	2	32	1	0	3	1	4	.20	14	.252	.303	.372
1989 Minnesota	AL	14	20	6	2	0	0	(0	0)	8	3	1	3	0	2	0	0	0	0	0	.00	0	.300	.391	.400
1990 Minnesota	AL	2	6	2	1	0	0	(0	0)	3	1	0	1	0	1	0	0	0	0	0	.00	0	.333	.429	.500
1991 Minnesota	AL	18	34	10	1	0	3	(1	2)	20	7	8	6	0	10	0	0	1	0	0	.00	2	.294	.390	.588
3 ML YEARS		34	60	18	4	0	3	(1	2)	31	11	9	10	0	13	0	0	1	0	0	.00	2	.300	.394	.517

Mitch Webster

Bats: Both **Throws:** Left **Pos:** RF/LF/CF **Ht:** 6' 1" **Wt:** 185 **Born:** 05/16/59 **Age:** 33

								BATTING												BASERUNNING				PERCENTAGES		
Year Team	Lg	G	AB	H	2B	3B	HR	(Hm	Rd)	TB	R	RBI	TBB	IBB	SO	HBP	SH	SF	SB	CS	SB%	GDP	Avg	OBP	SLG
1983 Toronto	AL	11	11	2	0	0	0	(0	0)	2	2	0	1	0	1	0	0	0	0	0	.00	0	.182	.250	.182
1984 Toronto	AL	26	22	5	2	1	0	(0	0)	9	4	1	0	0	7	0	0	0	0	0	.00	1	.227	.261	.409
1985 2 ML Teams		78	213	58	8	2	11	(3	8)	103	32	30	20	3	33	0	1	1	15	10	.60	3	.272	.333	.484
1986 Montreal	NL	151	576	167	31	13	8	(2	6)	248	89	49	57	4	78	4	3	5	36	15	.71	9	.290	.355	.431
1987 Montreal	NL	156	588	165	30	8	15	(9	6)	256	101	63	70	5	95	6	8	4	33	10	.77	6	.281	.361	.435
1988 2 ML Teams		151	523	136	16	8	6	(3	3)	186	69	39	55	2	87	8	5	4	22	14	.61	5	.260	.337	.356

215

Year Team	Lg	G	AB	H	2B	3B	HR	(Hm	Rd)	TB	R	RBI	TBB	IBB	SO	HBP	SH	SF	SB	CS	SB%	GDP	Avg	OBP	SLG
1989 Chicago	NL	98	272	70	12	4	3	(1	2)	99	40	19	30	5	55	1	3	2	14	2	.88	3	.257	.331	.364
1990 Cleveland	AL	128	437	110	20	6	12	(6	6)	178	58	55	20	1	61	3	11	6	22	6	.79	5	.252	.285	.407
1991 3 ML Teams		107	203	42	8	5	2	(2	0)	66	23	19	21	1	61	0	2	0	2	3	.40	3	.207	.281	.325
1985 Toronto	AL	4	1	0	0	0	0	(0	0)	0	0	0	0	0	0	0	0	0	0	1	.00	0	.000	.000	.000
Montreal	NL	74	212	58	8	2	11	(3	8)	103	32	30	20	3	33	0	1	1	15	9	.63	3	.274	.335	.486
1988 Montreal	NL	81	259	66	5	2	2	(0	2)	81	33	13	36	2	37	5	4	2	12	10	.55	3	.255	.354	.313
Chicago	NL	70	264	70	11	6	4	(3	1)	105	36	26	19	0	50	3	1	2	10	4	.71	2	.265	.319	.398
1991 Cleveland	AL	13	32	4	0	0	0	(0	0)	4	2	0	3	0	9	0	1	0	2	2	.50	0	.125	.200	.125
Pittsburgh	NL	36	97	17	3	4	1	(1	0)	31	9	9	9	1	31	0	0	0	0	0	.00	0	.175	.245	.320
Los Angeles	NL	58	74	21	5	1	1	(1	0)	31	12	10	9	0	21	0	1	0	0	1	.00	0	.284	.361	.419
9 ML YEARS		906	2845	755	127	47	57	(26	31)	1147	423	278	275	21	478	22	33	22	144	60	.71	35	.265	.332	.403

Eric Wedge

Bats: Right **Throws:** Right **Pos:** PH **Ht:** 6'3" **Wt:** 215 **Born:** 01/27/68 **Age:** 24

								BATTING											BASERUNNING				PERCENTAGES		
Year Team	Lg	G	AB	H	2B	3B	HR	(Hm	Rd)	TB	R	RBI	TBB	IBB	SO	HBP	SH	SF	SB	CS	SB%	GDP	Avg	OBP	SLG
1989 Elmira	A	41	145	34	6	2	7	--	--	65	20	22	15	0	21	0	0	0	1	1	.50	3	.234	.306	.448
New Britain	AA	14	40	8	2	0	0	--	--	10	3	2	5	0	10	0	2	0	0	0	.00	1	.200	.289	.250
1990 New Britain	AA	103	339	77	13	1	5	--	--	107	36	48	51	2	54	1	0	5	1	3	.25	14	.227	.326	.316
1991 New Britain	AA	2	8	2	0	0	0	--	--	2	0	2	0	0	2	0	0	0	1	0	.00	0	.250	.222	.250
Winter Havn	A	8	21	5	0	0	1	--	--	8	2	1	3	0	7	0	1	0	1	0	1.00	1	.238	.333	.381
Pawtucket	AAA	53	163	38	14	1	5	--	--	69	24	18	25	0	26	1	2	5	1	2	.33	3	.233	.330	.423
1991 Boston	AL	1	1	1	0	0	0	(0	0)	1	0	0	0	0	0	0	0	0	0	0	.00	0	1.000	1.000	1.000

Bill Wegman

Pitches: Right **Bats:** Right **Pos:** SP **Ht:** 6'5" **Wt:** 220 **Born:** 12/19/62 **Age:** 29

			HOW MUCH HE PITCHED					WHAT HE GAVE UP												THE RESULTS					
Year Team	Lg	G	GS	CG	GF	IP	BFP	H	R	ER	HR	SH	SF	HB	TBB	IBB	SO	WP	Bk	W	L	Pct.	ShO	Sv	ERA
1985 Milwaukee	AL	3	3	0	0	17.2	73	17	8	7	3	0	1	0	3	0	6	0	1	2	0	1.000	0	0	3.57
1986 Milwaukee	AL	35	32	2	1	198.1	836	217	120	113	32	4	5	7	43	2	82	5	2	5	12	.294	0	0	5.13
1987 Milwaukee	AL	34	33	7	0	225	934	229	113	106	31	4	6	6	53	2	102	0	2	12	11	.522	0	0	4.24
1988 Milwaukee	AL	32	31	4	0	199	847	207	104	91	24	3	10	4	50	5	84	1	1	13	13	.500	1	0	4.12
1989 Milwaukee	AL	11	8	0	1	51	240	69	44	38	6	0	4	0	21	2	27	2	0	2	6	.250	0	0	6.71
1990 Milwaukee	AL	8	5	1	0	29.2	132	37	21	16	6	1	1	0	6	1	20	0	0	2	2	.500	1	0	4.85
1991 Milwaukee	AL	28	28	7	0	193.1	785	176	76	61	16	6	4	7	40	0	89	6	0	15	7	.682	2	0	2.84
7 ML YEARS		151	140	21	2	914	3847	952	486	432	118	18	31	24	216	12	410	14	6	51	51	.500	4	0	4.25

John Wehner

Bats: Right **Throws:** Right **Pos:** 3B **Ht:** 6'3" **Wt:** 204 **Born:** 06/29/67 **Age:** 25

								BATTING											BASERUNNING				PERCENTAGES		
Year Team	Lg	G	AB	H	2B	3B	HR	(Hm	Rd)	TB	R	RBI	TBB	IBB	SO	HBP	SH	SF	SB	CS	SB%	GDP	Avg	OBP	SLG
1988 Watertown	A	70	265	73	6	0	3	--	--	88	41	31	21	0	39	2	1	4	18	6	.75	4	.275	.329	.332
1989 Salem	A	137	515	155	32	6	14	--	--	241	69	73	42	4	81	1	0	1	21	10	.68	14	.301	.354	.468
1990 Harrisburg	AA	138	511	147	27	1	4	--	--	188	72	62	40	4	51	4	4	6	24	11	.69	12	.288	.340	.368
1991 Carolina	AA	61	234	62	5	1	3	--	--	78	30	21	24	1	32	2	3	5	17	5	.77	7	.265	.332	.333
Buffalo	AAA	31	112	34	9	2	1	--	--	50	18	15	14	1	12	0	0	2	6	4	.60	5	.304	.375	.446
1991 Pittsburgh	NL	37	106	36	7	0	0	(0	0)	43	15	7	7	0	17	0	0	0	3	0	1.00	0	.340	.381	.406

Walt Weiss

Bats: Both **Throws:** Right **Pos:** SS **Ht:** 6'0" **Wt:** 175 **Born:** 11/28/63 **Age:** 28

								BATTING											BASERUNNING				PERCENTAGES		
Year Team	Lg	G	AB	H	2B	3B	HR	(Hm	Rd)	TB	R	RBI	TBB	IBB	SO	HBP	SH	SF	SB	CS	SB%	GDP	Avg	OBP	SLG
1987 Oakland	AL	16	26	12	4	0	0	(0	0)	16	3	1	2	0	2	0	1	0	1	2	.33	0	.462	.500	.615
1988 Oakland	AL	147	452	113	17	3	3	(0	3)	145	44	39	35	1	56	9	8	7	4	4	.50	9	.250	.312	.321
1989 Oakland	AL	84	236	55	11	0	3	(2	1)	75	30	21	21	0	39	1	5	0	6	1	.86	5	.233	.298	.321
1990 Oakland	AL	138	445	118	17	1	2	(1	1)	143	50	35	46	5	53	4	6	4	9	3	.75	8	.265	.337	.321
1991 Oakland	AL	40	133	30	6	1	0	(0	0)	38	15	13	12	0	14	0	1	2	6	0	1.00	3	.226	.286	.286
5 ML YEARS		425	1292	328	55	5	8	(3	5)	417	142	109	116	6	164	14	21	13	26	10	.72	25	.254	.319	.323

Bob Welch

Pitches: Right **Bats:** Right **Pos:** SP **Ht:** 6'3" **Wt:** 198 **Born:** 11/03/56 **Age:** 35

			HOW MUCH HE PITCHED					WHAT HE GAVE UP												THE RESULTS					
Year Team	Lg	G	GS	CG	GF	IP	BFP	H	R	ER	HR	SH	SF	HB	TBB	IBB	SO	WP	Bk	W	L	Pct.	ShO	Sv	ERA
1978 Los Angeles	NL	23	13	4	6	111	439	92	28	25	6	4	6	1	26	2	66	2	2	7	4	.636	3	3	2.03
1979 Los Angeles	NL	25	12	1	10	81	349	82	42	36	7	4	1	3	32	4	64	0	0	5	6	.455	0	5	4.00
1980 Los Angeles	NL	32	32	3	0	214	889	190	85	78	15	12	10	3	79	6	141	7	5	14	9	.609	2	0	3.28
1981 Los Angeles	NL	23	23	2	0	141	601	141	56	54	11	9	4	3	41	0	88	2	0	9	5	.643	1	0	3.36
1982 Los Angeles	NL	36	36	9	0	235.2	965	199	94	88	19	7	4	5	81	5	176	5	1	16	11	.593	3	0	3.36

Year	Team	Lg	G	GS	CG	GF	IP	BFP	H	R	ER	HR	SH	SF	HB	TBB	IBB	SO	WP	Bk	W	L	Pct.	ShO	Sv	ERA
1983	Los Angeles	NL	31	31	4	0	204	828	164	73	60	13	8	7	3	72	4	156	4	6	15	12	.556	3	0	2.65
1984	Los Angeles	NL	31	29	3	0	178.2	771	191	86	75	11	10	2	2	58	7	126	4	2	13	13	.500	1	0	3.78
1985	Los Angeles	NL	23	23	8	0	167.1	675	141	49	43	16	6	2	6	35	2	96	7	4	14	4	.778	3	0	2.31
1986	Los Angeles	NL	33	33	7	0	235.2	981	227	95	86	14	7	8	7	55	6	183	2	1	7	13	.350	3	0	3.28
1987	Los Angeles	NL	35	35	6	0	251.2	1027	204	94	90	21	10	6	4	86	6	196	4	4	15	9	.625	4	0	3.22
1988	Oakland	AL	36	36	4	0	244.2	1034	237	107	99	22	12	8	10	81	1	158	3	13	17	9	.654	2	0	3.64
1989	Oakland	AL	33	33	1	0	209.2	884	191	82	70	13	3	4	6	78	3	137	5	0	17	8	.680	0	0	3.00
1990	Oakland	AL	35	35	2	0	238	979	214	90	78	26	6	5	5	77	4	127	2	2	27	6	.818	2	0	2.95
1991	Oakland	AL	35	35	7	0	220	950	220	124	112	25	6	6	11	91	3	101	3	2	12	13	.480	1	0	4.58
14 ML YEARS			431	406	61	16	2732.1	11372	2493	1105	994	219	104	73	69	892	53	1815	50	42	188	122	.606	28	8	3.27

David Wells

Pitches: Left **Bats:** Left **Pos:** SP/RP **Ht:** 6' 4" **Wt:** 225 **Born:** 05/20/63 **Age:** 29

	HOW MUCH HE PITCHED						WHAT HE GAVE UP													THE RESULTS					
Year Team	Lg	G	GS	CG	GF	IP	BFP	H	R	ER	HR	SH	SF	HB	TBB	IBB	SO	WP	Bk	W	L	Pct.	ShO	Sv	ERA
1987 Toronto	AL	18	2	0	6	29.1	132	37	14	13	0	1	0	0	12	0	32	4	0	4	3	.571	0	1	3.99
1988 Toronto	AL	41	0	0	15	64.1	279	65	36	33	12	2	2	2	31	9	56	6	2	3	5	.375	0	4	4.62
1989 Toronto	AL	54	0	0	19	86.1	352	66	25	23	5	3	2	0	28	7	78	6	3	7	4	.636	0	2	2.40
1990 Toronto	AL	43	25	0	8	189	759	165	72	66	14	9	2	2	45	3	115	7	1	11	6	.647	0	3	3.14
1991 Toronto	AL	40	28	2	3	198.1	811	188	88	82	24	6	6	2	49	1	106	10	3	15	10	.600	0	1	3.72
5 ML YEARS		196	55	2	51	567.1	2333	521	235	217	55	21	12	6	165	20	387	33	9	40	28	.588	0	11	3.44

David West

Pitches: Left **Bats:** Left **Pos:** SP **Ht:** 6' 6" **Wt:** 231 **Born:** 09/01/64 **Age:** 27

	HOW MUCH HE PITCHED						WHAT HE GAVE UP													THE RESULTS					
Year Team	Lg	G	GS	CG	GF	IP	BFP	H	R	ER	HR	SH	SF	HB	TBB	IBB	SO	WP	Bk	W	L	Pct.	ShO	Sv	ERA
1988 New York	NL	2	1	0	0	6	25	6	2	2	0	0	0	0	3	0	3	0	2	1	0	1.000	0	0	3.00
1989 2 ML Teams		21	7	0	4	63.2	294	73	49	48	9	2	3	3	33	3	50	2	0	3	4	.429	0	0	6.79
1990 Minnesota	AL	29	27	2	0	146.1	646	142	88	83	21	6	4	4	78	1	92	4	1	7	9	.438	0	0	5.10
1991 Minnesota	AL	15	12	0	0	71.1	305	66	37	36	13	2	3	1	28	0	52	3	0	4	4	.500	0	0	4.54
1989 New York	NL	11	2	0	0	24.1	112	25	20	20	4	0	1	1	14	2	19	1	0	0	2	.000	0	0	7.40
Minnesota	AL	10	5	0	4	39.1	182	48	29	28	5	2	2	2	19	1	31	1	0	3	2	.600	0	0	6.41
4 ML YEARS		67	47	2	4	287.1	1270	287	176	169	43	10	10	8	142	4	197	9	3	15	17	.469	0	0	5.29

Mickey Weston

Pitches: Right **Bats:** Right **Pos:** RP **Ht:** 6' 1" **Wt:** 180 **Born:** 03/26/61 **Age:** 31

	HOW MUCH HE PITCHED						WHAT HE GAVE UP													THE RESULTS					
Year Team	Lg	G	GS	CG	GF	IP	BFP	H	R	ER	HR	SH	SF	HB	TBB	IBB	SO	WP	Bk	W	L	Pct.	ShO	Sv	ERA
1989 Baltimore	AL	7	0	0	2	13	55	18	8	8	1	0	0	1	2	0	7	0	0	1	0	1.000	0	1	5.54
1990 Baltimore	AL	9	2	0	4	21	94	28	20	18	6	1	0	0	6	1	9	1	0	0	1	.000	0	0	7.71
1991 Toronto	AL	2	0	0	2	2	8	1	0	0	0	0	0	0	1	1	1	0	0	0	0	.000	0	0	0.00
3 ML YEARS		18	2	0	8	36	157	47	28	26	7	1	0	1	9	2	17	1	0	1	1	.500	0	1	6.50

John Wetteland

Pitches: Right **Bats:** Right **Pos:** RP **Ht:** 6' 2" **Wt:** 195 **Born:** 08/21/66 **Age:** 25

	HOW MUCH HE PITCHED						WHAT HE GAVE UP													THE RESULTS					
Year Team	Lg	G	GS	CG	GF	IP	BFP	H	R	ER	HR	SH	SF	HB	TBB	IBB	SO	WP	Bk	W	L	Pct.	ShO	Sv	ERA
1989 Los Angeles	NL	31	12	0	7	102.2	411	81	46	43	8	4	2	0	34	4	96	16	1	5	8	.385	0	1	3.77
1990 Los Angeles	NL	22	5	0	7	43	190	44	28	23	6	1	1	4	17	3	36	8	0	2	4	.333	0	0	4.81
1991 Los Angeles	NL	6	0	0	3	9	36	5	2	0	0	0	1	1	3	0	9	1	0	1	0	1.000	0	0	0.00
3 ML YEARS		59	17	0	17	154.2	637	130	76	66	14	5	4	5	54	7	141	25	1	8	12	.400	0	1	3.84

Lou Whitaker

Bats: Left **Throws:** Right **Pos:** 2B **Ht:** 5'11" **Wt:** 180 **Born:** 05/12/57 **Age:** 35

	BATTING																	BASERUNNING				PERCENTAGES		
Year Team	Lg	G	AB	H	2B	3B	HR	(Hm	Rd)	TB	R	RBI	TBB	IBB	SO	HBP	SH	SF	SB	CS	SB%	GDP	Avg	OBP	SLG
1977 Detroit	AL	11	32	8	1	0	0	(0	0)	9	5	2	4	0	6	0	1	0	2	2	.50	0	.250	.333	.281
1978 Detroit	AL	139	484	138	12	7	3	(2	1)	173	71	58	61	0	65	1	13	8	7	7	.50	9	.285	.361	.357
1979 Detroit	AL	127	423	121	14	8	3	(3	0)	160	75	42	78	2	66	1	14	4	20	10	.67	10	.286	.395	.378
1980 Detroit	AL	145	477	111	19	1	1	(1	0)	135	68	45	73	0	79	0	12	6	8	4	.67	9	.233	.331	.283
1981 Detroit	AL	109	335	88	14	4	5	(4	1)	125	48	36	40	3	42	1	3	3	5	3	.63	5	.263	.340	.373
1982 Detroit	AL	152	560	160	22	8	15	(9	6)	243	76	65	48	4	58	1	6	4	11	3	.79	9	.286	.341	.434
1983 Detroit	AL	161	643	206	40	6	12	(7	5)	294	94	72	67	8	70	0	2	8	17	10	.63	9	.320	.380	.457
1984 Detroit	AL	143	558	161	25	1	13	(8	5)	227	90	56	62	5	63	0	4	5	6	5	.55	9	.289	.357	.407
1985 Detroit	AL	152	609	170	29	8	21	(11	10)	278	102	73	80	9	56	2	5	5	6	4	.60	3	.279	.362	.456
1986 Detroit	AL	144	584	157	26	6	20	(8	12)	255	95	73	63	5	70	0	0	4	13	8	.62	20	.269	.338	.437

217

Year	Team	Lg	G	AB	H	2B	3B	HR	(Hm	Rd)	TB	R	RBI	TBB	IBB	SO	HBP	SH	SF	SB	CS	SB%	GDP	Avg	OBP	SLG
1987	Detroit	AL	149	604	160	38	6	16	(10	6)	258	110	59	71	2	108	1	4	4	13	5	.72	5	.265	.341	.427
1988	Detroit	AL	115	403	111	18	2	12	(8	4)	169	54	55	66	5	61	0	6	2	2	0	1.00	8	.275	.376	.419
1989	Detroit	AL	148	509	128	21	1	28	(17	11)	235	77	85	89	6	59	3	1	9	6	3	.67	7	.251	.361	.462
1990	Detroit	AL	132	472	112	22	2	18	(8	10)	192	75	60	74	7	71	0	1	5	8	2	.80	10	.237	.338	.407
1991	Detroit	AL	138	470	131	26	2	23	(15	8)	230	94	78	90	6	45	2	2	8	4	2	.67	3	.279	.391	.489
	15 ML YEARS		1965	7163	1962	327	62	190	(111	79)	2983	1134	859	966	62	919	12	74	75	128	68	.65	115	.274	.358	.416

Devon White

Bats: Both   Throws: Right   Pos: CF　　　　**Ht: 6' 2"   Wt: 172   Born: 12/29/62   Age: 29**

										BATTING										BASERUNNING				PERCENTAGES		
Year	Team	Lg	G	AB	H	2B	3B	HR	(Hm	Rd)	TB	R	RBI	TBB	IBB	SO	HBP	SH	SF	SB	CS	SB%	GDP	Avg	OBP	SLG
1985	California	AL	21	7	1	0	0	0	(0	0)	1	7	0	1	0	3	1	0	0	3	1	.75	0	.143	.333	.143
1986	California	AL	29	51	12	1	1	1	(0	1)	18	8	3	6	0	8	0	0	0	6	0	1.00	0	.235	.316	.353
1987	California	AL	159	639	168	33	5	24	(11	13)	283	103	87	39	2	135	2	14	2	32	11	.74	8	.263	.306	.443
1988	California	AL	122	455	118	22	2	11	(3	8)	177	76	51	23	1	84	2	5	1	17	8	.68	5	.259	.297	.389
1989	California	AL	156	636	156	18	13	12	(9	3)	236	86	56	31	3	129	2	7	2	44	16	.73	12	.245	.282	.371
1990	California	AL	125	443	96	17	3	11	(5	6)	152	57	44	44	5	116	3	10	3	21	6	.78	6	.217	.290	.343
1991	Toronto	AL	156	642	181	40	10	17	(9	8)	292	110	60	55	1	135	7	5	6	33	10	.77	7	.282	.342	.455
	7 ML YEARS		768	2873	732	131	34	76	(37	39)	1159	447	301	199	12	610	17	41	14	156	52	.75	38	.255	.306	.403

Wally Whitehurst

Pitches: Right   Bats: Right   Pos: SP/RP　　　　**Ht: 6' 3"   Wt: 185   Born: 04/11/64   Age: 28**

				HOW MUCH HE PITCHED					WHAT HE GAVE UP								THE RESULTS					
Year	Team	Lg	G	GS	CG	GF	IP	BFP	H	R	ER	HR	SH	SF	HB	TBB	IBB	SO	WP	Bk	W	L	Pct.	ShO	Sv	ERA
1989	New York	NL	9	1	0	4	14	64	17	7	7	2	0	1	0	5	0	9	1	0	0	1	.000	0	0	4.50
1990	New York	NL	38	0	0	16	65.2	263	63	27	24	5	3	0	0	9	2	46	2	0	1	0	1.000	0	2	3.29
1991	New York	NL	36	20	0	6	133.1	556	142	67	62	12	6	3	4	25	3	87	3	4	7	12	.368	0	1	4.18
	3 ML YEARS		83	21	0	26	213	883	222	101	93	19	9	4	4	39	5	142	6	4	8	13	.381	0	3	3.93

Mark Whiten

Bats: Both   Throws: Right   Pos: RF　　　　**Ht: 6' 3"   Wt: 215   Born: 11/25/66   Age: 25**

										BATTING										BASERUNNING				PERCENTAGES		
Year	Team	Lg	G	AB	H	2B	3B	HR	(Hm	Rd)	TB	R	RBI	TBB	IBB	SO	HBP	SH	SF	SB	CS	SB%	GDP	Avg	OBP	SLG
1986	Medicne Hat	R	70	270	81	16	3	10	--	--	133	53	44	29	2	56	6	1	2	22	3	.88	2	.300	.378	.493
1987	Myrtle Bch	A	139	494	125	22	5	15	--	--	202	90	64	76	10	149	16	0	1	49	14	.78	1	.253	.370	.409
1988	Dunedin	A	99	385	97	8	5	7	--	--	136	61	37	41	6	69	3	2	3	17	14	.55	8	.252	.326	.353
	Knoxville	AA	28	108	28	3	1	2	--	--	39	20	9	12	1	20	1	0	0	6	0	1.00	5	.259	.339	.361
1989	Knoxville	AA	129	423	109	13	6	12	--	--	170	75	47	60	1	114	11	0	2	11	10	.52	7	.258	.363	.402
1990	Syracuse	AAA	104	390	113	19	4	14	--	--	182	65	48	37	5	72	3	0	4	14	5	.74	8	.290	.353	.467
1990	Toronto	AL	33	88	24	1	1	2	(1	1)	33	12	7	7	0	14	0	0	1	2	0	1.00	2	.273	.323	.375
1991	2 ML Teams		116	407	99	18	7	9	(4	5)	158	46	45	30	2	85	3	0	5	4	3	.57	12	.243	.297	.388
1991	Toronto	AL	46	149	33	4	3	2	(2	0)	49	12	19	11	1	35	1	0	3	0	1	.00	5	.221	.274	.329
	Cleveland	AL	70	258	66	14	4	7	(2	5)	109	34	26	19	1	50	2	0	2	4	2	.67	7	.256	.310	.422
	2 ML YEARS		149	495	123	19	8	11	(5	6)	191	58	52	37	2	99	3	0	6	6	3	.67	14	.248	.301	.386

Ed Whitson

Pitches: Right   Bats: Right   Pos: SP　　　　**Ht: 6' 3"   Wt: 202   Born: 05/19/55   Age: 37**

				HOW MUCH HE PITCHED					WHAT HE GAVE UP								THE RESULTS					
Year	Team	Lg	G	GS	CG	GF	IP	BFP	H	R	ER	HR	SH	SF	HB	TBB	IBB	SO	WP	Bk	W	L	Pct.	ShO	Sv	ERA
1977	Pittsburgh	NL	5	2	0	1	16	66	11	6	6	0	1	2	0	9	1	10	0	0	1	0	1.000	0	0	3.38
1978	Pittsburgh	NL	43	0	0	14	74	318	66	31	27	5	3	4	2	37	5	64	1	0	5	6	.455	0	4	3.28
1979	2 ML Teams		37	24	2	5	158	702	151	83	72	11	10	3	5	75	9	93	5	2	7	11	.389	0	1	4.10
1980	San Francisco	NL	34	34	6	0	212	898	222	88	73	7	10	9	4	56	7	90	1	1	11	13	.458	2	0	3.10
1981	San Francisco	NL	22	22	2	0	123	534	130	61	55	10	6	2	2	47	5	65	3	2	6	9	.400	1	0	4.02
1982	Cleveland	AL	40	9	1	18	107.2	467	91	43	39	6	7	8	0	58	3	61	4	1	4	2	.667	1	2	3.26
1983	San Diego	NL	31	21	2	4	144.1	617	143	73	69	23	3	4	1	50	1	81	2	0	5	7	.417	0	1	4.30
1984	San Diego	NL	31	31	1	0	189	773	181	72	68	16	10	7	3	42	1	103	3	1	14	8	.636	0	0	3.24
1985	New York	AL	30	30	2	0	158.2	705	201	100	86	19	3	7	2	43	0	89	1	0	10	8	.556	2	0	4.88
1986	2 ML Teams		31	16	0	6	112.2	526	139	85	78	13	4	5	0	60	1	73	3	0	6	9	.400	0	0	6.23
1987	San Diego	NL	36	34	3	0	205.2	858	197	113	108	36	4	2	3	64	3	135	2	1	10	13	.435	1	0	4.73
1988	San Diego	NL	34	33	0	0	205.1	846	202	89	86	17	13	8	1	45	1	118	2	2	13	11	.542	1	0	3.77
1989	San Diego	NL	33	33	5	0	227	914	198	77	67	22	12	8	5	48	6	117	2	0	16	11	.593	1	0	2.66
1990	San Diego	NL	32	32	6	0	228.2	918	215	73	66	13	9	6	1	47	8	127	2	0	14	9	.609	3	0	2.60
1991	San Diego	NL	13	12	2	0	78.2	337	93	47	44	13	6	3	0	12	3	40	1	1	4	6	.400	0	0	5.03
1979	Pittsburgh	NL	19	7	0	4	58	263	53	36	28	6	3	0	1	36	3	31	2	1	2	3	.400	0	1	4.34
	San Francisco	NL	18	17	2	1	100	439	98	47	44	5	7	3	4	39	6	62	3	1	5	8	.385	0	0	3.96

Year	Team	Lg	G	AB	H	2B	3B	HR	IP	BFP	H	R	ER	HR	SH	SF	TBB	IBB	SO	WP	Bk	W	L	Pct.	ShO	Sv	ERA
1986	New York	AL	14	4	0	6	37	189	54	37	31	5	2	3	0	23	1	27	2	0	5	2	.714	0	0	7.54
	San Diego	NL	17	12	0	0	75.2	337	85	48	47	8	2	2	0	37	0	46	1	0	1	7	.125	0	0	5.59
15 ML YEARS			452	333	35	48	2240.2	9479	2240	1045	944	211	101	78	29	698	54	1266	32	14	126	123	.506	12	8	3.79

Ernie Whitt

Bats: Left **Throws:** Right **Pos:** C **Ht:** 6' 2" **Wt:** 205 **Born:** 06/13/52 **Age:** 40

							BATTING													BASERUNNING				PERCENTAGES		
Year	Team	Lg	G	AB	H	2B	3B	HR	(Hm	Rd)	TB	R	RBI	TBB	IBB	SO	HBP	SH	SF	SB	CS	SB%	GDP	Avg	OBP	SLG
1976	Boston	AL	8	18	4	2	0	1	(1	0)	9	4	3	2	0	2	0	0	0	0	0	.00	0	.222	.300	.500
1977	Toronto	AL	23	41	7	3	0	0	(0	0)	10	4	6	2	0	12	0	0	2	0	0	.00	1	.171	.200	.244
1978	Toronto	AL	2	4	0	0	0	0	(0	0)	0	0	0	1	0	1	0	0	0	0	0	.00	0	.000	.200	.000
1980	Toronto	AL	106	295	70	12	2	6	(2	4)	104	23	34	22	0	30	0	5	3	1	3	.25	11	.237	.288	.353
1981	Toronto	AL	74	195	46	9	0	1	(0	1)	58	16	16	20	3	30	0	7	0	5	2	.71	2	.236	.307	.297
1982	Toronto	AL	105	284	74	14	2	11	(8	3)	125	28	42	26	5	34	0	1	5	3	1	.75	5	.261	.317	.440
1983	Toronto	AL	123	344	88	15	2	17	(11	6)	158	53	56	50	5	55	0	1	5	1	1	.50	9	.256	.346	.459
1984	Toronto	AL	124	315	75	12	1	15	(5	10)	134	35	46	43	7	49	1	0	5	0	3	.00	7	.238	.327	.425
1985	Toronto	AL	139	412	101	21	2	19	(7	12)	183	55	64	47	9	59	1	3	2	3	6	.33	7	.245	.323	.444
1986	Toronto	AL	131	395	106	19	2	16	(7	9)	177	48	56	35	3	39	0	0	0	0	1	.00	11	.268	.326	.448
1987	Toronto	AL	135	446	120	24	1	19	(11	8)	203	57	75	44	4	50	1	0	3	0	1	.00	17	.269	.334	.455
1988	Toronto	AL	127	398	100	11	2	16	(9	7)	163	63	70	61	4	38	1	2	6	4	2	.67	9	.251	.348	.410
1989	Toronto	AL	129	385	101	24	1	11	(8	3)	160	42	53	52	2	53	0	1	2	5	4	.56	9	.262	.349	.416
1990	Atlanta	NL	67	180	31	8	0	2	(2	0)	45	14	10	23	2	27	0	0	1	0	2	.00	5	.172	.265	.250
1991	Baltimore	AL	35	62	15	2	0	0	(0	0)	17	5	3	8	0	12	0	0	0	0	0	.00	3	.242	.329	.274
15 ML YEARS			1328	3774	938	176	15	134	(71	63)	1546	447	534	436	44	491	4	20	37	22	26	.46	97	.249	.324	.410

Curt Wilkerson

Bats: Both **Throws:** Right **Pos:** 2B/3B/SS **Ht:** 5' 9" **Wt:** 173 **Born:** 04/26/61 **Age:** 31

							BATTING													BASERUNNING				PERCENTAGES		
Year	Team	Lg	G	AB	H	2B	3B	HR	(Hm	Rd)	TB	R	RBI	TBB	IBB	SO	HBP	SH	SF	SB	CS	SB%	GDP	Avg	OBP	SLG
1983	Texas	AL	16	35	6	0	1	0	(0	0)	8	7	1	2	0	5	0	0	0	3	0	1.00	0	.171	.216	.229
1984	Texas	AL	153	484	120	12	0	1	(0	1)	135	47	26	22	0	72	2	12	2	12	10	.55	7	.248	.282	.279
1985	Texas	AL	129	360	88	11	6	0	(0	0)	111	35	22	22	0	63	4	6	3	14	7	.67	7	.244	.293	.308
1986	Texas	AL	110	236	56	10	3	0	(0	0)	72	27	15	11	0	42	1	0	1	9	7	.56	2	.237	.273	.305
1987	Texas	AL	85	138	37	5	3	2	(1	1)	54	28	14	6	0	16	2	0	0	6	3	.67	2	.268	.308	.391
1988	Texas	AL	117	338	99	12	5	0	(0	0)	121	41	28	26	3	43	2	3	2	9	4	.69	7	.293	.345	.358
1989	Chicago	NL	77	160	39	4	2	1	(1	0)	50	18	10	8	0	33	0	1	1	4	2	.67	3	.244	.278	.313
1990	Chicago	NL	77	186	41	5	1	0	(0	0)	48	21	16	7	2	36	0	3	0	2	2	.50	4	.220	.249	.258
1991	Pittsburgh	NL	85	191	36	9	1	2	(2	0)	53	20	18	15	0	40	0	0	4	2	1	.67	2	.188	.243	.277
9 ML YEARS			849	2128	522	68	22	6	(4	2)	652	244	150	119	5	350	11	25	13	61	36	.63	34	.245	.287	.306

Dean Wilkins

Pitches: Right **Bats:** Right **Pos:** RP **Ht:** 6' 1" **Wt:** 170 **Born:** 08/24/66 **Age:** 25

				HOW MUCH HE PITCHED					WHAT HE GAVE UP											THE RESULTS					
Year	Team	Lg	G	GS	CG	GF	IP	BFP	H	R	ER	HR	SH	SF	TBB	IBB	SO	WP	Bk	W	L	Pct.	ShO	Sv	ERA
1986	Oneonta	A	15	12	1	3	83.1	337	64	32	29	5	5	1	8	24	0	80	4	1	9	0	1.000	0	1	3.13
1987	Albany	AA	2	2	0	0	12	55	18	11	9	3	0	1	1	1	0	8	0	0	0	0	.000	0	0	6.75
	Ft.Laudrdle	A	15	14	5	1	105.2	435	95	41	32	2	1	1	1	39	0	76	7	4	8	5	.615	2	0	2.73
	Winston-Sal	A	13	6	3	1	50.1	224	49	31	23	3	2	3	1	24	0	29	1	0	4	4	.500	0	1	4.11
1988	Pittsfield	AA	59	0	0	49	71.2	295	53	25	13	0	6	1	2	30	5	59	9	0	5	7	.417	0	26	1.63
1989	Iowa	AAA	38	16	0	17	138	604	149	74	65	5	3	4	4	58	5	82	15	1	8	11	.421	0	3	4.24
1990	Iowa	AAA	52	2	0	33	73	325	75	37	30	4	2	3	6	38	5	61	10	2	6	2	.750	0	11	3.70
1991	Tucson	AAA	65	0	0	47	83.2	375	84	47	39	2	6	4	5	43	5	65	5	0	8	7	.533	0	20	4.20
1989	Chicago	NL	11	0	0	1	15.2	67	13	9	9	2	1	0	0	9	2	14	0	0	1	0	1.000	0	0	5.17
1990	Chicago	NL	7	0	0	3	7.1	41	11	8	8	1	0	0	1	7	0	3	3	0	0	0	.000	0	1	9.82
1991	Houston	NL	7	0	0	3	8	51	16	14	10	0	2	0	0	10	2	4	1	0	2	1	.667	0	1	11.25
3 ML YEARS			25	0	0	7	31	159	40	31	27	3	3	0	1	26	4	21	4	0	3	1	.750	0	2	7.84

Rick Wilkins

Bats: Left **Throws:** Right **Pos:** C **Ht:** 6' 2" **Wt:** 210 **Born:** 07/04/67 **Age:** 24

							BATTING													BASERUNNING				PERCENTAGES		
Year	Team	Lg	G	AB	H	2B	3B	HR	(Hm	Rd)	TB	R	RBI	TBB	IBB	SO	HBP	SH	SF	SB	CS	SB%	GDP	Avg	OBP	SLG
1987	Geneva	A	75	243	61	8	2	8	--	--	97	35	43	58	8	40	1	0	0	7	2	.78	3	.251	.397	.399
1988	Peoria	A	137	490	119	30	1	8	--	--	175	54	63	67	6	110	1	2	9	4	6	.40	12	.243	.337	.357
1989	Winston-Sal	A	132	445	111	24	1	12	--	--	173	61	54	50	6	87	8	2	7	6	3	.67	11	.249	.331	.389
1990	Charlotte	AA	127	449	102	17	1	17	--	--	172	48	71	43	5	97	5	1	3	4	5	.44	9	.227	.300	.383
1991	Iowa	AAA	38	107	29	3	1	5	--	--	49	12	14	11	1	17	1	2	2	1	2	.33	1	.271	.339	.458
1991	Chicago	NL	86	203	45	9	0	6	(2	4)	72	21	22	19	2	56	6	7	0	3	3	.50	2	.222	.307	.355

Jerry Willard

Bats: Left   **Throws:** Right   **Pos:** C   **Ht:** 6' 2"   **Wt:** 195   **Born:** 03/14/60   **Age:** 32

Year Team	Lg	G	AB	H	2B	3B	HR	(Hm	Rd)	TB	R	RBI	TBB	IBB	SO	HBP	SH	SF	SB	CS	SB%	GDP	Avg	OBP	SLG
1984 Cleveland	AL	87	246	55	8	1	10	(5	5)	95	21	37	26	0	55	0	0	3	1	0	1.00	6	.224	.295	.386
1985 Cleveland	AL	104	300	81	13	0	7	(4	3)	115	39	36	28	1	59	1	4	1	0	0	.00	3	.270	.333	.383
1986 Oakland	AL	75	161	43	7	0	4	(2	2)	62	17	26	22	0	28	2	4	4	0	1	.00	4	.267	.354	.385
1987 Oakland	AL	7	6	1	0	0	0	(0	0)	1	1	0	2	0	1	0	0	0	0	0	.00	0	.167	.375	.167
1990 Chicago	AL	3	3	0	0	0	0	(0	0)	0	0	0	0	0	2	0	0	0	0	0	.00	0	.000	.000	.000
1991 Atlanta	NL	17	14	3	0	0	1	(1	0)	6	1	4	2	0	5	0	0	0	0	0	.00	0	.214	.313	.429
6 ML YEARS		293	730	183	28	1	22	(12	10)	279	79	103	80	1	150	3	8	8	1	1	.50	13	.251	.324	.382

Bernie Williams

Bats: Both   **Throws:** Right   **Pos:** CF   **Ht:** 6' 2"   **Wt:** 180   **Born:** 09/13/68   **Age:** 23

Year Team	Lg	G	AB	H	2B	3B	HR	(Hm	Rd)	TB	R	RBI	TBB	IBB	SO	HBP	SH	SF	SB	CS	SB%	GDP	Avg	OBP	SLG
1986 Yankees	R	61	230	62	5	3	2	--	--	79	45	25	40	1	1	3	33	12	.73	3	.270	.374	.343
1987 Ft.Laudrdle	A	25	71	11	3	0	0	--	--	14	11	4	18	1	22	3	2	0	9	1	.90	1	.155	.348	.197
Oneonta	A	25	93	32	4	0	0	--	--	36	13	15	10	0	14	1	1	1	9	3	.75	0	.344	.410	.387
1988 Pr William	A	92	337	113	16	7	7	--	--	164	72	45	66	6	66	4	0	1	29	11	.73	5	.335	.449	.487
1989 Columbus	AAA	50	162	35	8	1	2	--	--	51	21	16	25	1	38	2	3	2	11	5	.69	3	.216	.325	.315
Albany	AA	91	314	79	11	8	11	--	--	139	63	42	60	4	72	6	3	1	26	13	.67	9	.252	.381	.443
1990 Albany	AA	134	466	131	28	5	8	--	--	193	91	54	98	6	97	4	1	2	39	18	.68	12	.281	.409	.414
1991 Columbus	AAA	78	306	90	14	6	8	--	--	140	52	37	38	2	43	2	4	3	9	8	.53	5	.294	.372	.458
1991 New York	AL	85	320	76	19	4	3	(1	2)	112	43	34	48	0	57	1	2	3	10	5	.67	4	.238	.336	.350

Brian Williams

Pitches: Right   **Bats:** Right   **Pos:** SP   **Ht:** 6' 2"   **Wt:** 195   **Born:** 02/15/69   **Age:** 23

| | | HOW MUCH HE PITCHED | | | | | | WHAT HE GAVE UP | | | | | | | | | THE RESULTS | | | | | |
Year Team	Lg	G	GS	CG	GF	IP	BFP	H	R	ER	HR	SH	SF	HB	TBB	IBB	SO	WP	Bk	W	L	Pct.	ShO	Sv	ERA
1990 Auburn	A	3	3	0	0	6.2	34	6	5	3	0	1	0	1	6	0	7	1	1	0	0	.000	0	0	4.05
1991 Osceola	A	15	15	0	0	89.2	378	72	41	29	0	3	6	2	40	1	67	3	5	6	4	.600	0	0	2.91
Jackson	AA	3	3	0	0	15	66	17	8	7	1	0	0	0	7	0	15	3	0	2	1	.667	0	0	4.20
Tucson	AAA	7	7	0	0	38.1	177	39	25	21	3	4	0	2	22	0	29	3	4	0	1	.000	0	0	4.93
1991 Houston	NL	2	2	0	0	12	49	11	5	5	2	0	0	1	4	0	4	0	0	0	1	.000	0	0	3.75

Ken Williams

Bats: Right   **Throws:** Right   **Pos:** RF   **Ht:** 6' 1"   **Wt:** 195   **Born:** 04/06/64   **Age:** 28

Year Team	Lg	G	AB	H	2B	3B	HR	(Hm	Rd)	TB	R	RBI	TBB	IBB	SO	HBP	SH	SF	SB	CS	SB%	GDP	Avg	OBP	SLG
1986 Chicago	AL	15	31	4	0	0	1	(1	0)	7	2	1	1	0	11	1	0	0	1	1	.50	1	.129	.182	.226
1987 Chicago	AL	116	391	110	18	2	11	(4	7)	165	48	50	10	0	83	9	3	1	21	10	.68	5	.281	.314	.422
1988 Chicago	AL	73	220	35	4	2	8	(3	5)	67	18	28	10	0	64	8	3	2	6	5	.55	2	.159	.221	.305
1989 Detroit	AL	94	258	53	5	1	6	(3	3)	78	29	23	18	0	63	5	2	2	9	4	.69	6	.205	.269	.302
1990 2 ML Teams		106	155	25	8	1	0	(0	0)	35	23	13	10	0	42	2	0	2	9	4	.69	1	.161	.219	.226
1991 2 ML Teams		47	99	25	7	2	1	(0	1)	39	16	4	7	0	27	2	0	1	3	1	.75	2	.253	.312	.394
1990 Detroit	AL	57	83	11	2	0	0	(0	0)	13	10	5	3	0	24	1	0	1	2	2	.50	0	.133	.170	.157
Toronto	AL	49	72	14	6	1	0	(0	0)	22	13	8	7	0	18	1	0	1	7	2	.78	1	.194	.272	.306
1991 Toronto	AL	13	29	6	2	0	1	(0	1)	11	5	3	4	0	5	1	0	1	1	0	1.00	1	.207	.314	.379
Montreal	NL	34	70	19	5	2	0	(0	0)	28	11	1	3	0	22	1	0	0	2	1	.67	1	.271	.311	.400
6 ML YEARS		451	1154	252	42	8	27	(11	16)	391	136	119	56	0	290	27	8	8	49	25	.66	17	.218	.269	.339

Matt D. Williams

Bats: Right   **Throws:** Right   **Pos:** 3B   **Ht:** 6' 2"   **Wt:** 205   **Born:** 11/28/65   **Age:** 26

Year Team	Lg	G	AB	H	2B	3B	HR	(Hm	Rd)	TB	R	RBI	TBB	IBB	SO	HBP	SH	SF	SB	CS	SB%	GDP	Avg	OBP	SLG
1987 San Francisco	NL	84	245	46	9	2	8	(5	3)	83	28	21	16	4	68	1	3	1	4	3	.57	5	.188	.240	.339
1988 San Francisco	NL	52	156	32	6	1	8	(7	1)	64	17	19	8	0	41	2	3	1	0	1	.00	7	.205	.251	.410
1989 San Francisco	NL	84	292	59	18	1	18	(10	8)	133	31	50	14	1	72	2	1	2	1	2	.33	5	.202	.242	.455
1990 San Francisco	NL	159	617	171	27	2	33	(20	13)	301	87	122	33	9	138	7	2	5	7	4	.64	13	.277	.319	.488
1991 San Francisco	NL	157	589	158	24	5	34	(17	17)	294	72	98	33	6	128	6	0	7	5	5	.50	11	.268	.310	.499
5 ML YEARS		536	1899	466	84	11	101	(59	42)	875	235	310	104	20	447	18	9	16	17	15	.53	41	.245	.289	.461

Mitch Williams

Pitches: Left **Bats:** Left **Pos:** RP **Ht:** 6' 4" **Wt:** 205 **Born:** 11/17/64 **Age:** 27

Year Team	Lg	G	GS	CG	GF	IP	BFP	H	R	ER	HR	SH	SF	HB	TBB	IBB	SO	WP	Bk	W	L	Pct.	ShO	Sv	ERA
1986 Texas	AL	80	0	0	38	98	435	69	39	39	8	1	3	11	79	8	90	5	5	8	6	.571	0	8	3.58
1987 Texas	AL	85	1	0	32	108.2	469	63	47	39	9	4	3	7	94	7	129	4	2	8	6	.571	0	6	3.23
1988 Texas	AL	67	0	0	51	68	296	48	38	35	4	3	4	6	47	3	61	5	6	2	7	.222	0	18	4.63
1989 Chicago	NL	76	0	0	61	81.2	365	71	27	24	6	2	5	8	52	4	67	6	4	4	4	.500	0	36	2.64
1990 Chicago	NL	59	2	0	39	66.1	310	60	38	29	4	5	3	1	50	6	55	4	2	1	8	.111	0	16	3.93
1991 Philadelphia	NL	69	0	0	60	88.1	386	56	24	23	4	4	4	8	62	5	84	4	1	12	5	.706	0	30	2.34
6 ML YEARS		436	3	0	281	511	2261	367	213	189	35	19	22	41	384	33	486	28	20	35	36	.493	0	114	3.33

Mark Williamson

Pitches: Right **Bats:** Right **Pos:** RP **Ht:** 6' 0" **Wt:** 171 **Born:** 07/21/59 **Age:** 32

Year Team	Lg	G	GS	CG	GF	IP	BFP	H	R	ER	HR	SH	SF	HB	TBB	IBB	SO	WP	Bk	W	L	Pct.	ShO	Sv	ERA
1987 Baltimore	AL	61	2	0	36	125	520	122	59	56	12	5	3	3	41	15	73	3	0	8	9	.471	0	3	4.03
1988 Baltimore	AL	37	10	2	11	117.2	507	125	70	64	14	4	2	2	40	4	69	5	3	5	8	.385	0	2	4.90
1989 Baltimore	AL	65	0	0	38	107.1	445	105	35	35	4	7	3	2	30	9	55	0	0	10	5	.667	0	9	2.93
1990 Baltimore	AL	49	0	0	15	85.1	343	65	25	21	8	6	7	0	28	2	60	1	0	8	2	.800	0	1	2.21
1991 Baltimore	AL	65	0	0	21	80.1	357	87	42	40	9	1	5	0	35	7	53	7	0	5	5	.500	0	4	4.48
5 ML YEARS		277	12	2	121	515.2	2172	504	231	216	47	23	20	7	174	41	310	16	3	36	29	.554	0	19	3.77

Carl Willis

Pitches: Right **Bats:** Left **Pos:** RP **Ht:** 6' 4" **Wt:** 212 **Born:** 12/28/60 **Age:** 31

Year Team	Lg	G	GS	CG	GF	IP	BFP	H	R	ER	HR	SH	SF	HB	TBB	IBB	SO	WP	Bk	W	L	Pct.	ShO	Sv	ERA
1984 2 ML Teams		17	2	0	5	25.2	113	33	17	17	2	1	0	0	7	2	7	0	0	0	3	.000	0	1	5.96
1985 Cincinnati	NL	11	0	0	6	13.2	69	21	18	14	3	1	2	0	5	0	6	1	0	1	0	1.000	0	1	9.22
1986 Cincinnati	NL	29	0	0	7	52.1	233	54	29	26	4	5	1	1	32	9	24	3	1	1	3	.250	0	0	4.47
1988 Chicago	AL	6	0	0	0	12	55	17	12	11	3	0	1	0	7	1	6	2	0	0	0	.000	0	0	8.25
1991 Minnesota	AL	40	0	0	9	89	355	76	31	26	4	3	4	1	19	2	53	4	1	8	3	.727	0	2	2.63
1984 Detroit	AL	10	2	0	4	16	74	25	13	13	1	0	0	0	5	2	4	0	0	0	2	.000	0	0	7.31
Cincinnati	NL	7	0	0	1	9.2	39	8	4	4	1	1	0	0	2	0	3	0	0	0	1	.000	0	1	3.72
5 ML YEARS		103	2	0	27	192.2	825	201	107	94	16	10	8	2	70	14	96	10	2	10	9	.526	0	4	4.39

Frank Wills

Pitches: Right **Bats:** Right **Pos:** RP **Ht:** 6' 2" **Wt:** 220 **Born:** 10/26/58 **Age:** 33

Year Team	Lg	G	GS	CG	GF	IP	BFP	H	R	ER	HR	SH	SF	HB	TBB	IBB	SO	WP	Bk	W	L	Pct.	ShO	Sv	ERA
1983 Kansas City	AL	6	4	0	1	34.2	152	35	17	16	2	0	2	0	15	0	23	3	0	2	1	.667	0	0	4.15
1984 Kansas City	AL	10	5	0	2	37	161	39	21	21	3	0	4	0	13	0	21	2	0	2	3	.400	0	0	5.11
1985 Seattle	AL	24	18	1	2	123	541	122	85	82	18	4	8	3	68	3	67	9	1	5	11	.313	0	1	6.00
1986 Cleveland	AL	26	0	0	16	40.1	182	43	23	22	6	6	2	0	16	4	32	2	0	4	4	.500	0	4	4.91
1987 Cleveland	AL	6	0	0	4	5.1	26	3	3	3	0	1	1	0	7	0	4	0	0	0	1	.000	0	1	5.06
1988 Toronto	AL	10	0	0	4	20.2	89	22	12	12	2	1	1	0	6	2	19	1	0	0	0	.000	0	0	5.23
1989 Toronto	AL	24	4	0	6	71.1	302	65	31	29	4	1	1	1	30	2	41	4	0	3	1	.750	0	0	3.66
1990 Toronto	AL	44	4	0	6	99	422	101	54	52	13	2	1	1	38	7	72	1	0	6	4	.600	0	0	4.73
1991 Toronto	AL	4	0	0	3	4.1	27	8	8	8	2	2	0	1	5	0	2	0	0	0	0	.000	0	0	16.62
9 ML YEARS		154	35	1	44	435.2	1902	438	254	245	50	17	20	6	198	18	281	22	1	22	26	.458	0	6	5.06

Craig Wilson

Bats: Right **Throws:** Right **Pos:** 3B **Ht:** 5'11" **Wt:** 175 **Born:** 11/28/64 **Age:** 27

Year Team	Lg	G	AB	H	2B	3B	HR	(Hm	Rd)	TB	R	RBI	TBB	IBB	SO	HBP	SH	SF	SB	CS	SB%	GDP	Avg	OBP	SLG
1989 St. Louis	NL	6	4	1	0	0	0	(0	0)	1	1	1	1	0	2	0	0	0	0	0	.00	0	.250	.400	.250
1990 St. Louis	NL	55	121	30	2	0	0	(0	0)	32	13	7	8	0	14	0	0	2	0	2	.00	7	.248	.290	.264
1991 St. Louis	NL	60	82	14	2	0	0	(0	0)	16	5	13	6	2	10	0	0	2	0	0	.00	2	.171	.222	.195
3 ML YEARS		121	207	45	4	0	0	(0	0)	49	19	21	15	2	26	0	0	4	0	2	.00	9	.217	.265	.237

Mookie Wilson

Bats: Both **Throws:** Right **Pos:** LF/DH   **Ht:** 5'10" **Wt:** 174 **Born:** 02/09/56 **Age:** 36

								BATTING											BASERUNNING				PERCENTAGES		
Year Team	Lg	G	AB	H	2B	3B	HR	(Hm Rd)	TB	R	RBI	TBB	IBB	SO	HBP	SH	SF	SB	CS	SB%	GDP	Avg	OBP	SLG
1980 New York	NL	27	105	26	5	3	0	(0 0)	37	16	4	12	0	19	0	2	0	7	7	.50	0	.248	.325	.352
1981 New York	NL	92	328	89	8	8	3	(2 1)	122	49	14	20	3	59	2	0	0	24	12	.67	3	.271	.317	.372
1982 New York	NL	159	639	178	25	9	5	(2 3)	236	90	55	32	4	102	2	1	3	58	16	.78	5	.279	.314	.369
1983 New York	NL	152	638	176	25	6	7	(4 3)	234	91	51	18	3	103	4	2	1	54	16	.77	6	.276	.300	.367
1984 New York	NL	154	587	162	28	10	10	(7 3)	240	88	54	26	2	90	2	2	2	46	9	.84	5	.276	.308	.409
1985 New York	NL	93	337	93	16	8	6	(2 4)	143	56	26	28	6	52	0	1	1	24	9	.73	9	.276	.331	.424
1986 New York	NL	123	381	110	17	5	9	(4 5)	164	61	45	32	5	72	1	0	1	25	7	.78	5	.289	.345	.430
1987 New York	NL	124	385	115	19	7	9	(5 4)	175	58	34	35	8	85	2	2	1	21	6	.78	2	.299	.359	.455
1988 New York	NL	112	378	112	17	5	8	(1 7)	163	61	41	27	2	63	2	1	2	15	4	.79	12	.296	.345	.431
1989 2 ML Teams		134	487	122	19	2	5	(2 3)	160	54	35	13	3	84	3	3	3	19	5	.79	5	.251	.273	.329
1990 Toronto	AL	147	588	156	36	4	3	(0 3)	209	81	51	31	0	102	0	6	4	23	4	.85	10	.265	.300	.355
1991 Toronto	AL	86	241	58	12	4	2	(1 1)	84	26	28	8	0	35	5	2	2	11	3	.79	4	.241	.277	.349
1989 New York	NL	80	249	51	10	1	3	(1 2)	72	22	18	10	3	47	1	0	2	7	4	.64	0	.205	.237	.289
Toronto		54	238	71	9	1	2	(1 1)	88	32	17	3	0	37	2	3	1	12	1	.92	5	.298	.311	.370
12 ML YEARS		1403	5094	1397	227	71	67	(30 37)	1967	731	438	282	36	866	23	22	20	327	98	.77	66	.274	.314	.386

Steve Wilson

Pitches: Left **Bats:** Left **Pos:** RP   **Ht:** 6'4" **Wt:** 195 **Born:** 12/13/64 **Age:** 27

				HOW MUCH HE PITCHED				WHAT HE GAVE UP										THE RESULTS					
Year Team	Lg	G	GS	CG	GF	IP	BFP	H	R	ER	HR	SH	SF	HB	TBB	IBB	SO	WP	Bk	W	L	Pct.	ShO	Sv	ERA
1988 Texas	AL	3	0	0	1	7.2	31	7	5	5	1	0	0	0	4	1	1	0	0	0	0	.000	0	0	5.87
1989 Chicago	NL	53	8	0	9	85.2	364	83	43	40	6	5	4	1	31	5	65	0	1	6	4	.600	0	2	4.20
1990 Chicago	NL	45	15	1	5	139	592	140	77	74	17	9	3	2	43	6	95	2	1	4	9	.308	0	1	4.79
1991 2 ML Teams		19	0	0	5	20.2	81	14	7	6	1	0	1	0	9	1	14	0	0	0	0	.000	0	2	2.61
1991 Chicago	NL	8	0	0	2	12.1	53	13	7	6	1	0	1	0	5	1	9	0	0	0	0	.000	0	0	4.38
Los Angeles	NL	11	0	0	3	8.1	28	1	0	0	0	0	0	0	4	0	5	0	0	0	0	.000	0	2	0.00
4 ML YEARS		120	23	1	20	253	1073	244	132	125	25	14	8	3	87	13	175	2	2	10	13	.435	0	5	4.45

Trevor Wilson

Pitches: Left **Bats:** Left **Pos:** SP/RP   **Ht:** 6'0" **Wt:** 175 **Born:** 06/07/66 **Age:** 26

				HOW MUCH HE PITCHED				WHAT HE GAVE UP										THE RESULTS					
Year Team	Lg	G	GS	CG	GF	IP	BFP	H	R	ER	HR	SH	SF	HB	TBB	IBB	SO	WP	Bk	W	L	Pct.	ShO	Sv	ERA
1988 San Francisco	NL	4	4	0	0	22	96	25	14	10	1	3	1	0	8	0	15	0	1	0	2	.000	0	0	4.09
1989 San Francisco	NL	14	4	0	2	39.1	167	28	20	19	2	3	1	4	24	0	22	0	1	2	3	.400	0	0	4.35
1990 San Francisco	NL	27	17	3	3	110.1	457	87	52	49	11	6	2	1	49	3	66	5	2	8	7	.533	2	0	4.00
1991 San Francisco	NL	44	29	2	6	202	841	173	87	80	13	14	5	5	77	4	139	5	3	13	11	.542	1	0	3.56
4 ML YEARS		89	54	5	11	373.2	1561	313	173	158	27	26	9	10	158	7	242	10	7	23	23	.500	3	0	3.81

Willie Wilson

Bats: Both **Throws:** Right **Pos:** LF/CF/RF   **Ht:** 6'3" **Wt:** 200 **Born:** 07/09/55 **Age:** 36

								BATTING											BASERUNNING				PERCENTAGES		
Year Team	Lg	G	AB	H	2B	3B	HR	(Hm Rd)	TB	R	RBI	TBB	IBB	SO	HBP	SH	SF	SB	CS	SB%	GDP	Avg	OBP	SLG
1976 Kansas City	AL	12	6	1	0	0	0	(0 0)	1	0	0	0	0	2	0	0	0	2	1	.67	0	.167	.167	.167
1977 Kansas City	AL	13	34	11	2	0	0	(0 0)	13	10	1	1	0	8	0	2	0	6	3	.67	1	.324	.343	.382
1978 Kansas City	AL	127	198	43	8	2	0	(0 0)	55	43	16	16	0	33	2	5	2	46	12	.79	2	.217	.280	.278
1979 Kansas City	AL	154	588	185	18	13	6	(3 3)	247	113	49	28	3	92	7	13	4	83	12	.87	1	.315	.351	.420
1980 Kansas City	AL	161	705	230	28	15	3	(2 1)	297	133	49	28	3	81	6	5	1	79	10	.89	4	.326	.357	.421
1981 Kansas City	AL	102	439	133	10	7	1	(0 1)	160	54	32	18	3	42	4	3	1	34	8	.81	5	.303	.335	.364
1982 Kansas City	AL	136	585	194	19	15	3	(2 1)	252	87	46	26	2	81	6	2	2	37	11	.77	4	.332	.365	.431
1983 Kansas City	AL	137	576	159	22	8	2	(2 0)	203	90	33	33	2	75	1	1	0	59	8	.88	4	.276	.316	.352
1984 Kansas City	AL	128	541	163	24	9	2	(1 1)	211	81	44	39	2	56	3	2	3	47	5	.90	7	.301	.350	.390
1985 Kansas City	AL	141	605	168	25	21	4	(1 3)	247	87	43	29	3	94	5	2	1	43	11	.80	6	.278	.316	.408
1986 Kansas City	AL	156	631	170	20	7	9	(5 4)	231	77	44	31	1	97	9	3	1	34	8	.81	6	.269	.313	.366
1987 Kansas City	AL	146	610	170	18	15	4	(0 4)	230	97	30	32	2	88	6	4	1	59	11	.84	9	.279	.320	.377
1988 Kansas City	AL	147	591	155	17	11	1	(0 1)	197	81	37	22	1	106	2	8	5	35	7	.83	5	.262	.289	.333
1989 Kansas City	AL	112	383	97	17	7	3	(1 2)	137	58	43	27	0	78	1	6	6	24	6	.80	8	.253	.300	.358
1990 Kansas City	AL	115	307	89	13	3	2	(1 1)	114	49	42	30	1	57	2	3	3	24	6	.80	4	.290	.354	.371
1991 Oakland	AL	113	294	70	14	4	0	(0 0)	92	38	28	18	1	43	4	1	1	20	5	.80	11	.238	.290	.313
16 ML YEARS		1900	7093	2038	255	137	40	(18 22)	2687	1098	537	378	24	1033	58	60	31	632	124	.84	77	.287	.327	.379

Dave Winfield

Bats: Right **Throws:** Right **Pos:** RF/DH **Ht:** 6' 6" **Wt:** 246 **Born:** 10/03/51 **Age:** 40

								BATTING										BASERUNNING				PERCENTAGES		
Year	Team	Lg	G	AB	H	2B	3B	HR	(Hm | Rd)	TB	R	RBI	TBB	IBB	SO	HBP	SH	SF	SB	CS	SB%	GDP	Avg	OBP	SLG
1973	San Diego	NL	56	141	39	4	1	3	(2 | 1)	54	9	12	12	1	19	0	0	1	0	0	.00	5	.277	.331	.383
1974	San Diego	NL	145	498	132	18	4	20	(12 | 8)	218	57	75	40	2	96	1	0	5	9	7	.56	14	.265	.318	.438
1975	San Diego	NL	143	509	136	20	2	15	(7 | 8)	205	74	76	69	14	82	3	3	7	23	4	.85	11	.267	.354	.403
1976	San Diego	NL	137	492	139	26	4	13	(4 | 9)	212	81	69	65	8	78	3	2	5	26	7	.79	14	.283	.366	.431
1977	San Diego	NL	157	615	169	29	7	25	(12 | 13)	287	104	92	58	10	75	0	0	5	16	7	.70	12	.275	.335	.467
1978	San Diego	NL	158	587	181	30	5	24	(11 | 13)	293	88	97	55	20	81	2	0	5	21	9	.70	13	.308	.367	.499
1979	San Diego	NL	159	597	184	27	10	34	(16 | 18)	333	97	118	85	24	71	2	0	2	15	9	.63	9	.308	.395	.558
1980	San Diego	NL	162	558	154	25	6	20	(7 | 13)	251	89	87	79	14	83	2	0	4	23	7	.77	13	.276	.365	.450
1981	New York	AL	105	388	114	25	1	13	(4 | 9)	180	52	68	43	3	41	1	1	7	11	1	.92	13	.294	.360	.464
1982	New York	AL	140	539	151	24	8	37	(14 | 23)	302	84	106	45	7	64	0	5	8	5	3	.63	20	.280	.331	.560
1983	New York	AL	152	598	169	26	8	32	(13 | 19)	307	99	116	58	2	77	2	0	6	15	6	.71	30	.283	.345	.513
1984	New York	AL	141	567	193	34	4	19	(9 | 10)	292	106	100	53	9	71	0	0	6	6	4	.60	14	.340	.393	.515
1985	New York	AL	155	633	174	34	6	26	(15 | 11)	298	105	114	52	8	96	0	0	4	19	7	.73	11	.275	.328	.471
1986	New York	AL	154	565	148	31	5	24	(12 | 12)	261	90	104	77	9	106	2	2	6	6	5	.55	20	.262	.349	.462
1987	New York	AL	156	575	158	22	1	27	(11 | 16)	263	83	97	76	5	96	0	1	3	5	6	.45	20	.275	.358	.457
1988	New York	AL	149	559	180	37	2	25	(12 | 13)	296	96	107	69	10	88	2	0	1	9	4	.69	19	.322	.398	.530
1990	2 ML Teams		132	475	127	21	2	21	(13 | 8)	215	70	78	52	3	81	2	1	7	0	1	.00	18	.267	.338	.453
1991	California	AL	150	568	149	27	4	28	(13 | 15)	268	75	86	56	4	109	1	2	6	7	2	.78	21	.262	.326	.472
1990	New York	AL	20	61	13	3	0	2	(0 | 2)	22	7	6	4	0	13	1	0	1	0	0	.00	2	.213	.269	.361
	California	AL	112	414	114	18	2	19	(13 | 6)	193	63	72	48	3	68	1	1	6	0	1	.00	16	.275	.348	.466
18 ML YEARS			2551	9464	2697	460	80	406	(187 | 219)	4535	1459	1602	1044	153	1414	23	17	88	216	89	.71	283	.285	.354	.479

Herm Winningham

Bats: Left **Throws:** Right **Pos:** CF **Ht:** 5'11" **Wt:** 190 **Born:** 12/01/61 **Age:** 30

								BATTING										BASERUNNING				PERCENTAGES		
Year	Team	Lg	G	AB	H	2B	3B	HR	(Hm | Rd)	TB	R	RBI	TBB	IBB	SO	HBP	SH	SF	SB	CS	SB%	GDP	Avg	OBP	SLG
1984	New York	NL	14	27	11	1	1	0	(0 | 0)	14	5	5	1	0	7	0	0	0	2	1	.67	0	.407	.429	.519
1985	Montreal	NL	125	312	74	6	5	3	(0 | 3)	99	30	21	28	3	72	0	1	4	20	9	.69	1	.237	.297	.317
1986	Montreal	NL	90	185	40	6	3	4	(1 | 3)	64	23	11	18	3	51	0	1	0	12	7	.63	4	.216	.286	.346
1987	Montreal	NL	137	347	83	20	3	4	(2 | 2)	121	34	41	34	7	68	0	1	4	29	10	.74	10	.239	.304	.349
1988	2 ML Teams		100	203	47	3	4	0	(0 | 0)	58	16	21	17	1	45	0	3	2	12	8	.60	2	.232	.288	.286
1989	Cincinnati	NL	115	251	63	11	3	3	(1 | 2)	89	40	13	24	1	50	0	3	0	14	5	.74	5	.251	.316	.355
1990	Cincinnati	NL	84	160	41	8	5	3	(0 | 3)	68	20	17	14	1	31	0	2	1	6	4	.60	2	.256	.314	.425
1991	Cincinnati	NL	98	169	38	6	1	1	(1 | 0)	49	17	4	11	1	40	0	2	0	4	4	.50	2	.225	.272	.290
1988	Montreal	NL	47	90	21	2	1	0	(0 | 0)	25	10	6	12	1	18	0	0	1	4	5	.44	2	.233	.320	.278
	Cincinnati	NL	53	113	26	1	3	0	(0 | 0)	33	6	15	5	0	27	0	3	1	8	3	.73	0	.230	.261	.292
8 ML YEARS			763	1654	397	61	25	18	(5 | 13)	562	185	133	147	17	364	0	13	11	99	48	.67	24	.240	.300	.340

Ron Witmeyer

Bats: Left **Throws:** Left **Pos:** 1B **Ht:** 6' 3" **Wt:** 215 **Born:** 06/28/67 **Age:** 25

								BATTING										BASERUNNING				PERCENTAGES		
Year	Team	Lg	G	AB	H	2B	3B	HR	(Hm	Rd)	TB	R	RBI	TBB	IBB	SO	HBP	SH	SF	SB	CS	SB%	GDP	Avg	OBP	SLG
1989	Modesto	A	134	457	93	22	1	8	--	--	141	54	43	70	1	101	4	5	4	5	1	.83	3	.204	.312	.309
1990	Tacoma	AAA	10	31	9	2	0	1	--	--	14	5	7	1	0	3	0	0	0	0	0	.00	1	.290	.313	.452
	Modesto	A	92	333	78	14	5	10	--	--	132	38	45	41	2	74	1	1	4	0	4	.00	4	.234	.317	.396
	Huntsville	AA	27	91	29	4	0	5	--	--	48	18	18	15	0	16	2	0	0	0	0	.00	2	.319	.426	.527
1991	Tacoma	AAA	122	431	113	18	4	15	--	--	184	64	80	57	5	59	2	2	5	2	5	.29	13	.262	.347	.427
1991	Oakland	AL	11	19	1	0	0	0	(0	0)	1	0	0	0	0	5	0	0	0	0	0	.00	1	.053	.053	.053

Bobby Witt

Pitches: Right **Bats:** Right **Pos:** SP **Ht:** 6' 2" **Wt:** 205 **Born:** 05/11/64 **Age:** 28

				HOW MUCH HE PITCHED					WHAT HE GAVE UP								THE RESULTS					
Year	Team	Lg	G	GS	CG	GF	IP	BFP	H	R	ER	HR	SH	SF	HB	TBB	IBB	SO	WP	Bk	W	L	Pct.	ShO	Sv	ERA
1986	Texas	AL	31	31	0	0	157.2	741	130	104	96	18	3	9	3	143	2	174	22	3	11	9	.550	0	0	5.48
1987	Texas	AL	26	25	1	0	143	673	114	82	78	10	5	5	3	140	1	160	7	2	8	10	.444	0	0	4.91
1988	Texas	AL	22	22	13	0	174.1	736	134	83	76	13	7	6	1	101	2	148	16	8	8	10	.444	2	0	3.92
1989	Texas	AL	31	31	5	0	194.1	869	182	123	111	14	11	8	2	114	3	166	7	4	12	13	.480	1	0	5.14
1990	Texas	AL	33	32	7	1	222	954	197	98	83	12	5	6	4	110	3	221	11	2	17	10	.630	1	0	3.36
1991	Texas	AL	17	16	1	0	88.2	413	84	66	60	4	3	4	1	74	1	82	8	0	3	7	.300	1	0	6.09
6 ML YEARS			160	157	27	1	980	4386	841	556	504	71	34	38	14	682	12	951	71	19	59	59	.500	5	0	4.63

Mike Witt

Pitches: Right **Bats:** Right **Pos:** SP **Ht:** 6' 7" **Wt:** 203 **Born:** 07/20/60 **Age:** 31

			HOW MUCH HE PITCHED						WHAT HE GAVE UP										THE RESULTS					
Year	Team	Lg	G	GS	CG	GF	IP	BFP	H	R	ER	HR	SH	SF	HB	TBB	IBB	SO	WP	Bk	W	L	Pct.	ShO	Sv	ERA
1981	California	AL	22	21	7	1	129	555	123	60	47	9	3	4	11	47	4	75	2	0	8	9	.471	1	0	3.28
1982	California	AL	33	26	5	2	179.2	748	177	77	70	8	8	5	7	47	2	85	8	1	8	6	.571	1	0	3.51
1983	California	AL	43	19	2	15	154	683	173	90	84	14	5	7	6	75	7	77	8	0	7	14	.333	0	5	4.91
1984	California	AL	34	34	9	0	246.2	1032	227	103	95	17	7	7	5	84	3	196	7	1	15	11	.577	2	0	3.47
1985	California	AL	35	35	6	0	250	1049	228	115	99	22	4	5	4	98	6	180	11	1	15	9	.625	1	0	3.56
1986	California	AL	34	34	14	0	269	1071	218	95	85	22	3	5	3	73	2	208	6	0	18	10	.643	3	0	2.84
1987	California	AL	36	36	10	0	247	1065	252	128	110	34	6	6	4	84	4	192	6	0	16	14	.533	0	0	4.01
1988	California	AL	34	34	12	0	249.2	1080	263	130	115	14	11	10	5	87	7	133	9	2	13	16	.448	2	0	4.15
1989	California	AL	33	33	5	0	220	937	252	119	111	26	10	13	2	48	1	123	7	0	9	15	.375	0	0	4.54
1990	2 ML Teams		26	16	2	4	117	498	106	62	52	9	1	6	5	47	4	74	7	0	5	9	.357	1	1	4.00
1991	New York	AL	2	2	0	0	5.1	26	8	7	6	1	0	0	0	1	0	0	1	0	0	1	.000	0	0	10.13
1990	California	AL	10	0	0	4	20.1	92	19	9	4	1	1	1	1	13	2	14	1	0	0	3	.000	0	1	1.77
	New York	AL	16	16	2	0	96.2	406	87	53	48	8	0	5	4	34	2	60	6	0	5	6	.455	1	0	4.47
	11 ML YEARS		332	290	72	22	2067.1	8744	2027	986	874	176	58	68	52	691	40	1343	72	5	114	114	.500	11	6	3.80

Mark Wohlers

Pitches: Right **Bats:** Right **Pos:** RP **Ht:** 6' 4" **Wt:** 207 **Born:** 01/23/70 **Age:** 22

			HOW MUCH HE PITCHED						WHAT HE GAVE UP										THE RESULTS					
Year	Team	Lg	G	GS	CG	GF	IP	BFP	H	R	ER	HR	SH	SF	HB	TBB	IBB	SO	WP	Bk	W	L	Pct.	ShO	Sv	ERA
1988	Pulaski	R	13	9	1	4	59.2	275	47	37	22	0	1	3	0	50	0	49	6	2	5	3	.625	0	0	3.32
1989	Sumter	A	14	14	0	0	68	326	74	55	49	3	3	3	4	59	0	51	10	1	2	7	.222	0	0	6.49
	Pulaski	R	14	8	0	2	46	219	48	36	28	5	1	0	2	28	0	50	2	0	1	1	.500	0	0	5.48
1990	Sumter	A	37	2	0	16	52.2	208	27	13	11	1	1	2	4	20	0	85	0	2	5	4	.556	0	5	1.88
	Greenville	AA	14	0	0	11	15.2	72	14	7	7	0	0	1	1	14	0	20	1	0	0	1	.000	0	6	4.02
1991	Greenville	AA	28	0	0	27	31.1	116	9	4	2	0	3	2	0	13	0	44	3	0	0	0	.000	0	21	0.57
	Richmond	AAA	23	0	0	21	26.1	111	23	4	3	1	4	0	1	12	1	22	1	1	1	0	1.000	0	11	1.03
1991	Atlanta	NL	17	0	0	4	19.2	89	17	7	7	1	2	1	2	13	3	13	0	0	3	1	.750	0	2	3.20

Ted Wood

Bats: Left **Throws:** Left **Pos:** RF **Ht:** 6' 2" **Wt:** 178 **Born:** 01/04/67 **Age:** 25

			BATTING																	BASERUNNING				PERCENTAGES		
Year	Team	Lg	G	AB	H	2B	3B	HR	(Hm	Rd)	TB	R	RBI	TBB	IBB	SO	HBP	SH	SF	SB	CS	SB%	GDP	Avg	OBP	SLG
1989	Shreveport	AA	114	349	90	13	1	0	--	--	105	44	43	51	2	72	6	10	3	9	7	.56	8	.258	.359	.301
1990	Shreveport	AA	131	456	121	22	11	17	--	--	216	81	72	74	5	76	7	4	2	17	8	.68	8	.265	.375	.474
1991	Phoenix	AAA	137	512	159	38	6	11	--	--	242	90	109	86	4	96	4	0	10	12	7	.63	13	.311	.407	.473
1991	San Francisco	NL	10	25	3	0	0	0	(0	0)	3	0	1	2	0	11	0	1	0	0	0	.00	0	.120	.185	.120

Craig Worthington

Bats: Right **Throws:** Right **Pos:** 3B **Ht:** 6' 0" **Wt:** 200 **Born:** 04/17/65 **Age:** 27

			BATTING																	BASERUNNING				PERCENTAGES		
Year	Team	Lg	G	AB	H	2B	3B	HR	(Hm	Rd)	TB	R	RBI	TBB	IBB	SO	HBP	SH	SF	SB	CS	SB%	GDP	Avg	OBP	SLG
1988	Baltimore	AL	26	81	15	2	0	2	(0	2)	23	5	4	9	0	24	0	0	0	1	0	1.00	2	.185	.267	.284
1989	Baltimore	AL	145	497	123	23	0	15	(12	3)	191	57	70	61	2	114	4	3	1	1	2	.33	10	.247	.334	.384
1990	Baltimore	AL	133	425	96	17	0	8	(3	5)	137	46	44	63	2	96	3	7	3	1	2	.33	13	.226	.328	.322
1991	Baltimore	AL	31	102	23	3	0	4	(1	3)	38	11	12	12	0	14	1	1	0	0	1	.00	3	.225	.313	.373
	4 ML YEARS		335	1105	257	45	0	29	(16	13)	389	119	130	145	4	248	8	11	4	3	5	.38	28	.233	.325	.352

Eric Yelding

Bats: Right **Throws:** Right **Pos:** SS **Ht:** 5'11" **Wt:** 165 **Born:** 02/22/65 **Age:** 27

			BATTING																	BASERUNNING				PERCENTAGES		
Year	Team	Lg	G	AB	H	2B	3B	HR	(Hm	Rd)	TB	R	RBI	TBB	IBB	SO	HBP	SH	SF	SB	CS	SB%	GDP	Avg	OBP	SLG
1989	Houston	NL	70	90	21	2	0	0	(0	0)	23	19	9	7	0	19	1	2	2	11	5	.69	2	.233	.290	.256
1990	Houston	NL	142	511	130	9	5	1	(0	1)	152	69	28	39	1	87	0	4	5	64	25	.72	12	.254	.305	.297
1991	Houston	NL	78	276	67	11	1	1	(0	1)	83	19	20	13	3	46	0	3	1	11	9	.55	4	.243	.276	.301
	3 ML YEARS		290	877	218	22	6	2	(0	2)	258	107	57	59	4	152	1	9	8	86	39	.69	18	.249	.294	.294

Mike York

Pitches: Right **Bats:** Right **Pos:** RP/SP **Ht:** 6' 1" **Wt:** 190 **Born:** 09/06/64 **Age:** 27

			HOW MUCH HE PITCHED						WHAT HE GAVE UP										THE RESULTS					
Year	Team	Lg	G	GS	CG	GF	IP	BFP	H	R	ER	HR	SH	SF	HB	TBB	IBB	SO	WP	Bk	W	L	Pct.	ShO	Sv	ERA
1984	White Sox	R	5	1	0	0	14.2	70	18	9	6	1	1	0	0	9	0	19	0	0	1	0	1.000	0	0	3.68
1985	Bristol	R	21	0	0	18	38	168	24	12	10	1	5	2	2	34	2	31	6	1	9	2	.818	0	2	2.37

Year	Team	Lg	G	GS	CG	GF	IP	BFP	H	R	ER	HR	SH	SF	HB	TBB	IBB	SO	WP	Bk	W	L	Pct.	ShO	Sv	ERA
1986	Lakeland	A	16	0	0	13	40.2	214	49	42	29	2	1	3	3	43	0	29	9	0	1	3	.250	0	1	6.42
	Gastonia	A	22	0	0	20	34	153	26	15	13	0	3	6	2	27	1	27	5	0	2	2	.500	0	9	3.44
1987	Macon	A	28	28	3	0	165.2	700	129	71	56	11	5	3	2	88	1	169	9	3	17	6	.739	2	0	3.04
1988	Salem	A	13	13	2	0	84	360	65	31	25	3	2	2	1	52	0	77	5	4	9	2	.818	1	0	2.68
	Harrisburg	AA	13	13	2	0	82.1	381	92	43	34	5	5	5	1	45	2	61	3	2	0	5	.000	0	0	3.72
1989	Harrisburg	AA	18	18	3	0	121	492	105	37	31	6	1	5	2	40	2	106	8	0	11	5	.688	2	0	2.31
	Buffalo	AAA	8	8	0	0	41	193	48	29	27	3	2	0	1	25	0	28	1	0	1	3	.250	0	0	5.93
1990	Buffalo	AAA	27	26	3	0	158.2	707	165	87	74	6	7	2	5	78	2	130	7	5	8	7	.533	1	0	4.20
1991	Buffalo	AAA	7	7	1	0	43.1	181	36	17	14	0	1	2	0	23	0	22	2	0	5	1	.833	0	0	2.91
	Colo Sprngs	AAA	5	5	0	0	26	130	40	19	17	2	0	1	1	16	0	13	1	0	0	1	.000	0	0	5.88
1990	Pittsburgh	NL	4	1	0	0	12.2	56	13	5	4	0	2	1	1	5	0	4	0	1	1	1	.500	0	0	2.84
1991	Cleveland	AL	14	4	0	3	34.2	163	45	29	26	2	3	4	2	19	3	19	2	0	1	4	.200	0	0	6.75
	2 ML YEARS		18	5	0	3	47.1	219	58	34	30	2	5	5	3	24	3	23	2	1	2	5	.286	0	0	5.70

Anthony Young

Pitches: Right **Bats:** Right **Pos:** SP **Ht:** 6' 2" **Wt:** 200 **Born:** 01/19/66 **Age:** 26

			HOW MUCH HE PITCHED						WHAT HE GAVE UP											THE RESULTS					
Year	Team	Lg	G	GS	CG	GF	IP	BFP	H	R	ER	HR	SH	SF	HB	TBB	IBB	SO	WP	Bk	W	L	Pct.	ShO	Sv	ERA
1987	Little Fls	A	14	9	0	0	53.2	247	58	37	27	6	2	2	1	25	1	48	4	0	3	4	.429	0	0	4.53
1988	Little Fls	A	15	10	4	2	73.2	304	51	33	18	1	1	3	0	34	0	75	9	1	3	5	.375	0	0	2.20
1989	Columbia	A	21	17	8	2	129	548	115	60	50	5	1	3	4	55	1	127	7	3	9	6	.600	1	0	3.49
1990	Jackson	AA	23	23	3	0	158	633	116	38	29	3	6	1	3	52	5	95	7	1	15	3	.833	1	0	1.65
1991	Tidewater	AAA	25	25	3	0	164	702	172	74	68	13	9	5	1	67	2	93	6	1	7	9	.438	1	0	3.73
1991	New York	NL	10	8	0	2	49.1	202	48	20	17	4	1	1	1	12	1	20	1	0	2	5	.286	0	0	3.10

Cliff Young

Pitches: Left **Bats:** Left **Pos:** RP **Ht:** 6' 4" **Wt:** 210 **Born:** 08/02/64 **Age:** 27

			HOW MUCH HE PITCHED						WHAT HE GAVE UP											THE RESULTS					
Year	Team	Lg	G	GS	CG	GF	IP	BFP	H	R	ER	HR	SH	SF	HB	TBB	IBB	SO	WP	Bk	W	L	Pct.	ShO	Sv	ERA
1984	Gastonia	A	24	24	7	0	144.1	614	117	77	67	10	7	7	1	68	2	121	9	0	8	10	.444	2	0	4.18
1985	Wst Plm Bch	A	25	25	7	0	153.2	664	149	77	68	13	3	6	6	57	0	112	6	4	15	5	.750	0	0	3.98
1986	Knoxville	AA	31	31	1	0	203.2	880	232	111	88	25	3	4	2	71	1	121	3	5	12	14	.462	0	0	3.89
1987	Knoxville	AA	42	12	0	10	119.1	541	148	76	59	15	5	4	3	43	5	81	12	2	8	9	.471	0	1	4.45
1988	Syracuse	AAA	33	18	4	7	147.1	608	133	68	56	13	2	5	3	32	0	75	3	4	9	6	.600	1	1	3.42
1989	Edmonton	AAA	31	21	2	3	139	591	158	80	74	16	6	4	5	32	1	89	3	4	8	9	.471	1	0	4.79
1990	Edmonton	AAA	30	0	0	14	52	208	45	15	14	1	6	1	1	10	1	30	0	2	7	4	.636	0	4	2.42
1991	Edmonton	AAA	34	8	0	15	71.2	328	88	53	39	2	4	3	4	25	1	39	8	0	4	8	.333	0	5	4.90
1990	California	AL	17	0	0	5	30.2	137	40	14	12	2	2	4	1	7	1	19	1	0	1	1	.500	0	0	3.52
1991	California	AL	11	0	0	6	12.2	49	12	6	6	3	0	0	0	3	1	6	0	0	1	0	1.000	0	0	4.26
	2 ML YEARS		28	0	0	11	43.1	186	52	20	18	5	2	4	1	10	2	25	1	0	2	1	.667	0	0	3.74

Curt Young

Pitches: Left **Bats:** Right **Pos:** RP **Ht:** 6' 1" **Wt:** 180 **Born:** 04/16/60 **Age:** 32

			HOW MUCH HE PITCHED						WHAT HE GAVE UP											THE RESULTS					
Year	Team	Lg	G	GS	CG	GF	IP	BFP	H	R	ER	HR	SH	SF	HB	TBB	IBB	SO	WP	Bk	W	L	Pct.	ShO	Sv	ERA
1983	Oakland	AL	8	2	0	0	9	50	17	17	16	1	0	0	1	5	0	5	1	0	0	1	.000	0	0	16.00
1984	Oakland	AL	20	17	2	0	108.2	475	118	53	49	9	1	4	8	31	0	41	3	0	9	4	.692	1	0	4.06
1985	Oakland	AL	19	7	0	5	46	214	57	38	37	15	0	1	1	22	0	19	1	0	0	4	.000	0	0	7.24
1986	Oakland	AL	29	27	5	0	198	826	176	88	76	19	8	9	7	57	1	116	7	2	13	9	.591	2	0	3.45
1987	Oakland	AL	31	31	6	0	203	828	194	102	92	38	6	4	3	44	0	124	2	1	13	7	.650	0	0	4.08
1988	Oakland	AL	26	26	1	0	156.1	651	162	77	72	23	3	5	4	50	3	69	3	6	11	8	.579	0	0	4.14
1989	Oakland	AL	25	20	1	2	111	495	117	56	46	10	1	0	3	47	2	55	4	4	5	9	.357	0	0	3.73
1990	Oakland	AL	26	21	0	0	124.1	527	124	70	67	17	4	2	2	53	1	56	3	0	9	6	.600	0	0	4.85
1991	Oakland	AL	41	0	0	6	68.1	306	74	38	38	8	3	1	2	34	2	27	2	1	4	2	.667	0	0	5.00
	9 ML YEARS		225	152	15	13	1024.2	4372	1039	539	493	140	26	26	31	343	9	512	26	14	64	50	.561	3	0	4.33

Gerald Young

Bats: Both **Throws:** Right **Pos:** CF **Ht:** 6' 2" **Wt:** 185 **Born:** 10/22/64 **Age:** 27

			BATTING																	BASERUNNING				PERCENTAGES		
Year	Team	Lg	G	AB	H	2B	3B	HR	(Hm	Rd)	TB	R	RBI	TBB	IBB	SO	HBP	SH	SF	SB	CS	SB%	GDP	Avg	OBP	SLG
1987	Houston	NL	71	274	88	9	2	1	(0	1)	104	44	15	26	0	27	1	0	2	26	9	.74	1	.321	.380	.380
1988	Houston	NL	149	576	148	21	9	0	(0	0)	187	79	37	66	1	66	3	5	5	65	27	.71	10	.257	.334	.325
1989	Houston	NL	146	533	124	17	3	0	(0	0)	147	71	38	74	4	60	2	6	5	34	25	.58	7	.233	.326	.276
1990	Houston	NL	57	154	27	4	1	1	(1	0)	36	15	4	20	0	23	0	4	1	6	3	.67	3	.175	.269	.234
1991	Houston	NL	108	142	31	3	1	1	(0	1)	39	26	11	24	0	17	0	1	2	16	5	.76	3	.218	.327	.275
	5 ML YEARS		531	1679	418	54	16	3	(1	2)	513	235	105	210	5	193	6	16	15	147	69	.68	24	.249	.332	.306

Matt Young

Pitches: Left **Bats:** Left **Pos:** SP **Ht:** 6' 3" **Wt:** 205 **Born:** 08/09/58 **Age:** 33

Year	Team	Lg	G	GS	CG	GF	IP	BFP	H	R	ER	HR	SH	SF	HB	TBB	IBB	SO	WP	Bk	W	L	Pct.	ShO	Sv	ERA
1983	Seattle	AL	33	32	5	0	203.2	851	178	86	74	17	4	8	7	79	2	130	4	2	11	15	.423	2	0	3.27
1984	Seattle	AL	22	22	1	0	113.1	524	141	81	72	11	1	5	1	57	3	73	3	1	6	8	.429	0	0	5.72
1985	Seattle	AL	37	35	5	2	218.1	951	242	135	119	23	7	3	7	76	3	136	6	2	12	19	.387	2	1	4.91
1986	Seattle	AL	65	5	1	32	103.2	458	108	50	44	9	4	3	8	46	2	82	7	1	8	6	.571	0	13	3.82
1987	Los Angeles	NL	47	0	0	31	54.1	234	62	30	27	3	1	1	0	17	5	42	3	0	5	8	.385	0	11	4.47
1989	Oakland	AL	26	4	0	1	37.1	183	42	31	28	2	4	1	0	31	2	27	5	0	1	4	.200	0	0	6.75
1990	Seattle	AL	34	33	7	0	225.1	963	198	106	88	15	7	7	6	107	7	176	16	0	8	18	.308	1	0	3.51
1991	Boston	AL	19	16	0	1	88.2	404	92	55	51	4	1	2	2	53	2	69	5	0	3	7	.300	0	0	5.18
8 ML YEARS			283	147	19	67	1044.2	4568	1063	574	503	84	29	30	31	466	26	735	49	6	54	85	.388	5	25	4.33

Robin Yount

Bats: Right **Throws:** Right **Pos:** CF/DH **Ht:** 6' 0" **Wt:** 180 **Born:** 09/16/55 **Age:** 36

Year	Team	Lg	G	AB	H	2B	3B	HR	(Hm	Rd)	TB	R	RBI	TBB	IBB	SO	HBP	SH	SF	SB	CS	SB%	GDP	Avg	OBP	SLG
1974	Milwaukee	AL	107	344	86	14	5	3	(3	0)	119	48	26	12	0	46	1	5	2	7	7	.50	4	.250	.276	.346
1975	Milwaukee	AL	147	558	149	28	2	8	(4	4)	205	67	52	33	3	69	1	10	5	12	4	.75	8	.267	.307	.367
1976	Milwaukee	AL	161	638	161	19	3	2	(1	1)	192	59	54	38	3	69	0	8	6	16	11	.59	13	.252	.292	.301
1977	Milwaukee	AL	154	605	174	34	4	4	(2	2)	228	66	49	41	1	80	2	11	4	16	7	.70	11	.288	.333	.377
1978	Milwaukee	AL	127	502	147	23	9	9	(5	4)	215	66	71	24	1	43	1	13	5	16	5	.76	5	.293	.323	.428
1979	Milwaukee	AL	149	577	154	26	5	8	(4	4)	214	72	51	35	3	52	1	10	3	11	8	.58	15	.267	.308	.371
1980	Milwaukee	AL	143	611	179	49	10	23	(13	10)	317	121	87	26	1	67	1	6	3	20	5	.80	8	.293	.321	.519
1981	Milwaukee	AL	96	377	103	15	5	10	(1	9)	158	50	49	22	1	37	2	4	6	4	1	.80	4	.273	.312	.419
1982	Milwaukee	AL	156	635	210	46	12	29	(9	20)	367	129	114	54	2	63	1	4	10	14	3	.82	19	.331	.379	.578
1983	Milwaukee	AL	149	578	178	42	10	17	(6	11)	291	102	80	72	6	58	3	1	8	12	5	.71	11	.308	.383	.503
1984	Milwaukee	AL	160	624	186	27	7	16	(8	8)	275	105	80	67	7	67	1	1	9	14	4	.78	22	.298	.362	.441
1985	Milwaukee	AL	122	466	129	26	3	15	(11	4)	206	76	68	49	3	56	2	1	9	10	4	.71	8	.277	.342	.442
1986	Milwaukee	AL	140	522	163	31	7	9	(4	5)	235	82	46	62	7	73	4	5	2	14	5	.74	9	.312	.388	.450
1987	Milwaukee	AL	158	635	198	25	9	21	(12	9)	304	99	103	76	10	94	1	6	5	19	9	.68	9	.312	.384	.479
1988	Milwaukee	AL	162	621	190	38	11	13	(7	6)	289	92	91	63	10	63	3	2	7	22	4	.85	21	.306	.369	.465
1989	Milwaukee	AL	160	614	195	38	9	21	(14	7)	314	101	103	63	9	71	6	3	4	19	3	.86	9	.318	.384	.511
1990	Milwaukee	AL	158	587	145	17	5	17	(8	9)	223	98	77	78	6	89	6	4	8	15	8	.65	7	.247	.337	.380
1991	Milwaukee	AL	130	503	131	20	4	10	(8	2)	189	66	77	54	6	79	4	1	9	6	4	.60	13	.260	.332	.376
18 ML YEARS			2579	9997	2878	518	120	235	(120	115)	4341	1499	1278	869	81	1176	40	95	105	247	97	.72	196	.288	.344	.434

Todd Zeile

Bats: Right **Throws:** Right **Pos:** 3B **Ht:** 6' 1" **Wt:** 190 **Born:** 09/09/65 **Age:** 26

Year	Team	Lg	G	AB	H	2B	3B	HR	(Hm	Rd)	TB	R	RBI	TBB	IBB	SO	HBP	SH	SF	SB	CS	SB%	GDP	Avg	OBP	SLG
1989	St. Louis	NL	28	82	21	3	1	1	(0	1)	29	7	8	9	1	14	0	1	1	0	0	.00	1	.256	.326	.354
1990	St. Louis	NL	144	495	121	25	3	15	(8	7)	197	62	57	67	3	77	2	0	6	2	4	.33	11	.244	.333	.398
1991	St. Louis	NL	155	565	158	36	3	11	(7	4)	233	76	81	62	3	94	5	0	6	17	11	.61	15	.280	.353	.412
3 ML YEARS			327	1142	300	64	7	27	(15	12)	459	145	146	138	7	185	7	1	13	19	15	.56	27	.263	.342	.402

Eddie Zosky

Bats: Right **Throws:** Right **Pos:** SS **Ht:** 6' 0" **Wt:** 175 **Born:** 02/10/68 **Age:** 24

Year	Team	Lg	G	AB	H	2B	3B	HR	(Hm	Rd)	TB	R	RBI	TBB	IBB	SO	HBP	SH	SF	SB	CS	SB%	GDP	Avg	OBP	SLG
1989	Knoxville	AA	56	208	46	5	3	2	--	--	63	21	14	10	0	32	0	2	1	1	1	.50	1	.221	.256	.303
1990	Knoxville	AA	115	450	122	20	7	3	--	--	165	53	45	26	1	73	5	6	3	3	13	.19	7	.271	.316	.367
1991	Syracuse	AAA	119	511	135	18	4	6	--	--	179	69	39	35	1	82	5	7	5	9	4	.69	11	.264	.315	.350
1991	Toronto	AL	18	27	4	1	1	0	(0	0)	7	2	2	0	0	8	0	1	0	0	0	.00	1	.148	.148	.259

Bob Zupcic

Bats: Right **Throws:** Right **Pos:** CF　　　　　**Ht:** 6' 4" **Wt:** 220 **Born:** 08/18/66 **Age:** 25

							BATTING												BASERUNNING				PERCENTAGES		
Year	Team	Lg	G	AB	H	2B	3B	HR	(Hm	Rd)	TB	R	RBI	TBB	IBB	SO	HBP	SH	SF	SB	CS	SB%	GDP	Avg	OBP	SLG
1987	Elmira	A	66	238	72	12	2	7	--	--	109	39	37	17	0	35	2	3	2	5	4	.56	5	.303	.351	.458
1988	Lynchburg	A	135	482	143	33	5	13	--	--	225	69	97	60	4	64	8	7	8	10	6	.63	6	.297	.378	.467
1989	Pawtucket	AAA	27	94	24	7	1	1	--	--	36	8	11	3	0	15	0	0	2	1	3	.25	2	.255	.273	.383
	New Britain	AA	94	346	75	12	2	2	--	--	97	37	28	19	0	55	1	7	2	15	1	.94	7	.217	.258	.280
1990	New Britain	AA	132	461	98	26	1	2	--	--	132	45	41	36	2	63	6	6	7	10	8	.56	7	.213	.275	.286
1991	Pawtucket	AAA	129	429	103	27	1	18	--	--	186	70	70	55	2	58	1	12	8	10	6	.63	5	.240	.323	.434
1991	Boston	AL	18	25	4	0	0	1	(1	0)	7	3	3	1	0	6	0	1	0	0	0	.00	0	.160	.192	.280

Paul Zuvella

Bats: Right **Throws:** Right **Pos:** 3B　　　　　**Ht:** 6' 0" **Wt:** 180 **Born:** 10/31/58 **Age:** 33

							BATTING												BASERUNNING				PERCENTAGES		
Year	Team	Lg	G	AB	H	2B	3B	HR	(Hm	Rd)	TB	R	RBI	TBB	IBB	SO	HBP	SH	SF	SB	CS	SB%	GDP	Avg	OBP	SLG
1982	Atlanta	NL	2	1	0	0	0	0	(0	0)	0	0	0	0	0	0	0	0	0	0	0	.00	0	.000	.000	.000
1983	Atlanta	NL	3	5	0	0	0	0	(0	0)	0	0	0	2	0	1	1	0	0	0	0	.00	0	.000	.375	.000
1984	Atlanta	NL	11	25	5	1	0	0	(0	0)	6	2	1	2	0	3	0	0	0	0	0	.00	0	.200	.259	.240
1985	Atlanta	NL	81	190	48	8	1	0	(0	0)	58	16	4	16	1	14	0	4	0	2	0	1.00	3	.253	.311	.305
1986	New York	AL	21	48	4	1	0	0	(0	0)	5	2	2	5	0	4	0	4	0	0	0	.00	1	.083	.170	.104
1987	New York	AL	14	34	6	0	0	0	(0	0)	6	2	0	0	0	4	0	2	0	0	0	.00	1	.176	.176	.176
1988	Cleveland	AL	51	130	30	5	1	0	(0	0)	37	9	7	8	0	13	0	8	0	0	0	.00	3	.231	.275	.285
1989	Cleveland	AL	24	58	16	2	0	2	(2	0)	24	10	6	1	0	11	1	0	0	0	0	.00	0	.276	.300	.414
1991	Kansas City	AL	2	0	0	0	0	0	(0	0)	0	0	0	0	0	0	0	0	0	0	0	.00	0	.000	.000	.000
9 ML YEARS			209	491	109	17	2	2	(2	0)	136	41	20	34	1	50	2	18	0	2	0	1.00	8	.222	.275	.277

Team Statistics

American League Batting

							BATTING												BASERUNNING				PERCENTAGES		
Team	G	AB	H	2B	3B	HR	(Hm	Rd)	TB	R	RBI	TBB	IBB	SO	HBP	SH	SF	SB	CS	SB%	GDP	Avg	OBP	SLG
Texas	162	5703	1539	288	31	177	(79	98)	2420	829	774	596	51	1039	42	59	41	102	50	.67	129	.270	.341	.424
Detroit	162	5547	1372	259	26	209	(109	100)	2310	817	778	699	40	1185	31	38	44	109	47	.70	90	.247	.333	.416
Milwaukee	162	5611	1523	247	53	116	(62	54)	2224	799	750	556	48	802	23	52	66	106	68	.61	136	.271	.336	.396
Minnesota	162	5556	1557	270	42	140	(62	78)	2331	776	733	526	38	747	40	44	49	107	68	.61	157	.280	.344	.420
Oakland	162	5410	1342	246	19	159	(76	83)	2103	760	716	642	56	981	50	41	49	151	64	.70	130	.248	.331	.389
Chicago	162	5594	1464	226	39	139	(74	65)	2185	758	722	610	45	896	37	76	41	134	74	.64	131	.262	.336	.391
Boston	162	5530	1486	305	25	126	(69	57)	2219	731	691	593	49	820	32	50	51	59	39	.60	144	.269	.340	.401
Kansas City	162	5584	1475	290	41	117	(47	70)	2198	727	689	523	47	969	35	53	47	119	68	.64	127	.264	.328	.394
Seattle	162	5494	1400	268	29	126	(69	57)	2104	702	665	588	57	811	37	55	62	97	44	.69	139	.255	.328	.383
Baltimore	162	5604	1421	256	29	170	(80	90)	2245	686	660	528	33	974	33	47	45	50	33	.60	146	.254	.319	.401
Toronto	162	5489	1412	295	45	133	(75	58)	2196	684	649	499	49	1043	58	56	65	148	53	.74	108	.257	.322	.400
New York	162	5541	1418	249	19	147	(82	65)	2146	674	630	473	38	861	39	37	50	109	36	.75	126	.256	.316	.387
California	162	5470	1396	245	29	115	(59	56)	2044	653	607	448	28	928	38	63	31	94	56	.63	114	.255	.314	.374
Cleveland	162	5470	1390	236	26	79	(22	57)	1915	576	546	449	24	888	43	62	46	84	58	.59	145	.254	.313	.350
American	2268	77603	20195	3680	453	1953	(965	988)	30640	10172	9610	7730	603	12944	538	733	687	1469	758	.66	1822	.260	.329	.395

American League Pitching

	HOW MUCH THEY PITCHED						WHAT THEY GAVE UP											THE RESULTS					
Team	G	GS	CG	GF	IP	BFP	H	R	ER	HR	SH	SF	HB	TBB	IBB	SO	WP	Bk	W	L	Pct.	ShO	Sv	ERA
Toronto	162	162	10	162	1462.2	6136	1301	622	569	121	53	45	43	523	41	971	55	8	91	71	.562	16	60	3.50
California	162	162	18	162	1441.2	6059	1351	649	591	141	43	35	38	543	29	990	49	11	81	81	.500	10	50	3.69
Minnesota	162	162	21	162	1449.1	6101	1402	652	595	139	46	49	27	488	39	876	57	5	95	67	.586	12	53	3.69
Seattle	162	162	10	162	1464.1	6261	1387	674	616	136	51	49	47	628	50	1003	82	7	83	79	.512	13	48	3.79
Chicago	162	162	28	162	1478	6194	1302	681	622	154	64	50	31	601	25	923	44	6	87	75	.537	8	40	3.79
Boston	162	162	15	162	1439.2	6126	1405	712	642	147	42	46	31	530	59	999	42	4	84	78	.519	13	45	4.01
Kansas City	162	162	17	162	1466	6310	1473	722	639	105	55	41	43	529	44	1004	47	5	82	80	.506	12	41	3.92
Milwaukee	162	162	23	162	1463.2	6302	1498	744	674	147	60	47	45	527	31	859	53	5	83	79	.512	11	41	4.14
Cleveland	162	162	22	162	1441.1	6231	1551	759	678	110	59	69	39	441	61	862	48	6	57	105	.352	8	33	4.23
Oakland	162	162	14	162	1444.1	6299	1425	776	734	155	51	54	55	655	30	892	60	7	84	78	.519	10	49	4.57
New York	162	162	3	162	1444	6209	1510	777	709	152	49	38	42	506	29	936	53	14	71	91	.438	11	37	4.42
Detroit	162	162	18	162	1450.1	6343	1570	794	726	148	65	63	24	593	88	739	50	5	84	78	.519	8	38	4.51
Baltimore	162	162	8	162	1457.2	6247	1534	796	743	147	43	45	28	504	40	868	49	8	67	95	.414	8	42	4.59
Texas	162	162	9	162	1479	6487	1486	814	734	151	52	56	45	662	37	1022	77	12	85	77	.525	10	41	4.47
American	2268	2268	216	2268	20382	87305	20195	10172	9272	1953	733	687	538	7730	603	12944	766	103	1134	1134	.500	150	618	4.09

National League Batting

Team	G	AB	H	2B	3B	HR	(Hm	Rd)	TB	R	RBI	TBB	IBB	SO	HBP	SH	SF	SB	CS	SB%	GDP	Avg	OBP	SLG
Pittsburgh	162	5449	1433	259	50	126	(61	65)	2170	768	725	620	62	901	35	99	66	124	46	.73	110	.263	.338	.398
Atlanta	162	5456	1407	255	30	141	(83	58)	2145	749	704	563	55	906	32	86	45	165	76	.68	104	.258	.328	.393
Chicago	160	5522	1395	232	26	159	(93	66)	2156	695	654	442	41	879	36	75	55	123	64	.66	86	.253	.309	.390
Cincinnati	162	5501	1419	250	27	164	(104	60)	2215	689	654	488	54	1006	32	72	41	124	56	.69	85	.258	.320	.403
Los Angeles	162	5408	1366	191	29	108	(57	51)	1939	665	605	583	50	957	28	94	46	126	68	.65	110	.253	.326	.359
St. Louis	162	5362	1366	239	53	68	(32	36)	1915	651	599	532	48	857	21	58	47	202	110	.65	94	.255	.322	.357
San Francisco	162	5463	1345	215	48	141	(69	72)	2079	649	605	471	59	973	40	90	33	95	57	.63	92	.246	.309	.381
New York	161	5359	1305	250	24	117	(57	60)	1954	640	605	578	53	789	27	60	52	153	70	.69	99	.244	.317	.365
San Diego	162	5408	1321	204	36	121	(65	56)	1960	636	591	501	60	1069	32	78	38	101	64	.61	121	.244	.310	.362
Philadelphia	162	5521	1332	248	33	111	(61	50)	1979	629	590	490	48	1026	21	52	49	92	30	.75	114	.241	.303	.358
Houston	162	5504	1345	240	43	79	(27	52)	1908	605	570	502	45	1027	35	63	43	125	68	.65	87	.244	.309	.347
Montreal	161	5412	1329	236	42	95	(35	60)	1934	579	536	484	51	1056	28	64	47	221	100	.69	97	.246	.308	.357
National	1940	65365	16363	2819	441	1430	(744	686)	24354	7955	7438	6254	626	11446	367	891	562	1651	809	.67	1199	.250	.317	.373

National League Pitching

Team	G	GS	CG	GF	IP	BFP	H	R	ER	HR	SH	SF	HB	TBB	IBB	SO	WP	Bk	W	L	Pct.	ShO	Sv	ERA
Los Angeles	162	162	15	162	1458	6089	1312	565	496	96	74	39	28	500	77	1028	48	12	93	69	.574	14	40	3.06
Pittsburgh	162	162	18	162	1456.2	6046	1411	632	557	117	59	34	30	401	34	919	40	12	98	64	.605	11	51	3.44
Atlanta	162	162	18	162	1452.2	6051	1304	644	563	118	74	39	28	481	39	969	66	13	94	68	.580	7	48	3.49
New York	161	161	12	161	1437.1	6030	1403	646	568	108	83	46	25	410	41	1028	59	14	77	84	.478	11	39	3.56
San Diego	162	162	14	162	1452.2	6092	1385	646	577	139	72	50	13	457	56	921	49	13	84	78	.519	11	47	3.57
St. Louis	162	162	9	162	1435.1	5996	1367	648	588	114	75	52	47	454	52	822	33	7	84	78	.519	5	51	3.69
Montreal	161	161	12	161	1440.1	6061	1304	655	583	111	67	33	32	584	42	909	51	9	71	90	.441	14	39	3.64
Philadelphia	162	162	16	162	1463	6332	1346	680	628	111	78	61	43	670	58	988	81	6	78	84	.481	11	35	3.86
Cincinnati	162	162	7	162	1440	6133	1372	691	613	127	73	52	28	560	41	997	60	9	74	88	.457	11	43	3.83
San Francisco	162	162	10	162	1442	6132	1397	697	646	143	71	46	36	544	60	905	44	14	75	87	.463	10	45	4.03
Houston	162	162	7	162	1453	6255	1347	717	646	129	69	52	29	651	62	1033	46	17	65	97	.401	13	36	4.00
Chicago	160	160	12	160	1456.2	6224	1415	734	653	117	96	58	28	542	64	927	48	12	77	83	.481	4	40	4.03
National	1940	1940	150	1940	17387.2	73441	16363	7955	7118	1430	891	562	367	6254	626	11446	625	138	970	970	.500	122	514	3.68

1991 Fielding Stats

Last year we gave'em to you. This year we organized them. This section is, without a doubt, the most rethought, revised, and rebuilt section for 1992.

There are subtle changes. The Games and Innings columns have been flip-flopped, since an inning is a subset of a game. The Range Factor calculation no longer credits a fielder for reaching a ball on which he committed an error, making it consistent will Bill James' original definition. Full first names have been added for easier readability. (Five C. Martinez's played first base this year?! Yikes!).

There are major changes. All positions have been divided into "Regulars" and "The Rest," with the divider being 600 innings at a position. We listed the Regulars in descending order by Range Factor, which is a better indicator of defensive skills than Fielding Percentage. We also included a final line average of all Regulars for all categories. The Rest are simply in alphabetical order. Catchers now have separate sections for traditional fielding and special fielding. In the special fielding section, catchers are ranked by Catcher ERA (CERA). CERA measures the ERA of all pitchers on the mound while that catcher is behind the plate. It's an indicator of a catcher's ability to call a game and handle pitchers. It is most useful when the catcher's pitching staff and team ERA are also taken into consideration. PCS stands for Pitcher Caught Stealings and allows the reader to make an alternate calculation of Caught Stealing Percentage for catchers by subtracting these from total CS. These major changes make this section the most complete and unique collection of fielding data available to the general public and, hopefully, will help bring more understanding to the nebulous area of fielding evaluation. Love those Range Factors or hate'em, there's argument fodder aplenty lurking in the pages ahead.

Finally, there are clarifications. Again, like last year, these fielding statistics are unofficial. However, at the expense of a few differences, we'd rather give you this book in November, rather than wait until December for the "official" fielding numbers. First Basemen are ranked by Fielding Percentage, without Range Factors, to make the point that, even though a Range can be calculated for First Basemen, it is meaningless. Ties in Range or Percentage are, in reality, not ties at all, just numbers that don't show enough digits to be unique. Pitchers' fielding numbers have been eliminated for 1992, since there are so many of them and only the extremes are interesting (kind of like pitchers' batting). These pages are better spent elsewhere in this book.

First Basemen - Regulars

Player	Tm	G	Inn	PO	A	E	DP	Pct.	Rng
Kruk,John	Phi	103	809.2	734	49	2	54	.997	---
O'Brien,Pete	Sea	132	1063.0	1049	84	3	124	.997	---
Clark,Will	SF	144	1234.1	1273	107	4	118	.997	---
McGwire,Mark	Oak	152	1262.2	1190	99	4	119	.997	---
Bream,Sid	Atl	85	640.2	668	51	3	54	.996	---
Olerud,John	Tor	135	1126.1	1121	77	5	80	.996	---
Mattingly,Don	NYA	127	1090.2	1118	78	5	136	.996	---
Magadan,Dave	NYN	122	1029.0	1033	91	5	74	.996	---
Grace,Mark	ChN	160	1404.1	1519	166	8	109	.995	---
Murray,Eddie	LA	149	1301.1	1327	129	7	96	.995	---
Joyner,Wally	Cal	141	1238.0	1334	96	8	126	.994	---
Benzinger,Todd	TOT	96	792.1	774	50	5	65	.994	---
Hrbek,Kent	Min	129	1082.1	1140	95	8	110	.994	---
Fielder,Cecil	Det	122	1037.0	1054	82	8	110	.993	---
Quintana,Carlos	Bos	138	1042.2	1025	101	8	104	.993	---
Morris,Hal	Cin	128	1067.1	975	101	9	88	.992	---
Palmeiro,Rafael	Tex	157	1366.0	1303	93	12	119	.991	---
Bagwell,Jeff	Hou	155	1331.2	1271	103	12	96	.991	---
Stubbs,Franklin	Mil	92	789.0	824	82	8	79	.991	---
Galarraga,Andres	Mon	105	865.1	886	79	9	68	.991	---
McGriff,Fred	SD	153	1347.0	1371	84	14	112	.990	---
Milligan,Randy	Bal	106	902.0	927	82	10	92	.990	---
Merced,Orlando	Pit	105	870.1	911	60	12	64	.988	---
Jordan,Ricky	Phi	72	600.1	624	37	9	38	.987	---
Guerrero,Pedro	StL	112	922.1	953	66	16	73	.985	---
Average	---	124	1048.1	1056	85	7	92	.993	---

First Basemen - The Rest

Player	Tm	G	Inn	PO	A	E	DP	Pct.	Rng
Aldrete,Mike	Cle	47	312.1	313	22	2	31	.994	---
Allanson,Andy	Det	2	4.0	7	0	0	2	1.000	---
Amaral,Rich	Sea	1	3.0	6	1	0	1	1.000	---
Anderson,Dave	SF	16	87.2	85	9	0	3	1.000	---
Azocar,Oscar	SD	1	4.0	5	0	0	0	1.000	---
Barberie,Bret	Mon	1	5.0	1	0	0	0	1.000	---
Barnes,Skeeter	Det	9	20.0	24	1	0	2	1.000	---
Bell,Mike	Atl	14	68.0	72	5	2	7	.975	---
Benzinger,Todd	Cin	21	143.0	124	12	2	8	.986	---
Benzinger,Todd	KC	75	649.1	650	38	3	57	.996	---
Bergman,Dave	Det	49	379.1	364	29	1	42	.997	---
Bonilla,Bobby	Pit	4	28.0	28	2	0	6	1.000	---
Bradley,Scott	Sea	1	2.0	3	0	1	0	.750	---
Brett,George	KC	10	84.0	87	5	1	6	.989	---
Brewer,Rod	StL	15	30.2	27	3	0	2	1.000	---
Brock,Greg	Mil	25	158.0	150	10	0	19	1.000	---
Bullock,Eric	Mon	3	13.0	11	3	1	0	.933	---
Bush,Randy	Min	12	46.0	35	4	2	6	.951	---
Cabrera,Francisco	Atl	14	60.0	66	5	2	3	.973	---
Calderon,Ivan	Mon	4	25.1	28	2	0	4	1.000	---
Canale,George	Mil	18	107.0	100	15	2	9	.983	---
Carter,Gary	LA	10	54.2	47	7	0	3	1.000	---
Clark,Jerald	SD	16	96.2	86	5	1	4	.989	---
Cochrane,Dave	Sea	4	20.0	21	1	0	3	1.000	---
Coles,Darnell	SF	1	3.0	4	0	0	0	1.000	---
Cromartie,Warren	KC	29	222.0	216	8	1	20	.996	---
Cron,Chris	Cal	5	42.0	32	6	0	1	1.000	---

First Basemen - The Rest

Player	Tm	G	Inn	PO	A	E	DP	Pct.	Rng
Daugherty,Jack	Tex	11	55.0	68	3	0	4	1.000	---
Davis,Alvin	Sea	14	115.0	116	7	0	14	1.000	---
Davis,Glenn	Bal	36	299.1	289	38	8	35	.976	---
de los Santos,Luis	Det	2	2.0	2	0	0	0	1.000	---
Dempsey,Rick	Mil	1	0.0	0	0	0	0	.000	---
Donnels,Chris	NYN	15	126.1	123	12	0	10	1.000	---
Doran,Billy	Cin	4	16.1	19	0	0	3	1.000	---
Dorsett,Brian	SD	2	5.0	4	1	0	0	1.000	---
Eisenreich,Jim	KC	15	105.0	99	11	1	12	.991	---
Fisk,Carlton	ChA	12	94.0	90	9	2	8	.980	---
Fitzgerald,Mike	Mon	3	23.2	15	3	0	1	1.000	---
Foley,Tom	Mon	31	134.2	148	9	1	8	.994	---
Gomez,Leo	Bal	3	12.0	16	0	0	0	1.000	---
Gonzales,Rene	Tor	2	2.1	4	0	0	0	1.000	---
Gregg,Tommy	Atl	13	89.0	105	9	0	6	1.000	---
Harper,Brian	Min	1	1.0	1	0	0	0	1.000	---
Heep,Danny	Atl	1	1.0	1	0	0	0	1.000	---
Hill,Donnie	Cal	3	16.0	15	3	1	2	.947	---
Hoiles,Chris	Bal	2	9.0	10	1	0	1	1.000	---
Hollins,Dave	Phi	6	40.0	42	3	1	4	.978	---
Howell,Jack	Cal	3	16.0	18	2	0	2	1.000	---
Howitt,Dann	Oak	1	7.0	8	0	0	0	1.000	---
Hudler,Rex	StL	12	31.0	30	0	0	5	1.000	---
Hunter,Brian	Atl	85	594.0	622	46	8	45	.988	---
Jacoby,Brook	Cle	55	425.0	379	31	4	27	.990	---
Jacoby,Brook	Oak	3	22.0	25	3	0	3	1.000	---
James,Chris	Cle	15	110.0	95	8	0	7	1.000	---
Javier,Stan	LA	2	18.0	20	3	2	1	.920	---
Jefferson,Reggie	Cin	2	11.1	15	1	0	4	1.000	---
Jefferson,Reggie	Cle	26	227.1	252	24	2	28	.993	---
Karros,Eric	LA	10	30.0	33	2	0	5	1.000	---
Kennedy,Terry	SF	2	3.0	3	0	0	0	1.000	---
Kingery,Mike	SF	6	26.0	21	2	0	2	1.000	---
Kittle,Ron	ChA	15	99.0	101	5	2	8	.981	---
Larkin,Gene	Min	39	241.0	284	19	1	22	.997	---
Law,Vance	Oak	1	1.0	2	0	0	0	1.000	---
Lee,Terry	Cin	2	12.0	8	4	0	0	1.000	---
Leyritz,Jim	NYA	3	5.0	5	0	0	1	1.000	---
Lindeman,Jim	Phi	1	4.0	4	0	0	1	1.000	---
Litton,Greg	SF	15	85.0	75	11	1	11	.989	---
Lopez,Luis	Cle	10	68.0	74	7	2	6	.976	---
Lyons,Barry	Cal	2	10.0	10	1	0	0	1.000	---
Lyons,Steve	Bos	2	2.0	0	0	0	0	.000	---
Maas,Kevin	NYA	36	314.1	317	22	6	22	.983	---
Manto,Jeff	Cle	14	71.0	75	3	2	4	.975	---
Marshall,Mike	Bos	5	37.0	45	0	1	4	.978	---
Marshall,Mike	Cal	1	9.0	14	1	0	2	1.000	---
Martinez,Carlos	Cle	31	227.2	229	12	8	32	.968	---
Martinez,Carmelo	Pit	8	41.0	51	1	3	2	.945	---
Martinez,Carmelo	KC	43	317.2	306	35	3	31	.991	---
Martinez,Carmelo	Cin	25	190.0	187	11	3	13	.985	---
Martinez,Chito	Bal	1	2.0	4	0	0	0	1.000	---
Martinez,Tino	Sea	29	236.1	248	23	2	24	.993	---
Maurer,Rob	Tex	4	10.0	7	3	0	2	1.000	---
McClendon,Lloyd	Pit	22	136.2	132	10	2	12	.986	---
McIntosh,Tim	Mil	1	2.0	1	0	0	0	1.000	---
McKnight,Jeff	Bal	2	16.0	14	1	0	1	1.000	---
Merullo,Matt	ChA	16	76.2	80	6	1	10	.989	---

231

First Basemen - The Rest

Player	Tm	G	Inn	PO	A	E	DP	Pct.	Rng
Meulens,Hensley	NYA	7	34.0	35	1	1	6	.973	---
Mitchell,Kevin	SF	1	3.0	0	0	0	0	.000	---
Molitor,Paul	Mil	46	407.2	389	33	6	52	.986	---
Morman,Russ	KC	8	43.0	45	3	0	2	1.000	---
Newman,Al	Min	1	7.0	7	0	0	0	1.000	---
Noboa,Junior	Mon	1	1.0	1	0	0	0	1.000	---
Oberkfell,Ken	Hou	13	68.2	66	8	0	6	1.000	---
Oquendo,Jose	StL	3	3.1	0	0	0	0	.000	---
Pagnozzi,Tom	StL	3	7.0	9	0	0	1	1.000	---
Parrish,Lance	Cal	3	17.0	12	0	0	0	1.000	---
Pasqua,Dan	ChA	83	542.0	510	43	5	46	.991	---
Pecota,Bill	KC	8	37.0	39	0	0	3	1.000	---
Pedre,Jorge	KC	1	8.0	6	0	0	0	1.000	---
Perry,Gerald	StL	61	426.2	407	27	5	30	.989	---
Powell,Alonzo	Sea	7	21.0	18	2	0	4	1.000	---
Prince,Tom	Pit	1	1.0	1	0	0	0	1.000	---
Quirk,Jamie	Oak	8	42.0	44	6	0	4	1.000	---
Redus,Gary	Pit	47	366.2	377	25	4	36	.990	---
Riles,Ernest	Oak	5	27.2	32	5	0	3	1.000	---
Rohde,David	Hou	1	2.2	3	0	0	0	1.000	---
Rose,Bobby	Cal	3	19.0	21	1	0	1	1.000	---
Salas,Mark	Det	5	7.0	6	1	0	0	1.000	---
Salazar,Luis	ChN	7	33.1	30	1	1	2	.969	---
Santovenia,Nelson	Mon	7	35.0	31	3	0	4	1.000	---
Sasser,Mackey	NYN	10	72.1	80	5	1	5	.988	---
Schu,Rick	Phi	1	9.0	13	1	0	0	1.000	---
Segui,David	Bal	42	217.1	205	22	1	22	.996	---
Sharperson,Mike	LA	10	53.0	46	12	1	5	.983	---
Snyder,Cory	ChA	18	93.1	107	6	1	10	.991	---
Snyder,Cory	Tor	4	17.0	26	3	0	1	1.000	---
Sorrento,Paul	Min	13	72.0	70	7	0	7	1.000	---
Sprague,Ed	Tor	22	143.0	143	9	0	13	1.000	---
Stanley,Mike	Tex	12	48.0	48	6	0	1	1.000	---
Steinbach,Terry	Oak	9	48.0	45	5	2	4	.962	---
Stevens,Lee	Cal	11	74.2	85	6	1	5	.989	---
Tabler,Pat	Tor	20	174.0	182	14	3	11	.985	---
Templeton,Garry	NYN	25	168.0	152	12	1	9	.994	---
Tettleton,Mickey	Det	1	1.0	2	0	0	0	1.000	---
Teufel,Tim	NYN	6	40.2	47	2	0	1	1.000	---
Thomas,Frank	ChA	56	476.2	459	27	2	44	.996	---
Tolentino,Jose	Hou	10	50.0	49	5	1	3	.982	---
Torve,Kelvin	NYN	1	1.0	0	2	0	0	1.000	---
Valle,Dave	Sea	2	4.0	7	0	0	0	1.000	---
Varsho,Gary	Pit	3	13.0	11	0	0	0	1.000	---
Vaughn,Mo	Bos	49	358.0	378	26	6	42	.985	---
Ventura,Robin	ChA	31	96.1	91	4	0	8	1.000	---
Villanueva,Hector	ChN	6	19.0	17	1	0	2	1.000	---
Walker,Larry	Mon	39	337.1	313	30	4	29	.988	---
Webster,Mitch	LA	1	1.0	2	0	0	1	1.000	---
Wilson,Craig	StL	4	14.1	14	1	0	2	1.000	---
Witmeyer,Ron	Oak	8	34.0	32	3	0	2	1.000	---

Second Basemen - Regulars

Player	Tm	G	Inn	PO	A	E	DP	Pct.	Rng
Oquendo,Jose	StL	118	904.2	244	344	7	60	.988	5.85
Baerga,Carlos	Cle	75	633.2	164	239	11	61	.973	5.72
Lind,Jose	Pit	149	1242.1	348	436	9	80	.989	5.68
Sojo,Luis	Cal	107	899.1	228	326	11	78	.981	5.54
Randolph,Willie	Mil	121	997.1	236	378	20	97	.968	5.54
Thompson,Robby	SF	144	1204.0	322	403	11	98	.985	5.42
Lemke,Mark	Atl	110	605.1	159	205	8	41	.978	5.41
Ripken,Billy	Bal	103	827.0	200	287	7	75	.986	5.30
Whitaker,Lou	Det	135	1063.2	254	362	4	90	.994	5.21
Reynolds,Harold	Sea	159	1402.1	348	463	18	133	.978	5.20
Treadway,Jeff	Atl	93	629.1	155	208	15	35	.960	5.19
Reed,Jody	Bos	152	1320.2	314	444	14	109	.982	5.17
Candaele,Casey	Hou	109	868.0	196	300	9	52	.982	5.14
Gallego,Mike	Oak	135	1073.1	245	368	7	69	.989	5.14
Morandini,Mickey	Phi	97	766.2	183	254	6	46	.986	5.13
Sandberg,Ryne	ChN	157	1374.2	267	516	4	68	.995	5.13
Knoblauch,Chuck	Min	148	1240.1	247	458	18	94	.975	5.12
Fletcher,Scott	ChA	86	647.1	177	190	3	49	.992	5.10
Shumpert,Terry	KC	144	1092.2	250	368	16	81	.975	5.09
Samuel,Juan	LA	153	1317.2	300	442	17	72	.978	5.07
Sax,Steve	NYA	149	1305.1	275	443	7	107	.990	4.95
Alomar,Roberto	Tor	160	1420.2	333	447	15	81	.981	4.94
DeShields,Delino	Mon	148	1297.1	285	405	27	73	.962	4.79
Jefferies,Gregg	NYN	77	611.2	144	177	6	15	.982	4.72
Franco,Julio	Tex	146	1283.1	295	374	14	79	.980	4.69
Doran,Billy	Cin	88	704.2	153	208	7	47	.981	4.61
Average	---	125	1028.0	243	347	11	72	.981	5.17

Second Basemen - The Rest

Player	Tm	G	Inn	PO	A	E	DP	Pct.	Rng
Alicea,Luis	StL	11	61.1	17	22	0	3	1.000	5.72
Amaral,Rich	Sea	5	20.0	4	11	0	4	1.000	6.75
Amaro,Ruben	Cal	4	22.0	6	5	1	1	.917	4.50
Anderson,Dave	SF	6	20.1	6	3	0	1	1.000	3.98
Backman,Wally	Phi	36	222.0	50	52	2	12	.981	4.14
Barberie,Bret	Mon	10	85.0	22	25	0	7	1.000	4.98
Barnes,Skeeter	Det	7	39.0	5	10	0	0	1.000	3.46
Barrett,Marty	SD	2	12.0	7	5	0	2	1.000	9.00
Bell,Juan	Bal	77	516.1	105	189	8	39	.974	5.12
Benavides,Freddie	Cin	3	17.0	7	4	0	1	1.000	5.82
Bernazard,Tony	Det	2	10.2	3	6	1	3	.900	7.59
Biggio,Craig	Hou	3	25.0	5	8	1	1	.929	4.68
Blankenship,Lance	Oak	45	265.0	70	100	3	22	.983	5.77
Blauser,Jeff	Atl	33	218.0	48	66	2	15	.983	4.71
Bordick,Mike	Oak	5	15.0	9	4	1	2	.929	7.80
Briley,Greg	Sea	1	2.0	0	0	0	0	.000	.00
Brosius,Scott	Oak	18	21.0	4	5	0	1	1.000	3.86
Browne,Jerry	Cle	47	327.0	80	109	7	17	.964	5.20
Brumley,Mike	Bos	7	42.0	12	21	0	8	1.000	7.07
Buechele,Steve	Tex	13	93.0	13	35	0	3	1.000	4.65
Cole,Stu	KC	5	10.0	1	4	0	0	1.000	4.50
Cora,Joey	ChA	80	565.0	103	184	9	33	.970	5.20
Diaz,Mario	Tex	20	73.2	22	26	0	5	1.000	5.86
Disarcina,Gary	Cal	7	58.0	12	11	0	2	1.000	3.57
Duncan,Mariano	Cin	63	475.0	118	144	7	29	.974	4.96
Escobar,Jose	Cle	4	22.0	10	8	0	4	1.000	7.36

Second Basemen - The Rest

Player	Tm	G	Inn	PO	A	E	DP	Pct.	Rng
Faries,Paul	SD	36	244.0	67	92	2	18	.988	5.86
Fariss,Monty	Tex	4	22.0	4	9	0	3	1.000	5.32
Felder,Mike	SF	1	2.0	0	2	0	0	1.000	9.00
Flora,Kevin	Cal	3	24.0	8	3	2	1	.846	4.13
Foley,Tom	Mon	2	15.0	6	8	0	3	1.000	8.40
Gantner,Jim	Mil	59	456.1	110	190	7	31	.977	5.92
Garcia,Carlos	Pit	1	3.1	2	0	0	0	1.000	5.40
Gardner,Jeff	NYN	3	23.0	4	9	0	0	1.000	5.09
Gonzales,Rene	Tor	11	42.0	4	12	0	1	1.000	3.43
Grebeck,Craig	ChA	36	263.2	62	96	1	20	.994	5.39
Harris,Lenny	LA	27	124.1	32	49	1	12	.988	5.86
Hemond,Scott	Oak	7	31.0	7	12	0	3	1.000	5.52
Henderson,Dave	Oak	1	1.0	0	0	0	0	.000	.00
Herr,Tommy	NYN	57	378.0	100	121	0	29	1.000	5.26
Herr,Tommy	SF	15	98.2	14	27	0	4	1.000	3.74
Hill,Donnie	Cal	39	281.2	76	89	5	23	.971	5.27
Howard,Dave	KC	26	165.0	36	60	1	10	.990	5.24
Howell,Jack	Cal	12	86.2	25	36	2	5	.968	6.33
Hudler,Rex	StL	5	8.0	3	2	0	1	1.000	5.63
Huff,Mike	Cle	2	17.0	1	3	0	1	1.000	2.12
Huff,Mike	ChA	2	2.0	0	0	0	0	.000	.00
Hulett,Tim	Bal	26	113.1	29	31	2	5	.968	4.76
Huson,Jeff	Tex	2	7.0	0	2	0	1	1.000	2.57
Jones,Tim	StL	4	14.0	0	3	0	0	1.000	1.93
Kelly,Pat	NYA	18	124.0	34	41	2	14	.974	5.44
Larkin,Gene	Min	1	0.1	0	0	0	0	.000	.00
Lewis,Mark	Cle	50	432.2	87	140	8	29	.966	4.72
Liriano,Nelson	KC	10	55.0	11	23	0	3	1.000	5.56
Litton,Greg	SF	15	86.0	28	23	0	6	1.000	5.34
Lyons,Steve	Bos	16	72.0	18	25	1	8	.977	5.38
Manrique,Fred	Oak	2	8.0	3	6	0	1	1.000	10.13
McLemore,Mark	Hou	19	150.2	26	54	2	9	.976	4.78
Miller,Keith	NYN	60	421.2	129	147	8	28	.972	5.89
Mota,Andy	Hou	27	220.1	30	66	3	11	.970	3.92
Mota,Jose	SD	13	89.2	24	27	2	5	.962	5.12
Naehring,Tim	Bos	1	5.0	1	2	0	0	1.000	5.40
Newman,Al	Min	35	208.0	52	76	1	15	.992	5.54
Noboa,Junior	Mon	6	43.0	11	14	1	3	.962	5.23
Pagliarulo,Mike	Min	1	0.2	0	0	0	0	.000	.00
Paredes,Johnny	Det	7	40.0	11	12	1	5	.958	5.18
Pecota,Bill	KC	34	143.1	46	34	0	8	1.000	5.02
Pena,Geronimo	StL	83	444.1	95	146	6	28	.976	4.88
Perezchica,Tony	SF	6	31.0	6	7	0	3	1.000	3.77
Perezchica,Tony	Cle	2	9.0	1	6	0	0	1.000	7.00
Phillips,Tony	Det	36	297.0	108	118	1	34	.996	6.85
Quinones,Luis	Cin	33	243.1	45	74	3	15	.975	4.40
Ramirez,Rafael	Hou	27	161.1	35	52	2	9	.978	4.85
Ready,Randy	Phi	66	474.1	127	145	3	22	.989	5.16
Riles,Ernest	Oak	7	30.0	10	12	0	4	1.000	6.60
Roberts,Bip	SD	68	563.1	128	185	7	36	.978	5.00
Rodriguez,Carlos	NYA	3	5.0	0	1	0	0	1.000	1.80
Rohde,David	Hou	4	27.2	7	12	0	1	1.000	6.18
Rose,Bobby	Cal	8	70.0	12	26	0	6	1.000	4.89
Sanchez,Rey	ChN	2	10.0	1	8	0	0	1.000	8.10
Schaefer,Jeff	Sea	11	39.0	10	13	0	6	1.000	5.31
Sharperson,Mike	LA	5	15.0	5	8	0	3	1.000	7.80
Shipley,Craig	SD	14	86.0	19	36	1	8	.982	5.76
Smith,Greg	LA	1	1.0	0	0	0	0	.000	.00

Second Basemen - The Rest

Player	Tm	G	Inn	PO	A	E	DP	Pct.	Rng
Surhoff,B.J.	Mil	1	1.0	0	0	0	0	.000	.00
Sveum,Dale	Mil	2	9.0	3	2	0	0	1.000	5.00
Teufel,Tim	NYN	1	3.0	1	2	0	0	1.000	9.00
Teufel,Tim	SD	65	457.2	99	122	3	22	.987	4.35
Turner,Shane	Bal	1	1.0	0	1	0	0	1.000	9.00
Velarde,Randy	NYA	1	9.2	0	6	0	1	1.000	5.59
Vizcaino,Jose	ChN	9	38.0	8	18	2	4	.929	6.16
Vizquel,Omar	Sea	1	1.0	0	0	0	0	.000	.00
Walker,Chico	ChN	6	34.0	11	16	0	1	1.000	7.15
Wilkerson,Curt	Pit	30	211.0	51	79	1	14	.992	5.55
Wilson,Craig	StL	3	3.0	0	2	0	1	1.000	6.00

Third Basemen - Regulars

Player	Tm	G	Inn	PO	A	E	DP	Pct.	Rng
Pendleton,Terry	Atl	149	1283.2	109	348	24	32	.950	3.20
Gaetti,Gary	Cal	152	1339.2	111	351	17	38	.965	3.10
Buechele,Steve	TOT	142	1195.0	109	302	7	24	.983	3.10
Baerga,Carlos	Cle	89	698.2	54	181	15	14	.940	3.03
Gruber,Kelly	Tor	111	977.1	97	230	13	17	.962	3.01
Pagliarulo,Mike	Min	118	913.1	56	248	11	30	.965	3.00
Ventura,Robin	ChA	151	1275.2	135	287	18	29	.959	2.98
Caminiti,Ken	Hou	152	1308.2	129	292	23	29	.948	2.90
Williams,Matt D.	SF	155	1317.2	131	292	16	29	.964	2.89
Wallach,Tim	Mon	150	1321.1	108	305	14	29	.967	2.81
Zeile,Todd	StL	154	1325.1	124	290	25	18	.943	2.81
Martinez,Edgar	Sea	144	1239.2	85	298	15	26	.962	2.78
Hayes,Charlie	Phi	138	1043.2	85	237	14	24	.958	2.78
Boggs,Wade	Bos	141	1196.2	89	274	12	33	.968	2.73
Kelly,Pat	NYA	81	671.0	45	156	16	14	.926	2.70
Pecota,Bill	KC	102	762.0	69	157	4	15	.983	2.67
Harris,Lenny	LA	113	781.2	77	154	14	16	.943	2.66
Salazar,Luis	ChN	86	673.2	46	151	9	6	.956	2.63
Fryman,Travis	Det	86	702.0	45	147	11	12	.946	2.46
Gantner,Jim	Mil	90	764.0	51	155	5	15	.976	2.43
Gomez,Leo	Bal	105	915.1	62	184	7	20	.972	2.42
Sabo,Chris	Cin	151	1303.1	88	255	12	24	.966	2.37
Johnson,Howard	NYN	104	878.0	54	172	18	11	.926	2.32
Average	---	124	1038.1	85	237	13	21	.959	2.80

Third Basemen - The Rest

Player	Tm	G	Inn	PO	A	E	DP	Pct.	Rng
Alicea,Luis	StL	2	3.0	1	0	0	0	1.000	3.00
Amaral,Rich	Sea	2	2.0	0	1	0	0	1.000	4.50
Anderson,Dave	SF	11	47.0	8	7	3	0	.833	2.87
Backman,Wally	Phi	20	120.2	4	27	2	1	.939	2.31
Barberie,Bret	Mon	10	82.0	11	17	0	1	1.000	3.07
Barnes,Skeeter	Det	17	91.1	9	21	2	2	.938	2.96
Barrett,Marty	SD	2	9.0	0	2	0	0	1.000	2.00
Benjamin,Mike	SF	1	3.0	0	0	0	0	.000	.00
Berry,Sean	KC	30	182.0	13	52	2	3	.970	3.21
Bichette,Dante	Mil	1	1.0	0	0	0	0	.000	.00
Blankenship,Lance	Oak	14	81.0	7	21	0	2	1.000	3.11
Blauser,Jeff	Atl	18	125.1	13	28	4	1	.911	2.94
Blowers,Mike	NYA	14	90.0	4	16	3	1	.870	2.00

Third Basemen - The Rest

Third Basemen - The Rest

Player	Tm	G	Inn	PO	A	E	DP	Pct.	Rng
Bonilla,Bobby	Pit	67	520.0	43	134	13	13	.932	3.06
Booker,Rod	Phi	3	12.0	1	4	0	0	1.000	3.75
Bordick,Mike	Oak	1	1.0	0	0	0	0	.000	.00
Bradley,Scott	Sea	4	17.0	0	2	1	0	.667	1.06
Briley,Greg	Sea	1	2.0	0	0	0	0	.000	.00
Brosius,Scott	Oak	7	50.0	3	10	0	1	1.000	2.34
Browne,Jerry	Cle	15	113.0	7	32	6	4	.867	3.11
Brumley,Mike	Bos	17	80.0	10	19	2	3	.935	3.26
Buechele,Steve	Tex	111	926.0	87	238	3	19	.991	3.16
Buechele,Steve	Pit	31	269.0	22	64	4	5	.956	2.88
Candaele,Casey	Hou	11	64.0	7	16	1	1	.958	3.23
Cochrane,Dave	Sea	13	97.0	11	14	5	1	.833	2.32
Coolbaugh,Scott	SD	54	457.1	32	108	7	8	.952	2.76
Cooper,Gary	Hou	4	30.0	3	2	1	0	.833	1.50
Cooper,Scott	Bos	13	84.0	6	22	2	1	.933	3.00
de los Santos,Luis	Det	2	9.0	0	1	1	0	.500	1.00
Diaz,Mario	Tex	8	34.0	3	7	0	1	1.000	2.65
Disarcina,Gary	Cal	2	12.0	2	6	0	1	1.000	6.00
Donnels,Chris	NYN	11	75.0	8	22	2	3	.938	3.60
Escobar,Jose	Cle	1	1.0	0	0	0	0	.000	.00
Espinoza,Alvaro	NYA	2	17.0	2	3	0	0	1.000	2.65
Faries,Paul	SD	12	54.0	5	13	0	0	1.000	3.00
Felder,Mike	SF	3	8.0	1	5	1	1	.857	6.75
Fletcher,Scott	ChA	4	7.0	1	1	0	0	1.000	2.57
Foley,Tom	Mon	6	23.0	1	5	1	0	.857	2.35
Garcia,Carlos	Pit	2	20.0	4	4	0	0	1.000	3.60
Giannelli,Ray	Tor	9	66.0	0	12	1	2	.923	1.64
Gonzales,Rene	Tor	26	110.1	7	41	4	3	.923	3.92
Grebeck,Craig	ChA	49	195.1	22	49	5	6	.934	3.27
Hamilton,Jeff	LA	33	203.2	21	43	5	2	.928	2.83
Hansen,Dave	LA	21	69.2	4	18	0	1	1.000	2.84
Hemond,Scott	Oak	2	9.1	3	0	0	0	1.000	2.89
Hernandez,Carlos	LA	1	0.1	0	0	0	0	.000	.00
Hernandez,Jose	Tex	1	3.0	1	1	0	1	1.000	6.00
Herr,Tommy	SF	3	11.0	2	3	0	0	1.000	4.09
Hollins,Dave	Phi	36	273.0	25	58	7	2	.922	2.74
Howard,Dave	KC	1	1.0	0	0	0	0	.000	.00
Howell,Jack	Cal	8	64.0	4	17	0	1	1.000	2.95
Howell,Jack	SD	54	380.0	33	98	2	7	.985	3.10
Hulett,Tim	Bal	39	289.0	18	64	2	8	.976	2.55
Humphreys,Mike	NYA	6	37.0	1	8	1	0	.900	2.19
Huson,Jeff	Tex	1	1.0	0	0	0	0	.000	.00
Jacoby,Brook	Cle	15	114.0	11	28	1	3	.975	3.08
Jacoby,Brook	Oak	52	421.1	38	71	2	9	.982	2.33
Jefferies,Gregg	NYN	51	438.1	26	94	11	7	.916	2.46
King,Jeff	Pit	33	281.0	15	62	2	0	.975	2.47
Lansford,Carney	Oak	4	26.0	0	3	0	1	1.000	1.04
Larkin,Gene	Min	1	0.2	0	0	0	0	.000	.00
Law,Vance	Oak	67	369.2	36	61	5	7	.951	2.36
Leius,Scott	Min	79	442.2	41	100	7	8	.953	2.87
Lemke,Mark	Atl	15	43.2	3	10	2	1	.867	2.68
Leyritz,Jim	NYA	18	140.1	10	21	3	2	.912	1.99
Litton,Greg	SF	11	55.1	5	17	1	1	.957	3.58
Livingstone,Scott	Det	43	316.0	31	67	2	6	.980	2.79
Lopez,Luis	Cle	1	2.0	0	0	0	0	.000	.00
Lovullo,Torey	NYA	22	134.0	14	33	3	1	.940	3.16
Lyons,Steve	Bos	12	67.0	9	17	2	0	.929	3.49
Manto,Jeff	Cle	32	260.1	21	57	6	13	.929	2.70
Miller,Keith	NYN	2	8.2	2	1	0	0	1.000	3.12
Mulliniks,Rance	Tor	5	29.0	2	3	0	0	1.000	1.55
Murray,Eddie	LA	1	1.0	0	0	0	0	.000	.00
Naehring,Tim	Bos	2	12.0	0	2	0	1	1.000	1.50
Newman,Al	Min	35	92.2	8	18	1	1	.963	2.53
Noboa,Junior	Mon	2	14.0	1	3	0	1	1.000	2.57
Oberkfell,Ken	Hou	4	36.1	4	5	2	0	.818	2.23
Palmer,Dean	Tex	50	400.0	27	74	6	5	.944	2.27
Paredes,Johnny	Det	1	1.0	0	0	0	0	.000	.00
Perezchica,Tony	Cle	3	10.0	0	1	0	0	1.000	0.90
Petralli,Geno	Tex	7	29.0	1	5	2	2	.750	1.86
Phillips,Tony	Det	46	331.0	26	84	5	7	.957	2.99
Presley,Jim	SD	16	139.0	14	22	3	0	.923	2.33
Quinones,Luis	Cin	19	136.2	12	20	3	2	.914	2.11
Quirk,Jamie	Oak	1	1.0	0	0	0	0	.000	.00
Ramirez,Rafael	Hou	2	2.0	0	1	0	0	1.000	4.50
Redfield,Joe	Pit	9	46.0	4	7	1	3	.917	2.15
Richardson,Jeff	Pit	3	3.0	0	0	0	0	.000	.00
Riles,Ernest	Oak	69	485.0	54	101	10	14	.939	2.88
Rohde,David	Hou	3	12.0	0	3	0	0	1.000	2.25
Rose,Bobby	Cal	4	18.0	2	4	0	0	1.000	3.00
Royer,Stan	StL	5	38.0	5	4	0	0	1.000	2.13
Sax,Steve	NYA	5	43.0	3	10	3	0	.813	2.72
Schaefer,Jeff	Sea	30	106.2	4	20	1	3	.960	2.03
Schu,Rick	Phi	3	13.2	2	0	1	0	.667	1.32
Scott,Gary	ChN	31	235.0	13	50	2	7	.969	2.41
Seitzer,Kevin	KC	68	519.0	45	126	11	9	.940	2.97
Sharperson,Mike	LA	68	401.2	31	70	2	5	.981	2.26
Sheffield,Gary	Mil	43	369.0	29	65	8	7	.922	2.29
Slaught,Don	Pit	1	2.0	0	0	0	0	.000	.00
Snyder,Cory	Tor	3	20.0	0	7	1	0	.875	3.15
Sojo,Luis	Cal	1	8.0	1	3	0	0	1.000	4.50
Sprague,Ed	Tor	35	260.0	19	61	12	2	.870	2.77
Stanley,Mike	Tex	6	26.0	1	4	1	1	.833	1.73
Strange,Doug	ChN	3	27.0	1	3	1	0	.800	1.33
Surhoff,B.J.	Mil	5	22.0	3	3	0	0	1.000	2.45
Sveum,Dale	Mil	38	307.2	26	62	4	9	.957	2.57
Templeton,Garry	SD	15	87.2	2	17	1	2	.950	1.95
Templeton,Garry	NYN	2	17.0	2	8	0	1	1.000	5.29
Teufel,Tim	NYN	5	20.1	1	5	0	0	1.000	2.66
Teufel,Tim	SD	48	325.2	28	74	6	4	.944	2.82
Thome,Jim	Cle	27	242.1	12	60	8	6	.900	2.67
Velarde,Randy	NYA	49	311.2	29	86	8	8	.935	3.32
Vizcaino,Jose	ChN	57	144.1	10	26	2	1	.947	2.24
Walker,Chico	ChN	57	376.2	22	69	7	7	.929	2.17
Walling,Denny	Tex	14	60.0	6	13	1	0	.950	2.85
Wehner,John	Pit	36	231.1	23	65	6	10	.936	3.42
Wilkerson,Curt	Pit	14	84.1	14	24	1	4	.974	4.06
Wilson,Craig	StL	12	69.0	8	11	2	3	.905	2.48
Worthington,Craig	Bal	30	253.1	26	50	2	3	.974	2.70
Zuvella,Paul	KC	2	2.0	0	0	0	0	.000	.00

Shortstops - Regulars

Player	Tm	G	Inn	PO	A	E	DP	Pct.	Rng
Larkin,Barry	Cin	120	1032.0	225	370	15	65	.975	5.19
Griffin,Alfredo	LA	109	933.2	184	347	22	45	.960	5.12
Vizquel,Omar	Sea	138	1134.1	224	421	13	104	.980	5.12
Ripken,Cal	Bal	162	1427.2	269	526	11	114	.986	5.01
Trammell,Alan	Det	92	771.0	131	295	9	60	.979	4.97
Espinoza,Alvaro	NYA	147	1197.0	222	437	21	113	.969	4.95
Bell,Jay	Pit	156	1347.1	239	492	24	79	.968	4.88
Fernandez,Tony	SD	145	1262.2	248	437	20	79	.972	4.88
Dunston,Shawon	ChN	142	1192.0	261	383	21	71	.968	4.86
Fermin,Felix	Cle	129	1092.1	215	374	12	73	.980	4.85
Guillen,Ozzie	ChA	149	1286.0	250	439	21	89	.970	4.82
Huson,Jeff	Tex	116	765.1	141	266	15	40	.964	4.79
Belliard,Rafael	Atl	145	990.0	166	360	18	53	.967	4.78
Owen,Spike	Mon	133	1066.0	189	377	8	65	.986	4.78
Gagne,Greg	Min	137	1067.2	182	378	9	68	.984	4.72
Fryman,Travis	Det	71	604.2	110	207	12	48	.964	4.72
Elster,Kevin	NYN	107	865.0	151	299	14	39	.970	4.68
Schofield,Dick	Cal	133	1140.0	188	398	15	82	.975	4.63
Rivera,Luis	Bos	129	1103.2	181	386	24	90	.959	4.62
Uribe,Jose	SF	87	620.1	98	219	11	37	.966	4.60
Bordick,Mike	Oak	84	683.2	137	210	10	43	.972	4.57
Thon,Dickie	Phi	146	1277.0	237	411	21	66	.969	4.57
Smith,Ozzie	StL	150	1253.1	244	387	8	78	.987	4.53
Spiers,Bill	Mil	128	1104.0	200	344	17	93	.970	4.43
Lee,Manuel	Tor	138	1155.1	194	360	19	54	.967	4.32
Stillwell,Kurt	KC	118	911.0	163	262	18	65	.959	4.20
Average	---	127	1049.1	194	360	15	69	.973	4.76

Shortstops - The Rest

Player	Tm	G	Inn	PO	A	E	DP	Pct.	Rng
Alicea,Luis	StL	1	1.0	1	1	0	1	1.000	18.00
Amaral,Rich	Sea	2	18.0	3	3	2	1	.750	3.00
Anderson,Dave	SF	63	327.2	68	107	8	26	.956	4.81
Baerga,Carlos	Cle	2	9.0	0	0	1	0	.000	.00
Barberie,Bret	Mon	19	132.1	19	48	5	7	.931	4.56
Batiste,Kim	Phi	7	59.0	10	22	1	4	.970	4.88
Bell,Juan	Bal	15	29.0	3	10	1	1	.929	4.03
Beltre,Esteban	ChA	8	24.0	1	5	0	1	1.000	2.25
Benavides,Freddie	Cin	20	143.1	26	49	2	5	.974	4.71
Benjamin,Mike	SF	51	308.0	65	123	3	24	.984	5.49
Blauser,Jeff	Atl	85	435.0	75	123	11	23	.947	4.10
Booker,Rod	Phi	20	115.0	16	29	0	2	1.000	3.52
Brumley,Mike	Bos	31	188.0	19	76	5	9	.950	4.55
Buechele,Steve	Tex	4	4.0	0	1	0	0	1.000	2.25
Castilla,Vinny	Atl	12	26.2	6	6	0	1	1.000	4.05
Cedeno,Andujar	Hou	66	577.1	89	152	18	35	.931	3.76
Clayton,Royce	SF	8	60.0	16	6	3	1	.880	3.30
Cole,Stu	KC	1	8.0	1	0	0	0	1.000	1.13
Cora,Joey	ChA	5	23.0	4	8	1	3	.923	4.70
Diaz,Mario	Tex	65	359.2	68	110	7	25	.962	4.45
Disarcina,Gary	Cal	10	89.0	14	29	4	2	.915	4.35
Duncan,Mariano	Cin	32	223.0	46	68	2	12	.983	4.60
Escobar,Jose	Cle	5	29.0	5	5	0	0	1.000	3.10
Faries,Paul	SD	8	42.0	8	13	0	2	1.000	4.50
Foley,Tom	Mon	43	234.0	45	71	4	12	.967	4.46
Gallego,Mike	Oak	55	272.0	42	76	5	22	.959	3.90

Shortstops - The Rest

Player	Tm	G	Inn	PO	A	E	DP	Pct.	Rng
Garcia,Carlos	Pit	9	36.0	5	13	1	3	.947	4.50
Gardner,Jeff	NYN	8	66.1	7	20	6	2	.818	3.66
Gonzales,Rene	Tor	36	222.1	46	64	3	13	.973	4.45
Grebeck,Craig	ChA	26	145.0	20	38	4	9	.935	3.60
Green,Gary	Tex	8	53.0	10	20	1	5	.968	5.09
Hamilton,Jeff	LA	1	1.0	0	0	0	0	.000	.00
Hansen,Dave	LA	1	1.0	1	1	0	1	1.000	18.00
Harris,Lenny	LA	20	117.0	16	46	5	7	.925	4.77
Hayes,Charlie	Phi	2	12.0	3	3	1	0	.857	4.50
Hemond,Scott	Oak	1	1.0	0	1	0	0	1.000	9.00
Hernandez,Jose	Tex	44	297.0	48	110	4	17	.975	4.79
Hill,Donnie	Cal	29	201.2	37	82	2	12	.983	5.31
Howard,Dave	KC	63	515.0	93	190	11	30	.963	4.95
Hulett,Tim	Bal	1	1.0	0	0	0	0	.000	.00
Johnson,Howard	NYN	28	218.0	45	88	11	16	.924	5.49
Jones,Tim	StL	14	57.0	5	13	0	3	1.000	2.84
Knoblauch,Chuck	Min	2	4.0	0	0	0	0	.000	.00
Law,Vance	Oak	3	11.0	1	4	0	0	1.000	4.09
Leius,Scott	Min	19	77.0	15	28	0	7	1.000	5.03
Lewis,Mark	Cle	36	281.0	42	91	1	18	.993	4.26
Litton,Greg	SF	9	41.1	7	12	0	3	1.000	4.14
Lyons,Steve	Bos	1	1.0	1	1	0	0	1.000	18.00
Magallanes,Ever	Cle	2	3.0	0	1	0	0	1.000	3.00
Manrique,Fred	Oak	7	51.0	7	14	1	2	.955	3.71
Miller,Keith	NYN	2	9.0	1	3	2	1	.667	4.00
Mota,Jose	SD	3	9.0	1	2	1	0	.750	3.00
Naehring,Tim	Bos	17	134.0	15	50	3	7	.956	4.37
Newman,Al	Min	55	300.2	63	90	2	24	.987	4.58
Noboa,Junior	Mon	2	8.0	0	2	0	0	1.000	2.25
Offerman,Jose	LA	50	351.1	50	121	10	17	.945	4.38
Oquendo,Jose	StL	22	124.0	27	22	2	5	.961	3.56
Paredes,Johnny	Det	1	1.0	0	0	0	0	.000	.00
Pecota,Bill	KC	9	32.0	8	14	0	3	1.000	6.19
Perezchica,Tony	SF	13	70.2	14	22	2	3	.947	4.58
Perezchica,Tony	Cle	6	27.0	2	4	0	1	1.000	2.00
Phillips,Tony	Det	13	73.2	21	32	1	10	.981	6.48
Quinones,Luis	Cin	5	41.2	11	12	1	5	.958	4.97
Ramirez,Rafael	Hou	45	268.2	51	71	6	13	.953	4.09
Reed,Jody	Bos	6	13.0	2	5	0	1	1.000	4.85
Richardson,Jeff	Pit	2	6.1	0	1	0	0	1.000	1.42
Riles,Ernest	Oak	20	101.0	17	25	1	5	.977	3.74
Rodriguez,Carlos	NYA	11	83.0	11	33	2	9	.957	4.77
Rohde,David	Hou	3	20.0	3	8	0	1	1.000	4.95
Rossy,Rico	Atl	1	1.0	0	0	0	0	.000	.00
Sanchez,Rey	ChN	10	64.2	10	17	0	1	1.000	3.76
Schaefer,Jeff	Sea	46	312.0	64	86	5	24	.968	4.33
Sharperson,Mike	LA	16	54.0	8	16	1	2	.960	4.00
Shipley,Craig	SD	19	135.0	21	34	6	6	.902	3.67
Sojo,Luis	Cal	2	11.0	2	6	0	0	1.000	6.55
Sveum,Dale	Mil	51	359.2	56	125	6	24	.968	4.53
Templeton,Garry	SD	1	4.0	1	0	0	0	1.000	2.25
Templeton,Garry	NYN	40	279.0	53	104	6	18	.963	5.06
Velarde,Randy	NYA	31	164.0	32	64	7	16	.932	5.27
Vizcaino,Jose	ChN	33	200.0	31	74	3	14	.972	4.72
Weiss,Walt	Oak	40	324.2	64	99	5	21	.970	4.52
Wilkerson,Curt	Pit	15	67.0	9	20	0	5	1.000	3.90
Williams,Matt D.	SF	4	14.0	2	2	0	1	1.000	2.57
Yelding,Eric	Hou	72	587.0	114	166	18	31	.940	4.29

Shortstops - The Rest

Player	Tm	G	Inn	PO	A	E	DP	Pct.	Rng
Zosky,Eddie	Tor	18	85.0	12	26	0	6	1.000	4.02

Left Fielders - Regulars

Player	Tm	G	Inn	PO	A	E	DP	Pct.	Rng
Gilkey,Bernard	StL	74	604.1	163	6	1	1	.994	2.52
Gonzalez,Luis	Hou	133	1084.2	293	6	5	1	.984	2.48
Vaughn,Greg	Mil	135	1164.1	315	5	2	1	.994	2.47
Orsulak,Joe	Bal	85	651.1	161	13	0	2	1.000	2.40
Henderson,Rickey	Oak	119	982.1	249	11	8	1	.970	2.38
Bonds,Barry	Pit	150	1295.2	313	13	3	1	.991	2.26
Calderon,Ivan	Mon	122	1038.0	257	3	7	2	.974	2.25
McReynolds,Kevin	NYN	125	959.1	230	7	2	1	.992	2.22
Gladden,Dan	Min	126	990.0	239	4	3	1	.988	2.21
Raines,Tim	ChA	133	1165.1	273	12	3	3	.990	2.20
Belle,Albert	Cle	88	726.2	168	8	9	1	.951	2.18
Chamberlain,Wes	Phi	95	841.2	195	4	3	0	.985	2.13
Mitchell,Kevin	SF	100	824.0	188	6	6	0	.970	2.12
Greenwell,Mike	Bos	143	1219.2	263	9	3	3	.989	2.01
Daniels,Kal	LA	132	1041.1	220	9	5	0	.979	1.98
Bell,George	ChN	146	1191.1	249	6	10	0	.962	1.93
Gibson,Kirk	KC	91	759.1	157	3	4	0	.976	1.90
Clark,Jerald	SD	85	693.0	139	3	1	1	.993	1.84
Polonia,Luis	Cal	143	1249.2	246	8	5	0	.981	1.83
Smith,Lonnie	Atl	99	725.0	134	5	5	2	.965	1.73
Average	---	116	960.1	222	7	4	1	.982	2.15

Left Fielders - The Rest

Player	Tm	G	Inn	PO	A	E	DP	Pct.	Rng
Aldrete,Mike	SD	5	24.2	8	1	0	0	1.000	3.28
Aldrete,Mike	Cle	16	111.0	21	1	0	0	1.000	1.78
Allred,Beau	Cle	20	121.1	42	1	0	0	1.000	3.19
Amaro,Ruben	Cal	3	24.0	3	1	0	0	1.000	1.50
Anderson,Brady	Bal	75	392.1	84	2	3	0	.966	1.97
Azocar,Oscar	SD	12	63.0	12	0	1	0	.923	1.71
Baines,Harold	Oak	1	6.0	0	0	0	0	.000	.00
Barnes,Skeeter	Det	13	96.0	24	3	0	0	1.000	2.53
Bass,Kevin	SF	23	163.2	35	5	1	0	.976	2.20
Bell,Derek	Tor	7	57.0	10	0	1	0	.909	1.58
Bell,Juan	Bal	1	1.0	0	0	0	0	.000	.00
Benzinger,Todd	Cin	15	94.1	23	0	0	0	1.000	2.19
Bergman,Dave	Det	4	6.0	1	0	0	0	1.000	1.50
Biggio,Craig	Hou	1	0.2	0	0	0	0	.000	.00
Blankenship,Lance	Oak	18	79.2	34	0	0	0	1.000	3.84
Boston,Daryl	NYN	9	53.0	17	0	0	0	1.000	2.89
Braggs,Glenn	Cin	55	408.1	102	1	4	1	.963	2.27
Briley,Greg	Sea	95	524.0	122	3	3	0	.977	2.15
Brosius,Scott	Oak	5	24.0	8	0	0	0	1.000	3.00
Brown,Jarvis	Min	3	10.0	4	0	0	0	1.000	3.60
Browne,Jerry	Cle	17	122.0	26	0	1	0	.963	1.92
Bullett,Scott	Pit	1	1.0	1	0	0	0	1.000	9.00
Bullock,Eric	Mon	6	31.0	6	0	0	0	1.000	1.74
Bush,Randy	Min	7	30.0	8	0	0	0	1.000	2.40
Candaele,Casey	Hou	18	112.0	30	0	0	0	1.000	2.41
Capra,Nick	Tex	1	2.0	1	0	0	0	1.000	4.50

Left Fielders - The Rest

Player	Tm	G	Inn	PO	A	E	DP	Pct.	Rng
Carreon,Mark	NYN	43	303.2	69	3	0	0	1.000	2.13
Carrillo,Matias	Mil	3	3.0	0	0	0	0	.000	.00
Carter,Joe	Tor	56	464.1	94	1	5	0	.950	1.84
Castillo,Carmen	Min	1	1.0	1	0	0	0	1.000	9.00
Cochrane,Dave	Sea	23	141.0	28	0	1	0	.966	1.79
Cole,Alex	Cle	8	46.0	11	0	1	0	.917	2.15
Cotto,Henry	Sea	38	184.0	51	0	1	0	.981	2.49
Cromartie,Warren	KC	5	15.0	4	0	0	0	1.000	2.40
Dascenzo,Doug	ChN	32	69.1	16	0	0	0	1.000	2.08
Daugherty,Jack	Tex	34	236.0	51	1	1	0	.981	1.98
Davidson,Mark	Hou	32	143.0	38	0	0	0	1.000	2.39
Davis,Chili	Min	2	3.0	2	0	0	0	1.000	6.00
Davis,Eric	Cin	6	36.0	8	0	0	0	1.000	2.00
de los Santos,Luis	Det	3	17.0	6	0	0	0	1.000	3.18
Doran,Billy	Cin	6	42.1	11	0	0	0	1.000	2.34
Ducey,Rob	Tor	19	124.0	26	1	2	0	.931	1.96
Duncan,Mariano	Cin	6	30.0	4	0	0	0	1.000	1.20
Eisenreich,Jim	KC	59	377.1	75	1	3	0	.962	1.81
Espy,Cecil	Pit	2	5.0	1	0	0	0	1.000	1.80
Fariss,Monty	Tex	8	47.0	21	0	0	0	1.000	4.02
Felder,Mike	SF	44	241.1	60	2	1	2	.984	2.31
Finley,Steve	Hou	1	2.0	0	0	0	0	.000	.00
Gallagher,Dave	Cal	7	51.0	9	1	0	0	1.000	1.76
Gonzalez,Jose	LA	8	20.0	5	0	0	0	1.000	2.25
Gonzalez,Jose	Pit	3	8.1	4	1	0	0	1.000	5.40
Gonzalez,Jose	Cle	5	29.0	7	0	0	0	1.000	2.17
Gonzalez,Juan	Tex	92	505.1	112	1	2	0	.983	2.01
Goodwin,Tom	LA	2	3.0	0	0	0	0	.000	.00
Gregg,Tommy	Atl	9	58.2	9	0	0	0	1.000	1.38
Griffey Sr.,Ken	Sea	26	181.0	31	0	0	0	1.000	1.54
Grissom,Marquis	Mon	3	6.0	1	0	0	0	1.000	1.50
Gwynn,Chris	LA	30	125.0	28	0	0	0	1.000	2.02
Hall,Mel	NYA	63	484.2	111	4	0	1	1.000	2.14
Hamilton,Daryl	Mil	25	143.0	32	1	0	0	1.000	2.08
Harper,Brian	Min	1	1.0	0	0	0	0	.000	.00
Harris,Donald	Tex	2	3.0	1	0	0	0	1.000	3.00
Harris,Lenny	LA	1	1.0	0	0	0	0	.000	.00
Hatcher,Billy	Cin	83	554.0	132	4	2	0	.986	2.21
Hayes,Charlie	Phi	1	0.0	0	0	0	0	.000	.00
Hayes,Von	Phi	20	184.0	55	1	0	0	1.000	2.74
Heep,Danny	Atl	1	1.0	0	0	0	0	.000	.00
Henderson,Dave	Oak	3	25.0	8	0	0	0	1.000	2.88
Hill,Glenallen	Tor	9	76.1	23	0	0	0	1.000	2.71
Hill,Glenallen	Cle	12	51.1	18	0	0	0	1.000	3.16
Howard,Thomas	SD	34	188.1	49	1	1	0	.980	2.39
Howell,Jack	Cal	1	5.0	2	0	0	0	1.000	3.60
Howitt,Dann	Oak	5	18.0	7	0	0	0	1.000	3.50
Hudler,Rex	StL	27	176.0	43	3	0	0	1.000	2.35
Huff,Mike	Cle	7	11.0	6	0	0	0	1.000	4.91
Huff,Mike	ChA	9	41.2	11	0	0	0	1.000	2.38
Humphreys,Mike	NYA	8	29.0	6	0	0	0	1.000	1.86
Hunter,Brian	Atl	5	16.0	2	0	0	0	1.000	1.13
Incaviglia,Pete	Det	50	396.0	90	4	2	1	.979	2.14
Jackson,Darrin	SD	21	141.0	34	0	1	0	.971	2.17
James,Chris	Cle	26	184.0	48	1	0	0	1.000	2.40
Javier,Stan	LA	52	172.2	42	0	0	0	1.000	2.19
Jefferson,Stan	Cin	4	19.2	2	0	0	0	1.000	0.92
Jennings,Doug	Oak	6	22.0	8	0	0	0	1.000	3.27

Left Fielders - The Rest

Player	Tm	G	Inn	PO	A	E	DP	Pct.	Rng
Jones,Chris	Cin	18	106.0	21	0	0	0	1.000	1.78
Jones,Tracy	Sea	35	191.1	47	0	0	0	1.000	2.21
Karkovice,Ron	ChA	1	1.0	0	0	0	0	.000	.00
Kelly,Roberto	NYA	52	452.0	101	7	1	1	.991	2.15
Kingery,Mike	SF	14	32.1	7	0	1	0	.875	1.95
Kirby,Wayne	Cle	5	6.1	1	0	0	0	1.000	1.42
Komminsk,Brad	Oak	7	25.0	5	0	0	0	1.000	1.80
Kruk,John	Phi	36	315.2	79	4	1	1	.988	2.37
Landrum,Ced	ChN	25	78.1	19	0	1	0	.950	2.18
Law,Vance	Oak	3	4.0	0	0	0	0	.000	.00
Lennon,Patrick	Sea	1	2.0	2	0	0	0	1.000	9.00
Leonard,Mark	SF	24	162.1	27	0	0	0	1.000	1.50
Lindeman,Jim	Phi	14	74.2	15	1	0	0	1.000	1.93
Litton,Greg	SF	2	4.2	0	0	0	0	.000	.00
Lopez,Luis	Cle	1	2.0	0	0	0	0	.000	.00
Lusader,Scott	NYA	1	1.0	0	0	0	0	.000	.00
Lyons,Steve	Bos	8	21.0	6	0	0	0	1.000	2.57
Mack,Shane	Min	49	347.0	103	0	4	0	.963	2.67
Maldonado,Candy	Mil	14	108.1	29	0	1	0	.967	2.41
Maldonado,Candy	Tor	52	445.0	98	2	1	0	.990	2.02
Manto,Jeff	Cle	1	2.0	0	0	0	0	.000	.00
Marshall,Mike	Bos	1	7.0	0	0	0	0	.000	.00
Martinez,Carmelo	Cin	16	115.2	35	1	0	0	1.000	2.80
Martinez,Chito	Bal	1	7.0	4	0	0	0	1.000	5.14
Martinez,Dave	Mon	36	181.2	30	2	1	0	.970	1.59
May,Derrick	ChN	7	40.1	11	1	0	0	1.000	2.68
McClendon,Lloyd	Pit	14	51.2	7	1	0	1	1.000	1.39
McCray,Rodney	ChA	4	7.1	4	0	0	0	1.000	4.91
McDaniel,Terry	NYN	7	18.1	8	0	0	0	1.000	3.93
McDowell,Roger	LA	2	1.1	0	0	0	0	.000	.00
McIntosh,Tim	Mil	4	5.0	0	0	0	0	.000	.00
McKnight,Jeff	Bal	6	44.0	7	1	0	0	1.000	1.64
Mercedes,Luis	Bal	13	93.0	12	0	0	0	1.000	1.16
Meulens,Hensley	NYA	61	459.1	115	3	5	0	.959	2.31
Miller,Keith	NYN	14	59.0	11	1	0	0	1.000	1.83
Milligan,Randy	Bal	9	67.0	18	0	1	0	.947	2.42
Mitchell,Keith	Atl	24	67.1	19	1	0	0	1.000	2.67
Moore,Bobby	KC	9	18.0	3	0	0	0	1.000	1.50
Morman,Russ	KC	2	11.0	3	0	0	0	1.000	2.45
Morris,Hal	Cin	1	9.0	0	0	0	0	.000	.00
Morris,John	Phi	12	47.0	7	0	0	0	1.000	1.34
Moseby,Lloyd	Det	64	530.2	125	1	6	0	.955	2.14
Moses,John	Det	11	56.1	13	0	0	0	1.000	2.08
Munoz,Pedro	Min	10	61.1	15	0	0	0	1.000	2.20
Newman,Al	Min	1	6.0	0	0	0	0	.000	.00
Newson,Warren	ChA	16	100.1	15	1	1	0	.941	1.44
Nixon,Otis	Atl	55	348.0	84	3	0	1	1.000	2.25
Noboa,Junior	Mon	1	1.0	0	0	0	0	.000	.00
O'Brien,Pete	Sea	13	93.0	18	1	2	1	.905	1.84
Olander,Jim	Mil	2	8.0	5	0	0	0	1.000	5.63
Ortiz,Javier	Hou	15	83.1	19	0	0	0	1.000	2.05
Palmer,Dean	Tex	29	182.2	42	1	3	0	.935	2.12
Parker,Rick	SF	4	13.2	5	0	0	0	1.000	3.29
Pasqua,Dan	ChA	10	72.1	16	0	0	0	1.000	1.99
Pecota,Bill	KC	1	7.0	1	0	0	0	1.000	1.29
Pena,Geronimo	StL	4	19.0	6	0	0	0	1.000	2.84
Perry,Gerald	StL	4	33.0	5	1	0	0	1.000	1.64
Phillips,Tony	Det	25	176.0	53	0	0	0	1.000	2.71

Left Fielders - The Rest

Player	Tm	G	Inn	PO	A	E	DP	Pct.	Rng
Plantier,Phil	Bos	17	124.0	29	0	1	0	.967	2.10
Powell,Alonzo	Sea	24	148.0	31	0	1	0	.969	1.89
Puhl,Terry	KC	1	1.0	0	0	0	0	.000	.00
Pulliam,Harvey	KC	11	50.2	5	1	1	0	.857	1.07
Quintana,Carlos	Bos	1	8.0	2	0	0	0	1.000	2.25
Redus,Gary	Pit	11	50.0	8	1	0	0	1.000	1.62
Reimer,Kevin	Tex	61	452.0	109	0	5	0	.956	2.17
Roberts,Bip	SD	19	126.2	39	0	2	0	.951	2.77
Romine,Kevin	Bos	9	49.1	5	0	0	0	1.000	0.91
Rose,Bobby	Cal	6	40.0	9	0	0	0	1.000	2.03
Russell,John	Tex	6	21.2	4	0	0	0	1.000	1.66
Salazar,Luis	ChN	1	2.0	0	0	0	0	.000	.00
Sanders,Deion	Atl	41	236.2	52	3	3	0	.948	2.09
Santiago,Benito	SD	1	2.0	0	0	0	0	.000	.00
Sasser,Mackey	NYN	7	44.0	9	0	0	0	1.000	1.84
Scruggs,Tony	Tex	5	9.0	3	0	0	0	1.000	3.00
Segui,David	Bal	28	202.0	47	1	2	0	.960	2.14
Shelby,John	Det	26	170.1	42	4	1	0	.979	2.43
Sheridan,Pat	NYA	3	12.0	1	0	0	0	1.000	0.75
Simms,Mike	Hou	1	1.0	0	0	0	0	.000	.00
Smith,Dwight	ChN	5	30.0	8	0	0	0	1.000	2.40
Snyder,Cory	ChA	13	89.2	18	0	1	0	.947	1.81
Sojo,Luis	Cal	1	9.0	2	0	0	0	1.000	2.00
Sosa,Sammy	ChA	1	1.0	0	0	0	0	.000	.00
Stanley,Mike	Tex	1	1.0	0	0	0	0	.000	.00
Stevens,Lee	Cal	1	8.0	4	0	0	0	1.000	4.50
Stubbs,Franklin	Mil	4	32.0	4	0	1	0	.800	1.13
Tabler,Pat	Tor	1	1.0	1	0	0	0	1.000	9.00
Tettleton,Mickey	Det	2	2.0	0	0	0	0	.000	.00
Thompson,Milt	StL	72	578.2	164	5	2	0	.988	2.63
Thurman,Gary	KC	39	226.2	68	1	1	0	.986	2.74
Tolentino,Jose	Hou	1	8.0	4	0	0	0	1.000	4.50
VanderWal,John	Mon	17	124.0	29	0	0	0	1.000	2.10
Varsho,Gary	Pit	5	36.0	11	0	0	0	1.000	2.75
Vatcher,Jim	SD	2	3.0	0	0	0	0	.000	.00
Velarde,Randy	NYA	2	6.0	1	0	0	0	1.000	1.50
Venable,Max	Cal	13	55.0	17	0	1	0	.944	2.78
Walker,Chico	ChN	20	45.1	10	0	1	0	.909	1.99
Walling,Denny	Tex	3	19.1	4	0	0	0	1.000	1.86
Ward,Kevin	SD	31	211.0	52	0	1	0	.981	2.22
Ward,Turner	Tor	1	2.0	0	0	0	0	.000	.00
Webster,Mitch	Cle	6	28.2	10	0	0	0	1.000	3.14
Webster,Mitch	Pit	2	9.0	1	1	0	0	1.000	2.00
Webster,Mitch	LA	29	93.2	25	0	0	0	1.000	2.40
Williams,Ken	Tor	1	2.0	0	0	0	0	.000	.00
Williams,Ken	Mon	9	58.2	20	1	1	0	.955	3.22
Wilson,Craig	StL	5	24.1	8	0	0	0	1.000	2.96
Wilson,Mookie	Tor	36	291.0	60	2	2	0	.969	1.92
Wilson,Willie	Oak	41	258.1	81	1	2	0	.976	2.86
Winningham,Herm	Cin	11	24.2	8	0	0	0	1.000	2.92
Young,Gerald	Hou	6	18.1	7	0	0	0	1.000	3.44
Zupcic,Bob	Bos	3	10.2	3	0	1	0	.750	2.53

Center Fielders - Regulars

Player	Tm	G	Inn	PO	A	E	DP	Pct.	Rng
Cuyler,Milt	Det	151	1229.1	415	6	6	3	.986	3.08
Johnson,Lance	ChA	158	1332.1	424	11	2	4	.995	2.94
Devereaux,Mike	Bal	148	1261.0	399	9	3	1	.993	2.91
White,Devon	Tor	156	1384.0	438	8	1	2	.998	2.90
Pettis,Gary	Tex	126	782.0	247	4	6	2	.977	2.89
Jackson,Darrin	SD	79	654.2	208	2	1	1	.995	2.89
Cole,Alex	Cle	101	800.0	245	6	7	1	.973	2.82
McRae,Brian	KC	150	1301.1	405	2	3	0	.993	2.81
Grissom,Marquis	Mon	130	1140.2	344	12	5	2	.986	2.81
Yount,Robin	Mil	117	1021.0	315	1	2	1	.994	2.79
Williams,Bernie	NYA	85	754.1	230	3	5	0	.979	2.78
Henderson,Dave	Oak	136	1179.1	354	10	1	2	.997	2.78
Lankford,Ray	StL	149	1217.1	368	7	6	2	.984	2.77
Gonzalez,Juan	Tex	93	651.0	192	5	3	0	.985	2.72
Griffey Jr,Ken	Sea	152	1271.2	361	15	4	4	.989	2.66
Davis,Eric	Cin	77	633.0	182	5	3	4	.984	2.66
Puckett,Kirby	Min	144	1216.2	345	13	5	5	.986	2.65
Finley,Steve	Hou	124	948.0	266	11	3	2	.989	2.63
McGee,Willie	SF	89	700.1	189	5	3	4	.985	2.49
Butler,Brett	LA	161	1409.0	372	8	0	3	1.000	2.43
Gant,Ron	Atl	148	1293.1	338	7	6	1	.983	2.40
Burks,Ellis	Bos	126	1074.0	283	2	2	1	.993	2.39
Kelly,Roberto	NYA	73	641.0	167	1	3	0	.982	2.36
Van Slyke,Andy	Pit	135	1137.1	273	8	1	1	.996	2.22
Coleman,Vince	NYN	70	603.0	132	5	3	1	.979	2.04
Average	---	123	1025.1	299	6	3	1	.989	2.69

Center Fielders - The Rest

Player	Tm	G	Inn	PO	A	E	DP	Pct.	Rng
Abner,Shawn	SD	36	258.0	84	1	0	0	1.000	2.97
Abner,Shawn	Cal	31	236.0	71	3	0	1	1.000	2.82
Anderson,Brady	Bal	26	190.2	54	1	0	0	1.000	2.60
Barnes,Skeeter	Det	5	32.0	9	1	0	0	1.000	2.81
Bell,Derek	Tor	6	28.0	6	0	1	0	.857	1.93
Bichette,Dante	Mil	7	41.0	20	0	1	0	.952	4.39
Biggio,Craig	Hou	1	1.0	0	1	0	0	1.000	9.00
Bonds,Barry	Pit	4	11.0	7	0	0	0	1.000	5.73
Boston,Daryl	NYN	74	425.2	119	1	2	0	.984	2.54
Briley,Greg	Sea	4	26.0	6	1	0	0	1.000	2.42
Brown,Jarvis	Min	11	53.1	13	0	1	0	.929	2.19
Brumley,Mike	Bos	4	19.0	5	0	0	0	1.000	2.37
Brunansky,Tom	Bos	1	1.0	0	0	0	0	.000	.00
Buhner,Jay	Sea	3	8.0	1	0	0	0	1.000	1.13
Bullett,Scott	Pit	1	7.0	1	0	0	0	1.000	1.29
Campusano,Sil	Phi	15	90.0	27	1	0	0	1.000	2.80
Candaele,Casey	Hou	5	25.1	6	0	0	0	1.000	2.13
Capra,Nick	Tex	1	4.0	3	0	0	0	1.000	6.75
Carr,Chuck	NYN	9	22.0	9	0	0	0	1.000	3.68
Carreon,Mark	NYN	22	126.0	19	1	3	1	.870	1.43
Castillo,Braulio	Phi	24	142.0	39	2	1	1	.976	2.60
Cotto,Henry	Sea	19	126.2	41	1	1	1	.977	2.98
Dascenzo,Doug	ChN	59	401.1	109	0	2	0	.982	2.44
Davidson,Mark	Hou	4	7.0	0	0	0	0	.000	.00
Ducey,Rob	Tor	1	1.0	0	0	0	0	.000	.00
Duncan,Mariano	Cin	2	9.0	3	0	0	0	1.000	3.00
Dykstra,Lenny	Phi	63	545.2	167	3	4	1	.977	2.80

Center Fielders - The Rest

Player	Tm	G	Inn	PO	A	E	DP	Pct.	Rng
Eisenreich,Jim	KC	14	79.0	26	0	0	0	1.000	2.96
Espy,Cecil	Pit	25	130.1	41	0	1	0	.976	2.83
Felder,Mike	SF	38	232.1	70	1	1	0	.986	2.75
Felix,Junior	Cal	63	521.2	125	1	2	0	.984	2.17
Gallagher,Dave	Cal	61	468.0	135	6	0	1	1.000	2.71
Gonzalez,Jose	LA	1	1.0	0	0	0	0	.000	.00
Gonzalez,Jose	Pit	6	30.0	11	0	0	0	1.000	3.30
Gonzalez,Jose	Cle	10	50.0	15	0	1	0	.938	2.70
Goodwin,Tom	LA	4	15.0	8	0	0	0	1.000	4.80
Gwynn,Chris	LA	2	8.0	1	0	0	0	1.000	1.13
Hamilton,Daryl	Mil	55	383.2	108	0	0	0	1.000	2.53
Harris,Donald	Tex	7	19.0	6	0	0	0	1.000	2.84
Hatcher,Billy	Cin	53	394.0	117	0	3	0	.975	2.67
Hayes,Von	Phi	49	424.1	134	2	2	2	.986	2.88
Herr,Tommy	NYN	1	1.1	0	0	0	0	.000	.00
Hill,Glenallen	Cle	26	214.2	70	0	2	0	.972	2.93
Housie,Wayne	Bos	4	18.0	3	0	0	0	1.000	1.50
Howard,Thomas	SD	41	321.1	105	1	0	1	1.000	2.97
Howitt,Dann	Oak	7	29.0	15	0	0	0	1.000	4.66
Hudler,Rex	StL	21	153.0	44	0	2	0	.957	2.59
Huff,Mike	Cle	39	302.2	86	3	1	1	.989	2.65
Huff,Mike	ChA	13	51.0	19	0	0	0	1.000	3.35
Javier,Stan	LA	7	19.0	6	0	1	0	.857	2.84
Jefferson,Stan	Cin	1	9.0	2	0	0	0	1.000	2.00
Jones,Chris	Cin	3	3.2	0	0	0	0	.000	.00
Kingery,Mike	SF	2	3.0	1	0	0	0	1.000	3.00
Kirby,Wayne	Cle	1	2.0	2	0	0	0	1.000	9.00
Komminsk,Brad	Oak	8	25.0	10	0	0	0	1.000	3.60
Kruk,John	Phi	11	85.1	18	0	0	0	1.000	1.90
Landrum,Ced	ChN	18	129.0	40	0	1	0	.976	2.79
Leius,Scott	Min	2	2.0	0	0	0	0	.000	.00
Lewis,Darren	SF	68	505.2	160	3	0	1	1.000	2.90
Lindeman,Jim	Phi	6	30.0	6	0	0	0	1.000	1.80
Lofton,Kenny	Hou	20	151.1	41	1	1	0	.977	2.50
Lusader,Scott	NYA	3	11.0	3	0	0	0	1.000	2.45
Lyons,Steve	Bos	36	258.2	80	0	0	0	1.000	2.78
Mack,Shane	Min	37	177.1	58	2	0	1	1.000	3.05
Martinez,Dave	Mon	30	258.1	67	0	2	0	.971	2.33
McCray,Rodney	ChA	2	10.0	4	0	0	0	1.000	3.60
McDaniel,Terry	NYN	5	33.1	7	0	0	0	1.000	1.89
McReynolds,Kevin	NYN	33	223.1	50	2	0	0	1.000	2.10
Miller,Keith	NYN	2	2.2	1	0	0	0	1.000	3.38
Mitchell,Keith	Atl	1	9.0	0	0	0	0	.000	.00
Moore,Bobby	KC	5	22.0	8	0	0	0	1.000	3.27
Morris,John	Phi	27	145.2	44	0	2	0	.957	2.72
Newson,Warren	ChA	1	1.0	0	0	0	0	.000	.00
Nixon,Otis	Atl	17	130.0	45	1	0	0	1.000	3.18
Olander,Jim	Mil	6	11.0	2	0	0	0	1.000	1.64
Orsulak,Joe	Bal	1	6.0	1	0	0	0	1.000	1.50
Parker,Rick	SF	1	0.2	0	0	0	0	.000	.00
Phillips,Tony	Det	9	51.0	16	0	0	0	1.000	2.82
Polonia,Luis	Cal	1	5.0	0	1	0	0	1.000	1.80
Powell,Alonzo	Sea	6	32.0	7	0	1	0	.875	1.97
Raines,Tim	ChA	1	1.0	0	0	0	0	.000	.00
Redus,Gary	Pit	12	49.2	15	0	2	0	.882	2.72
Roberts,Bip	SD	29	218.2	72	0	1	0	.986	2.96
Romine,Kevin	Bos	4	29.0	10	0	0	0	1.000	3.10
Sanders,Deion	Atl	5	20.1	5	0	0	0	1.000	2.21

238

Center Fielders - The Rest

Player	Tm	G	Inn	PO	A	E	DP	Pct.	Rng
Sanders,Reggie	Cin	9	78.1	22	0	0	0	1.000	2.53
Scruggs,Tony	Tex	1	8.0	2	0	0	0	1.000	2.25
Shelby,John	Det	26	138.0	56	0	1	0	.982	3.65
Sheridan,Pat	NYA	6	37.2	15	1	0	0	1.000	3.82
Sierra,Ruben	Tex	3	15.0	4	1	0	0	1.000	3.00
Smith,Dwight	ChN	13	84.0	22	0	2	0	.917	2.36
Sosa,Sammy	ChA	14	82.2	19	1	0	0	1.000	2.18
Spiers,Bill	Mil	1	2.0	0	0	0	0	.000	.00
Surhoff,B.J.	Mil	1	5.0	2	0	0	0	1.000	3.60
Thompson,Milt	StL	12	65.0	24	3	0	1	1.000	3.74
Thurman,Gary	KC	9	63.2	23	1	2	0	.923	3.39
Varsho,Gary	Pit	5	27.0	4	1	1	0	.833	1.67
Venable,Max	Cal	27	211.0	34	3	0	0	1.000	1.58
Walker,Chico	ChN	36	265.0	62	4	0	1	1.000	2.24
Walker,Larry	Mon	4	24.1	5	0	0	0	1.000	1.85
Walton,Jerome	ChN	100	577.1	170	1	3	1	.983	2.67
Ward,Turner	Cle	2	16.0	4	0	0	0	1.000	2.25
Webster,Mitch	Cle	1	7.0	1	0	0	0	1.000	1.29
Webster,Mitch	Pit	9	64.1	18	0	0	0	1.000	2.52
Webster,Mitch	LA	4	6.0	3	0	0	0	1.000	4.50
Whiten,Mark	Cle	8	49.0	20	0	0	0	1.000	3.67
Williams,Ken	Tor	1	5.0	2	0	0	0	1.000	3.60
Williams,Ken	Mon	4	17.0	5	0	0	0	1.000	2.65
Wilson,Mookie	Tor	5	44.2	11	0	0	0	1.000	2.22
Wilson,Willie	Oak	32	211.0	66	0	1	0	.985	2.82
Winningham,Herm	Cin	56	313.0	90	2	5	0	.948	2.65
Yelding,Eric	Hou	3	5.0	1	0	1	0	.500	1.80
Young,Gerald	Hou	78	315.1	89	4	0	1	1.000	2.65
Zupcic,Bob	Bos	7	40.0	7	0	1	0	.875	1.58

Right Fielders - Regulars

Player	Tm	G	Inn	PO	A	E	DP	Pct.	Rng
Sosa,Sammy	ChA	103	699.2	195	5	6	0	.971	2.57
Whiten,Mark	TOT	105	881.2	236	13	7	1	.973	2.54
Walker,Larry	Mon	100	790.0	216	6	2	2	.991	2.53
Barfield,Jesse	NYA	81	677.2	178	10	0	3	1.000	2.50
Deer,Rob	Det	132	1146.0	307	8	7	4	.978	2.47
Bichette,Dante	Mil	121	981.0	249	14	6	7	.978	2.41
Buhner,Jay	Sea	131	1011.1	242	14	5	5	.981	2.28
Gwynn,Tony	SD	134	1175.2	290	7	3	3	.990	2.27
O'Neill,Paul	Cin	150	1258.2	301	13	2	2	.994	2.25
Brunansky,Tom	Bos	136	1099.2	265	6	3	2	.989	2.22
Murphy,Dale	Phi	147	1235.2	287	6	5	0	.983	2.13
Carter,Joe	Tor	101	871.0	190	12	3	2	.985	2.09
Canseco,Jose	Oak	131	1084.1	245	5	9	0	.965	2.08
Bonilla,Bobby	Pit	104	810.2	176	8	2	0	.989	2.04
Justice,Dave	Atl	106	957.1	205	9	7	0	.968	2.01
Sierra,Ruben	Tex	161	1405.0	300	14	7	3	.978	2.01
Brooks,Hubie	NYN	100	791.1	166	6	5	1	.972	1.96
Jose,Felix	StL	153	1308.1	268	14	3	2	.989	1.94
Bass,Kevin	SF	79	606.0	124	4	3	1	.977	1.90
Dawson,Andre	ChN	138	1192.1	243	7	3	3	.988	1.89
Winfield,Dave	Cal	115	984.0	198	7	2	0	.990	1.88
Tartabull,Danny	KC	124	1035.2	190	4	7	0	.965	1.69
Strawberry,Darryl	LA	136	1185.2	209	11	5	2	.978	1.67
Average	---	121	1008.0	229	8	4	1	.982	2.13

Right Fielders - The Rest

Player	Tm	G	Inn	PO	A	E	DP	Pct.	Rng
Abner,Shawn	SD	3	8.0	2	0	0	0	1.000	2.25
Abner,Shawn	Cal	7	13.0	1	0	0	0	1.000	0.69
Allred,Beau	Cle	27	209.0	63	0	3	0	.955	2.71
Amaro,Ruben	Cal	2	3.0	0	0	0	0	.000	.00
Anderson,Brady	Bal	9	39.0	11	0	0	0	1.000	2.54
Anthony,Eric	Hou	37	280.2	64	5	1	1	.986	2.21
Azocar,Oscar	SD	1	8.0	2	0	1	0	.667	2.25
Baines,Harold	Oak	10	63.0	11	1	1	0	.923	1.71
Barnes,Skeeter	Det	17	74.2	21	1	0	0	1.000	2.65
Belle,Albert	Cle	2	10.0	2	0	0	0	1.000	1.80
Blankenship,Lance	Oak	11	30.2	10	0	0	0	1.000	2.93
Boston,Daryl	NYN	37	106.1	20	1	1	1	.955	1.78
Braggs,Glenn	Cin	26	141.1	36	1	1	0	.974	2.36
Brewer,Rod	StL	3	9.0	3	0	1	0	.750	3.00
Briley,Greg	Sea	46	317.1	59	1	1	1	.984	1.70
Brosius,Scott	Oak	10	65.0	16	1	0	1	1.000	2.35
Brown,Jarvis	Min	19	43.1	4	0	0	0	1.000	0.83
Bullett,Scott	Pit	1	1.0	0	0	0	0	.000	.00
Bullock,Eric	Mon	3	16.1	5	0	0	0	1.000	2.76
Bush,Randy	Min	33	193.0	42	1	0	2	1.000	2.01
Candaele,Casey	Hou	4	15.0	4	1	0	0	1.000	3.00
Carreon,Mark	NYN	22	62.0	8	0	0	0	1.000	1.16
Castillo,Braulio	Phi	2	8.1	1	0	0	0	1.000	1.08
Castillo,Carmen	Min	3	9.0	2	0	0	0	1.000	2.00
Chamberlain,Wes	Phi	3	12.2	4	0	0	0	1.000	2.84
Clark,Dave	KC	1	1.0	0	0	0	0	.000	.00
Clark,Jerald	SD	13	89.1	20	2	0	1	1.000	2.22
Cochrane,Dave	Sea	3	19.2	3	0	0	0	1.000	1.37
Coles,Darnell	SF	3	13.1	0	0	0	0	.000	.00
Cotto,Henry	Sea	8	45.0	12	1	0	0	1.000	2.60
Cromartie,Warren	KC	1	1.0	2	0	0	0	1.000	18.00
Dascenzo,Doug	ChN	15	48.1	9	0	0	0	1.000	1.68
Daugherty,Jack	Tex	3	7.0	1	0	0	0	1.000	1.29
Davidson,Mark	Hou	32	139.0	31	1	0	0	1.000	2.07
Davis,Mark	Cal	3	6.0	1	0	1	0	.500	1.50
Devereaux,Mike	Bal	1	0.2	0	0	0	0	.000	.00
Ducey,Rob	Tor	5	28.0	6	0	2	0	.750	1.93
Eisenreich,Jim	KC	42	223.0	42	0	1	0	.977	1.70
Espy,Cecil	Pit	11	56.2	12	3	1	2	.938	2.38
Evans,Dwight	Bal	67	523.1	115	6	2	2	.984	2.08
Felder,Mike	SF	44	220.0	61	0	1	0	.984	2.50
Felix,Junior	Cal	2	18.0	0	0	1	0	.000	.00
Finley,Steve	Hou	72	324.2	58	2	2	0	.968	1.66
Fitzgerald,Mike	Mon	3	23.2	10	0	0	0	1.000	3.80
Gallagher,Dave	Cal	23	160.0	36	1	0	0	1.000	2.08
Gibson,Kirk	KC	3	21.0	5	0	0	0	1.000	2.14
Gonzalez,Jose	LA	19	47.2	15	0	0	0	1.000	2.83
Gonzalez,Jose	Pit	5	9.0	3	0	0	0	1.000	3.00
Gonzalez,Jose	Cle	17	120.0	30	1	0	0	1.000	2.33
Gonzalez,Juan	Tex	8	31.0	6	0	1	0	.857	1.74
Gregg,Tommy	Atl	5	18.0	7	0	0	0	1.000	3.50
Grissom,Marquis	Mon	6	36.1	5	2	1	1	.875	1.73
Gwynn,Chris	LA	14	76.1	8	2	0	0	1.000	1.18
Hall,Mel	NYA	64	487.2	109	4	3	1	.974	2.09
Hamilton,Daryl	Mil	48	390.2	94	2	1	0	.990	2.21
Hare,Shawn	Det	6	29.0	9	1	0	0	1.000	3.10
Harris,Donald	Tex	5	7.0	1	0	0	0	1.000	1.29
Hayes,Von	Phi	6	30.0	12	0	0	0	1.000	3.60

Right Fielders - The Rest

Player	Tm	G	Inn	PO	A	E	DP	Pct.	Rng
Henderson,Dave	Oak	1	4.0	0	0	0	0	.000	.00
Hill,Glenallen	Tor	4	29.0	4	0	1	0	.800	1.24
Hill,Glenallen	Cle	1	3.0	1	0	0	0	1.000	3.00
Howard,Dave	KC	1	1.0	0	0	0	0	.000	.00
Howard,Thomas	SD	14	115.2	27	2	0	0	1.000	2.26
Howell,Jack	Cal	4	24.0	6	0	0	0	1.000	2.25
Howitt,Dann	Oak	10	39.2	6	0	0	0	1.000	1.36
Hudler,Rex	StL	11	46.0	10	1	0	0	1.000	2.15
Huff,Mike	Cle	6	22.0	4	0	0	0	1.000	1.64
Huff,Mike	ChA	36	176.0	41	1	1	0	.977	2.15
Humphreys,Mike	NYA	2	12.0	3	0	0	0	1.000	2.25
Hunter,Brian	Atl	1	1.0	0	0	0	0	.000	.00
Incaviglia,Pete	Det	4	38.0	15	0	1	0	.938	3.55
James,Chris	Cle	18	135.0	30	1	0	0	1.000	2.07
Javier,Stan	LA	18	126.1	22	1	0	0	1.000	1.64
Jefferson,Stan	Cin	1	1.0	0	0	0	0	.000	.00
Johnson,Howard	NYN	30	273.1	61	3	2	0	.970	2.11
Johnson,Lance	ChA	2	0.2	0	0	0	0	.000	.00
Jones,Chris	Cin	9	35.1	6	1	0	0	1.000	1.78
Jones,Tracy	Sea	3	8.0	2	0	0	0	1.000	2.25
Kingery,Mike	SF	22	115.0	31	0	0	0	1.000	2.43
Kirby,Wayne	Cle	17	118.0	37	1	0	0	1.000	2.90
Komminsk,Brad	Oak	8	30.0	3	1	0	0	1.000	1.20
Kruk,John	Phi	6	35.0	15	0	0	0	1.000	3.86
Landrum,Ced	ChN	8	11.1	2	0	0	0	1.000	1.59
Larkin,Gene	Min	48	312.2	59	1	2	1	.968	1.73
Leonard,Mark	SF	12	72.2	14	0	0	0	1.000	1.73
Lindeman,Jim	Phi	10	57.2	10	0	0	0	1.000	1.56
Litton,Greg	SF	4	12.0	2	0	0	0	1.000	1.50
Lyons,Steve	Bos	3	23.0	5	0	0	0	1.000	1.96
Mack,Shane	Min	80	540.2	132	4	3	1	.978	2.26
Maldonado,Candy	Mil	12	81.0	12	0	0	0	1.000	1.33
Maldonado,Candy	Tor	1	1.0	0	0	0	0	.000	.00
Marshall,Mike	Bos	3	15.0	3	0	0	0	1.000	1.80
Martinez,Chito	Bal	53	433.0	106	4	2	2	.982	2.29
Martinez,Dave	Mon	58	437.2	115	8	1	0	.992	2.53
McClendon,Lloyd	Pit	18	109.2	19	1	1	0	.952	1.64
McCray,Rodney	ChA	2	4.2	2	0	0	0	1.000	3.86
McDaniel,Terry	NYN	4	5.1	3	0	0	0	1.000	5.06
McGee,Willie	SF	48	348.0	69	0	3	0	.958	1.78
McKnight,Jeff	Bal	1	7.0	1	0	0	0	1.000	1.29
McReynolds,Kevin	NYN	2	17.0	1	0	0	0	1.000	0.53
Merced,Orlando	Pit	7	12.2	5	0	0	0	1.000	3.55
Mercedes,Luis	Bal	3	20.0	8	0	0	0	1.000	3.60
Meulens,Hensley	NYA	13	105.0	29	1	0	1	1.000	2.57
Miller,Keith	NYN	17	75.0	21	1	0	1	1.000	2.64
Mitchell,Keith	Atl	10	73.0	12	0	1	0	.923	1.48
Morris,John	Phi	24	83.2	22	1	0	0	1.000	2.47
Moses,John	Det	1	3.0	0	0	0	0	.000	.00
Munoz,Pedro	Min	39	261.1	72	3	1	2	.987	2.58
Newson,Warren	ChA	34	170.1	33	2	1	0	.972	1.85
Nixon,Otis	Atl	48	394.1	88	1	3	0	.967	2.03
Noboa,Junior	Mon	6	42.0	7	0	0	0	1.000	1.50
Olander,Jim	Mil	1	9.0	2	0	0	0	1.000	2.00
Orsulak,Joe	Bal	67	397.2	109	9	1	2	.992	2.67
Ortiz,Javier	Hou	11	69.2	8	2	0	1	1.000	1.29
Pasqua,Dan	ChA	51	318.0	60	3	1	2	.984	1.78
Perry,Gerald	StL	1	1.0	1	0	0	0	1.000	9.00

Right Fielders - The Rest

Player	Tm	G	Inn	PO	A	E	DP	Pct.	Rng
Phillips,Tony	Det	23	135.1	45	3	1	0	.980	3.19
Plantier,Phil	Bos	26	169.0	50	1	1	0	.981	2.72
Powell,Alonzo	Sea	14	63.0	10	0	0	0	1.000	1.43
Puckett,Kirby	Min	19	89.1	27	0	1	0	.964	2.72
Pulliam,Harvey	KC	5	39.0	16	0	1	0	.941	3.69
Quintana,Carlos	Bos	12	72.0	13	1	1	0	.933	1.75
Raines,Tim	ChA	1	0.0	0	0	0	0	.000	.00
Redus,Gary	Pit	11	23.0	3	0	0	0	1.000	1.17
Reimer,Kevin	Tex	6	12.0	2	0	1	0	.667	1.50
Rhodes,Karl	Hou	44	350.1	87	4	4	1	.958	2.34
Riesgo,Nikco	Mon	2	18.0	0	1	1	0	.500	0.50
Romine,Kevin	Bos	11	41.0	12	0	1	0	.923	2.63
Rose,Bobby	Cal	1	1.0	0	0	0	0	.000	.00
Russell,John	Tex	2	4.0	0	0	0	0	.000	.00
Sanders,Deion	Atl	1	9.0	0	0	0	0	.000	.00
Sasser,Mackey	NYN	14	103.0	17	3	1	1	.952	1.75
Segui,David	Bal	5	37.0	11	0	0	0	1.000	2.68
Shelby,John	Det	3	21.1	10	0	0	0	1.000	4.22
Sheridan,Pat	NYA	26	161.2	30	2	0	1	1.000	1.78
Simms,Mike	Hou	41	267.2	44	4	6	0	.889	1.61
Smith,Dwight	ChN	28	183.0	43	3	1	1	.979	2.26
Snyder,Cory	ChA	17	108.2	32	1	0	0	1.000	2.73
Snyder,Cory	Tor	14	83.1	12	1	0	0	1.000	1.40
Stevens,Lee	Cal	8	61.0	11	0	0	0	1.000	1.62
Surhoff,B.J.	Mil	1	1.0	0	0	0	0	.000	.00
Templeton,Garry	NYN	2	4.0	0	0	0	0	.000	.00
Tettleton,Mickey	Det	1	3.0	2	0	0	0	1.000	6.00
Thompson,Milt	StL	11	71.0	19	0	0	0	1.000	2.41
Thurman,Gary	KC	29	144.1	38	0	1	0	.974	2.37
Varsho,Gary	Pit	45	291.0	70	1	0	1	1.000	2.20
Vatcher,Jim	SD	9	43.0	8	1	1	0	.900	1.88
Vaughn,Greg	Mil	1	1.0	1	0	0	0	1.000	9.00
Venable,Max	Cal	30	171.2	34	0	2	0	.944	1.78
Walker,Chico	ChN	8	20.2	1	0	0	0	1.000	0.44
Walling,Denny	Tex	2	13.0	0	0	0	0	.000	.00
Walton,Jerome	ChN	1	1.0	0	0	0	0	.000	.00
Ward,Kevin	SD	2	13.0	2	0	0	0	1.000	1.38
Ward,Turner	Cle	36	249.0	61	1	0	0	1.000	2.24
Ward,Turner	Tor	5	31.0	5	0	0	0	1.000	1.45
Webster,Mitch	Cle	6	50.0	13	0	0	0	1.000	2.34
Webster,Mitch	Pit	20	143.0	31	1	2	0	.941	2.01
Webster,Mitch	LA	7	22.0	7	0	0	0	1.000	2.86
Whiten,Mark	Tor	42	356.1	90	2	0	0	1.000	2.32
Whiten,Mark	Cle	63	525.1	146	11	7	1	.957	2.69
Williams,Ken	Tor	8	63.0	14	1	0	0	1.000	2.14
Williams,Ken	Mon	12	76.1	17	2	1	0	.950	2.24
Wilson,Willie	Oak	19	127.2	29	1	0	0	1.000	2.11
Winningham,Herm	Cin	1	3.2	1	0	0	0	1.000	2.45
Wood,Ted	SF	8	55.0	10	0	1	0	.909	1.64
Yelding,Eric	Hou	1	2.0	0	0	1	0	.000	.00
Young,Gerald	Hou	2	4.0	1	0	0	0	1.000	2.25
Zupcic,Bob	Bos	6	20.0	4	0	0	0	1.000	1.80

Catchers - Regulars

Player	Tm	G	Inn	PO	A	E	DP	PB	Pct.
LaValliere,Mike	Pit	105	852.2	565	46	1	4	5	.998
Hoiles,Chris	Bal	89	728.2	433	42	1	5	3	.998
Parrish,Lance	Cal	111	912.2	657	58	2	12	19	.997
Olson,Greg	Atl	127	1010.1	721	48	4	10	5	.995
Pena,Tony	Bos	140	1156.2	864	58	5	14	5	.995
Surhoff,B.J.	Mil	127	1055.0	660	67	4	11	11	.995
Fisk,Carlton	ChA	106	794.1	535	53	4	5	11	.993
Borders,Pat	Tor	102	700.2	505	48	4	4	13	.993
Nokes,Matt	NYA	130	1001.2	690	47	6	7	11	.992
Valle,Dave	Sea	129	926.1	670	52	6	10	15	.992
Reed,Jeff	Cin	89	690.2	526	29	5	7	7	.991
Skinner,Joel	Cle	99	790.0	504	37	5	4	6	.991
Pagnozzi,Tom	StL	139	1156.1	673	81	7	8	5	.991
Scioscia,Mike	LA	115	907.1	677	47	7	7	3	.990
Tettleton,Mickey	Det	125	1013.2	557	56	6	2	9	.990
Biggio,Craig	Hou	139	1175.1	889	62	10	10	13	.990
Harper,Brian	Min	119	990.0	642	31	8	7	9	.988
Mayne,Brent	KC	80	607.0	426	34	6	4	2	.987
Santiago,Benito	SD	151	1305.1	830	99	14	14	8	.985
Daulton,Darren	Phi	88	717.0	493	32	8	5	2	.985
Rodriguez,Ivan	Tex	88	684.0	517	61	10	6	8	.983
Steinbach,Terry	Oak	117	949.1	593	48	13	7	6	.980
Oliver,Joe	Cin	90	676.1	497	40	11	6	10	.980
Myers,Greg	Tor	104	752.0	484	37	11	7	9	.979
Average	---	112	898.0	608	50	6	7	8	.990

Catchers - The Rest

Player	Tm	G	Inn	PO	A	E	DP	PB	Pct.
Afenir,Troy	Oak	4	27.1	18	1	0	1	0	1.000
Allanson,Andy	Det	56	396.2	212	22	5	1	3	.979
Alomar Jr,Sandy	Cle	46	395.1	280	18	4	5	5	.987
Berryhill,Damon	ChN	48	346.2	211	24	8	2	8	.967
Berryhill,Damon	Atl	1	3.0	3	0	0	0	0	1.000
Bilardello,Dann	SD	13	67.1	59	6	0	1	0	1.000
Bradley,Scott	Sea	65	404.2	284	16	2	4	3	.993
Cabrera,Francisco	Atl	17	111.0	72	5	1	0	3	.987
Carter,Gary	LA	68	497.1	355	45	5	2	4	.988
Cerone,Rick	NYN	81	573.0	424	35	6	0	6	.987
Cochrane,Dave	Sea	19	77.1	42	10	1	0	6	.981
Decker,Steve	SF	78	578.1	385	41	7	4	7	.984
Dempsey,Rick	Mil	56	408.2	246	23	2	5	5	.993
Eusebio,Tony	Hou	9	58.0	49	4	1	0	1	.981
Fitzgerald,Mike	Mon	54	421.2	306	24	2	3	2	.994
Fletcher,Darrin	Phi	45	334.0	244	20	2	1	1	.992
Gedman,Rich	StL	43	251.0	192	13	5	3	3	.976
Geren,Bob	NYA	63	375.2	255	18	3	2	1	.989
Girardi,Joe	ChN	21	134.0	95	11	3	1	1	.972
Hassey,Ron	Mon	34	274.1	172	12	2	1	4	.989
Heath,Mike	Atl	45	324.1	192	33	2	1	6	.991
Hemond,Scott	Oak	8	31.0	17	1	1	0	0	.947
Hernandez,Carlos	LA	13	37.2	24	4	1	0	1	.966
Howard,Chris	Sea	9	30.0	13	2	0	1	0	1.000
Hundley,Todd	NYN	20	150.0	85	10	0	1	1	1.000
Karkovice,Ron	ChA	69	455.1	309	28	4	6	2	.988
Kennedy,Terry	SF	58	390.1	237	36	6	3	2	.978
Knorr,Randy	Tor	3	4.0	6	1	0	0	0	1.000

Catchers - The Rest

Player	Tm	G	Inn	PO	A	E	DP	PB	Pct.
Kreuter,Chad	Tex	1	6.0	5	0	0	0	0	1.000
Lake,Steve	Phi	58	403.0	277	24	2	1	5	.993
Lampkin,Tom	SD	11	80.0	49	5	0	0	1	1.000
Leyritz,Jim	NYA	5	25.2	24	0	0	0	0	1.000
Lindsey,Doug	Phi	1	9.0	8	0	0	0	1	1.000
Litton,Greg	SF	1	2.0	3	0	0	0	0	1.000
Lopez,Luis	Cle	12	59.0	34	3	0	0	2	1.000
Lyons,Barry	LA	6	15.2	13	1	0	1	0	1.000
Macfarlane,Mike	KC	69	578.2	389	30	3	4	4	.993
Manto,Jeff	Cle	5	16.0	13	1	0	0	2	1.000
Manwaring,Kirt	SF	67	471.1	315	27	4	7	0	.988
Marzano,John	Bos	48	283.0	174	20	3	0	6	.985
McClendon,Lloyd	Pit	2	7.1	5	0	0	0	0	1.000
Melvin,Bob	Bal	72	580.2	383	31	1	8	3	.998
Merullo,Matt	ChA	27	136.2	79	8	1	1	3	.989
Nichols,Carl	Hou	17	125.2	86	14	3	2	2	.971
O'Brien,Charlie	NYN	67	488.0	396	37	4	7	2	.991
Ortiz,Junior	Min	60	370.2	202	18	1	2	3	.995
Orton,John	Cal	28	205.2	145	22	1	3	1	.994
Pappas,Erik	ChN	6	36.2	35	1	0	0	0	1.000
Parent,Mark	Tex	3	5.0	5	0	0	0	0	1.000
Pedre,Jorge	KC	9	50.0	29	4	1	0	0	.971
Petralli,Geno	Tex	66	403.0	294	19	9	3	3	.972
Prince,Tom	Pit	19	87.2	52	9	1	0	1	.984
Quirk,Jamie	Oak	54	436.2	294	31	6	2	2	.982
Ramos,John	NYA	5	41.0	23	1	0	0	1	1.000
Reyes,Gil	Mon	80	568.1	375	61	11	4	10	.975
Rowland,Rich	Det	2	2.0	2	1	0	0	0	1.000
Russell,John	Tex	5	25.0	20	0	0	1	1	1.000
Salas,Mark	Det	11	38.0	22	1	0	0	0	1.000
Santovenia,Nelson	Mon	30	176.0	109	12	3	3	6	.976
Sasser,Mackey	NYN	43	226.1	165	13	1	0	3	.994
Scott,Donnie	Cin	8	41.0	19	0	0	2	1	1.000
Servais,Scott	Hou	14	94.0	77	4	1	0	0	.988
Sinatro,Matt	Sea	5	26.0	18	3	0	0	0	1.000
Slaught,Don	Pit	69	509.0	338	30	5	4	3	.987
Spehr,Tim	KC	37	230.1	190	17	3	2	5	.986
Sprague,Ed	Tor	2	6.0	5	0	2	0	0	.714
Stanley,Mike	Tex	58	356.0	240	9	5	1	3	.980
Stephens,Ray	StL	6	28.0	16	2	0	0	1	1.000
Sutko,Glenn	Cin	9	32.0	16	5	3	0	1	.875
Tackett,Jeff	Bal	6	30.1	22	0	0	0	1	1.000
Taubensee,Eddie	Cle	25	181.0	89	6	2	1	4	.979
Tingley,Ron	Cal	45	323.1	222	32	3	2	3	.988
Villanueva,Hector	ChN	55	400.0	259	26	6	2	4	.979
Wakamatsu,Don	ChA	18	91.2	47	2	0	2	4	1.000
Webster,Lenny	Min	17	88.2	61	10	1	1	0	.986
Whitt,Ernie	Bal	20	118.0	72	8	0	0	1	1.000
Wilkins,Rick	ChN	82	539.1	373	42	3	6	6	.993
Willard,Jerry	Atl	1	4.0	3	0	0	0	0	1.000

Catchers - Regulars - Special

Player	Tm	G	Inn	SBA	CS	PCS	CS%	ER	CERA
Scioscia,Mike	LA	115	907.1	112	30	6	.27	322	3.19
Olson,Greg	Atl	127	1010.1	132	37	15	.28	376	3.35
Borders,Pat	Tor	102	700.2	78	28	4	.36	266	3.42
Parrish,Lance	Cal	111	912.2	92	39	8	.42	355	3.50
LaValliere,Mike	Pit	105	852.2	129	39	11	.30	336	3.55
Myers,Greg	Tor	104	752.0	93	25	10	.27	298	3.57
Santiago,Benito	SD	151	1305.1	150	57	13	.38	519	3.58
Reed,Jeff	Cin	89	690.2	85	28	9	.33	276	3.60
Valle,Dave	Sea	129	926.1	77	31	6	.40	376	3.65
Harper,Brian	Min	119	990.0	126	28	6	.22	412	3.75
Pagnozzi,Tom	StL	139	1156.1	156	70	2	.45	482	3.75
Mayne,Brent	KC	80	607.0	76	23	2	.30	255	3.78
Biggio,Craig	Hou	139	1175.1	172	46	6	.27	513	3.93
Oliver,Joe	Cin	90	676.1	98	28	6	.29	296	3.94
Fisk,Carlton	ChA	106	794.1	91	37	5	.41	349	3.95
Pena,Tony	Bos	140	1156.2	121	40	7	.33	512	3.98
Daulton,Darren	Phi	88	717.0	102	18	1	.18	322	4.04
Hoiles,Chris	Bal	89	728.2	75	26	1	.35	339	4.19
Surhoff,B.J.	Mil	127	1055.0	121	35	5	.29	493	4.21
Skinner,Joel	Cle	99	790.0	82	28	4	.34	370	4.22
Rodriguez,Ivan	Tex	88	684.0	70	34	0	.49	334	4.39
Nokes,Matt	NYA	130	1001.2	135	36	6	.27	501	4.50
Tettleton,Mickey	Det	125	1013.2	104	40	15	.38	513	4.55
Steinbach,Terry	Oak	117	949.1	111	35	3	.32	495	4.69
Average	---	112	898.0	107	34	6	.32	387	3.88

Catchers - The Rest - Special

Player	Tm	G	Inn	SBA	CS	PCS	CS%	ER	CERA
Afenir,Troy	Oak	4	27.1	1	0	0	0	18	5.93
Allanson,Andy	Det	56	396.2	36	16	4	.44	199	4.52
Alomar Jr,Sandy	Cle	46	395.1	33	12	2	.36	172	3.92
Berryhill,Damon	ChN	48	346.2	43	10	0	.23	139	3.61
Berryhill,Damon	Atl	1	3.0	0	0	0	0	0	0.00
Bilardello,Dann	SD	13	67.1	10	4	0	.40	19	2.54
Bradley,Scott	Sea	65	404.2	43	7	1	.16	182	4.05
Cabrera,Francisco	Atl	17	111.0	14	4	0	.29	52	4.22
Carter,Gary	LA	68	497.1	87	28	3	.32	155	2.80
Cerone,Rick	NYN	81	573.0	71	32	8	.45	215	3.38
Cochrane,Dave	Sea	19	77.1	3	3	0	1.00	44	5.12
Decker,Steve	SF	78	578.1	77	28	5	.36	242	3.77
Dempsey,Rick	Mil	56	408.2	41	12	0	.29	186	4.10
Eusebio,Tony	Hou	9	58.0	6	2	1	.33	38	5.90
Fitzgerald,Mike	Mon	54	421.2	82	21	9	.26	180	3.84
Fletcher,Darrin	Phi	45	334.0	46	13	1	.28	110	2.96
Gedman,Rich	StL	43	251.0	40	10	0	.25	93	3.33
Geren,Bob	NYA	63	375.2	45	14	2	.31	175	4.19
Girardi,Joe	ChN	21	134.0	20	6	0	.30	54	3.63
Hassey,Ron	Mon	34	274.1	42	9	0	.21	82	2.69
Heath,Mike	Atl	45	324.1	62	18	5	.29	132	3.66
Hemond,Scott	Oak	8	31.0	2	1	0	.50	14	4.06
Hernandez,Carlos	LA	13	37.2	5	2	1	.40	12	2.87
Howard,Chris	Sea	9	30.0	4	3	0	.75	11	3.30
Hundley,Todd	NYN	20	150.0	22	6	1	.27	51	3.06
Karkovice,Ron	ChA	69	455.1	44	19	4	.43	185	3.66
Kennedy,Terry	SF	58	390.1	79	35	9	.44	195	4.50
Knorr,Randy	Tor	3	4.0	0	0	0	0	1	2.25

Catchers - The Rest - Special

Player	Tm	G	Inn	SBA	CS	PCS	CS%	ER	CERA
Kreuter,Chad	Tex	1	6.0	0	0	0	0	4	6.00
Lake,Steve	Phi	58	403.0	51	17	2	.33	189	4.22
Lampkin,Tom	SD	11	80.0	14	4	0	.29	40	4.50
Leyritz,Jim	NYA	5	25.2	1	0	0	0	15	5.26
Lindsey,Doug	Phi	1	9.0	0	0	0	0	7	7.00
Litton,Greg	SF	1	2.0	1	0	0	0	0	0.00
Lopez,Luis	Cle	12	59.0	8	3	1	.38	31	4.73
Lyons,Barry	LA	6	15.2	1	0	0	0	8	4.60
Macfarlane,Mike	KC	69	578.2	38	17	2	.45	261	4.06
Manto,Jeff	Cle	5	16.0	4	1	0	.25	10	5.63
Manwaring,Kirt	SF	67	471.1	55	20	4	.36	209	3.99
Marzano,John	Bos	48	283.0	29	13	3	.45	131	4.17
McClendon,Lloyd	Pit	2	7.1	2	0	0	0	4	4.91
Melvin,Bob	Bal	72	580.2	67	19	0	.28	314	4.87
Merullo,Matt	ChA	27	136.2	23	8	4	.35	61	4.02
Nichols,Carl	Hou	17	125.2	17	9	0	.53	58	4.15
O'Brien,Charlie	NYN	67	488.0	81	26	1	.32	192	3.54
Ortiz,Junior	Min	60	370.2	28	13	2	.46	150	3.64
Orton,John	Cal	28	205.2	27	11	1	.41	85	3.72
Pappas,Erik	ChN	6	36.2	6	2	2	.33	21	5.15
Parent,Mark	Tex	3	5.0	0	0	0	0	3	5.40
Pedre,Jorge	KC	9	50.0	9	2	0	.22	23	4.14
Petralli,Geno	Tex	66	403.0	53	17	3	.32	202	4.51
Prince,Tom	Pit	19	87.2	16	8	2	.50	45	4.62
Quirk,Jamie	Oak	54	436.2	62	24	2	.39	207	4.27
Ramos,John	NYA	5	41.0	3	0	0	0	20	4.39
Reyes,Gil	Mon	80	568.1	81	43	4	.53	244	3.86
Rowland,Rich	Det	2	2.0	0	0	0	0	0	0.00
Russell,John	Tex	5	25.0	1	0	0	0	8	2.88
Salas,Mark	Det	11	38.0	6	2	1	.33	19	4.50
Santovenia,Nelson	Mon	30	176.0	25	8	2	.32	77	3.94
Sasser,Mackey	NYN	43	226.1	34	10	1	.29	111	4.41
Scott,Donnie	Cin	8	41.0	8	0	0	0	27	5.93
Servais,Scott	Hou	14	94.0	8	3	1	.38	37	3.54
Sinatro,Matt	Sea	5	26.0	1	0	0	0	4	1.38
Slaught,Don	Pit	69	509.0	69	27	4	.39	172	3.04
Spehr,Tim	KC	37	230.1	27	14	3	.52	100	3.91
Sprague,Ed	Tor	2	6.0	0	0	0	0	4	6.00
Stanley,Mike	Tex	58	356.0	41	7	2	.17	184	4.65
Stephens,Ray	StL	6	28.0	6	1	0	.17	13	4.18
Sutko,Glenn	Cin	9	32.0	9	4	1	.44	14	3.94
Tackett,Jeff	Bal	6	30.1	3	0	0	0	6	1.78
Taubensee,Eddie	Cle	25	181.0	22	3	1	.14	96	4.77
Tingley,Ron	Cal	45	323.1	42	22	3	.52	151	4.20
Villanueva,Hector	ChN	55	400.0	58	16	3	.28	153	3.44
Wakamatsu,Don	ChA	18	91.2	4	2	1	.50	29	2.85
Webster,Lenny	Min	17	88.2	7	2	0	.29	33	3.35
Whitt,Ernie	Bal	20	118.0	17	6	1	.35	84	6.41
Wilkins,Rick	ChN	82	539.1	76	30	5	.39	288	4.81
Willard,Jerry	Atl	1	4.0	0	0	0	0	4	9.00

1991 Lefty-Righty Stats

Our Lefty-Righty stats are now presented in a more easily readable, vertical format. The notation below each player's name tells how the player bats or pitches. The **vs** column labels each statistical line based on what he did against lefties and righties. Now, the fact that Tony Bernazard bashed lefties yet was powerless against righties, while Sean Berry was equally helpless against either, jumps right out at the reader! All kidding aside, we think you'll agree that **this** is the way such data was meant to be read.

Batters vs. Left-Handed and Right-Handed Pitchers

Batter	vs	Avg	AB	H	2B	3B	HR	BI	BB	SO	OBP	SLG
Abner,Shawn	L	.179	84	15	4	0	3	8	3	14	.216	.333
Bats Right	R	.205	132	27	6	2	0	6	8	29	.248	.280
Afenir,Troy	L	.000	1	0	0	0	0	0	0	0	.000	.000
Bats Right	R	.100	10	1	0	0	0	0	0	2	.100	.100
Aldrete,Mike	L	.167	12	2	0	1	0	1	0	5	.154	.333
Bats Left	R	.247	186	46	6	0	1	19	39	36	.376	.296
Alicea,Luis	L	.250	16	4	1	0	0	0	2	3	.333	.313
Bats Both	R	.173	52	9	2	0	0	0	6	16	.259	.212
Allanson,Andy	L	.217	115	25	7	0	0	10	4	26	.244	.278
Bats Right	R	.278	36	10	3	0	1	6	3	5	.333	.444
Allred,Beau	L	.167	12	2	1	0	0	1	4	2	.375	.250
Bats Left	R	.239	113	27	2	0	3	11	21	33	.358	.336
Alomar,R	L	.246	191	47	12	3	5	27	11	35	.295	.419
Bats Both	R	.316	446	141	29	8	4	42	46	51	.379	.444
Alomar Jr,S	L	.214	42	9	1	0	0	1	4	3	.283	.238
Bats Right	R	.218	142	31	8	0	0	6	4	21	.258	.275
Amaral,Rich	L	.143	7	1	0	0	0	0	0	3	.143	.143
Bats Right	R	.000	9	0	0	0	0	0	1	2	.182	.000
Amaro,Ruben	L	.000	4	0	0	0	0	0	1	0	.200	.000
Bats Both	R	.263	19	5	1	0	0	2	2	3	.333	.316
Anderson,B	L	.139	36	5	0	1	0	5	11	12	.347	.194
Bats Left	R	.245	220	54	12	2	2	22	27	32	.336	.345
Anderson,Dave	L	.148	81	12	0	1	1	3	6	12	.207	.210
Bats Right	R	.303	145	44	5	1	1	10	6	23	.331	.372
Anthony,Eric	L	.138	29	4	0	0	0	1	4	9	.242	.138
Bats Left	R	.157	89	14	6	0	1	6	8	32	.222	.258
Azocar,Oscar	L	.000	2	0	0	0	0	1	0	0	.000	.000
Bats Left	R	.255	55	14	2	0	0	8	1	9	.276	.291
Backman,Wally	L	.083	24	2	1	0	0	3	2	3	.148	.125
Bats Both	R	.267	161	43	11	0	0	12	28	27	.372	.335
Baerga,Carlos	L	.329	161	53	8	0	2	20	8	14	.376	.416
Bats Both	R	.273	432	118	20	2	9	49	40	60	.335	.391
Bagwell,Jeff	L	.320	206	66	10	0	7	37	33	37	.417	.471
Bats Right	R	.279	348	97	16	4	8	45	42	79	.369	.417
Baines,Harold	L	.301	83	25	5	0	4	18	5	14	.348	.506
Bats Left	R	.294	405	119	20	1	16	72	67	53	.390	.467
Banister,Jeff	L	.000	0	0	0	0	0	0	0	0	.000	.000
Bats Right	R	1.000	1	1	0	0	0	0	0	0	1.000	1.000
Barberie,Bret	L	.270	37	10	3	0	1	5	6	5	.364	.432
Bats Both	R	.384	99	38	9	2	1	13	14	17	.462	.545
Barfield,J	L	.315	108	34	4	0	9	24	17	22	.408	.602
Bats Right	R	.170	176	30	8	0	8	24	19	58	.250	.352
Barnes,S	L	.282	85	24	6	2	3	11	6	12	.330	.506
Bats Right	R	.297	74	22	7	0	2	6	3	12	.321	.473
Barrett,Marty	L	.167	6	1	0	0	1	3	0	2	.167	.667
Bats Right	R	.200	10	2	1	0	0	0	0	1	.273	.300
Bass,Kevin	L	.239	113	27	5	0	6	15	5	15	.276	.442
Bats Both	R	.230	248	57	5	4	4	25	31	41	.320	.331
Batiste,Kim	L	.333	12	4	0	0	0	1	0	2	.333	.333
Bats Right	R	.133	15	2	0	0	0	0	1	6	.188	.133
Bell,Derek	L	.150	20	3	0	0	0	0	3	4	.292	.150
Bats Right	R	.125	8	1	0	0	0	1	3	1	.364	.125
Bell,George	L	.288	208	60	8	0	15	34	17	19	.341	.543
Bats Right	R	.283	350	99	19	0	10	52	15	43	.313	.423
Bell,Jay	L	.289	194	56	13	5	6	28	26	18	.371	.500
Bats Right	R	.261	414	108	19	3	10	39	26	81	.309	.394
Bell,Juan	L	.104	48	5	1	0	0	0	0	16	.104	.125
Bats Both	R	.193	161	31	8	2	1	15	8	35	.228	.286
Bell,Mike	L	.000	4	0	0	0	0	0	0	2	.000	.000
Bats Left	R	.154	26	4	0	0	1	1	2	5	.214	.269
Belle,Albert	L	.288	132	38	11	1	8	34	5	27	.312	.568
Bats Right	R	.280	329	92	20	1	20	61	20	72	.327	.529
Belliard,R	L	.242	95	23	2	0	0	4	6	14	.287	.263
Bats Right	R	.252	258	65	7	2	0	23	16	49	.300	.295
Beltre,E	L	.000	1	0	0	0	0	0	0	0	.000	.000
Bats Right	R	.200	5	1	0	0	0	0	1	1	.333	.200
Benavides,F	L	.278	18	5	0	0	0	0	0	2	.316	.278
Bats Right	R	.289	45	13	1	0	0	3	1	13	.298	.311
Benjamin,Mike	L	.167	30	5	1	0	1	1	3	6	.242	.300
Bats Right	R	.105	76	8	2	0	1	7	4	20	.167	.171
Benzinger,T	L	.252	143	36	6	0	1	16	6	13	.280	.315
Bats Both	R	.267	273	73	12	5	2	35	21	53	.324	.370
Bergman,Dave	L	.053	19	1	1	0	0	1	3	11	.182	.105
Bats Left	R	.257	175	45	9	1	7	28	32	29	.368	.440
Bernazard,T	L	1.000	1	1	0	0	0	0	0	0	1.000	1.000
Bats Both	R	.091	11	1	0	0	0	0	0	4	.091	.091
Berry,Sean	L	.167	30	5	1	0	0	0	2	10	.219	.200
Bats Right	R	.100	30	3	2	0	0	1	3	13	.206	.167
Berryhill,D	L	.051	39	2	0	0	0	3	2	8	.095	.051
Bats Both	R	.231	121	28	7	0	5	11	9	34	.290	.413
Bichette,D	L	.253	154	39	5	2	6	18	11	37	.299	.429
Bats Right	R	.230	291	67	13	1	9	41	11	70	.257	.375
Biggio,Craig	L	.274	186	51	10	2	1	11	21	19	.346	.366
Bats Right	R	.306	360	110	13	2	3	35	32	52	.364	.378
Bilardello,D	L	.167	6	1	0	0	0	0	1	0	.286	.167
Bats Right	R	.300	20	6	2	1	0	5	2	4	.364	.500
Blankenship,L	L	.222	63	14	2	0	1	10	8	9	.301	.302
Bats Right	R	.262	122	32	6	0	2	11	15	33	.355	.361
Blauser,Jeff	L	.305	128	39	5	3	4	26	25	20	.416	.484
Bats Right	R	.232	224	52	9	0	7	28	29	39	.323	.366
Blowers,Mike	L	.250	16	4	0	0	1	1	3	1	.368	.438
Bats Right	R	.158	19	3	0	0	0	0	1	2	.200	.158
Boggs,Wade	L	.265	166	44	6	2	2	13	17	10	.333	.361
Bats Left	R	.361	380	137	36	0	6	38	72	22	.456	.503
Bonds,Barry	L	.284	201	57	13	2	7	39	32	30	.385	.473
Bats Left	R	.298	309	92	15	3	18	77	75	43	.425	.540
Bonilla,Bobby	L	.284	232	66	13	1	14	47	25	23	.349	.530
Bats Both	R	.313	345	108	31	5	4	53	65	44	.418	.467
Booker,Rod	L	.000	5	0	0	0	0	0	0	3	.000	.000
Bats Left	R	.250	48	12	1	0	0	7	1	4	.260	.271

Batters vs. Left-Handed and Right-Handed Pitchers

Batter	vs	Avg	AB	H	2B	3B	HR	BI	BB	SO	OBP	SLG
Borders,Pat	L	.238	147	35	9	0	1	14	7	19	.271	.320
Bats Right	R	.250	144	36	8	0	4	22	4	26	.272	.389
Bordick,Mike	L	.224	58	13	1	0	0	6	4	6	.274	.241
Bats Right	R	.243	177	43	4	1	0	15	10	31	.293	.277
Boston,Daryl	L	.194	31	6	3	0	1	1	0	11	.194	.387
Bats Left	R	.286	224	64	13	4	3	20	30	31	.369	.420
Bradley,Scott	L	.182	11	2	0	0	0	2	2	2	.308	.182
Bats Left	R	.205	161	33	7	0	0	9	17	17	.278	.248
Braggs,Glenn	L	.282	124	35	6	0	5	23	14	22	.352	.452
Bats Right	R	.238	126	30	4	0	6	16	9	24	.292	.413
Bream,Sid	L	.150	40	6	0	0	1	7	0	9	.150	.225
Bats Right	R	.271	225	61	12	0	10	38	25	22	.339	.458
Brett,George	L	.234	167	39	12	1	2	18	20	28	.309	.353
Bats Left	R	.266	338	90	28	1	8	43	38	47	.337	.426
Brewer,Rod	L	.200	5	1	0	0	0	1	0	3	.200	.200
Bats Left	R	.000	8	0	0	0	0	0	0	2	.000	.000
Briley,Greg	L	.231	39	9	2	1	0	9	1	10	.250	.333
Bats Left	R	.263	342	90	15	2	2	17	26	41	.313	.336
Brock,Greg	L	.400	15	6	1	0	1	4	2	1	.471	.667
Bats Left	R	.244	45	11	3	0	0	2	12	8	.404	.311
Brooks,Hubie	L	.248	121	30	5	0	5	17	18	13	.343	.413
Bats Right	R	.233	236	55	6	1	11	33	26	49	.315	.407
Brosius,Scott	L	.208	24	5	1	0	0	1	3	2	.296	.250
Bats Right	R	.250	44	11	4	0	2	3	0	9	.250	.477
Brown,Jarvis	L	.000	9	0	0	0	0	0	0	0	.000	.000
Bats Right	R	.286	28	8	0	0	0	0	2	8	.333	.286
Browne,Jerry	L	.231	78	18	1	0	0	6	8	9	.310	.244
Bats Both	R	.226	212	48	4	2	1	23	19	20	.285	.278
Brumley,Mike	L	.308	39	12	2	0	0	2	3	9	.357	.359
Bats Both	R	.165	79	13	3	0	0	3	7	13	.233	.203
Brunansky,Tom	L	.254	142	36	7	1	5	22	16	12	.321	.423
Bats Right	R	.218	317	69	17	0	11	48	33	60	.294	.375
Buechele,S	L	.298	131	39	7	1	9	26	22	23	.404	.573
Bats Right	R	.251	399	100	15	2	13	59	27	74	.305	.396
Buhner,Jay	L	.240	146	35	5	2	9	26	28	28	.371	.486
Bats Right	R	.246	260	64	9	2	18	51	25	89	.316	.504
Bullett,Scott	L	.000	0	0	0	0	0	0	0	0	.000	.000
Bats Both	R	.000	4	0	0	0	0	0	0	3	.200	.000
Bullock,Eric	L	.500	2	1	1	0	0	0	2	1	.750	1.000
Bats Left	R	.214	70	15	3	0	1	6	7	12	.282	.300
Burks,Ellis	L	.259	135	35	12	2	5	23	11	21	.313	.489
Bats Right	R	.248	339	84	21	1	9	33	28	60	.315	.395
Bush,Randy	L	.000	2	0	0	0	0	0	0	1	.000	.000
Bats Left	R	.307	163	50	10	1	6	23	24	24	.405	.491
Butler,Brett	L	.281	256	72	2	3	0	14	49	41	.397	.313
Bats Left	R	.306	359	110	11	2	2	24	58	38	.404	.365
Cabrera,F	L	.222	54	12	3	0	1	9	2	12	.246	.333
Bats Right	R	.268	41	11	3	0	3	14	4	8	.333	.561
Calderon,Ivan	L	.354	161	57	9	1	11	31	20	22	.423	.627
Bats Right	R	.272	309	84	13	2	8	44	33	42	.339	.405

Batter	vs	Avg	AB	H	2B	3B	HR	BI	BB	SO	OBP	SLG
Caminiti,Ken	L	.310	232	72	14	2	9	44	12	27	.347	.504
Bats Both	R	.213	342	73	16	1	4	36	34	58	.289	.301
Campusano,Sil	L	.053	19	1	0	0	0	0	1	4	.100	.053
Bats Right	R	.188	16	3	0	0	1	2	0	6	.188	.375
Canale,George	L	.000	6	0	0	0	0	1	2	0	.222	.000
Bats Left	R	.214	28	6	2	0	3	9	6	6	.343	.607
Candaele,C	L	.285	158	45	7	1	1	13	15	15	.347	.361
Bats Both	R	.251	303	76	13	6	3	37	25	34	.305	.363
Canseco,Jose	L	.250	136	34	9	0	8	21	24	41	.370	.493
Bats Right	R	.271	436	118	23	1	36	101	54	111	.356	.576
Capra,Nick	L	.000	0	0	0	0	0	0	0	0	.000	.000
Bats Right	R	.000	0	0	0	0	0	0	1	0	1.000	.000
Carr,Chuck	L	.400	5	2	0	0	0	1	0	1	.400	.400
Bats Both	R	.000	6	0	0	0	0	0	0	1	.000	.000
Carreon,Mark	L	.242	165	40	4	0	3	14	8	15	.286	.321
Bats Right	R	.292	89	26	2	0	1	7	4	11	.319	.348
Carrillo,M	L	.000	0	0	0	0	0	0	0	0	.000	.000
Bats Left	R	.000	0	0	0	0	0	0	0	0	.000	.000
Carter,Gary	L	.252	151	38	9	0	3	14	18	16	.347	.371
Bats Right	R	.237	97	23	5	0	3	12	4	10	.282	.381
Carter,Joe	L	.335	188	63	12	1	10	32	11	28	.366	.569
Bats Right	R	.247	450	111	30	2	23	76	38	84	.315	.476
Castilla,V	L	.000	0	0	0	0	0	0	0	0	.000	.000
Bats Right	R	.200	5	1	0	0	0	0	0	2	.200	.200
Castillo,B	L	.167	24	4	1	0	0	1	1	7	.200	.208
Bats Right	R	.179	28	5	2	0	0	1	0	8	.179	.250
Castillo,C	L	.111	9	1	0	0	0	0	0	2	.111	.111
Bats Right	R	.333	3	1	0	1	0	0	0	0	.500	1.000
Cedeno,A	L	.213	80	17	4	0	0	10	1	24	.220	.263
Bats Right	R	.257	171	44	9	2	9	26	8	50	.293	.491
Cerone,Rick	L	.315	111	35	8	0	0	8	11	13	.377	.387
Bats Right	R	.233	116	27	5	0	2	8	19	11	.346	.328
Chamberlain,W	L	.271	140	38	8	1	7	26	16	18	.350	.493
Bats Right	R	.222	243	54	8	2	6	24	15	55	.270	.346
Clark,Dave	L	.000	0	0	0	0	0	0	0	0	.000	.000
Bats Left	R	.200	10	2	0	0	0	1	1	1	.273	.200
Clark,Jack	L	.325	117	38	6	0	6	20	34	22	.465	.530
Bats Right	R	.225	364	82	12	1	22	67	62	111	.342	.445
Clark,Jerald	L	.175	126	22	3	0	4	13	10	31	.239	.294
Bats Right	R	.255	243	62	13	0	6	34	21	59	.324	.383
Clark,Will	L	.239	197	47	11	2	9	40	14	35	.291	.452
Bats Left	R	.334	368	123	21	5	20	76	37	56	.394	.582
Clayton,Royce	L	.200	5	1	0	0	0	0	0	1	.200	.200
Bats Right	R	.095	21	2	1	0	0	2	1	5	.136	.143
Cochrane,Dave	L	.245	49	12	5	0	0	10	3	3	.302	.347
Bats Both	R	.248	129	32	8	0	2	12	6	35	.279	.357
Cole,Alex	L	.387	62	24	5	1	0	8	14	7	.500	.500
Bats Left	R	.277	325	90	12	2	0	13	44	40	.362	.326
Cole,Stu	L	.000	4	0	0	0	0	0	0	1	.000	.000
Bats Right	R	.333	3	1	0	0	0	0	2	1	.600	.333

Batters vs. Left-Handed and Right-Handed Pitchers

Batter	vs	Avg	AB	H	2B	3B	HR	BI	BB	SO	OBP	SLG
Coleman,Vince	L	.248	105	26	3	0	1	4	9	11	.307	.305
Bats Both	R	.260	173	45	4	5	0	13	30	36	.369	.341
Coles,Darnell	L	.429	7	3	0	0	0	0	0	1	.429	.429
Bats Right	R	.000	7	0	0	0	0	0	0	1	.000	.000
Coolbaugh,S	L	.231	52	12	4	0	1	7	7	11	.317	.365
Bats Right	R	.211	128	27	4	1	1	8	12	34	.284	.281
Cooper,Gary	L	.000	3	0	0	0	0	0	2	1	.400	.000
Bats Right	R	.308	13	4	1	0	0	2	1	5	.357	.385
Cooper,Scott	L	.667	6	4	0	1	0	2	1	1	.714	1.000
Bats Left	R	.414	29	12	4	1	0	5	1	1	.433	.621
Cora,Joey	L	.298	57	17	0	0	0	1	5	6	.365	.298
Bats Both	R	.222	171	38	2	3	0	17	15	15	.295	.269
Cotto,Henry	L	.323	96	31	2	1	4	13	5	15	.359	.490
Bats Right	R	.284	81	23	4	1	2	10	5	12	.333	.432
Cromartie,W	L	.313	16	5	0	0	0	4	1	3	.353	.313
Bats Left	R	.313	115	36	7	2	1	16	14	15	.385	.435
Cron,Chris	L	.250	8	2	0	0	0	0	1	2	.333	.250
Bats Right	R	.000	7	0	0	0	0	0	1	3	.125	.000
Cuyler,Milt	L	.270	122	33	6	1	0	8	13	19	.345	.336
Bats Both	R	.252	353	89	9	6	3	25	39	73	.332	.337
Daniels,Kal	L	.252	206	52	8	0	6	36	19	52	.309	.379
Bats Left	R	.247	255	63	7	1	11	37	44	64	.359	.412
Dascenzo,Doug	L	.299	87	26	4	0	0	8	5	7	.340	.345
Bats Both	R	.230	152	35	7	0	1	10	19	19	.320	.296
Daugherty,J	L	.233	30	7	1	1	0	2	4	7	.324	.333
Bats Both	R	.184	114	21	2	1	1	9	12	16	.256	.246
Daulton,D	L	.146	96	14	4	0	2	9	9	31	.224	.250
Bats Left	R	.222	189	42	8	0	10	33	32	35	.332	.423
Davidson,Mark	L	.186	97	18	6	0	1	12	10	16	.275	.278
Bats Right	R	.200	45	9	0	0	1	3	2	12	.234	.267
Davis,Alvin	L	.238	101	24	2	0	4	14	16	19	.339	.376
Bats Left	R	.216	361	78	13	1	8	55	40	59	.288	.324
Davis,Butch	L	.000	0	0	0	0	0	0	0	0	.000	.000
Bats Right	R	.000	1	0	0	0	0	0	0	0	.000	.000
Davis,Chili	L	.270	174	47	9	0	11	32	25	36	.358	.511
Bats Both	R	.281	360	101	25	1	18	61	70	81	.397	.506
Davis,Eric	L	.229	105	24	5	0	3	11	20	31	.359	.362
Bats Right	R	.239	180	43	5	0	8	22	28	61	.349	.400
Davis,Glenn	L	.255	47	12	3	0	5	7	3	7	.314	.638
Bats Right	R	.217	129	28	6	1	5	21	13	22	.304	.395
Davis,Mark	L	.000	0	0	0	0	0	0	0	0	.000	.000
Bats Right	R	.000	2	0	0	0	0	0	0	0	.000	.000
Dawson,Andre	L	.296	223	66	8	1	16	47	7	27	.319	.556
Bats Right	R	.256	340	87	13	3	15	57	15	53	.291	.444
de los Santos,L	L	.167	24	4	2	0	0	0	1	2	.200	.250
Bats Right	R	.167	6	1	0	0	0	0	1	2	.286	.167
Decker,Steve	L	.221	86	19	2	1	3	13	2	11	.231	.372
Bats Right	R	.197	147	29	5	0	2	11	14	33	.279	.272
Deer,Rob	L	.196	138	27	6	1	9	18	27	46	.327	.449
Bats Right	R	.171	310	53	8	1	16	46	62	129	.307	.358
Dempsey,Rick	L	.237	97	23	4	0	3	15	15	14	.330	.371
Bats Right	R	.220	50	11	1	0	1	6	8	6	.328	.300
DeShields,D	L	.217	189	41	2	0	3	14	33	58	.338	.275
Bats Left	R	.249	374	93	13	4	7	37	62	93	.352	.361
Devereaux,M	L	.293	167	49	7	6	6	16	14	30	.350	.515
Bats Right	R	.247	441	109	20	4	13	43	33	85	.299	.399
Diaz,Mario	L	.268	82	22	5	0	0	12	8	6	.333	.329
Bats Right	R	.260	100	26	2	0	1	10	7	12	.306	.310
Disarcina,G	L	.222	18	4	1	0	0	1	0	1	.222	.278
Bats Right	R	.205	39	8	1	0	0	2	3	3	.295	.231
Donnels,Chris	L	.294	34	10	1	0	0	2	5	7	.385	.324
Bats Left	R	.182	55	10	1	0	0	3	9	12	.297	.200
Doran,Billy	L	.263	80	21	4	1	2	8	13	8	.362	.413
Bats Both	R	.285	281	80	8	1	4	27	33	31	.358	.363
Dorsett,Brian	L	.167	6	1	0	0	0	1	0	0	.167	.167
Bats Right	R	.000	6	0	0	0	0	0	0	3	.000	.000
Downing,Brian	L	.281	139	39	5	0	9	17	25	24	.401	.511
Bats Right	R	.276	268	74	12	2	8	32	33	46	.364	.425
Ducey,Rob	L	.333	12	4	0	1	1	2	1	5	.385	.750
Bats Left	R	.214	56	12	2	1	0	2	5	21	.279	.286
Duncan,M	L	.314	140	44	6	2	5	19	7	22	.347	.493
Bats Right	R	.218	193	42	1	2	7	21	5	35	.244	.352
Dunston,S	L	.232	194	45	7	2	5	19	10	23	.269	.366
Bats Right	R	.279	298	83	15	5	7	31	13	41	.308	.433
Dykstra,Lenny	L	.309	94	29	6	3	2	6	16	13	.414	.500
Bats Left	R	.289	152	44	7	2	1	6	21	7	.376	.382
Eisenreich,J	L	.322	87	28	2	1	1	16	4	12	.351	.402
Bats Left	R	.295	288	85	20	2	1	31	16	23	.328	.389
Elster,Kevin	L	.296	159	47	9	0	1	14	17	16	.362	.371
Bats Right	R	.196	189	37	7	2	5	22	23	37	.282	.333
Escobar,Jose	L	.143	7	1	0	0	0	0	1	2	.250	.143
Bats Right	R	.250	8	2	0	0	0	1	0	2	.250	.250
Espinoza,A	L	.261	161	42	10	0	1	15	7	11	.294	.342
Bats Right	R	.254	319	81	13	2	4	18	9	46	.276	.345
Espy,Cecil	L	.188	16	3	0	0	0	1	0	3	.188	.188
Bats Both	R	.258	66	17	4	0	1	10	5	14	.301	.364
Eusebio,Tony	L	.111	9	1	0	0	0	0	0	5	.111	.111
Bats Right	R	.100	10	1	1	0	0	0	6	3	.438	.200
Evans,Dwight	L	.308	107	33	3	0	1	10	32	15	.468	.364
Bats Right	R	.245	163	40	6	1	5	28	22	39	.339	.387
Faries,Paul	L	.239	46	11	3	0	0	1	4	2	.300	.304
Bats Right	R	.143	84	12	0	1	0	6	10	19	.242	.167
Fariss,Monty	L	.261	23	6	0	0	1	3	6	8	.414	.391
Bats Right	R	.250	8	2	0	0	0	3	1	3	.333	.375
Felder,Mike	L	.271	107	29	5	1	0	4	7	8	.316	.336
Bats Both	R	.261	241	63	5	5	0	14	23	23	.328	.324
Felix,Junior	L	.291	55	16	3	1	0	9	0	17	.286	.382
Bats Both	R	.280	175	49	7	1	2	17	11	38	.332	.366
Fermin,Felix	L	.281	121	34	4	0	0	8	10	6	.341	.314
Bats Right	R	.254	303	77	9	0	0	23	16	21	.293	.297

Batters vs. Left-Handed and Right-Handed Pitchers

Batter	vs	Avg	AB	H	2B	3B	HR	BI	BB	SO	OBP	SLG
Fernandez,T	L	.261	184	48	7	1	2	13	17	22	.323	.342
Bats Both	R	.278	374	104	20	4	2	25	38	52	.344	.369
Fielder,Cecil	L	.296	159	47	9	0	13	31	25	29	.399	.597
Bats Right	R	.249	465	116	16	0	31	102	53	122	.328	.484
Finley,Steve	L	.250	184	46	6	1	1	16	11	25	.290	.310
Bats Left	R	.301	412	124	22	9	7	38	31	40	.350	.449
Fisk,Carlton	L	.229	157	36	8	0	5	28	9	24	.274	.376
Bats Right	R	.248	303	75	17	0	13	46	23	62	.312	.432
Fitzgerald,M	L	.233	86	20	3	1	3	19	9	13	.302	.395
Bats Right	R	.179	112	20	2	1	1	9	13	22	.260	.241
Fletcher,D	L	.273	22	6	2	0	0	4	0	6	.273	.364
Bats Left	R	.219	114	25	6	0	1	8	5	9	.252	.298
Fletcher,S	L	.188	101	19	3	0	0	5	6	13	.248	.218
Bats Right	R	.218	147	32	7	1	1	23	11	13	.272	.299
Flora,Kevin	L	.000	1	0	0	0	0	0	0	1	.000	.000
Bats Right	R	.143	7	1	0	0	0	0	1	4	.250	.143
Foley,Tom	L	.150	20	3	1	0	0	2	1	4	.217	.200
Bats Left	R	.216	148	32	10	1	0	13	13	26	.276	.297
Franco,Julio	L	.368	155	57	10	3	8	29	16	19	.424	.626
Bats Right	R	.332	434	144	17	0	7	49	49	59	.402	.419
Fryman,Travis	L	.296	152	45	9	2	5	23	11	43	.349	.480
Bats Right	R	.244	405	99	27	1	16	68	29	106	.293	.435
Gaetti,Gary	L	.239	159	38	7	0	6	26	13	25	.303	.396
Bats Right	R	.248	427	106	15	1	12	40	20	79	.289	.372
Gagne,Greg	L	.280	118	33	8	2	2	12	12	17	.348	.432
Bats Right	R	.259	290	75	15	1	6	30	14	55	.294	.379
Galarraga,A	L	.180	128	23	1	2	6	17	7	35	.222	.359
Bats Right	R	.239	247	59	12	0	3	16	16	51	.291	.324
Gallagher,D	L	.300	110	33	7	0	0	9	8	14	.353	.364
Bats Right	R	.288	160	46	10	0	1	21	16	29	.356	.369
Gallego,Mike	L	.311	122	38	6	1	5	13	20	16	.408	.500
Bats Right	R	.225	360	81	9	3	7	36	47	68	.320	.325
Gant,Ron	L	.287	164	47	16	0	10	37	25	23	.383	.567
Bats Right	R	.237	397	94	19	3	22	68	46	81	.318	.466
Gantner,Jim	L	.266	139	37	3	0	0	13	6	8	.304	.288
Bats Left	R	.289	387	112	24	4	2	34	21	26	.325	.388
Garcia,Carlos	L	.400	5	2	0	2	0	1	1	2	.500	1.200
Bats Right	R	.211	19	4	0	0	0	0	0	6	.211	.211
Gardner,Jeff	L	.000	8	0	0	0	0	0	0	3	.000	.000
Bats Left	R	.207	29	6	0	0	0	1	4	3	.294	.207
Gedman,Rich	L	.000	10	0	0	0	0	1	1	1	.091	.000
Bats Left	R	.119	84	10	1	0	3	7	3	12	.146	.238
Geren,Bob	L	.257	105	27	2	0	2	11	7	21	.304	.333
Bats Right	R	.043	23	1	1	0	0	1	2	10	.120	.087
Giannelli,Ray	L	.500	2	1	0	0	0	0	0	0	.500	.500
Bats Left	R	.136	22	3	1	0	0	0	5	9	.296	.182
Gibson,Kirk	L	.197	132	26	2	3	2	11	16	31	.307	.303
Bats Left	R	.252	330	83	15	3	14	44	53	72	.355	.442
Gilkey,B	L	.190	137	26	5	0	2	9	20	15	.297	.270
Bats Right	R	.244	131	32	2	2	3	11	19	18	.336	.359

Batter	vs	Avg	AB	H	2B	3B	HR	BI	BB	SO	OBP	SLG
Girardi,Joe	L	.229	35	8	2	0	0	6	5	3	.325	.286
Bats Right	R	.083	12	1	0	0	0	0	1	3	.154	.083
Gladden,Dan	L	.254	118	30	5	4	1	19	16	10	.341	.390
Bats Right	R	.245	343	84	9	5	5	33	20	50	.293	.344
Gomez,Leo	L	.219	114	25	4	0	6	16	13	20	.288	.412
Bats Right	R	.238	277	66	13	2	10	29	27	62	.308	.408
Gonzales,Rene	L	.212	33	7	1	0	0	2	7	6	.366	.242
Bats Right	R	.188	85	16	2	0	1	4	5	16	.255	.247
Gonzalez,Jose	L	.059	68	4	1	1	0	2	6	20	.145	.103
Bats Right	R	.184	49	9	1	0	2	5	7	22	.286	.327
Gonzalez,Juan	L	.299	147	44	7	0	9	27	16	28	.366	.531
Bats Right	R	.251	398	100	27	1	18	75	26	90	.304	.460
Gonzalez,Luis	L	.172	122	21	7	1	1	13	12	31	.257	.270
Bats Left	R	.282	351	99	21	8	12	56	28	70	.342	.490
Goodwin,Tom	L	.000	2	0	0	0	0	0	0	0	.000	.000
Bats Left	R	.200	5	1	0	0	0	0	0	0	.200	.200
Grace,Mark	L	.270	252	68	7	3	2	19	23	33	.333	.345
Bats Left	R	.275	367	101	21	2	6	39	47	20	.355	.392
Grebeck,Craig	L	.304	115	35	8	2	5	21	20	22	.404	.539
Bats Right	R	.257	109	28	8	1	1	10	18	18	.367	.376
Green,Gary	L	.077	13	1	0	0	0	0	1	5	.143	.077
Bats Right	R	.286	7	2	1	0	0	1	0	1	.286	.429
Greenwell,M	L	.327	168	55	9	2	4	34	8	12	.357	.476
Bats Left	R	.287	376	108	17	4	5	49	35	23	.347	.394
Gregg,Tommy	L	.000	5	0	0	0	0	0	0	4	.000	.000
Bats Left	R	.196	102	20	8	1	1	4	12	20	.287	.324
Griffey Jr,K	L	.314	159	50	10	0	5	26	20	30	.386	.472
Bats Left	R	.332	389	129	32	1	17	74	51	52	.404	.550
Griffey Sr,K	L	.333	3	1	1	0	0	0	0	1	.333	.667
Bats Left	R	.280	82	23	6	0	1	9	13	12	.381	.390
Griffin,A	L	.270	148	40	1	1	0	9	10	19	.319	.291
Bats Both	R	.223	202	45	5	1	0	18	12	30	.261	.257
Grissom,M	L	.284	211	60	11	1	3	18	18	35	.341	.389
Bats Right	R	.256	347	89	12	8	3	21	16	54	.291	.363
Gruber,Kelly	L	.277	112	31	4	0	8	18	8	15	.323	.527
Bats Right	R	.243	317	77	14	2	12	47	23	55	.303	.413
Guerrero,P	L	.256	160	41	5	1	0	15	17	14	.326	.300
Bats Right	R	.281	267	75	7	0	8	55	20	32	.327	.397
Guillen,Ozzie	L	.211	161	34	3	0	1	9	1	15	.213	.248
Bats Left	R	.300	363	109	17	3	2	40	10	23	.315	.380
Gwynn,Chris	L	.182	11	2	0	0	0	1	0	2	.182	.182
Bats Left	R	.258	128	33	5	1	5	21	10	21	.310	.430
Gwynn,Tony	L	.294	211	62	7	4	2	19	13	7	.332	.393
Bats Left	R	.332	319	106	20	7	2	43	21	12	.370	.458
Hall,Mel	L	.309	162	50	5	1	5	27	9	9	.353	.444
Bats Left	R	.273	330	90	18	1	14	53	17	31	.305	.461
Hamilton,D	L	.276	87	24	2	1	0	11	4	12	.308	.322
Bats Left	R	.321	318	102	13	5	1	46	29	26	.374	.403
Hamilton,Jeff	L	.192	78	15	4	0	0	9	3	19	.222	.244
Bats Right	R	.375	16	6	0	0	1	5	1	2	.412	.563

Batters vs. Left-Handed and Right-Handed Pitchers

Batter	vs	Avg	AB	H	2B	3B	HR	BI	BB	SO	OBP	SLG	Batter	vs	Avg	AB	H	2B	3B	HR	BI	BB	SO	OBP	SLG
Hansen,Dave	L	.167	6	1	1	0	0	0	0	2	.167	.333	Howard,Thomas	L	.286	28	8	0	1	1	2	5	5	.394	.464
Bats Left	R	.280	50	14	3	0	1	5	2	10	.308	.400	Bats Both	R	.245	253	62	12	2	3	20	19	52	.299	.344
Hare,Shawn	L	.000	0	0	0	0	0	0	0	0	.000	.000	Howell,Jack	L	.103	29	3	1	0	0	0	1	10	.133	.138
Bats Left	R	.053	19	1	1	0	0	0	2	1	.143	.105	Bats Left	R	.222	212	47	4	1	8	23	28	34	.313	.363
Harper,Brian	L	.316	114	36	7	1	2	14	5	8	.344	.447	Howitt,Dann	L	.000	2	0	0	0	0	0	0	1	.000	.000
Bats Right	R	.309	327	101	21	0	8	55	9	14	.333	.446	Bats Left	R	.175	40	7	1	0	1	3	1	11	.190	.275
Harris,Donald	L	.333	3	1	0	0	0	0	1	1	.500	.333	Hrbek,Kent	L	.281	128	36	3	0	6	25	14	19	.352	.445
Bats Right	R	.400	5	2	0	0	1	2	0	2	.400	1.000	Bats Left	R	.284	334	95	17	1	14	64	53	29	.380	.467
Harris,Lenny	L	.241	87	21	0	0	1	9	6	8	.309	.276	Hudler,Rex	L	.252	155	39	9	2	1	10	7	21	.282	.355
Bats Left	R	.298	342	102	16	1	2	29	31	24	.359	.368	Bats Right	R	.154	52	8	1	0	0	5	3	8	.196	.173
Hassey,Ron	L	.333	3	1	0	0	0	1	2	1	.600	.333	Huff,Mike	L	.231	121	28	4	1	3	9	16	21	.333	.355
Bats Left	R	.224	116	26	8	0	1	13	11	15	.289	.319	Bats Right	R	.270	122	33	6	1	0	16	21	27	.388	.336
Hatcher,Billy	L	.277	130	36	7	1	1	11	8	20	.324	.369	Hulett,Tim	L	.139	72	10	2	0	2	8	5	17	.205	.250
Bats Right	R	.256	312	80	18	2	3	30	18	35	.307	.356	Bats Right	R	.239	134	32	7	0	5	10	8	32	.282	.403
Hayes,Charlie	L	.258	190	49	14	0	4	22	6	30	.283	.395	Humphreys,M	L	.250	20	5	0	0	0	3	6	5	.423	.250
Bats Right	R	.211	270	57	9	1	8	31	10	45	.239	.341	Bats Right	R	.150	20	3	0	0	0	0	3	2	.261	.150
Hayes,Von	L	.267	90	24	4	1	0	8	11	15	.355	.333	Hundley,Todd	L	.105	19	2	0	0	0	3	3	9	.250	.105
Bats Left	R	.206	194	40	11	0	0	13	20	27	.278	.263	Bats Both	R	.146	41	6	0	1	1	4	3	5	.205	.268
Heath,Mike	L	.167	54	9	2	0	1	3	1	11	.182	.259	Hunter,Brian	L	.273	121	33	4	0	6	22	6	17	.305	.455
Bats Right	R	.235	85	20	1	1	0	9	6	15	.290	.271	Bats Right	R	.233	150	35	12	1	6	28	11	31	.288	.447
Heep,Danny	L	.000	0	0	0	0	0	0	0	0	.000	.000	Huson,Jeff	L	.074	27	2	0	0	0	0	4	6	.194	.074
Bats Left	R	.417	12	5	1	0	0	3	1	4	.462	.500	Bats Left	R	.228	241	55	8	3	2	26	35	26	.325	.311
Hemond,Scott	L	.273	11	3	0	0	0	0	1	2	.333	.273	Incaviglia,P	L	.206	97	20	3	1	0	5	8	20	.264	.258
Bats Right	R	.167	12	2	0	0	0	0	0	5	.167	.167	Bats Right	R	.217	240	52	9	0	11	33	28	72	.300	.392
Henderson,D	L	.354	144	51	14	0	8	24	15	23	.416	.618	Jackson,Bo	L	.231	26	6	1	0	2	6	4	13	.323	.500
Bats Right	R	.250	428	107	19	0	17	61	43	90	.322	.414	Bats Right	R	.222	45	10	3	0	1	8	8	12	.340	.356
Henderson,R	L	.289	114	33	3	0	8	17	21	19	.401	.526	Jackson,D	L	.264	163	43	5	0	11	26	12	24	.311	.497
Bats Right	R	.261	356	93	14	1	10	40	77	54	.399	.390	Bats Right	R	.260	196	51	7	1	10	23	15	42	.318	.459
Hernandez,C	L	.333	6	2	1	0	0	1	0	1	.375	.500	Jacoby,Brook	L	.250	116	29	4	1	1	13	12	14	.326	.328
Bats Right	R	.125	8	1	0	0	0	0	0	4	.125	.125	Bats Right	R	.215	303	65	17	0	3	31	15	40	.252	.300
Hernandez,J	L	.241	29	7	1	1	0	2	0	4	.241	.345	James,Chris	L	.198	131	26	5	1	2	12	7	20	.239	.298
Bats Right	R	.159	69	11	1	0	0	2	3	27	.194	.174	Bats Right	R	.255	306	78	11	1	3	29	11	41	.288	.327
Herr,Tommy	L	.217	83	18	3	1	0	14	18	11	.356	.277	Javier,Stan	L	.247	97	24	3	2	0	9	10	18	.315	.320
Bats Both	R	.205	132	27	5	0	1	7	27	17	.335	.265	Bats Both	R	.152	79	12	2	1	1	2	6	18	.209	.241
Hill,Donnie	L	.257	35	9	3	1	0	4	8	5	.395	.400	Jefferies,G	L	.293	174	51	10	1	1	18	15	9	.353	.379
Bats Both	R	.236	174	41	5	0	1	16	22	16	.321	.282	Bats Both	R	.260	312	81	9	1	8	44	32	29	.328	.372
Hill,G	L	.281	96	27	7	1	4	12	12	17	.361	.500	Jefferson,R	L	.160	25	4	1	0	0	3	0	7	.160	.200
Bats Right	R	.240	125	30	1	1	4	13	11	37	.295	.360	Bats Both	R	.205	83	17	2	0	3	10	4	17	.239	.337
Hoiles,Chris	L	.257	113	29	6	0	6	8	11	16	.320	.469	Jefferson,S	L	.000	5	0	0	0	0	0	0	0	.000	.000
Bats Right	R	.237	228	54	9	0	5	23	18	45	.296	.342	Bats Both	R	.071	14	1	0	0	0	0	1	3	.133	.071
Hollins,Dave	L	.444	45	20	1	2	3	10	5	9	.510	.756	Jennings,Doug	L	.000	0	0	0	0	0	0	0	0	.000	.000
Bats Both	R	.236	106	25	9	0	3	11	12	17	.322	.406	Bats Left	R	.111	9	1	0	0	0	0	2	2	.273	.111
Horn,Sam	L	.111	18	2	0	0	1	1	1	7	.158	.278	Johnson,H	L	.253	217	55	9	1	14	40	24	59	.320	.498
Bats Left	R	.241	299	72	16	0	22	60	40	92	.335	.515	Bats Both	R	.262	347	91	25	3	24	77	54	61	.355	.559
Housie,Wayne	L	.500	2	1	1	0	0	0	0	0	.500	1.000	Johnson,Lance	L	.244	164	40	3	1	0	8	10	21	.291	.274
Bats Both	R	.167	6	1	0	0	0	0	1	3	.286	.167	Bats Left	R	.285	424	121	11	12	0	41	16	37	.309	.368
Howard,Chris	L	.200	5	1	1	0	0	0	1	1	.333	.400	Jones,Chris	L	.283	46	13	1	1	1	5	2	20	.306	.413
Bats Right	R	.000	1	0	0	0	0	0	0	1	.000	.000	Bats Right	R	.302	43	13	0	1	1	1	0	11	.302	.419
Howard,Dave	L	.225	80	18	2	0	1	10	6	12	.276	.288	Jones,Ron	L	.000	1	0	0	0	0	0	0	1	.000	.000
Bats Both	R	.212	156	33	5	0	0	7	10	33	.262	.244	Bats Left	R	.160	25	4	2	0	0	3	2	8	.222	.240

Batters vs. Left-Handed and Right-Handed Pitchers

Batter	vs	Avg	AB	H	2B	3B	HR	BI	BB	SO	OBP	SLG
Jones,Tim	L	.000	3	0	0	0	0	1	0	1	.000	.000
Bats Left	R	.190	21	4	2	0	0	1	2	5	.261	.286
Jones,Tracy	L	.203	118	24	3	0	1	15	15	16	.289	.254
Bats Right	R	.351	57	20	5	1	2	9	3	6	.393	.579
Jordan,Ricky	L	.310	126	39	12	0	4	19	6	15	.338	.500
Bats Right	R	.246	175	43	9	3	5	30	8	34	.280	.417
Jose,Felix	L	.298	262	78	18	2	2	30	23	51	.354	.405
Bats Both	R	.310	306	95	22	4	6	47	27	62	.365	.467
Joyner,Wally	L	.275	189	52	15	1	5	28	9	31	.308	.444
Bats Left	R	.315	362	114	19	2	16	68	43	35	.384	.511
Justice,Dave	L	.277	155	43	6	1	7	39	14	24	.333	.465
Bats Left	R	.274	241	66	19	0	14	48	51	57	.403	.527
Karkovice,Ron	L	.295	61	18	3	0	3	8	7	13	.368	.492
Bats Right	R	.217	106	23	10	0	2	14	8	29	.276	.368
Karros,Eric	L	.000	10	0	0	0	0	0	1	4	.091	.000
Bats Right	R	.250	4	1	1	0	0	1	0	2	.250	.500
Kelly,Pat	L	.263	99	26	5	0	1	7	4	13	.292	.343
Bats Right	R	.231	199	46	7	4	2	16	11	39	.285	.337
Kelly,Roberto	L	.296	159	47	4	1	9	26	20	18	.372	.503
Bats Right	R	.254	327	83	18	1	11	43	25	59	.313	.416
Kennedy,Terry	L	.300	10	3	0	1	1	3	0	2	.273	.800
Bats Left	R	.230	161	37	7	0	2	10	11	29	.283	.311
King,Jeff	L	.323	31	10	0	0	1	4	11	2	.500	.419
Bats Right	R	.205	78	16	1	1	3	14	3	13	.241	.359
Kingery,Mike	L	.077	13	1	0	1	0	0	1	4	.143	.231
Bats Left	R	.196	97	19	2	1	0	8	14	17	.297	.237
Kirby,Wayne	L	.000	7	0	0	0	0	1	0	3	.000	.000
Bats Left	R	.250	36	9	2	0	0	4	2	3	.282	.306
Kittle,Ron	L	.188	16	3	0	0	1	2	2	2	.316	.375
Bats Right	R	.194	31	6	0	0	1	5	3	7	.278	.290
Knoblauch,C	L	.257	148	38	8	1	0	6	14	10	.325	.324
Bats Right	R	.290	417	121	16	5	1	44	45	30	.360	.360
Knorr,Randy	L	.000	1	0	0	0	0	0	0	1	.000	.000
Bats Right	R	.000	0	0	0	0	0	0	1	0	1.000	.000
Komminsk,Brad	L	.143	14	2	0	0	0	1	0	4	.143	.143
Bats Right	R	.091	11	1	1	0	0	1	2	5	.231	.182
Kreuter,Chad	L	.000	2	0	0	0	0	0	0	1	.000	.000
Bats Both	R	.000	2	0	0	0	0	0	0	0	.000	.000
Kruk,John	L	.297	202	60	12	2	4	35	18	38	.350	.436
Bats Left	R	.292	336	98	15	4	17	57	49	62	.378	.512
Lake,Steve	L	.245	110	27	3	1	0	7	2	16	.259	.291
Bats Right	R	.188	48	9	1	0	1	4	0	10	.188	.271
Lampkin,Tom	L	.000	0	0	0	0	0	0	0	0	.000	.000
Bats Left	R	.190	58	11	3	1	0	3	3	9	.230	.276
Landrum,Ced	L	.385	13	5	0	1	0	2	2	4	.467	.538
Bats Left	R	.205	73	15	2	0	0	4	8	14	.284	.233
Lankford,Ray	L	.236	220	52	11	7	0	26	16	48	.290	.350
Bats Left	R	.260	346	90	12	8	9	43	25	66	.308	.419
Lansford,C	L	.000	9	0	0	0	0	0	0	2	.000	.000
Bats Right	R	.143	7	1	0	0	0	1	0	0	.143	.143
Larkin,Barry	L	.326	135	44	7	2	8	22	28	15	.436	.585
Bats Right	R	.292	329	96	20	2	12	47	27	49	.351	.474
Larkin,Gene	L	.273	88	24	8	0	1	6	13	7	.363	.398
Bats Both	R	.293	167	49	6	1	1	13	17	14	.360	.359
LaValliere,M	L	.222	54	12	2	1	0	14	3	9	.259	.296
Bats Left	R	.301	282	85	9	1	3	27	30	18	.368	.372
Law,Vance	L	.259	54	14	5	0	0	7	9	11	.365	.352
Bats Right	R	.175	80	14	2	1	0	2	9	16	.258	.225
Lee,Manuel	L	.285	144	41	9	0	0	11	10	25	.333	.347
Bats Both	R	.209	301	63	9	3	0	18	14	82	.245	.259
Lee,Terry	L	.000	5	0	0	0	0	0	0	1	.000	.000
Bats Right	R	.000	1	0	0	0	0	0	0	1	.000	.000
Leius,Scott	L	.305	128	39	5	2	3	13	28	17	.427	.445
Bats Right	R	.254	71	18	2	0	2	7	2	18	.274	.366
Lemke,Mark	L	.254	114	29	7	1	0	11	11	7	.313	.333
Bats Both	R	.219	155	34	4	1	2	12	18	20	.299	.297
Lennon,P	L	.125	8	1	1	0	0	1	1	1	.222	.250
Bats Right	R	.000	0	0	0	0	0	0	2	0	1.000	.000
Leonard,Mark	L	.100	10	1	1	0	0	0	1	2	.182	.200
Bats Left	R	.252	119	30	6	1	2	14	11	23	.316	.370
Lewis,Darren	L	.280	75	21	4	1	1	6	12	8	.386	.400
Bats Right	R	.231	147	34	1	2	0	9	24	22	.343	.265
Lewis,Mark	L	.276	87	24	3	0	0	7	5	12	.305	.310
Bats Right	R	.260	227	59	12	1	0	23	10	33	.289	.322
Leyritz,Jim	L	.243	37	9	2	0	0	2	5	9	.333	.297
Bats Right	R	.125	40	5	1	0	0	2	8	6	.271	.150
Lind,Jose	L	.269	167	45	2	1	2	15	14	20	.326	.329
Bats Right	R	.263	335	88	14	5	1	39	16	36	.295	.343
Lindeman,Jim	L	.426	61	26	3	0	0	8	10	10	.507	.475
Bats Right	R	.176	34	6	2	0	0	4	3	4	.237	.235
Lindsey,Doug	L	.000	0	0	0	0	0	0	0	0	.000	.000
Bats Right	R	.000	3	0	0	0	0	0	0	3	.000	.000
Liriano,N	L	.000	1	0	0	0	0	0	0	0	.000	.000
Bats Both	R	.429	21	9	0	0	0	1	0	2	.429	.429
Litton,Greg	L	.159	44	7	4	0	0	3	3	5	.213	.250
Bats Right	R	.193	83	16	3	1	1	12	8	20	.269	.289
Livingstone,S	L	.417	12	5	1	0	1	1	2	1	.500	.750
Bats Left	R	.278	115	32	4	0	1	10	8	24	.323	.339
Lofton,Kenny	L	.250	20	5	0	0	0	0	2	8	.318	.250
Bats Left	R	.185	54	10	1	0	0	0	3	11	.228	.204
Lopez,Luis	L	.234	47	11	2	1	0	5	3	1	.275	.319
Bats Right	R	.200	35	7	2	0	0	2	1	6	.243	.257
Lovullo,Torey	L	.167	6	1	0	0	0	0	0	1	.167	.167
Bats Both	R	.178	45	8	2	0	0	2	5	6	.260	.222
Lusader,Scott	L	.000	0	0	0	0	0	0	0	0	.000	.000
Bats Left	R	.143	7	1	0	0	0	1	1	3	.250	.143
Lyons,Barry	L	.000	8	0	0	0	0	0	0	2	.000	.000
Bats Right	R	.167	6	1	0	0	0	0	0	1	.167	.167
Lyons,Steve	L	.167	12	2	0	0	1	2	1	5	.231	.417
Bats Left	R	.245	200	49	10	1	3	15	10	30	.280	.350

Batters vs. Left-Handed and Right-Handed Pitchers

Batter	vs	Avg	AB	H	2B	3B	HR	BI	BB	SO	OBP	SLG	Batter	vs	Avg	AB	H	2B	3B	HR	BI	BB	SO	OBP	SLG
Maas,Kevin	L	.221	181	40	7	0	9	31	30	51	.338	.409	McGriff,Fred	L	.272	213	58	7	1	14	48	39	56	.380	.512
Bats Left	R	.219	319	70	7	1	14	32	53	77	.330	.379	Bats Left	R	.283	315	89	12	0	17	58	66	79	.406	.483
Macfarlane,M	L	.321	112	36	10	1	5	14	7	19	.372	.563	McGwire,Mark	L	.200	130	26	5	0	5	19	23	28	.316	.354
Bats Right	R	.245	155	38	8	1	8	27	10	33	.301	.465	Bats Right	R	.201	353	71	17	0	17	56	70	88	.336	.394
Mack,Shane	L	.350	137	48	13	4	9	29	14	19	.412	.701	McIntosh,Tim	L	.444	9	4	1	0	1	1	0	2	.444	.889
Bats Right	R	.292	305	89	14	4	9	45	20	60	.341	.452	Bats Right	R	.000	2	0	0	0	0	0	0	2	.000	.000
Magadan,Dave	L	.245	151	37	4	0	0	12	24	14	.347	.272	McKnight,Jeff	L	.150	20	3	0	0	0	1	1	3	.190	.150
Bats Left	R	.266	267	71	19	0	4	39	59	36	.395	.382	Bats Both	R	.190	21	4	1	0	0	1	1	4	.227	.238
Magallanes,E	L	.000	0	0	0	0	0	0	0	0	.000	.000	McLemore,Mark	L	.179	28	5	1	0	0	1	2	8	.233	.214
Bats Left	R	.000	2	0	0	0	0	0	1	1	.333	.000	Bats Both	R	.121	33	4	0	0	0	1	4	5	.211	.121
Maldonado,C	L	.276	76	21	5	0	3	12	15	13	.398	.461	McRae,Brian	L	.294	204	60	13	2	2	19	9	16	.326	.407
Bats Right	R	.241	212	51	10	0	9	36	21	63	.321	.415	Bats Both	R	.245	425	104	15	7	6	45	15	83	.270	.355
Manrique,Fred	L	.100	10	1	0	0	0	0	0	1	.100	.100	McReynolds,K	L	.259	189	49	10	1	6	21	14	17	.311	.418
Bats Right	R	.182	11	2	0	0	0	0	2	0	.308	.182	Bats Right	R	.258	333	86	22	0	10	53	35	29	.329	.414
Manto,Jeff	L	.222	45	10	2	0	0	5	4	7	.280	.267	Medina,Luis	L	.000	10	0	0	0	0	0	0	6	.000	.000
Bats Right	R	.205	83	17	5	0	2	8	10	15	.320	.337	Bats Right	R	.167	6	1	0	0	0	0	1	1	.286	.167
Manwaring,K	L	.308	65	20	5	0	0	9	3	9	.333	.385	Melvin,Bob	L	.269	78	21	5	0	0	5	10	14	.348	.333
Bats Right	R	.177	113	20	4	0	0	10	6	13	.236	.212	Bats Right	R	.240	150	36	5	0	1	18	1	32	.239	.293
Marshall,Mike	L	.313	16	5	1	0	0	2	0	5	.313	.375	Merced,O	L	.208	53	11	3	1	0	6	3	10	.263	.302
Bats Right	R	.245	53	13	3	0	1	5	0	15	.245	.358	Bats Both	R	.285	358	102	14	1	10	44	61	71	.388	.413
Martinez,Carlos	L	.338	80	27	5	0	4	13	6	11	.367	.550	Mercedes,Luis	L	.212	33	7	0	0	0	0	1	8	.235	.212
Bats Right	R	.260	177	46	9	0	1	17	4	32	.283	.328	Bats Right	R	.190	21	4	2	0	0	2	3	1	.292	.286
Martinez,C'rm'lo	L	.221	131	29	7	0	2	16	23	32	.335	.321	Merullo,Matt	L	.125	8	1	0	0	0	1	1	0	.222	.125
Bats Right	R	.222	144	32	4	0	8	20	20	32	.313	.417	Bats Left	R	.235	132	31	1	0	5	20	8	18	.271	.356
Martinez,Chito	L	.207	29	6	1	0	1	1	2	10	.258	.345	Meulens,H	L	.236	178	42	6	1	5	19	12	54	.297	.365
Bats Left	R	.278	187	52	11	1	12	32	9	41	.310	.540	Bats Right	R	.200	110	22	2	0	1	10	6	43	.239	.245
Martinez,Dave	L	.237	93	22	6	1	0	8	5	22	.287	.323	Miller,Keith	L	.247	146	36	11	0	1	7	9	26	.297	.342
Bats Left	R	.314	303	95	12	4	7	34	15	32	.346	.449	Bats Right	R	.318	129	41	11	1	3	16	14	18	.397	.488
Martinez,E	L	.359	156	56	13	0	2	12	24	11	.442	.481	Milligan,R	L	.229	140	32	3	1	5	19	26	35	.347	.371
Bats Right	R	.286	388	111	22	1	12	40	60	61	.390	.441	Bats Right	R	.277	343	95	14	1	11	51	58	73	.384	.420
Martinez,Tino	L	.257	35	9	2	0	1	1	4	7	.333	.400	Mitchell,Keith	L	.345	29	10	0	0	0	1	4	3	.424	.345
Bats Left	R	.182	77	14	0	0	3	8	7	17	.244	.299	Bats Right	R	.297	37	11	0	0	2	4	4	9	.366	.459
Marzano,John	L	.300	30	9	3	0	0	2	1	3	.333	.400	Mitchell,Kevin	L	.272	114	31	4	0	7	22	17	7	.370	.491
Bats Right	R	.250	84	21	5	0	0	7	0	13	.247	.310	Bats Right	R	.249	257	64	9	1	20	47	26	50	.323	.525
Mattingly,Don	L	.264	227	60	12	0	5	29	18	20	.321	.383	Molitor,Paul	L	.322	174	56	8	3	5	17	24	13	.405	.489
Bats Left	R	.303	360	109	23	0	4	39	28	22	.350	.400	Bats Right	R	.326	491	160	24	10	12	58	53	49	.397	.489
Maurer,Rob	L	.000	0	0	0	0	0	0	0	0	.000	.000	Moore,Bobby	L	.455	11	5	1	0	0	0	1	0	.500	.545
Bats Left	R	.063	16	1	1	0	0	2	2	6	.211	.125	Bats Right	R	.000	3	0	0	0	0	0	0	2	.000	.000
May,Derrick	L	.000	1	0	0	0	0	0	1	0	.500	.000	Morandini,M	L	.185	65	12	0	0	0	3	3	11	.221	.185
Bats Left	R	.238	21	5	2	0	1	3	1	1	.261	.476	Bats Left	R	.265	260	69	11	4	1	17	26	34	.334	.350
Mayne,Brent	L	.091	22	2	0	0	0	3	3	8	.179	.091	Morman,Russ	L	.238	21	5	0	0	0	1	1	5	.273	.238
Bats Left	R	.268	209	56	8	0	3	28	20	34	.332	.349	Bats Right	R	.500	2	1	0	0	0	0	0	0	.500	.500
McClendon,L	L	.350	117	41	5	0	6	19	14	17	.429	.547	Morris,Hal	L	.252	103	26	8	1	1	12	6	25	.288	.379
Bats Right	R	.130	46	6	2	0	1	5	4	6	.200	.239	Bats Left	R	.336	375	126	25	0	13	47	40	36	.397	.507
McCray,Rodney	L	.000	1	0	0	0	0	0	0	0	.000	.000	Morris,John	L	.333	12	4	0	0	0	0	1	2	.429	.333
Bats Right	R	.333	6	2	0	0	0	0	0	2	.333	.333	Bats Left	R	.209	115	24	2	1	1	6	11	23	.278	.270
McDaniel,T	L	.267	15	4	0	0	0	0	1	4	.313	.267	Moseby,Lloyd	L	.239	46	11	4	0	1	9	5	11	.327	.391
Bats Both	R	.143	14	2	1	0	0	2	0	7	.143	.214	Bats Left	R	.266	214	57	11	1	5	26	16	32	.319	.397
McGee,Willie	L	.338	154	52	11	0	2	20	10	24	.380	.448	Moses,John	L	.000	3	0	0	0	0	0	0	1	.000	.000
Bats Both	R	.300	343	103	19	3	2	23	24	50	.347	.391	Bats Both	R	.056	18	1	1	0	0	0	2	6	.150	.111

Batters vs. Left-Handed and Right-Handed Pitchers

Batter	vs	Avg	AB	H	2B	3B	HR	BI	BB	SO	OBP	SLG
Mota,Andy	L	.114	35	4	0	0	0	1	1	11	.139	.114
Bats Right	R	.236	55	13	2	0	1	5	0	6	.236	.327
Mota,Jose	L	.444	9	4	0	0	0	0	0	0	.444	.444
Bats Both	R	.148	27	4	0	0	0	2	2	7	.233	.148
Mulliniks,R	L	.083	12	1	0	0	0	0	0	3	.083	.083
Bats Left	R	.259	228	59	12	1	2	24	44	41	.376	.346
Munoz,Pedro	L	.295	44	13	2	1	3	16	3	12	.333	.591
Bats Right	R	.277	94	26	5	0	4	10	6	19	.324	.457
Murphy,Dale	L	.297	192	57	13	0	5	25	17	33	.351	.443
Bats Right	R	.227	352	80	20	1	13	56	31	60	.286	.401
Murray,Eddie	L	.217	254	55	10	0	6	40	20	30	.269	.327
Bats Both	R	.295	322	95	13	1	13	56	35	44	.361	.463
Myers,Greg	L	.171	35	6	1	0	1	3	2	7	.211	.286
Bats Left	R	.274	274	75	21	0	7	33	19	38	.319	.427
Naehring,Tim	L	.125	16	2	0	0	0	0	2	6	.222	.125
Bats Right	R	.103	39	4	1	0	0	3	4	9	.186	.128
Newman,Al	L	.242	66	16	4	0	0	8	2	7	.265	.303
Bats Both	R	.172	180	31	1	0	0	11	21	14	.259	.178
Newson,Warren	L	.143	7	1	0	0	0	0	1	3	.250	.143
Bats Left	R	.304	125	38	5	0	4	25	27	31	.428	.440
Nichols,Carl	L	.200	25	5	0	0	0	0	4	9	.310	.200
Bats Right	R	.192	26	5	3	0	0	1	1	8	.222	.308
Nixon,Otis	L	.305	95	29	5	0	0	7	14	7	.400	.358
Bats Both	R	.294	306	90	5	1	0	19	33	33	.362	.317
Noboa,Junior	L	.253	79	20	3	0	1	2	1	7	.263	.329
Bats Right	R	.188	16	3	0	0	0	0	0	1	.188	.188
Nokes,Matt	L	.261	111	29	1	0	7	23	6	12	.303	.459
Bats Left	R	.270	345	93	19	0	17	54	19	37	.310	.472
O'Brien,C	L	.167	78	13	2	0	1	7	6	10	.233	.231
Bats Right	R	.200	90	18	4	0	1	7	11	15	.305	.278
O'Brien,Pete	L	.235	179	42	11	0	4	27	11	22	.280	.363
Bats Left	R	.255	381	97	18	3	13	61	33	39	.309	.420
O'Neill,Paul	L	.201	169	34	9	0	3	15	11	52	.254	.308
Bats Left	R	.281	363	102	27	0	25	76	62	55	.385	.562
Oberkfell,Ken	L	.333	3	1	0	0	0	0	0	1	.333	.333
Bats Left	R	.224	67	15	4	0	0	14	14	7	.358	.284
Offerman,Jose	L	.300	50	15	1	0	0	2	7	11	.386	.320
Bats Both	R	.111	63	7	1	0	0	1	18	21	.317	.127
Olander,Jim	L	.000	8	0	0	0	0	0	2	5	.200	.000
Bats Right	R	.000	1	0	0	0	0	0	0	0	.000	.000
Olerud,John	L	.217	83	18	3	1	3	16	17	19	.358	.386
Bats Left	R	.264	371	98	27	0	14	52	51	65	.352	.450
Oliver,Joe	L	.229	131	30	5	0	8	27	15	24	.308	.450
Bats Right	R	.203	138	28	6	0	3	14	3	29	.220	.312
Olson,Greg	L	.290	100	29	8	0	2	17	10	12	.348	.430
Bats Right	R	.225	311	70	17	0	4	27	34	36	.306	.318
Oquendo,Jose	L	.240	150	36	8	1	1	15	29	21	.365	.327
Bats Both	R	.241	216	52	3	3	0	11	38	27	.352	.282
Orsulak,Joe	L	.234	64	15	3	0	0	6	4	8	.286	.281
Bats Left	R	.284	422	120	19	1	5	37	24	37	.326	.370

Batter	vs	Avg	AB	H	2B	3B	HR	BI	BB	SO	OBP	SLG
Ortiz,Javier	L	.250	48	12	2	0	0	2	10	10	.379	.292
Bats Right	R	.314	35	11	2	1	1	3	4	4	.385	.514
Ortiz,Junior	L	.143	42	6	0	1	0	5	4	5	.217	.190
Bats Right	R	.239	92	22	5	0	0	6	11	7	.327	.293
Orton,John	L	.316	19	6	1	0	0	1	2	2	.381	.368
Bats Right	R	.160	50	8	3	0	0	2	8	15	.288	.220
Owen,Spike	L	.305	200	61	18	2	1	12	14	25	.350	.430
Bats Both	R	.210	224	47	4	6	2	14	28	36	.296	.308
Pagliarulo,M	L	.188	16	3	1	0	0	1	3	1	.316	.250
Bats Left	R	.284	349	99	19	0	6	35	18	54	.323	.390
Pagnozzi,Tom	L	.254	201	51	11	2	2	25	18	29	.311	.358
Bats Right	R	.271	258	70	13	3	0	32	18	34	.326	.345
Palmeiro,R	L	.274	186	51	8	1	9	26	14	26	.333	.473
Bats Left	R	.342	445	152	41	2	17	62	54	46	.411	.557
Palmer,Dean	L	.247	81	20	3	0	9	16	11	30	.337	.617
Bats Right	R	.160	187	30	6	2	6	21	21	68	.256	.310
Pappas,Erik	L	.100	10	1	0	0	0	1	1	3	.182	.100
Bats Right	R	.286	7	2	0	0	0	1	0	2	.286	.286
Paredes,J	L	.357	14	5	0	0	0	0	0	1	.357	.357
Bats Right	R	.250	4	1	0	0	0	0	0	0	.250	.250
Parent,Mark	L	.000	1	0	0	0	0	0	0	1	.000	.000
Bats Right	R	.000	0	0	0	0	0	0	0	0	.000	.000
Parker,Dave	L	.233	133	31	6	1	4	17	3	26	.259	.383
Bats Left	R	.241	369	89	20	1	7	42	30	72	.299	.358
Parker,Rick	L	.000	3	0	0	0	0	0	0	1	.000	.000
Bats Right	R	.091	11	1	0	0	0	1	1	4	.167	.091
Parrish,Lance	L	.219	105	23	1	0	3	10	12	25	.297	.314
Bats Right	R	.215	297	64	11	0	16	41	23	92	.281	.414
Pasqua,Dan	L	.265	49	13	2	1	3	8	9	12	.379	.531
Bats Left	R	.258	368	95	20	4	15	58	53	74	.355	.457
Pecota,Bill	L	.336	128	43	10	0	2	17	17	13	.414	.461
Bats Right	R	.263	270	71	13	2	4	28	24	32	.328	.370
Pedre,Jorge	L	.231	13	3	1	1	0	2	0	4	.231	.462
Bats Right	R	.333	6	2	0	0	0	1	3	1	.556	.333
Pena,Geronimo	L	.301	93	28	7	1	4	13	6	24	.358	.527
Bats Both	R	.185	92	17	1	2	1	4	12	21	.286	.272
Pena,Tony	L	.283	106	30	4	0	4	17	9	11	.336	.434
Bats Right	R	.215	358	77	19	2	1	31	28	42	.278	.288
Pendleton,T	L	.299	177	53	10	3	4	23	15	9	.351	.458
Bats Both	R	.328	409	134	24	5	18	63	28	61	.368	.543
Perezchica,T	L	.250	20	5	1	0	0	1	3	4	.348	.300
Bats Right	R	.280	50	14	5	1	0	2	2	13	.308	.420
Perry,Gerald	L	.240	104	25	3	2	2	13	7	14	.286	.365
Bats Left	R	.239	138	33	5	2	4	23	15	20	.310	.391
Petralli,Geno	L	.111	9	1	0	0	0	2	0	3	.100	.111
Bats Left	R	.279	190	53	8	1	2	18	21	22	.351	.363
Pettis,Gary	L	.195	77	15	1	1	0	6	14	17	.315	.234
Bats Both	R	.224	205	46	6	4	0	13	40	74	.351	.293
Phillips,Tony	L	.357	154	55	7	0	11	25	32	18	.466	.617
Bats Both	R	.256	410	105	21	4	6	47	47	77	.333	.371

Batters vs. Left-Handed and Right-Handed Pitchers

Batter	vs	Avg	AB	H	2B	3B	HR	BI	BB	SO	OBP	SLG	Batter	vs	Avg	AB	H	2B	3B	HR	BI	BB	SO	OBP	SLG
Plantier,Phil	L	.320	25	8	1	0	3	13	3	11	.367	.720	Riesgo,Nikco	L	.167	6	1	0	0	0	0	3	1	.444	.167
Bats Left	R	.333	123	41	6	1	8	22	20	27	.431	.593	Bats Right	R	.000	1	0	0	0	0	0	0	0	.000	.000
Polonia,Luis	L	.238	168	40	8	1	0	17	11	25	.283	.298	Riles,Ernest	L	.143	21	3	0	0	0	1	0	2	.143	.143
Bats Left	R	.319	436	139	20	7	2	33	41	49	.377	.411	Bats Left	R	.219	260	57	8	4	5	31	31	40	.301	.338
Powell,Alonzo	L	.250	68	17	5	0	3	7	8	16	.325	.456	Ripken,Billy	L	.270	100	27	4	0	0	7	5	9	.302	.310
Bats Right	R	.163	43	7	1	1	0	5	3	8	.229	.233	Bats Right	R	.187	187	35	7	1	0	7	10	22	.227	.235
Presley,Jim	L	.130	23	3	0	0	1	1	1	6	.167	.261	Ripken,Cal	L	.348	164	57	14	2	12	31	19	15	.411	.677
Bats Right	R	.139	36	5	0	0	0	4	3	10	.220	.139	Bats Right	R	.315	486	153	32	3	22	83	34	31	.361	.529
Prince,Tom	L	.375	16	6	2	0	1	2	4	1	.500	.688	Rivera,Luis	L	.315	108	34	10	1	4	16	6	25	.356	.537
Bats Right	R	.167	18	3	1	0	0	0	3	2	.318	.222	Bats Right	R	.239	306	73	12	2	4	24	29	61	.305	.330
Puckett,Kirby	L	.406	155	63	8	5	7	24	8	19	.436	.658	Roberts,Bip	L	.252	119	30	3	1	0	8	7	13	.299	.294
Bats Right	R	.289	456	132	21	1	8	65	23	59	.324	.393	Bats Both	R	.292	305	89	10	2	3	24	30	58	.358	.367
Puhl,Terry	L	.000	2	0	0	0	0	0	0	0	.000	.000	Rodriguez,C	L	.500	8	4	0	0	0	1	0	0	.500	.500
Bats Left	R	.250	16	4	0	0	0	3	3	2	.368	.250	Bats Both	R	.103	29	3	0	0	0	1	1	2	.133	.103
Pulliam,H	L	.267	30	8	1	0	3	4	3	8	.333	.600	Rodriguez,I	L	.239	71	17	6	0	1	9	2	9	.260	.366
Bats Right	R	.333	3	1	0	0	0	0	0	1	.333	.333	Bats Right	R	.273	209	57	10	0	2	18	3	33	.282	.349
Quinones,Luis	L	.172	64	11	2	0	1	4	8	9	.264	.250	Rohde,David	L	.000	17	0	0	0	0	0	1	5	.056	.000
Bats Both	R	.243	148	36	2	3	3	16	13	22	.311	.358	Bats Both	R	.208	24	5	0	0	0	0	4	3	.321	.208
Quintana,C	L	.340	153	52	7	0	5	26	26	21	.436	.484	Romine,Kevin	L	.176	34	6	1	0	0	3	2	4	.222	.206
Bats Right	R	.274	325	89	14	1	6	45	35	45	.345	.378	Bats Right	R	.143	21	3	1	0	1	4	1	6	.182	.333
Quirk,Jamie	L	.313	16	5	0	0	0	2	3	2	.421	.313	Rose,Bobby	L	.359	39	14	3	1	1	6	2	9	.381	.564
Bats Left	R	.257	187	48	4	0	1	15	13	26	.312	.294	Bats Right	R	.154	26	4	2	0	0	2	1	4	.185	.231
Raines,Tim	L	.279	208	58	6	1	2	17	21	21	.343	.346	Rossy,Rico	L	.000	0	0	0	0	0	0	0	0	.000	.000
Bats Both	R	.262	401	105	14	5	3	33	62	47	.366	.344	Bats Right	R	.000	1	0	0	0	0	0	0	1	.000	.000
Ramirez,R	L	.245	110	27	4	0	1	14	8	20	.294	.309	Rowland,Rich	L	.333	3	1	0	0	0	0	1	1	.400	.333
Bats Right	R	.228	123	28	6	0	0	6	5	20	.256	.276	Bats Right	R	.000	1	0	0	0	0	0	0	1	.000	.000
Ramos,John	L	.333	15	5	1	0	0	1	1	2	.375	.400	Royer,Stan	L	.250	8	2	0	0	0	1	0	1	.250	.250
Bats Right	R	.273	11	3	0	0	0	2	0	1	.231	.273	Bats Right	R	.308	13	4	1	0	0	0	1	1	.357	.385
Randolph,W	L	.358	148	53	5	1	0	21	27	10	.457	.405	Russell,John	L	.133	15	2	0	0	0	0	0	4	.133	.133
Bats Right	R	.311	283	88	9	2	0	33	48	28	.407	.357	Bats Right	R	.083	12	1	0	0	0	0	1	3	.143	.083
Ready,Randy	L	.265	147	39	10	1	1	18	39	17	.418	.367	Sabo,Chris	L	.358	193	69	17	1	9	29	16	23	.412	.596
Bats Right	R	.207	58	12	0	0	0	2	8	8	.294	.207	Bats Right	R	.272	389	106	18	2	17	59	28	56	.325	.460
Redfield,Joe	L	.125	16	2	0	0	0	0	1	1	.176	.125	Salas,Mark	L	.000	3	0	0	0	0	2	0	0	.000	.000
Bats Right	R	.000	2	0	0	0	0	0	3	0	.600	.000	Bats Left	R	.093	54	5	1	0	1	5	0	10	.125	.167
Redus,Gary	L	.249	173	43	7	2	5	15	15	27	.302	.399	Salazar,Luis	L	.271	166	45	8	0	10	25	8	18	.309	.500
Bats Right	R	.241	79	19	5	0	2	9	13	12	.368	.380	Bats Right	R	.246	167	41	6	1	4	13	7	27	.276	.365
Reed,Jeff	L	.192	26	5	2	0	0	5	3	6	.281	.269	Samuel,Juan	L	.252	250	63	11	2	7	27	14	59	.294	.396
Bats Left	R	.275	244	67	13	2	3	26	20	32	.326	.381	Bats Right	R	.285	344	98	11	4	5	31	35	74	.352	.384
Reed,Jody	L	.267	165	44	9	0	0	6	16	11	.331	.321	Sanchez,Rey	L	.000	5	0	0	0	0	1	2	1	.286	.000
Bats Right	R	.289	453	131	33	2	5	54	44	42	.355	.404	Bats Right	R	.333	18	6	0	0	0	1	2	2	.400	.333
Reimer,Kevin	L	.222	36	8	1	0	1	4	2	9	.275	.333	Sandberg,Ryne	L	.359	209	75	19	0	8	27	39	23	.456	.565
Bats Left	R	.274	358	98	21	0	19	65	31	84	.338	.492	Bats Right	R	.253	376	95	13	2	18	73	48	66	.335	.441
Reyes,Gil	L	.186	97	18	2	0	0	4	8	26	.248	.206	Sanders,Deion	L	.125	16	2	1	0	0	1	3	8	.263	.188
Bats Right	R	.245	110	27	7	0	0	9	11	25	.317	.309	Bats Left	R	.202	94	19	0	2	4	12	9	15	.272	.372
Reynolds,H	L	.264	174	46	7	0	1	16	17	14	.326	.322	Sanders,R	L	.125	16	2	0	0	0	1	0	3	.125	.125
Bats Both	R	.249	457	114	27	6	2	41	55	49	.334	.348	Bats Right	R	.250	24	6	0	0	1	2	0	6	.250	.375
Rhodes,Karl	L	.242	33	8	2	0	0	4	3	7	.306	.303	Santiago,B	L	.284	204	58	12	2	8	35	10	41	.318	.480
Bats Left	R	.204	103	21	1	1	1	8	11	19	.284	.262	Bats Right	R	.258	376	97	10	1	9	52	13	73	.284	.362
Richardson,J	L	.333	3	1	0	0	0	0	0	2	.333	.333	Santovenia,N	L	.265	49	13	2	0	2	8	2	7	.283	.429
Bats Right	R	.000	1	0	0	0	0	0	0	1	.000	.000	Bats Right	R	.234	47	11	3	0	0	6	0	11	.224	.298

Batters vs. Left-Handed and Right-Handed Pitchers

Batter	vs	Avg	AB	H	2B	3B	HR	BI	BB	SO	OBP	SLG	Batter	vs	Avg	AB	H	2B	3B	HR	BI	BB	SO	OBP	SLG
Sasser,Mackey	L	.172	29	5	2	0	0	2	0	5	.167	.241	Smith,Greg	L	.000	0	0	0	0	0	0	0	0	.000	.000
Bats Left	R	.286	199	57	12	2	5	33	9	14	.316	.442	Bats Both	R	.000	3	0	0	0	0	0	0	2	.000	.000
Sax,Steve	L	.344	215	74	20	0	5	20	17	6	.390	.507	Smith,Lonnie	L	.339	115	39	9	1	0	11	18	22	.435	.435
Bats Right	R	.284	437	124	18	2	5	36	24	32	.322	.368	Bats Right	R	.244	238	58	10	0	7	33	32	42	.348	.374
Schaefer,Jeff	L	.263	95	25	5	0	1	4	3	14	.286	.347	Smith,Ozzie	L	.262	248	65	18	2	3	25	35	20	.356	.387
Bats Right	R	.232	69	16	2	1	0	7	2	11	.254	.290	Bats Both	R	.305	302	92	12	1	0	25	48	16	.399	.351
Schofield,D	L	.183	115	21	1	0	0	8	22	15	.314	.191	Snyder,Cory	L	.164	116	19	4	0	3	10	4	42	.192	.276
Bats Right	R	.240	312	75	8	3	0	23	28	54	.309	.285	Bats Right	R	.200	50	10	0	1	0	7	5	18	.268	.240
Schu,Rick	L	.133	15	2	0	0	0	1	0	5	.125	.133	Sojo,Luis	L	.298	114	34	7	1	0	5	5	6	.328	.377
Bats Right	R	.000	7	0	0	0	0	1	1	2	.125	.000	Bats Right	R	.240	250	60	7	0	3	15	9	20	.280	.304
Schulz,Jeff	L	.000	0	0	0	0	0	0	0	0	.000	.000	Sorrento,Paul	L	.600	5	3	1	0	1	2	0	0	.600	1.400
Bats Left	R	.000	3	0	0	0	0	0	0	2	.000	.000	Bats Left	R	.214	42	9	1	0	3	11	4	11	.283	.452
Scioscia,Mike	L	.189	106	20	2	0	3	13	11	12	.276	.292	Sosa,Sammy	L	.227	128	29	5	0	5	11	8	39	.277	.383
Bats Left	R	.297	239	71	14	2	5	27	36	20	.388	.435	Bats Right	R	.186	188	35	5	1	5	22	6	59	.214	.303
Scott,Donnie	L	.154	13	2	0	0	0	0	0	0	.154	.154	Spehr,Tim	L	.209	43	9	2	0	3	10	6	11	.314	.465
Bats Both	R	.167	6	1	0	0	0	0	0	2	.167	.167	Bats Right	R	.161	31	5	3	0	0	4	3	7	.235	.258
Scott,Gary	L	.200	25	5	3	0	0	2	9	4	.412	.320	Spiers,Bill	L	.222	117	26	1	0	2	12	13	16	.305	.282
Bats Right	R	.148	54	8	0	0	1	3	4	10	.246	.204	Bats Left	R	.306	297	91	12	6	6	42	21	39	.350	.448
Scruggs,Tony	L	.000	5	0	0	0	0	0	0	1	.000	.000	Sprague,Ed	L	.267	90	24	3	0	3	11	10	24	.347	.400
Bats Right	R	.000	1	0	0	0	0	0	0	0	.000	.000	Bats Right	R	.286	70	20	4	0	1	9	9	19	.378	.386
Segui,David	L	.337	98	33	4	0	1	12	4	8	.363	.408	Stanley,Mike	L	.277	94	26	8	1	3	15	21	21	.405	.479
Bats Both	R	.228	114	26	3	0	1	10	8	11	.276	.281	Bats Right	R	.218	87	19	5	0	0	10	13	23	.333	.276
Seitzer,Kevin	L	.333	66	22	3	0	1	7	11	3	.429	.424	Steinbach,T	L	.266	139	37	11	0	3	15	7	17	.302	.410
Bats Right	R	.238	168	40	8	3	0	18	18	18	.317	.321	Bats Right	R	.278	317	88	20	1	3	52	15	53	.316	.375
Servais,Scott	L	.143	7	1	0	0	0	1	1	2	.250	.143	Stephens,Ray	L	.167	6	1	0	0	0	0	0	3	.167	.167
Bats Right	R	.167	30	5	3	0	0	5	3	6	.242	.267	Bats Right	R	1.000	1	1	0	0	0	0	1	0	1.000	1.000
Sharperson,M	L	.323	158	51	10	2	2	15	18	19	.392	.449	Stephenson,P	L	.000	0	0	0	0	0	0	0	0	.000	.000
Bats Right	R	.155	58	9	1	0	0	5	7	5	.258	.172	Bats Left	R	.286	7	2	0	0	0	0	2	3	.444	.286
Sheffield,G	L	.140	43	6	2	1	0	4	7	2	.264	.233	Stevens,Lee	L	.294	17	5	1	0	0	5	0	3	.294	.353
Bats Right	R	.212	132	28	10	1	2	18	12	13	.282	.348	Bats Left	R	.293	41	12	6	0	0	4	6	9	.375	.439
Shelby,John	L	.175	63	11	5	0	2	4	3	9	.212	.349	Stillwell,K	L	.266	109	29	6	1	1	15	6	17	.304	.367
Bats Both	R	.138	80	11	3	1	1	4	5	14	.198	.238	Bats Both	R	.264	276	73	11	0	5	36	27	39	.328	.359
Sheridan,Pat	L	.200	15	3	0	0	0	1	0	6	.200	.200	Strange,Doug	L	.400	5	2	0	0	0	0	0	0	.400	.400
Bats Left	R	.204	98	20	3	0	4	6	13	24	.297	.357	Bats Both	R	.500	4	2	1	0	0	1	0	1	.500	.750
Shipley,Craig	L	.318	44	14	2	0	1	2	2	8	.348	.432	Strawberry,D	L	.276	228	63	9	2	11	43	34	59	.370	.478
Bats Right	R	.234	47	11	1	0	0	4	0	6	.250	.255	Bats Left	R	.256	277	71	13	2	17	56	41	66	.353	.502
Shumpert,T	L	.207	135	28	6	0	2	12	9	25	.277	.296	Stubbs,F	L	.218	87	19	7	0	2	10	1	19	.236	.368
Bats Right	R	.222	234	52	10	4	3	22	21	50	.286	.338	Bats Left	R	.211	275	58	9	2	9	28	34	52	.295	.356
Sierra,Ruben	L	.335	188	63	15	2	7	32	20	22	.393	.548	Surhoff,B.J.	L	.255	102	26	2	1	0	11	6	12	.291	.294
Bats Both	R	.296	473	140	29	3	18	84	36	69	.342	.484	Bats Left	R	.298	403	120	17	3	5	57	20	21	.326	.392
Simms,Mike	L	.212	52	11	3	0	2	9	10	19	.333	.385	Sutko,Glenn	L	.250	4	1	0	0	0	1	1	2	.400	.250
Bats Right	R	.197	71	14	2	0	1	7	8	19	.275	.268	Bats Right	R	.000	6	0	0	0	0	0	1	4	.143	.000
Sinatro,Matt	L	.000	3	0	0	0	0	0	0	1	.000	.000	Sveum,Dale	L	.246	118	29	6	1	2	16	15	35	.331	.364
Bats Right	R	.400	5	2	0	0	0	1	1	0	.500	.400	Bats Both	R	.236	148	35	13	0	2	27	17	43	.312	.365
Skinner,Joel	L	.307	88	27	3	0	0	7	2	19	.319	.341	Tabler,Pat	L	.190	147	28	5	1	0	15	19	10	.275	.238
Bats Right	R	.214	196	42	11	0	1	17	12	48	.262	.286	Bats Right	R	.316	38	12	0	0	1	6	10	11	.469	.395
Slaught,Don	L	.262	126	33	10	0	0	11	14	20	.345	.341	Tackett,Jeff	L	.333	3	1	0	0	0	0	1	0	.500	.333
Bats Right	R	.340	94	32	7	1	1	18	7	12	.388	.468	Bats Right	R	.000	5	0	0	0	0	0	1	2	.167	.000
Smith,Dwight	L	.000	5	0	0	0	0	0	1	2	.167	.000	Tartabull,D	L	.296	142	42	9	1	8	22	27	31	.408	.542
Bats Left	R	.235	162	38	7	2	3	21	10	30	.283	.358	Bats Right	R	.325	342	111	26	2	23	78	38	90	.392	.614

Batters vs. Left-Handed and Right-Handed Pitchers

Batter	vs	Avg	AB	H	2B	3B	HR	BI	BB	SO	OBP	SLG
Taubensee,E	L	.400	10	4	0	0	0	0	1	2	.455	.400
Bats Left	R	.214	56	12	2	1	0	8	4	14	.258	.286
Templeton,G	L	.344	96	33	4	2	1	13	6	10	.379	.458
Bats Both	R	.156	180	28	6	0	2	13	4	28	.172	.222
Tettleton,M	L	.248	109	27	4	0	9	25	17	32	.349	.532
Bats Both	R	.268	392	105	13	2	22	64	84	99	.397	.480
Teufel,Tim	L	.271	133	36	8	0	7	27	23	23	.376	.489
Bats Right	R	.183	208	38	8	0	5	17	28	54	.282	.293
Thomas,Frank	L	.376	170	64	9	0	11	35	42	27	.500	.624
Bats Right	R	.293	389	114	22	2	21	74	96	85	.432	.522
Thome,Jim	L	.050	20	1	0	0	0	0	0	5	.050	.050
Bats Left	R	.308	78	24	4	2	1	9	5	11	.357	.449
Thompson,Milt	L	.216	74	16	3	0	1	6	3	17	.247	.297
Bats Left	R	.333	252	84	13	5	5	28	29	36	.401	.484
Thompson,R	L	.281	135	38	8	1	7	16	20	26	.378	.511
Bats Right	R	.255	357	91	16	4	12	32	43	69	.342	.423
Thon,Dickie	L	.259	205	53	7	2	2	14	14	23	.306	.341
Bats Right	R	.249	334	83	11	2	7	30	11	61	.269	.356
Thurman,Gary	L	.267	120	32	7	0	1	9	6	23	.302	.350
Bats Right	R	.297	64	19	2	0	1	4	5	19	.352	.375
Tingley,Ron	L	.212	33	7	2	0	0	3	1	7	.235	.273
Bats Right	R	.195	82	16	5	0	1	10	7	27	.267	.293
Tolentino,J	L	.500	6	3	2	0	0	1	1	0	.571	.833
Bats Left	R	.229	48	11	2	0	1	5	3	9	.269	.333
Torve,Kelvin	L	.000	0	0	0	0	0	0	0	0	.000	.000
Bats Left	R	.000	8	0	0	0	0	0	0	1	.000	.000
Trammell,Alan	L	.212	113	24	6	0	4	17	8	10	.268	.372
Bats Right	R	.263	262	69	14	0	5	38	29	29	.341	.374
Treadway,Jeff	L	.250	20	5	0	0	0	0	0	2	.250	.250
Bats Left	R	.325	286	93	17	2	3	32	23	17	.376	.430
Turner,Shane	L	.000	0	0	0	0	0	0	0	0	.000	.000
Bats Left	R	.000	1	0	0	0	0	0	0	0	.000	.000
Uribe,Jose	L	.250	60	15	2	1	0	3	7	8	.328	.317
Bats Both	R	.211	171	36	6	3	1	9	13	25	.266	.298
Valle,Dave	L	.232	112	26	1	0	6	17	10	14	.320	.402
Bats Right	R	.175	212	37	7	1	2	15	24	35	.269	.245
Van Slyke,A	L	.195	185	36	9	2	4	23	23	40	.287	.330
Bats Left	R	.307	306	94	15	5	13	60	48	45	.396	.516
VanderWal,J	L	.063	16	1	0	0	0	1	0	8	.059	.063
Bats Left	R	.267	45	12	4	1	1	7	1	10	.283	.467
Varsho,Gary	L	.200	5	1	0	0	0	0	0	1	.333	.200
Bats Left	R	.275	182	50	11	2	4	23	19	33	.345	.423
Vatcher,Jim	L	.273	11	3	0	0	0	1	1	3	.333	.273
Bats Right	R	.111	9	1	0	0	0	1	3	3	.333	.111
Vaughn,Greg	L	.227	154	35	6	1	5	22	19	35	.307	.377
Bats Right	R	.250	388	97	18	4	22	76	43	90	.323	.487
Vaughn,Mo	L	.212	33	7	2	0	0	7	2	8	.257	.273
Bats Left	R	.269	186	50	10	0	4	25	24	35	.352	.387
Velarde,Randy	L	.253	75	19	4	0	0	3	10	17	.349	.307
Bats Right	R	.239	109	26	7	1	1	12	8	26	.303	.349

Batter	vs	Avg	AB	H	2B	3B	HR	BI	BB	SO	OBP	SLG
Venable,Max	L	.211	19	4	0	0	0	0	1	5	.286	.211
Bats Left	R	.250	168	42	8	2	3	21	10	25	.293	.375
Ventura,Robin	L	.260	192	50	6	0	5	20	31	29	.364	.370
Bats Left	R	.295	414	122	19	1	18	80	49	38	.369	.476
Villanueva,H	L	.280	100	28	5	1	6	16	17	16	.385	.530
Bats Right	R	.272	92	25	5	0	7	16	4	14	.299	.554
Vizcaino,Jose	L	.216	37	8	0	0	0	2	1	5	.231	.216
Bats Both	R	.278	108	30	5	0	0	8	4	13	.301	.324
Vizquel,Omar	L	.230	87	20	4	0	0	11	7	5	.284	.276
Bats Both	R	.230	339	78	12	4	1	30	38	32	.306	.298
Wakamatsu,Don	L	.313	16	5	0	0	0	0	0	2	.313	.313
Bats Right	R	.133	15	2	0	0	0	0	1	4	.188	.133
Walker,Chico	L	.210	119	25	2	1	3	12	8	17	.256	.319
Bats Both	R	.278	255	71	8	0	3	22	25	40	.342	.345
Walker,Larry	L	.288	160	46	9	0	4	25	13	39	.352	.419
Bats Left	R	.291	327	95	21	2	12	39	29	63	.348	.477
Wallach,Tim	L	.222	185	41	8	0	5	21	18	29	.293	.346
Bats Right	R	.227	392	89	14	1	8	52	32	71	.292	.329
Walling,Denny	L	.000	6	0	0	0	0	0	0	1	.000	.000
Bats Left	R	.105	38	4	1	0	0	2	3	7	.209	.132
Walton,Jerome	L	.195	128	25	6	0	0	6	10	23	.261	.242
Bats Right	R	.239	142	34	7	1	5	11	9	32	.288	.408
Ward,Kevin	L	.294	68	20	7	2	2	7	5	17	.351	.544
Bats Right	R	.154	39	6	0	0	0	1	4	10	.233	.154
Ward,Turner	L	.250	32	8	2	0	0	3	5	4	.351	.313
Bats Both	R	.235	81	19	5	0	0	4	6	14	.287	.296
Webster,Lenny	L	.400	10	4	0	0	0	2	2	1	.462	.400
Bats Right	R	.250	24	6	1	0	3	6	4	9	.357	.667
Webster,Mitch	L	.240	104	25	2	3	2	12	11	27	.313	.375
Bats Both	R	.172	99	17	6	2	0	7	10	34	.248	.273
Wedge,Eric	L	.000	0	0	0	0	0	0	0	0	.000	.000
Bats Right	R	1.000	1	1	0	0	0	0	0	0	1.000	1.000
Wehner,John	L	.346	52	18	3	0	0	1	2	7	.370	.404
Bats Right	R	.333	54	18	4	0	0	6	5	10	.390	.407
Weiss,Walt	L	.194	31	6	2	0	0	1	1	0	.219	.258
Bats Both	R	.235	102	24	4	1	0	12	11	14	.304	.294
Whitaker,Lou	L	.247	97	24	3	0	2	14	15	15	.354	.340
Bats Left	R	.287	373	107	23	2	21	64	75	30	.400	.528
White,Devon	L	.302	199	60	15	2	8	20	16	32	.350	.518
Bats Both	R	.273	443	121	25	8	9	40	39	103	.339	.427
Whiten,Mark	L	.257	109	28	7	2	2	10	9	26	.311	.413
Bats Both	R	.238	298	71	11	5	7	35	21	59	.291	.379
Whitt,Ernie	L	.200	5	1	0	0	0	0	0	1	.200	.200
Bats Left	R	.246	57	14	2	0	0	3	8	11	.338	.281
Wilkerson,C	L	.224	49	11	4	0	0	5	5	6	.286	.306
Bats Both	R	.176	142	25	5	1	2	13	10	34	.227	.268
Wilkins,Rick	L	.237	38	9	1	0	1	5	3	14	.326	.342
Bats Left	R	.218	165	36	8	0	5	17	16	42	.303	.358
Willard,Jerry	L	.000	0	0	0	0	0	0	0	0	.000	.000
Bats Left	R	.214	14	3	0	0	1	4	2	5	.313	.429

Batters vs. Left-Handed and Right-Handed Pitchers

Batter	vs	Avg	AB	H	2B	3B	HR	BI	BB	SO	OBP	SLG
Williams,B	L	.202	104	21	6	0	2	13	17	11	.309	.317
Bats Both	R	.255	216	55	13	4	1	21	31	46	.349	.366
Williams,Ken	L	.267	75	20	5	2	1	4	4	19	.309	.427
Bats Right	R	.208	24	5	2	0	0	0	3	8	.321	.292
Williams,M	L	.279	165	46	8	0	7	25	9	34	.315	.455
Bats Right	R	.264	424	112	16	5	27	73	24	94	.309	.517
Wilson,Craig	L	.231	52	12	2	0	0	10	4	8	.276	.269
Bats Right	R	.067	30	2	0	0	0	3	2	2	.125	.067
Wilson,Mookie	L	.209	43	9	2	0	0	1	0	8	.209	.256
Bats Both	R	.247	198	49	10	4	2	27	8	27	.291	.369
Wilson,Willie	L	.253	99	25	4	0	0	6	6	13	.302	.293
Bats Both	R	.231	195	45	10	4	0	22	12	30	.284	.323
Winfield,Dave	L	.300	160	48	9	1	11	27	20	24	.381	.575
Bats Right	R	.248	408	101	18	3	17	59	36	85	.304	.431
Winningham,H	L	.154	13	2	0	0	0	0	1	2	.214	.154
Bats Left	R	.231	156	36	6	1	1	4	10	38	.277	.301
Witmeyer,Ron	L	.000	1	0	0	0	0	0	0	0	.000	.000
Bats Left	R	.056	18	1	0	0	0	0	0	5	.056	.056
Wood,Ted	L	.333	3	1	0	0	0	0	0	0	.333	.333
Bats Left	R	.091	22	2	0	0	0	1	2	11	.167	.091
Worthington,C	L	.258	31	8	2	0	1	4	4	3	.343	.419
Bats Right	R	.211	71	15	1	0	3	8	8	11	.300	.352
Yelding,Eric	L	.299	97	29	3	1	0	5	6	15	.337	.351
Bats Right	R	.212	179	38	8	0	1	15	7	31	.242	.274
Young,Gerald	L	.244	78	19	2	1	1	4	10	8	.326	.333
Bats Both	R	.188	64	12	1	0	0	7	14	9	.329	.203
Yount,Robin	L	.256	129	33	5	0	2	18	26	16	.377	.341
Bats Right	R	.262	374	98	15	4	8	59	28	63	.314	.388
Zeile,Todd	L	.304	237	72	15	1	5	33	26	44	.375	.439
Bats Right	R	.262	328	86	21	2	6	48	36	50	.337	.393
Zosky,Eddie	L	.167	6	1	1	0	0	0	0	2	.167	.333
Bats Right	R	.143	21	3	0	1	0	2	0	6	.143	.238
Zupcic,Bob	L	.182	11	2	0	0	0	2	1	1	.250	.182
Bats Right	R	.143	14	2	0	0	1	1	0	5	.143	.357
Zuvella,Paul	L	.000	0	0	0	0	0	0	0	0	.000	.000
Bats Right	R	.000	0	0	0	0	0	0	0	0	.000	.000

Pitchers vs. Left-Handed and Right-Handed Batters

Pitcher	vs	Avg	AB	H	2B	3B	HR	BI	BB	SO	OBP	SLG
Abbott,Jim	L	.303	142	43	9	0	3	18	9	25	.348	.430
Throws Left	R	.233	768	179	26	3	11	57	64	133	.293	.318
Abbott,Kyle	L	.308	13	4	0	0	0	2	2	3	.400	.308
Throws Left	R	.300	60	18	4	0	2	7	11	9	.417	.467
Abbott,Paul	L	.186	59	11	1	0	3	12	19	15	.375	.356
Throws Right	R	.257	105	27	9	1	2	14	17	28	.358	.419
Acker,Jim	L	.294	126	37	6	0	5	18	17	10	.372	.460
Throws Right	R	.202	198	40	4	1	11	39	19	34	.275	.399
Agosto,Juan	L	.271	96	26	6	2	0	14	14	12	.393	.375
Throws Left	R	.300	220	66	11	2	4	42	25	22	.373	.423
Aguilera,Rick	L	.184	136	25	4	1	2	14	19	36	.285	.272
Throws Right	R	.183	104	19	5	1	1	13	11	25	.259	.279
Akerfelds,D	L	.233	90	21	4	1	1	11	14	13	.349	.333
Throws Right	R	.277	101	28	1	1	4	17	13	18	.360	.426
Aldred,Scott	L	.242	33	8	1	0	1	3	6	2	.359	.364
Throws Left	R	.270	185	50	5	1	8	26	24	33	.351	.438
Alexander,G	L	.226	164	37	2	2	5	22	24	18	.321	.354
Throws Right	R	.315	178	56	13	1	6	32	24	32	.403	.500
Allison,Dana	L	.421	19	8	2	0	0	4	1	0	.429	.526
Throws Left	R	.348	23	8	0	1	0	5	4	4	.444	.435
Alvarez,W	L	.222	18	4	0	0	0	0	1	3	.263	.222
Throws Left	R	.231	186	43	7	1	9	18	28	29	.330	.425
Andersen,L	L	.281	89	25	4	0	0	10	9	13	.340	.326
Throws Right	R	.179	78	14	1	0	0	6	4	27	.220	.192
Anderson,A	L	.225	111	25	4	0	2	9	6	5	.265	.315
Throws Left	R	.296	416	123	22	2	22	65	36	46	.354	.517
Appier,Kevin	L	.268	403	108	25	1	8	41	37	61	.327	.395
Throws Right	R	.243	399	97	16	0	5	38	24	97	.288	.321
Aquino,Luis	L	.263	289	76	16	4	2	32	26	42	.318	.367
Throws Right	R	.244	312	76	17	1	8	35	21	38	.299	.381
Armstrong,J	L	.279	297	83	13	4	13	48	35	35	.355	.481
Throws Right	R	.309	243	75	11	0	12	36	19	58	.352	.502
Arnsberg,Brad	L	.200	10	2	0	0	1	2	1	2	.273	.500
Throws Right	R	.276	29	8	0	0	4	7	4	6	.364	.690
Ashby,Andy	L	.247	93	23	2	2	3	14	10	15	.317	.409
Throws Right	R	.269	67	18	7	0	2	11	9	11	.370	.463
Assenmacher,P	L	.179	134	24	6	1	1	14	10	49	.247	.261
Throws Left	R	.247	247	61	7	3	9	33	21	68	.304	.409
August,Don	L	.318	302	96	12	3	10	50	27	20	.375	.477
Throws Right	R	.281	249	70	10	0	8	29	20	42	.336	.418
Austin,Jim	L	.231	13	3	0	0	0	4	8	1	.583	.231
Throws Right	R	.313	16	5	2	0	1	3	3	2	.400	.625
Avery,Steve	L	.183	164	30	4	2	3	10	12	33	.237	.287
Throws Left	R	.255	624	159	29	2	18	70	53	104	.315	.394
Bailes,Scott	L	.247	77	19	4	0	3	16	6	13	.318	.416
Throws Left	R	.198	111	22	3	1	2	9	16	28	.305	.297
Ballard,Jeff	L	.182	88	16	4	1	1	9	6	13	.232	.284
Throws Left	R	.328	418	137	29	3	15	72	22	24	.363	.519
Bankhead,S	L	.313	112	35	10	0	2	17	9	11	.366	.455
Throws Right	R	.284	134	38	6	1	6	18	12	17	.345	.478
Banks,Willie	L	.313	32	10	1	0	0	7	2	7	.353	.344
Throws Right	R	.268	41	11	1	0	1	4	10	9	.412	.366
Bannister,F	L	.258	31	8	1	0	2	4	4	5	.343	.484
Throws Left	R	.270	63	17	2	2	3	8	6	11	.333	.508
Barfield,John	L	.269	52	14	4	0	0	7	1	5	.273	.346
Throws Left	R	.293	280	82	15	3	11	36	21	22	.340	.486
Barnes,Brian	L	.240	104	25	5	2	3	13	22	19	.380	.413
Throws Left	R	.231	476	110	19	2	13	57	62	98	.322	.361
Bautista,Jose	L	.400	15	6	2	0	0	5	3	3	.500	.533
Throws Right	R	.538	13	7	3	0	1	6	2	0	.625	1.000
Beasley,C	L	.275	40	11	4	0	2	8	4	5	.341	.525
Throws Right	R	.246	61	15	1	0	0	7	6	9	.319	.262
Beatty,Blaine	L	.500	10	5	1	0	0	1	2	2	.538	.600
Throws Left	R	.154	26	4	2	0	0	3	2	5	.214	.231
Beck,Rod	L	.292	89	26	6	1	4	10	6	19	.337	.517
Throws Right	R	.257	105	27	5	1	0	16	7	19	.304	.324
Bedrosian,S	L	.260	123	32	8	1	4	17	22	20	.365	.439
Throws Right	R	.230	165	38	8	0	7	23	13	24	.297	.406
Belcher,Tim	L	.274	445	122	16	1	4	33	46	82	.343	.342
Throws Right	R	.195	344	67	10	2	6	33	29	74	.258	.288
Belinda,Stan	L	.203	123	25	3	0	4	12	14	25	.298	.325
Throws Right	R	.168	149	25	2	2	6	26	21	46	.272	.329
Bell,Eric	L	.045	22	1	0	0	0	0	2	4	.125	.045
Throws Left	R	.121	33	4	0	0	0	0	3	3	.216	.121
Benes,Andy	L	.230	466	107	11	4	13	38	32	93	.281	.354
Throws Right	R	.235	370	87	13	2	10	32	27	74	.289	.362
Berenguer,J	L	.198	106	21	3	0	1	2	15	22	.303	.255
Throws Right	R	.180	122	22	4	2	4	14	5	31	.221	.344
Bielecki,Mike	L	.275	345	95	16	3	10	42	36	37	.343	.426
Throws Right	R	.247	308	76	15	6	8	41	20	38	.292	.412
Bitker,Joe	L	.333	27	9	3	0	3	8	2	6	.379	.778
Throws Right	R	.229	35	8	1	0	1	3	6	10	.341	.343
Black,Bud	L	.274	175	48	5	0	6	27	15	20	.326	.406
Throws Left	R	.245	625	153	26	5	19	65	56	84	.309	.394
Blair,Willie	L	.392	74	29	6	0	3	11	4	7	.430	.595
Throws Right	R	.363	80	29	2	0	4	16	6	6	.398	.538
Boddicker,M	L	.301	355	107	29	5	7	43	29	22	.365	.470
Throws Right	R	.240	337	81	12	2	6	37	30	57	.314	.341
Boever,Joe	L	.257	171	44	7	1	4	25	30	41	.361	.380
Throws Right	R	.234	197	46	8	2	6	26	24	48	.314	.386
Bohanon,Brian	L	.265	34	9	2	0	0	5	1	2	.286	.324
Throws Left	R	.275	207	57	11	0	4	27	22	32	.343	.386
Bolton,Tom	L	.247	81	20	6	0	2	10	5	11	.295	.395
Throws Left	R	.322	360	116	16	4	14	50	46	53	.396	.506
Bones,Ricky	L	.267	116	31	3	0	2	19	11	13	.323	.345
Throws Right	R	.271	96	26	4	1	1	11	7	18	.317	.365
Bosio,Chris	L	.251	418	105	16	3	6	39	30	53	.303	.347
Throws Right	R	.236	348	82	12	1	9	33	28	64	.300	.353
Boskie,Shawn	L	.320	291	93	18	6	10	43	36	27	.393	.526
Throws Right	R	.259	220	57	11	0	4	22	16	35	.315	.364

Pitchers vs. Left-Handed and Right-Handed Batters

Pitcher	vs	Avg	AB	H	2B	3B	HR	BI	BB	SO	OBP	SLG	Pitcher	vs	Avg	AB	H	2B	3B	HR	BI	BB	SO	OBP	SLG
Boucher,Denis	L	.344	32	11	3	0	1	1	3	1	.400	.531	Casian,Larry	L	.138	29	4	2	0	0	2	0	5	.138	.207
Throws Left	R	.303	208	63	18	1	11	34	21	28	.371	.558	Throws Left	R	.480	50	24	7	0	4	12	7	1	.552	.860
Bowen,Ryan	L	.288	160	46	9	0	2	25	22	30	.365	.381	Castillo,F	L	.282	273	77	11	2	5	28	27	49	.344	.392
Throws Right	R	.241	112	27	4	0	2	9	14	19	.336	.330	Throws Right	R	.197	152	30	12	0	0	16	6	24	.226	.276
Boyd,Oil Can	L	.264	367	97	25	4	5	30	32	56	.322	.395	Castillo,Tony	L	.176	34	6	2	0	1	3	0	9	.171	.324
Throws Right	R	.290	341	99	19	3	16	52	25	59	.337	.504	Throws Left	R	.340	100	34	3	0	3	12	11	9	.405	.460
Brantley,C	L	.216	74	16	1	0	0	4	14	14	.337	.230	Cerutti,John	L	.188	69	13	2	1	2	16	9	8	.275	.333
Throws Right	R	.250	40	10	3	1	0	7	5	11	.347	.375	Throws Left	R	.299	271	81	9	3	7	44	28	21	.368	.432
Brantley,Jeff	L	.205	185	38	6	0	3	16	36	42	.338	.286	Chapin,Darrin	L	.071	14	1	0	0	0	0	0	4	.071	.071
Throws Right	R	.248	161	40	7	1	5	20	16	39	.324	.398	Throws Right	R	.400	5	2	2	0	0	2	6	1	.727	.800
Briscoe,John	L	.222	18	4	1	0	0	3	5	3	.391	.278	Charlton,Norm	L	.253	87	22	4	0	0	16	11	19	.359	.299
Throws Right	R	.242	33	8	2	0	3	11	5	6	.333	.576	Throws Left	R	.231	303	70	9	4	6	30	23	58	.290	.347
Bross,Terry	L	.125	16	2	0	0	0	0	1	3	.176	.125	Chiamparino,S	L	.387	31	12	0	1	0	2	6	2	.486	.452
Throws Right	R	.263	19	5	1	0	1	2	2	2	.333	.474	Throws Right	R	.246	57	14	2	0	1	7	6	6	.317	.333
Brown,Keith	L	.227	22	5	0	0	0	1	5	2	.370	.227	Chitren,Steve	L	.292	96	28	4	1	4	18	15	16	.400	.479
Throws Right	R	.370	27	10	3	1	0	6	1	2	.393	.556	Throws Right	R	.233	133	31	6	2	4	25	17	31	.322	.398
Brown,Kevin	L	.273	410	112	22	2	8	52	47	51	.349	.395	Christopher,M	L	.000	6	0	0	0	0	0	1	1	.143	.000
Throws Right	R	.294	411	121	18	2	9	48	43	45	.375	.414	Throws Right	R	.333	6	2	1	0	0	0	2	1	.500	.500
Brown,Kevin D.	L	.170	47	8	0	0	1	7	6	3	.264	.234	Clancy,Jim	L	.224	147	33	11	2	2	21	17	22	.305	.367
Throws Left	R	.294	197	58	16	1	5	26	28	27	.383	.462	Throws Right	R	.222	180	40	6	2	6	18	17	28	.286	.378
Browning,Tom	L	.203	212	43	14	2	4	22	19	41	.269	.344	Clark,Mark	L	.227	44	10	1	0	2	5	7	9	.327	.386
Throws Left	R	.285	694	198	26	3	28	92	37	74	.321	.452	Throws Right	R	.200	35	7	1	0	1	4	4	4	.268	.314
Burba,Dave	L	.288	59	17	3	0	2	4	8	5	.373	.441	Clemens,Roger	L	.218	563	123	26	6	3	45	47	121	.279	.302
Throws Right	R	.213	80	17	4	2	4	11	6	11	.267	.463	Throws Right	R	.223	430	96	20	2	12	37	18	120	.258	.363
Burke,Tim	L	.297	192	57	13	2	2	26	15	20	.346	.417	Clements,Pat	L	.174	23	4	2	0	0	4	2	6	.240	.261
Throws Right	R	.202	193	39	3	1	6	15	11	39	.257	.321	Throws Left	R	.321	28	9	1	0	0	6	7	2	.421	.357
Burkett,John	L	.293	467	137	25	1	14	62	39	72	.347	.441	Combs,Pat	L	.209	43	9	1	0	1	3	10	7	.382	.302
Throws Right	R	.255	337	86	6	1	5	39	21	59	.312	.323	Throws Left	R	.263	209	55	12	0	6	27	33	34	.361	.407
Burns,Todd	L	.083	24	2	1	0	0	0	2	2	.154	.125	Comstock,K	L	1.000	1	1	1	0	0	0	0	0	1.000	2.000
Throws Right	R	.364	22	8	2	0	2	11	6	1	.467	.727	Throws Right	R	.500	2	1	0	0	0	1	1	0	.667	.500
Cadaret,Greg	L	.246	118	29	7	0	0	11	12	25	.313	.305	Cone,David	L	.248	545	135	20	6	7	47	50	123	.311	.345
Throws Left	R	.246	329	81	14	4	8	43	47	80	.342	.386	Throws Right	R	.214	323	69	9	1	6	31	23	118	.270	.303
Campbell,K	L	.129	31	4	1	0	1	2	9	5	.325	.258	Cook,Dennis	L	.160	25	4	1	0	0	3	2	5	.214	.200
Throws Right	R	.191	47	9	2	0	3	8	5	11	.283	.426	Throws Left	R	.235	34	8	2	0	0	3	5	3	.325	.294
Candelaria,J	L	.138	58	8	1	0	1	4	5	25	.206	.207	Corbin,Archie	L	.250	4	1	0	0	0	0	1	0	.400	.250
Throws Left	R	.354	65	23	8	1	2	14	6	13	.392	.600	Throws Right	R	.333	6	2	0	0	0	1	1	1	.429	.333
Candiotti,Tom	L	.243	449	109	16	8	6	40	35	63	.295	.354	Cormier,Rheal	L	.146	48	7	0	0	0	2	1	10	.163	.146
Throws Right	R	.212	438	93	25	2	6	27	38	104	.280	.320	Throws Left	R	.306	219	67	16	1	5	25	7	28	.329	.457
Capel,Mike	L	.278	72	20	5	0	2	15	12	11	.376	.431	Corsi,Jim	L	.288	153	44	5	1	5	18	15	25	.351	.431
Throws Right	R	.250	52	13	5	0	1	3	3	12	.291	.404	Throws Right	R	.227	141	32	4	0	1	16	8	28	.265	.277
Carman,Don	L	.300	50	15	3	0	1	8	5	7	.368	.420	Costello,John	L	.241	58	14	1	1	1	9	14	8	.378	.345
Throws Left	R	.278	90	25	5	0	7	15	14	8	.375	.567	Throws Right	R	.303	76	23	3	0	1	9	3	16	.329	.382
Carpenter,C	L	.228	123	28	13	0	0	13	14	21	.304	.333	Cox,Danny	L	.275	189	52	11	1	7	32	24	15	.350	.455
Throws Right	R	.212	118	25	4	0	6	17	6	26	.248	.398	Throws Right	R	.241	191	46	5	2	7	21	15	31	.295	.398
Carreno,A	L	.222	9	2	0	0	1	5	2	0	.364	.556	Crawford,S	L	.359	92	33	5	2	1	15	9	17	.416	.489
Throws Right	R	.500	6	3	1	1	0	3	1	2	.667	1.000	Throws Right	R	.267	101	27	3	2	2	14	9	21	.325	.396
Carter,Jeff	L	.158	19	3	1	0	1	2	3	1	.273	.368	Crews,Tim	L	.303	142	43	12	1	3	19	9	13	.340	.465
Throws Right	R	.200	25	5	2	0	0	4	2	1	.259	.280	Throws Right	R	.212	151	32	5	0	4	17	10	44	.261	.325
Cary,Chuck	L	.324	37	12	2	0	2	9	11	8	.479	.541	Crim,Chuck	L	.293	184	54	7	0	7	30	16	19	.355	.446
Throws Left	R	.277	177	49	11	1	4	23	21	26	.354	.418	Throws Right	R	.316	193	61	8	0	2	25	9	20	.347	.389

Pitchers vs. Left-Handed and Right-Handed Batters

Pitcher	vs	Avg	AB	H	2B	3B	HR	BI	BB	SO	OBP	SLG	Pitcher	vs	Avg	AB	H	2B	3B	HR	BI	BB	SO	OBP	SLG
Dalton,Mike	L	.286	14	4	0	1	1	2	1	2	.333	.643	Erickson,S	L	.295	417	123	26	2	8	38	45	40	.363	.424
Throws Left	R	.364	22	8	1	0	1	1	1	2	.391	.545	Throws Right	R	.191	345	66	13	3	5	34	26	68	.255	.290
Darling,Ron	L	.238	391	93	15	4	8	42	37	76	.303	.358	Fajardo,H	L	.298	47	14	3	1	0	3	6	11	.370	.404
Throws Right	R	.274	336	92	15	6	14	47	34	53	.351	.479	Throws Right	R	.368	57	21	3	0	2	7	5	12	.415	.526
Darwin,Danny	L	.245	139	34	12	0	3	12	10	24	.301	.396	Farr,Steve	L	.241	116	28	6	0	2	10	11	23	.333	.345
Throws Right	R	.282	131	37	5	1	12	21	5	18	.319	.611	Throws Right	R	.201	144	29	6	0	2	15	9	37	.248	.285
Davis,Mark	L	.304	56	17	2	0	0	6	8	11	.394	.339	Fassero,Jeff	L	.243	70	17	2	2	0	11	5	19	.293	.329
Throws Left	R	.220	173	38	9	1	6	30	31	36	.332	.387	Throws Left	R	.171	129	22	5	0	1	9	12	23	.246	.233
Davis,Storm	L	.335	227	76	13	3	6	45	26	30	.402	.498	Fernandez,A	L	.252	330	83	20	1	4	32	42	64	.331	.355
Throws Right	R	.277	231	64	8	0	5	28	20	23	.333	.377	Throws Right	R	.265	389	103	13	5	12	54	46	81	.342	.416
Dayley,Ken	L	.300	10	3	0	0	0	3	3	2	.467	.300	Fernandez,Sid	L	.371	35	13	0	0	1	3	1	9	.389	.457
Throws Left	R	.444	9	4	0	0	0	0	2	1	.545	.444	Throws Left	R	.181	127	23	3	1	3	13	8	22	.228	.291
de la Rosa,F	L	.500	8	4	1	0	0	0	0	0	.500	.625	Fetters,Mike	L	.273	88	24	2	0	1	13	12	11	.360	.330
Throws Right	R	.222	9	2	1	0	0	2	2	1	.333	.333	Throws Right	R	.337	86	29	5	0	3	14	16	13	.457	.500
DeJesus,Jose	L	.231	376	87	20	3	1	41	89	65	.377	.309	Finley,Chuck	L	.257	109	28	6	0	4	8	13	22	.336	.422
Throws Right	R	.215	279	60	12	1	6	23	39	53	.318	.330	Throws Left	R	.242	730	177	37	3	19	80	88	149	.329	.379
DeLeon,Jose	L	.252	326	82	18	3	9	25	43	44	.339	.408	Flanagan,Mike	L	.181	127	23	1	0	2	10	6	27	.221	.236
Throws Right	R	.224	277	62	11	2	6	21	18	74	.281	.343	Throws Right	R	.266	229	61	12	0	4	20	19	28	.327	.371
Delucia,Rich	L	.288	320	92	14	3	11	42	54	34	.386	.453	Fleming,Dave	L	.333	9	3	3	0	0	2	1	0	.455	.667
Throws Right	R	.235	358	84	21	0	20	54	24	64	.282	.461	Throws Left	R	.276	58	16	3	1	3	11	2	11	.323	.517
Deshaies,Jim	L	.279	104	29	6	1	4	19	19	18	.386	.471	Fossas,Tony	L	.190	84	16	3	0	2	13	8	15	.277	.298
Throws Left	R	.255	498	127	30	4	15	59	53	80	.324	.422	Throws Left	R	.266	124	33	7	0	1	18	20	14	.372	.347
Dibble,Rob	L	.197	173	34	5	1	2	14	14	75	.255	.272	Foster,Steve	L	.200	25	5	0	0	1	3	2	2	.259	.320
Throws Right	R	.258	128	33	4	2	3	20	11	49	.312	.391	Throws Right	R	.083	24	2	1	0	0	0	2	9	.154	.125
Dopson,John	L	.500	2	1	0	0	0	2	1	0	.500	.500	Franco,John	L	.340	53	18	2	1	0	6	4	7	.397	.415
Throws Right	R	.500	2	1	1	0	0	0	0	0	.500	1.000	Throws Left	R	.250	172	43	6	2	2	24	14	38	.306	.343
Downs,Kelly	L	.264	220	58	9	2	6	31	26	20	.341	.405	Fraser,Willie	L	.246	134	33	2	1	5	19	15	16	.329	.388
Throws Right	R	.210	195	41	7	0	6	26	27	42	.310	.338	Throws Right	R	.280	157	44	10	0	8	34	17	21	.361	.497
Drabek,Doug	L	.287	530	152	29	1	8	49	41	59	.337	.391	Freeman,M	L	.259	81	21	3	0	0	9	9	10	.333	.296
Throws Right	R	.255	364	93	12	4	8	30	21	83	.298	.376	Throws Right	R	.174	92	16	3	0	2	11	4	24	.222	.272
Drahman,Brian	L	.242	33	8	2	1	2	7	4	2	.316	.545	Frey,Steve	L	.268	56	15	2	0	1	11	7	15	.354	.357
Throws Right	R	.171	76	13	1	0	2	13	9	16	.259	.263	Throws Left	R	.289	97	28	3	0	2	12	16	6	.386	.381
Drees,Tom	L	.286	7	2	0	0	2	5	1	1	.333	1.143	Frohwirth,T	L	.223	130	29	8	2	0	16	18	26	.320	.315
Throws Left	R	.364	22	8	1	0	2	6	5	1	.481	.682	Throws Right	R	.169	207	35	6	1	2	20	11	51	.211	.237
Dressendorfer,K	L	.268	71	19	5	0	1	12	12	12	.373	.380	Gakeler,Dan	L	.302	116	35	5	1	2	14	19	17	.397	.414
Throws Right	R	.219	64	14	2	0	4	14	9	5	.311	.438	Throws Right	R	.225	169	38	7	0	3	27	20	26	.307	.320
Eckersley,D	L	.227	150	34	4	0	5	18	6	34	.261	.353	Garcia,Ramon	L	.274	135	37	8	0	4	16	19	18	.359	.422
Throws Right	R	.188	138	26	4	2	6	15	3	53	.206	.377	Throws Right	R	.264	159	42	6	0	9	22	12	22	.324	.472
Edens,Tom	L	.250	64	16	3	2	1	4	5	11	.304	.406	Gardiner,Mike	L	.259	247	64	12	1	4	23	22	39	.317	.364
Throws Right	R	.261	69	18	5	0	1	10	5	8	.311	.377	Throws Right	R	.288	264	76	14	1	14	41	25	52	.348	.508
Edwards,Wayne	L	.308	26	8	0	0	0	4	5	1	.419	.308	Gardner,Chris	L	.100	40	4	1	0	2	2	12	7	.308	.275
Throws Left	R	.237	59	14	4	0	2	10	12	11	.356	.407	Throws Right	R	.319	47	15	1	0	3	8	2	5	.347	.532
Egloff,Bruce	L	.273	11	3	1	0	0	1	1	5	.333	.364	Gardner,Mark	L	.228	381	87	13	2	10	41	51	61	.321	.352
Throws Right	R	.385	13	5	1	0	0	2	3	3	.500	.462	Throws Right	R	.233	223	52	8	0	7	27	24	46	.313	.363
Eichhorn,Mark	L	.262	126	33	8	1	2	13	4	15	.280	.389	Gardner,Wes	L	.386	44	17	2	2	1	8	10	3	.500	.591
Throws Right	R	.185	162	30	8	1	0	14	9	34	.236	.247	Throws Right	R	.224	67	15	0	0	0	5	4	9	.268	.224
Eiland,Dave	L	.270	148	40	9	3	3	15	10	7	.314	.432	Garrelts,S	L	.405	42	17	2	1	2	10	5	2	.458	.643
Throws Right	R	.336	140	47	11	2	7	34	13	11	.399	.593	Throws Right	R	.211	38	8	1	0	3	4	4	6	.286	.474
Eldred,Cal	L	.222	36	8	0	0	1	2	1	7	.243	.306	George,Chris	L	.429	14	6	3	0	0	2	0	1	.400	.643
Throws Right	R	.387	31	12	1	0	1	5	5	3	.472	.516	Throws Right	R	.200	10	2	0	0	0	0	0	1	.200	.200

Pitchers vs. Left-Handed and Right-Handed Batters

Pitcher	vs	Avg	AB	H	2B	3B	HR	BI	BB	SO	OBP	SLG	Pitcher	vs	Avg	AB	H	2B	3B	HR	BI	BB	SO	OBP	SLG
Gibson,Paul	L	.345	113	39	1	2	6	30	11	12	.405	.549	Hammaker,A	L	.250	4	1	0	0	0	0	0	0	.250	.250
Throws Left	R	.277	264	73	9	2	4	29	37	40	.368	.371	Throws Left	R	.389	18	7	1	0	0	4	3	1	.476	.444
Glavine,Tom	L	.294	170	50	8	2	4	18	17	37	.356	.435	Hammond,Chris	L	.184	98	18	2	1	1	11	13	14	.286	.255
Throws Left	R	.205	735	151	27	4	13	56	52	155	.258	.306	Throws Left	R	.274	270	74	15	1	3	31	35	36	.358	.370
Gleaton,J	L	.263	76	20	1	3	1	12	5	14	.301	.395	Haney,Chris	L	.183	60	11	2	1	0	6	14	12	.347	.250
Throws Left	R	.271	199	54	10	1	6	27	34	33	.374	.422	Throws Left	R	.301	276	83	18	1	6	35	29	39	.366	.438
Gooden,Dwight	L	.252	412	104	22	2	4	35	42	75	.321	.345	Hanson,Erik	L	.239	355	85	21	5	10	47	18	84	.275	.411
Throws Right	R	.262	309	81	11	4	8	38	14	75	.298	.401	Throws Right	R	.302	321	97	15	2	6	22	38	59	.374	.417
Gordon,Tom	L	.248	302	75	7	5	4	31	42	81	.340	.344	Harkey,Mike	L	.256	39	10	2	0	1	7	4	10	.326	.385
Throws Right	R	.191	283	54	9	3	12	32	45	86	.307	.371	Throws Right	R	.289	38	11	2	0	2	4	2	5	.317	.500
Gossage,Goose	L	.188	48	9	3	0	1	8	5	5	.264	.313	Harnisch,Pete	L	.234	457	107	16	4	10	35	55	88	.319	.352
Throws Right	R	.247	97	24	3	1	3	23	11	23	.342	.392	Throws Right	R	.183	339	62	12	1	4	28	28	84	.247	.260
Gott,Jim	L	.191	141	27	1	2	2	9	17	35	.278	.270	Harris,Gene	L	.227	22	5	3	0	0	2	7	3	.414	.364
Throws Right	R	.255	141	36	5	0	3	15	15	38	.329	.355	Throws Right	R	.303	33	10	1	0	1	2	3	3	.361	.424
Gozzo,Mauro	L	.357	14	5	3	0	0	4	3	2	.471	.571	Harris,Greg	L	.244	303	74	14	2	5	35	34	58	.322	.353
Throws Right	R	.667	6	4	2	0	0	2	4	1	.727	1.000	Throws Right	R	.243	342	83	16	2	8	40	35	69	.314	.371
Grahe,Joe	L	.301	143	43	13	1	1	20	15	22	.365	.427	Harris,Greg W.	L	.252	309	78	9	0	12	27	16	64	.288	.398
Throws Right	R	.275	149	41	7	2	1	21	18	18	.365	.369	Throws Right	R	.201	189	38	8	0	4	13	11	31	.248	.307
Grater,Mark	L	.333	9	3	0	0	0	0	1	0	.400	.333	Harris,Reggie	L	.500	4	2	0	0	0	2	1	0	.500	.500
Throws Right	R	.500	4	2	0	0	0	1	1	0	.600	.500	Throws Right	R	.429	7	3	1	0	0	1	2	2	.556	.571
Gray,Jeff	L	.200	95	19	5	0	2	12	2	15	.216	.316	Hartley,Mike	L	.239	159	38	4	2	5	18	25	24	.346	.384
Throws Right	R	.165	121	20	6	1	5	14	8	26	.221	.355	Throws Right	R	.235	153	36	6	0	6	26	22	39	.348	.392
Greene,Tommy	L	.256	453	116	23	4	12	52	45	82	.321	.404	Harvey,Bryan	L	.183	164	30	6	0	4	14	11	62	.233	.293
Throws Right	R	.194	315	61	12	0	7	30	21	72	.244	.298	Throws Right	R	.172	122	21	1	0	2	11	6	39	.215	.230
Grimsley,J	L	.262	130	34	6	1	2	11	29	29	.398	.369	Hawkins,Andy	L	.244	176	43	7	2	4	22	33	14	.363	.375
Throws Right	R	.215	93	20	6	1	2	12	12	13	.315	.366	Throws Right	R	.281	171	48	9	2	6	31	9	31	.330	.462
Gross,Kevin	L	.313	233	73	9	2	6	32	35	42	.400	.446	Heaton,Neal	L	.354	82	29	3	0	2	12	4	16	.382	.463
Throws Right	R	.234	214	50	4	0	4	16	15	53	.288	.308	Throws Left	R	.239	180	43	12	0	4	24	17	18	.313	.372
Gross,Kip	L	.304	184	56	3	0	6	26	24	22	.383	.418	Henke,Tom	L	.179	95	17	5	1	3	10	8	24	.243	.347
Throws Right	R	.248	149	37	9	1	2	15	16	18	.319	.362	Throws Right	R	.190	84	16	3	0	1	6	3	29	.218	.262
Gubicza,Mark	L	.326	258	84	14	3	3	36	28	43	.394	.438	Henneman,Mike	L	.268	127	34	9	0	0	11	23	17	.373	.339
Throws Right	R	.293	287	84	13	0	7	45	14	46	.330	.411	Throws Right	R	.251	187	47	8	2	2	24	11	44	.290	.348
Guetterman,L	L	.175	97	17	5	0	2	8	7	13	.250	.289	Henry,Doug	L	.133	60	8	6	0	0	3	8	14	.229	.233
Throws Left	R	.305	243	74	14	2	4	31	18	22	.348	.428	Throws Right	R	.133	60	8	0	0	1	4	6	14	.212	.183
Gullickson,B	L	.275	487	134	31	3	15	55	25	35	.312	.444	Henry,Dwayne	L	.226	133	30	5	1	4	23	25	30	.350	.368
Throws Right	R	.303	403	122	20	4	7	47	19	56	.333	.424	Throws Right	R	.210	100	21	5	0	3	16	14	21	.310	.350
Gunderson,E	L	.000	2	0	0	0	0	0	1	0	.333	.000	Hentgen,Pat	L	.333	6	2	0	0	1	2	1	0	.500	.833
Throws Left	R	.400	15	6	2	0	0	5	0	2	.400	.533	Throws Right	R	.167	18	3	2	0	0	0	2	3	.286	.278
Guthrie,Mark	L	.337	86	29	2	0	4	10	7	14	.383	.500	Heredia,Gil	L	.239	67	16	1	1	2	6	3	5	.271	.373
Throws Left	R	.293	297	87	17	5	7	36	34	58	.365	.455	Throws Right	R	.224	49	11	2	0	2	7	4	8	.278	.388
Guzman,Johnny	L	.500	6	3	1	0	0	3	0	1	.500	.667	Hernandez,J	L	.115	26	3	0	0	0	1	4	4	.233	.115
Throws Left	R	.500	16	8	3	0	0	2	2	2	.556	.688	Throws Right	R	.200	25	5	2	0	0	1	1	5	.231	.280
Guzman,Jose	L	.244	283	69	15	1	6	30	47	52	.353	.367	Hernandez,R	L	.212	33	7	1	0	1	7	4	5	.297	.333
Throws Right	R	.234	354	83	18	0	4	21	37	73	.310	.319	Throws Right	R	.379	29	11	3	0	0	5	3	1	.438	.483
Guzman,Juan	L	.193	238	46	6	1	1	15	36	49	.299	.239	Hernandez,X	L	.217	129	28	5	0	1	17	20	31	.322	.279
Throws Right	R	.201	259	52	7	1	5	30	30	74	.289	.293	Throws Right	R	.311	122	38	7	0	5	14	12	24	.370	.492
Haas,Dave	L	.143	7	1	0	0	0	1	2	0	.333	.143	Hershiser,O	L	.284	208	59	9	2	2	20	18	27	.345	.375
Throws Right	R	.269	26	7	1	0	1	7	10	6	.462	.423	Throws Right	R	.236	225	53	9	0	1	20	14	46	.289	.289
Habyan,John	L	.272	114	31	7	1	0	16	6	16	.306	.351	Hesketh,Joe	L	.241	87	21	7	0	2	9	12	18	.327	.391
Throws Right	R	.200	210	42	10	2	2	19	14	54	.257	.295	Throws Left	R	.252	481	121	25	5	17	44	41	86	.310	.430

Pitchers vs. Left-Handed and Right-Handed Batters

Pitcher	vs	Avg	AB	H	2B	3B	HR	BI	BB	SO	OBP	SLG
Hibbard,Greg	L	.250	120	30	2	0	5	19	4	10	.283	.392
Throws Left	R	.269	617	166	25	2	18	71	53	61	.326	.404
Hickerson,B	L	.234	47	11	1	0	0	2	4	10	.294	.255
Throws Left	R	.288	146	42	10	0	3	14	13	33	.346	.418
Hickey,Kevin	L	.321	28	9	1	2	2	9	2	7	.355	.714
Throws Left	R	.231	26	6	3	0	1	3	4	3	.323	.462
Higuera,Teddy	L	.219	32	7	2	0	0	3	1	11	.242	.281
Throws Left	R	.275	109	30	6	0	2	15	9	22	.333	.385
Hill,Ken	L	.237	367	87	8	3	8	36	37	62	.307	.341
Throws Right	R	.208	289	60	15	3	7	33	30	59	.288	.353
Hill,Milt	L	.254	63	16	4	0	0	6	6	11	.310	.317
Throws Right	R	.339	59	20	4	1	1	10	2	9	.355	.492
Hillegas,S	L	.225	142	32	6	0	1	14	20	34	.315	.289
Throws Right	R	.222	158	35	6	1	6	29	26	32	.332	.386
Holman,Brian	L	.284	391	111	21	2	6	42	46	48	.362	.394
Throws Right	R	.250	352	88	15	2	10	35	31	60	.322	.389
Holmes,Darren	L	.275	149	41	8	0	2	20	14	27	.339	.369
Throws Right	R	.314	156	49	7	1	4	29	13	32	.363	.449
Honeycutt,R	L	.204	54	11	3	0	1	4	8	11	.306	.315
Throws Left	R	.295	88	26	3	2	2	10	12	15	.388	.443
Horsman,Vince	L	.333	3	1	0	0	0	2	2	0	.600	.333
Throws Left	R	.111	9	1	0	0	0	0	1	2	.200	.111
Hough,Charlie	L	.237	355	84	11	7	8	45	44	48	.323	.375
Throws Right	R	.222	374	83	17	3	13	45	50	59	.317	.388
Howe,Steve	L	.128	47	6	1	0	0	2	1	13	.160	.149
Throws Left	R	.256	129	33	7	0	1	9	6	21	.299	.333
Howell,Jay	L	.175	97	17	6	1	1	11	7	21	.234	.289
Throws Right	R	.256	86	22	2	1	2	8	4	19	.289	.372
Huismann,Mark	L	.455	11	5	0	1	0	2	0	2	.455	.636
Throws Right	R	.167	12	2	1	0	0	4	2	3	.286	.250
Hunter,Jim	L	.378	74	28	5	0	0	13	11	8	.465	.446
Throws Right	R	.309	55	17	3	0	3	12	6	6	.400	.527
Hurst,Bruce	L	.176	136	24	3	0	1	10	13	31	.247	.221
Throws Left	R	.253	699	177	27	1	16	65	46	110	.301	.363
Ignasiak,Mike	L	.150	20	3	0	0	1	2	6	1	.346	.300
Throws Right	R	.174	23	4	0	1	1	4	2	9	.240	.391
Innis,Jeff	L	.250	124	31	5	1	1	15	10	17	.301	.331
Throws Right	R	.197	178	35	5	2	1	21	13	30	.247	.264
Irvine,Daryl	L	.273	33	9	4	1	0	6	5	6	.368	.455
Throws Right	R	.356	45	16	4	0	2	13	4	2	.431	.578
Jackson,Danny	L	.300	60	18	3	1	0	12	12	7	.417	.383
Throws Left	R	.311	228	71	12	0	8	37	36	24	.404	.469
Jackson,Mike	L	.252	119	30	6	2	2	12	17	23	.355	.387
Throws Right	R	.170	200	34	4	1	3	21	17	51	.249	.245
Jeffcoat,Mike	L	.289	121	35	3	3	2	15	7	17	.323	.413
Throws Left	R	.338	204	69	10	2	6	31	18	26	.399	.495
Johnson,Dave	L	.405	200	81	10	2	10	42	13	17	.439	.625
Throws Right	R	.280	164	46	10	0	8	26	11	21	.341	.488
Johnson,Jeff	L	.231	52	12	1	0	1	7	7	7	.344	.308
Throws Left	R	.313	460	144	20	5	14	70	26	55	.352	.470
Johnson,Randy	L	.212	85	18	2	0	2	14	15	25	.337	.306
Throws Left	R	.213	623	133	30	1	13	67	137	203	.361	.327
Johnston,Joel	L	.125	32	4	1	0	0	0	2	6	.176	.156
Throws Right	R	.116	43	5	0	0	0	1	7	15	.240	.116
Jones,Barry	L	.255	141	36	6	2	2	15	21	15	.348	.369
Throws Right	R	.238	168	40	4	0	6	29	12	31	.291	.369
Jones,Calvin	L	.164	67	11	2	0	0	4	14	17	.309	.194
Throws Right	R	.242	91	22	2	1	0	11	15	25	.355	.286
Jones,Doug	L	.341	132	45	11	1	4	25	9	20	.380	.530
Throws Right	R	.300	140	42	12	1	3	20	8	28	.336	.464
Jones,Jimmy	L	.302	348	105	13	4	6	40	37	57	.371	.414
Throws Right	R	.209	182	38	5	1	3	19	14	31	.268	.297
Jones,Stacy	L	.320	25	8	4	0	1	5	3	4	.393	.600
Throws Right	R	.167	18	3	2	0	0	3	2	6	.238	.278
Juden,Jeff	L	.222	36	8	0	0	2	4	3	8	.268	.389
Throws Right	R	.333	33	11	3	0	1	9	4	3	.395	.515
Kaiser,Jeff	L	.375	8	3	0	0	1	4	1	2	.444	.750
Throws Left	R	.231	13	3	1	0	0	1	4	2	.412	.308
Kamieniecki,S	L	.267	116	31	6	2	5	13	13	21	.341	.483
Throws Right	R	.242	95	23	6	1	3	10	9	13	.324	.421
Key,Jimmy	L	.286	112	32	2	0	2	9	6	19	.325	.357
Throws Left	R	.249	703	175	34	2	10	57	38	106	.288	.346
Kiecker,Dana	L	.311	74	23	1	0	1	11	12	6	.407	.365
Throws Right	R	.371	89	33	7	0	5	23	11	15	.447	.618
Kiely,John	L	.444	9	4	1	0	0	4	5	0	.643	.556
Throws Right	R	.450	20	9	3	0	0	5	4	1	.538	.600
Kile,Darryl	L	.262	343	90	20	3	7	36	56	64	.365	.399
Throws Right	R	.223	242	54	8	2	9	34	28	36	.314	.384
Kilgus,Paul	L	.232	82	19	6	0	1	16	7	12	.301	.341
Throws Left	R	.270	152	41	7	0	7	23	17	20	.343	.454
King,Eric	L	.285	326	93	12	4	5	44	26	33	.334	.393
Throws Right	R	.272	268	73	21	0	2	28	18	26	.321	.373
Kipper,Bob	L	.321	78	25	2	0	4	15	3	19	.341	.500
Throws Left	R	.255	161	41	10	2	3	17	19	19	.331	.398
Kiser,Garland	L	.308	13	4	0	0	0	3	2	3	.438	.308
Throws Left	R	.500	6	3	0	0	0	0	2	0	.625	.500
Klink,Joe	L	.224	98	22	3	1	2	9	5	18	.276	.337
Throws Left	R	.284	134	38	7	0	2	20	16	16	.373	.381
Knudson,Mark	L	.357	84	30	8	1	4	19	5	12	.385	.619
Throws Right	R	.353	68	24	4	0	4	12	10	11	.438	.588
Kramer,Tom	L	.455	11	5	1	1	0	6	3	1	.500	.727
Throws Right	R	.500	10	5	2	0	1	5	3	3	.571	1.000
Krueger,Bill	L	.307	140	43	7	1	2	16	10	19	.351	.414
Throws Left	R	.284	532	151	27	3	13	56	50	72	.345	.419
LaCoss,Mike	L	.330	112	37	4	2	3	17	14	14	.398	.482
Throws Right	R	.293	82	24	6	0	1	12	10	16	.383	.402
Lamp,Dennis	L	.333	129	43	6	2	2	19	18	22	.419	.457
Throws Right	R	.243	235	57	15	2	6	41	13	35	.286	.400
Lancaster,Les	L	.261	310	81	15	1	6	36	34	46	.337	.374
Throws Right	R	.249	277	69	11	2	7	36	15	56	.290	.379

Pitchers vs. Left-Handed and Right-Handed Batters

Pitcher	vs	Avg	AB	H	2B	3B	HR	BI	BB	SO	OBP	SLG	Pitcher	vs	Avg	AB	H	2B	3B	HR	BI	BB	SO	OBP	SLG
Landrum,Bill	L	.273	139	38	4	1	2	18	13	19	.336	.360	Martinez,D	L	.233	489	114	17	2	4	34	51	73	.304	.301
Throws Right	R	.235	162	38	3	1	2	18	6	26	.260	.302	Throws Right	R	.215	340	73	15	4	5	28	11	50	.247	.326
Langston,Mark	L	.217	129	28	5	1	1	7	14	27	.294	.295	Martinez,R	L	.225	453	102	21	0	7	39	48	81	.302	.318
Throws Left	R	.215	755	162	29	1	29	75	82	156	.291	.371	Throws Right	R	.235	375	88	12	1	11	40	21	69	.282	.360
LaPoint,Dave	L	.000	0	0	0	0	0	0	0	0	.000	.000	Mason,Roger	L	.212	52	11	1	1	1	6	5	9	.276	.327
Throws Left	R	.435	23	10	3	0	0	9	6	3	.548	.565	Throws Right	R	.189	53	10	2	0	1	4	1	12	.218	.283
Layana,Tim	L	.324	37	12	1	0	0	9	4	6	.390	.351	Mathews,Terry	L	.305	82	25	7	1	2	8	11	15	.394	.488
Throws Right	R	.239	46	11	0	0	1	6	7	8	.340	.304	Throws Right	R	.218	133	29	12	0	3	14	7	36	.257	.376
Leach,Terry	L	.367	128	47	12	0	1	20	5	5	.388	.484	Mauser,Tim	L	.500	18	9	2	0	1	4	2	0	.550	.778
Throws Right	R	.240	146	35	7	0	2	20	9	27	.284	.329	Throws Right	R	.290	31	9	2	0	2	6	1	6	.313	.548
Leary,Tim	L	.303	267	81	19	2	9	38	30	42	.371	.491	May,Scott	L	.667	3	2	1	0	0	1	0	0	.667	1.000
Throws Right	R	.322	214	69	13	0	11	37	27	41	.408	.537	Throws Right	R	.500	8	4	1	0	0	0	1	1	.556	.625
Lee,Mark	L	.304	92	28	3	0	3	18	10	11	.379	.435	McCaskill,K	L	.313	351	110	17	2	11	50	22	24	.355	.467
Throws Left	R	.272	162	44	8	1	7	26	21	32	.353	.463	Throws Right	R	.252	330	83	19	3	8	33	44	47	.338	.400
Lefferts,C	L	.281	64	18	2	2	1	17	3	16	.309	.422	McClellan,P	L	.273	143	39	6	0	7	20	16	19	.350	.462
Throws Left	R	.286	196	56	9	1	4	25	11	32	.321	.403	Throws Right	R	.228	127	29	6	1	5	15	9	25	.277	.409
Leibrandt,C	L	.274	190	52	14	1	2	20	13	31	.319	.389	McClure,Bob	L	.230	61	14	0	1	1	10	8	13	.319	.311
Throws Left	R	.237	674	160	24	4	16	71	43	97	.285	.356	Throws Left	R	.354	65	23	3	0	3	11	5	7	.397	.538
Leiter,Al	L	.333	6	2	1	0	0	2	1	1	.429	.500	McDonald,Ben	L	.215	256	55	8	1	8	30	26	50	.285	.348
Throws Left	R	1.000	1	1	1	0	0	1	4	0	1.000	2.000	Throws Right	R	.313	227	71	14	2	8	32	17	35	.362	.498
Leiter,Mark	L	.239	230	55	10	2	9	26	26	33	.322	.417	McDowell,Jack	L	.225	485	109	23	2	7	40	42	84	.289	.324
Throws Right	R	.249	281	70	10	3	7	41	24	70	.311	.381	Throws Right	R	.231	445	103	21	3	12	49	40	107	.295	.373
Lewis,Jim	L	.200	20	4	0	1	0	2	6	6	.385	.300	McDowell,R	L	.270	196	53	10	2	2	26	36	25	.383	.372
Throws Right	R	.323	31	10	3	0	2	5	5	4	.417	.613	Throws Right	R	.254	185	47	10	0	2	21	12	25	.302	.341
Lewis,Scott	L	.286	126	36	9	0	2	20	11	15	.348	.405	McElroy,Chuck	L	.172	122	21	3	0	3	15	19	42	.280	.270
Throws Right	R	.346	130	45	7	0	7	22	10	22	.397	.562	Throws Left	R	.231	225	52	7	1	4	23	38	50	.337	.324
Lilliquist,D	L	.333	18	6	2	0	1	4	1	2	.368	.611	McGaffigan,A	L	.471	17	8	1	1	0	3	1	1	.474	.647
Throws Left	R	.396	48	19	4	0	2	8	3	5	.431	.604	Throws Right	R	.316	19	6	1	0	0	1	1	2	.350	.368
Long,Bill	L	.000	2	0	0	0	0	1	3	0	.600	.000	Meacham,Rusty	L	.404	47	19	3	0	3	12	5	3	.444	.660
Throws Right	R	.667	6	4	2	0	0	3	1	0	.714	1.000	Throws Right	R	.250	64	16	5	0	1	4	6	11	.310	.375
MacDonald,Bob	L	.325	77	25	4	0	2	18	12	9	.416	.455	Melendez,Jose	L	.227	176	40	6	0	6	17	16	32	.284	.364
Throws Left	R	.208	125	26	3	0	3	17	13	15	.279	.304	Throws Right	R	.215	172	37	10	1	5	15	8	28	.253	.372
Machado,Julio	L	.219	151	33	5	0	8	25	27	48	.341	.411	Mercker,Kent	L	.194	72	14	1	0	1	6	13	20	.318	.250
Throws Right	R	.204	157	32	6	0	4	19	28	50	.328	.318	Throws Left	R	.216	194	42	8	2	4	18	22	42	.297	.340
Maddux,Greg	L	.252	587	148	18	7	14	65	44	113	.306	.378	Mesa,Jose	L	.302	258	78	15	0	4	28	34	23	.380	.407
Throws Right	R	.214	392	84	16	2	4	29	22	85	.262	.296	Throws Right	R	.312	234	73	18	2	7	36	28	41	.390	.496
Maddux,Mike	L	.246	171	42	5	2	0	12	13	27	.296	.298	Milacki,Bob	L	.256	360	92	19	0	5	41	28	56	.307	.350
Throws Right	R	.198	182	36	5	1	4	14	14	30	.259	.302	Throws Right	R	.250	332	83	20	0	12	41	25	52	.303	.419
Magnante,Mike	L	.260	73	19	6	0	1	9	9	15	.337	.384	Miller,Paul	L	.500	6	3	2	0	0	0	3	0	.667	.833
Throws Left	R	.263	137	36	9	1	2	15	14	27	.331	.387	Throws Right	R	.083	12	1	0	0	0	0	0	2	.083	.083
Mahler,Rick	L	.250	132	33	11	1	1	18	14	11	.320	.371	Mills,Alan	L	.326	43	14	2	0	1	6	6	6	.400	.442
Throws Right	R	.301	123	37	4	1	3	21	14	16	.381	.423	Throws Right	R	.100	20	2	0	0	0	2	2	5	.182	.100
Maldonado,C	L	.353	17	6	1	0	0	4	3	0	.450	.412	Minutelli,G	L	.333	27	9	3	1	1	5	8	6	.459	.630
Throws Right	R	.313	16	5	2	0	0	2	6	1	.500	.438	Throws Left	R	.273	77	21	2	1	4	9	10	15	.356	.481
Mallicoat,Rob	L	.263	38	10	2	0	1	9	6	7	.378	.395	Monteleone,R	L	.324	74	24	4	0	2	12	5	6	.367	.459
Throws Left	R	.255	47	12	3	0	1	7	7	11	.351	.383	Throws Right	R	.173	104	18	6	0	3	16	14	28	.267	.317
Manuel,Barry	L	.087	23	2	1	0	0	1	3	2	.192	.130	Montgomery,J	L	.262	168	44	9	1	4	31	15	33	.323	.399
Throws Right	R	.192	26	5	0	0	0	3	3	3	.250	.192	Throws Right	R	.229	170	39	6	1	2	12	13	44	.288	.312
Manzanillo,J	L	.500	2	1	1	0	0	0	1	0	.667	1.000	Moore,Mike	L	.228	394	90	19	0	4	32	56	65	.322	.307
Throws Right	R	.333	3	1	0	0	0	2	2	1	.600	.333	Throws Right	R	.230	374	86	16	0	7	33	49	88	.327	.329

Pitchers vs. Left-Handed and Right-Handed Batters

Pitcher	vs	Avg	AB	H	2B	3B	HR	BI	BB	SO	OBP	SLG
Morgan,Mike	L	.228	495	113	13	3	9	41	43	78	.290	.321
Throws Right	R	.223	376	84	9	3	3	29	18	62	.262	.287
Morris,Jack	L	.281	456	128	18	3	9	52	58	63	.359	.393
Throws Right	R	.210	466	98	10	3	9	45	34	100	.269	.303
Morton,Kevin	L	.268	41	11	2	0	2	5	6	8	.375	.463
Throws Left	R	.286	287	82	21	2	7	36	34	37	.354	.446
Moyer,Jamie	L	.520	25	13	3	0	3	8	2	4	.556	1.000
Throws Left	R	.266	94	25	5	1	2	12	14	16	.360	.404
Mulholland,T	L	.255	157	40	3	2	6	20	6	19	.280	.414
Throws Left	R	.262	730	191	39	5	9	69	43	123	.303	.366
Munoz,Mike	L	.357	14	5	2	0	0	6	1	1	.400	.500
Throws Left	R	.346	26	9	0	0	0	4	4	2	.419	.346
Murphy,Rob	L	.203	74	15	3	1	2	11	1	9	.224	.351
Throws Left	R	.281	114	32	9	2	2	17	18	25	.379	.447
Mussina,Mike	L	.214	182	39	7	0	3	17	14	29	.273	.302
Throws Right	R	.271	140	38	7	1	4	12	7	23	.304	.421
Mutis,Jeff	L	.000	3	0	0	0	0	0	1	1	.250	.000
Throws Left	R	.418	55	23	5	2	1	11	6	5	.468	.636
Myers,Randy	L	.287	122	35	6	1	3	18	26	38	.407	.426
Throws Left	R	.226	358	81	12	2	5	40	54	70	.326	.313
Nabholz,Chris	L	.232	95	22	6	2	2	8	10	26	.305	.400
Throws Left	R	.238	471	112	29	1	3	43	47	73	.307	.323
Nagy,Charles	L	.289	460	133	26	6	7	47	37	62	.341	.417
Throws Right	R	.258	368	95	19	2	8	42	29	47	.316	.386
Navarro,Jaime	L	.271	480	130	17	1	13	59	43	52	.328	.392
Throws Right	R	.250	428	107	22	2	5	45	30	62	.305	.346
Neagle,Denny	L	.238	21	5	4	0	0	2	0	5	.238	.429
Throws Left	R	.359	64	23	4	1	3	5	7	9	.423	.594
Nelson,Gene	L	.355	76	27	5	3	3	18	15	5	.453	.618
Throws Right	R	.275	120	33	4	1	9	34	8	18	.328	.550
Nichols,Rod	L	.298	272	81	13	1	2	35	20	34	.349	.375
Throws Right	R	.246	260	64	5	0	4	25	10	42	.281	.312
Nolte,Eric	L	.276	29	8	2	0	2	9	3	2	.314	.552
Throws Left	R	.400	80	32	3	1	4	19	10	14	.467	.613
Nunez,Edwin	L	.283	53	15	3	1	3	18	8	13	.371	.547
Throws Right	R	.271	48	13	2	0	3	7	5	11	.333	.500
Ojeda,Bobby	L	.257	136	35	4	1	1	11	7	36	.301	.324
Throws Left	R	.257	569	146	27	3	14	61	63	84	.328	.388
Olin,Steve	L	.330	103	34	4	1	1	11	12	10	.400	.417
Throws Right	R	.225	120	27	6	0	1	18	11	28	.295	.300
Olivares,Omar	L	.235	345	81	9	3	5	32	42	48	.321	.322
Throws Right	R	.254	264	67	13	1	8	32	19	43	.309	.402
Oliveras,F	L	.272	151	41	6	1	5	21	15	25	.335	.424
Throws Right	R	.209	134	28	1	0	7	17	7	23	.250	.373
Olson,Gregg	L	.230	139	32	2	0	1	15	17	39	.316	.266
Throws Right	R	.296	142	42	3	2	0	21	12	33	.351	.345
Orosco,Jesse	L	.286	63	18	3	0	1	8	3	14	.313	.381
Throws Left	R	.286	119	34	5	0	3	22	12	22	.351	.403
Osuna,Al	L	.239	109	26	3	0	3	21	10	24	.298	.349
Throws Left	R	.179	184	33	10	1	2	17	36	44	.318	.277

Pitcher	vs	Avg	AB	H	2B	3B	HR	BI	BB	SO	OBP	SLG
Otto,Dave	L	.304	69	21	2	0	0	11	4	3	.347	.333
Throws Left	R	.278	313	87	12	4	7	31	23	44	.330	.409
Palacios,V	L	.234	137	32	6	0	2	13	18	24	.321	.321
Throws Right	R	.223	166	37	4	1	10	24	20	40	.310	.440
Pall,Donn	L	.189	106	20	3	0	1	4	10	19	.259	.245
Throws Right	R	.262	149	39	3	0	6	21	10	21	.321	.403
Parrett,Jeff	L	.362	47	17	4	1	0	11	6	5	.434	.489
Throws Right	R	.292	48	14	0	0	2	3	6	9	.370	.417
Patterson,Bob	L	.181	83	15	4	0	1	8	4	25	.218	.265
Throws Left	R	.310	168	52	8	1	6	28	11	32	.348	.476
Patterson,Ken	L	.270	63	17	2	2	1	12	10	7	.360	.413
Throws Left	R	.193	161	31	5	0	4	20	25	25	.305	.298
Pavlas,Dave	L	.500	2	1	0	0	0	1	0	0	.500	.500
Throws Right	R	1.000	2	2	0	0	1	1	0	0	1.000	2.500
Pena,A	L	.193	150	29	4	0	3	14	13	35	.256	.280
Throws Right	R	.296	152	45	5	1	3	16	9	27	.329	.401
Perez,Melido	L	.202	223	45	9	1	6	25	24	66	.279	.332
Throws Right	R	.243	272	66	7	0	9	25	28	62	.315	.368
Perez,Mike	L	.333	24	8	2	1	0	2	4	2	.429	.500
Throws Right	R	.262	42	11	4	0	1	5	3	5	.326	.429
Perez,Pascual	L	.279	140	39	5	2	5	15	14	24	.344	.450
Throws Right	R	.220	132	29	1	1	2	10	10	17	.275	.288
Perez,Yorkis	L	.167	6	1	1	0	0	2	0	3	.143	.333
Throws Left	R	.167	6	1	1	0	0	1	2	0	.333	.333
Peterson,Adam	L	.278	115	32	6	3	8	20	13	16	.349	.591
Throws Right	R	.196	92	18	1	0	2	11	15	21	.306	.272
Petkovsek,M	L	.476	21	10	3	0	2	7	3	0	.542	.905
Throws Right	R	.407	27	11	0	0	2	9	1	6	.414	.630
Petry,Dan	L	.292	168	49	9	1	7	29	19	14	.362	.482
Throws Right	R	.286	234	67	13	2	7	40	26	25	.363	.449
Piatt,Doug	L	.316	57	18	3	0	3	9	10	13	.418	.526
Throws Right	R	.159	69	11	4	0	0	6	7	16	.237	.217
Plesac,Dan	L	.297	64	19	2	0	4	14	7	12	.361	.516
Throws Left	R	.255	286	73	18	2	8	38	32	49	.330	.416
Plunk,Eric	L	.291	223	65	9	4	10	30	35	44	.385	.502
Throws Right	R	.280	225	63	13	1	8	40	27	59	.357	.453
Plympton,Jeff	L	.143	7	1	0	0	0	1	0	0	.125	.143
Throws Right	R	.333	12	4	1	0	0	0	4	2	.500	.417
Poole,Jim	L	.188	69	13	0	0	2	10	1	18	.200	.275
Throws Left	R	.203	79	16	4	0	1	6	11	20	.290	.291
Portugal,Mark	L	.243	366	89	14	3	10	45	37	79	.313	.380
Throws Right	R	.273	271	74	15	0	9	34	22	41	.326	.428
Power,Ted	L	.292	171	50	14	1	4	20	23	23	.378	.456
Throws Right	R	.236	157	37	4	1	2	16	8	28	.272	.312
Radinsky,S	L	.205	78	16	2	0	3	11	2	18	.220	.346
Throws Left	R	.207	179	37	7	0	1	13	21	31	.291	.263
Rasmussen,D	L	.231	104	24	2	1	2	10	8	19	.286	.327
Throws Left	R	.280	468	131	15	5	10	53	41	56	.337	.397
Reardon,Jeff	L	.299	127	38	6	1	7	17	10	17	.348	.528
Throws Right	R	.157	102	16	5	1	2	7	6	27	.209	.284

Pitchers vs. Left-Handed and Right-Handed Batters

Pitcher	vs	Avg	AB	H	2B	3B	HR	BI	BB	SO	OBP	SLG	Pitcher	vs	Avg	AB	H	2B	3B	HR	BI	BB	SO	OBP	SLG
Reed,Rick	L	.417	12	5	1	0	1	3	0	1	.417	.750	Saberhagen,B	L	.215	354	76	11	2	9	36	27	68	.270	.333
Throws Right	R	.375	8	3	2	0	0	1	1	1	.444	.625	Throws Right	R	.241	370	89	17	2	3	27	18	68	.290	.322
Remlinger,M	L	.250	20	5	0	0	1	2	4	2	.375	.400	Sampen,Bill	L	.256	180	46	10	1	7	25	30	23	.357	.439
Throws Left	R	.274	113	31	9	0	4	12	16	17	.362	.460	Throws Right	R	.291	172	50	12	0	6	25	16	29	.359	.465
Renfroe,L	L	.167	12	2	0	0	1	3	2	2	.286	.417	Sanderson,S	L	.261	437	114	24	4	15	54	17	74	.290	.437
Throws Right	R	.692	13	9	2	0	0	6	0	2	.692	.846	Throws Right	R	.240	358	86	22	1	7	35	12	56	.265	.366
Reuschel,Rick	L	.417	24	10	4	0	0	5	5	3	.517	.583	Sanford,Mo	L	.203	59	12	0	0	2	6	13	14	.347	.305
Throws Right	R	.318	22	7	1	0	0	3	2	1	.375	.364	Throws Right	R	.163	43	7	2	0	1	6	2	17	.217	.279
Reynoso,A	L	.286	42	12	3	3	2	9	4	6	.362	.643	Sauveur,R	L	.500	4	2	1	0	0	0	0	1	.500	.750
Throws Right	R	.311	45	14	1	0	2	7	6	4	.415	.467	Throws Left	R	.455	11	5	0	1	1	5	2	3	.538	.909
Rhodes,Arthur	L	.154	13	2	0	0	0	1	3	3	.313	.154	Scanlan,Bob	L	.258	225	58	12	3	2	25	21	20	.321	.364
Throws Left	R	.336	134	45	8	1	4	27	20	20	.414	.500	Throws Right	R	.283	198	56	7	2	3	30	19	24	.345	.384
Rice,Pat	L	.222	36	8	0	0	0	1	5	4	.317	.222	Schatzeder,D	L	.455	11	5	1	0	0	6	1	0	.500	.545
Throws Right	R	.244	41	10	0	0	3	10	5	8	.320	.463	Throws Left	R	.316	19	6	2	0	0	6	6	4	.480	.421
Righetti,Dave	L	.167	72	12	0	0	0	9	2	13	.197	.167	Schilling,C	L	.255	149	38	8	1	1	14	27	40	.367	.342
Throws Left	R	.267	195	52	12	0	4	23	26	38	.357	.390	Throws Right	R	.289	142	41	7	2	1	24	12	31	.344	.387
Rijo,Jose	L	.252	436	110	21	4	5	45	38	92	.312	.353	Schiraldi,C	L	.286	7	2	0	0	1	4	0	0	.286	.714
Throws Right	R	.172	319	55	12	0	3	16	17	80	.215	.238	Throws Right	R	.250	12	3	0	0	2	3	5	1	.471	.750
Ritchie,Wally	L	.161	62	10	2	1	1	7	4	13	.221	.274	Schmidt,Dave	L	.800	10	8	1	0	2	5	0	0	.800	1.500
Throws Left	R	.270	126	34	5	0	3	13	13	13	.336	.381	Throws Right	R	.091	11	1	0	0	0	0	2	3	.231	.091
Ritz,Kevin	L	.333	24	8	2	0	0	3	12	3	.556	.417	Schooler,Mike	L	.175	57	10	1	1	1	7	6	10	.254	.281
Throws Right	R	.257	35	9	1	0	1	11	10	6	.429	.371	Throws Right	R	.217	69	15	1	0	1	9	4	21	.257	.275
Robinson,Don	L	.279	251	70	15	3	5	36	39	46	.371	.422	Schourek,Pete	L	.264	110	29	4	2	2	18	13	18	.336	.391
Throws Right	R	.248	214	53	10	2	7	26	11	32	.286	.411	Throws Left	R	.240	221	53	10	4	5	34	30	49	.333	.389
Robinson,Jeff	L	.276	98	27	6	0	4	16	8	22	.327	.459	Scott,Mike	L	.417	12	5	2	0	0	4	2	0	.500	.583
Throws Right	R	.246	118	29	7	0	5	17	21	35	.366	.432	Throws Right	R	.333	18	6	1	0	2	6	2	3	.429	.722
Robinson,Jeff M	L	.350	214	75	14	0	11	31	31	28	.437	.570	Scott,Tim	L	.000	2	0	0	0	0	0	0	1	.000	.000
Throws Right	R	.222	198	44	8	1	1	19	20	37	.306	.288	Throws Right	R	.667	3	2	1	0	0	1	0	0	.667	1.000
Robinson,Ron	L	.357	14	5	1	1	0	1	2	0	.438	.571	Scudder,Scott	L	.251	215	54	13	3	3	23	38	30	.368	.381
Throws Right	R	.333	3	1	1	0	0	1	1	0	.600	.667	Throws Right	R	.239	155	37	6	0	3	18	18	21	.328	.335
Rodriguez,Rich	L	.221	95	21	4	0	3	12	17	13	.339	.358	Seanez,Rudy	L	.455	11	5	1	0	0	4	2	1	.538	.545
Throws Left	R	.241	187	45	7	1	5	22	27	27	.333	.369	Throws Right	R	.333	15	5	1	0	2	6	5	6	.500	.800
Rodriguez,Ros	L	.250	20	5	0	0	0	0	1	4	.286	.250	Searcy,Steve	L	.242	66	16	1	1	2	9	13	13	.358	.379
Throws Left	R	.243	37	9	2	0	1	6	7	6	.378	.378	Throws Left	R	.302	215	65	13	2	8	41	31	40	.386	.493
Rogers,Kenny	L	.224	98	22	4	0	3	16	16	19	.342	.357	Segura,Jose	L	.400	30	12	0	1	1	9	1	3	.419	.567
Throws Left	R	.298	332	99	18	3	11	50	45	54	.385	.470	Throws Right	R	.222	36	8	0	0	0	2	4	7	.300	.222
Rojas,Mel	L	.247	89	22	6	3	2	15	9	15	.310	.449	Shaw,Jeff	L	.286	105	30	2	1	2	12	10	8	.347	.381
Throws Right	R	.211	95	20	3	0	2	7	4	22	.250	.305	Throws Right	R	.247	170	42	8	0	4	28	17	23	.323	.365
Rosenberg,S	L	.308	13	4	1	0	1	5	1	4	.357	.615	Sherrill,Tim	L	.294	17	5	0	0	0	3	2	1	.381	.294
Throws Left	R	.226	31	7	0	0	2	6	4	2	.314	.419	Throws Left	R	.357	42	15	1	0	2	10	1	3	.378	.524
Rosenthal,W	L	.269	119	32	5	2	3	20	13	22	.341	.420	Show,Eric	L	.358	95	34	11	4	1	17	14	9	.436	.621
Throws Right	R	.248	161	40	11	0	6	27	23	39	.340	.429	Throws Right	R	.248	113	28	6	0	1	14	3	11	.261	.327
Ruffin,Bruce	L	.252	111	28	6	0	1	12	6	22	.291	.333	Simons,Doug	L	.195	87	17	3	1	0	9	7	23	.250	.253
Throws Left	R	.279	348	97	22	3	5	35	32	63	.338	.402	Throws Left	R	.277	137	38	10	0	5	25	12	15	.340	.460
Ruskin,Scott	L	.275	91	25	6	1	0	10	10	18	.347	.363	Sisk,Doug	L	.394	33	13	2	2	1	11	7	3	.488	.667
Throws Left	R	.219	146	32	9	1	4	17	20	32	.325	.377	Throws Right	R	.267	30	8	0	0	0	3	1	2	.290	.267
Russell,Jeff	L	.241	145	35	2	0	2	28	17	20	.317	.297	Slocumb,H	L	.290	107	31	5	1	3	14	12	10	.361	.439
Throws Right	R	.229	157	36	4	0	9	24	9	32	.271	.427	Throws Right	R	.180	122	22	5	0	0	16	18	24	.288	.221
Ryan,Nolan	L	.183	345	63	13	3	5	27	34	105	.257	.281	Slusarski,Joe	L	.296	253	75	10	3	7	25	22	29	.350	.443
Throws Right	R	.157	249	39	12	0	7	27	38	98	.271	.289	Throws Right	R	.264	174	46	7	0	7	28	30	31	.383	.425

Pitchers vs. Left-Handed and Right-Handed Batters

Pitcher	vs	Avg	AB	H	2B	3B	HR	BI	BB	SO	OBP	SLG
Smiley,John	L	.196	153	30	4	3	3	12	5	30	.220	.320
Throws Left	R	.264	621	164	34	3	14	59	39	99	.309	.396
Smith,Bryn	L	.272	441	120	28	4	7	50	28	41	.317	.401
Throws Right	R	.221	308	68	11	1	9	34	17	53	.268	.351
Smith,Dave	L	.378	74	28	4	3	4	21	10	7	.459	.676
Throws Right	R	.200	55	11	0	1	2	7	9	9	.313	.345
Smith,Lee	L	.255	165	42	5	2	3	19	11	43	.301	.364
Throws Right	R	.241	116	28	3	1	2	12	2	24	.252	.336
Smith,Pete	L	.309	97	30	9	1	3	15	10	13	.364	.515
Throws Right	R	.209	86	18	4	1	2	12	12	16	.303	.349
Smith,Roy	L	.280	157	44	10	2	4	24	12	14	.329	.446
Throws Right	R	.342	161	55	8	0	5	17	12	11	.387	.484
Smith,Zane	L	.267	146	39	0	2	1	12	5	32	.291	.315
Throws Left	R	.268	727	195	36	2	14	76	24	88	.292	.381
Smoltz,John	L	.288	486	140	23	6	10	56	60	69	.363	.422
Throws Right	R	.182	363	66	15	1	6	33	17	79	.221	.278
St. Claire,R	L	.238	42	10	2	0	1	3	5	13	.319	.357
Throws Right	R	.309	68	21	4	0	3	10	4	17	.342	.500
Stanton,Mike	L	.194	103	20	1	0	1	4	8	26	.252	.233
Throws Left	R	.230	183	42	8	2	5	31	13	28	.284	.377
Stewart,Dave	L	.302	444	134	22	5	8	71	46	51	.361	.428
Throws Right	R	.255	436	111	22	3	16	55	59	93	.350	.429
Stieb,Dave	L	.239	117	28	5	0	2	11	13	15	.318	.333
Throws Right	R	.247	97	24	3	1	2	10	10	14	.324	.361
Stottlemyre,T	L	.242	422	102	9	3	11	33	40	51	.310	.355
Throws Right	R	.228	404	92	18	2	10	51	35	65	.300	.356
Sutcliffe,R	L	.289	218	63	12	4	4	30	30	24	.366	.436
Throws Right	R	.226	146	33	8	1	0	14	15	28	.294	.295
Swan,Russ	L	.193	119	23	1	0	1	9	10	13	.254	.227
Throws Left	R	.319	182	58	16	0	7	24	18	20	.380	.522
Swift,Bill	L	.236	123	29	2	0	1	9	9	15	.288	.276
Throws Right	R	.217	207	45	4	1	2	22	17	33	.280	.275
Swindell,Greg	L	.275	153	42	8	2	1	14	7	28	.309	.373
Throws Left	R	.261	763	199	40	2	20	88	24	141	.283	.397
Tanana,Frank	L	.233	159	37	5	1	5	17	11	25	.282	.371
Throws Left	R	.273	660	180	29	3	21	70	67	82	.338	.421
Tapani,Kevin	L	.235	520	122	26	3	8	42	16	69	.257	.342
Throws Right	R	.259	397	103	22	1	15	34	24	66	.302	.433
Taylor,Wade	L	.325	206	67	13	1	6	30	31	29	.415	.485
Throws Right	R	.304	253	77	15	3	7	43	22	43	.365	.470
Telford,A	L	.271	48	13	1	0	1	6	2	10	.300	.354
Throws Right	R	.259	54	14	4	0	2	9	4	14	.305	.444
Terrell,Walt	L	.306	461	141	27	4	9	55	50	31	.371	.440
Throws Right	R	.295	393	116	21	4	7	44	29	49	.342	.422
Terry,Scott	L	.240	171	41	6	1	1	18	23	29	.330	.304
Throws Right	R	.261	134	35	5	1	0	13	9	23	.308	.313
Tewksbury,Bob	L	.278	406	113	28	3	4	38	31	31	.326	.392
Throws Right	R	.284	327	93	14	5	9	41	7	44	.305	.440
Thigpen,Bobby	L	.258	124	32	4	2	6	23	21	18	.363	.468
Throws Right	R	.233	133	31	4	0	4	19	17	29	.333	.353

Pitcher	vs	Avg	AB	H	2B	3B	HR	BI	BB	SO	OBP	SLG
Timlin,Mike	L	.296	169	50	2	1	3	22	27	27	.392	.373
Throws Right	R	.187	235	44	4	0	3	30	23	58	.260	.243
Tomlin,Randy	L	.172	134	23	3	0	1	10	13	30	.261	.216
Throws Left	R	.275	535	147	25	6	8	53	41	74	.329	.389
Valdez,Efrain	L	.444	9	4	0	0	0	0	3	0	.615	.444
Throws Left	R	.083	12	1	0	0	0	0	1	1	.077	.083
Valdez,Sergio	L	.267	30	8	1	0	1	3	4	3	.353	.400
Throws Right	R	.212	33	7	0	0	2	5	1	8	.229	.394
Valenzuela,F	L	.500	6	3	0	0	1	1	0	0	.500	1.000
Throws Left	R	.440	25	11	3	0	2	6	3	5	.483	.800
Valera,Julio	L	.500	2	1	0	0	0	0	3	1	.800	.500
Throws Right	R	.000	5	0	0	0	0	1	1	2	.167	.000
Van Poppel,T	L	.385	13	5	0	1	0	2	1	3	.429	.538
Throws Right	R	.333	6	2	0	0	1	3	1	3	.429	.833
Viola,Frank	L	.233	193	45	8	1	5	22	11	35	.273	.363
Throws Left	R	.301	712	214	33	3	20	77	43	97	.339	.440
Wagner,Hector	L	.320	25	8	1	0	1	3	2	3	.370	.480
Throws Right	R	.381	21	8	4	0	1	5	1	2	.409	.714
Wainhouse,D	L	.000	2	0	0	0	0	0	2	0	.500	.000
Throws Right	R	.286	7	2	0	0	0	2	2	1	.400	.286
Walk,Bob	L	.258	244	63	14	1	5	24	21	30	.323	.385
Throws Right	R	.217	189	41	7	0	5	24	14	37	.274	.333
Walker,Mike	L	.500	4	2	1	0	0	0	0	0	.500	.750
Throws Right	R	.267	15	4	1	0	0	1	2	2	.389	.333
Walton,Bruce	L	.067	15	1	0	0	0	0	1	2	.176	.067
Throws Right	R	.303	33	10	2	0	3	9	5	8	.385	.636
Wapnick,Steve	L	.250	8	2	1	0	0	0	0	0	.250	.375
Throws Right	R	.000	10	0	0	0	0	1	4	1	.286	.000
Ward,Duane	L	.193	187	36	5	1	3	18	21	76	.275	.278
Throws Right	R	.221	199	44	5	0	0	20	12	56	.266	.246
Wayne,Gary	L	.308	13	4	2	0	0	3	0	4	.333	.462
Throws Left	R	.219	32	7	1	0	1	4	4	3	.306	.344
Weathers,Dave	L	.294	17	5	2	0	1	1	5	4	.455	.588
Throws Right	R	.250	40	10	2	0	0	9	12	9	.436	.300
Wegman,Bill	L	.221	384	85	13	1	6	34	26	33	.271	.307
Throws Right	R	.265	344	91	16	2	10	28	14	56	.303	.410
Welch,Bob	L	.272	430	117	17	2	8	57	51	49	.348	.377
Throws Right	R	.254	406	103	17	2	17	55	40	52	.333	.431
Wells,David	L	.208	130	27	3	1	3	9	6	14	.246	.315
Throws Left	R	.261	618	161	34	1	21	61	43	92	.307	.421
West,David	L	.343	35	12	1	1	2	4	5	8	.415	.600
Throws Left	R	.229	236	54	16	0	11	32	23	44	.298	.436
Weston,Mickey	L	.000	0	0	0	0	0	0	1	0	1.000	.000
Throws Right	R	.143	7	1	1	0	0	0	0	1	.143	.286
Wetteland,J	L	.188	16	3	1	0	0	2	1	6	.263	.250
Throws Right	R	.133	15	2	0	0	0	1	2	3	.235	.133
Whitehurst,W	L	.296	270	80	15	3	7	30	15	46	.334	.452
Throws Right	R	.250	248	62	9	2	5	30	10	41	.285	.363
Whitson,Ed	L	.283	180	51	7	3	5	15	12	18	.326	.439
Throws Right	R	.321	131	42	4	0	8	28	5	22	.341	.534

Pitchers vs. Left-Handed and Right-Handed Batters

Pitcher	vs	Avg	AB	H	2B	3B	HR	BI	BB	SO	OBP	SLG
Wilkins,Dean	L	.440	25	11	2	1	0	6	5	2	.533	.600
Throws Right	R	.357	14	5	3	0	0	6	5	2	.526	.571
Williams,B	L	.208	24	5	0	0	1	3	4	2	.321	.333
Throws Right	R	.300	20	6	0	0	1	2	0	2	.333	.450
Williams,M	L	.191	68	13	4	1	0	6	12	17	.353	.279
Throws Left	R	.179	240	43	8	0	4	21	50	67	.323	.263
Williamson,M	L	.248	121	30	4	1	2	16	15	21	.326	.347
Throws Right	R	.292	195	57	12	1	7	35	20	32	.353	.472
Willis,Carl	L	.285	130	37	8	1	0	10	10	15	.333	.362
Throws Right	R	.197	198	39	4	0	4	19	9	38	.232	.278
Wills,Frank	L	.333	6	2	1	0	0	1	4	2	.600	.500
Throws Right	R	.462	13	6	0	0	2	7	1	0	.533	.923
Wilson,Steve	L	.182	22	4	1	0	0	6	5	4	.321	.227
Throws Left	R	.204	49	10	2	0	1	5	4	10	.264	.306
Wilson,Trevor	L	.169	160	27	2	1	1	13	22	39	.270	.213
Throws Left	R	.252	580	146	30	4	12	62	55	100	.319	.379
Witt,Bobby	L	.232	151	35	5	2	2	21	37	40	.381	.331
Throws Right	R	.272	180	49	13	0	2	33	37	42	.394	.378
Witt,Mike	L	.385	13	5	2	0	0	1	0	0	.385	.538
Throws Right	R	.250	12	3	0	0	1	5	1	0	.308	.500
Wohlers,Mark	L	.321	28	9	1	1	1	4	7	5	.457	.536
Throws Right	R	.186	43	8	4	0	0	7	6	8	.308	.279
York,Mike	L	.301	73	22	4	1	0	12	11	7	.386	.384
Throws Right	R	.371	62	23	3	3	2	13	8	12	.444	.613
Young,Anthony	L	.295	112	33	6	1	3	11	6	10	.328	.446
Throws Right	R	.200	75	15	2	0	1	8	6	10	.268	.267
Young,Cliff	L	.250	8	2	0	0	1	2	1	1	.333	.625
Throws Left	R	.263	38	10	1	0	2	5	2	5	.300	.447
Young,Curt	L	.229	109	25	2	1	2	10	9	19	.298	.321
Throws Left	R	.312	157	49	9	1	6	18	25	8	.407	.497
Young,Matt	L	.255	51	13	2	0	1	4	7	8	.356	.353
Throws Left	R	.268	295	79	10	0	3	33	46	61	.366	.332

Leader Boards

Last year, these Leader Boards were opposite a page labelled "This page intentionally left blank." Now, despite such a modest introduction, we felt that the Leader Boards were of more than sufficient interest and merit, so we provided 12 pages of them. We still feel that way, so here they are.

The format and contents should be familiar to those readers who were wise enough to have purchased last year's edition, but here's a brief summary of what you'll find in the following pages:

1991 Batting and Pitching Leaders: the tops in 46 standard statistical categories (23 batting and 23 pitching) are listed. Did you know that Expos teammates Marquis Grissom (76 stolen bases) and Delino Deshields (56 stolen bases) accounted for more stolen bases (132) than 19 other major league teams?

1991 Special Batting and Pitching Leaders: the best in 46 non-standard statistical categories (23 batting and 23 pitching), answering this question, among others: could Kirby Puckett become the next .400 hitter? (Answer: Yes, if the American League became the "left-handers" league and banished all right-handed pitchers.) Note: many of the uncommon categories listed here and in some of the other Leader Boards are explained fully in the Glossary (the thing at the end of this book).

1991 Active Career Batting Leaders: we've doubled the number of pages devoted to Career Leaders (and at no additional cost to you, the consumer!). There were six lists that covered the Top 10 players in a category: they now cover the Top 25. The other lists have been expanded to include the Top 15 in each category. Prediction: Rickey Henderson will become one of the few men to get 1,000 of anything in their major league career by swiping base #1,000 on April 19, 1992 (please, no wagering).

1991 Bill James Leader Boards: while Bill has yet to lend his name to a spaghetti sauce or a line of men's clothing (that's no knock on his taste in either, by the way), he has given his permission to label a chart of the top players in various statistical categories of his own ingenious invention "Bill James Leader Boards." Here you'll find the real league MVPs and some unsung players who turned in unheralded but unusually fine seasons. You'll also be cajoled into remembering the year's best pitching performances: was David Cone's 19-strikeout game really better than Randy Johnson's near no-hitter against the A's?

Go digging around in the next dozen or so pages and we guarantee you'll find something that'll pique your interest or simply tell you something interesting that you may not have known at all. Or, if you're looking for just the facts, all the facts, and nothing but the facts, there are a lot of those in here, too.

Who's the best RBI man in the business? See: **Active Career Batting Leaders**: *"AB per RBI"*

1991 American League Batting Leaders

Batting Average

Player, Team	AB	H	AVG
J FRANCO, Tex	**589**	**201**	**.341**
W Boggs, Bos	546	181	.331
W Randolph, Mil	431	141	.327
K Griffey Jr, Sea	548	179	.327
P Molitor, Mil	665	216	.325
C Ripken, Bal	650	210	.323
R Palmeiro, Tex	631	203	.322
K Puckett, Min	611	195	.319
F Thomas, ChA	559	178	.318
D Tartabull, KC	484	153	.316

On-Base Percentage

Player, Team	PA*	OB	OBP
F THOMAS, ChA	**700**	**317**	**.453**
W Randolph, Mil	509	216	.424
W Boggs, Bos	641	270	.421
J Franco, Tex	659	269	.408
E Martinez, Sea	640	259	.405
R Henderson, Oak	578	231	.400
P Molitor, Mil	749	299	.399
K Griffey Jr, Sea	629	251	.399
D Tartabull, KC	557	221	.397
L Whitaker, Det	570	223	.391

Slugging Percentage

Player, Team	AB	TB	SLG
D TARTABULL, KC	**484**	**287**	**.593**
C Ripken, Bal	650	368	.566
J Canseco, Oak	572	318	.556
F Thomas, ChA	559	309	.553
R Palmeiro, Tex	631	336	.533
K Griffey Jr, Sea	548	289	.527
C Fielder, Det	624	320	.513
C Davis, Min	534	271	.507
J Carter, Tor	638	321	.503
R Sierra, Tex	661	332	.502

Games

J CARTER, Tor	**162**
C RIPKEN, Bal	**162**
C FIELDER, Det	**162**
R Alomar, Tor	161
R Sierra, Tex	161
H Reynolds, Sea	161

Plate Appearances

P MOLITOR, Mil	**752**
H Reynolds, Sea	728
R Sierra, Tex	726
R Alomar, Tor	719
C Ripken, Bal	717

At Bats

P MOLITOR, Mil	**665**
R Sierra, Tex	661
S Sax, NYA	652
C Ripken, Bal	650
D White, Tor	642

Hits

P MOLITOR, Mil	**216**
C Ripken, Bal	210
R Palmeiro, Tex	203
R Sierra, Tex	203
J Franco, Tex	201

Singles

J FRANCO, Tex	**156**
P Molitor, Mil	154
S Sax, NYA	148
K Puckett, Min	145
L Polonia, Cal	141

Doubles

R PALMEIRO, Tex	**49**
C Ripken, Bal	46
R Sierra, Tex	44
J Carter, Tor	42
J Reed, Bos	42
W Boggs, Bos	42
K Griffey Jr, Sea	42

Triples

P MOLITOR, Mil	**13**
L JOHNSON, ChA	**13**
R Alomar, Tor	11
D White, Tor	10
M Devereaux, Bal	10

Home Runs

J CANSECO, Oak	**44**
C FIELDER, Det	**44**
C Ripken, Bal	34
J Carter, Tor	33
F Thomas, ChA	32

Total Bases

C RIPKEN, Bal	**368**
R Palmeiro, Tex	336
R Sierra, Tex	332
P Molitor, Mil	325
J Carter, Tor	321

Runs Scored

P MOLITOR, Mil	**133**
R Palmeiro, Tex	115
J Canseco, Oak	115
D White, Tor	110
R Sierra, Tex	110

Runs Batted In

C FIELDER, Det	**133**
J Canseco, Oak	122
R Sierra, Tex	116
C Ripken, Bal	114
F Thomas, ChA	109

Ground Double Play

K PUCKETT, Min	**27**
A Belle, Cle	24
T Pena, Bos	23
R Milligan, Bal	23
R Ventura, ChA	22

Sacrifice Hits

L SOJO, Cal	**19**
R Alomar, Tor	16
H Reynolds, Sea	14
3 players with	13

Sacrifice Flies

J OLERUD, Tor	**10**
A DAVIS, Sea	**10**
9 players with	9

Stolen Bases

R HENDERSON, Oak	**58**
R Alomar, Tor	53
T Raines, ChA	51
L Polonia, Cal	48
M Cuyler, Det	41

Caught Stealing

L POLONIA, Cal	**23**
R Henderson, Oak	18
A Cole, Cle	17
T Raines, ChA	15
O Guillen, ChA	15

Walks

F THOMAS, ChA	**138**
M Tettleton, Det	101
R Henderson, Oak	98
J Clark, Bos	96
C Davis, Min	95

Intentional Walks

W BOGGS, Bos	**25**
H Baines, Oak	22
K Griffey Jr, Sea	21
P Molitor, Mil	16
C Ripken, Bal	15

Hit by Pitch

J CARTER, Tor	**10**
J Canseco, Oak	9
D Valle, Sea	9
B Downing, Tex	8
E Martinez, Sea	8
G Gaetti, Cal	8

Strikeouts

R DEER, Det	**175**
J Canseco, Oak	152
C Fielder, Det	151
T Fryman, Det	149
D White, Tor	135

1991 National League Batting Leaders

Batting Average

Player, Team	AB	H	AVG
T PENDLETON, Atl	586	187	.319
H Morris, Cin	478	152	.318
T Gwynn, SD	530	168	.317
W McGee, SF	497	155	.312
F Jose, StL	568	173	.305
B Larkin, Cin	464	140	.302
B Bonilla, Pit	577	174	.302
W Clark, SF	565	170	.301
C Sabo, Cin	582	175	.301
I Calderon, Mon	470	141	.300

On-Base Percentage

Player, Team	PA*	OB	OBP
B BONDS, Pit	634	260	.410
B Butler, LA	726	291	.401
F McGriff, SD	642	254	.396
B Bonilla, Pit	680	266	.391
J Bagwell, Hou	649	251	.387
O Smith, StL	635	241	.380
R Sandberg, ChN	683	259	.379
D Magadan, NYN	510	193	.378
B Larkin, Cin	524	198	.378
H Morris, Cin	532	199	.374

Slugging Percentage

Player, Team	AB	TB	SLG
W CLARK, SF	565	303	.536
H Johnson, NYN	564	302	.535
T Pendleton, Atl	586	303	.517
B Bonds, Pit	510	262	.514
B Larkin, Cin	464	235	.507
C Sabo, Cin	582	294	.505
M Williams, SF	589	294	.499
R Gant, Atl	561	278	.495
F McGriff, SD	528	261	.494
B Bonilla, Pit	577	284	.492

Games

B BUTLER, LA	161
M Grace, ChN	160
S Finley, Hou	159
R Sandberg, ChN	158
3 players with	157

Plate Appearances

B BUTLER, LA	730
M Grace, ChN	703
J Bell, Pit	697
R Sandberg, ChN	684
B Bonilla, Pit	680

At Bats

M GRACE, ChN	619
B Butler, LA	615
J Bell, Pit	608
S Finley, Hou	596
J Samuel, LA	594

Hits

T PENDLETON, Atl	187
B Butler, LA	182
C Sabo, Cin	175
B Bonilla, Pit	174
F Jose, StL	173

Singles

B BUTLER, LA	162
C Biggio, Hou	130
M Grace, ChN	128
T Gwynn, SD	126
S Finley, Hou	124

Doubles

B BONILLA, Pit	44
F Jose, StL	40
T Zeile, StL	36
P O'Neill, Cin	36
C Sabo, Cin	35
R Gant, Atl	35

Triples

R LANKFORD, StL	15
T Gwynn, SD	11
S Finley, Hou	10
L Gonzalez, Hou	9
M Grissom, Mon	9

Home Runs

H JOHNSON, NYN	38
M Williams, SF	34
R Gant, Atl	32
F McGriff, SD	31
A Dawson, ChN	31

Total Bases

T PENDLETON, Atl	303
W CLARK, SF	303
H Johnson, NYN	302
C Sabo, Cin	294
M Williams, SF	294

Runs Scored

B BUTLER, LA	112
H Johnson, NYN	108
R Sandberg, ChN	104
B Bonilla, Pit	102
R Gant, Atl	101

Runs Batted In

H JOHNSON, NYN	117
B Bonds, Pit	116
W Clark, SF	116
F McGriff, SD	106
R Gant, Atl	105

Ground Double Play

B SANTIAGO, SD	21
D Murphy, Phi	20
J Lind, Pit	19
K Caminiti, Hou	18
L Harris, LA	17
E Murray, LA	17

Sacrifice Hits

J BELL, Pit	30
T Glavine, Atl	15
R Tomlin, Pit	13
Z Smith, Pit	13
3 players with	12

Sacrifice Flies

H JOHNSON, NYN	15
B Bonds, Pit	13
B Bonilla, Pit	11
A Van Slyke, Pit	11
S Dunston, ChN	11

Stolen Bases

M GRISSOM, Mon	76
O Nixon, Atl	72
D DeShields, Mon	56
R Lankford, StL	44
B Bonds, Pit	43

Caught Stealing

B BUTLER, LA	28
D DeShields, Mon	23
O Nixon, Atl	21
R Lankford, StL	20
S Finley, Hou	18

Walks

B BUTLER, LA	108
B Bonds, Pit	107
F McGriff, SD	105
D DeShields, Mon	95
B Bonilla, Pit	90

Intentional Walks

F McGRIFF, SD	26
B Bonds, Pit	25
E Murray, LA	17
J Kruk, Phi	16
P O'Neill, Cin	14

Hit by Pitch

J BAGWELL, Hou	13
L Smith, Atl	9
L Gonzalez, Hou	8
B Hatcher, Cin	7
G Carter, LA	7

Strikeouts

D DeSHIELDS, Mon	151
F McGriff, SD	135
J Samuel, LA	133
M Williams, SF	128
D Strawberry, LA	125

1991 American League Pitching Leaders

Earned Run Average

Pitcher, Team	IP	ER	ERA
R CLEMENS, Bos	**271.1**	**79**	**2.62**
T Candiotti, Tor	238.0	70	2.65
B Wegman, Mil	193.1	61	2.84
J Abbott, Cal	243.0	78	2.89
N Ryan, Tex	173.0	56	2.91
M Moore, Oak	210.0	69	2.96
K Tapani, Min	244.0	81	2.99
M Langston, Cal	246.1	82	3.00
J Key, Tor	209.1	71	3.05
B Saberhagen, KC	196.1	67	3.07

Won-Lost Percentage

Pitcher, Team	W	L	WL%
J HESKETH, Bos	**12**	**4**	**.750**
S Erickson, Min	20	8	.714
M Langston, Cal	19	8	.704
B Gullickson, Det	20	9	.690
M Moore, Oak	17	8	.680
B Wegman, Mil	15	7	.682
C Finley, Cal	18	9	.667
N Ryan, Tex	12	6	.667
T Stottlemyre, Tor	15	8	.652
J Guzman, Tex	13	7	.650

Opposition Average

Pitcher, Team	AB	H	AVG
N RYAN, Tex	**594**	**102**	**.172**
R Johnson, Sea	708	151	.213
M Langston, Cal	884	190	.215
R Clemens, Bos	993	219	.221
T Candiotti, Tor	887	202	.228
J McDowell, ChA	930	212	.228
B Saberhagen, KC	724	165	.228
C Hough, ChA	729	167	.229
M Moore, Oak	768	176	.229
T Stottlemyre, Tor	826	194	.235

Games

D WARD, Tor	**81**
G Olson, Bal	72
M Jackson, Sea	72
B Swift, Sea	71
2 pitchers with	70

Games Started

B GULLICKSON, Det	**35**
B WELCH, Oak	**35**
D STEWART, Oak	**35**
J MORRIS, Min	**35**
J McDOWELL, ChA	**35**
R CLEMENS, Bos	**35**

Complete Games

J McDOWELL, ChA	**15**
R Clemens, Bos	13
J Morris, Min	10
J Navarro, Mil	10
W Terrell, Det	8

Games Finished

B HARVEY, Cal	**63**
G Olson, Bal	62
R Aguilera, Min	60
D Eckersley, Oak	59
B Thigpen, ChA	58

Wins

S ERICKSON, Min	**20**
B GULLICKSON, Det	**20**
M Langston, Cal	19
J Abbott, Cal	18
J Morris, Min	18
C Finley, Cal	18
R Clemens, Bos	18

Losses

K McCASKILL, Cal	**19**
G Swindell, Cle	16
C Nagy, Cle	15
3 pitchers with	14

Saves

B HARVEY, Cal	**46**
D Eckersley, Oak	43
R Aguilera, Min	42
J Reardon, Bos	40
J Montgomery, KC	33

Shutouts

R CLEMENS, Bos	**4**
J McDowell, ChA	3
K Appier, KC	3
B Holman, Sea	3
S Erickson, Min	3

Hits Allowed

W TERRELL, Det	**257**
B Gullickson, Det	256
D Stewart, Oak	245
G Swindell, Cle	241
J Navarro, Mil	237

Doubles Allowed

B GULLICKSON, Det	**51**
W Terrell, Det	48
K Tapani, Min	48
G Swindell, Cle	48
R Clemens, Bos	46
S Sanderson, NYA	46

Triples Allowed

T CANDIOTTI, Tor	**10**
C HOUGH, ChA	**10**
5 pitchers with	8

Home Runs Allowed

R DELUCIA, Sea	**31**
M Langston, Cal	30
F Tanana, Det	26
B Welch, Oak	25
3 pitchers with	24

Batters Faced

R CLEMENS, Bos	**1077**
J Morris, Min	1032
J McDowell, ChA	1028
D Stewart, Oak	1014
2 pitchers with	1002

Innings Pitched

R CLEMENS, Bos	**271.1**
J McDowell, ChA	253.2
J Morris, Min	246.2
M Langston, Cal	246.1
K Tapani, Min	244.0

Runs Allowed

D STEWART, Oak	**135**
B Welch, Oak	124
J Navarro, Mil	117
K Brown, Tex	116
W Terrell, Det	115

Strikeouts

R CLEMENS, Bos	**241**
R Johnson, Sea	228
N Ryan, Tex	203
J McDowell, ChA	191
M Langston, Cal	183

Walks Allowed

R JOHNSON, Sea	**152**
M Moore, Oak	105
D Stewart, Oak	105
C Finley, Cal	101
M Langston, Cal	96

Hit Batters

K BROWN, Tex	**13**
M BODDICKER, KC	**13**
R Johnson, Sea	12
T Stottlemyre, Tor	12
2 pitchers with	11

Wild Pitches

J MORRIS, Min	**15**
E Hanson, Sea	14
M Moore, Oak	14
D Stewart, Oak	13
K Brown, Tex	12
R Johnson, Sea	12

Balks

D BOUCHER, Cle	**4**
J ABBOTT, Cal	**4**
6 pitchers with	3

1991 National League Pitching Leaders

Earned Run Average

Pitcher, Team	IP	ER	ERA
D MARTINEZ, Mon	222.0	59	2.39
J Rijo, Cin	204.1	57	2.51
T Glavine, Atl	246.2	70	2.55
T Belcher, LA	209.1	61	2.62
P Harnisch, Hou	216.2	65	2.70
J DeLeon, StL	162.2	49	2.71
M Morgan, LA	236.1	73	2.78
R Tomlin, Pit	175.0	58	2.98
A Benes, SD	223.0	75	3.03
D Drabek, Pit	234.2	80	3.07

Won-Lost Percentage

Pitcher, Team	W	L	WL%
J SMILEY, Pit	20	8	.714
J Rijo, Cin	15	6	.714
M Williams, Phi	12	5	.706
S Avery, Atl	18	8	.692
B Hurst, SD	15	8	.652
T Greene, Phi	13	7	.650
D Gooden, NYN	13	7	.650
T Glavine, Atl	20	11	.645
Z Smith, Pit	16	10	.615
O Olivares, StL	11	7	.611

Opposition Average

Pitcher, Team	AB	H	AVG
P HARNISCH, Hou	796	169	.212
J Rijo, Cin	755	165	.219
T Glavine, Atl	905	201	.222
K Hill, StL	656	147	.224
J DeJesus, Phi	655	147	.224
D Martinez, Mon	829	187	.226
M Morgan, LA	871	197	.226
R Martinez, LA	828	190	.229
M Gardner, Mon	604	139	.230
T Greene, Phi	768	177	.230

Games

B JONES, Mon	77
P Assenmacher, ChN	75
M Stanton, Atl	74
T Burke, NYN	72
J Agosto, StL	72

Games Started

G MADDUX, ChN	37
C Leibrandt, Atl	36
J Smoltz, Atl	36
T Browning, Cin	36
4 pitchers with	35

Complete Games

T GLAVINE, Atl	9
D MARTINEZ, Mon	9
T Mulholland, Phi	8
G Maddux, ChN	7
Z Smith, Pit	6
R Martinez, LA	6

Games Finished

L SMITH, StL	61
M Williams, Phi	60
R Dibble, Cin	57
D Righetti, SF	49
J Franco, NYN	48

Wins

J SMILEY, Pit	20
T GLAVINE, Atl	20
S Avery, Atl	18
R Martinez, LA	17
Z Smith, Pit	16
T Mulholland, Phi	16

Losses

B BLACK, SF	16
F Viola, NYN	15
D Drabek, Pit	14
T Browning, Cin	14
D Cone, NYN	14

Saves

L SMITH, StL	47
R Dibble, Cin	31
J Franco, NYN	30
M Williams, Phi	30
D Righetti, SF	24

Shutouts

D MARTINEZ, Mon	5
R Martinez, LA	4
B Black, SF	3
Z Smith, Pit	3
T Mulholland, Phi	3

Hits Allowed

F VIOLA, NYN	259
D Drabek, Pit	245
T Browning, Cin	241
Z Smith, Pit	234
G Maddux, ChN	232

Doubles Allowed

B TEWKSBURY, StL	42
T M'LHOLLAND, Phi	42
D Drabek, Pit	41
F Viola, NYN	41
T Browning, Cin	40

Triples Allowed

G MADDUX, ChN	9
M BIELECKI, Atl	9
B Tewksbury, StL	8
R Darling, Oak	8
3 pitcxhers tied with	7

Home Runs Allowed

T BROWNING, Cin	32
F Viola, NYN	25
B Black, SF	25
J Armstrong, Cin	25
A Benes, SD	23

Batters Faced

G MADDUX, ChN	1070
T Glavine, Atl	989
T Browning, Cin	983
F Viola, NYN	980
D Drabek, Pit	977

Innings Pitched

G MADDUX, ChN	263.0
T Glavine, Atl	246.2
M Morgan, LA	236.1
D Drabek, Pit	234.2
D Cone, NYN	232.2

Runs Allowed

T BROWNING, Cin	124
G Maddux, ChN	113
F Viola, NYN	112
C Leibrandt, Atl	105
B Black, SF	104

Strikeouts

D CONE, NYN	241
G Maddux, ChN	198
T Glavine, Atl	192
P Harnisch, Hou	172
J Rijo, Cin	172

Walks Allowed

J DeJESUS, Phi	128
B Barnes, Mon	84
D Kile, Hou	84
P Harnisch, Hou	83
R Myers, Cin	80

Hit Batters

J BURKETT, SF	10
J Agosto, StL	8
M Williams, Phi	8
B Smith, StL	7
R Martinez, LA	7
R Darling, Oak	7

Wild Pitches

J SMOLTZ, Atl	20
D Cone, NYN	17
J Grimsley, Phi	14
R Darling, Oak	13
2 pitchers with	11

Balks

B BLACK, SF	6
J Deshaies, Hou	5
7 pitchers with	4

1991 American League Special Batting Leaders

Scoring Position

Player, Team	AB	H	AVG
D TARTABULL, KC	**123**	**46**	**.374**
W Randolph, Mil	110	41	.373
D Hamilton, Mil	106	39	.368
F Thomas, ChA	147	51	.347
R Sierra, Tex	187	64	.342
R Ventura, ChA	150	50	.333
L Polonia, Cal	132	44	.333
W Joyner, Cal	139	46	.331
K Griffey Jr, Sea	167	55	.329
P Molitor, Mil	138	45	.326

Leadoff On-Base%

Player, Team	PA*	OB	OBP
W BOGGS, Bos	**500**	**220**	**.440**
E Martinez, Sea	309	125	.405
R Henderson, Oak	571	229	.401
P Molitor, Mil	736	294	.400
A Cole, Cle	432	165	.382
B Downing, Tex	410	154	.376
T Phillips, Det	568	209	.368
J Reed, Bos	166	60	.361
T Raines, ChA	695	251	.361
L Polonia, Cal	653	231	.354

Cleanup Slugging%

Player, Team	AB	TB	SLG
D TARTABULL, KC	**444**	**271**	**.610**
J Carter, Tor	165	87	.527
A Belle, Cle	382	201	.526
C Fielder, Det	624	320	.513
R Sierra, Tex	279	143	.512
K Maas, NYA	201	100	.498
J Franco, Tex	198	98	.495
D Pasqua, ChA	261	128	.490
C Davis, Min	201	97	.483
K Hrbek, Min	357	169	.473

Vs LHP

K PUCKETT, Min	**.407**
F Thomas, ChA	.377
J Franco, Tex	.368
E Martinez, Sea	.359
W Randolph, Mil	.358

Vs RHP

W BOGGS, Bos	**.361**
R Palmeiro, Tex	.342
J Franco, Tex	.332
K Griffey Jr, Sea	.332
P Molitor, Mil	.326

Late & Close

C QUINTANA, Bos	**.394**
D Hamilton, Mil	.389
K Hrbek, Min	.389
K Puckett, Min	.378
K Reimer, Tex	.357

Bases Loaded

G VAUGHN, Mil	**.636**
W Randolph, Mil	.545
F Thomas, ChA	.500
D Bichette, Mil	.500
W Joyner, Cal	.500
T Steinbach, Oak	.500

OBP vs LHP

F THOMAS, ChA	**.500**
D Evans, Bal	.468
T Phillips, Det	.466
J Clark, Bos	.465
W Randolph, Mil	.457

OBP vs RHP

W BOGGS, Bos	**.456**
F Thomas, ChA	.432
R Palmeiro, Tex	.411
K Griffey Jr, Sea	.405
J Franco, Tex	.403

BA at Home

W BOGGS, Bos	**.389**
F Thomas, ChA	.371
K Griffey Jr, Sea	.365
J Franco, Tex	.343
R Palmeiro, Tex	.339

BA on the Road

C RIPKEN, Bal	**.358**
P Molitor, Mil	.354
J Franco, Tex	.339
L Polonia, Cal	.332
W Joyner, Cal	.325

SLG vs LHP

S MACK, Min	**.701**
C Ripken, Bal	.677
K Puckett, Min	.658
J Franco, Tex	.626
F Thomas, ChA	.623

SLG vs RHP

D TARTABULL, KC	**.614**
J Canseco, Oak	.576
R Palmeiro, Tex	.557
K Griffey Jr, Sea	.550
C Ripken, Bal	.529

SB Success %

C KNOBL'CH, Min	**83.3**
R Alomar, Tor	82.8
K Gibson, KC	81.8
J Canseco, Oak	81.3
M Cuyler, Det	80.4

% CS by Catchers

L PARRISH, Cal	**42.4**
C Fisk, ChA	40.7
D Valle, Sea	40.3
M Tettleton, Det	38.5
P Borders, Tor	35.9

AB per HR

J CANSECO, Oak	**13.0**
C Fielder, Det	14.2
D Tartabull, KC	15.6
M Tettleton, Det	16.2
J Clark, Bos	17.2

Ground/Fly Ratio

C QUINTANA, Bos	**2.79**
L Johnson, ChA	2.64
M Cuyler, Det	2.55
B Surhoff, Mil	2.40
W Boggs, Bos	2.27

% GDP/GDP Opp

L WHITAKER, Det	**2.6**
R DEER, Det	**2.6**
K Maas, NYA	3.4
D Schofield, Cal	3.6
G Vaughn, Mil	4.2

Times on Base

F THOMAS, ChA	**317**
P Molitor, Mil	299
R Palmeiro, Tex	277
W Boggs, Bos	270
J Franco, Tex	269

Pitches Seen

F THOMAS, ChA	**3014**
D White, Tor	2761
R Ventura, ChA	2709
H Reynolds, Sea	2703
R Alomar, Tor	2698

Pitches per PA

R HENDERSON, Oak	**4.34**
F Thomas, ChA	4.30
R Deer, Det	4.25
J Clark, Bos	4.25
R Milligan, Bal	4.16

% Pitches Taken

R HENDERSON, Oak	**68.1**
F Thomas, ChA	65.2
A Davis, Sea	64.2
A Cole, Cle	64.0
W Boggs, Bos	63.6

Steals of Third

R HENDERSON, Oak	**21**
R ALOMAR, Tor	**21**
L Polonia, Cal	17
M Cuyler, Det	10
4 players with	5

1991 National League Special Batting Leaders

Scoring Position

Player, Team	AB	H	AVG
T GWYNN, SD	130	49	.377
P Guerrero, StL	143	50	.350
D Justice, Atl	124	43	.347
B Bonds, Pit	148	51	.345
W McGee, SF	105	36	.343
F Jose, StL	143	49	.343
B Hatcher, Cin	94	32	.340
R Sandberg, ChN	136	46	.338
W Clark, SF	152	51	.336
O Merced, Pit	95	31	.326

Leadoff On-Base%

Player, Team	PA*	OB	OBP
B BUTLER, LA	725	291	.401
L Smith, Atl	150	59	.393
L Dykstra, Phi	279	108	.387
O Merced, Pit	436	164	.376
D Dascenzo, ChN	151	56	.371
B Doran, Cin	208	77	.370
O Nixon, Atl	435	160	.368
D Lewis, SF	249	89	.357
D DeShields, Mon	545	191	.350
V Coleman, NYN	315	110	.349

Cleanup Slugging%

Player, Team	AB	TB	SLG
H JOHNSON, NYN	152	90	.592
R Gant, Atl	226	133	.589
K Mitchell, SF	357	187	.524
D Justice, Atl	338	176	.521
P O'Neill, Cin	214	110	.514
D Strawberry, LA	193	97	.503
M Williams, SF	148	74	.500
J Kruk, Phi	313	156	.498
B Bonilla, Pit	575	284	.494
F McGriff, SD	486	236	.486

Vs LHP

R SANDBERG, ChN	.359
C Sabo, Cin	.357
I Calderon, Mon	.354
L McClendon, Pit	.350
L Smith, Atl	.339

Vs RHP

H MORRIS, Cin	.336
W Clark, SF	.334
T Pendleton, Atl	.328
B Bonilla, Pit	.313
B Butler, LA	.306

Late & Close

J BAGWELL, Hou	.361
M Lemke, Atl	.359
S Dunston, ChN	.357
O Nixon, Atl	.352
F Jose, StL	.352

Bases Loaded

T ZEILE, StL	.600
R Gant, Atl	.556
F Jose, StL	.500
D Justice, Atl	.444
J Blauser, Atl	.444

OBP vs LHP

R SANDBERG, ChN	.456
B Larkin, Cin	.436
L Smith, Atl	.435
L McClendon, Pit	.429
I Calderon, Mon	.423

OBP vs RHP

B BONDS, Pit	.425
B Bonilla, Pit	.418
F McGriff, SD	.406
B Butler, LA	.404
H Morris, Cin	.397

BA at Home

C BIGGIO, Hou	.343
T Pendleton, Atl	.340
C Sabo, Cin	.339
B Larkin, Cin	.326
O Smith, StL	.323

BA on the Road

W McGEE, SF	.345
T Gwynn, SD	.325
W Clark, SF	.319
H Morris, Cin	.317
B Bonds, Pit	.313

SLG vs LHP

I CALDERON, Mon	.627
C Sabo, Cin	.596
B Larkin, Cin	.585
R Gant, Atl	.567
R Sandberg, ChN	.565

SLG vs RHP

W CLARK, SF	.581
P O'Neill, Cin	.562
H Johnson, NYN	.559
T Pendleton, Atl	.543
B Bonds, Pit	.540

SB Success %

L DYKSTRA, Phi	85.7
G Redus, Pit	85.0
C Landrum, ChN	84.4
G Jefferies, NYN	83.9
M Grissom, Mon	81.7

% CS by Catchers

G REYES, Mon	53.1
T Pagnozzi, StL	44.9
T Kennedy, SF	44.3
R Wilkins, ChN	39.5
B Santiago, SD	38.0

AB per HR

H JOHNSON, NYN	14.8
F McGriff, SD	17.0
M Williams, SF	17.3
R Gant, Atl	17.5
D Strawberry, LA	18.0

Ground/Fly Ratio

W McGEE, SF	3.97
B Butler, LA	3.74
T Gwynn, SD	3.07
D DeShields, Mon	2.08
O Smith, StL	1.99

% GDP/GDP Opp

C BIGGIO, Hou	1.8
H Johnson, NYN	3.0
G Perry, StL	3.6
R Lankford, StL	3.7
A Van Slyke, Pit	4.0

Times on Base

B BUTLER, LA	291
B Bonilla, Pit	266
B Bonds, Pit	260
R Sandberg, ChN	259
F McGriff, SD	254

Pitches Seen

B BUTLER, LA	3064
D DeShields, Mon	2846
R Sandberg, ChN	2716
J Samuel, LA	2553
T Zeile, StL	2552

Pitches per PA

D DeSHIELDS, Mon	4.23
B Butler, LA	4.20
D Strawberry, LA	4.04
T Zeile, StL	4.00
D Magadan, NYN	4.00

% Pitches Taken

D MAGADAN, NYN	63.6
D DeShields, Mon	63.3
O Merced, Pit	63.1
T Zeile, StL	62.4
B Butler, LA	61.8

Steals of Third

M GRISSOM, Mon	18
O Nixon, Atl	13
B Larkin, Cin	10
C Landrum, ChN	9
B Bonds, Pit	9

1991 American League Special Pitching Leaders

Baserunners Per 9 IP

Player, Team	IP	BR	BR/9
N RYAN, Tex	173.0	179	9.31
R Clemens, Bos	271.1	289	9.59
K Tapani, Min	244.0	267	9.85
S Sanderson, NYA	208.0	232	10.04
B Saberhagen, KC	196.1	219	10.04
B Wegman, Mil	193.1	223	10.38
G Swindell, Cle	238.0	275	10.40
M Langston, Cal	246.1	288	10.52
J McDowell, ChA	253.2	298	10.57
T Candiotti, Tor	238.0	281	10.63

Run Support Per 9 IP

Player, Team	IP	R	R/9
D STEWART, Oak	226.0	154	6.13
B Gullickson, Det	226.1	146	5.81
S Erickson, Min	204.0	130	5.74
J McDowell, ChA	253.2	156	5.53
R Delucia, Sea	182.0	111	5.49
C Finley, Cal	227.1	136	5.38
K Tapani, Min	244.0	144	5.31
B Wegman, Mil	193.1	112	5.21
J Guzman, Tex	169.2	98	5.20
F Tanana, Det	217.1	125	5.18

Save Percentage

Player, Team	OP	SV	SV%
T HENKE, Tor	35	32	.914
B Harvey, Cal	52	46	.885
M Henneman, Det	24	21	.875
D Ward, Tor	27	23	.852
J Montgomery, KC	39	33	.846
D Eckersley, Oak	51	43	.843
R Aguilera, Min	51	42	.823
J Reardon, Bos	49	40	.816
G Olson, Bal	39	31	.795
S Farr, NYA	29	23	.793

Hits per 9 IP

N RYAN, Tex	5.31
R Johnson, Sea	6.75
M Langston, Cal	6.94
R Clemens, Bos	7.26
J McDowell, ChA	7.52

Home Runs per 9 IP

T CANDIOTTI, Tor	.45
M Moore, Oak	.47
R Clemens, Bos	.50
J Key, Tor	.52
J Abbott, Cal	.52

Strikeouts per 9 IP

N RYAN, Tex	10.6
R Johnson, Sea	10.2
R Clemens, Bos	8.0
E Hanson, Sea	7.4
K Appier, KC	6.8

GDP per 9 IP

W TERRELL, Det	1.4
K Brown, Tex	1.3
G Hibbard, ChA	1.3
K McCaskill, Cal	1.1
B Holman, Sea	1.0

Vs LHB

M FLANAGAN, Bal	.181
N Ryan, Tex	.183
B Harvey, Cal	.183
R Aguilera, Min	.184
D Ward, Tor	.192

Vs RHB

S ERICKSON, Min	.191
J Morris, Min	.210
T Candiotti, Tor	.212
R Johnson, Sea	.213
M Langston, Cal	.215

OBP Leadoff Inning

N RYAN, Tex	.225
R Clemens, Bos	.260
J McDowell, ChA	.260
K Appier, KC	.267
T Candiotti, Tor	.269

BA Allowed ScPos

J HESKETH, Bos	.141
J Guzman, Tex	.162
T Candiotti, Tor	.189
T Gordon, KC	.200
C Hough, ChA	.201

SLG Allowed

N RYAN, Tex	.285
M Moore, Oak	.318
R Johnson, Sea	.325
B Saberhagen, KC	.327
R Clemens, Bos	.328

OBP Allowed

N RYAN, Tex	.263
R Clemens, Bos	.270
K Tapani, Min	.277
S Sanderson, NYA	.279
B Saberhagen, KC	.280

PkOf Throw/Runner

C HOUGH, ChA	2.42
B Saberhagen, KC	1.29
M Boddicker, KC	1.28
F Tanana, Det	1.27
A Fernandez, ChA	1.23

SB% Allowed

G HARRIS, Bos	14.3
S Erickson, Min	28.6
R Delucia, Sea	30.8
K Brown, Tex	31.3
D Wells, Tor	38.1

Pitches per Batter

B GULLICKS'N, Det	3.27
G Swindell, Cle	3.34
W Terrell, Det	3.42
C Bosio, Mil	3.42
K Tapani, Min	3.46

Grd/Fly Ratio Off

K BROWN, Tex	2.82
S Erickson, Min	2.35
J Abbott, Cal	2.10
C Nagy, Cle	1.84
M Moore, Oak	1.77

K/BB Ratio

G SWINDELL, Cle	5.45
S Sanderson, NYA	4.48
R Clemens, Bos	3.71
K Tapani, Min	3.38
B Saberhagen, KC	3.02

Wins in Relief

M HENNEMAN, Det	10
J KLINK, Oak	10
M TIMLIN, Tor	10
C Crim, Mil	8
C Willis, Min	8

Holds

M EICHHORN, Cal	25
J Habyan, NYA	20
J Gray, Bos	19
T Fossas, Bos	18
D Ward, Tor	17

Blown Saves

J RUSSELL, Tex	10
B Thigpen, ChA	9
R Aguilera, Min	9
J Reardon, Bos	9
3 pitchers with	8

% Inherited Scored

J KLINK, Oak	15.2
S Bedrosian, Min	16.3
K Rogers, Tex	18.0
R Swan, Sea	19.0
M Jackson, Sea	19.2

1st Batter OBP

T FROHWIRTH, Bal	.109
C Willis, Min	.114
R Aguilera, Min	.127
T Fossas, Bos	.130
S Bedrosian, Min	.135

1991 National League Special Pitching Leaders

Baserunners Per 9 IP

Player, Team	IP	BR	BR/9
J RIJO, Cin	204.1	223	9.82
T Glavine, Atl	246.2	272	9.92
M Morgan, LA	236.1	261	9.94
D Martinez, Mon	222.0	253	10.26
A Benes, SD	223.0	257	10.37
G Maddux, ChN	263.0	304	10.40
J Smiley, Pit	207.2	241	10.44
Z Smith, Pit	228.0	265	10.46
C Leibrandt, Atl	229.2	272	10.66
T Greene, Phi	207.2	246	10.66

Run Support Per 9 IP

Player, Team	IP	R	R/9
J RIJO, Cin	204.1	128	5.64
B Smith, StL	198.2	121	5.48
S Avery, Atl	210.1	126	5.39
Z Smith, Pit	228.0	130	5.13
D Gooden, NYN	190.0	108	5.12
M Bielecki, Atl	173.2	97	5.03
R Martinez, LA	220.1	121	4.94
D Drabek, Pit	234.2	126	4.83
J Smiley, Pit	207.2	110	4.77
T Browning, Cin	230.1	122	4.77

Save Percentage

Player, Team	OP	SV	SV%
L SMITH, StL	53	47	.887
R Dibble, Cin	36	31	.861
J Franco, NYN	35	30	.857
D Righetti, SF	29	24	.828
S Belinda, Pit	20	16	.800
B Landrum, Pit	22	17	.773
M Williams, Phi	39	30	.769
C Lefferts, SD	30	23	.767
A Pena, Atl	20	15	.750
D Smith, ChN	23	17	.739

Hits per 9 IP

P HARNISCH, Hou	7.02
J Rijo, Cin	7.27
J DeJesus, Phi	7.28
K Hill, StL	7.30
T Glavine, Atl	7.33

Home Runs per 9 IP

J DeJESUS, Phi	.35
J Rijo, Cin	.35
D Martinez, Mon	.36
T Belcher, LA	.43
M Morgan, LA	.46

Strikeouts per 9 IP

D CONE, NYN	9.3
J Rijo, Cin	7.6
P Harnisch, Hou	7.1
D Gooden, NYN	7.1
T Glavine, Atl	7.0

GDP per 9 IP

Z SMITH, Pit	1.1
B Tewksbury, StL	.9
M Morgan, LA	.9
B Black, SF	.8
T Wilson, SF	.8

Vs LHB

T WILSON, SF	.169
R Tomlin, Pit	.172
C McElroy, ChN	.172
B Hurst, SD	.176
P Assenmacher, ChN	.179

Vs RHB

J SMOLTZ, Atl	.182
P Harnisch, Hou	.183
T Belcher, LA	.195
T Glavine, Atl	.205
G Maddux, ChN	.214

OBP Leadoff Inning

T GLAVINE, Atl	.232
J Rijo, Cin	.238
B Hurst, SD	.244
M Morgan, LA	.247
T Greene, Phi	.254

BA Allowed ScPos

J BRANTLEY, SF	.161
P Harnisch, Hou	.188
A Benes, SD	.196
D Martinez, Mon	.197
J DeJesus, Phi	.204

SLG Allowed

J RIJO, Cin	.305
M Morgan, LA	.306
D Martinez, Mon	.311
P Harnisch, Hou	.313
J DeJesus, Phi	.318

OBP Allowed

J RIJO, Cin	.272
T Glavine, Atl	.277
M Morgan, LA	.278
D Martinez, Mon	.282
A Benes, SD	.285

PkOf Throw/Runner

J DESHAIES, Hou	2.89
D Cone, NYN	2.31
J Burkett, SF	1.78
T Wilson, SF	1.70
B Black, SF	1.67

SB% Allowed

F VIOLA, NYN	27.3
T Wilson, SF	40.0
M Gardner, Mon	43.3
A Benes, SD	47.6
O Olivares, StL	47.6

Pitches per Batter

B TEWKSB'RY, StL	3.10
B Smith, StL	3.26
B Hurst, SD	3.36
T Browning, Cin	3.42
G Maddux, ChN	3.42

Grd/Fly Ratio Off

Z SMITH, Pit	2.69
M Morgan, LA	2.58
G Maddux, ChN	2.41
D Gooden, NYN	2.12
T Wilson, SF	1.97

K/BB Ratio

Z SMITH, Pit	4.14
D Cone, NYN	3.30
J Rijo, Cin	3.13
G Maddux, ChN	3.00
J Smiley, Pit	2.93

Wins in Relief

M WILLIAMS, Phi	12
C Carpenter, StL	10
R McDowell, LA	9
A Pena, Atl	8
4 pitchers tied with	7

Holds

J CANDELARIA, LA	19
S Terry, StL	15
M Stanton, Atl	15
P Assenmacher, ChN	14
B Patterson, Pit	13

Blown Saves

T BURKE, NYN	10
A Osuna, Hou	9
P Assenmacher, ChN	9
M Williams, Phi	9
B Jones, Mon	8

% Inherited Scored

D RIGHETTI, SF	15.6
S Ruskin, Mon	16.7
J Candelaria, LA	18.3
R Dibble, Cin	19.1
M Maddux, SD	19.2

1st Batter OBP

D RIGHETTI, SF	.071
S Belinda, Pit	.120
M Williams, Phi	.145
H Slocumb, ChN	.146
B Landrum, Pit	.155

1991 Active Career Batting Leaders

Batting Average				On-Base Percentage				Slugging Percentage			
Player, Team	AB	H	AVG	Player, Team	PA*	OB	OBP	Player, Team	AB	TB	SLG
W BOGGS	**5699**	**1965**	**.345**	**W BOGGS**	**6702**	**2913**	**.435**	**C FIELDER**	**1703**	**898**	**.527**
T Gwynn	5181	1699	.328	R Henderson	7756	3123	.403	F McGriff	2472	1291	.522
K Puckett	5006	1602	.320	D Magadan	2090	817	.391	J Canseco	3216	1666	.518
D Mattingly	5003	1570	.314	F McGriff	2962	1157	.391	K Mitchell	2749	1420	.517
M Greenwell	2800	870	.311	R Milligan	1576	614	.390	D Strawberry	4408	2276	.516
G Brett	9197	2836	.308	E Martinez	1486	578	.389	D Tartabull	2919	1500	.514
R Palmeiro	2662	805	.302	K Daniels	2497	970	.388	W Clark	3265	1673	.512
P Guerrero	5246	1586	.302	T Raines	6843	2649	.387	E Davis	2857	1453	.509
J Franco	5309	1605	.302	J Kruk	2844	1090	.383	G Brett	9197	4566	.496
L Polonia	2163	653	.302	T Gwynn	5684	2171	.382	D Mattingly	5003	2457	.491
P Molitor	6911	2086	.302	A Davis	4890	1863	.381	K Hrbek	5132	2517	.490
W Clark	3265	985	.302	J Clark	7896	3000	.380	A Dawson	8348	4086	.489
K Griffey Jr	1600	478	.299	K Seitzer	3150	1196	.380	K Daniels	2126	1039	.489
W McGee	5195	1548	.298	M Greenwell	3143	1189	.378	M McGwire	2656	1297	.488
T Raines	5914	1761	.298	G Brett	10349	3882	.375	E Murray	8573	4181	.488
E Martinez	1277	380	.298	W Randolph	9033	3375	.374	P Guerrero	5246	2545	.485
M Grace	2204	655	.297	P Guerrero	5947	2216	.373	B Bonds	3111	1509	.485
K Griffey Sr	7229	2143	.296	W Clark	3698	1377	.372	G Bell	5086	2462	.484
B Larkin	2589	762	.294	M Grace	2503	932	.372	J Clark	6590	3176	.482
K Seitzer	2749	809	.294	D Tartabull	3353	1247	.372	G Davis	3208	1544	.481
D Magadan	1767	519	.294	B Butler	6439	2394	.372	K Griffey Jr	1600	767	.479
S Mack	1112	325	.292	L Smith	5396	2002	.371	D Winfield	9464	4535	.479
E Murray	8573	2502	.292	D Evans	10517	3890	.370	B Jackson	1908	910	.477
C Lansford	6662	1944	.292	K Hrbek	5869	2167	.369	M Greenwell	2800	1333	.476
B Harper	1861	543	.292	E Murray	9762	3601	.369	R Sierra	3543	1680	.474

Games		Runs Scored		Runs Batted In		Stolen Bases	
D EVANS	**2606**	**R YOUNT**	**1499**	**D WINFIELD**	**1602**	**R HENDERSON**	**994**
R Yount	2579	D Evans	1470	D Parker	1493	T Raines	685
D Winfield	2551	G Brett	1459	E Murray	1469	W Wilson	632
D Parker	2466	D Winfield	1459	G Brett	1459	V Coleman	586
C Fisk	2412	R Henderson	1395	D Evans	1384	O Smith	499
G Brett	2410	E Murray	1279	A Dawson	1335	S Sax	407
E Murray	2288	D Parker	1272	C Fisk	1305	B Butler	396
B Downing	2237	C Fisk	1262	R Yount	1278	P Molitor	381
G Carter	2201	W Randolph	1210	D Murphy	1252	L Smith	356
A Dawson	2167	A Dawson	1199	G Carter	1196	J Samuel	341
D Murphy	2136	D Murphy	1191	J Clark	1147	G Pettis	340
W Randolph	2112	P Molitor	1186	B Downing	1034	M Wilson	327
K Griffey Sr	2097	B Downing	1135	L Parrish	998	G Redus	307
G Templeton	2079	L Whitaker	1134	H Baines	990	A Dawson	304
O Smith	2076	K Griffey Sr	1129	C Ripken	942	R Sandberg	297

276

Hits		Home Runs		Strikeouts		AB per HR	
R YOUNT	2878	D WINFIELD	406	D MURPHY	1720	C FIELDER	13.5
G Brett	2836	E Murray	398	D Evans	1697	M McGwire	14.9
D Parker	2712	D Murphy	396	D Parker	1537	R Kittle	15.4
D Winfield	2697	D Evans	385	D Winfield	1414	J Canseco	15.4
E Murray	2502	A Dawson	377	L Parrish	1372	D Strawberry	15.7
D Evans	2446	C Fisk	372	J Clark	1354	F McGriff	15.8
A Dawson	2354	D Parker	339	C Fisk	1337	E Davis	16.1
C Fisk	2303	J Clark	335	A Dawson	1279	K Mitchell	17.0
K Griffey Sr	2143	G Carter	319	J Barfield	1207	B Jackson	17.0
W Randolph	2138	L Parrish	304	R Yount	1176	R Deer	17.2
G Templeton	2096	G Brett	291	J Samuel	1159	G Davis	18.2
D Murphy	2095	D Strawberry	280	E Murray	1150	M Williams	18.8
P Molitor	2086	B Downing	265	L Moseby	1135	J Buhner	18.9
W Wilson	2038	C Ripken	259	G Templeton	1092	D Tartabull	19.2
G Carter	2030	K Hrbek	243	D Strawberry	1085	J Barfield	19.5

Doubles		Walks		K/BB Ratio		AB per GDP	
G BRETT	599	D EVANS	1391	W BOGGS	.47	D VALLE	23.8
D Parker	526	J Clark	1206	M Scioscia	.52	C Quintana	26.2
R Yount	518	W Randolph	1203	W Randolph	.53	R Milligan	26.9
D Evans	483	R Henderson	1191	O Smith	.55	B Harper	27.0
D Winfield	460	B Downing	1135	T Gwynn	.60	T Pena	27.8
E Murray	425	E Murray	1081	K Oberkfell	.65	J Franco	27.8
A Dawson	417	D Winfield	1044	M Barrett	.69	P Borders	27.9
C Fisk	417	G Brett	1022	D Magadan	.70	F Fermin	29.5
W Boggs	400	D Murphy	980	J Reed	.71	R Hassey	31.3
P Molitor	369	L Whitaker	966	M Grace	.71	S Bradley	31.6
K Griffey Sr	364	W Boggs	930	M Greenwell	.72	G Petralli	31.6
G Carter	353	O Smith	890	R Henderson	.73	L Harris	31.7
A Trammell	349	R Yount	869	M LaValliere	.73	R Jordan	32.3
D Murphy	348	T Raines	858	T Raines	.74	T Steinbach	32.5
B Downing	342	C Fisk	824	G Brett	.76	C Ripken	32.7

Triples		Intentional Walks		SB Success %		AB per RBI	
W WILSON	137	G BRETT	214	E DAVIS	87.0	C FIELDER	4.9
G Brett	129	E Murray	193	T Raines	85.0	J Canseco	5.0
R Yount	120	D Parker	170	M Grissom	83.9	M McGwire	5.3
G Templeton	106	D Murphy	158	W Wilson	83.6	D Strawberry	5.3
A Dawson	92	D Winfield	153	H Cotto	82.7	E Davis	5.4
B Butler	88	G Templeton	144	B Larkin	82.1	D Tartabull	5.5
T Raines	87	W Boggs	131	V Coleman	82.0	G Vaughn	5.7
W McGee	81	A Dawson	127	R Henderson	81.3	K Mitchell	5.7
J Samuel	81	T Raines	127	L Dykstra	80.9	J Clark	5.7
D Winfield	80	J Clark	124	O Smith	80.6	K Hrbek	5.8
P Molitor	79	H Baines	121	G Redus	80.4	W Clark	5.8
A Griffin	78	T Gwynn	116	K Gibson	79.8	J Buhner	5.8
K Griffey Sr	77	P Guerrero	112	M Felder	79.6	B Jackson	5.8
D Parker	75	D Strawberry	112	A Van Slyke	79.4	E Murray	5.8
D Evans	73	C Davis	107				

1991 Active Career Pitching Leaders

Wins		Losses		Saves		Shutouts	
N RYAN	314	N RYAN	278	J REARDON	327	N RYAN	61
F Tanana	220	F Tanana	208	L Smith	312	F Tanana	34
J Morris	216	R Reuschel	191	G Gossage	308	D Stieb	30
R Reuschel	214	C Hough	179	D Righetti	248	F Valenzuela	29
C Hough	195	J Clancy	167	D Smith	216	R Clemens	29
B Welch	188	J Morris	162	J Franco	211	B Welch	28
D Martinez	177	D Martinez	145	D Eckersley	188	R Reuschel	26
J Candelaria	175	D Eckersley	144	T Henke	186	J Morris	26
D Eckersley	174	M Flanagan	143	S Bedrosian	184	O Hershiser	23
D Stieb	170	F Bannister	142	B Thigpen	178	D Martinez	23
M Flanagan	167	R Honeycutt	131	J Howell	149	M Scott	22
F Viola	150	M Moore	130	R McDowell	135	D Gooden	21
F Valenzuela	141	D Stieb	126	D Plesac	132	D Eckersley	20
J Clancy	140	F Viola	125	D Jones	128	M Flanagan	19
R Sutcliffe	139	E Whitson	123	J Orosco	121	B Hurst	19

Games		Games Started		CG Freq		Innings Pitched	
G GOSSAGE	897	N RYAN	733	J MORRIS	0.37	N RYAN	5163.1
C Hough	776	F Tanana	553	F Valenzuela	0.33	F Tanana	3797.1
N Ryan	767	R Reuschel	529	R Clemens	0.32	R Reuschel	3549.2
J Reardon	751	J Morris	443	N Ryan	0.30	C Hough	3306.0
L Smith	717	D Martinez	410	C Hough	0.28	J Morris	3290.0
D Eckersley	671	B Welch	406	B Saberhagen	0.28	D Martinez	2933.1
D Lamp	618	M Flanagan	404	D Eckersley	0.28	D Eckersley	2891.1
B McClure	613	D Stieb	391	T Higuera	0.27	M Flanagan	2735.1
S Bedrosian	608	J Clancy	381	O Hershiser	0.27	B Welch	2732.1
J Orosco	598	F Bannister	363	D Stieb	0.26	D Stieb	2726.2
D Smith	598	D Eckersley	361	F Tanana	0.25	J Clancy	2518.2
D Righetti	583	C Hough	358	M Flanagan	0.25	J Candelaria	2481.1
C Lefferts	582	J Candelaria	356	D Martinez	0.25	F Valenzuela	2355.1
F Tanana	574	F Viola	341	M Witt	0.25	F Bannister	2350.2
L Andersen	572	E Whitson	333	B Hurst	0.25	F Viola	2339.0

Batters Faced		Home Runs Allowed		Walks Allowed		Strikeouts	
N RYAN	21609	F TANANA	398	N RYAN	2686	N RYAN	5511
F Tanana	15951	J Morris	339	C Hough	1476	F Tanana	2566
R Reuschel	14888	C Hough	327	J Morris	1178	J Morris	2143
C Hough	14028	N Ryan	307	F Tanana	1110	C Hough	2095
J Morris	13777	D Eckersley	302	D Stieb	960	D Eckersley	2025
D Martinez	12290	F Bannister	288	J Clancy	947	R Reuschel	2015
D Eckersley	11904	D Martinez	274	R Reuschel	935	B Welch	1815
M Flanagan	11504	F Viola	258	F Valenzuela	918	F Valenzuela	1764
B Welch	11372	M Flanagan	248	R Sutcliffe	901	F Bannister	1693
D Stieb	11322	J Clancy	244	B Welch	892	R Clemens	1665
J Clancy	10772	J Candelaria	242	M Langston	868	J Candelaria	1633
J Candelaria	10166	B Hurst	227	M Flanagan	867	M Langston	1631
F Bannister	10014	R Reuschel	221	D Martinez	866	F Viola	1601
F Valenzuela	9893	B Welch	219	D Petry	852	D Stieb	1586
F Viola	9797	D Petry	218	F Bannister	825	D Martinez	1546

Earned Run Average

Player, Team	IP	ER	ERA
D SMITH	**795.1**	**236**	**2.67**
O Hershiser	1594.1	490	2.77
J Orosco	836.2	262	2.82
L Smith	992.1	313	2.84
R Clemens	1784.1	565	2.85
A Pena	927.1	299	2.90
D Gooden	1713.2	554	2.91
G Gossage	1676.1	547	2.94
T Belcher	806.0	268	2.99
C Lefferts	831.1	280	3.03
J Reardon	1003.0	338	3.03
L Andersen	866.2	299	3.11
D Righetti	1207.2	420	3.13
N Ryan	5163.1	1810	3.15
D Cone	1017.1	359	3.18

Winning Percentage

Player, Team	W	L	W%
D GOODEN	**132**	**53**	**.714**
R Clemens	134	61	.687
T Higuera	92	56	.622
D Cone	67	41	.620
O Hershiser	106	67	.613
B Welch	188	122	.606
J Candelaria	175	114	.606
J Key	103	68	.602
J Smiley	60	42	.588
T Browning	107	75	.588
D Drabek	84	59	.587
B Saberhagen	110	78	.585
D Stewart	134	96	.583
D Stieb	170	126	.574
B Walk	82	61	.573

Opposition Batting

Player, Team	AB	H	AVG
N RYAN	**18444**	**3731**	**.202**
S Fernandez	4547	930	.205
J DeLeon	5773	1286	.223
J Orosco	3059	685	.224
R Clemens	6629	1500	.226
D Cone	3768	858	.228
J Reardon	3725	850	.228
T Belcher	2977	680	.228
C Hough	12201	2803	.230
J Berenguer	4160	957	.230
S Bedrosian	3959	911	.230
D Gooden	6364	1467	.231
O Hershiser	5940	1378	.232
S Garrelts	3511	815	.232
B Witt	3618	841	.232

Hits Per 9 Innings

Player, Team	IP	H	H/9
N RYAN	**5163.1**	**3731**	**6.50**
S Fernandez	1256.1	930	6.66
J DeLeon	1579.2	1286	7.33
G Gossage	1676.1	1372	7.37
J Orosco	836.2	685	7.37
R Clemens	1784.1	1500	7.57
D Cone	1017.1	858	7.59
T Belcher	806.0	680	7.59
J Reardon	1003.0	850	7.63
C Hough	3306.0	2803	7.63
J Berenguer	1127.2	957	7.64
S Garrelts	959.1	815	7.65
S Bedrosian	1067.0	911	7.68
D Gooden	1713.2	1467	7.70
B Witt	980.0	841	7.72

Homeruns Per 9 Innings

Player, Team	IP	HR	HR/9
D SMITH	**795.1**	**34**	**.38**
B Swift	759.0	37	.44
O Hershiser	1594.1	79	.45
D Gooden	1713.2	87	.46
M LaCoss	1739.2	99	.51
D Righetti	1207.2	69	.51
Z Smith	1344.1	77	.52
L Andersen	866.2	50	.52
M Gubicza	1540.1	89	.52
A Pena	927.1	54	.52
L Smith	992.1	59	.54
N Ryan	5163.1	307	.54
G Gossage	1676.1	102	.55
D Jackson	1277.0	78	.55
R Reuschel	3549.2	221	.56

Baserunners Per 9 Innings

Player, Team	IP	BR	BR/9
R CLEMENS	**1784.1**	**2034**	**10.26**
B Saberhagen	1660.1	1909	10.35
S Fernandez	1256.1	1460	10.46
D Gooden	1713.2	2000	10.50
D Eckersley	2891.1	3415	10.63
O Hershiser	1594.1	1885	10.64
T Belcher	806.0	954	10.65
J Candelaria	2481.1	2960	10.74
C Lefferts	831.1	993	10.75
D Drabek	1237.2	1486	10.81
J Reardon	1003.0	1206	10.82
J Smiley	854.0	1028	10.83
D Cone	1017.1	1227	10.85
J Key	1479.0	1784	10.86
T Higuera	1291.1	1558	10.86

Strikeouts per 9 Innings

Player, Team	IP	K	K/9
N RYAN	**5163.1**	**5511**	**9.61**
L Smith	992.1	990	8.98
B Witt	980.0	951	8.73
D Cone	1017.1	966	8.55
S Fernandez	1256.1	1184	8.48
R Clemens	1784.1	1665	8.40
D Gooden	1713.2	1541	8.09
M Langston	1843.2	1631	7.96
M Davis	989.2	874	7.95
J Rijo	1076.1	925	7.73
J Orosco	836.2	719	7.73
J DeLeon	1579.2	1343	7.65
G Gossage	1676.1	1407	7.55
J Berenguer	1127.2	930	7.42
D Righetti	1207.2	991	7.39

Walks per 9 Innings

Player, Team	IP	BB	BB/9
B SABERHAGEN	**1660.1**	**331**	**1.79**
G Swindell	1043.0	226	1.95
J Candelaria	2481.1	570	2.07
D Eckersley	2891.1	668	2.08
J Key	1479.0	345	2.10
B Wegman	914.0	216	2.13
B Smith	1740.1	416	2.15
B Gullickson	2063.1	503	2.19
S Sanderson	2034.1	507	2.24
C Bosio	958.2	245	2.30
A Anderson	818.2	211	2.32
D Schmidt	899.0	234	2.34
A Hammaker	1071.0	279	2.34
R Reuschel	3549.2	935	2.37
O Boyd	1389.2	368	2.38

Strikeout to Walk Ratio

Player, Team	K	BB	K/BB
R CLEMENS	**1665**	**490**	**3.40**
G Swindell	756	226	3.35
B Saberhagen	1093	331	3.30
D Gooden	1541	505	3.05
D Eckersley	2025	668	3.03
J Candelaria	1633	570	2.86
D Cone	966	349	2.77
S Sanderson	1339	507	2.64
L Smith	990	376	2.63
T Higuera	1019	391	2.61
C Bosio	629	245	2.57
A Pena	709	288	2.46
B Smith	1010	416	2.43
T Belcher	633	261	2.43
F Viola	1601	662	2.42

Bill James Leaders: American League

Top Game Scores of the Year

Pitcher	Date	Opp	IP	H	R	ER	BB	K	SC	Pitcher	Date	Opp	IP	H	R	ER	BB	K	SC
Ryan, Tex	5/1	Tor	9.0	0	0	0	2	16	101	Clemens, Bos	8/26	Oak	9.0	3	0	0	1	10	90
Johnson R, Sea	8/14	Oak	9.0	1	0	0	3	12	94	Erickson S, Min	5/1	Bos	9.0	2	0	0	1	7	89
Clemens, Bos	4/13	Cle	9.0	3	0	0	0	11	92	King E, Cle	8/5	Tex	9.0	2	0	0	1	7	89
Ryan, Tex	7/7	Cal	8.1	2	0	0	1	14	92	Alvarez W, ChA	8/11	Bal	9.0	0	0	0	5	7	89
Finley C, Cal	4/19	Min	9.0	2	0	0	2	9	90	Finley C, Cal	6/4	Bos	9.0	2	0	0	4	9	88
Sanderson, NYA	5/3	Sea	9.0	3	0	0	0	9	90	Key, Tor	6/13	Cle	9.0	2	0	0	0	5	88
Saberhagen, KC	8/4	Cle	9.0	3	0	0	0	9	90	Erickson S, Min	6/24	NYA	9.0	2	0	0	1	6	88
Saberhagen, KC	8/26	ChA	9.0	0	0	0	2	5	90	Clemens, Bos	9/10	Det	9.0	2	0	0	1	6	88

Offensive Winning%

F Thomas, ChA	.822
D Tartabull, KC	.801
K Griffey Jr, Sea	.762
C Ripken, Bal	.747
P Molitor, Mil	.740
J Franco, Tex	.748
R Palmeiro, Tex	.742
L Whitaker, Det	.739
W Boggs, Bos	.731
C Davis, Min	.718

Runs Created

F Thomas, ChA	144
C Ripken, Bal	134
P Molitor, Mil	131
R Palmeiro, Tex	129
K Griffey JR, Sea	118
J Franco, Tex	118
R Sierra, Tex	117
J Canseco, Oak	116
D Tartabull, KC	116
C Fielder, Det	110

Isolated Power

J Canseco, Oak	.290
D Tartabull, KC	.277
C Fielder, Det	.252
C Ripken, Bal	.243
F Thomas, ChA	.234
C Davis, Min	.230
J Carter, Tor	.230
M Tettleton, Det	.228
J Clark, Bos	.216
G Vaughn, Mil	.212

Power/Speed

J Canseco, Oak	32.7
R Henderson, Oak	27.5
J Carter, Tor	24.9
R Kelly, NYA	24.6
D White, Tor	22.4
J Franco, Tex	21.2
K Griffey JR, Sea	19.8
R Sierra, Tex	19.5
P Molitor, Mil	17.9
M Devereaux, Bal	17.4

Secondary Average

R Henderson, Oak	.487
F Thomas, ChA	.483
J Canseco, Oak	.472
M Tettleton, Det	.435
D Tartabull, KC	.424
C Davis, Min	.418
J Clark, Bos	.416
L Whitaker, Det	.411
R Deer, Det	.408
M McGwire, Oak	.379

Cheap Wins

B Gullickson, Det	5
M Gardiner, Bos	5
M Gubicza, KC	5
K Rogers, Tex	4
8 pitchers with	3

Tough Losses

J Abbott, Cal	8
C Nagy, Cle	7
F Tanana, Det	6
G Swindell, Cle	6
J Key, Tor	6
J Morris, Min	6

Slow Hooks

Rangers	20
Royals	19
White Sox	15
Athletics	14
Angels	13
Indians	13
Orioles	12
Red Sox	12
Brewers	11
Twins	11
Yankees	11
Blue Jays	7
Mariners	7
Tigers	7

Quick Hooks

Brewers	30
Royals	26
Yankees	25
Blue Jays	22
Athletics	21
Red Sox	21
Mariners	20
Orioles	20
Tigers	18
White Sox	18
Rangers	17
Twins	16
Indians	11
Angels	9

Bill James Leaders: National League

Top Game Scores of the Year

Pitcher	Date	Opp	IP	H	R	ER	BB	K	SC	Pitcher	Date	Opp	IP	H	R	ER	BB	K	SC
Cone, NYN	10/6	Phi	9.0	3	0	0	1	19	99	Schourek, NYN	9/10	Mon	9.0	1	0	0	2	7	90
Cone, NYN	9/20	StL	9.0	1	0	0	1	11	95	Smiley, Pit	4/17	NYN	9.0	1	0	0	0	4	89
Mulholland, Phi	9/18	Mon	9.0	2	0	0	0	10	93	Glavine, Atl	4/23	LA	9.0	4	0	0	0	10	89
Martinez De, Mon	7/28	LA	9.0	0	0	0	0	5	92	Smith Z, Pit	5/29	StL	9.0	1	0	0	1	5	89
Benes, SD	8/29	StL	9.0	2	0	0	1	10	92	Harnisch, Hou	6/9	NYN	9.0	3	0	0	3	11	89
Rijo, Cin	8/24	NYN	9.0	2	0	0	1	9	91	Belcher, LA	8/30	ChN	9.0	4	0	0	0	10	89
Greene, Phi	5/23	Mon	9.0	0	0	0	7	10	90	Greene, Phi	5/28	Mon	9.0	3	0	0	0	9	90

Offensive Winning%

B Bonds, Pit	.795
B Larkin, Cin	.762
W Clark, SF	.762
F McGriff, SD	.754
B Bonilla, Pit	.751
R Sandberg, ChN	.743
H Morris, Cin	.742
T Pendelton, Atl	.729
J Kruk, Phi	.727
C Sabo, Cin	.710

Runs Created

B Bonds, Pit	118
R Sandberg, ChN	114
B Bonilla, Pit	114
W Clark, SF	110
T Pendleton, Atl	107
F McGriff, SD	107
H Johnson, NYN	107
C Sabo, Cin	103
J Kruk, Phi	99
J Bagwell, Hou	98

Isolated Power

H Johnson, NYN	.277
R Gant, Atl	.244
W Clark, SF	.235
M Williams, SF	.231
D Strawberry, LA	.226
P O'Neill, Cin	.226
B Bonds, Pit	.222
A Dawson, ChN	.217
F McGriff, SD	.216
B Larkin, Cin	.205

Power/Speed

H Johnson, NYN	33.5
R Gant, Atl	33.0
B Bonds, Pit	31.6
I Calderon, Mon	23.6
R Sandberg, ChN	23.8
C Sabo, Cin	22.0
B Larkin, Cin	21.8
D DeShields, Mon	17.0
R Thompson, SF	16.1
P O'Neill, Cin	16.8

Secondary Average

B Bonds, Pit	.516
H Johnson, NYN	.468
R Gant, Atl	.431
F McGriff, SD	.422
D Strawberry, LA	.394
R Sandberg, ChN	.381
P O'Neill, Cin	.385
B Larkin, Cin	.375
D DeShields, Mon	.362
I Calderon, Mon	.360

Cheap Wins

J Smiley, Pit	5
S Avery, Atl	4
B Hurst, SD	3
J Rijo, Cin	3
M Bielecki, Atl	3
O Hershiser, LA	3
R Martinez, LA	3
T Wilson, SF	3
12 pitchers with	2

Tough Losses

B Black, SF	7
D Drabek, Pit	7
M Morgan, LA	7
A Benes, SD	6
D Cone, NYN	6
G Maddux, ChN	6
J Rijo, Cin	6
R Myers, Cin	6
T Glavine, Atl	6

Slow Hooks

Giants	10
Mets	10
Astros	8
Cubs	7
Reds	7
Padres	6
Braves	5
Expos	5
Pirates	5
Cardinals	4
Dodgers	4
Phillies	4

Quick Hooks

Pirates	29
Giants	25
Phillies	25
Braves	22
Cubs	21
Expos	20
Astros	17
Reds	17
Cardinals	16
Dodgers	15
Mets	15
Padres	13

Player Profiles

In last year's Handbook, we took an in-depth look at four of baseball's most well-known players. We turned them inside out and upside down, and the results were the most comprehensive detail of any player's season found anywhere.

In this edition, based on suggestions from Bill, our readers, and the staff here at the office, we've made some changes in the Profiles:

The biggest change is that the numbers for all the breakdowns in the following pages are career totals, not just 1991 totals. Often, the data for batting and pitching splits over the course of one season are so small as to be meaningless. However, totals over a four or five year period begin to take on some real value .

Another shift is in the players themselves. Last year, as it turned out, we wound up selecting four established veteran stars: Carlton Fisk, Dennis Eckersley, Ryne Sandberg, and Doug Drabek. This year we selected six of baseball's youngest stars:

The Hitters:

Ken Griffey Jr (Seattle Mariners), only 22 years old, already the best centerfielder in the American League; **Roberto Alomar** (Toronto Blue Jays), 24, a defensive whiz at second base — and no slouch at the plate, either; and **Ron Gant** (Atlanta Braves), 27, who returned from the minors with back to back 30 Home Run/30 Stolen Base seasons.

The Pitchers:

Bryan Harvey (California Angels), 28, who cut his walks in half and nearly doubled his saves, was an unhittable closer behind the Angels' trio of lefties in 1991; **Tom Glavine** (Atlanta Braves), 26, 20-game winner, the anchor of one of baseball's best young pitching staffs; and **Ramon Martinez** (Los Angeles Dodgers), 24, who may be the skinniest pitcher in baseball, but one of the best.

Player Profile Definitions:

- **Avg, OBP** and **SLG** are Batting Average, On-Base Percentage and Slugging Percentage, respectively.

- **FLY** is the number of Flyballs (hits and outs); it excludes line drives.

- **GDP Opp** indicates a record of performance in plate appearances in which there was a Double Play Opportunity (Runner on 1st and less than 2 outs).

- **GRD** indicates the number of Groundball hits and outs.

- **HD** indicates Holds.

- **OP** indicates Save Opportunities.

- **RF** indicates the total number of Runs scored For a pitcher while he was in the game.

- **SB Atd** indicates a record of performance in plate appearances in which there was a Stolen Base Attempt.

- **SB Opp** indicates a record of performance in plate appearances in which there was a Stolen Base Opportunity (man on first, second base open).

- **SUP** indicates Run Support Per 9 Innings Pitched.

- **#Pit** is the number of Pitches Thrown.

- **#PK** is the number of Pickoff Throws Made.

Player Profile Notes:

- You may notice some walks being given up with less than a 3-ball count. These are intentional walks. We don't count pitches as true pitches if they are intentional.

- There are two sets of count information. The first set shows performance when the play happens on that pitch. For example, a .231 Avg on the **0-1** line indicates a batting average when hitting that exact pitch. The second set of count info shows performance anytime after that count. For example, **After (0-1)** tells what a guy does after he receives a first pitch strike, whether or not he actually hits the ball on the very next pitch or any subsequent pitch in that at bat.

- Batter vs. Pitcher Information. For The Hitters, any pitcher against whom a batter has a total of 7 or more at bats is shown; for The Pitchers, any batter who has 14 or more at bats against the pitcher and is still in the same league is shown, except if the pitcher is primarily a reliever, in which case the minimum number of at bats is 5.

Roberto Alomar

Split	Avg	G	AB	R	H	2B	3B	HR	RBI	SB	CS	SH	SF	BB	IW	HP	K	GRD	FLY	DP	#PIT	OBP	SLG
Total	.286	609	2391	334	685	119	23	31	226	143	41	54	18	205	13	10	317	968	624	47	9749	.343	.394

Split	Avg	G	AB	R	H	2B	3B	HR	RBI	SB	CS	SH	SF	BB	IW	HP	K	GRD	FLY	DP	#PIT	OBP	SLG
vs.Bal	.250	13	52	9	13	3	0	1	2	5	1	2	0	7	0	0	7	20	16	0	203	.339	.365
vs.Bos	.196	13	46	5	9	0	0	0	2	4	1	3	0	7	0	0	5	22	13	2	215	.302	.196
vs.Cal	.256	11	43	7	11	4	0	0	7	6	1	1	0	4	0	1	8	19	8	0	190	.333	.349
vs.ChA	.311	12	45	7	14	0	0	2	6	3	0	0	1	6	0	0	6	16	17	0	212	.385	.444
vs.Cle	.283	13	53	11	15	4	1	0	6	4	0	2	0	2	0	0	4	21	14	0	181	.309	.396
vs.Det	.250	13	56	8	14	4	0	1	4	4	0	1	1	2	0	1	8	19	15	1	250	.283	.375
vs.KC	.327	12	52	5	17	1	1	1	8	1	0	2	2	2	0	1	7	19	16	0	225	.351	.500
vs.Mil	.259	13	54	5	14	6	1	0	4	4	1	1	0	5	2	0	8	19	16	1	213	.322	.407
vs.Min	.342	12	38	4	13	2	1	1	5	2	3	1	0	5	0	1	4	12	10	0	178	.432	.526
vs.NYA	.412	13	51	7	21	4	3	1	9	6	0	0	1	3	0	0	7	18	16	1	200	.436	.667
vs.Oak	.300	12	50	9	15	3	2	1	4	4	1	0	0	6	0	0	8	13	18	0	221	.375	.500
vs.Sea	.375	12	48	4	18	4	0	0	5	6	1	2	0	4	1	0	6	17	9	0	183	.423	.458
vs.Tex	.286	12	49	7	14	3	2	1	7	4	2	1	0	4	0	0	8	19	15	0	227	.340	.490
vs.Atl	.296	50	199	34	59	15	1	2	25	8	4	9	1	18	0	1	21	86	53	1	814	.356	.412
vs.ChN	.283	34	127	19	36	5	2	1	13	5	2	2	1	10	2	0	11	59	30	5	509	.333	.378
vs.Cin	.291	48	182	27	53	8	3	3	12	15	6	5	2	22	0	0	26	71	42	4	770	.364	.418
vs.Hou	.318	52	214	43	68	10	4	4	25	9	2	1	1	14	1	2	40	79	54	2	837	.364	.458
vs.LA	.282	46	177	21	50	6	0	1	13	10	3	5	2	13	2	0	24	66	45	6	740	.328	.333
vs.Mon	.221	34	140	13	31	0	1	5	7	1	5	0	0	11	1	0	21	59	33	5	562	.278	.286
vs.NYN	.309	35	139	17	43	6	1	3	17	6	2	0	0	11	1	0	19	57	32	2	518	.360	.432
vs.Phi	.312	35	138	25	43	2	0	2	15	14	2	5	1	19	1	1	15	60	32	4	602	.396	.420
vs.Pit	.289	35	135	18	39	9	0	3	10	5	4	1	2	9	2	0	20	59	35	1	503	.329	.422
vs.StL	.315	35	130	7	41	8	1	0	10	5	2	3	1	5	0	1	18	58	35	5	510	.343	.392
vs.SF	.197	44	173	22	34	3	0	2	12	6	2	2	2	16	0	1	16	80	50	7	686	.266	.249

Split	Avg	G	AB	R	H	2B	3B	HR	RBI	SB	CS	SH	SF	BB	IW	HP	K	GRD	FLY	DP	#PIT	OBP	SLG
at Bal	.258	7	31	4	8	0	0	0	1	4	1	1	0	1	0	0	5	11	9	0	112	.281	.258
at Bos	.208	6	24	1	5	0	0	0	1	1	1	1	0	0	0	0	5	10	6	0	88	.208	.208
at Cal	.261	6	23	4	6	3	0	0	5	3	0	1	0	1	0	1	4	8	5	0	98	.320	.391
at ChA	.333	6	21	3	7	0	0	0	3	2	0	0	1	4	0	0	3	7	7	0	103	.423	.333
at Cle	.286	7	28	6	8	1	0	0	5	2	0	2	0	1	0	0	3	12	6	0	107	.310	.321
at Det	.192	6	26	4	5	2	0	1	1	0	0	0	0	2	0	0	3	8	8	0	135	.250	.385
at KC	.346	6	26	3	9	2	1	1	1	1	0	1	0	1	0	1	4	9	7	0	125	.393	.615
at Mil	.240	6	25	4	6	3	0	0	2	2	1	1	0	2	0	0	3	9	7	1	106	.296	.360
at Min	.375	6	16	2	6	0	1	1	4	2	1	0	0	4	0	0	1	5	6	0	87	.500	.688
at NYA	.393	7	28	2	11	2	1	0	1	2	0	0	0	0	0	0	6	9	5	0	107	.393	.536
at Oak	.217	6	23	2	5	0	0	0	1	1	1	0	0	4	0	0	3	9	7	0	109	.333	.217
at Sea	.444	6	27	2	12	2	0	0	2	4	1	1	0	2	1	0	4	12	3	0	90	.483	.519
at Tex	.269	6	26	4	7	3	0	0	2	1	0	1	0	0	0	0	6	10	7	0	114	.269	.385
at Tor	.297	80	313	47	93	23	8	6	40	28	5	7	4	35	2	2	36	115	100	4	1317	.367	.479
at Atl	.311	24	103	19	32	10	0	1	11	5	1	3	0	7	0	0	13	39	29	1	399	.355	.437
at ChN	.303	18	66	7	20	5	0	0	4	2	1	1	0	3	1	0	8	25	18	2	251	.333	.379
at Cin	.305	22	82	15	25	6	2	3	5	9	3	3	0	13	0	0	13	27	23	2	364	.400	.537
at Hou	.330	25	112	25	37	7	2	3	13	6	0	0	1	7	1	0	21	45	25	2	424	.367	.509
at LA	.253	25	95	12	24	4	0	0	6	6	3	1	1	6	0	0	16	32	27	4	391	.294	.295
at Mon	.176	18	74	7	13	4	0	1	2	4	0	4	0	6	0	0	11	36	20	3	288	.237	.270
at NYN	.271	18	70	5	19	2	1	0	5	3	0	0	0	7	1	0	8	27	18	2	265	.338	.329
at Phi	.329	17	70	11	23	1	0	1	7	9	1	3	0	10	1	0	6	27	19	2	288	.412	.386
at Pit	.261	18	69	9	18	4	0	0	2	3	3	1	0	5	1	0	8	29	22	1	261	.311	.319
at StL	.333	18	69	5	23	6	0	0	5	1	1	1	1	2	0	0	8	35	17	2	260	.347	.420
at SD	.290	225	863	123	250	27	7	12	91	39	15	21	9	75	5	5	112	374	195	19	3530	.347	.379
at SF	.160	20	81	8	13	2	0	1	6	3	2	0	1	7	0	1	7	38	28	2	330	.233	.222

Split	Avg	G	AB	R	H	2B	3B	HR	RBI	SB	CS	SH	SF	BB	IW	HP	K	GRD	FLY	DP	#PIT	OBP	SLG
April	.262	73	290	34	76	13	1	2	20	16	8	8	3	21	2	1	37	125	74	3	1187	.311	.334
May	.288	109	444	53	128	19	4	9	48	21	6	4	2	36	0	1	53	182	120	5	1805	.342	.410
June	.263	107	422	58	111	25	5	4	37	23	6	9	3	41	0	2	55	160	122	11	1774	.329	.374
July	.292	104	384	46	112	18	4	1	32	21	5	11	6	29	5	1	49	173	104	9	1589	.338	.367
August	.282	110	443	67	125	23	6	6	40	26	6	10	3	40	3	4	79	169	97	13	1810	.345	.402
September	.325	96	382	66	124	20	3	8	46	34	8	12	1	34	4	1	41	146	100	6	1477	.380	.455
October	.346	10	26	10	9	1	0	1	3	2	2	0	0	4	0	0	3	13	7	0	107	.433	.500

Split	Avg	G	AB	R	H	2B	3B	HR	RBI	SB	CS	SH	SF	BB	IW	HP	K	GRD	FLY	DP	#PIT	OBP	SLG
As 2b	.287	595	2366	-	678	118	22	31	222	53	11	54	18	204	12	10	315	958	614	46	9650	.343	.394
As ss	.350	5	20	-	7	1	1	0	4	0	0	0	0	1	1	0	2	7	8	0	77	.381	.500
As ph	.000	5	5	-	0	0	0	0	0	0	0	0	0	0	0	0	0	3	2	1	22	.000	.000

Split	Avg	G	AB	R	H	2B	3B	HR	RBI	SB	CS	SH	SF	BB	IW	HP	K	GRD	FLY	DP	#PIT	OBP	SLG
Batting #1	.294	86	354	52	104	14	2	5	24	20	9	3	1	24	0	1	50	154	73	7	1384	.339	.387
Batting #2	.281	433	1722	242	484	82	17	24	163	103	28	51	14	148	6	9	231	679	458	34	7051	.339	.390
Batting #3	.315	43	168	23	53	14	2	1	22	10	2	0	1	15	1	0	19	69	44	2	707	.370	.440
Batting #4	.250	4	16	0	4	0	1	0	1	0	0	0	0	0	0	0	3	6	5	0	51	.250	.375
Batting #5	.273	8	33	5	9	2	0	0	1	4	1	0	0	2	0	0	6	13	11	0	140	.314	.333
Batting #6	.292	15	48	8	14	3	0	1	5	2	1	0	2	7	2	0	3	25	17	1	207	.368	.417
Batting #7	.444	2	9	1	4	1	1	0	3	1	0	0	0	0	0	0	2	2	3	0	31	.444	.778
Batting #8	.382	11	34	3	13	3	0	0	7	3	0	0	0	9	4	0	3	16	10	2	148	.512	.471
Batting #9	.000	7	7	0	0	0	0	0	0	0	0	0	0	0	0	0	0	4	3	1	30	.000	.000

Split	Avg	G	AB	R	H	2B	3B	HR	RBI	SB	CS	SH	SF	BB	IW	HP	K	GRD	FLY	DP	#PIT	OBP	SLG
Home	.292	305	1176	170	343	50	15	18	131	67	20	28	13	110	7	7	148	489	295	23	4847	.352	.406
Away	.281	304	1215	164	342	69	8	13	95	76	21	26	5	95	6	3	169	479	329	24	4902	.334	.384
Day	.283	179	689	85	195	46	2	8	77	49	11	14	5	64	4	2	86	274	185	15	2800	.343	.390
Night	.288	430	1702	249	490	73	21	23	149	94	30	40	13	141	9	8	231	694	439	32	6949	.343	.396
Grass	.278	393	1533	208	426	64	9	15	145	76	26	33	12	120	7	7	205	628	382	31	6245	.331	.361
Turf	.302	216	858	126	259	55	14	16	81	67	15	21	6	85	6	3	112	340	242	16	3504	.364	.455

Split	Avg	G	AB	R	H	2B	3B	HR	RBI	SB	CS	SH	SF	BB	IW	HP	K	GRD	FLY	DP	#PIT	OBP	SLG
vs. Left	.255	367	768	-	196	41	6	16	81	32	7	20	5	66	1	7	130	264	234	15	3210	.318	.387
vs. Right	.301	540	1623	-	489	78	17	15	145	111	34	34	13	139	12	3	187	704	390	32	6539	.355	.398
Groundball	.307	303	762	-	234	46	8	10	84	29	16	19	5	46	6	4	79	337	198	15	2926	.348	.428
Flyball	.263	310	623	-	164	17	8	9	48	46	12	12	3	63	3	2	95	254	164	11	2643	.331	.360
Ave G:F	.285	392	1006	-	287	56	7	12	94	68	13	23	10	96	4	4	143	377	262	21	4180	.347	.391
Finesse	.275	283	639	-	176	39	7	14	50	38	7	16	5	57	5	7	90	290	147	18	2563	.336	.377
Power	.280	273	615	-	172	22	4	13	64	34	14	11	2	38	1	1	107	192	189	7	2499	.322	.392
Ave F:P	.296	425	1137	-	337	58	12	14	112	71	20	27	11	110	7	5	131	486	288	22	4687	.358	.405

Split	Avg	G	AB	R	H	2B	3B	HR	RBI	SB	CS	SH	SF	BB	IW	HP	K	GRD	FLY	DP	#PIT	OBP	SLG
Inning 1-6	.301	594	1675	246	505	88	20	23	162	117	33	38	12	132	5	7	213	683	431	35	6848	.353	.419
Inning 7+	.251	582	716	88	180	31	3	8	64	26	8	16	6	73	8	3	104	285	193	12	2901	.321	.337

Split	Avg	G	AB	R	H	2B	3B	HR	RBI	SB	CS	SH	SF	BB	IW	HP	K	GRD	FLY	DP	#PIT	OBP	SLG
Close & Late	.274	332	398	53	109	16	3	4	39	14	6	11	4	47	6	2	63	156	105	8	1683	.350	.359
Close	.267	519	951	126	254	49	8	14	97	48	14	23	7	95	12	3	139	373	265	10	3901	.333	.380
Not Close	.299	596	1440	208	431	70	15	17	129	95	27	31	11	110	1	7	178	595	359	37	5848	.349	.404

Split	Avg	G	AB	R	H	2B	3B	HR	RBI	SB	CS	SH	SF	BB	IW	HP	K	GRD	FLY	DP	#PIT	OBP	SLG
None on	.278	591	1430	23	398	72	13	23	23	0	0	0	0	121	0	4	197	577	374	0	5947	.336	.395
None on/out	.294	427	561	14	165	34	4	14	14	0	0	0	0	52	0	2	67	227	148	0	2283	.356	.444
None on:1/2 Out	.268	520	869	9	233	38	9	9	9	0	0	0	0	69	0	2	130	350	226	0	3664	.323	.364

Split	Avg	G	AB	R	H	2B	3B	HR	RBI	SB	CS	SH	SF	BB	IW	HP	K	GRD	FLY	DP	#PIT	OBP	SLG
Runners on	.299	563	961	-	287	47	10	8	203	143	41	54	18	84	13	6	120	391	250	47	3802	.353	.393
Scoring Posn	.297	470	529	-	157	28	5	4	183	51	7	31	18	51	13	2	75	208	141	11	2211	.350	.391
OnBase: 2	.306	252	222	-	68	11	3	4	51	18	2	24	0	21	6	0	37	83	47	0	945	.366	.437
OnBase: 3	.242	120	62	-	15	2	1	0	21	0	1	0	5	10	4	0	10	31	18	0	266	.325	.306
OnBase: 12	.287	172	122	-	35	7	1	0	29	16	2	7	0	10	0	1	15	40	34	5	515	.346	.361
OnBase: 13	.386	102	44	-	17	3	0	0	30	15	2	0	7	4	0	0	5	18	18	3	192	.382	.455
OnBase: 23	.318	85	44	-	14	4	0	0	32	2	0	0	4	5	3	1	4	21	14	0	159	.370	.409
Bases Loaded	.229	89	35	-	8	1	0	0	20	0	0	0	2	1	0	0	4	15	10	3	134	.237	.257
SB Opp	.309	453	476	-	147	22	5	4	50	107	36	23	7	37	0	4	50	201	127	39	1783	.359	.401
SB Atd	.305	147	131	-	40	6	2	2	20	15	3	4	0	17	2	1	28	51	30	1	662	.389	.427
GDP Opp	.320	421	422	-	135	21	5	2	57	75	31	30	9	30	0	4	42	178	106	47	1552	.363	.408

Split	Avg	G	AB	R	H	2B	3B	HR	RBI	SB	CS	SH	SF	BB	IW	HP	K	GRD	FLY	DP	#PIT	OBP	SLG
0-0 count	.342	273	278	-	95	17	3	6	38	33	10	23	7	2	2	2	0	117	80	9	320	.343	.489
0-1 Count	.331	277	293	-	97	17	4	3	26	20	2	14	2	1	1	2	0	132	97	5	622	.336	.447
0-2 Count	.178	157	174	-	31	7	0	4	14	7	1	0	0	0	0	1	75	50	29	4	580	.183	.287
1-0 Count	.333	193	174	-	58	7	6	3	16	25	7	7	2	2	2	1	0	73	46	4	369	.341	.494
1-1 Count	.336	260	283	-	95	22	1	2	22	16	3	6	2	0	0	0	0	155	67	9	868	.333	.442
1-2 Count	.223	298	355	-	79	9	0	3	30	11	3	1	1	0	0	3	104	116	81	4	1570	.228	.273
2-0 Count	.391	64	64	-	25	1	1	1	15	5	4	1	2	1	1	0	0	29	22	2	201	.388	.484
2-1 Count	.404	200	188	-	76	16	2	4	20	7	4	2	0	0	0	0	0	95	46	4	766	.404	.574
2-2 Count	.177	272	327	-	58	10	2	2	21	5	3	0	2	0	0	0	105	101	79	5	1822	.176	.239
3-0 Count	1.00	52	1	-	1	0	0	0	0	1	0	0	0	58	1	0	0	1	0	0	237	1.000	1.000
3-1 Count	.254	117	63	-	16	2	1	1	7	1	1	0	0	66	0	0	0	31	17	0	649	.636	.365
3-2 Count	.279	224	190	-	53	11	3	2	16	3	0	0	0	69	0	0	32	68	59	1	1745	.471	.400

Split	Avg	G	AB	R	H	2B	3B	HR	RBI	SB	CS	SH	SF	BB	IW	HP	K	GRD	FLY	DP	#PIT	OBP	SLG
After (0-1)	.258	565	1091	-	281	59	5	12	95	53	11	18	7	33	1	6	208	425	277	16	4363	.281	.354
After (0-2)	.196	328	393	-	77	15	0	6	34	16	4	1	2	8	0	2	135	121	93	5	1785	.215	.280
After (1-0)	.302	563	1021	-	308	43	15	13	92	51	19	13	4	164	4	1	109	426	266	22	5066	.397	.411
After (1-1)	.282	530	910	-	257	49	4	8	71	33	10	6	3	58	0	2	155	379	209	18	4377	.326	.371
After (1-2)	.217	422	584	-	127	19	1	4	47	16	5	1	2	17	0	3	175	189	139	5	3105	.243	.274
After (2-0)	.292	341	342	-	100	14	6	5	40	15	7	3	2	128	2	0	27	146	98	6	2276	.483	.412
After (2-1)	.289	395	478	-	138	28	5	8	42	14	6	2	1	82	0	0	64	197	121	9	2908	.392	.418
After (2-2)	.206	351	436	-	90	16	3	4	33	8	3	0	2	37	0	0	126	138	113	6	2866	.267	.284
After (3-0)	.290	131	62	-	18	1	2	0	5	1	1	0	0	94	1	0	3	26	22	0	777	.718	.371
After (3-1)	.259	203	143	-	37	7	3	1	11	1	2	0	0	97	0	0	11	62	42	0	1349	.558	.371
After (3-2)	.279	227	190	1	53	11	3	2	16	5	1	0	0	69	0	0	32	68	59	1	1753	.471	.400

What He Does on Each Pitch Count

Result	0-0	0-1	0-2	1-0	1-1	1-2	2-0	2-1	2-2	3-0	3-1	3-2
Taken Ball	1226	446	245	478	316	264	161	141	148	59	65	70
Taken Strike	787	79	16	317	56	23	202	40	17	97	40	6
Swung & Missed	92	105	60	54	94	77	15	44	85	0	11	26
Fouled Off	311	242	102	189	236	227	30	145	176	0	60	110
Put In Play	307	309	99	183	290	251	66	190	222	1	63	158

Pitcher	Avg	AB	H	2B	3B	HR	BI	W	K	SB	CS
ACKER, Ji.	.286	7	2	1	0	0	0	0	1	0	0
AGOSTO, Ju.	.444	9	4	1	0	0	1	1	2	0	0
ANDERSEN, La.	.455	11	5	1	0	0	1	0	3	0	0
APPIER, Ke.	.429	7	3	1	0	1	2	0	0	1	0
ARMSTRONG, Ja.	.455	11	5	1	0	0	3	3	3	1	0
ASSENMACHER, P.	.125	8	1	1	0	0	0	2	1	0	0
BARFIELD, Jo.	.143	7	1	0	0	0	1	0	1	0	0
BEDROSIAN, St.	.300	10	3	1	0	0	1	1	2	1	0
BELCHER, Ti.	.292	24	7	0	0	0	1	2	2	1	2
BIELECKI, Mi.	.462	13	6	0	0	0	3	1	1	1	0
BODDICKER, Mi.	.714	7	5	1	1	0	1	0	0	0	0
BOEVER, Jo.	.400	10	4	0	0	0	1	1	2	2	0
BOSIO, Ch.	.182	11	2	0	1	0	0	0	1	0	0
BOYD, Oi.	.231	13	3	0	0	0	0	1	0	0	0
BRANTLEY, Je.	.200	10	2	0	0	0	1	2	0	1	0
BROWN, Ke.	.143	7	1	0	0	0	0	0	1	0	0
BROWNING, To.	.290	31	9	1	0	1	2	3	1	2	2
CANDIOTTI, To.	.000	7	0	0	0	0	0	0	0	0	0
CARMAN, Do.	.214	14	3	0	0	0	1	2	1	0	0
CERUTTI, Jo.	.273	11	3	1	0	0	2	0	2	3	0
CHARLTON, No.	.333	15	5	1	0	0	0	5	1	2	0
CLANCY, Ji.	.273	22	6	0	1	0	3	1	3	1	0
CLEMENS, Ro.	.154	13	2	0	0	0	1	0	1	1	0
CONE, Da.	.167	24	4	2	0	0	3	1	1	1	1
COOK, De.	.250	8	2	1	0	0	2	0	0	0	0
CREWS, Ti.	.143	7	1	0	0	0	0	1	0	0	0
DARLING, Ro.	.429	21	9	1	0	0	4	1	2	2	1
DARWIN, Da.	.300	20	6	1	0	1	3	0	1	1	0
DAVIS, St.	.364	11	4	1	0	0	3	0	1	0	0
DeJESUS, Jo.	.429	7	3	0	0	0	2	0	1	1	0
DeLEON, Jo.	.318	22	7	0	0	0	1	1	3	3	0
DESHAIES, Ji.	.278	36	10	0	0	1	4	2	11	2	0
DIBBLE, Ro.	.154	13	2	0	1	0	1	1	2	1	1
DOWNS, Ke.	.111	9	1	0	0	0	0	1	0	0	0
DRABEK, Do.	.300	20	6	1	0	0	2	2	3	0	1
FERNANDEZ, Si.	.250	20	5	0	1	2	3	1	6	0	0
FINLEY, Ch.	.429	7	3	2	0	0	3	0	2	0	0
FRANCO, Jo.	.111	9	1	0	0	0	1	0	0	0	0
GARDNER, Ma.	.200	10	2	0	0	0	0	1	2	1	0
GARRELTS, Sc.	.167	18	3	0	0	0	1	0	0	1	0
GLAVINE, To.	.371	35	13	3	0	0	5	0	4	1	0
GOODEN, Dw.	.167	18	3	0	0	0	0	0	3	2	0
GROSS, Ke.	.412	17	7	0	0	1	1	1	3	2	0
GULLICKSON, Bi.	.250	20	5	1	0	1	2	0	1	1	0
HAMMAKER, At.	.000	10	0	0	0	0	1	1	2	0	0
HANSON, Er.	.375	8	3	0	0	0	1	0	2	0	0
HARKEY, Mi.	.143	7	1	0	0	0	1	1	0	1	0
HARRIS, Gr.	.091	11	1	0	0	0	0	2	2	0	1
HEATON, Ne.	.400	20	8	3	0	2	4	2	4	0	0
HERSHISER, Or.	.261	23	6	0	0	0	0	2	5	2	0
HESKETH, Jo.	.273	11	3	0	0	0	0	1	1	0	0
HILL, Ke.	.500	8	4	3	0	0	2	0	1	0	0
HOLMAN, Br.	.500	18	9	2	0	0	1	8	4	0	0
HOUGH, Ch.	.000	12	0	0	0	0	2	0	1	0	0
HOWELL, Ja.	.125	8	1	0	0	0	1	0	1	0	0
JACKSON, Da.	.364	22	8	2	1	1	1	3	4	2	0
JOHNSON, Je.	.308	13	4	0	0	1	2	0	3	1	0
JOHNSON, Ra.	.222	9	2	0	0	0	0	0	4	1	1
KILGUS, Pa.	.308	13	4	1	0	0	0	1	0	0	0
LaCOSS, Mi.	.200	15	3	1	0	0	1	3	0	2	0
LANCASTER, Le.	.286	7	2	2	0	0	1	0	0	0	0
LANGSTON, Ma.	.188	16	3	1	0	0	2	1	3	1	1
LEACH, Te.	.429	7	3	1	0	0	2	0	0	0	0
LEARY, Ti.	.481	27	13	1	0	0	2	4	5	6	1
LEFFERTS, Cr.	.091	11	1	0	0	0	0	0	3	0	0
LEIBRANDT, Ch.	.222	9	2	2	0	0	0	1	1	0	0
LILLIQUIST, De.	.333	9	3	0	0	1	2	2	1	0	0
MACHADO, Ju.	.143	7	1	0	0	0	0	0	1	1	0
MADDUX, Gr.	.261	23	6	1	1	0	2	1	1	2	0
MAHLER, Ri.	.310	29	9	1	1	0	2	0	2	2	0
MARTINEZ, De.	.250	24	6	1	0	0	2	0	2	1	1
MARTINEZ, Ra.	.450	20	9	1	0	0	3	1	1	3	1
McDOWELL, Ja.	.667	9	6	0	0	0	0	0	1	2	0
McDOWELL, Ro.	.300	10	3	0	0	0	0	2	0	3	0
McGAFFIGAN, An.	.125	8	1	1	0	0	0	1	1	0	0
MILACKI, Bo.	.143	7	1	0	0	0	0	0	1	0	1
MOORE, Mi.	.154	13	2	1	0	0	0	0	4	1	0
MORGAN, Mi.	.286	7	2	2	0	0	0	1	0	0	0
MORRIS, Ja.	.429	7	3	1	0	0	1	2	1	2	0
MYERS, Ra.	.429	7	3	0	0	0	0	0	1	4	0
NAGY, Ch.	.429	14	6	1	0	0	0	0	1	4	0
OJEDA, Bo.	.176	17	3	1	0	0	1	0	4	0	0
PENA, Al.	.250	8	2	0	0	0	0	0	0	1	0
PEREZ, Pa.	.167	12	2	0	0	0	0	1	5	2	0
PLESAC, Da.	.125	8	1	0	0	0	1	0	2	0	0
PORTUGAL, Ma.	.313	16	5	0	0	1	1	2	3	0	0
REUSCHEL, Ri.	.259	27	7	0	0	1	3	4	1	0	0
RIJO, Jo.	.211	19	4	0	1	0	0	2	5	0	1
ROBINSON, Do.	.222	18	4	0	0	0	0	1	1	0	2
ROBINSON, Je.	.222	9	2	1	0	0	0	0	2	2	0
ROBINSON, Ro.	.444	9	4	2	0	0	0	0	2	0	1
RUFFIN, Br.	.222	9	2	0	0	0	0	0	2	3	0
RUSKIN, Sc.	.125	8	1	0	0	0	0	0	2	0	0
RYAN, No.	.261	23	6	0	2	0	3	1	6	2	2
SANDERSON, Sc.	.417	12	5	2	0	0	2	0	3	2	0
SCHIRALDI, Ca.	.333	12	4	0	0	1	2	0	2	0	1
SCOTT, Mi.	.444	27	12	3	1	1	5	2	7	3	0
SMILEY, Jo.	.111	9	1	0	0	0	0	0	3	0	0
SMITH, Br.	.182	33	6	2	0	0	0	0	3	1	0
SMITH, Da.	.286	7	2	0	0	0	0	0	2	0	0
SMITH, Pe.	.320	25	8	2	0	0	3	2	1	2	1
SMITH, Za.	.571	7	4	0	0	2	2	1	1	0	0
SMOLTZ, Jo.	.231	26	6	2	0	1	3	0	4	0	0
SUTCLIFFE, Ri.	.400	10	4	0	0	0	2	1	0	1	0
SWINDELL, Gr.	.200	10	2	2	0	0	3	0	1	0	0
TAPANI, Ke.	.300	10	3	0	0	0	1	0	2	0	1
TERRELL, Wa.	.273	11	3	1	0	0	0	0	0	0	0
TERRY, Sc.	.375	8	3	0	0	0	2	1	1	0	1
VALENZUELA, Fe.	.148	27	4	1	0	0	2	2	4	1	0
VIOLA, Fr.	.500	12	6	0	0	0	3	2	2	0	0
WALK, Bo.	.276	29	8	2	0	0	3	3	1	2	1
WELCH, Bo.	.364	11	4	1	0	1	1	0	0	0	1
WETTELAND, Jo.	.385	13	5	0	0	0	0	1	4	0	0
WILSON, Tr.	.091	11	1	0	0	0	0	0	1	0	0

Ron Gant

Split	Avg	G	AB	R	H	2B	3B	HR	RBI	SB	CS	SH	SF	BB	IW	HP	K	GRD	FLY	DP	#PIT	OBP	SLG
Total	.259	548	2042	328	529	109	17	94	283	99	49	6	16	188	12	10	382	611	743	24	8438	.322	.467

Split	Avg	G	AB	R	H	2B	3B	HR	RBI	SB	CS	SH	SF	BB	IW	HP	K	GRD	FLY	DP	#PIT	OBP	SLG
vs.ChN	.216	37	125	21	27	3	1	4	13	5	1	0	3	10	0	1	28	39	41	3	519	.273	.352
vs.Cin	.235	60	221	35	52	14	3	14	31	8	4	0	1	25	3	0	46	59	80	1	930	.312	.516
vs.Hou	.265	65	257	37	68	16	5	10	38	14	3	1	1	20	0	0	44	84	96	6	1092	.317	.482
vs.LA	.248	62	222	37	55	7	3	5	22	12	6	1	1	16	1	3	46	63	76	2	930	.306	.374
vs.Mon	.235	37	149	21	35	5	1	5	18	9	2	0	2	10	0	0	34	49	51	1	586	.280	.383
vs.NYN	.275	37	138	18	38	9	1	6	24	9	4	1	2	11	1	1	19	36	58	0	543	.329	.486
vs.Phi	.280	39	150	30	42	13	1	7	23	6	7	0	2	15	1	1	23	48	56	2	616	.345	.520
vs.Pit	.246	37	134	19	33	5	0	8	18	7	6	1	0	12	0	0	26	46	48	0	560	.308	.463
vs.StL	.289	41	159	30	46	12	0	9	22	6	2	1	1	13	1	0	30	43	58	2	604	.341	.535
vs.SD	.263	66	243	39	64	12	1	12	29	7	9	1	2	33	3	0	47	74	81	4	1023	.349	.469
vs.SF	.283	67	244	45	69	13	1	14	45	16	5	0	1	23	2	4	39	70	98	3	1035	.353	.516

Split	Avg	G	AB	R	H	2B	3B	HR	RBI	SB	CS	SH	SF	BB	IW	HP	K	GRD	FLY	DP	#PIT	OBP	SLG
at Atl	.267	265	986	171	263	47	11	49	142	44	19	3	4	95	7	6	177	275	398	10	4000	.334	.486
at ChN	.176	20	68	9	12	1	0	2	9	3	0	0	3	5	0	0	20	23	19	1	292	.224	.279
at Cin	.214	29	112	15	24	11	1	5	14	4	1	0	1	11	1	0	24	29	39	1	465	.282	.464
at Hou	.260	33	123	14	32	9	1	5	17	5	2	1	0	11	0	0	22	44	36	4	549	.321	.472
at LA	.278	33	126	20	35	5	2	3	14	10	4	0	1	6	1	2	23	38	36	2	513	.319	.421
at Mon	.254	18	71	8	18	3	1	2	8	7	2	0	2	5	0	0	16	30	21	1	290	.295	.408
at NYN	.235	19	68	7	16	3	1	3	9	3	4	0	0	6	0	0	13	16	25	0	279	.297	.441
at Phi	.318	20	85	19	27	9	0	4	15	4	5	0	2	8	1	1	13	26	31	1	360	.375	.565
at Pit	.237	21	76	7	18	3	0	2	8	4	4	1	0	5	0	0	15	29	24	0	330	.284	.355
at StL	.306	21	85	17	26	8	0	5	10	6	0	0	1	8	1	0	9	26	34	0	306	.362	.576
at SD	.205	33	112	18	23	5	0	4	13	3	4	1	1	16	1	0	28	36	28	2	488	.302	.357
at SF	.269	36	130	23	35	5	0	10	24	6	4	0	1	12	0	1	22	39	52	2	566	.333	.538

Split	Avg	G	AB	R	H	2B	3B	HR	RBI	SB	CS	SH	SF	BB	IW	HP	K	GRD	FLY	DP	#PIT	OBP	SLG
April	.159	59	195	18	31	10	2	4	14	9	5	0	0	22	0	0	43	51	76	4	844	.244	.292
May	.251	102	378	63	95	18	1	21	59	16	7	1	6	21	0	1	79	112	136	4	1489	.288	.471
June	.273	92	337	53	92	18	6	17	48	8	7	1	2	26	1	2	60	105	124	2	1366	.327	.513
July	.286	83	332	60	95	20	3	16	51	15	10	1	2	29	3	1	61	108	108	3	1349	.343	.509
August	.267	88	329	62	88	18	3	16	44	21	7	2	2	39	4	4	57	83	135	4	1378	.350	.486
September	.257	110	417	61	107	21	2	16	55	25	11	1	2	45	3	2	72	135	148	6	1782	.330	.432
October	.389	14	54	11	21	4	0	4	12	5	2	0	2	6	1	0	10	17	16	1	230	.435	.685

Split	Avg	G	AB	R	H	2B	3B	HR	RBI	SB	CS	SH	SF	BB	IW	HP	K	GRD	FLY	DP	#PIT	OBP	SLG
As 2b	.256	142	554	-	142	26	8	17	59	0	0	3	5	35	4	3	115	158	197	9	2191	.302	.424
As 3b	.210	74	286	-	60	11	2	10	30	0	0	2	2	28	2	1	60	88	98	1	1227	.281	.367
As lf	.295	38	132	-	39	7	1	9	20	0	0	0	2	14	0	0	18	46	48	3	541	.358	.568
As cf	.273	273	1041	-	284	63	6	58	172	34	15	1	7	107	8	6	177	310	394	11	4336	.342	.512
As rf	.500	2	2	-	1	0	0	0	0	0	0	0	0	0	0	0	1	0	0	0	6	.500	.500
As ph	.111	31	27	-	3	2	0	0	2	0	0	0	0	4	0	0	11	9	6	0	137	.226	.185

Split	Avg	G	AB	R	H	2B	3B	HR	RBI	SB	CS	SH	SF	BB	IW	HP	K	GRD	FLY	DP	#PIT	OBP	SLG
Batting #1	.271	157	650	105	176	36	5	30	68	29	20	3	3	48	3	4	115	200	236	4	2645	.323	.480
Batting #2	.238	52	202	35	48	11	0	8	25	13	4	1	1	10	0	0	33	54	76	7	726	.272	.411
Batting #3	.271	149	584	93	158	32	4	28	85	32	10	1	4	58	1	2	92	188	204	8	2422	.336	.483
Batting #4	.281	62	228	48	64	15	2	17	56	14	7	0	2	29	4	2	46	64	92	2	1004	.364	.588
Batting #5	.237	40	131	12	31	6	2	3	18	6	5	0	2	21	3	1	27	35	51	1	588	.342	.382
Batting #6	.130	14	46	4	6	2	0	1	3	2	2	0	0	8	0	0	16	12	15	0	235	.259	.239
Batting #7	.190	8	21	3	4	1	0	1	2	1	0	1	1	2	0	1	5	8	6	0	91	.280	.381
Batting #8	.248	46	161	24	40	5	4	6	25	2	1	0	3	10	1	0	40	43	59	2	639	.287	.441
Batting #9	.105	20	19	3	2	1	0	0	1	0	0	0	0	2	0	0	8	7	4	0	88	.190	.158

Split	Avg	G	AB	R	H	2B	3B	HR	RBI	SB	CS	SH	SF	BB	IW	HP	K	GRD	FLY	DP	#PIT	OBP	SLG
Home	.267	265	986	171	263	47	11	49	142	44	19	3	4	95	7	6	177	275	398	10	4000	.334	.486
Away	.252	283	1056	157	266	62	6	45	141	55	30	3	12	93	5	4	205	336	345	14	4438	.312	.450
Day	.242	134	483	68	117	19	1	20	68	30	17	2	2	51	1	5	105	150	170	6	2073	.320	.410
Night	.264	414	1559	260	412	90	16	74	215	69	32	4	14	137	11	5	277	461	573	18	6365	.323	.485
Grass	.258	406	1490	248	384	66	14	71	211	69	35	4	10	140	9	9	283	427	558	17	6138	.323	.464
Turf	.263	142	552	80	145	43	3	23	72	30	14	2	6	48	3	1	99	184	185	7	2300	.320	.476

Split	Avg	G	AB	R	H	2B	3B	HR	RBI	SB	CS	SH	SF	BB	IW	HP	K	GRD	FLY	DP	#PIT	OBP	SLG
vs. Left	.265	312	664	-	176	45	4	30	98	34	19	3	5	78	9	2	105	215	236	4	2862	.342	.480
vs. Right	.256	468	1378	-	353	64	13	64	185	65	30	3	11	110	3	8	277	396	507	20	5576	.313	.461
Groundball	.265	242	562	-	149	32	3	29	77	21	15	1	4	40	3	4	89	178	204	9	2205	.316	.488
Flyball	.247	280	502	-	124	24	7	18	59	27	11	4	2	59	5	3	120	141	170	6	2146	.329	.430
Ave G:F	.262	359	978	-	256	53	7	47	147	50	23	1	10	89	4	3	173	292	369	9	4087	.322	.474
Finesse	.282	270	599	-	169	32	5	26	83	19	12	1	4	58	4	3	98	212	200	13	2422	.346	.482
Power	.242	264	553	-	134	33	2	23	72	36	12	3	3	59	3	3	107	147	223	7	2393	.317	.434
Ave F:P	.254	349	890	-	226	44	10	45	128	44	25	2	9	71	5	4	177	252	320	4	3623	.309	.478

Split	Avg	G	AB	R	H	2B	3B	HR	RBI	SB	CS	SH	SF	BB	IW	HP	K	GRD	FLY	DP	#PIT	OBP	SLG
Inning 1-6	.265	509	1388	226	368	77	12	69	196	76	40	1	13	129	4	7	260	412	509	15	5765	.328	.487
Inning 7+	.246	524	654	102	161	32	5	25	87	23	9	5	3	59	8	3	122	199	234	9	2673	.310	.425

Split	Avg	G	AB	R	H	2B	3B	HR	RBI	SB	CS	SH	SF	BB	IW	HP	K	GRD	FLY	DP	#PIT	OBP	SLG
Close & Late	.203	263	311	46	63	11	2	10	44	9	6	4	3	33	5	2	67	89	113	4	1345	.281	.347
Close	.241	444	783	112	189	37	7	28	117	40	24	5	8	72	7	5	138	238	279	9	3226	.306	.414
Not Close	.270	514	1259	216	340	72	10	66	166	59	25	1	8	116	5	5	244	373	464	15	5212	.332	.500

Split	Avg	G	AB	R	H	2B	3B	HR	RBI	SB	CS	SH	SF	BB	IW	HP	K	GRD	FLY	DP	#PIT	OBP	SLG
None on	.271	506	1205	64	326	60	11	64	64	0	0	0	0	101	0	8	226	341	439	0	4918	.331	.498
None on/out	.293	395	556	37	163	30	4	37	37	0	0	0	0	41	0	3	89	158	218	0	2195	.345	.561
None on:1/2 Out	.251	419	649	27	163	30	7	27	27	0	0	0	0	60	0	5	137	183	221	0	2723	.319	.444

Split	Avg	G	AB	R	H	2B	3B	HR	RBI	SB	CS	SH	SF	BB	IW	HP	K	GRD	FLY	DP	#PIT	OBP	SLG
Runners on	.243	495	837	-	203	49	6	30	219	99	49	6	16	87	12	2	156	270	304	24	3520	.310	.423
Scoring Posn	.246	412	499	-	123	32	3	12	175	13	0	2	16	61	12	1	93	169	175	5	2173	.321	.395
OnBase: 2	.209	210	177	-	37	8	1	4	30	1	0	1	0	26	7	0	42	58	53	0	784	.310	.333
OnBase: 3	.229	96	70	-	16	5	0	1	25	0	0	0	6	7	1	0	16	22	28	0	343	.277	.343
OnBase: 12	.244	154	127	-	31	9	2	4	42	4	0	1	0	13	0	1	18	48	45	5	528	.319	.441
OnBase: 13	.315	101	54	-	17	4	0	3	30	8	0	0	6	4	1	0	9	20	19	0	211	.328	.556
OnBase: 23	.300	57	30	-	9	2	0	0	15	0	0	0	1	6	3	0	4	10	11	0	130	.405	.367
Bases Loaded	.317	74	41	-	13	4	0	0	33	0	0	0	3	5	0	0	4	11	19	0	177	.367	.415
SB Opp	.247	379	392	-	97	21	3	21	74	94	49	4	6	30	1	1	72	121	148	19	1558	.298	.477
SB Atd	.080	69	50	-	4	1	0	1	5	4	4	0	1	13	0	0	18	16	14	1	336	.266	.160
GDP Opp	.281	341	320	-	90	21	2	20	101	61	32	5	9	26	1	2	48	101	132	24	1258	.331	.547

Split	Avg	G	AB	R	H	2B	3B	HR	RBI	SB	CS	SH	SF	BB	IW	HP	K	GRD	FLY	DP	#PIT	OBP	SLG
0-0 count	.351	285	299	-	105	23	4	18	64	38	11	4	6	0	0	2	0	105	129	3	312	.349	.635
0-1 Count	.293	143	133	-	39	7	4	6	14	11	5	1	1	0	0	1	0	45	62	3	272	.296	.541
0-2 Count	.209	131	153	-	32	7	0	2	8	1	1	0	0	0	0	1	62	41	32	3	486	.214	.294
1-0 Count	.308	185	185	-	57	10	2	18	40	16	8	0	2	1	0	1	0	66	86	1	379	.312	.676
1-1 Count	.320	183	175	-	56	11	0	8	29	7	7	0	3	0	0	3	0	67	75	2	544	.326	.520
1-2 Count	.168	236	292	-	49	9	2	8	32	3	6	0	3	0	0	0	121	72	75	5	1268	.166	.295
2-0 Count	.338	73	68	-	23	7	0	4	11	3	0	0	0	0	0	0	0	26	31	1	204	.338	.618
2-1 Count	.356	147	135	-	48	13	1	4	17	11	3	0	0	0	0	0	0	51	59	0	538	.356	.556
2-2 Count	.160	250	319	-	51	9	2	7	19	5	1	0	0	0	0	1	119	77	90	4	1730	.162	.266
3-0 Count	.273	52	11	-	3	1	0	0	4	1	0	0	0	46	0	0	0	2	6	1	228	.860	.364
3-1 Count	.365	129	63	-	23	5	1	8	22	0	0	1	0	62	0	0	0	17	35	0	633	.680	.857
3-2 Count	.207	217	208	-	43	7	1	11	23	1	0	0	1	67	0	1	79	42	63	1	1838	.401	.409

Split	Avg	G	AB	R	H	2B	3B	HR	RBI	SB	CS	SH	SF	BB	IW	HP	K	GRD	FLY	DP	#PIT	OBP	SLG
After (0-1)	.212	473	882	-	187	41	6	30	82	24	19	2	6	42	0	4	238	245	293	15	3904	.249	.374
After (0-2)	.175	286	359	-	63	15	1	8	28	5	5	0	3	6	0	1	142	87	98	6	1608	.190	.290
After (1-0)	.275	487	861	-	237	45	7	46	137	36	16	0	4	134	0	4	144	261	321	6	4221	.374	.504
After (1-1)	.232	473	805	-	187	32	2	32	92	19	13	1	3	83	0	5	198	226	270	9	4237	.307	.396
After (1-2)	.171	375	551	-	94	16	3	20	51	6	7	0	3	26	0	1	213	124	159	8	2979	.208	.319
After (2-0)	.298	274	262	-	78	22	4	12	45	9	3	0	1	86	0	0	43	82	98	2	1634	.470	.550
After (2-1)	.258	360	430	-	111	25	3	15	55	15	4	1	1	85	0	1	100	125	146	2	2731	.381	.435
After (2-2)	.177	342	458	-	81	14	2	16	37	5	1	0	1	48	0	2	173	105	128	4	3005	.257	.321
After (3-0)	.245	99	49	-	12	3	1	3	11	2	0	0	0	64	0	0	8	12	23	1	538	.673	.531
After (3-1)	.271	177	133	-	36	7	2	10	27	1	0	1	0	81	0	0	26	31	60	1	1199	.547	.579
After (3-2)	.208	226	207	-	43	7	1	11	23	2	0	0	1	67	0	1	79	42	62	1	1844	.402	.411

What He Does at Each Pitch Count

Result	0-0	0-1	0-2	1-0	1-1	1-2	2-0	2-1	2-2	3-0	3-1	3-2
Taken Ball	1046	448	220	356	368	293	110	160	192	46	63	67
Taken Strike	538	130	23	211	128	30	60	79	31	41	23	22
Swung & Missed	207	125	42	110	110	90	42	60	89	6	19	58
Fouled Off	243	121	57	159	131	147	68	90	139	7	44	111
Put In Play	309	135	90	189	178	172	68	134	200	11	64	129

Pitcher	Avg	AB	H	2B	3B	HR	BI	W	K	SB	CS	Pitcher	Avg	AB	H	2B	3B	HR	BI	W	K	SB	CS
AGOSTO, Ju.	.278	18	5	1	0	0	2	0	1	0	0	HURST, Br.	.267	30	8	3	0	2	4	1	7	1	0
ANDERSEN, La.	.214	14	3	0	2	0	1	1	2	1	0	JACKSON, Da.	.300	20	6	2	0	2	3	3	3	0	0
ARMSTRONG, Ja.	.389	18	7	0	0	3	5	0	3	1	0	JONES, Ji.	.214	14	3	1	0	0	1	0	2	0	0
BEDROSIAN, St.	.125	8	1	0	0	0	0	0	1	0	0	KIPPER, Bo.	.500	8	4	1	0	1	1	0	0	1	1
BELCHER, Ti.	.217	23	5	0	2	1	5	2	4	4	2	LaCOSS, Mi.	.429	7	3	0	0	0	0	0	1	0	0
BENES, An.	.176	17	3	0	0	0	1	11	4	0	1	LANCASTER, Le.	.308	13	4	1	0	1	2	1	1	1	1
BIELECKI, Mi.	.222	9	2	0	0	0	1	1	2	0	0	LEARY, Ti.	.444	9	4	0	0	0	1	0	1	0	1
BLACK, Bu.	.278	18	5	1	0	1	2	0	2	2	0	LEFFERTS, Cr.	.111	18	2	0	0	1	3	2	2	0	1
BOYD, Oi.	.000	8	0	0	0	0	0	0	3	0	0	MADDUX, Gr.	.214	14	3	0	0	1	2	2	3	0	0
BRANTLEY, Je.	.364	11	4	1	0	2	3	1	2	0	0	MADDUX, Mi.	.267	15	4	1	0	2	2	1	4	1	2
BROWNING, To.	.216	37	8	2	0	4	6	1	3	1	1	MAHLER, Ri.	.429	7	3	1	0	0	1	0	0	0	0
BURKE, Ti.	.273	11	3	0	1	0	1	0	2	0	0	MARTINEZ, De.	.278	18	5	3	0	1	3	0	3	1	0
BURKETT, Jo.	.222	27	6	0	0	1	6	1	7	2	0	MARTINEZ, Ra.	.346	26	9	3	0	1	1	0	6	0	1
CARMAN, Do.	.227	22	5	2	0	3	3	1	3	1	0	McDOWELL, Ro.	.250	8	2	1	0	0	3	1	2	2	0
CARPENTER, Cr.	.286	7	2	2	0	0	2	0	0	0	0	MORGAN, Mi.	.160	25	4	0	0	1	1	0	0	1	0
CHARLTON, No.	.154	13	2	0	0	0	1	2	5	0	1	MULHOLLAND, Te.	.400	20	8	1	0	2	4	0	1	0	3
COMBS, Pa.	.286	7	2	0	0	0	0	1	1	0	1	MYERS, Ra.	.182	11	2	1	0	1	1	1	3	1	0
CONE, Da.	.261	23	6	1	0	1	2	0	5	1	0	OJEDA, Bo.	.263	19	5	1	0	0	4	1	3	2	0
COOK, De.	.222	9	2	1	0	0	0	2	0	1	0	OLIVERAS, Fr.	.429	7	3	0	0	0	0	0	0	1	1
CREWS, Ti.	.313	16	5	1	0	0	0	1	5	2	0	PALACIOS, Vi.	.286	7	2	0	0	2	4	0	4	0	0
DARLING, Ro.	.400	20	8	2	1	1	7	0	1	0	0	PARRETT, Je.	.400	10	4	2	0	0	0	1	2	0	2
DARWIN, Da.	.364	22	8	2	0	0	5	1	4	3	1	PENA, Al.	.000	11	0	0	0	0	0	0	3	0	0
DAVIS, Ma.	.143	7	1	0	0	0	0	1	3	0	0	PEREZ, Pa.	.429	7	3	0	0	1	2	0	0	0	0
DeJESUS, Jo.	.200	10	2	0	0	0	1	0	3	0	0	PORTUGAL, Ma.	.471	17	8	1	0	1	3	2	2	1	0
DeLEON, Jo.	.176	34	6	2	0	1	2	2	12	2	0	RASMUSSEN, De.	.318	22	7	3	0	1	4	4	4	3	1
DESHAIES, Ji.	.270	37	10	3	0	3	8	1	5	2	0	REUSCHEL, Ri.	.286	14	4	2	0	2	4	0	3	0	0
DIBBLE, Ro.	.167	12	2	0	1	0	0	0	5	0	0	RIJO, Jo.	.214	28	6	2	1	2	5	1	9	1	0
DOWNS, Ke.	.368	19	7	2	0	1	5	3	4	2	1	ROBINSON, Do.	.185	27	5	0	1	1	3	3	5	2	1
DRABEK, Do.	.130	23	3	0	0	1	4	0	9	0	1	RUFFIN, Br.	.357	14	5	3	0	1	4	0	1	0	0
FERNANDEZ, Si.	.000	8	0	0	0	0	0	2	4	0	1	RYAN, No.	.273	11	3	0	0	2	2	0	5	1	0
FRANCO, Jo.	.125	8	1	0	0	1	2	1	2	0	0	SAMPEN, Bi.	.333	9	3	0	0	1	1	0	2	1	0
GARDNER, Ma.	.375	8	3	0	0	1	2	0	2	0	1	SCHIRALDI, Ca.	.077	13	1	0	0	1	1	2	6	1	0
GARRELTS, Sc.	.200	20	4	1	0	2	6	2	3	0	0	SCOTT, Mi.	.207	29	6	2	1	2	4	1	8	1	0
GOODEN, Dw.	.286	28	8	1	0	1	2	1	3	4	0	SCUDDER, Sc.	.000	7	0	0	0	0	0	2	2	1	1
GOTT, Ji.	.182	11	2	0	0	0	2	0	3	0	0	SHOW, Er.	.240	25	6	2	0	2	3	1	3	1	0
GREENE, To.	.333	9	3	0	0	1	2	0	1	0	1	SMILEY, Jo.	.211	19	4	1	0	0	1	1	2	1	0
GROSS, Ke.	.118	17	2	1	0	0	0	1	3	1	0	SMITH, Br.	.095	21	2	1	0	1	1	1	7	0	0
GROSS, Ki.	.286	7	2	1	0	0	1	0	1	0	1	SMITH, Da.	.375	8	3	0	0	0	2	1	0	0	0
HAMMAKER, At.	.308	13	4	0	0	0	0	1	1	1	1	SMITH, Za.	.300	10	3	1	0	0	2	0	2	0	0
HARKEY, Mi.	.300	10	3	0	1	0	0	0	3	1	0	TERRY, Sc.	.375	16	6	1	0	0	0	1	3	1	0
HARNISCH, Pe.	.235	17	4	1	0	0	0	0	2	1	0	TEWKSBURY, Bo.	.500	12	6	0	0	0	1	0	2	1	0
HARRIS, Gr.	.154	13	2	0	0	0	1	2	7	1	2	VALENZUELA, Fe.	.263	19	5	1	1	0	0	3	4	1	0
HARTLEY, Mi.	.250	8	2	1	0	0	3	0	2	1	0	VIOLA, Fr.	.313	16	5	1	0	0	1	0	1	1	1
HAWKINS, An.	.353	17	6	0	0	1	1	0	4	0	0	WALK, Bo.	.154	13	2	0	0	0	0	0	0	1	1
HEATON, Ne.	.333	12	4	1	0	1	1	4	3	1	1	WHITEHURST, Wa.	.300	10	3	0	0	2	5	0	1	0	1
HERSHISER, Or.	.273	22	6	1	0	0	1	1	6	1	0	WHITSON, Ed.	.320	25	8	2	0	0	1	2	2	0	1
HILL, Ke.	.313	16	5	1	0	2	7	1	2	0	0	WILSON, Tr.	.286	14	4	1	0	1	3	0	1	1	0
HOLMAN, Br.	.077	13	1	0	0	0	0	0	2	1	0												

Ken Griffey Jr.

Split	Avg	G	AB	R	H	2B	3B	HR	RBI	SB	CS	SH	SF	BB	IW	HP	K	GRD	FLY	DP	#PIT	OBP	SLG
Total	.299	436	1600	228	478	93	8	60	241	50	24	5	17	178	41	5	246	570	458	26	6394	.367	.479

Split	Avg	G	AB	R	H	2B	3B	HR	RBI	SB	CS	SH	SF	BB	IW	HP	K	GRD	FLY	DP	#PIT	OBP	SLG
vs.Bal	.382	36	131	22	50	10	1	4	30	4	2	0	3	15	6	0	13	56	35	0	494	.436	.565
vs.Bos	.261	36	134	13	35	8	1	2	14	6	2	1	1	14	1	1	22	53	38	3	526	.333	.381
vs.Cal	.314	29	105	16	33	9	0	4	16	3	2	1	1	9	2	0	20	39	28	3	402	.365	.514
vs.ChA	.240	30	104	17	25	1	2	4	16	1	0	1	4	10	0	1	14	37	36	2	431	.303	.404
vs.Cle	.263	33	114	20	30	7	1	3	14	2	1	0	2	17	6	0	18	41	34	0	484	.353	.421
vs.Det	.320	34	122	17	39	10	0	3	16	5	3	0	1	24	8	0	14	44	37	4	535	.429	.475
vs.KC	.246	34	126	15	31	4	1	5	17	4	1	0	0	16	2	1	23	44	32	5	480	.336	.413
vs.Mil	.333	35	135	19	45	9	0	5	19	4	2	0	1	10	2	0	23	49	34	1	536	.377	.511
vs.Min	.328	36	137	24	45	9	0	7	19	5	2	0	1	13	5	0	22	41	46	1	531	.384	.547
vs.NYA	.328	34	125	17	41	9	1	7	21	5	3	1	0	12	2	0	24	30	42	1	515	.387	.584
vs.Oak	.275	31	120	15	33	7	0	7	21	1	2	1	3	9	2	1	14	44	41	3	497	.323	.508
vs.Tex	.254	36	126	18	32	3	1	6	24	5	1	0	0	17	1	0	21	46	29	1	515	.343	.437
vs.Tor	.322	32	121	15	39	7	0	3	14	5	3	0	0	12	4	1	18	46	26	2	448	.388	.455

Split	Avg	G	AB	R	H	2B	3B	HR	RBI	SB	CS	SH	SF	BB	IW	HP	K	GRD	FLY	DP	#PIT	OBP	SLG
at Bal	.413	18	63	9	26	3	0	3	12	1	2	0	2	9	5	0	7	31	14	0	235	.473	.603
at Bos	.275	18	69	8	19	5	0	0	7	3	0	0	0	8	1	1	12	28	17	3	289	.359	.348
at Cal	.265	14	49	7	13	2	0	4	10	1	2	1	0	3	0	0	10	15	17	3	180	.308	.551
at ChA	.228	15	57	9	13	0	1	1	8	0	0	0	3	4	0	1	9	17	21	1	243	.277	.316
at Cle	.224	17	58	10	13	2	1	2	3	1	1	0	0	6	4	0	11	20	16	0	233	.297	.397
at Det	.381	17	63	7	24	4	0	0	6	3	1	0	1	12	5	0	8	19	21	2	273	.474	.444
at KC	.213	17	61	6	13	3	1	2	7	3	1	0	0	10	1	0	10	28	13	4	250	.324	.393
at Mil	.338	17	65	10	22	3	0	3	10	2	1	0	0	4	2	0	13	24	14	1	249	.377	.523
at Min	.328	17	67	11	22	7	0	3	8	2	0	0	1	3	2	0	13	17	25	1	258	.352	.567
at NYA	.288	16	59	5	17	2	1	3	11	3	1	0	0	4	1	0	11	14	23	0	254	.333	.508
at Oak	.270	16	63	6	17	4	0	2	11	0	2	1	2	6	0	0	5	23	22	2	254	.324	.429
at Sea	.309	221	805	122	249	53	4	34	136	30	10	3	8	94	18	3	116	289	228	7	3200	.380	.512
at Tex	.221	19	68	11	15	2	0	3	10	1	1	0	0	10	0	0	13	22	17	1	287	.321	.382
at Tor	.283	14	53	7	15	3	0	0	2	0	2	0	0	5	2	0	8	23	10	1	192	.345	.340

Split	Avg	G	AB	R	H	2B	3B	HR	RBI	SB	CS	SH	SF	BB	IW	HP	K	GRD	FLY	DP	#PIT	OBP	SLG
April	.336	62	232	34	78	10	1	10	32	7	4	2	2	22	5	0	37	72	68	3	899	.391	.517
May	.301	81	286	44	86	16	1	15	42	12	5	0	2	33	13	0	44	111	81	3	1113	.371	.521
June	.264	78	276	36	73	19	0	5	30	8	2	0	2	38	6	0	40	95	74	5	1143	.351	.388
July	.336	66	247	41	83	17	1	10	47	8	2	2	4	27	4	1	38	90	73	2	992	.398	.534
August	.310	67	261	34	81	19	2	11	38	8	4	1	2	26	7	1	41	89	76	7	1037	.372	.525
September	.263	76	281	37	74	12	3	9	51	6	5	0	5	30	6	3	46	104	81	6	1132	.335	.423
October	.176	6	17	2	3	0	0	0	1	1	2	0	0	2	0	0	0	9	5	0	78	.263	.176

Split	Avg	G	AB	R	H	2B	3B	HR	RBI	SB	CS	SH	SF	BB	IW	HP	K	GRD	FLY	DP	#PIT	OBP	SLG
As ph for dh	.000	1	1	-	0	0	0	0	0	0	0	0	0	0	0	0	0	0	1	0	7	.000	.000
As lf	.000	0	0	-	0	0	0	0	0	0	0	0	0	0	0	0	0	0	0	0	0	.000	.000
As cf	.300	422	1578	-	474	93	8	58	236	18	6	5	17	175	40	5	242	560	452	25	6289	.368	.480
As dh (not ph)	.083	3	12	-	1	0	0	0	0	1	0	0	0	1	0	0	1	6	5	0	59	.154	.083
As ph (not dh)	.300	12	10	-	3	0	0	2	5	0	0	0	0	2	1	0	3	4	2	1	48	.417	.900

Split	Avg	G	AB	R	H	2B	3B	HR	RBI	SB	CS	SH	SF	BB	IW	HP	K	GRD	FLY	DP	#PIT	OBP	SLG
Batting #1	.286	2	7	1	2	0	0	1	1	0	0	1	0	2	0	0	1	3	1	0	37	.444	.714
Batting #2	.238	29	101	13	24	3	0	4	11	1	2	1	0	7	1	0	24	28	29	1	413	.287	.386
Batting #3	.313	232	880	126	275	58	5	31	143	26	9	2	11	102	22	3	127	312	268	18	3540	.382	.495
Batting #4	.154	9	26	3	4	1	1	1	3	0	0	1	1	3	1	0	8	7	7	1	110	.233	.385
Batting #5	.290	123	458	65	133	25	2	18	60	18	10	0	3	48	12	1	60	171	125	5	1768	.357	.472
Batting #6	.307	35	114	16	35	6	0	3	16	5	3	0	2	15	5	1	23	45	25	1	465	.386	.439
Batting #7	.333	4	12	3	4	0	0	1	4	0	0	0	0	1	0	0	2	4	2	0	52	.385	.583
Batting #8	1.00	1	1	1	1	0	0	1	3	0	0	0	0	0	0	0	0	0	1	0	5	1.000	4.000
Batting #9	.000	1	1	0	0	0	0	0	0	0	0	0	0	0	0	0	0	1	0	0	0	4	.000	.000

Split	Avg	G	AB	R	H	2B	3B	HR	RBI	SB	CS	SH	SF	BB	IW	HP	K	GRD	FLY	DP	#PIT	OBP	SLG
Home	.309	221	805	122	249	53	4	34	136	30	10	3	8	94	18	3	116	289	228	7	3200	.380	.512
Away	.288	215	795	106	229	40	4	26	105	20	14	2	9	84	23	2	130	281	230	19	3194	.354	.447
Day	.306	113	418	68	128	22	3	20	64	12	8	0	7	40	11	1	75	134	132	8	1607	.363	.517
Night	.296	323	1182	160	350	71	5	40	177	38	16	5	10	138	30	4	171	436	326	18	4787	.369	.466
Grass	.292	167	614	82	179	27	3	21	88	15	11	2	8	66	18	2	99	213	182	13	2494	.358	.448
Turf	.303	269	986	146	299	66	5	39	153	35	13	3	9	112	23	3	147	357	276	13	3900	.373	.499

Split	Avg	G	AB	R	H	2B	3B	HR	RBI	SB	CS	SH	SF	BB	IW	HP	K	GRD	FLY	DP	#PIT	OBP	SLG
vs. Left	.286	272	496	-	142	30	1	13	60	9	6	4	6	46	5	3	106	169	124	6	2028	.347	.429
vs. Right	.304	387	1104	-	336	63	7	47	181	41	18	1	11	132	36	2	140	401	334	20	4366	.376	.502
Groundball	.331	203	495	-	164	37	2	20	85	13	6	0	8	53	16	0	59	198	133	6	1899	.390	.535
Flyball	.280	221	378	-	106	20	0	20	64	15	6	3	2	51	12	0	84	115	103	5	1517	.364	.492
Ave G:F	.286	288	727	-	208	36	6	20	92	22	12	2	7	74	13	5	103	257	222	15	2978	.353	.435
Finesse	.300	168	300	-	90	20	1	6	36	13	2	1	2	40	10	1	41	122	85	7	1171	.382	.433
Power	.339	174	339	-	115	19	1	21	64	9	4	1	6	33	11	0	52	99	122	4	1311	.392	.587
Ave F:P	.284	354	961	-	273	54	6	33	141	28	18	3	9	105	20	4	153	349	251	15	3912	.354	.456

Split	Avg	G	AB	R	H	2B	3B	HR	RBI	SB	CS	SH	SF	BB	IW	HP	K	GRD	FLY	DP	#PIT	OBP	SLG
Inning 1-6	.309	424	1115	164	344	64	5	44	181	41	18	2	11	112	12	3	150	415	311	17	4440	.370	.493
Inning 7+	.276	411	485	64	134	29	3	16	60	9	6	3	6	66	29	2	96	155	147	9	1954	.361	.447

Split	Avg	G	AB	R	H	2B	3B	HR	RBI	SB	CS	SH	SF	BB	IW	HP	K	GRD	FLY	DP	#PIT	OBP	SLG
Close & Late	.242	225	248	31	60	9	2	8	33	7	4	3	3	35	12	1	63	82	69	5	1081	.334	.391
Close	.292	357	617	88	180	39	4	27	88	16	8	5	3	79	31	3	109	215	172	10	2439	.373	.499
Not Close	.303	425	983	140	298	54	4	33	153	34	16	0	14	99	10	2	137	355	286	16	3955	.363	.467

Split	Avg	G	AB	R	H	2B	3B	HR	RBI	SB	CS	SH	SF	BB	IW	HP	K	GRD	FLY	DP	#PIT	OBP	SLG
None on	.296	414	881	36	261	50	4	36	36	0	0	0	0	77	0	1	122	305	268	0	3583	.353	.485
None on/out	.267	279	330	13	88	11	3	13	13	0	0	0	0	17	0	1	38	110	112	0	1264	.305	.436
None on:1/2 Out	.314	353	551	23	173	39	1	23	23	0	0	0	0	60	0	0	84	195	156	0	2319	.381	.514

Split	Avg	G	AB	R	H	2B	3B	HR	RBI	SB	CS	SH	SF	BB	IW	HP	K	GRD	FLY	DP	#PIT	OBP	SLG
Runners on	.302	405	719	-	217	43	4	24	205	50	24	5	17	101	41	4	124	265	190	26	2811	.383	.473
Scoring Posn	.313	343	412	-	129	26	2	11	171	11	5	1	17	79	41	2	86	145	109	5	1730	.412	.466
OnBase: 2	.314	163	121	-	38	9	1	1	28	3	1	1	0	45	27	0	26	38	27	0	577	.500	.430
OnBase: 3	.391	77	46	-	18	4	0	2	32	0	0	0	9	5	2	1	8	17	19	0	210	.393	.609
OnBase: 12	.259	152	139	-	36	4	1	3	32	3	3	0	0	13	0	1	31	56	31	4	553	.327	.367
OnBase: 13	.436	86	55	-	24	5	0	2	36	5	1	0	4	2	1	0	12	18	15	1	184	.426	.636
OnBase: 23	.222	59	27	-	6	3	0	0	20	0	0	0	3	12	11	0	6	7	11	0	119	.429	.333
Bases Loaded	.292	48	24	-	7	1	0	3	23	0	0	0	1	2	0	0	3	9	6	0	87	.333	.708
SB Opp	.309	308	362	-	112	22	2	15	70	44	20	4	4	24	1	2	50	138	96	22	1265	.352	.506
SB Atd	.259	61	54	-	14	5	0	0	11	3	1	1	2	10	1	0	18	15	12	0	322	.364	.352
GDP Opp	.316	272	320	-	101	19	2	16	83	17	14	4	5	19	0	3	43	127	86	26	1098	.354	.538

Split	Avg	G	AB	R	H	2B	3B	HR	RBI	SB	CS	SH	SF	BB	IW	HP	K	GRD	FLY	DP	#PIT	OBP	SLG
0-0 count	.391	204	238	-	93	17	1	15	58	7	6	4	5	6	6	4	0	101	77	9	260	.407	.660
0-1 Count	.345	141	145	-	50	15	2	5	22	4	1	0	2	1	1	0	0	62	43	7	294	.345	.579
0-2 Count	.231	102	117	-	27	7	1	3	9	1	1	0	0	0	0	0	49	33	20	2	374	.231	.385
1-0 Count	.373	152	158	-	59	9	0	4	22	7	2	0	2	2	2	0	0	63	50	1	324	.377	.506
1-1 Count	.337	156	163	-	55	10	2	4	24	6	1	1	1	0	0	0	0	80	49	2	495	.335	.497
1-2 Count	.189	178	227	-	43	11	0	5	22	3	4	0	2	0	0	0	93	56	49	1	987	.188	.304
2-0 Count	.349	67	63	-	22	1	0	2	14	2	1	0	1	2	2	0	0	24	26	0	197	.364	.460
2-1 Count	.326	105	89	-	29	6	0	8	18	8	2	0	1	0	0	0	0	33	38	3	362	.322	.663
2-2 Count	.207	173	208	-	43	7	0	4	13	5	2	0	3	0	0	1	71	52	53	1	1148	.208	.298
3-0 Count	.667	53	9	-	6	1	0	2	7	1	0	0	0	47	3	0	0	2	4	0	225	.946	1.444
3-1 Count	.290	72	31	-	9	1	0	2	5	1	0	0	0	44	0	0	0	11	13	0	379	.707	.516
3-2 Count	.284	163	148	-	42	8	2	6	27	1	2	0	0	49	0	0	31	53	34	0	1335	.462	.486

Split	Avg	G	AB	R	H	2B	3B	HR	RBI	SB	CS	SH	SF	BB	IW	HP	K	GRD	FLY	DP	#PIT	OBP	SLG
After (0-1)	.268	385	708	-	190	48	4	24	86	11	12	0	7	26	3	0	149	239	196	16	2935	.291	.449
After (0-2)	.209	214	254	-	53	15	1	3	19	3	4	0	3	5	1	0	92	73	59	3	1105	.221	.311
After (1-0)	.298	392	654	-	195	28	3	21	97	30	6	1	5	122	8	1	97	230	186	1	3202	.407	.446
After (1-1)	.262	360	600	-	157	29	4	22	77	20	9	1	4	38	0	0	124	202	167	6	2961	.304	.433
After (1-2)	.185	281	378	-	70	17	0	9	36	8	4	0	5	9	0	0	136	118	99	2	1976	.202	.302
After (2-0)	.325	235	206	-	67	8	0	11	43	5	1	0	1	101	6	1	30	70	62	0	1455	.547	.524
After (2-1)	.282	260	298	-	84	14	2	14	42	13	6	0	1	50	0	1	55	93	91	3	1864	.386	.483
After (2-2)	.235	245	306	-	72	11	1	10	35	8	4	0	3	27	0	1	90	85	76	1	2017	.297	.376
After (3-0)	.439	116	41	-	18	3	0	4	14	1	1	0	0	82	4	0	6	15	11	0	613	.813	.805
After (3-1)	.262	130	84	-	22	5	1	2	11	1	0	0	0	66	0	0	14	31	25	0	863	.587	.417
After (3-2)	.280	173	150	-	42	8	2	6	27	3	2	0	0	49	0	0	32	53	35	0	1346	.457	.480

What He Does at Each Pitch Count

Result	0-0	0-1	0-2	1-0	1-1	1-2	2-0	2-1	2-2	3-0	3-1	3-2
Taken Ball	800	327	147	310	236	167	126	87	132	47	44	50
Taken Strike	404	81	11	172	64	22	66	49	18	56	24	5
Swung & Missed	115	66	41	51	71	71	10	40	54	6	16	28
Fouled Off	226	119	54	101	118	108	43	90	107	5	36	100
Put In Play	246	146	68	161	163	137	64	90	138	9	30	116

294

Pitcher	Avg	AB	H	2B	3B	HR	BI	W	K	SB	CS
ABBOTT, Ji.	.364	11	4	2	0	0	1	0	1	0	0
ANDERSON, Al.	.308	13	4	0	0	1	3	1	3	0	1
APPIER, Ke.	.286	21	6	0	0	2	4	1	1	1	0
AQUINO, Lu.	.375	8	3	1	0	0	1	0	0	1	1
BAILES, Sc.	.200	10	2	0	0	0	1	1	2	0	0
BALLARD, Je.	.500	14	7	2	0	0	6	0	0	1	0
BARFIELD, Jo.	.143	7	1	0	0	0	0	0	1	0	0
BLACK, Bu.	.182	11	2	2	0	0	2	2	1	0	0
BODDICKER, Mi.	.143	21	3	0	0	0	1	2	4	2	0
BOLTON, To.	.333	9	3	0	0	1	1	0	1	0	0
BOSIO, Ch.	.286	14	4	2	0	0	0	2	1	1	0
BROWN, Ke.	.273	11	3	0	0	0	2	0	0	0	0
CADARET, Gr.	.455	11	5	1	0	0	0	0	1	1	1
CANDIOTTI, To.	.222	18	4	0	0	0	4	2	2	1	0
CERUTTI, Jo.	.222	9	2	0	0	0	0	1	3	0	0
CLEMENS, Ro.	.400	15	6	3	0	0	4	1	1	1	0
CRIM, Ch.	.143	7	1	0	0	0	0	0	2	0	0
DAVIS, St.	.182	11	2	1	0	0	1	0	2	0	0
DOPSON, Jo.	.125	8	1	0	0	0	0	0	2	0	0
ERICKSON, Sc.	.462	13	6	2	0	0	0	0	0	0	1
FARR, St.	.091	11	1	1	0	0	0	2	5	0	0
FINLEY, Ch.	.133	15	2	0	0	0	1	0	4	0	0
FLANAGAN, Mi.	.462	13	6	1	0	0	0	1	1	1	0
FOSSAS, To.	.125	8	1	0	0	0	1	0	3	0	0
GIBSON, Pa.	.583	12	7	2	0	1	1	1	0	0	0
GLEATON, Je.	.125	8	1	0	0	0	0	1	2	0	0
GORDON, To.	.389	18	7	0	0	3	6	8	3	0	0
GUBICZA, Ma.	.571	7	4	0	0	0	1	2	2	0	0
GUETTERMAN, Le.	.273	11	3	0	1	1	4	0	3	0	0
GULLICKSON, Bi.	.231	13	3	2	0	0	1	8	3	1	0
GUTHRIE, Ma.	.455	11	5	0	0	1	2	2	2	1	1
HARNISCH, Pe.	.375	16	6	0	0	1	3	1	1	0	0
HARRIS, Gr.	.250	8	2	0	0	1	2	3	2	2	0
HAWKINS, An.	.353	17	6	0	0	0	1	3	2	0	1
HIBBARD, Gr.	.091	11	1	0	0	0	1	0	2	0	0
HIGUERA, Te.	.364	11	4	0	0	0	2	0	3	1	0
HONEYCUTT, Ri.	.125	8	1	0	0	0	1	0	1	0	0
HOUGH, Ch.	.333	24	8	0	0	2	4	1	2	2	0
JEFFCOAT, Mi.	.250	12	3	0	0	2	2	0	1	0	0
JOHNSON, Da.	.500	14	7	1	0	1	3	0	0	0	0
JONES, Do.	.125	8	1	0	0	0	0	0	1	0	0
KEY, Ji.	.250	12	3	0	0	1	2	1	2	0	0
KIECKER, Da.	.500	8	4	0	1	0	1	0	0	0	1
KING, Er.	.154	13	2	0	0	1	2	0	1	0	0
KNUDSON, Ma.	.429	14	6	0	0	1	2	0	0	1	0
LANGSTON, Ma.	.429	14	6	3	0	0	2	1	4	0	0
LEARY, Ti.	.250	16	4	1	0	1	1	0	4	0	0
McCASKILL, Ki.	.250	20	5	1	0	1	2	0	0	1	0
McDOWELL, Ja.	.214	14	3	0	1	0	0	1	1	0	0
MILACKI, Bo.	.667	9	6	1	0	0	3	2	0	0	0
MONTGOMERY, Je.	.143	7	1	0	0	0	1	0	2	1	0
MOORE, Mi.	.308	13	4	0	0	1	6	1	1	0	0
MORRIS, Ja.	.313	16	5	2	0	1	3	2	3	2	0
MURPHY, Ro.	.143	7	1	1	0	0	0	2	3	0	0
NAGY, Ch.	.455	11	5	2	1	1	4	1	3	0	0
NAVARRO, Ja.	.409	22	9	1	0	1	4	0	3	0	0
NICHOLS, Ro.	.444	9	4	2	0	0	0	0	0	0	0
OROSCO, Je.	.400	10	4	0	0	0	0	1	3	0	0
PEREZ, Me.	.231	13	3	0	0	1	2	0	3	0	0
PLESAC, Da.	.111	9	1	1	0	0	1	0	2	0	0
RADINSKY, Sc.	.000	7	0	0	0	0	0	0	3	0	0
ROBINSON, Je.	.300	10	3	1	0	1	3	1	0	0	0
ROBINSON, Ro.	.143	7	1	1	0	0	0	0	1	0	0
ROGERS, Ke.	.333	15	5	2	0	0	1	1	4	0	0
RYAN, No.	.250	24	6	1	0	2	8	3	5	3	0
SABERHAGEN, Br.	.083	12	1	0	0	0	0	1	3	0	0
SANDERSON, Sc.	.444	18	8	2	0	2	6	1	1	0	0
SMITH, Ro.	.533	15	8	3	0	1	9	0	2	0	0
STEWART, Da.	.458	24	11	4	0	1	4	2	1	1	0
STIEB, Da.	.500	8	4	2	0	0	2	0	0	1	0
STOTTLEMYRE, T.	.200	20	4	0	0	0	2	0	1	0	1
SWINDELL, Gr.	.333	9	3	0	0	2	2	0	2	0	0
TANANA, Fr.	.316	19	6	2	0	0	2	1	1	0	0
TAPANI, Ke.	.182	22	4	1	0	1	2	0	2	0	0
TERRELL, Wa.	.250	12	3	2	0	0	1	1	0	0	0
WARD, Du.	.556	9	5	1	0	1	1	0	1	2	0
WEGMAN, Bi.	.444	9	4	0	0	2	4	3	2	1	0
WELCH, Bo.	.150	20	3	0	0	0	0	1	2	0	1
WELLS, Da.	.429	14	6	1	0	1	1	0	3	0	0
WEST, Da.	.462	13	6	1	0	2	3	1	3	0	0
WILLS, Fr.	.200	10	2	0	0	0	1	0	2	0	1
WITT, Bo.	.231	13	3	0	0	1	5	3	2	0	0
WITT, Mi.	.133	15	2	0	0	0	1	2	2	1	0
YOUNG, Cu.	.300	10	3	1	0	0	0	0	1	0	1

Tom Glavine

Split	W	L	S	ERA	SUP	Avg	G	GS	CG	SO	GF	OP	HD	IP	H	HR	BFP	R	ER	RF
Total	53	52	0	3.81	4.47	.255	139	139	17	5	0	0	0	893.0	861	72	3766	427	378	444

Split	W	L	S	ERA	SUP	Avg	G	GS	CG	SO	GF	OP	HD	IP	H	HR	BFP	R	ER	RF
Starting	53	52	0	3.81	4.47	.255	139	139	17	5	0	0	0	893.0	861	72	3766	427	378	444

Split	W	L	S	ERA	SUP	Avg	G	GS	CG	SO	GF	OP	HD	IP	H	HR	BFP	R	ER	RF
vs.ChN	2	3	0	3.42	3.99	.231	8	8	1	0	0	0	0	47.1	42	4	198	24	18	21
vs.Cin	10	3	0	3.02	5.77	.221	14	14	1	0	0	0	0	98.1	78	6	387	35	33	63
vs.Hou	0	8	0	4.15	1.57	.267	13	13	1	0	0	0	0	80.1	82	3	343	40	37	14
vs.LA	6	9	0	3.96	2.85	.292	18	18	5	3	0	0	0	113.2	129	8	493	57	50	36
vs.Mon	2	8	0	4.66	2.54	.233	13	13	1	0	0	0	0	85.0	74	12	352	45	44	24
vs.NYN	2	2	0	3.64	3.64	.249	7	7	1	0	0	0	0	47.0	44	6	194	20	19	19
vs.Phi	8	1	0	3.19	6.59	.239	13	13	2	1	0	0	0	84.2	76	4	352	35	30	62
vs.Pit	6	5	0	3.78	5.83	.266	13	13	0	0	0	0	0	83.1	82	5	355	45	35	54
vs.StL	3	2	0	3.96	4.11	.259	10	10	1	0	0	0	0	61.1	62	5	263	27	27	28
vs.SD	9	6	0	3.82	5.80	.262	19	19	2	1	0	0	0	122.2	124	10	529	62	52	79
vs.SF	5	5	0	4.28	5.71	.256	11	11	2	0	0	0	0	69.1	68	9	300	37	33	44

Split	W	L	S	ERA	SUP	Avg	G	GS	CG	SO	GF	OP	HD	IP	H	HR	BFP	R	ER	RF
at Atl	25	25	0	4.12	4.84	.260	65	65	6	2	0	0	0	415.0	414	49	1752	211	190	223
at ChN	1	1	0	3.22	5.24	.256	4	4	1	0	0	0	0	22.1	23	1	97	14	8	13
at Cin	8	0	0	1.74	6.53	.201	8	8	1	0	0	0	0	62.0	44	2	233	14	12	45
at Hou	0	8	0	4.15	0.97	.271	11	11	1	0	0	0	0	65.0	68	1	285	33	30	7
at LA	4	5	0	4.09	2.86	.305	11	11	3	2	0	0	0	66.0	80	3	290	34	30	21
at Mon	1	4	0	4.15	2.27	.222	7	7	1	0	0	0	0	47.2	38	6	199	22	22	12
at NYN	1	1	0	3.33	4.00	.250	4	4	0	0	0	0	0	27.0	26	1	112	11	10	12
at Phi	4	0	0	1.96	7.85	.205	5	5	1	0	0	0	0	36.2	27	2	149	10	8	32
at Pit	0	5	0	6.15	2.67	.318	6	6	0	0	0	0	0	33.2	41	1	158	27	23	10
at StL	1	1	0	5.12	2.27	.254	6	6	0	0	0	0	0	31.2	31	1	142	18	18	8
at SD	6	2	0	3.02	6.03	.227	9	9	2	1	0	0	0	62.2	51	5	251	23	21	42
at SF	2	0	0	2.31	7.33	.212	3	3	1	0	0	0	0	23.1	18	0	98	10	6	19

Split	W	L	S	ERA	SUP	Avg	G	GS	CG	SO	GF	OP	HD	IP	H	HR	BFP	R	ER	RF
April	6	7	0	3.10	3.88	.245	13	17	4	2	0	0	0	116.0	105	9	468	43	40	50
May	11	5	0	3.45	5.63	.229	23	23	5	1	0	0	0	140.2	120	13	584	64	54	88
June	9	10	0	4.23	4.54	.285	23	23	2	1	0	0	0	146.2	163	14	625	79	69	74
July	6	6	0	3.62	3.62	.250	20	20	2	0	0	0	0	134.1	127	14	560	58	54	54
August	9	15	0	4.44	4.07	.273	28	28	2	1	0	0	0	170.1	181	10	746	95	84	77
September	11	9	0	3.86	4.83	.242	27	27	2	0	0	0	0	177.0	160	12	753	85	76	95
October	1	0	0	1.13	6.75	.185	1	1	0	0	0	0	0	8.0	5	0	30	3	1	6

Split	W	L	S	ERA	SUP	Avg	G	GS	CG	SO	GF	OP	HD	IP	H	HR	BFP	R	ER	RF
Home	25	25	0	4.12	4.84	.260	65	65	6	2	0	0	0	415.0	414	49	1752	211	190	223
Away	29	27	0	3.54	4.29	.250	74	74	11	3	0	0	0	478.0	447	23	2014	216	188	228
Day	12	13	0	4.28	4.41	.267	34	34	4	1	0	0	0	208.1	215	17	903	112	99	102
Night	41	39	0	3.67	4.50	.251	101	105	13	4	0	0	0	684.2	646	55	2863	315	279	342
Grass	39	34	0	3.87	4.82	.259	96	96	13	5	0	0	0	616.1	612	59	2600	303	265	330
Turf	14	18	0	3.68	3.71	.243	43	43	4	0	0	0	0	276.2	249	13	1166	124	113	114

Days Rest	W	L	S	ERA	SUP	Avg	G	GS	CG	SO	GF	OP	HD	IP	H	HR	BFP	R	ER	RF
0-3	2	6	0	5.46	2.50	.311	10	10	2	2	0	0	0	57.2	71	3	254	35	35	16
4	34	30	0	3.66	4.73	.250	82	82	10	3	0	0	0	525.2	497	35	2220	254	214	276
5	9	8	0	3.82	4.91	.259	28	28	1	0	0	0	0	181.1	178	19	755	82	77	99
6+	7	8	0	3.78	3.71	.243	18	18	4	0	0	0	0	121.1	111	14	511	55	51	50

Split	2B	3B	RBI	SH	SF	BB	IW	HB	K	WP	Bk	SB	CS	DP	GRD	FLY	#PIT	#PK	OBP	SLG
Total	148	18	359	58	26	283	30	16	515	23	6	70	45	75	1350	960	13493	934	.313	.373

Split	2B	3B	RBI	SH	SF	BB	IW	HB	K	WP	Bk	SB	CS	DP	GRD	FLY	#PIT	#PK	OBP	SLG
Starting	148	18	359	58	26	283	30	16	515	23	6	70	45	75	1350	960	13493	934	.313	.373

Split	2B	3B	RBI	SH	SF	BB	IW	HB	K	WP	Bk	SB	CS	DP	GRD	FLY	#PIT	#PK	OBP	SLG
vs.ChN	10	2	19	5	0	11	3	0	29	2	0	5	0	1	74	51	682	33	.275	.374
vs.Cin	16	3	27	5	1	27	2	1	62	1	0	5	4	11	141	111	1401	80	.277	.334
vs.Hou	8	5	36	6	3	24	3	3	45	1	0	14	3	5	121	81	1202	118	.323	.355
vs.LA	15	1	53	11	5	33	2	2	68	3	1	7	2	12	183	117	1754	138	.340	.385
vs.Mon	12	0	41	7	3	25	2	0	66	4	0	10	8	3	119	80	1309	102	.287	.385
vs.NYN	9	0	20	3	1	12	3	1	22	0	0	1	3	1	54	61	673	44	.298	.401
vs.Phi	18	2	26	3	1	28	1	2	38	3	0	5	4	10	141	92	1273	78	.304	.346
vs.Pit	10	2	36	4	7	35	4	1	37	2	0	6	9	10	126	99	1273	100	.336	.360
vs.StL	16	0	22	2	1	20	2	1	41	1	4	11	2	4	85	63	958	67	.318	.389
vs.SD	19	1	50	9	2	42	5	2	55	3	1	3	7	14	202	129	1882	100	.323	.369
vs.SF	15	2	29	3	2	26	3	3	52	3	0	3	3	4	104	76	1086	74	.327	.429

Split	2B	3B	RBI	SH	SF	BB	IW	HB	K	WP	Bk	SB	CS	DP	GRD	FLY	#PIT	#PK	OBP	SLG
at Atl	77	6	174	26	7	119	14	7	229	7	2	22	25	38	639	476	6178	433	.313	.408
at ChN	4	1	10	2	0	5	3	0	18	1	0	2	0	1	34	19	306	14	.295	.356
at Cin	5	2	11	0	0	14	0	0	38	1	0	4	2	9	88	70	859	46	.249	.269
at Hou	8	5	29	5	2	24	3	3	40	1	0	14	3	3	98	61	999	106	.339	.355
at LA	9	1	31	7	4	16	1	1	50	3	1	3	1	7	109	63	1058	82	.343	.382
at Mon	9	0	20	6	2	20	1	0	35	2	0	7	4	1	71	38	745	42	.301	.380
at NYN	4	0	11	1	1	6	1	0	13	0	0	1	2	1	34	36	408	29	.288	.317
at Phi	5	0	9	2	0	14	0	1	18	2	0	3	0	5	52	41	532	37	.286	.288
at Pit	5	2	25	3	6	20	3	0	14	1	0	4	4	1	51	38	589	52	.394	.411
at StL	11	0	15	1	1	17	2	1	20	1	3	10	1	1	44	31	529	38	.348	.369
at SD	6	1	18	3	2	19	1	2	26	3	0	0	3	7	93	63	940	44	.290	.329
at SF	5	0	6	2	1	9	1	1	14	1	0	0	0	1	37	24	350	11	.292	.271

Split	2B	3B	RBI	SH	SF	BB	IW	HB	K	WP	Bk	SB	CS	DP	GRD	FLY	#PIT	#PK	OBP	SLG
April	20	2	36	11	1	26	1	2	62	2	1	5	4	10	168	137	1681	101	.291	.364
May	17	2	51	4	5	50	6	1	91	5	1	17	4	12	209	150	2143	141	.295	.344
June	24	1	69	12	2	36	2	3	95	8	0	5	6	14	222	163	2189	166	.330	.404
July	25	3	50	9	5	34	5	3	82	2	2	11	11	11	201	135	2030	139	.298	.393
August	36	6	78	13	5	62	10	3	85	3	2	16	11	10	262	186	2620	205	.336	.391
September	25	4	72	9	8	72	6	4	95	3	0	15	9	15	276	182	2718	173	.317	.347
October	1	0	3	0	0	3	0	0	5	0	0	1	0	3	12	7	112	9	.267	.222

Split	2B	3B	RBI	SH	SF	BB	IW	HB	K	WP	Bk	SB	CS	DP	GRD	FLY	#PIT	#PK	OBP	SLG
Home	77	6	193	26	7	119	14	7	229	7	2	22	25	38	639	476	6178	433	.313	.408
Away	71	12	166	32	19	164	16	9	286	16	4	48	20	37	711	484	7315	501	.313	.341
Day	30	7	94	18	3	73	12	3	127	4	2	12	9	16	285	230	3192	223	.329	.385
Night	118	11	265	40	23	210	18	13	388	19	4	58	36	59	1065	730	10301	711	.308	.369
Grass	105	9	250	41	15	174	21	11	350	15	3	28	31	55	946	681	9240	613	.311	.387
Turf	43	9	109	17	11	109	9	5	165	8	3	42	14	20	404	279	4253	321	.316	.341

Days Rest	2B	3B	RBI	SH	SF	BB	IW	HB	K	WP	Bk	SB	CS	DP	GRD	FLY	#PIT	#PK	OBP	SLG
0-3	9	2	31	4	3	19	6	0	32	2	0	5	3	5	91	55	861	80	.360	.408
4	93	11	209	33	18	173	17	8	321	13	3	45	26	42	795	539	8067	521	.310	.361
5	27	3	68	14	3	49	2	3	92	4	2	12	11	19	265	225	2637	185	.310	.391
6+	18	2	50	7	2	40	5	5	66	4	1	8	5	8	189	132	1833	140	.310	.383

Split	H	HR	BFP	R	ER	2B	3B	RBI	SH	SF	BB	IW	HB	K	WP	Bk	SB	CS	DP	GRD	FLY	Avg	OBP	SLG
vs. Left	143	9	665	-	-	20	4	52	13	2	64	1	4	113	1	0	10	8	16	251	125	.246	.324	.340
vs. Right	718	63	3101	-	-	128	14	307	45	24	219	29	12	402	22	6	60	37	59	1099	835	.256	.311	.380

Split	H	HR	BFP	R	ER	2B	3B	RBI	SH	SF	BB	IW	HB	K	WP	Bk	SB	CS	DP	GRD	FLY	Avg	OBP	SLG
vs 1st Batr	21	0	72	0	0	3	1	0	0	0	3	0	2	10	0	0	0	0	0	18	19	.313	.361	.388
1st IP	150	7	618	84	77	22	8	81	7	5	62	5	3	92	5	1	26	9	11	209	137	.277	.352	.386
Inning 1-6	713	55	3178	355	314	119	15	306	52	24	249	27	14	450	22	5	66	41	64	1137	781	.251	.312	.362
Inning 7+	148	17	588	73	65	29	3	53	6	2	34	3	2	65	1	1	4	4	11	213	179	.272	.316	.430

Split	H	HR	BFP	R	ER	2B	3B	RBI	SH	SF	BB	IW	HB	K	WP	Bk	SB	CS	DP	GRD	FLY	Avg	OBP	SLG
Close & Late	76	6	301	34	31	16	2	27	6	2	18	2	0	32	0	1	4	4	8	116	83	.276	.319	.415
Close	256	24	1130	122	108	54	6	98	22	8	77	12	6	128	8	1	18	15	25	423	306	.252	.306	.387
Not Close	605	48	2636	305	270	94	12	261	36	18	206	18	10	387	15	5	52	30	50	927	654	.256	.316	.366

Split	H	HR	BFP	R	ER	2B	3B	RBI	SH	SF	BB	IW	HB	K	WP	Bk	SB	CS	DP	GRD	FLY	Avg	OBP	SLG
None on	505	52	2213	-	-	87	8	52	0	0	117	0	9	319	2	0	0	0	0	840	585	.242	.285	.366
None on/out	225	17	951	-	-	42	5	17	0	0	42	0	7	117	1	0	0	0	0	349	279	.249	.288	.364
None on:1/2 Out	280	35	1262	-	-	45	3	35	0	0	75	0	2	202	1	0	0	0	0	491	306	.236	.283	.368

Split	H	HR	BFP	R	ER	2B	3B	RBI	SH	SF	BB	IW	HB	K	WP	Bk	SB	CS	DP	GRD	FLY	Avg	OBP	SLG
Runners on	356	20	1553	-	-	61	10	307	58	26	166	30	7	196	21	6	70	45	75	510	375	.275	.354	.383
Scoring Posn	198	10	918	-	-	35	5	272	21	26	134	30	6	120	14	1	23	9	33	305	199	.271	.377	.373
SB Opp	188	10	761	-	-	27	6	89	38	11	46	1	2	87	11	6	50	38	51	259	203	.283	.326	.387
SB Atd	23	1	136	-	-	3	1	11	7	2	22	2	0	24	1	0	11	1	1	36	32	.219	.349	.295
GDP Opp	171	10	658	-	-	29	6	129	50	18	38	1	3	66	8	4	35	29	75	220	161	.311	.349	.441

Split	H	HR	BFP	R	ER	2B	3B	RBI	SH	SF	BB	IW	HB	K	WP	Bk	SB	CS	DP	GRD	FLY	Avg	OBP	SLG
0-0 Count	153	7	572	-	-	38	1	59	26	7	17	17	1	0	4	2	14	8	12	236	175	.294	.313	.411
0-1 Count	101	6	336	-	-	17	3	35	5	0	0	0	1	0	4	1	8	10	13	162	102	.306	.308	.430
0-2 Count	25	3	187	-	-	2	1	15	1	1	0	0	3	90	0	0	5	0	6	44	33	.137	.151	.209
1-0 Count	111	8	370	-	-	21	3	46	9	4	1	1	1	0	1	0	9	11	7	165	123	.313	.313	.456
1-1 Count	85	8	331	-	-	15	2	39	6	4	0	0	0	0	2	0	7	6	12	150	117	.265	.262	.399
1-2 Count	77	8	457	-	-	14	1	29	5	0	0	0	5	187	4	1	9	1	12	143	71	.172	.181	.262
2-0 Count	41	8	134	-	-	8	0	21	2	2	3	3	0	0	1	0	2	0	1	55	47	.323	.333	.575
2-1 Count	64	2	219	-	-	8	1	28	0	3	0	0	1	0	2	1	7	3	4	99	73	.298	.297	.372
2-2 Count	93	10	489	-	-	9	3	41	1	4	0	0	4	161	4	0	6	4	4	147	118	.194	.199	.287
3-0 Count	4	0	88	-	-	2	0	1	0	0	75	6	0	0	0	0	1	1	0	6	7	.308	.898	.462
3-1 Count	33	3	177	-	-	4	0	15	2	0	80	1	0	0	0	0	1	1	0	38	38	.347	.646	.484
3-2 Count	69	4	404	-	-	10	3	29	1	1	106	1	0	77	1	0	1	0	4	114	56	.233	.434	.328

Split	H	HR	BFP	R	ER	2B	3B	RBI	SH	SF	BB	IW	HB	K	WP	Bk	SB	CS	DP	GRD	FLY	Avg	OBP	SLG
After (0-1)	332	25	1545	-	-	52	9	128	13	10	66	1	10	314	14	1	26	18	36	526	375	.230	.266	.330
After (0-2)	87	7	526	-	-	15	1	30	3	2	12	0	8	201	3	0	12	0	14	144	98	.174	.205	.250
After (1-0)	376	40	1647	-	-	58	8	171	19	9	199	11	5	201	5	2	31	19	27	587	410	.266	.356	.403
After (1-1)	288	28	1388	-	-	40	8	136	9	10	108	1	2	268	9	1	19	13	27	478	334	.229	.289	.340
After (1-2)	161	15	914	-	-	24	5	63	5	5	51	0	6	312	8	0	14	4	18	271	168	.190	.240	.283
After (2-0)	120	15	572	-	-	17	2	52	6	3	144	10	3	46	2	1	10	3	2	174	128	.288	.472	.447
After (2-1)	157	14	727	-	-	19	2	72	2	3	102	2	4	104	3	1	11	6	6	241	171	.255	.363	.360
After (2-2)	142	14	773	-	-	16	5	63	1	5	76	0	4	219	5	0	8	4	8	226	155	.207	.288	.310
After (3-0)	25	1	193	-	-	4	1	8	2	0	108	6	0	9	0	0	1	1	0	35	24	.301	.696	.410
After (3-1)	56	5	298	-	-	7	1	22	3	0	110	2	0	19	0	1	1	1	0	74	57	.303	.563	.432
After (3-2)	69	4	402	-	-	10	3	29	1	1	104	0	1	77	2	0	1	0	4	114	56	.234	.434	.329

Split	H	HR	BFP	R	ER	2B	3B	RBI	SH	SF	BB	IW	HB	K	WP	Bk	SB	CS	DP	GRD	FLY	Avg	OBP	SLG
Pitch 1-15	147	11	527	90	83	15	8	47	5	2	42	0	3	75	4	1	21	9	10	184	130	.309	.368	.444
Pitch 16-30	124	7	586	88	79	22	0	57	13	4	41	7	2	86	1	1	5	8	11	204	142	.236	.291	.317
Pitch 31-45	128	9	567	59	48	23	2	57	10	4	53	4	3	98	3	2	6	7	14	207	121	.258	.330	.366
Pitch 46-60	118	12	560	54	50	22	1	47	5	4	42	5	3	64	5	0	13	4	14	223	144	.233	.294	.352
Pitch 61-75	109	11	543	57	46	29	4	45	11	3	32	5	2	77	1	1	8	9	11	189	147	.220	.269	.362
Pitch 76-90	113	7	499	57	26	20	1	46	7	5	36	3	0	48	7	1	7	6	7	179	144	.251	.303	.346
Pitch 91-105	85	11	338	34	30	12	1	47	5	4	23	3	3	53	2	0	8	1	7	114	91	.281	.333	.436
Pitch 106-20	34	3	123	12	12	5	1	11	2	0	11	3	0	10	0	0	1	1	1	43	37	.309	.372	.455
Pitch 121-35	3	1	22	3	3	0	0	2	0	0	3	0	0	4	0	0	1	0	0	7	4	.158	.273	.316
Pitch 136-50	0	0	1	1	1	0	0	0	0	0	0	0	0	0	0	0	0	0	0	0	0	.000	.000	.000

Earned Run Average with Each Catcher

Catcher	ERA	IP	BFP	H	HR	R	ER	SH	SF	BB	IW	HB	K	WP	Bk	2B	3B	RBI	SB	CS	DP	GRD	FLY
BENEDICT, Br.	3.83	213.2	900	213	19	101	91	18	7	57	8	7	112	1	1	37	5	88	13	11	20	328	244
DAVIS, Jo.	3.34	89.0	357	75	8	36	33	3	1	18	0	2	29	1	0	8	2	27	3	4	8	141	106
HEATH, Mi.	9.00	2.0	9	3	0	2	2	0	0	0	0	0	2	0	0	1	0	2	0	0	0	2	3
KREMERS, Ji.	3.92	20.2	83	19	3	9	9	0	0	4	1	0	12	0	0	3	0	9	2	1	1	31	27
MANN, Ke.	4.15	13.0	58	14	1	6	6	1	0	7	0	0	9	0	0	2	0	3	0	2	2	17	17
MIZEROCK, Jo.	1.50	6.0	24	4	0	3	1	0	1	1	0	0	3	0	0	0	0	3	0	0	0	10	5
OLSON, Gr.	2.98	372.0	1531	335	26	144	123	22	8	118	12	3	267	16	2	59	8	123	25	15	37	530	358
RUSSELL, Jo.	3.75	24.0	100	25	1	14	10	2	2	5	1	0	11	0	0	4	0	10	3	4	2	40	23
VIRGIL, Oz.	6.27	93.1	437	102	8	73	65	6	7	52	5	4	36	3	2	18	1	60	11	5	3	149	117
WHITT, Er.	5.76	59.1	267	71	6	39	38	6	0	21	3	0	34	2	1	16	2	34	13	3	2	102	60

Pitcher	Avg	AB	H	2B	3B	HR	BI	W	K	SB	CS
BASS, Ke.	.310	29	9	1	0	3	7	2	3	2	0
BELL, Ja.	.429	21	9	0	0	0	1	0	3	1	0
BIGGIO, Cr.	.333	21	7	0	1	1	3	0	1	3	0
BONDS, Ba.	.214	14	3	0	0	0	0	3	3	1	2
BONILLA, Bo.	.235	34	8	0	1	0	4	2	3	0	0
BROOKS, Hu.	.440	25	11	2	0	1	6	2	4	0	0
BUTLER, Br.	.290	31	9	0	0	0	1	3	4	2	1
CAMINITI, Ke.	.222	27	6	0	0	1	3	1	5	0	0
CANDAELE, Ca.	.300	20	6	2	2	0	6	0	4	0	0
CARTER, Ga.	.296	27	8	2	0	1	2	2	4	0	0
CLARK, Wi.	.226	31	7	2	0	0	2	3	7	1	0
COLEMAN, Vi.	.238	21	5	1	0	0	2	3	4	0	0
DANIELS, Ka.	.417	24	10	4	0	1	5	2	0	0	0
DAVIS, Er.	.323	31	10	3	1	1	4	3	5	1	1
DAWSON, An.	.286	21	6	1	2	1	2	1	2	0	0
DeSHIELDS, De.	.176	17	3	0	0	0	0	0	7	0	1
DORAN, Bi.	.435	23	10	1	0	0	2	4	1	0	0
DUNCAN, Ma.	.190	21	4	0	1	0	2	0	3	0	0
DUNSTON, Sh.	.111	18	2	0	0	0	0	4	1	0	0
DYKSTRA, Le.	.375	16	6	2	0	0	2	4	2	1	0
ELSTER, Ke.	.250	16	4	2	0	0	3	1	1	0	0
FITZGERALD, Mi.	.190	21	4	0	0	0	2	1	5	0	0
GALARRAGA, An.	.167	30	5	2	0	2	6	2	11	0	0
GONZALEZ, Jo.	.318	22	7	2	0	0	3	0	3	0	1
GRACE, Ma.	.261	23	6	1	0	0	2	1	4	0	0
GRIFFIN, Al.	.289	38	11	1	0	0	3	2	7	0	0
GRISSOM, Ma.	.188	16	3	1	0	0	0	0	3	0	0
GUERRERO, Pe.	.455	22	10	3	0	2	6	0	2	0	0
GWYNN, To.	.255	55	14	0	0	1	4	3	2	0	1
HAMILTON, Je.	.167	24	4	0	0	0	2	0	2	0	0
HATCHER, Bi.	.314	51	16	0	1	2	8	4	4	5	2
HAYES, Ch.	.381	21	8	3	0	1	4	1	2	1	1
HAYES, Vo.	.370	27	10	2	0	0	3	3	2	0	0
HERR, To.	.176	17	3	0	0	0	0	3	1	0	0
HUDLER, Re.	.190	21	4	0	0	1	3	1	2	1	0
JACKSON, Da.	.269	26	7	1	0	1	4	1	6	1	0
JEFFERIES, Gr.	.429	14	6	1	0	1	2	0	2	1	0
JOHNSON, Ho.	.158	19	3	1	0	0	1	0	2	0	1
JORDAN, Ri.	.300	20	6	3	0	0	3	0	0	0	0

Pitcher	Avg	AB	H	2B	3B	HR	BI	W	K	SB	CS
KRUK, Jo.	.150	20	3	0	0	0	2	1	3	1	1
LAKE, St.	.125	16	2	2	0	0	1	1	3	0	0
LARKIN, Ba.	.303	33	10	3	0	1	5	5	1	0	1
LIND, Jo.	.258	31	8	1	0	0	3	1	0	2	0
MARTINEZ, Ca.	.290	31	9	2	0	2	6	0	2	0	0
McCLENDON, Ll.	.529	17	9	0	0	2	6	2	3	1	1
McGEE, Wi.	.333	24	8	1	0	1	4	0	2	1	1
McREYNOLDS, Ke.	.333	18	6	2	0	0	2	0	1	0	1
MITCHELL, Ke.	.321	28	9	2	0	2	7	3	6	0	0
MURRAY, Ed.	.270	37	10	0	0	0	4	0	4	1	0
NIXON, Ot.	.263	19	5	0	0	0	0	2	2	5	1
O'NEILL, Pa.	.050	20	1	0	0	0	0	0	7	0	1
OLIVER, Jo.	.190	21	4	2	0	0	1	0	7	0	0
OQUENDO, Jo.	.240	25	6	0	0	0	0	1	3	0	0
OWEN, Sp.	.120	25	3	1	0	0	2	2	0	1	
RAMIREZ, Ra.	.310	29	9	1	0	0	1	0	3	1	0
READY, Ra.	.353	34	12	2	1	1	4	4	2	1	1
REDUS, Ga.	.267	15	4	1	0	1	2	0	3	1	1
ROBERTS, Bi.	.357	28	10	3	0	0	1	2	1	2	2
SABO, Ch.	.314	35	11	2	0	0	2	2	3	3	0
SALAZAR, Lu.	.133	15	2	0	0	1	3	0	2	0	0
SAMUEL, Ju.	.314	35	11	1	0	2	5	4	11	0	2
SANDBERG, Ry.	.320	25	8	4	1	1	3	0	1	1	0
SANTIAGO, Be.	.167	30	5	0	0	0	1	3	2	0	1
SHARPERSON, Mi.	.368	19	7	3	0	0	0	1	3	3	0
SMITH, Oz.	.346	26	9	5	0	0	2	3	1	1	1
STRAWBERRY, Da.	.250	28	7	0	1	2	4	0	8	0	0
TEMPLETON, Ga.	.262	42	11	1	0	0	6	1	6	0	1
TEUFEL, Ti.	.211	19	4	1	0	1	2	2	3	0	0
THOMPSON, Ro.	.333	24	8	4	1	1	3	1	5	0	0
THON, Di.	.162	37	6	2	0	0	1	0	3	0	0
URIBE, Jo.	.250	20	5	1	0	0	2	0	2	0	0
VAN SLYKE, An.	.344	32	11	2	1	0	5	6	1	0	0
WALKER, La.	.313	16	5	0	0	2	6	0	2	0	0
WALLACH, Ti.	.294	34	10	2	0	5	8	3	2	0	1
WALTON, Je.	.235	17	4	2	0	0	0	1	3	1	0
WILLIAMS, Ma.	.167	24	4	3	0	0	2	1	7	0	1
YOUNG, Ge.	.118	17	2	1	0	0	0	1	3	0	0
ZEILE, To.	.429	14	6	1	0	0	1	1	3	0	0

Bryan Harvey

Split	W	L	S	ERA	SUP	Avg	G	GS	CG	SO	GF	OP	HD	IP	H	HR	BFP	R	ER	RF
Total	16	16	113	2.45	2.61	.196	225	0	0	0	192	138	2	279.0	197	20	1146	87	76	81

Split	W	L	S	ERA	SUP	Avg	G	GS	CG	SO	GF	OP	HD	IP	H	HR	BFP	R	ER	RF
Relief	16	16	113	2.45	2.61	.196	225	0	0	0	192	138	2	279.0	197	20	1146	87	76	81

Split	W	L	S	ERA	SUP	Avg	G	GS	CG	SO	GF	OP	HD	IP	H	HR	BFP	R	ER	RF
vs.Bal	2	2	7	3.38	2.11	.171	16	0	0	0	14	10	0	21.1	13	2	86	8	8	5
vs.Bos	0	2	12	1.78	1.42	.176	21	0	0	0	20	13	0	25.1	15	2	99	6	5	4
vs.ChA	1	1	16	1.04	2.42	.200	24	0	0	0	22	20	0	26.0	19	0	106	5	3	7
vs.Cle	3	1	9	2.63	5.63	.179	18	0	0	0	15	11	0	24.0	15	0	97	9	7	15
vs.Det	1	2	10	5.18	3.33	.195	20	0	0	0	14	12	1	24.1	17	3	107	14	14	9
vs.KC	1	0	7	2.77	2.08	.184	14	0	0	0	14	8	0	13.0	9	1	55	5	4	3
vs.Mil	0	1	6	4.80	1.20	.250	12	0	0	0	9	7	0	15.0	14	2	67	8	8	2
vs.Min	1	0	12	0.44	3.48	.118	18	0	0	0	18	12	0	20.2	8	0	74	4	1	8
vs.NYA	1	2	4	3.57	0.51	.212	16	0	0	0	13	7	0	17.2	14	3	76	7	7	1
vs.Oak	1	0	4	0.42	1.27	.129	14	0	0	0	12	4	0	21.1	9	0	78	1	1	3
vs.Sea	0	3	9	2.70	2.25	.260	15	0	0	0	13	11	0	20.0	20	4	85	6	6	5
vs.Tex	1	0	13	1.66	2.08	.190	20	0	0	0	17	15	0	21.2	15	1	91	4	4	5
vs.Tor	4	2	4	2.51	4.40	.261	17	0	0	0	11	8	1	28.2	29	2	125	10	8	14

Split	W	L	S	ERA	SUP	Avg	G	GS	CG	SO	GF	OP	HD	IP	H	HR	BFP	R	ER	RF
at Bal	1	1	2	3.00	2.25	.103	8	0	0	0	6	3	0	12.0	4	1	44	4	4	3
at Bos	0	1	5	2.79	1.86	.156	10	0	0	0	10	6	0	9.2	5	1	39	3	3	2
at Cal	10	7	54	2.56	2.08	.209	116	0	0	0	97	67	0	151.1	115	12	630	48	43	35
at ChA	0	1	10	1.17	3.52	.182	12	0	0	0	12	11	0	15.1	10	0	60	2	2	6
at Cle	1	0	6	3.18	6.35	.220	9	0	0	0	6	8	0	11.1	9	0	45	4	4	8
at Det	0	2	5	5.68	4.97	.178	11	0	0	0	8	7	1	12.2	8	1	58	8	8	7
at KC	0	0	4	0.00	1.80	.200	6	0	0	0	6	4	0	5.0	4	0	21	1	0	1
at Mil	0	0	2	4.91	0.00	.259	6	0	0	0	4	3	0	7.1	7	1	33	4	4	0
at Min	0	0	5	0.00	5.00	.129	8	0	0	0	8	5	0	9.0	4	0	34	3	0	5
at NYA	0	1	2	3.00	0.00	.217	7	0	0	0	7	3	0	6.0	5	1	25	2	2	0
at Oak	1	0	3	0.00	2.70	.094	8	0	0	0	8	3	0	10.0	3	0	37	0	0	3
at Sea	0	2	5	2.25	1.13	.290	7	0	0	0	6	6	0	8.0	9	2	34	2	2	1
at Tex	0	0	7	0.00	0.00	.077	9	0	0	0	9	7	0	8.0	2	0	29	0	0	0
at Tor	3	1	3	2.70	6.75	.240	8	0	0	0	5	5	1	13.1	12	1	57	6	4	10

Split	W	L	S	ERA	SUP	Avg	G	GS	CG	SO	GF	OP	HD	IP	H	HR	BFP	R	ER	RF
April	3	1	10	1.87	4.54	.202	27	0	0	0	25	11	1	33.2	23	2	137	8	7	17
May	3	3	14	2.22	1.91	.202	40	0	0	0	32	18	1	56.2	41	3	229	16	14	12
June	0	2	24	1.90	1.71	.178	40	0	0	0	34	26	0	47.1	30	1	198	13	10	9
July	6	5	15	3.80	4.80	.231	36	0	0	0	29	22	0	45.0	40	5	195	19	19	24
August	2	1	21	0.75	2.44	.145	35	0	0	0	30	23	0	48.0	24	3	180	4	4	13
September	2	3	26	4.57	1.25	.208	42	0	0	0	37	34	0	43.1	33	6	186	25	22	6
October	0	1	3	0.00	0.00	.300	5	0	0	0	5	4	0	5.0	6	0	21	2	0	0

Split	W	L	S	ERA	SUP	Avg	G	GS	CG	SO	GF	OP	HD	IP	H	HR	BFP	R	ER	RF
Home	10	7	54	2.56	2.08	.209	117	0	0	0	98	67	0	151.1	115	12	630	48	43	35
Away	6	9	59	2.33	3.24	.181	109	0	0	0	95	71	2	127.2	82	8	516	39	33	46
Day	3	3	28	2.22	3.45	.201	55	0	0	0	49	33	1	73.0	53	6	300	20	18	28
Night	13	13	85	2.53	2.32	.195	170	0	0	0	143	105	1	206.0	144	14	846	67	58	53
Grass	13	13	96	2.59	2.36	.193	196	0	0	0	167	118	1	243.2	168	17	1000	75	70	64
Turf	3	3	17	1.53	4.33	.220	29	0	0	0	25	20	1	35.1	29	3	146	12	6	17

Days Rest	W	L	S	ERA	SUP	Avg	G	GS	CG	SO	GF	OP	HD	IP	H	HR	BFP	R	ER	RF
0	3	0	25	0.66	2.41	.140	39	0	0	0	36	26	0	41.0	20	1	157	7	3	11
1	5	7	27	2.80	1.95	.201	59	0	0	0	49	37	0	74.0	54	5	313	29	23	16
2	3	5	17	4.47	3.31	.249	41	0	0	0	33	23	0	54.1	51	4	243	27	27	20
3-5	3	4	26	2.09	2.82	.181	77	0	0	0	66	28	1	99.0	63	10	389	24	23	31
6+	5	2	1	1.00	2.75	.214	25	0	0	0	22	1	0	36.0	28	2	142	4	4	11

Split	2B	3B	RBI	SH	SF	BB	IW	HB	K	WP	Bk	SB	CS	DP	GRD	FLY	#PIT	#PK	OBP	SLG
Total	26	3	105	15	11	115	16	2	331	21	4	32	5	13	276	268	4469	109	.278	.288

Split	2B	3B	RBI	SH	SF	BB	IW	HB	K	WP	Bk	SB	CS	DP	GRD	FLY	#PIT	#PK	OBP	SLG
Relief	26	3	105	15	11	115	16	2	331	21	4	32	5	13	276	268	4469	109	.278	.288

Split	2B	3B	RBI	SH	SF	BB	IW	HB	K	WP	Bk	SB	CS	DP	GRD	FLY	#PIT	#PK	OBP	SLG
vs.Bal	0	0	12	0	0	10	0	0	28	4	0	5	1	2	26	15	348	8	.267	.250
vs.Bos	1	1	7	3	2	9	1	0	26	3	0	0	1	2	20	25	362	10	.250	.282
vs.ChA	3	0	8	2	1	8	1	0	27	2	1	3	0	0	31	23	410	5	.260	.232
vs.Cle	2	0	10	3	0	9	1	1	27	2	2	0	0	1	22	20	375	10	.266	.202
vs.Det	5	0	13	2	2	16	1	0	27	0	1	3	0	0	20	29	457	3	.314	.356
vs.KC	3	0	5	0	0	6	2	0	23	0	0	1	0	0	9	12	221	2	.273	.306
vs.Mil	4	1	10	2	1	7	3	1	20	2	0	6	0	1	18	13	267	14	.338	.464
vs.Min	0	0	2	0	0	6	0	0	19	0	0	1	0	4	25	20	274	8	.189	.118
vs.NYA	1	0	9	2	0	8	4	0	23	0	0	4	0	0	18	13	288	3	.297	.364
vs.Oak	0	0	3	0	1	7	1	0	27	0	0	3	2	1	11	23	296	12	.205	.129
vs.Sea	1	0	9	1	1	6	0	0	24	1	0	1	0	1	24	21	317	7	.310	.429
vs.Tex	1	0	7	0	1	11	0	0	27	1	0	3	0	0	22	23	361	18	.286	.241
vs.Tor	5	1	10	0	2	12	2	0	33	6	0	2	1	1	30	31	493	9	.328	.378

Split	2B	3B	RBI	SH	SF	BB	IW	HB	K	WP	Bk	SB	CS	DP	GRD	FLY	#PIT	#PK	OBP	SLG
at Bal	0	0	7	0	0	5	0	0	14	2	0	4	1	1	13	10	182	3	.205	.179
at Bos	0	0	4	1	1	5	1	0	13	1	0	0	1	0	7	9	150	5	.263	.250
at Cal	13	1	53	13	4	61	8	1	171	10	3	16	1	6	155	152	2374	69	.287	.301
at ChA	2	0	4	0	1	4	1	0	19	1	1	3	0	0	16	13	246	3	.233	.218
at Cle	0	0	5	0	0	4	0	0	14	2	0	0	0	1	8	9	185	5	.289	.220
at Det	3	0	8	0	1	12	0	0	16	0	0	0	0	0	8	14	268	0	.345	.311
at KC	2	0	0	0	0	1	1	0	8	0	0	0	0	0	6	3	81	0	.238	.300
at Mil	3	1	6	1	1	3	2	1	10	1	0	3	0	1	10	6	132	4	.344	.556
at Min	0	0	1	0	0	3	0	0	9	0	0	0	0	2	7	11	133	2	.206	.129
at NYA	1	0	4	0	0	2	1	0	7	0	0	3	0	0	8	4	110	0	.280	.391
at Oak	0	0	2	0	1	4	0	0	15	0	0	2	1	0	4	11	142	9	.189	.094
at Sea	1	0	5	0	1	2	0	0	8	1	0	0	0	1	11	8	119	2	.324	.516
at Tex	0	0	0	0	0	3	0	0	9	0	0	0	0	0	9	6	115	2	.172	.077
at Tor	1	1	6	0	1	6	2	0	18	3	0	1	1	1	14	12	232	5	.316	.360

Split	2B	3B	RBI	SH	SF	BB	IW	HB	K	WP	Bk	SB	CS	DP	GRD	FLY	#PIT	#PK	OBP	SLG
April	2	0	11	4	2	16	3	1	33	1	1	2	1	5	34	36	523	12	.301	.272
May	5	1	18	2	5	19	3	0	58	8	2	7	1	2	63	52	878	9	.264	.281
June	6	1	12	3	2	23	3	1	63	4	1	7	0	1	41	47	821	25	.277	.243
July	7	1	30	2	1	19	3	0	48	3	0	6	1	1	50	52	730	18	.306	.370
August	1	0	7	2	0	13	0	0	71	2	0	3	1	3	34	36	701	18	.208	.206
September	4	0	26	2	1	24	4	0	51	3	0	5	0	1	49	41	735	22	.310	.346
October	1	0	1	0	0	1	0	0	7	0	0	2	1	0	5	4	81	5	.333	.350

Split	2B	3B	RBI	SH	SF	BB	IW	HB	K	WP	Bk	SB	CS	DP	GRD	FLY	#PIT	#PK	OBP	SLG
Home	13	1	53	13	4	61	8	1	171	10	3	16	1	6	155	152	2374	69	.287	.301
Away	13	2	52	2	7	54	8	1	160	12	1	16	4	7	121	116	2095	40	.267	.272
Day	8	1	28	3	4	28	3	1	93	6	0	10	1	3	74	64	1191	18	.276	.307
Night	18	2	77	12	7	87	13	1	238	15	4	22	4	10	202	204	3278	91	.278	.281
Grass	22	2	93	15	9	103	13	2	288	17	4	31	4	9	238	234	3904	100	.277	.281
Turf	4	1	12	0	2	12	3	0	43	4	0	1	1	4	38	34	565	9	.281	.333

Days Rest	2B	3B	RBI	SH	SF	BB	IW	HB	K	WP	Bk	SB	CS	DP	GRD	FLY	#PIT	#PK	OBP	SLG
0	2	0	7	2	0	12	2	0	30	0	0	2	0	2	49	42	582	7	.206	.175
1	6	0	32	5	5	34	3	1	99	9	2	6	1	2	71	67	1257	30	.289	.280
2	10	2	31	5	3	29	10	1	72	4	2	10	0	3	49	55	930	23	.340	.376
3-5	5	1	33	3	3	35	1	0	118	6	0	14	3	6	95	94	1527	48	.254	.287
6+	3	0	8	0	0	11	0	0	36	3	0	4	3	2	34	41	545	14	.275	.282

Split	H	HR	BFP	R	ER	2B	3B	RBI	SH	SF	BB	IW	HB	KWP	Bk	SB	CS	DP	GRD	FLY	Avg	OBP	SLG
vs. Left	93	10	600	-	-	16	2	58	4	6	67	12	0	185 10	4	15	1	7	148	123	.178	.268	.273
vs. Right	104	10	546	-	-	10	1	47	11	5	48	4	2	146 11	0	17	4	6	128	145	.217	.288	.304

Split	H	HR	BFP	R	ER	2B	3B	RBI	SH	SF	BB	IW	HB	KWP	Bk	SB	CS	DP	GRD	FLY	Avg	OBP	SLG
vs 1st Batr	45	6	224	6	6	8	0	24	1	1	26	0	0	64 2	1	3	2	0	56	49	.230	.318	.362
1st IP	137	13	846	30	28	19	2	84	10	9	94	10	1	236 16	2	26	4	11	210	202	.187	.278	.272
Inning 1-6	3	0	13	1	1	0	0	1	0	1	0	0	0	3 0	0	1	0	1	3	4	.250	.231	.250
Inning 7+	194	20	1133	86	75	26	3	104	15	10	115	16	2	328 21	4	31	5	12	273	264	.196	.278	.289

Split	H	HR	BFP	R	ER	2B	3B	RBI	SH	SF	BB	IW	HB	KWP	Bk	SB	CS	DP	GRD	FLY	Avg	OBP	SLG
Close & Late	135	15	784	59	49	16	2	87	13	7	84	12	2	235 16	4	24	4	8	180	171	.199	.287	.295
Close	158	17	942	76	66	17	2	90	14	9	103	16	2	274 18	4	28	4	10	226	211	.194	.283	.283
Not Close	42	3	212	11	10	10	1	15	1	2	12	0	0	58 3	0	4	1	3	53	60	.213	.256	.320

Split	H	HR	BFP	R	ER	2B	3B	RBI	SH	SF	BB	IW	HB	KWP	Bk	SB	CS	DP	GRD	FLY	Avg	OBP	SLG
None on	104	13	546	-	-	10	0	13	0	0	39	0	1	163 1	0	0	0	0	151	121	.206	.264	.302
None on/out	43	6	229	-	-	7	0	6	0	0	19	0	1	63 1	0	0	0	0	67	51	.206	.275	.325
None on:1/2 Out	61	7	317	-	-	3	0	7	0	0	20	0	0	100 0	0	0	0	0	84	70	.205	.256	.286

Split	H	HR	BFP	R	ER	2B	3B	RBI	SH	SF	BB	IW	HB	KWP	Bk	SB	CS	DP	GRD	FLY	Avg	OBP	SLG
Runners on	93	7	600	-	-	16	3	92	15	11	76	16	1	168 20	4	32	5	13	125	147	.187	.291	.274
Scoring Posn	52	6	396	-	-	9	3	88	6	11	63	15	1	113 13	3	10	3	5	84	91	.165	.297	.270
SB Opp	45	1	245	-	-	8	0	10	9	2	19	2	0	66 7	2	28	3	9	48	67	.209	.271	.260
SB Atd	4	1	45	-	-	0	0	6	1	1	8	2	0	17 1	0	3	0	0	7	9	.114	.273	.200
GDP Opp	48	3	250	-	-	7	1	40	12	6	27	2	0	56 7	1	15	3	13	52	66	.234	.315	.322

Split	H	HR	BFP	R	ER	2B	3B	RBI	SH	SF	BB	IW	HB	KWP	Bk	SB	CS	DP	GRD	FLY	Avg	OBP	S LG
0-0 count	24	2	117	-	-	4	0	9	6	1	13	13	0	0 3	0	12	2	3	37	40	.247	.333	.351
0-1 Count	22	2	87	-	-	1	0	8	2	2	0	0	0	0 5	0	3	0	3	43	27	.265	.259	.349
0-2 Count	17	0	131	-	-	2	1	4	1	0	0	0	0	80 2	0	1	1	0	21	12	.131	.131	.162
1-0 Count	15	2	58	-	-	1	1	11	2	2	0	0	1	0 2	1	5	0	1	15	32	.283	.286	.453
1-1 Count	26	4	80	-	-	5	1	9	2	0	0	0	0	0 2	0	5	1	2	23	35	.333	.333	.577
1-2 Count	26	3	225	-	-	3	0	14	0	1	0	0	0	127 2	0	0	0	0	44	35	.116	.116	.170
2-0 Count	7	2	19	-	-	2	0	12	0	0	0	0	0	0 1	0	2	0	0	8	9	.368	.368	.789
2-1 Count	17	2	57	-	-	3	0	10	1	0	2	2	0	0 1	1	1	0	2	20	25	.315	.339	.481
2-2 Count	25	1	149	-	-	5	0	11	0	1	0	0	0	81 1	0	2	0	0	28	23	.169	.168	.223
3-0 Count	1	0	35	-	-	0	0	2	0	0	32	1	1	0 0	1	0	0	0	0	1	.500	.971	.500
3-1 Count	3	1	40	-	-	0	0	6	1	3	22	0	0	0 0	0	1	0	0	5	9	.214	.641	.429
3-2 Count	14	1	148	-	-	0	0	9	0	1	46	0	0	43 2	1	0	1	2	32	20	.139	.405	.168

Split	H	HR	BFP	R	ER	2B	3B	RBI	SH	SF	BB	IW	HB	KWP	Bk	SB	CS	DP	GRD	FLY	Avg	OBP	SLG
After (0-1)	97	9	544	-	-	11	2	42	3	4	18	0	0	210 11	0	8	2	5	121	114	.187	.213	.268
After (0-2)	34	1	252	-	-	4	1	10	1	0	6	0	0	145 4	0	2	2	0	37	31	.139	.159	.176
After (1-0)	75	9	483	-	-	11	1	54	6	6	84	3	2	121 7	4	12	1	5	117	113	.195	.338	.299
After (1-1)	80	9	461	-	-	12	1	43	2	4	35	1	0	159 6	1	7	1	6	106	104	.190	.251	.288
After (1-2)	42	4	344	-	-	5	0	18	0	1	17	0	0	187 4	0	2	1	0	57	54	.129	.172	.181
After (2-0)	21	4	169	-	-	4	0	24	2	2	61	2	1	27 1	2	3	0	0	37	33	.204	.497	.359
After (2-1)	40	4	242	-	-	6	0	30	1	3	38	2	0	61 2	1	2	1	4	65	52	.200	.324	.290
After (2-2)	33	2	246	-	-	5	0	17	0	1	32	0	0	112 3	0	2	1	2	44	35	.155	.264	.207
After (3-0)	4	0	67	-	-	0	0	4	1	2	47	1	1	3 0	0	1	0	0	7	6	.250	.788	.250
After (3-1)	9	1	90	-	-	0	0	9	1	4	36	0	0	12 0	1	1	0	0	20	17	.184	.506	.245
After (3-2)	14	1	147	-	-	0	0	10	0	1	46	0	0	43 2	0	0	1	2	31	20	.140	.408	.170

Split	H	HR	BFP	R	ER	2B	3B	RBI	SH	SF	BB	IW	HB	K	WP	Bk	SB	CS	DP	GRD	FLY	Avg	OBP	SLG
Pitch 1-15	133	15	706	30	27	15	2	63	7	6	68	2	1	203	14	2	24	3	11	177	179	.213	.289	.316
Pitch 16-30	53	5	358	37	30	9	1	29	7	3	37	9	1	108	5	1	6	2	2	83	69	.171	.259	.255
Pitch 31-45	10	0	75	20	19	1	0	12	0	1	9	4	0	20	2	1	1	0	0	13	19	.154	.253	.169
Pitch 46-60	1	0	6	0	0	1	0	1	1	1	1	1	0	0	0	0	1	0	0	3	1	.333	.400	.667
Pitch 61-75	0	0	1	0	0	0	0	0	0	0	0	0	0	0	0	0	0	0	0	0	0	.000	.000	.000

Earned Run Average with Each Catcher

Catcher	ERA	IP	BFP	H	HR	R	ER	SH	SF	BB	IW	HB	K	WP	Bk	2B	3B	RBI	SB	CS	DP	GRD	FLY
BOONE, Bo.	2.08	43.1	175	38	3	13	10	1	0	13	2	0	36	3	0	5	0	14	5	1	4	41	54
DORSETT, Br.	0.00	1.0	3	0	0	0	0	0	0	0	0	0	2	0	0	0	0	0	0	0	0	0	1
MILLER, Da.	2.55	24.2	103	21	1	7	7	1	2	7	3	1	21	4	0	1	2	13	5	1	1	24	35
ORTON, Jo.	1.85	24.1	99	17	0	9	5	1	2	7	2	0	25	5	1	3	1	5	1	0	1	33	17
PARRISH, La.	2.91	145.1	615	98	13	50	47	10	4	80	7	1	192	9	2	13	0	62	15	3	5	141	129
SCHROEDER, Bi.	2.61	10.1	40	6	1	3	3	0	1	4	0	0	20	0	0	1	0	4	2	0	1	5	7
TINGLEY, Ro.	1.50	18.0	67	11	2	3	3	1	1	2	1	0	24	0	0	2	0	6	3	0	0	19	13
WYNEGAR, Bu.	0.75	12.0	44	6	0	2	1	1	1	2	1	0	11	0	1	1	0	1	1	0	1	13	12

Pitcher	Avg	AB	H	2B	3B	HR	BI	W	K	SB	CS
ANDERSON, Br.	.000	5	0	0	0	0	0	0	3	2	0
BAERGA, Ca.	.000	5	0	0	0	0	0	0	2	0	0
BAINES, Ha.	.167	6	1	0	0	0	0	1	2	0	0
BARFIELD, Je.	.333	9	3	0	0	2	3	1	4	0	0
BARRETT, Ma.	.000	5	0	0	0	0	0	0	2	0	0
BELL, Ge.	.375	8	3	0	0	0	1	1	1	0	0
BENZINGER, To.	.200	5	1	0	0	0	0	0	1	0	0
BERGMAN, Da.	.125	8	1	1	0	0	1	1	1	0	0
BOGGS, Wa.	.375	8	3	1	1	0	1	2	2	0	0
BRADLEY, Sc.	.000	6	0	0	0	0	1	0	3	0	0
BRILEY, Gr.	.375	8	3	0	0	0	0	2	0	0	0
BUECHELE, St.	.000	5	0	0	0	0	4	2	0	0	0
BURKS, El.	.125	8	1	0	0	0	1	0	4	0	0
BUSH, Ra.	.000	5	0	0	0	0	1	1	0	0	0
CANSECO, Jo.	.222	9	2	0	0	0	2	5	1	2	
CARTER, Jo.	.222	9	2	0	0	0	2	3	4	0	0
CLARK, Da.	.167	6	1	0	0	0	0	2	0	0	0
CLARK, Ja.	.000	5	0	0	0	0	0	2	0	0	0
DAUGHERTY, Ja.	.200	5	1	0	0	0	0	3	0	0	0
DAVIS, Al.	.250	8	2	0	0	0	1	0	1	0	0
ESPINOZA, Al.	.200	5	1	0	0	0	1	0	0	1	0
EVANS, Dw.	.000	7	0	0	0	0	0	3	1	0	0
FERNANDEZ, To.	.375	8	3	2	0	0	0	2	0	0	1
FIELDER, Ce.	.000	5	0	0	0	0	1	2	2	0	0
FISK, Ca.	.100	10	1	0	0	0	0	1	5	0	0
FLETCHER, Sc.	.000	5	0	0	0	0	0	1	1	0	0
FRANCO, Ju.	.500	10	5	1	0	0	2	0	1	0	0
GAETTI, Ga.	.333	6	2	0	0	0	1	0	2	0	0
GANTNER, Ji.	.000	6	0	0	0	0	0	0	2	0	0
GEDMAN, Ri.	.400	5	2	0	0	0	0	1	0	0	0
GLADDEN, Da.	.000	5	0	0	0	0	0	1	0	0	0
GREENWELL, Mi.	.000	10	0	0	0	0	1	0	2	0	0
GRIFFEY JR, Ke.	.333	6	2	0	0	1	3	0	2	0	0
GRUBER, Ke.	.200	10	2	1	0	0	0	1	1	0	0
GUILLEN, Oz.	.273	11	3	1	0	0	2	1	1	0	0
HALL, Me.	.100	10	1	1	0	0	1	0	4	0	0
HENDERSON, Da.	.273	11	3	0	0	0	0	1	2	0	0
HORN, Sa.	.200	5	1	0	0	0	0	2	0	0	0
HRBEK, Ke.	.000	9	0	0	0	0	0	1	2	0	0

Pitcher	Avg	AB	H	2B	3B	HR	BI	W	K	SB	CS
JACKSON, Bo.	.200	5	1	0	0	0	0	1	2	1	0
JACOBY, Br.	.125	8	1	0	0	0	1	2	1	0	0
JOHNSON, La.	.375	8	3	0	0	0	0	0	3	2	0
KELLY, Ro.	.200	5	1	0	0	1	1	0	2	0	0
LANSFORD, Ca.	.167	6	1	0	0	0	2	1	1	0	0
LARKIN, Ge.	.333	6	2	0	0	0	0	1	1	0	0
LEE, Ma.	.000	6	0	0	0	0	0	1	3	0	0
LIRIANO, Ne.	.375	8	3	0	1	1	4	1	3	0	0
LYONS, St.	.000	6	0	0	0	0	0	1	0	0	0
MACFARLANE, Mi.	.000	6	0	0	0	0	0	3	0	0	0
McGRIFF, Fr.	.000	6	0	0	0	0	0	2	4	0	0
McGWIRE, Ma.	.000	6	0	0	0	0	0	1	0	0	0
MOSEBY, Ll.	.167	6	1	0	0	0	0	1	0	0	0
MULLINIKS, Ra.	.222	9	2	0	0	1	1	1	2	0	0
NEWMAN, Al.	.200	5	1	0	0	0	0	0	0	0	0
O'BRIEN, Pe.	.200	15	3	0	0	2	5	1	6	0	0
OLERUD, Jo.	.200	5	1	0	0	0	0	4	0	0	0
PALMEIRO, Ra.	.000	5	0	0	0	0	0	2	0	0	0
PASQUA, Da.	.200	5	1	0	0	0	0	2	0	0	0
PENA, To.	.200	5	1	0	0	0	0	4	0	0	0
PETTIS, Ga.	.167	6	1	0	0	0	0	1	1	3	0
PHILLIPS, To.	.000	5	0	0	0	0	0	0	4	0	0
PUCKETT, Ki.	.100	10	1	0	0	0	0	0	4	0	0
REED, Jo.	.200	5	1	0	0	1	1	1	0	0	0
REYNOLDS, Ha.	.200	10	2	0	0	0	0	0	5	0	0
RIPKEN, Ca.	.111	9	1	0	0	0	0	0	3	0	1
SAX, St.	.286	7	2	0	0	0	1	0	0	2	0
SIERRA, Ru.	.286	7	2	0	0	0	1	0	0	2	0
SNYDER, Co.	.167	6	1	0	0	0	0	0	2	0	0
STEINBACH, Te.	.000	5	0	0	0	0	1	2	3	0	0
STILLWELL, Ku.	.200	5	1	1	0	0	0	0	2	0	0
SURHOFF, B..	.375	8	3	0	0	2	4	0	3	1	0
TETTLETON, Mi.	.125	8	1	0	0	1	2	2	3	0	0
TRAMMELL, Al.	.143	7	1	1	0	0	0	1	3	0	0
WHITAKER, Lo.	.100	10	1	0	0	1	2	1	4	0	0
WHITT, Er.	.222	9	2	0	0	0	1	4	0	0	
WILSON, Mo.	.500	6	3	1	0	0	2	0	0	0	0
YOUNT, Ro.	.333	6	2	0	1	0	2	0	1	0	0

Ramon Martinez

Split	W	L	S	ERA	SUP	Avg	G	GS	CG	SO	GF	OP	HD	IP	H	HR	BFP	R	ER	RF
Total	44	26	0	3.15	5.01	.223	90	87	20	9	0	0	1	589.0	487	51	2427	234	206	328

Split	W	L	S	ERA	SUP	Avg	G	GS	CG	SO	GF	OP	HD	IP	H	HR	BFP	R	ER	RF
Starting	44	26	0	3.18	5.06	.225	87	87	20	9	0	0	0	583.0	486	51	2405	233	206	328
Relief	0	0	0	0.00	0.00	.053	3	0	0	0	0	0	0	6.0	1	0	22	1	0	0

Split	W	L	S	ERA	SUP	Avg	G	GS	CG	SO	GF	OP	HD	IP	H	HR	BFP	R	ER	RF
vs.Atl	8	2	0	1.41	4.23	.185	11	10	4	3	0	0	1	76.2	50	6	292	15	12	36
vs.ChN	4	1	0	3.56	7.74	.230	6	6	1	0	0	0	0	43.0	37	5	176	18	17	37
vs.Cin	4	4	0	5.88	6.06	.274	8	8	2	1	0	0	0	49.0	54	6	213	32	32	33
vs.Hou	2	1	0	3.64	3.43	.224	7	7	1	1	0	0	0	42.0	36	5	176	21	17	16
vs.Mon	3	3	0	2.50	3.18	.246	6	6	0	0	0	0	0	39.2	35	2	163	15	11	14
vs.NYN	3	4	0	3.98	3.64	.234	9	9	1	0	0	0	0	54.1	47	4	226	25	24	22
vs.Phi	4	2	0	3.00	5.50	.224	8	8	2	1	0	0	0	54.0	45	4	225	19	18	33
vs.Pit	1	2	0	4.60	5.83	.252	5	5	0	0	0	0	0	29.1	28	7	133	19	15	19
vs.StL	3	1	0	1.95	3.65	.235	5	5	2	0	0	0	0	37.0	32	0	150	10	8	15
vs.SD	7	1	0	2.69	6.14	.205	11	10	4	1	0	0	0	70.1	52	3	287	24	21	48
vs.SF	5	5	0	2.98	5.28	.206	14	13	3	1	0	0	0	93.2	71	9	386	36	31	55

Split	W	L	S	ERA	SUP	Avg	G	GS	CG	SO	GF	OP	HD	IP	H	HR	BFP	R	ER	RF
at Atl	3	1	0	2.25	5.14	.229	4	4	2	1	0	0	0	28.0	24	3	110	10	7	16
at ChN	2	1	0	3.43	8.14	.256	3	3	0	0	0	0	0	21.0	21	2	86	8	8	19
at Cin	3	2	0	5.01	6.96	.258	5	5	1	1	0	0	0	32.1	33	3	136	18	18	25
at Hou	0	0	0	3.18	1.59	.210	3	3	0	0	0	0	0	17.0	13	2	70	7	6	3
at LA	24	12	0	2.90	4.44	.204	46	44	12	5	0	0	1	310.0	229	25	1263	111	100	153
at Mon	1	2	0	3.18	3.18	.274	3	3	0	0	0	0	0	17.0	17	0	72	10	6	6
at NYN	1	2	0	5.09	4.30	.253	4	4	0	0	0	0	0	23.0	22	3	100	14	13	11
at Phi	2	1	0	4.50	7.13	.250	4	4	1	0	0	0	0	24.0	23	3	101	12	12	19
at Pit	1	1	0	3.50	6.50	.246	3	3	0	0	0	0	0	18.0	17	4	81	10	7	13
at StL	3	0	0	0.36	3.60	.184	3	3	2	1	0	0	0	25.0	16	0	94	2	1	10
at SD	3	0	0	1.69	6.99	.212	6	5	1	1	0	0	0	37.1	29	1	150	9	7	29
at SF	1	4	0	5.20	5.94	.297	6	6	1	0	0	0	0	36.1	43	5	164	23	21	24

Split	W	L	S	ERA	SUP	Avg	G	GS	CG	SO	GF	OP	HD	IP	H	HR	BFP	R	ER	RF
April	5	1	0	2.21	5.84	.194	8	8	4	3	0	0	0	57.0	41	4	223	17	14	37
May	8	4	0	3.84	5.76	.245	12	12	2	0	0	0	0	75.0	70	7	315	36	32	48
June	7	1	0	1.94	4.94	.213	12	12	5	3	0	0	0	93.0	71	4	368	23	20	51
July	9	3	0	2.60	5.20	.217	14	14	3	1	0	0	0	97.0	77	9	393	36	28	56
August	6	10	0	3.93	4.47	.248	21	21	1	0	0	0	0	135.0	126	15	573	64	59	67
September	8	6	0	3.78	5.09	.207	20	18	4	2	0	0	1	116.2	89	9	494	54	49	66
October	1	1	0	2.35	1.76	.241	3	2	1	0	0	0	0	15.1	13	3	61	4	4	3

Split	W	L	S	ERA	SUP	Avg	G	GS	CG	SO	GF	OP	HD	IP	H	HR	BFP	R	ER	RF
Home	24	12	0	2.90	4.44	.204	46	44	12	5	0	0	1	310.0	229	25	1263	111	100	153
Away	20	14	0	3.42	5.65	.244	44	43	8	4	0	0	0	279.0	258	26	1164	123	106	175
Day	14	7	0	2.90	4.69	.222	27	26	4	2	0	0	0	176.2	141	15	716	66	57	92
Night	30	19	0	3.25	5.15	.224	63	61	16	7	0	0	1	412.1	346	36	1711	168	149	236
Grass	34	20	0	3.08	4.98	.219	69	66	16	7	0	0	1	455.2	368	39	1873	175	156	252
Turf	10	6	0	3.38	5.13	.238	21	21	4	2	0	0	0	133.1	119	12	554	59	50	76

Days Rest	W	L	S	ERA	SUP	Avg	G	GS	CG	SO	GF	OP	HD	IP	H	HR	BFP	R	ER	RF
0-3	1	1	0	6.10	2.61	.275	2	2	0	0	0	0	0	10.1	11	2	48	7	7	3
4	25	14	0	3.26	5.48	.235	49	49	11	5	0	0	0	328.1	288	31	1372	137	119	200
5	13	7	0	2.98	4.47	.220	23	23	7	3	0	0	0	163.0	134	12	663	60	54	81
6+	5	4	0	2.88	4.87	.187	13	13	2	1	0	0	0	81.1	53	6	322	29	26	44
3-5 (Relief)	0	0	0	0.00	0.00	.053	3	0	0	0	0	0	0	6.0	1	0	22	1	0	0
6+ (Relief)	0	0	0	0.00	0.00	.059	2	0	0	0	0	0	0	5.0	1	0	19	1	0	0

Split	2B	3B	RBI	SH	SF	BB	IW	HB	K	WP	Bk	SB	CS	DP	GRD	FLY	#PIT	#PK	OBP	SLG
Total	86	10	205	23	9	199	11	16	485	11	3	45	35	24	635	690	9605	354	.292	.342

Split	2B	3B	RBI	SH	SF	BB	IW	HB	K	WP	Bk	SB	CS	DP	GRD	FLY	#PIT	#PK	OBP	SLG
Starting	85	10	205	23	9	196	11	16	483	11	3	45	34	24	629	682	9509	350	.293	.344
Relief	1	0	0	0	0	3	0	0	2	0	0	0	1	0	6	8	96	4	.182	.105

Split	2B	3B	RBI	SH	SF	BB	IW	HB	K	WP	Bk	SB	CS	DP	GRD	FLY	#PIT	#PK	OBP	SLG
vs.Atl	8	1	13	1	1	19	0	1	84	1	0	4	5	2	58	87	1146	35	.241	.289
vs.ChN	6	0	18	2	0	11	0	2	31	2	0	2	1	0	55	51	693	24	.287	.360
vs.Cin	14	2	30	2	0	13	1	1	36	1	1	5	1	2	66	63	826	32	.322	.457
vs.Hou	7	1	19	0	0	12	1	3	39	1	0	5	4	2	44	46	708	34	.290	.373
vs.Mon	3	1	13	3	1	17	0	0	37	1	0	6	6	4	45	41	646	36	.325	.324
vs.NYN	11	0	19	5	1	18	1	1	30	0	1	5	1	2	59	72	914	22	.299	.348
vs.Phi	8	2	18	0	1	22	1	1	44	1	0	3	4	3	64	53	906	33	.302	.343
vs.Pit	5	1	19	1	2	17	1	1	30	1	0	2	1	1	29	37	547	24	.351	.505
vs.StL	2	2	8	1	0	13	1	0	30	1	1	6	3	3	46	35	590	46	.302	.279
vs.SD	13	0	18	4	1	26	0	2	54	0	0	4	4	3	70	81	1133	28	.283	.291
vs.SF	9	0	30	4	2	31	5	4	70	2	0	3	5	2	99	124	1496	40	.277	.310

Split	2B	3B	RBI	SH	SF	BB	IW	HB	K	WP	Bk	SB	CS	DP	GRD	FLY	#PIT	#PK	OBP	SLG
at Atl	4	0	8	0	0	4	0	1	24	0	0	2	1	1	21	37	413	14	.264	.352
at ChN	5	0	8	1	0	2	0	1	11	1	0	0	0	0	29	28	312	8	.282	.390
at Cin	8	1	18	1	0	6	0	1	24	1	0	2	0	2	43	40	518	18	.296	.406
at Hou	3	0	5	0	0	6	1	2	12	0	0	4	2	1	21	16	285	17	.300	.355
at LA	29	5	97	10	5	119	5	6	286	6	1	24	26	11	310	348	5126	182	.283	.305
at Mon	2	1	10	2	1	7	0	0	13	1	0	3	2	1	19	19	289	20	.343	.339
at NYN	7	0	10	2	1	9	1	1	9	0	1	3	0	0	26	37	375	12	.327	.437
at Phi	4	1	12	0	1	8	0	0	15	0	0	1	0	1	34	31	394	10	.307	.413
at Pit	5	1	10	0	0	11	1	0	19	1	0	1	0	1	18	22	330	20	.350	.522
at StL	1	1	1	1	0	6	0	0	20	1	1	3	2	2	26	28	371	23	.237	.218
at SD	9	0	7	2	0	10	0	1	29	0	0	2	1	2	42	36	586	10	.270	.299
at SF	9	0	19	4	1	11	3	3	23	0	0	0	1	2	46	48	606	20	.356	.462

Split	2B	3B	RBI	SH	SF	BB	IW	HB	K	WP	Bk	SB	CS	DP	GRD	FLY	#PIT	#PK	OBP	SLG
April	7	0	17	0	1	10	2	1	49	0	0	3	3	1	54	74	839	30	.233	.284
May	16	2	35	3	0	25	1	0	69	2	1	11	6	4	79	89	1277	53	.305	.388
June	12	2	22	2	0	29	1	3	91	3	0	4	8	4	95	95	1484	70	.281	.296
July	14	1	32	3	6	27	1	2	70	1	0	12	2	4	113	119	1524	45	.272	.338
August	17	3	54	8	2	50	2	4	99	2	1	4	8	7	166	147	2217	77	.319	.381
September	18	2	41	5	0	54	3	5	102	3	1	11	5	3	114	140	2022	70	.303	.321
October	2	0	4	2	0	4	1	1	5	0	0	0	3	1	14	26	242	9	.305	.444

Split	2B	3B	RBI	SH	SF	BB	IW	HB	K	WP	Bk	SB	CS	DP	GRD	FLY	#PIT	#PK	OBP	SLG
Home	29	5	97	10	5	119	5	6	286	6	1	24	26	11	310	348	5126	182	.283	.305
Away	57	5	108	13	4	80	6	10	199	5	2	21	9	13	325	342	4479	172	.303	.382
Day	29	3	58	10	2	63	2	5	144	2	1	17	14	7	173	207	2865	118	.296	.347
Night	57	7	147	13	7	136	9	11	341	9	2	28	21	17	462	483	6740	236	.291	.340
Grass	63	5	149	19	7	155	9	13	382	7	2	31	29	16	474	534	7418	246	.289	.332
Turf	23	5	56	4	2	44	2	3	103	4	1	14	6	8	161	156	2187	108	.302	.376

Days Rest	2B	3B	RBI	SH	SF	BB	IW	HB	K	WP	Bk	SB	CS	DP	GRD	FLY	#PIT	#PK	OBP	SLG
0-3	4	0	7	1	0	6	0	1	12	0	0	0	0	1	4	17	199	3	.383	.525
4	54	6	119	11	6	115	8	11	290	6	3	28	20	15	344	388	5396	184	.304	.364
5	19	4	56	7	2	42	2	3	125	5	0	10	10	6	201	182	2674	114	.273	.323
6+	8	0	23	4	1	33	1	1	56	0	0	7	4	2	80	95	1240	49	.274	.279
3-5 Relief	1	0	0	0	0	3	0	0	2	0	0	0	1	0	6	8	96	4	.182	.105
6+ Relief	1	0	0	0	0	2	0	0	2	0	0	0	0	0	6	6	76	4	.158	.118

Split	H	HR	BFP	R	ER	2B	3B	RBI	SH	SF	BB	IW	HB	K	WP	Bk	SB	CS	DP	GRD	FLY	Avg	OBP	SLG
vs. Left	291	26	1391	-	-	54	5	117	10	6	142	7	9	252	4	3	33	21	14	370	384	.238	.320	.354
vs. Right	196	25	1036	-	-	32	5	88	13	3	57	4	7	233	7	0	12	14	10	265	306	.205	.254	.328

Split	H	HR	BFP	R	ER	2B	3B	RBI	SH	SF	BB	IW	HB	K	WP	Bk	SB	CS	DP	GRD	FLY	Avg	OBP	SLG
vs 1st Batr	4	0	24	0	0	1	1	0	0	0	2	0	0	3	0	0	0	0	0	6	9	.182	.250	.318
1st IP	73	11	380	33	32	12	3	39	0	1	39	1	3	66	3	1	7	7	3	94	118	.217	.303	.369
Inning 1-6	405	43	1991	200	177	75	10	181	16	8	163	11	15	401	9	3	41	28	19	526	561	.226	.295	.352
Inning 7+	82	8	436	34	29	11	0	24	7	1	36	0	1	84	2	0	4	7	5	109	129	.210	.277	.299

Split	H	HR	BFP	R	ER	2B	3B	RBI	SH	SF	BB	IW	HB	K	WP	Bk	SB	CS	DP	GRD	FLY	Avg	OBP	SLG
Close & Late	37	3	229	20	18	6	0	9	7	0	18	0	1	44	1	0	3	7	2	59	71	.182	.252	.256
Close	154	15	776	60	55	24	2	46	11	2	66	2	3	140	3	0	10	13	8	208	221	.222	.292	.327
Not Close	333	36	1651	174	151	62	8	159	12	7	133	9	13	345	8	3	35	22	16	427	469	.224	.292	.349

Split	H	HR	BFP	R	ER	2B	3B	RBI	SH	SF	BB	IW	HB	K	WP	Bk	SB	CS	DP	GRD	FLY	Avg	OBP	SLG
None on	283	32	1465	-	-	57	5	32	0	0	124	0	10	318	0	0	0	0	0	364	423	.213	.285	.335
None on/out	131	18	628	-	-	25	3	18	0	0	52	0	7	125	0	0	0	0	0	151	195	.230	.303	.380
None on:1/2 Out	152	14	837	-	-	32	2	14	0	0	72	0	3	193	0	0	0	0	0	213	228	.199	.271	.302

Split	H	HR	BFP	R	ER	2B	3B	RBI	SH	SF	BB	IW	HB	K	WP	Bk	SB	CS	DP	GRD	FLY	Avg	OBP	SLG
Runners on	204	19	962	-	-	29	5	173	23	9	75	11	6	167	11	3	45	35	24	271	267	.241	.304	.354
Scoring Posn	105	9	540	-	-	16	2	145	6	9	47	11	5	104	5	1	8	6	6	151	145	.222	.294	.321
SB Opp	122	12	496	-	-	17	3	63	18	4	33	0	1	73	6	2	44	31	20	140	145	.278	.327	.412
SB Atd	25	1	115	-	-	5	1	15	1	2	14	1	0	26	1	0	3	2	3	30	26	.258	.345	.361
GDP Opp	91	10	406	-	-	11	3	65	21	5	26	0	2	61	3	1	25	26	24	112	116	.259	.310	.393

Split	H	HR	BFP	R	ER	2B	3B	RBI	SH	SF	BB	IW	HB	K	WP	Bk	SB	CS	DP	GRD	FLY	Avg	OBP	SLG
0-0 count	74	11	279	-	-	13	2	38	10	0	8	8	3	0	2	2	16	10	3	95	111	.287	.316	.481
0-1 Count	53	3	179	-	-	5	0	18	2	0	0	0	3	0	1	0	7	7	3	62	58	.305	.316	.385
0-2 Count	24	1	170	-	-	4	1	7	2	0	0	0	4	78	0	0	3	1	2	34	32	.146	.167	.201
1-0 Count	48	5	181	-	-	9	2	19	2	4	1	1	1	0	0	0	7	4	2	62	80	.277	.279	.439
1-1 Count	43	0	210	-	-	8	0	8	3	0	0	0	2	0	1	0	2	3	4	82	78	.211	.218	.250
1-2 Count	35	3	342	-	-	6	0	13	1	0	0	0	2	193	5	0	3	1	2	67	50	.103	.109	.147
2-0 Count	22	6	58	-	-	4	0	14	0	0	0	0	0	0	0	1	0	1	2	19	25	.379	.379	.759
2-1 Count	42	7	127	-	-	6	1	16	1	2	0	0	0	0	0	0	2	5	0	45	50	.339	.333	.573
2-2 Count	66	9	374	-	-	10	1	29	1	2	0	0	1	141	2	0	4	1	3	94	93	.178	.180	.284
3-0 Count	0	0	49	-	-	0	0	1	0	0	46	2	0	0	0	0	0	0	0	1	2	.000	.939	.000
3-1 Count	22	2	122	-	-	7	0	13	0	0	56	0	0	0	0	0	1	1	0	22	28	.333	.639	.530
3-2 Count	58	4	335	-	-	14	3	29	1	1	88	0	0	73	0	0	0	1	3	51	83	.237	.437	.367

Split	H	HR	BFP	R	ER	2B	3B	RBI	SH	SF	BB	IW	HB	K	WP	Bk	SB	CS	DP	GRD	FLY	Avg	OBP	SLG
After (0-1)	192	16	1076	-	-	29	3	72	6	2	48	0	11	322	6	0	19	14	14	264	259	.190	.235	.273
After (0-2)	59	6	442	-	-	10	2	29	3	2	15	0	7	207	5	0	6	2	3	94	74	.142	.185	.219
After (1-0)	221	24	1072	-	-	44	5	95	7	7	143	3	2	163	3	1	10	11	7	276	320	.242	.344	.380
After (1-1)	173	15	949	-	-	32	3	58	5	2	61	0	2	233	3	0	8	8	10	249	260	.197	.250	.292
After (1-2)	97	10	707	-	-	17	2	43	2	2	33	0	3	310	7	0	5	2	5	139	143	.145	.189	.222
After (2-0)	80	11	397	-	-	17	1	43	1	1	114	2	0	45	0	0	1	5	3	73	107	.285	.490	.470
After (2-1)	108	13	497	-	-	22	3	45	2	3	77	0	0	83	0	0	4	6	3	122	142	.260	.374	.422
After (2-2)	104	12	597	-	-	20	4	50	2	3	61	0	1	192	2	0	4	2	6	126	145	.196	.279	.317
After (3-0)	18	2	145	-	-	4	0	13	0	0	80	2	0	13	0	0	1	1	0	20	21	.277	.676	.431
After (3-1)	42	3	235	-	-	11	0	21	0	0	83	0	0	22	0	0	1	1	0	42	59	.276	.532	.408
After (3-2)	58	4	336	-	-	14	3	29	1	1	88	0	0	73	0	0	0	1	3	52	83	.236	.436	.366

Split	H	HR	BFP	R	ER	2B	3B	RBI	SH	SF	BB	IW	HB	K	WP	Bk	SB	CS	DP	GRD	FLY	Avg	OBP	SLG
Pitch 1-15	58	9	285	35	32	8	2	21	0	1	26	0	2	55	1	1	7	6	3	70	92	.227	.303	.380
Pitch 16-30	60	8	316	32	25	14	2	26	2	0	24	2	3	67	3	1	3	5	2	73	91	.209	.277	.355
Pitch 31-45	56	5	331	32	30	10	2	21	6	1	22	0	6	87	2	0	10	5	2	92	81	.189	.258	.287
Pitch 46-60	89	8	355	31	28	17	1	39	4	3	26	3	1	61	1	1	7	4	3	91	113	.277	.330	.411
Pitch 61-75	56	6	320	31	29	12	1	34	2	2	28	4	1	68	2	0	10	4	2	89	84	.195	.267	.307
Pitch 76-90	65	3	308	27	23	10	2	25	2	1	25	0	2	51	1	0	2	2	4	91	82	.234	.301	.317
Pitch 91-105	51	5	244	16	14	8	0	18	3	1	21	2	0	45	0	0	6	4	5	67	69	.233	.299	.338
Pitch 106-20	32	3	177	20	16	2	0	10	3	0	19	0	1	33	1	0	0	4	2	42	49	.208	.299	.279
Pitch 121-35	14	2	77	7	7	4	0	6	1	0	7	0	0	16	0	0	1	1	1	17	24	.203	.276	.348
Pitch 136-50	4	2	14	0	0	1	0	5	0	0	1	0	0	2	0	0	0	0	0	3	5	.308	.357	.846
Pitch 151+	0	0	1	3	2	0	0	0	0	0	0	0	0	0	0	0	0	0	0	1	0	.000	.000	.000

Earned Run Average with Each Catcher

Catcher	ERA	IP	BFP	H	HR	R	ER	SH	SF	BB	IW	HB	K	WP	Bk	2B	3B	BI	SB	CS	DP	GRD	FLY
CARTER, Ga.	2.91	77.1	320	60	4	32	25	2	2	30	1	2	51	4	0	9	0	27	8	5	0	94	94
DEMPSEY, Ri.	7.17	42.2	193	44	4	37	34	3	0	24	1	3	36	0	1	11	3	27	7	5	2	49	46
HERNANDEZ, Ca.	2.00	18.0	68	12	2	5	4	0	0	3	0	0	13	0	0	2	0	5	0	2	1	19	22
LYONS, Ba.	0.00	2.0	9	2	0	0	0	0	0	1	0	0	1	0	0	0	0	0	0	0	0	4	1
REYES, Gi.	0.00	3.0	11	1	0	1	0	0	0	0	0	0	1	0	0	1	0	0	0	0	0	5	2
SCIOSCIA, Mi.	2.89	446.0	1826	368	41	159	143	18	7	141	9	11	383	7	2	63	7	146	30	23	21	464	525

Pitcher	Avg	AB	H	2B	3B	HR	BI	W	K	SB	CS
BIGGIO, Cr.	.125	16	2	0	0	1	1	0	2	0	0
BLAUSER, Je.	.176	17	3	0	0	1	1	1	11	0	0
BONDS, Ba.	.357	14	5	1	0	1	4	0	2	1	1
BONILLA, Bo.	.286	14	4	0	1	2	4	1	4	0	0
BUTLER, Br.	.208	24	5	0	0	0	2	1	4	1	1
CARTER, Jo.	.313	16	5	2	0	0	2	1	1	0	1
CLARK, Ja.	.063	16	1	0	0	0	0	3	6	0	1
CLARK, Wi.	.400	30	12	2	0	3	6	1	3	0	0
COLEMAN, Vi.	.250	16	4	0	0	0	1	1	5	4	0
DAULTON, Da.	.235	17	4	1	0	0	0	4	6	0	0
DAVIS, Er.	.263	19	5	1	0	1	4	1	5	1	1
DAWSON, An.	.313	16	5	1	0	1	3	0	1	0	0
DORAN, Bi.	.167	12	2	2	0	0	0	2	4	0	1
DUNCAN, Ma.	.286	14	4	0	1	1	2	1	1	0	0
DYKSTRA, Le.	.286	21	6	1	1	0	1	4	2	2	1
FELDER, Mi.	.214	14	3	0	0	0	0	0	4	0	1
GALARRAGA, An.	.250	16	4	0	1	0	0	0	5	0	0
GANT, Ro.	.346	26	9	3	0	1	1	0	6	0	1
GRACE, Ma.	.350	20	7	1	0	1	3	0	3	0	0
GREGG, To.	.350	20	7	2	0	1	1	0	3	1	1
GUERRERO, Pe.	.267	15	4	0	0	0	3	1	1	0	1
GWYNN, To.	.333	15	5	1	0	0	0	3	0	0	0
HATCHER, Bi.	.529	17	9	2	0	0	8	0	2	3	0
HAYES, Ch.	.118	17	2	1	0	1	1	0	6	0	0
HAYES, Vo.	.267	15	4	0	0	2	4	0	1	0	1
HERR, To.	.250	16	4	1	0	0	2	2	1	0	1
JEFFERIES, Gr.	.318	22	7	2	0	0	2	1	3	1	0
JOHNSON, Ho.	.350	20	7	4	0	2	5	3	3	0	0
JORDAN, Ri.	.429	14	6	2	0	1	4	0	1	0	0
JUSTICE, Da.	.200	15	3	1	0	0	1	0	6	1	0
KENNEDY, Te.	.211	19	4	1	0	0	3	0	2	0	0
KRUK, Jo.	.227	22	5	0	1	0	2	3	6	1	0
LARKIN, Ba.	.125	16	2	0	1	0	1	0	1	0	0
MAGADAN, Da.	.238	21	5	0	0	0	2	1	1	1	0
MARTINEZ, Da.	.333	15	5	1	0	0	3	1	2	1	2
McGEE, Wi.	.286	21	6	0	0	0	0	1	7	0	0
McREYNOLDS, Ke.	.174	23	4	0	0	2	2	1	0	0	0
MITCHELL, Ke.	.219	32	7	1	0	1	4	5	5	0	0
MORRIS, Ha.	.350	20	7	2	0	0	3	0	1	1	0
MURPHY, Da.	.296	27	8	1	0	0	0	2	5	1	0
O'NEILL, Pa.	.217	23	5	1	0	1	4	1	5	0	0
PENDLETON, Te.	.250	20	5	0	0	1	1	0	3	0	0
RAMIREZ, Ra.	.214	14	3	2	0	0	1	0	1	0	0
REED, Je.	.263	19	5	1	0	0	1	0	4	0	0
ROBERTS, Bi.	.211	19	4	1	0	0	0	4	6	0	1
SABO, Ch.	.316	19	6	2	0	2	6	1	4	0	0
SANDBERG, Ry.	.100	20	2	0	0	1	1	0	4	0	0
SANTIAGO, Be.	.231	26	6	1	0	1	5	0	6	0	0
TEMPLETON, Ga.	.300	20	6	2	0	0	0	0	3	0	0
THOMPSON, Mi.	.211	19	4	0	1	0	1	1	4	0	0
THOMPSON, Ro.	.138	29	4	2	0	0	0	0	8	1	0
THON, Di.	.222	18	4	1	0	0	1	0	2	0	0
TREADWAY, Je.	.300	20	6	1	0	0	2	2	4	0	0
URIBE, Jo.	.200	20	4	1	0	0	1	0	3	0	0
WALLACH, Ti.	.429	14	6	0	0	0	2	1	3	0	2
WILLIAMS, Ma.	.300	40	12	2	0	4	7	1	6	0	0

1992 Player Projections

This is our third annual attempt to project statistics a year into the future, and it is perhaps time to revisit a few of our assumptions. Our initial position was that we don't make any claim at all that these projections will be accurate; it's just fun. It's fun to do this and we're going to do it; we don't claim to know anything.

After two years of hits and misses, we are in a better position to evaluate our product. We were not quite as accurate last year (1991) as we were in the projections for 1990, at least as we measure it. On the whole, I am — as I was a year ago — shocked by how often we are right, how often the player will produce essentially the numbers that we project for him.

It's just luck; sometimes we get lucky. I'm just saying I'm amazed how often we get lucky.

The luckiest projection of last year's book was for Kirby Puckett. In the charts below I'll compare the projected 1991 statistics, which appeared in this book last year, to the player's actual 1991 statistics. This is the comparison for Kirby Puckett:

Kirby Puckett (987)

	G	AB	R	H	2B	3B	HR	RBI	BB	SO	SB	CS	Avg	SLG
Projected	153	628	86	200	34	5	15	92	43	73	8	5	.318	.460
Actual	152	611	92	195	29	6	15	89	31	78	11	5	.319	.460

We evaluate our projections by the use of similarity scores; the similarity between what we projected for Puckett and what he did is 987, which is the best we have done yet. We had 41 projections with a similarity of 950 or better, which is down from last year but still astonishingly good, compared to my own expectations. Another guy we projected very accurately was George Bell:

George Bell (972)

	G	AB	R	H	2B	3B	HR	RBI	BB	SO	SB	CS	Avg	SLG
Projected	144	550	72	152	29	3	23	93	31	63	3	2	.276	.465
Actual	149	558	63	159	27	0	25	86	32	62	2	6	.285	.468

Sometimes the similarity score is different than it looks. Almost anyone, glancing at last year's projection for Matt Williams, would conclude that we made an accurate projection:

Matt Williams (930)

	G	AB	R	H	2B	3B	HR	RBI	BB	SO	SB	CS	Avg	SLG
Projected	160	605	78	152	26	2	32	98	33	130	8	6	.251	.460
Actual	157	589	72	158	24	5	34	98	33	128	5	5	.268	.499

At first glance you think it's a spectacularly good projection, since we're almost perfect on home runs, RBI, walks and strikeouts, and reasonably close on everything else. What you don't notice at first glance, though, is that Williams had six more hits and two more homers in sixteen less at bats; consequently, his slugging percentage is 39 points higher than we projected it to be, which is a significant deviation. In the system of similarity scores used here, we penalize a difference in slugging percentage at 1 point per .001, so that's a 39-point penalty. But any reasonable person would say that our projection was an accurate one.

Terry Pendleton, of course, was an atrocious projection — we had him at .249 with 5 homers, and he's probably going to win the MVP award. It scores at 720:

Terry Pendleton (720)

	G	AB	R	H	2B	3B	HR	RBI	BB	SO	SB	CS	Avg	SLG
Projected	117	430	51	107	19	3	5	51	30	56	6	4	.249	.342
Actual	153	586	94	187	34	8	22	86	43	70	10	2	.319	.517

If we couldn't do better than that 99% of the time, we'd give up. But there were three candidates for the NL batting title — Pendleton, Hal Morris and Tony Gwynn. On the other two, we did great:

Tony Gwynn (956)

	G	AB	R	H	2B	3B	HR	RBI	BB	SO	SB	CS	Avg	SLG
Projected	146	562	73	178	27	5	6	67	51	31	28	13	.317	.415
Actual	134	530	69	168	27	11	4	62	34	19	8	8	.317	.432

Hal Morris (927)

	G	AB	R	H	2B	3B	HR	RBI	BB	SO	SB	CS	Avg	SLG
Projected	135	490	67	153	23	3	10	59	38	62	8	4	.312	.433
Actual	136	478	72	152	33	1	14	59	46	61	10	4	.318	.479

This happened, of course, because Gwynn and (to an extent) Morris had seasons which were consistent with their previous production, as most players do most of the time. Pendleton did not; he had a year which was inconsistent with his previous performance, and so our projections were wrong. That's about all there is to this, really; we just take samples of what the player has done in the past, and predict that he'll do it again. There's nothing profound about it. We just take what the player has done, and modify it in a few common-sense ways. As a player ages, we take stolen bases away from him. We take doubles and triples and a few base hits away from him (as he ages), and give him walks and homers. Up to the age of 27 these adjustments tend to make a player's projected performance better than his past performance; after age 27 they tend to make him worse, but very slowly.

There is research supporting these adjustments, of course, but the way in which the research is applied to the adjustments is somewhat intuitive. In some areas of performance we base the projections primarily on what the player has done over the last two or three years; in other areas we use the player's entire career record, and modify it in consideration of his age.

There's a lot of things we don't know when we make these projections. This is an early book, of course; this is the first statistical summary of the season, so we have to do the work in early October, long before any free agents sign with their new teams. We would have done a little better with Terry Pendleton if we had known he was going to be playing in Atlanta. As we write this, we have no idea whether Danny Tartabull will be playing next year in Fenway Park or the Astrodome, so we project him as if he were going to continue playing in Kansas City. We could do a little better with it if we could do this in late March, when we know who has a job locked up. We could do a hell of a lot better if we could wait until next August, and just have to project the last two months.

The tough part is to project playing time; as a rule, if we get the system to guess right on the playing time, 90% of the time everything else will fall into place. But in modern baseball there are only about three players per team who bat 550 or more times in a season; everybody else is, to one extent or another, a part-time player — and if we project a player to bat 150 times and he bats 425 times, then we're going to be out in left field.

At times we "intervene" in the system. A few times, when we first look at the numbers, we say "that's not right", so we intervene. The system projected Todd Zeile to hit 16 home runs next year — but the system doesn't know that the Cardinals are pulling in their fences. We intervened in the system, and gave Zeile four extra homers, making similar adjustments to a few other Cardinals. We may be wrong; he may hit only 16, as we would otherwise have projected, or he may hit 35. All we're saying is that we'd rather take our chances at 20 than 16.

We'd don't intervene in that way very often, and we don't do it without a specific reason. The computer would project Cal Ripken to play 159 games; we moved that to 162, for an obvious reason. Only very rarely do we intervene to move a batting average up or down; basically, we assume that each player will follow a normal rising and falling pattern as he ages.

But we do very often have to intervene to correct the playing time. Things very often happen in baseball that the system has no knowledge of. A young player will be given a job in August. An injury occurs, or another one heals. A player announces the intention of going through free agency. We look at the projected playing time, and then we change it when it doesn't look right. John Dewan and I argue it out; we had a long argument about how much playing time to project for Paul Molitor.

Anyway, as I was saying:

a) There's an awful lot of luck in getting the playing time right, and

b) If you get the playing time right everything else will be OK. Take, for example, Jim Eisenreich:

Jim Eisenreich (953)

	G	AB	R	H	2B	3B	HR	RBI	BB	SO	SB	CS	Avg	SLG
Projected	120	370	46	101	23	3	5	40	27	36	15	8	.273	.392
Actual	135	375	47	113	22	3	2	47	20	35	5	3	.301	.392

It's pretty good, but if you look carefully you realize we missed his batting average by 28 points, which is a lot. But we got the playing time right, so of course everything else is proportional; if he bats 375 times there's no way he's going to drive in or score 80 runs, and it's unlikely he'll be in the 60s. If we get the playing time right we're almost certain to be close on the runs scored and RBI, and then we're OK. Or maybe a better example is Brian Downing or Rich Gedman:

310

Brian Downing (855)

	G	AB	R	H	2B	3B	HR	RBI	BB	SO	SB	CS	Avg	SLG
Projected	119	393	48	96	16	1	11	43	55	62	1	1	.244	.374
Actual	123	407	76	113	17	2	17	49	58	70	1	1	.278	.455

Rich Gedman (788)

	G	AB	R	H	2B	3B	HR	RBI	BB	SO	SB	CS	Avg	SLG
Projected	43	106	11	25	7	0	3	12	10	20	0	0	.236	.387
Actual	43	94	7	10	1	0	3	8	4	15	0	1	.106	.213

In both cases, we really weren't very accurate in projecting the quality of the player's production; after all, we had Gedman projected to have a higher slugging percentage than Downing. But you don't notice it, at a glance, because we got the playing time right. If we get the playing time right we're certain to get lucky in several of the other elements.

Or, on the other hand, look at Lloyd Moseby or Pete O'Brien:

Lloyd Moseby (896)

	G	AB	R	H	2B	3B	HR	RBI	BB	SO	SB	CS	Avg	SLG
Projected	134	487	76	120	23	4	14	50	62	94	26	8	.246	.396
Actual	74	260	37	68	15	1	6	35	21	43	8	1	.262	.396

Pete O'Brien (905)

	G	AB	R	H	2B	3B	HR	RBI	BB	SO	SB	CS	Avg	SLG
Projected	101	342	38	87	16	1	10	38	47	37	1	1	.254	.395
Actual	152	560	58	139	29	3	17	88	44	61	0	1	.248	.402

If you look carefully you'll realize that we projected the performance levels accurately — but it doesn't look right, because the playing time was all wrong. Another one of those was Marquis Grissom:

Marquis Grissom (925)

	G	AB	R	H	2B	3B	HR	RBI	BB	SO	SB	CS	Avg	SLG
Projected	111	359	52	97	16	4	4	29	52	47	24	7	.270	.370
Actual	148	558	73	149	23	9	6	39	34	89	76	17	.267	.373

In this case we were extremely accurate in projecting the batting average and slugging percentage, and generally accurate in most other areas, but we missed on the playing time, and also Grissom decided to steal bases. Stolen bases, because they represent an element of decision and because the manager has input into those, are among the most unpredictable elements of a player's record. If you look at the comparisons I've given here, you'll notice that we're way off on stolen bases more often than we're way off on anything else. We had Tony Gwynn projected for 28 stolen bases; he stole 8. We had Jim Eisenreich projected for 15; he stole 5. We had Lloyd Moseby predicted for 26; he stole 8. Marquis Grissom picked up the slack for all three.

As I mentioned, our average prediction similarity declined last year, despite some improvements to the system. We knew this would happen, and I so stated in this essay last year (page 300; "Statistically, we won't do as well on the average next year as we did this year because we're trying to do more.") We have decided to project more playing time than exists; this is a conscious decision, and it is the right decision. What we are trying to tell you is, if Royce Clayton plays, how will he hit? The answer we give you to that question will be proven to be correct, because we know how to do that — but we cannot tell you whether or not he will play. What we have to try to tell you is how he will do if he plays.

This problem — speculative projections of players who may or may not play — results in virtually all of the least successful projections. The lowest projections of any season are for players who are projected to play but do not; in 1991 this included Eric Anthony, Carney Lansford, Tim Naehring, Jose Offerman and Jim Presley. Those were:

Eric Anthony (617)

	G	AB	R	H	2B	3B	HR	RBI	BB	SO	SB	CS	Avg	SLG
Projected	155	550	73	136	17	1	27	81	53	163	14	7	.247	.429
Actual	39	118	11	18	6	0	1	7	12	41	1	0	.153	.229

Carney Lansford (645)

	G	AB	R	H	2B	3B	HR	RBI	BB	SO	SB	CS	Avg	SLG
Projected	122	461	63	132	21	2	9	50	38	33	21	10	.286	.399
Actual	5	16	0	1	0	0	0	1	0	2	0	0	.063	.063

Tim Naehring (600)

	G	AB	R	H	2B	3B	HR	RBI	BB	SO	SB	CS	Avg	SLG
Projected	155	570	74	158	28	1	19	76	62	93	3	2	.277	.430
Actual	20	55	1	6	1	0	0	3	6	15	0	0	.109	.127

Jose Offerman (684)

	G	AB	R	H	2B	3B	HR	RBI	BB	SO	SB	CS	Avg	SLG
Projected	155	600	91	162	9	3	2	51	62	98	53	32	.270	.305
Actual	52	113	10	22	2	0	0	3	25	32	3	2	.195	.212

Jim Presley (629)

	G	AB	R	H	2B	3B	HR	RBI	BB	SO	SB	CS	Avg	SLG
Projected	137	507	54	123	27	2	19	65	31	121	2	2	.243	.416
Actual	20	59	3	8	0	0	1	5	4	16	0	1	.136	.186

My standard line here is that I take responsibility for the accuracy of the projections if the player bats 250 times; if he doesn't, then there is a very high probability that his batting line simply doesn't represent his ability. None of these players got to one-half of the level at which their stats would begin to indicate their ability. Tim Naehring's 1991 performance was very frustrating for the Red Sox — but it's 55 at bats. Probably one-third or one-fourth of the players in the American League last year had 6-for-55 slumps; that certainly is not unusual. Mark Lewis last year started out 34-for-81, hitting .420. Suppose that he had been injured at that point; people certainly could have said that we missed the boat on him, that our system had failed to spot his hitting ability. But it's 81 at bats; it doesn't mean anything. We had him projected to hit .256; in the end he hit .264.

The worst projection for a player that we had projected to play 100 games who did play 100 games was for Terry Pendleton, which I showed before (720). The others below 800 were Jerry Browne (753), Alvin Davis (770), Andres Galarraga (769), Brook Jacoby (783), Mark McGwire (775), Cal Ripken (785), Sammy Sosa (761), Robin Ventura (790), and Jerome Walton (770). Ripken and Ventura, of course, played much better than we had projected; the other players played much worse. I'll run a couple of those:

Jerry Browne (753)

	G	AB	R	H	2B	3B	HR	RBI	BB	SO	SB	CS	Avg	SLG
Projected	149	524	81	148	25	5	4	47	69	55	14	8	.282	.372
Actual	107	290	28	66	5	2	1	29	27	29	2	4	.228	.269

Cal Ripken (785)

	G	AB	R	H	2B	3B	HR	RBI	BB	SO	SB	CS	Avg	SLG
Projected	162	619	88	165	32	3	24	93	86	70	3	2	.267	.444
Actual	162	650	99	210	46	5	34	114	53	46	6	1	.323	.566

Those are the least accurate projections that we made. The ten most accurate projections:

Kirby Puckett	987
Jody Reed	979
Gary Redus	978
Dave Anderson	978
Juan Gonzalez	976
Dickie Thon	973
Brian McRae	972
George Bell	972
Milt Cuyler	971
Brady Anderson	970
Ozzie Guillen	970

Gary Redus, I'll throw in because he's one of my favorite players:

Gary Redus (978)

	G	AB	R	H	2B	3B	HR	RBI	BB	SO	SB	CS	Avg	SLG
Projected	97	296	43	72	16	3	7	31	44	59	22	6	.243	.389
Actual	98	252	45	62	12	2	7	24	28	39	17	3	.246	.393

We did have more really good projections this year than last year, but then there's a lot of luck in that.

What we are most proud of in this system is our success in projecting the performance of young players, first-year players and players in their first full years. Three of these — Juan Gonzalez, Brian McRae and Milt Cuyler — made the top ten list, and I will run those here:

Juan Gonzalez (976)

	G	AB	R	H	2B	3B	HR	RBI	BB	SO	SB	CS	Avg	SLG
Projected	151	551	74	145	30	4	26	90	30	114	3	4	.263	.474
Actual	142	545	78	144	34	1	27	102	42	118	4	4	.264	.479

Brian McRae (972)

	G	AB	R	H	2B	3B	HR	RBI	BB	SO	SB	CS	Avg	SLG
Projected	149	565	76	146	29	8	8	68	41	84	18	10	.258	.381
Actual	152	629	86	164	28	9	8	64	24	99	20	11	.261	.372

Milt Cuyler (971)

	G	AB	R	H	2B	3B	HR	RBI	BB	SO	SB	CS	Avg	SLG
Projected	125	450	77	113	11	6	5	43	54	82	36	11	.251	.336
Actual	154	475	77	122	15	7	3	33	52	92	41	10	.257	.337

Our projections for most other young players were generally accurate, or at least no less accurate than the projections for veterans. Travis Fryman didn't quite make the list:

Travis Fryman (952)

	G	AB	R	H	2B	3B	HR	RBI	BB	SO	SB	CS	Avg	SLG
Projected	152	575	70	150	32	2	19	78	30	107	7	6	.261	.423
Actual	149	557	65	144	36	3	21	91	40	149	12	5	.259	.447

The celebrated Jeff Bagwell projection, although it was not spectacularly accurate, was more right than wrong:

Jeff Bagwell (915)

	G	AB	R	H	2B	3B	HR	RBI	BB	SO	SB	CS	Avg	SLG
Projected	140	500	65	159	34	6	3	62	68	64	3	5	.318	.436
Actual	156	554	79	163	26	4	15	82	75	116	7	4	.294	.437

In the case of Frank Thomas, we would have done even better if we had adjusted for the new park, where Thomas hit spectacularly well — but we ain't apologizing:

Frank Thomas (950)

	G	AB	R	H	2B	3B	HR	RBI	BB	SO	SB	CS	Avg	SLG
Projected	155	525	105	164	34	7	25	87	121	133	5	5	.312	.547
Actual	158	559	104	178	31	2	32	109	138	112	1	2	.318	.553

We projected him to have an on-base percentage of .441 and a slugging percentage of .547; his actual (and phenomenal) figures were .453 and .553. This was based mostly on his Major League Equivalencies, his MLEs.

In reviews of this book last year, the projections for young players were belittled by any number of people. This is very natural, because we are claiming here to be able to do something which most people couldn't do, which is to evaluate a major league hitter by his minor league batting stats. People are very disinclined to believe that other people know something that they don't know, and this is good and normal. We are not asking all of the people who poked fun at us a year ago for saying that Jeff Bagwell might hit .318 or that Frank Thomas would be the best hitter in the American League to apologize.

But the fact is that we do know what we are talking about in this one area. We have done research, lots of research, over a long period of time. We were right about Thomas. We were right about Milt Cuyler, and right about McRae, and basically right about Bagwell. We're not always right, and sometimes when we are it takes three years before the truth emerges at the major league level, but we were right about Juan Gonzalez and Travis Fryman, and we're going to go on being right about young players until people realize that we're not just making this stuff up. And that's why the real value of these projections is in the projections for young players.

The MLEs are useful not only in projecting first-year performance, but in understanding whether or not a rookie was performing at his best. Steve Decker hit .206 last year; we know that he is a better hitter than that. Another guy might hit .290, when we know that he is only a .270 hitter.

Well, I don't want to start bragging. I hope you enjoy the projections; it's a lot of work doing these, and sort of a digression from what this book is really about. It's just supposed to be fun.

Bill James

Projections for 1992 Batters

Batter	Age	Avg	G	AB	R	H	2B	3B	HR	RBI	BB	SO	SB	CS	OBP	SLG
Abner,Shawn	26	.223	77	175	20	39	8	1	3	17	9	35	2	2	.261	.331
Aldrete,Mike	31	.243	64	103	12	25	7	0	1	11	19	22	1	1	.361	.340
Allanson,Andy	30	.232	60	155	13	36	5	0	2	13	11	23	2	1	.283	.303
Allred,Beau	27	.257	53	148	23	38	8	1	3	20	19	31	3	2	.341	.385
Alomar,Roberto	24	.296	158	624	88	185	34	5	11	68	56	77	41	13	.354	.420
Alomar Jr,Sandy	26	.269	134	450	51	121	21	3	7	57	26	49	2	2	.309	.376
Amaro,Ruben	27	.275	70	200	30	55	13	1	2	18	18	24	8	8	.335	.380
Anderson,Brady	28	.235	85	179	28	42	8	2	2	18	28	32	10	4	.338	.335
Anderson,Dave	31	.237	91	156	17	37	7	1	1	11	11	27	2	1	.287	.314
Anthony,Eric	24	.245	60	188	23	46	9	0	6	25	15	53	4	3	.300	.388
Backman,Wally	32	.259	94	247	35	64	12	1	1	21	33	40	3	2	.346	.328
Baerga,Carlos	23	.267	158	581	71	155	26	1	10	69	36	90	3	4	.310	.367
Bagwell,Jeff	24	.315	155	550	74	173	32	6	11	76	72	88	7	6	.394	.455
Baines,Harold	33	.273	140	465	63	127	25	3	15	71	71	78	1	1	.369	.437
Barberie,Bret	24	.265	135	400	60	106	20	3	7	54	69	67	12	6	.373	.383
Barfield,Jesse	32	.234	133	436	62	102	20	2	19	64	71	129	4	3	.341	.420
Barnes,Skeeter	35	.255	52	149	20	38	8	0	2	16	11	20	7	3	.306	.349
Bass,Kevin	33	.252	81	246	29	62	12	2	5	30	21	36	5	3	.311	.378
Batiste,Kim	24	.256	80	180	18	46	11	2	1	14	3	29	6	4	.268	.356
Bell,Derek	23	.270	65	200	29	54	9	2	5	29	14	34	7	4	.318	.410
Bell,George	32	.276	147	572	70	158	29	2	22	92	33	67	3	3	.316	.449
Bell,Jay	26	.263	159	578	88	152	27	5	13	64	58	100	12	7	.330	.394
Bell,Juan	24	.241	85	220	29	53	8	2	3	19	17	46	7	6	.295	.336
Belle,Albert	25	.275	155	550	71	151	28	3	26	104	33	117	7	5	.316	.478
Belliard,Rafael	30	.226	119	248	24	56	5	2	1	19	16	43	4	2	.273	.274
Benjamin,Mike	26	.191	43	110	11	21	5	1	1	8	5	27	2	1	.226	.282
Benzinger,Todd	29	.252	130	420	46	106	23	3	9	53	28	75	4	4	.299	.386
Bergman,Dave	39	.247	87	194	18	48	6	1	3	20	28	27	1	1	.342	.335
Berry,Sean	26	.258	90	260	36	67	15	4	5	34	23	51	5	4	.318	.404
Berryhill,Damon	28	.241	76	241	26	58	11	0	7	29	14	47	1	1	.282	.373
Bichette,Dante	28	.230	116	374	44	86	18	2	11	48	21	81	8	5	.271	.377
Biggio,Craig	26	.282	153	550	72	155	25	3	8	56	58	74	24	9	.350	.382
Blankenship,Lance	28	.222	107	243	40	54	12	1	2	20	32	52	11	5	.313	.305
Blauser,Jeff	26	.266	134	410	55	109	21	3	10	48	46	77	5	4	.340	.405
Boggs,Wade	34	.323	147	573	92	185	39	3	8	54	93	50	2	2	.417	.443
Bonds,Barry	27	.278	155	550	103	153	33	5	27	98	105	85	45	14	.394	.504
Bonilla,Bobby	29	.281	159	602	100	169	35	6	23	95	73	87	5	5	.359	.473
Borders,Pat	29	.262	124	332	30	87	19	1	9	43	16	56	1	1	.296	.407
Bordick,Mike	26	.214	81	224	23	48	7	0	1	18	22	29	2	3	.285	.259
Boston,Daryl	29	.257	100	226	38	58	13	2	6	25	23	33	11	5	.325	.412
Bradley,Scott	32	.240	62	121	8	29	7	0	1	15	10	11	0	0	.298	.322
Braggs,Glenn	29	.255	110	345	50	88	16	2	10	47	35	71	11	5	.324	.400
Bream,Sid	31	.251	110	350	36	88	20	1	11	55	44	54	5	5	.335	.409
Brett,George	39	.272	107	393	53	107	23	3	9	55	46	53	6	2	.349	.415
Briley,Greg	27	.257	119	346	43	89	19	3	6	36	34	55	17	7	.324	.382

Projections for 1992 Batters

Batter	Age	Avg	G	AB	R	H	2B	3B	HR	RBI	BB	SO	SB	CS	OBP	SLG
Brooks,Hubie	35	.252	95	306	36	77	16	1	8	42	25	60	3	3	.308	.389
Brosius,Scott	25	.253	65	150	21	38	11	0	4	19	14	21	2	1	.317	.407
Browne,Jerry	26	.276	100	275	42	76	14	3	2	27	34	26	6	4	.356	.371
Brumley,Mike	29	.232	85	194	31	45	10	2	2	15	17	39	5	3	.294	.335
Brunansky,Tom	31	.235	134	456	54	107	22	2	17	67	53	87	4	6	.314	.404
Buechele,Steve	30	.231	139	441	55	102	18	2	14	56	41	93	2	2	.297	.376
Buhner,Jay	27	.251	145	470	65	118	23	1	24	78	60	139	4	4	.336	.457
Burks,Ellis	27	.285	144	551	84	157	34	5	19	79	48	81	14	11	.342	.468
Bush,Randy	33	.242	113	260	33	63	14	2	8	31	34	45	3	3	.330	.404
Butler,Brett	35	.274	150	576	96	158	19	6	3	36	82	69	35	19	.365	.344
Cabrera,Francisco	25	.269	60	145	16	39	9	0	5	23	6	24	1	1	.298	.434
Calderon,Ivan	30	.282	147	554	78	156	32	3	18	78	50	77	23	12	.341	.448
Caminiti,Ken	29	.248	153	557	62	138	27	3	9	66	50	90	6	4	.310	.355
Candaele,Casey	31	.237	126	384	34	91	15	3	3	32	35	55	8	5	.301	.315
Canseco,Jose	27	.264	150	561	103	148	28	1	38	114	79	167	22	10	.355	.520
Carreon,Mark	28	.260	88	204	27	53	12	1	5	25	15	27	3	2	.311	.402
Carter,Gary	38	.247	90	223	21	55	12	1	6	26	21	27	1	1	.311	.390
Carter,Joe	32	.251	157	621	79	156	31	2	27	103	45	102	18	8	.302	.438
Castillo,Braulio	24	.247	65	150	19	37	11	1	2	17	8	39	6	4	.285	.373
Cedeno,Andujar	22	.242	141	479	47	116	24	7	12	56	19	126	6	7	.271	.397
Cerone,Rick	38	.229	92	236	18	54	11	1	3	24	25	30	0	0	.303	.322
Chamberlain,Wes	26	.258	140	520	58	134	25	2	14	68	34	82	14	13	.303	.394
Clark,Jack	36	.220	130	410	61	90	21	2	17	66	109	130	3	2	.383	.405
Clark,Jerald	28	.240	87	263	28	63	14	2	8	33	17	62	1	1	.286	.399
Clark,Will	28	.306	153	581	93	178	32	5	26	106	65	96	6	3	.376	.513
Clayton,Royce	22	.242	130	430	58	104	18	4	3	48	36	101	20	8	.300	.323
Cochrane,Dave	29	.236	51	140	15	33	8	1	3	17	9	36	1	0	.282	.371
Cole,Alex	26	.271	117	399	59	108	8	4	1	25	52	62	35	19	.355	.318
Coleman,Vince	30	.262	107	412	64	108	12	6	3	28	40	69	58	15	.327	.342
Coolbaugh,Scott	26	.221	68	208	20	46	8	1	4	19	18	48	1	1	.283	.327
Cooper,Scott	24	.265	115	275	30	73	20	1	6	30	24	44	1	0	.324	.411
Cora,Joey	27	.257	88	179	29	46	5	2	1	14	15	14	10	5	.314	.324
Cotto,Henry	31	.260	111	304	41	79	12	1	6	31	17	45	16	5	.299	.365
Cron,Chris	28	.253	90	225	27	57	16	0	8	34	14	54	2	2	.297	.431
Cuyler,Milt	23	.256	155	550	86	141	14	6	6	46	61	106	44	15	.331	.336
Daniels,Kal	28	.275	142	473	77	130	25	2	21	81	80	111	8	4	.380	.469
Dascenzo,Doug	28	.247	95	219	30	54	12	1	2	20	20	21	11	8	.310	.338
Daulton,Darren	30	.221	121	366	41	81	15	1	10	44	56	64	4	2	.325	.350
Davis,Alvin	31	.270	105	344	44	93	19	1	12	56	58	46	1	1	.376	.436
Davis,Chili	32	.254	141	504	70	128	24	2	17	74	74	105	3	3	.349	.411
Davis,Eric	30	.262	135	450	75	118	19	3	25	80	69	116	21	6	.360	.484
Davis,Glenn	31	.245	125	440	61	108	22	1	22	68	52	84	6	3	.325	.450
Dawson,Andre	37	.267	145	525	64	140	27	4	21	89	35	79	9	4	.313	.453
Decker,Steve	26	.253	110	320	30	81	15	0	8	41	21	57	2	2	.299	.375
Deer,Rob	31	.208	119	395	56	82	14	1	21	57	63	140	3	4	.317	.408

Projections for 1992 Batters

Batter	Age	Avg	G	AB	R	H	2B	3B	HR	RBI	BB	SO	SB	CS	OBP	SLG
DeShields,Delino	23	.264	155	552	83	146	22	6	7	53	85	127	53	25	.363	.364
Devereaux,Mike	29	.253	160	596	80	151	25	4	16	66	50	96	24	16	.311	.389
Diaz,Mario	30	.254	93	201	24	51	11	1	1	20	11	16	1	2	.292	.333
Disarcina,Gary	24	.229	50	140	16	32	5	1	1	13	7	16	2	2	.265	.300
Doran,Billy	34	.254	128	425	56	108	19	2	6	42	63	56	16	6	.350	.351
Downing,Brian	41	.244	82	283	34	69	11	1	7	29	37	49	0	0	.331	.364
Duncan,Mariano	29	.258	122	387	51	100	15	4	8	41	17	66	10	6	.290	.380
Dunston,Shawon	29	.261	148	522	63	136	26	5	12	60	25	82	22	9	.294	.398
Dykstra,Lenny	29	.285	154	590	96	168	32	5	10	50	86	53	39	11	.376	.407
Eisenreich,Jim	33	.284	115	306	39	87	24	4	4	37	23	31	9	6	.334	.428
Elster,Kevin	27	.233	121	374	41	87	19	2	8	44	36	61	3	2	.300	.358
Espinoza,Alvaro	30	.247	152	485	43	120	15	2	3	33	16	58	3	2	.271	.305
Espy,Cecil	29	.252	50	115	15	29	5	1	1	10	10	24	8	4	.312	.339
Eusebio,Tony	25	.233	60	150	15	35	7	0	1	14	12	39	2	2	.290	.300
Evans,Dwight	40	.254	90	252	35	64	15	1	7	40	46	47	2	2	.369	.405
Faries,Paul	27	.232	85	220	27	51	11	1	2	18	18	25	11	6	.290	.318
Fariss,Monty	24	.265	80	200	28	53	13	3	4	24	24	57	2	2	.344	.420
Felder,Mike	29	.250	119	284	43	71	8	4	2	23	25	27	21	7	.311	.327
Felix,Junior	24	.276	130	450	71	124	21	7	12	59	38	94	17	11	.332	.433
Fermin,Felix	28	.249	92	301	29	75	7	1	1	22	22	17	3	3	.300	.289
Fernandez,Tony	30	.271	153	606	79	164	29	8	7	59	56	67	26	11	.332	.380
Fielder,Cecil	28	.263	161	601	101	158	21	1	45	123	89	167	0	0	.358	.526
Finley,Steve	27	.272	156	584	76	159	21	6	6	55	41	68	36	15	.320	.360
Fisk,Carlton	44	.243	103	341	35	83	16	1	10	47	35	63	2	1	.314	.384
Fitzgerald,Mike	31	.226	77	199	21	45	9	1	4	25	30	38	4	2	.328	.342
Fletcher,Darrin	25	.239	62	176	16	42	8	0	3	19	12	19	0	1	.287	.335
Fletcher,Scott	33	.244	70	225	25	55	9	1	1	22	22	27	1	1	.312	.307
Foley,Tom	32	.230	64	139	12	32	8	1	2	14	14	21	1	1	.301	.345
Franco,Julio	30	.295	153	579	92	171	27	4	11	74	75	77	29	9	.376	.413
Fryman,Travis	23	.262	155	550	66	144	33	2	21	83	32	115	8	7	.302	.444
Gaetti,Gary	33	.240	128	483	53	116	23	1	16	66	28	88	5	3	.282	.391
Gagne,Greg	30	.250	145	424	52	106	23	5	8	44	24	77	11	7	.290	.384
Galarraga,Andres	31	.252	101	361	42	91	20	1	12	50	27	98	6	3	.304	.413
Gallagher,Dave	31	.266	85	252	30	67	13	1	1	22	20	34	2	3	.320	.337
Gallego,Mike	31	.231	146	412	47	95	12	1	6	36	47	59	7	6	.309	.308
Gant,Ron	27	.271	156	565	94	153	30	4	27	81	60	104	30	15	.341	.481
Gantner,Jim	38	.263	98	342	36	90	13	1	2	27	21	25	10	4	.306	.325
Gardner,Jeff	28	.250	65	180	19	45	6	0	0	14	25	17	1	1	.341	.283
Geren,Bob	30	.232	75	151	14	35	5	0	4	17	9	34	0	0	.275	.344
Gibson,Kirk	35	.252	96	322	56	81	15	2	11	39	46	73	17	4	.345	.413
Gilkey,Bernard	25	.252	90	210	33	53	14	3	2	20	27	21	14	9	.338	.376
Girardi,Joe	27	.253	70	190	16	48	10	0	2	18	10	25	3	1	.290	.337
Gladden,Dan	34	.265	123	452	59	120	20	3	6	41	27	58	19	8	.307	.363
Gomez,Leo	25	.255	147	487	69	124	23	2	19	72	72	100	2	2	.351	.427
Gonzales,Rene	30	.213	71	122	15	26	4	1	1	10	12	19	2	2	.284	.287

Projections for 1992 Batters

Batter	Age	Avg	G	AB	R	H	2B	3B	HR	RBI	BB	SO	SB	CS	OBP	SLG
Gonzalez,Jose	27	.238	72	126	17	30	7	1	2	12	11	31	5	3	.299	.357
Gonzalez,Juan	22	.263	145	560	74	147	32	3	27	93	34	124	3	4	.305	.475
Gonzalez,Luis	24	.249	151	507	63	126	31	7	15	72	41	104	16	9	.305	.426
Goodwin,Tom	23	.236	70	110	16	26	6	1	0	8	8	19	8	5	.288	.309
Grace,Mark	28	.294	155	578	79	170	30	3	11	75	74	50	11	6	.374	.413
Grebeck,Craig	27	.256	135	410	55	105	18	2	6	48	45	63	6	8	.330	.354
Greenwell,Mike	28	.307	154	589	83	181	33	5	16	90	59	42	12	6	.370	.462
Gregg,Tommy	28	.262	67	130	13	34	7	1	3	15	11	23	2	2	.319	.400
Griffey Jr,Ken	22	.307	156	573	85	176	35	3	25	91	67	80	19	10	.380	.510
Griffin,Alfredo	35	.225	85	258	22	58	10	2	1	19	16	35	4	3	.270	.291
Grissom,Marquis	25	.269	155	550	77	148	23	6	7	49	42	76	54	13	.321	.371
Gruber,Kelly	30	.264	135	526	75	139	22	3	21	79	38	75	13	6	.314	.437
Guerrero,Pedro	36	.291	105	368	33	107	18	1	11	66	40	53	2	1	.360	.435
Guillen,Ozzie	28	.268	157	548	60	147	21	5	2	55	18	41	25	17	.292	.336
Gwynn,Chris	27	.246	109	179	22	44	9	2	3	22	10	28	1	1	.286	.369
Gwynn,Tony	32	.317	144	567	74	180	27	5	5	63	45	24	22	11	.368	.409
Hall,Mel	31	.277	130	423	57	117	23	2	15	64	19	43	0	0	.308	.447
Hamilton,Daryl	27	.278	124	371	52	103	14	2	2	38	27	36	15	9	.327	.342
Hansen,Dave	23	.265	80	200	25	53	8	0	3	23	22	24	2	1	.338	.350
Hare,Shawn	25	.247	92	227	29	56	17	1	6	31	23	43	2	2	.316	.410
Harper,Brian	32	.294	132	446	49	131	24	1	9	57	16	22	3	2	.318	.413
Harris,Lenny	27	.272	145	460	60	125	16	2	4	38	34	38	16	10	.322	.341
Hatcher,Billy	31	.254	115	389	46	99	19	2	4	32	25	43	18	8	.300	.344
Hayes,Charlie	27	.254	131	452	40	115	23	1	10	51	19	78	4	3	.285	.376
Hayes,Von	33	.249	100	346	54	86	18	2	9	44	60	63	14	5	.360	.390
Heath,Mike	37	.227	45	110	9	25	5	1	2	10	6	22	1	1	.267	.345
Henderson,Dave	33	.250	142	527	70	132	26	1	18	70	51	119	6	4	.317	.406
Henderson,Rickey	33	.276	140	496	106	137	24	3	15	53	108	69	66	15	.406	.427
Hernandez,Carlos	25	.271	60	140	13	38	7	0	2	13	5	18	1	2	.297	.364
Hernandez,Jose	22	.213	70	150	14	32	6	1	0	8	8	47	1	1	.253	.267
Herr,Tommy	36	.254	100	228	23	58	16	2	1	21	26	28	4	2	.331	.355
Hill,Donnie	31	.247	96	283	35	70	11	1	3	27	33	25	2	1	.326	.325
Hill,Glenallen	27	.262	98	317	46	83	14	3	10	37	23	75	10	5	.312	.420
Hoiles,Chris	27	.241	125	410	48	99	19	0	13	49	42	80	2	2	.312	.383
Hollins,Dave	26	.242	87	231	27	56	12	2	6	29	25	45	2	1	.316	.390
Horn,Sam	28	.240	121	329	39	79	16	0	21	59	43	94	0	0	.328	.480
Howard,Dave	25	.225	65	178	15	40	4	1	1	16	14	33	3	2	.281	.275
Howard,Thomas	27	.252	89	270	29	68	13	2	3	23	20	58	12	7	.303	.348
Howell,Jack	30	.233	75	202	26	47	11	1	7	23	25	45	1	1	.317	.401
Hrbek,Kent	32	.284	132	454	65	129	25	1	21	86	66	44	4	2	.375	.482
Hudler,Rex	31	.252	66	111	14	28	7	1	2	10	5	16	8	4	.284	.387
Huff,Mike	28	.270	92	281	41	76	14	3	4	34	32	49	13	7	.345	.384
Hulett,Tim	32	.230	41	100	11	23	5	1	2	9	8	21	0	1	.287	.360
Humphreys,Mike	25	.247	65	150	25	37	9	1	3	19	18	26	9	4	.327	.380
Hundley,Todd	23	.241	115	382	40	92	17	2	6	42	36	75	2	2	.306	.343

318

Projections for 1992 Batters

Batter	Age	Avg	G	AB	R	H	2B	3B	HR	RBI	BB	SO	SB	CS	OBP	SLG
Hunter,Brian	24	.241	78	253	28	61	10	0	11	37	17	41	2	2	.289	.411
Huson,Jeff	27	.244	133	365	52	89	14	2	2	30	46	41	15	9	.328	.310
Incaviglia,Pete	28	.247	99	332	39	82	16	2	15	54	30	94	3	3	.309	.443
Jackson,Bo	29	.255	105	345	58	88	14	2	20	63	35	112	14	8	.324	.481
Jackson,Darrin	28	.244	116	312	38	76	13	1	12	38	21	62	4	3	.291	.407
Jacoby,Brook	32	.269	112	383	39	103	18	2	9	48	40	52	2	2	.338	.397
James,Chris	29	.257	93	338	35	87	15	2	8	42	18	47	3	2	.295	.385
Javier,Stan	28	.251	91	195	30	49	7	2	1	17	22	32	8	3	.327	.323
Jefferies,Gregg	24	.283	147	544	82	154	34	3	15	69	47	41	20	6	.340	.439
Jefferson,Reggie	23	.267	120	420	55	112	17	2	9	59	29	72	2	2	.314	.381
Johnson,Howard	31	.251	153	569	90	143	27	2	28	90	75	114	38	13	.339	.453
Johnson,Lance	28	.279	155	563	77	157	18	8	1	48	39	54	35	19	.326	.345
Jones,Tracy	31	.259	62	139	17	36	6	0	3	20	11	15	1	1	.313	.367
Jordan,Ricky	27	.273	114	385	44	105	22	1	9	55	17	52	2	2	.303	.405
Jose,Felix	27	.264	156	557	63	147	28	2	14	72	44	112	16	11	.318	.397
Joyner,Wally	30	.279	133	498	65	139	26	2	16	72	50	54	2	1	.345	.436
Justice,Dave	26	.286	145	510	90	146	30	2	30	97	80	95	13	9	.383	.529
Karkovice,Ron	28	.241	95	228	31	55	12	0	6	27	18	59	1	0	.297	.373
Karros,Eric	24	.288	80	250	34	72	17	1	7	34	21	43	2	3	.343	.448
Kelly,Pat	24	.260	88	273	39	71	13	3	4	27	17	46	14	7	.303	.374
Kelly,Roberto	27	.284	144	529	74	150	24	3	15	61	42	106	38	15	.336	.425
Kennedy,Terry	36	.253	79	198	13	50	12	0	3	18	19	32	1	1	.318	.359
King,Jeff	27	.240	86	246	34	59	12	1	7	32	20	32	4	2	.297	.382
Knoblauch,Chuck	23	.289	155	554	84	160	29	7	3	59	64	35	23	9	.362	.383
Kruk,John	31	.289	151	506	68	146	21	3	13	72	69	84	7	3	.374	.419
Landrum,Ced	28	.252	120	230	39	58	10	2	1	18	19	36	21	8	.309	.326
Lankford,Ray	25	.268	155	555	78	149	27	10	14	80	56	86	37	15	.336	.429
Lansford,Carney	35	.283	85	300	38	85	14	1	4	30	27	22	13	7	.343	.377
Larkin,Barry	28	.299	142	521	80	156	24	4	12	63	48	50	23	7	.359	.430
Larkin,Gene	29	.264	100	265	35	70	18	1	3	27	32	32	3	2	.343	.374
LaValliere,Mike	31	.268	106	302	24	81	13	0	3	33	40	28	1	2	.354	.341
Lee,Manuel	27	.246	129	410	41	101	12	3	4	38	27	93	5	2	.293	.320
Leius,Scott	26	.271	99	269	34	73	13	2	3	27	28	46	3	3	.340	.368
Lemke,Mark	26	.251	126	335	40	84	17	2	4	36	34	31	2	3	.320	.349
Leonard,Mark	27	.259	70	170	21	44	10	1	5	24	20	34	1	1	.337	.418
Lewis,Darren	24	.264	113	386	56	102	10	3	3	34	39	46	21	11	.332	.329
Lewis,Mark	22	.264	129	417	49	110	22	2	4	52	21	50	5	5	.299	.355
Lind,Jose	28	.251	154	550	52	138	22	4	3	52	38	59	10	3	.299	.322
Litton,Greg	27	.226	53	106	10	24	6	1	2	12	7	24	1	1	.274	.358
Livingstone,Scott	26	.242	63	198	23	48	7	0	4	25	17	29	1	1	.302	.338
Lofton,Kenny	25	.255	151	560	64	143	16	11	0	30	35	118	28	23	.299	.323
Lyons,Steve	32	.244	102	242	27	59	13	1	2	24	17	44	6	3	.293	.331
Maas,Kevin	27	.256	135	450	66	115	20	1	22	64	72	110	4	3	.358	.451
Macfarlane,Mike	28	.257	130	440	45	113	27	2	11	61	27	72	1	0	.300	.402
Mack,Shane	28	.292	155	520	80	152	20	4	15	69	47	104	19	11	.351	.433

319

Projections for 1992 Batters

Batter	Age	Avg	G	AB	R	H	2B	3B	HR	RBI	BB	SO	SB	CS	OBP	SLG
Magadan,Dave	29	.289	131	409	59	118	22	2	5	52	71	47	1	1	.394	.389
Maldonado,Candy	31	.239	130	426	49	102	21	1	13	59	43	97	4	2	.309	.385
Manto,Jeff	27	.246	72	203	33	50	12	1	6	30	35	38	2	2	.357	.404
Manwaring,Kirt	26	.218	59	147	11	32	5	1	1	13	9	20	1	1	.263	.286
Martinez,Carlos	26	.280	100	322	35	90	15	1	6	41	17	51	5	3	.316	.388
Martinez,Carmelo	31	.224	88	205	22	46	11	0	7	30	29	43	1	0	.321	.380
Martinez,Chito	26	.245	135	400	54	98	17	2	20	58	43	135	4	4	.318	.448
Martinez,Dave	27	.287	132	408	53	117	15	5	8	40	27	57	20	9	.331	.407
Martinez,Edgar	29	.291	152	550	88	160	30	1	12	58	84	73	3	3	.385	.415
Martinez,Tino	24	.261	65	207	25	54	12	1	6	27	24	22	2	1	.338	.415
Marzano,John	29	.231	71	182	18	42	12	0	3	18	8	26	1	1	.263	.346
Mattingly,Don	31	.298	137	534	64	159	35	1	16	82	42	30	1	1	.349	.457
Maurer,Rob	25	.283	115	321	43	91	29	2	14	52	46	110	2	2	.373	.517
May,Derrick	23	.276	75	170	21	47	14	1	3	23	7	21	2	2	.305	.424
Mayne,Brent	24	.253	135	475	48	120	16	1	5	57	47	66	5	4	.320	.322
McClendon,Lloyd	33	.255	88	204	27	52	9	0	6	25	26	30	3	2	.339	.387
McGee,Willie	33	.284	121	451	60	128	21	5	4	44	33	76	19	8	.333	.379
McGriff,Fred	28	.284	155	550	94	156	26	2	35	97	112	126	5	3	.405	.529
McGwire,Mark	28	.235	155	502	79	118	22	1	32	96	101	109	2	1	.363	.474
McIntosh,Tim	27	.257	60	140	18	36	9	1	4	21	7	20	1	1	.293	.421
McRae,Brian	24	.245	162	620	80	152	25	8	7	61	34	101	19	12	.284	.345
McReynolds,Kevin	32	.263	138	498	65	131	25	2	18	74	53	57	9	5	.334	.430
Melvin,Bob	30	.232	97	297	23	69	12	1	4	33	14	56	1	1	.267	.320
Merced,Orlando	25	.257	107	350	51	90	13	3	6	42	37	65	7	4	.328	.363
Mercedes,Luis	24	.310	135	455	73	141	15	3	3	41	46	76	26	17	.373	.376
Merullo,Matt	26	.256	76	207	23	53	10	0	4	25	15	26	1	1	.306	.362
Meulens,Hensley	25	.244	80	250	35	61	9	1	8	32	28	78	2	2	.320	.384
Miller,Keith	29	.253	112	312	47	79	16	1	3	24	26	49	17	5	.311	.340
Milligan,Randy	30	.265	140	464	69	123	24	3	17	66	99	96	6	5	.394	.440
Mitchell,Keith	22	.306	65	170	28	52	8	0	6	26	15	26	5	4	.362	.459
Mitchell,Kevin	30	.271	142	505	82	137	24	3	32	91	69	91	4	5	.359	.521
Molitor,Paul	35	.290	146	596	91	173	31	4	12	56	64	66	21	8	.359	.416
Morandini,Mickey	26	.260	139	470	63	122	22	4	3	37	45	77	13	6	.324	.343
Morris,Hal	27	.302	145	490	68	148	28	2	12	58	38	60	10	5	.352	.441
Moseby,Lloyd	32	.247	112	393	57	97	19	3	10	44	42	73	16	5	.320	.387
Mota,Andy	26	.252	80	230	23	58	11	1	2	22	8	44	6	4	.277	.335
Mota,Jose	27	.231	60	130	15	30	3	0	1	9	14	20	2	2	.306	.277
Mulliniks,Rance	36	.250	67	136	14	34	10	1	2	17	23	25	0	0	.358	.382
Munoz,Pedro	23	.291	125	423	52	123	24	3	12	59	25	74	12	7	.330	.447
Murphy,Dale	36	.244	133	480	51	117	21	2	18	72	51	114	3	2	.316	.408
Murray,Eddie	36	.271	126	458	58	124	23	1	16	73	61	64	6	3	.356	.430
Myers,Greg	26	.253	116	336	32	85	19	0	9	38	22	44	0	0	.299	.390
Naehring,Tim	25	.247	60	150	16	37	11	0	4	18	14	27	0	0	.311	.400
Newman,Al	32	.224	100	255	29	57	8	1	0	20	28	24	10	6	.300	.263
Newson,Warren	27	.286	110	290	46	83	15	1	8	37	50	72	8	6	.391	.428

Projections for 1992 Batters

Batter	Age	Avg	G	AB	R	H	2B	3B	HR	RBI	BB	SO	SB	CS	OBP	SLG
Nixon,Otis	33	.247	122	288	52	71	7	1	1	21	36	37	50	16	.330	.288
Noboa,Junior	27	.282	80	195	19	55	7	1	1	18	7	15	5	4	.307	.344
Nokes,Matt	28	.262	142	424	41	111	17	1	19	63	27	52	2	2	.306	.441
O'Brien,Pete	34	.253	109	379	42	96	18	1	9	45	45	38	1	1	.333	.377
O'Neill,Paul	29	.256	153	550	65	141	30	1	21	85	68	103	17	10	.338	.429
Offerman,Jose	23	.258	145	485	70	125	9	3	2	38	60	93	38	30	.339	.301
Olander,Jim	29	.251	85	275	32	69	13	2	3	29	26	56	4	4	.316	.345
Olerud,John	23	.269	155	554	76	149	29	1	22	80	89	98	1	2	.370	.444
Oliver,Joe	26	.243	118	350	30	85	18	0	10	48	26	64	0	0	.295	.380
Olson,Greg	31	.244	98	279	32	68	13	0	5	31	31	34	1	1	.319	.344
Oquendo,Jose	28	.266	143	444	42	118	13	2	2	36	74	49	2	2	.371	.318
Orsulak,Joe	30	.266	110	346	43	92	15	3	5	40	32	34	5	4	.328	.370
Orton,John	26	.200	60	145	17	29	7	0	3	15	12	44	1	1	.261	.310
Owen,Spike	31	.231	145	441	46	102	20	4	4	32	64	55	5	5	.329	.322
Pagliarulo,Mike	32	.237	130	389	33	92	21	1	11	38	34	70	2	2	.298	.380
Pagnozzi,Tom	29	.263	140	460	38	121	22	2	6	54	36	66	8	8	.317	.359
Palmeiro,Rafael	27	.303	159	604	90	183	37	4	18	83	61	60	4	3	.367	.467
Palmer,Dean	23	.231	145	490	64	113	24	4	25	74	36	172	5	5	.283	.449
Parker,Dave	41	.260	70	246	24	64	13	1	7	35	17	47	1	1	.308	.407
Parrish,Lance	36	.223	121	412	41	92	18	1	15	50	40	113	1	1	.292	.381
Pasqua,Dan	30	.257	136	416	57	107	19	2	18	67	55	89	2	2	.344	.442
Pecota,Bill	32	.252	106	298	45	75	14	1	5	30	34	39	12	5	.328	.356
Pena,Geronimo	25	.257	97	257	45	66	15	4	5	27	33	64	14	7	.341	.405
Pena,Tony	35	.256	128	410	43	105	20	1	6	44	35	49	6	4	.315	.354
Pendleton,Terry	31	.261	147	551	69	144	26	3	15	72	40	70	9	5	.311	.401
Perry,Gerald	31	.252	84	242	27	61	12	1	4	28	24	29	11	5	.320	.360
Petralli,Geno	32	.268	81	190	18	51	8	1	2	17	24	26	1	1	.350	.353
Pettis,Gary	34	.225	77	218	33	49	7	2	1	12	38	61	20	9	.340	.289
Phillips,Tony	33	.268	145	519	71	139	19	3	10	56	79	84	11	7	.365	.374
Plantier,Phil	23	.281	143	545	92	153	27	2	32	91	81	155	4	4	.374	.514
Polonia,Luis	27	.307	159	592	88	182	20	8	4	56	44	66	39	20	.355	.389
Powell,Alonzo	27	.259	69	205	26	53	13	2	5	27	19	50	5	4	.321	.415
Puckett,Kirby	31	.313	152	595	79	186	33	4	14	83	44	70	9	5	.360	.452
Quinones,Luis	30	.229	90	179	18	41	11	2	4	20	14	26	1	1	.285	.380
Quintana,Carlos	26	.287	135	450	58	129	23	1	10	63	57	64	2	1	.367	.409
Quirk,Jamie	37	.215	65	130	10	28	6	0	2	16	13	29	1	1	.287	.308
Raines,Tim	32	.283	145	530	83	150	27	5	8	61	84	53	47	15	.381	.398
Ramirez,Rafael	33	.245	85	249	22	61	12	1	2	23	14	32	3	2	.285	.325
Randolph,Willie	37	.257	127	440	51	113	18	2	2	37	63	43	5	3	.350	.320
Ready,Randy	32	.250	106	248	36	62	16	2	4	28	44	36	3	2	.363	.379
Redus,Gary	35	.246	85	203	31	50	13	2	5	20	28	36	13	4	.338	.404
Reed,Jeff	29	.232	104	280	18	65	13	1	3	26	33	42	0	0	.313	.318
Reed,Jody	29	.279	156	596	79	166	39	1	6	53	75	56	5	5	.359	.378
Reimer,Kevin	28	.253	125	376	37	95	24	3	15	58	27	81	1	1	.303	.452
Reyes,Gil	28	.208	66	178	13	37	7	0	3	17	14	45	1	1	.266	.298

Projections for 1992 Batters

Batter	Age	Avg	G	AB	R	H	2B	3B	HR	RBI	BB	SO	SB	CS	OBP	SLG
Reynolds,Harold	31	.257	156	619	87	159	27	5	3	48	70	53	28	15	.332	.331
Riles,Ernest	31	.245	60	143	19	35	6	1	3	18	17	23	1	1	.325	.364
Ripken,Billy	27	.252	100	282	29	71	14	1	2	23	19	35	2	1	.299	.330
Ripken,Cal	31	.276	162	635	84	175	34	2	25	96	66	62	4	2	.344	.454
Rivera,Luis	28	.245	135	437	54	107	25	2	7	44	32	79	5	4	.296	.359
Roberts,Bip	28	.287	136	463	86	133	19	4	5	37	52	64	34	14	.359	.378
Rodriguez,Ivan	20	.258	135	450	36	116	22	1	5	49	9	75	0	3	.272	.344
Rohde,David	28	.258	45	120	13	31	4	1	0	10	15	17	4	2	.341	.308
Rose,Bobby	25	.269	45	130	17	35	6	1	3	18	10	23	1	0	.321	.400
Royer,Stan	24	.239	65	180	17	43	12	1	4	24	12	38	0	0	.286	.383
Sabo,Chris	30	.271	154	584	88	158	38	2	21	73	54	67	23	11	.332	.450
Salazar,Luis	36	.252	80	230	22	58	9	1	5	23	11	38	1	1	.286	.365
Samuel,Juan	31	.249	146	543	71	135	28	7	13	57	49	127	33	14	.311	.398
Sandberg,Ryne	32	.279	153	588	98	164	28	4	23	80	65	84	20	7	.351	.457
Sanders,Deion	24	.234	48	128	21	30	4	2	3	12	12	23	9	4	.300	.367
Sanders,Reggie	24	.272	140	470	63	128	19	6	11	57	40	112	16	4	.329	.409
Santiago,Benito	27	.265	148	521	60	138	23	3	16	77	30	96	10	8	.305	.413
Santovenia,Nelson	30	.240	50	125	12	30	6	0	3	16	8	19	1	1	.286	.360
Sasser,Mackey	29	.280	114	282	27	79	17	1	4	37	14	20	1	1	.314	.390
Sax,Steve	32	.282	154	624	74	176	24	3	6	50	47	42	38	13	.332	.359
Schaefer,Jeff	32	.224	56	116	12	26	7	0	1	8	6	14	3	3	.262	.310
Schofield,Dick	29	.227	121	384	48	87	12	3	4	31	50	66	7	4	.316	.305
Scioscia,Mike	33	.248	132	400	40	99	19	1	7	46	53	32	3	2	.336	.353
Segui,David	25	.287	61	178	20	51	11	0	2	22	17	16	1	1	.349	.382
Seitzer,Kevin	30	.284	123	437	62	124	21	4	5	38	63	49	9	5	.374	.384
Servais,Scott	25	.218	70	170	15	37	8	1	1	16	8	31	1	1	.253	.294
Sharperson,Mike	30	.270	125	322	42	87	14	2	2	32	43	41	10	8	.356	.345
Sheffield,Gary	23	.269	125	490	62	132	25	2	13	62	44	38	20	11	.330	.408
Shumpert,Terry	25	.238	145	450	57	107	26	5	5	38	32	80	24	11	.288	.351
Sierra,Ruben	26	.298	161	635	94	189	35	7	27	111	52	84	11	3	.351	.502
Simms,Mike	25	.231	50	130	17	30	8	1	3	18	15	42	2	2	.310	.377
Skinner,Joel	31	.228	84	206	16	47	9	0	2	18	10	52	1	1	.264	.301
Slaught,Don	33	.264	106	292	28	77	19	2	5	34	29	44	1	1	.330	.394
Smith,Dwight	28	.283	85	212	27	60	13	2	5	27	19	34	6	4	.342	.434
Smith,Lonnie	36	.271	95	284	42	77	16	2	6	31	41	54	9	6	.363	.405
Smith,Ozzie	37	.246	140	516	66	127	22	2	2	42	63	36	27	7	.328	.308
Snyder,Cory	29	.226	66	212	23	48	10	1	8	28	11	60	2	1	.265	.396
Sojo,Luis	26	.258	99	337	37	87	12	1	4	29	14	25	5	5	.288	.335
Sorrento,Paul	26	.278	135	418	56	116	31	1	19	75	58	83	1	1	.366	.493
Sosa,Sammy	23	.246	104	338	46	83	16	3	9	39	21	82	18	11	.290	.391
Spiers,Bill	26	.267	135	419	61	112	13	4	6	48	30	56	13	7	.316	.360
Sprague,Ed	24	.240	71	225	23	54	11	1	7	28	15	48	1	1	.288	.391
Stanley,Mike	29	.263	114	205	25	54	11	1	4	25	33	37	1	0	.366	.385
Steinbach,Terry	30	.262	134	458	42	120	21	2	9	59	26	72	2	1	.302	.376
Stevens,Lee	24	.249	135	490	61	122	27	1	17	71	46	119	3	3	.313	.412

Projections for 1992 Batters

Batter	Age	Avg	G	AB	R	H	2B	3B	HR	RBI	BB	SO	SB	CS	OBP	SLG
Stillwell,Kurt	27	.259	138	467	54	121	23	4	6	54	41	62	5	4	.319	.364
Strawberry,Darryl	30	.261	148	529	89	138	25	4	32	99	75	118	13	8	.353	.505
Stubbs,Franklin	31	.230	78	204	24	47	8	1	8	25	23	47	8	3	.308	.397
Surhoff,B.J.	27	.275	146	509	57	140	23	3	7	65	35	36	14	10	.322	.373
Sveum,Dale	28	.237	98	287	33	68	16	2	5	36	30	77	2	3	.309	.359
Tabler,Pat	34	.271	56	129	13	35	8	1	1	17	14	15	0	0	.343	.372
Tartabull,Danny	29	.280	129	447	63	125	27	2	22	78	64	122	4	2	.370	.497
Templeton,Garry	36	.251	80	239	20	60	12	3	3	24	11	36	1	1	.284	.364
Tettleton,Mickey	31	.236	139	462	71	109	17	1	20	62	97	139	3	3	.369	.407
Teufel,Tim	33	.231	105	264	35	61	19	1	7	30	36	60	3	2	.323	.390
Thomas,Frank	24	.325	155	550	111	179	32	4	34	108	137	112	4	4	.460	.584
Thome,Jim	21	.291	140	525	63	153	27	5	5	68	45	104	7	3	.347	.390
Thompson,Milt	33	.270	136	429	50	116	17	4	5	41	37	71	23	9	.328	.364
Thompson,Robby	30	.249	149	522	79	130	26	5	14	52	53	110	14	6	.318	.398
Thon,Dickie	34	.248	137	483	43	120	19	3	8	45	31	80	9	4	.294	.350
Thurman,Gary	27	.271	77	192	28	52	7	3	1	14	16	42	16	6	.327	.354
Tingley,Ron	33	.225	50	120	12	27	5	0	2	15	9	29	1	1	.279	.317
Trammell,Alan	34	.268	126	467	59	125	22	2	9	62	52	49	11	5	.341	.381
Treadway,Jeff	29	.286	126	423	53	121	21	2	7	45	28	33	3	3	.330	.395
Uribe,Jose	32	.232	90	233	20	54	8	2	1	14	17	32	3	4	.284	.296
Valle,Dave	31	.221	106	290	33	64	12	1	7	32	34	39	1	1	.302	.341
Van Slyke,Andy	31	.259	139	498	72	129	23	5	14	70	64	93	14	5	.343	.410
VanderWal,John	26	.264	135	375	50	99	28	3	8	46	40	84	3	2	.335	.419
Varsho,Gary	31	.242	90	178	22	43	10	1	2	18	13	31	7	4	.293	.343
Vaughn,Greg	26	.245	155	550	83	135	28	3	27	97	63	128	11	5	.323	.455
Vaughn,Mo	24	.280	100	300	35	84	20	0	11	46	37	60	1	1	.359	.457
Velarde,Randy	29	.242	94	260	30	63	16	2	5	27	23	64	2	3	.304	.377
Venable,Max	35	.224	49	98	11	22	4	1	1	9	9	19	2	1	.290	.316
Ventura,Robin	24	.268	157	594	79	159	24	1	17	87	81	61	5	5	.356	.397
Villanueva,Hector	27	.248	89	266	25	66	15	0	9	34	18	56	0	0	.296	.406
Vizcaino,Jose	24	.254	75	181	17	46	5	1	1	15	10	19	4	4	.293	.309
Vizquel,Omar	25	.228	128	372	37	85	12	3	2	28	32	33	4	3	.290	.293
Walker,Chico	34	.234	82	252	31	59	8	1	6	25	25	45	8	4	.303	.345
Walker,Larry	25	.263	142	463	65	122	23	3	17	62	50	108	23	9	.335	.436
Wallach,Tim	34	.254	123	461	50	117	24	1	12	62	40	70	3	4	.313	.388
Walton,Jerome	26	.281	109	360	57	101	18	2	4	31	31	59	15	6	.338	.375
Ward,Kevin	30	.243	51	140	18	34	7	2	3	14	16	30	5	3	.321	.386
Ward,Turner	27	.269	68	212	29	57	10	1	3	21	26	29	6	5	.349	.368
Webster,Mitch	33	.248	50	113	15	28	6	2	2	12	9	23	4	2	.303	.389
Wehner,John	25	.273	59	194	25	53	9	0	2	20	14	22	8	5	.322	.351
Weiss,Walt	28	.251	130	430	51	108	16	1	3	38	43	55	11	4	.319	.314
Whitaker,Lou	35	.258	136	469	77	121	22	3	15	66	84	59	6	3	.371	.414
White,Devon	29	.248	159	588	85	146	26	6	14	55	47	130	34	13	.304	.384
Whiten,Mark	25	.259	96	316	45	82	11	4	7	34	28	64	6	5	.320	.386
Wilkerson,Curt	31	.221	60	140	15	31	4	1	1	12	8	28	2	1	.264	.286

Projections for 1992 Batters

Batter	Age	Avg	G	AB	R	H	2B	3B	HR	RBI	BB	SO	SB	CS	OBP	SLG
Wilkins,Rick	24	.226	84	239	22	54	9	0	8	29	18	51	2	2	.280	.364
Williams,Bernie	23	.248	145	500	78	124	25	4	9	54	72	96	24	17	.343	.368
Williams,Matt D.	26	.259	159	587	76	152	27	3	33	100	35	126	7	5	.301	.484
Wilson,Mookie	36	.252	75	202	24	51	11	2	2	18	8	37	7	2	.281	.356
Wilson,Willie	36	.252	75	147	22	37	9	3	1	18	11	29	8	3	.304	.374
Winfield,Dave	40	.249	131	481	59	120	21	2	16	66	51	96	3	2	.321	.401
Winningham,Herm	30	.238	80	147	19	35	6	2	2	11	13	31	6	4	.300	.347
Wood,Ted	25	.250	50	120	16	30	7	1	2	16	14	23	2	2	.328	.375
Worthington,Craig	27	.232	85	271	31	63	12	0	7	32	37	58	1	1	.325	.354
Yelding,Eric	27	.249	80	225	27	56	7	1	1	16	16	35	22	11	.299	.302
Young,Gerald	27	.249	95	189	28	47	10	3	1	17	28	23	12	8	.346	.349
Yount,Robin	36	.258	138	523	75	135	27	4	11	73	61	80	11	5	.336	.388
Zeile,Todd	26	.265	154	554	73	147	32	3	21	85	64	89	7	5	.341	.448
Zosky,Eddie	24	.247	95	215	26	53	13	3	2	19	11	34	2	3	.283	.363

These Guys Can Play Too and Might Get A Shot

Batter	Age	Avg	G	AB	R	H	2B	3B	HR	RBI	BB	SO	SB	CS	OBP	SLG
Bret Boone	23	.237	139	464	57	110	17	0	17	67	54	135	6	8	.317	.384
Bernardo Brito	28	.239	46	138	17	33	5	0	7	22	6	35	0	0	.283	.428
Jeromy Burnitz	23	.204	135	445	67	91	14	7	25	71	74	137	22	14	.318	.436
Jim Campanis	24	.230	118	378	32	87	9	0	13	43	28	70	0	0	.283	.357
Cheo Garcia	24	.282	55	163	17	46	8	1	3	23	10	16	3	1	.343	.399
Juan Guerrero	25	.300	128	456	61	137	35	1	14	73	30	94	9	8	.344	.474
Steve Hosey	23	.264	50	129	20	34	6	1	4	19	9	31	5	3	.333	.419
Mark Howie	29	.307	130	473	64	145	23	0	12	78	29	52	3	6	.347	.431
John Jaha	26	.283	120	421	73	119	27	1	18	81	36	96	6	5	.368	.480
Ryan Klesko	21	.274	126	409	51	112	19	1	12	53	48	63	8	16	.350	.413
Dave Nilsson	22	.314	93	318	42	100	25	1	3	48	27	30	2	1	.368	.428
Dave Silvestri	24	.233	56	163	26	38	9	1	5	22	13	44	5	4	.313	.393
Matt Stairs	23	.307	129	486	73	149	27	7	9	65	46	50	17	10	.367	.447
Jimmy Tatum	24	.272	130	460	67	125	22	4	12	87	36	84	3	7	.325	.415

About STATS, Inc.

It all starts with the **system**. The STATS scoring method, which includes pitch-by-pitch information and the direction, distance, and velocity of each ball hit into play, yields an immense amount of information. Sure, we have all the statistics you're used to seeing, but where other statistical sources stop, STATS is just getting started.

Then, there's the **network**. Our information is timely because our game reporters send their information by computer as soon as the game is over. Statistics are checked, rechecked, updated, and are available daily.

Analysis comes next. STATS constantly searches for new ways to use this wealth of information to open windows into the workings of Baseball. Accurate numbers, intelligent computer programming, and a large dose of imagination all help coax the most valuable information from its elusive cover.

Finally, distribution!

For 12 years now STATS has served Major League teams including the White Sox, Athletics and Yankees. The box scores that STATS provides to the *Associated Press* and *USA Today* have revolutionized what Baseball fans expect from a box score. *Sports Illustrated* and *The Sporting News* regularly feature STATS, Inc. while *ESPN's* nightly baseball coverage is supported by a full-time STATS statistician. We provide statistics for *Earl Weaver Baseball*, *Rotisserie Baseball*, the syndicated newspaper game *Dugout Derby*, and many other baseball games and fantasy leagues all over the country.

For the baseball fan, STATS publishes monthly and year-end reports on each Major League team. We offer a host of year-end statistical breakdowns on paper or disk that cover hitting, pitching, catching, baserunning, throwing, and more. STATS even produces custom reports on request.

Computer users with modems can access the STATS computer for information with **STATS On-line**. If you own a computer with a modem, there is no other source with the scope of baseball information that STATS can offer.

STATS and Bill James enjoy an on-going affiliation that has produced the book you are now holding. We also administer *Bill James Fantasy Baseball*, the ultimate baseball game designed by Bill James himself which allows you to manage your own team and compete with other team owners around the country. STATS also produces a similarly-designed head-to-head fantasy football game, *STATS Fantasy Football*.

Always looking for innovative approaches, STATS has other exciting future projects underway for sports fans nationwide. It is the purpose of STATS, Inc. to make the best possible sports information available to all interests: fans, players, teams, or media. For more information write to:

STATS, Inc.
7366 North Lincoln Ave.
Lincolnwood, IL 60646-1708

. . . or call us at 1-708-676-3322. We can send you a STATS brochure, a free Bill James Fantasy Baseball or STATS Fantasy Football information kit, and/or information on STATS On-line.

To maintain our information, STATS hires people around the country to cover games using the STATS scoring method. If you are interested in applying for a game reporter's position, please write or call STATS.

For the story behind the numbers, check out STATS' other publications: *The STATS 1992 Baseball Scoreboard* : The first edition of this book in 1990 took the nation's Baseball fans by storm. This all new 1992 edition, available in many bookstores or directly from STATS, is back with the same great writing, great graphics and stats you won't find anywhere else. There is also our newest publication, the *STATS 1992 Minor League Handbook,* complete with Bill James' unique Major League Equivalencies that allow YOU to scout the players destined to be big league stars. In addition, STATS continues a tradition with *The Scouting Report:1992*, available in book stores in the Spring of 1992. You'll find scouting reports on over 700 players, including new team prospect reports, backed by statistical findings you can only get from STATS, Inc.

Turn to the last pages in this book to find a handy order form and additional information about the fine products from STATS.

Glossary

% Inherited Scored
A Relief Pitching statistic indicating the percentage of runners on base at the time a relief pitcher enters a game that he allows to score.

1st Batter OBP
The On-Base Percentage allowed by a relief pitcher to the first batter he faces in a game.

Active Career Batting Leaders
Minimum of 1,000 At Bats required for Batting Average, On-Base Percentage, Slugging Percentage, At Bats Per HR, At Bats Per GDP, At Bats Per RBI, and K/BB Ratio. One hundred (100) Stolen Base Attempts required for Stolen Base Success %. Any player who appeared in 1991 is eligible for inclusion provided he meets the category's minimum requirements.

Active Career Pitching Leaders
Minimum of 750 Innings Pitched required for Earned Run Average, Opponent Batting Average, all of the "Per 9 Innings" categories, and Strikeout to Walk Ratio. Two hundred fifty (250) Games Started required for Complete Game Frequency. One hundred (100) decisions required for Win-Loss Percentage. Any player who appeared in 1991 is eligible for inclusion provided he meets the category's minimum requirements.

BA ScPos Allowed
Batting Average Allowed with Runners in Scoring Position.

Batting Average
Hits divided by At Bats.

Catcher's ERA
The Earned Run Average of a catcher. To figure this for a catcher, multiply the Earned Runs Allowed by the pitchers while he was catching times nine and divide that by his number of Innings Caught.

Cheap Wins/Tough Losses/Top Game Scores
First determine the starting pitcher's Game Score as follows: (1)Start with 50. (2)Add 1 point for each out recorded by the starting pitcher. (3)Add 2 points for each inning the pitcher completes afer the fourth inning. (4)Add 1 point for each strikeout. (5)Subtract 2 points for each hit allowed. (6)Subtract 4 points for each earned run allowed. (7)Subtract 2 points for an unearned run. (8)Subtract 1 point for each walk.

If the starting pitcher scores over 50 and loses, it's a Tough Loss. If he wins with a game score under 50, it's a Cheap Win. All Game Scores of 90 or above are listed.

Cleanup Slugging%
The Slugging Percentage of a player when batting fourth in the batting order.

Complete Game Frequency
Complete Games divided by Games Started.

Earned Run Average
(Earned Runs times 9) divided by Innings Pitched.

Fielding Percentage
(Putouts plus Assists) divided by (Putouts plus Assists plus Errors).

Hold

A Hold is credited anytime a relief pitcher enters a game in a Save Situation (see definition below), records at least one out, and leaves the game never having relinquished the lead. Note: a pitcher cannot finish the game and receive credit for a Hold.

Isolated Power

Slugging Percentage minus Batting Average.

K/BB Ratio

Strikeouts divided by Walks.

Late & Close

A Late & Close situation meets the following requirements: (1)the game is in the seventh inning or later, and (2)the batting team is either leading by one run, tied, or has the potential tying run on base, at bat, or on deck. Note: this situation is very similar to the characteristics of a Save Situation.

Leadoff On Base%

The On-Base Percentage of a player when batting first in the batting order.

Offensive Winning Percentage

The Winning Percentage a team of nine Will Clarks (or anybody) would compile against average pitching and defense. The formula: (Runs Created per 27 outs) divided by the League average of runs scored per game. Square the result and divide it by (1+itself).

On Base Percentage

(Hits plus Walks plus Hit by Pitcher) divided by (At Bats plus Walks plus Hit by Pitcher plus Sacrifice Flies).

Opponent Batting Average

Hits Allowed divided by (Batters Faced minus Walks minus Hit Batsmen minus Sacrifice Hits minus Sacrifice Flies minus Catcher's Interference).

PA*

The divisor for On Base Percentage: At Bats plus Walks plus Hit By Pitcher plus Sacrifice Flies; or Plate Appearances minus Sacrifice Hits and Times Reached Base on Defensive Interference.

PCS (Pitchers' Caught Stealing)

The number of runners officially counted as Caught Stealing where the initiator of the fielding play was the pitcher, not the catcher. Note: such plays are often referred to as "pickoffs", but appear in official records as Caught Stealings. The most common "pitcher caught stealing scenario" is a 1-3-6 fielding play, where the runner is officially charged a Caught Stealing because he broke for second base. "Pickoff" (fielding play 1-3 being the most common) is not an official statistical category.

PkOf Throw/Runner

The number of pickoff throws made by a pitcher divided by the number of runners on first base.

Plate Appearances

At Bats plus Total Walks plus Hit By Pitcher plus Sacrifice Hits plus Sacrifice Flies plus Times Reached on Defensive Interference.

Power/Speed Number

A way to look at power and speed in one number. A player must score high in both areas to earn a high Power/Speed Number. The formula: (HR x SB x 2) divided by (HR + SB).

Quick Hooks and Slow Hooks

A Quick Hook is the removal of a pitcher who has pitched less than 6 innings and given up 3 runs or less. A Slow Hook goes to a pitcher who pitches more than 9 innings, or allows 7 or more runs, or whose combined innings pitched and runs allowed totals 13 or more.

Range Factor

The number of Chances (Putouts plus Assists) times nine divided by the number of Defensive Innings Played. The average for a Regular Player at each position in 1991:

Second Base: 5.17

Left Field: 2.15

Third Base: 2.80

Center Field: 2.69

Shortstop: 4.76

Right Field: 2.13

Run Support Per 9 IP

The number of runs scored by a pitcher's team while he was still in the game times nine divided by his Innings Pitched.

Runs Created

A way to combine a batter's total offensive contributions into one number. The formula: (H + BB + HBP - CS - GIDP) times (Total Bases + .26(TBB - IBB + HBP) + .52(SH + SF + SB)) divided by (AB + TBB + HBP +SH + SF).

Save Percentage

Saves (SV) divided by Save Opportunities (OP).

Save Situation

A Relief Pitcher is in a Save Situation when:

upon entering the game with his club leading, he has the opportunity to be the finishing pitcher (and is not the winning pitcher of record at the time), and meets any one of the three following conditions:

(1) he has a lead of no more than three runs and has the opportunity to pitch for at least one inning, or;

(2) he enters the game, regardless of the count, with the potential tieing run either on base, at bat, or on deck; or

(3) has the opportunity to pitch three or more innings and not be the winning pitcher.

SB Success%

Stolen Bases divided by (Stolen Bases plus Caught Stealing).

Secondary Average

A way to look at a player's extra bases gained, independent of Batting Average. The formula: (Total Bases - Hits + TBB + SB) divided by At Bats.

Slugging Percentage

Total Bases divided by At Bats.

Total Bases

Hits plus Doubles plus (2 times Triples) plus (3 times Homeruns).

Win-Loss Percentage or Winning Percentage

Wins divided by (Wins plus Losses).

Two More Hits from
Bill James and STATS, Inc.

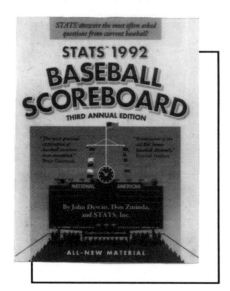

STATS 1992 Baseball Scoreboard

All New for 1992!

- The Unique STATS Analysis Used by the Teams, Networks, and NOW YOU!

- Find Out the Answers to Questions Like:

    "Who Has the Best Zone Ratings?"
    "Does AstroTurf Really Affect Hitting?"
    "Which Pitchers Eat Lefties?"

- Over 100 Questions Answered Using Baseball's Most In-Depth Database

- Available February, 1992

"Brilliant . . . reminiscent of the old Bill James Abstracts!" — *Baseball America*

Bill James/STATS 1992 Minor League Handbook

New in 1992! **Available November 15, 1991!**

- Exclusive Bill James' Major League Equivalencies

- Official Minor League Stats from Howe Sportsdata International

- Minor League Career Records

- Minor League Leader Boards

"The Next Step for the Serious Baseball Fan!"

Order Now! Use the STATS Order Form on the last page of this book.

Bill James
FANTASY
BASEBALL

If You Like Fantasy Baseball, You'll Love Bill James Fantasy Baseball . . .

"Hi. This is Bill James. A few years ago I designed a set of rules for a new fantasy baseball league, which has been updated with the benefit of experience and the input of a few thousand owners.

The idea of a fantasy league, of course, is that it forges a link between you and your ballplayers; YOU win or lose based on how the players that you picked have performed. My goal was to develop a fantasy league based on the simplest and yet most realistic principles possible — a league in which the values are as nearly as possible what they ought to be, without being distorted by artificial category values or rankings, but which at the same time are so simple that you can keep track of how you've done just by checking box scores. There are a lot of different rules around for fantasy leagues, but none of them before this provided exactly what I was looking for. Here's what we want:

1) *We want it to be realistic.* We don't want the rules to make David Cone the MVP because of his strikeouts. We don't want Vince Coleman to be worth more than Bobby Bonilla because he steals lots of bases. We want good ballplayers to be good ballplayers.

2) *We prefer it simple.* We want you to be able to look up your players in the morning paper, and know how you've done.

3) *We want you to have to develop a real team.* We don't want somebody to win by stacking up starting pitchers and leadoff men. We don't want somebody to corner the market on home run hitters.

I made up the rules and I'll be playing the game with you. STATS, Inc. is running the leagues. They'll run the draft, man the computers, keep the rosters straight and provide you with weekly updates. Of course you can make trades, pick up free agents and move players on and off the inactive list; that's not my department, but there are rules for that, too. It all starts with a draft. . ."

- Draft Your Own Team and Play vs. Other Owners! Play by Mail or With a Computer On-Line!

- Manage Your Roster All Season With Daily Transactions! Live Fantasy Phone Lines Every Day of the Baseball Season!

- Realistic Team and Individual Player Totals That Even Take Fielding Into Account!

- The Best Weekly Reports in the Business!

- Play Against Bill James' Own Drafted Teams!

- Get Discounted Prices by Forming Your Own Private League of 11 or 12 Owners! (Call or write for more information)

- Money-Back Guarantee! Play one month, and if not satisfied, we'll return your franchise fee!

All This, All Summer Long — For Less Than An Average of $5 per week.

Reserve your BJFB team now! Sign up with the STATS Order Form on the next page, or send for additional Free Information.

STATS Order Form

Product	Quantity	Your price	Total
Bill James Fantasy Baseball Franchise		$25 deposit	
STATS 1992 Baseball Scoreboard		$12.95	
Bill James/STATS 1992 Minor League Handbook		17.95	
The Scouting Report: 1992		15.95	
Bill James/STATS 1992 Major League Handbook		17.95	
Discounts on previous editions while supplies last:			
Bill James/STATS 1991 Major League Handbook		9.95	
Bill James/STATS 1990 Major League Handbook		9.95	
STATS 1991 Baseball Scoreboard		9.95	
The STATS Baseball Scoreboard (1990)		7.95	
U.S. – For First Class Mailing – add $2.50 per book		2.50	
Canada – all orders – add $3.50 per book		3.50	
Subtotal			
Subtract $1.00 per book if you order 2 or more		– $1.00	–
Total			

☐ Yes, I can't wait! Sign me up to play Bill James Fantasy Baseball in 1992. Enclosed is my deposit of $25.00 on the franchise fee of $85.00. A processing fee of $1.00 per player is charged during the season for roster moves.

Team Nickname: _____ _____ (example: Dayton Mutants)

Would you like to play in a league with a team drafted by Bill James? Yes No (circle one)

Would you like to receive information on playing BJFB on-line by computer? Yes No (circle one)

Please Rush Me These Free Informational Brochures:

☐ **Bill James Fantasy Baseball Info Kit**

☐ **STATS Fantasy Football Info Kit**

☐ **STATS On-Line Brochure**

☐ **STATS Year-End Reports Brochure**

☐ **STATS Reporter Brochure**

Please Print:

Name_____ Phone_____

Address_____

City_____ State_____ Zip_____

Method of Payment (U.S. Funds only):

☐ Check (no Candian checks) ☐ Money Order ☐ Visa ☐ MasterCard

Credit Card Information:

Cardholder Name_____

Visa/MC #_____ Exp. Date_____

Signature_____

Return this form (don't tear your book; copy this page) to:

**STATS, Inc.
7366 N. Lincoln Ave
Lincolnwood, IL
60646-1708**

For faster credit card service: call 1-800-63-STATS to place your order, or fax this page to 1-708-676-0821.

HB92